Rogers

France

Quality camping & caravanning sites

2007

Alan

Alan
Rogers

Celebrating 40 Years

Compiled by: Alan Rogers Guides Ltd

Designed by: Paul Effenberg, Vine Design Ltd

Maps created by Customised Mapping (01769 540044)
contain background data provided by GisDATA Ltd
Maps are © Alan Rogers Guides and Gis DATA Ltd 2006

© Alan Rogers Guides Ltd 2007

Published by: Alan Rogers Guides Ltd,
Spelmonden Old Oast, Goudhurst, Kent TN17 1HE
www.alanrogers.com Tel: 01580 214000

British Library Cataloguing-in-Publication Data:
A catalogue record for this book is available from the
British Library.

ISBN-13 978-0-9550486-4-7
ISBN-10 0-9550486-4-8

Printed in Great Britain by J H Haynes & Co Ltd

Contents

the Alan Rogers
approach

THIS YEAR WE CELEBRATE THE PUBLICATION OF THE FORTIETH EDITIONS OF THE ALAN ROGERS GUIDES. SINCE ALAN ROGERS PUBLISHED THE FIRST CAMPSITE GUIDE THAT BORE HIS NAME, THE RANGE HAS EXPANDED TO SIX TITLES COVERING 27 COUNTRIES. NO FEWER THAN 20 OF THE CAMPSITES SELECTED BY ALAN FOR THE FIRST GUIDE ARE STILL FEATURED IN OUR 2007 EDITIONS – LOOK OUT FOR THE 'CELEBRATING 40 YEARS' SYMBOL BESIDE OUR REPORTS.

THERE ARE OVER 11,000 CAMPSITES IN FRANCE OF VARYING QUALITY: THIS GUIDE CONTAINS IMPARTIALLY WRITTEN REPORTS ON ALMOST 900 (300 MORE THAN LAST YEAR), INCLUDING SOME OF THE VERY FINEST, EACH BEING INDIVIDUALLY INSPECTED AND SELECTED. ALL THE USUAL MAPS AND INDEXES ARE ALSO INCLUDED, DESIGNED TO HELP YOU FIND THE CHOICE OF CAMPSITE THAT'S RIGHT FOR YOU. WE HOPE YOU ENJOY SOME HAPPY AND SAFE TRAVELS – AND SOME PLEASURABLE 'ARMCHAIR TOURING' IN THE MEANTIME!

A question of quality

The criteria we use when inspecting and selecting sites are numerous, but the most important by far is the question of good quality. People want different things from their choice of campsite so we try to include a range of campsite 'styles' to cater for a wide variety of preferences: from those seeking a small peaceful campsite in the heart of the countryside, to visitors looking for an 'all singing, all dancing' site in a popular seaside resort. Those with more specific interests, such as sporting facilities, cultural events or historical attractions, are also catered for.

The size of the site, whether it's part of a chain or privately owned, makes no difference in terms of it being required to meet our exacting standards in respect of its quality and it being 'fit for purpose'. In other words, irrespective of the size of the site, or the number of facilities it offers, we consider and evaluate the welcome, the pitches, the sanitary facilities, the cleanliness, the general maintenance and even the location.

" ...the campsites included in this book have been chosen entirely on merit, and no payment of any sort is made by them for their inclusion."

Alan Rogers, 1968

Independent and honest

Whilst the content and scope of the Alan Rogers guides have expanded considerably since the early editions, our selection of campsites still employs exactly the same philosophy and criteria as defined by Alan Rogers in 1968.

'telling it how it is'

Firstly, and most importantly, our selection is based entirely on our own rigorous and independent inspection and selection process. Campsites cannot buy their way into our guides – indeed the extensive Site Report which is written by us, not by the site owner, is provided free of charge so we are free to say what we think and to provide an honest, 'warts and all' description. This is written in plain English and without the use of confusing icons or symbols.

Expert opinions

We rely on our dedicated team of Site Assessors, all of whom are experienced campers, caravanners or motorcaravanners, to visit and recommend sites. Each year they travel some 100,000 miles around Europe inspecting new campsites for the guide and re-inspecting the existing ones. Our thanks are due to them for their enthusiastic efforts, their diligence and integrity.

We also appreciate the feedback we receive from many of our readers and we always make a point of following up complaints, suggestions or recommendations for possible new sites. Of course we get a few grumbles too – but it really is a few, and those we do receive usually relate to overcrowding or to poor maintenance during the peak school holiday period.

Please bear in mind that, although we are interested to hear about any complaints, we have no contractual relationship with the campsites featured in our guides and are therefore not in a position to intervene in any dispute between a reader and a campsite.

Highly respected by site owners and readers alike, there is no better guide when it comes to forming an independent view of a campsite's quality. When you need to be confident in your choice of campsite, you need the Alan Rogers Guide.

- ☑ Parks only included on merit
- ☑ Parks cannot pay to be included
- ☑ Independently inspected, rigorously assessed
- ☑ Impartial reviews
- ☑ **40** years of expertise

Region

The Site Reports – *Example of an entry*

Site Number Site name
Postal Address (including département)
Telephone number. Email address

A description of the site in which we try to give an idea of its general features – its size, its situation, its strengths and its weaknesses. This section should provide a picture of the site itself with reference to the facilities that are provided and if they impact on its appearance or character. We include details on pitch numbers, electricity (with amperage), hardstandings etc. in this section as pitch design, planning and terracing affects the site's overall appearance. Similarly we include reference to pitches used for caravan holiday homes, chalets, and the like. Importantly at the end of this column we indicate if there are any restrictions, e.g. no tents, no children, naturist sites.

Facilities
Lists more specific information on the site's facilities and amenities and, where available, the dates when these facilities are open (if not for the whole season). Off site: here we give distances to various local amenities, for example, local shops, the nearest beach, plus our featured activities (bicycle hire, fishing, horse riding, boat launching). Where we have space we list suggestions for activities and local tourist attractions.

Open: Site opening dates.

Directions
Separated from the main text in order that they may be read and assimilated more easily by a navigator en-route. Bear in mind that road improvement schemes can result in road numbers being altered.

GPS: references are provided as we obtain them for satellite navigation systems (in degrees and minutes).

Charges 2007

Regions and départements

For administrative purposes France is actually divided into 23 official regions covering the 95 départements (similar to our counties). However, these do not always coincide with the needs of tourists. For example the area we think of as the Dordogne is split between two of the official regions. We have, therefore, opted to feature our campsites within unofficial 'tourist regions', and the relevant départements are stated in our introduction to each region with their official number (eg. the département of Manche is number 50) included. We use these département numbers as the first two digits of our campsite numbers, so any campsite in the Manche département will start with the number 50, prefixed with FR.

Indexes

Our three indexes allow you to find sites by their number and name, by region and site name or by the town or village where the site is situated.

Campsite Maps

The maps relate to our tourist regions and will help you to identify the approximate position of each campsite. The colour of the campsite number indicates whether it is open all year or not. You will certainly need more detailed maps and we have found the Michelin atlas to be particularly useful.

Facilities

Toilet blocks

We assume that toilet blocks will be equipped with a reasonable amount of British style WCs, washbasins with hot and cold water and hot showers with dividers or curtains, and will have all necessary shelves, hooks, plugs and mirrors. We also assume that there will be an identified chemical toilet disposal point, and that the campsite will provide water and waste water drainage points and bin areas. If not the case, we comment. We do mention certain features that some readers find important: washbasins in cubicles, facilities for babies, facilities for those with disabilities and motorcaravan service points. Readers with disabilities are advised to contact the site of their choice to ensure that facilities are appropriate to their needs.

Shop

Basic or fully supplied, and opening dates.

Bars, restaurants, takeaway facilities and entertainment

We try hard to supply opening and closing dates (if other than the campsite opening dates) and to identify if there are discos or other entertainment.

Children's play areas

Fenced and with safety surface (e.g. sand, bark or pea-gravel).

Swimming pools

If particularly special, we cover in detail in our main campsite description but reference is always included under our Facilities listings. Opening dates, charges and levels of supervision are provided where we have been notified. There is a regulation whereby Bermuda shorts may not be worn in swimming pools (for health reasons). It is worth ensuring that you do take 'proper' swimming trunks with you.

Leisure facilities

E.g. playing fields, bicycle hire, organised activities and entertainment.

Dogs

If dogs are not accepted or restrictions apply, we state it here. Check the quick reference list at the back of the guide.

Off site

This briefly covers leisure facilities, tourist attractions, restaurants etc nearby.

Charges

These are the latest provided to us by the sites. In those few cases where 2006 or 2007 prices are not given, we try to give a general guide.

Reservations

Necessary for high season (roughly mid-July to mid-August) in popular holiday areas (ie beach resorts). You can reserve via our own Alan Rogers Travel Service or through tour operators. Or be wholly independent and contact the campsite(s) of your choice direct, using the phone or e-mail numbers shown in the site reports, but please bear in mind that many sites are closed all winter.

Telephone numbers

All numbers assume that you are phoning from within France. To phone France from outside that country, prefix the number shown with the relevant International Code (00 33) and drop the first 0, shown as (0) in the numbers indicated.

Opening dates

Are those advised to us during the early autumn of the previous year – sites can, and sometimes do, alter these dates before the start of the following season, often for good reasons. If you intend to visit shortly after a published opening date, or shortly before the closing date, it is wise to check that it will actually be open at the time required. Similarly some parks operate a restricted service during the low season, only opening some of their facilities (e.g. swimming pools) during the main season; where we know about this, and have the relevant dates, we indicate it – again if you are at all doubtful it is wise to check.

Some French site owners are very laid back when it comes to opening and closing dates. They may not be fully ready by their stated opening dates – grass and hedges may not all be cut or perhaps only limited sanitary facilities open. At the end of the season they also tend to close down some facilities and generally wind down prior to the closing date. Bear this in mind if you are travelling early or late in the season – it is worth phoning ahead.

The Camping Cheque low season touring system goes some way to addressing this in that participating campsites are encouraged to have all key facilities open and running by the opening date and to remain fully operational until the closing date.

Our Accommodation Section

Mobile homes page 452

Over recent years, more and more campsites have added high quality mobile home and chalet accommodation. In response to feedback from many of our readers, and to reflect this evolution in campsites, we have now decided to include a separate section on mobile homes and chalets. If a site offers this accommodation, it is indicated above the site report with a page reference where full details are given. We have chosen a number of sites offering some of the best accommodation available and have included full details of one or two accommodation types at these sites. Please note however that many other campsites listed in this guide may also have a selection of accommodation for rent.

Whether you're an 'old hand' in terms of camping and caravanning or are contemplating your first trip, a regular reader of our Guides or a new 'convert', we wish you well in your travels and hope we have been able to help in some way. We are, of course, also out and about ourselves, visiting sites, talking to owners and readers, and generally checking on standards and new developments.

We wish all our readers thoroughly enjoyable Camping and Caravanning in 2007 – favoured by good weather of course!

THE ALAN ROGERS TEAM

Regions

Northern France

Eastern France

Normandy

Paris & Ile de France

Brittany

Loire Valley

Burgundy

Franche Comté

Vendée & Charente

Savoy & Dauphiny Alps

Limousin & Auvergne

Rhône Valley

Dordogne & Aveyron

Provence

Atlantic Coast

Mediterranean East

Midi-Pyrénées

Mediterranean West

Corsica

In 2004 we introduced the first ever Alan Rogers Campsite Awards.

BEFORE MAKING OUR AWARDS, WE CAREFULLY CONSIDER MORE THAN 2000 CAMPSITES FEATURED IN OUR GUIDES, TAKING INTO ACCOUNT COMMENTS FROM OUR SITE ASSESSORS, OUR HEAD OFFICE TEAM AND, OF COURSE, OUR READERS.

OUR AWARD WINNERS COVER A MASSIVE GEOGRAPHICAL AREA FROM THE IBERIAN PENINSULA TO HUNGARY, AND THIS YEAR WE ARE MAKING AWARDS TO CAMPSITES IN 12 DIFFERENT COUNTRIES.

NEEDLESS TO SAY, IT'S AN EXTREMELY DIFFICULT TASK TO CHOOSE OUR EVENTUAL WINNERS, BUT WE BELIEVE THAT WE HAVE IDENTIFIED A NUMBER OF CAMPSITES WITH TRULY OUTSTANDING CHARACTERISTICS.

IN EACH CASE, WE HAVE SELECTED AN OUTRIGHT WINNER, ALONG WITH TWO HIGHLY COMMENDED RUNNERS-UP.

Listed below are full details of each of our award categories and our winners for 2006.

Alan Rogers Progress Award 2006

This award reflects the hard work and commitment undertaken by particular site owners to improve and upgrade their site.

WINNER

Camping International Marina, Spain

RUNNERS-UP

Camping La Grande Métairie, France

Newlands Caravan Park, England

Alan Rogers Welcome Award 2006

This award takes account of sites offering a particularly friendly welcome and maintaining a friendly ambience throughout reader's holidays.

WINNER

Mannix Point Caravan Park, Ireland

RUNNERS-UP

Castel Camping Sequoia Park, France

Balatontourist Napfeny, Hungary

Alan Rogers Active Holiday Award 2006

This award reflects sites in outstanding locations which are ideally suited for active holidays, notably walking or cycling, but which could extend to include such activities as winter sports or water sports

WINNER

Sportcamp Woferlgut, Austria

RUNNERS-UP

Klim Strand Camping, Denmark

Camping Bijela Uvala, Croatia

Alan Rogers Motorhome Award 2006

Motorhome sales are increasing and this award acknowledges sites which, in our opinion, have made outstanding efforts to welcome motorhome clients.

WINNER

Spessart-Camping Schönrain, Germany

RUNNERS-UP

Camping El Astral, Spain

Gaasper Camping, Netherlands

Alan Rogers 4 Seasons Award 2006

This award is made to outstanding sites with extended opening dates and which welcome clients to a uniformly high standard throughout the year.

WINNER

Komfort-Campingpark Burgstaller, Austria

RUNNERS-UP

Recreatiecentrum de Schatberg, Netherlands

Caravaning La Manga, Spain

Alan Rogers Seaside Award 2006

This award is made for sites which we feel are outstandingly suitable for a really excellent seaside holiday.

WINNER

Playa Montroig Camping Resort, Spain

RUNNERS-UP

Camping Baia Blu La Tortuga, Italy

Camping Bois Soleil, France

Alan Rogers Country Award 2006

This award contrasts with our former award and acknowledges sites which are attractively located in delightful, rural locations.

WINNER
Stowford Farm Meadows, England

RUNNERS-UP
Castel Camping La Paille Basse, France
Camping Romantische Strasse, Germany

Alan Rogers Rented Accommodation Award 2006

Given the increasing importance of rented accommodation on many campsites, and the inclusion in many Alan Rogers guides, of a rented accommodation section, we feel that it is important to acknowledge sites which have made a particular effort in creating a high quality 'rented accommodation' park.

WINNER
Camping Cambrils Park, Spain

RUNNERS-UP
Castel Camping Caravaning Esterel, France
Camping Kovacine, Croatia

Alan Rogers Unique Site Award 2006

This award acknowledges sites with unique, outstanding features – something which simply cannot be found elsewhere and which is an important attraction of the site.

WINNER
Camping Jésolo International, Italy

RUNNERS-UP
The Plassey Touring Park, Wales
Vakantiepark Duinrell, Netherlands

Alan Rogers Family Site Award 2006

Many sites claim to be child friendly but this award acknowledges the sites we feel to be the very best in this respect.

WINNER
Camping Capalonga, Italy

RUNNERS-UP
Beverley Park Holiday Centre, England
Domaine Le Pommier, France

Alan Rogers Readers' Award 2006

In 2005 we introduced a new award, which we believe to be the most important, our Readers' Award. We simply invited our readers (by means of an on-line poll at www.alanrogers.com) to nominate the site they enjoyed most. The outright winner for 2006 is:

WINNER
Camping Le Paradis, France

Alan Rogers.travel

The Alan Rogers Travel Service was set up to provide a low cost booking service for readers. We pride ourselves on being able to put together a bespoke holiday, taking advantage of our experience, knowledge and contacts. We can tailor-make a holiday to suit your requirements, giving you maximum choice and flexibility: exactly what we have been offering for some 7 years now.

2007 PRICE CRASH

For 2007 we offer more choice than ever before (around 500 campsites) and have thousands of holidays at significantly reduced prices - guaranteed.

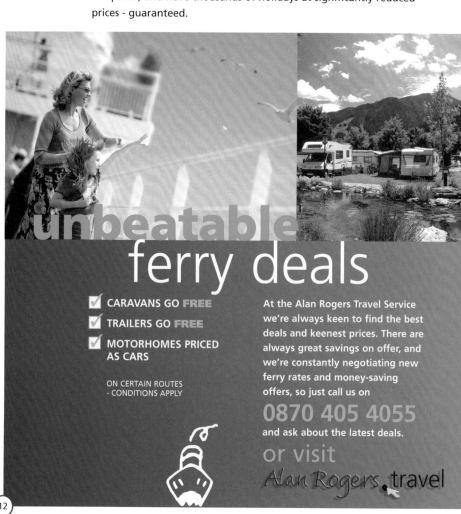

unbeatable ferry deals

- ☑ CARAVANS GO FREE
- ☑ TRAILERS GO FREE
- ☑ MOTORHOMES PRICED AS CARS

ON CERTAIN ROUTES
- CONDITIONS APPLY

At the Alan Rogers Travel Service we're always keen to find the best deals and keenest prices. There are always great savings on offer, and we're constantly negotiating new ferry rates and money-saving offers, so just call us on

0870 405 4055

and ask about the latest deals.

or visit
Alan Rogers.travel

Whether you book on-line or book by phone, you will be allocated an experienced Personal Travel Consultant to provide you with personal advice and manage every stage of your booking. Our Personal Travel Consultants have first-hand experience of many of our campsites and access to a wealth of information. They can 'paint a picture' of individual campsites, check availability, provide a competitive price and tailor your holiday arrangements to your specific needs.

- Discuss your holiday plans with a friendly person with first-hand experience

- Let us reassure you that your holiday arrangements really are taken care of

- Tell us about your special requests and allow us to pass these on

- Benefit from advice which will save you money – the latest ferry deals and more

- Remember, our offices are in Kent not overseas and we do NOT operate a queuing system!

THE AIMS OF THE TRAVEL SERVICE ARE SIMPLE

- To provide convenience - a one-stop shop to make life easier.

- To provide peace of mind - when you need it most.

- To provide a friendly, knowledgeable, efficient service – when this can be hard to find.

- To provide a low cost means of organising your holiday – when prices can be so complicated.

HOW IT WORKS

1 Choose your campsite(s) – we can book around 500 across Europe. Look for the yellow coloured campsite entries in this book. You'll find more info and images at www.alanrogers.travel.

Please note: the list of campsites we can book for you varies from time to time.

2 Choose your dates – choose when you arrive, when you leave.

3 Choose your ferry crossing – we can book most routes with most operators at extremely competitive rates.

Then just call us for an instant quote

0870 405 4055
or visit

Alan Rogers.travel

LOOK FOR A CAMPSITE ENTRY LIKE THIS TO INDICATE WHICH CAMPSITES WE CAN BOOK FOR YOU.

THE LIST IS GROWING SO PLEASE CALL FOR UP TO THE MINUTE INFORMATION.

Leave The Hassle To Us

- All site fees paid in advance (nominal local tourist taxes may be payable on arrival).

- Your pitch is reserved for you – travel with peace of mind.

- No endless overseas phone calls or correspondence with foreign site owners.

- No need to pay foreign currency deposits and booking fees.

- Take advantage of our expert advice and experience of camping in Europe.

Already Booked Your Ferry?

We're confident that our ferry inclusive booking service offers unbeatable value. However, if you have already booked your ferry then we can still make a pitch-only reservation for you (minimum 5 nights). Since our prices are based on our ferry inclusive service, you need to be aware that a non-ferry booking may result in slightly higher prices than if you were to book direct with the site.

book on-line
and save money

www.alanrogers.travel is a website designed to give you everything you need to know when it comes to booking your Alan Rogers inspected and selected campsite, and your low cost ferry.

Our friendly, expert team of travel consultants is always happy to help on **0870 405 4055** – but they do go home sometimes!

Visit www.alanrogers.travel and you'll find constantly updated information, latest ferry deals, special offers from campsites and much more. And you can visit it at any time of day or night!

www.alanrogers.travel

Campsite Information

☑ Details of all Travel Service campsites - **instantly**

☑ Find latest special offers on campsites - **instantly**

☑ Check campsite availability - **instantly**

Ferry Information

☑ Check ferry availability - **instantly**

☑ Find latest ferry deals - **instantly**

☑ Book your ferry online - **instantly**

☑ Save money - **instantly**

Crossing the Channel

MAP 1

Rolling sandy beaches, hidden coves, pretty villages and a picturesque coastline all combine to make Brittany a very popular holiday destination. Full of Celtic culture steeped in myths and legends, Brittany is one of the most distinctive regions of France.

DÉPARTEMENTS: 22 CÔTES D'ARMOR, 29 FINISTÈRE, 35 ILLE-ET-VILAINE, 56 MORBIHAN, 44 LOIRE ATLANTIQUE

MAJOR CITIES: RENNES AND BREST

Brittany's 800 miles of rocky coastline offers numerous bays, busy little fishing villages and broad sandy beaches dotted with charming seaside resorts. The coastline to the north of Brittany is rugged with a maze of rocky coves, while to the south, the shore is flatter with long sandy beaches. Inland you'll find wooded valleys, rolling fields, moors and giant granite boulders, but most impressive is the wealth of prehistoric sites, notably the Carnac standing stones.

Breton culture offers a rich history of menhirs, crosses, cathedrals and castles. Strong Celtic roots provide this region with its own distinctive traditions, evident in the local Breton costume and music, traditional religious festivals and the cuisine, featuring crêpes and cider. Many castles and manor houses, countless chapels and old towns and villages provide evidence of Brittany's eventful history and wealth of traditions. The abbey fortress of Mont-St-Michel on the north coast should not be missed and Concarneau in the south is a lovely walled town enclosed by granite rocks.

Places of interest

Cancale: small fishing port famous for oysters.

Carnac: 3,000 standing stones (menhirs).

Concarneau: fishing port, old walled town.

Dinan: historical walled town.

La Baule: resort with lovely, sandy bay.

Le Croisic: fishing port, Naval museum.

Guérande: historic walled town.

Perros-Guirec: leading resort of the 'Pink Granite Coast'.

Quiberon: boat service to three islands: Belle Ile (largest of the Breton islands), Houat, Hoedic.

Rennes: capital of Brittany, medieval streets, half timbered houses; Brittany Museum.

St Malo: historical walled city, fishing port.

Cuisine of the region

Fish and shellfish are commonplace; traditional *crêperies* abound and welcome visitors with a cup of local cider.

Agneau de pré-salé: leg of lamb from animals pastured in the salt marshes and meadows.

Beurre blanc: sauce for fish dishes made with shallots, wine vinegar and butter.

Cotriade: fish soup with potatoes, onions, garlic and butter.

Crêpes Bretonnes: the thinnest of pancakes with a variety of sweet fillings.

Galette: can be a biscuit, cake or pancake; with sweet or savoury fillings.

Gâteau Breton: rich cake.

Poulet blanc Breton: free-range, quality, white Breton chicken.

FR22000 Camping des Vallées

Chemin des Vallées, Parc de Brézillet, F-22000 St Brieuc (Côtes d'Armor)

Tel: 02 96 94 05 05. Email: campingdesvallees@wanadoo.fr

Previously run by the municipality, this site is now privately managed. Neat and tidy, it has 106 good size pitches, 70 with electrical connections (10A), set mainly on flat terraced grass and separated by shrubs and bushes. There are 14 pitches with hardstanding and electricity, water and sewage connections. Mature trees are plentiful, providing shade if required, and a small stream winds through the middle of the site creating a quiet, peaceful atmosphere. A key system operates the access gate (closed 22.30-07.00 hrs).

Facilities

The two main toilet blocks include some washbasins in cabins, facilities for disabled people and baby room. Laundry facilities. Motorcaravan services. Two further smaller blocks are at the bottom of the site. Shop with basic provisions. Compact bar with snacks. Play area. Volley and basketball, arcade games. Bicycle hire. Animation organised in peak season, also weekly pony days for children. Off site: Aquatic centre, gym and fitness centre (part of a holiday village). Saint Brieuc 800 m. Beach 10 km.

Open: Easter - 15 October.

Directions

From the east, on entering St Brieuc, look for the sign to the railway station and from there, signs for Brézillet or site.

Charges 2006

Per pitch incl. car and 1 person	€ 9,20 - € 11,50
extra person	€ 3,50 - € 4,40
child (under 7 yrs)	€ 2,30 - € 2,90
electricity (10A)	€ 3,90
water and drainage	€ 5,90 - € 7,80

FR22010 Camping les Capucines

Kervourdon, F-22300 Tredrez-Locquémeau (Côtes d'Armor)

Tel: 02 96 35 72 28. Email: les.capucines@wanadoo.fr

A warm welcome awaits at Les Capucines which is quietly situated about a kilometre from the village of Saint Michel with its good, sandy beach and also very near Locquémeau, a pretty fishing village. This attractive, family run site has 100 pitches on flat or slightly sloping ground. All are well marked out by hedges, with mature trees and with more recently planted. There are 70 pitches with electricity, water and drainage, including 10 for larger units. A good value restaurant/crêperie can be found at Trédrez; others at Saint Michel. A 'Sites et Paysages' member.

Facilities

Two modern toilet blocks, clean and very well kept, include washbasins mainly in cabins, facilities for babies and disabled people. Laundry with washing machines and dryer. Small shop for essentials (bread to order). Takeaway. Bar with TV. General room with table tennis and table football. Swimming and paddling pools. Playground. Tennis. Minigolf. New multisport area. Chalets and mobile homes to rent. Off site: Fishing 1 km. Riding 2 km. Golf 15 km. Beach 1 km.

Open: 15 March - 5 November.

Directions

Turn off main D786 road northeast of St Michel where site is signed, and 1 km. to site.

Charges 2006

Per unit incl. 2 persons	€ 13,80 - € 19,50
incl. electiricty (7A) and water	€ 18,40 - € 26,00
extra person	€ 3,80 - € 5,30
child	€ 2,70 - € 3,40

FR22020 Camping Fleur de Bretagne

Kerandouaron, F-22110 Rostrenen (Côtes d'Armor)

Tel: 02 96 29 16 45. Email: info@fleurdebretagne.com

With British owners, this small, rural site is set in the heart of the Brittany countryside, only one kilometre from the small town of Rostrenen. Well kept pitches are laid out in groups of seven or eight and these groups are separated by small trees and shrubs. The site is terraced and slopes gently down to a fishing lake. This site lends itself to a quiet holiday spent with friends and it is particularly suitable for campers using tents.

Facilities

Two well kept toilet blocks provide showers and washbasins, some in cubicles. Facilities for disabled visitors. Small bar which serves snacks and has a terrace overlooking a grassy area where children can play. Bread to order. Small unheated swimming pool. Football field. Boules. Fishing.

Open: All year.

Directions

Rostrenen is in the heart of Brittany, about halfway between St Brieuc and Quimper. From N164 Loudéac - Carhaix-Plouguer road, turn south to Rostrenen and take D764 Route de Pontivy to site on the southeast edge of the town.

Charges 2006

Per person	€ 3,00 - € 5,00
child (3-11 yrs)	€ 2,00 - € 3,00
pitch incl. electricity	€ 5,00 - € 7,00

FR22030 Camping Nautic International

Route de Beau-Rivage, F-22530 Caurel (Côtes d'Armor)

Tel: 02 96 28 57 94. Email: contact@campingnautic.fr

This friendly family site is on the northern shore of the Lac de Guerledan. The lake is popular for all manner of watersports and there are some pleasant walks around the shores and through the surrounding Breton countryside and forests. The site is terraced down to the lake shore and offers 100 large pitches, all with electrical connections. A number of 'super pitches' (160-200 sq.m.) are also available. There is an imaginatively designed swimming pool and smaller children's pool, both heated by a wood burning stove (15/5-25/9). Small boats can be launched from the site, and other boating activities are available on the lake. A member of 'Sites et Paysages'.

Facilities

Washing and drying machines. Small shop (7/7-31/8). Swimming pools. Gym. Giant chess. Play area. Fishing. Tennis. Table tennis. Games room. Mobile homes for rent. Off site: Watersports. Riding. Canal from Nantes to Brest. Sea 50 minutes by car.

Open: 15 May - 25 September.

Directions

From N164 Rennes - Brest road, turn off between Mur-de-Bretagne and Gouarec to the village of Caurel. Site is well signed from there. GPS: N48:12.533 E03:03.050

Charges 2007

Per person	€ 3,30 - € 6,00
child (0-7 yrs)	€ 1,90 - € 3,30
pitch	€ 5,40 - € 8,00
electricity (10A)	€ 4,30 - € 4,50

FR22040 Camping le Châtelet

Rue des Nouettes, F-22380 St Cast-le-Guildo (Côtes d'Armor)

Tel: 02 96 41 96 33. Email: chateletcp@aol.com

Carefully developed over the years from a former quarry, Le Châtelet is pleasantly and quietly situated with lovely views over the estuary from many pitches. It is well laid out, mainly in terraces with fairly narrow access roads. There are 216 good-sized pitches separated by hedges, all with electricity and 70 with water and drainage. Some pitches are around a little lake (unfenced) which can be used for fishing. Used by three different tour operators (73 pitches).

Facilities

Four toilet blocks with access at different levels include washbasins in cabins and facilities for children. Three small toilet blocks on the lower terraces. Some facilities are closed outside July/Aug. Motorcaravan services. Heated swimming and paddling pools. Shop for basics, takeaway, bar lounge and general room with satellite TV and pool table. Games room. Play area. Organised games and activities in season. Dancing (high season). Off site: Beach 200 m. Bicycle hire, riding and golf within 1.5 km.

Open: 1 May - 11 September.

Directions

Best approach is to turn off D786 road at Matignon towards St Cast; just inside St Cast limits turn left at sign for 'campings' and follow camp signs on C90.

Charges 2006

Per person	€ 4,10 - € 6,10
child (under 7 yrs)	€ 2,80 - € 4,10
pitch	€ 12,10 - € 19,60
electricity (6/8A)	€ 4,20 - € 5,20
animal	€ 2,80 - € 3,80

FR22050 Camping le Vieux Moulin

14 rue des Moulins, F-22430 Erquy (Côtes d'Armor)

Tel: 02 96 72 34 23. Email: camp.vieux.moulin@wanadoo.fr

Le Vieux Moulin is a family run site, just two kilometres from the little fishing port of Erquy on Brittany's Emerald Coast on the edge of a pine forest and nature reserve. It is about 900 metres from a beach of sand and shingle. Taking its name from the old mill opposite, the site has 173 pitches all with electricity (6/9A) and some with electricity, water and drainage. One section of 39 pitches is arranged around a pond. Most pitches are of a fair size in square boxes with trees giving shade.

Facilities

Two good quality toilet blocks have mostly British style toilets and plenty of individual washbasins, facilities for disabled people and babies. A further small block provides toilets and dishwashing only. Washing machines and dryer. Motorcaravan service point. Shop. Pizzeria and takeaway. Bar and terrace. Heated pool complex. Play areas. Tennis. Fitness gym. TV room (with satellite) and games room with table tennis. Bicycle hire. No electric barbecues. Off site: Beach 900 m. Fishing 1.2 km. Golf and riding 7 km.

Open: 30 April - 10 September.

Directions

Site is 2 km. east of Erquy. Take minor road towards Les Hôpitaux and site is signed from junction of D786 and D34 roads.

Charges 2006

Per person	€ 4,50 - € 5,60
child (under 7 yrs)	€ 3,20 - € 4,20
pitch incl. electricity	€ 14,50 - € 18,50
dog	€ 3,00 - € 4,00

FR22060 Camping Municipal la Hallerais

6 Bourg de Taden, F-22100 Taden (Côtes d'Armor)

Tel: 02 96 39 15 93. Email: camping.la.hallerais@wanadoo.fr

As well as being an attractive old medieval town, Dinan is quite a short run from the resorts of the Côte d'Armor. This useful municipal site, open for a long season, is just outside Dinan, beyond and above the little harbour on the Rance estuary. There is a pleasant riverside walk where the site slopes down towards the Rance. The 226 pitches, all with electricity (6A) and most with water and drainaway, are mainly on level, shallow terraces connected by tarmac roads, with trees and hedges giving a park-like atmosphere. This is a clean efficiently run and well organised site.

Facilities

Two traditional toilet blocks, of good quality and heated in cool weather, have some private cabins with shower and washbasin. Unit for disabled people. Laundry room. Shop. Attractive bar/restaurant with outside terrace and takeaway (all season). Swimming and paddling pools (15/5-30/9). Tennis. Minigolf. Games room with table tennis. TV room with satellite. Playground. Fishing. Mobile homes for rent. Off site: Bus in Taden, 15 minutes walk. Riding 2 km. Bicycle hire 5 km. Beach 20 km.

Open: 15 March - 4 November.

Directions

Taden is northeast of Dinan. On leaving Dinan on D766, turn right to Taden and site before reaching large bridge and N176 junction. From N176 take Taden/Dinan exit.

Charges 2006

Per person	€ 3,20 - € 3,80
child (under 7 yrs)	€ 1,35 - € 1,65
pitch incl. electricity	€ 6,90 - € 11,90

FR22070 Camping les Plages de Beg-Léguer

Route de La Côte, Beg-Léguer, F-22300 Lannion (Côtes d'Armor)

Tel: 02 96 47 25 00. Email: info@campingdesplages.com

This site is spacious, tranquil and well managed with an enthusiastic and friendly new owner. Comprising five hectares, the campsite provides 229 pitches of which 34 are used for mobile homes. There are no tour operators. There is plenty of shade and young hedges are growing to provide separation. Some pitches have sea views. Amenities include a play area, table tennis and trampoline for children and in high season, music, karaoke and magic shows provide entertainment.

Facilities

A very clean toilet block includes private cabins and facilities for disabled visitors. Shop. Bar, restaurant and takeaway (all from Easter). Heated, covered swimming pool (from 1/6). Play area. Some entertainment in high season. Off site: Beach 400 m.

Open: Easter - 31 October.

Directions

From the bypass at Lannion take the D65 towards Trébeurden. Turn left (southwest) signed Beg-Léguer, then Plages Beg-Léguer until signs for site appear.

Charges 2006

Per person	€ 3,00 - € 6,00
child (0-10 yrs)	€ 2,00 - € 4,00
pitch incl. electricity (6A)	€ 10,00 - € 12,00

FR22080 Yelloh! Village le Ranolien

Ploumanach, F-22700 Perros Guirec (Côtes d'Armor)

Tel: 02 96 91 65 65. Email: leranolien@yellohvillage.fr

Le Ranolien has been attractively developed around a former Breton farm – everything here is either made from, or placed on or around the often massive pink rocks. The 560 pitches are of a variety of sizes and types, mostly large and flat but some quite small. Some are formally arranged in rows with hedge separators, but most are either on open ground or under trees, amongst large boulders. With many holiday caravans and tour operator tents around the site (318 pitches), there are 70 pitches for tourists, all with electricity and some with water and drainage.

Facilities

The main toilet block, heated in cool weather, is supplemented by several other more open type blocks around the site. Washbasins in cabins, mostly British style WCs and good showers. Dishwashing facilities are mainly in the open. Laundry. Motorcaravan service facilities. Supermarket and gift shop (1/5-18/9). Restaurant, crêperie and bar (all open over a long season). Disco some nights in high season. Minigolf. Table tennis. Games room. Play area. Cinema. Gym and steam room. Mobile homes for hire. Off site: Beach 150 m. Beach 300 m. Bicycle hire 1 km. Riding 3 km. Golf 10 km.

Open: 7 April - 17 September.

Directions

From Lannion take D788 to Perros Guirec. Follow signs to 'Centre Ville' past main harbour area and then signs to Ploumanach, La Clarté. Pass through village of La Clarté and around sharp left hand bend. Site is immediately on the right.

Charges 2006

Per unit incl. 2 persons and electricity	€ 12,00 - € 30,00
with water and drainage	€ 16,00 - € 39,00
extra person	€ 5,00 - € 8,00
child (2-7 yrs)	free - € 6,00

FR22090 Castel Camping le Château de Galinée

La Galinée, F-22380 St Cast-le-Guildo (Côtes d'Armor)

Tel: **02 96 41 10 56**. Email: chateaugalinee@wanadoo.fr

Situated a few kilometres back from St Cast and owned and managed by the Vervel family, Galinée is in a parkland setting on level grass with numerous and varied mature trees. It has 273 pitches, all with electricity, water and drainage and separated by many mature shrubs and bushes. The top section is mostly for mobile homes. An attractive pool complex has swimming and paddling pools, two new pools with a water slide and a 'magic stream'. Entertainment is organised during peak season featuring traditional Breton music at times or weekly discos.

Facilities

The main tiled, modern sanitary block includes washbasins in private cabins, facilities for babies and a good unit for disabled people. Dishwashing under cover. Laundry room. Shop for basics, bar and excellent takeaway menu (both 1/7-30/8). Attractive, heated pool complex (26/5-2/9) with swimming and paddling pools. Three tennis courts. Fishing. Play area and field for ball games. Off site: Golf 3.5 km. Riding 6 km. Beach 6 km.

Open: 12 May - 9 September.

Directions

From D168 Ploubalay - Plancoet road turn onto D786 towards Matignon and St Cast. Site is very well signed 1 km. after leaving Notre Dame de Guildo.

Charges 2007

Per person	€ 4,00 - € 6,00
child (under 7 yrs)	€ 2,50 - € 4,20
pitch incl. water and drainage	€ 8,50 - € 15,00
electricity (10A)	€ 4,80
animal	€ 3,50

Camping Cheques accepted.

FR22100 Camping L'Abri Côtier

Ville Es Rouxel, F-22680 Etables-sur-Mer (Côtes d'Armor)

Tel: **02 96 70 61 57**. Email: camping.abricotier@wanadoo.fr

L'Abri Côtier is a well-cared-for, family run site 500 metres from a sandy beach. Small and tranquil, it is arranged in two sections separated by a lane. The pitches are marked out on part level, part sloping grass, divided by mature trees and shrubs with some in a charming walled area with a quaint, old-world atmosphere. The second section has an orchard type setting. The evening bar forms a good social centre. In total there are 140 pitches, all with electrical connections (long leads useful) and 60 fully serviced.

Facilities

Good clean sanitary facilities, heated in low season, include some washbasins in cabins, two units for disabled visitors and a baby bath/shower. Dishwashing under cover. Laundry room. Well stocked shop, set menu and simple takeaway service. Bar (with TV) and outdoor terrace area. Sheltered, heated swimming pool with paddling pool and outdoor jacuzzi. Playground. Games room. Some entertainment in peak season. Off site: Restaurants and indoor pool in the village. Riding 1 km. Fishing 2 km. Bicycle hire 4 km. Golf 10 km. Beach 500 m.

Open: 6 May - 15 September.

Directions

From N12 (Saint Brieuc bypass) take D786 towards St Quay Portrieux. After 12 km. pass Aire de la Chapelle on the right and take second left on D47 towards Etables-sur-Mer. Take second right to site at crossroads in 100 m.

Charges 2006

Per person	€ 4,10 - € 4,60
child (under 7 yrs)	€ 2,50 - € 3,00
pitch	€ 6,20 - € 7,20
serviced pitch	€ 6,80 - € 8,00

FR22110 Camping les Madières

Le Vau Madec, F-22590 Pordic (Côtes d'Armor)

Tel: **02 96 79 02 48**. Email: campinglesmadieres@wanadoo.fr

Les Madières is well placed for exploring the Go'lo coast with its seaside resorts of St Quay-Portrieux, Binic and Etables-sur-Mer – ports used in the past by fishing schooners and now used by pleasure boats and a few coastal fishing boats. The young and enthusiastic owners here have already made their mark on this quiet campsite. With plenty of open spaces and set in the countryside, yet near the sea (800 m), it has 83 pitches of which 10 are used for mobile homes. There are no tour operators.

Facilities

Two refurbished heated toilet blocks include facilities for disabled visitors. Basic provisions are kept all season. Bar, restaurant and takeaway (all season). Swimming pool (1/6-20/9). Some entertainment (high season). Off site: Beach 800 m. Bus service nearby. Riding 2.5 km. Bicycle hire 3 km.

Open: 1 April - 31 October.

Directions

From St Brieuc ring-road (N12), turn north on D786 signed Paimpol (by the coast). Les Madières is at Pordic, 3 km. from the ring-road. Site is well signed from the D786. GPS: N48:34.944 W02:48.288

Charges 2006

Per person	€ 4,80
child 90-10 yrs)	€ 3,00
pitch incl. electricity (10A)	€ 11,00

(21)

TO BOOK CALL **0870 405 4055** TRAVEL SERVICE SITE
Advice & low ferry-inclusive prices

FR22120 Camping du Port

3 chemin des Douaniers, Landrellec, F-22560 Pleumeur-Bodou (Côtes d'Armor)

Tel: **02 96 23 87 79**. Email: **renseignments@camping-du-port.com**

Camping du Port is situated beside the beach at Landrellec with magnificent views of the estuary and islands. It is a well maintained, family run site with 103 pitches of varied size, 80 of which are for touring. The pitches are marked and numbered on level grass with hedging and most have electricity, water and drainage. The site is within ten minutes of the village Pleumeur-Bodou and centrally located for visiting the Pink Granite Coast at Perros-Guinec, Ploumanach, Trégastel and Trébeurdon. This is an area ideal for watersports enthusiasts with sailing, windsurfing, canoeing, fishing and scuba diving available.

Facilities

Sanitary facilities are centrally located in one large block with modern toilets, washbasins in cabins and showers. Small toilets and basins for children. Excellent facilities for babies. Provision for disabled people. Laundry and dishwashing facilities. Motorcaravn service point. Shop for basics. Restaurant. Takeaway. Bar with TV. Small play area. Children's club. Organised entertainment in high season.

Open: 1 April - 30 September.

Directions

From Lannion head north to Pleumeur-Bodou, then follow signs to Landrellec. Site is signed.

Charges 2006

Per pitch incl. 2 persons	€ 13,50 - € 16,60
extra person	€ 4,50 - € 5,50
child (2-7 yrs)	€ 2,00 - € 3,00
electricity	€ 2,60

FR22130 Camping de Port l'Epine

Venelle de Pors Garo, F-22660 Trélévern (Côtes d'Armor)

Tel: **02 96 23 71 94**. Email: **camping-de-port-lepine@wanadoo.fr**

Port L'Epine is a pretty little site in a unique situation on a promontory. There is access to the sea, therefore, on the south side of the site, with views across to Perros Guirec. The area covered by the site is not large but there are 160 grass pitches, all with electricity, which are divided by pretty hedging and trees. Some are used for mobile homes. Access is a little tight in parts. This site is ideal for families with young children (probably not for teenagers).

Facilities

The original toilet block is well equipped and a second block has been refurbished in modern style. Unusual dishwashing sinks in open air stone units. Shop and bar/restaurant (1/4-22/9) with takeaway (1/7-31/8). Small heated swimming pool and paddling pool (May-Sept). Fenced play area near the bar/restaurant. Table tennis and video games. Bicycle hire. Off site: Riding or golf 15 km. Useful small supermarket up-hill from site. Many coastal paths to enjoy.

Open: 1 April - 22 September.

Directions

From roundabout south of Perros Guirec take D6 towards Tréguier. After passing through Louannec, take left turn at crossroads for Trélévern. Go through village following camp signs – Port L'Epine is clearly marked as distinct from the municipal site.

Charges 2006

Per pitch incl. 2 persons and electricity	€ 14,50 - € 27,00
serviced pitch	€ 2,50

Camping Cheques accepted.

FR22140 Camping de Port la Chaine

F-22610 Pleubian (Côtes d'Armor)

Tel: **02 96 22 92 38**. Email: **info@portlachaine.com**

The Suquet family has worked hard to establish this comfortable, quiet, family site. In a beautiful location on the 'Untamed Peninsula' between Paimpol and Perros Guirec, attractive trees and shrubs provide a balance of sun and shade, edging the central road and the grassy bays or fields which branch off on the gradual decline towards the bay and the sea (a sandy bay with rocks). Most of the bays have a slight slope, so those with motorcaravans will need to choose their pitch carefully. More open, level pitches nearer the sea are useful for tents.

Facilities

Two traditional style toilet blocks are comfortable and fully equipped, both now completely renovated. Washbasins in cabins, British and Turkish style toilets. Cabins for families or disabled visitors. Washing machines and dryer. Bar/restaurant with terrace and takeaway (23/6-25/8). Heated swimming pool (17/5-9/9). Play area. Games room. Children's entertainer in July/Aug. Beach, fishing and sailing. Off site: Bus 1 km. Village 2 km. for market, shops and restaurants. Fishing and diving. Boat launching 1 km. Bicycle hire 2 km. Riding 6 km. Golf 18 km.

Open: 7 April - 16 September.

Directions

Leave D786 between Lézardrieux and Tréguier to go north to village of Pleubian (about 8 km). Continue on D20 towards Larmor Pleubian and site signed on left, 2 km. from Pleubian.

Charges 2007

Per person	€ 5,60
child (under 7 yrs)	€ 3,60
pitch	€ 9,80
electricity	€ 4,00
dog	€ 2,80

FR22200 Camping Au Bocage du Lac

Rue du Bocage, F-22270 Jugon-les Lacs (Côtes d'Armor)

Tel: 02 96 31 60 16

This well kept former municipal site has been updated over the past few years by the current owners M. and Mme. Riviere. It is on the edge of the village beside a lake, 25 km. from the sea. It offers 181 good size pitches, all with electrical connections, set on gently sloping grass and divided by shrubs and bushes, with mature trees providing shade. Some 40 wooden chalets and mobile homes are intermingled with the touring pitches. On-site facilities include a good pool with children's section and sunbathing patio. There is also a small animal park.

Facilities

Two main sanitary blocks include facilities for disabled visitors. British and Turkish style WCs and some washbasins in cabins. Washing machine. Small shop. Bar. Swimming pool (15/6-10/9). Table tennis, tennis, football. Play area. Activity programmes July/Aug. Fishing. Bicycle hire. Off site: Supermarket in village 1 km. River 1 km.

Open: 1 April - 31 October.

Directions

From N176 (E401) Lamballe - Dinan road, approx. 15 km. from Lamballe take turning for Jugon-les-Lacs. Site is signed shortly after.

Charges 2006

Per person	€ 3,50 - € 4,30
child (under 7 yrs)	€ 2,50 - € 3,00
pitch	€ 5,50 - € 6,90
electricity (5A)	€ 2,80

Camping ★★★
Au Bocage du Lac
AU BOCAGE DU LAC
Hôtel de Plein Air

On the lakeside, for both relaxation and leisure, you will find a wide range of activities : heated pool, water slide, paddling pool, childrens' mini camp, tennis, minigolf, sailing, fishing, walking. One new sanitary block includes private cabins, facilities for babies. WELCOME IN BRITTANY !
22270 Jugon les Lacs
Tél : 02.96.31.60.16
Fax : 02.96.31.75.04

Open from 1st April to 31st October

FR22160 Camping le Neptune

Kerguistin, F-22580 Lanloup (Côtes d'Armor)

Tel: 02 96 22 33 35. Email: contact@leneptune.com

Situated on the Côte de Goelo at Lanloup, Le Neptune offers a peaceful, rural retreat for families. The friendly new owners, M. and Mme. Camard, keep the site neat and tidy and there is a regular programme of renovation. There are 84 level, grass pitches (65 for touring units) separated by trimmed hedges providing privacy and all with electricity. There are also 13 mobile homes to rent. A heated swimming pool has a retractable roof so can be open for a long season. Within walking distance is the local village, with a restaurant and shop, and sandy beaches. The site is also a good base for cycling and walking.

Facilities

The modern toilet block is of a good standard, clean and well maintained. Laundry room with washing machine and dryer. No restaurant but good takeaway (all season). Small shop well stocked for basic needs. Bar with indoor and outdoor seating. Heated swimming pool (Easter - end Oct). Petanque. Volleyball. Table tennis, table football. Animation in season. Off site: Tennis 300 m. Fishing and beach 2 km. Golf 4 km. Riding 8 km. Restaurant and shop within walking distance. Beach 2.5 km.

Open: 1 April - 31 October.

Directions

From Saint Brieuc (N12) take D786 Paimpol ('par la Côte'). After 28 km. on approaching Lanloup, site is well signed.
GPS: N48:42.49 W02:58.00

Charges 2006

Per person	€ 4,70
child (under 7 yrs)	€ 3,00
pitch	€ 7,50
electricity (6A)	€ 3,50
dog	€ 1,90

Camping Cheques accepted.

Check real time availability and at-the-gate prices...
www.alanrogers.com

FR22210 Camping Bellevue

Route de Pléneuf Val-André, F-22430 Erquy (Côtes d'Armor)

Tel: **02 96 72 33 04**. Email: **campingbellevue@yahoo.fr**

Situated a mile from the beaches between Erquy and Pléneuf Val-André, Camping Bellevue offers a quiet country retreat with easy access to the cliffs of Cap Fréhel, Sables d'Or and St Cast. There are 140 pitches of which 120 are available for touring units, most with electricity (6/10A) and 15 with water and drainage. The site also has 20 mobile homes, chalets and bungalows to rent. A 'Sites et Paysages' member. Children are well catered for at this campsite – there are heated swimming and paddling pools, three play areas and minigolf, petanque and volleyball. Indoor entertainment for all includes theme evenings, Breton dancing and visits to a local cider house. There are numerous walks in the area and a vast range of aquatic sports at nearby Erquy.

Facilities

Two modern, unisex toilet blocks are of a high standard. Some washbasins in cubicles. Facilities for disabled visitors. Dishwashing and laundry facilities. Shop and bar (15/6-10/9). Restaurant and takeaway (12/6-31/8). Swimming and paddling pools (10/5-10/9). Play areas. Pool table. TV room. Table football, video games and library. Minigolf. Petanque. Volleyball. Entertainment and organised activities in high season. Off site: Beach and fishing 2 km. Golf 3 km. Bicycle hire and boat launching 5 km. Riding 6 km.

Open: 31 March - 30 September.

Directions

From St Brieuc road take D786 towards Erquy. Site is adjacent to the D786 at St Pabu and is well signed.

Charges 2006

extra person	€ 3,80 - € 4,80
child (2-13 yrs)	free - € 4,20
Per unit incl. 2 persons	€ 14,20 - € 18,00
electricity	€ 3,20 - € 4,50
dog	€ 1,20 - € 1,60

FR22180 Camping le Coq Hardi

Chef du Bois, F-22450 Hengoat (Côtes d'Armor)

Tel: **02 96 91 55 69**. Email: **campinglecoqhardi@chello.nl**

A small, simple campsite set in the heart of the French countryside. The Dutch owners are sympathetically developing the site which has 21 large touring pitches, all marked and numbered on level grass and with 6A electricity connection. You are made to feel very welcome here and it is a good base from which to explore the Côte d'Armor. Entertainment is provided for children every day in high season by the owner's wife who is a former children's nurse.

Facilities

Modern well equipped sanitary facilities include open style washbasins and spacious showers. Facilities for disabled people and babies. Laundry and dishwashing facilities. Small bar with TV in barn. Small play area. Games room. Entertainment in high season. Off site: Shops, bars, cafés within 2 km. in local villages. Fishing 5km. Golf 10 km.

Open: 1 May – 30 September.

Directions

From the D786 Treguier to Paimpol road take the D20 south to Pouldouran and on to Hengoat. Follow blue camp signs. Site is approx. 3 km. from the D786.

Charges 2006

Per person	€ 4,00
child	€ 2,50
pitch	€ 2,50 - € 6,50
electricity	€ 2,50

FR22230 Camping Bellevue

68 boulevard du Littoral, F-22410 Saint Quay-Portrieux (Côtes d'Armor)

Tel: 02 96 70 41 84. Email: campingbellevue@free.fr

With magnificent coastal views, this attractive and well cared for site lives up to its name. Family-owned for many years, it is situated on the outskirts of the popular seaside resort of St Quay-Portrieux and you will be made to feel most welcome by the friendly owners. There are 173 numbered touring pitches which vary in size, 140 with 6A electricity. Some are separated by hedges, whilst others are in groups of four. Entertainment on site is limited but there is plenty to do and see around the area and a great opportunity for exploring the Goëlo coast.

Facilities

Two clean sanitary blocks provide both open and cubicled washbasins and controllable showers. Facilities for disabled visitors and babies. Laundry and dishwashing facilities. Motorcaravan service point. Shop for basics. Simple snack bar (1/7-16/9). Outdoor pool (1/6-16/9; no Bermuda shorts). Paddling pool. Boules. Play area. Off site: Bicycle hire 1 km. Riding 8 km. Golf 10 km.

Open: 29 April - 16 September.

Directions

From N12 St Brieuc by-pass, take D786 north towards Paimpol. Site is well signed north west of St Quay-Portrieux, 13 km from the by-pass.

Charges 2006

Per person over 7 yrs	€ 3,80 - € 4,65
child	€ 2,80 - € 3,00
pitch	€ 5,50 - € 7,40
electricity (6A)	€ 3,00

FR29000 Yelloh! Village les Mouettes

La Grande Grève, F-29660 Carantec (Finistère)

Tel: 02 98 67 02 46. Email: camping@les-mouettes.com

Les Mouettes is a sheltered site on the edge of an attractive bay with access to the sea at the front of the site. In a wooded setting with many attractive trees and shrubs, the 434 pitches include just 70 for touring units, the remainder being taken by tour operators and around 131 site-owned mobile homes and tents (located together at the top of the site). The touring pitches, mostly arranged in hedged areas in the lower section, are of a good size and all have electricity. The focal point of the site is an impressive heated pool complex.

Facilities

Three clean unisex sanitary blocks include washbasins in cabins, mainly British toilets and baby bathrooms. Facilities for disabled people. Laundry. Motorcaravan services. Shop (limited hours outside the main season). Takeaway. Bar. Pool complex. Games and TV rooms. Play area. Volleyball, two half-courts for tennis and minigolf (in peak season). Table tennis. Entertainment in main season. Large units should phone first. Dogs are not accepted after 26/6. Off site: Fishing 1 km. Golf 2 km. Riding 6 km. Bicycle hire 10 km. Beach 2 km.

Open: 1 May - 9 September.

Directions

From D58 Roscoff - Morlaix road, turn to Carantec on D173. Site is 4 km. from here on the outskirts of the village, signed to the left at roundabout immediately after passing supermarket on right. GPS: N48:39.384 W03:55.484

Charges 2007

Per unit incl. 2 persons, electricity and water	€ 17,00 - € 43,00
extra person	€ 5,00 - € 8,00
child (under 7 yrs)	free - € 4,20

FR29030 Camping du Letty

F-29950 Bénodet (Finistère)

Tel: 02 98 57 04 69. Email: reception@campingduletty.com

The Guyader family have ensured that this excellent and attractive site has plenty to offer for all the family. The site on the outskirts of the popular resort of Bénodet spreads over 22 acres with 493 pitches, all for touring units. Groups of four to eight pitches are set in cul-de-sacs, each group divided by mature hedging and trees. Most pitches have electricity, water and drainage. The site has direct access to a small sandy beach with a floating pontoon (safe bathing depends on the tides).

Facilities

Six well placed toilet blocks are of good quality and include mixed style WCs, washbasins in large cabins and controllable hot showers (charged). Baby rooms. Separate facility for disabled visitors. Launderette. Hairdressing room. Motorcaravan services. Mini-market. Extensive snack bar and takeaway (22/6-30/8). Bar with games room and night club. Fitness centre (no charge). Saunas, jacuzzi and solarium (all on payment). Two tennis and two squash courts (charged). Play area.

Open: 15 June - 6 September.

Directions

From N165 take D70 Concarneau exit. At first roundabout take D44 to Fouesnant. Turn right at T-junction. After 2 km. turn left to Fouesnant (still D44). Continue through La Forêt Fouesnant and Fouesnant, picking up signs for Bénodet. Shortly before Bénodet at roundabout turn left (signed Le Letty). GPS: N47:52.02 W04:05.27

Charges 2007

Per person	€ 5,40
pitch	€ 9,00 - € 11,00

FR29020 Yelloh! Village le Club Saint Laurent

Kerleven, F-29940 La Forêt-Fouesnant (Finistère)

Tel: **02 98 56 97 65**. Email: **info@camping-du-saint-laurent.fr**

Saint Laurent is a well established site, situated on a sheltered wooded slope bordering one of the many attractive little inlets that typify the Brittany coastline. The 260 pitches are on level terraces, under tall trees. All are of average size (100 sq.m.) and divided by hedges and partly shaded, all with electricity connections. Around 50% of the pitches are occupied by tour operators or site owned mobile homes. Pitches with the best sea views tend to be adjacent to the cliff edge and may not be suitable for families with young children. Access to some places can be a little difficult, but the friendly site owners ensure that this is not a problem by offering to site any caravan using their own 4 x 4 vehicle. The swimming pool complex is overlooked by the bar terrace. With organised activities and entertainment in high season, this site is an ideal choice for a lively family holiday, particularly for older children. There is direct access to two small sandy bays, which empty at low tide to reveal numerous rock pools , and the site is on the coastal footpath leading from Kerleven to Concarneau.

Facilities

Two sanitary blocks provide combined shower and washbasin cubicles, separate washbasin cubicles, baby changing and facilities for disabled people. Washing machines, dryers and ironing. Small shop at reception. Bar, snack bar and takeaway. Swimming pools. Gym and sauna. Canoe and boat hire. Basketball. Two tennis courts (no charge). Table tennis. Play area. Entertainment in July/Aug. for adults and children (in English as well as in French), with discos in the bar each evening.

Open: 2 May - 9 September.

Directions

From N165 take D70 Concarneau exit. At first roundabout take first exit D44 (Fouesnant). After 2.5 km. turn right at T-junction, follow for 2.5 km. then turn left (Port La Forêt). Continue to roundabout, straight ahead (Port La Forêt) and after 1 km. turn left (site signed here). In 400 m. left turn to site. GPS: N47:53.770 W03:57.305

Charges 2006

Per unit incl. 1 or 2 persons, electricity and water	€ 16,00 - € 37,00
extra person	€ 2,50 - € 5,50

FR29040 Camping Ar Kleguer

Plage Sainte Anne, F-29250 Saint-Pol-de-Léon (Finistère)

Tel: **02 98 69 18 81**. Email: **info@camping-ar-kleguer.com**

Ar Kleguer is located 20 minutes from the Roscoff ferry terminal in the heart of the Pays du Léon in north Finistère. The site is in two sections – one is in a quiet woodland setting which incorporates a small domestic animal and bird park. The other section is divided into several more open areas at the edge of the sea with spectacular views overlooking the Bay of Morlaix. There are 173 large and well kept pitches, all with 10A electricity connections. Of these, 125 are for touring units. This neat site is decorated with attractive flowers, shrubs and trees and there are tarmac roads.

Facilities

Three modern, tiled toilet blocks are bright, clean and heated when required. Facilities for babies, children and disabled visitors. Laundry room. Shop (July/Aug). Bar and takeaway (July/Aug). Good heated pool complex with paddling pools and slide. Table tennis. Pool table. Tennis. Bicycle hire. Animal park. Play area. Activities for children and some entertainment in high season. Beach adjacent with fishing and sailing. Off site: Restaurant at site entrance. Sailing 800 m. Riding 3 km. Golf 5 km.

Open: Easter - 30 September.

Directions

From Roscoff take D58 to Morlaix. From Morlaix follow signs to Saint-Pol-de-Léon (centre). In the centre follow white 'campings' signs or Plage de Sainte Marie until site signs appear.

Charges 2006

Per person	€ 3,60 - € 4,60
child (2-7 yrs)	€ 2,00 - € 3,00
pitch	€ 4,70 - € 6,50
car	€ 1,60 - € 2,00
electricity (5A)	€ 3,50

FR29010 Castel Camping le Ty Nadan

Route d'Arzano, F-29310 Locunolé (Finistère)
Tel: 02 98 71 75 47. Email: infos@camping-ty-nadan.fr

Mobile homes ▶ page 454

Ty Nadan is a well organised site set amongst wooded countryside along the bank of the River Elle. The 183 pitches for touring units are grassy, many with shade and 99 are fully serviced. The pool complex with slides and paddling pool is very popular as is the large indoor pool complex and an indoor games area with a climbing wall. There is also an adventure play park and a 'Minikids' park for 5-8 year olds, not to mention tennis courts, table tennis, pool tables, archery and trampolines. This is a wonderful site for families with children. Several tour operators use the site. An exciting and varied programme of activities is offered throughout the season – canoe and sea kayaking expeditions, rock climbing, mountain biking, aqua-gym, paintball, riding or walking – all supervised by qualified staff. A full programme of entertainment for all ages is provided in high season including concerts, Breton evenings with pig roasts, dancing, etc. (be warned, you will be actively encouraged to join in!)

Facilities

Two older, split-level toilet blocks are of fair quality and include washbasins in cabins and baby rooms. A newer block provides easier access for disabled people. Washing machines and dryers. Restaurant, takeaway, bar and well stocked shop. Crêperie (July/Aug). Heated outdoor pool (17 x 8 m.) and new indoor pool. Small river beach (unfenced). Indoor badminton and rock climbing facility. Activity and entertainment programmes (high season). Bicycle hire. Boat hire. Fishing. Off site: Beaches 20 minutes by car. Golf 12 km.

Open: 1 April - 7 September.

Directions

Make for Arzano which is northeast of Quimperlé on the Pontivy road and turn off D22 just west of village at camp sign. Site is about 3 km.

Charges 2006

Per person	€ 4,30 - € 8,40
child (under 7 yrs)	€ 1,70 - € 5,20
pitch	€ 8,70 - € 21,00
electricity (10A)	€ 2,60 - € 6,30
dog	€ 1,70 - € 5,20

Less 15-20% outside July/Aug.
Camping Cheques accepted.

kawan
VILLAGES CAMPINGS

tel: 00 333 59 59 03 59   kawan-villages.com

FR29060 Camping Caravaning le Pil-Koad

Route de Douarnenez, Poullan-sur-Mer, F-29100 Douarnenez (Finistère)

Tel: 02 98 74 26 39. Email: info@pil-koad.com

Pil-Koad is an attractive, family run site just back from the sea near Douarnenez in Finistère. It has 190 pitches on fairly flat ground, marked out by separating hedges and of quite good quality, though varying in size and shape. With 100 pitches used for touring units, the site also has a number of mobile homes and chalets. Nearly all pitches have electrical connections and the original trees provide shade in some areas. A large room, the 'Woodpecker Bar', is used for entertainment with discos and cabaret in July/Aug. Weekly outings and clubs for children are organised (30/6-30/8) with a charge included in the tariff. A variety of beaches is within easy reach, with the coast offering some wonderful scenery and good for walking.

Facilities

Two main toilet blocks in modern style include mainly British style WCs and washbasins mostly in cabins. Laundry facilities. Motorcaravan service point. Gas supplies. Small shop for basics (1/4-30/9). Bar, new restaurant and takeaway (all 1/6-5/9). Heated swimming and paddling pools (1/4-30/9, no Bermuda-style shorts). Tennis court. Table tennis. Minigolf. Volleyball. Fishing. Bicycle hire. Playground. Off site: Restaurants in village 500 m. Riding 4 km. Nearest sandy beach 5 km. Douarnenez 6 km.

Open: 1 April - 30 September.

Directions

Site is 500 m. east from the centre of Poullan on D7 road towards Douarnenez. From Douarnenez take circular bypass route towards Audierne; if you see road for Poullan sign at roundabout, take it, otherwise there is a camping sign at turning to Poullan from the D765 road.

Charges 2006

Per person	€ 3,00 - € 4,50
child (under 7 yrs)	€ 1,50 - € 3,00
pitch	€ 6,50 - € 15,00
electricity (10A)	€ 3,50

FR29070 Camping Plage de Trez Rouz

Route de Camaret á la Pointe des Espagnol, Camaret sur Mer, F-29160 Crozon (Finistère)

Tel: 0298 279 396. Email: camping-plage-de-trez-rouz@wanadoo.fr

If you are looking for a restful holiday without swimming pools, televisions and noisy games, Trez Rouz could be just the place for you. Yannick and Isabelle Trouplin aim to keep their campsite, to use their own words, calm and peaceful. The 80 pitches vary in size, trees give shade on many and electricity is a generous 16A. Some are hedged, others have superb views across the bay to Camaret. The site has a comfortable, rural feel. There is a small bar and terrace where Yannick will be pleased to make you a crêpe or a pizza.

Facilities

One toilet block with British style toilets, showers and washing cubicles. Separate building for disabled campers. Washing machine and dryers. Fridges for hire. Bread can be ordered. Very basic groceries from reception. Small bar with snacks lunch and evening. Bicycle hire. Play area with trampoline. Kayak hire. Off site: Camaret 3 km. Riding 5 km. Beach 20 m.

Open: 15 March - 15 October.

Directions

From the RN165 (Brest - Quimper) turn west on D971 at Le Frou towards Corzon. Continue to Camaret and just before town turn right on D355 coast road. Site is signed to right after 3 km. GPS: N48:17.19 W04:33.57

Charges 2006

Per person	€ 3,80 - € 4,60
child (2-7 yrs)	€ 2,20 - € 2,80
pitch	€ 3,20 - € 4,00
electricity (10A)	€ 3,00

FR29050 Castel Camping L'Orangerie de Lanniron

Mobile homes ▶ page 454

Château de Lanniron, F-29336 Quimper (Finistère)
Tel: 02 98 90 62 02. Email: camping@lanniron.com

L'Orangerie is a beautiful and peaceful, family site set in 10 acres of a XVIIth century, 42 acre country estate on the banks of the Odet river, formerly the home of the Bishops of Quimper. The site has 200 grassy pitches (146 for touring units) of three types varying in size and services. They are on flat ground laid out in rows alongside access roads with shrubs and bushes providing pleasant pitches. All have electricity and 88 have all three services. With lovely walks within the grounds, the restaurant and the gardens are both open to the public and in Spring the rhododendrons and azaleas are magnificent. The site is just to the south of Quimper and about 15 km. from the sea and beaches at Bénodet. The family owner's five year programme to restore the park, the original canal, fountains, ornamental 'Bassin de Neptune', the boathouse, the gardens and avenues is very well advanced. The original outbuildings have been attractively converted around a walled courtyard. Used by tour operators (30 pitches). All facilities are available when the site is open.

Facilities

Excellent heated block in the courtyard and second modern block serving the top areas of the site. Facilities for disabled people and babies. Washing machines and dryers. Motorcaravan services. Shop (15/5-9/9). Gas supplies. Bar, snacks and takeaway. New restaurant (open daily). New pool complex of pools. New golf driving range and 9 hole course (with academy). Small play area. Tennis. Minigolf. Table tennis. Fishing. Archery. Bicycle hire. General reading, games and billiards rooms. TV/video room. Karaoke. Outdoor activities. Large room for indoor activities. Off site: Two hypermarkets 1 km. Historic town of Quimper under 3 km. Activities in the area include golf, cycling, walking, fishing, canoeing, surfing and sailing. Beach 15 km.

Open: 15 May - 15 September.

Directions

From Quimper follow 'Quimper Sud' signs, then 'Toutes Directions' and general camping signs, finally signs for Lanniron.

Charges 2006

Per person	€ 4,20 - € 6,50
child (2-10 yrs)	€ 2,70 - € 4,20
pitch (100 sq.m.)	€ 10,20 - € 15,80
with electricity (10A)	€ 13,20 - € 20,00
special pitch (120/150 sq.m.)	
with water and electricity	€ 16,80 - € 25,20
Less 15% outside July/Aug.	

Camping Cheques accepted.

Check real time availability and at-the-gate prices...

www.alanrogers.com

FR29080 Camping le Panoramic

Mobile homes ▶ page 454

Route de la Plage-Penker, F-29560 Telgruc-sur-Mer (Finistère)

Tel: **02 98 27 78 41**. Email: info@camping-panoramic.com

This medium sized traditional site is situated on quite a steep, ten acre hillside with fine views. It is personally run by M. Jacq and his family who all speak good English. The 200 pitches are arranged on flat, shady terraces, in small groups with hedges and flowering shrubs and 20 pitches have services for motorcaravans. Divided into two parts, the main upper site is where most of the facilities are located, with the swimming pool, its terrace and a playground located with the lower pitches across the road. A 'Sites et Paysages' member. Some up-and-down walking is therefore necessary, but this is a small price to pay for such pleasant and comfortable surroundings. This area provides lovely coastal footpaths.

Facilities

The main site has two well kept toilet blocks with another very good block opened for main season across the road. All three include British and Turkish style WCs, washbasins in cubicles, facilities for disabled people, baby baths, plus laundry facilities. Motorcaravan services. Small shop (1/7-31/8). Bar/restaurant with takeaway (1/7-31/8). Barbecue area. Heated pool, paddling pool and jacuzzi (1/6-15/9). Playground. Games and TV rooms. Tennis. Volleyball. Bicycle hire. Off site: Beach and fishing 700 m. Riding 6 km. Golf 14 km. Sailing school nearby.

Open: 1 June - 15 September.

Directions

Site is just south of Telgruc-sur-Mer. On D887 pass through Ste Marie du Ménez Horn. Turn left on D208 signed Telgruc-sur-Mer. Continue straight on through town and site is on right within 1 km. GPS: N48:13.428 W04:22.382

Charges 2006

Per person	€ 5,00
child (under 7 yrs)	€ 3,00
pitch	€ 12,00
electricity (6-10A)	€ 3,10 - € 4,50
water and drainage connection	€ 2,50

Less 20% outside July/Aug.

FR29120 Yelloh! Village le Manoir de Kerlut

F-29740 Plobannalec-Lesconil (Finistère)

Tel: **02 98 82 23 89**. Email: info@yellohvillage-manoir-de-kerlut.com

Le Manoir de Kerlut is a comfortable site in the grounds of a manor house on a river estuary near Pont l'Abbe. The campsite itself has neat, modern buildings and is laid out on flat grass providing 240 pitches (90 for touring units). All have electricity connections, some also have water and drainage and around ten pitches have hardstanding. One area is rather open with separating hedges planted, the other part being amongst more mature bushes and some trees which provide shade. Site amenities are of good quality. A 'Yelloh! Village' member.

Facilities

Toilet facilities in two good blocks (each with several rooms, not all open outside July/Aug), include washbasins all in cabins, and facilities for babies and disabled people. Laundry. Small shop. Takeaway. Large modern bar with TV (satellite) and entertainment all season. Two heated swimming pools, paddling pool and water slide. Sauna, solarium and small gym. Play area. Tennis, badminton and petanque. Games room. Bicycle hire. Off site: Beach 2 km. Fishing 2 km. Riding 5 km. Golf 15 km.

Open: 5 May - 16 September, with all services.

Directions

From Pont l'Abbé, on D785, take D102 road towards Lesconil. Site is signed on the left, shortly after the village of Plobannalec.

Charges 2007

Per unit incl. 2 persons and 5A electricity	€ 17,00 - € 37,00
extra person	€ 5,00 - € 7,00
child (under 10 yrs)	free
electricity (10A)	free - € 2,00

See advertisement on page 32

FR29090 Camping le Raguenès Plage

Mobile homes ▶ page 455

19 rue des Iles, Raguenés, F-29920 Névez (Finistère)
Tel: **02 98 06 80 69**. Email: **info@camping-le-raguenes-plage.com**

Madame Guyader and her family will ensure you receive a warm welcome on arrival at this well kept and pleasant site. Le Raguenès Plage is an attractive and well laid out campsite with many shrubs and trees. The 287 pitches are a good size, flat and grassy, separated by trees and hedges. All have electricity, water and drainage. The site is used by one tour operator (50 pitches), and has 44 mobile homes of its own. A pool complex complete with water toboggan is a key feature and is close to the friendly bar, restaurant, shop and takeaway. From the far end of the campsite a delightful five minute walk along a path and through a cornfield takes you down to a pleasant, sandy beach looking out towards the Ile Verte and the Presqu'île de Raguenès.

Facilities

Two clean, well maintained sanitary blocks include mixed style toilets, washbasins in cabins, baby baths and facilities for disabled visitors. Laundry room. Motorcaravan service point. Small shop (from 15/5). Bar and restaurant (from 1/6) with outside terrace and takeaway. Reading and TV room, internet access point. Heated pool with sun terrace and paddling pool. Sauna (charged). Play areas, table tennis, games room and volleyball. Various activities are organised in July/Aug. Off site: Beach, fishing and watersports 300 m. Supermarket 3 km. Riding 4 km.

Open: 1 April - 16 October.

Directions

From N165 take D24 Kerampaou exit. After 3 km. turn right towards Nizon and bear right at church in village following signs to Névez (D77). Continue through Névez, following signs to Raguenès. Continue for 3 km. to site entrance on left (entrance is quite small and easy to miss). GPS: N47:47. W03:48

Charges 2007

Per unit incl. 2 persons	€ 16,50 - € 28,50
extra person	€ 4,40 - € 5,70
child (under 7 yrs)	€ 2,20 - € 3,30
electricity (2-10A)	€ 3,20 - € 4,60

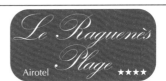

Airotel **Le Raguenès Plage** ★★★★

19, rue des Îles 29920 RAGUENÈZ EN NÉVEZ
Tel : 0033 298 06 80 69 Fax : 0033 298 06 89 05

✓ Heated swimming pool
✓ New water slide
✓ Direct and private access to the beach
✓ Renting of mobil-homes

Low season : 40% reduction

www.camping-le-raguenes-plage.com
info@camping-le-raguenes-plage.com

Direct access to the beach 300 meters

FR29140 Siblu Camping Domaine de Kerlann

Land Rosted, F-29930 Pont-Aven (Finistère)
Tel: **02 98 06 01 77**. Email: **kerlann@siblu.fr**

Haven Europe have, with careful and imaginative planning, ensured that their mobile homes pitches blend naturally into the environment here. The remaining 20% of around 110 touring pitches (80 or 120 sq.m.) have been left in a more natural situation on rough grass with some mature trees providing shade. Land drainage is poor due to the park being situated on low lying ground. Much evening holiday camp style entertainment takes place on the bar terrace with its raised stage.

Facilities

The main large toilet block on the centre of the mobile home area includes washbasins in cubicles. Good laundry. A second block in the touring section opens in high season. Mini-market. Restaurant, snacks and takeaway. Bar. Indoor and outdoor pools. Play areas. Multi-sports court, tennis, minigolf. Video games room and satellite TV in the bar. Children's clubs. Off site: Beach 5 km.

Open: 1 April - 29 October.

Directions

From Tregunc - Pont-Aven road, turn south towards Névez and site is on right.

Charges guide

Per pitch incl. up to 2 persons	
with electricity	€ 13,00 - € 34,00
extra person	€ 3,00 - € 6,00

FR29110 Yelloh! Village la Plage

F-29730 Le Guilvinec (Finistère)

Tel: **02 98 58 61 90**. Email: **info@yellohvillage-la-plage.com**

La Plage is a spacious site located beside a long sandy beach between the fishing town of Le Guilvinec and the watersports beaches of Penmarc'h on the southwest tip of Brittany. It is surrounded by tall trees which provide shelter and is made up of several flat, sandy meadows. The 410 pitches (100 for touring units) are arranged on either side of sandy access roads, mostly not separated but all numbered. There is less shade in the newer areas. Electricity is available on most pitches. Like all beach-side sites, the facilities receive heavy use. Used by tour operators (176 pitches). There is plenty to occupy one at this friendly site but the bustling fishing harbour at Le Guilvinec and the water sports of Penmarc'h and Pointe de la Torche are within easy travelling distance.

Facilities

Five sanitary blocks are of differing designs but all provide modern, bright facilities including washbasins in cabins, good facilities for children and toilets for disabled people. Laundry facilities. Motorcaravan service point. Shop with gas supplies. Bright, airy well furnished bar, crêperie and takeaway. Heated swimming pool with paddling pool and slide. Sauna. Play area. TV room. Tennis courts. Volleyball, basketball, minigolf, badminton, petanque, table tennis, giant chess/draughts. Bicycle hire. Beach. Off site: Fishing and watersports near. Riding 5 km. Golf 20 km.

Open: 31 March - 16 September, with all facilities.

Directions

Site is west of Guilvinec. From Pont l'Abbé, take the D785 road towards Penmarc'h. In Plomeur, turn left on D57 signed Guilvinec. On entering Guilvinec fork right signed Port and camping. Follow road along coast to site on left.

Charges 2007

Per unit incl. 2 persons and 5A electricity	€ 17,00 - € 38,00
extra person	€ 5,00 - € 7,00
child (under 10 yrs)	free - € 5,00
electricity (10A)	free - € 2,00
dog	€ 3,50

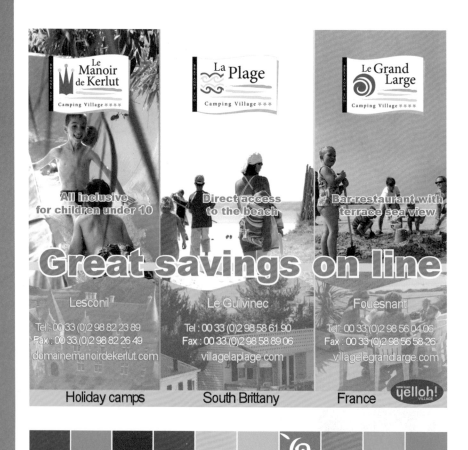

FR29130 Camping des Abers

Dunes de Sainte Marguerite, F-29870 Landéda (Finistère)

Tel: **02 98 04 93 35**. Email: **camping-des-abers@wanadoo.fr**

The location of this delightful twelve acre site is beautiful. Almost at the tip of the Sainte Marguerite peninsula on the north-western shores of Brittany, it is on a wide bay formed between the mouths (abers) of two rivers, L'Aber Wrac'h and L'Aber Benoit. Camping des Abers is set just back from the beach, the lower pitches sheltered from the wind by high hedges or with panoramic views of the bay from the higher places and the new orientation table. There are 180 pitches arranged in distinct areas, many partly shaded and sheltered by mature hedges, trees and flowering shrubs, all planted and carefully tended for over 30 years by the Le Cuff family. Landscaping and terracing where appropriate on the different levels avoids any regimentation or crowding.

Facilities

Three toilet blocks are very clean, with washbasins in cubicles and roomy showers (token from reception €0.80). Good facilities for disabled visitors and babies. Fully equipped laundry. Motorcaravan services. Mini-market (25/5-22/9). Simple takeaway (1/7-31/8). Pizzeria and restaurant next door. Good play area (on sand). Massage. Live music, Breton dancing and Breton cooking classes, and guided walks. Splendid beach. Off site: Miles of coastal walks. Tennis close. Riding 10 km. Golf 30 km.

Open: 28 April - 30 September.

Directions

From Roscoff (D10, then D13), cross river bridge (L'Aber Wrac'h) to Lannilis. Go through town taking road to Landéda and from there signs for Dunes de Ste Marguerite, 'camping' and des Abers. GPS: N48:35.584 W40:36.183

Charges 2007

Per person	€ 3,30
pitch with electricity	€ 8,50

Less 10% outside 15/6-31/8.
Camping Cheques accepted.

FR29440 Camping La Baie du Kernic

Rue de Pen An Theven, 29430 Plouescat, (Finistère)

Tel: **02 98 69 86 60**. Email: **etoplouescat@wanadoo.fr**

This campsite has been recommended by our agent in France and we intend to undertake a full inspection in 2007. La Baie du Kernic is located just 15 minutes from Roscoff, a popular beach resort in Brittany and its white sandy beaches.

Facilities

Bar, Snack bar, Shop, Laundry room. Swimming pool complex with heated outdoor and indoor pool. Paddling pool. TV-Room. Multi-sports ground. Play area. Miniclub for children. Organised activities during the high season. Off site: Tennis. Football. Fishing. Riding. Watersports. Walking. Bicycle hire. Thalassotherapy. Casino.

Open: 7 April - 15 September.

Directions

Site is located on the D788 between Brignogan-Plage and Roscoff and is well signed from Plouescat centre.

Charges 2006

Per unit incl 2 persons and electricity	€ 14.00 - € 29,00
extra person	€ 2,00 - € 4,50
child (under 7 years)	€ 1,70 - € 3,75

33

TRAVEL SERVICE SITE
TO BOOK CALL **0870 405 4055**
Advice & low ferry-inclusive prices

FR29160 Camping les Genets d'Or

Kermerour, Pont Kereon, F-29380 Bannalec (Finistère)

Tel: **02 98 39 54 35**. Email: **Enquiries@holidaybrittany.com**

A jewel of a small site, Les Genets d'Or is situated in a tiny country hamlet at the end of a road from Bannalec, 12 km. from Pont-Aven in Finistère. The spacious surroundings offer a safe haven for young children and a rural, tranquil environment for adults. The gently sloping, grassy site is edged with mature trees and divided into hedged glades with the odd apple tree providing shade. There are only 52 pitches (46 for touring units), all of a good size – some of over 100 sq.m. – and most pitches have electricity, each glade having a water point.

Facilities

The good quality toilet block provides all the necessary amenities and washing facilities, including a shower for disabled campers. Washing machine and dryer. Bar area. Bread delivered in season. Ice pack service. Indoor room with snooker and table tennis. Bicycle hire. Play and picnic area. Caravan storage. Off site: Riding 3 km. Beach 12 km. The village is 15 minutes walk with bars, shop, baker, etc.

Open: Easter/1 April - 30 September.

Directions

Take exit D4 from N165 towards Bannalec. In Bannalec turn right into Rue Lorec (signed Quimperlé) and follow camp signs for 1 km.

Charges 2007

Per person	€ 3,50
child (under 6 yrs)	€ 2,50
pitch	€ 6,00
electricity (6A)	€ 3,00
animal	€ 1,50

FR29170 Camping de la Piscine

Kerleya B.P.12, Beg-Meil, F-29170 Fouesnant (Finistère)

Tel: **02 98 56 56 06**. Email: **contact@campingdelapiscine.com**

There are many campsites in this area but La Piscine is notable for the care and attention to detail that contributes to the well-being of its visitors. Created by the Caradec family from an apple orchard, the 185 level, grass pitches are of generous size and are separated by an interesting variety of hedges and trees. Water, waste and electricity points are provided, normally one stand between two pitches. A quiet site, set back from the sea, La Piscine will appeal to families looking for good quality without too many on site activities.

Facilities

Two refurbished toilet units include British and Turkish style toilets and washbasins in cabins. Facilities for disabled people. Laundry facilities. Motorcaravan service point. Shop. Takeaway (high season). Pool complex with three slides, waterfall and jacuzzi. Sauna and solarium. Play area. BMX track. Football pitch, volleyball, half-court tennis and table tennis. TV room. Entertainment organised in high season. Off site: Beach 1 km. Bicycle hire, fishing and riding within 4 km. Golf 7 km.

Open: 15 May - 15 September.

Directions

Site is 5 km. south of Fouesnant. Turn off the N165 expressway at Coat Conq signed Concarnau and Fouesnant. At Fouesnant join D45 signed Beg Meil and shortly turn left on D145 signed Mousterlin. In 1 km. turn left and follow signs to site. GPS: N47:51.941 W04:00.932

Charges 2007

Per person	€ 3,90 - € 5,75
pitch	€ 7,80 - € 11,50
electricity (3-10A)	€ 3,00 - € 4,40

FR29210 Camping Municipal Bois de la Palud

F-29250 Plougoulm (Finistère)

Tel: **02 98 29 81 82**

This delightful, small municipal site is on the edge of the little village of Plougoulm, about 10 km. southwest of Roscoff. It sits on the brow of a hill with lovely views across the Guillec valley and the sandy bay and estuary to which there is access by footpath. There are 34 reasonably level, numbered pitches grouped in small hedged bays and most have access to 6A electricity (although long leads may be necessary). A small building near the entrance houses reception and sanitary facilities. The season is short – only 15 June - 15 September.

Facilities

All necessary toilet facilities are provided. Play area. Off site: Fishing, bicycle hire, riding and golf, all within 4 km.

Open: 15 June - 15 September.

Directions

On leaving Roscoff, follow signs for Morlaix. After 6 km. take D10 (westward) signed Plouescat and after 3 km. watch for clear camp signs in the village of Plougoulm.

Charges guide

per person	€ 3,00
pitch incl. electricity	€ 5,50
No credit cards.	

FR29190 Camping les Prés Verts

B.P. 612, Kernous-Plage, F-29186 Concarneau Cedex (Finistère)

Tel: **02 98 97 09 74**. Email: **info@presverts.com**

What sets this family site apart from the many others in this region are its more unusual features – its stylish pool complex with Romanesque style columns and statue, and its plants and flower tubs. The 150 pitches are mostly arranged on long, open, grassy areas either side of main access roads. Specimen trees, shrubs or hedges divide the site into smaller areas. There are a few individual pitches and an area towards the rear of the site where the pitches have sea views. A 'Sites et Paysages' member. Concarneau is just 2.5 km. and there are many marked coastal walks to enjoy in the area, plus watersports or boat and fishing trips available nearby.

Facilities

Two toilet blocks provide unisex WCs, but separate washing facilities for ladies and men. Pre-set hot showers and washbasins in cabins for ladies, both closed 9 pm - 8 am. Some child-size toilets. Laundry facilities. Pizza service twice weekly. Heated swimming pool (1/7-31/8) and paddling pool. Playground (0-5 yrs only). Minigolf (charged). Off site: Path to sandy/rocky beach (300 m.) and coastal path. Riding 1 km. Supermarket 2 km. Bicycle hire 3 km. Golf 5 km.

Open: 1 April - 22 September.

Directions

Turn off C7 road, 2.5 km. north of Concarneau, where site is signed. Take third left after Hotel de l'Océan. GPS: N47:53. W03:56

Charges 2007

Per unit incl. 2 persons	€ 16,00 - € 22,00
extra person	€ 4,70 - € 6,50
child (2-7 yrs)	€ 3,10 - € 4,30
electricity (2-6A)	€ 3,20 - € 6,00

Check real time availability and at-the-gate prices...

www.**alanrogers**.com

FR29180 Camping les Embruns

Mobile homes ▶ page 455

Rue du Philosophe Alain, Le Pouldu, F-29360 Clohars-Carnoét (Finistère)

Tel: **02 98 39 91 07**. Email: **camping-les-embruns@wanadoo.fr**

This site is unusual in that it is located in the heart of a village, yet is only 250 metres from a sandy cove. The entrance with its card operated barrier and wonderful floral displays, is the first indication that this is a well tended and well organised site, and the owners have won numerous regional and national awards for its superb presentation. The 180 pitches (100 occupied by mobile homes) are separated by trees, shrubs and bushes, and most have electricity, water and drainage. There is a covered, heated swimming pool, a circular paddling pool and a water play pool. It is only a short walk to the village centre with all its attractions and services. It is also close to beautiful countryside and the Carnoét Forest which are good for walking and cycling.

Facilities

Two modern sanitary blocks, recently completely renewed, include mainly British style toilets, some washbasins in cubicles, baby baths and good facilities for disabled visitors. Family bathrooms. Laundry facilities. Motorcaravan service point. Mini-market and restaurant by site entrance. Bar and terrace (1/7-31/8). Takeaway (20/6-5/9). Covered, heated swimming and paddling pools. Large games hall. Play area. Football field, volleyball and minigolf. Communal barbecue area. Daily activities for children and adults organised in July/Aug.
Off site: Nearby sea and river fishing and watersports. Bicycle hire 50 m. Beach 250 m. Riding 2 km.

Open: 7 April - 15 September.

Directions

From N165 take either 'Kervidanou, Quimperlé Ouest' exit or 'Kergostiou, Quimperlé Centre, Clohars Carnoét' exit and follow D16 to Clohars Carnoét. Then take D24 for Le Pouldu and follow site signs in village. GPS: N47:46 W03:32

Charges 2007

Per unit incl. 2 persons	€ 10,50 - € 15,40
fully serviced pitch	€ 15,90 - € 28,20
extra person	€ 3,90 - € 5,30
child (under 7 yrs)	€ 2,60 - € 3,20
electricity on ordinary pitch	€ 3,90
Less in low seasons.	
Use of motorcaravan services € 4.	

Les Embruns ★★★★

250 m from one of Brittany's sandy beaches Mr & Mrs Leguennou welcome you in their particularly well maintained campsite where you are assured of a good holiday.
• First class facilities and amenities in a green and floral environment • Mobile homes to let
• Motorcaravan service point • Covered heated swimming pool right from the opening •

LE POULDU - F-29360 CLOHARS-CARNOET
TEL: 0033 298 39 91 07 - FAX: 0033 298 39 97 87
www.camping-les-embruns.com
E-mail: camping-les-embruns@wanadoo.fr

FR29220 Camping Municipal de Kerisole

Kerisole, F-29390 Scaer (Finistère)

Tel: **02 98 57 60 91**. Email: **mairie@ville-scaer.fr**

Within walking distance of the pleasant little town of Scaër, Kerisole is an attractive and well kept site, ideal for exploring inland Brittany and yet only 32 km. from the coast. There are 80 mostly level, grass pitches, not hedged, but individually numbered (28 have electricity). Throughout the season the managers, in conjunction with the local council, organise walks, local visits and various activities, many of which are free of charge. With its delightful park-like setting, reasonable charges, and proximity to both town facilities and countryside walks, this site makes an ideal base.

Facilities

Central, clean and tidy sanitary blocks include washbasins in cubicles and separate facilities for men and ladies. Facilities for disabled people. Laundry with free use of washing machine and dryer. Dishwashing sinks. Bread to order and delivered to your pitch. Adjacent play area in grassy field. Marked woodland footpath, which also has a range of 'assault course' obstacles along the way.
Off site: Tennis, basketball and petanque, and indoor swimming pool (free for campers). Scaër with shops, bars and restaurants is a short walk away. Beach 25 km.

Open: 15 June - 15 September.

Directions

From N165 take D70 to Rosporden, then D782 to Scaër. Drive through town centre, following signs for Faouet, and site is on left at traffic lights on leaving town centre. GPS: N48:01 W003:41

Charges 2006

Per person	€ 2,40
child (under 7 yrs)	€ 1,70
pitch	€ 2,90
car	€ 1,60
No credit cards.	

FR29240 Camping de Kéranterec

Route de Port la Forêt, F-29940 La Forêt Fouesnant (Finistère)

Tel: 02 98 56 98 11. Email: info@camping-keranterec.com

A well established family run site with a very French ambience (unlike some of the neighbouring sites which have a much higher UK presence), Keranterec has 265 grassy pitches in two distinct areas. The upper part of the site is more open and has little shade, and is also largely taken up by private mobile homes. The lower and more mature area is predominantly for tourers, with terraced pitches set in a former orchard. Spacious and divided by mature hedging, all pitches have electrical connections (25 m. cable advised) and most also offer water and drainage.

Facilities

Two modern, fully equipped toilet blocks kept very clean include washbasins in cubicles, baby baths and facilities for disabled visitors. Laundry facilities. Small shop and bar (15/6-10/9) and takeaway (1/7-31/8). TV room with satellite. Heated swimming pool (1/6-10/9) with paddling pool, jacuzzi and three slides. Tennis court, boules, volleyball and basketball, table tennis. Play area. In July/Aug. organised events and activities for all the family, and a free children's club. Off site: Attractive sandy beach of Kerleven 10 minutes walk. Golf 1 km. Riding 3 km.

Open: 8 April - 17 September.

Directions

From N165 take D70 Concarneau exit. At first roundabout take D44 signed Fouesnant. After 2.5 km. turn right at T-junction, and follow for 2.5 km. and turn left (Port La Forêt). Continue to roundabout and take second exit (straight ahead), signed Port La Forêt. After 1 km. turn left (site signed), then in 400 m. turn left to site on left. GPS: N47:53.930 W03:57.375

Charges 2006

Per person	€ 7,00 - € 8,00
pitch incl. electricity	€ 12,00 - € 16,00
No credit cards.	

FR29250 Camping Bois des Ecureuils

F-29300 Guilligomarc'h (Finistère)

Tel: 02 98 71 70 98. Email: bois-des-ecureuils@tiscali.fr

Situated in beautiful countryside between the rivers Scorff and Elle, this two star site provides rural camping for those seeking an ideal base from which to explore southern and central Brittany. The site is set in nine acres of natural woodland and open field with oak, chestnut, birch and beech trees providing a leafy backdrop to many of the 40 pitches. With a choice of sunny or shady pitches bordered by shrubs and trees, many pitches have electrical connections.

Facilities

Small toilet block with showers, British and Turkish style WCs, dishwashing and laundry facilities. Reception/shop provides basic groceries and bread to order. Play area. Large grass leisure area with boules pitch, table tennis and badminton net. Bicycle and kayak hire. Off site: Beach 17 km.

Open: 15 May - 15 September.

Directions

From south on N165 take D769 (Lorient) to Carhaix Plouguer - Morlaix road. After 24 km. turn right on D6(E) to Meslan/Arzano. In 700 m. turn left on D6 towards Arzano. After 1 km. turn left on C2 to Guilligomarch and site is on left in 1.1 km. GPS: N47:57. W03:25.

Charges 2006

Per person	€ 3,00
pitch incl. electricity (5A)	€ 7,50
No credit cards.	

FR29260 Camping les Genêts

Rue de Gouesnac'h Nevez, F-29760 Penmarc'h (Finistère)

Tel: 02 98 58 66 93. Email: nohartp@wanadoo.fr

Des Genêts' present owners, Bridgette and Pascal Rohart, bought this old, rural campsite a few years ago and have transformed it beyond recognition. The modem reception is in front of a modestly sized swimming pool that has a section for small children. The toilet block although old but adequate is to be replaced by two new blocks. There are 100 pitches which are divided by trees and hedges and vary in both size and quality. Some in one corner of the site appear to have poor drainage. Around 40 pitches are used for mobile homes which are placed to one side of the campsite.

Facilities

One old but very clean toilet block (with no facilities for disabled visitors) has both British and Turkish style toilets, showers and wash cubicles. This is to be replaced with two new blocks. Laundry room. Bar and snack bar (July/Aug). Bread available (July/Aug). Swimming pool. Play area. Off site: Shops and restaurants 1.5 km. Beach, fishing, boat launching, riding 1.5 km. Golf 3 km.

Open: 1 April - 31 October.

Directions

From Pont l'Abbé, take the D785 southwest towards Penmarc'h. Before the town turn left eastwards on the D53 (Loc Tody) and site is on left in about 2 km. GPS: N47:49.05 W04:18.32

Charges 2006

Per unit incl. 2 persons	€ 10,60 - € 13,60
extra person	€ 3,00 - € 3,60
electricity (10A)	€ 2,50 - € 2,70

37

FR29270 Camping des Dunes

67 rue Paul Langevin, F-29740 Lesconil (Finistère)

Tel: **02 98 58 62 82**. Email: **info@campingdelatorche.fr**

On the edge of the sand dunes near the village of Lesconil, this campsite has the great advantage of providing direct access to an excellent sandy beach. The 120 sandy and grassy pitches have little shade, but are quite spacious and all have electricity. The site is only 800 m. from the village of Lesconil, a delightfully unspoilt fishing port where you can still see the little fishing fleet return each day. There is a good choice of restaurants and cafés, and a 'Centre Nautique' offering range of watersports.

Facilities

Two central, unisex toilet blocks have predominantly British style toilets and washbasins, both open and in cubicles. Baby area. Two toilet/shower rooms for disabled people. Laundry and dishwashing sinks. Washing machine and dryer. Baker's van visits every morning in high season. Play area for younger children. Two trampolines, bowling alley game, volleyball and table tennis. Off site: Tennis nearby. Beach 100 m.

Open: 1 June - 15 September.

Directions

From Pont L'Abbé follow D102 to Lesconil. Just before village (sports stadium on right) - site signed just past stadium. Site approx. 1.5 km. on right, just past Camping de la Grande Plage. GPS: N47:47.49 W04:13.42

Charges 2006

Per unit incl. 2 persons incl. electricity	€ 23,30
extra person	€ 4,60
child (under 7 yrs)	€ 2,85

FR29280 La Pointe Superbe Camping

Route de St Coulitz, F-29150 Châteaulin (Finistère)

Tel: **02 98 86 51 53**. Email: **lapointecamping@aol.com**

La Pointe, just outside Châteaulin, has been lovingly and impressively brought back to life by its delightful English owners Colin Grewer and Sue Dodds. Châteaulin is a bustling market town, 15 km. from the beach at Pentrez and within easy reach of Quimper, medieval Locronan and the Crozon peninsula. Although not endowed with a great deal in terms of amenities, this very tranquil site does boast particularly large, grassy pitches in a quiet valley leading down to the River Aulne, which makes up part of the Nantes - Brest canal. The 60 pitches all have electricity with water close by.

Facilities

The first-class toilet block, kept very clean at all times, has many washbasins in cubicles. Shower cubicles are somewhat small but have full adjustable hot and cold taps. Large room with facilities for disabled visitors. Baby bathroom. Motorcaravan service point. Play area. Table tennis, volleyball and large activity room with basketball, badminton and children's corner. Off site: Châteaulin 700 m. Riding and tennis nearby. Fishing in the Aulne (permit needed). Beach 9 km.

Open: 6 March - 31 October.

Directions

Site is just southeast of Châteaulin. From the bridge over the river in town centre follow signs for St Coulitz and Quimper. Shortly turn left signed St Coulitz. Site is clearly signed at this point and is 100 m. on the right.

Charges 2006

Per unit incl. 2 persons	€ 14,00
extra person	€ 3,00
electricity (10A)	€ 2,50
No credit cards.	

FR29290 Yelloh! Village le Grand Large

48 route du Grand Large, Mousterlin, F-29170 Fouesnant (Finistère)

Tel: **02 98 56 04 06**. Email: **info@yellohvillage-grand-large.com**

Le Grand Large is a beach-side site situated on the Pointe de Mousterlin in natural surroundings. The site is separated from the beach by the road that follows the coast around the point. It is also protected from the wind by an earth bank with trees and a fence. There are 300 pitches with just 54 rather small uneven places used for tourers. Tour operators take 70 pitches and the site itself has tents and mobile homes to rent. Electricity is available everywhere (long leads useful) and some pitches have drainage. A small river runs through the site but it is fenced.

Facilities

Two neat toilet blocks, the largest only opened in high season, include plenty of washbasins in cabins. Facilities for children in the larger block, for disabled people in both. Laundry facilities. Bar overlooking the sea with attractive terrace. Crêperie/grill restaurant including takeaway. Swimming pool with paddling pool, water slides in separate pool. Tennis court and multi-sport court. Small play area. TV and games rooms. Bicycle hire. Off site: Beach and fishing 100 m. Golf and riding 5 km.

Open: 31 March - 16 September (with all services).

Directions

Site is 7 km. south of Fouesnant. Turn off N165 expressway at Coat Conq, signed Concarneau and Fouesnant. At Fouesnant take A45 signed Beg Meil, then follow signs to Mousterlin, then camping signs.

Charges 2007

Per unit incl. 2 persons and 5A electricity	€ 17,00 - € 37,00
extra person	€ 5,00 - € 7,00
electricity (10A)	€ 1,00

See advertisement on page 32

FR29310 Camping la Roche Percée

Hent Kerveltrec, Beg-Meil, F-29170 Fouesnant (Finistère)
Tel: **02 98 94 94 15**. Email: **contact@camping-larochepercee.com**

Close to the beautiful Brittany coastline, La Roche Percée combines a tranquil setting with a friendly and active family environment, only 400 metres from the beach. There are 123 pitches, of which 80 are for touring units, the rest being for privately owned or site owned mobile homes. Pitches are arranged in cul-de-sacs off a central area and are of a good size, grassy and flat, all with electrical connections (some may require a long lead). All pitches are separated by mature hedging, and some benefit from the shade of the variety of trees planted around the site.

Facilities

The clean, tidy central toilet block includes mostly British style toilets, washbasins in cubicles, dishwashing and laundry sinks. Baby bath and changing area. Wheelchair access provided on request. Motorcaravan service point. Small shop, snack bar and bar (open 15/5-15/9, with bread to order outside these dates, which can be flexible if busy.) Swimming pools (all season). Two play areas. Football and volleyball. Large trampoline (parental supervision essential!) Bicycle hire. Off site: Beach 400 m. Sailing school, golf and riding nearby.

Open: 2 April - 26 September.

Directions

From N165 take D70 Concarneau exit. At first roundabout take first exit on D44 (signed Fouesnant, Benodet). Following D44, turning right at T-junction, after 2 km. turn left and follow through Forêt Fouesnant. About 2 km. after village are two roundabouts. Go straight over first (smaller) one and turn left at second on D45 to Beg-Meil. After 3 km. site is signed on left.

Charges 2006

Per adult	€ 3,50 - € 4,50
child (under 7 yrs)	€ 2,50
pitch incl. electricity	€ 12,50 - € 14,50

FR29340 Camping de la Côte des Légendes

Keravezan BP 36, F-29890 Brignogan-Plages (Finistère)
Tel: **02 98 83 41 65**. Email: **camping-cote-des-legendes@wanadoo.fr**

Located just behind a safe, sandy beach on the Bay of Brignogan and adjacent to a Centre Nautique (sailing, windsurfing, kayak), this site is ideal for a family seaside holiday. It is a quiet site with 147 level pitches arranged in rows and protected by hedges. There are a few mobile homes and chalets for rent but no tour operators. A shop, bar and takeaway are open in high season when activities are arranged for adults and children by the helpful owner (good English is spoken). The beach of fine sand can be reached directly from the site.

Facilities

Main toilet facilities are at the rear of the site in a large block that provides washbasins in cubicles, baby baths and facilities for disabled visitors. Dishwashing and laundry sinks. Motorcaravan service point. The upper floor provides a games room with views of the sea. Further toilet facilities are at the reception building, also a laundry. Bar, small shop and takeaway (July/Aug). Playground and playing field. Table tennis. Off site: Watersports centre. Village services 700 m. Bicycle hire 1 km. Riding 6 km.

Open: Easter - 1 November.

Directions

From Roscoff take the D58 towards Morlaix and after 6 km. turn right on the D10 towards Plouescat and then Plouguerneau. Turn right on the D770 to Brignogan-Plages. In the main street go straight on following signs for site and Club Nautique.

Charges 2006

Per unit incl. 2 persons	€ 9,90 - € 12,50
extra person	€ 3,05 - € 3,75
child (1-13 yrs)	€ 2,80 - € 3,75
electricity	€ 1,00 - € 3,10

FR29370 Camping de la Torche

Roz an Tremen, F-29120 Plomeur (Finistère)
Tel: **02 98 58 62 82**. Email: **info@campingdelatorche.fr**

Probably a 'must stay' site for surfers, this rural, wooded campsite, like so many in this part of Brittany, comes to life in July and August. The natural beauty of the wide sandy beaches of La Torche can be accessed direct from the site via a footpath. La Torche is internationally renowned as a paradise for all boardsports, particularly windsurfing. The site has 155 pitches (115 for tourers), divided by trees and hedges and tending to the generous in size. Around 40 chalets and mobile homes are discreetly positioned amongst the trees.

Facilities

The single, very good toilet block provides British style toilets, showers, washing cubicles and good facilities for disabled visitors. Washing machine and dryer. Play area. Shop (1/7-31/8). Bar and terrace, with snacks (1/7-31/8). Swimming pool (20/6-15/9). Animation in July/Aug. Off site: Plomeur 3 km. Beach and fishing 1.5 km.

Open: 1 April - 30 September.

Directions

From Pont l'Abbé the D785 south to Plomeur, then follow signs for Pointe de La Torche. After 3 km. site is signed to left. GPS: N47:49.58 W04:19.32

Charges 2006

Per person	€ 3,20 - € 4,50
child (0-7 yrs)	€ 2,00 - € 2,80
pitch incl. electricity (5A)	€ 8,80 - € 11,20

39

FR29330 Camping la Corniche

F-29710 Plozévet (Finistère)

Tel: **02 98 91 33 94**. Email: **infos@campinglacorniche.com**

A well presented site, La Corniche is conveniently placed for both coast – with some sandy beaches – and the delights of inland Brittany. The owners speak minimal English, but are good at sign language! Large level fields are divided into smaller areas by mature hedging and there is some shade from trees. There are 120 grass pitches with 6A electricity available to touring units, with some mobile homes as well. The town of Plozévet is a ten minute stroll away. There are several restaurants, most specialising in galettes and other typically Breton food, bars and a small supermarket. This site would be ideal for those wishing to get away from the busiest tourist areas.

Facilities

Toilet facilities are excellent, one block having being completely rebuilt. Comprehensively equipped, they include individual wash cubicles. Roof lights create a light and airy feel. Provision for those with disabilities. Small shop (from May). Bar (from May) and takeaway (July/Aug). Swimming pool and paddling pool. Off site: Village within walking distance. Beach 2 km.

Open: 31 March - 30 September.

Directions

Head west from Quimper and pick up the D784 towards Landudec and Plozévet. After 26 km. where the road makes a sharp right in the centre of Plozévet, take a left (caravan site sign partially obscured on the corner) towards the coast (Plage). The site is on the right after 1 km.

Charges 2007

Per pitch with electricity	€ 8,40 - € 9,20
person	€ 3,80 - € 4,50
child (under 7 yrs)	€ 2,20 - € 3,00

Camping La Corniche

In an attractive landscaped setting at Audierne Bay, half way between Quimper and the Raz headland, the Penmarch headland and Locronan, camp site La Corniche offers a high standard of comfort and a friendly atmosphere.

Camping La Corniche - Route de la Corniche - 29710 Plozévet - France
Tel: +33 (0)2 98 91 33 94 - Fax: +33 (0)2 98 91 41 53
info@campinglacorniche.com
www.campinglacorniche.com

FR29390 Camping de Keranquernat

Rue des Grandes Sables, Le Pouldu, F-29360 Clohars-Carnöet (Finistère)

Tel: **02 98 39 92 32**. Email: **camping.keranquernat@wanadoo.fr**

The first impression that one gets when arriving at this simple, immaculate campsite is of flowers everywhere, even in the toilet block. The second impression will be the warm welcome that you will receive from Nicole and Michel Le Guennou. The 90 touring pitches are immaculate and clearly divided with bushes and flowering shrubs. Pitch size ranges from medium to large, many having shade from the numerous trees and 60 with electricity (3/5A). There is a basic, well kept pool and paddling pool. On site entertainment is simple with a games room, a small play area and a TV set.

Facilities

The single, very clean toilet block has been modernised. British style WCs, showers and washbasins in cubicles but no facilities for disabled people. Laundry with washing machine and dryer. Swimming and paddling pools (heated July/Aug). Games room with billiards, table tennis and TV. Off site: Shop in nearby Le Pouldu. Beach and fishing 700 m. Riding 800 m. Bicycle hire 500 m. Golf 12 km.

Open: 20 May - 5 September.

Directions

On the N165 travelling northwest from Lorient, take exit for Guidel. In 1 km. turn west on D224, then follow signs for Le Pouldu, Site is signed at entrance to town. GPS: N47:46.21 W03:32.36

Charges 2006

Per person	€ 3,50
child (0-7 yrs)	€ 2,50
pitch	€ 7,50
electricity (3/5A)	€ 3,00 - € 3,50

FR29410 Camping Domaine de Ker Ys

Pentrez Plage, F-29550 Saint Nic (Finistère)

Tel: 02 98 26 53 95. Email: camping-kerys@wanadoo.fr

Domaine De Ker Ys is a site especially suited to families with young children. Here there are many imaginative play areas on the site and miles of wide sandy beach 20 metres away. The site has no bar or restaurant, but the pool complex is very good with its slides, fountains and paddling pools, and a little entertainment is organised in high season. The 121 touring pitches vary in size, some being in open groups of four or five, others being divided by hedges. The site is pleasantly laid out with many trees giving shade. This site's main attraction is its close proximity to the magnificent beaches.

Facilities

Three unisex toilet blocks have British style toilets, showers and washbasins in cabins. Facilities for disabled visitors. Washing machines and dryers. Some groceries in reception, bread (July/Aug). Play area. Mini-tennis. TV and games rooms. Off site: Shops, bars and restaurants nearby (but not many). Riding 15 km. Beach 20 m.

Open: 1 May - 24 September.

Directions

From the N165 (Quimper – Brest) take exit west at Châteaulin on D887 towards Crozon. Turn left to Saint Nic, then follow signs for Penthez Plage and site. At the promenade turn left and site is 300 m. on the left. GPS: N48:11.32 W04:18.04

Charges 2006

Per unit incl. 1 or 2 persons	€ 12,00 - € 20,00
extra person	€ 3,60 - € 5,30
child (2-7 yrs)	€ 2,10 - € 3,00
electricity	€ 3,20

FR29380 Yelloh! Village Port de Plaisance

7 route de Quimper, F-29950 Bénodet (Finistère)

Tel: 02 98 57 02 38. Email: info@campingbenodet.fr

Sometimes larger campsites can lack ambiance, but it is not so with Port de Plaisance. This is a delightful, family run site with 340 pitches of which 100 are for touring campers. The pitches are mostly in two areas, where they are hedged and positioned in small groups amongst the many mature trees and flowering shrubs. Although there are five holiday tour operators on site, their presence is unobtrusive because of careful positioning amongst the trees. This is truly a campsite with something for everybody, with a wide range of entertainment and activities provided over a long season. The restaurant that overlooks the pool complex boasts a very good menu. There is entertainment suitable for all ages, from up-to-date films to taster aquadiving lessons in the pool. An additional covered pool is planned for the 2007 season. The marina at the mouth of the Odet river is 500 m. away, and from here you can enjoy a boat trip up to Quimper. The large seaside town of Benodet, with all the shops, bars and restaurants that you could wish for is just 1 km.

Facilities

Three toilet blocks, older and simple in style, include British style toilets, showers and washing cubicles. Baby room. Facilities for disabled visitors. Laundry room. Shop (15/5-15/9). Bar. Restaurant and takeaway (15/5-15/9). Swimming pool complex with flumes and toboggan. Games room. Programme of entertainment. Taster diving lessons in the pool. Multi-sports court. Bicycle hire. Off site: Benodet 1 km. Beach and fishing 1 km. Riding 2 km. Golf 3 km.

Open: 15 May - 23 September.

Directions

Take the D34 south from Quimper. Site is on the left just as you enter Benodet. GPS: N47:52.56 W04:06.12

Charges 2006

Per unit incl. 2 persons and electricity (6A)	€ 16,00 - € 33,00
extra person	€ 3,00 - € 7,00
child (0-7 yrs)	free - € 3,50

Check real time availability and at-the-gate prices...

www.alanrogers.com

FR35010 Camping le Bois Coudrais

F-35270 Cuguen (Ille-et-Vilaine)

Tel: **02 99 73 27 45**. Email: **info@vacancebretagne.com**

This gem of a campsite, owned and run by a delightful couple from Jersey, is the kind of small, rural site that is becoming a rarity in France. It has 25 medium to large, well kept, grassy pitches, some divided by young shrubs, others by mature trees. They are spread over three small fields, one of which has an area set aside for ball games and is also home to a group of friendly goats and some chickens – a magnet for children. Electrical connections are possible in most areas. In the small bar, Claire is happy to prepare and serve a selection of home-made meals.

Facilities

The toilet block beside the house provides washbasins in cubicles, showers and sinks for dishwashing and laundry, plus facilities for disabled visitors. Bar with meals (May-Sept). Small heated swimming pool. Play area on grass. Animal enclosure. Table tennis. Bicycle hire. Games field. Internet access. Off site: Shop in village 0.5 km. Comborug 5 km. Fishing 5 km. Golf and riding 15 km. Beach 20 km.

Open: 1 May - 30 September.

Directions

From St Malo take the N137 (in the direction of Rennes) to Combourg. Follow signs on D83 for Fougères and Mont St Michel. Site is 0.5 km. past Cuguen on the left, well signed. GPS: N48:27.237 W01:39.08

Charges 2006

Per person	€ 2,75
child (0-12 yrs)	€ 2,35
pitch incl. electricity	€ 11,00

FR35000 Camping le Vieux Chêne

Mobile homes ▶ page 455

Baguer-Pican, F-35120 Dol-de-Bretagne (Ille-et-Vilaine)

Tel: **02 99 48 09 55**. Email: **vieux.chene@wanadoo.fr**

This attractive, family owned site is situated between Saint Malo and Mont Saint Michel. Developed in the grounds of a country farmhouse dating from 1638, its young and enthusiastic owner has created a really pleasant, traditional atmosphere. In spacious, rural surroundings it offers 199 good sized pitches on gently sloping grass, most with 10A electricity, water tap and light. They are separated by bushes and flowers, with mature trees for shade. A very attractive tenting area (without electricity) is in the orchard. Used by a Dutch tour operator (10 pitches). There are three lakes in the grounds and centrally located leisure facilities include a restaurant with a terrace overlooking an attractive pool complex. Some entertainment is provided in high season, which is free for children.

Facilities

Three very good, unisex toilet blocks, which can be heated, include washbasins in cabins, a baby room and facilities for disabled people. Small laundry. Motorcaravan services. Shop, takeaway and restaurant (15/5-15/9). Heated swimming pool, paddling pool, slides (15/5-15/9; lifeguard July/Aug). TV room (satellite) and games room. Tennis court. Minigolf. Giant chess. Play area. Riding in July/Aug. Fishing. Off site: Supermarket in Dol 3 km. Golf 12 km. Beach 20 km.

Open: 31 March - 22 September.

Directions

Site is by the D576 Dol-de-Bretagne - Pontorson road, just east of Baguer-Pican. It can be reached from the new N176 taking exit for Dol-Est and Baguer-Pican. GPS: N48:32.972 W01:41.03

Charges 2007

Per person	€ 4,50 - € 5,75
child (under 13 yrs)	free - € 3,90
pitch with electricity	€ 10,00 - € 21,50

FR35040 Camping le P'tit Bois

Saint Malo, F-35430 Saint Jouan des Guerets (Ille-et-Vilaine)

Tel: 02 99 21 14 30. Email: camping.ptitbois@wanadoo.fr

On the outskirts of Saint Malo, this neat, family oriented site is very popular with British visitors, being ideal for one night stops or for longer stays in this interesting area. Le P'tit Bois provides 274 large level pitches with 114 for touring units. In two main areas, either side of the entrance lane, these are divided into groups by mature hedges and trees, separated by shrubs and flowers and with access from tarmac roads. Nearly all have electrical hook-ups and over half have water taps. Behind reception, an attractive, sheltered terraced area around the complex of heated indoor and outdoor pools provides a focus during the day along with a bar and snack bar. There are site-owned mobile homes and chalets but this does mean that the facilities are open over a long season (if only for limited hours).

Facilities

Two fully equipped toilet blocks, include washbasins in cabins. Baby baths. Laundry facilities. Simple facilities for disabled people. Motorcaravan service point. Small shop (from 1/5). Bar with entertainment in July-Aug. Snack bar with takeaway. TV room. Games rooms. Heated swimming pool, paddling pool and two water slides (from 1/5). Heated indoor pool (from 8/4). Playground. Multi-sports court. Tennis court, minigolf. Charcoal barbecues not permitted. Off site: Beach, fishing 1.5 km. Buses 2 km. Bicycle hire or riding 5 km. Golf 15 km.

Open: 7 April - 8 September.

Directions

St Jouan is west off the St Malo - Rennes road (N137) just outside St Malo. Site is signed from the N137 (exit St Jouan on the D4).
GPS: N48:36.579 W01:59.27

Charges 2007

Per person	€ 5,00 - € 8,00
child (under 7 yrs)	€ 3,00 - € 6,00
pitch and car	€ 8,00 - € 19,00
electricity (6A)	€ 4,00

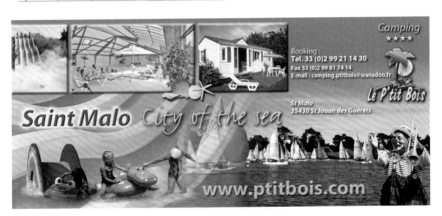

FR35020 Castel Camping le Domaine des Ormes

Epiniac, F-35120 Dol-de-Bretagne (Ille-et-Vilaine)

Tel: 02 99 73 53 00. Email: info@lesormes.com

This impressive site is in the northern part of Brittany, about 30 km. from the old town of Saint Malo, in the grounds of the Château des Ormes. In an estate of wooded parkland and lakes it has a pleasant atmosphere, busy in high season but peaceful at other times, with a wide range of facilities. The 800 pitches are divided into a series of different sections, each with its own distinctive character and offering a choice of terrain – flat or gently sloping, wooded or open. Only 150 pitches, all with electricity, are used for touring units and there is a variety of other accommodation available.

Facilities

The toilet blocks are of fair standard, including washbasins in cabins and ample facilities for disabled people. Motorcaravan services. Shop, bar, restaurant, pizzeria and takeaway. Games room, bar and disco. Two traditional heated swimming pools and Aqua park. Adventure play area. Golf. Bicycle hire. Fishing. Equestrian centre with riding. Minigolf. Two tennis courts. Sports ground with volleyball, etc. Paintball, Archery. Cricket club.

Open: 19 May - 9 September, with all services.

Directions

Access road leads off main D795 about 7 km. south of Dol-de-Bretagne, north of Combourg.
GPS: N48:29 W01:43

Charges 2006

Per person	€ 4,95 - € 7,25
child (under 13 yrs)	free - € 4,00
pitch incl. vehicle	€ 19,95 - € 29,25
electricity 3/6A	€ 3,80 - € 4,30
water and drainage	free - € 2,00
Less 10% outside July/Aug.	

43

FR35050 Domaine de la Ville Huchet

Route de la Passagère, Quelmer, F-35400 Saint Malo (Ille-et-Vilaine)

Tel: **02 99 73 53 00**. Email: info@villehuchet.com

Domaine de la Ville Huchet is a friendly, former municipal site which has been taken over by the owners of FR35020 Les Ormes. It is being progressively overhauled by its new owners and is a useful site on the edge of St Malo, with easy access to the ferry terminal, old town and beaches. Some road noise is audible from the St Malo by-pass. Pitches are on level ground set around the old manor house at the centre of the site. Most pitches have electricity (6A), and there is shade from mature trees in some areas. Amenities include a small, well-stocked shop and a bar. The large pool is attractively landscaped and has a number of water slides. Mobile homes for rent.

Facilities	Directions
The sanitary blocks are old and undergoing renovation but were clean when we visited. Facilities for disabled visitors. Bar and snack bar. Shop. Aqua park with water slides. Football pitch. Bicycle hire. Animation programme in peak season (including live bands). Play area. Off site: Aquarium 700 m. St Malo (beaches, ferry terminal and old town) 4 km.	From St Malo take D301 heading south. Join D165 signed Quelmer and the site is well signed (2 km).

Open: 1 May - 15 September.

Charges 2007

Per person	€ 3,45 - € 5,20
child (1-7 yrs)	€ 2,30 - € 3,10
pitch	€ 9,00 - € 12,40
electricity	€ 3,65 - € 4,40

Holiday resort in Saint-Malo

For your events, rent a room full of character.
On a 6 hectare estate, 4 km from the beaches.

- Campsite *** • Aquatic Park
- Renting of Mobile-homes O'HARA
- Renting of Apartments

Rte de la Passagère. 35400 St Malo
Tél. 33(0)2 99 81 11 83 • Fax 33(0)2 99 81 51 89
E-mail : info@lavillehuchet.com
Internet : www.lavillehuchet.com

Domaine de la Ville Huchet***

FR35060 Camping la Touesse

F-35800 St Lunaire (Ille-et-Vilaine)

Tel: **02 99 46 61 13**. Email: camping.la.touesse@wanadoo.fr

This family campsite was purpose built and has been developed since 1987 by Alain Clement who is keen to welcome more British visitors. Set just back from the coast road, 300 metres from a sandy beach, it is in a semi-residential area. It is, nevertheless, an attractive, sheltered site with a range of trees and shrubs. The 142 level, grass pitches in bays (95 for touring units) have electricity and are accessed by circular tarmac roads. The plus factor of this site, besides its proximity to Dinard, is the fine sandy beach which is sheltered – so useful in early season – and safe for children. The owners speak English.

Facilities	Directions
The central toilet block is well maintained, heated in low season with all modern facilities. Part of it may not be open outside July/Aug. Baby bath and toilet for disabled people. Dishwashing sinks. Laundry facilities. Motorcaravan service point. Shop for basics (1/4-20/9). Pleasant bar/restaurant with TV. Volleyball, table tennis and video games for children. Sauna. Off site: Buses 100 m. Sandy beach, fishing 300 m. Riding 500 m. Bicycle hire 1 km. Golf 4 km. Many amenities near.	From Dinard take D786 coast road towards St Lunaire; watch for site signs to the left.

Open: 1 April - 30 September.

Charges 2007

Per person	€ 4,00 - € 5,10
child (under 7 yrs)	€ 2,40 - € 2,90
pitch with electricity	€ 8,20 - € 9,80
dog	€ 1,50

No credit cards.

44

FR35070 Camping Longchamp

Boulevard de Saint Cast, F-35800 Saint Lunaire (Ille-et-Vilaine)

Tel: 02 99 46 33 98. Email: contact@camping-longchamp.com

Michel Roult is justifiably proud of his campsite which lies on the 'Emerald Coast', just 100 m. from a magnificent sandy beach. Set in a wooded area and divided into three sections, this site feels like being in a large landscaped garden. Pitches are large and well kept with 240 for touring. Some hedging and shade is provided by Cypress trees and 140 have electricity. The restaurant on site has a cosy atmosphere, an extensive menu and is run by a 'Michelin' recommended chef. Mr Roult's aim is to keep the site simple and peaceful and as a result many families return year after year.

Facilities

Two very clean toilet blocks with washbasins in cabins and open-style and large showers. Covered dishwashing area. Laundry facilities. Restaurant, bar and takeaway. Small shop. Games room and TV. Play area with bouncy castle (Juy/Aug). Minigolf and tennis. Boules. Some entertainment in high season. Torches useful. Off site: Golf 2 km. Riding 4 km. Bicycle hire 6 km.

Open: Easter - 10 September.

Directions

Leave St Maloon D301 and follow signs for Dinard. Turn west onto D168. Keep west onto D603 and in approx. 3 km. turn north on D503 (St Lunaire). Site signed from village. GPS: N48:31.01 W02:07.15

Charges 2006

Per person	€ 5,20
child (under 7 yrs)	€ 3,00
pitch	€ 5,80
electricity (4/10A)	€ 2,70 - € 3,90

FR44020 Camping Municipal du Moulin

Route de Nantes, F-44190 Clisson (Loire-Atlantique)

Tel: 02 40 54 44 48

This good value, small site is conveniently located on one of the main north - south routes on the edge of the interesting old town of Clisson. A typical municipal site, it is useful for short stays. There are 45 good sized, marked and level pitches with electricity and divided by hedges and trees giving a good degree of privacy and some shade. There is also an unmarked area for small tents. A barbecue and camp fire area is to the rear of the site above the river where one can fish or canoe.

Facilities

The fully equipped toilet block, cleaned each afternoon, includes some washbasins in cabins and others in a separate large room, with hot and cold water. Unit for disabled visitors. Dishwashing and laundry facilities. Bread delivered daily. Table tennis, volleyball, and small playground. No double axle or commercial vehicles accepted. Off site: Supermarket with cheap fuel just across the road. Bicycle hire, riding 5 km. Sailing 15 km. Golf 30 km.

Open: Mid April - mid October.

Directions

From N249 Nantes - Cholet road, take exit for Vallet/Clisson and D763 south for 7 km. then fork right towards Clisson town centre. At roundabout after passing Leclerc supermarket on your right take second exit (into site). GPS: N47:05.742 W01:16.965

Charges 2006

Per unit incl. 1 person and electricity	€ 7,58 - € 8,00
extra person	€ 2,37 - € 2,50
child (0-7 yrs)	€ 1,58 - € 1,67

FR44050 Camping les Ecureuils

24, avenue Gilbert Burlot, F-44760 La Bernerie en Retz (Loire-Atlantique)

Tel: 02 40 82 76 95. Email: contact@camping-les-ecurevils.com

Just 350 metres from both the sea and the centre of the little town of La Bernerie, Les Ecureuils is a family run site. The sandy beach here is great for children; swimming is restricted to high tide, since the sea goes out a long way, but at low tide you can join the locals in collecting shellfish from the rocks. The site has 167 touring pitches, all with electricity (10A) close by and 19 with their own water tap and drain. There are also 80 mobile homes and chalets for rent and a further 70 privately owned.

Facilities

Four toilet blocks are in traditional French style; some have controllable showers and washbasins in cubicles. Facilities for disabled visitors are not all easily accessible. Very basic baby room. All is kept fairly clean but lacking attention to detail. Bar with terrace - also sells bread (15/6-31/8). Snack bar and takeaway (July/Aug). Swimming pools (15/5-15/9). Playground. Off site: Shops, restaurants and bars 350 m. Also beach, fishing, sailing and boat launching. Golf, riding and bicycle hire 6 km.

Open: 1 May - 15 September.

Directions

La Bernerie-en-Retz is 5 km. south of Pornic and 26 km. south of the Saint Nazaire bridge. From the D213/D13 (St Nazaire - Noirmoutier) turn west on D66 to La Bernerie. Site is signed to right by railway station before reaching town. GPS: N47:05.070 W02:02.200

Charges 2006

Per unit incl. 2 persons	€ 14,00 - € 26,00
extra person	€ 4,00 - € 6,50
child 92-10 yrs)	€ 3,00 - € 5,00
electricity (10A)	€ 4,00

45

FR44060 Camping de la Madrague

Sainte Marie de la Mer, F-44210 Pornic (Loire-Atlantique)

Tel: **02 40 82 06 73**. Email: **campinglamadrague@wanadoo.fr**

Close to the fishing village of Pornic, this pleasant site has direct access to two attractive rocky coves below – indeed it boasts that it is the only campsite in Pornic that is close to the seashore. The 89 touring pitches are on land sloping gently towards the cliff edge and all have sea views, whilst 137 mobile homes, of which 37 are for rent, lie further back. Electricity (3, 6 or 10A) is available to all. This is not a sophisticated site, but everything is neat and well cared for and all the information in reception is beautifully presented.

Facilities

The main sanitary block is kept very clean. Pre-set showers and some washbasins in cabins; washbasins have either cold or warm water (clearly labelled); En-suite unit for disabled visitors. Baby room. Washing machine and dryer. Small shop (all season). Bar with snack bar and takeaway (July/Aug). Play area. Good programme of activities for children and adults (July/Aug). Bicycle hire. Off site: Sailing and golf 3 km. Riding 4 km. Freshwater fishing 10 km.

Open: 1 April - 30 September.

Directions

From D213 (St Nazaire - Noirmoutier) north of Pornic turn south on D286 towards Ste Marie de la Mer but avoid village centre. Take first exit at roundabout, then turn left on Rue du Moulin Neuf and right along Rue des Bougrenets (site signed). Continue ahead at roundabout to site on left. GPS: N47:06.966 W02:09.354

Charges 2006

Per unit incl. 2 persons	€ 15,00 - € 20,00
extra person	€ 3,00 - € 4,50
child (under 7 yrs)	€ 2,00 - € 3,50
electricity (3/6A)	€ 3,00 - € 3,50

FR44040 Castel Camping le Parc Sainte-Brigitte

Domaine de Bréhet, F-44420 La Turballe (Loire-Atlantique)

Tel: **02 40 24 88 91**. Email: **saintebrigitte@wanadoo.fr**

Le Parc Sainte-Brigitte is a well established site in the attractive grounds of a manor house, three kilometres from the beaches. It is a spacious site with 150 good pitches, 110 with electricity and 25 also with water and drainage. Some are arranged in a circular, park-like setting near the entrance, others are in wooded areas under tall trees and the remainder are on more open grass in an unmarked area near the pool. This is a quiet place to stay outside the main season, whilst in high season, it can become very busy. Used by a tour operator (12 pitches). In high season it is mainly used by families with its full share of British visitors. One can walk around many of the areas of the estate not used for camping; there are farm animals to see and a fishing lake is very popular.

Facilities

The main toilet block, supplemented by a second block, is of good quality. They include washbasins in cabins and two bathrooms. Laundry facilities and lines provided. Motorcaravan services. Small shop. Pleasant restaurant/bar with takeaway (both 15/5-15/9). Heated swimming pool with retractable roof and paddling pool. Playground. Bicycle hire. Boules, volleyball, pool and 'baby-foot'. TV room and traditional 'salle de reunion'. Fishing. Off site: Riding 2 km. Nearest beach 2.5 km. Golf 15 km.

Open: 1 April - 1 October.

Directions

Entrance is off the busy La Turballe-Guérande D99 road, 3 km. east of La Turballe. A one-way system operates - in one lane, out via another. GPS: N47:20. W02:28.

Charges 2007

Per person	€ 5,90
child (under 7 yrs)	€ 4,80
pitch	€ 6,70
with water and electricity	€ 13,40
car	€ 3,10

No credit cards.

FR44070 Camping Parc du Guibel

Route de Kerdrien, F-44420 Piriac sur Mer (Loire-Atlantique)

Tel: 02 40 23 52 67. Email: camping@parcduguibel.com

This very large site, situated in an extensive wood, describes itself as 'un Hôtel de Plein Air' and prides itself on its spaciousness and its trees. A keen birdwatcher told the owner that he had seen 50 different species of birds. There are 450 pitches of which 307 are for touring scattered among the 14 hectares of woodland, mainly shaded but some in clearings. One section at the top of the site across a minor road is always quiet and peaceful. 110 pitches have electricity of which 67 also have water tap and drain. There are also 134 mobile homes and chalets for rent. A long room houses the bar, snack bar with takeaway and a small restaurant. A small shop sells bread and a few basics. There is a heated pool and two paddling pools linked by a small water slide. A programme of activities and entertainment for children and adults is olrganised in high season. The sea is just over a kilometre away and nearby are the salt-marshes producing the famous 'Sel de Guérande'.

Facilities

Five sanitary blocks: the newest is smart and well equipped, with controllable showers and washbasins. Two others have been partially refurbished to the same standards. The others are rather old-fashioned, with preset showers and washbasins in cubicles. Facilities for disabled visitors. Baby room. Dishwashing and laundry facilities. Motorcaravan service point. Heated swimming and paddling pools (1/5-15/9). Bar, snack bar, takeaway and restaurant (July-Aug only). Off site: Riding 400 m. Fishing 1 km. Beach 1.2 km. Sailing 3.5 km. Golf 18 km.

Open: 1 April - 30 September.

Directions

On N165 from Vannes, leave at exit 15 towards La Roche Bernard, turn left to join D774 towards La Baule. 8 km. after Herbignac, turn right on D52 to St Molt and Mesquer towards Piriac. Turn left on D52. Site signed on right in 3 km. From Nantes on N165, take N171 to Guérande. Then D99/D333 for Centre Aquatique at St Sebastien, past Centre and cross D52 to site. GPS: N47:23.177 W02:30.604

Charges 2006

Per person	€ 3,00 - € 4,50
child (under 7 yrs)	€ 2,00 - € 3,00
pitch incl. electricity	€ 5,70 - € 8,60

CAMPING CARAVANING ★★★★
Rental of mobiles homes and chalets

14 ha. wooded park
450 pitches

Route de Kerdrien - 44420 PIRIAC SUR MER
Tél. 02 40 23 52 67 - Fax 02 40 15 50 24
E-mail : camping@parcduguibel.com
www.parcduguibel.com

FR44080 Camping la Chênaie

36 rue du Patisseau, F-44210 Pornic (Loire-Atlantique)

Tel: 02 40 82 07 31. Email: la.chenaie@Free.fr

La Chênaie is a pleasant, family run campsite in countryside close to the fishing port of Pornic and less than three kilometres from the nearest beach. There are 94 touring pitches in two areas on gently sloping ground, with the pool and other leisure facilities in the dip between. All the pitches are well tended with electricity available (6/10A; longer leads may be needed in places) and there is some shade in places from maturing trees and bushes. Some of the 70 mobile homes (20 for rent) are scattered among the touring pitches, others are at the top of the site.

Facilities

Two good sanitary blocks, one central to each area. Some washbasins in cubicles. Baby room. Facilities for disabled visitors. Large washing machines and dryer. Motorcaravan service point. Heated swimming pools and paddling pool (3/6-16/9). Bar and shop selling bread and a few basics (July/Aug). Restaurant and snack bar with takeaway (8/7-26/8). Play area. Some activities for children and adults. Off site: Fishing 300 m. Sailing and boat launching 3 km. Golf 4 km. Riding 5 km.

Open: 1 May - 15 September.

Directions

Road to site is at junction of D751 (Nantes - Pornic) with the D213 (St Nazaire – Noirmoutier) 'Route Bleue'. From north take exit for D751 Nantes. From south follow D751 Clion. At roundabout north of D213 exit for Le Patisseau and follow signs to site. Avoid Pornic centre. GPS: N47:07.109 W02:04.249

Charges 2006

Per unit incl. 2 persons	€ 11,00 - € 19,00
extra person	€ 4,00 - € 5,00
electricity (6/10A)	€ 3,50 - € 4,50

FR44090 Camping Château du Deffay

Mobile homes ▶ page 456

B.P. 18 Le Deffay, Ste Reine de Bretagne, F-44160 Pontchâteau (Loire-Atlantique)

Tel: **02 40 88 00 57**. Email: **campingdudeffay@wanadoo.fr**

A family managed site, Château de Deffay is a refreshing departure from the usual formula in that it is not over organised or supervised and has no tour operator units. The 142 good sized, fairly level pitches have pleasant views and are either on open grass, on shallow terraces divided by hedges, or informally arranged in a central, slightly sloping wooded area. Most have electricity. The facilities are located within the old courtyard area of the smaller château (that dates from before 1400). With the temptation of free pedaloes and the fairly deep, unfenced lake, parents should ensure that children are supervised. The landscape is natural right down to the molehills, and the site blends well with the rural environment of the estate, lake and farmland which surround it. For these reasons it is enjoyed by many. The larger château (built 1880) and another lake stand away from this area providing pleasant walking. The reception has been built separately to contain the camping area. Alpine type chalets overlook the lake and fit well with the environment. The site is close to the Brière Regional Park, the Guérande Peninsula, and La Baule with its magnificent beach is 20 km.

Facilities

The main toilet block is well equipped including washbasins in cabins, provision for disabled people and a baby bathroom. Laundry facilities. Maintenance can be variable and hot water can take time to reach temperature in low season. Shop, bar, small restaurant with takeaway and solar heated swimming pool and paddling pool (all 15/5-15/9). Play area. TV. Animation in season including children's miniclub. Torches useful. Off site: Golf and riding 5 km.

Open: 1 May - 30 September.

Directions

Site is signed from D33 Pontchâteau - Herbignac road near Ste Reine. Also signed from the D773 and N165.

Charges 2006

Per person	€ 3,00 - € 4,90
child (2-12 yrs)	€ 2,00 - € 3,30
pitch	€ 7,20 - € 11,00
with electricity (6A)	€ 10,40 - € 14,90
with 3 services	€ 12,20 - € 16,80

Camping Cheques accepted.

kawan-villages.com **tel: 00 333 59 59 03 59**

FR44130 Camping L'Hermitage

36 avenue du Paradis, F-44290 Guemene-Penfao (Loire-Atlantique)

Tel: **02 40 79 23 48**. Email: **contact@campinglhermitage.com**

L'Hermitage is a pretty wooded site set in the Vallée du Don and would be useful for en-route stops or for longer stays. The enthusiastic staff, even though their English is a little limited, provide a warm welcome and maintain this reasonably priced site to a good standard. There are 110 pitches of which 80 are a good size for touring and camping. Some are formally arranged on open, level grass pitches, whereas others are informal amongst light woodland. Electricity (6A) is available to all (a long lead may be useful). Both Nantes and Rennes are 30 minutes away, La Baule with its beaches is 40 minutes.

Facilities

A clean and well serviced toilet block includes some washbasins in cabins with warm water. Laundry and dishwashing sinks under cover (cold water but a hot tap is provided). Smallish pool, paddling pool and slide, nicely maintained and carefully fenced. Small play area. Table tennis. Petanque. Games room with video games. Off site: Leisure complex with indoor pool opposite. Fishing 500 m. Village 1 km. for all facilities. Riding 2 km. Many walking trails.

Open: 1 April - 31 October.

Directions

Exit N137 at Derval (signed Châteaubriant) but take D775 for Redon. Guémené-Penfao is approx. 13 km. Watch for site signs before village centre. Site is on the outskirts in a semi-residential area to the northeast.

Charges 2007

Per unit incl. 2 persons	€ 11,50
extra person	€ 3,50
child (under 10 yrs)	€ 2,50
electricity	€ 2,80
dog	€ 2,00

CAMPING • GÎTE D'ÉTAPE

L'HERMITAGE ★★★

Sun, calm and uncovered

New 2004: water slide

36 avenue du Paradis
44290 GUÉMENÉ-PENFAO
Tél. : 02 40 79 23 48
Fax : 02 40 51 11 87
contact@campinglhermitage.com
www.campinglhermitage.com

FR44100 Sunêlia le Patisseau

Mobile homes ▶ page 456

29 rue du Patisseau, F-44210 Pornic (Loire-Atlantique)

Tel: **02 40 82 10 39**. Email: **contact@lepatisseau.com**

Le Patisseau is situated in the countryside just a short drive from the fishing village of Pornic. It is a relaxed site with a large number of mobile homes and chalets, and popular with young families and teenagers. The 115 touring pitches all with electrical connections (6A), are divided between the attractive 'forest' area with plenty of shade from mature trees and the more open 'prairie' area some are on a slight slope and access to others might be tricky for larger units. A railway runs along the bottom half of the site with trains several times a day, (but none overnight) and the noise is minimal. The Morice family works very hard to maintain a friendly atmosphere.

Facilities

The modern heated toilet block is very spacious and well fitted; most washbasins are open style, but the controllable showers are all in large cubicles which have washbasins; these are very popular, so it is best to avoid busy times! Also good facilities for disabled visitors and babies, laundry rooms and dishwashing facilities. Shop (15/5 - 8/9). Bar, restaurant and takeaway (1/7-31/9). Indoor heated pool with sauna, jacuzzi and spa (all season). Small heated outdoor pools and water slides (15/5-3/9). Play area. Multisport court. Bicycle hire. Off site: Fishing and beach 2.5 km. Riding, golf, sailing and boat launching all 5 km.

Open: 8 April - 6 November.

Directions

Pornic is 19 km. south of the St Nazaire bridge. Access to site is at junction of D751 Nantes - Pornic road with the D213 St Nazaire - Noirmoutier 'Route Bleue'. From north take exit for D751 Nantes. From south follow D751 Clion-sur-Mer. At roundabout north of D213 take exit for Le Patisseau and follow signs to site. Avoid Pornic town centre. GPS: N47:07.183 W02:04.397

Charges 2006

Per unit incl. 2 persons	€ 20,00 - € 30,50
incl. electricity (6A)	€ 24,00 - € 34,50
extra person	€ 5,50 - € 7,50
child (1-7 yrs)	€ 3,00 - € 5,00
animal	€ 5,00

49

FR44150 Camping la Tabardière

F-44770 La Plaine-sur-Mer (Loire-Atlantique)

Tel: 02 40 21 58 83. Email: **info@camping-la-tabardiere.com**

Owned and managed by the Barre family, this campsite lies next to the family farm. Pleasant, peaceful and immaculate, it will suit those who want to enjoy the local coast and towns but return to an 'oasis' for relaxation. It still, however, provides activities and fun for those with energy remaining. The pitches are mostly terraced either side of a narrow valley. Care needs to be taken in manoeuvring caravans into position – although the effort is well worth it. Most pitches have access to electricity and water taps are conveniently situated. The site is probably not suitable for wheelchair users. A 'Sites et Paysages' member.

Facilities

Two good, clean toilet blocks are well equipped and include laundry facilities. Motorcaravan service point. Bar. Shop. Snacks and takeaway. Good sized swimming pool, paddling pool and slides (supervised). Playground. Minigolf. Table tennis. Volleyball and basketball. Half size tennis courts. Boules. Overnight area for motorcaravans (€ 9 per night). Off site: Beach 3 km. Sea fishing, golf, riding all 5 km.

Open: 1 April - 30 September.

Directions

Site is well signed, situated inland off the D13 Pornic - La Plaine sur Mer road.

Charges 2006

Per unit incl. 2 persons	€ 12,50 - € 21,00
extra person	€ 3,30 - € 5,50
child (2-10 yrs)	€ 2,50 - € 3,50
dog	€ 2,70
electricity (3/8A)	€ 2,80 - € 4,20

FR44160 Camping Armor-Héol

Route de Guérande, F-44420 Piriac-sur-Mer (Loire-Atlantique)

Tel: 02 40 23 57 80. Email: **armor.heol@wanadoo.fr**

Situated only 700 metres from Piriac town and the beach, and 14 km. from Guérande, this campsite makes an ideal base for a beach holiday or for touring this beautiful corner of southern Brittany. There are 98 good sized level pitches all with 5A electricity and a further 164 are occupied by mobiles and chalets, half privately-owned, the rest available for rent. As the site is attractively laid out with plenty of trees and hedges, these do not feel intrusive. With an impressive leisure complex and programme of activities and entertainment in high season, the site can be very lively, but it is very well run and becomes quiet after 11pm. With considerable recent investment, the site now offers excellent facilities for visitors of all ages. This is a friendly site with English speaking reception and good amenities.

Facilities

Two clean and well maintained toilet blocks include washbasins in cabins, baby rooms, facilities for disabled visitors and family rooms with shower, basin and toilet (free except July/Aug when they are for hire). At busy times facilities may be under pressure. Washing machines and dryers. Bar, takeaway and restaurant (1/6-15/9). Indoor pool with water movement. Outdoor heated pools and water slides (1/6-15/9). Multisports area, tennis, volleyball. Playground. Off site: Beach and town, fishing, boat launching, surfing and bicycle hire 700 m. Sailing 1 km. Golf and riding 2 km.

Open: 8 April - 24 September.

Directions

Piriac is 90 km. west of Nantes and 11 km. northwest of Guérande. By-pass Guérande and take D99 then D333 signed Piriac sur Mer. Site on left before Piriac. GPS: N47:22.481 W02:32.131

Charges 2006

Per unit incl. 2 persons	€ 14,95 - € 29,75
extra person	€ 4,00 - € 7,45
child (under 4 yrs)	€ 2,40 - € 4,60
animal	€ 2,30 - € 4,00
electricity	€ 3,50

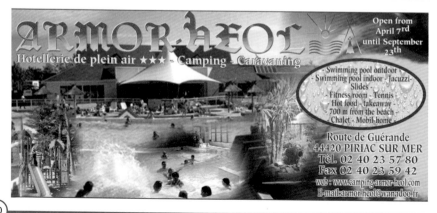

Check real time availability and at-the-gate prices...

www.alanrogers.com

FR44190 Camping le Fief

Mobile homes ▶ page 457

57, chemin du Fief, F-44250 St Brévin-les-Pins (Loire-Atlantique)

Tel: 02 40 27 23 86. Email: camping@lefief.com

If you are a family with young children or lively teenagers, this could be the campsite for you. Le Fief is a well established site only 800 metres from sandy beaches on the southern Brittany coast. It has a magnificent 'aqua park' with outdoor and covered swimming pools, paddling pools, slides, river rapids, fountains, jets and more. The site has 220 pitches for touring units (out of 413). Whilst these all have electricity (5A), they vary in size and many are worn and may be untidy. There are also 143 mobile homes and chalets to rent and 55 privately owned units. This is a lively site in high season with a variety of entertainment and organised activity for all ages. This ranges from a miniclub for 5-12 year olds, to 'Tonic Days' with aquagym, jogging and sports competitions, and to evening events which include karaoke, themed dinners and cabaret. There are plenty of sporting facilities for active youngsters.

Facilities

One excellent new toilet block and three others of a lower standard. Laundry facilities. Shop (15/5-15/9). Bar, restaurant and takeaway (15/4-15/9) with terrace overlooking the pool complex. Outdoor pools, etc. (15/5-15/9). Covered pool (all season). Play area. Tennis. Archery. Games room. Internet access. Organised entertainment and activities (July/Aug). Off site: Beach, bicycle hire 800 m. Bus stop 1 km. Riding 1 km. Golf 15 km.

Open: 1 April - 15 October.

Directions

From the St Nazaire bridge take the fourth exit from the D213 signed St Brévin - L'Océan. Continue over first roundabout and bear right at the second to join Chemin du Fief. The site is on the right, well signed.

Charges 2006

Per pitch incl. 2 persons	€ 14,00 - € 35,00
extra person	€ 4,00 - € 8,50
child (0-7 yrs)	€ 2,00 - € 4,25
electricity	€ 4,00 - € 5,00

FR44170 Camping les Ajoncs d'Or

Chemin du Rocher, F-44500 La Baule (Loire-Atlantique)

Tel: **02 40 60 33 29**. Email: **contact@ajoncs.com**

This site is situated in pine woods, 1.5 km. on the inland side of La Baule and its beautiful bay. A well maintained, natural woodland setting provides a wide variety of pitch types (just over 200), some level and bordered with hedges and tall trees to provide shade and many others that maintain the natural characteristics of the woodland. Most pitches have electricity and water nearby and are usually of a larger size. A central building provides a shop and open friendly bar that serve snacks and takeaways. The English speaking Bazillails family (the owners) who live on site will welcome you to their campsite.

Facilities

Two good quality sanitary blocks are clean and well maintained providing plenty of facilities including a baby room. Washing machines and dryers. Shop and bar (July/Aug). Snack bar (July/Aug). Good size swimming pool and paddling pool (1/6-5/9). Sports and playground areas. Bicycle hire. Reception with security barrier (closed 22.30 - 7.30 hrs). Off site: Everything for an enjoyable holiday can be found in nearby La Baule. Fishing and riding 1.5 km. Golf 3 km. Beach 1.5 km.

Open: 1 April - 30 September.

Directions

From N171 take exit for La Baule les Pins. Follow signs for 'La Baule Centre', then left at roundabout in front of Champion supermarket and follow site signs.

Charges 2006

Per unit incl. 2 persons	€ 19,00
with electricity	€ 22,00
with water and drainage	€ 24,00
extra person	€ 6,00
child (2-7 yrs)	free - € 3,00

FR44180 Camping de la Boutinardière

Mobile homes ▶ page 456

Rue de la Plage de la Boutinardière, F-44210 Pornic (Loire-Atlantique)

Tel: **02 40 82 05 68**. Email: **info@laboutinardiere.com**

This is truly a holiday site to suit all the family whatever their age, just 200 m. from the beach. It has 250 individual good sized pitches, 100-120 sq.m. in size, many bordered by three metre high, well maintained hedges for shade and privacy. All pitches have electricity available. It is a family owned site and English is spoken by the helpful, obliging reception staff. Beside reception is the excellent site shop and across the road is a complex of indoor and outdoor pools, paddling pool and a twin toboggan water slide. On site there are sports and entertainment areas. Facing the water complex, the bar, restaurant and terraces are new and serve excellent food, be it a snack or in the restaurant or perhaps a takeaway. This site is difficult to better in the South Brittany, Loire-Atlantique area. This campsite has it all – two kilometres from the beautiful harbour town of Pornic and 200 metres from the sea, together with the very best of amenities and facilities.

Facilities

Toilet facilities are in three good blocks, one large and centrally situated and two supporting blocks. The quality, maintenance and cleanliness are amongst the best. Washbasins are in cabins, dishwashing is under cover. Laundry facilities. Shop (15/6-15/9). New complex of bar, restaurant, terraces (1/4-30/9). Three heated swimming pools, one indoor (1/4-15/9), a paddling pool and water slides (15/5-22/9). Games room. Sports area. Playground. Off site: Sandy cove 200 m. Restaurants, cafés, golf, riding, fishing, sailing and windsurfing, all within 5 km.

Open: 1 April - 30 September.

Directions

From north or south on D213, take Nantes D751 exit. At roundabout (with McDonalds) take D13 signed Bemarie-en-Retz. After 4 km. site is signed to right. Note: do NOT exit from D213 at Pornic Ouest or Centre.

Charges 2006

Per unit incl. 2 persons	€ 14,00 - € 32,00
extra person	€ 3,00 - € 6,00
child (2-10 yrs)	€ 2,00 - € 4,50
electricity (6-10A)	€ 3,50 - € 5,00

See advertisement on page 55

Check real time availability and at-the-gate prices...
www.**alanrogers**.com

FR44300 Camping Les Pierres Couchées

L'Hermitage, F-44250 Saint Brévin les Pins (Loire-Atlantique)

Tel: 02 40 27 85 64

In high season this is a lively and bustling site, just 300 metres from the beach and close to the 'Route Bleue' running south from St Nazaire towards the Vendée. Most of the site is devoted to mobile homes and chalets either privately-owned or for rent. There are 79 touring pitches on the hilly part of the complex, 53 with electricity available (5A) and access to some is not easy. There are no water taps, so a sometimes lengthy trek to the toilet block is necessary. There is a full programme of activities for children, young people and families in July and August and good leisure facilities, including a good heated pool complex with water slides and paddling pool, supervised in high season.

Facilities

Several sanitary blocks, but only one serving the touring pitches. It has pre-set showers, washbasins in cubicles and facilities for disabled visitors, although the latter would have great difficulty in getting there as it is on top of a hillock. Washing machines and dryers in another block some distance away. Bar/restaurant (all season). Shop, bakery and takeaway (July-Aug). Multisport court, tennis courts, boules. Bicycle hire. Play areas. Large covered amphitheatre. Off site: Beach 300 m. Riding 1 km. Shops, restaurants and bars nearby. Fishing, sailing and boat launching 4 km. Golf 12 km.

Open: 1 April - 8 October.

Directions

The site is south of the town just off the D213 between St Brévin-l'Océan and St Michel-Chef-Chef, on a brief section where the road narrows (a difficult crossing from the south and the sign for Les Pierres Couchées is concealed until the last second from the north). GPS: N47:12.282 W02:09.091

Charges 2006

Per unit with 2 persons and electricity	€ 20,00 - € 30,00
extra person	€ 4,00 - € 6,50
child (3-6 yrs)	€ 2,50 - € 4,00
dog	€ 3,00

53

FR44210 Camping L'Océan

Mobile homes ▶ page 457

44490 Le Croisic (Loire-Atlantique)

Tel: **02 40 23 07 69**. Email: **info@camping-ocean.com**

Camping de l'Océan is located on the Le Croisic peninsula, an area which enjoys a microclimate, thanks to the gulf stream. The site is within walking distance of the Atlantic Ocean and the white sandy the beaches of the Côte d'Amor. L'Océan has been recommended by our French agent and we hope to undertake a full inspection in 2007. There are many facilities here including a large swimming pool complex with water slides, an indoor pool and paddling pool.

Facilities

Laundry and ironing facilities. Restaurant. Takeaway food. Bar. Supermarket. Motorcaravan service point. Swimming pool complex comprising an indoor pool, outdoor pool and paddling pool. Volleyball. Football. Basketball. Tennis. Off site: Archery. Sailing. Scuba diving. Cycling. Fishing.

Open: April - September.

Directions

From Nantes take the N165 and then the N171 to Guérande. At the roundabout before Guérande follow signs to Le Croisic using the D774. Just before the centre of Le Croisic, the site is signed.

Charges 2007

Per unit incl 2 persons and electricity	€ 16,50 - € 36.50
extra person	€ 3,00 - € 7,00
child (under 7 years)	€ 2,00 - € 5,50

FR44220 Parc de Léveno

Mobile homes ▶ page 457

Route de Sandun, F-44350 Guérande (Loire-Atlantique)

Tel: **02 40 24 79 30, or 02 40 24 79**. Email: **domaine.leveno@wanadoo.fr**

There have been many changes to this extensive site over the past three years and considerable investment has been made to provide some excellent new facilities. The number of mobile homes and chalets has increased considerably, leaving just 47 touring pitches. However, these are mainly grouped at the far end of the site. Pitches are divided by hedges and trees which offer a good deal of shade and all have electricity (10A). Access is tricky to some and the site is not recommended for larger units. Twin axle caravans and American motorhomes are not accepted. The site is close to the historic town of Guérande, its salt marshes, some good beaches and the Natural Reserve of La Brière.

Facilities

Main refurbished toilet block offers pre-set showers, washbasins in cubicles and facilities for disabled visitors. Laundry facilities. Small shop selling basics and takeaway snacks. Bar with TV and games (all July/Aug). Indoor pool. Heated outdoor pool complex with water slides and a flume, paddling pool (15/5-15/9). Aquatic Centre. Fitness room. Play area. Multisport court. Programme of activities and events (high season). Off site: Hypermarket 1 km. Fishing 2 km. Beach, golf and riding all 5 km.

Open: Easter - 30 September.

Directions

Site is less than 3 km. from the centre of Guérande. From D774 and from D99/N171 take D99E Guérande by-pass. Turn east following signs for Villejames and Leclerc Hypermarket and continue on D247 to site on right. GPS: N47:19.987 W02:23.478

Charges 2006

Per unit incl. 2 persons, electricity and water	€ 15,00 - € 25,00
extra person	€ 3,00 - € 5,00
child (under 7 yrs)	€ 1,80 - € 3,00

Check real time availability and at-the-gate prices...

www.**alanrogers**.com

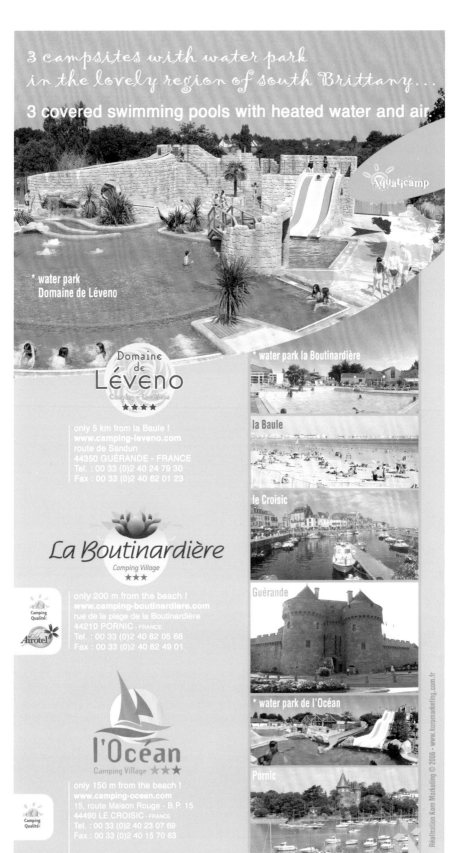

3 campsites with water park
in the lovely region of south Brittany...

3 covered swimming pools with heated water and air

Aquaticamp

* water park
Domaine de Léveno

Domaine de **Léveno**
Camping - location
★★★★

only 5 km from la Baule !
www.camping-leveno.com
route de Sandun
44350 GUÉRANDE - FRANCE
Tel. : 00 33 (0)2 40 24 79 30
Fax : 00 33 (0)2 40 62 01 23

* water park la Boutinardière

la Baule

le Croisic

La Boutinardière
Camping Village
★★★

Camping Qualité

Airotel

only 200 m from the beach !
www.camping-boutinardiere.com
rue de la plage de la Boutinardière
44210 PORNIC - FRANCE
Tel. : 00 33 (0)2 40 82 05 68
Fax : 00 33 (0)2 40 82 49 01

Guérande

* water park de l'Océan

l'Océan
Camping Village ★★★

Camping Qualité

only 150 m from the beach !
www.camping-ocean.com
15, route Maison Rouge - B.P. 15
44490 LE CROISIC - FRANCE
Tel. : 00 33 (0)2 40 23 07 69
Fax : 00 33 (0)2 40 15 70 63

Pornic

Réalisation Koro Marketing © 2006 - www.koromarketing.com.tr

FR44200 Camping Saint Clair

F-44530 Guenrouet (Loire-Atlantique)

Tel: 02 40 87 61 52. Email: chabliny@wanadoo.fr

This is a very well maintained campsite in a lovely position next to the Brest - Nantes canal, making it suitable for anyone interested in boating or fishing. There are about 100 pitches of varying sizes, many within a wooded area, and most with electricity (10A). The site would be ideal for an overnight stop or for a longer stay.

Facilities

Three well maintained, modern toilet blocks provide toilets (mixed British and Turkish style), washbasins in cabins and showers. Facilities for disabled visitors. Small play area. Tennis. Petanque. Games room. Off site: Leisure complex with outdoor pool, restaurant and crêperie opposite site. Village with small supermarket and other facilities 500 m.

Open: 15 April - 30 September.

Directions

On the N165 from Nantes, take D773 signed St Gildas de Bois. At St Gildas, turn right on D2 for Guenrouet. Site is on right after village, just before river.

Charges 2006

Per person	€ 2,80 - € 4,10
pitch	€ 4,00 - € 5,00
electricity	€ 2,80

FR44240 Camping le Ranch

Les Hautes Raillères, F-44770 La Plaine sur Mer (Loire-Atlantique)

Tel: 02 40 21 52 62. Email: info@camping-le-ranch.com

This is a pleasant, family-run campsite with a friendly atmosphere, close to the beaches of the 'Jade Coast' between Pornic and St Brévin-les-Pins, yet not right on the seashore. The 99 touring pitches all have access to electricity (6A) although on some a long cable may be required; these occupy the central part of the site, with the fringe areas taken up by mobile homes and chalets (several for rent). The rows of pitches are separated by well-kept hedges, and small trees mark the corners of most.

Facilities

The central sanitary block has pre-set showers, facilities for disabled visitors, washbasins in cubicles, and a fairly basic baby room. Further small toilet block. Pool (1/5-30/9, heated 15/6-15/9). Bar has small shop selling basics. Good takeaway (July/Aug). Activities and entertainment in high season. Off site: Beach 800 m. Bicycle hire 1.5 km. Fishing 5 km. Golf, riding and sailing 9 km.

Open: April - September.

Directions

La Plaine-sur-Mer is 16 km. south of the St Nazaire bridge. Site is on D96 5 km. northeast of the town. From D213 (Route Bleue) just south of St Michel-Chef-Chef turn southwest on D96 towards La Plaine. GPS: N47:09.313 W02:09.894

Charges 2006

Per unit incl. 2 persons	€ 12,00 - € 20,10
electricity	€ 3,60

FR44230 Camping EléoVic

Route de la Pointe Saint Gildas, Préfailles, F-44216 Pornic (Loire-Atlantique)

Tel: 02 40 21 61 60. Email: contact@camping-eleovic.com

This is a delightful site overlooking the sea on the attractive Jade Coast west of Pornic. There are 80 touring pitches, some with wonderful views of the sea, and a similar number of mobile homes, many of which are available for rent. All pitches have access to electricity (6, 10 or 16A), though on some you may need a long cable. Much of the ground is sloping, so a really level pitch may not be available and access for larger units to some pitches may be tricky.

Facilities

Central sanitary block has spacious pre-set showers and washbasins in cabins. Facilities for disabled visitors. Excellent room for dishwashing and laundry. Further facilities are in the pool building and another smaller block should be ready for 2007. Good restaurant (July-Aug. - not Wednesdays) with small bar and terrace. Fitness room. Playground. Table tennis. Boules. Children's activities and entertainment and sporting events for families (high season). Off site: Sailing and boat launching 800 m. Bicycle hire and golf 7 km. Horse riding 10 km.

Open: 8 April - 1 November.

Directions

Préfailles is 20 km. south of the St Nazaire bridge and 9 km. west of Pornic. From north on D213 (Route Bleue) turn southwest just south of St Michel-Chef-Chef on D96 to La Plaine-sur-Mer and follow signs for Préfailles. From Pornic take D13 to La Plaine but do not enter town. Follow signs for Préfailles. Continue on D313 past village towards La Pointe Saint-Gildas and at 50 km. sign turn left, then left again to site on right. GPS: N47:07.957 W02:13.890

Charges 2006

Per unit incl. 2 persons	€ 15,70 - € 26,30
extra person	€ 4,90 - € 7,00
electricity (6A)	€ 4,10

FR44250 Camping Trémondec

48 rue du Château Careil, F-44350 Guérande (Loire-Atlantique)

Tel: 02 40 60 00 07. Email: camping.tremondec@wanadoo.fr

This is a delightful site close to the sophisticated resort of La Baule, the more relaxed beaches of La Turballe, the salt marshes of the historic town of Guérande and the Natural Reserve of Brière. It is lovingly cared for by the very friendly Schgier family. There are 60 touring pitches on gently sloping ground, divided by hedges and with plenty of trees offering some shade to many; almost all have electricity (6A) nearby. A further 40 pitches are occupied by mobile homes, chalets and family tents either for rent or leased to individuals and a small tour operator.

Facilities	Directions
Two well-equipped and clean sanitary blocks with push-button showers and some washbasins in cubicles. Facilities for disabled visitors. Bar, snack bar/takeaway and restaurant all July/Aug. Good heated swimming pool and paddling pool (1/5-30/9). Small games room. Children's activities and evening events for families in high season. Off site: Supermarkets, bicycle hire, sailing and beach all within 2.5 km. Riding 5 km. Fishing and golf 10 km.	From east on N171 (St Nazaire - Guérande), turn south for La Baule Centre. Turn right at roundabout signed to Château Careil and then turn right signed to château and site. From west on D99E Guérande by-pass, take D92 towards La Baule, then turn left signed to site. GPS: N47:17.856 W02:23.998

Open: 1 April - 24 September.

Charges 2006

Per person	€ 3,10 - € 5,50
pitch incl. electricity	€ 9,30 - € 11,50

FR44270 Camping le Château du Petit Bois

F-44420 Mesquer (Loire-Atlantique)

Tel: 02 40 42 68 77. Email: info@campingdupetitbois.com

This pleasant campsite is located in the wooded grounds of a small château. The 125 good-sized touring pitches, all with electricity (3 or 6A) have varying degrees of shade and a few are in the open for those who like a sunny plot. Reception is housed in the converted outbuildings of the château, and is welcoming and informative. The Marin family and their staff are friendly and helpful, and the site is very well run. The sea is just over a kilometre away, as is the village of Mesquer and nearby are the salt marshes which produce the famous Sel de Guérande.

Facilities	Directions
The main sanitary block has pre-set showers and open style washbasins together with some cubicles with controllable shower and a washbasin. Dishwashing and laundry facilities. Facilities for disabled visitors. Combined bar, snack bar and takeaway (with TV, pool table and 'babyfoot'). Small shop selling bread and basics (July/Aug). Pool complex with heated main pool and paddling pool and pool with water slides (only open when supervised). Programme of activities (all July/Aug). Off site: Fishing, bicycle hire, riding and sailing all nearby. Golf 12 km.	Mesquer is 80 km. northwest of Nantes and 16 km. north of La Baule. From N165 Nantes - Vannes road, leave at exit 15 towards La Roche Bernard, turn left to join D774 towards La Baule. 8 km. after Herbignac, turn right on D52 to St Molt and Mesquer. Site is on D52 just west of village (do not go into village). GPS: N47:23.941 W02:28.279

Open: 1 April - 30 October.

Charges 2006

Per unit incl. 2 persons	€ 15,40 - € 19,20
extra person	€ 4,90 - € 6,10
electricity (3/6A)	€ 4,30 - € 5,40

FR56080 Camping Municipal le Pâtis

3 chemin du Pâtis, F-56130 La Roche Bernard (Morbihan)

Tel: 02 99 90 60 13

This is another of those excellent municipal sites one comes across in France. Situated beside the River Vilaine, a 5 minute walk from the centre of the very attractive old town of La Roche Bernard and beside the port and marina, it provides 69 level grass, part-hedged pitches in bays of four, with 10A electricity and water. 10 special pitches for motorcaravans have been created at the entrance (€ 9.40 incl. 2 persons and electricity). Next door is a sailing school, boats to hire, fishing, tennis, archery, etc. A restaurant and bar are on the quayside, with others uphill in the town.

Facilities	Directions
There are two fully equipped sanitary blocks, one new and very modern, the other fully refurbished. Laundry room behind reception with washing machine and dryer. Small play area. Bicycle hire. Off site: Bicycle hire 500 m. Riding 5 km. Golf 15 km.	Go into town centre and follow signs for the Port around a one-way system and then a sharp turn down hill.

Open: Easter/April - 30 September.

Charges 2006

Per pitch with 2 persons and electricity	€ 13,00
extra person	€ 3,00
child (under 9 yrs)	€ 1,50
No credit cards.	

FR56010 Castel Camping la Grande Métairie

Route des Alignements de Kermario, B.P. 85, F-56342 Carnac (Morbihan)

Tel: **02 97 52 24 01**. Email: **info@lagrandemetairie.com**

La Grande Métairie is a good quality site situated a little back from the sea, close to the impressive rows of the famous 'menhirs' (giant prehistoric standing stones). The site has 575 individual pitches (108 for touring units), surrounded by hedges and trees. All have electricity (some long leads needed). The site is well known and popular and has many British visitors with 358 pitches taken by tour operators. It is ideal for families with children of all ages, but not suitable for those with walking difficulties. The site has a great deal to offer and is lively and busy over a long season. Outside amphitheatre for musical evenings and barbecues. Organised events. Occasional dances (pitches near these facilities may be noisy late at night - the bar closes at midnight). Paddocks with ponds are home for ducks, goats and ponies to watch and feed. There are also pony rides around the site. A super swimming pool complex comprises heated indoor and outdoor pools, water slides and toboggans and a jacuzzi. A local market takes place at Carnac on Wednesdays and Sundays.

Facilities

Three large well maintained toilet blocks, with washbasins in cabins. Facilities for babies and disabled people. Laundry facilities. Motorcaravan service points. Shops. Restaurant. Takeaway. Bar lounge and terrace. TV and games rooms. Pool complex with bar. Playgrounds and playing field. Tennis courts. Volleyball and basketball. Minigolf. BMX track. Bicycle hire. Fishing. Amphitheatre. Zip-wire. Paintball. Helicopter rides (July/Aug). Organised events. American motorhomes accepted up to 27 ft. Off site: Riding 1 km. Nearest beach 3 km. Golf 12 km.

Open: 1 April - 9 September (all services from 20/5).

Directions

From N165 take Quiberon/Carnac exit onto the D768. After 5 km. turn south onto D119 towards Carnac. At roundabout and after 4 km. turn left (north east) onto D196 to the site.
GPS: N47:35.837 W03:03.646

Charges 2006

Per person	€ 4,00 - € 7,20
child (under 4-7 yrs)	€ 3,50 - € 5,40
pitch incl. car	€ 8,00 - € 23,90
6A electricity	€ 2,00 - € 3,50

Less 20% 22/5-29/6 and after 1/9.

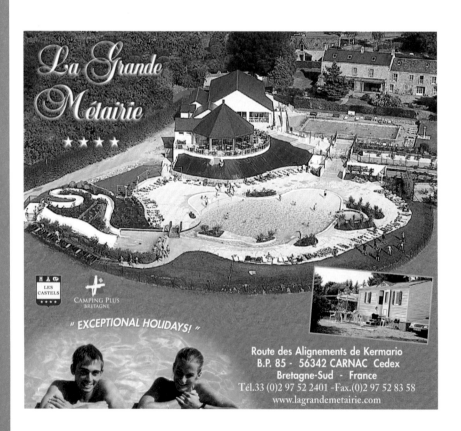

FR56020 Camping de la Plage

Plage de Kervilaine, F-56470 La Trinité-sur-Mer (Morbihan)

Tel: 02 97 55 73 28. Email: camping@camping-plage.com

The Carnac/La Trinité area of Brittany is popular with British holiday makers. Camping de la Plage is one of two sites, close to each other and owned by members of the same family, with direct access to the safe sandy beach of Kervillen Plage. There are 198 grass pitches of which 112 are for touring (64 are used by tour operators). All are hedged and have electricity (6/10A), water and drainage. The site has a pronounced slope and some pitches reflect this. With narrow roads and sharp bends, it is not suitable for large units. The shop, restaurant and bar, 200 m. along the coast opposite Camping de la Baie, are used by local residents and provide excellent value. The restaurant and takeaway have extensive menus. A lively entertainment programme for all ages in high season makes this an attractive site for family holidays.

Facilities

Toilet blocks have washbasins in cubicles and facilities for disabled people and small children. Laundry facilities. Small swimming pool with water slides. Play areas including ball pool. Tennis, basketball, table tennis. TV. Entertainment programme in high season for all ages. Bicycle hire. Beach. Guided tours. Internet access. Communal barbecue areas (gas or electric only on pitches). Off site: Fishing 50 m. Shop with bakery. Bar, restaurant, crêperie, takeaway (all 200 m). Sailing 1.5 km. Riding 3.5 km. Golf 5 km.

Open: 12 May - 16 September.

Directions

From N165 at Auray take D28 (La Trinité-sur-Mer). On through town following signs to Carnac-Plage on D186. Site signed off this road to the south. Take care to take road signed to Kervillen Plage where it forks. At sea front turn right. Site is 300 m. on right. GPS: N47:34.538 W03:01.734

Charges 2006

Per unit incl. 2 persons	€ 16,90 - € 32,30
extra person	€ 5,00
child (2-18 yrs)	€ 3,00 - € 4,00
electricity (6/10A)	€ 2,20 - € 3,20

www.camping-plage.com
our holiday at La Plage
56470 La Trinité sur Mer
Tel 33 2 97 55 73 28
Fax 33 2 97 55 88 31
email : contact@camping-plage.com
CAMPING CARAVANING LA TRINITE SUR MER

FR56030 Camping de la Baie

Plage de Kervillan, F-56470 La Trinité-sur-Mer (Morbihan)

Tel: 02 97 55 73 42. Email: contact@campingdelabaie.com

This site is one of two owned by members of the same family. It is situated on the coast overlooking the safe, sandy beach of Kervillen Plage, with its little rocky outcrops providing a naturally enclosed swimming area. This is a very friendly site, which is ideal for quiet or family holidays in an area with lots of local interest. There are 170 pitches, of which 60 are used by tour operators. The 91 touring pitches are all of good size, hedged and all have electricity (6/10A) water and drainage.

Facilities

Two modern, very clean toilet blocks include well equipped baby rooms and full en-suite facilities for disabled visitors. Laundry facilities. Bar, restaurant and takeaway (open to the public - all season). Well stocked shop (all season). Small (12 m.) swimming pool with slide. Play areas. TV room. Indoor games room. Bicycle hire. Internet access. Off site: Beach, fishing 50 m. Tennis and minigolf 200 m. (shared with Camping de la Plage). Riding 3 km. Sailing school 1.5 km. Golf 5 km.

Open: 20 May - 17 September.

Directions

From the N165 at Auray take D28 signed La Trinité-sur-Mer. Keep on through the town following signs to Carnac Plage on D186. Site is well signed off this road to the south. Be careful to take the road signed to Kervillen Plage where it forks.

Charges 2006

Per person (over 2 yrs)	€ 2,80 - € 6,85
small pitch	€ 7,70 - € 11,95
serviced pitch	€ 11,30 - € 21,65
electricity (6/10A)	€ 2,20 - € 4,20

FR56040 Camping de Penboch

9, chemin de Penboch, F-56610 Arradon (Morbihan)

Tel: 02 97 44 71 29. Email: camping.penboch@wanadoo.fr

Penboch is 200 metres by footpath from the shores of the Golfe du Morbihan with its many islands, and plenty to do including watersports, fishing and boat trips. The site, in a peaceful, rural area, is divided into two – the main part, on open ground, with hedges and young trees, the other across a minor road in woodland with lots of shade. Penboch offers 175 pitches on flat grass, 95 are for touring and mostly divided into groups. Electricity (6/10A) is available on all pitches and most also have water and drainage. British tour operator (12 pitches). A 'Sites et Paysages' member. There are also old towns with weekly markets nearby and it is 30 minutes walk to Arradon which has a good range of shops and restaurants.

Facilities

Three toilet blocks, two on the main part (one heated) and one on the annex, include washbasins in cabins. Facilities can be under pressure in peak season. Laundry facilities. Motorcaravan service point. Bar with satellite TV, snacks and takeaway, shop (all 20/5-11/9). Heated pool with water slide and children's pool (1/5-17/9). Good playground. Games room. Caravan storage. American motorhomes accepted in low season. Off site: Beach, fishing 200 m. Sailing, windsurfing 2 km. Bicycle hire 2 km. Golf and riding 6 km.

Open: 8 April - 23 September.

Directions

From N165 at Auray or Vannes, take D101 along northern shores of the Golfe du Morbihan; or leave N165 at D127 signed Ploeren and Arradon. Take turn to Arradon and site is signed.
GPS: N47:37.336 W02:48.074

Charges 2006

Per unit incl. 2 persons	€ 9,95 - € 29,80
extra person	€ 3,00 - € 5,90
child (2-7 yrs)	€ 2,50 - € 4,20
electricity (6/10A)	€ 3,20 - € 4,20
dog	free - € 3,50

FR56090 Camping Moulin de Kermaux

F-56340 Carnac (Morbihan)

Tel: 02 97 52 15 90. Email: moulin-de-kermaux@wanadoo.fr

Only 100 metres from the famous Carnac megaliths, Le Moulin de Kermaux is an excellent base from which to see these ancient stones as they portray their ever changing mood, colour and profile. The family run site has 150 pitches (120 with 6-10A electricity) and its compact nature offers a safe environment for parents and children. The 70 pitches for touring units are mostly separated by hedges and numerous mature trees offer welcome shade. Keen walkers and families with young children alike, will enjoy the footpaths in the area. This is a well run, quiet and comfortable site.

Facilities

The fully equipped toilet block (a few Turkish style) has washbasins in cabins. Facilities for disabled visitors. Baby bath. Laundry and dishwashing facilities. Motorcaravan service point. Shop (26/6-31/8). Bar (12/6-31/8) evenings only in low season. Swimming and paddling pools. Sauna and jacuzzi. Adventure playground. Volleyball, basketball and minigolf. Organised activities. Internet access (both July/Aug). Not suitable for American motorhomes or twin axle caravans. Off site: Fishing, bicycle hire and riding 2 km. Beaches 3 km.

Open: 8 April - 15 September.

Directions

From N165 take Quiberon/Carnac exit onto D768. After 5 km. turn left on D119 and then, after 3 km. turn left on D196 (Route de Kerlescan). Site is on right in 1 km. opposite the centre of the standing stones.

Charges 2006

Per person	€ 4,50
child (under 7 yrs)	€ 3,00
pitch and car	€ 14,00
electricity 6A	€ 3,50
Less 10-40% outside high season.	

FR56050 Camping de Kervilor

F-56470 La Trinité-sur-Mer (Morbihan)

Tel: 02 97 55 76 75. Email: **ebideau@camping-kervilor.com**

Kervilor may be a good alternative for those who find the beach-side sites in La Trinité too busy and lively. In a village on the outskirts of the town, it has 230 pitches on flat grass and is attractively landscaped with trees (silver birch) and flowers giving a sense of spaciousness. The pitches are in groups divided by hedges, separated by shrubs and trees and 200 have electricity (6/10A). Around 116 are used for touring units. Used by tour operators (10 pitches). The site has an inviting, well designed pool complex with swimming and paddling pools, slides and fountains. Activities and entertainment are organised in high season. The pleasant port is only 1.5 km. with sandy beaches within 2 km.

Facilities

Two modern toilet blocks of a good standard with further facilities in an older block. They include many washbasins in cabins, facilities for disabled people and babies. Dishwashing. Small laundry. Small shop and takeaway in season. Bar with terrace (28/5-9/9). Pool complex. Play area. Minigolf, pétanque, tennis and volleyball. Table tennis. Bicycle hire. Only charcoal barbecues are permitted. Off site: Town facilities 1.5 km. Sandy beach, fishing or riding 2 km. Golf 12 km.

Open: 1 May - 9 September.

Directions

Site is north of La Trinité-sur-Mer and is signed in the town centre. From Auray take D186 Quiberon road; turn left at camp sign at Kergroix on D186 to La Trinité-sur-Mer, and left again at outskirts of town.

Charges 2007

Per person	€ 4,90
child (under 7 yrs)	€ 3,20
pitch	€ 13,00 - € 16,00
electricity	€ 3,40 - € 3,90

Less 25% outside high season.

camping **Kervilor**

Near to the port and beaches, Camping de Kervilor will welcome you to its calm, shaded setting - with heated swimming pools, waterslides (including multi-track), spa bath, bar, entertainment tennis court, multi-sport terrain - divertissement room and billards, multi-sport terrain - everything on site. Mobile home rental.

56470 La Trinité sur Mer - Tel. 0297557675 - Fax. 0297558726
www.camping-kervilor.com - ebideau@camping-kervilor.com

FR56100 Camping de Moulin Neuf

F-56220 Rochefort-en-Terre (Morbihan)

Tel: **02 97 43 37 52**

This quiet family site is in wooded countryside, 600 m. from the town. Ian and Norma Hetherington have worked hard to develop Moulin Neuf into a neat, tidy and organised site. There are 72 pitches (60 for tourers, 44 with 10A electricity) of good size (120 sq.m.) on neat grass, with two levels. The top level, with a limited number of electrical hook-ups, is flat and pitches are divided by young shrubs. The entrance is here and reception is located just beyond the security gate. The lower level is partly sloping with mature trees, shade and electricity on all pitches.

Facilities

The modern heated sanitary block is kept very clean and includes large, comfortable showers, cabins with washbasins and British and Turkish style WCs. Provision for disabled people. Baby room. Dishwashing and laundry facilities with washing lines. Bread delivered each morning. Heated swimming pool (1/6-31/8). Tennis court, football area. Two play areas. Off site: Lake 500 m. with watersports. Shop 600 m. Riding and golf. Vannes and the beaches of Golfe du Morbihan.

Open: 15 May - 16 September.

Directions

From Redon take D775 Vannes road west for 25 km. Branch north on D774 signed Rochefort en Terre. Follow road past the lake on left, in 800 m. Turn left and follow sign to site.

Charges 2006

Per unit incl. 2 persons	€ 20,60
extra person	€ 6,30
child (under 8 yrs)	€ 5,00
electricity	€ 4,50

FR56130 Camping Mané Guernehué

52 rue Mané er Groez, F-56870 Baden (Morbihan)
Tel: **02 97 57 02 06**. Email: **mane-guernehue@wanadoo.fr**

Located close to the Morbihan Gulf, Mané Guernehué is a smart, modern site with excellent amenities and a variety of pitches. Some are terraced beneath pine trees, others in a former orchard with delightful views of the surrounding countryside. The 377 pitches are generally large, 200 being occupied by mobile homes and chalets. Most pitches have 10A electricity and a few also have water and drainage. Many are level but others, particularly in the centre of the site, slope to varying degrees. There is a well stocked fishing lake one edge of the site. Used by tour operators (around 146 pitches).

Facilities

Two modern toilet blocks include washbasins in cabins. The maintenance of the blocks does seem to be under some pressure. Facilities for disabled visitors. Washing machines and dryers. Small shop, bar and takeaway. Heated swimming pool, waterslide, jacuzzi and gym. Fishing. Teenagers' room with table tennis, pool, billiards and TV. Play area. Varied entertainment programme in high season, based around a large purpose built hall. Off site: Beach, golf 3 km.

Open: 8 April - 30 September.

Directions

From Auray or Vannes use the D101 to Baden and watch for signs to site.

Charges 2006

Per person	€ 3,10 - € 6,60
child (2-6 yrs)	€ 2,00 - € 4,70
pitch	€ 10,50 - € 18,60
electricity (10A)	€ 4,30
dog	€ 1,70 - € 3,50
Camping Cheques accepted.	

Situated in a 10 hectares wooded park
During the season: rental of chalets, cottages and mobile homes
Year-round: rental of gîtes

Mané Guernehué CAMPING ★★★★
Golfe du Morbihan

52 Rue Mané Er Groëz - 56870 BADEN
Tel. 33 (0)2 97 57 02 06 Fax 33 (0)2 97 57 15 43
www.mane-guernehue.com
E mail : mane-guernehue@wanadoo.fr

Morbihan

FR56110 Camping le Moustoir

Route du Moustoir, F-56340 Carnac (Morbihan)
Tel: **02 97 52 16 18**. Email: **info@lemoustoir.com**

Camping du Moustoir is a friendly, family run site situated about three kilometres inland from the many beaches of the area and close to the famous 'alignments' of standing stones. Pitches are grassy and separated by shrubs and hedges, with several shaded by tall pine trees. There is a popular pool area with slides, a separate swimming pool and a paddling pool with 'mushroom' fountain. The bar and terrace become the social centre of the site in the evenings. A high season entertainment programme includes a daily 'Kid's club' attracting children of several nationalities. Several small tour operators use the site.

Facilities

The substantial, traditional style toilet block is well maintained (outside peak season some sections may be closed). Motorcaravan service facilities. Shop. Bar and takeaway (from 20/5). Heated swimming pool (21 x 8 m.), water slides, and paddling pool (from 20/5). Adventure playground. Tennis. Boules. Volleyball, football and basketball. Table tennis and pool. 'Kids Club'. Barrier deposit € 20. Off site: Watersports at Carnac Plage. Fishing, bicycle hire, riding 2 km. Beach 3 km. Golf 10 km.

Open: 6 June - 22 September.

Directions

From N165, take exit to D768 (Carnac and Quiberon). At second crossroads after 5 km. turn left (D119) towards Carnac. After 3 km. turn left (oblique turning) after a hotel. Site is 500 m. on left. GPS: N47:36 W03:03

Charges 2006

Per person (over 2 yrs)	€ 4,40
pitch incl. car	€ 5,00 - € 16,00
electricity	€ 3,20
animal	€ 1,50
Camping Cheques accepted.	

kawan-villages.com tel: **00 333 59 59 03 59**

kawan VILLAGES CAMPINGS

FR56150 Camping du Haras

Aérodrome Vannes-Meucon, F-56250 Vannes-Meucon / Monterblanc (Morbihan)

Tel: **02 97 44 66 06**. Email: **camping-vannes@wanadoo.fr**

Close to Vannes and the Golfe du Morbihan in southern Brittany, Le Haras is a small, family run, rural site that is open all year. There are just 50 pitches at the moment, although there are plans to extend the site. With a variety of settings, both open and wooded, the pitches are well kept and of a good size, all with electricity (4-10A) and most with water and drainage. Whilst M. Danard intends keeping the site quiet and in keeping with its rural setting, he provides plenty of activities for lively youngsters, including some organised games and evening parties. There is a good pool with waves, a long slide, fountains and plenty of sunbathing space. Small animals are kept at the animal park on site and there is a riding school nearby. The site is close to a small airfield, where there are opportunities for leisure flights over the Morbihan, Vannes and Carnac areas, all of which are also easily accessible by car. The beaches are 25 km.

Facilities

The small modern toilet block (heated in winter) provides a few washbasins in cabins and controllable showers. Facilities for babies and disabled visitors. Laundry facilities. No shop but basics are kept in the bar. Bar with snacks (May - Oct). Swimming pool with waves and slide (1/5-31/10). Play area. Animal park. Table tennis. Trampoline. Minigolf. Bicycle hire. Organised activities (high season). Off site: Riding 400 m. Fishing 3 km. Beach, golf 25 km.

Open: All year.

Directions

From Vannes on N165 take exit signed Pontivy and airport on the D767. Follow signs for airport and Meucon. Turn right on the D778, follow airport and yellow campsite signs. GPS: N47:43. W02:43

Charges 2006

Per person	€ 3,00 - € 4,00
child (0-7 yrs)	€ 2,00 - € 3,00
pitch	€ 2,00 - € 3,00
electricity	€ 3,00 - € 6,00

FR56120 Camping les Iles

La Pointe du Bile, F-56760 Pénestin-sur-Mer (Morbihan)

Tel: **02 99 90 30 24**. Email: **contact@camping-des-iles.fr**

You will receive a warm and friendly welcome at this family run campsite. The owner, Madame Communal, encourages everyone to make the most of this beautiful region. Of the 189 pitches, 112 are for touring. Most are flat, hedged and of a reasonable size (larger caravans and American motorhomes are advised to book) and all have electricity. Some pitches have sea views and overlook the beach. All services are fully open 15/5-15/9, with a limited service at other times. There is direct access to cliff-top walks and local beaches (you can even walk to small off-shore islands at low tide).

Facilities

The new large central toilet block is spotlessly clean with washbasins in cabins and showers. Dishwashing and laundry facilities. Facilities for disabled people and baby room. Shop. Bar and restaurant with takeaway (15/5-15/9). Pool complex (15/5-15/9). Bicycle hire. Riding. Activities and entertainment in July/Aug. Across the road in Parc des Iles (mobile home section of site) - TV room, multisports pitch, tennis court and motorcaravan service point. Off site: Windsurfing 500 m. Sailing school 3 km. Golf 3.5 km.

Open: 1 April - 1 October.

Directions

From D34 (La Roche-Bernard), at roundabot just after entering Pénestin take D201 south (Assérac). Take right fork to Pointe du Bile after 2 km. Turn right at crossroads just before beach. Site is on left. GPS: N47:26.735 W02:29.040

Charges 2006

Per unit incl. 2 persons	€ 15,00 - € 34,00
extra person (over 7 yrs)	€ 2,30 - € 5,00
child (2-7 yrs)	€ 1,30 - € 2,50
pet	€ 1,50 - € 3,00
electricity (6A)	€ 3,20

FR56200 Camping la Ferme de Lann Hoedic

Route du Roaliguen, F-56370 Sarzeau (Morbihan)

Tel: **02 97 48 01 73**. Email: **contact@camping-lannhoedic.fr**

'Camping la Ferme' is an attractively landscaped site with many flowering shrubs and trees. The 108 touring pitches, all with electricity (10A) are large and mostly level, with maturing trees which are beginning to offer some shade. The 20 pitches with mobile homes are in a separate area. Families are welcome to visit the working farm which produces cereal crops and raises sheep. Mireille and Timothy Prouten, the owners, go out of their way to make this a welcoming and happy site. Located in the countryside on the Rhuys Peninsula, Golfe du Morbihan, it is an ideal base for cycling, walking and water based activities.

Facilities	Directions
Two new, high quality toilet blocks with facilities for disabled people and babies. Washing machines and dryers. Playground with modern well designed equipment. Volleyball and petanque. Bread delivery. Ice creams and soft drinks available at reception. Takeaway meals and traditional Breton 'soirées' (high season). Bicycle hire. Off site: Beach, fishing and boating 800 m. Sarzeau 2 km. Riding 2 km. Golf 6 km.	East of Vannes on the N165, join the D780 in the direction of Sarzeau. Exit D780 at the 'Super U'; roundabout south of Sarzeau, following signs for Le Roaliguen. Campsite is signed. GPS: N47:30.447 W02.45.655

Open: 1 April - 31 October.

Charges 2006

Per person	€ 3,30 - € 4,20
child (under 7 yrs)	€ 1,60 - € 2,00
pitch incl. electricity	€ 8,10 - € 10,20

No credit cards.
Camping Cheques accepted.

FR56230 Camping Plijadur Park

94 route de Carnac, F-56470 La Trinité-sur-Mer (Morbihan)

Tel: **02 97 55 72 05**. Email: **parkphiljadur@wanadoo.fr**

Plijadur is Breton for pleasure. The owners of the campsite, M. and Mme. Prevosto, have spent many years developing the site to make an attractive, welcoming place for a quiet family holiday with the added benefits of being close to La Trinité-sur-Mer with its lively waterfront and the beaches along the coast. Of a total of 198 pitches 171 are touring pitches, all of good size, level, and separated by low hedges. Most have electricity (6/10A). The saltwater lake, controlled by sluices, makes a pleasant focal point – the bar overlooks it – and provides fishing. The adjacent woods have deer and there are views over the salt marshes to the sea.

Facilities	Directions
Four toilet blocks, three small and one more modern, heated large block, have washbasins in cabins, baby rooms and facilities for disabled visitors. Motorcaravan service point. Small shop (15/6-15/9). Bar with TV and terrace (1/7-31/8). Takeaway (5/7-24/8). Heated swimming and paddling pools (15/5-15/9). Indoor fitness facilities include multi-gym and sauna. Jacuzzi. Bicycle hire. Fishing. Minigolf. Boules. Play area. Off site: Port area, with shops, bars and restaurants, 1 km. Beach and sailing 1 km. Riding 4 km. Golf 12 km.	From La Trinité-sur-Mer take D781 to Carnac. Site is well signed on right 100 m. past the end of town sign for La Trinité-sur-Mer. GPS: N47:35.273 W03:02.613

Open: 1 April - 30 September.

Charges 2006

Per person	€ 3,50 - € 4,30
child (2-7 yrs)	€ 2,00 - € 2,50
pitch	€ 5,50 - € 12,95
electricity (6/10A)	€ 2,50 - € 3,50

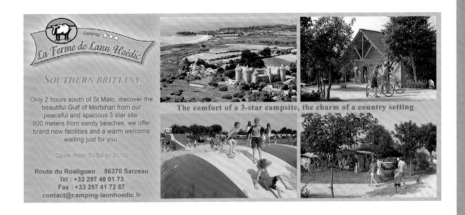

FR56250 Domaine le Bohat

Route d'Arzon, F-56370 Sarzeau (Morbihan)

Tel: 02 97 41 78 68. Email: brekelmans.famille@neuf.fr

Camping Le Bohat is a quiet site close to the Gulf of Morbihan and the medieval towns of Vannes and Auray. It is divided into two main parts by a wooded gully. The larger area by the entrance (some 120 pitches) was an orchard and some mature apple trees have been left to mark the pitches and provide some shade. On the other part, the 80 pitches are divided into small groups by hedges. There are 10 shaded pitches in the gully. All the pitches, except those in the gully, are flat and of good size, and most have electricity (10A). There is a pleasant bar overlooking the swimming pool in the converted farm building, which also houses the reception area.

Facilities

Three toilet blocks, one fairly new, with some washbasins in cabins, baby rooms and facilities for disabled visitors. Washing machines and dryer. Motorcaravan service point. Shop (all season). Bar and takeaway (1/7-31/8). Heated swimming and paddling pools (20/5-16/9). Games room. TV room. Three graded play areas. Children's club (1/7-31/8). Off site: Supermarket and town centre 2 km. Bicycle hire 2 km. Riding 2 km. Fishing, Sailing 3 km. Beach 6 km. Golf 6 km. Daily market in Aurey.

Open: 1 April - 1 November.

Directions

East of Vannes on the N165, join the D780 in the direction of Sarzeau. Bypass Sarzeau, keeping on D780, following signs to Arzon. Turn left (south) at site sign after 2 km. and site is 300 m. on right. GPS: N47:31.350 W02:47.824

Charges 2007

Per pitch with 2 persons	
and electricity	€ 18,50 - € 25,70
extra person	€ 4,60
child (3-13 yrs)	€ 3,00

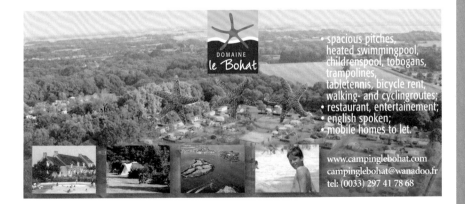

FR56180 Camping le Cénic

F-56760 Pénestin-sur-Mer (Morbihan)

Tel: **02 99 90 33 14**. Email: **info@lecenic.com**

Le Cénic is attractively set amidst trees and flowers, providing activities for all tastes. An attractive covered aquatic complex has water slides, bridges, rivers and a jacuzzi, whilst the outdoor pool comes complete with water slide, 'mushroom' fountain and sunbathing areas. You may fish in the lake or use inflatables, watched by the peacock, the geese and the turkeys. There is a hall for table tennis and a range of indoor games. There are 183 pitches, 100 of which are for touring. 90 have electricity (6A), but long leads will be required. The area has much to offer from the beaches of La Mine d'Or, the harbour at Trébiguier-Pénestin, the Golf du Morbihan with its numerous islands, La Baule with its magnificent beach and the medieval city of Guérande to the unique Brière nature reserve.

Facilities

Good new toilet block includes washbasins in cabins, facilities for disabled visitors, baby room and a separate laundry. Bar and shop (1/7-15/9). TV and games rooms (1/7-31/8). Indoor (15/4-15/9) and outdoor (1/7-31/8) swimming pools. Play area. Fishing. Off site: Riding 500 m. Bicycle hire 1 km. Sailing 2 km. Pénestin town 2 km. Sandy beaches 2.5 km. Golf 30 km.

Open: 1 May - 30 September.

Directions

From D34 (La Roche-Bernard), at roundabout just after entering Pénestin take D201 south (Assérac). After 100 m. take first turning on left. After 800 m. turn left and campsite is 300 m. on right down the narrow winding lane. GPS: N47:28.746 W02:27.386

Charges 2006

Per person	€ 4,50 - € 6,00
child (under 7 yrs.)	€ 2,00 - € 3,00
pitch	€ 5,00 - € 12,00
electricity	€ 4,00

Camping Cheques accepted.

Covered Aquatic Centre (heated swimming pool, balneotherapy area, children's pool), outdoor pool, water chute, games room, bar), fishing in the lake.
Le Cénic offers a range of accommodation : static caravans, chalets to rent.

www.lecenic.com
56760 Pénestin-sur-Mer   Tél : +33 (0)2 99 90 33 14   Fax : +33 (0)2 99 90 45 05

info@lecenic.com

FR56140 Camping Municipal du Bas de la Lande

F-56120 Guégon-Josselin (Morbihan)

Tel: **02 97 22 22 20**. Email: **campingbasdulalande@wanadoo.fr**

Bas de la Lande is a municipal site, ideally located for overnight stops. The Oust river, which makes up part of the Nantes - Brest canal, runs opposite the site and provides good fishing (permit needed). Bas de la Lande has 53 pitches, of which 49 are for touring and four are for mobile homes. 38 have electricity (6/10A). The pitches are on a number of flat terraces up a steep incline, and most are large, grassy and lightly shaded. As the site is situated close to the N24, a busy dual-carriageway, road noise can be audible in all parts of the site.

Facilities

The principal toilet block just behind reception has washbasins in cabins and large showers. Unit for disabled people (with shower, washbasin and toilet). Washing machine and dryer. A second, much older block is only used at peak periods. Motorcaravan service point. Play area. Fishing. Games and TV room. Table tennis. Off site: Minigolf (opposite site - free to campers). Nearest shops are in Josselin (2 km.), where there is also bicycle hire and tennis.

Open: 1 April - 31 October.

Directions

Leave N24 Rennes - Lorient road to west of Josselin following signs to Guégon, then Josselin. Site is clearly signed from the N24.

Charges 2006

Per person	€ 2,50 - € 3,00
child (under 7 yrs)	€ 1,30 - € 1,50
pitch	€ 2,10 - € 3,00
car or motorcaravan	€ 1,60 - € 2,00
motorcycle	€ 0,80 - € 1,00

Less 5% for stays over 5 nights, 10% for over 7 days. No credit cards.

FR56160 Camping la Vallée du Ninian

Le Rocher, F-56800 Taupont (Morbihan)

Tel: 02 97 93 53 01. Email: info@camping-ninian.com

M. and Mme. Joubaud have developed this peaceful family run site in central Brittany from a former farm and they continue to make improvements to ensure that their visitors have an enjoyable holiday. The level site falls into the three areas – the orchard with 32 large, hedged pitches with electricity, the wood with about 13 pitches more suited to tents, and the meadow by the river providing a further 35 pitches delineated by small trees and shrubs, some with electricity. The bar has as its centre-piece; a working cider press with which M. Joubaud makes his own 'potion magique'.

Facilities

A central building houses unisex toilet facilities including washbasins in cubicles, large cubicle with facilities for disabled visitors and laundry area with washing machines, dryer and ironing board. Covered dishwashing area with hot water. Shop (July/Aug) selling freshly cooked bread. Small (7 x 12 m.) heated swimming pool and children's pool with slide and fountain. Swings, slides and large trampoline. Fishing. Off site: Riding and bicycle hire 4 km. Golf 7 km.

Open: 15 April - 30 September.

Directions

From Plo'rmel follow signs to Taupont north on N8. Continue through Taupont and turn left (east) signed Vallée du Ninian. Follow road for 3 km. to site on left. From Josselin follow signs for Hellean. Through village, sharp right after river bridge. Site is 400 m.

Charges 2007

Per person	€ 2,80 - € 3,50
child (under 7 yrs)	€ 2,00 - € 2,50
pitch incl. electricity	€ 6,20 - € 8,80

Credit cards accepted in July/Aug. only.

FR56270 Camping les Menhirs

Allée St Michel, F-56340 Carnac (Morbihan)

Tel: 02 97 52 94 67. Email: contad@lesmenhirs.com

Although located within the built-up area of the popular resort of Carnac, and only 300 m. from the beach, this campsite feels much more rural. Catering for all ages, this is a friendly site and lively in high season with plenty of activities including evening entertainment and a club for children. There are 350 pitches; 154 touring pitches and the remainder used for mobile homes and chalets, of which the majority are used by tour operators. The touring pitches are in groups and are large, level and hedged. All have electricity (10A), water and drainage, and 14 have hardstanding. The central complex containing the pools and games areas, all overlooked by the bar and its terrace, makes a convivial focal point. The town and seafront can be explored on foot and the Brittany coast and the Gulf of Morbihan are within easy reach by car or bicycle.

Facilities

Three spotless, modern, light toilet blocks with washbasins in cabins, facilities for children, babies and disabled people. A further en-suite unit for disabled people. Laundry. Shop. Comfortable bar with satellite TV and takeaway (13/5-17/9). Heated indoor and outdoor swimming pools, the latter with slides (all season). Fitness complex with free massage, multi-gym, jacuzzi, sauna and solarium. Multisports pitch. Riding (1/7-31/8). Play areas. Children's club and evening entertainment (July/August). Off site: Beach 300 m. Bicycle hire 500 m. Golf 800 m. Sailing 1 km. Town centre 1 km.

Open: 1 May - 30 September.

Directions

From Auray take D786 to Carnac and Quiberon. After 5 km. turn south on D119 towards Carnac at roundabout. 600 m. beyond next roundabout fork left, signed La Trinité-sur-Mer and Plages. Keep straight on at lights. Fork left at first roundabout. Turn left at next roundabout (T-junction) and site is signed at 250 m. on left.

Charges 2006

Per person	€ 7,58
child (0-6 yrs)	€ 5,63
pitch	€ 28,97
electricity	€ 3,60

Check real time availability and at-the-gate prices...

www.alanrogers.com

FR56260 Camping le Conguel

Boulevard de la Teignouse, B.P. 20599, F-56170 Quiberon (Morbihan)

Tel: **02 97 50 19 11**. Email: **info@campingducongel.com**

Camping Le Conguel is situated on the coast near the southern tip of the Quiberon peninsula, about 2 km. from the town centre. The beach is just across the road (not busy except at weekends) and a national sailing school is 500 m. along the coast. The 75 touring pitches are in two groups along the seaward side of the site. They are flat and hedged, and all have electricity (10A), water and drainage. The remaining 175 pitches are taken up by mobile homes, some for tour operators. The site has a good range of facilities, as well as a children's club. There are separate activities for teenagers in July and August.

Facilities

Three modern, well-designed toilet blocks with baby rooms and facilities for the disabled. Laundry with washing machines and dryers. Heated swimming pool complex with slides (1/4-30/9). Bar (with TV). Restaurant, takeaway and shop (all 1/5-20/9). Tennis. Multi-gym. Sauna. Jacuzzis. Bicycle hire. Internet access. Off site: Beach and fishing 50 m. Boat ramp 200 m. Sailing school 500 m. Golf 500 m.

Open: 1 April - 31 October.

Directions

From N165 take Quiberon/Carnac exit onto D768. Follow road south to Quiberon town centre. At church turn left (east) signed Port Haliguen. At the port follow road round to the right towards the aerodrome. Site is on the right 1.5 km. along the coast.

Charges 2006

Per unit incl. 1 or 2 persons	€ 12,20 - € 41,80
extra person	€ 2,55 - € 6,80
electricity	€ 3,55

FR56280 Airotel les Sept Saints

Mobile homes ▶ page 458

B.P. 14, F-56410 Erdeven (Morbihan)

Tel: **02 97 55 52 65**. Email: **info@septsaints.com**

One is attracted to this campsite on arrival, with a well-tended shrubbery and reception to the left of the entrance and a landscaped pool complex on the right. The 200 pitches are divided equally between mobile homes and touring pitches, arranged in three separate groups: 60 normal touring pitches with electricity (10A), mobile homes, and an area under the trees across the play area for tents. Touring pitches are separated by manicured hedges and are level grass. The heated swimming pool complex, with its slides, jacuzzi and padding pool, and overlooked by the bar terrace, provides a focal point. In July and August there are separate children's clubs for younger children and teenagers and a variety of entertainment in the evenings. The site offers a complete holiday within itself as well as access to the Brittany coast.

Facilities

Two modern toilet blocks include en-suite facilities for disabled visitors and attractive baby rooms. Two laundry rooms. Bar, takeaway and shop (10/6-9/9). Heated swimming pool with slides, Jacuzzi and paddling pool with mushroom and baby slide (15/5-15/9). Excellent play areas. Multisports pitch. Boules. Grass area for ball games. Bicycle hire. Games room. TV room. Gas supplies. Internet. Off site: Fishing 1.5 km. Riding 3 km. Golf 3 km. Beach and sailing 3 km.

Open: 15 May - 15 September.

Directions

From N165 at Auray take exit for D768 to Carnac and Quiberon. At roundabout entering Plouharnel turn west on D781, following signs to Erdeven and L'Orient. Continue through Erdeven, turn left where site is signed after 1.5 km. and site is 150 m. on the right. GPS: N47:39.317 W03:10.307

Charges 2006

Per person	€ 4,00 - € 6,00
child (under 7 yrs)	€ 3,00 - € 5,00
pitch incl. electricity	€ 15,00 - € 22,00

MAP 2

Normandy

A striking area whose beauty lies not only in the landscape. Famed for its seafood and Celtic tradition, certain areas of Normandy remain untouched and wonderfully old fashioned.

DÉPARTEMENTS: 14 CALVADOS, 27 EURE, 50 MANCHE, 61 ORNE, 76 SEINE MARITIME

MAJOR CITIES: CAEN AND ROUEN

Normandy has a rich landscape full of variety. From the wild craggy granite coastline of the northern Cotentin to the long sandy beaches and chalk cliffs of the south. It also boasts a superb coastline including the Cotentin Peninsula, cliffs of the Côte d'Albâtre and the fine beaches and fashionable resorts of the Côte Fleurie. Plus a wealth of quiet villages and unspoilt countryside for leisurely exploration.

The history of Normandy is closely linked with our own. The famous Bayeux Tapestry chronicles the exploits of the Battle of Hastings and there are many museums, exhibitions, sites and monuments, including the Caen Memorial Museum, which commemorate operations that took place during the D-Day Landings of 1944.

Known as the dairy of France you'll also find plenty of fresh fish, rich cream, butter, and fine cheeses such as Camembert and Pont l'Evêque. The many apple orchards are used in producing cider and the well known Calvados, Normandy's apple brandy.

Places of interest

Bayeux: home to the famous tapestry; 15th-18th century houses, cathedral, museums.

Caen: feudal castle, Museum of Normandy, Museum for Peace.

Omaha Beach: D-Day beaches, Landing site monuments, American Cemetery.

Deauville: seaside resort, horse racing centre.

Giverny: home of impressionist painter Claude Monet, Monet Museum.

Honfleur: picturesque port city with old town.

Lisieux: pilgrimage site, shrine of Ste Thérèse.

Mont St Michel: world famous abbey on island.

Rouen: Joan of Arc Museum; Gothic churches, cathedrals, abbey, clock tower.

Cuisine of the region

Andouillette de Vire: small chitterling (tripe) sausage.

Barbue au cidre: brill cooked in cider and Calvados.

Douillons de pommes à la Normande: baked apples in pastry.

Escalope (Vallée d'Auge): veal sautéed and flamed in Calvados and served with cream and apples.

Ficelle Normande: pancake with ham, mushrooms and cheese.

Poulet (Vallée d'Auge): chicken cooked in the same way as Escalope Vallée d'Auge.

Tripes à la Mode de Caen: stewed beef tripe with onions, carrots, leeks, garlic, cider and Calvados.

FR14010 Camping de la Côte de Nacre

Rue du Général Moulton, F-14750 Saint Aubin sur Mer (Calvados)

Tel: **02 31 97 14 45**. Email: **camping-cote-de-nacre@wanadoo.fr**

De la Côte de Nacre is a large, commercial site with many facilities, all of a high standard. This could be an ideal holiday location for families with older children and teenagers. Two thirds of the site is given over to mobile homes and there are five tour operators on the site. The touring pitches are reasonable, both in size and condition. With pleasant, well cared for flowerbeds, there is some hedging to the pitches, but not much, and a few trees, so little shade. There is a 'state of the art' pool complex which includes a covered pool (lifeguards in attendance).

Facilities	Directions
One open toilet block has showers and washbsins in cubicles. New block under construction for 07. Laundry room. Bar, restaurant and takeaway. Pool complex with outdoor and indoor pools, slides, etc. Play area. Library. Games room. Children's club. Multisports area. Off site: Town 1 km.	Travel west from Ouistreham on D514 to St Aubin-sur-Mer. Site is well signed, just off the main road in a residential area. GPS: N49:19.34 W00:23.24

Open: 1 April - 17 September.

Charges 2006

Per unit incl. 2 persons and electricity	€ 16,00 - € 38,00
extra person	€ 5,00 - € 8,00
child (2-7 yrs)	free - € 5,00

FR14020 Camping Municipal du Bayeux

Boulevard Eindhoven, F-14400 Bayeux (Calvados)

Tel: **02 31 92 08 43**

Only a few kilometres from the coast and the landing beaches this site makes a very useful night stop on the way to or from Cherbourg, whether or not you want to see the tapestry. The 140 pitches are in two areas (many on hardstanding), well marked and generally of good size with electricity. The site is busy over a long season – early arrival is advised as reservations are not taken. There is a full time warden from 15/6-15/9, otherwise reception is open from 08.00-10.00 and 17.00-19.00 hrs. There may be some road noise on one side of the site.

Facilities	Directions
The two good quality toilet blocks have British and Turkish style WCs, washbasins in cabins in main block, and units for disabled people. Motorcaravan service point. Laundry room. Takeaway food and snacks. Two playgrounds. Volleyball. Reading room with TV. Games room. Off site: Large public indoor swimming pool adjoins site with children's pool and jacuzzi. Supermarket nearby (closes 8 pm). Bicycle hire 1 km. Riding 5 km. Beach, golf or fishing 8 km.	Site is on the south side of northern ring road (D613) to town, and just west of the junction with the D516 to autoroute. GPS: N49:17.037 W00:41.857

Open: 1 May - 30 September.

Charges 2006

Per person	€ 3,10
child (under 7 yrs)	€ 1,65
pitch and car	€ 3,83
electricity	€ 3,14

Less 10% for stay over 5 days.

FR14030 Castel Camping le Château de Martragny

F-14740 Martragny (Calvados)

Tel: **02 31 80 21 40**. Email: **chateau.martragny@wanadoo.fr**

Martragny is an attractive site in a parkland setting adjoining the château. Close to D-Day beaches, it is also convenient for the ports of Caen and Cherbourg, and has the facilities and charm to encourage both long stays and stopovers. The pleasant lawns surrounding and approaching the château take 160 units, with electricity connections for 140. Most pitches are divided by either a small hedge or a few trees. Bed and breakfast are available in the château all year (reservation essential). Madame de Chassey takes great pride in the site and takes care that peace and quiet is preserved.

Facilities	Directions
Three modernised sanitary blocks include washbasins in cabins, sinks for dishes and clothes and two baby baths. Disabled people are well catered for. Good laundry. Shop and takeaway food bar open 21/5-15/9. Bar. Swimming pool (20 x 6 m.) and paddling pool heated in poor weather. Play areas. Tennis courts. Minigolf. Games and TV room. Table tennis and billiards. Fishing. Bicycle and buggy hire. Off site: Riding 1 km. Beach 15 km. Golf 20 km.	Site is off N13, 8 km. southeast of Bayeux. Take Martragny exit from dual carriageway. GPS: N49:14.595 W00:36.348

Open: 1 May - 15 September.

Charges 2006

Per person	€ 4,50 - € 5,00
child (under 7 yrs)	€ 2,50 - € 2,70
pitch	€ 9,00 - € 11,00
electricity (6/10A)	€ 2,70 - € 3,00

Less 15% outside 1/7-31/8.
Camping Cheques accepted.

FR14060 Camping les Hautes Coutures

Route de Ouistreham, F-14970 Bénouville (Calvados)

Tel: 02 31 44 73 08. Email: camping-hautes-coutures@wanadoo.fr

Les Hautes Coutures is a useful site for overnight stays and near the Caen-Portsmouth ferry terminal. It is beside the Caen ship canal, 2 km. from the sea (and ferry port) and 10 km. from Caen. Gates open at 6 am. for early ferries and there can be movement on site late into the evening. There are 120 grass touring pitches of 100 sq.m. and clearly marked by mature hedges with tarmac roads. All have electrical connections (up to 10A). An area close to the canal is being developed to provide further pitches. There are also around 150 mobile homes.

Facilities

Two toilet blocks include showers, washbasins in cabins (warm water). Facilities can be under pressure at peak times with variable hot water supply. In low season only one block may be open. Dishwashing and laundry facilities. Motorcaravan service point. Small shop. Bar and takeaway. Small heated swimming pool (from June). Small lounge/TV area and games room. Play area. Tennis courts. Volleyball. Minigolf. Boules. Off site: Beach and riding 2 km. Golf 4 km.

Open: 1 April - 30 September.

Directions

Site is just off the D514 dual-carriageway, north of Bénouville. From Caen, follow Ouistreham car ferry signs and take first exit from D514 after Bénouville. GPS: N49:15.003 W00:16.396

Charges 2007

Per person	€ 8,20
child (under 7 yrs)	€ 5,50
pitch	€ 8,20
electricity (4/10A)	€ 6,40 - € 8,50

FR14070 Camping de la Vallée

Mobile homes ▶ page 458

88 rue de la Vallée, F-14510 Houlgate (Calvados)

Tel: 02 31 24 40 69. Email: camping.lavallee@wanadoo.fr

Camping de la Vallée is an attractive site with good, well maintained facilities, situated on one of the rolling hillsides overlooking the seaside resort of Houlgate. The original farmhouse building has been converted to house a good bar and comfortable TV lounge and billiards room overlooking the pool. The site has 373 pitches with around 100 for touring units. Large, open and separated by hedges, all the pitches have 4 or 6A electricity. Part of the site is sloping, the rest level, with gravel or tarmac roads. Shade is provided by a variety of well kept trees and shrubs.

Facilities

Three good toilet blocks include washbasins in cabins, mainly British style toilets, facilities for disabled people and baby bathrooms. Laundry facilities (no washing lines allowed). Motorcaravan services. Shop (from 1/5). Bar. Snack bar with takeaway in season (from 15/5). Heated swimming pool (15/5-20/9; no shorts). Games room. Playground. Bicycle hire. Volleyball, football, tennis, petanque. Entertainment in Jul/Aug. Internet access. Off site: Riding 500 m. Beach, town 1 km. Golf 2 km.

Open: 1 April - 30 September.

Directions

From A13 take exit for Cabourg following signs for Dives/Houlgate. Go straight on at two roundabouts, then four sets of traffic lights. Turn left along sea front. After 1 km. at lights turn right, after about 1 km. go over mini-roundabout - look for site sign and flag poles on right. Site well signed around town especially from the D513 coast road. GPS: N49:17.644 W00:04.097

Charges 2006

Per unit incl. 2 persons and electricity	€ 21,00 - € 30,00
extra person	€ 5,00 - € 6,00
child (under 7 yrs)	€ 3,00 - € 4,00

Credit card minimum € 50.
Camping Cheques accepted.

www.campinglavallee.com
Tél.: +33 (0)2 31 24 40 69
88, rue de la Vallée
14510 HOULGATE

Authentic Normandy... 900 m away from the beaches

FR14090 Castel Camping du Brévedent

Le Brévedent, F-14130 Pont-l'Evêque (Calvados)

Tel: 02 31 64 72 88. Email: contact@campinglebrevedent.com

Le Brévedent is a well established, traditional site with 144 pitches (109 for tourists) set in the grounds of an elegant 18th century hunting pavilion. Level pitches are either around the fishing lake, in the lower gardens, or in the old orchard. Most have electricity. The site is used by a tour operator (31 pitches). It is an excellent holiday destination within easy reach of the Channel ports. Apart from the church bells ringing at 07.00 hrs, the otherwise peaceful, friendly environment makes it ideal for mature campers or families with younger children (note: the lake is unfenced).

Facilities

Three toilet blocks include washbasins in cubicles and facilities for babies and disabled people. Dishwashing and laundry facilities. Motorcaravan service point. Shop. Baker each morning. Bar open evenings (1/5-25/9). Restaurant (24/5-19/9). Takeaway (1/5-25/9). Clubroom. Internet access. TV and library. Heated swimming pool (1/5-25/9). Playground. Minigolf. Boules. Games room. Fishing. Rowing. Bicycle and buggy hire. Dogs are not accepted. Off site: Riding 1 km. Golf. Beach 25 km.

Open: 28 April - 23 September.

Directions

From Pont-L'Evêque take D579 toward Lisieux for 4 km. then D51 towards Moyaux. At Blangy le Château turn right (still on D51) to Le Brévedent. GPS: N49:13.528 E00:18.342

Charges 2007

Per person	€ 5,20 - € 6,70
child (1-6 yrs)	€ 2,20 - € 3,50
child (7-12 yrs)	€ 3,35 - € 4,50
pitch incl. electricity	€ 9,45 - € 11,45

Camping Cheques accepted.

FR14100 Camping Municipal du Château

3 rue du Val d'Ante, F-14700 Falaise (Calvados)

Tel: 02 31 90 16 55. Email: camping@falaise.fr

The location of this site is really quite spectacular, lying in the shadow of the Château de Falaise, in the old part of the town, in the 'coeur de Normandie'. The site itself is small, with only 66 pitches (all with 6A electricity). It has a rather intimate 'up-market' feel about it, different from the average municipal site. With good shade, tarmac roads and easy access, it was well recommended by the British campers we met there. Whatever this site lacks in size and facilities it makes up for in its situation. Charges are reasonable and the reception friendly.

Facilities

The quantity of sanitary facilities could be insufficient when the site is full - perhaps it never is and campers we met there felt they were adequate. Although dated, quality is good and cleanliness reasonable. Unit for disabled visitors (shower room and separate WC). Access to showers, laundry and dishwashing closed 22.00-07.30. Motorcaravan service point. Play area. TV room. Fishing. Off site: Tennis. Bicycle hire 300 m. Riding 500 m.

Open: 1 May - 30 September.

Directions

Site on western side of town, well signed from ring road. From N158 heading south take first roundabout into Falaise (site signed),through residential suburb to site. GPS: N48:53.734 W00:12.288

Charges 2007

Per person	€ 3,30
child (3-12 yrs)	€ 2,20
pitch incl. electricity	€ 6,50

FR14130 Camping le Fanal

Rue de Fanal, F-14230 Isigny-sur-Mer (Calvados)

Tel: 02 31 21 33 20. Email: info@camping-le-fanal.com

A useful, informal, spacious site, Le Fanal is 400 m. from the centre of a fairly typical small town. There are 186 pitches, of which 93 are for touring (100 sq.m.), all on grass with around 42 electric hook-ups (16A), arranged in several large bays, surrounded by mature trees. Some areas could be a little soft in inclement weather, so the site is not really suitable for American RVs. The small, heated and covered swimming pool (10 x 4 m.) may look like a child's pool, but is in fact between one and two metres deep – only supervised children are permitted.

Facilities

The main sanitary unit provides washbasins in cubicles, pre-set hot showers, plus facilities for disabled people. Motorcaravan service point. Bar and restaurant with takeaway (from 15/06). The reception building has a dining room with microwave and soft drink machines, a lounge with TV, laundry facilities, plus more toilets and washbasins. Small swimming pool (July and Aug). Playground. Off site: Fishing and boating in the lake.

Open: 31 March - 30 September.

Directions

Isigny-sur-Mer is just off N13, midway between Cherbourg and Caen, (10 km. east of Carentan). Site is west of town centre off D197A, and is well signed. GPS: N49:19.194 W01:06.589

Charges 2007

Per person	€ 2,00 - € 4,60
child (2-12 yrs)	€ 1,80 - € 3,85
pitch incl.	€ 15,00 - € 25,80

No credit cards.

FR14140 Camping Municipal Pont Farcy

F-14380 Pont Farcy (Calvados)

Tel: 02 31 68 32 06

This well tended, riverside site is in a tranquil location within easy walking distance of the small village. Just off the A84 motorway it is within easy driving distance of Cherbourg or Caen. A warden lives on site. The 60 numbered pitches are on grass, some separated by small hedges, with electricity (5A) available to all (long leads may be needed). Activities either on-site or at the adjacent 'base plein air' include tennis, minigolf, volleyball, petanque, canoe/kayak, pedaloes and cycle hire, walking and fishing. Swimming is not permitted and the river is well fenced with access gates for anglers.

Facilities	Directions
A rather stylish modern building houses all the facilities, including some washbasins in cubicles and a suite for disabled campers. First floor 'salle' with dining tables for campers, table tennis and other games (ask the warden). There is a lift from the ground floor. Adventure style playground (5-12 yrs). Off site: Village garage with a small shop, bakery, butcher, post office. Bar/hotel. Attractions include the Gorges de la Vire and opportunities in the area for riding, climbing and parachuting.	Pont Farcy is about 25 km. due south of St Lô. From A84, exit 39, take D21 south for 1 km. Site is on left at entrance to village. GPS: N48:56.395 W01:02.120

Open: 1 April - 30 September.

Charges 2006

Per unit incl. 1 or 2 persons	€ 9,00
extra person	€ 2,15
child (under 7 yrs)	€ 1,00
electricity	€ 1,85
No credit cards.	

FR14150 Sunelia Port'land

Chemin du Castel, F-14520 Port en Bessin (Calvados)

Tel: 02 31 51 07 06. Email: campingportland@wanadoo.fr

Port'land is a newly built site lying 700 metres to the east of the little resort of Port en Bessin, one of Normandy's busiest fishing ports. The 300 pitches are large and grassy with 202 available for touring units. Most offer 10A electricity although there is a separate area for tents without electricity. The camping area has been imaginatively designed into distinct zones, some overlooking small fishing ponds and another radiating out from a central barbecue area. An attractive building houses reception and the amenities which include a shop, and a bar and restaurant with views over the Normandy coastline. There are site-owned mobile homes for rent. A member of the Sunelia group.

Facilities	Directions
The two sanitary blocks are modern and well maintained. Special disabled facilities. Heated swimming pool (covered in low season) and paddling pool. Bar, restaurant, takeaway (all open all season). Large TV and games room. Multisports pitch. Fishing. Play area. Off site: Beach 4 km. 27 hole Omaha Beach International golf course adjacent. D-Day beaches. Colleville American war Cemetery. Bayeux.	Site is clearly signed off the D514 4 km. west of Port en Bessin.

Open: 1 April - 5 November.

Charges 2006

Per unit incl. 2 persons	€ 15,50 - € 32,30
extra person	€ 4,80 - € 7,30
child (2-10 yrs)	€ 2,80 - € 4,20
dog	€ 4,00

FR14160 Camping Bellevue

Mobile homes ▶ page 458

Route des Dives, F-14640 Villers–sur-Mer (Calvados)

Tel: 02 31 87 05 21. Email: contact@camping-bellevue.com

Bellevue is located just west of Villers-sur-Mer with its sandy beach, and 9.5 km. west of fashionable Deauville. A fairly large site with 249 pitches in total, but including 190 privately owned mobile homes and 20 units for rent, there are only 59 pitches left for tourists. Many of these are on terraces, individual and relatively small with restricted access, so suitable only for smaller units. Double axle caravans will have difficulty and will only be able to access pitches adjacent to the road. There are around half a dozen, further level pitches behind reception mostly used by motorcaravans (unsuitable for American RVs).

Facilities	Directions
Two sanitary units provide unisex facilities, all in individual cubicles, with some wide door cubicles for disabled visitors. Baby changing room. Laundry facilities and dishwashing sinks. Swimming pool complex (15/6-15/9). Bar (1/7-15/9). Takeaway van (July/Aug). Video games machines. Pool table. Playground. Organised activities in peak season. Off site: Golf 4 km. Riding 2 km. Beach and town 1.5 km.	Villers-sur-Mer is about 8 km. west of Deauville. The site is 1.5 km. west of Villers on the D513; be ready to turn right into lane (site signed) at the crest of a hill, where the road bends to the right. GPS: N49:18.562 W00:1.178

Open: 1 April - 31 October.

Charges 2006

Per person	€ 6,00
child (0-7 yrs)	€ 3,50
pitch incl. electricity	€ 11,00

FR14170 Camping la Capricieuse

2 rue Brummel, F-14530 Luc-sur-Mer (Calvados)

Tel: **02 31 97 34 43**. Email: **info@campinglacapricieuse.com**

La Capricieuse is situated on the edge of the delightful small seaside town of Luc-sur-Mer. It is an ideal location for those looking for a superb municipal site just a few minutes drive from the Ouistreham car ferry. This immaculate site has 204 touring pitches of varying size, on level grass with hedges and a variety of trees give some shade. There are 105 with electricity and 52 also have water and drainage. Although the site does not have its own shop, bar or restaurant, these can be found within walking distance in Luc-sur-Mer.

Facilities

Three modern toilet blocks with washbasins in cubicles and showers are kept very clean. Fully equipped facilities for disabled visitors. Laundry and dishwashing facilities. Motorcaravan service point. Large TV room. Games room. Adventure playground (unfenced). Tennis. Boules. Off site: Fishing and bicycle hire nearby. Riding 3 km. Golf 30 km.

Open: 1 April - 30 September.

Directions

Take the D514 from Ouistreham car ferry and head west to Luc-sur-Mer. Campsite is well signed from the western end of St Luc.

Charges 2006

Per person	€ 4,20
pitch	€ 5,00
child (0-7 yrs)	€ 2,20
electricity (6/10A)	€ 3,80 - € 5,20

FR14180 Camping la Briquerie

Equemauville, F-14600 Honfleur (Calvados)

Tel: **02 31 89 28 32**. Email: **info@campinglabriquerie.com**

La Briquerie is a large, neat municipal site on the outskirts of the attractive and popular harbour town of Honfleur. Very well cared for and efficiently run by a family team, the site has 420 pitches, many of which are let on a seasonal basis. There are also 130 medium to large, hedged touring pitches. All have electricity (5/10A), water and drainage. One of the main attractions here is the close proximity to Honfleur where one can watch the fishing boats from the quay or browse the work of the artists who display their work in the galleries around the town.

Facilities

Two toilet blocks with washbasins in cubicles and showers. Good facilities for disabled visitors. Laundry room with washing machines and dryers. Large restaurant (July/Aug). Takeaway (1/6-15/9). Bar (1/6-30/9). Small shop (July/Aug). Large pool complex with two flumes (15/5-15/9). Sauna. Jacuzzi. Fitness room. Boules, table tennis and minigolf. TV and internet access. Off site: Supermarket adjacent. Riding and bicycle hire 1 km. Beach 2 km. Fishing 5 km. Golf 7 km.

Open: 1 April - 30 September.

Directions

Site is well signed from Honfleur on the D579, beside the Intermarche on the D62. GPS: N49:23.868 E00:12.514

Charges 2006

Per person	€ 5,50
child (0-7 yrs)	€ 3,00
pitch incl. water and drainage	€ 6,00
electricity (5/10A)	€ 4,50 - € 5,50
animal	€ 2,00

FR14200 Camping la Vallée de Deauville

Route de Beaumont, F-14800 St Arnoult (Calvados)

Tel: 02 31 88 58 17. Email: campinglavalleededeauville@wannadoo.fr

Close to the traditional seaside resorts of Deauville and Trouville, this large, modern site is owned and run by a delightful Belgian couple. With a total of 450 pitches, there are many mobile homes, both for rent and privately owned, and 150 used for touring units. These pitches are level, of a reasonable size and mostly hedged, and 100 have 10A electricity connections. A brand new pool complex complete with flumes, lazy river, jacuzzi and fun pool makes an attractive focal point near the entrance and there is a large fishing lake. The bar and restaurant are large and comfortable and there is a very good shop on the site. The wide sandy beaches of this coast are 3 km. With the various new developments at this site, it promises to be a good choice in the Deauville and Caen area.

Facilities

Two new heated toilet blocks with showers and washbasins in cubicles. Good facilities for babies and disabled visitors. Laundry facilities. Small shop, bar and restaurant (high season). Takeaway (July/Aug). New swimming pool complex. Good play area and play room. Table tennis. Entertainment in high season. Off site: Golf and riding 2 km. Bicycle hire 3 km. Beach 3 km.

Open: 1 April - 31 October.

Directions

From the north, take the A29, then the A13 at Pont l'Eveque. Join the N177 (Deauville/Trouville) and after 9 km. take the D27 signed St Arnoult. Site is well signed on edge of village.

Charges 2006

Per person	€ 7,00
child (0-7 yrs)	€ 5,00
pitch	€ 12,00
electricity (16A)	€ 3,00
animal	€ 4,00

Camping La Vallee de Deauville

Route de Beaumont
14800 Deauville-St-Arnoult

Tél: (33) 02 31 88 11 57
Fax: (33) 2 31 88 11 57

FR14190 Camping les Peupliers

Allée des Pins, F-14810 Merville-Franceville (Calvados)

Tel: 02 31 24 05 07. Email: asl-mondeville@wanadoo.fr

Les Peupliers is run by friendly, family managers who keep this site attractive and tidy. It is just 300 metres from a long, wide, sandy beach. The touring pitches, of which there are 85, are on level open ground, all with 10A electricity. Those in the newest part are hedged but, with just a few trees on the edge of the site, there is little shade. The campsite amenities are near the entrance, housed in neat modern buildings. An animation programme for children and various activities are organised in high season. This site is ideally located for visiting Caen, Bayeux and the traditional seaside towns of Deauville and Trouville.

Facilities

Two excellent heated toilet blocks with washbasins in cabins and showers. Good facilities for disabled visitors and for babies. Laundry room. Small shop, bar with terrace and takeaway (all July/Aug). Heated swimming pool and paddling pool (May-Sept). Play area. Games room. Entertainment in high season. Off site: Fishing, riding and golf all within 1 km. Bicycle hire 2 km.

Open: 1 April - 30 October.

Directions

From Ouistreham take the D514 to Merville-Franceville. Site is well signed off Allée des Pins. From Rouen on A13 (exit 29B), take D400 to Cabourg then the D514 to Merville-Franceville.

Charges 2006

Per person	€ 6,45
child (0-7 yrs)	€ 3,80
pitch incl. electricity	€ 12,10

FR27010 Camping Caravaning des Etangs Risle-Seine

19 route des Etangs, Toutainville, F-27500 Pont Audemer (Eure)

Tel: **02 32 42 46 65**. Email: **camping@ville-pont-audemer.fr**

This attractive and well maintained site is owned by the Pont Audemer Council and run by an enthusiastic manager. It is well laid out with 61 hedged pitches on level grass and electricity connections for 28 of them. Fishing and watersports are possible as the site is positioned next to some large lakes, but swimming is not allowed. In high season a shuttle bus goes to Pont-Audemer where you will find shops, restaurants and a good swimming complex.

Facilities

Two well equipped and maintained toilet blocks with facilities for disabled visitors. They include washbasins in cabins and pre-set showers. Laundry and dishwashing facilities. Bar area with terrace (soft drinks only as there is no alcohol licence, visitors may bring their own). Bread and milk available. Paddling pool. Playing field. TV. Bicycle hire. Fishing. Takeaway food and courtesy bus (high season).

Open: 15 March - 15 November.

Directions

Approaching from north or south on D810, at the bridge over the River Risle, turn to the west on south side of river and travel 1.5 km. on Rue des Etangs. Site is well signed.

Charges 2006

Per person	€ 2,81
child (under 7 yrs)	€ 1,48
pitch incl. electricity	€ 8,57 - € 10,39
with water and drainage	€ 7,24

FR27020 Camping du Domaine Catinière

Route de Honfleur, F-27210 Fiquefleur-Equainville (Eure)

Tel: **02 32 57 63 51**. Email: **info@camping-catiniere.com**

A peaceful, friendly site, close to the Normandy coast, in the countryside yet in the middle of a very long village, this site is steadily achieving a modern look, whilst retaining its original French flavour. There are 14 rental and 30 privately owned mobile homes, but there should be around 88 pitches for tourists including a large open field for tents and units not needing electricity. Caravan pitches are separated, some with shade, others are more open and all have electricity hook-ups. The site is divided by well fenced streams, popular with young anglers.

Facilities

Toilet facilities include mostly British style WCs, some washbasins in cubicles, and facilities for disabled people and babies (cleaning can be variable). Dishwashing sinks. Washing machine and dryer. Reception with shop. Small bar/restaurant with regional dishes and snacks. Heated swimming pool (1/6-31/8). Two playgrounds, trampoline. Table tennis. Boules. Barrier (card deposit). Off site: Large supermarket close to southern end of the bridge. Smaller supermarket in Beuzeville 7 km. Beach 7 km.

Open: 7 April - 24 September.

Directions

From the Pont de Normandie (toll bridge). Take first exit on leaving bridge (exit 3, A29) signed Honfleur. At roundabout turn left under motorway in direction of Le Mans and Alencon on D180. Take second exit on right after 2.5 km, onto D22 (Beuzeville). Site on right after 1 km. GPS: N49:24.054 E00:18.365

Charges 2007

Per pitch incl. 1 or 2 persons	€ 14,00 - € 18,00
with electricity	€ 18,00 - € 23,00
extra person	€ 4,00 - € 5,00
Credit cards accepted (minimum of € 70).	

FR27050 Camping Municipal Saint Paul

2 route de Saint Paul, F-27480 Lyons la Foret (Eure)

Tel: **02 32 49 42 02**

The village of Lyons La Foret, with its medieval covered market and magnificently preserved half-timbered buildings is regarded as one of the most beautiful in France. Within walking distance (900 metres), next to the stadium and public swimming pool, this quiet municipal campsite provides a pleasant respite. The site has 100 level grass, numbered pitches, separated by hedges or mature trees providing shade. 60 are available for tourists and each has access to electricity (6A), water and drainage. The site is edged by fast-flowing, shallow (unfenced) streams.

Facilities

Two reasonable toilet blocks include facilities for people with disabilities. These facilities could be stretched in peak season and cleaning may be variable. Laundry and dishwashing sinks. Washing machine. Drying lines. Play area. Separate tent area. Off site: All facilities in nearby village. Many walking and cycling routes.

Open: 1 April - 31 October.

Directions

Site is to the north of Lyons-La-Foret on the D921 road. GPS: N49:24.185 E01:28.693

Charges guide

Per unit incl. 2 persons	€ 15,00
tent pitch incl. 2 persons	€ 13,00
extra person	€ 2,50
No credit cards.	

FR27030 Camping Saint Nicolas

F-27800 Le Bec-Hellouin (Eure)

Tel: **02 32 44 83 55**

This lovely site (formerly a municipal site and still run by the same resident wardens) is located on a forested hillside above the interesting and attractive small town of Le Bec-Hellouin. The town is quite photogenic, has the usual tourist shops, several bars and restaurants and horse drawn carriage rides. There are 90 marked grassy pitches, 30 used for seasonal units, leaving about 60 for tourists all with 10A hook-ups and some with water taps. There is limited shade from a few mature trees. A rather steep footpath leads down to the town and the imposing Abbey of Bec. This is still a working monastery, which was founded in 1034, at the time of William the Conqueror, and has links to the archbishops of Canterbury – well worth a visit. The surrounding area is very popular with artists and photographers and there is a wealth of interesting historical and cultural places to visit.

Facilities

A modern heated unit has good showers, British style WCs, open and cubicled washbasins, and a dishwashing area. Extra facilities in the old unit by reception, where you will find the laundry. Reception keeps soft drinks and ices. The baker calls each morning. Playground. Playing field and tennis courts. Off site: Le Bec-Hellouin and its Abbey 1.5 km. Fishing 1.5 km. Riding 2 km. Swimming pool at Brionne 6 km. Golf 7 km.

Open: 1 April - 30 September.

Directions

Le Bec-Hellouin is about 30 km. southwest of Rouen, 24 km. southeast of Pont Audemer, just off the D130 between Pont Authou and Brionne. Turn east onto D39 to Le Bec-Hellouin, pass through edge of town. At far end of one-way section, turn left on minor road. Continue for 1 km. Take left fork, for about 500 m. to site. GPS: N49:14.086 E00:43.519

Charges 2006

Per unit incl. 2 persons and electricity	€ 10,40
extra person	€ 2,85
child under 7 yrs	€ 1,45

No credit cards.

FR27060 Domaine de Marcilly

Mobile homes ▶ page 459

F-27810 Marcilly-sur-Eure (Eure)

Tel: **02 37 48 51 11**. Email: **domainedemarcilly@wanadoo.fr**

FR27070 Camping l'Ile de Trois Rois

Mobile homes ▶ page 459

FR27700 Les Andelys (Eure)

Tel: **02 32 54 23 79**. Email: campingtroisrois@aol.com

One hour from Paris and 30 minutes from Rouen, L'Ile des Trois Rois has an attractive setting on the banks of the Seine and has a private fishing lake within the grounds of Château-Gaillard. The site has 300 spacious, shady pitches all with electricity. There are also mobile homes for rent. Recommended by our French agent and we plan to undertake a full inspection in 2007.

Facilities

Swimming pool. Fishing in the Seine or in the private lake. Volleyball. Games room. Animation, evening entertainment in peak season. Off site: Day trips to Paris and Rouen. Cycling and walking trails. Golf, riding.

Open: March - November.

Directions

From the A13 motorway, take exit 17 and join the D316 to Les Andelys. In Les Andelys follow signs to Evreux, and the campsite is located before passing the bridge over the Seine.

Charges 2007

Per unit (incl 2 persons	
and electricity	€ 15,00
extra person	€ 10,00
child (under 3 years)	free

L'Ile des Trois Rois

swimming pool opens during summer of 2007

The park Ile des Trois Rois is situated in the most beautiful bend of the Seine nearby Castle Gaillard in Normandy and is a haven of peace. Paris is situated of less than than an hour and Rouen is half an hour driving from the camp site.

Facilities: two heated swimming pools, ping pong, camper service, bar and restaurant (high season) and play area

1, Rue Gilles Nicole - F-27700 Les Andelys - France
Tel. 0033 (0) 2 32 54 23 79 - Fax 0033 (0) 2 32 51 14 54 - Email campingtroisrois@aol.com

FR50010 Camping la Gallouette

F-50550 Saint Vaast La Hougue (Manche)

Tel: **02 33 54 20 27**. Email: contact@camping-logallouette.fr

Claudine and Jean Luc Boblin will give you a warm welcome at their seaside campsite which is ideally placed for visiting Barfleur, Ste Mère-Eglise and the Normandy landing beaches. There are 192 level pitches in total, 132 of which are for touring and all have 6A electricity. Some are separated by hedges and there are many colourful flower beds, shrubs and trees but little shade. A light and airy bar faces onto a terrace and swimming pool and there is also a state-of-the-art multisports court.

Facilities

Three modern sanitary blocks, one open and two enclosed, have British style toilets, showers and washbasins (some in cabins). Area for disabled visitors and for babies. Laundry facilities. Small shop. Snack bar. Bar with terrace. Swimming pool. Multisports court. Play area. Petanque. Fishing. Internet access. Entertainment in high season. Off site: Beach 300m. Shops and restaurant in Saint-Vaast. Riding 5 km. Golf 12 km.

Open: 1 April - 30 September.

Directions

The D902 runs between Barfleur and Valognes on the eastern side of the Cherbourg peninsula. About half way along at Quettehou take the D1 to Saint-Vaast. Site signed on right on entering town. GPS: N49:35.04 W01:16.07

Charges 2006

Per person	€ 4,50 - € 5,50
child (1-7 yrs)	€ 2,80 - € 3,50
pitch	€ 6,20 - € 9,80
electricity (4/6A)	€ 2,50 - € 3,70

FR50000 Camping L'Etang des Haizes

43 rue Cauticotte, F-50250 Saint Symphorien-le-Valois (Manche)

Tel: 02 33 46 01 16. Email: etang.des.haizes@wanadoo.fr

This is an attractive and very friendly site with a swimming pool complex with four-lane slides, jacuzzi and a paddling pool. L'Etang des Haizes has 98 good size pitches, of which 60 are for touring units, on fairly level ground and all with electricity (10A). They are set in a mixture of conifers, orchard and shrubbery, with some very attractive, slightly smaller pitches overlooking the lake and 38 mobile homes inconspicuously sited. The fenced lake has a small beach (swimming is permitted), ducks and pedaloes, and offers good coarse fishing for huge carp (we are told). Believe it or not, a turtle can sometimes be seen on a fine day! Just one kilometre away is La Haye-du-Puits with two supermarkets, good restaurants and a market on Wednesdays. A good sandy beach is within 10 km. and the Normandy landing beaches are 25 km.

Facilities

Two well kept and modern unisex toilet blocks have British style toilets, washbasins in cabins, units for disabled people and two family cabins. Small laundry. Motorcaravan services. Milk, bread and takeaway snacks available (no gas). Snackbar/bar with TV and terrace. Pool complex (all 20/5-10/9). Play areas. Bicycle hire. Table tennis, pool table, petanque and volleyball. Organised activities including treasure hunts, archery and food tasting (10/7-25/8). Off site: Beach 10 km.

Open: 1 April - 16 October.

Directions

Site is just north of La Haye du Puits on the primary route from Cherbourg to Mont St Michel, St Malo and Rennes. It is 24 km. south of N13 at Valognes and 29 km. north of Coutances: leave D900 at roundabout at northern end of by-pass (towards town). Site signed on right.
GPS: N49:18.031 W01:32.729

Charges 2006

Per person (over 4 yrs)	€ 4,00 - € 6,00
pitch	€ 5,00 - € 17,00
electricity (10A)	€ 3,00 - € 5,00

Camping Cheques accepted.

FR50060 Camping le Grand Large

F-50340 Les Pieux (Manche)

Tel: **02 33 52 40 75**. Email: **le-grand-large@wanadoo.fr**

Le Grand Large is a well established, quality family site with direct access to a long sandy beach and within a 20 kilometre drive of Cherbourg. It is a neat and tidy site with 174 touring pitches divided and separated by hedging giving an orderly, well laid out appearance. A separate area has 40 mobile homes for rent. The reception area is at the entrance (with a security barrier) and the forecourt is decorated with flower beds. To the rear of the site and laid out in the sand-hills is an excellent play area with swings, slides and climbing frame. A 'Sites et Paysages' member. Not surprisingly the sandy beach is the big attraction. Roads around the site are tarmac and there are pleasant views across the bay to the tip of the Cherbourg peninsula.

Facilities

Two well maintained toilet blocks. The main one is modern and includes washbasins in cubicles and some family rooms. WCs are mostly to the outside of the building. Provision for disabled people. Baby bathroom. Laundry area. Motorcaravan services. Shop for basics, bar (all season), snacks (1/7-26/8). Swimming pool and children's pool. Play area. Tennis. Boules. TV room. Animation in July/Aug. Off site: Bicycle hire and riding 5 km. Golf 15 km.

Open: 8 April - 17 September.

Directions

From Cherbourg port take N13 south for about 2 km. Branch right on D650 (previously D904) signed Cartaret. Continue for 18 km. to Les Pieux. Take the D4 in town and turn left just after 'Super U' supermarket. Follow site signs via D117/517. GPS: N49:29.665 W01:50.544

Charges 2006

Per unit incl. 2 persons	€ 17,00 - € 28,00
extra person	€ 4,00 - € 6,00
child (under 7 yrs)	€ 2,50 - € 3,50
electricity (6A)	€ 4,00

Less 20% in low seasons (excl. electricity). Camping Cheques accepted.

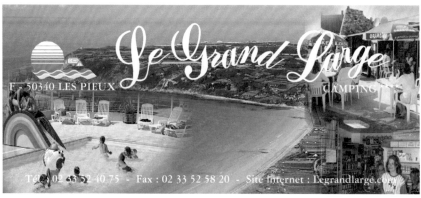

FR50030 Castel Camping le Château de lez Eaux

Saint Aubin des Préaux, F-50380 Saint Pair sur Mer (Manche)

Tel: **02 33 51 66 09**. Email: **bonjour@lez-eaux.com**

Set in the spacious grounds of a château, Lez Eaux lies in a rural situation just off the main route south, under two hours from Cherbourg. There are 229 pitches of which 113 are for touring, all with electricity (5/10A) and 70 fully serviced. Most of the pitches are of a very good size, partly separated by trees and shrubs on either flat or very slightly sloping, grassy ground overlooking Normandy farmland or beside a small lake (with carp and other fish). There is a considerable tour operator presence, but these units by no means dominate, being generally tucked away in their own areas.

Facilities

Three modern clean toilet blocks include hot showers and washbasins in cabins, facilities for children and babies, and for disabled people. Shop, small bar, snacks and takeaway (all from 1/5). Small heated swimming pool and indoor tropical-style fun pool (from 1/5, no T-shirts or Bermuda style shorts). Play area. Tennis. Football. Games and TV rooms. Bicycle hire. Lake fishing. Torches useful. Only one dog per pitch. Off site: Beach 4 km. Riding 5 km. Golf 7 km.

Open: 1 April - 15 September.

Directions

Lez-Eaux is just to the west of the D973 about 17 km. northwest of Avranches and 7 km. southeast of Granville. Site is between the two turnings east to St Aubin des Préaux and well signed. GPS: N48:47.764 W01:31.480

Charges 2006

Per unit incl. 2 persons	€ 13,50 - € 31,00
extra person	€ 8,50
child (under 7 yrs)	€ 6,50
electricity (5A)	€ 7,00
all services	€ 10,00

FR50070 Castel Camping Caravaning L'Anse du Brick

Route du Val de Saire, F-50330 Maupertus sur Mer (Manche)

Tel: 02 33 54 33 57. Email: welcome@anse-du-brick.com

A friendly, family site, L'Anse du Brick overlooks a picturesque bay on the northern tip of the Cotentin peninsula, eight kilometres east of Cherbourg port. This quality site makes a pleasant night halt or an ideal longer stay destination for those not wishing to travel too far. Its pleasing location offers direct access to a small sandy beach and a woodland walk. This is a mature, terraced site with magnificent views from certain pitches. Tarmac roads lead to the 117 touring pitches (all with 10A electricity) which are level, separated and mostly well shaded by many trees, bushes and shrubs. Beyond the site lie miles of walking tracks through the gorse-covered hills which, together with a stark rock face, surround the site and make it a sheltered sun-trap. A gourmet restaurant is conveniently located just outside the site gates.

Facilities

Two sanitary blocks, although not ultra-modern, are kept spotlessly clean and are well maintained. British style toilets, washbasins mainly in cubicles and push-button showers, provision for disabled visitors, laundry and dishwashing areas, motorcaravan service point. Heated swimming pool (1/5-15/9). Shop (1/4-30/9). Restaurant and bar/pizzeria (1/5-10/9). Tennis. Play area. Organised entertainment in season. Miniclub (6-12 yrs). Bicycle and kayak hire. Off site: Fishing 100 m. Riding 4 km. Golf 10 km.

Open: 1 April - 30 September.

Directions

From Cherbourg port follow for Caen and Rennes. After third roundabout, take road to right, towards Bretteville (D116). From southeast on N13 at first (Auchan) roundabout, take slip road to right towards Tourlaville (N13 car ferry), ahead at next roundabout, right at third lights on D116 to Bretteville. Site signed to right in 7 km. GPS: N49:40.044 W01:29.293

Charges 2006

Per pitch, 2 persons	€ 17,40 - € 30,40
extra person	€ 4,00 - € 6,00
child (3-12 yrs)	€ 3,00 - € 4,00

Camping Cheques accepted.

Beach at 100 m

FR50050 Camping le Cormoran

Ravenoville-Plage, F-50480 Sainte Mère Eglise (Manche)

Tel: 02 33 41 33 94. Email: lecormoran@wanadoo.fr

Set in a flat, open landscape and separated from the beach by the coast road, Le Cormoran is ideal for a holiday or short break quite near Cherbourg (33 km.) and the Landing Beaches close by. It does get full in peak season. Mobile homes, many privately owned, take 136 places and include 40 for rent. The remaining 80 pitches for touring units are sheltered from the wind by neat hedges and have 6A electricity available. If staying for one night you may be asked to pitch on the overflow area adjacent to the main site. A 'Sites et Paysages' member.

Facilities

Four toilet blocks of varying styles and ages. Washbasins in cabins. Dishwashing sinks. Laundry facilities. A sanitary block serves 15 extra large pitches (150 sq.m.) at the back of the site. Small shop, bar with snacks and takeaway. Swimming pool (heated 1/5-15/9, unsupervised). Play areas. Tennis. Boules. Entertainment, TV and games room. Bicycle and shrimp net hire. Communal barbecue. Off site: Beach 50 m. Utah Beach, golf 5 km.

Open: 1 April - 24 September.

Directions

From N13 take Ste Mère Eglise exit and in centre of town take road to Ravenoville (6 km), then Ravenoville-Plage (3 km). Just before beach turn right and site is 500 m. GPS: N49:27.960 W01:14.104

Charges 2006

Per unit incl. 1 or 2 persons	€ 16,20 - € 25,00
extra person	€ 4,60 - € 7,00
electricity (6A)	€ 3,80

Camping Cheques accepted.

kawan
VILLAGES CAMPINGS

tel: 00 333 59 59 03 59 *kawan-villages.com*

Check real time availability and at-the-gate prices...

www.alanrogers.com

TRAVEL SERVICE SITE
TO BOOK CALL 0870 405 4055
Advice & low ferry-inclusive prices

FR50080 Camping Haliotis

Chemin des Soupirs, F-50170 Pontorson (Manche)

Tel: **02 33 68 11 59**. Email: **info@camping-haliotis-mont-saint-michel.com**

The Duchesne family have achieved a remarkable transformation of this former municipal site. Situated on the edge of the little town of Pontorson and next to the river Couesnon, Camping Haliotis is within walking, cycling and canoeing distance of Mont Saint Michel. The site has 154 pitches, including 110 for touring units. Most pitches have electricity and several really large ones also have water and drainage. The large, comfortable reception area has been developed to incorporate a bar and restaurant. A 'Sites et Paysages' member.

Facilities

Very clean, renovated and well-equipped toilet block. Laundry facilities. Bar and restaurant. No shop or takeaway on site, facilities available in nearby town. Swimming pool (cleaned daily) with jacuzzi, separate paddling pool. Sauna and solarium. Good fenced play area. Large games room. Tennis court. Bicycle hire. Fishing in the River Couesnon. Japanese garden and animal park. Off site: Local services in Pontorson within walking distance. Riding 5 km. Golf 18 km. Beach 30 km.

Open: 1 April - 5 November.

Directions

Site is 300 m. from the town centre, west of D976, alongside the river, and is well signed from the town. GPS: N48:33.424 W01:30.67

Charges 2007

Per person	€ 4,50 - € 6,00
child (under 7 yrs)	€ 2,00 - € 3,50
pitch	€ 5,00 - € 7,00
electricity	€ 2,50 - € 3,00

No credit cards.
Camping Cheques accepted.

kawan-villages.com **tel: 00 333 59 59 03 59**

FR50090 Camping la Gerfleur

Rue Guillaume Le Conquérant, F-50270 Barneville Carteret (Manche)

Tel: **02 33 04 38 41**. Email: **alabouriau@aol.com**

La Gerfleur is a pleasant little site with a relaxed atmosphere and a warm welcome. It is a good holiday base, being an easy cycle ride from the sandy beach at Barneville Plage, or from the harbour and smaller cove at Carteret, both only 1.5 km. There are 44 mobile homes and chalets (13 to rent), but these are separated from 49 individual touring pitches. These are on grass with small dividing hedges and are arranged around a small lake which is used for fishing (and with a resident turtle). All the pitches have electricity hook-ups (6/10A) and some shade from mature trees. Day trips to the Channel Islands are possible from the nearby port. French and a little English are spoken by the friendly family owners.

Facilities

Clean and reasonable facilities include British style WCs, chain operated showers and some washbasins, all in unisex cubicles, units for disabled visitors. Laundry facilities. Motorcaravan service point. Heated swimming pool (6.5 x 14 m.) and paddling pool. Fishing lake. Table tennis, boules, games room. Small playground. Extra services (July/Aug) include a bar, 'frites' and bread supplies. Off site: Barneville 300 m. Beach 1.5 km. Golf 4 km. Riding 7 km.

Open: 1 April - 31 October.

Directions

Barneville Carteret is 37 km. SSW of Cherbourg. From the north turn off the D904 Barneville Carteret by-pass, and use the old road to town. After 1 km. at roundabouts, continue on D903E towards Barneville centre. Site is immediately on right. From south, continue round by-pass and approach as from north. GPS: N49:22.974 W01:45.341

Charges 2006

Per person	€ 4,30
child (under 13 yrs)	€ 5,00
pitch incl. electricity	€ 8,00

FR50110 Camping Saint Michel

35 Route du Mont Saint Michel, F-50220 Courtils (Manche)

Tel: **02 33 70 96 90**. Email: **infos@campingsaintmichel.com**

This delightful site is owned and run by an enthusiastic young couple, the Duchesnes. It is located in a peaceful, rural setting, yet is only 8 km. from busy tourist attraction of Mont St Michel. The site has 100 pitches which include 36 for touring units and 25 for mobile homes and chalets to rent. Electricity connections (6A) are available and many trees and shrubs provide shade to the pitches. From the restaurant and its terrace overlooking the pool, the site slopes gently down to a small enclosure of farm animals. The animals are kept to entertain children and adults alike. Meet Nestor and Napoléon, the donkeys, Linotte the pony and Dédé and Dedette, the Vietnamese potbellied pigs, as well as miniature goats, sheep, chickens and ducks. It is M. and Mme. Duschesne's intention to maintain a quiet and peaceful site, hence there are no discos or organised clubs.

Facilities

The modern, well maintained toilet block has washbasins in cubicles and showers. Separate laundry. Facilities for disabled visitors in the new reception building. All is of an excellent standard. Motorcaravan service point. Shop. Bar (1/4-30/9). Restaurant (15/6-10/9). Heated swimming pool (1/5-30/9). Animal farm. Play area. Games room. Bicycle hire. Off site: Fishing 2 km. Riding 3 km.

Open: 15 March - 15 October.

Directions

From St Malo take the N137 south and join the N176 east to Pontorson where it becomes the N175. In 20 km. turn northwest on D43 signed Courtils. Site is through village on left.
GPS: N48:37.657 W01:24.96

Charges 2006

Per person	€ 3,00 - € 5,00
child (0-7 yrs)	€ 1,50 - € 2,00
pitch incl. car	€ 10,00 - € 14,50
electricity (6A)	€ 2,60

83

FR50150 Camping la Route Blanche

F-50290 Breville sur Mer (Manche)

Tel: **02 33 50 23 31**. Email: **larouteblanche@camping-breville.com**

La Route Blanche has a bright and cheerful atmosphere and Philippe and Corinne, the owners, are working continually to make an excellent site even better.The 140 pitches for touring are generous and numbered on well-cut grass and divided by young conifers. There are many shrubs and flowers and mature trees give shade to some areas. There are 67 pitches with electricity and long leads may be necessary for some. Although the site does not have its own restaurant, there are five to choose from within a short distance and the beaches of Breville-sur-Mer are within a ten minute walk.

Facilities

Well maintained sanitary facilities with British style toilets, washbasins in cabins and showers. Good provision for disabled visitors. Laundry and dishwashing facilities. Bread available all season. Bar and takeaway (July/Aug). New large swimming pool complex with flumes, toboggan and bubble pool. Play area. Multisports court. Entertainment in high season. Off site: Golf (opposite). Fishing 500 m. Riding 1 km.

Open: 1 April - 31 October.

Directions

Take D971 that runs between Granville and Coutance. Then one of the roads west to Breville sur Mer. Site is well signposted.

Charges 2006

Per pitch incl. 2 persons	€ 16,00 - € 24,00
electricity (6/10A)	€ 2,60 - € 3,60
extra person	€ 3,50 - € 4,50
child (2-7 yrs)	€ 1,80 - € 2,20
dog	€ 2,00 - € 2,50

Camp site La Route Blanche ★★★

Flowered camp site full with charme and exceptional nature. At 5 km distance from the sea resort of Granville. Located in the bay of the Mount Saint Michel facing the Channel Islands: Jersey and Guernesey.

6, La Route Blanche, 50290 Breville sur Mer
Tel: 0033 (0)2 33 50 23 31
Fax: 0033 (0)2 33 50 26 47
larouteblanche@camping-breville.com
www.camping-breville.com

FR50100 Camping Municipal le Pont-Roulland

F-50370 Brécey (Manche)

Tel: **02 33 48 60 60**. Email: **office-tourisme@brecey.com**

Comfortable and good value, this little site is set in an old orchard and is ideal for a relaxing short break, perhaps before heading further south or west. The 50 numbered tourist pitches are on lush grass, all with electric hook-ups (6A), although some may need long leads. The entire site has a slight slope, so motorcaravans will probably need levelling blocks. There is good site lighting and tarmac roads. The guardienne lives on site and reception is open 9.00-22.00 (July/Aug), 17.00-22.00 (low season) – just choose your pitch and pay later if she is not around.

Facilities

A traditional Normandy stone building houses toilet facilities with modern fittings including British style toilets, spacious hot showers, some basins in cubicles, dishwashing and laundry sinks, and a washing machine, but no dedicated facilities for disabled visitors. Table tennis. Playground for young children. Off site: Town centre, shops 1 km. Small park with free paddling pool adjacent. River fishing. Golf 18 km. Beaches 25 km.

Open: 1 April - 30 September.

Directions

Brécey is 16 km. east of Avranches. Site is 1 km. east of town just off D911. Turn south on D79 towards Les Cresnays. Site entrance is adjacent to swimming pool, off a public car park.
GPS: N48:43.366 W01:09.154

Charges 2006

Per person	€ 2,35
child (under 7 yrs)	€ 1,20
pitch INCL. electricity	€ 4,20

No credit cards.

FR61010 Camping Municipal la Campière

Boulevard du Docteur Dentu, F-61120 Vimoutiers (Orne)

Tel: **02 33 39 18 86**. Email: **mairie.vimoutiers@wanadoo.fr**

This small, well kept site is situated in a valley to the north of the town, which is on both the Normandy Cheese and Cider routes. Indeed the town is famous for its cheese and has a Camembert Museum, five minutes walk away in the town centre. The 40 pitches here are flat and grassy, separated by laurel hedging and laid out amongst attractive and well maintained flower and shrub beds. There is some shade around the perimeter and all pitches have electricity.

Facilities

The single central sanitary block is clean and heated, providing open washbasins, good sized, well designed showers, children's toilets and a bathroom for disabled visitors. Dishwashing and laundry facilities under cover. Off site: No shop but a large supermarket is 300 m. Tennis courts and a park are adjacent. Water sports facilities or riding 2 km.

Open: March - October.

Directions

Site is on northern edge of town, signed from main Lisieux-Argentan road next to large sports complex. GPS: N48:55.954 E00:11.805

Charges guide

Per person	€ 2,30 - € 2,75
child (under 10 yrs)	€ 1,34 - € 1,60
pitch	€ 1,63 - € 1,95

FR61040 Camping Municipal du Champ Passais

F-61700 Domfront (Orne)

Tel: **02 33 37 37 66**. Email: **mairie@domfront.com**

Situated on the edge of the fascinating fortified town of Domfront, this small site has 34 individual pitches on a series of level terraces and a separate open grassy area for tents. The nine pitches nearest the entrance are all hardstandings separated by grass and with 10A electricity. Grass pitches on the lower levels, divided by shrubs and hedges, have 5A electricity and most have water and waste water points. The site is cared for by a lady warden who keeps everything immaculate and is justifiably proud of the entries in her visitors' book.

Facilities

Excellent sanitary facilities include British style toilets, some washbasins in cubicles, facilities for disabled people, dishwashing and laundry sinks plus a washing machine. No separate chemical waste disposal point, but a notice tells visitors where to empty toilet cassettes. Boules. Play area. Double axle caravans are not accepted under any circumstances; American RVs can be accommodated. Off site: Sports centre adjacent. Supermarket 800 m. Fishing 1 km.

Open: 1 April - 30 September.

Directions

Domfront is on the N176 Alençon-Mont St Michel road and site is just off this to the south of town; signed to the right up the hill towards town centre - or the left as you leave town heading west. GPS: N48:35.491 W00:39.146

Charges 2006

Per unit incl. 1 person	€ 3,70
extra person	€ 2,00
electricity (10A)	€ 3,00
No credit cards.	

FR76040 Camping la Source

Petit Appeville, F-76550 Hautot-sur-Mer (Seine-Maritime)

Tel: **02 35 84 27 04**. Email: **info@camping-la-source.fr**

This friendly, attractive site with a new heated pool is just four kilometres from Dieppe and is useful for those using the Newhaven - Dieppe ferry crossing either as a one-night stop-over or for a few days' break before heading on. The 120 pitches are flat and there is some shade. There are good hardstandings for motorcaravans and electricity is available. The site is quietly located in a valley with the only disturbance from the occasional passing train. A fast-flowing small river runs along one border (not protected for young children).

Facilities

A good, clean single toilet block (men - left, ladies - right) includes washbasins in cubicles and mainly British style WCs. En-suite unit for disabled people but the unmade gravel roads may cause problems. Laundry facilities. Small bar and terrace (15/3-15/10). Swimming pool. Play field. TV and games rooms. Fishing. Bicycle hire. Off site: Riding 2 km. Beach 3 km. Golf 4 km.

Open: 15 March - 15 October.

Directions

From Dieppe follow D925 west to Fécamp. At foot of descent at traffic lights in Petit Appeville turn left. From west, turn right (signed D153 St Aubin). Just after railway, turn left under bridge and ahead on narrow road. Site is shortly on left. GPS: N49:53.925 E01:03.398

Charges 2006

Per person	€ 3,20 - € 4,80
child (under 7 yrs)	€ 2,00 - € 3,00
pitch incl. electricity (6A)	€ 7,50 - € 10,50
Camping Cheques accepted.	

FR76090 Camping Municipal d'Etennemare

Hameau d'Etennemare, F-76460 St Valery-en-Caux (Seine-Maritime)

Tel: **02 35 97 15 79**

This comfortable, neat municipal site is two kilometres from the harbour and town, 30 km. west of Dieppe. Quietly located, it has 116 pitches of which 49 are available for touring units. The grassy pitches are all on a slight slope, all with electricity (6A), water and drain, but there is very little shade. Reception is open all day in July and August, but in low season is closed 12.00-15.00 hrs daily and all day Wednesdays: there is a card operated security barrier.

Facilities

Two modern, clean and well maintained sanitary buildings are side by side, one containing showers and the other, more recently refitted, has cubicled washbasins and facilities for disabled people. Both blocks can be heated in winter. Dishwashing and laundry sinks. Washing machines. Small shop (July/Aug). Playground. Table tennis. Off site: Hypermarket 1.5 km. Harbour and beach (pebbles) 2 km.

Open: All year.

Directions

From Dieppe keep to D925 Fécamp road (not through town). At third roundabout turn right on D925E towards hypermarket. From Fécamp turn left on D925E as before. Take first right (site signed) to site on left in 1 km. GPS: N49:51.515 E00:42.279

Charges 2006

Per unit incl. 2 persons and electricity	€ 13,40
extra person	€ 2,75
child (under 10 yrs)	€ 1,75

FR76100 Camping Municipal Cany-Barville

Route de Barville, F-76450 Cany-Barville (Seine-Maritime)

Tel: **02 35 97 70 37**. Email: **mairie.cany-barville@cote-albatre.com**

This good quality site, first opened in 1997 next to the municipal sports stadium, has a floral entrance and tarmac roads. Of the 100 individual hedged pitches 75 are available for tourists. There are around 40 concrete hardstandings (awnings can be a problem) and the remainder are on grass: all are fully serviced with water, drain and electric hook-ups (10A). Shade from new specimen trees is still very limited. Cany-Barville is a bustling small town with a traditional Normandy market on Monday mornings.

Facilities

The modern, centrally located, sanitary unit can be heated and has British style toilets, controllable showers and washbasins in cubicles. Dishwashing and laundry sinks. Copious hot water. Separate suites for disabled people. Drive-over motorcaravan service point with chemical disposal facility. Table tennis, volleyball, boules. Games room with pin-ball machine and ski-simulator. Off site: Bakery, restaurants 600 m. Supermarket 1 km. Sailing and windsurfing centre 2 km. Beach 10 km.

Open: 1 April - 1 October.

Directions

Cany-Barville is 20 km. east of Fécamp on D925 to Dieppe. From traffic lights on east of town turn south on D268 towards Yvetot. Go under railway. Site is 600 m. from town on right, after stadium. GPS: N49:46.990 E00:38.546

Charges 2006

Per person	€ 2,71 - € 2,85
child (under 14 yrs)	€ 1,14 - € 1,20
pitch	€ 1,80 - € 1,90
electricity (10A)	€ 2,71 - € 2,85

FR76110 Camping Municipal les Boucaniers

Rue Pierre Mendès France, F-76470 Le Tréport (Seine-Maritime)

Tel: **02 35 86 35 47**. Email: **ville.le.treport@wanadoo.fr**

This large, good quality, municipal site has an attractive entrance and some floral displays, tarmac roads and site lighting. The 300 pitches are on level grass, some with dividing hedges, and trees to provide a little shade. There are 22 good quality wooden chalets for rent, and some privately owned mobile homes, which leaves around 262 pitches for tourists, all with electric hook-ups (6A). A small unit acts as shop, bar and takeaway all season, the baker calls daily in high season, and every day except Monday in low season.

Facilities

Three well equipped sanitary blocks (one can be heated) provide mainly British style WCs, washbasins in cubicles, pre-set hot showers, with facilities for small children and disabled persons in one block. Multisport court. Minigolf. Boules. Off site: Tennis, football and gymnasium nearby. Fishing, golf and beach 2 km. Riding 3 km. Markets at Le Tréport (Mon and Sat) and at Eu (Fri).

Open: Easter weekend - 30 September.

Directions

Site is just north of the D925 Abbeville - Dieppe road; take D1915 towards Le Tréport centre, (from Dieppe, at second roundabout) at traffic lights (multi-way junction), turn right into Rue Pierre Mendès-France. Site is on corner (entrance immediately on right - not signed from main road). GPS: N50:03.463 E01:23.322

Charges 2006

Per person	€ 2,90
child (2-10 yrs)	€ 1,70
pitch incl. electricity	€ 9,70

FR76130 Camping de la Forêt

Rue Mainberthe, F-76480 Jumieges (Seine-Maritime)

Tel: 02 35 37 93 43. Email: info@campinglaforet.com

This is a pretty family site with a friendly laid back atmosphere. It is located just 10 km. from the A13 Paris - Caen autoroute, and is best accessed by ferry across the River Seine. The site was formerly a municipal and has recently been taken on by the Joret family. The 111 grassy pitches (94 for tourers) are attractively located in woodland. Many pitches have some shade and all have 10A electrical connections. There is a separate area for tents. Jumieges is just 600 m. away. The site organises some activities in high season and these include treasure hunts and guided walks. The great abbey at Jumieges was founded in 654 by St Philibert, rebuilt by the Normans and consecrated in the presence of William the Conqueror – well worth a visit! A good range of shops, cafes, restaurants etc. can also be found here.

Facilities

Two toilet blocks, both of modern construction and maintained to a good standard with British toilets, some basins in cubicles and pre-set showers. Baby room. Facilities for disabled visitors. Laundry facilities. Shop. Baker calls daily and pizzas are available on Friday and Saturday evenings 18.30 hrs. Small swimming pool and children's pool (heated 15/6-15/9). Playground. Boules. Games room with TV. Cycle hire. Motorcaravan service point. Chalets and mobile homes to let.

Open: 7 April - 28 October.

Directions

Jumieges is around 10 km. north of A13 Paris - Caen autoroute (Bourg-Achard exit). Take D313 towards Caudebec-en-Caux. Then, either ferry across the Seine from Heurtauville to Jumieges, or continue over Pont de Brotonne and double back on D982 to Jumieges. Site clearly signed.
GPS: N49:26.092 E00:49.738

Charges 2007

Per unit incl. 2 persons	€ 15,50 - € 18,00
extra person	€ 4,00 - € 4,50
child (under 7 yrs)	€ 1,50
electricity	€ 3,80

Camping Cheques accepted.

CAMPING DE LA FORÊT ★ ★ ★

Rue Mainberte
74480 JUMIÈGES
Tél 02 35 37 93 43
Fax 02 35 37 76 48

FR76120 Camping Municipal Veulettes sur Mer

8 Rue de Greenock, F-76450 Veulettes sur Mer (Seine-Maritime)

Tel: 02 35 97 53 44

A good value, well kept municipal site in an attractive little coastal town, just 500 m. from the beach and all town services. There are 116 marked pitches on open level grass, 40 of which are seasonal pitches, which leaves 76 pitches for tourists, all with electric hook-ups, water and waste water drain. Reception keeps soft drinks and ices during July/August. Also on site is an attractive 'salle' (open all day in July/August) with a library and TV, a games area, table tennis, babyfoot and further toilet facilities. There is a traffic free cycle path to the next village 4 km. away.

Facilities

Three good modern sanitary units in traditional style buildings are of varying ages (one can be heated). These provide pre-set hot showers, washbasins in cubicles, and facilities for disabled people in the smallest unit on the far side of the site. Laundry room. Playground. TV, library and table tennis. Off site: Public park with tennis courts and large playground, beach (pebble), watersports centre and all shops and services are within 500 m.

Open: 1 April - 31 October.

Directions

Veulettes sur Mer is on the coast approx. 45 km. west of Dieppe. Site is central in town, lying about 500 m. back from the main promenade (signed).
GPS: N49:50.967 E00:35.791

Charges 2006

per person	€ 2,65
child (4-10 yrs)	€ 1,33
pitch	€ 2,30

Check real time availability and at-the-gate prices...

www.alanrogers.com

TRAVEL SERVICE SITE
TO BOOK CALL 0870 405 4055
Advice & low ferry-inclusive prices

MAP 3

Northern France, with its lush countryside and market towns, is much more than just a stop off en-route to or from the ports. The peaceful rural unspoilt charms of the region provide a real breath of fresh air.

NORD/PAS DE CALAIS: 59 NORD, 62 PAS-DE-CALAIS
MAJOR CITY: LILLE

PICARDY: 02 AISNE, 60 OISE, 80 SOMME
MAJOR CITY: AMIENS

This is a region where centuries of invaders have left their mark. At Vimy Ridge near Arras, World War One trenches have been preserved intact, a most poignant sight. Elsewhere almost every village between Arras and Amiens has its memorial. It is also the birthplace of Gothic architecture with six cathedrals, including Laon, Beauvais and Amiens, arguably the grandest in France.

The area however is predominately rural. Inland and south are long vistas of rolling farmland broken by little rivers and well scattered with pockets of forest woodland. The coastline is characterised by sandy beaches, shifting dunes and ports. It is a quiet and sparsely populated area with peaceful villages and churches that provide evidence of the glorious achievements of French Gothic architecture. Boulogne is home to Nausicaa, the world's largest sea-life centre and from Cap Griz-Nez you may be able to see the White Cliffs of Dover. There are also many huge hypermarkets where you may stock up on wine, beer and cheese.

Places of interest

Amiens: Notre Dame cathedral, monument to 1918 Battle of the Somme.

Chantilly: Château of Chantilly with a 17th century stable with a 'live' Horse museum.

Compiègne: Seven miles east of the town is Clairière de l'Armistice. The railway coach here is a replica of the one in which the 1918 Armistice was signed and in which Hitler received the French surrender in 1942.

Laon: 12th century cathedral, WW1 trenches, Vauclair Abbey.

Marquenterre: one of Europe's most important bird sanctuaries.

Cuisine of the region

Carbonnade de Boeuf à la Flamande: braised beef with beer, onions and bacon.

Caudière (Chaudière, Caudrée): versions of fish and potato soup.

Ficelles Picardes: ham pancakes with mushroom sauce.

Flamiche aux poireaux: puff pastry tart with cream and leeks.

Hochepot: a thick Flemish soup with virtually everything in it but the kitchen sink.

Soupe courquignoise: soup with white wine, fish, moules, leeks and Gruyère cheese.

Tarte aux Maroilles: a hot creamy tart based on Maroilles cheese.

Waterzooï: a cross between soup and stew, usually of fish or chicken.

FR02060 Camping Municipal Guignicourt

14 bis rue Godins, F-02190 Guignicourt (Aisne)

Tel: 03 23 79 74 58. Email: mairie-guignicourt@wanadoo.fr

This very pleasant little municipal site has 100 pitches, 50 for long stay units and 50 for tourists. These two sections are separated by the main facilities on a higher terrace. Pitches are generally large and level, although you might need an extra long electricity lead for some, but there are few dividing hedges. Pitches along the river bank have most shade, with a few specimen trees providing a little shade to some of the more open pitches.

Facilities

The modern sanitary unit has British and Turkish style toilets, washbasins (cold only except for the one in a cubicle), push-button hot showers, dishwashing and laundry sinks. Bar (1/4-30/9). Playground. Tennis and boules courts. Fishing. Off site: The town has all services including a supermarket and bank. Golf 3 km. Beach 15 km.

Open: 1 April - 30 September.

Directions

Guignicourt is about 20 km. north of Reims, just east of the A26, junction 14. The site is well signed from D925 in the village. GPS: N49:25.922 E03:58.223

Charges 2006

Per person	€ 2,00
child (2-10 yrs)	€ 1,20
pitch incl. electricity (6/10A)	€ 11,50 - € 12,50
animal	€ 1,50

FR02000 Camping Caravaning du Vivier aux Carpes

10 rue Charles Voyeux, F-02790 Seraucourt-le-Grand (Aisne)

Tel: 03 23 60 50 10. Email: camping.du.vivier@wanadoo.fr

Vivier aux Carpes is a small quiet site, close to the A26, two hours from Calais, so is an ideal overnight stop but is also worthy of a longer stay. The 60 well spaced pitches, are at least 100 sq.m. on flat grass with dividing hedges. The 45 for touring units all have electricity (6A), some also with water points, and there are special pitches for motorcaravans. This is a neat, purpose designed site imaginatively set out with a comfortable feel. The enthusiastic owners and manager speak excellent English and are keen to welcome British visitors.

Facilities

The spacious, clean toilet block has separate, heated facilities for disabled visitors, made available to other campers in the winter. Laundry facilities. Motorcaravan service point (fresh water for large vans is charged). Large TV/games room. Small play area. Bicycle hire. Petanque. Fishing (about € 5.50 p/day). Gates close 22.00 hrs, office open 09.00-21.30. Rallies welcome. Off site: Village has post office, doctor, chemist and small supermarket. Riding 500 m. Golf 12 km.

Open: 1 March - 30 October.

Directions

Leave A26 (Calais - Reims) at exit 11. Take D1 left towards Soissons for 4 km. Take D8, on entering Essigny-le-Grand (4 km.) turn sharp right on D72 signed Seraucourt-le-Grand (5 km). Site signed. GPS: N49:46.915 E03:12.850

Charges 2006

Per unit incl. 2 persons and electricity	€ 16,50
extra person	€ 3,30
child (under 10 yrs)	€ 2,50

Monthly, weekly or weekend rates available. Discounts for students with tents. No credit cards.

FR02030 Caravaning la Croix du Vieux Pont

F-02290 Berny-Riviere (Aisne)

Tel: 03 23 55 50 02. Email: info@la-croix-du-vieux-pont.com

Located on the banks of the River Aisne, La Croix du Vieux Pont is a very smart, modern 34 hectare site offering a high standard of facilities. Many pitches are occupied by mobile homes and tour operator tents, but there are 60 pleasant touring pitches, some on the banks of the Aisne. Maintained to a high standard, the excellent amenities include four heated swimming pools, one indoors with a waterslide and jacuzzi. At the heart of the site is a well-stocked fishing lake.

Facilities

The six toilet blocks are modern and kept very clean, with washbasins in cabins and free hot showers. Laundry facilities. Facilities for disabled visitors. Large supermarket. Bar, takeaway and good value restaurant (most amenities 1/4-30/9). Swimming pool complex (covered pool 1/4-30/10, outdoor 1/5-30/9). Play area. Fishing. Bicycle hire. Apartments to let. Dogs are not accepted. Off site: Riding 100 m. Golf 30 km.

Open: 8 April - 31 October.

Directions

From Compiegne take N31 towards Soissons. At Vic-sur-Aisne turn right, towards Berny-Riviere and site is on right after 400 m. GPS: N49:24.292 E03:07.704

Charges 2006

Per unit incl. 2 persons and electricity	€ 22,50
incl. 4 persons	€ 31,00

Camping Cheques accepted.

TO BOOK CALL 0870 405 4055 Advice & low ferry-inclusive prices — TRAVEL SERVICE SITE

TO BOOK CALL 0870 405 4055 Advice & low ferry-inclusive prices — TRAVEL SERVICE SITE

FR59010 Camping Caravaning la Chaumière

529 Langhemast Straete, F-59285 Buysscheure (Nord)

Tel: **03 28 43 03 57**. Email: **camping.LaChaumiere@wanadoo.fr**

This is a very friendly, pleasant site, in the département du Nord with a strong Flanders influence, There is a real welcome here. Set just behind the village of Buysscheure, the site has 29 touring pitches separated by trees and bushes. Each pair shares a light, electricity connections, water points and rubbish container. Access from narrow site roads can be difficult. A small, fenced fishing lake contains some large carp (seen!). A bonus is that Bernadette works for the local vet and can arrange all the documentation for British visitors' pets. English is spoken.

Facilities

Modern unisex toilet facilities are simple and small in number, with two WCs, one shower and one washbasin cabin. Facilities for disabled visitors may also be used (a toilet and separate washbasin/shower room). Dishwashing and laundry facilities. Motorcaravan services. Basic chemical disposal. Bar (daily) and restaurant (weekends only, all day, in season). Dog exercise area. Heated outdoor pools. Play area. Gates closed 22.00-08.00 but parking by entrance. Off site: Local market (Monday) at Bergues. St Omer. Cycling. Beach 30 km. Lille 60 km.

Open: 1 April - 30 September.

Directions

From Calais take N43 (St Omer) for 25 km. Just beyond Nordausques take D221 left (Watten). In Watten turn left for centre, then right on D26 (Cassel). Soon after Lederzeele site signed to right. On reaching Buysscheure turn left, then right, site signed. Single track road (1 km.) with bend.

Charges 2006

Per unit incl. 2 persons and electricity	€ 16,00
extra person	€ 7,00
child (under 7 yrs)	€ 3,50

No credit cards.

FR59050 Camp Municipal du Clair de Lune

Route de Mons, F-59600 Maubeuge (Nord)

Tel: **03 27 62 25 48**

This is an attractive site convenient for a night-stop or for longer stays close to the RN2 road. It is a neat and tidy municipal site with 92 marked pitches of fair size. Mainly on level ground and separated by trim hedges, most have electrical connections (6 or 10A) and some have hardstanding. A variety of trees provides shade when needed. Reception staff were friendly and helpful. Although there are few amenities on site, the interesting town centre of Maubeuge itself is only about 1 km.

Facilities

Two circular sanitary blocks provide good modern facilities. A new block should now be ready. Dishwashing sinks under cover and washing machines. The block used in winter can be heated. Motorcaravan service point. Small adventure-style playground. Fishing. Bicycle hire. Off site: Riding and bicycle hire 2 km. Golf 2.5 km.

Open: 1 February - 22 December.

Directions

Site is on the RN2 road (known as the N6 in Belgium) north of the town, on the right going towards Mons.

Charges 2006

Per person	€ 3,30
child (3-16 yrs)	€ 2,20
pitch	€ 3,20
electricity (3/10A)	€ 2,70 - € 5,15

FR62010 Castel Camping Caravaning la Bien-Assise

D231, F-62340 Guines (Pas-de-Calais)

Tel: **03 21 35 20 77**. Email: **castel@bien-assise.com**

A mature and well developed site, the history of La Bien-Assise goes back to the 1500s. There are 198 grass pitches mainly set among mature trees with others on a newer field. Connected by gravel roads and of a good size (up to 300 sq.m.), shrubs and bushes divide most of the pitches. Being close to Calais, the Channel Tunnel exit and Boulogne, makes it a good stopping point en-route, but it is well worth a longer stay. The site can have heavy usage at times (when maintenance can be variable). Used by tour operators (40 pitches).

Facilities

Three well equipped toilet blocks provide many washbasins in cabins, mostly British style WCs and provision for babies, laundry and dishwashing. The main block is in four sections, two unisex. Motorcaravan service point. Shop. Restaurant. Bar/grill and takeaway (evenings from 1/5). TV room. Pool complex (1/5-20/9) with a toboggan, covered paddling pool and outdoor pool. Play areas. Minigolf. Tennis court. Bicycle hire. Off site: Fishing 8 km. Beach 9 km. Riding 10 km.

Open: 25 April - 20 September.

Directions

From ferry or tunnel follow signs for A16 Boulogne. Take exit 11 (Frethun, Gare TGV) and RD215 (Frethun). At first roundabout take third exit (Guines). Pass under the TGV. In Frethun take RD246 towards Guines and St Tricat and at roundabout take exit for Guines. Pass through St Tricat and Hames Boucres, and in Guines follow site signs turning right towards Marquise for 120 m.

Charges 2006

Per unit incl. 2 persons and electricity	€ 17,00 - € 28,00
extra person	€ 3,00 - € 5,00

Check real time availability and at-the-gate prices...

www.alanrogers.com

FR62030 Camping Château du Gandspette

F-62910 Eperlecques (Pas-de-Calais)

Tel: 03 21 93 43 93. Email: contact@chateau-gandspette.com

This spacious family-run site, in the grounds of a 19th century château, conveniently situated for the Channel ports and tunnel, provides overnight accommodation together with a range of facilities for longer stays. There are 100 touring pitches, all with electric hook-ups, inter-mingled with 50 French-owned mobile homes and caravans, and a further 18 for hire. Pitches are delineated by trees and hedging. Mature trees form the perimeter of the site, through which there is access to woodland walks. A 'Sites et Paysages' member.

Facilities

Two sanitary blocks with a mixture of open and cubicled washbasins. Good facilities for disabled people and babies. Dishwashing sinks. Laundry facilities. Motorcaravan service point. Bar, grill restaurant and takeaway (all 15/5-15/9). Swimming pools (15/5-30/9). Playground and field. Tennis, petanque and a children's room. Entertainment in season. Off site: Supermarket 1 km. Fishing 3 km. Riding, golf 5 km. Bicycle hire 9 km. Beach 30 km.

Open: 1 April - 30 September.

Directions

From Calais follow N43 (St Omer) for 25 km. Southeast of Nordausques take D221 (east). Follow camp signs for 5-6 km. From St Omer follow N43 to roundabout at junction with D600. Turn right on D600 (Dunkirk). After 5 km. turn left on D221. Site is 1.5 km. on right. GPS: N50:49.137 E02:10.740

Charges 2006

Per unit incl. 2 persons	€ 16,00 - € 22,00
extra person (over 6 yrs)	€ 5,00 - € 6,00
electricity (6A)	€ 4,00

Camping Cheques accepted.

tel: 00 333 59 59 03 59 *kawan-villages.com*

FR62050 Camping Caravaning Saint Louis

Rue Leulène, F-62610 Autingues par Ardres (Pas-de-Calais)

Tel: 03 21 35 46 83. Email: domirine@aol.com

Convenient for the ferry port at Calais, this is a peaceful little site with 84 pitches. Many are taken by privately owned holiday homes, but there are around 25 pitches for tourists. In a garden-like setting, they are individual and grassy with some shade. Electricity hook-ups are available for all. In high season the site is usually full by 17.00 hrs, so arrive early.

Facilities

New unisex toilet block with free showers, washbasins and baby changing area. Facilities for disabled people. Dishwashing, laundry sinks and washing machine. Motorcaravan service point. Snack bar and takeaway (1/5-30/9). Playground. Games room with table football, table tennis. Off site: Supermarket on N34. Golf 6 km. Beach 20 km.

Open: 1 April - 20 October.

Directions

From Calais take N43 to Ardres. At traffic lights, on through town and left on D224 (Autingues). Site on right. From St Omer, follow N43 north until Le Plat d'Or, turn left on local road. Site is signed.

Charges 2006

Per unit incl. 2 persons and electricity	€ 18,00
extra person	€ 3,00
child (2-7 yrs)	€ 1,50

FR62060 Caravaning L'Orée du Bois

Chemin Blanc, F-62180 Rang-du-Fliers (Pas-de-Calais)

Tel: 03 21 84 28 51. Email: oree.du.bois@wanadoo.fr

A fairly peaceful, extensive campsite in a natural woodland setting, 3 km. from a large sandy beach. From reception you pass through the mobile home (privately owned) section, then through an area of preserved woodland which separates the touring area. This has 80 individual, touring pitches on sandy grass which can be slightly undulating, all with shade and electric hook-ups and most are separated by hedges and bushes. There are also 67 wooden camping lodges and a clearing in the woodland is reserved for tents. Site and area are well suited to disabled visitors.

Facilities

Facilities with open and cubicle washbasins and hot showers. Laundry facilities. Good facilities for disabled persons, small children and babies. Note: water for toilets is from a borehole, and has a slight brownish colour. Motorcaravan service point. Bar/brasserie (30/3-20/10). Animation in July/Aug. Multi-court tennis. Playgrounds. Woodland area with fitness trail, course for quads and all terrain bikes, and a fishing lake. Off site: Supermarket. Beach 3 km. Cycle hire 2 km. Riding 1.5 km. Golf 8 km.

Open: 30 March - 20 October.

Directions

Rang-du-Fliers is just east of Berck Plage, 15 km. south of Le Touquet. From Berck Plage take D917 east to roundabout by supermarket, turn left (north) at next roundabout (site signed), entrance is 500 m. on left. From A16 exit 25, follow D917 towards Berck Plage. GPS: N50:25.024 E01:36.694

Charges 2006

Per unit incl. 2 persons and electricity	€ 16,00 - € 22,00
extra person	€ 4,00 - € 5,50

FR62080 Camping de la Paille Haute

FR62156 Boiry Notre Dame (Pas-de-Calais)

Tel: **03 21 48 15 40**. Email: **lapaillehaute@wanadoo.fr**

This campsite has been recommended by our French agent and we intend to undertake a full inspection in 2007. La Paille Haute is small family run campsite in Northern France offering just 47 touring pitches, some with beautiful views over the surrounding countryside and others on the edge of the site's small fishing lake. Thanks to its location close to several motorways this site is a good choice for an overnight stops, but it is a pleasant choice for longer stays too. During high season an entertainment team organises many activities for all ages.

Facilities

Toilet block with laundry room and facilities for disabled people. Restaurant. Bar. Takeaway food. Swimming pool and paddling pool. Play area. Sports field. Fishing. Entertainment during high season. Supermarket 500 m.

Open: April - October.

Directions

The site can be easily accessed from the A1, A2 and A26 motorways. From the A1 take exit 15 and follow signs for Boiry Notre Dame. From the A26 take exit 8 and follow signs for Boiry Notre Dame.

Charges year

Per unit incl 2 persons	€ 14,50 - € 17,50
extra person	€ 3,00 - € 3,50
child (under 7 years)	€ 2,00 - € 2,50
electricity	€ 3,00

La Paille Haute

Ideal overnight stop for your journey. At only 5 minutes from A1. You will love the amazing facilities!

146, rue de Sailly - 62156 Boiry-Notre-Dame - France
Tel: 0033 (0)3 21 48 15 40 - Fax: 0033 (0)3 21 22 07 24

E-mail: lapaillehaute@wanadoo.fr
Website: www.la-paille-haute.com

FR80020 Camping Caravaning le Champ Neuf

Rue du Champ Neuf, F-80120 St Quentin en Tourmont (Somme)

Tel: **03 22 25 07 94**. Email: **contact@camping-lechampneuf.com**

Part of a large farm, the campsite was started in 1995 and all the charming family are now involved (although Mama is firmly in charge). There are 157 pitches with 59 for touring, of which 30 are in a new field with the remainder scattered amongst more permanent mobile homes and caravans. All pitches are on level grass with 3 or 6A electricity. The site is only 75 minutes from Calais, 18 km. off the motorway. This is a quiet site with home-made cooking and soirées, and with the famous Marquenterre bird reserve next door, bird-watching enthusiasts will appreciate the dawn chorus and migrating birds.

Facilities

Two toilet blocks have British style toilets, washbasins in cubicles, family cubicles and facilities for disabled visitors. Laundry facilities. Motorcaravan service point. Bar, entertainment area and snack bar. Games room. Tennis. Off site: Shops, restaurants, bars in Rue 7 km.

Open: 1 April - 1 November.

Directions

From A16 exit 24, take D32 towards and around Rue. At second roundabout take second exit on D940, then left on D4 for 1.5 km. before turning right on D204 to Le Bout des Crocs. Site is signed to the left.

Charges 2006

Per unit incl. 2 persons	€ 11,60
extra person	€ 4,10
child (0-5 yrs)	€ 2,60
electricity (3-6A)	€ 3,00 - € 3,60

FR80060 Camping le Val de Trie

Bouillancourt-sous-Miannay, F-80870 Moyenneville (Somme)

Tel: **03 22 31 48 88**. Email: **raphael@camping-levaldetrie.fr**

Mobile homes ▶ page 460

Le Val de Trie is a natural countryside site in woodland, near a small village. The 100 numbered, grassy pitches are of a good size, divided by hedges and shrubs with mature trees providing good shade in most areas, and all have electricity (6A) and water. Access roads are gravel (site is possibly not suitable for the largest motorcaravans). It can be very quiet in April, June, September and October. If there is no-one on site, just choose a pitch or call at farm to book in. There are a few Dutch tour operator tents (5). This is maturing into a well managed site with modern facilities and a friendly, relaxed atmosphere. There are good walks around the area and a notice board keeps campers up to date with local market, shopping and activity news. English is spoken.

Facilities

Two clean sanitary buildings include washbasins in cubicles, units for disabled people, babies and children. Laundry and dishwashing facilities. Motorcaravan services. Shop (from 1/4), bread to order and butcher visits in season. Bar with TV (1/4-31/10), snack-bar with takeaway (29/4-10/9). Children's club (high season). Small heated pool (29/4-10/9), paddling pool and jacuzzi. Table tennis, boules and volleyball. Fishing. Play areas and animal enclosure. Off site: Riding 2 km. Golf 10 km. Beach 12 km.

Open: 1 April - 1 November.

Directions

From exit 2 on A28 near Abbeville take D925 to Miannay and turn left on D86 to Bouillancourt-sous-Miannay: site is signed in village.
GPS: N50:05.038 E01:42.779

Charges 2007

Per unit incl. 2 persons	€ 14,60 - € 19,60
with electricity	€ 16,70 - € 23,60
extra person	€ 3,10 - € 4,90
child (under 7 yrs)	€ 1,90 - € 2,90
dog	€ 0,80 - € 1,30

Camping Cheques accepted.

FR80010 Castel Camping le Château de Drancourt

B.P. 80022, F-80230 St Valéry-sur-Somme (Somme)

Tel: **03 22 26 93 45**. Email: **chateau.drancourt@wanadoo.fr**

This is a popular, busy and lively site within easy distance of the Channel ports, between Boulogne and Dieppe. There are 356 pitches in total, of which 220 are occupied by several tour operators; 30 units for rent, and 26 privately owned. The 80 touring pitches are on level grass, of good size, some in shade and others in the open, all with electricity. Fully-serviced pitches are available on reservation. The site is well landscaped and, in spite of the numbers in high season, does not feel over-crowded. It can be dusty around the reception buildings and the château in dry weather. English is spoken and the site is run personally by the energetic owner and his staff. Nearby medieval St Valéry-sur-Somme has a fête each year to celebrate William the Conqueror's embarkation in 1066. The reserve of Le Marquenterre is a must for bird enthusiasts. Pony riding is avaiable in season (stables 15 km).

Facilities

Three toilet blocks include washbasins in cubicles, family bathrooms and facilities for disabled visitors. Laundry facilities. Drainage difficulties can cause occasional problems. Shop, restaurant and takeaway. Several bars. TV rooms, one for children. Games room. Heated pools, one indoor, one outside and paddling pool. Tennis court, golf practise range and minigolf. Bicycle hire. Fishing. Off site: Beach 14 km.

Open: Easter - 5 November.

Directions

Site is 2.5 km. south of St Valéry and signed from the D940 Berck - Le Tréport road. Turn south on D48 Estreboeuf road. Turn immediately left to Drancourt and site. GPS: N50:09.228 E01:38.156

Charges 2006

Per unit incl. 2 persons	€ 12,00 - € 29,00
extra person	€ 4,00 - € 6,50
child (under 5 yrs)	€ 2,00 - € 4,50
electricity (6A)	€ 3,00

Camping le Château de Drancourt - BP 80022, 80230 St. Valéry-sur-Somme
Tel.: (33) 3 22 26 93 45 - Fax: (33) 3 22 26 85 87 - E-mail: chateau.drancourt@wanadoo.fr
www.chateau-drancourt.com

FR80030 Camping du Port de Plaisance

Route de Paris, F-80200 Péronne (Somme)

Tel: **03 22 84 19 31**. Email: **contact@camping-plaisance.com**

Formerly a municipal site, it is informally laid out beside the Canal du Nord on the outskirts of the small town of Péronne, on the river Somme. Only some two or three hours drive from the Channel ports and Tunnel, Péronne is convenient for overnight stops en-route to or from destinations further south or east. The site itself is attractive, being surrounded by trees, with 90 marked pitches (87 have 6/10A electricity hook-up) of varying shapes and sizes on mainly level grass, some being seasonal.

Facilities

The modernised toilet block is kept spotlessly clean, well maintained and heated in winter. Excellent provision for people with disabilities. Laundry area with washing machine and dryer. Motorcaravan service point. New reception building includes a small shop (1/5-31/8), bar and TV room (bread orders are taken). Attractive swimming pool (June-Sept). Play area. Fishing. Off site: Bicycle hire 2 km. Riding 10 km.

Open: 1 March - 31 October.

Directions

From north and ferries, on A1 autoroute, take exit 14. Follow N17 south to Péronne. Take signs for town centre, continue through (look for camp signs). Pass over river Somme and Canal du Nord. Site is on right just past garage at Porte du Plaisance. Or use exit 13. From south use exit 13 and RN29 to Villers Carbonnel to pick up N17 going north. Site signs on left after traffic lights. GPS: N49:55.078 E02:55.975

Charges 2006

Per unit incl. 1-3 persons	€ 13,50 - € 20,00
extra person	€ 3,40 - € 4,30
child (under 7 yrs)	free
electricity (6/10A)	€ 3,50 - € 7,20

FR80070 Camping la Ferme des Aulnes

Mobile homes ▶ page 460

1 rue du Marais, Fresne-sur-Authie, F-80120 Nampont-St Martin (Somme)
Tel: **03 22 29 22 69**. Email: **contact@fermedesaulnes.com**

This peaceful site, with 120 pitches, has been developed on the meadows of a small, 17th century farm on the edge of Fresne and is lovingly cared for by its enthusiastic owner and his hard-working team. Restored outbuildings house reception and the facilities, around a central courtyard that boasts a fine heated swimming pool. A new development outside, facing the main gate, has 20 large level grass pitches for touring. There is also an area for tents. In the centre, a warden lives above a new facility building. The remaining 22 touring pitches are in the main complex, hedged and fairly level. From here you can visit Crécy, Agincourt, St Valéry and Montreuil (where Victor Hugo wrote 'Les Misérables'). The nearby Bay of the Somme has wonderful sandy beaches and many watersports.

Facilities

Both sanitary areas are heated and include washbasins in cubicles with a large cubicle for disabled people. Dishwashing and laundry sinks. Shop. Piano bar and restaurant. Motorcaravan service point. TV room. Swimming pool (16 x 9 m. heated and with cover for cooler weather). Fitness room. Aquagym and Balneo therapy. Playground. Beach volleyball, table tennis, boules and archery. Rooms with play stations and videos. Off site: River fishing 100 m. Golf 3 km. Riding 8 km.

Open: 1 April - early November.

Directions

From Calais, take A16 to exit 25 and turn for Arras for 2 km. and then towards Abbeville on N1. At Nampont St Martin turn west on D485 and site will be found in 2 km. GPS: N50:20.157 E01:42.740

Charges 2006

Per person	€ 7,00
child (under 7 yrs)	€ 4,00
pitch	€ 7,00
electricity (6/10A)	€ 6,00 - € 12,00

Camping Cheques accepted.

FR80040 Camping le Royon

1271 route de Quend, F-80120 Fort-Mahon-Plage (Somme)

Tel: **03 22 23 40 30**. Email: **info@campingleroyon.com**

This busy site, some two kilometres from the sea, has 300 pitches of which 100 are used for touring units. The marked and numbered pitches (of either 95 or 120 sq.m.) are divided by hedges and arranged either side of access roads. Electricity (6A) and water points are available to all. The site is well lit, fenced and guarded at night (€ 30 deposit for barrier card). Entertainment is organised for adults and children in July/Aug when it will be very full. The site is close to the Baie de l'Authie which is an area noted for migrating birds. Nearby there are opportunities for windsurfing, sailing, sand yachting, canoeing, swimming, climbing and shooting.

Facilities

Slightly dated toilet blocks provide unisex facilities with British WCs and washbasins in cubicles. Units for disabled people. Baby baths. Dishwashing and laundry sinks. Shop. Mobile takeaway calls evenings in July/Aug. Clubroom and bar. Heated, covered pool (16 x 8 m). Open air children's pool and sun terrace. Playground. Table tennis, multi-court, tennis court and boules. Bicycle hire. Off site: Fishing, riding, golf within 1 km.

Open: 10 March - 1 November.

Directions

From A16 exit 24, take D32 around Rue (road becomes D940 for a while)then continues as D32 (Fort-Mahon-Plage). Site is on right after 19 km. GPS: N50:19.98 E01:34.811

Charges 2006

Per pitch 95 sq.m. incl. caravan, car, water tap, electricity (6A) and 3 persons	€ 17,00 - € 27,00
extra person (over 1 yr)	€ 7,00

FR80080 Camping Municipal le Bois des Pêcheurs

Route de Forges Les Eaux, F-80290 Poix-de-Picardie (Somme)

Tel: **03 22 90 11 71**. Email: **camping@ville-poix-de-picardie.fr**

The municipal site at Poix-de-Picardie is excellent for a one night stop, or even a few days to explore the region, especially the Somme Battlefields. The 135 pitches are on level, neatly mown grass, either individual or in hedged bays of four. The pitches at one end are often occupied by long stay or holiday groups, but there are up to 125 pitches available for tourists, all with electricity (6A). The city of Amiens (28 km.) is worth visiting for its famous cathedral and quayside market (Thursday and Saturday) in the old, restored St Leu quarter.

Facilities

The old but well maintained, central toilet block includes pushbutton showers, and some washbasins in cubicles. Two separate rooms provide ample dishwashing and laundry sinks. Washing machine and dryer. Small playground. Volleyball, boules and table tennis. TV in Reception. Off site: Supermarket 200 m. Fishing 1 km. Shops, services and swimming pool in Poix de Picardie approx. 1.5 km.

Open: 1 April - 30 September.

Directions

The town is 27 km. south west of Amiens just off the N29. Site is south west of the town on the D919 road, and is signed from the D901 Grandvilliers road. GPS: N49:46.588 E01:58.479

Charges 2006

Per unit incl. 1 or 2 persons	€ 11,00
extra person	€ 2,00
child (under 12 yrs)	€ 1,00
electricity	€ 3,80
No credit cards.	

FR80090 Camping Caravaning le Val d'Authie

20 route de Vercourt, F-80120 Villers-sur-Authie (Somme)

Tel: **03 22 29 92 47**. Email: **camping@valdauthie.fr**

In a village location, this well organised site is fairly close to several beaches, but also has its own excellent pool complex, small restaurant and bar. The owner has carefully controlled the size of the site, leaving space for a leisure area with an indoor pool complex. There are 170 pitches in total, but with many holiday homes and chalets, there are only 60 for touring units. These are on grass, some are divided by small hedges, with 3 or 6A electric hook-ups, and 15 have full services. A 'Sites et Paysages' member.

Facilities

Good toilet facilities include some shower and washbasin units, washbasins in cubicles, and limited facilities for disabled people and babies. Facilities may be under pressure in high season and cleaning variable. Shop (not October). Bar/restaurant (8/4-15/10; hours vary). Swimming and paddling pools (8/4-15/10, with lifeguards in July/Aug). Playground, club room with TV. Weekend entertainment in season (discos may be noisy until midnight, once weekly). Multi-court, beach volleyball, football, boules and tennis court.

Open: 31 March - 15 October.

Directions

Villers-sur-Authie is about 25 km. NNW of Abbéville. From A16 junction 24 take N1 to Vron, then left on D175 to Villers-sur-Authie. Or use D85 from Rue, or D485 from Nampont St Martin. Site is at southern end of village at road junction.
GPS: N50:18.815 E01:41.729

Charges 2007

Per person	€ 6,00
child (under 7 yrs)	€ 3,00
pitch	€ 5,50
electricity (4-10A)	€ 4,00 - € 8,00

Camping Cheques accepted.

tel: 00 333 59 59 03 59 *kawan-villages.com*

FR80100 Camping Parc des Cygnes

111 rue de Montières, F-80080 Amiens (Somme)

Tel: **03 22 43 29 28**. Email: **camping.amiens@wanadoo.fr**

Formerly Camping de L'Ecluse, this is now a 3.2 hectare site which has been completely levelled and attractively landscaped. Bushes and shrubs divide the site into areas some 20 mature trees are planned to provide some shade. The 145 pitches are for touring, with plans for a handful of mobile homes for rent. All pitches are grassed with plenty of space on the tarmac roads in front of them for motorcaravans to park in wet conditions. There are 42 pitches with electricity (6/16A), water and drainage and further water points throughout the rest of the site.

Facilities

Two toilet blocks (one open only when site is busy) with separate toilet facilities but unisex shower and washbasin area. Dishwashing sinks. Facilities for disabled people. Reception building also has toilets, showers and washbasins (heated when necessary). Laundry facilities. Shop (1/4-15/9). Bar and takeaway (1/5-15/9; weekends only in low season). Games and TV room. Bicycle hire. Fishing. Off site: Golf and riding 5 km. Beaches 70 km.

Open: 1 April - 31 October.

Directions

From A16, leave at exit 20. Take the Rocade Nord (northern bypass) to exit 40, follow signs for Amiens Longpré. At roundabout take second exit to Parc de Loisirs, then right to site (signs all the way).
GPS: N49:55.255 E02:15.53

Charges guide

Per person	€ 5,40
child (0-7 yrs)	€ 4,40
pitch	€ 6,10 - € 8,90
car	€ 2,90
electricity	€ 3,10

Low season price for 2 persons and pitch € 13.

Check real time availability and at-the-gate prices...
www.**alanrogers**.com

FR80110 Camping le Ridin

Lieu-dit Mayocq, F-80550 Le Crotoy (Somme)

Tel: **03 22 27 03 22**. Email: **contact@campingleridin.com**

Le Ridin is a popular family site just 2 km. from Le Crotoy and 6 km. from the famous bird reserve of Le Marquenterre. The site has 162 pitches, some of which are occupied by mobile homes and chalets (for rent) and 47 for touring. Pitches are on the small size (roads not suitable for large units) and reasonably shaded. Amenities housed in beautifully converted barns across the road include a heated pool, fitness centre, bar/restaurant and bicycles for hire.

Facilities

Toilet blocks with special facilities for children. Swimming and paddling pools. Restaurant/Bar. Small shop. Games room. Playground. TV room. Bicycle hire. Entertainment programme. Off site: Birdwatching 6 km. Golf 10 km.

Open: 1 April - 1 November.

Directions

Take exit 24 from the A16 (Calais - Abbeville autoroute). Follow signs to Le Crotoy. Site is 1 km. from Le Crotoy on the road to Rue. GPS: N50:14.364 E01:37.893

Charges 2006

Per unit incl. 2 persons	€ 16,00 - € 23,00
extra person	€ 5,00
electricity (6-10A)	€ 2,50 - € 5,50

Camping Cheques accepted.

FR80120 Camping les Aubépines

Saint Firmin, F-80550 Le Crotoy (Somme)

Tel: **03 22 27 01 34**. Email: **contact@campingl-lesaubepines.com**

This peaceful, family-run site is on the edge of the Parc Ornithologique du Marquenterre and is just 1 km. from a beach on the Baie de Somme, a river estuary famous for its resident population of seals. There are 196 pitches, although around 100 are occupied by privately-owned mobile homes with a few available for rent. Consequently there are just 76 touring pitches scattered throughout the site. All on level ground, they are of a reasonable to good size, separated by hedges and trees and with water taps and electricity (3-10A) close by.

Facilities

Two unisex toilet blocks, fairly basic but clean and in good order. British style toilets (seatless), washbasins in cubicles, push-button showers and some larger cubicles with shower and basin. Baby bath and toilet. Facilities for disabled visitors are minimal (no grab-rails). Dishwashing sinks. Laundry room. Shop. Indoor games. Small play area. Bicycle hire. Off site: Riding adjacent. Nautical base 500 m. Beaches: 1 km and 10 km. Fishing 2 km. Bird sanctuary, tennis 3 km. Golf 10 km.

Open: 1 April - 1 November.

Directions

Le Crotoy is on the D940 Berck - Le Tréport road. At roundabout for town, take D4 to St Firmin, turn right at next roundabout. After village sign, turn left to site (signed) on right in about 500 m. GPS: N50:15.004 E01:36.747

Charges 2006

Per unit incl. 2 persons and 3A electricity	€ 19,00 - € 23,00
extra person	€ 4,30 - € 4,70
child (2-7 yrs)	€ 3,30 - € 3,60
electricity 6/10A	€ 5,00

FR80130 Camping les Vertes Feuilles

25 route de la Plage Monchaux, F-80120 Quend Plage les Pins (Somme)

Tel: **03 22 23 55 12**. Email: **contact@lesvertesfeuilles.com**

Situated on the Picardy coast, three kilometres from the beach, this small 1.5 hectare site provides 30 touring pitches out of a total of 106. The remainder accommmodate a mix of mobile homes and semi-residential caravans. It is a charming campsite where a pleasant welcome awaits you. The site roads are slightly narrow, so larger units cannot be accommodated. This whole area is bustling in high season with many campsites and holiday villages but this makes for a wonderful French style seaside holiday. Don't forget to visit the nearby Aquaclub, the Abbey and Gardens of Valloires and the bird reserve of Le Marquenterre.

Facilities

One large toilet block, old but renovated, has unisex showers, washbasins in cubicles and 3 family rooms. Ramped facilities for disabled visitors. Snack bar in season. Covered heated swimming pool (1/6-31/8). Play areas. Bicycle hire. Off site: Beach 3 km. Golf 2 km. Riding 5 km. Local markets.

Open: 1 April - 1 November.

Directions

From A16 Rue exit, take D32 around Rue, when road becomes D940 for a while, then continues again as D32 towards Fort-Mahon-Plage. After left turn for Quend Plage, site on left.

Charges 2006

Per unit incl. 2 persons	€ 14,00 - € 23,00
incl. electricity	€ 17,00 - € 23,00
extra person	€ 3,50 - € 4,00

MAP 3

With its tree lined boulevards, museums, art galleries, the Arc de Triomphe and of course the famous Eiffel Tower, this cosmopolitan city has plenty to offer. Less than 30 miles from the heart of the capital, a fun-packed trip to Disneyland Paris is also within reach.

Paris & Ile de France

DÉPARTEMENTS: 75 PARIS, 77 SEINE-ET-MARNE, 78 YVELINES, 91 ESSONE, 92 HAUTS-DE-SEINE, 93 SEINE-ST-DENIS, 94 VAL DE MARNE, 95 VAL D'OISE

MAJOR CITIES: PARIS, VERSAILLES, IVRY, MELUN, NANTERRE, BOBIGNY, CRETEIL AND PONTOISE.

One of the most chic and culturally rewarding cities in the world, Paris has something for everyone. The list of things to do is virtually endless and could easily fill many holidays - window shopping, the Eiffel Tower, Notre Dame, Montmartre, trips on the Seine, pavement cafés and the Moulin Rouge, the list goes on.

As a peaceful retreat, you can relax and enjoy the lush scenery of surrounding hills and secret woodlands of the Ile de France. Square bell towers in gentle valleys, white silos on endless plains of wheat; soft and harmonious landscapes painted and praised by La Fontaine, Corot and all the landscape painters. Paris is surrounded by forests, Fontainebleau, Compiègne, Saint-Germain-en-Laye and majestic châteaux such as Fontainbleau and Vaux-le-Vicomte.

Disneyland Resort Paris provides a great day out for all the family with two fantastic theme parks with over 70 attractions and shows to choose from. On the outskirts of Paris is Parc Asterix. with one of Europe's most impressive roller-coasters.

Places of interest

Fontainebleau: château and national museum, history of Napoléon from 1804-1815.

Malmaison: château and national museum.

Meaux: agricultural centre, Gothic cathedral, chapter house and palace.

Paris: obviously! The list of places is too extensive to include here.

St Germain-en-Laye: château, Gallo-roman and Merovingian archeological museum.

Sèvres: ceramics museum.

Thoiry: château and Parc Zoologique, 450-hectare park with gardens and African reserve containing 800 animals.

Versailles: Royal Castle, Royal Apartments, Hall of Mirrors, Royal Opera and French History Museum.

Cuisine of the region

Although without a specific cuisine of its own, Paris and Ile de France offer a wide selection of dishes from all the regions of France. Paris also has a wide choice of foreign restaurants, such as Vietnamese and North African.

FR91010 Camping Caravaning le Beau Village

1 voie des Prés, F-91700 Villiers-sur-Orge (Essonne)

Tel: **01 60 16 17 86**. Email: **le-beau-village@wanadoo.fr**

This is a pleasant, typically French campsite just 25 km. south of Paris and conveniently located at the centre of a triangle formed by the A6 motorway, the N20/A10 to Orleans and the N104 east/west link road 'La Francilienne'. Half of its 100 pitches are occupied on a seasonal basis by Parisians; the remainder are touring pitches, all hedged and with electricity. Trees provide some shade. Reception, in a traditional style building, also has a pleasant little bar, a games room and an attractive terrace.

Facilities

The main toilet block has controllable showers and some washbasins in cabins. A second (older) block has adequate facilities for disabled visitors, the third (in a 'portacabin') has laundry facilities and a very tired unit for children. All three can be heated. Small bar. Games room with internet access (charged). Play area. Loan of canoes. Off site: Tennis and football. Shops and restaurants. Golf, riding 2 km. River beach and sailing 3 km. Boat launching 4 km.

Open: All year.

Directions

From N20 at Ballainvillers take exit for La Ville du Bois on D35 southeast to Villiers-sur-Orge. In village turn right along river bank to site on left. From A6 leave at exit 6 (Savigny-sur-Orge). Turn west, follow signs (Quartier Latin) then D25 to Villiers-sur-Orge. Turn left after river and as above. From A10 turn east on N104. From N104 take N20 north, then as above.

Charges 2006

Per person	€ 4,50
pitch incl. electricity	€ 7,00

FR91020 Le Parc des Roches

La Petite Beauce, F-91530 Saint-Chéron (Essonne)

Tel: **01 64 56 65 50**. Email: **contact@parcdesroches.com**

This large site with 400 pitches occupying a wooded hill-top is principally dedicated to providing Parisians with somewhere to escape from city life, but also offers 80 touring pitches on gently sloping ground near the entrance. These are reasonably well tended and all have 5A electricity. A convenient location for a night's break if travelling north or south on the N20. The bar/restaurant is pleasant and offers basic food at reasonable prices.

Facilities

The main toilet block provides pre-set showers, washbasins in cabins (warm water only). Dishwashing and laundry facilities. Several separate toilets, washbasins in cubicles and showers (with detachable shower-heads) for disabled visitors. An older block is more basic with open style washbasins. Both can be heated when necessary. Swimming pool (1/6-15/9). Bar/restaurant and takeaway (15/6-15/9) also sells basics. Tennis. Play area (in residential part). Off site: Train station 3 km. (Paris, Versailles). Fishing 6 km. Riding 10 km. Golf 15 km.

Open: 15 April - 1 November.

Directions

From N20, 5 km. south of junction with N104 (La Francilienne) turn west at Arpajon on D97. At roundabout turn south on D116 (St Chéron and Dourdan). In St Chéron at first traffic lights turn left past railway, then left on D132 for 3 km. to la Petite Beauce. After hamlet turn left to campsite. GPS: N48:32.717 E02:08.22

Charges 2007

Per person	€ 6,60
child (0-18 yrs)	€ 3,80 - € 5,00
pitch incl. electricity	€ 10,20

FR75020 Camping du Bois de Boulogne

2 allée du Bord de l'eau, F-75016 Paris (Paris)

Tel: **01 45 24 30 00**. Email: **camping-boulogne@stereau.fr**

A busy site and the nearest to the city, set in a wooded area between the Seine and the Bois de Boulogne. The site is quite extensive but nevertheless becomes very full with many international visitors. There are 510 pitches (including mobile homes and a few chalets) of which 280 are marked, with electricity (10A), water, drainage and TV aerial connections. The site has undergone a huge improvement and re-development programme including the refurbishment of all toilet blocks. Reservations are made for pitches – if not booked, arrive early in season (mornings).

Facilities

Toilet blocks have British style WCs, washbasins in cubicles and showers with divider and seat (hot water throughout). All these facilities suffer from heavy use in season. Laundry facilities. Five motorcaravan service points. Mini-market. Bar and restaurant (1/4-15/10). Bar open 7 am. - midnight at most times and until 2 am. in peak season. Pizza bar. Takeaway. Information service. Playground. Off site: Fishing 1 km. Bicycle hire 2 km.

Open: All year.

Directions

Site is on east side of Seine between the river and the Bois de Boulogne, just north of the Pont de Suresnes. Easiest approach is from Port Maillot. Traffic lights at site entrance. Follow signs closely and use a good map. GPS: N48:52.06 E02:14.05

Charges 2006

Per unit incl. 2 persons	€ 20,00 - € 27,50
with electricity, water and drain	€ 24,00 - € 34,50
extra person	€ 4,50 - € 6,50

Check real time availability and at-the-gate prices...

www.alanrogers.com

FR77020 Camping le Chêne Gris

Mobile homes ▶ page 460

24, place de la Gare de Faremoutiers, F-77515 Pommeuse (Seine-et-Marne)
Tel: 01 64 04 21 80. Email: info@lechenegris.com

This site is currently being developed by a new Dutch/Italian company and when we visited in July 2006, work was very much behind schedule. A new building which houses reception on the ground floor and an airy restaurant/bar plus a takeaway is of high quality. Of the 190 pitches, 134 are for touring many of which are on rough aggregate stone, the rest (higher up the hill on which the site is built) being occupied by mobile homes and tents of a Dutch tour operator. Terraces look out onto the heated leisure pool complex and an adventure-type play area for over-fives, whilst the play area for under-fives is at the side of the bar with picture windows overlooking it. The site is next to a railway station with trains to Paris (45 minutes). Disneyland is 20 km.

Facilities

One basic toilet block with push-button showers, washbasins in cubicles and a dishwashing and laundry area. At busy times these facilities may be under pressure. Facilities for disabled visitors (although grab-rail only for WC and shower seemed to be set too high). Children's area with toilets and baby bath but showers at adult height! Bar, restaurant and takeaway. Pool complex (all season). Off site: Shops, bars and restaurants within walking distance. Fishing and riding 2 km.

Open: 28 April - 31 October.

Directions

Pommeuse is 55 km. east of Paris. From A4 at exit 16 take N34 towards Coulommiers. In 10 km. turn south for 2 km. on D25 to Pommeuse; site on right after level-crossing. Also signed from south on D402 Guignes - Coulommiers road, taking D25 to Faremoutiers. GPS: N48:48.514 E02:59.530

Charges 2006

Per unit incl. 2 persons and electricity	€ 29,00 - € 35,00
extra person	€ 2,00 - € 3,50
child (3-11 yrs)	€ 2,00 - € 3,00

FR77040 Caravaning des 4 Vents

Rue de Beauregard, F-77610 Crèvecoeur-en-Brie (Seine-et-Marne)
Tel: 01 64 07 41 11. Email: f.george@free.fr

This peaceful, pleasant site has been owned and run by the same family for over 35 years. There are around 200 pitches, with many permanent or seasonal units, however, there are 130 spacious grassy pitches for tourists, well separated by good hedges, all with 6A electricity and most with a water tap. The whole site is well landscaped with flowers and trees everywhere. This is a great family site with pool and games facilities located at the top end of the site so that campers are not disturbed.

Facilities

Three modern sanitary units provide British style WCs, washbasins (mainly in cubicles) and pushbutton showers. Facilities for disabled people. Laundry facilities. Motorcaravan service point. In high season (July/Aug) a mobile snack bar and pizzeria (open from 16.00-23.00), and a baker from 07.30-11.00. Well fenced, circular swimming pool (16 m. diameter; June to Sept). Playground, games room, volleyball court, billiard hall and boules court. Off site: La Houssaye 1 km. Fontenay 5 km.

Open: 1 March - 1 November.

Directions

Crèvecoeur is just off the D231 between A4 exit 13 and Provins. From north, pass obelisk and turn right in 3 km. From south 19 km. after junction with N4, turn left at signs to village. Follow site signs. GPS: N48:45.044 E02:53.775

Charges 2007

Per unit incl. 2 persons and electricity	€ 23,00
extra person (over 5 yrs)	€ 5,00

FR77030 Camping International de Jablines

Base de Loisirs, F-77450 Jablines (Seine-et-Marne)

Tel: **01 60 26 09 37**. Email: **welcome@camping-jablines.com**

Jablines is a modern site which, with the accompanying leisure facilities of the adjacent 'Espace Loisirs', provides an interesting, if a little impersonal alternative to other sites in the region. Man-made lakes provide marvellous water activities. The 'Great Lake' as it is called, is said to have the largest beach in the Ile-de-France! The site itself provides 150 pitches, of which 132 are for touring units. Most are of a good size with gravel hardstanding and grass, accessed by tarmac roads and marked by fencing panels and shrubs. All have 10A electrical connections, 60 with water and waste connections also. The whole complex close to the Marne has been developed around old gravel workings. Water activities include dinghy sailing, windsurfing, canoeing, fishing and supervised bathing, plus a large equestrian centre. In season the activities at the leisure complex are supplemented by a bar/restaurant and a range of very French style group activities.

Facilities

Two toilet blocks, heated in cool weather, include push-button showers, some washbasins in cubicles. Dishwashing and laundry facilities. Motorcaravan service (charged). Shop. Play area. Bar/restaurant adjacent at leisure centre/lake complex with watersports including 'water cable ski', riding activities, tennis and minigolf. Whilst staying on the campsite, admission to the leisure complex is free. Internet point. Ticket sales for Disneyland and Asterix. Off site: Golf 24 km.

Open: 31 March - 28 October.

Directions

From A4 Paris - Rouen turn north on A104. Take exit 8 on D404 Meaux and Base de Loisirs Jablines. From A1 going south, follow signs for Marne-la-Vallée using A104. Take exit 6A Clay-Souilly on the N3 (Meaux). After 6 km. turn south on D404 and follow signs. At park entry keep left for campsite. GPS: N48:54.817 E02:44.051

Charges 2007

Per pitch incl. 2 persons and 10A electricity	€ 20,00 - € 23,00
incl. water and drain	€ 22,00 - € 25,00
extra person	€ 5,00 - € 6,00
child (3-11 yrs)	€ 3,50 - € 4,50

Camping Cheques accepted.

102
Check real time availability and at-the-gate prices...
www.alanrogers.com

FR77070 Camping la Belle Etoile

Quai Joffre, La Rochette, F-77000 Melun (Seine-et-Marne)

Tel: **01 64 39 48 12**. Email: **info@campinglabelleetoile.com**

Alongside the River Seine, this site has an overall mature and neat appearance, although the approach road is somewhat off-putting with several industrial plants. However, you'll discover that La Belle Etoile enjoys a pleasant position with pitches to the fore of the site within view of the barges which continually pass up and down. The 170 touring pitches, with electricity connections (6/10A), are on grass and laid out between the many shrubs and trees. There are ten units for hire. A friendly, family run site with pleasant and helpful English speaking owners. Ideally situated for visiting Fontainebleau and Paris.

Facilities

The toilet blocks are not new but they are kept very clean and the water is very hot. Laundry room. Baby bath. Facilities for disabled visitors (shower, washbasin and WC). Motorcaravan service point. Small bar, snacks and shop (28/6-30/8). Takeaway (1/5-15/9). Swimming pool (1/5-15/9). Play area. Fishing. Bicycle hire. Tickets for Disney and Vaux le Vicomte are sold by the site. Off site: Fontainebleau and Paris. Golf 15 km.

Open: 1 April - 22 October.

Directions

Travelling north on N6 Fontainebleau - Melun road, on entering La Rochette, pass petrol station on left. Turn immediately right into Ave de la Seine. At end of road turn left at river, site on left in 500 m.
GPS: N48:31.501 E02:40.164

Charges 2006

Per person	€ 4,90 - € 5,40
baby (0-2 yrs)	€ 2,20 - € 2,40
child (3-11 yrs)	€ 3,00 - € 3,40
pitch	€ 5,00 - € 5,40
Camping Cheques accepted.	

FR77090 Camping les Etangs Fleuris

Route Couture, F-77131 Touquin (Seine-et-Marne)

Tel: **01 64 04 16 36**. Email: **contact@etangs-fleuris.com**

This is a pleasant, peaceful site which has a very French feel despite the presence of a fair number of tour operator mobile homes, since these occupy their own areas round the periphery. The 60 touring pitches are grouped on the level ground around the attractive lakes, all with electricity (10A) and water, separated by hedges and with shade from mature trees. The life of the site centres round a smart bar/function room which doubles as reception and a shop, as well as the lakes and an attractive, irregularly shaped pool.

Facilities

Basic toilet has push-button showers, and open washbasins (with dividers and hooks) for men but mainly in cubicles for ladies. Cleaning can be variable at busy times. No facilities for disabled visitors. Another heated block is only opened in cold weather or when site is very busy. Laundry facilities. Shop for basics in bar. Heated pool with paddling section (15/5-15/9). Takeaway meals and snacks (15/5-15/9). Internet access. Off site: Riding 5 km. Golf 15 km.

Open: 15 April - 15 September.

Directions

Touquin is off the D231, 21 km. from exit 13 of A4 motorway and 30 km. northeast of Provins. From D231 follow signs for Touquin, then Etangs Fleuris. Site is 2.5 km. west of village.
GPS: N48:43.867 E03:02.845

Charges 2006

Per person	€ 7,00 - € 8,00
child (0-9 yrs)	€ 3,50 - € 4,00

FR94000 Camping du Tremblay – Paris Est

Boulevard des Alliés, F-94507 Champigny-sur-Marne (Val-de-Marne)

Tel: **01 43 97 43 97**. Email: **champigny@campingparis.fr**

This site is on flat land beside the River Marne with 450 pitches, 76 of which are occupied by mobile homes and chalets to rent. The 220 touring pitches are on gravel and are separated by hedges. All have electricity (10A) but water has to be fetched from the toilet blocks except for the 32 serviced pitches which have taps and waste water points. There is also a large area of grass pitches for camping where there are water points but no electricity. It is very much a short-stay site.

Facilities

Three toilet blocks are old-fashioned but apparently cleaned three times a day. Toilets are mainly segregated with many Turkish-style but some British (with occasional seat!) One block has unisex toilets (seat-less British-style). Showers are pre-set and washbasins in cubicles with warm and cold water. Facilities for disabled visitors (some en-suite) are basic and there are no grab rails. Dishwashing sinks. Laundry facilities. Small shop, bar and snack bar (15/3-15/10). Fishing.

Open: All year.

Directions

From A4 take exit 5 on D45 south (towards Champigny). At lights, turn right on N303 (St Maur). At next lights continue on (now N4 to Vincennes) and immediately right at next lights (Boulevard de Polangis).Before flyover, turn right along Boulevard des Allies. Site on left (pass under motorway). Signs for Camping IDF. GPS: N48:49.777 E02:28.624

Charges 2006

Per unit incl. 2 persons	€ 17,50 - € 29,90
extra person	€ 4,40 - € 5,70

FR95000 Parc de Séjour de L'Etang

10 chemin des Bellevues, F-95690 Nesles-la-Vallée (Val-d'Oise)

Tel: **01 34 70 62 89**. Email: **brehinier1@hotmail.com**

Parc de Séjour de L'Etang is small, informal site 33 km. northwest of Paris. It is situated on the southern outskirts of the village of Nesles-la-Vallée in a pretty, tree-lined river valley not far from L'Isle-Adam, which is a popular destination for Parisians at weekends. Many of the 165 pitches are occupied by seasonal caravans but there are 65 large, flat pitches available for touring units of which 25 have electricity (3/9A). The site is informally arranged around a duck pond with many trees.

Facilities

The main, central toilet block (heated in cooler weather) includes washbasins in rather small cubicles and, in separate rooms, rather older style British and Turkish WCs. Washing machine. Smaller, much older unit includes fairly basic facilities for disabled people. Playground and play barn. Off site: Village within walking distance. Riding 500 m. Golf 7 km.

Open: 1 March - 15 November.

Directions

From A15 exit 10 take D915 (Pontoise), avoiding town centre, then D27 (Beauvais) which joins D927, then D79 to Nesles-la-Vallée. Site on left as you leave village (D64). GPS: N49:07.647 E02:11.047

Charges 2006

Per person	€ 4,00
pitch incl. electricity	€ 7,15 - € 8,10
No credit cards.	

FR78010 Camping Caravaning International

1 rue Johnson, F-78600 Maisons-Laffitte (Yvelines)

Tel: **01 39 12 21 91**. Email: **ci.mlaffitte@wanadoo.fr**

This site on the banks of the Seine is consistently busy, has multilingual, friendly reception staff and occupies a grassy, tree covered area bordering the river. There are 351 pitches, 66 occupied by mobile homes and 90 used by tour operators, plus two areas dedicated to tents. Most pitches are separated by hedges, are of a good size with some overlooking the Seine (unfenced access), and all 195 touring pitches have electricity hook-ups (6A). The roads leading to the site are a little narrow so large vehicles need to take care. Train noise can be expected.

Facilities

Three sanitary blocks, two insulated for winter use and one more open (only used in July/August). Facilities are clean with constant supervision necessary, due to volume of visitors. Provision for people with disabilities. Laundry and dishwashing areas. Motorcaravan service point. Self-service shop. Restaurant/bar. Takeaway food and pizzeria. TV room, table tennis, football area. Internet point. SNCF rep each morning 15/6-15/8 for travel advice. Off site: Sports complex adjoining. Riding 500 m. Bicycle hire 5 km.

Open: 1 April - 31 October.

Directions

Best approached from A13 or A15 autoroute. From A13 take exit 7 (Poissy) and follow D153 (Poissy), the D308 (Maisons-Laffitte), then site signs on right before town centre. From A15 exit 7 take D184 towards St Germain, after 11 km. turn left on D308 (Maisons-Laffitte). Follow site signs. From A1 take A86, then at exit 2 (Bezons) take D308 (Maisons-Laffitte). Follow signs to site on left. GPS: N48:56.394 E02:08.740

Charges 2007

Per unit incl. 2 persons	€ 13,00 - € 26,00
electricity	€ 3,00
extra person	€ 5,40 - € 6,00

Check real time availability and at-the-gate prices...

www.**alanrogers**.com

FR78040 Huttopia Rambouillet

Route du Château d'Eau, F-78120 Rambouillet (Yvelines)

Tel: **01 30 41 07 34**. Email: **rambouillet@huttopia.com**

This pleasant site has recently been taken over by the Huttopia group who will be developing it, starting with an outdoor, heated swimming pool. It is in a peaceful forest location beside a lake, with good tarmac access roads, site lighting and 190 touring pitches of varying size and surfaces. Some of the individual pitches are divided by hedges, others are more open and sunny. All have electricity, 83 also have water and drainage, with a few hardstandings. There are many good cycle and footpaths in the area. It is possible to visit Paris by rail; the Mobilis 'transport package' ticket is available from the railway station. Rambouillet itself is an interesting town and Chartres and Versailles are within reach.

Facilities

Two heated sanitary buildings include British and Turkish style WCs, washbasins (some in cubicles), dishwashing and laundry sinks, plus basic facilities for baby changing and for disabled persons. Washing machine and dryer. Motorcaravan service point. Café/bar and boutique. Good playground. Swimming pool. Off site: Large supermarket at southern end of the town.

Open: 1 July - 30 September.

Directions

Rambouillet is 52 km. southwest of Paris. Site is southeast of town: from N10 southbound take Rambouillet/Les Eveuses exit, northbound take Rambouillet centre exit, loop round and rejoin N10 southbound, taking next exit. Pass under N10, following site signs. GPS: N48:37.623 E01:50.727

Charges 2007

Per person	€ 5,00 - € 6,00
pitch	€ 6,00 - € 17,00
electricity (6-10A)	€ 4,00 - € 6,20

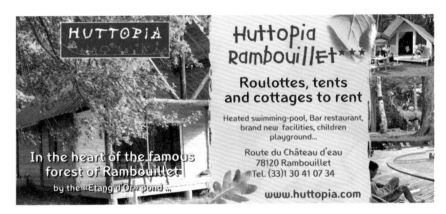

FR78050 Camping le Val de Seine

Base de Loisirs, Chemin du Rouillard, F-78480 Verneuil-sur-Seine (Yvelines)

Tel: **01 39 28 16 20**. Email: **sce-client@valdeseine78.com**

This is an excellent little site, completely refurbished to high standards and located in a large leisure and country park on the western outskirts of Paris. Campers have free access to the huge country park (800 m. from site) with its three large lakes, one with a beach for swimming, others for sailing and pedalo hire. The site has 87 pitches in two sections, one end for campers (mainly groups) with its own toilet block, the other for caravans and tents. Here there are 37 level pitches each with electricity (6A), water and drainage.

Facilities

Two modern toilet blocks have controllable showers and some washbasins in cubicles. Facilities for disabled visitors. Dishwashing provision. Small block for children plus baby room. Laundry facilities. Motorcaravan service point. Reception sells bread (to order) and basics. Country park with lakes, fishing, sailing, many other sports facilities, a self-service restaurant and brasserie. Tennis courts, 18 hole minigolf. Off site: Riding adjacent. Golf 7 km.

Open: 1 April - 30 September.

Directions

From A13 take exit 8 (Meulan-les Mureaux). Follow signs for 'Base de Loisirs du Val de Seine'. Go through Les Mureaux and bear right on D154 towards Verneuil. At roundabout turn left (signed 'Base de Loisirs') to site. GPS: N48:59.762 E01:57.548

Charges 2006

Per person (4 yrs and over)	€ 3,25 - € 4,80
pitch	€ 3,70 - € 5,00
car	€ 1,60
electricity	€ 4,25

FR78060 Huttopia Versailles

31 rue Berthelot, F-78000 Versailles (Yvelines)

Tel: **01 39 51 23 61**. Email: **versailles@huttopia.com**

This Huttopia site is rather different. When the French owners visited Canada and experienced 'back to nature' camping, they were so impressed that they decided to introduce the idea to France. This is probably a little like camping as it used to be, but with some big differences. Gone are the formal pitches with neatly trimmed hedges and instead there are 145 places of ample size arranged informally amongst the trees. The terrain is as nature intended with very little grass and much of it steep and rugged (there are plans to introduce some terracing). Long electricity leads are required and be prepared to use blocks and corner steadies on many pitches, most of which have good shade. All the site buildings are designed and built to fit into the natural concept. Attractive wooden huts, tents and gypsy style caravans can be rented. This is a different but popular site that will suit campers who, while still wanting their creature comforts, would like to be in more natural surroundings.

Facilities

Three well designed toilet blocks (wood cabin style) are evenly dispersed around the site and provide basic facilities. Special bivouacs set up for cooking and washing up. Restaurant with takeaway food (1/7-31/8 and weekends). Bar. Games room. Simple swimming and paddling pools (June-Sept). Playground. Bicycle hire. Children's club. Off site: Versailles and its château. Hiking. Cycling trails. Fishing 1 km. Golf 3 km. Riding 5 km. Paris 20 minutes by RER express train from Versailles.

Open: 1 April - 31 December.

Directions

From the front of the château of Versailles take the Avenue de Paris and the site is signed after 2 km. GPS: N48:47.38 E02:09.38

Charges 2006

Per person	€ 6,00 - € 7,00
child (2-7 yrs)	€ 3,00 - € 3,50
pitch	€ 10,00 - € 20,00
electricity (6/10A)	€ 4,00 - € 6,00

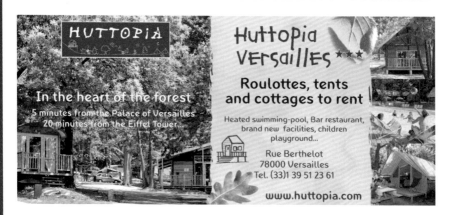

FR60010 Camping Campix

B.P. 37, F-60340 St Leu-d'Esserent (Oise)

Tel: **03 44 56 08 48**. Email: **campixfr@aol.com**

This informal site has been unusually developed in a former sandstone quarry on the outskirts of the small town. The quarry walls provide a sheltered, peaceful environment and trees soften the slopes. Not a neat, manicured site, the 160 pitches are in small groups on the different levels with stone and gravel access roads (some fairly steep and possibly muddy in poor weather). Electricity (6A) is available to about 140 pitches. There are many secluded corners mostly for smaller units and tents and space for children to explore (parents must supervise – some areas, although fenced, could be dangerous). Torches are advised.

Facilities

A large building houses reception and two clean, heated sanitary units - one for tourers, the other usually reserved for groups. Two suites for disabled people double as baby rooms. Laundry facilities. At quieter times only one unit open but facilities may be congested at peak times. Motorcaravan service facilities. Daily bread and milk. Pizza and other Italian food delivery in the evenings. Off site: Fishing 1 or 5 km. Riding, golf 5 km.

Open: 7 March - 30 November.

Directions

St Leu-d'Esserent is 11 km. west of Senlis, 5 km. northwest of Chantilly. From north on A1 autoroute take Senlis exit, from Paris the Chantilly exit. Site north of town off D12 towards Cramoisy, and signed in village. GPS: N49:13.509 E02:25.638

Charges 2007

Per person	€ 3,00 - € 5,50
child (under 9 yrs)	€ 2,00 - € 3,00
pitch	€ 3,50 - € 5,50
electricity	€ 2,50 - € 3,50

MAP 4

Home to the Champagne region, the varied landscapes of Eastern France include dense forests, vineyards and winding rivers. The whole area is dotted with fascinating ancient churches and castles, towns and villages.

EASTERN FRANCE IS DEFINED AS:
CHAMPAGNE-ARDENNE: 08 ARDENNES, 51 MARNE, 10 AUBE, 52 HAUTE-MARNE. LORRAINE VOSGES: 54 MEURTHE-ET-MOSELLE, 55 MEUSE, 57 MOSELLE, 88 VOSGES. ALSACE: 67 BAS-RHIN, 68 HAUT-RHIN

Situated on the flatlands of Champagne are the most northerly vineyards in France where special processing turns the light, dry wine into 'le Champagne' and names such as Moet et Chandon and Veuve Clicquot spring to mind. Nowhere else in the world are you allowed to make sparkling wine and call it champagne. Travelling further east you come across the spa towns such as Vittel, Bains-les-Bains and Plombières and the birth place of St Joan of Arc at Domrémy.

Today you can descend from the mountains into the Alsace vineyards and fairy tale wine villages. The 'Route des Vins' follows the vineyards along the Rhine valley from Mulhouse to Colmar and north almost to Strasbourg. Alsace and Lorraine have been frequently fought over and today there are many poignant reminders of the turbulent past. You'll find noticeable German influence in architecture, cuisine and language. There are also numerous little wine towns, medieval villages and a host of ruined castles stretching along the north eastern margins of the Vosges.

Places of interest

Épernay: home of champagne production.

Le Linge: trenches including rusty barbed wire have been left as they were.

Reims: 13th century Gothic cathedral.

Riquewihr: traditional town, fortifications and medieval houses.

Verdun: hill forts such as Fort de Vaux and Fort de Douaumont, large military cemetery at Douaumont.

Cuisine of the region

Quiche Lorraine: made only in the classical manner with cream, eggs and bacon.

Potage Lorraine: potato, leek and onion soup.

Tarte (aux mirabelles): golden plum tart. Also made with other fruits.

Tarte à l'oignon Alsacienne: onion and cream tart.

FR08010 Camping Municipal du Mont Olympe

Rue des Paquis, F-08000 Charleville-Mezieres (Ardennes)

Tel: **03 24 33 23 60**. Email: **camping-charlevillemezieres@wanadoo.fr**

Attractively situated alongside the Meuse River, within easy walking distance across a footbridge to the centre of the pleasant large town, this site was completely rebuilt in 2002. It now offers excellent facilities, with 129 grass pitches, all with electricity (10A), water and waste water connections. There are 66 from 108 to 219 sq.m. in size, 49 up to 106 sq.m. and 7 hardstandings for motorcaravans.

Facilities

Two heated buildings provide first class showers, private cabins, baby rooms and facilities for the disabled, plus inside dishwashing (including one for the disabled) and a well-equipped laundry room. Motorcaravan service point. Shop (July/Aug). Play area. TV and games room. Barbecues allowed at communal area only. Off site: Municipal pool next door. Boat trips on the river. Attractive town centre close by. Bicycle hire 1 km. Golf 20 km.

Open: 1 April - 15 October.

Directions

Site north of Charleville on island of Montcy St Pierre. From north D988/D1 follow river, over bridge, then immediately left. From southeast (A203, N51, N43) take 'centre' exit, head for 'Gare' then Avenue Forest north and sharp left after bridge. Site is 150 m. on from old site. GPS: N49:46.741 E04:43.246

Charges 2006

Per person	€ 3,15
child (2-10 yrs)	€ 1,60
pitch incl. electricity	€ 7,30 - € 9,30

FR08040 Camping la Samaritaine

F-08240 Buzancy (Ardennes)

Tel: **03 24 30 08 88**. Email: **info@campinglasamaritaine.com**

A delightful new site in the heart of the Ardennes. It is peacefully situated just outside the village beside a stream. There may be some high season noise from a nearby lake where you can swim or fish. Flowers decorate the entrance and bushes and saplings separate the pitches. The 101 numbered touring pitches all have electricity (10A) and are on level grass off hard access roads. They vary in size up to 130 sq.m. 55 have water and waste water, and there are small wooden containers for waste. There are also 10 mobile homes and 9 chalets for rent.

Facilities

Sanitary facilities provide private cabins, baby bath, laundry facilities, dishwashing and facilities for the disabled. A large recreation room has some games and tables to sit at. Bread delivered daily. A few essentials are kept in reception. Snack bar/takeaway (mid-May - end-Sept). High season accompanied walks and entertainment programme. Motorcaravan service point and an 'Aire Exterieur' are beside the entrance road to the site. Off site: Restaurant in village.

Open: 4 May - 30 September.

Directions

Buzancy is about 22 km. east of Vouziers on RD947 towards Stenay and Montmédy. Site is just over 1.5 km. from centre of village down a small road. Well signed. GPS: N49:25.584 E04:56.406

Charges 2007

Per person	€ 3,00 - € 4,00
child (under 10 yrs)	€ 2,00 - € 3,00
pitch	€ 4,50 - € 5,50
water and waste water	€ 2,00
electricity (10A)	€ 3,50

FR10010 Camping Municipal de Troyes

1 rue de Roger Salengro, F-10150 Pont-Sainte-Marie (Aube)

Tel: **03 25 81 02 64**. Email: **info@troyescamping.net**

This municipal campsite, within the Troyes city boundary and about 4 km. from the centre, has been taken over by two young enthusiastic managers who are turning it into an attractive place to stay. There are 110 level grassy pitches (6 with hardstanding), all for tourers, about equally shaded and open. All have electrical connections (5A), and there are plenty of water taps. Being on one of the main routes from Luxembourg to the southwest of France, and on the main route from Calais to the Mediterranean, Troyes makes a good night stop.

Facilities

Two modern toilet blocks contain British style WCs, washbasins and pre-set showers. Facilities for disabled people. Motorcaravan services. Washing machines and dryer. Shop for basics (all season). Gas supplies. Restaurant, snack bar and takeaway (15/6-15/9). TV room. Games room. Playground. Minigolf. Table tennis. Volleyball. Boules. Bicycle hire. Off site: Bus to Troyes centre 50 m. Supermarket 100 m. Other shops, restaurants, bars, ATM 300 m. Riding 8 km.

Open: 1 April - 15 October.

Directions

From north, leave A26 at exit 22 (Charmont). Turn right (southwest) on D15 (Troyes). In 4 km. turn left (south) at roundabout on N77 (Troyes). After 6 km. pass over ring road, towards town. After 2 km. road swings left, then right. Sign for site on right. From Troyes, follow road north (Nancy). In 2 km. site sign on left. GPS: N48:18.666 E04:05.817

Charges 2006

Per person	€ 4,20
pitch incl. electricity	€ 8,50

FR10030 Camping du Tertre

Route de Radonvilliers, F-10500 Dienville (Aube)

Tel: 03 25 92 26 50. Email: campingdutertre@wanadoo.fr

This medium sized site is situated near the lakes of the Parc l'Orient, 40 km. east of Troyes in the Champagne-Ardenne region. You will receive a warm welcome from Michel at this family owned site and some English is spoken. Of the 156 pitches, 113 are for touring units. Laid out in groups of four to six, with dividing hedges and ornamental trees providing shade, all the pitches have 10A electricity and water nearby. The small reception is part of the bar/restaurant and is modern and well kept. Adjacent to this building are the swimming pools, which are enclosed with fencing.

Facilities

Three small sanitary blocks provide basic facilities. Washing machine in each. Bar/restaurant open July/August and also during reception hours. Play area (unfenced). Heated outdoor pool and small paddling pool with large paved terrace. Off site: Walking distance to water sports centre. Bicycle hire and fishing 200 m. Golf and riding 20 km.

Open: 23 March -17 October.

Directions

From A5 exit 22, head north via Vendeuvre-sur-Barse to Dienville. Cross first roundabout at harbour for Lac Amance and site is immediately on right.

Charges 2006

Per person	€ 3,00 - € 3,80
child (4-10 yrs)	€ 2,10 - € 2,60
pitch	€ 6,20 - € 7,80
electricity	€ 2,10 - € 2,60

FR67010 Camping l'Oasis

3 rue du Frohret, F-67110 Oberbronn (Bas-Rhin)

Tel: 03 88 09 71 96. Email: oasis.oberbronn@laregie.fr

This is an attractively situated, inexpensive site, amidst the mountains and forests of northern Alsace, not far from the German border. There are good views over the valley to one side and the pretty village with trees sheltering the other. The circular internal road has pitches around the outside (120 for touring units, 30 for seasonal units), and space in the centre where there is a playground. The solar-heated swimming pool and children's pool are of excellent quality. A 'Centre de Vacances' was added for 2004, with a covered swimming pool, sauna and fitness room.

Facilities

The first well appointed toilet block, heated in cool weather, has some washbasins in cabins for ladies, washing machines and dryers, a baby room and facilities for disabled people. The second block is unisex and small. Small shop. General room with table football and air hockey. Swimming pool and children's pool (July/Aug). Indoor pool next to site. Playground. Tennis court. Off site: Riding 700 m. Supermarket 1 km. Fishing 3 km. Fitness circuit in forest.

Open: 14 March - 13 November.

Directions

Travel northwest from Haguenau on N62 for 20 km. South of Niederbronn turn left on D28 for Oberbronn-Zinswiller - site is signed from here. From A4 take exit 42 to Sarreguemines, then N62 and D620 towards Haguenau and as above. GPS: N48:55.746 E07:36.244

Charges 2006

Per person	€ 3,70
child (under 7 yrs)	€ 2,20
pitch incl. electricity	€ 6,30

No credit cards.

FR67030 Camping Caravaning du Ried

Route de Rhinau, F-67860 Boofzheim (Bas-Rhin)

Tel: 03 88 74 68 27. Email: info@camping-ried.com

Camping du Ried is situated on the edge of a small, picturesque village and has 100 tourist pitches (with 5A electricity) amongst the 120 rental and 55 private static caravans. Most are under tall trees, on grass and separated by hedges. There is an excellent pool complex near the site entrance with an attractive outdoor pool for use in July and August and a heated indoor one open from May to September. There is also a lake and small beach. A pleasant site with very friendly management who would like to welcome more British visitors, although no English is spoken.

Facilities

The main, heated toilet block has usual facilities including those for disabled people. Laundry facilities. Additional units by lake or reception. Bar/restaurant (weekends 1/4-30/6 and 1/9-30/9, daily 1/7-31/8). Outdoor and heated indoor (1/5-30/9) pools (toilets and showers). Motorcaravan services. Playground. Minigolf. Fishing. Fitness trail. Excursions, canoe trips and competitions. Off site: Supermarket. Bicycle hire 1 km. Riding 4 km.

Open: 1 April - 30 September.

Directions

Leave N83 Strasbourg - Colmar road at Benfeld and go east on D5 to Boofzheim. Site is 500 m. beyond village towards Rhinau. GPS: N48:19.753 E07:41.640

Charges 2007

Per unit incl. 2 persons	€ 13,00 - € 17,50
extra person	€ 3,00 - € 5,50
electricity (5A)	€ 5,00

Security barrier card deposit €30.
Discount for longer stays.

FR67050 Camping Municipal Wasselonne

Route de Romanswiller, F-67310 Wasselonne (Bas-Rhin)

Tel: **03 88 87 00 08**. Email: **camping-wasselonne@wanadoo.fr**

A good quality municipal site with a resident warden. Facilities include a well stocked small shop, a crêperie in season and the added bonus of free admission to the superb indoor heated swimming pool adjacent to the site. There are 70 tourist pitches and around 30 seasonal units, on grass with a slight slope, all with electricity hook-ups (5/10A). Four new rental chalets are in a separate fenced area. This could be an excellent base from which to visit Strasbourg.

Facilities

The single, large, and well maintained sanitary unit has unisex facilities with ample sized showers and washbasins in cubicles. Laundry facilities and covered dishwashing sinks. No specific facilities for disabled visitors but the rooms are spacious and should be accessible to many. Motorcaravan service point. Off site: Heated pool, hotel with restaurant, tennis courts, plus athletics stadium all adjacent. Supermarket 500 m. Fitness trail, riding 1 km.

Open: 15 April - 15 October.

Directions

Wasselonne is 25 km. west of Strasbourg. Site lies southwest of town centre on D224 towards Romanswiller, and is well signed.
GPS: N48:38.264 E07:25.907

Charges 2006

Per unit incl. 1 person	€ 7,20
extra person	€ 3,30
child (0-10 yrs)	€ 1,60
electricity	€ 2,30 - € 3,70

FR52020 Castel Camping la Forge de Sainte Marie

Mobile homes ▶ **page 461**

F-52230 Thonnance-les-Moulins (Haute-Marne)

Tel: **03 25 94 42 00**. Email: **info@laforgedesaintemarie.com**

This is a most attractive campsite, entered through an arched gateway, and created in 1995 by careful conservation of original forge buildings to create modern facilities in this secluded valley. A picturesque bridge links the upper part with a lower road to the section near the river. Another old building has been converted into gites for letting. Grass pitches, 165 for touring units, are of a very generous size on terraces amongst trees or in more open areas. Electricity (6A) and water are available and 120 pitches are fully serviced. There are also 30 mobile homes and chalets, and 22 tour operator units. The département of Haute-Marne is situated between the better known areas of Champagne and the Vosges. It is a sleepy land of rolling hills, forests and farmland. In the heart of this lies Thonnance-les-Moulins, a small village 12 km. east of Joinville and the north-south N67 main road between St Dizier and Chaumont. There is much of interest in the area – Joan d'Arc and General de Gaulle lived near and it is not too far to the Champagne vineyards and cellars at Reims. The British and Dutch managers and their staff are enthusiastic.

Facilities

Two sanitary blocks (under pressure at peak times). Additional facilities at reception or pool complex. Shop, restaurant and bar with terrace. Pizzeria in high season. Heated indoor pool and one for children (28/4-12/9). Play areas. Bicycle hire. Fishing on payment. Games room. Internet terminal. Organized games for children (high season). Programme for adults including farm visit with barbecue, music, dancing and excursions. Golfing holidays arranged. Off site: Riding 15 km. Golf 45 km.

Open: 28 April - 12 September.

Directions

Site is about 12 km. southeast of Joinville between Poissons and Germay on road D427. The site entrance may be a little tight for large units.
GPS: N48:24.392 E05:16.270

Charges 2006

Per unit incl. 2 persons and electricity	€ 18,00 - € 29,00
extra person	€ 3,50 - € 7,00
child (2-9 yrs)	€ 1,75 - € 3,50

Less 20% outside July/Aug.
Camping Cheques accepted.

110
Check real time availability and at-the-gate prices...
www.alanrogers.com

FR52030 Camping Lac de la Liez

Mobile homes ▶ page 462

Peigney, F-52200 Langres (Haute-Marne)
Tel: 03 25 90 27 79. Email: campingliez@free.fr

Managed by the enthusiastic Baude family, this newly renovated lakeside site is near the city of Langres. Only 10 minutes from the A5, Camping Lac de la Liez provides an ideal spot for an overnight stop en-route to the south of France. There is also a lot on offer for a longer stay. The site provides 131 fully serviced pitches, some with panoramic views of the 200 hectare lake with its sandy beach and small harbour where boats and pedaloes may be hired. Lake access is down steps and across quite a fast road (in total 150 m). With its old ramparts and ancient city centre, Langres was elected one of the 50 most historic cities in France.

Facilities

Two toilet blocks have all facilities in cabins (only one is open in low season). Facilities for disabled people and babies. Laundry facilities. Motorcaravan services. Shop, bar and restaurant (with takeaway food). Indoor pool complex with spa and sauna. Heated outdoor pool (1/6-30/9). Games room. Playground. Extensive games area and tennis court (free in low season). Off site: Lake with beach. Boat and bicycle hire and cycle tracks around lake. Fishing 100 m. Riding 5 km. Golf 40 km.

Open: 1 April - 1 November

Directions

From Langres take the N19 towards Vesoul. After approximately 3 km. turn right, straight after the large river bridge, then follow site signs.
GPS: N47:52.44 E05:22.628

Charges 2006

Per person	€ 4,50 - € 6,00
child (2-12 yrs)	€ 3,00 - € 4,50
pitch	€ 15,00 - € 20,00
electricity	€ 3,00 - € 4,50

Camping Cheques accepted.

kawan

tel: **00 333 59 59 03 59** *kawan-villages.com*

Camping du Lac de la Liez ★★★★

In the heart of the Champagne and Ardennes region, this lakeside site is a top quality 4 star site, ideal for the whole family

Open 01st April - 01st November.

Peigney, F-52200 Langres • tel 0033 (0)325 90 27 79 • fax 0033 (0)325 90 66 79
e-mail campingliez@free.fr • http://campingliez.free.fr

FR52040 Camping de la Croix d'Arles

RN 74, Bourg, F-52200 Langres (Haute-Marne)
Tel: 03 25 88 24 02. Email: croix.arles@wanadoo.fr

This quiet site is only 8 km. south of Langres. There are 100 pitches, of which 81 are for tourers. Most facilities are near the entrance, as is a flat grassy area mostly used by caravans and motorcaravans. There are electrical points and water taps, but no pitch markings or shade. A wooded area, where nature has been worked with rather than controlled, provides groups of numbered pitches with lots of shade (leads for electricity of up to 40 m. could be needed). Further on is an area without electricity supply. A tour operator uses the site.

Facilities

Two modern toilet blocks contain British style WCs, washbasins (some in cabins) and controllable showers. Facilities for disabled people. Baby room. Washing machines, dryer, ironing board and washing lines. Shop for basics. Restaurant, bar, snack bar and takeaway (1/4 - 31/10). Games rooms. Swimming and paddling pools (15/5-15/9). Playground. Table tennis. Boules. Off site: Town 2 km. Fishing 8 km. Riding 10 km. Bicycle hire 5 km. Boat launching 8 km.

Open: 15 March - 31 October.

Directions

From north, take N74 from Langres (towards Dijon). After 8 km. site is on right. From south, turning left from N74 into site is forbidden. Go 2 km. north, take right hand slip road towards trading estate (signed to A31), turn left, pass under N74, then left to rejoin N74 going south.

Charges 2007

Per person	€ 2,50 - € 4,00
child	€ 2,00 - € 3,00
pitch	€ 6,00 - € 6,50
electricity	€ 3,50

Check real time availability and at-the-gate prices...

www.**alanrogers**.com

FR68030 Camping de Masevaux

3 rue du Stade, F-68290 Masevaux (Haut-Rhin)

Tel: **03 89 82 42 29**. Email: **camping-masevaux@tv-com.net**

Masevaux is a pleasant little town in the Haut-Rhin département of Alsace, just north of the A36 Belfort - Mulhouse motorway. The neatly mown 120 pitches for tourists are on level grass, of reasonable size, marked by trees and hedges, and all have electricity (3/6A). Most are well shaded with good views of the surrounding hills. The pleasant and helpful Scottish managers, who take pride in the site, would like to welcome more British visitors. A good choice for one night or a longer stay to explore this interesting region, and an ideal destination for serious walkers.

Facilities

A modern, well designed and well equipped sanitary block has most washbasins in private cabins. Baby room. Laundry and covered dishwashing area. Café/bar serving snacks. Baker calls in high season. Ice-creams and soft drinks available at reception. TV room, small library. Boules. Children's play area. Tennis courts (extra charge), volleyball, table tennis. Off site: Supermarket, restaurants and indoor pool. Fishing. Market in Masevaux Wednesdays.

Open: 15 February - 31 December.

Directions

From D466 in Masevaux follow signs for Belfort and then 'Camping Complexe Sportif'.
GPS: N47:46.677 E06:59.462

Charges 2006

Per person	€ 3,00
child (under 13 yrs)	€ 1,50
pitch	€ 3,00
electricity (3/6A)	€ 2,70 - € 3,90
dog	€ 0,75

FR68040 Camping Municipal les Trois Châteaux

10 rue du Bassin, F-68420 Eguisheim (Haut-Rhin)

Tel: **03 89 23 19 39**. Email: **camping.eguisheim@wanadoo.fr**

The village of Eguisheim is on the Alsace 'Rue du Vin' to the west of Colmar. The three châteaux from which the site gets its name are clearly visible on the distant hills. About 400 m. from the village, Les Trois Châteaux is busy and popular. Flowers, shrubs and trees, and well tended grass areas make this a very pleasant place. The 121 pitches, 115 with electricity (6A), are either on a slight slope or a terrace, and are marked and numbered, most with good shade. Around 80% of pitches have some gravel hardstandings, most of irregular shape and size.

Facilities

The single sanitary block in the centre of the site has hot showers and warm water only to washbasins. Some washbasins in cubicles and facilities for disabled people. Playground. Caravans over 7 m. and/or 1 ton in weight are not accepted. Motorcaravan service point. Off site: Fishing 3 km.

Open: 1 April - 30 September.

Directions

Eguisheim is just off the N83 and the site is well signed in the village.

Charges 2006

Per person	€ 3,60
child (under 7 yrs)	€ 1,80
pitch	€ 3,90
electricity (6A)	€ 3,40
No credit cards.	

FR68050 Camping Municipal Pierre de Coubertin

23, rue de Landau, F-68150 Ribeauvillé (Haut-Rhin)

Tel: **03 89 73 66 71**. Email: **camping.ribeauville@wanadoo.fr**

The fascinating medieval town of Ribeauvillé on the Alsace Wine Route is within walking distance of this attractive, quietly located site. Popular and well run, it has 226 tourist pitches, all with electricity hook-ups (2/6A) and some separated by shrubs or railings. There are tarmac or gravel access roads. This is a site solely for tourists – there are no mobile homes or seasonal units here. The small shop is open daily for most of the season (hours vary) providing bread, basic supplies and some wines. Only breathable groundsheets permitted.

Facilities

Large, heated block provides modern facilities with washbasins in cubicles. Baby changing facilities. Large laundry and dishwashing rooms with a generous supply of sinks. A smaller unit at the far end of the site is opened for July/Aug. Very good facilities for disabled campers at both units. Recycling. Excellent adventure style playground with a rubber base. Tennis court. Boules. Table tennis. TV room. Off site: Outdoor pool (June-Aug). Sports complex.

Open: 15 March - 15 November.

Directions

Ribeauvillé is about 13 km. southwest of Sèlestat. Site is well signed, turn north off D106 at traffic lights by large car park, east of town centre.
GPS: N48:11.697 E07:20.198

Charges 2007

Per person	€ 3,80
child (0-7 yrs)	€ 1,90
pitch	€ 4,00
electricity	€ 2,50 - € 4,00

Check real time availability and at-the-gate prices...
www.alanrogers.com

FR68060 Camping Intercommunal Riquewihr

Route des Vins, F-68340 Riquewihr (Haut-Rhin)

Tel: **03 89 47 90 08**. Email: **camping.riquewihr@tiscali.fr**

Surrounded by vineyards and minutes from the delightful village of Riquewihr, this is a well run site which has earned its good reputation. Situated in the heart of the Alsace wine region the site covers three hectares with views across the open countryside. To the right of the security barrier stands a modern, part-timbered building housing reception and information. The 161 spacious individual pitches, many with shade and divided by hedging, have electrical connections (6/10A). Most are on grass but there are also a few with hardstandings. Wine caves are just 200 m. away.

Facilities

Three sanitary blocks, one of a more modern design (not all open in low season). Facilities include private cabins with basins, good nursery room with baby bath, child's WC and changing mat, and excellent facilities for disabled people. Dishwashing and laundry areas. Motorcaravan service point. Campers' room with tables and chairs. Shop for basics, drinks and papers (from 1/7-31/8). TV room. Playground. Off site: Ball games area and sports field. Fishing 3 km. Swimming pool 4 km. Bicycle hire 5 km.

Open: Easter - 31 December.

Directions

From N83 north of Colmar take D4 westwards (Bennwihr). Turn north on D1bis for 2 km. towards Ribeauvillé. Site signed off roundabout at southern end of Riquewihr bypass. Do not enter village. GPS: N48:09.731 E07:19.014

Charges 2007

Per person	€ 3,25 - € 3,60
child (under 7 yrs)	€ 1,55 - € 1,70
pitch	€ 3,60 - € 4,00
electricity (6/10A)	€ 3,50 - € 4,00

FR68100 Parc de la Fecht

FR-68140 Munster (Haut-Rhin)

Tel: **03 89 77 31 08**. Email: **contact@village-center.com**

This campsite has been recommended by our agent in France and we intend to undertake a full inspection in 2007. Parc de la Fecht is a popular site located close to Colmar and Munster, along the famous Alsace wine route.

Facilities

Children's playground. Table tennis. Snack bar. TV room. Grocery shop. Excursions and competitions are organised during high season. Off site: Restaurant 200 m. Swimming pool with water slides nearby

Open: 12 May - 15 September.

Directions

Site is east of Munster on D417 (Gérardmer - Colmar). From Munster take the D417 towards Turkheim, then head for Colmar on the D10. The site is 2.2 km from Munster.

Charges 2007

Per unit incl. 2 persons and electricity	€ 8,00 - € 16,00
extra person	€ 1,90 - € 4,00
child (under 7 yrs)	€ 1,50 - € 3,25

FR68080 Camping Clair Vacances

Route de Herrlisheim, F-68127 Saint Croix-en-Plaine (Haut-Rhin)

Tel: **03 89 49 27 28**. Email: **clairvacances@wanadoo.fr**

Clair Vacances, extended in 2003, is a very neat, tidy and pretty site with 130 level pitches of generous size which are numbered and most are separated by trees and shrubs. All have electricity connections (8-13A) and 10 are fully serviced with water and drainage. The site has been imaginatively laid out with the pitches reached from hard access roads. This is a quiet family site. The friendly couple who own and run it will be pleased to advise on the attractions of the area. The site is 1 km. from the A35 exit, not far from Colmar.

Facilities

Two excellent, modern toilet blocks include washbasins in cabins, well equipped baby rooms and good facilities for disabled visitors. Laundry and dishwashing facilities. Shop with limited supplies. Swimming pool and children's pool (heated) with sunbathing area (15/6-15/9). Playground. Dogs are not accepted. No barbecues or football. American motorhomes and twin axle caravans are not accepted. Off site: Colmar with restaurants and shops.

Open: Week before Easter - 15 October.

Directions

Site is signed from exit 27 of the A35 south of Colmar on the Herrlisheim road (D1).
GPS: N48:00.957 E07:20.989

Charges 2006

Per unit incl. 2 persons and electricity	€ 12,00 - € 20,00
extra person	€ 5,00 - € 7,00
child (0-7 yrs)	€ 0,20 - € 3,00
child (8-12 yrs)	€ 4,00 - € 6,00

FR51020 Camping Municipal en Champagne

Rue de Plaisance, F-51000 Châlons-en Champagne (Marne)

Tel: **03 26 68 38 00**. Email: **camping.mairie.chalons@wanadoo.fr**

The location of Châlons, south of Reims and near the A4 and A26 autoroutes, about 200 miles from Calais and Boulogne, make this an ideal stopover. This site on the southern edge of town is an example of a good municipal site. The wide entrance with its neatly mown grass and flower beds sets the tone for the rest of the site; 95 of the 148 pitches, accessed from tarmac roads, are on a gravel base with the rest on grass. Most have electricity (10A). The generously sized gravel pitches are separated by hedges and 48 of these are multi-serviced.

Facilities

Two toilet blocks (one can be heated) are of varying standards due to an ongoing programme of refurbishment. Some washbasins in cabins, baby room and hairdressing station. Facilities for disabled visitors. Laundry and dishwashing facilities. Refuse bins. Bread to order. Bar, snack bar and takeaway (1/6-31/9 evenings, lunchtime July/Aug). Gas supplies. Games and TV rooms. Playground. Mini golf, tennis, volleyball, boules, mini-football. Motorcaravan service point. Off site: Bus stop. Fishing.

Open: 1 April - 31 October.

Directions

From north on A4, take La Veuve exit (27) onto N44 which by-passes town. Leave at last exit (St Memmie), follow camping signs. From south on A26, take exit 18 on N77 and towards town. Site well signed 'Camping', (south of town on D60).
GPS: N48:56.156 E04:22.994

Charges 2006

Per person	€ 4,70
child (under 7 yrs)	€ 1,80
pitch incl. electricity	€ 7,80
vehicle	€ 3,10

FR54000 Camping le Brabois

Avenue Paul Muller, F-54600 Villers les Nancy (Meurthe-et-Moselle)

Tel: **03 83 27 18 28**. Email: **campeoles.brabois@wanadoo.fr**

This former municipal site is within the Nancy city boundary and 5 km. from the centre. Situated within a forest area, there is shade in most parts and, although the site is on a slight slope, the 185 good-sized, numbered and separated pitches are level. Of these, 160 pitches have electrical connections (5/15A) and 30 also have water and drainage. Being on one of the main routes from Luxembourg to the south of France, Le Brabois makes a good night stop. However, Nancy is a delightful city in the heart of Lorraine and well worth a longer stay.

Facilities

Six sanitary blocks (old and due for refurbishment over the next few years) with a mix of British and Turkish style WCs and some washbasins in cubicles. One can be heated in cool weather. Units for disabled visitors. Laundry facilities. Motorcaravan service point. Shop. Bread to order. Restaurant with bar and small shop (15/6-31/8). Library. Playground. Ball games. Table tennis. Off site: Restaurants, shops 1 km. Walking and cycling. Regular buses to Nancy.

Open: 1 April - 15 October.

Directions

Take exit 2b 'Brabois' from autoroute A33, continue for 500 m. to 'Quick' restaurant on left. Turn left, pass racetrack to T-junction, turn right and after 400 m. turn right on to site entrance road.

Charges guide

Per unit incl. 2 persons	€ 11,00 - € 12,90
extra person	€ 4,00 - € 5,00
electricity	€ 3,90
Credit cards minimum € 15.	

FR54010 Camping de Villey-le-Sec

34 rue de La Gare, F-54840 Villey-le-Sec (Meurthe-et-Moselle)

Tel: 03 83 63 64 28. Email: info@campingvilleylesec.com

This neat campsite is a popular overnight stop, but the area is worth a longer stay. Villey-le-Sec has its own fortifications, part of the defensive system built along France's frontiers after the 1870 war, and a long cycle track passes near the site. On a bank of the Moselle river, there are 64 level grassy marked touring pitches, with electricity (6A) and plenty of water taps. There are also individual water taps and waste water drainage for 8 of these pitches. Another area without electricity accommodates 11 tents. Just outside the site is an overnight stopping place for motorcaravans.

Facilities

Two modern toilet blocks (one heated) contain British style WCs, washbasins in cabins and controllable showers. Facilities for disabled people and babies. Motorcaravan services. Washing machine and dryer. Gas supplies. Shop. Bar/restaurant. Snack bar and takeaway. Games room. Playground. Playing field. Table tennis. Boules. Fishing. Off site: Riding 2 km. Rock climbing 4 km. Golf 15 km.

Open: 1 April - 30 September.

Directions

Villey-le-Sec is 20 km. west of Nancy, and 7 km. east of Toul. From Toul head east (towards Nancy), crossing bridge over the Moselle, Pass under A31 motorway, turn right on D909 to Villey-le-Sec. Follow sings signs, turn left after old railway.

Charges 2006

Per person	€ 2,80
child (0-7 yrs)	€ 1,70
pitch incl. electricity (6A)	€ 5,30 - € 7,40

FR55010 Camping les Breuils

Allée des Breuils, F-55100 Verdun (Meuse)

Tel: 03 29 86 15 31. Email: contact@camping-lesbreuils.com

Thousands of soldiers of many nations are buried in the cemeteries around this famous town and the city is justly proud of its determined First World War resistance. Les Breuils is a neat, attractive site beside a small fishing lake and close to the town and Citadel. It provides 166 flat pitches of varying sizes on two levels (144 for touring units), many with shade. Separated by trees or hedges, they are beside the lake and 120 offer electricity connection (6A) - long leads will be necessary for some.

Facilities

Two sanitary blocks are a mixture of old and new, including washbasins in cabins for ladies. Laundry facilities. Facilities for the disabled and babies. Dishwashing sinks (cold water). Cleaning variable. Motorcaravan services. Shop (1/5-30/9). Guide books on sale at reception (1/5-31/8). Restaurant and takeaway (mid June-31/8), bar (evenings 1/5-30/9). Pool (200 sq.m). Children's pool (1/6-31/8). Fenced play area. Multi-sports complex. Off site: Bicycle hire, town 1 km. Riding 5 km.

Open: 1 April - 30 September.

Directions

The RN3 forms a sort of ring road round the north of the town. Site is signed from this on the west side of the town (500 m. to site).
GPS: N49:09.222 E05:21.938

Charges 2006

Per person	€ 5,00
child (under 10 yrs)	€ 3,00
caravan or motorcaravan	€ 4,40
double axle caravan	€ 15,00
Credit cards accepted for minimum of € 15.	

FR57010 Camping Municipal Ramstein-Plage

F-57230 Baerenthal (Moselle)

Tel: 03 87 06 50 73. Email: camping.ramstein@wanadoo.fr

Located at the edge of town beside a small lake in a peaceful position, this site would make a good base from which to explore the area. Ramstein-Plage is a large site with mostly permanent holiday units, 12 small chalets and an area for groups. However, it also has a more recently developed touring area of 62 individual grassy pitches all with water, drainage and electric hook-ups. The 300 assorted long stay units, mostly touring caravans with miscellaneous additions, most having been in position for many years, are impossible to ignore and do rather detract from the atmosphere of the site.

Facilities

One modern unit in the touring area includes facilities for disabled campers, some washbasins in cubicles, and spacious showers. Washing machines and dryers. A smaller older unit is close to the motorcaravan parking area. Motorcaravan service point. Restaurant, bar and takeway (1/4-30/9). Heated swimming pool (25 x 10 m. July/Aug). Multi-court and tennis. Boules. Small lake and beach with picnic area and playgrounds. Off site: Riding 0.8 km. Bicycle hire 2 km. Golf 20 km. Fishing on the adjacent Baerenthal Lake which is also a nature reserve.

Open: 1 April - 30 September.

Directions

Baerenthal is just west of the N62 between Hagenau and Bitche. At Philippsbourg (22 km. from Bitche, 27 km. from Hagenau), turn west on D36 to Baerenthal. Continue through town, site is well signed on right at northern end of town.
GPS: N48:58.887 E07:30.868

Charges 2006

Per person	€ 3,80
child (2-7 yrs)	€ 1,90
pitch	€ 5,30
incl. electricity	€ 9,50

115

FR57030 Camping le Felsberg

Le Felsberg, F-57500 Saint Avold (Moselle)

Tel: 03 87 92 75 05. Email: cis.stavold@free.fr

This neat little site with a resident manager, is situated on a wooded hilltop above the town of Saint Avold. There are 33 mostly shady, hedged pitches, 21 for caravans or motorcaravans with electricity. An attractive small bar is open daily in the main season, on demand at other times. Groups of young people are taken in low season (generally using the rooms in the chalet house). St Avold has 18th century fountains, an Abbey church, chapel and Basilica. The largest WW2 American cemetery in Europe lies just north of the town and a British WW1 cemetery is in the town.

Facilities

A functional sanitary unit with fairly standard facilities, below the chalet style building housing reception and 16 bedrooms for rent. Facilities for disabled visitors. Bar with TV. Basic motorcaravan service point. Bicycle hire. Play area. WiFi. No double-axle caravans. American RVs should book in advance. Off site: Town with all services 800 m. via steep footpath, further by road. Riding 1 km. Fishing 10 km. Golf 18 km.

Open: All year.

Directions

St Avold is about 30 km. east of Metz. From A4 junction turn south, then left (after Novotel), right at roundabout, under bridge and right again opposite Record supermarket (site signed). Site is also signed from the N3.

Charges 2006

Per person	€ 3,20
child (under 12 yrs)	€ 1,50
pitch incl. electricity (6/10A)	€ 9,00 - € 11,00

FR57050 Camping Municipal de Metz-Plage

Allée de Metz-Plage, F-57000 Metz (Moselle)

Tel: 03 87 68 26 48. Email: campingmetz@mairie-metz.fr

As this site is just a short way from the autoroute exit and within easy walking distance for the city centre, it could make a useful night stop if travelling from Luxembourg to Nancy or for a longer stay if exploring the area. By the Moselle river, the 151 pitches are on fairly level grass and most are under shade from tall trees. 65 pitches are fully serviced and 84 have electricity (10A). Tent pitches have a separate place beside the river.

Facilities

The two sanitary blocks, one newer than the other, are acceptable if not luxurious. Facilities for disabled visitors. Baby room. Laundry and dishwashing facilities. Motorcaravan service point. Shop. Bar, restaurant and takeaway. Hardstanding pitches for over night stops for motorcaravans without electricity. Off site: Indoor pool adjacent. Fishing. Riding 5 km. Golf 8 km.

Open: 5 May - 23 September.

Directions

From autoroute take Metz-Nord - Pontiffray exit (no. 33) and follow camp signs. GPS: N49:07.430 E06:10.135

Charges 2006

Per person	€ 2,50
child (4-10 yrs)	€ 1,20
pitch incl. electricity	€ 6,00
with water and drainage	€ 7,00
tent and vehicle	€ 2,50

FR57070 Camping Centre de Loisirs et Culture

Route de Luttange, F-57940 Volstroff (Moselle)

Tel: 03 82 56 93 40. Email: campingvol@aol.com

This site is located in a fairly remote, rural setting but does have a full range of services and activities in July/August. Outside this period it may feel rather too empty and quiet for some. There are 28 chalet style gites on-site and a fair number of seasonal caravans. Set in one corner of what is a very large park with a lake, the camping area is fan shaped, with 162 individual pitches divided by hedges and shrubs. These are in rows back to back between fairly narrow gravel access roads which can be very dusty in dry weather.

Facilities

Two modern toilet blocks (not heated) are fairly stylish, clean and well appointed; some cubicles and corridors are cramped in the smaller block. Washbasins in cubicles. Facilities for babies and disabled campers. Washing machine and dryer. Bar. Shop and takeaway. Outdoor swimming pool (25 x 18 m.) and children's pool (July/Aug). Sauna. Tennis. Minigolf. Play area. Fishing. Pedaloes. Animation. Internet access. Off site: Golf 15 km. Riding 10 km. Bicycle hire 10 km.

Open: 16 April - 23 October.

Directions

Best approached from A31 junction 37. Cross first river bridge on D8, at second (blue bridge) turn right on D8bis. After 2 km. turn left on D1 to Bousse. At Bousse take D8 for about 7 km. and turn left towards Volstroff on D2bis. Site is signed. GPS: N49:17.905 E06:16.329

Charges 2006

Per unit incl. up to 4 persons and 3A electricity	€ 14,00 - € 16,20
6A electricity	€ 3,20

Check real time availability and at-the-gate prices...

www.alanrogers.com

FR88010 Camping les Deux Ballons

17 rue du Stade, F-88560 St Maurice sur Moselle (Vosges)

Tel: 03 29 25 17 14. Email: vero@camping-deux-ballons.fr

St Maurice-sur-Moselle is in a narrow valley seven kilometres from the source of the River Moselle in the massif de Haute-Vosges, on the main N66 which leads to the Col de Bussang. This is a pleasant leafy area for winter skiing and summer outdoor activities. Les Deux Ballons lies in a small valley surrounded by mountains with a stream running through the site and a cover of trees giving deep shade in most parts. The 180 pitches are on stony ground with sparse grass under the firs or on two terraces, and all have electrical connections (4A). Some long leads may be required. English is spoken (ask for Véronique). Torches recommended.

Facilities

Unisex sanitary facilities in 4 units of varying ages (only two open in low season). Washbasins and some showers are rather small. Facilities for disabled people and babies. Laundry facilities. Motorcaravan service point. Shop. Gas supplies. Bar (30/6-25/8). Snack bar and takeaway (1/7-27/8). Large heated swimming pool with slide and children's pool (15/6-31/8). Walks, fishing, bowls, riding, paragliding (high season). TV. Internet point. Volleyball and basketball. Fishing. Off site: Bicycle hire 5 km.

Open: 10 April - 15 September.

Directions

Site is on main N66 Le Thillot - Bussang road on western edge of St Maurice behind Avia filling station (entrance partly obscured - keep a look out). GPS: N47:51.320 E06:48.671

Charges 2006

Per unit incl. 2 persons	€ 13,60 - € 21,50
extra person	€ 4,35 - € 4,70
child (2-7 yrs)	€ 3,20 - € 3,50
electricity (4/15A)	€ 4,00 - € 5,00

No credit cards (except for on-line bookings).

FR88020 Camping de Belle-Hutte

1 bis Vouille de Belle-Hutte, F-88250 La Bresse (Vosges)

Tel: 03 29 25 49 75. Email: camping-belle-hutte@wanadoo.fr

Belle-Hutte is a pleasant family-run site in the heart of the Vosges mountains on one of the southern routes to the Col de la Schlucht. Attractively situated surrounded by mountains and trees, it occupies an open hill slope (900 m. above sea level) with 125 numbered grass pitches (95 for touring) on six terraces. Pitches of about 90 sq.m. (some are larger) are divided by hedges and all have electrical connections. To reach the site you would have to depart from the usual main through routes but access is easy via good roads.

Facilities

The central sanitary block is of excellent quality and heated in cool weather. Facilities for disabled people and babies. Laundry facilities. Motorcaravan service point. Shop for basics. Takeaway and bar (hours vary). TV. New pool complex (June - Sept; no Bermuda shorts). Play areas. Fishing. Ski storage room. Internet access. Off site: Ski lift 100 m. Village 400 m. Fishing 4 km. Riding 10 km.

Open: All year.

Directions

Site is about 9 km. from La Bresse on the D34 road towards the Col de la Schlucht. GPS: N48:02.095 E06:57.758

Charges 2006

Per person	€ 3,10 - € 5,95
child (under 7 yrs)	€ 1,95 - € 3,10

Higher prices are for winter.

FR88030 Camping de Noirrupt

5 chemin de l'Etang, F-88530 Le Tholy (Vosges)

Tel: 03 29 61 81 27. Email: info@jpvacances.com

An attractive, modern, family run site, Camping de Noirrupt has a commanding mountainside position with some magnificent views especially from the upper terraces. This is a very comfortable and high quality site and one that is sure to please. The tarmac site road winds up through the site with pitches being terraced and cars parked in separate small car parks close by. The 70 lawn-like tourist pitches are generally spacious, and the site is beautifully landscaped and divided with shrubs, flower beds, decking and trees. Paths and steps take more direct routes between levels.

Facilities

Two very modern buildings at different levels, plus a small unit behind reception, all immaculate with modern fittings. Washbasins in cubicles, facilities for babies, children and disabled campers. Washing machines and dryer. Shop. Bar, snack bar and takeaway (4/7-20/8). Swimming pool (15 x 10m. 1/6-15/9). TV room (1/6-15/9). Tennis. Animation in season. No double axle caravans or American RVs. Off site: Riding 300 m. Fishing 2 or 5 km. Golf 30 km. Le Tholy 2 km. Gérardmer 10 km.

Open: 15 April - 15 October.

Directions

From Gérardmer take D417 west towards Remiremont. In Le Tholy turn right on D11, continue up hill for 2 km., and site is signed to your left. GPS: N48:05.334 E06:43.709

Charges 2006

Per person	€ 5,20
child (under 7 yrs)	€ 3,00
pitch	€ 8,60
electricity (2/6A)	€ 3,00 - € 5,00

117

FR88040 Camping Club Lac de Bouzey

Mobile homes ▶ page 462

19 rue du Lac, F-88390 Sanchey (Vosges)

Tel: 03 29 82 49 41. Email: **camping.lac.de.bouzey@wanadoo.fr**

Camping-Club Lac de Bouzey is eight kilometres west of Épinal, overlooking the lake, at the beginning of the Vosges Massif. The 125 individual 100 sqm. back-to-back grass pitches are arranged on either side of tarmac roads with electricity (6-10A); 100 are fully serviced. They are on a gentle slope, divided by trees and hedging and some overlook the 130 haectare lake with its sandy beaches. Units can be close when site is busy. An 'all year' site, with lots going on for all ages especially teenagers. English is spoken. A 'Sites et Paysages' member.

Facilities

Sanitary block includes a baby room and one for disabled people (there is up and down hill walking). In winter a small, heated section in main building with toilet, washbasin and shower is used. Laundry and dishwashing facilities. Motorcaravan service point. Shop. Bar and restaurant. Heated pool (1/5-30/9). Fishing, riding, volleyball, games room, archery and bicycle hire. Internet access. Cinema shows and discos. Off site: Golf 8 km.

Open: All year.

Directions

Site is 8 km. west of Épinal on D460 and is signed from some parts of Épinal. Follow signs for Lac de Bouzey and Sanchey. GPS: N48:10.015 E06:21.594

Charges 2007

Per unit incl. 2 persons	€ 15,00 - € 25,00
extra person	€ 5,00 - € 9,00
child (4-10 yrs)	free - € 6,00
electricity (6-10A)	€ 5,00 - € 6,00

Camping Cheques accepted.

kawan-villages.com tel: **00 333 59 59 03 59**

kawan
VILLAGES CAMPINGS

FR88050 Domaine de Champé

14 rue des Champs-Navés, F-88540 Bussang (Vosges)

Tel: **03 29 61 61 51**. Email: **info@domaine-de-champ.com**

Bordered by the Moselle river and located just off the town square, this site is open all year making it a good base from which to explore in summer, and ideal for skiing in winter, when you might be tempted to rent one of the 12 chalets. Domaine de Champé is a level site with 110 touring pitches, all with electricity (4-12A), spread over a fairly large area on both sides of a tributary stream, so some are a distance from the facilities. An improving site where you will receive a hospitable welcome.

Facilities

Two sanitary units, one behind reception, with a smaller one in a more central position, are adequate rather than luxurious. Facilities for disabled campers. Motorcaravan services. Bar (all year). Restaurant and takeaway (weekends only in low season). Swimming pool (1/5-30/9). Sauna, steam room, jacuzzi and massage. Tennis. Small play area. Fishing. Internet access and WiFi. Off site: Shops and all other services in town. Lake fishing 3.5 km. Riding 4 km. Skiing 3 km.

Open: All year.

Directions

Bussang is about midway between Remiremont and Mulhouse on N66, almost due north of Belfort. Site is signed from town centre. GPS: N47:53.317 E06:51.429

Charges 2006

Per person	€ 4,60 - € 5,00
child (4-10 yrs)	€ 2,40 - € 2,70
pitch	€ 5,20 - € 6,60
electricity (4A)	€ 3,40 - € 3,90

FR88060 Camping la Vologne

Rue Retournermer, F-88400 Xonrupt-Longemer (Vosges)

Tel: **03 29 60 87 23**. Email: **paulette@lavologne.com**

Lac de Longemer, in the heart of the Vosges massif, lies south of Xonrupt-Longemer. A short walk from the southern end of the lake, is suited to those wanting a quiet, simple, inexpensive campsite with good basic facilities. There are 103 grassy pitches of which 99 are for tourers, all with electricity (2/5A) although long leads would be required in some places. They lie either side of the river Vologne. Pitches on the far side of the river have most shade; until trees mature the others will be in the open.

Facilities

Two modern toilet blocks contain 12 British and 4 Turkish style WCs, washbasins (some in cabins) and pre-set showers. Facilities for disabled people, children and babies. Motorcaravan services. Laundry. Shop (July/Aug). Gas supplies. Games and TV room. Playground. Playing field. Trampoline. Off site: Beach, windsurfing, sailing, canoe hire 700 m. Restaurant and bar 1 km. ATM 5 km. Xonrupt-Longemer 7 km. Bicycle hire. Riding 10 km.

Open: 1 May - 15 September.

Directions

Xonrupt-Longemer is just east of Gerardmer, and 46 km. west of Colmar, on D470. Take D67 or D67A, which run southeast from Xonrupt near Lac de Longemer. Just after junction of these roads, site on right.

Charges 2006

Per person	€ 3,00
child (0-7 yrs)	€ 1,50
pitch incl. electricity	€ 5,80

FR88120 Camping le Clos de la Chaume

21, rue d'Alsace, F-88430 Corcieux (Vosges)

Tel: 03 29 50 76 76. Email: **info@camping-closdelachaume.com**

This pleasant site is within walking distance of the town, on level ground with a small stream adjacent. The friendly family owners live on site and do their best to ensure campers have an enjoyable relaxing stay. There are 100 level grassy pitches of varying sizes, with some holiday homes (private and rental) leaving 70 pitches for tourists. All have electricity hook-ups (6/10A) and some are divided by shrubs and trees. Access roads are sandy and large units or American RVs should telephone first to check pitch availability. The site boasts an attractive, well fenced, small swimming pool and an excellent small adventure style playground. The site has some excellent and informative leaflets (available in several languages) which give details of walks and mountain biking routes in the surrounding countryside. Corcieux is in the heart of the 'Ballons des Vosges' and this site would make a good base to explore the area.

Facilities

Two units provide well maintained facilities including a laundry with washing machines and dryers, a dual purpose family/disabled room and dishwashing sinks. Motorcaravan service point. Recycling. Reception keeps basic supplies (July/August). Campingaz stocked. Swimming pool (13 x 7 m. June-Sept). Games room with table football and a pool table. Table tennis, boules and volleyball. Off site: Bicycle hire 800 m. Riding 2 km. Fishing 3, 10 km. Golf 30 km. Corcieux market (Mondays).

Open: 15 April - 20 September.

Directions

Corcieux is about 17 km. southwest of St Dié des Vosges. Site is on D60, east of town centre, by the town boundary sign. GPS: N48:10.094 E06:53.401

Charges 2007

Per unit incl. 2 persons	€ 11,80
extra person	€ 3,40
child (0-7 yrs)	€ 1,80
electricity	€ 2,90
animal	€ 1,25

Camping le Clos de la Chaume

Le Clos de la Chaume - 21 rue d'Alsace - F-88430 Corcieux - France
Tél.: (33) 03 29 50 76 76 - Fax: (33) 03 29 50 76 76

info@camping-closdelachaume.com
www.camping-closdelachaume.com

FR88080 Yelloh! Village Domaine des Bans

Rue James Wiese, F-88430 Corcieux (Vosges)

Tel: 03 29 51 64 67. Email: **les-bans@domaine-des-bans.com**

Domaine des Bans is a large, busy campsite with 630 pitches in a country setting, with plenty of opportunities to be active. There is a very high percentage of static and tour operator units, but room for about 80 tourist units. Pitches (with electricity, water and drainage), numbered and separated by hedges, vary in size with some on low terraces. There is good shade. Some are tucked away in quiet areas with others nearer to where activities take place. This is not really a site for short stays, but is a base for exploring the varied and interesting countryside.

Facilities

Three functional toilet blocks. Some washbasins are in cabins. Shop (30/5-30/9). Bar (1/6-15/9). Restaurant (1/5-15/9). Takeaway (30/4-15/9). Swimming pools (outdoor 1/6-15/9, indoor 1/5-15/9). Playground and area for ball games. Tennis, table tennis, badminton, minigolf, volleyball and archery. Bicycle hire. Riding. Lakes for fishing and boating. High season entertainment including discos (sound-proof building), theatre performances and live music. 'Goats Castle' with about two dozen goats. Off site: Restaurant outside site. Others nearby in village.

Open: 26 April - 30 September.

Directions

From D8 St Dié - Gerardmer road, turn west on D60 just north of Gerbepal to Corcieux. GPS: N48:10.142 E06:52.817

Charges guide

Per person	€ 5,00 - € 7,00
child (3-7 yrs)	free - € 7,00
pitch incl. electricity	€ 15,00 - € 33,00

FR88090 Base de Loisirs du Lac de la Moselotte

Les Amias - B.P. 34, F-88290 Saulxures-sur-Moselotte (Vosges)

Tel: 03 29 24 56 56. Email: lac-moselotte@ville-saulxures-mtte.fr

This neat, well run, spacious lakeside site, part of a leisure village complex, has 75 generously sized, grassy and individual hedged pitches. All have electricity (10A) and 25 of these are multi-serviced with electricity, water and waste water drainage. The trees currently provide no more than a little shade. The site is fully fenced with security barrier and key for the gates (to site and lakeside). All facilities are modern and well maintained. The adjacent 'Base de Loisirs' has a wide variety of activities on offer, and the area is very good for walking and cycling.

Facilities

The heated toilet block has controllable hot showers, some washbasins in cubicles and good facilities for babies and disabled campers. Laundry facilities. Shop (July/Aug). Bread to order all year. Bar/snack bar and terrace. Bicycle hire. Play area. 30 chalets for rent. Off site: Town an easy walk. The 'base de loisirs' with lake (supervised swimming July/Aug), beach, fishing and hire of canoes and kayaks.

Open: All year.

Directions

Saulxures-sur-Moselotte is 20 km. east of Remiremont. From Remiremont take D417 east (St Ame), then right (east) on D43 towards La Bresse for 10.5 km. Turn left into Saulxures (site signed). GPS: N47:57.164 E06:45.127

Charges guide

Per person	€ 4,00 - € 5,00
pitch incl. electricity	€ 9,00 - € 11,00

FR88130 Camping Vanne de Pierre

Mobile homes ▶ page 462

5, rue du camping, F-88100 Saint Dié-des-Vosges (Vosges)

Tel: 03 29 56 23 56. Email: vannedepierre@wanadoo.fr

La Vanne de Pierre is a neat and attractive site with 118 pitches, many of which are individual with trimmed hedges giving plenty of privacy. There are 9 chalets and mobile homes (for rent) and a few seasonal units, leaving around 105 tourist pitches, all multi-serviced with water, drainage and electricity (6/10A). The reception building has been refitted and provides a small shop and a bar that includes a restaurant and takeaway (all year, opening hours vary). A 'Sites et Paysages' member.

Facilities

Main unit is heated with good facilities including washbasins in cubicles. Three family rooms each with WC, basin, and shower and two similar units fully equipped for disabled campers. Dishwashing and laundry rooms. A second, older unit (opened July/Aug). Shop. Bar/restaurant and takeaway. Swimming pool (1/4-30/9, weather permitting). Internet terminal. Bicycle hire. Off site: Golf, tennis, archery, riding all 1 km. Fishing. Supermarkets (some have 2.5 m. height barriers).

Open: All year.

Directions

St Dié is south east of Nancy. Site is east of town on north bank of river Meurthe and south of D82 to Nayemont les Fosses. Site well signed. GPS: N48:17.160 E06:58.199

Charges 2007

Per unit incl. 2 persons	€ 15,00 - € 22,00
extra person	€ 4,00 - € 6,00
electricity	€ 4,00 - € 5,00
Camping Cheques accepted.	

kawan-villages.com **tel: 00 333 59 59 03 59**

kawan
VILLAGES CAMPINGS

FR88140 Camping les Lacs

F-88110 Celles-sur-Plaine (Vosges)

Tel: 03 29 41 28 00. Email: camping@sma-lacs-piette-percee.fr

This is a well organised site with its own pool, close to the town centre, with many water-based and sporting activities available at the nearby Base Nautique and adjacent Lac de la Plaine. There are 129 hedged touring pitches and 10 chalets and, unlike many sites in the area, there are virtually no seasonal caravans. Some shady pitches border the tiny Plaine river, some pitches have gravel hardstanding, others are on grass, but all are surrounded by mature hedges. The site is owned by a collaboration of regional and local organisations, with a very enthusiastic resident manageress.

Facilities

Three good sanitary units provide adequate facilities including some Turkish toilets. Facilities for disabled visitors. Swimming pool (25 x 10 m.) and paddling pool. Small shop. Bar, snack bar and takeaway (all season, hours may vary). Entertainment in high season. Off site: Many activities at Base Nautique adjacent. Adventure Parc at Lake Pierre-Percée (8 km). Beach and lake swimming area. Tennis. Minigolf. Riding 22 km.

Open: 1 April - 30 September.

Directions

From Nancy take N59 southeast towards St Dié, turning into Raon l'Etape, then take D392a northeast for 10 km. to Celles-sur-Plaine, and follow camping signs. GPS: N48:27.296 E06:56.835

Charges 2006

Per person	€ 4,00 - € 5,15
child (under 7 yrs)	€ 2,50 - € 3,30
pitch	€ 5,00 - € 5,15
electricity (4/10A)	€ 2,60 - € 4,00

FR88150 Camping de Ramberchamp

21 chemin du Tour du Lac, F-88150 Gérardmer (Vosges)

Tel: **03 29 63 03 82**. Email: **boespflug.helene@wanadoo.fr**

A long established, family run site in a beautiful location on the southern side of Lake Gérardmer, de Ramberchamp is very peaceful. It benefits from a bar and restaurant adjacent to reception, which is on one side of the D69, with mostly long stay units on the pitches around it. Most of the 200 touring pitches are on the opposite side of the road by the lakeside, with the larger sanitary building. Pitches here vary in size, larger ones being further from the lake, all with 4A electricity and quite level. Those by the lakeside are mostly on gravel and are very popular.

Facilities

The main sanitary unit is fairly central and has been refurbished with modern fittings, whilst retaining some its old French style and character. Baby room. Unit for disabled campers. Laundry. Motorcaravan service point. A second smaller older unit serves pitches on the other side of the road. Bar/restaurant with takeaway (15/4-15/9). Small play area. Max length of unit 8.5 m. Off site: Fishing, riding and bicycle hire 500 m. Town with shops, banks, buses and railway station 1.5 km.

Open: 15 April - 15 September.

Directions

Site is west of Gérardmer, on D69 on southern side of the lake. Best approached from N417 towards Le Tholy, turning on D69, passing Lido. Site reception on right hand side, site entrance opposite. GPS: N48:03.860 E06:51.222

Charges 2006

Per unit incl. 2 persons	€ 14,00 - € 16,00
extra person	€ 5,00
electricity (4A)	€ 3,00 - € 3,50

No credit cards.

FR88160 Camping les Jonquilles

Route du Lac, F-88400 Xonrupt-Longemer (Vosges)

Tel: **03 29 63 34 01**

Les Jonquilles is a traditional, family run, lakeside site with a friendly reception and some terrific views of the surrounding countryside and lake. The site has an overall slope (blocks advised), with 240 pitches entirely for tourists and no mobile homes, chalets or rental units. All the pitches are marked, many by very small trees and have access to electricity hook-ups (6A), but the site is generally quite open. There are a number of special pitches for motorcaravans by the lakeside, with a full 'aire de service' facility alongside and this area is very popular.

Facilities

Two traditional buildings, modernised at various times, give a good provision and include some Turkish toilets, washbasins in cubicles and spacious showers. Baby bath in ladies. Facilities for disabled campers. Washing machines and dryer. Playground. Petanque. Off site: Opposite reception is a food shop, bar, snack bar and creperie, with takeaway, all operated by the site owner's brother. Bar has internet terminal and satellite TV.

Open: 15 April - 10 October.

Directions

Xonrupt-Longemer is just to the east of Gérardmer. From centre of town take D67a that runs around the southern side of the lake and site is on left opposite a bar/restaurant. GPS: N48:04.057 E06:56.944

Charges 2006

Per unit incl. 2 persons	€ 8,00 - € 13,80
extra person	€ 2,00 - € 3,00
child (under 7 yrs)	€ 1,30 - € 1,50
electricity (6A)	€ 2,80

FR88170 Camping les Pinasses

215 route de Bruyères, F-88600 La Chapelle-devant-Bruyères (Vosges)

Tel: **03 29 58 51 10**. Email: **pinasses@dial.oleane.com**

Les Pinasses is an orderly, well run family site with a small outdoor swimming pool. Traditional in style, the site is long and narrow with pitches on two levels. The sanitary facilities are good. However the site is fronted by a fairly busy road and a railway track runs immediately behind it, and this is quite close to some pitches. There are around 125 grassy, individual, hedged pitches of varying sizes, all with 4/6A electricity under trees plus 14 units to rent. There are also a number of seasonal units on site. The site organises a little low key animation in July and August.

Facilities

Four blocks of varying styles, upgraded at different times, include a mix of seated and Turkish style toilets, some washbasins in cubicles. Facilities for disabled campers at one block only (ramped entrance). Washing machines, dryers and spin dryer. Small shop (15/4-15/9). Bar and restaurant (July/Aug). Swimming and paddling pools (1/6-15/9). Playground. TV room. Boule. Minigolf. Tennis. Fishing. Some entertainment in high season. American RVs not accepted. Off site: Golf 30 km. Bicycle hire 8 km.

Open: 15 April - 15 September.

Directions

La Chapelle-devant-Bruyères is about 25 km. southwest of St Dié. Site is beside D60 Corcieux to Bruyeres road, 2 km. east of its junction with D423. GPS: N48:11.399 E06:46.538

Charges 2006

Per unit incl. 2 persons	€ 17,80
extra person	€ 4,90
child (under 7 yrs)	€ 2,50
electricity (4/6A)	€ 3,50 - € 4,50

MAP 5

It's not only the fine beaches that make this holiday region so appealing. Sleepy fishing harbours, historic ports and charming towns all create a great holiday atmosphere.

WE HAVE EXERCISED A LITTLE TOURISM LICENSE WITH THIS AREA TAKING ONE DÉPARTEMENT FROM THE OFFICIAL WESTERN LOIRE REGION, 85 VENDÉE, AND ONE FROM THE POITOU-CHARENTES REGION, 17 CHARENTE-MARITIME

With a sunshine record to rival the south of France, the Vendée and Charente regions are among the most popular areas in France. Running alongside the coastal area stretching down from La Rochelle past Rochefort to Royan, it boasts gently shelving sandy beaches, warm shallow waters and fragrant pine forests. Explore the coasts for traditional fishing villages or head inland for fields of sunflowers and unspoilt rural villages.

The Vendée was the centre of the counter-revolutionary movement between 1793 and 1799 and a 'son et lumière' held at Le Puy-du-Fou tells the whole story. Les Sables d'Olonne is its main resort renowned for its excellent sandy beach. The area between the Vendée and Charente, the Marais Poitevin, is one of the most unusual in France – a vast tract of marshland with a thousand or more tree-lined canals and slow moving streams. The port of La Rochelle, with massive medieval towers, buzzes with life and the island of Ré is popular with those seeking beaches and small, quiet ports.

Places of interest

Marais Poitevin: marshes known as the 'Green Venice'.

Angoulême: Hill-top town surrouded by ramparts, cathedral, Renaissance château.

La Rochelle: port, Porte de la Grosse Horloge (clock gate), Museum of the New World.

Le Puy-du-Fou: 15th-16th century castle, sound and light show involving over 700 participants.

Les Sables d'Olonne: fishing port and seaside resort.

Noirmoutier: linked to the mainland by a 3 mile bridge.

Saint Savin: 17th century abbey, mural painting.

Cuisine of the region

Fish predominates, both fresh water (eel, trout, pike), sea water (shrimps, mussels, oysters). Light fruity wines from Haut-Poitou, Deux-Sèvres and Charente, and Cognac and Pineau des Charentes – an aperitif of grape juice and Cognac.

Cagouilles: snails from Charentes.

Chaudrée: ragout of fish cooked in white wine, shallots and butter.

Mouclade: mussels cooked in wine, egg and cream, served with Pineau des Charentes.

Soupe de moules à la Rochelaise: soup of various fish, mussels, saffron, garlic, tomatoes, onions and red wine.

Sourdons: cockles from the Charentes.

FR17020 Airotel le Puits de L'Auture

151 avenue de La Grande-Côte, F-17420 St Palais-sur-Mer (Charente-Maritime)

Tel: **05 46 23 20 31**. Email: **camping-lauture@wanadoo.fr**

Le Puits de l'Auture is well situated with the sea just across the road, and a long sandy beach starting 400 m. away, at the start of a pleasant coastal development down to Royan and beyond. There are 240 level touring pitches, all with electricity (10A). Some are separated by bushes with some trees giving shade and all have access to water and drainage. Mobile homes occupy the rest of the site, a few used by a tour operator.

Facilities

Well maintained toilet blocks. Most WCs are British type and all washbasins are in cabins, showers are adjustable with hot water. Facilities for disabled people and babies. Laundry and dishwashing facilities. Shop (1/5-30/9). Takeaway and bar (1/6-15/9). Swimming pool complex. Volleyball. Table tennis. Games room. Play area. Bicycle hire. Internet access. Barbecues (in a special area only). Dogs not accepted. Off site: Riding and golf 800 m. Restaurants specialising in sea food. Sea fishing.

Open: 1 May - 30 September.

Directions

Site is 2 km. from St Palais and 8 km. from Royan. From Royan take D25 past St Palais following signs for La Palmyre. At two lane junction turn back left signed Grande-Côte and St Palais. Site is 800 m. GPS: N45:38.948 W01:07.050

Charges 2006

Per unit incl. 2 persons	€ 16,00 - € 31,00
with 10A electricity	€ 23,00 - € 37,00
with water and drainage	€ 30,00 - € 43,00
extra person (over 3 yrs)	€ 5,00 - € 7,00

FR17030 Camping le Bois Roland

82 Route Royan - Saujon, F-17600 Medis (Charente-Maritime)

Tel: **05 46 05 47 58**. Email: **bois.roland@wanadoo.fr**

This campsite is in an urban area on a busy N-road but, nevertheless, has some unique features. Over the past 30 years, M. Dupont, the owner, has planted a very large number of tree varieties to mark and separate the pitches and they provide some shade. The site has 88 pitches for touring units, mainly between 80-90 sq.m. All have electricity (some may need long leads) and access to water close at hand. The family run a bar and provide simple takeaway food in July and August and there is a welcoming swimming pool.

Facilities

Two modernised toilet blocks contain a mixture of Turkish and British style toilets (no seats and no paper). Modern showers. Baby changing room. Special facilities for disabled campers. Dishwashing under cover. Laundry room with washing machines. Play area for young children. Off site: Buses pass the gate. Riding 1 km. Fishing 4 km. Bicycle hire 5 km. Golf 10 km. Supermarket with ATM 2 km. Beach 5 km.

Open: 23 April - 30 September.

Directions

Site is clearly signed on the west side of the N150, 600 m. north of the village of Medis (the N150 runs between Saujon and Royan).

Charges 2006

Per unit incl. 2 persons	€ 14,00 - € 17,00
extra person	€ 4,50
child (0-5 yrs)	€ 3,50
electricit (5A)	€ 4,00
dog (max. 1)	€ 2,50

FR17040 Camping International Bonne Anse Plage

La Palmyre, F-17570 Les Mathes - La Palmyre (Charente-Maritime)

Tel: **05 46 22 40 90**. Email: **Bonne.Anse@wanadoo.fr**

On the edge of the Forêt de la Coubre, just beyond La Palmyre, Bonne Anse is set amongst pines, just a short stroll from a tidal inlet. It is a spacious, gently undulating site, providing 850 level, marked pitches, of which 460 are for touring units (300 with electricity). Most are shaded, the ones nearer the sea less so and are rather more sandy. The reception, restaurant and bar with a spacious outdoor terrace and an impressive pool complex form the social focus. English and Dutch are spoken. Used by tour operators (35 pitches).

Facilities

Seven sanitary blocks include some washbasins in cabins, British style toilets with a few Turkish. Facilities for disabled visitors and babies. Dishwashing and laundry facilities. Motorcaravan service point. Shopping centre. Restaurant and bar (20/6-30/8). Takeaway. Pool complex. Playground. Video games. TV. Minigolf. Football. Trampolines. Bicycle hire. Entertainment in season. Internet access. Gas barbecues only. Dogs not accepted. Off site: Supervised, safe beaches 500 m. Fishing, riding 1 km. Zoo 3 km. Golf 5 km. Watersports.

Open: 24 May - 4 September.

Directions

Leave A10 autoroute at Saintes. Head for Royan (N150). In Royan take signs for La Palmyre (D25). At La Palmyre roundabout follow signs for Ronce-les-Bains. Site is 1 km. on left.

Charges 2006

Per unit incl. 2 persons	€ 26,00 - € 31,00
extra person (over 1 yr)	€ 7,00 - € 8,50
electricity (6A)	€ 5,00 - € 6,00

FR17010 Camping Bois Soleil

Mobile homes ▶ page 464

2 avenue de Suzac, F-17110 St Georges-de-Didonne (Charente-Maritime)

Tel: **05 46 05 05 94**. Email: **camping.bois.soleil@wanadoo.fr**

Close to the sea, Bois Soleil is a fairly large site in three parts, with 165 serviced pitches for touring units and a few for tents. All touring pitches are hedged, and have electricity, with water and a drain between two. The main part, 'Les Pins', is attractive with trees and shrubs providing shade. Opposite is 'La Mer' with direct access to the beach, some areas with less shade and an area for tents. The third part, 'La Forêt', is for static holiday homes. It is best to book your preferred area and can be full mid-June - late August. There are a few pitches with lockable gates. The areas are well tended with the named pitches (not numbered) cleared and raked between visitors and with an all-in charge including electricity and water. This lively site offers something for everyone, whether they like a beach-side spot or a traditional pitch, plenty of activities or the quiet life. The sandy beach here is a wide public one, sheltered from the Atlantic breakers although the sea goes out some way at low tide.

Facilities

Each area has one large sanitary block, and smaller blocks with toilets only. Heated block near reception. Cleaned twice daily, they include washbasins in cubicles, facilities for disabled people and babies. Launderette. Nursery. Supermarket, bakery (July/Aug). Beach shop. Restaurant and bar. Takeaway. Pool (heated 15/6-15-9). Steam room. Tennis. Bicycle hire. Play area. TV room and library. Internet terminal. Charcoal barbecues not permitted. Pets not accepted 24/6-2/9). Off site: Fishing, riding 500 m. Golf 20 km.

Open: 1 April - 4 November.

Directions

From Royan centre take coast road (D25) along the sea-front of St Georges-de-Didonne towards Meschers. Site is signed at roundabout at end of the main beach. GPS: N45:35.13 W00:59.128

Charges 2006

Per unit incl. 2 persons, 6A electricity	€ 19,00 - € 33,00
3 persons	€ 22,00 - € 33,00
tent incl. 2 persons	€ 14,00 - € 29,00
extra person	€ 3,50 - € 6,50
child (3-7 yrs)	€ 1,50 - € 4,50

Less 20% outside July/Aug.
Camping Cheques accepted.

FR17050 Camping L'Orée du Bois

225 route de la Bouverie, La Fouasse, F-17570 Les Mathes (Charente-Maritime)

Tel: **05 46 22 42 43**. Email: **info@camping-oree-du-bois.fr**

L'Orée du Bois has 388 pitches of about 100 sq.m. in a very spacious, pinewood setting. There are 150 for touring units, mainly scattered amongst the permanent chalets and tents. They include 40 large pitches with hardstanding and individual sanitary facilities (in blocks of four with shower, toilet, washbasin and dishwashing sink). Pitches are on flat, fairly sandy ground, separated by trees, shrubs and hedges and all have electrical connections (6A). The forest pines offer some shade. Used by several tour operators. A lively site in high season which can be noisy but is tranquil in low season.

Facilities

Four main toilet blocks include some washbasins in cabins. Three have a laundry and facilities for disabled people. Shop. Excellent bar, restaurant, crêperie and takeaway service. Swimming pools, water slide and paddling pool (trunks, not shorts). Play areas. Tennis court, boules, volleyball, table tennis, football and basketball. Games room and TV lounge. Bicycle hire. Discos. Entertainment in July/Aug. Internet access. Barbecues in special areas only. Off site: Riding 300 m. Fishing 4 km. Golf 20 km.

Open: 6 May - 30 September.

Directions

From north follow D14 La Tremblade. At roundabout before Arvert turn on D268 (Les Mathes and La Palmyre). Site on right in Fouasse. From south, at Royan take D25 (La Palmyre). In town turn north to Les Mathes. At first roundabout in Les Mathes follow sign (Fouasse and La Tremblade). Site on left after 2 km.

Charges 2006

Per unit incl. 2 persons	€ 16,00 - € 32,00
with private sanitary facility	€ 23,00 - € 40,00
extra person (over 3 yrs)	€ 6,00

Min. stay 7 days in high season.
Camping Cheques accepted.

Check real time availability and at-the-gate prices...

www.**alanrogers**.com

Bois Soleil

Camping ★★★★
Charente-Maritime

...rrounded by pine trees and a sandy beach on the Atlantic ...ast, with one direct access to the beach, Bois Soleil ...oposes to you many attractions like tennis, tabletennis, ...ildren playgrounds and entertainment. ...ops, take-away and snack-bar with big TV screen.

Camping-Caravaning
Les pieds dans l'eau
www.lespiedsdansleau.com

Camping Cheque

Camping Qualité

Spring and Summer 2007

2, avenue de Suzac - 17110 ST GEORGES DE DIDONNE
Tel: 0033 546 05 05 94 - Fax: 0033 546 06 27 43
...w.bois-soleil.com / e-mail: camping.bois.soleil@wanadoo.fr

FR17060 Airotel Oléron

Domaine de Montravail, F-17480 Le Château d'Oléron (Charente-Maritime)

Tel: 05 46 47 61 82. Email: info@camping-airotel-oleron.com

This family run site offers a friendly, attentive, laid-back atmosphere on the outskirts of Le Château d'Oléron. Appearing to be in a residential area, the site itself is surrounded by paddocks and backs onto the Marais. This is a mature site with about 270 pitches of medium to large size, with varying degrees of shade provided by trees and shrubs. It is well laid out with the touring pitches (130) and mobile homes each in several separate groups. Most touring pitches have electricity (10A) and four have their own water and drainage.

Facilities

Two clean toilet blocks with toilets of both styles, and washbasins in cabins. Laundry and dishwashing facilities. Motorcaravan service point. Fridge hire. Well stocked shop with pleasant staff. Bar, restaurant and takeaway (15/6-15/9). TV and games room. Internet access. Heated swimming and paddling pools. Tennis courts. Table tennis and play area. Bicycle hire. Riding (hard hats supplied, but best to take your own).

Open: 15 April - 30 September.

Directions

Immediately after the viaduct turn right onto the D734 to Le Château and follow camp signs at junctions.

Charges 2006

Per unit incl. 2 persons	€ 13,50 - € 22,00
extra person	€ 4,00 - € 6,50
electricity (8A)	€ 3,90
dog	€ 2,50

FR17070 Camping les Gros Joncs

Mobile homes ► page 464

850 Route de Ponthezieres, Les Sables Vignier, F-17190 St-Georges-d'Oléron (Charente-Maritime)

Tel: 05 46 76 52 29. Email: camping.gros.joncs@wanadoo.fr

Situated on the west coast of the island of Ile d'Oléron, Les Gros Joncs is owned and run by the Cavel family who strive to keep the site up to date and of high quality. There are 50 or so touring pitches of a good size (some extra large) providing a choice between full sun and varying degrees of shade. All have water and electricity (10A) to hand. Much attention has been given to the needs of disabled visitors including chalets where space and equipment is specially adapted. The restaurant and takeaway are of a standard unusual in a campsite. The shop with its own bakery and patisserie stocks a wide range of foods, drinks and every day essentials. The site has a heated swimming pool, recently renovated and now including a water slide (1/4- 15/9) with hydrotherapy and beauty treatments available. New indoor pool and fitness room. The Ile d'Oléron has much history to explore and the French are justifiably proud of the oyster and mussel production on the island – probably the best in Europe and well worth a visit (and tasting!).

Facilities

Toilet facilities are of traditional design, kept very clean and very adequate in number. Laundry facilities. Motorcaravan services. Well stocked shop with bakery (1/4-15/9). Bar with TV, restaurant and snack bar with takeaway (all 1/4-15/9). Swimming pool (1/4-15/9) with hydrotherapy and beauty treatments. Bicycle hire. Children's club (1/7-15/9). WiFi internet access. No barbecues. Off site: Beach 200 or 400 m. Bus service from Chéray. Fishing 2 km. Riding 6 km. Golf 8 km.

Open: All year.

Directions

Cross the viaduct onto the Ile d'Oléron. Take D734 (St George d'Oléron). At traffic lights in Chéray turn left. Follow signs for camping and Sable Vignier. Soon signs indicate direction of Les Gros Joncs.

Charges 2006

Per unit incl. 2 persons	€ 13,40 - € 36,50
incl. 3 persons	€ 15,60 - € 36,50
extra person	€ 5,10 - € 10,20
child (0-7 yrs)	€ 2,20 - € 6,30

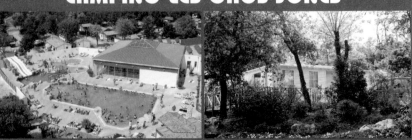

CAMPING LES GROS JONCS

850 Route de Ponthezieres - F-17190 St Georges-d'Oléron - France
Tél: 05 46 76 52 29 - Fax: 05 46 76 67 74 - E-mail: camping.gros.joncs@wanadoo.fr

FR17080 Camping le Royan

10 rue des Bleuets, F-17200 Royan (Charente-Maritime)

Tel: **05 46 39 09 06**. Email: **camping.le.royan@wanadoo.fr**

Camping Le Royan is a well established family site located close to the resort of Royan and its beaches. There are 186 good size grassy pitches, of which 80 are for touring. All but 16 have 10A electricity (Euro plugs). Some pitches may suffer from road noise from the nearby Royan by-pass. The site has tarmac access roads and well maintained toilet blocks. The swimming pool is particularly attractive with a jacuzzi and a number of slides. A lively entertainment programme and children's club are organised in peak season.

Facilities

Two sanitary buildings with facilities for disabled people. Snack bar and pizzeria. Shop. Swimming pool with waterslides and other features. Paddling pool. Games room. Playground. Table tennis. Volleyball. Bicycle hire. Children's club. Entertainment. Mobile homes and chalets for rent. Gas barbecues allowed. Only small dogs accepted. Off site: Beach 2.5 km. Royan centre 2 km. La Palmyre zoo. Riding, golf 7 km.

Open: 1 April - 15 October.

Directions

Site is close to the Royan by-pass to the northwest of the town heading towards La Palmyre. It is well signed. GPS: N45:38.708 W001:02.48

Charges 2006

Per unit including 3 people	
and electricity	€ 21,50 - € 32,50
extra person	€ 3,50 - € 7,00
child (3-9 yrs)	€ 3,50 - € 6,00

Camping Le Royan

Located in parkland at on the edge of Royan, this quality site offers you a warm welcome in a family friendly setting. Only 2.5 km away from beautiful sandy beaches, Camping Le Royan offers you high quality chalets and mobile homes during the whole season. There are 100 grassy pitches reserved for caravans and tents. The site's heated pool complex is open from 1st May

Camping Le Royon • 10 Rue Des Bleuets • 17200 Des Bleuets
Tel.: 05 46 39 09 06 • fax: 05 46 38 12 05
Email: camping.le.royan@wanadoo.fr • www.le-royan.com

FR17110 Camping Caravaning Monplaisir

Route de la Palmyre, F-17570 Les Mathes - La Palmyre (Charente-Maritime)

Tel: **05 46 22 50 31**

Monplaisir provides a small, quiet haven in an area with some very hectic campsites. It is ideal for couples or families with young children. Quite close to the town and set back from the road, the entrance leads through an avenue of trees, past the owners home to a well kept, garden-like site with many trees and shrubs. There are only 114 level, marked pitches and all but 9 have electrical connections (6A). On 14 there are caravans for rent and a modern building provides flats and studios for rent. Visitors return year after year.

Facilities

The toilet block has good facilities including some washbasins in cabins and excellent facilities for disabled people. Laundry and dishwashing facilities. Ice pack service in reception. Bread delivered daily. TV, games room and library. Heated swimming pool and paddling pool (early May - 30/9). Small play area. Winter caravan storage. Off site: Supermarket short walk. Minigolf adjacent (owned by the site). Fishing 500 m. Riding 1 km. Golf 5 km.

Open: 1 April - 1 October.

Directions

Follow D25 to La Palmyre. In town, turn north to Les Mathes. At roundabout turn right to town centre. Site on left. From north on the D14 (La Tremblade) turn onto D268 (Les Mathes and La Palmyre) at roundabout just before Arvert. Keep straight on to Les Mathes, road becomes D141 and turn left (north) at roundabout. Site is 600 m. on left.

Charges guide

Per unit incl. 2 persons	€ 16,00
incl. 3 persons	€ 18,00
extra person	€ 4,50
electricity	€ 3,00
Less 20% outside July/Aug.	

FR17140 Castel Camping Séquoia Parc

La Josephtrie, F-17320 St Just-Luzac (Charente-Maritime)

Tel: **05 46 85 55 55**. Email: **sequoia.parc@wanadoo.fr**

This is definitely a site not to be missed. Approached by an avenue of flowers, shrubs and trees, Séquoia Parc is a Castel site set in the grounds of La Josephtrie, a striking château with beautifully restored outbuildings and courtyard area with a bar and restaurant. Most pitches are 140 sq.m. with 6A electricity connections and separated by mature shrubs providing plenty of privacy. The site has 300 mobile homes and chalets, with 125 used by tour operators. This is a popular site with a children's club and entertainment throughout the season and reservation is necessary in high season. Member of Leading Campings Group. The site itself is designed to a high specification with reception in a large, light and airy room retaining its original beams and leading to the courtyard area where you find the bar and restaurant. The pool complex with water slides, large paddling pool and sunbathing area is impressive.

Facilities

Three spotlessly clean luxurious toilet blocks, include units with washbasin and shower and facilities for disabled visitors and children. Dishwashing sinks. New large laundry. Motorcaravan service point. Gas supplies. Large new supermarket. Restaurant/bar and takeaway. Impressive swimming pool complex with water slides and large paddling pool. Tennis, volleyball, football field. Games and TV rooms. Bicycle hire. Pony trekking. Organised entertainment all season. Off site: Sailing, fishing, golf 25 km. Flying trips.

Open: 13 May - 10 September, with all services.

Directions

Site is 5 km. southeast of Marennes. From Rochefort take D733 south for 12 km. Turn west on D123 to Ile d'Oléron. Continue for 12 km. Turn southeast on D728 (Saintes). Site signed, in 1 km. on left. GPS: N45:48.699 W01:03.637

Charges 2006

Per unit incl. 2 persons	
and electricity	€ 15,00 - € 37,00
extra person	€ 6,00 - € 8,00
child (3-12 yrs)	€ 3,00 - € 5,00

FROM AQUAPARK TILL ATLANTIC OCEAN: MAGNIFICENT

Large separated pitches 140 m², modern and comfortable cottages, 3 heated pools, 2000 m² water, lazy river and water slides, Ocean and sandy beaches nearby, Kid's club during the whole season.

Séquoia Parc

Bookings:
www.sequoiaparc.com
Address: Séquoia Parc,
17320 St.Just-Luzac
France
Tel: 00 33 546 85 55 55

FR17150 Camping Municipal du Château Benon

F-17170 Benon (Charente-Maritime)

Tel: **05 46 01 61 48**. Email: **mairie-benon@smic17.fr**

This municipal campsite is beautifully kept, with open and shady areas and is ideal for those wanting a peaceful stay, and to stroll or cycle through the fields and woods which surround Benon. There are 70 pitches on neat grass, 40 with 10A electricity, although many are sloping or uneven. This is a pretty, quiet site where visitors are made welcome. Benon was once the capital of this area with strong English connections, its castle being built in 1096, but just a single round tower remains. The mayor and villagers are still anxious to welcome English visitors.

Facilities

The reasonably modern toilet block is fully equipped, with hot water always available and facilities for disabled visitors. Tennis court. Reception may only be open in the mornings. Off site: Auberge, general shop and post office in village, 250 m. La Rochelle is within easy reach (25 minutes) for shopping, beaches, etc. Riding 5 km. Fishing or bicycle hire 7 km. Golf 13 km.

Open: 1 May - 30 September.

Directions

Benon is 28 km. east of La Rochelle on the N11. Turn south at 'Relais de Benon', Benon 2 km. and site in centre of village.

Charges 2006

Per person	€ 2,70
child (under 11 yrs)	€ 1,60
pitch	€ 1,60
electricity	€ 2,20
No credit cards.	

FR17160 Camping le Clos Fleuri

8 impasse du Clos Fleuri, F-17600 Médis (Charente-Maritime)

Tel: **05 46 05 62 17**. Email: **clos-fleuri@wanadoo.fr**

Camping Le Clos Fleuri really does live up to its name. The profusion of different trees and the lawns and flower beds give this small site a very rural atmosphere. There is always a warm welcome from the Devais family who created this pretty site in 1974. The 125 touring pitches are mostly of generous size (a little uneven in places). They vary from being in full sun to well shaded and 110 have electrical connections. The bar/restaurant is a converted barn providing a cool haven on hot days and a very convivial venue for evening gatherings and entertainment. There is occasional noise from light aircraft. The surrounding countryside is very pleasant with crops of sunflowers, wheat and maize, while beaches of all sorts are within easy reach. All in all the Clos Fleuri combines a great deal of charm, beauty and friendliness with a location from which the attractions of the Charente-Maritime may be discovered.

Facilities

Toilet facilities are kept scrupulously clean. One block is segregated male and female, the other is unisex with each unit in its own cubicle. Facility for disabled visitors. Baby baths. Laundry facilities. Small pool and paddling pool. Sauna. Shop (1/7-15/9). Restaurant (1/7-31/8) and bar (1/7-15/9). In high season there are twice weekly 'soirées' and boules and archery competitions. Minigolf. Small football pitch. Security barrier closed at night. Off site: Médis 2 km.

Open: 1 June - 18 September.

Directions

Médis is on the N150 from Saintes, halfway between Saujon and Royan. Drive into village. Site signed to south at various points in Médis and is about 2 km. outside village. GPS: N45:37.782 W00:56.768

Charges 2007

Per pitch incl. 2 persons	€ 17,90 - € 25,50
extra person	€ 6,00 - € 7,70
child (2-7 yrs)	€ 4,00 - € 5,20
electricity (5/10A)	€ 3,00 - € 5,60

Less 25% in June and Sept.

In the land of Sun, Pineau, Cognac, Oysters, Mussels and Melons.

nr.ROYAN

Le Clos Fleuri

www.le-clos-fleuri.com ☆ ☆ ☆ ☆

Trees, bushes, flowers and birds.....
Beauty and peace. Smart & large
grassy pitches & now chalets !
Bar & restaurant set in
a old stone built barn

country camping

Family barbecues are...recommended !

FR17200 Camping Municipal Au Fil de l'Eau

6 rue de Courbiac, F-17100 Saintes (Charente-Maritime)

Tel: **05 46 93 08 00**. Email: **contact@camping-saintes-17.com**

Saintes is a 2,000 year old Gallo-Roman city, well worth a couple of days to visit the Cathedral, the Abbey, the Arch of Germanicus, the Amphitheatre and several museums, all within walking distance of the site (city map from reception). Do take a stroll through the well tended public gardens by the riverside. This pleasant site is well run as a franchise from the local municipality and has 214 mostly shady and generally grassy level pitches, with 132 electric hook-ups, and six mobile homes for rent.

Facilities

The main toilet block is a large building, with two smaller older units opened at peak times. Washbasins in cubicles. Facilities for disabled people. Laundry building. Motorcaravan service point. Shop. Bar. Restaurant and takeaway (July/Aug). TV room. Boules pitch, table tennis, badminton, volleyball and minigolf. Playground. Barrier system, with gates locked 22.00-07.00 hrs (22.30-7.00 July/Aug), and guardian lives on site. Off site: Adjacent open air Olympic sized swimming pool complex - free for campers (23/6-10/9).

Open: 1 April - 30 October.

Directions

From east and northeast follow signs for town and site, turning right after river. Avoiding centre, use bypass following signs for N137 La Rochelle to large roundabout at northern end. Turn right (town centre and Camping Municipal) (at this roundabout coming from La Rochelle N137, go straight on). Left at next roundabout, ahead at two more, right at next. Left at mini roundabout. Site is 200 m. on right. GPS: N45:45.317 W00:37.688

Charges 2006

Per person	€ 4,30
child (under 7 yrs)	€ 2,10
pitch incl. electricity (5A)	€ 7,80

FR17170 Domaine des Charmilles

St Laurent de la Prée, F-17450 Fouras (Charente-Maritime)

Tel: **08 20 20 23 27**. Email: **charmilles17@wanadoo.fr**

Les Charmilles is about a mile from the town centre. There are 270 large pitches, of which only 60 are touring pitches. The remainder are occupied by mobile homes, chalets and tour operators. All touring pitches have electricity (10A) and many have water and drainage. Ten are specially for disabled visitors. A third are well shaded, with the remainder in a sunnier, more open setting. The latter area is also away from the busy road which runs past the front of the site. Entertainment in high season can mean that the site is noisy until at least midnight. Recent improvements include the attractive refurbishment of the bar and restaurant, the upgrading of the main pool with extra slides and a new pool with sliding doors. These changes have created a high quality focal point for the site. Fouras is a relatively little known resort situated between La Rochelle and Rochefort which retains much of the charm missing from larger, more heavily commercialised resorts in the area.

Facilities

Three modern toilet blocks provide most washbasins in cubicles and facilities for babies and disabled people. Laundry facilities. Shop (1/6-15/9). Bar and takeaway (15/5-15/9). Restaurant (1/6-15/9). Heated swimming pools (one covered), water slides and sunbathing terrace (15/5-30/9). Playground. Table tennis and multisports court. Bicycle hire. Entertainment. Minibus service to beach in July/Aug. Communal barbecues. Off site: Fishing 3 km. Golf 5 km. Riding 15 km.

Open: 7 April - 22 September.

Directions

Leave N137 at exit for Fouras and St Laurent de la Prée, joining D937 towards Fouras. Site is on left in about 800 m. GPS: N45:59.233 W01:03.150

Charges 2006

Per pitch incl. 2 persons	€ 15,00 - € 30,00
extra person	€ 6,00
child (under 5 yrs)	€ 4,00
electricity	€ 4,00
animal	€ 5,00 - € 6,00

Domaine des Charmilles

St. Laurent de la Prée
F-17450 Fouras
Tel.: (33) 5 46 84 00 05
Fax: (33) 5 46 84 02 84
Email: charmilles17@wanadoo.fr

FR17210 Sunêlia Interlude

Plage de Gros Jonc, F-17580 Le Bois-Plage-en-Ré (Charente-Maritime)

Tel: **05 46 09 18 22**. Email: **infos@interlude.fr**

Camping Interlude enjoys a pleasant location with access to an excellent beach. A popular site even in low season, (may become very crowded with overstretched facilities in high season), it has 387 pitches, 136 of which are for touring units. Pitches are sand based, vary in size from 80-120 sq.m. and are mostly divided by hedges on part undulating, sandy terrain. Many are placed to the left of the site in a pine forest setting, others mingle with the tour operators and mobile homes. Choosing a shady pitch is not a problem for there are many trees.

Facilities

Two modern, clean and well equipped sanitary blocks provide washbasins in cabins and some shower units suitable for families with twin washbasins. Baby room, child size toilets, en suite facilities for disabled visitors, laundry and dishwashing service. Motorcaravan service point. Restaurant/bar and shop. Fresh bread. Swimming pools, one outdoor and one inside. Play area. Volleyball, boules. Organised events and entertainment. Games/TV room. Tennis courts. Bicycle hire. Communal barbecues. Multi-sport area.

Open: 9 April - 2 November.

Directions

After toll bridge to the Ile de Ré follow sign for (Le Bois-Plage). Turn left at first roundabout, straight on at next two, then left at fourth roundabout. Site signed. GPS: N46:10.440 W01:22.701

Charges 2006

Per unit incl. 2 persons	
and electricity	€ 22,00 - € 39,00
with water and waste	€ 24,00 - € 43,00
extra person	€ 5,00 - € 10,00

FR17190 Le Logis du Breuil

F-17570 St Augustin-sur-Mer (Charente-Maritime)

Tel: **05 46 23 23 45**. Email: **camping.Logis-du-Breuil@wanadoo.fr**

The first impression on arrival at this impressive campsite is space. The camping area is a 200 m. expanse of farm pasture where (on different areas) cattle graze and children play. The camping areas are set among rows of mature and shady trees giving a dappled effect to the tents, caravans and grassy pitches. The 320 pitches (250 with 3/6A electricity) are very large and have direct access to wide, unpaved alleys, which lead on to the few tarmac roads around the site. The amenities are centred around the reception area and pool complex. The area around the site is very pleasant agricultural land and the beaches of the Atlantic coast are nearby, as are the oyster and the mussel beds of Marennes and La Tremblade. The Gagnard family started the campsite about 25 years ago and obviously takes great pride in what it has now become; a peaceful, friendly and very pleasant site from which to explore a delightful holiday area. A 'Sites et Paysages' member.

Facilities

Four well maintained toilet blocks are spaced around the camping area. Dishwashing and laundry facilities. Swimming pools. Shop, bar and snacks and takeaway (franchised) are well run. No evening entertainment. Play area. Indoor area providing archery, pool and table tennis. Bicycle hire. Tennis and basketball. Excursions organised. Internet access. Off site: A 50 minute walk leads to the sea near St Palais-sur-Mer, another to the 'Cote Sauvage'.

Open: 1 May - 30 September.

Directions

Approaching Royan follow signs to St Palais sur Mer. Go straight on past first set of traffic lights and two roundabouts. At second set of lights turn right (St Augustin). Site is approx. 2 km. on left, just before village. GPS: N45:40.463 W01:05.768

Charges 2007

Per unit incl. 2 persons	€ 14,10 - € 19,20
with electricity	€ 17,55 - € 23,30
extra person	€ 3,85 - € 6,10
child (under 7 yrs)	€ 3,30 - € 4,51
dog	€ 1,80 - € 2,25

Quiet and space

Le Logis du Breuil

★ ★ ★

CAMPING   CARAVANING

17570 SAINT-AUGUSTIN-SUR-MER
Tel : (33) 05 46 23 23 45
Fax : (33) 05 46 23 43 33

Chalet and Mobilhomes to rent

www.logis-du-breuil.com
camping.logis-du-breuil@wanadoo.fr

FR17220 Camping la Brande

Route des Huitres, F-17480 Le Château-d'Oléron (Charente-Maritime)

Tel: **05 46 47 62 37**. Email: **info@camping-labrande.com**

A quality site, run and maintained to the highest standard, La Brande offers an ideal holiday environment on the delightful Ile d'Oléron, famed for its oysters. La Brande is situated on the oyster route and close to a sandy beach. Pitches here are generous and mostly separated by hedges and trees, the greater number for touring outfits. All are on level grassy terrain and have electricity hook-ups, some are fully serviced. The many activities during the high season, plus the natural surroundings, make this an ideal choice for families.

Facilities

Three heated, clean sanitary blocks have spacious, well equipped showers and washbasins (mainly in cabins). Baby facilities. Excellent facilities for people with disabilities (separate large shower, washbasin and WC). Laundry room. Motorcaravan service point. Shop. Restaurant/takeaway and bar (July/Aug). Grass play area. Football field, tennis, minigolf, fishing and archery. Bicycle hire. Canoe hire. Internet access. Off site: Beach 300 m.

Open: 15 March - 15 November.

Directions

After crossing bridge to L'Ile d'Oléron turn right towards Le Château d'Oléron. Continue through village and follow sign for Route des Huitres. Site is on left after 3 km. GPS: N45:90.353 W01:21.53

Charges 2007

Per unit incl. 2 persons	
and electricity	€ 19,20 - € 39,00
extra person	€ 5,00 - € 8,00
Camping Cheques accepted.	

FR17230 Camping de L'Océan

La Passe, La Couarde-sur-Mer, F-17670 Ile de Ré (Charente-Maritime)

Tel: 05 46 29 87 70. Email: campingdelocean@wanadoo.fr

L'Océan lies close to the centre of the Ile de Ré, just 50 m. from a sandy beach. There are 338 pitches here with 161 for touring units, the remainder occupied by mobile homes and chalets. The camping area is well shaded and pitches are of a reasonable size, all with electricity (10A). A pleasant bar/restaurant overlooks the large heated swimming pool which is surrounded by an attractive sunbathing terrace. Bicycle hire is popular here as the island offers over 100 km. of cycle routes.

Facilities

The new toilet blocks are modern and well maintained with facilities for disabled visitors. Motorcaravan services. Shop. Bar/restaurant and takeaway (all season). Swimming pool. Riding. Bicycle hire. Tennis court. Fishing pond adjacent. Basketball. Play area. Minigolf (free). Helicopter rides, subaqua diving and pony riding (high season). Entertainment in high season. No charcoal barbecues. Internet access. Off site: Beach 50 m. La Couarde 2.5 km. Golf 5 km.

Open: 25 March - 24 September.

Directions

After toll bridge, join D735 which runs along the north side of the island until you pass La Couarde. The site is 2.5 km. beyond village (in direction of Ars-en-Re). GPS: N46:12.260 W01:28.06

Charges 2006

Per unit incl. 1-3 persons	€ 14,65 - € 37,08
extra person	€ 4,25 - € 9,37
electricity	€ 5,05
dog	€ 1,77 - € 4,42

Camping Cheques accepted.

kawan-villages.com **tel: 00 333 59 59 03 59**

FR17270 Camping L'Anse des Pins

Chemin du Râteau - Domino, F-17190 Saint-Georges-d'Oléron (Charente-Maritime)

Tel: 05 46 76 55 97. Email: camping-apv@wanadoo.fr.

Rock pools, sand dunes and spectacular sun sets, with sea views from many of the pitches, help to make this site attractive to those seeking an away from it all holiday in a quiet part of the island of the Ile d'Oléron. The campsite is arranged in three areas, some parts having good shade, but with a fair proportion in full sun. There are 350 pitches including 188 for touring units, the remainder used for mobile homes. Electricity connections are available (3-10A) and 22 pitches also have water and drainage. Mobile home numbers at this site increase each year.

Facilities

Two main toilet blocks (plus two small blocks for high season use) with mainly British style toilets. Showers and washbasins in cabins. Laundry facilities. Gas supplies. Bar. Shop with limited takeaway and snack bar. Swimming and paddling pools. Play area. Activities in high season (1/7- 31/8). Tennis. Boules courts. Table tennis. No TV. Barbecues only permitted in a communal area. Off site: Beach 50 m. Bicycle hire 1 km. Riding 10 km. St Georges 5 km.

Open: April - September.

Directions

Cross the bridge onto Ile d'Oléron and follow D734 (St Dennis). In Chéray, turn left at traffic lights (signed Camping). Stay on this road to Domino (avoid side roads). Follow green signs to Rex and L'Anse des Pins Camping. Narrow roads. GPS: N45:58.226 W01:23.213

Charges guide

Per unit incl. 2 persons	€ 16,00 - € 28,00
extra person	€ 6,00 - € 7,00
electricity	€ 2,50 - € 4,00

FR17300 Camping Au Petit Port de l'Houmeau

F-17137 L'Houmeau (Charente-Maritime)

Tel: 05 46 50 90 82. Email: info@aupetitport.com

Au Petit Port de l'Houmeau is a pretty, quiet and rural site on the edge of the small seaside village of L'Houmeau. The friendly English speaking owners ensure high standards of maintenance. Pitches (clustered in groups of four or five) are of a good size, and are all equipped with 5A electrical connections. Virtually all offer some degree of shade. Larger motorcaravans may have difficulty finding a suitable pitch. There are relatively few amenities here, but the village shops, bars and a good restaurant are very close by.

Facilities

Two well maintained toilet blocks. Washing machines and dryers. Snack bar (July/Aug). Internet point. Bicycle hire. Play area. 'Moules/frites' evenings in high season. Mobile homes and chalets for rent (all year). Off site: Beach 800 m. Hourly bus to La Rochelle from village centre. Shops, bars, restaurant.

Open: 1 April - 30 September.

Directions

From northbound N137 dual-carriageway (La Rochelle bypass), leave at Lagord exit, then follow signs to L'Houmeau. On reaching L'Houmeau, site is well signed.

Charges 2007

Per unit incl. 2 persons	€ 12,50 - € 15,50
extra person	€ 3,50 - € 4,50
electricity (5/10A)	€ 3,50 - € 4,20

FR17260 Camping le Cormoran

Route de Radia, Ars-en-Ré, F-17590 Ile de Ré (Charente-Maritime)

Tel: **05 46 29 46 04**. Email: **info@cormoran.com**

Just outside Ars-en-Ré, Le Cormoran offers a quiet rural holiday for families with young children. Pitches vary in size and are a mixture of sand and grass. All have electricity. The restaurant and bar overlook the pool (covered in April and May and heated throughout the season) and are open during the season until June. Basic provisions are stocked in the bar. There are the usual shops in Ars, which is some 800 m. away. Le Cormoran is close to the local oyster beds. The sister site, Camping La Plage, is about 3 km. away and concentrates mainly on its 144 mobile homes. There are 44 pitches for touring units but the facilities for them are a little old fashioned.

Facilities

Unisex toilet facilities are in two blocks with toilets (British and Turkish style), showers and washbasins mainly in cabins. Provision for disabled visitors. Dishwashing and laundry facilities. Motorcaravan service point. Bar, restaurant and takeaway meals. Swimming pool (covered in low season). Fitness centre. Tennis. Volleyball. Games room. Play area. Entertainment programme in high season. Bicycle hire. Off site: Nearest beach 500 m. Ars-en-Ré 800 m. Fishing 500 m. Boat launching 1 km. Riding 3 km. Golf 10 km.

Open: 1 April - 30 September.

Directions

Cross the toll bridge from La Rochelle onto the Ile de Ré and continue on D735 to Ars-en-Ré from where site is well signed.

Charges 2006

Per unit incl. 2 persons	€ 16,30 - € 23,50
extra person	€ 5,40 - € 11,00
child (0-9 yrs)	€ 3,25 - € 11,00
electricity (10A)	€ 5,00
animal	€ 2,65 - € 5,50

Ile de Ré

www.cormoran.com

Le cormoran ★★★★
www.airotel.com
Club
Airotel
LA PLAGE ★★★★

Camping
Qualité

At 500 m of the beach, adjacent to a big forest and at 800 m from the lovely town of Ars, campsite Le Cormoran is truly a paradise for the young and adults.

E-mail : info@cormoran.com
E-mail : info@la-plage.com
Tél. 05 46 29 46 04 - Fax 05 46 29 29 36
Paradis en Ré Route de Radia 17590 ARS EN RÉ

At 100 m from the beach

At 100 m from the beach 'La Plage de la Conche' and 500 m from the lighthouse of Baleines. This campsite is particularly good for family holidays and boat trips with a skipper.

www.la-plage.com

FR17280 Camping la Grainetière

Mobile homes ▶ page 464

Route de Saint-Martin, F-17630 La Flotte-en-Ré (Charente-Maritime)
Tel: **05 46 09 68 86**. Email: **la-grainetiere@free.fr**

A truly friendly welcome awaits you from the owners, Isabelle and Eric, at La Grainetière. It is a peaceful campsite set in almost three hectares of pine trees which provide some shade for the 65 touring pitches of various shapes and sizes. There are also 50 well spaced chalets for rent. Some pitches are suitable for units up to 7 metres (book in advance). There are no hedges for privacy and the pitches are sandy with some grass. Ample new water points and electricity (10A) hook-ups (Euro plugs) serve the camping area. The site is well lit.

Facilities

The unisex sanitary block is first class, with washbasins in cubicles, showers, British style WCs, facilities for children and people with disabilities. Shop (1/4-30/9). Takeaway (July/Aug). Swimming pool (heated 1/4-30/9). Bicycle hire. Fridge hire. TV room. Charcoal barbecues are not permitted. Off site: Beach and sailing 2 km. Fishing and boat launching 2 km. Riding 3 km. Golf 10 km. Bar and restaurant 2 km.

Open: 1 April - 30 September.

Directions

Follow camping signs from La Flotte, 1 km. from the village. GPS: N46:11.253 W01:20.696

Charges 2006

Per unit incl. 2 persons	€ 14,00 - € 22,00
extra person	€ 3,00 - € 6,00
child (0-7 yrs)	€ 2,00 - € 3,00
electricity (10A)	€ 3,50

La Grainetiere

Between St. Martin harbor and la Flotte. All kinds of shops at proximity. Isabelle and Eric welcome you in a wooded park. Friendly family atmosphere.

Route de Saint Martin - 17630 La Flotte - France - Tel: 0033 (0)5 46 09 68 86 - Fax: 0033 (0)5 46 09 53 13
lagrainetiere@free.fr - www.la-grainetiere.com

FR17290 Camping les Peupliers

RD 735, F-17630 La Flotte-en-Ré (Charente-Maritime)
Tel: **05 46 09 62 35**. Email: **camping@les-peupliers.com**

On the Ile de Ré, you are never far from the sea and the location of this campsite is no exception. It is just 800 metres from the sea with sea views from some of the pitches. English is spoken at reception and the staff go out of their way to make your stay enjoyable. The 46 level touring pitches are in a separate area from 98 chalets for rent, in an area of light woodland. There are few water points. The trees provide some shade, but the very low hedges provide little privacy as the width and length of the pitches varies.

Facilities

Two new but traditionally designed sanitary blocks are clean and well maintained. Both have unisex facilities including showers and vanity type units in cabins. Separate facilities for people with disabilities. Laundry facilities. Shop, restaurant, takeaway and bar with TV (all 8/4-23/9). Outdoor swimming pool (15/5-15/9). Play area. Children's club and entertainment (high season). Fridge hire. Bicycle hire. Off site: Riding 500 m. Boat launching and saling 5 km. Beach 800 m. Fishing 5 km. Golf 20 km.

Open: 8 April - 23 September.

Directions

Over the toll bridge (€15 in 2006) and turn left at second roundabout. Site is well signed. GPS: N46:10.969 W01:18.050

Charges 2006

Per unit incl. 2 persons	€ 15,00 - € 28,00
incl. electricity	€ 19,00 - € 33,00
extra person	€ 5,00 - € 8,00
child (0-5 yrs)	free - € 5,00
Camping Cheques accepted.	

FR17310 Camping le Val Vert

108 avenue Frederic Garnier, F-17640 Vaux-sur-Mer (Charente-Maritime)
Tel: **05 46 38 25 51**. Email: **camping-val-vert@wanadoo.fr**

Situated in seven acres of lush countryside (hence its name 'Green Valley'), this is a charming campsite, just 200 metres from the village of Vaux-sur-Mer, and 900 metres from the sandy beach at Nouzon. There are 95 touring pitches, all with 6 or 10A electricity (French connections – adaptors available). Extra long cables are required for some pitches, which are of average size (100 sq.m.) with good access, even for larger units. Some are terraced. Although entertainment is organised in high season, facilities on the site are minimal as the accent here is on peace and tranquillity.

Facilities

There are ample toilet and shower facilities. Separate facilities for people with disabilities. Laundry facilities. Shop, bar, restaurant and takeaway (all 10/6-10/9). Swimming and paddling pools (29/4-10/9; supervised in high season). Play area. Volleyball. Petanque. Off site: Village facilities 200 m. Fishing 1 km. Boat launching 5 km. Golf 10 km. Riding 10 km. Beach 900 m.

Open: 8 April - 30 September.

Directions

Follow camping signs from the village of Vaux-sur-Mer. GPS: N45:38.640 W01:03:768

Charges 2006

Per unit incl. 1-3 persons	€ 16,00 - € 24,50
extra person	€ 4,00 - € 5,20
child (1-7 yrs)	€ 3,40 - € 4,20
electricity (6/10A)	€ 4,00 - € 4,60

FR17340 Camping Port-Punay

Allée Bernard Moreau, Les Boucholeurs, F-17340 Châtelaillon-Plage (Charente-Maritime)
Tel: **05 46 56 01 53**. Email: **contact@camping-port-punay.com**

Port-Punay is a friendly, well run site just 200 metres from the beach and 3 km. from the centre of the resort of Chatelaillon-Plage. There are 190 pitches laid out on well trimmed grass, with many mature poplars and low shrubs. The site has a well stocked shop, open all season and a small bar and restaurant only open in high season. A heated swimming pool has a separate gated area for paddling. There is a good range of activities available and in high season some entertainment is arranged. This is a family run site (Famille Moreau) and the son of the family speaks excellent English, as does his Dutch wife. Rochefort to the south and La Rochelle to the north are well worth a visit (buses from outside the site), as is the nearby town of Chatelaillon-Plage, which has an all-year covered market and, in summer, a street market every day. Port-Punay has just one large toilet block, centrally positioned on the site, with very good facilities.

Facilities

One large toilet block with good facilities including washbasins in cubicles and large shower cubicles. Facilities for disabled visitors and babies. Washing machines. Shop. Bar, restaurant and takeaway (1/7-31/8). Swimming pool. Games area. Play area. Bicycle hire. Internet access. Free WiFi all over site. Off site: Chatelaillon-Plage 3 km. by road, 1.5 km. along the seafront on foot or bike. Buses to Rochefort and La Rochelle from outside site. Riding 2 km. Beach 200 m.

Open: 1 April - 30 September.

Directions

From N137 (La Rochelle - Rochefort) take exit for Chatelaillon-Plage. Just after the town sign, the site (and the Hippodrome) are signed to the left. Follow signs to the site at the seaside hamlet of Les Boucholeurs. Here drive to the sea-wall then turn left through village to site. Take care, as the road has traffic-calming measures and can be narrow in places.

Charges 2006

Per unit incl. 2 persons	€ 14,50 - € 20,00
extra person	€ 4,30 - € 5,50
child (0-3 yrs)	€ 3,20 - € 4,20
electricity (6/10A)	€ 4,00 - € 5,00

FR85000 Camping le Petit Rocher

1250 avenue de Docteur Mathevet, F-85560 Longeville-sur-Mer (Vendée)

Tel: **02 51 90 31 57**. Email: **rocher@free.fr**

A former municipal site, Le Petit Rocher is now under the same management (M. Guignard) as another local campsite, Les Brunelles. With its seaside location set in a pine forest, there is an air of peace and tranquillity. Although the area is undulating, the 178 good size touring pitches are flat and arranged in terraces throughout the wooded area. Electricity hook-ups are available (Euro style plugs) and there are adequate water points. A grassy play area for children is thoughtfully situated in a hollow, but has limited equipment. A swimming pool is planned for 2007.

Facilities

Three new, spacious sanitary blocks are clean and well maintained with showers, British style WCs. Facilities for people with disabilities. Washing machine and dryer. Tennis court. Off site: Bars, restaurant, and small shops nearby. Riding and bicycle hire 3 km. Boat launching 11 km. Fishing 15 km. Golf 20 km. Beach 200 m.

Open: 29 April - 23 September.

Directions

From Longeville-sur-Mer follow signs for Le Rocher towards La Tranche-sur-Mer. Turn right at first roundabout, following campsite signs to site on right. GPS: N46:24.226 W01:30.431

Charges 2006

Per person	€ 3,80
child (0-7 yrs)	€ 2,20
pitch incl. electricity	€ 8,20

FR17350 Camping Les Catalpas

45 chemin Enlias, FR17110 Saint Georges de Didonne (Charente-Maritime)

Tel: **05 46 64 45 52**. Email: **contact@village-center.com**

This campsite has been recommended by our French agent and we intend to undertake a full inspection in 2007. This campsite is located close to the beach near Saint Georges de Didonne and is well located for a seaside holiday in a region rich with history and culture.

Facilities

Swimming pool with paddling pool. Playground. Table tennis. Snack bar. TV room. Grocery shop.
Off site: Watersports. Bicycle hire. Tennis. Riding.

Open: May - September.

Directions

From the A10 take the Saintes exit. Then the N150 towards Royan. Before Royan take the D25 to St Georges. Site is signed from this point.

Charges 2007

Per unit incl 2 persons and electricity	€ 8,00 - € 16,00
extra person	€ 1,90 - € 4,00
child (under 7 yrs)	€ 1,50 - € 3,25

FR85010 Camping le Zagarella

Route de La Tranche, F-85560 Longeville-sur-Mer (Vendée)

Tel: **02 51 33 30 60**. Email: **contact@campingzagarella.com**

This pleasant campsite is set in a wooded, six hectare area, 900 metres walk from the beach (or 1.5 km by road). As well as 100 chalets to rent, there are 45 small touring pitches (the site is probably unsuitable for units over 6 metres). On well drained grass and shaded, the pitches are hedged and all have water and 10A electricity (French connections). Access around the site is by tarmac roads. The site has a landscaped pool complex including slides and a covered pool. An area for sports and games including tennis is across the road via an underpass.

Facilities

Two well maintained toilet blocks of traditional design include British style WCs, washbasins in cubicles and free pre-set showers. Separate baby room and facilities for people with disabilities. Washing machines. Shop (25/5-5/9). Bar (20/5-5/9). Restaurant and takeaway (1/5-30/9). Swimming pool (1/6-30/9) and indoor pool (heated 1/4-30/9). Playground. Tennis. Bicycle hire. Gas barbecues permitted (available for rent). Off site: Beach 900 m. Riding 1 km. Golf 30 km.

Open: 1 April - 30 September.

Directions

From Longeville-sur-Mer take road to Tranche-sur-Mer and site is on the left (follow green camping signs).

Charges 2006

Per unit incl. 3 persons	€ 25,00 - € 32,50
extra person	€ 5,00 - € 5,30
child (0-5 yrs)	€ 2,50 - € 2,70
dog	€ 3,00

Domaine de Zagarella

Pitches, mobile homes and chalets. Indoor pool and heated outdoor pool in a natural setting, waterfall, Jacuzzi, waterslide, play area, tennis...
At 900m from the beach

Le Rocher - Route de la Tranche
85560 Longeville Sur Mer
Tél : 33 (0) 251 33 30 60
Fax : 33 (0) 251 33 37 09
www.campings-franceloc.com

Vendée

FR85020 Camping du Jard

123 Mal de Lattre de Tassigny, F-85360 La Tranche-sur-Mer (Vendée)

Tel: **02 51 27 43 79**. Email: **info@campingdujard.fr**

Camping du Jard is a well maintained site between La Rochelle and Les Sables d'Olonne. First impressions are good, with a friendly welcome from M. Marton or his staff. The 242 touring pitches are level and grassy, hedged on two sides by bushes. The smallest are 100 sq.m. (the majority larger) and most are equipped with electricity, half with water and drainage. It is a comparatively new site, but the large variety of trees is beginning to provide a little shade.

Facilities

Three toilet blocks with facilities for babies and disabled people and most washbasins are in cabins. Laundry facilities. Shop (1/6-10/9), restaurant and bar (25/5-10/9). Heated pool with toboggan and paddling pool, plus heated indoor pool with jacuzzi (no Bermuda-style shorts in pools). Sauna, solarium and fitness room. Tennis. Minigolf. Bicycle hire. Play area, games and TV rooms. American motorhomes are not accepted. Internet access. Pets are not accepted.

Open: 25 May - 15 September.

Directions

Site is east of La Tranche-sur-Mer on D46. From D747 (La Roche-sur-Yon to La Tranche) follow signs (La Faute-sur-mer) along bypass. Take exit for La Grière and then turn east to site. GPS: N46:23.280 W001:28.69

Charges 2006

Per unit incl. 2 persons, electricity (10A)	€ 27,60
extra person	€ 5,10
child (under 5 yrs)	€ 3,60

FR85030 Camping la Loubine

1 route de la Mer, F-85340 Olonne-sur-Mer (Vendée)

Tel: **02 51 33 12 92**. Email: **camping.la.loubine@wanadoo.fr**

Situated on the edge of a forest, this campsite is just 1.8 kilometres from a sandy beach and five minutes from Les Sables d'Olonne. The 60 grass touring pitches are mostly shaded, all with 6A electricity connections and adequate water points. Only a limited number of pitches is available for large units (over 7 m.) because of difficulties with manoeuvring. It is best to confirm availability and book in advance. The focal point of the site is an excellent bar and entertainment area for karaoke and discos with a patio overlooking the splendid pool complex with its water slides. There are many chalets and mobile homes on the site, both privately owned and to rent.

Facilities

Toilet blocks are clean with British style WCs, washbasins in cubicles and controllable showers. Shop. Bar and restaurant (15/5-15/9). Indoor pool (all season). Outdoor swimming pools (15/5-15/9). Tennis. Fitness room. Minigolf. Play area. Bicycle hire. Off site: Beach 1.8 km. Fishing and boat launching 6.5 km. Golf 5 km. Riding 1 km.mile. Boat launching 4 miles. Restaurant, shop, bar within 1.5 km.

Open: 5 April - September.

Directions

Site is west of Olonne beside the D80 road. Turn towards the coast at roundabout, signed La Forêt d'Olonne and site (75 m).

Charges 2006

Per pitch incl. 2 persons	€ 15,30 - € 26,10
extra person	€ 3,20 - € 5,00
child (under 7 yrs)	€ 2,15 - € 2,85
electricity (6A)	€ 3,55

Camping La Loubine

Traditional-style facilities set in the grounds of an old farm; La Loubine is a lively site with one of the best pool complexes in the area. (2 outdoor swimming pools with 5 waterslides, 1 heated indoor pool with whirlpool bath and sauna).

Bar - Restaurant - Take Away - Shop - Tennis Court - Crazy Golf - Playground - Fitness Room - Multi Sport Pitch - Bicycle Hire - Entertainment in high season.

1, Route de la Mer - 85340 Olonne Sur mer - France
Tel.: 0033 (0)2 51 33 12 92 - Fax: 0033 (0)2 51 33 12 71

camping.la.loubine@wanadoo.fr
www.campinglaloubine.com

FR85040 Castel Camping Caravaning la Garangeoire

Saint Julien-des-Landes, F-85150 La Mothe-Achard (Vendée)

Tel: **02 51 46 65 39**. Email: **info@garangeoire.com**

La Garangeoire is a stunning campsite, situated some 15 km. inland near the village of Saint Julien-des-Landes. Set in 200 ha. of parkland surrounding the small château of La Garangeoire of which there is an outstanding view as you approach through the gates. With a spacious, relaxed atmosphere, the main camping areas are on either side of the old road which is edged with mature trees. The 360 pitches, all named after birds, are individually hedged, some with shade. They are well spaced and are especially large (most 150-200 sq.m.), most with electricity (12A) and some with water and drainage also.

Facilities

Ample, first class sanitary facilities. All have washbasins in cabins. Facilities for babies and disabled people. Laundry facilities. Motorcaravan service point. Shop. Full restaurant, takeaway and a crêperie with bars and terrace. Pool complex with water slides, fountains and a children's pool. Play field with play equipment. Games room. Tennis courts. Bicycle hire. Table tennis, crazy golf, archery and volleyball. Riding (July/Aug). Fishing and boating. Off site: Golf 10 km. Beaches 15 km.

Open: 5 April - 24 September.

Directions

Site is signed from St Julien; entrance is to the east off the D21 road, 2.5 km. north of St Julian-des-Landes. GPS: N46:39.936 W001:42.80

Charges 2006

Per unit incl. 2 persons	€ 14,00 - € 27,00
with electricity	€ 17,00 - € 33,00
with services	€ 18,50 - € 35,50
extra person	€ 4,50 - € 7,00
child (under 10 yrs)	€ 2,50 - € 3,50
Camping Cheques accepted.	

FR85080 Hotellerie de Plein Air la Puerta del Sol

Les Borderies, Chemin de Hommeaux, F-85270 St Hilaire-de-Riez (Vendée)

Tel: **02 51 49 10 10**. Email: **info@campinglapuentadepsop.com**

La Puerta del Sol is a good quality campsite a short distance away from the busy coast. It is suitable not only for families with teenage children to entertain, but also for those seeking a more peaceful and relaxing holiday. There are 216 pitches, of which 102 are used for touring units. Pitches are level with dividing hedges and many receive shade from the mature trees on the site. Each pitch is fully serviced with water, waste water point and electricity. There is one small French tour operator on site (20 pitches). A self-service restaurant and takeaway with reasonably priced food overlooks the pool and terrace. In July and August a range of activities is provided for adults and children, including a club for children, aqua-aerobics, swimming lessons, tournaments and games, with evening entertainment in the bar.

Facilities

Three heated toilet blocks have a mix of Turkish and British style WCs, washbasins in cabins and baby baths. Dishwashing and laundry facilities. Facilities for disabled visitors. Shop (1/5-31/8). Bar (1/5-15/9). Self-service restaurant and takeaway (1/5-31/8). Swimming pool, slide and paddling pool (1/5-30/9; no Bermuda style shorts). Play area. Tennis court. Bicycle hire. Volleyball, table tennis and video games. American motorhomes accepted with reservation. Off site: Beach, riding, fishing and golf 5 km. St Jean-de-Monts 7 km.

Open: 1 April - 30 September.

Directions

From Le Pissot (7 km. north of St Gilles Croix-de-Vie on D38) take D59 (Le Perrier). Site is 2 km. along this road on the right down a short side road. Site signed.

Charges 2006

Per unit incl. up to 2 persons	
and services	€ 18,50 - € 28,00
extra person	€ 5,00 - € 6,50
child (under 7 yrs)	free - € 4,50
animal	€ 3,50

FR85050 Camping le Village de Florine

La Grouinière, FR85220 Coëx (Vendée)

Tel: **02 51 60 19 51**. Email: **le-village-de-florine@wanadoo,fr**

Le Village de Florine is a pleasant new site set 13 km. from the sandy beaches at St Gilles Croix de Vie. This is a rural site with some very large, grassy pitches all of which are equipped with 10A electrical connections. The principal site buildings are converted farm buildings and lend to the rural ambience. The site boasts a limited range of amenities including a swimming pool with separate children's pool. During the peak season, activities and events are organised including themed meals and discos. The site lies 2 km. from the attractive small town of Coëx where there is a good selection of cafés, restaurants and shops. The town is also home to Les Jardins d'Olfacties and close to the châteaux of Apremont and Commequiers.

Facilities

Toilet block with special facilities for disabled visitors and for babies. Bar. Takeaway. Swimming and paddling pools. TV room. Play area. Entertainment in high season. Mobile homes for rent. Off site: Coëx 2 km. (shops, restaurants etc). Golf. Tennis. Fishing.

Open: 15 May - 30 September.

Directions

From St Gilles-Croix-de-Vie take the D6 to Coëx. Then take the D40 towards La Chaize-Giraud – the site is on the right after 2 km.

Charges 2007

Per unit incl. 2 persons	
extra person	€ 10,00 - € 18,00
child (to 13 yrs)	€ 4,00 - € 4,50
electricity (10A)	€ 3,00 - € 3,50
	€ 4,00

FR85090 Camping L'Abri des Pins

Route de Notre-Dame-de-Monts, F-85160 St Jean-de-Monts (Vendée)

Tel: **02 51 58 83 86**. Email: **contact@abridespins.com**

L'Abri des Pins is situated on the outskirts of St Jean-de-Monts and is separated from the sea and long sandy beach by a strip of pinewood. The site has 218 pitches, 78 of which are for touring units with 30 larger than average, with electricity, water and drainage. Electricity is also available for the other pitches which are around 100 sq.m, fully marked out with dividing hedges and shade. Many pitches are occupied by privately owned mobile homes, but there are no tour operators on the site. From the site, it is a pleasant 15 minute walk to the beach.

Facilities

The two sanitary blocks include washbasins in cabins, laundry and dishwashing sinks. Good small shop (1/7-31/8) and bar/restaurant provides good quality, value for money meals, both to eat in and take away. Outdoor, heated swimming pool and water slide, small pool for children, with sunbathing area (all season; no Bermuda style shorts). Children's club, petanque, aquarobics. Off site: Supermarket. Restaurants. Beach 700 m. Walking, cycling and fishing 1 km. Riding 2 km. Golf 5 km.

Open: 15 June - 16 September.

Directions

Site is 4 km. from town centre on St Jean-de-Monts - Notre Dame-de-Monts road (D38), on left heading north, just after Camping les Amiaux. GPS: N46:48.562 W02:06.540

Charges 2007

Per unit incl. 3 persons and electricity	€ 22,50 - € 33,70
extra person	€ 3,60 - € 6,10
child (under 5 yrs)	€ 2,55 - € 4,10
dog	free - € 3,50

FR85110 Camping l'Océan

Rue des Gabelous, F-85470 Brem-sur-Mer (Vendée)

Tel: **02 51 90 59 16**. Email: **contact@campingdelocean.fr**

Set amongst grapevines and fir trees, Camping L'Océan is situated between the fishing port of St Gilles-Croix-de-Ville and Brem-sur-Mer, only 600 metres (15 minutes walk) from beautiful sandy beaches and the clear Atlantic Ocean. The campsite is family managed (Helen is English) and a very warm welcome awaits at the reception area which is well stocked with local information. The touring pitches are an average of 100 sq.m. in size have 6A French style electric hook-ups (some require long leads). They are divided by hedges and centrally located with mobile homes to rent on either side.

Facilities

Three old style but very clean unisex toilet blocks have free pre-set showers, British style WCs, and washbasins in cubicles. Shop (July/Aug). Bar and restaurant (weekends only May, June, Sept). Swimming pool (heated 15/6-30/8) with slide. Indoor pool (15/4-30/9). Fitness room. Bicycle hire. Play areas (ages 2-6 yrs and 6-12yrs). Organised activities. Children's club. Off site: Brem-sur-Mer 15 minutes walk. Supermarket 5 minute drive. Fishing 1 km. Riding 9 km. Golf 15 km.

Open: 1 April - 15 October.

Directions

Take N160 from La Roche-sur-Yon towards Les Sables d'Olonne. Take exit for La Mothe-Achard and Bretignolles-sur-Mer. Follow D54 to Brem-sur-Mer then D38 Bretignolles-sur-Mer. Site is signed on left before Activity Centre.

Charges 2006

Per unit incl. 2 persons incl. electricity (6A)	€ 13,00 - € 18,00
	€ 15,60 - € 21,00
extra person	€ 3,40 - € 4,20
child (0-7 yrs)	€ 2,20 - € 2,60

FR85120 Siblu Camping le Bois Masson

149 rue des Sables, F-85160 St Jean-de-Monts (Vendée)

Tel: **02 51 58 62 62**. Email: **boismasson@siblu.fr**

Le Bois Masson is a large, lively site in the resort of St Jean-de-Monts. The long, sandy beach is a few minutes away by car. This site, popular with tour operators, offers 500 good sized pitches, all with electricity. Most are occupied by mobile homes. Pitches are of sandy grass, mostly separated by hedges, with trees providing some shade. There are some pitches with water and drainage and an area kept for those who prefer a quieter pitch. A very busy site in high season, not for those seeking somewhere quiet. Plenty to do for those perhaps with older children.

Facilities

Four sanitary blocks provide modern showers with mixer taps, washbasins in cabins and British style WCs. Facilities for disabled visitors and babies. Dishwashers. Laundry. Comprehensive amenities include a good supermarket, a large, lively bar with entertainment room above, a restaurant and a crêperie. Tennis. Bicycle hire. Off site: Riding, golf, squash, watersports.

Open: 19 March - 23 September.

Directions

From roundabout at southeast end of St Jean de Monts bypass, turn into town following signs to 'Centre Ville' and site, which is on right after 400 m.

Charges guide

Per unit incl. 2 persons and electricity	€ 13,00 - € 34,00

Check real time availability and at-the-gate prices...

www.**alanrogers**.com

FR85150 Camping la Yole

Mobile homes ▶ page 463

Chemin des Bosses, Orouet, F-85160 St Jean-de-Monts (Vendée)

Tel: **02 51 58 67 17**. Email: **contact@la-yole.com**

La Yole is an attractive and well run site, 2 kilometres from a sandy beach. It offers 278 pitches, the majority of which are occupied by tour operators and mobile homes to rent. There are 100 touring pitches, most with shade and separated by bushes and trees. A newer area at the rear of the site is more open. All the pitches are of at least 100 sq.m. and have electricity (10A), water and drainage. The pool complex includes an outdoor pool, a paddling pool, slide and an indoor heated pool with jacuzzi. Entertainment is organised in high season.

Facilities

Two toilet blocks include washbasins in cabins and facilities for disabled people and babies. A third block has a baby room. Laundry facilities. Shop. Bar, restaurant and takeaway (18/5-10/9). Outdoor pool and paddling pool. Indoor heated pool with jacuzzi. Play area. Ball games. Club room. Tennis. Table tennis, pool and video games. Entertainment in high season. Gas barbecues only. Off site: Beach, bus service, bicycle hire 2 km. Riding 3 km. Fishing, golf and watersports 6 km.

Open: 2 April - 28 September.

Directions

Signed off the D38, 6 km. south of St Jean de Monts in the village of Orouet.
GPS: N46:45.383 W02:00.466

Charges 2007

Per unit incl. 2 persons, electricity	€ 16,00 - € 29,00
extra person	€ 3,70 - € 6,00
child (2-9 yrs)	€ 2,15 - € 4,50
baby (0-2 yrs)	free - € 3,30
dog	€ 4,00 - € 5,00

Camping Cheques accepted.

Camping La Yole ★★★★

Wake up to the sound of birdsong in a wooded park of 17 acres with four star comfort. Space, security, informal atmosphere: la yole, tucked away between fields and pine trees, only 2 km from the beach.

– Chemin des Bosses - Orouet - F 85160 Saint Jean de Monts –
– Tel: 0033 251 58 67 17 - Fax: 0033 251 59 05 35 –
– contact@la-yole.com / www.la-yole.com –

FR85130 Camping Pong

Rue du Stade, F-85220 Landevieille (Vendée)

Tel: **02 51 22 92 63**. Email: **info@lepong.com**

A comfortable family run site, in a rural situation 12 km. southeast of St Gilles-Croix-de-Vie, and 5 km. from the coast at Brétignolles. It has 229 pitches with 187 used for touring units, the remainder for mobile homes and chalets. All have electricity connections (4/6A) and are of a good size. The bar, restaurant, function room, games room, gym and shop have all recently been rebuilt. The original part of the site around the small, lightly fenced fishing lake (there are warning signs) has mature trees, whereas, in the newer areas trees and shrubs are developing well.

Facilities

Four modern, unisex sanitary blocks provide toilets of mixed styles and some washbasins in cabins. Facilities for disabled people, baby room, dishwashing and laundry room. Shop, takeaway, bar and restaurant (15/6-15/9). Swimming pools including heated pool with jacuzzi, toboggan and paddling pool (from 15/5). Gym, TV lounge and games room. Bicycle hire. Fishing. Fenced play area and children's club. Off site: Tennis 200 m. Lac du Jaunay 2.5 km. Beach, golf, riding 5 km.

Open: 1 April - 19 September.

Directions

Site is on the edge of Landevieille and is signed from the D32 (Challans-Les Sables d'Olonne) and D12 (La Mothe Achard-St Gilles Croix de Vie).

Charges 2006

Per unit incl. 2 persons	€ 12,00 - € 19,00
extra person	€ 3,00 - € 4,80
child (under 5 yrs)	€ 2,25 - € 3,50
electricity 4-6A	€ 3,00 - € 4,00
water and drainage	€ 1,50

FR85140 Camping Naturiste le Colombier

'Le Colombier', F-85210 St Martin-Lars-en-St Hermine (Vendée)

Tel: **02 51 27 83 84**. Email: **lecolombier.nat@wanadoo.fr**

A countryside site for naturists near La Roche sur Yon, just right for those seeking a peaceful holiday. It provides around 160 pitches in seven very natural fields on different levels linked by informal tracks. There are level, terraced areas for caravans and a feeling of spaciousness with pitches around the edges of fields, unmarked and with electricity (6/10A, some may require long leads). The bar/restaurant is in a converted barn. The site's 125 acres provide many walks throughout the attractive, wooded valley and around the lake.

Facilities

Fully equipped toilet blocks are good, providing some showers in cubicles. Dishwashing sinks. Motorcaravan service point. Grocer/baker calls daily. Bar/restaurant with à la carte and full menu (order before 1 pm), home baked bread and pizzas. Heated swimming pool. Fishing. Volleyball. Boules Playground. Pony and trap rides and one day a week children can make their own bread. Plans for a sauna and aquagym. Off site: Shop 1 km.

Open: 1 April - 30 October.

Directions

From N148, La Roche sur Yon - Niort road, at St Hermine, turn onto D8 eastward for 4 km. Turn left on D10 to St Martin-Lars. Site is signed. GPS: N46:35.859 W001:58.16

Charges 2006

Per unit incl. 2 persons	
and electricity	€ 18,50 - € 21,50
child (3-9 yrs)	€ 3,40 - € 3,50
child (10-16 yrs)	€ 4,70 - € 4,80

FR85200 Camping la Petite Boulogne

12 rue du Stade, F-85670 St Etienne-du-Bois (Vendée)

Tel: **02 51 34 54 51**. Email: **la.petite.boulogne@wanadoo.fr**

Set in countryside 24 km. northwest of La Roche sur Yon, St Etienne-du-Bois is a quiet village, well away from the big Vendée resorts. This delightful campsite, owned by the local council, has 40 grassy pitches (most slightly sloping), all with electricity, water and drainage. Pitches are marked by low hedges giving the site an open and sunny aspect. Although inland, it is only 20 km. to the coast with its large sandy beaches. There are also many places to visit inland in the Vendée, and this excellent value municipal site provides a great base for exploring the whole region.

Facilities

The modern, heated toilet block includes some washbasins in cabins. Laundry and dishwashing facilities. Room for disabled people with toilet and shower. Reception sells a few essentials. Small unheated pool (June - Aug). TV room. Table tennis. Small play area. Two free tennis courts. Bicycle hire. Daily events listed and occasional animation in high season. Off site: Outside, heated pool. Bar and restaurant. Fishing. Sports centre 300 m. Supermarket 8 km. Beach 30 km.

Open: 1 April - 30 September.

Directions

From Legé take D978 south (Palluau) for 7 km. Turn left on D94 (St Etienne-du-Bois). Go through village and, out the other side, cross bridge over river. Site is 50 m. further, on right.

Charges 2006

Per unit incl. 2 persons	€ 12,25
extra person	€ 3,05
child (under 7 yrs)	€ 2,05
No credit cards.	

FR85210 Camping les Ecureuils

Mobile homes ▶ page 463

Route des Goffineaux, F-85520 Jard-sur-Mer (Vendée)
Tel: **02 51 33 42 74**. Email: **camping-ecureuils@wanadoo.fr**

Les Ecureuils is a wooded site in a quieter part of the southern Vendée. It is undoubtedly one of the prettiest sites on this stretch of coast, with an elegant reception area, attractive vegetation and large pitches separated by low hedges with plenty of shade. Of the 261 pitches, some 128 are for touring units, each with water and drainage, as well as easy access to 10A electricity. This site is very popular with tour operators (103 pitches). Jard is rated among the most pleasant and least hectic of Vendée towns. The harbour is home to some fishing boats and rather more pleasure craft, and has a public slipway for those bringing their own boats.

Facilities

Two toilet blocks, well equipped and kept very clean, include baby baths, and laundry rooms. Small shop (bread baked on site). New snack-bar. Takeaway service (pre-order 1/6-15/9). Snacks and ice-creams available from the friendly bar. Good sized L-shaped swimming pool and separate paddling pool (30/5-15/9). Indoor pool and fitness centre (all season). Two play areas for different age groups. Modern play area. Minigolf, table tennis and a pool table. Club for children (5-10 yrs) daily in July/Aug. Bicycle hire. Only gas barbecues are allowed. Dogs are not accepted. Internet access. Off site: Beach, fishing 400 m. Marina and town.

Open: 1 April - 30 September.

Directions

Jard-sur-Mer is on D21 between Talmont St Hilaire and Longeville sur Mer. Site is signed from main road – caravanners follow signs to avoid tight bends and narrow roads. GPS: N46:24.683 W01:35.382

Charges 2006

Per person	€ 5,00 - € 6,50
child (0-4 yrs)	€ 1,50 - € 2,00
child (5-9 yrs)	€ 4,00 - € 4,50
pitch with water and drainage	€ 13,00 - € 15,50

Less 10% outside 30/6-1/9.

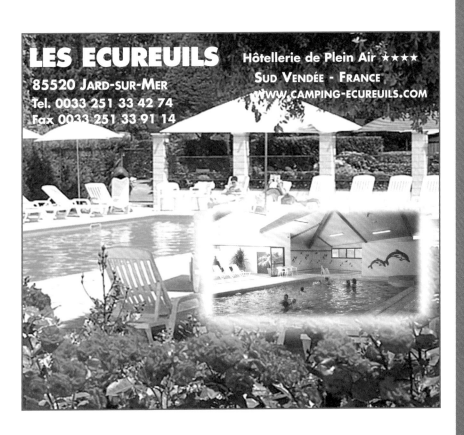

FR85220 Camping Acapulco

Avenue des Epines, F-85160 St Jean-de-Monts (Vendée)

Tel: **02 51 59 20 64**. Email: **info@sunmarina.com**

Ideal for family beach holidays, this friendly site is situated mid-way between St Jean-de-Monts and St Hilaire-de-Riez, and is 600 m. from the beach. It is one of four sites on the Vendée coast owned by the Sunmarina group. Most of the pitches here are taken by mobile homes, leaving about 20 for touring. All are about 100 sq.m. on grass and divided by hedges which give some shade. The central part of the site has an excellent pool complex complete with five slides, a children's pool and a terrace for sunbathing. Adjacent to this is a spacious bar, restaurant and a safe play area.

Facilities

Two sanitary blocks are clean and include washbasins in cabins and showers. Facilities for disabled visitors. Laundry facilities. Motorcaravan service point. Shop with basic supplies. Bar, restaurant and takeaway. Large heated pool complex with five water slides and paddling pool. Play area. Entertainment in high season. Off site: Shopping centre 400 m. Sancy beach 600 m.

Open: 15 May - 15 September.

Directions

Follow the coastal road of St Jean de Monts south towards St Hilaire-de-Riez. Just past signs of Commune St Hilaire, turn left at first roundabout. Site is 400 m. on right (signed).

Charges 2006

Per unit incl. 3 persons and electricity	€ 30,00
extra person	€ 9,00
child (under 5 yrs)	€ 5,00

FR85230 Camping les Ecureuils

100 avenue de la Pège, F-85270 St Hilaire-de-Riez (Vendée)

Tel: **02 51 54 33 71**. Email: **info@camping-aux-ecureuils.com**

Of the seaside sites on the Vendée, Les Ecureuils has to be one of the best, run by a friendly and most helpful family. Just 300 m. from a superb beach, the site is ideally situated for exploring from Les Sables d'Olonne to Noirmoutier. Developed on what was originally a farm, there are 230 pitches (55 for touring units). On sandy grass, all have electricity (6A, Euro adaptors avalable), water and drainage. Well kept hedges and mature trees give shade and privacy, although some more open pitches are also available for sun lovers. The site is popular with British tour operators (60%).

Facilities

The two main sanitary blocks are spacious, and include some washbasins in cubicles, and facilities for babies and disabled people. Laundry and dishwashing facilities. Small shop (25/5-6/9). Restaurant. Large, airy bar with screened terrace. Pool complex including pool for small children with its own 'mini aqua park', large heated pool, and water slide with separate splash pool. New indoor pool, paddling pool and jacuzzi. Off site: Bicycle hire 200 m. Fishing 4 km. Riding 5 km. Golf 6 km.

Open: 1 May - 15 September.

Directions

Driving south D38 (St Jean-de-Monts - St Gilles), turn right at L'Oasis hotel/restaurant in Orouet (6 km. outside St Jean-de-Monts), signed Les Mouettes. After 1.5 km. at roundabout turn left (St Hilaire-de-Riez). Site is 500 m. on left.
GPS: N46:44.167 W001:00.57

Charges 2006

Per unit incl. 2 persons and 3 services	€ 24,50 - € 32,70
extra person	€ 4,60 - € 5,65
child (under 5 yrs)	€ 2,75 - € 3,60

FR85260 Village de la Guyonnière

La Guyonnière, F-85150 St Julien-des-Landes (Vendée)

Tel: **02 51 46 62 59**. Email: **info@laguyonniere.com**

La Guyonnière is a spacious, rural site. It is Dutch owned but English is spoken and all visitors are made very welcome. It is a farm type site with seven different fields, each being reasonably level and each having a toilet block. The 183 pitches have a mix of sun and shade. They are very large (a few smaller ones) and are separated by a tree and a few bushes. All have access to electricity connections. Bar and restaurant facilities are housed in the original farm buildings attractively converted. Entertainment is provided in the bar on high season evenings. A perfect place for families, with large play areas on sand and grass, and paddling pond with shower. Being in the country, it is a haven for cyclists and walkers, with many signed routes from the site. A pleasant 500 m. walk takes you to the Jaunay Lake where fishing is possible (permits from the village), canoeing (lifejackets from reception) and pedaloes to hire. There are no tour operators and, needless to say, no road noise. It is popular for many reasons, the main ones being the free and easy atmosphere and its reasonable pricing.

Facilities

Modern toilet blocks. Most cubicles are quite small. Washbasins are in cubicles. Limited provision for babies and disabled visitors. Dishwashing and laundry sinks. Shop (1/5-15/9). Bar with TV and pool table. Restaurant (1/5-15/9). Pizzeria with takeaway. Small pool and heated pool with jacuzzi and slide. Paddling pool. Play areas, sand pit. Volleyball, tennis and football fields. Bicycle hire. Car wash. Off site: Riding 3 km. Golf 8 km. Beaches 10 km.

Open: 1 May - 30 October.

Directions

Site is off the D12 road (La Mothe Achard - St Gilles-Croix de Vie), approx. 4 km. west of St Julien-des-Landes. It is signed about 1 km. from the main road.

Charges 2007

Per unit incl. 2 persons	
and electricity	€ 11,00 - € 29,40
extra person	€ 4,40 - € 5,40
child (3-9 yrs)	€ 2,80 - € 3,30
animal	€ 2,90

Less 10-20% outside high season.

FR85270 Chadotel Camping L'Oceano d'Or

58 rue Georges Clémenceau, B.P. 12, F-85520 Jard-sur-Mer (Vendée)

Tel: **02 51 33 05 05**. Email: **chadotel@wanadoo.fr**

This site should appeal to families with children of all ages. It is very lively in high season but appears to be well managed, with a full programme of activities (it can therefore be noisy, sometimes late at night). The site is only 999 metres from the excellent beach. There are 430 flat, grass and sand pitches of which 40% are occupied by tour operators and mobile homes. The 260 for touring units, all with 6A electricity, are quite large (about 100 sq.m). Some are separated by high hedges, others are more open with low bushes between them.

Facilities

Four modern, unisex toilet blocks include washbasins all in cabins. Dishwashing and facilities. Shop (1/6-10/9). Bar and snack bar (1/6-10/9, but limited hours outside high season). Swimming pool (15/5-15/9) with slides, 2 waterfalls and children's pool. Walled (three sides) play area. Tennis, petanque and minigolf. Electric barbecues are not allowed. Internet access. Off site: Excellent beach within walking distance. Golf, riding, karting within 15 km.

Open: 7 April - 23 September.

Directions

Site is on the D21 Talmont St Hilaire - Longeville, just east of the turning to the town centre.

Charges 2007

Per pitch incl. 2 persons	€ 14,50 - € 24,20
with electricity	€ 19,20 - € 28,90
extra person	€ 5,80
child (under 2 yrs)	€ 3,80
animal	€ 3,00

FR85280 Camping les Places Dorées

Route de Notre-Dame-de-Monts, F-85160 St Jean-de-Monts (Vendée)

Tel: **02 51 59 02 93**. Email: **abridespins@aol.com**

Les Places Dorées is owned by the same family as L'Abri des Pins (FR85090) which is just across the road. It is a much newer site with maturing trees gradually beginning to offer some shade. There are 245 grassy pitches, the quietest being towards the back of the site. Each one is separated, all have electrical connections (6A) and some are also equipped with water and drainage. One small Dutch tour operator is on site (22 pitches). In low season the site is quiet but it can be noisy in high season with the bar and disco closing late.

Facilities

Three modern toilet blocks include washbasins in cubicles. Facilities for disabled visitors. Laundry and dishwashing facilities. Pool complex with slides, jacuzzi area and waterfall (no Bermuda style shorts). Entertainment and children's club at L'Abri des Pins (high season), also adult activities (petanque, aqua aerobics). Facilities at L'Abri des Pins may be used - shop (July/Aug), tennis, fitness room, swimming pools and a games room. Off site: Fishing 500 m. Beach 700 m. Riding 2 km. Golf 5 km.

Open: 1 June - 1 September.

Directions

Site is 4 km. north of St Jean-de-Monts on the D38 St Jean-de-Monts - Notre Dames-de-Monts road on the right hand side, almost opposite L'Abri des Pins. GPS: N46:48.690 W02:06.685

Charges 2006

Per pitch incl. 3 persons and electricity	€ 22,00 - € 33,00
extra person	€ 3,50 - € 6,00
child	€ 2,50 - € 4,00

FR85300 Camping la Grand' Métairie

8 rue de la Vineuse en Plaine, F-85440 St Hilaire-la-Forêt (Vendée)

Tel: **02 51 33 32 38**. Email: **grand-metairie@wanadoo.fr**

Just five kilometres from the super sandy beach at Jard-sur-Mer, La Grand' Métairie offers many of the amenities of its seaside counterparts, but with the important advantage of being on the edge of a delightful, sleepy village, otherwise untouched by tourism. It is a busy well run site with a programme of lively entertainment in high season. The site has 180 pitches (69 touring pitches), all with electricity, water and drainage. The pitches as yet have little shade but are all separated by small trees and bushes and are reasonable in size.

Facilities

Two modern toilet blocks are very clean and include washbasins mainly in cabins. Units for disabled people. Washing machines and dryers. Fridge hire. Basic provisions on site, with useful village store just 100 m. Smart bar/restaurant (all 1/5-10/9). Attractive, heated pool, indoor pool, jacuzzi and paddling pool. Tennis, minigolf (both free in low season). Visiting hairdressing salon. Internet access. Not suitable for American motorhomes. Off site: Riding and fishing within 5 km.

Open: 1 April - 30 September.

Directions

From Les Sables d'Olonne take D949 (La Rochelle) towards Talmont St Hilaire and Luçon; 7 km. after Talmont turn right on D70 to St Hilaire-la-Forêt. Site is on left before village centre. GPS: N46:26.907 W01:31.580

Charges 2006

Per unit incl. 2 persons and electricity (6A)	€ 16,00 - € 26,00
extra person	€ 5,00 - € 8,00
child (2-5 yrs)	€ 3,00 - € 4,00

FR85310 Chadotel Camping la Trévillière

Rue de Bellevue, F-85470 Bretignolles-sur-Mer (Vendée)

Tel: **02 51 33 05 05**. Email: **chadotel@wanadoo.fr**

A member of the Chadotel group, La Trévillière has a pleasant semi-rural setting on the edge of the little resort town of Bretignolles. After an extension, there are now 203 pitches, all with easy access to electricity and water. The original area provides either level or slightly sloping pitches separated by hedges or low bushes either with shade or more open. The new area has no shade as yet. The site has around 50 mobile homes and chalets and is used by three small tour operators, but it remains very much a camping and caravanning site.

Facilities

Three modern, clean toilet blocks include washbasins in cubicles, a unit for disabled people and baby room with bath, shower and toilet. Washing machines and dryers. Bar (limited opening in low season). Small shop and snack bar with takeaway (20/6-8/9). New restaurant. Heated outdoor pool (15/5-15/9) with slide and paddling pool. Play area. Minigolf. No charcoal barbecues. Off site: Beach 2 km. Fishing 3 km. Riding 5 km. Golf 10 km.

Open: April - 23 September.

Directions

From north, after St Gilles go through Bretignolles-La Sauzaie (left fork) and before reaching Bretignolles turn left on sharp right bend, towards water tower. Site on right in 800 m. From south, after Bretignolles, turn right ('Ecoles'), then left. Site to left after stadium.

Charges 2007

Per unit incl. 2 persons	€ 14,50 - € 24,20
with electricity	€ 19,20 - € 28,90
extra person	€ 5,80

FR85320 Camping Caravaning Val de Vie

Rue du Stade, F-85190 Maché (Vendée)

Tel: **02 51 60 21 02**. Email: **campingvaldevie@aol.com**

Opened in 1999, Val de Vie is a small, good quality site run with enthusiasm and dedication by its English owners on the outskirts of a rural village back from the coast. There are 52 original pitches for touring units (42 with electricity; 4, 6 or 10A) that vary in size from 80-137 sq.m. on mostly level grass with newly planted hedging. There should now also be 12 new touring pitches (including 9 'super pitches' which must be booked for high season). The ground can become very hard so steel pegs are advised.

Facilities

The toilet block provides excellent, modern facilities including some washbasins in cabins, baby bath, facilities for disabled people, dishwashing and laundry facilities. Reception also offers wine, beer, soft drinks and ice cream. Small play area. Heated swimming pool (from mid May). Bicycle hire. Not suitable for American motorhomes. Off site: Tennis courts, shops, bar, tabac within walking distance. Lake d'Apremont (300 m). Apremont itself with Renaissance château 4 km. Vendée coast 20 km.

Open: 1 May - 30 September.

Directions

From La Roche sur Yon take D948 northwest. At end of Aizenay bypass continue for 2 km; cross River Vie and take next left (D40). Site signed in village. GPS: N46:45.180 W01:41.370

Charges 2007

Per unit incl. 2 persons	€ 18,00 - € 28,00
extra person	€ 4,25
child (under 10 yrs)	€ 3,20
electricity (4-10A)	€ 2,90 - € 3,50

FR85330 Camping Naturiste Cap Natur'

Mobile homes ▶ page 463

151 avenue de la Faye, F-85270 St Hilaire-de-Riez (Vendée)

Tel: **02 51 60 11 66**. Email: **info@cap-natur.com**

Situated on the northern outskirts of St Hilaire-de-Riez, this family campsite for naturists is in an area of undulating sand dunes and pine trees. The 140 touring pitches nestle among the dunes and trees and offer a wide choice to suit most tastes, including the possibility of electrical connections (10A), although in some cases long leads are needed. Despite the undulating terrain, some pitches are quite level and thus suitable for motorcaravans. The whole of the indoor complex is a designated non-smoking area. A number of apartments, tents and mobile homes are on site.

Facilities

Basic, but clean sanitary facilities, two indoor (heated) and one outdoor (roofed) block. Open plan hot showers, British style WCs, washbasins, baby baths and children's toilets. Shop (with takeaway pizzas) and restaurant, bar, with TV, indoor table games. Indoor and outdoor pools. Fitness classes (high season). Massage room. Play area. Volleyball. Torches useful. Bicycle hire. Not suitable for American motorhomes. Off site: Beach 2 km. Fishing 5 km. Naturist beach 6 km. Golf, riding 10 km.

Open: 1 April - 1 November.

Directions

From Le Pissot roundabout go south on D38, for St Hilaire. At roundabout (first exit), next roundabout turn right ('Les Plages'). At third Y-shaped junction turn right ('Parée Prèneau'). Site is 2 km. on left.

Charges 2006

Per unit incl. 2 persons	€ 14,80 - € 28,10
extra person	€ 2,60 - € 6,80
child (under 13 yrs)	€ 1,60 - € 5,10
electricity (10A)	€ 4,20

Camping Cheques accepted.

Check real time availability and at-the-gate prices...

www.alanrogers.com

FR85350 Camping Caravaning la Ningle

Chemin des Roselières 66, F-85270 St Hilaire-de-Riez (Vendée)

Tel: **02 51 54 07 11**. Email: **campingdelaningle@wanadoo.fr**

At Camping La Ningle you are guaranteed to receive a warm welcome from M. et Mme. Guibert, who have established a very pleasant campsite with a friendly, family atmosphere. There are 155 pitches, 80 available for touring units. All have electricity (6A) and a limited number are fully serviced (electricity, water and drainage). Pitches are spacious with dividing hedges and all have some shade. The nearest beach is a 500 m. walk through a pine forest, but there are also three small swimming pools on site. This site is well situated to explore the beautiful port of St Gilles-Croix-de-Vie, with its abundance of restaurants (where seafood is served direct from the morning's catch) and pedestrianised shopping area with a variety of individual boutiques.

Facilities

Two clean toilet blocks include some washbasins in cubicles. Toilet/shower room for disabled people and large family shower room. Laundry and dishwashing facilities. Bread (July/Aug). Takeaway three evenings per week. Bar (July/Aug). Main swimming pool, larger children's pool, paddling pool and slide. Fitness suite. Tennis court. Games field. Volleyball. Table tennis. Games room. Fishing lake. Children's activities (July/Aug), and regular petanque and tennis competitions. Off site: Small supermarket and takeaway 200 m.

Open: 20 May - 10 September.

Directions

Driving south on D38 (St Jean-de-Monts - St Gilles), turn right at L'Oasis hotel/restaurant in Orouet, signed Les Mouettes. After 1.5 km. at roundabout, turn left (St Hilaire-de-Riez). Pass two campsites, then next left, signed La Ningle.

Charges 2006

Per pitch incl. 2 persons	€ 14,80 - € 21,30
with 6A electricity	€ 17,10 - € 24,40
with 10A electricity	€ 19,50 - € 27,00
extra person	€ 3,10 - € 4,40
child (under 7 yrs)	€ 1,60 - € 2,75

No credit cards.

Camping la Ningle

Campsites for families in the heart of nature, at 500 m distance from beaches.
July-august: Animations in the evenings and animations for children.
2 heated swimming pools, 1 paddling pool, Tennis court and bar.
Mobile homes for rent with or without terrace.
All kinds of shops near the campsite.

Chemin des Roselières 66 - F-85270 St. Hilaire-de-Riez - France
Tel : +33 (0)2 51 54 07 11 - Fax : +33 (0)2 51 54 99 39
campingdelanigle@wanadoo.fr

FR85360 Camping la Forêt

190 chemin de la Rive, F-85160 St Jean-de-Monts (Vendée)

Tel: **02 51 58 84 63**. Email: **camping-la-foret@wanadoo.fr**

Camping La Forêt is owned by M. and Mme. Jolivet and they work hard to provide a small, quality site. Well run and attractive, with a friendly, family atmosphere, it provides just 63 pitches with 50 for touring units. Of 100 sq.m. in size, the pitches are surrounded by mature hedges and have water and electricity. Over 50 species of trees are planted, providing shade to every pitch. There is one tour operator on site (13 pitches), but their presence is not intrusive and the site has a quiet and relaxed atmosphere, ideal for couples or families with young children.

Facilities

The central toilet block includes washbasins in cubicles. Laundry and dishwashing facilities. Baby bath. Facilities for disabled people. Motorcaravan waste tanks can be emptied on request. Basic provisions sold in reception, including fresh bread. Takeaway. Small heated swimming pool (15/5-15/9). Play area. Table tennis. Bicycle hire. Only gas and electric barbecues allowed, communal barbecue in centre of site. Not suitable for American motorhomes. Off site: Beach 400 m. Network of cycle paths through the forest and local marshland.

Open: 15 May - 28 September.

Directions

Follow D38 out of St Jean de Monts, towards Notre Dame de Monts. After 5.5 km. turn left at sign for site and 'Plage de Pont d'Yeu'. Follow road and site is on left in about 100 m.

Charges 2006

Per pitch incl. 2 persons	€ 16,00 - € 26,00
extra person	€ 3,00 - € 5,00
child (under 7 yrs)	€ 3,50
electricity (6A)	€ 3,80

No credit cards.

FR85390 Camping des Batardières

F-85440 St Hilaire-la-Foret (Vendée)

Tel: **02 51 33 33 85**

Camping des Batardières is a haven of tranquillity on the edge of an unspoilt village, yet just 5 km. from the sea. It is an attractive, unsophisticated little site, lovingly maintained by its owners for the past 23 years. Many visitors return year after year. There are 75 good-sized pitches (a few up to 130 sq.m.) and all are available for touring units (there are no mobile homes and no tour operators!) All have access to water and electricity (6A, or 2A for tents). Otherwise there are few facilities on site.

Facilities

The sanitary block is kept very clean and visitors are encouraged to keep it that way (no shoes in the shower cubicles, for instance). Some washbasins in cubicles for ladies. Dishwashing and laundry facilities, including washing machine and dryer. TV room. Table tennis. Tennis court. Play area and field for games, kite-flying etc. Not suitable for American motorhomes. Off site: Village shop and bar 200 m. Jard-sur-Mer 5 km.

Open: 27 June - 2 September.

Directions

From Les Sables d'Olonne take D949 (la Rochelle) towards Talmont St Hilaire and Luçon. 7 km. after Talmont turn right on D70 to St Hilaire-la-Forêt. Site signed to the right approaching village.

Charges 2007

Per unit incl. 2 persons	€ 20,00
electricity	€ 3,50

FR85400 Camping Bois Soleil

Chemin des Barres, F-85340 Olonne-sur-Mer (Vendée)

Tel: **02 51 33 11 97**. Email: **camping.boissoleil@wanadoo.fr**

A traditionally laid out site with 199 marked pitches, separated by hedges, on flat or gently sloping ground. There are just two tour operators and a scattering of mobile homes and chalets, leaving some 87 pitches for tourers and tents. All have electricity (6A, French style sockets) and water points adjacent and many also have waste water pipes. The main buildings house a small reception and tourist information room as well as the bar and attached shop. There is an excellent swimming pool complex with slides and an impressive flume, plus an indoor pool.

Facilities

The two toilet blocks have hot water, mainly British style toilets, with washbasins in cubicles in new block. Locked overnight, but basic toilet facilities provided. Dishwashing and laundry facilities. Shop (July/Aug) – 'eat in'/takeaway service; bread to order. Bar (28/6-31/8). Indoor and outdoor pools. Play area, trampoline and table tennis. Bicycle hire. Barbecues are not permitted. Off site: Bus service in Olonne sur Mer. Riding 400 m. Fishing and golf 3 km. Beaches 2.5 km. Les Sables d'Olonne is 5 km.

Open: 5 April - 28 September.

Directions

Site is off D80 coast road between Olonne-sur-Mer and Brem-sur-Mer, clearly signed on the inland side.

Charges guide

Per unit incl. 2 persons	€ 15,00 - € 21,50
with electricity	€ 18,00 - € 24,50
extra person	€ 2,60 - € 3,70
child (under 7 yrs)	€ 2,10 - € 2,70
animal	€ 2,60

FR85420 Camping 'Bel

Rue du Bottereau, F-85360 La Tranche-sur-Mer (Vendée)

Tel: **02 51 30 47 39**. Email: **campbel@wanadoo.fr**

Camping Bel's owner, M. Guicau, takes an individual approach. The first priority is the contentment of the children, who receive various small gifts during their stay. A popular site with a large proportion of French clients, despite the large presence of British tour operators (130 pitches). The 85 touring pitches are on level, sandy grass. and separated by hedges with some trees giving shade. All pitches have electrical connections (6/10A). Being just 150 m. from a sandy beach this is a good site for a family beach holiday. La Tranche with all amenities is within walking distance.

Facilities

Two modern toilet blocks have washbasins in cabins, very good baby units and facilities for disabled visitors. Shop with basic provisions. Bar. Heated outdoor pool with jacuzzi. Plenty of entertainment for children aged 6-14 yrs (July/Aug). Table tennis. Fitness area. Tennis and badminton. Pets are not accepted. Not suitable for American motorhomes or twin axle caravans. Off site: Bicycle hire 100 m. Supermarket with fuel 200 m. Fishing 150 m. Watersports 150 m. Riding 5 km.

Open: 26 May - 2 September with all services.

Directions

Follow signs from roundabout on La Tranche bypass, near 'Super U' supermarket onto avenue General de Gaulle. Left after 50 m. onto rue du bottereau. Site on right after 100 m.

Charges 2007

Per unit with 2 persons and water	€ 22,00
with electricity (6A)	€ 26,00
extra person	€ 6,00
child (under 5 yrs)	€ 4,00

FR85440 Camping les Brunelles

Le Bouil, F-85560 Longeville-sur-Mer (Vendée)

Tel: **02 51 33 50 75**. Email: **camping@les-brunelles.com**

This is a well managed site with good facilities and a varied programme of high season entertainment for all the family. A busy site in high season, there are plenty of activities to keep chidren happy and occupied. For 2007 La Brunelles will be combined with an adjacent campsite to provide 600 pitches. Many of the new touring pitches will be with water, electricity and waste, and will be in excess of 100 sq.m. to allow easier access for larger units. On the original La Brunelles site, the touring pitches are all level on sandy grass and separated by hedges, away from most of the mobile homes.

Facilities

Four old, but well maintained and modernised toilet blocks have British and Turkish style toilets and washbasins, both open style and in cabins. Laundry facilities. Shop (enlarged for 2007). Takeaway and large modern, airy bar. Covered pool with jacuzzi (all season). Outdoor pool with slides and paddling pools (1/5-30/9). Tennis. Bicycle hire. Off site: Golf and riding within 15 km. Good supervised sandy beach 900 m. St Vincent-sur-Jard (2 km).

Open: 1 May - 29 September.

Directions

From D21 (Talmont - Longueville), between St Vincent and Longueville, site signed south from main road towards coast. Turn left in Le Bouil. Site is 800 m. on left. GPS: N46:24.798 W01:31.388

Charges 2006

Per unit incl. 2 persons	€ 15,00 - € 28,00
with electricity	€ 18,00 - € 33,00
extra person	€ 5,00
child (under 5 yrs)	free - € 5,00

Camping Cheques accepted.

FR85480 Camping Caravaning le Chaponnet

Mobile homes ▶ page 466

Rue du Chaponnet N16, F-85470 Brem sur Mer (Vendée)

Tel: **02 51 90 55 56**. Email: **campingchaponnet@wanadoo.fr**

This well established family run site is within five minutes walk of Brem village and 1.5 km. from a sandy beach. The 80 touring pitches are level with varying amounts of grass, some with shade from mature trees. Pitches are separated by tall hedges and serviced by tarmac or gravel roads and have frequent water and electricity points (long leads may be required). Tour operators have mobile homes and tents on 70 pitches and there are 55 privately owned mobile homes and chalets. The swimming pool complex also has a jacuzzi, slides and a children's pool, together with a sauna and fitness centre. It is overlooked by the spacious bar and snack bar. Entertainment is provided for all ages and three or four musical evenings a week provide family fun rather than teenage activities.

Facilities

The six sanitary blocks are well maintained with washbasins in cubicles, some showers and basins have controllable water temperature. Facilities for babies and disabled people. Laundry facilities. Bar (15/5-6/9), snack bar and takeaway (1/6-30/9). No shop but bread and croissants available. Indoor (heated) and outdoor pools. Play area with space for ball games. Table tennis, tennis and bicycle hire. Indoor games room. Off site: Shops and restaurants. Beach 1.5 km. Fishing 5 km. Golf 12 km. Riding 10 km.

Open: 1 May - 15 September.

Directions

Brem is on the D38 St Gilles - Les Sables d'Olonne road. Site is clearly signed, just off the one-way system in centre of village.

Charges 2006

Per unit incl. 3 persons	€ 17,70 - € 27,20
with electricity	€ 21,60 - € 30,90
extra person	€ 3,90 - € 5,00
child (under 5 yrs)	€ 2,40 - € 3,40
dog	€ 2,00

FR85510 Camping le Bois Joli

2 rue de Châteauneuf, F-85710 Bois de Céné (Vendée)

Tel: **02 51 68 20 05**. Email: **campingboisjoli@free.fr**

A warm welcome is given by the English speaking Malard family, who make every effort to make your stay enjoyable. On site is a small lake with fishing and a large sports field (with a portacabin style toilet block). The site also has a small swimming pool and paddling pool. The bar has been extended and includes a dancing area. There are 130 pitches of which 90 are for touring units. All pitches have 6A electricity, although not every pitch is serviced with water. An extra 60 pitches and a new toilet block are planned. A local farmer visits the site three times a week offering local produce. This site is a hidden gem in a small village away from the hustle and bustle of the seaside resorts. Suitable for people looking for a quiet holiday, it is still within driving distance of the Vendée coast (20 km).

Facilities

Three toilet blocks – old, but with modern, bright tiles and very clean. All are unisex with some washbasins in cubicles, some controllable showers, two baby baths, two washing machines, dishwashing and laundry sinks. Bar with evening entertainment. Takeaway (1/7-31/8). Children's activities. Good play area with swings. Table tennis. Tennis court. Volleyball. Petanque. Bicycle hire. Off site: Supermarket and bus service in village (two minutes walk). Walking, cycling and canoeing. Riding 5 km. Beach 18 km.

Open: 1 April - 25 September.

Directions

From Challans take D58 direct to Bois de Céné (10 km). Turn left at first road junction and site is immediately on right.

Charges 2006

Per pitch incl. 2 persons	€ 10,30 - € 14,10
with electricity (6A)	€ 12,60 - € 16,90
extra person	€ 2,90 - € 3,90
child (under 7 yrs)	€ 1,60 - € 2,50
animal	€ 2,00 - € 3,50

CAMPING LE BOIS JOLI

2 rue de Châteauneuf - F-85710 Bois de Céné - France
Tel: +33 (0)2 51 68 20 05 - Fax: +33 (0)2 51 68 46 40 - contact@camping-leboisjoli.com

FR85450 Camping les Roses

Rue des Roses, F-85100 Les Sables d'Olonne (Vendée)

Tel: **02 51 33 05 05**. Email: **info@chadotel.com**

Les Roses has an urban location, with the town centre and lovely beach just a short walk away. It has an informal air with the 210 pitches arranged interestingly on a knoll. Mature trees give good shade to some areas. There are 107 touring pitches of varying size, many being more suitable for tents than caravans. All pitches have access to electricity (10A) and water (long cables may be needed). In high season caravanners might find site access tricky at times due to overloaded town centre traffic systems. The site has 103 mobile homes and chalets, but no tour operators.

Facilities

Three well maintained toilet blocks have washbasins in cubicles, unit for disabled visitors, baby room, washing machines and dryers. Simple bar and takeaway (15/5-15/9). Simple shop. Small, attractively laid out, heated, outdoor pool with water slide and paddling pool (1/5-30/9). Play area. Volleyball, basketball, petanque and table tennis. Bicycle hire. Electric barbecues are not permitted. Off site: Beach 500 m. Golf, riding, karting, watersports, zoo, sea and river fishing all within 5 km.

Open: April - 31 October.

Directions

Site is signed from D949 Les Sables to La Rochelle road, north of the 'Géant Casino' roundabout. Turn south at minor junction.

Charges 2007

Per pitch incl. 2 persons	€ 14,50 - € 24,20
with electricity	€ 19,20 - € 28,90
extra person	€ 5,80
child (under 5 yrs)	€ 3,80
animal	€ 3,00

FR85520 Camping Domaine des Renardières

13 chemin du Chêne Vert, F-85270 Notre-Dame-de-Riez (Vendée)

Tel: **02 51 55 14 17**. Email: **caroline.raffin@free.fr**

Just 7 km. from the busy coastal strip, Domaine des Renardières is an oasis of calm in the traditional French manner. Converted from the family farm in 1970, the site consists of three fields with varying amounts of shade and two further open fields in full sun. Visitors are 65% French, many of whom, together with British visitors, return year after year. The 90 touring pitches are well grassed and level; torches and long cables are advisable. Mme. Raffin's benevolent authority is to be seen everywhere and the welfare of her clients is of paramount importance to her.

Facilities

The new unisex toilet block has private wash cubicles, baby changing room and a bathroom for disabled visitors. Showers are closed at night except for one cold shower. Dishwashing and laundry facilities. Shop, takeaway, air-conditioned bar with TV and video games (1/7-27/8). Small outdoor pool (1/5-4/9). Play area. Gas barbecues only. Motorhome service point. Not suitable for American motorhomes. Off site: Fishing 700 m. Bicycle hire 6 km. St Hilaire de Riez 7 km. Riding 9 km. Golf 11 km.

Open: 1 May - 4 September.

Directions

Site is well signed from the centre of the village of Notre Dame de Riez.

Charges 2007

Per unit incl. 2 persons	€ 14,50
with electricity (6A)	€ 17,50
extra person	€ 3,50
child (under 5 yrs)	€ 2,50
dog	€ 1,50 - € 3,00

Less 10-20% outside 15/7-21/8. No credit cards.

FR85530 Camping la Parée Préneau

23 avenue de la Parée Préneau, F-85270 St Hilaire-de-Riez (Vendée)

Tel: **02 51 54 33 84**. Email: **camplapareepreneau@wanadoo.fr**

This site was founded in 1968 by the grandfather of the present owner. It has been gradually and thoughtfully expanded to its present size (206 pitches). Of these, 150 are touring pitches of varying shapes and sizes. Mature trees proliferate to give varying amounts of shade to the undulating site, although the pitches are level. All have electricity (6A) and many also have water and drainage. The calm atmosphere is enhanced by the absence of tour operators. All amenities are very clean and well maintained. The friendly welcome is indicative of the caring attitude of those running the site.

Facilities

The two sanitary blocks include washbasins (some in cubicles), facilities for babies and disabled visitors. WCs are a mix of British, seatless and Turkish. Laundry and dishwashing facilities. Bread, milk and other essentials available. Mobile takeaway (high season). Heated indoor and outdoor pools with jacuzzi and paddling pool. Play area. Bicycle hire. Not suitable for American motorhomes or twin axle caravans. Off site: Beach 1 km. Riding 3 km. Shops, bars, restaurants 5 km. Fishing, golf, sailing 7 km.

Open: 15 May - 8 September.

Directions

From roundabout on D38 (north of St Hilaire-de-Riez), turn south (St Hilaire) for 400 m. First exit at next roundabout (Les Plages) and after 400 m. go on at junction. Site on left after 3 km.

Charges 2006

Per unit incl. 2 persons	€ 14,50 - € 18,90
with electricity	€ 16,60 - € 21,00
extra person	€ 3,70 - € 4,50
child	€ 2,20 - € 2,60
dog	€ 1,50 - € 2,00

FR85580 Camping les Blancs Chenes

Route de la Roche sur Yon, F-85360 La Tranche-sur-Mer (Vendée)

Tel: **02 51 30 41 70**. Email: **vagues.oceanes@wanadoo.fr**

Part of the Vagues Océanes group, this is a very well managed site with good facilities, excellent children's activities and a programme of high season entertainment for all. The manager and his staff take a real pride in their work. The 40 level touring pitches are on sandy grass, are separated by hedges and have access to electricity (10A). They are scattered around the site and some have shade. The site is 1.8 km. from the town of La Tranche with its many shops, restaurants and sandy beach.

Facilities

Three modern toilet blocks have washbasins in cabins, baby units and facilities for disabled visitors. Shop (15/4-15/9). Bar with TV (15/4-15/9). Restaurant and takeaway (1/7-30/8). Pool complex with sun terrace, indoor pool (15/4-15/9), outdoor pool (15/6- 15/9) with jacuzzi, paddling pool and slides. Good sports facilities. Bicycle hire. Key-operated barrier. Spa pool and sauna. Entertainment centre with bar. Fitness centre. Off site: Fishing 1.8 km. Riding 6 km. Golf 20 km.

Open: 15 April - 30 September.

Directions

Site is well signed on the western side of the D747 (La Tranche - La Roche) road, 2 km. north of La Tranche. GPS: N46:21.786 W01:25.230

Charges 2006

Per unit incl. 2 persons	€ 15,00 - € 24,00
extra person	€ 5,00 - € 7,00
child under 5 yrs	free - € 4,50
electricity	€ 5,00 - € 6,00
dog	€ 4,00

FR85590 Camping Plein Sud

246 route de Notre-Dame-de-Monts, F-85160 St Jean-de-Monts (Vendée)

Tel: **02 51 59 10 40**. Email: **camping-pleinsud@club-internet.fr**

Plein Sud is a small welcoming site with 110 grassy pitches, many with adequate shade and separated by hedges. All are of about 100 sq.m. and have electricity (4/6A), water and drainage. There is one main drive through the site and site owned and private mobile homes are mostly positioned nearer the entrance. Touring pitches are further from the main road and bar area and are more peaceful. Only 800 m. away is a long stretch of safe sandy beach. In high season there is a security guard and gate. There are no tour operators.

Facilities

Two modern, clean sanitary blocks provide washbasins in cabins. Baby room. Dishwashing and laundry facilities. Small bar with TV and terrace. Heated pool (no Bermuda style shorts). Play area with volleyball and table tennis. Bread and milk can be ordered daily at reception. Outside caterers provide regular takeaways. Bicycle hire. Pony and trap rides for young children. Children's entertainment in high season. Off site: Supermarket, bar and restaurants 500 m. Fishing 1 km. Riding 2 km. Golf 3 km.

Open: 1 May - 15 September.

Directions

Site is about 3 km. north of St Jean de Monts on the D38, Route de Notre Dame de Monts, on the right almost opposite Camping L'Abri des Pins.

Charges 2006

Per unit incl. 3 persons	€ 12,00 - € 23,00
incl. 4A electricity	€ 15,00 - € 25,00
incl. water and drainage	€ 18,00 - € 28,00
extra person	€ 2,50 - € 5,00
child (2-5 yrs)	free - € 3,00

FR85610 Camping les Aventuriers de la Calypso

Route de Notre-Dame-de-Monts, Les Tonnelles, F-85160 St Jean-de-Monts (Vendée)

Tel: **02 51 56 08 78**. Email: **camping-apv@wanadoo.fr**

This site is ideally situated within 700 metres of the beautiful, sandy Vendée beaches and close to St Jean de Monts (4 km.) with its shops and restaurants. Although there are 253 pitches, only a limited number are for touring units, and these are situated amongst the site's own mobile homes (there are no tour operators here). The pitches are level, grassy and of good size, and are either in the open or shade, with hedges providing privacy. All have electricity (3-10A) and some have water and drainage. The site is neatly maintained with an attractive pool complex and amenities.

Facilities

The modern sanitary block is fully equipped including facilities for babies and disabled campers. A 'portacabin' style block has WCs, showers and washbasins. Both are clean and well maintained. Laundry. Bar with restaurant area (high season). Very small shop with basics. Games area. Tennis. Bicycle hire. Entertainment (July and Aug). Off site: Commercial centre 150 m. Beach 700 m. Notre Dame de Monts 3 km. St Jean de Monts 4 km. Cycling.

Open: 31 March - 22 September.

Directions

Site is on the D38 St Jean de Monts - Notre Dame de Monts road, at the Les Tonnelles roundabout.

Charges 2006

Per unit incl. 2 persons	€ 15,50 - € 27,00
extra person	€ 6,50
child (under 5 yrs)	€ 2,50 - € 3,50
electricity	€ 2,50 - € 4,00

FR85620 Camping le Caravan'ile

B.P. 4, La Guérinière, F-85680 Ile de Noirmoutier (Vendée)

Tel: **02 51 39 50 29**. Email: **contact@caravanile.com**

This well appointed, family run site on the island of Noirmoutier has direct access to the dunes and an extensive sandy beach. It offers heated indoor and outdoor swimming pools with a paddling pool and flume, a sauna, steam room, jacuzzi and mini gym and a variety of entertainment in high season. Most of the 103 level touring pitches are near the beach (shielded by the dune). All have electricity (5A) and are separated by bushes and occasional maturing trees providing a little shade. The site has no tour operators, 90 mobile homes for rent and many more privately-owned.

Facilities

Three very clean sanitary blocks, each with showers, some washbasins in cabins and facilities for disabled people (showers are closed overnight). Laundry. Small supermarket at entrance (1/4-15/9). Bar, snack bar and takeaway (1/4-15/9). Indoor pool (all season) and outdoor pools (15/5-15/9; heated July/Aug). Games and sports area. Games room. Off site: Restaurant, bicycle hire, boat launching and minigolf all close by. Sailing 2 km. Riding 5 km. Golf 20 km.

Open: 1 March - 15 November.

Directions

The Ile de Noirmoutier is 70 km. southwest of Nantes. Take D38 road from the mainland, cross bridge to island and continue to fourth roundabout. Take exit for La Guérinière and immediately turn left to site. GPS: N46:57.980 W02:13.046

Charges 2006

Per unit incl. 2 persons	€ 11,50 - € 18,30
incl. 5A electricity	€ 13,50 - € 21,50
extra person	€ 2,90 - € 4,50
child (2-7 yrs)	€ 1,90 - € 2,90

FR85640 Camping les Chouans

108 avenue de la Faye, F-85270 St Hilaire-de-Riez (Vendée)

Tel: **02 51 54 34 90**. Email: **info@sunmarina.com**

This family run campsite is within a short drive of the wonderful Vendée beaches. A friendly greeting from Josée and Stephane is welcome before entering this well organized, smart site. Cleanliness is important here! In high season it is bustling and lively, with numerous activities available. The restaurant and bar area is attractive, and the pool with its slides is popular. The site mainly caters for mobile homes and touring pitches are minimal (early booking advised). Some are shaded, and smaller than average but with electricity. Late night discos may be noisy in July and August.

Facilities

Two sanitary blocks (one unisex) both have open, vanity style washbasins. Shower room and separate toilet for disabled campers. Baby room. Laundry facilites. Small shop (multi national newspapers available). Bicycle hire. Swimming pools and slides. Good sports area. Small fitness gym (charged). Good entertainment programme for all ages. Weekly excursions. Off site: Beach 1.6 km. St Hillaire de Riez 3 km. Riding, golf and fishing 6 km.

Open: 15 May - 15 September.

Directions

Travel south on D38 from St Jean-de-Monts and turn right at Oruet towards Les Mouettes. At the coast join D23 southwards and follow this road to first roundabout (2.5 km). Site is signed and is 2 km.

Charges guide

Per unit incl. 3 persons	€ 29,00
extra person	€ 7,00
child under 5 yrs	€ 4,00

FR85660 Camping le Pont Rouge

Rue Clémenceau, F-85220 St Révérend (Vendée)

Tel: **02 51 54 68 50**. Email: **camping.pontrouge@wanadoo.fr**

This small, tranquil site is situated down a short tree-lined lane just 600 metres from a small village. Suitable for people who prefer to be away from the nearby coastal resorts. The pitches are grassy, varied in shape and size with most near mature trees giving ample shade and separated by tall hedges, some flowering, ensuring peace and privacy. The 17 mobile homes are situated with some touring pitches, in an open sunny aspect. All pitches have electricity but long leads may be required on some. Ample water points are situated close to all pitches.

Facilities

Two toilet blocks, one in the main reception building with segregated showers, toilets, and wash cubicles. The second new block has segregated showers and wash cubicles with a unisex toilet section and includes laundry facilities. Play areas. Sports. Small, fenced-off pool complex with children's pool and slide. Bicycle hire. Snack bar. Basic provisions in reception. Off site: Village 600 m. Country walks, cycling. Golf and riding nearby.

Open: 1 April - 31 October.

Directions

From D6 Aizenay to St Gilles-Croix-de-Vie turn north onto D94 St Révérend about 4 km. west of Coëx. Site on left after 400 m., just before village. GPS: N46:41.790 W01:50.066

Charges 2006

Per unit incl. 2 persons	€ 13,70 - € 15,80
with electricity	€ 16,10 - € 18,50
extra person	€ 3,45 - € 3,90
child (under 8 yrs)	€ 2,50 - € 2,90

FR85680 Camping le Pin Parasol

Lac du Jaunay, F-85220 La Chapelle-Hermier (Vendée)

Tel: **02 51 34 64 72**. Email: **pinparasol@freesurf.fr**

Tucked away in the Vendée countryside yet just 15 minutes drive from the beach, the site enjoys a pleasant rural setting above the Lac du Jaunay, well away from the bustle of the coast. There are 284 good-sized touring pitches, all with electricity (6/10A) and 22 with water tap and drain. The established pitches have some shade, others are in the open with hedges and tress yet to mature. The enthusiastic family owners are very hands-on and the facilities are of a high standard, most notably the pool area with its new indoor pool, jacuzzi, steam room and fitness suite.

Facilities

Four fully equipped toilet blocks include facilities for babies and disabled visitors. Block in new area can be under some pressure at busy times. Washing machines and dryers. Shop. Restaurant and bar. Takeaway. (July - Aug). Heated outdoor pool with paddling pool and slides (15/6 - 15/9). Indoor pool. Play area. Multisports pitch. Bicycle hire. Entertainment in high season. Fishing. Internet boxes for hire. Off site: Tennis, golf and riding within 5 km. Beaches and sailing 12 km.

Open: 28 May - 25 September.

Directions

La Chapelle-Hermier is 26 km. west of La Roche-sur-Yon. Site is to the south of the D42 La Chapelle-Hermier - L'Aiguillon-sur-Vie, road, 2 km. east of the junction with the D40 Coex-La Chaize - Giraud road and is well signed. GPS: N46:39.973 W01:45.317

Charges 2006

Per unit incl. 2 persons	€ 10,50 - € 25,50
extra person	€ 4,50 - € 5,50
child (0-10 yrs)	€ 3,00
electricity (6/10A)	€ 3,50 - € 4,00

FR85740 Camping Aux Coeurs Vendéens

251 route de Notre-Dame-de-Monts, F-85160 St Jean-de-Monts (Vendée)

Tel: **02 51 58 84 91**. Email: **info@coeursvendeens.com**

This is a delightful little site, a real find for those wishing to enjoy the beaches and life-style of this stretch of coastline without the razzmatazz of some of the neighbouring sites. It is family run and everywhere there is attention to detail: flower tubs beside the road as you drive in, white-washed stones for the pitch numbers, engraved designs on the washbasin mirrors, even plugs for the dishwashing sinks! There are 57 touring pitches, all with electricity available (10A), and a further 60 with mobile homes and chalets, all but five available for rent.

Facilities

Two sanitary blocks are bright and cheerful and kept very clean. Controllable showers, washbasins in cubicles, two pleasant baby rooms. En-suite facilities for disabled visitors (wheel-chair users might have minor difficulties accessing this). Washing machines and dryer. Small shop with takeaway. Swimming pools (7/5-10/9). TV and games rooms. Playgrounds. Trampoline. Minigolf. Bicycle hire. Off site: Beach, sea fishing and boat launching 700 m. Sailing, riding and golf 3 km. Fresh water fishing 7 km.

Open: 8 April - 23 September.

Directions

Site is on the D38 just over 3 km. north of St Jean-de-Monts, roughly halfway between St Jean-de-Monts and Notre Dame-de-Monts, on the western side of the road. GPS: N46:48.548 W02:06.610

Charges 2006

Per unit incl. 2 persons	€ 14,50 - € 25,00
extra person	€ 2,50 - € 4,50
child (under 5 yrs)	free - € 3,00
electricity (10A)	free - € 3,20

Check real time availability and at-the-gate prices...

www.**alanrogers**.com

FR85720 Camping Indigo la Vendette

23 allée des Sableaux, Bois de la Chaize, F-85330 Noirmoutier en L'Ile (Vendée)

Tel: **02 51 39 06 24**. Email: **camping-indigo.com**

Located in woodland and on dunes along a two kilometre stretch of sandy beach just east of the attractive little town of Noirmoutier on the island of the same name, this could be paradise for those who enjoy a simple campsite in a natural setting. On land belonging to the ONF (France's forestry commission), this site is operated by Huttopia whose aim is to adapt to the environment rather than take it over. The 520 touring pitches, all with electricity, are situated among the pine trees and accessed along tracks. Those on the sand dunes have fantastic views across the Bay of Bourgneuf to Pornic and the Jade Coast. They cost a few euros extra - if you are lucky enough to get one! Cars are only allowed in these areas on arrival and departure and it is planned eventually to provide more car parking at strategic points so that this rule can apply to the whole site. There are no mobile homes, just ten large, traditional, but well equipped tents for rent. Nearby are salt marshes, an aquarium and a water theme park and there are opportunities to walk, cycle, sail and windsurf.

Facilities

Five sanitary blocks currently provide basic facilities including pre-set showers and some washbasins in cubicles. The central one is larger and more modern, two others will be refurbished for 2007, the others for 2008. All are kept clean and have facilities for disabled visitors. Washing machines and dryers. Motorcaravan service point. Playground and field for ball games. Bicycle hire. Off site: Riding 4 km. Golf 25 km.

Open: 8 April - 1 October.

Directions

The Ile de Noirmoutier is 70 km southwest of Nantes. Take D38 road from the mainland, cross bridge to island and continue to Noirmoutier en L'Ile. Go through town past three sets of traffic lights and at roundabout turn right following signs to 'Campings'. GPS: N46:59.815 W02:13.200

Charges 2006

Per unit incl. 2 persons	€ 11,90 - € 16,40
incl. electricity	€ 14,25 - € 19,20
extra person	€ 2,90 - € 4,00
child (2-7 yrs)	€ 1,45 - € 2,00

FR85730 Camping les Jardins de L'Atlantique

100 rue de la Caillauderie, Plage de Demoiselles, F-85164 St Jean-de-Monts (Vendée)

Tel: **02 51 58 05 74**. Email: **info@campingjardinsatlantique.com**

This very friendly, family run site is situated on the edge of an extensive pine forest and is just over a kilometre from the attractive beaches south of St Jean-de-Monts. The main area of the site is shaded by pine trees, whilst across the (fairly minor) road are the main amenities and access to a smaller camping and mobile home area that is given plenty of shade by deciduous trees. Access to most pitches might be tricky for really large units, as the tracks wind through the trees. In total there are 90 touring pitches, all with electricity (6A), and a further 213 occupied by mobile homes.

Facilities

Three main sanitary blocks are bright and cheerful and kept very clean. Pre-set showers and washbasins in cubicles. Facilities for disabled visitors. Motorcaravan service point. Shop (25/6-1/9). Bar (1/6-7/9). Restaurant, takeaway (July/Aug). Swimming pools (20/5-10/9). Playground. Minigolf. Multisport court. Bicycle hire. Family activities in high season. Off site: Beach 1.2 km. Fishing and riding 3 km. Sailing and golf 4 km.

Open: 1 April - 30 September.

Directions

From D38 (Noirmoutier - Sables d'Olonne) road at southern end of St Jean-de-Monts bypass (D38bis), turn west towards town and follow signs to site, turning left at first roundabout, cross next and bear left again at roundabout on Rue de la Chauderie. Site is on left. GPS: N46:46.225 W02:01.678

Charges 2006

Per unit incl. 2 persons	€ 13,60 - € 16,80
incl. electricity	€ 16,60 - € 20,70
extra person	€ 3,70 - € 5,00

With over one hundred of France's finest châteaux, this is a region to inspire the imagination. The Loire valley is a charming region of lush countryside, fields of sunflowers, rolling vineyards and of course the great river itself.

OUR TOURIST REGIONS INCLUDES ALL THE LOIRE VALLEY: 18 CHER, 28 EURE-ET-LOIR, 36 INDRE, 37 INDRE-ET-LOIRE, 41 LOIR-ET-CHER, 45 LOIRET. FROM WESTERN LOIRE: 49 MAINE-ET-LOIRE, 53 MAYENNE, 72 SARTHE. AND FROM POITOU-CHARENTES: 79 DEUX SÈVRES, 86 VIENNE

For centuries the Loire valley was frequented by French royalty and the great river winds its way past some of France's most magnificent châteaux: Amboise, Azay-le-Rideau, Chenonceau, with its famous arches that span the river and appear to 'float' on the water, and the fairytale Ussé with myriad magical turrets are just some of the highlights.

Known as the Garden of France, the Loire's mild climate and fertile landscape of soft green valleys, lush vineyards and fields of flowers makes it a favourite with the visitors. Renowned for its wines, with hundreds to choose from, all are produced from vineyards stretching along the main course of the River Loire. Imposing abbeys, troglodyte caves, tiny Romanesque churches, woodland areas such as the Sologne and sleepy, picturesque villages reward exploration. Cities like Blois and Tours are elegant with fine architecture and museums and Paris is only one hour by TGV. One of the oldest towns of Loire valley is Saumur. Its old quarter, grouped around the riverbank beneath the imposing château, is particularly pleasant to wander around.

Places of interest

Amboise: château, Leonardo da Vinci museum.

Beauregard: château with Delft tiled floors.

Blois: château with architecture from Middle Ages to Neo-Classical periods.

Chambord: Renaissance château.

Chartres: cathedral with stained glass windows.

Chinon: old town, Joan of Arc museum

Loches: old town, château and its fortifications.

Orléans: Holy Cross cathedral, house of Joan of Arc.

Tours: Renaissance and Neo-Classical mansions, cathedral of St Gatien.

Vendôme: Tour St Martin, La Trinité.

Villandry: famous renaissance gardens.

Cuisine of the region

Wild duck, pheasant, hare, deer, and quail are classics and fresh water fish such as salmon, perch and trout are favourite. Specialities include rillettes, andouillettes, tripes, mushrooms and the regional cheeses of Trappiste d'Entrammes and Cremet d'Angers, Petit Sable and Ardoises d'Angers cookies.

Bourdaines: apples stuffed with jam and baked.

Tarte a la citrouille: pumpkin tart.

Tarte Tatin: upside down tart of caramelised apples and pastry.

FR79020 Camping de Courte Vallée

F-79600 Airvault (Deux-Sèvres)

Tel: **05 49 64 70 65**. Email: **camping@caravanningfrance.com**

A warm welcome is given to all visitors with a glass of wine and a friendly chat from the British owners. This very attractive site, within walking distance of Airvault, has 65 pitches on level grass amongst trees and shrubs, all with electricity (8A). The owners have spent lots of time and work improving what was already a well laid out site, and have recently added several hardstanding pitches and four 'super' pitches. This is an ideal location for a short stay or as a base for touring the Poitou-Charentes region and the Loire valley. Nearby are Puy du Fou, Fontevraud Abbey, Doué la Fontaine zoo and the châteaux of Saumur and Oiron. From this peaceful site you can wander into the picturesque medieval town or venture further afield to enjoy one of the many excellent local restaurants.

Facilities

A modern unisex block has spacious cubicles for showers and washbasins, and shower and WC cubicles for disabled visitors, all kept to a very high standard of cleanliness. Dishwashing area under cover. Washing machine and dryers. Reception sells 'frites', snacks, a selection of beers and wine and ice cream. Internet access. Swimming pool. Boules. Table tennis. Play area. Caravan storage. Wine tasting events and barbecues. Coffee bar. Off site: Airvault (birthplace of Voltaire) is a 10-15 minute walk. Fishing 300 m. Riding 8 km.

Open: All year.

Directions

From D938 (Parthenay-Thouars) take D725 Airvault. On approaching village turn left over bridge. At T-junction turn sharp left, second exit at roundabout, left at junction to site on left. Note: caravans are not allowed in village. GPS: N46:49.937 W00:08.909

Charges 2006

Per person	€ 6,00 - € 7,00
child (under 7 yrs)	€ 2,00 - € 4,00
pitch	€ 9,00 - € 11,00
electricity (8A)	€ 11,00 - € 13,00

No credit cards.

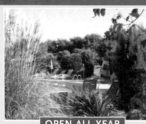

CAMPING de COURTE VALLEE

A small, beautifully landscaped camp site in the heart of rural France. Welcoming atmosphere. British owned.

- **Refurnished pool and sun lounging area**
- **New bar/coffee bar offering drinks and snacks**
- **New shaded terrace/dining area**

Walking distance of mediaeval town of Airvault. Riverside walks and cycle rides. Local wine caves and chateaux. Interesting local villages and restaurants. Near to Futuroscope and Puy du Fou.

OPEN ALL YEAR

Camping de Courte Vallée (Alistair & Johanna Ross) - 79600 Airvault - France
Tél. +33 (0)5 49 64 70 65 - camping@caravanningfrance.com - www.caravanningfrance.com

FR79040 Camping de la Venise Verte

178, route des Bords de Sèvre, F-79510 Coulon (Deux-Sèvres)

Tel: **05 49 35 90 36**. Email: **accueil@camping-laveniseverte.com**

This family run site on the edge of the Sevre Nortaise and the Marais Poitevin is ideal for short or long stays. With canoe and cycle hire on site you have no excuse for not exploring the local area. In the Deux-Sevres, the 'department of discovery', so named because it has two rivers named Sevre, the Noirtaise and Nantaise, the Venise Verte provides an excellent site. The flat pitches are of a good size with electricity, water and drainage and with some shade. A 'Sites et Paysages' member.

Facilities

Modern, heated toilet facilities are of a high standard with free showers. Washing machine and dryer. Motorcaravan services. Restaurant/bar. Heated swimming pool (high season) Bicycle and canoe hire. Boules area. Off site: Coulon 1.0 km. and boat trips in the Marais. Ideal for walking, cycling or canoeing.

Open: 1 April - 30 October.

Directions

From Niort take N11 towards La Rochelle. Turn on the D3 towards Sansais and then north on D1 (Coulon). At traffic lights head towards 'centre ville' (Coulon) at mini-roundabout turn slightly right. Follow Sevre Noirtaise for 1.5 km. to site right.

Charges 2007

Per unit incl. 2 persons and electricity	€ 16,50 - € 22,00
extra person	€ 4,00 - € 5,50
child (2-5 yrs)	€ 2,00

FR79050 Camping du Bois Vert

14 rue Boisseau, Le Tallud, F-79200 Parthenay (Deux-Sèvres)

Tel: 05 49 64 78 43. Email: bois-vert@wanadoo.fr

This former municipal site is now operated by a campsite group although so far it has changed little. There are 88 pitches of which 74 are for touring, all with electricity (10A) and 30 also with water and drainage. There are 14 mobile homes to rent. Pitches are separated by hedges and there are mature trees providing some shade. The site is on the River Thouet and although there is a secure fence, there is a steep drop to the river bank. Pleasant walkways along both sides and a footbridge close by enable you to walk into the old walled town.

Facilities

Two very traditional sanitary blocks both in need of attention. One has unisex toilets (a few British-style but seatless), showers and washbasins in cubicles. Primitive dishwashing and laundry sinks. The second is slightly better. Facilities for disabled visitors. Bar with snackbar and takeaway (1/5-30/9). Bread can be ordered. New swimming pool planned. TV. Table tennis and boules. Small play area. Tickets available for Futuroscope and Puy du Fou. Off site: Motorcaravan service point adjacent. Fishing 100 m. Base de Loisirs nearby. Riding and golf 15 km.

Open: 1 April - 30 September.

Directions

Parthenay is 50 km. west of Poitiers (and the A10) via the N149 to Bressuire and Nantes. Site is southwest of the town at Le Tallud on the D949 La Roche sur Yon road. Take ring road and site is on right as you join D949.
GPS: N46:38.486 W00:16.035

Charges 2006

Per unit incl. 2 persons	€ 12,50 - € 16,50
extra person	€ 4,00 - € 4,60
child (2-10 yrs)	€ 2,00
electricity	€ 3,00

Camping Cheques accepted.

Le Camping du Bois vert****

On the banks of the Thouet River, Camping du Bois Vert will charm you with its tranquillity and serenity.

This 88 pitch site is situated in the heart of Parthenay, a town full of art, culture and history. You will have many things to do and places to see: Visit Le quartier St Jacques, walks in the Poitevin Marsh, discovering the "Moutons Village" or even join one of the many festivals such as "Festival des Jeux"... Camping du Bois Vert sees the completion of its new heated swimming pool in 2007.

14 rue Boisseau - Le Tallud
79200 PARTHENAY
Tél. 0033 549 647 843
Fax : 0033 549 959 668
www.camping-boisvert.com
boisvert@cvtloisirs.fr

FR28110 Camping du Bois Chièvre

Route de Vouvray - St Maurice, F-28800 Bonneval (Eure-et-Loir)

Tel: 02 37 47 54 01. Email: camping.bonneval@wanadoo.fr

On the outskirts of Bonneval and within 20 minutes walk of the town, this municipal site offers good facilities in peaceful surroundings. It is set in woodland and the laerge pitches offer plenty of shade. Nearly all pitches are marked out in stony clearings or on hedged grass, many are sloping and 120 have 6A electricity. The indoor municipal swimming pool and tennis complex are adjacent (reduced rates for campers). A short path leads down the river which is good for fishing. Easy access makes this site ideal for overnight stops or short stays.

Facilities

Sanitary facilities consist of a large central block, plus three very small units without showers and hot water. The large block has mostly pre-set hot showers, some washbasins in cubicles and facilities for disabled people. Laundry facilities and dishwashing sinks. Small bar with snacks and shop for basics (July/Aug). Motorcaravan services. Large TV/games room. Playground. Fishing. Boules court. Table tennis, table football and pool table. Off site: Indoor pool and tennis courts adjacent.

Open: 1 April - 31 December.

Directions

Bonneval is on N10 between Châteaudun and Chartres (on Rte de Vouvray). Follow signs Camping and Piscine, south from town centre. D27 then fork right onto D144 then right again onto C1. Site entrance on right after swimming pool.
GPS: N48:10.244 E01:23.154

Charges 2006

Per person	€ 3,20
child (2-7 yrs)	€ 1,70
pitch	€ 3,50
electricity	€ 3,30 - € 4,00

No credit cards. Barrier card deposit € 15.

159

FR36050 Camping Municipal les Vieux Chênes

F-36310 Chaillac (Indre)

Tel: **02 54 25 61 39**

A small, delightful site on the outskirts of an attractive village, within walking distance of the centre, where there are shops, bars, cafés, restaurants, etc. The 40 grass pitches, all with electricity (16A), are very generous in size, slightly sloping, with hedging and some mature trees. The well manicured appearance and relaxed atmosphere add to the attraction of this peaceful environment. A warden lives on the site. The adjacent lake is for fishing only. There is a larger lake just 1 km. away where varied watersports can be enjoyed. The small water toboggan is free of charge.

Facilities

Heated sanitary facilities are insulated for winter use and include washbasins in private cabins. Limited facilities for disabled campers. Washing machine. Winter caravan storage. Off site: Tennis club adjacent. Fishing 25 m. Shops 200 m. Watersports 1 km.

Open: All year.

Directions

From north leave A20, south of Argenton sur Creuse, take D1 to St Benoit (16 km.) then west to Chaillac on D36 (8.5 km). From south leave A20 - exit 21, take D10 to St Benoit, then D36 as before. Through village and left by the Mairie. GPS: N46:25.921 E01:17.735

Charges guide

Per person	€ 1,65
pitch incl. electricity	€ 3,80 - € 5,40
No credit cards.	

FR37060 Camping L'Arada Parc

Mobile homes ▶ page 466

Rue de la Baratière, F-37360 Sonzay (Indre-et-Loire)

Tel: **02 47 24 72 69**. Email: **laradaparc@free.fr**

A good, well maintained site in a quiet location, Camping L'Arada Parc is a popular base from which to visit the numerous châteaux in this beautiful part of France. The 79 grass pitches all have electricity and 22 have water and drainage. The clearly marked pitches, some slightly sloping, are separated by trees and shrubs some of which are now providing a degree of shade. An attractive, heated pool is on a pleasant terrace beside the restaurant. Entertainment, themed evenings and activities for children are organised in July/August. A new site with modern facilities and developing well. A 'Sites et Paysages' member.

Facilities

Two modern toilet blocks provide unisex toilets, showers and washbasins in cubicles. Baby room. Facilities for disabled visitors (wheelchair users may find the gravel access difficult). Dishwashing and laundry facilities. Shop, bar, restaurant and takeaway (24/3-31/10). Swimming pool (no Bermuda style shorts; 1/5-13/9). Play area, games area. Boules, volleyball, badminton and table tennis. TV room. Bicycle hire. Internet access. Off site: Tennis 200 m. Riding 7 km. Fishing 9 km. Golf 12 km.

Open: 24 March - 1 November.

Directions

Sonzay is northwest of Tours. From the new A28 north of Tours take the exit to Neuillé-Pont-Pierre which is on the N139 Le Mans - Tours road. Then take D766 towards Château la Vallière and turn southwest to Sonzay. Follow campsite signs. GPS: N47:31.687 E00:27.18

Charges 2006

Per unit incl. 2 persons	€ 13,50 - € 17,50
extra person	€ 3,50 - € 4,50
child (2-10 yrs)	€ 2,75 - € 3,50
electricity (10A)	€ 3,50
Camping Cheques accepted.	

kawan-villages.com tel: **00 333 59 59 03 59**

Check real time availability and at-the-gate prices...

 www.**alanrogers**.com

FR37010 Camping de la Mignardière

22 avenue des Aubépines, F-37510 Ballan-Miré (Indre-et-Loire)
Tel: **02 47 73 31 00**. Email: **info@mignardiere.com**

Southwest of the city of Tours, this site is within easy reach of several of the Loire châteaux, notably Azay-le-Rideau. There are also many varied sports amenities on the site or very close by. The site has 177 numbered pitches of which 139 are for touring units, all with electricity (6/10A) and 37 with drainage and water. Pitches are of a good size on rather uneven grass with limestone gravel paths (which are rather 'sticky' when wet). The barrier gates (coded access) are closed 22.30 - 07.30 hrs. Reservation is essential for most of July/August.

Facilities

Two toilet blocks, one new, the other totally refurbished, include washbasins in private cabins, a unit for disabled people, baby bath and laundry facilities. Motorcaravan service point. Shop (15/5-15/9). Takeaway (1/7-31/8). Two large, heated swimming pools (15/5-15/9). Tennis court. Table tennis. Bicycle hire. Off site: Attractive lake good for windsurfing 300 m. (boards can be hired or use your own) and family fitness run. Fishing 500 m. Riding 1 km. Golf 3 km. Tours centre 8 km.

Open: 10 April - 25 September.

Directions

From A10 autoroute take exit 24 and D751 towards Chinon. Turn right after 5 km. at Campanile Hotel following signs to site. From Tours take D751 towards Chinon.

Charges 2006

Per unit incl. 2 persons	€ 14,00 - € 20,00
with electricity, water, drainage	€ 20,00 - € 27,50
extra person	€ 4,00 - € 5,00
child (2-10 yrs)	€ 2,60 - € 3,00

Camping Cheques accepted.

FR37050 Camping Caravanning la Citadelle

Avenue Aristide Briand, F-37600 Loches en Touraine (Indre-et-Loire)
Tel: **02 47 59 05 91**. Email: **camping@lacitadelle.com**

A pleasant, well maintained site, La Citadelle is within walking distance of Loches, noted for its perfect architecture and its glorious history, at the same time offering a rural atmosphere in the site itself. Most of the 128 level, good-sized touring pitches (all with 10A electricity and 42 fully serviced) offer some shade from trees, although sun lovers can opt for a more open spot. The most recent addition is an on-site outdoor swimming pool with paddling pool (solar heated). A 'Sites et Paysages' member. Loches, its château and dungeons, is 500 m.

Facilities

Three sanitary blocks provide British and Turkish style WCs, washbasins (mostly in cabins) and showers. Dishwashing and laundry facilities. Motorcaravan service area. Two excellent baby units and provision for disabled people. Play equipment. Boules, volleyball and games room. Small bar and snack bar offering a variety of food and drink in a lively environment (15/6-13/9). Internet access and TV. Off site: Riding 3 km. Supermarket 3 km. Market on Wednesday and Saturday mornings. Golf 7 km.

Open: 19 March - 19 October.

Directions

From any direction take town bypass (RN143) and leave via roundabout at southern end (supermarket). Site signed towards town centre on right in 800 m. Do not enter centre. GPS: N47:07.382 E01:00.134

Charges 2006

Per pitch incl. 2 adults with electricity, water	€ 15,20 - € 20,00
and drainage	€ 17,90 - € 25,50
extra person	€ 3,90 - € 4,80

Camping Cheques accepted.

awan
tel: 00 333 59 59 03 59 *kawan-villages.com*

FR37070 Camping de L'Ile Auger

Quai Danton, F-37500 Chinon (Indre-et-Loire)
Tel: **02 47 93 08 35**

This is a well-placed site for exploring the old medieval town of Chinon and its impressive castle that was a home of England's Henry II and includes a museum to Joan of Arc. Alongside the River Vienne, it is a five minute walk over the main bridge to the town centre. The 277 pitches are numbered but not separated, with electricity (4/8/12A). A number are shaded by tall trees. A warden lives on site.

Facilities

Six toilet blocks around the site have mostly British style WCs. A very good new block is next to the office building. Washing up sinks. Barrier locked 22.00 - 07.00 hrs. Motorcaravan service point. Playground. Boules court. Off site: Tennis. Swimming pools nearby. Bicycle hire 1 km. Shop 1 km. Fishing 3 km. Riding 10 km.

Open: 15 March - 15 October.

Directions

From Chinon town cross the river and turn right at the end of the bridge. Site entrance is about 100 m. on the right. GPS: N47:09.827 E00:14.121

Charges guide

Per person	€ 1,85
pitch incl. electricity	€ 7,05 - € 7,40

No credit cards.

FR37030 Camping le Moulin Fort

F-37150 Francueil-Chenonceaux (Indre-et-Loire)

Tel: **02 47 23 86 22**. Email: **lemoulinfort@wanadoo.fr**

Camping Le Moulin Fort is a tranquil, riverside site that has been redeveloped by British owners, John and Sarah Scarratt. The 137 pitches are enhanced by trees and shrubs offering some shade and 110 pitches have electricity (6A). The swimming pool (unheated) is accessed by a timber walkway over the mill race from the snack bar terrace adjacent to the restored mill building. Although not intrusive there is some noise from the railway across the river and a few trains run at night. The site is more suitable for couples and families with young children, although the river is unfenced. All over the campsite, visitors will find little information boards about local nature (birds, fish, trees and shrubs), about the history of the mill and fascinating facts about recycling. The owners are keen to encourage recycling on the site. The picturesque Château of Chenonceaux is little more than 1 km. along the Cher riverbank and many of the Loire châteaux are within easy reach, particularly Amboise and its famous Leonardo de Vinci museum.

Facilities

Two toilet blocks with all the usual amenities of a good standard, including washbasins in cubicles and baby baths. Shop (1/4-30/9). Bar, restaurant and takeaway (all 1/4-30/9). Swimming pool (15/5-30/9). Petanque. Minigolf. Games room and TV. Library. Regular family entertainment including wine tasting, quiz evenings, activities for children and light-hearted games and tournaments. Motorcaravan service point. Fishing. Bicycle and canoe hire. Petanque. Live music events. Off site: Riding 12 km. Golf 20 km.

Open: 1 April - 30 September.

Directions

Site signed from N76 Tours - Vierzon road. From D40 (Tours - Chenonceaux), go through village and after 2 km. right on D80 to cross river at Chisseaux. Site on left just after bridge. GPS: N47:19.637 E01:05.358

Charges 2007

Per unit incl. 2 persons	€ 9,00 - € 20,00
extra person	€ 3,00 - € 5,00
child (4-12 yrs)	€ 2,00 - € 4,00
electricity (6A)	€ 4,00

FR37100 Camping la Fritillaire

Rue Basse, F-37420 Savigny-en-Véron (Indre-et-Loire)

Tel: **02 47 58 03 79**. Email: **lafritillaire.veron@ffcc.fr**

Formerly a municipal site and now owned by the FFCC (France's Camping and Caravanning Federation), La Fritillaire is a pleasant, no-frills site offering excellent value. There are 94 touring pitches, marked by trees and bushes, on level ground and ringed by tall trees. There are 58 electric connections (10A) so for some of the shadier pitches a hook-up may not be available or you will need a long cable. The central pitches, however, all have electricity and water, and 22 also have drainage.

Facilities

A smart, modern building houses reception and the sanitary facilities which include push-button showers, washbasins in cabins, good provision for disabled visitors, dishwashing and laundry facilities. Motorcaravan service point. Play area. Boules, volleyball, table tennis and basketball. Internet access. Off site: Baker's 500 m. Shops, bar and restaurant in village. Fishing 200 m. Golf 3 km. Bicycle hire and boat launching 10 km. Riding 15 km.

Open: 1 April - 30 September.

Directions

Savigny-en-Véron is 20 km. east of Saumur via D947 to Montsoreau, then the D7 road along the south bank of the Loire. Village and campsite are both clearly signed from all approaches. GPS: N47:12.013 E00:08.366

Charges 2006

Per unit incl. 2 person	€ 7,10 - € 9,50
full services	€ 11,80 - € 13,35
extra person	€ 1,95 - € 2,40
child (under 10 yrs)	€ 0,95 - € 1,30
electricity (10A)	€ 2,95 - € 3,05

LE MOULIN FORT

CAMPING ★★★★
37150 FRANCUEIL-CHENONCEAUX

Téléphone: +33(0) 2 47 23 86 22 - Fax: +33(0) 2 47 23 80 93 - lemoulinfort@wanadoo.fr

Camping Le Moulin Fort

offers you:

- An unbeatable location within walking distance of Chenonceau Castle

- An ideal base for exploring the Loire region of France

- A warm welcome from the English owners

- A perfect place for relaxing by the river or enjoying the wide range of facilities and animation available on site

- A good stopover point within easy reach of the UK ports, well-signposted and easy to find

On-site facilities:
•Shop •Bar •Take-away •Restaurant •Swimming pool •TV room •Animation •Play-area •Themed evenings •Bicycle hire •Canoe hire •Barbecues permitted

Motorcaravan service area

•• Reservation recommended for high season ••

FR37090 Camping du Château de la Rolandière

F-37220 Trogues (Indre-et-Loire)

Tel: **02 47 58 53 71**. Email: **contact@larolandiere.com**

This is a charming site set in the grounds of a château. The owners, Sabine Toulemonde and her husband, offer a very warm welcome. There are 30 medium sized, flat pitches, some gently sloping front to rear, separated by hedges. All but four have 10A electricity and water taps nearby and parkland trees give shade. The château and adjoining buildings contain rooms to let. The site has a pleasant swimming pool (14 x 6 m.) with a sunny terrace and paddling pool, minigolf through the parkland and an area for ball games, swings and slides. Situated on the D760 between Ille Bouchard and St Maure-de-Touraine, the site is 5 km. west off the A10, convenient for an overnight break or for longer stays to explore the châteaux at Chinon, Loches or Azay-le-Rideau and the villages of Richelieu and Crissay-s-Manse. There are interesting excursions to gardens and grottos. In nearby Azay-le-Rideau visit the wicker craftsmen's workshops.

Facilities

The toilet block is older in style but has been refurbished to provide adequte facilities with shower, washbasin, dishwashing and laundry areas around central British style WCs. Provision for disabled visitors. Bar with terrace and snacks/takeaway. Small shop for basics (July/Aug). Swimming pool (15/5-30/9). Minigolf (no children under 12 yrs). Play area. Fitness room. Bicycle hire 25 km. Off site: Fishing 1 km. to River Vienne. Restaurant 5 km. St Maure 8 km.

Open: 15 April - 30 September.

Directions

Site is 5 km. west from exit 25 on A10 at St Maure-de-Touraine on D760 towards Chinon. Entrance is signed and marked by a model of the château. GPS: N47:06.460 E00:30.631

Charges 2006

Per person	€ 5,00 - € 6,00
child (under 7 yrs)	€ 2,50 - € 3,00
pitch	€ 7,00 - € 8,50
electricity	€ 3,50

No credit cards.

FR37110 Camping Municipal Au Bord du Cher

RN 76, F-37270 Veretz (Indre-et-Loire)

Tel: **02 47 50 50 48**. Email: **camping@veretz.com**

This is an inexpensive, well laid out site on the banks of the River Cher with views through tall elm trees to the Château of Veretz. The managers live in a caravan on site during the season and are always pleased to welcome British tourists. With 64 pitches, most divided by small hedges and all with at least 6A electricity, the site is just outside the town of Veretz where shops, restaurants, bars, etc. can be found. A wooden chalet houses reception and plenty of tourist information, with notice boards giving weather forecasts, etc.

Facilities

Large, modern sanitary block includes British and Turkish style WCs, dishwashing under cover, laundry and washing machine. Motorcaravan service point. Takeaway with covered area to sit and eat (from mid-June). Communal barbecue. Playground. Table tennis. Bicycle hire. Off site: Baker 700 m. Tennis 1 km. Riding 3 km. Outdoor swimming pool (July/Aug) 4 km. Bus service from Tours station to Bleré passes site entrance. Fishing.

Open: 22 May - 10 September.

Directions

Site is at Veretz, via the N76 road, 10 km. southeast of Tours (much better than the municipal at St Avertin en-route).

Charges 2006

Per person	€ 2,00

No credit cards.

FR37120 Castel Camping Parc de Fierbois

Sainte Catherine de Fierbois, F-37800 Saint Maure-de-Touraine (Indre-et-Loire)

Tel: **02 47 65 43 35**. Email: **parc.fierbois@wanadoo.fr**

Parc de Fierbois has an impressive entrance and a tree lined driveway and is set among 250 acres of lakes and forest in the heart of the Loire Valley. In all, there are 320 pitches including 100 for touring units, the remainder being used by tour operators and for chalets and mobile homes. There are 80 touring pitches, mostly level and separated by low hedging or small trees, with water, drainage and electricity hook-ups (2-8A). The other pitches are small or medium in size, many unmarked and some sloping and in the shade.

Facilities

Three toilet blocks provide British style WCs, hot showers and washbasins in cubicles. Baby room. Dishwashing and laundry facilities. Motorcaravan service point. Shop. Bar. Restaurant. Takeaway. Indoor heated pool. Water park complex (pools, slides, paddling pool, sunbathing areas). Indoor entertainment and games bar. Tennis. Volleyball. Badminton. Football. Petanque. Minigolf. Bicycle hire. Go-karts, electric cars on a circuit. TV/video room. Fishing. Pedaloes, canoeing and entertainment programme (July/Aug). Off site: Riding 10 km. Golf 30 km.

Open: 15 May - 15 September.

Directions

Travelling south on N10 from Tours, go through Montbazon and on towards St Maure and Chatellerault. Site signed 16 km. outside Montbazon near Ste Catherine. Turn off main road. Follow site signs. From A10 autoroute use Ste Maure exit and turn north up N10.

Charges 2006

Per unit incl. 2 persons	€ 16,00 - € 35,00
extra person	€ 6,00
electricity	€ 4,00

FR37130 Domaine Résidential Le Parc des Allais

Mobile homes ▶ page 466

FR37220 Trogues (Indre-et-Loir)

Tel: **05 38 50 70 90**. Email: **contact@parc-des-allais.com**

This campsite has been recommended by our French agent and we plan to undertake a full inspection in 2007. Parc des Allais was previously known as Chlorophylle Parc and it is well located in the heart of the Loire Valley, convenient for exploring the surrounding countryside and the region's world class chateaux. The site is situated within a 16 acre park and borders an attractive lake. Pitches here are large and grassy and the site also offers a range of mobile homes and chalets for rent.

Facilities

Modern toilet blocks include a laundry room and facilities for disabled visitors. Restaurant. Bar. Supermarket. Indoor heated swimming pool. Outdoor pool with water slide. Fitness facilities. Tennis. Mountain bike track. Lake and river fishing. Play areas. Games room. Bicycle and mountain bike rental. Small boat rental. Multisport court. Trampoline. Cycle excursions, pétanque. Theme evenings. Entertainment for children.

Open: February - November.

Directions

Take exit 25 from the A10 motorway (Ste Maure de Touraine). Then follow directions to Pouzay and the site is well signed.

Charges 2007

Per unit incl 2 persons and electricity	€ 21,95 - € 26,35
extra person	€ 3,95 - € 4,75
child (under 7 yrs)	€ 2,45 - € 3,20

FR37140 **Huttopia Rillé**

Lac de Rillé, F-37340 Rillé (Indre-et-Loire)

Tel: **02 47 24 62 97**. Email: **rille@huttopia.com**

This site in a forest by a lake has plenty of potential. It has recently been acquired by the Huttopia group which aims to provide a traffic-free environment. Cars are to be left in a carpark outside the barrier (allowed on site to unload and load). New arrivals must park outside and gain an entry code from reception. There are 120 pitches of which 32 are occupied by rental accommodation and 24 are for motorcaravans in a separate area. The touring pitches are numbered in groups amongst the trees but are not marked; they vary in size and cost. When we visited there were very few people on site so it is difficult to judge what sort of atmosphere it will have.

Facilities

The central toilet block has family rooms (with showers and basins), washbasins in cubicles and facilities for disabled visitors (shower/basin plus separate toilet) but there are no ramps and access for wheelchairs is very difficult. Another smaller block has separate showers, washbasins and slightly better facilities for disabled visitors. Motor caravan service point. Heated swimming pool with paddling area (April - Sept). Play area. Communal barbecue areas. Fishing. Canoes on lake. Off site: Riding 6 km. Golf 15 km.

Open: 7 April - 4 November.

Directions

Rillé is 40 km. west of Tours. From D766 Angers - Blois road at Château la Vallière take D749 southwest. From N152 Tours - Angers road go northwest at Langeais on D57. In Rillé turn west on D49. Site on right in a short distance.

Charges 2006

Per person	€ 4,50 - € 5,20
child (2-7 yrs)	€ 3,00 - € 3,50
pitch	€ 3,80 - € 14,00
electricity (6/10A)	€ 4,00 - € 6,00

HUTTOPIA
authenticity & nature

In the heart of the forest
around Lake Rillé
near the Châteaux of the Loire Valley...

Huttopia Rillé ★★★
Roulottes, tents and cottages to rent

Heated swimming-pool, Bar restaurant, tennis courts, beach, brand new facilities, children playground, hiking, biking......

Lac de Rillé -37340 Rillé
Tel. (33)2 47 24 62 97

www.huttopia.com

FR37150 **Camping les Coteaux du Lac**

Base de Loisirs, F-37460 Chemillé-sur-Indrois (Indre-et-Loire)

Tel: **02 47 92 77 83**. Email: **lescoteaux.dulac@wanadoo.fr**

This former municipal site has been completely refurbished to a high standard and is being operated efficiently by a private company owned by the present enthusiastic manager, Yves Joyaut. There are 49 touring pitches, all with electricity (10A) and individual water tap; four have hard standing for motorcaravans. At present there is little shade apart from that offered by a few mature trees, but new trees and bushes have been planted and flower beds are to be added. In a few years this promises to be a delightful site; meanwhile it is smart and very well tended.

Facilities

Excellent sanitary block with controllable showers, some washbasins in cabins and en-suite facilities for disabled visitors. Dishwashing and laundry facilities. Reception sells a few basic supplies and bread can be ordered. Swimming and paddling pools. Playing field. Play equipment for different ages. Chalets to rent (15) are grouped at far end of site, Off site: Fishing 100 m. Lakeside beach, sailing and other water sports 200 m. Horse riding 4 km. Bicycle hire and Golf 15 km.

Open: 7 April - 30 September.

Directions

Chemillé-sur-Indrois is 55 km. southeast of Tours and 14 km. east of Loches, just off the D760 from Loches to Montrésor. Site is to the north of this road and is signed just west of Montrésor.
GPS: N47:09.472 E01:09.592

Charges 2006

Per pitch incl. 2 persons	€ 11,50 - € 16,00
extra person	€ 3,50 - € 4,50
child (2-9 yrs)	€ 2,00 - € 3,00
electricity	€ 3,50

FR45010 Camping les Bois du Bardelet

Route de Bourges, Poilly, F-45500 Gien (Loiret)

Tel: 02 38 67 47 39. Email: contact@bardelet.com

This attractive, lively family site, in a rural setting, is well situated for exploring the less well known eastern part of the Loire Valley. Two lakes (one for boating, one for fishing) and a pool complex have been attractively landscaped in 12 hectares of former farmland, blending old and new with natural wooded areas and more open field areas with rural views. Bois du Bardelet provides 260 pitches with around 130 for touring units. All are larger than 100 sq.m. and have electrical connections, with some fully serviced. The communal areas are based on attractively converted former farm buildings with a wide range of leisure facilities. A family club card can be purchased to make use of the many activities on a daily basis (some high season only). Various activities and excursions are organised, the most popular being to Paris on Wednesdays, which can be pre-booked.

Facilities

Two sanitary blocks (only one open outside 15/6-31/8) include washbasins in cabins. Facilities for disabled visitors and babies. Washing machines. Shop (1/4-17/9). Bar. Snack bar, takeaway, restaurant (all 1/4-17/9) and pizzeria (8/7-21/8). Outside pool (1/5-31/8). Indoor children's pool. Indoor pool, heated (with purchased club card). Aqua gym, fitness and jacuzzi room. Games area. Archery. Canoeing and fishing. Tennis, minigolf, boules. Bicycle hire. Playground. Internet access. Off site: Supermarket 5 km. Riding 7 km. Golf 25 km. Walking and cycling.

Open: 1 April - 30 September.

Directions

From Gien take D940 (Bourges). After 5 km. turn right and right again to cross road and follow site signs. From Argent sur Sauldre take D940 (Gien). Site signed to right after 15 km. Entrance is 200 m. past what looks like the first opening to site. GPS: N47:38.497 E02:36.891

Charges 2006

Per unit incl. 2 persons incl. electricity	€ 18,00 - € 30,00

Less 15-25% in low seasons (20-40% for over 60s). Camping Cheques accepted.

FR45040 Camping Hortus

1 route d'Orléans, D60 Sully-sur-Loire, F-45600 St Père-sur-Loire (Loiret)

Tel: 02 38 36 35 94. Email: into@camping-hortus.com

Across the river from Sully-sur-Loire with its imposing château, this site makes a comfortable base for exploring this part of the Loire valley. The present owners acquired it from the local authority in 2005 and their drive and initiative have turned it into an attractive site with many facilities. There are 80 well-sized touring pitches, all with electricity, water and drainage, on level grass and divided into groups of four by hedges. Trees provide a degree of shade. New swimming pools, bar and (open air) restaurant make this an ideal site for a quiet family holiday.

Facilities

Two modern toilet blocks, one heated, are well equipped: some washbasins in cabins; separate suite for disabled visitors. Small shop for essentials. Bar and open-air restaurant (1/5-30/9). Heated, covered swimming pool (12 x 8 m.) and separate paddling pool (both 1/5-30/9). Fishing. Bicycle hire. Minigolf. Play areas. Off site: Town and Château 1.5 km. Two supermarkets 2 km. Golf 2 km. Riding 4 km.

Open: All year.

Directions

From Orleans take N60 then the D952 towards Gien. Turn south on D948 for Sully-sur-Loire. In St Père-sur-Loire, at roundabout just before bridge, turn west on D60 (St Benoit). Site is 300 m. on left.

Charges 2006

Per unit incl. 2 persons and electricity	€ 11,80 - € 18,50
extra person	€ 2,00 - € 5,00
child (3-12 yrs)	free - € 3,00

FR45030 Camping Touristique de Gien

Rue des Iris, Pouilly lez Gien, F-45500 Gien (Loiret)

Tel: **02 38 67 12 50**. Email: **camping-gien@wanadoo.fr**

This open, attractive site lies immediately across the river from Gien on the opposite bank of the Loire with views of the château and town. It has a long river frontage, which includes a good expanse of sandy beach. There are 150 well-sized, level, grassed touring pitches. All have electricity (4/6A), 18 have water and drainage (between two). Some are shaded by mature trees. The bar and restaurant, with a large outdoor area, are open to the public and provide a sociable gathering point. Soirées with different themes are held at least weekly in July and August. The town, with its château, is within a kilometre across the bridge. The site makes an excellent base for exploring the eastern end of the Loire valley, and the town of Gien itself is of interest. The festival celebrating the heritage of this part of the Loire at Ascensiontide is well worth a visit.

Facilities

Three toilet blocks (no paper or seats in toilets, some Turkish), one heated, and one new with an en-suite unit for disabled people. Laundry. Bar and restaurant (1/4-30/9), both open to the public. Shop 20 m. outside gates (all year). Swimming pool paddling pools (1/6-15/9). Play area and grassed games area. Minigolf. Bicycle hire. Canoe hire. Fishing. Off site: Town centre less than 1 km. Hypermarket 1 km. Riding 2 km. Golf 25 km.

Open: 6 March - 15 November.

Directions

North of the river, from north (A77 and RN7) take D940 to Gien; from southeast (A77 and RN7) and from west take D952 to Gien. Follow signs to Centre Ville and turn south over bridge. At traffic lights turn west on D951 towards Pouilly-lez-Gien. Site is signed 300 m. on right. If south of the river, from D940 turn west onto D951 and site is 300 m. on right.

Charges 2006

Per unit incl. 2 persons	€ 11,50 - € 18,00
extra person	€ 6,00
child (under 12 yrs)	€ 4,00
electricity (4/10A)	€ 3,00 - € 4,50

FR41020 Castel Camping Château La Grenouillère

Mobile homes ▶ page 467

F-41500 Suèvres (Loir-et-Cher)

Tel: **02 54 87 80 37**. Email: **la.grenouillere@wanadoo.fr**

Château de la Grenouillère is a comfortable site with good amenities. It is set in a 28-acre park and the 260 pitches (including 130 for tour operators and mobile homes) are in three distinct areas. The majority are in a wooded area, with about 60 in the old orchard and the remainder in open meadow, although all pitches are separated by hedges. There is one water point for every four pitches and all have electric hook-up (5A). Additionally, there are 14 'grand confort' pitches with a separate luxury sanitary block in the outbuildings of the château.

Facilities

Three sanitary blocks are modern and well appointed, including some washbasins in cabins. Laundry facilities. Shop. Bar. Pizzeria and pizza takeaway. Restaurant and Chicken Grill takeaway (1/6-5/9). Swimming complex of four pools (one covered) and slide. Tennis, table tennis, pool, baby foot and video games. Internet point. Bicycle and canoe hire (July/Aug). Off site: Suèvres 3 km. Fishing, riding, and aqua sports 5 km. Golf 10 km.

Open: 1 May - 5 September.

Directions

Site is between Suèvres and Mer on north side of N152 and is well signed.

Charges 2006

Per unit incl. 2 persons	€ 19,00 - € 31,00
with 6A electricity	€ 23,00 - € 35,00
with full services	€ 27,00 - € 43,00
extra person	€ 5,00 - € 8,00
child (under 7 yrs)	€ 3,00 - € 6,00

Less 10% during middle season, and 35% during low season.

FR41010 Le Parc du Val de Loire

Route de Fleuray, F-41150 Mesland (Loir-et-Cher)

Tel: **02 54 70 27 18**. Email: **parduvaldeloire@wanadoo.fr**

Between Blois and Amboise, quietly situated among vineyards away from the main roads and towns, this site is nevertheless centrally placed for visits to the châteaux; Chaumont, Amboise and Blois (21 km.) are the nearest in that order. There are 210 touring pitches of reasonable size, either in light woodland marked by trees or on open meadow with separators. All the pitches have electricity (10A) and 100 of them also have water and drainage. Sports and competitions are organised in July/August with a weekly disco and dance for adults and opportunities for wine tasting are arranged weekly. There are local walks and bike rides on marked paths (free maps available). Nearby there are balloon and helicopter flights over the Loire valley. New, experienced owners have recently taken over the site.

Facilities

Three original toilet blocks of varying ages are acceptable. Units for disabled visitors, babies and laundry facilities. Motorcaravan services. Shop with bakery (July/Aug). Bar. Restaurant, snack service, pizzeria and takeaway (July/Aug). TV and recreation rooms. Swimming pools, one heated all season, larger one with slide. Tennis. Playgrounds with skate board facilities. Bicycle hire. Table tennis. Minigolf. Football pitch. Volleyball, badminton and basketball. Barbecue area.
Off site: Fishing 2 km. Golf 4 km. Riding 10 km.

Open: 31 March - 29 September.

Directions

From A10 exit 18 (Château-Renault, Amboise) take D31 south to Autrèche (2 km). Turn left on D55 for 3.5 km. In Darne-Marie Les Bois turn left and then right onto D43 to Mesland. Follow site signs. Or, from south, site signed from Onzain.
GPS: N47:30.601 E01:06.286

Charges 2007

Per standard pitch (100 sq.m.) incl. 2 persons	€ 14,00 - € 24,50
large pitch (110-170 sq.m.) with electricity, water and drainage	€ 22,00 - € 38,50
extra person	€ 4,50 - € 7,00
child (4-10 yrs)	€ 3,50 - € 6,20

PARC DU VAL DE LOIRE
F-41 150 MESLAND
Tel. 33 (0)2 54 70 27 18 - Fax 33 (0)2 54 70 21 71
www.parcduvaldeloire.com
e-mail : parcduvaldeloire@wanadoo.fr

PARC DU VAL DE LOIRE - **Camping** ★★★★
«Au coeur des **châteaux de la Loire**»
Blois - Amboise

Nouveaux propriétaires

FR41030 Yelloh! Village le Parc des Alicourts

Domaine des Alicourts, F-41300 Pierrefitte-sur-Sauldre (Loir-et-Cher)

Tel: **02 54 88 63 34**. Email: **parcdesalicourts@wanadoo.fr**

A secluded holiday village set in the heart of the forest and with many sporting facilities, Parc des Alicourts is midway between Orléans and Bourges, to the east of the A71. There are 490 pitches, 150 for touring and the remainder occupied by mobile homes and chalets. All pitches have electricity connections (6A) and good provision for water, and most are 150 sq.m. (min. 100 sq.m). Locations vary from wooded to more open areas, thus giving a choice of amount of shade. All facilities are open all season and the leisure amenities are exceptional. Member of Leading Campings Group.

Facilities

Three modern sanitary blocks include some washbasins in cabins and baby bathrooms. Laundry facilities. Facilities for disabled visitors (shallow step to reach them).
Motorcaravan services. Shop. Restaurant. Takeaway in bar with terrace. Water complex. 7 hectare lake (fishing, bathing, canoes, pedaloes). 9-hole golf course. Play area. Football, volleyball, tennis, minigolf, table tennis, boules. Roller skating/skateboarding (bring own equipment). Bicycle hire. Internet access. Walk and cycle path.

Open: Mid May - 7 September.

Directions

From A71, take Lamotte Beuvron exit (no 3) or from N20 Orléans to Vierzon turn left on to D923 towards Aubigny. After 14 km. turn right at camping sign on to D24E. Site signed in about 4 km.
GPS: N47:32.639 E02:11.516

Charges 2006

Per unit incl. 2 persons and electricity	€ 15,00 - € 38,00
extra person	€ 6,00 - € 9,00
child (1-17 yrs)	free - € 7,00

(169)

FR41040 Camping Château des Marais

27 rue de Chambord, F-41500 Muides-sur-Loire (Loir-et-Cher)

Tel: **02 54 87 05 42**. Email: **chateau.des.marais@wanadoo.fr**

The Château des Marais campsite is well situated to visit the chateau at Chambord (its park is impressive) and the other châteaux in the 'Vallée des Rois'. The site, providing 133 large touring pitches, all with electricity (6/10A), water and drainage and with ample shade, is situated in the oak and hornbeam woods of its own small château. An excellent swimming complex offers pools and two flumes. English is spoken and the reception from the enthusiastic owners and the staff is very welcoming. Used by tour operators (90 pitches).

Facilities

Four modern sanitary blocks have good facilities including some large showers and washbasins en-suite. Washing machine. Motorcaravan service point. Shop and takeaway. Bar/restaurant with large terrace. Swimming complex with heated and unheated pools, slide and cover for cooler weather. TV room. Bicycle hire. Fishing pond. Excursions to Paris, an entertainment programme and canoe trips organised in high season. Internet access. Off site: Riding 5 km. Golf 12 km. Muides-sur-Loire (five minutes walk).

Open: 15 May - 15 September.

Directions

From A10 autoroute take exit 16 to Mer, cross the Loire to join D951 and follow signs. Site signed off D103 to southwest of village. 600 m. from junction with D112. GPS: N47:39.948 E01:31.726

Charges 2006

Per pitch incl. 2 persons	€ 23,00 - € 31,00
extra person	€ 6,00
child (under 5 yrs)	€ 5,00
electricity (6/10A)	€ 5,00 - € 7,00

Credit cards accepted for amounts over € 80.

FR41060 Domaine de Dugny

CD45 (La Cabinette), F-41150 Onzain (Loir-et-Cher)

Tel: **02 54 20 70 66**. Email: **info@dugny.fr**

This well organised campsite began as an 'a la ferme' back in 1976. Since then it has grown into an eight hectare site surrounded by acres of quiet farmland. Still under the same ownership, it opens all year round. There are 300 pitches, with mobile homes (privately owned and to rent) leaving 190 tourist pitches. Generously sized, they are partially separated, some with shade and others open. All but 30 have electricity (10A), water and drainage. This is a campsite for active people. Play areas and sports fields includes equipment for youngsters, a trampoline, minigolf, football and basket ball.

Facilities

Three sanitary units include some washbasins in cubicles and provision for disabled people. Dishwashing and laundry sinks. Bread, ices, soft drinks and gas are stocked. Restaurant and takeaway. Barbecue evenings. Heated outdoor pool complex (one pool with slides) and paddling pool. Play areas. Minigolf, volleyball, basketball and pétanque. Internet point. Pony and horse riding. Microlight flights. Pedaloes/row boats for hire. Children's disco, boules tournaments. Camp-fire evenings.

Open: All year.

Directions

Onzain is southwest of Blois (15 km.), on opposite side of river from Chaumont-sur-Loire. Take N152 (Blois Tours), turn right onto D1 (Onzain). Site signed after railway bridge. Turn right onto D58, then left onto D45. Follow signs.

Charges 2007

Per person	€ 7,00 - € 14,00
electricity	€ 5,50
pitch	€ 5,50 - € 9,00

Camping Cheques accepted.

FR41090 Camping Municipal de la Varenne

34 rue de Veillas, F-41210 Neung-sur-Beuvron (Loir-et-Cher)

Tel: **02 54 83 68 52**. Email: **camping.lavarenne@wanadoo.fr**

This is a particularly well organised site in a peaceful location, The site has a slight slope but most of the 69 grass touring pitches are fairly level, all with electricity hook-ups (10A). Some pitches are individual, others in bays of four, and some for tents amongst trees. There is good shade in most areas. To the rear is a large field which slopes down to the small river. Each evening the warden takes bread orders (available from reception at 08.00 next morning). Four mobile homes are for rent.

Facilities

An excellent, clean and well equipped modern building includes spacious showers, baby changing facilities, a suite for disabled people, and a washing machine. A second unit at the rear of the reception building has additional good facilities. Freezer for ice blocks. Motorcaravan service point. Playground. Volleyball. Two tennis courts. Table tennis. Bicycle hire. River fishing adjacent to site. Off site: The town has all services including restaurants, bars, small supermarket.

Open: Easter - 30 September.

Directions

Neung-sur-Beuvron is about 40 km. east of Blois, and 2 km. west of the D922 about 22 km. north of Romarantin-Lanthenay. Site is 1 km. northeast of town centre (well signed).
GPS: N47:32.293 E01:48.905

Charges 2006

Per person	€ 1,90
child (5-16 yrs)	€ 1,50
pitch	€ 1,85
electricity	€ 2,40

FR41070 Camping Caravaning la Grande Tortue

Mobile homes ▶ page 467

3 route de Pontlevoy, F-41120 Candé-sur-Beuvron (Loir-et-Cher)
Tel: 02 54 44 15 20. Email: **grandetortue@wanadoo.fr**

This is a pleasant, shady site that has been developed in the surroundings of an old forest. It provides 169 touring pitches the majority of which are more than 100 sq.m. 150 have 10A electricity and the remainder are fully serviced. The family owners continue to develop the site with a new multisports court already created. During July and August, they organise a programme of trips including wine/cheese tastings, canoeing and horse riding excursions. Used by tour operators. This site is well placed for visiting the châteaux of the Loire or the cities of Orléans and Tours. A 'Sites et Paysages' member.

Facilities

Three sanitary blocks offer British style WCs, washbasins in cabins and push-button showers. Laundry facilities. Shop selling provisions. Terraced bar and restaurant with reasonably priced food and drink (15/4-15/9). Swimming pool and two shallower pools for children (1/5-30/9). Trampolines, a ball crawl with slide and climbing wall, bouncy inflatable, table tennis. New multisport court. Off site: Walking and cycling. Bicycle hire 1 km. Fishing 500 m. Golf 10 km. Riding 12 km.

Open: 9 April - 30 September.

Directions

Site is just outside Candé-sur-Beuvron on D751, between Amboise and Blois. From Amboise, turn right just before Candé, then left into campsite. GPS: N47:29.389 E01:15.515

Charges 2007

Per unit incl. 2 persons	€ 15,00 - € 26,00
incl. electricity	€ 19,50 - € 30,00
extra person	€ 5,00 - € 7,50
child (3-9 yrs)	€ 3,50 - € 5,50

Camping Cheques accepted.

awan
AGES CAMPINGS

tel: 00 333 59 59 03 59 *kawan-villages.com*

FR41100 Camping les Saules

D102 route de Contres, F-41700 Cheverny (Loir-et-Cher)

Tel: **02 54 79 90 01**. Email: **contact@camping-cheverny.com**

Set in the heart of the châteaux region, has recently been revitalised and re-opened by a local family. The tastefully renovated traditional reception buildings in their lakeside setting give a very pleasant welcome. There are 166 good size, level pitches with 159 available for touring units. All have shade from the many trees on the site, 150 have electrical connections (a few will require leads longer than 25 m.), and there are ample water taps. Cheverny is considered to have the best interior and furnishings of all the châteaux in the Loire region, and many others are within easy reach. A 'Sites et Paysages' member.

Facilities

Two sanitary blocks with modern toilets, showers, washbasins in cubicles and facilities for disabled visitors. Dishwashing and laundry facilities. The older block should have been refurbished. Motorcaravan service point. Gas supplies. Shop. Restaurant. Bar. Snack bar and takeaway. Swimming and paddling pools. TV/social room with toys, board games, books. Two play areas. Large grass area for ball games. Minigolf (free), Table tennis. Fishing. Bicycle hire. Internet and WiFi. Off site: Golf 3 km. Riding 3 km.

Open: 1 April - 16 October.

Directions

From Cheverny take D102 south towards Contres. Site is on the right after about 2 km. GPS: N47:30.000 E01:27.668

Charges 2007

Per unit incl. 2 persons	€ 15,50 - € 25,50
extra person	€ 4,50
child (4-10 yrs)	€ 2,00
electricity	€ 3,50 - € 7,00

CHEVERNY CAMPING LES SAULES ★★★★

In the heart of the Kings Valley, next to the Château of Cheverny and its 18-hole golf course, just near the forest, welcome to the quiet atmosphere of the Camping Les Saules and its green and shady setting of 8 hectares. Excellent starting point for walking and cycling.

Rental of chalets.

CAMPING LES SAULES F. 41700 CHEVERNY
Tel. : 33 (0) 254 799 001
Fax : 33 (0) 254 792 834
www.camping-cheverny.com - contact@camping-cheverny.com

FR49000 Camping du Lac de Maine

Avenue du Lac de Maine, F-49000 Angers (Maine-et-Loire)

Tel: **02 41 73 05 03**. Email: **camping@lacdemaine.fr**

The Lac de Maine campsite is situated in the heart of the Anjou region. Most of the 141 level touring pitches are part grass and part gravel hardstanding, with the remainder all gravel. All have water, a drain and electricity (6/10A). The main entrance has a height restriction of 3.2 m, although there is an alternative gate for higher vehicles. This is a useful site, open for a long season and only five minutes from the centre of Angers. With wide access roads, it is also suitable for American RVs.

Facilities

Two sanitary blocks, one which can be heated and includes some washbasins in cubicles. British style WCs (no seats). Facilities for babies and visitors with disabilities. Dishwashing and laundry facilities. Motorcaravan service point. Reception stocks gas. Restaurant/bar (both 15/6-15/9). Heated L-shaped swimming pool (1/6-15/9). Volleyball. Petanque. Bicycle hire. Internet point. Barrier card deposit € 20. Off site: Lake beach 0.5 km. Fishing 1 km. Riding 3 km. Golf 5 km.

Open: 25 March - 10 October.

Directions

Site is just west of Angers near the N23 (Angers - Nantes road). Turn south at signs for Quartier de Maine and Lac de Maine. Follow signs for Pruniers and Bouchemaine. Site on D111 and signed. GPS: N47:27.277 W00:35.777

Charges 2006

Per unit incl. 2 persons	€ 11,20 - € 16,00
extra person	€ 2,50
child (under 13 yrs)	€ 1,80
electricity (10A)	€ 3,20
animal	€ 2,00
Camping Cheques accepted.	

FR49010 Castel Camping L'Etang de la Brèche

Route Nationale 152, 5 Impasse de la Breche, F-49730 Varennes-sur-Loire (Maine-et-Loire)

Tel: 02 41 51 22 92. Email: mail@etang-breche.com

The Saint Cast family have developed L'Etang de la Brèche with care and attention. The site provides 201 large, level pitches with shade from trees and bushes. Less shaded areas are used for recreation. There are electrical connections to all pitches (some long cable may be required), with water and drainage on 63 of them. The restaurant, bar and terrace, also open to the public, provides a social base and is popular with British visitors. The pool complex includes one with a removable cover, one outdoor, and one for toddlers. A Les Castels site used by tour operators (85 pitches).

Facilities

Three toilet blocks, modernised to good standards, include facilities for babies with two units for people with disabilities. Washing up sinks and laundry. Shop and epicerie. Restaurant, pizzeria and takeaway. Heated pools. Tennis, basketball, minigolf and a field for football. Bicycle hire. General room, games and TV rooms. Internet point. Varied sporting and entertainment programme (10/7-25/8). Pony riding. Child minding is arranged in afternoons. Torch useful. Off site: Golf 8 km.

Open: 12 May - 15 September.

Directions

Site is 100 m. north off the main N152, about 4 km. northeast of Saumur on the north bank of the Loire.

Charges 2007

Per unit incl. 2 persons	€ 18,50 - € 31,00
extra person	€ 5,00 - € 7,00
child (4-10 yrs)	€ 3,00 - € 3,50
electricity (10A)	free - € 3,00
water and drainage	€ 2,50

7th night free in low season.

FR49060 Camping Parc de Montsabert

Montsabert, F-49320 Coutures (Maine-et-Loire)

Tel: 02 41 57 91 63. Email: camping@parcdemontsabert.com

This extensive site has recently been taken over by a friendly French couple who already have plans for improvements. It has a rural atmosphere in the shadow of Montsabert château, from where visiting peacocks happily roam in the spacious surroundings. The main features are the heated swimming pool (with cover) and the adjoining refurbished, rustic style restaurant. There are 96 large, well marked touring pitches, divided by hedges and all with water tap, drain and electricity (5/10A). Picnic tables are provided near the entrance. Used by several small tour operators (30 pitches). Partially wooded by a variety of trees, this site offers the peace of the countryside and yet easy access to both Saumur and Angers. It is an ideal base for exploring the area, whether on foot or by bicycle or car.

Facilities

The main toilet block can be heated and has washbasins and bidets in cabins and a baby room. Laundry facilities. A second block serves the pool and another provides more WCs. Shop, bar and takeaway (2/6-29/8). Restaurant(16/6-20/8). Heated pool (no Bermuda style shorts) and paddling pool. Sports hall, minigolf, volleyball and basketball. Tennis. Play area. Bicycle hire. Entertainment (high season). Off site: Canoeing nearby. Fishing, riding 5 km. Golf 8 km.

Open: 14 April - 15 September.

Directions

Coutures is 25 km. southeast of Angers on the D751 to Saumur. From A11 take exit 14 and follow signs for Cholet/Poitiers, then Poitiers on D748. At Brissac-Quincé turn northeast on D55 and in 5 km. turn right to Coutures. Montsabert is north of village. GPS: N47:22.464 W00:20.709

Charges 2007

Per pitch incl. 2 persons	€ 15,60 - € 24,30
extra person	€ 4,60
child (1-10 yrs)	€ 3,10
electricity (5/10A)	€ 3,00 - € 4,20
dog	€ 3,30

FR49090 Camping l'Isle Verte

Avenue de la Loire, F-49730 Montsoreau (Maine-et-Loire)
Tel: 02 41 51 76 60. Email: isleverte@cutloisirs.fr

This friendly, natural site, with pitches overlooking the Loire, is just 100 m. from the centre of Montsoreau, an ideal starting point to visit the western Loire area. Most of the 90 shaded, level and good-sized tourist pitches are separated by low hedges but grass tends to be rather sparse during dry spells. All have electricity (16A). Excellent English is spoken in the reception and bar. Fishermen are particularly well catered for here, there being an area to store equipment and live bait (permits are available in Saumur). Attractions within walking distance of the campsite include the château, Troglodyte (mushroom caves and restaurant), both just 500 m. away, wine tasting in the cellars nearby, and a Sunday market in the town.

Facilities

A single building provides separate male and female toilets. Washbasins, some in cabins, and showers are unisex. Separate facilities for disabled campers. Baby room. Laundry and dishwashing facilities. Motorcaravan service point. Bar and snack bar (1/5-30/9). Swimming and paddling pools (15/5-30/9). Small play area. Table tennis, volleyball and boules. Bicycle hire (June - August or by special request). Fishing. Off site: Golf 6 km. Riding 15 km.

Open: 1 April - 30 September.

Directions

Take D947 from Saumur to Montsoreau and site is clearly signed on left along the road into town.
GPS: N47:13.092 E00:03.159

Charges 2007

Per unit incl. 1 or 2 persons	€ 12,90 - € 17,50
extra person	€ 3,00 - € 3,50
child (2-10 yrs)	€ 2,00 - € 2,50
electricity	€ 3,00

Camping Cheques accepted.

Le Camping Isle verte***

Residing on the banks of the Loire River, 100 m from centre of Montsoreau, this family campsite with 110 pitches is an excellent destination for discovering the Troglodytes (the champignonnière, wine caves within 500m) and Castles of the Loire.
Isle Verte is situated in natural settings, ideal for relaxing holidays. The site has direct access to the banks of the Loire and offers activities for all tastes and ages: excursions, fishing, walking and cycling.

Avenue de la Loire
49730 MONTSOREAU
Tél. : 0033 241 517 660
Fax : 0033 241 510 883
www.campingisleverte.com
isleverte@cvtloisirs.fr

FR49040 Camping de l'Etang

Mobile homes ▶ page 467

Route de St Mathurin, F-49320 Brissac (Maine-et-Loire)

Tel: **02 41 91 70 61**. Email: **info@campingetang.com**

At Camping de l'Etang many of the 150 level touring pitches have pleasant views across the countryside. Separated and numbered, some have a little shade and all have electricity with water and drainage nearby. 21 are fully serviced. A small bridge crosses the river Aubance which runs through the site (well fenced) and there are two lakes where fisherman can enjoy free fishing. The site has its own vineyard and the wine produced can be purchased on the campsite. Tour operators use 16 pitches. A 'Sites et Paysages' member. Originally the farm of the Château de Brissac (yet only 24 km. from the lovely town of Angers), this is an attractive campsite retaining much of its rural charm. The adjacent Parc de Loisirs is a paradise for young children with many activities including boating, pony rides, miniature train, water slide, bouncy castle and swings (free entry for campers).

Facilities

Three well maintained toilet blocks provide all the usual facilities. Laundry facilities. Baby room. Disabled visitors are well catered for. Motorcaravan service point. The farmhouse houses reception, small shop and takeaway snacks when bar is closed. A bar/restaurant serves crêpes, salads, etc (evenings June-August). Swimming pool (heated and covered) and paddling pool. Fishing. Play area. Bicycle hire. Wide variety of evening entertainment in high season. Off site: Golf and riding 10 km. Sailing 25 km.

Open: 15 May - 15 September.

Directions

Brissac-Quincé is 17 km. southeast of Angers on D748 towards Poitiers. Do not enter the town but turn north on D55 (site signed) in direction of St Mathurin. GPS: N47:21.560 W00:26.065

Charges 2006

Per unit incl. 2 persons	€ 15,00 - € 26,00
extra person	€ 4,50 - € 6,50
child (0-10 yrs)	€ 3,00 - € 3,50
electricity	€ 3,00
dog	€ 2,50

On the route of the châteaux of the Loire, 2 campsites welcome you

The same spirit of hospitality

CAMPING DE CHANTEPIE **
S'-Hilaire-S'-Florent - 49400 SAUMUR
Tél. +33 (0)2 41 67 95 34 - Fax +33 (0)2 41 67 95 85
e-mail : info@campingchantepie.com
www.campingchantepie.com

Association de
Chantepie et de l'Etang
N° 2002/DRTEFP/280

CAMPING DE L'ETANG **
Route de S'-Mathurin
49320 BRISSAC
Tél. +33 (0)2 41 91 70 61 - Fax +33 (0)2 41 91 72 65
e-mail : info@campingetang.com
www.campingetang.com

FR49020 Camping de Chantepie

St Hilaire-St Florent, F-49400 Saumur (Maine-et-Loire)

Tel: **02 41 67 95 34**. Email: **info@campingchantepie.com**

On arriving at Camping de Chantepie with its colourful, floral entrance, a friendly greeting awaits at reception, set beside a restored farmhouse. The site is owned by a charitable organisation which provides employment for local disabled people. Linked by gravel roads (which can be dusty), the 150 grass touring pitches are level and spacious, with some new larger ones (200 sq.m. at extra cost). All pitches have electricity (5/10A) and are separated by low hedges of flowers and trees which offer some shade. This is a good site for families. A 'Sites et Paysages' member. The panoramic views over the Loire from the pitches on the terraced perimeter of the meadow are stunning and from here a footpath leads to the river valley. Leisure activities are organised in July/August.

Facilities

The toilet block is clean and facilities are good with washbasins in cubicles, new showers (men and women separately) and facilities for disabled visitors. Dishwashing and laundry facilities. Baby area. Shop. Bar, terraced café and takeaway. Covered and heated pool, outdoor pool and paddling pool. Play area with apparatus. Terraced minigolf. Volleyball, TV, video games and table tennis. Pony rides. Bicycle hire. Internet access. Off site: Fishing 500 m. Golf, riding 2 km. Sailing 7 km.

Open: 15 May - 15 September.

Directions

St Hilaire-St Florent is 2 km. west of Saumur. Take D751 (Gennes). Right at roundabout in St Hilaire-St Florent and on until Le Poitrineau and campsite sign, then turn left. Continue for 3 km. then turn right into site road. GPS: N47:21.560 W00:08.580

Charges 2006

Per unit incl. 2 persons	€ 15,00 - € 26,00
extra person	€ 4,50 - € 6,50
child (0-10 yrs)	€ 3,00 - € 3,50
electricity	€ 3,00

FR49030 Camping Caroline

Route de la Bohalle, F-49800 Brain-sur-l'Authion (Maine-et-Loire)

Tel: **05 46 55 10 01**. Email: **info@campingterreoceane.com**

Camping Caroline is an attractive former municipal site, lying on the edge of the little village of Brain-sur-l'Authion at the heart of the Anjou. This is a relaxing site with 120 large grassy pitches, mostly with reasonable shade and electricity (6A). There are several leisure amenities, notably a heated pool and snack bar. The River Authion is just 200 metres away and is popular with anglers. This is a useful base for visiting the vineyards of the Anjou which are all around.

Facilities

The two sanitary blocks are of very different designs but are clean and well maintained. Facilities for disabled visitors. Heated swimming pool and paddling pool. Snack bar. Play area. Children's club in peak season. Mobile homes for hire. Off site: Tennis. Fishing (charge applies). Boating. Multisports pitch. Walking and cycle trails. Boat trips on the Loire.

Open: 26 March - 1 October.

Directions

From Angers take the N147 towards Saumur and then the D113 to the south of the village of Brain-sur-l'Authion. The site is clearly signed from the village.

Charges 2006

Per person	€ 2,10 - € 3,00
child (0-7 yrs)	€ 1,70 - € 2,50
pitch incl. electricity	€ 8,00 - € 12,00

Caroline ★★★
Maine et Loire - France

Le Candais ★★★
Maine et Loire - France

Documentation on request

www.village-center.com/caroline
caroline@village-center.com

Villagecenter
la vie plein air
+334 99 57 20 25

www.village-center.com/candais
candais@village-center.com

FR49070 Camping Caravaning la Vallée des Vignes

La Croix Patron, F-49700 Concourson-sur-Layon (Maine-et-Loire)

Tel: **02 41 59 86 35**. Email: **Campingvdv@wanadoo.fr**

The enthusiasm of the English owners here comes across instantly in the warm welcome received by their guests. Bordering the Layon river, the 54 good sized touring pitches are reasonably level and fully serviced (10A electricity, water tap and drain). Five pitches have a hardstanding for cars. Attractions include a newly enclosed bar and restaurant, a generously sized sun terrace surrounding the pool and high season activities for children and adults. These include wine tasting, a hog roast (or similar), competitions and treasure hunts. An ideal base for visiting the châteaux of the Loire and the many caves and vineyards.

Facilities

The toilet block includes washbasins in cabins, and dishwashing facilities at either end. Baby room. Facilities for disabled visitors. Laundry facilities. Bar (from 15/5 or on request) serving meals, snacks and takeaway (from 15/5). Swimming and paddling pools (from 15/5). Playground, games area and football pitch. Minigolf, volleyball, basketball, table tennis. Internet access. Fishing. Caravan storage. Off site: Zoo and rose gardens at Doué-la-Fontaine. Grand Parc Puy du Fou.

Open: 15 March - 20 October.

Directions

Site signed off D960 Doué - Vihiers road, just west of Concourson-sur-Layon.

Charges 2007

Per unit incl. 2 persons	€ 16,50 - € 22,00
extra person	€ 4,00 - € 5,00
child (2-12 yrs)	€ 2,50 - € 3,00
electricity (10A)	€ 4,00
dog	€ 3,00
Special offers available.	

FR49080 Camping Ile d'Offard

Rue de Verden, Ile d'Offard, F-49400 Saumur (Maine-et-Loire)

Tel: 02 41 40 30 00. Email: iledoffard@cutloisirs.fr

This site is situated on an island between the banks of the Loire. The 224 touring pitches are at present on grass at the far end or hardstanding nearer the entrance. Some 34 pitches are occupied by tour operators and caravan holiday homes and these can be intrusive in some areas. Pitches have access to electricity hook-ups (10A). A new heated outdoor swimming pool has been completed together with paddling and spa pools. Within walking distance of the centre of Saumur, this site is useful as an overnight stop en-route south or as a short-term base from which to visit the numerous châteaux in the region. Fishing is possible in the Loire (permits are available from Saumur).

Facilities

Three sanitary blocks, one heated in winter, include provision for disabled visitors. Toilet facilities are unisex. Block one has a well equipped laundry. The other blocks are only open in high season. Motorcaravan service point € 4.50 - € 7.50 (free to campers). Restaurant and bar (early May - late Sept) with takeaway. Internet access. Table tennis, volleyball. Play area. Some activities with a children's club, wine tastings, etc. in high season. Off site: Thursday market 500 m. Saturday morning market 2 km. Riding 5 km.

Open: 1 March - 31 October.

Directions

From north and A85 exit 3, take N147 south (Saumur). After 2.5 km. turn left (N147 bears right). Follow old road towards river and town. Cross bridge onto island, then first left. Site ahead. GPS: N47:15.457 W00:03.660

Charges 2007

Per unit incl. 2 persons	€ 15,50 - € 24,00
extra person	€ 4,00 - € 5,00
child (2-10 yrs)	€ 2,00 - € 2,50
electricity	€ 3,50

Camping Cheques accepted.

FR49110 Camping de l'Ile du Château

Avenue de la Boire Salée, F-49130 Les Ponts-de-Cé (Maine-et-Loire)

Tel: 02 41 44 62 05. Email: ile-du-chateau@wanadoo.fr

This could be a very useful site for those wishing to visit Angers and tour the surrounding vineyards and châteaux from a no-nonsense campsite offering good value for money. Just five kilometres from the city centre, the site is on an island in the Loire, though sadly one arm of the river is now dry in summer because of reservoirs up-stream. A camping field (25 pitches without electricity) overlooks this, while the main area has 89 touring pitches on generally level ground, with lots of mature trees offering shade, separated by hedges and all with electricity (6A).

Facilities

The main sanitary block is traditional, kept clean and offers reasonable provision. Mainly seatless WCs, some washbasins in cabins and pre-set showers. Facilities for disabled visitors. Baby bath. Dishwashing and laundry facilities. Motorcaravan service point. Small shop selling basics (bread can be ordered). Simple, open-air bar with snacks and takeaway (all 1/07-31/8). Minigolf. Boules. Bicycle hire. Adjacent open-air leisure pool, tennis courts and football field. Off site: Pizza takeaway 200 m. Fishing 200 m. Riding 2 km. Golf 5 km. Supermarket nearby.

Open: 3 April - 30 September.

Directions

Les Ponts-de-Cé is just off the N260 Angers eastern bypass. Take exit west onto D4 signed Ponts-de-Cé and Bouchemaine. In 1.5 km. turn south on N160 signed to town centre and campsite. After about 1 km. turn right at small roundabout into campsite road. GPS: N47:25.475 W00:31.746

Charges 2006

Per unit incl. 2 persons	€ 10,10 - € 12,60
extra person	€ 2,40 - € 2,80
child (2-10 yrs)	free - € 1,80
electricity	€ 2,80

FR49120 Centre Touristique Lac de Ribou

Allée Léon Mandin, F-49300 Cholet (Maine-et-Loire)

Tel: 02 41 49 74 30. Email: lacderibou@cholet-sports-loisirs.fr

Situated just 58 km. southeast of Nantes and a similar distance from the River Loire at Angers and Saumur, this could be a useful place to break a journey or to spend a few days relaxing. Camping Lac de Ribou, with the adjacent 'Village Vacances', forms a holiday complex in pleasant parkland next to an extensive lake on the outskirts of the busy market town of Cholet. 162 touring pitches are on undulating land (some are sloping), divided by hedges and with mature trees proving shade on many; most have electricity (10A) and 115 also have individual water tap and drainage.

Facilities

Two sanitary blocks provide pre-set showers, washbasins in cabins and excellent dishwashing and laundry sinks. Facilities for disabled visitors. Motorcaravan service points. Large heated swimming pool plus smaller pool with slide and a paddling pool (1/06-30/09 - supervised July/Aug). Restaurant and bar with a small shop (July/Aug) and very limited takeaway. Very full programme of activities for all ages (July/Aug). Off site: Fishing and small beach (no swimming) 500 m. Sailing 1 km. Supermarket 2 km. Riding 5 km. Golf 7 km.

Open: 1 April - 30 September.

Directions

From Cholet ring road east of town, turn east on D20 towards Maulévrier/Mauléon. At roundabout by Leclerc supermarket, take first exit signed to the Centre Touristique and campsite. GPS: N47:02.182 W00:50.624

Charges 2006

Per unit incl. 2 persons	€ 9,25 - € 18,90
extra person	€ 2,95 - € 4,69
electricity (10A)	€ 3,65 - € 5,10
dog	€ 1,38 - € 2,14

FR72020 Camping Municipal du Lac

Rue du Lac, F-72120 Saint Calais (Sarthe)

Tel: 02 43 35 04 81

Camping du Lac is a pleasant, traditional municipal site with 75 marked pitches (about 60 for touring), most are separated by hedges and all with electricity (3/6A), water and drainage. A separate area is for tents. In high season there are themed evening walks, competitions and communal meals (campers take their own food and can join in the dancing). Reception is welcoming, the value is excellent and this would make a good night stop or a base for visiting the Le Mans 24 hour race.

Facilities

Two sanitary blocks are old but kept very clean and provide showers and some washbasins in private cabins. Washing machine. Bread and croissants (to order). Two small play areas. Fishing in lake. Off site: Swimming pool adjacent (free). Local supermarket just a short walk. Riding 10 km. Bicycle hire 15 km. Golf 40 km.

Open: 1 April - 15 October.

Directions

St Calais is 45 km. east of Le Mans. Well signed from N157, site is beside lake north of the town, near the station. Follow signs for campsite and 'Plan d'eau'.

Charges 2006

Per person	€ 2,55
child (under 12 yrs)	€ 1,25 - € 2,50
pitch incl. electricity (3/6A)	€ 2,75 - € 4,85

FR72030 Castel Camping le Château de Chanteloup

F-72460 Sillé-le-Philippe (Sarthe)

Tel: 02 43 27 51 07. Email: chanteloup.souffront@wanadoo.fr

An attractive and peaceful site close to Le Mans, Chanteloup is situated in the park of a 19th century château in the heart of the Sarthe countryside. There are 100 pitches all with 6A electricity although long leads will be required in some places. Some are in the woods, many are around the edges of the lawns and completely open, and a few overlook the lake, so there are differing degrees of shade throughout the site.

Facilities

All sanitary facilities are in the château outbuildings and are well maintained and kept very clean. Washbasins are in cabins. Dishwashing and laundry facilities. Small shop, takeaway and restaurant with covered outdoor seating (all 5/7-24/8). Bar (1/6-3/9). Swimming pool (fenced). Play area (parental supervision essential). Games room, tennis, volleyball, table tennis. Mountain bike hire. Organised activities (high season). WiFi. Off site: Riding 7 km. Golf 10 km. Tennis club in Le Mans.

Open: 1 June - 3 September.

Directions

Sillé-le-Philippe is 18 km. northeast of Le Mans on the D301 to Bonnétable. From autoroute take exit 23, follow signs for Le Mans and Tours, then Le Mans and Savigné l'Evèque. Site is to the east just off main road and signed on southern edge of Sillé. GPS: N48:06.281 E00:20.424

Charges 2006

Per person	€ 5,50 - € 8,50
child (under 7 yrs)	€ 3,00
pitch	€ 8,00 - € 13,00
electricity	€ 3,00

Less 10% outside 24/6-20/8. Charges are higher during the 24 hr race week at Le Mans.

FR72040 Camping des Molières

Sillé-Plage, F-72140 Sillé le Guillaume (Sarthe)

Tel: **02 43 20 11 12**. Email: **campingsilleplage@wanadoo.fr**

This pleasant 'no frills' site is located in forestry commission land on the edge of an attractive lake. The 120 pitches are set among the trees and many have been grassed. There is electricity (10A) available to all (long leads may be needed in places). The ground is undulating, so finding a perfectly level pitch is difficult. The great attraction of this site is its location: the lake offers fishing, swimming and many water sports, whilst the surrounding forest is a maze of marked tracks used by walkers, cyclists and horse riders.

Facilities

Two new sanitary blocks are well maintained with push-button showers, some washbasins in cubicles and good indoor dishwashing and laundry sinks. Very limited facilities for disabled visitors. No chemical disposal or motorhome service points. Small shop in reception selling a few basics; bread can be ordered. Small club room with television. Some activities organised in conjunction with sister site and the local tourist board. Off site: Golf 30 km.

Open: 1 June - 31 August.

Directions

Sillé le Guillaume is 22 km. north-west of Le Mans on the D304/D35 to Mayenne. Approaching from Mayenne, turn north 2 km. before the town on C1 towards Sillé-Plage. Cross first junction and turn left at second (campsites signed). Site on right in less than 1 km. GPS: N48:12.203 W00:07.660

Charges 2006

Per unit incl. 2 persons	€ 8,20 - € 9,00
extra person	€ 2,90 - € 3,20
electricity (10A)	€ 2,40 - € 2,60

FR72060 Camping Municipal du Val de Sarthe

Rue de l'Abreuvoir, F-72170 Beaumont sur Sarthe (Sarthe)

Tel: **02 43 97 01 93**. Email: **beaumont.sur.sarthe@wanadoo.fr**

This delightful, inexpensive riverside site is conveniently located just a short walk from the town and its shops and services. The 73 level, grassy individual pitches are large, divided by hedges and all have electricity (5A). Some of the pitches including those along the river's edge may require a longer cable. An activity area provides swings and other play equipment, boules , tennis, netball, and a fitness trail. Those intending to stay longer than one night require a barrier card (refundable deposit). Reception opens 08.00-22.00 daily (high season), 10.00-20.00 (low season). Barrier opens at 07.00.

Facilities

The central sanitary unit is accessed by a flight of steps although there is a long and fairly steep ramp for disabled people. Facilities include some washbasins in cubicles and spacious showers. Motorcaravan service point. Bread and croissants to order. Activity area. River fishing. Room for campers' use (July/Aug). Double axle caravans are not accepted. Off site: Riding 10 km. Bicycle hire 15 km.

Open: 1 May - 30 September.

Directions

Beaumont is half way between Alençon and Le Mans on the N138. Turn east on D26 in town centre and follow signs to site. GPS: N48:13.533 E00:08.069

Charges 2006

Per person	€ 1,70
child (under 7 yrs)	€ 0,90
pitch incl. electricity	€ 3,55

FR86010 Castel Camping le Petit Trianon

Saint Ustre, 1 rue du Moulin de St Ustre, F-86220 Ingrandes-sur-Vienne (Vienne)

Tel: **05 49 02 61 47**. Email: **chateau@petit-trianon.fr**

A family owned site for many years, quaint and rustic are words that spring to mind on arrival here. Situated between Tours, Poitiers and Futuroscope, the approach to Le Petit Trianon is through a grand, narrow, gateway leading onto a slightly sloping meadow surrounded by trees in front of the château, plus a newer, large, more open field with a woodland area between. The 99 spacious, open but marked pitches are arranged to leave plenty of free space and there is shade in parts. All have electricity (13A). Reception is housed in the 18th century château.

Facilities

The original toilet unit includes washbasins in cabins, some washbasin and shower units, baby baths, laundry and dishwashing facilities. Smaller blocks for newer parts of site and one has facilities for disabled people. Motorcaravan service point. Shop (bread to order). Takeaway. Heated pool and paddling pools. Playground. Table tennis. Minigolf. Badminton, croquet, volleyball and boules. TV room, books and games. Bicycle hire. Wine tastings. Excursions. Internet access. Caravan storage. Off site: Restaurant 50 m. Fishing 3 km. Riding 15 km.

Open: 20 May - 20 September.

Directions

Ingrandes is signed from N10 north of town (between Dangé and Châtellerault). From autoroute A10 take exit 26 for Châtellerault-Nord, at roundabout follow signs for Tours to Ingrandes where site is signed.

Charges 2006

Per person	€ 7,00
child (0-6 yrs)	€ 1,10 - € 3,50
pitch	€ 4,20
electricity (5/10A)	€ 4,20 - € 4,60
dog	€ 2,10

FR86030 Camping le Relais du Miel

Route d'Antran, F-86100 Châtellerault (Vienne)

Tel: 05 49 02 06 27. Email: camping@lerelaisdumiel.com

With very easy access from the A10 and N10 roads, in the northern outskirts of Châtellerault, this site is in the 10 acre grounds of a grand house dating from Napoleonic times. It is surrounded by majestic old trees beside the River Vienne. There is also an orchard and stone gateposts leading onto ground, previously the home farm, that now forms 80 large, flat pitches. Divided by mature trees and bushes providing plenty of shade, all the pitches have electricity (10A) and water, 15 with drainage connections. Twin barns form two sides of a courtyard behind the house, one of which has been converted very stylishly into reception, a high ceilinged function and games room, and a bar and restaurant serving good value meals. Beams taken from the original ceiling now form part of the bar top and act as arm rests. The second barn is being developed into apartments.

Facilities

Excellent toilet facilities include washbasins in cabins, facilities for disabled visitors, dishwashing and laundry facilities. Basic essentials and gas. Bar and restaurant. Pizzas (from local pizzeria). Takeaway. Snack bar (open in evenings 1/7-30/8). Swimming and paddling pools (15 x 7 m). Playground. Tennis courts. Volleyball, basketball. Bicycle hire. Boules. Games room with electronic games. Fishing. Observatory. Internet access. Torch useful. Mobile homes and apartments to rent. Off site: Supermarket 400 m. Riding 5 km. Golf 11 km. Futuroscope 16 km.

Open: 15 May - 2 September.

Directions

Châtellerault is between Tours and Poitiers. Site is north of town close to A10 autoroute. Take exit 26 (Châtellerault-Nord) and site is signed just off roundabout. From N10 follow signs for motorway (Tours - Péage) and at roundabout take exit for Antran. GPS: N46:50.307 E00:32.071

Charges 2006

Per unit incl. 2 persons and electricity	€ 19,00 - € 24,00
extra person over 5 yrs	€ 3,00 - € 5,00

Less 15% for 1 week, 20% for 2 weeks.

FR86080 Camping Caravaning les Peupliers

F-86700 Couhé (Vienne)

Tel: 05 49 59 21 16. Email: info@lespeupliers.fr

Family owned and run since 1968, Les Peupliers is located in a valley south of Poitiers. The site is arranged on the banks of a river (unfenced), the 160 pitches on both sides or around a fishing lake. On level grass, most are separated and all have 16A electricity, while 50 are fully serviced. There is a good pool complex that includes water slides and toboggans, a heated main pool, a paddling pool and a lagoon with two slides for younger children, jacuzzi, plus water games. There is some noise from the N10 which runs fairly close to the site.

Facilities

Three toilet blocks of varying ages are in Mediterranean style, with washbasins in cubicles and facilities for babies and disabled people. The newest is in regular use and the other two open as the season progresses. Dishwashing and laundry facilities. TV and fridge rental. Shop. Snack bar, restaurant and bar. Entertainment in peak season. Pool complex. Playgrounds. Fishing lake. Minigolf, table tennis, football, volleyball and boules. Motorcaravan service point. Off site: Tennis 800 m. Bicycle hire 1 km. Riding 5 km.

Open: 2 May - 30 September. Chalets for hire all year.

Directions

Couhé is 30 km. south of Poitiers on N10. From north, follow signs (Couhé town centre) and campsite (a short distance from slip road on right). From south, take 2nd Couhé exit from N10. Site entrance is opposite end of slip road. GPS: N46:18.706 E00:10.670

Charges 2007

Per person	€ 7,00
child (2-10 yrs)	€ 3,50
pitch incl. electricity	€ 13,00

Camping Cheques accepted.

FR86040 Camping le Futuriste

F-86130 Saint Georges-les-Baillargeaux (Vienne)

Tel: 05 49 52 47 52. Email: camping-le-futuriste@wanadoo.fr

Mobile homes ▶ page 468

Le Futuriste is a neat, modern site, open all year and close to Futuroscope. With a busy atmosphere, there are early departures and late arrivals. The reception office is open 08.00-22.00 hrs. There are 118 individual, flat, grassy pitches divided by young trees and shrubs which are beginning to provide some shelter for this elevated and otherwise rather open site (possibly windy). 82 pitches have electricity (6A) and a further 30 have electricity, water, waste water and sewage connections. All are accessed via neat, level and firmly rolled gravel roads. On raised ground with panoramic views over the strikingly modern buildings and night-time bright lights that comprise the popular attraction of Futuroscope, this site is ideal for a short stay to visit the park which is only 1.5 km. away (tickets can be bought at the site) but it is equally good for longer stays to see the region. Details of attractions are available from the enthusiastic young couple who run the site. Note: it is best to see the first evening show at Futuroscope otherwise you will find yourself locked out of the site – the gates are closed at 23.30 hrs.

Facilities

Excellent, clean sanitary facilities in two insulated blocks (can be heated). Those in the newest block are unisex. and include some washbasins in cabins and facilities for disabled people. Dishwashing and laundry facilities. Shop (bread to order), bar/restaurant (all 1/5-30/9) . Snack bar and takeaway (1/7-31/8). Two heated outdoor pools, one with slide and paddling pool (1/5-30/9). Games room. TV. Volleyball, boules and table tennis. Lake fishing. Youth groups not accepted. Off site: Bicycle hire 500 m. Hypermarket 600 m. Golf 5 km. Riding 10 km.

Open: All year.

Directions

From either A10 autoroute or N10, take Futuroscope exit. Site is east of both roads, off D20 (St Georges-Les-Baillargeaux). Follow signs to St Georges. Site on hill; turn by water tower and site is on left. GPS: N46:39.928 E00:23.668

Charges 2007

Per pitch incl. 1-3 persons	€ 14,20 - € 19,50
extra person	€ 1,90 - € 2,60
electricity	€ 2,60 - € 3,50
animal	€ 1,80

Camping Cheques accepted.

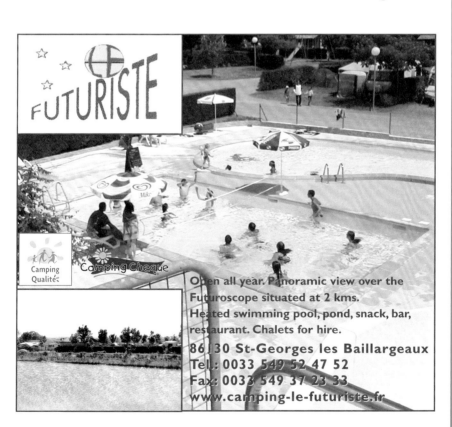

Open all year. Panoramic view over the Futuroscope situated at 2 kms.
Heated swimming pool, pond, snack, bar, restaurant. Chalets for hire.
86130 St-Georges les Baillargeaux
Tel: 0033 549 52 47 52
Fax: 0033 549 37 23 33
www.camping-le-futuriste.fr

FR86100 Camping du Futur

9 rue des Bois, F-86170 Avanton (Vienne)
Tel: 05 49 54 09 67. Email: campingdufutur@wanadoo.fr

This is a pleasant little site conveniently located close to Futuroscope, the remarkable theme park devoted to the moving image, and to the historic town of Poitiers. It is particularly popular as an en-route stop-over on journeys along the A10 and N10. There are 54 grassy touring pitches, marked by bushes, on flat land with a scattering of mature trees; all have electricity (10A) although long cables may be required in places. There are also 14 mobile homes to rent. There is a warm welcome from the British owners, Brian and Dianne Ford.

Facilities

The sanitary block is in a traditional style, open at each end. Well maintained and kept very clean with push-button showers and some washbasins in cubicles. Dishwashing and laundry facilities. Good little swimming pool. Basic supplies from reception; bread can be ordered. Bar (July and August – limited hours) serving continental breakfasts. TV, pool and electronic games in room next to bar. Off site: Futuroscope 5 km. Fishing 5 km. Poitiers airport 10 km. (occasional flights go over). Golf 10 km. Riding 20 km.

Open: 1 April - 30 September.

Directions

Avanton is 12 km. north of Poitiers, just west of A10 (exit 28 - follow signs for Martigny and Avanton). From north on N10 turn right north of Jaunay-Clan towards Neuville on new road to join D62; in about 3 km, turn south on D757 to Avanton. Site signed. GPS: N46:39.374 E00:18.044

Charges 2006

Per unit incl. 2 persons	€ 12,60 - € 18,00
extra person	€ 3,00 - € 3,50
child (3-12 yrs)	€ 2,00 - € 2,50
electricity (10A)	€ 3,00

FR86090 Camping Flower du Lac de Saint Cyr

F-86130 Saint Cyr (Vienne)
Tel: 05 49 62 57 22. Email: contact@parcdesaintcyr.com

This well organised, five hectare campsite is part of a 300 hectare leisure park, based around a large lake with sailing and associated sports, and an area for swimming (supervised July/Aug). Land-based activities include tennis, two half-courts, fishing, badminton, beach volleyball, petanque, table tennis, TV room, and a well equipped fitness suite, all of which are free of charge. The campsite has around 185 tourist pitches, 10 mobile homes and 3 'yurts' (canvas and wooden tents) for rent. The marked and generally separated pitches are all fully serviced with electricity (10A), water and drainage. In high season there are extra free activities including a kids club, beach club, archery and an entertainment programme. Also in high season but charged for are sailing school, aquatic toboggan, windsurfing, canoe, kayak and water bikes. Campers can also use the 9 and 18 hole golf courses (with 20% discount for the 18 hole).

Facilities

The main toilet block is modern and supplemented for peak season by a second unit, although they do attract some use by day-trippers to the leisure facilities. They include washbasins in cubicles, dishwashing and laundry facilities, and facilities for babies and disabled persons. Shop, restaurant and takeaway (April - Sept). Playground on beach. Bicycle hire. Barrier locked 22.00-07.00 hrs (€ 10 deposit for card). Off site: Riding 200 m. Golf 800 m.

Open: 1 April - 30 September.

Directions

Saint Cyr is about midway between Châtellerault and Poitiers. Site signed to east of N10 at Beaumont along D82 towards Bonneuil-Matours, and is part of the Parc de Loisirs de Saint Cyr.

Charges 2006

Per person	€ 2,50 - € 5,00
child (1-7 yrs)	€ 1,50 - € 2,00
pitch incl. electricity, water and drainage	€ 6,00 - € 12,00

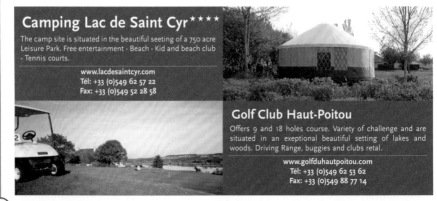

Check real time availability and at-the-gate prices...
www.alanrogers.com

MAP 8

Burgundy is a wonderfully evocative region offering breathtaking châteaux and cathedrals, rolling hills and heady mountain views, vineyards and superlative cuisine, not to mention of course, a wide variety of world renowned wines.

DÉPARTEMENTS: 21 CÔTE D'OR, 58 NIÈVRE, 71 SAÔNE-ET-LOIRE, 89 YONNE

MAJOR CITY: DIJON

In the rich heartland of France, Burgundy was once a powerful independent state and important religious centre. Its golden age is reflected in the area's magnificent art and architecture: the grand palaces and art collections of Dijon, the great pilgrimage church of Vézelay, the Cistercian Abbaye de Fontenay and the evocative abbey remains at Cluny, once the most powerful monastery in Europe.

However Burgundy is best known for its wine, including some of the world's finest, notably from the great vineyards of the Côte d'Or and Chablis, and also for its sublime cuisine. You'll also notice how driving through the country villages is like reading a wine merchant's list with plenty of opportunities for tasting and choosing your wine.

The area is criss-crossed by navigable waterways and includes the Parc Régional du Morvan; good walking country amidst lush, rolling wooded landscape.

Places of interest

Autun: 12th century St Lazare cathedral.

Beaune: medieval town; Museum of Burgundy Wine.

Cluny: Europe's largest Benedictine abbey.

Dijon: Palace of the Dukes, Fine Arts Museum, Burgundian Folklore Museum.

Fontenay: Fontenay Abbey and Cloister.

Joigny: medieval town.

Mâcon: Maison des Vins (wine centre).

Paray-le-Monial: Romanesque basilica, pilgrimage centre.

Sens: historic buildings, museum with fine Gallo-Roman collections.

Vézelay: fortified medieval hillside.

Cuisine of the region

Many dishes are wine based, including *Poulet au Meursault* and *Coq au Chambertin*. Dijon is known for its *pain d'épice* (spiced honey-cake) and spicy mustard.

Boeuf Bourguignon: braised beef simmered in a red wine-based sauce.

Garbure: heavy soup, a mixture of pork, cabbage, beans and sausages.

Gougère: cheese pastry based on Gruyère.

Jambon persillé: parsley-flavoured ham, served cold in jelly.

Matelote: fresh-water fish soup, usually based on a red wine sauce.

Meurette: red wine-based sauce with small onions, used with fish or poached egg dishes.

FR21000 Sunêlia Lac de Panthier

F-21320 Vandenesse-en-Auxois (Côte d'Or)

Tel: **03 80 49 21 94**. Email: **info@lac-de-panthier.com**

An attractively situated lakeside site in Burgundy countryside, Camping Lac de Panthier is divided into two distinct campsites. The first, smaller section houses the reception, shop, restaurant and other similar facilities. The second, larger area is 200 m. along the lakeside road and is where the site activities take place and the pool can be found. The 207 pitches (157 for touring units) all have electricity connections and are mostly on level grass, although in parts there are shallow terraces. The site's restaurant has panoramic views over the lake which has many watersports facilities. The site is used by tour operators.

Facilities

Two unisex toilet blocks per site also provide for babies and disabled people. Shop, bar and restaurant. Games and TV rooms. Pool, children's pool and water-slide (15/5-15/9). Indoor pool, sauna and fitness equipment. Fishing. Riding. Bicycle and canoe hire. Watersports. Entertainment and activities organised in high season and clubs for children and teenagers. Off site: Boat excursions from Pouilly en Auxois (8 km). Riding and golf 10 km. Dijon, Autun and Beaune. Bus to Dijon and Poilly 300 m.

Open: 8 April - 15 October.

Directions

From A6 join A38 and exit at junction 24. Take N81 towards Arnay Le Duc (back over A6), turn left on D977 for 5 km. Fork left for Vandenesse-en-Auxois. On through village on D977 for 2.5 km. then left again and site is on left.

Charges 2006

Per pitch incl. 2 persons and electricity	€ 19,90 - € 23,40
extra person	€ 5,00 - € 6,20

Camping Cheques accepted.

FR21010 Camping Municipal Louis Rigoly

Esplanade Saint Vorles, F-21400 Châtillon-sur-Seine (Côte d'Or)

Tel: **03 80 91 03 05**. Email: **tourism-chatillon-sur-seine@wanadoo.fr**

This well kept, small, hillside municipal site has 52 touring pitches. Mainly individual and separated, they are on fairly flat grass, all with electricity (4/6A) with mature trees providing shelter. Adjoining the site is the municipal swimming pool complex with both indoor and outdoor pools (free in July and August). There is no shop, but the town is close. The site, which has much transit trade, can become full by evening in season.

Facilities

The main toilet block at the lower end of the site is satisfactory. A smaller heated unit behind reception contains facilities for babies, a washing machine and dryer. Facilities for disabled visitors provided in a separate block. Snack bar July/Aug. Baker calls every morning (except Tuesday). Play area. Boules. Motorcaravan service point. Internet access. Off site: Fishing or bicycle hire 1 km. Riding 4 km.

Open: 1 April - 30 September.

Directions

On northeast outskirts of town; site is signed from centre (steep hills approaching site, narrow roads).

Charges 2007

Per person	€ 3,25
child (under 7 yrs)	€ 1,30
pitch	€ 3,15
vehicle	€ 1,35
motorcycle	€ 1,00

No credit cards.

FR21020 Camping Municipal les Cent Vignes

10 rue Auguste Dubois, F-21200 Beaune (Côte d'Or)

Tel: **03 80 22 03 91**

Les Cent Vignes is a very well kept site offering 116 individual pitches of good size, separated from each other by neat beech hedges high enough to keep a fair amount of privacy. Over half of the pitches are on grass, ostensibly for tents, the remainder on hardstandings with electricity for caravans. A popular site, within walking distance of the town centre, Les Cent Vignes becomes full mid-June to early Sept. but with many short-stay campers there are departures each day and reservations can be made.

Facilities

Two modern, fully equipped and well constructed, sanitary blocks, one of which can be heated, should be large enough. Nearly all washbasins are in cabins. Dishwashing and laundry sinks. Washing machines. Shop, restaurant with takeaway (all 1/4-15/10). Playground. Sports area with tennis, basketball, volleyball, boules and table tennis. TV room. Barbecue area. Off site: Bicycle hire 1 km. Fishing, golf or windsurfing 4 km. Beaune 1 km.

Open: 15 March - 31 October.

Directions

From autoroute exit 24 follow signs for Beaune centre on D2 road, camping signs to site in about 1 km. Well signed from other routes.

Charges 2006

Per person	€ 3,50
child (2-7 yrs)	€ 1,80
pitch	€ 4,30
electricity (6A)	€ 3,50

FR21030 Camping Municipal les Premier Pres

Route de Bouilland, F-21420 Savigny-lès-Beaune (Côte d'Or)

Tel: 03 80 26 15 06. Email: mairie.savigny-les-beaune@wanadoo.fr

This popular site is ideally located for visiting the Burgundy vineyards, for use as a transit site or for spending time in the town of Beaune. During the high season it is full every evening, so it is best to arrive by 4 pm. The 90 level pitches are marked and numbered, with electric hook-ups and room for an awning. If reception is closed when you arrive, you find a pitch and report later, otherwise 'Madame' will allocate a place.

Facilities

Well kept sanitary facilities are housed in a modern building behind reception. Additional WCs and water points are conveniently placed towards the middle of the site. Table tennis. Motorcaravan service point. Torch useful. Staff are pleasant and ice can be purchased. Off site: Sunday market in the village 1 km. Beaune 7 km.

Open: 29 April - 30 September.

Directions

From A6 autoroute take exit 24 signed Beaune and Savigny-lès-Beaune onto D2. Turn right towards Savigny-lès-Beaune (3 km) and follow signs to site.

Charges 2006

Per person	€ 2,10
child (under 7 yrs)	€ 1,10
pitch	€ 3,05
electricity	€ 3,35

No credit cards.

FR21040 Camping de l'Etang de Fouché

Rue du 8 Mai 1945, F-21230 Arnay le Duc (Côte d'Or)

Tel: 03 80 90 02 23. Email: info@campingfouche.com

Useful as an overnight stop en-route to or from the Mediterranean or indeed for longer stays, this quite large but peaceful, lakeside site has good facilities and the added advantage of being open all year. It can be very busy during the school holidays, and is probably better visited outside the main season. There are 190 good sized pitches, on fairly level grass and all with 10A electricity (some with water). Many are hedged and offer a choice of shade or more open aspect. In July/August there are regular activities for children and adults.

Facilities

At the time of the inspection, only two of the four sanitary blocks were open. They are reasonably modern and well maintained, including some British style WCs, washbasins in cabins, facilities for disabled visitors. Washing machines and dishwashing under cover. Shop (with bread), bar, restaurant, takeaway (all 15/5-15/9). TV/games room. New heated outdoor swimming pool. Boules. Table tennis. Playground. Off site: Town centre 800 m. Lakeside beach with playground, water slides, pedaloes, canoes.

Open: 15 April - 15 October.

Directions

Site is on east side of town (well signed), 15 km. from A6 (exit at péage de Pouilly-en-Auxois).

Charges 2006

Per unit incl. 2 persons	€ 10,10 - € 14,70
extra person	€ 3,10 - € 4,30
child (under 10 yrs)	€ 1,60 - € 2,30
electricity	€ 3,50
animal	€ 1,70

FR21050 Camping la Grappe d'Or

2 route de Volnay, F-21190 Meursault (Côte d'Or)

Tel: 03 80 21 22 48. Email: info@camping-meursault.com

Meursault, the capital of the great white wines of Burgundy, is southwest of Beaune and Camping de la Grappe d'Or offers terraced pitches overlooking acres of vineyards. Most of the 125 touring pitches are flat, of varying sizes, and some have shade from mature trees. They all have electrical connections (15A). There is an outdoor pool and flume and, during July and August, aqua gym and other water activities are organised. There is a fenced play area for youngsters and, just across the road from the entrance, there are two tennis courts for campers.

Facilities

Sanitary facilities are in three blocks with some washbasins in cabins. Child/baby room, facilities for visitors with disabilities, laundry and undercover dishwashing sinks. Shop, bar, restaurant, takeaway and swimming pool, all open from 1/5 - 30/9 (pool heated 15/6 - 15/9) although hours may vary. Play area, volleyball, tennis courts. Bicycle hire. Off site: Golf or riding 7 km. Indoor swimming pool 7 km. Fishing 8 km. Beaune 9 km.

Open: 1 April - 15 October.

Directions

Site is north of Meursault. Take N74 from Beaune and follow the sign for Meursault; campsite is well signed from the town.

Charges 2007

Per unit incl. 2 persons	€ 13,50
extra person	€ 3,00
child (under 7 yrs)	€ 1,50
electricity	€ 3,50

Camping Cheques accepted.

FR21060 Camping les Bouleaux

F-21200 Vignoles (Côte d'Or)

Tel: **03 80 22 26 88**

Camping Les Bouleaux is an excellent little campsite located at Vignoles, northeast of Beaune. There are just 46 pitches, all with an electrical connection (3-6A, long leads may be required on some pitches). The large flat pitches are attractively laid out and most are separated by hedges and trees giving some shade. Monsieur Rossignal takes great pride in his campsite, keeping the grounds and facilities exceptionally clean and tidy, and by planting bright flowers near the reception. The nearest shops are 3 km.

Facilities

An older unisex building provides Turkish style WCs, while the adjacent modern block houses British style WCs (no paper). Washbasins in cabins or communal; push-button controllable showers, excellent facilities for visitors with disabilities. No shop, but wine and basic groceries can be bought at reception. Gas exchange. Off site: Beaune 3 km. Bicycle hire, fishing or golf 3 km. Riding 6 km.

Open: All year.

Directions

Leave A6 at junction 24.1 south of Beaune. Turn right at roundabout, straight on at traffic lights (centre lane), then right at next roundabout. Cross autoroute, left (Vignole). Follow campsite signs.

Charges 2006

Per person	€ 3,35
child (under 7 yrs)	€ 2,40
pitch incl. electricity (3/6A)	€ 4,80 - € 6,00

No credit cards.

FR21070 Camping Municipal les Grèbes

F-21330 Marcenay (Côte d'Or)

Tel: **03 80 81 61 72**. Email: **marcenay@club-internet.fr**

This attractive, peacefully located and very spacious lakeside site has 90 level, grassy pitches all with 6A electricity hook-ups. They are arranged in small clearings with dividing shrubs and hedges. The stylish reception building has a small shop, a snack bar with drinks, a small library, some games machines and a pool table. The site has access via pedestrian gates onto the lakeside path, there is a small beach and marked swimming area and one can use non-powered boats or fish. The nearby Haut Fourneau is worth a visit.

Facilities

Two good quality modern sanitary units. The main one can be heated, the second is open only for peak season. Both provide washbasins in cubicles and spacious hot showers. Good units for disabled people. Laundry. Motorcaravan service point. Shop. Snack bar. Games and TV rooms. Small pool for children. Canoe hire. Playground. Boules. Internet access. Off site: Restaurant, pony and donkey rides 500 m.

Open: 1 April - 15 October.

Directions

Marcenay is about 35 km. east of Tonnerre and 14 km. west of Chatillon-sur-Seine, just north of the D965 road joining these towns. Site is signed from Marcenay. GPS: N47:52.195 E04:24.276

Charges guide

Per person	€ 2,50
child (under 7 yrs)	€ 1,40
pitch incl. electricity	€ 7,50

Reductions for stays over 15 days.

FR21080 Camping des Sources

Avenue des Sources, F-21590 Santenay (Côte d'Or)

Tel: **03 80 20 66 55**

Santenay lies in the heart of the Côte de Beaune, a region renowned for its wine and châteaux, and within easy reach of Beaune. After a day's sightseeing or 'dégustation', there is a casino and a spa to visit. It is also alongside a long distance track for cycling, rollerskating and walking, from which start a number of shorter circular routes. This relatively new site is next to the village sports and leisure area, with access to the swimming pool and paddling pool (free 1/6-31/8). There are 110 comfortable level grassy touring pitches. All have electrical connections (6A) and a water tap is never far.

Facilities

The modern toilet block contains British style WCs, washbasins and pre-set showers. Facilities for disabled people. Motorcaravan services. Laundry facilities. Gas supplies. Shop. Bar, restaurant, snack bar and takeaway (15/5-15/9). Games room. Internet terminal. Playground. Playing field. Table tennis. Minigolf. Boules. Skittles. Off site: Tennis courts, skateboarding. Casino 300 m. Spa 400 m. Santenay 1.5 km. Bicycle hire 1.5 km. Riding 2 km. Fishing, boat launching 4 km.

Open: 15 April - 1 November.

Directions

From Beaune take N74 (Autun and Montceau-les-Mines). After 2 km., at roundabout, continue on N74. After 11 km. pass under N6 and in 3 km. turn right into Santenay. Site signed from village. GPS: N46:54.26 E04:41.06

Charges 2006

Per unit incl. 2 persons and electricity	€ 16,00 - € 19,50
extra person	€ 3,00 - € 3,70
child (0-7 yrs)	€ 1,40 - € 1,90

FR58010 Camping des Bains

15 avenue Jean Mermoz, F-58360 St Honoré-les-Bains (Nièvre)

Tel: 03 86 30 73 44. Email: camping-les-bains@wanadoo.fr

You are assured of a warm welcome at this attractive family run site, in an area of rolling countryside, woods, rivers and country villages, ideal for walking or cycling. The spacious 130 level grassed pitches (all with 6A electricity) are mostly separated by hedges with mature trees offering shade. Next to the camping is the 'thermal spa' where there are opportunities to 'take the waters' for a three day session or a full blown cure of three weeks! Reception has details. There is an excellent restaurant almost opposite the campsite entrance. A 'Sites et Paysages' member.

Facilities

Two main sanitary units have mostly British style WCs, washbasins in cabins and showers (one block may be closed in low season). Baby bath. Laundry. Facilities for disabled people. Bar provides food and a takeaway. Swimming pool, slide and paddling pool (15/6-10/10). Play area. Streams for children to fish. Minigolf. Children's entertainment (July/Aug). TV and DVDs. Internet access. Off site: Bicycle hire or riding 500 m. Fishing 5 km.

Open: 1 April - 10 October.

Directions

From Nevers, travel east on D978; turn right onto D985 (St Honoré-les-Bains). Site is signed on entering town. Care is needed at narrow site entrance.

Charges 2006

Per unit incl. 2 persons	€ 15,50
extra person	€ 4,50
child (2-7 yrs)	€ 2,85
electricity (6A)	€ 3,20

FR58030 Manoir de Bezolle

F-58110 Saint Pereuse-en-Morvan (Nièvre)

Tel: 03 86 84 42 55. Email: info@bezolle.com

Manoir de Bezolle is well situated to explore the Morvan Natural Park and the Nivernais area. It has been attractively landscaped to provide a number of different areas, some giving pleasant views over the surrounding countryside. The touring pitches of good size are on level grass with shade, some with terracing and access to electricity (10A). There are two small lakes, stocked with many fish for anglers. This site is good for families, with a range of activities provided for them.

Facilities

Two main toilet blocks (opened as needed) provide washbasins in cabins, mostly British style WCs, bath, provision for disabled visitors and a baby bath. A fibreglass unit contains two tiny family WC/basin/shower suites for rent. An older block is by the pools. Laundry. Motorcaravan services. Shop. Bar and restaurant. Pizza and takeaway (main season). Internet point. Two pools (1/6-15/9). Pony rides (July-Aug). Table tennis, minigolf and boules. Mini zoo. Fishing.

Open: 15 May - 15 September.

Directions

Site is between Nevers and Autun (mid-way between Châtillon-en-Bazois and Château-Chinon), just north of the D978.

Charges 2007

Per unit incl. 2 persons	€ 20,00 - € 27,00
extra person	€ 6,00
child (3-7 yrs)	€ 4,00
electricity (10A)	€ 4,00
animal	free - € 2,00

Camping Cheques accepted.

FR58040 Camping l'Etang de la Fougeraie

Hameau de Champs, F-58120 St Léger de Fougeret (Nièvre)

Tel: 03 86 85 11 85. Email: campingfougeraie@aol.com

This is a straightforward, unpretentious camping site with no 'glitz and glamour', just a small bar and restaurant serving good quality regional meals, and a well stocked shop with local produce. There are 70 pitches, 3 chalets for rent, and only 36 electric hook-ups (6A). Some of the newer pitches are more spacious and terraced, but many of the outlying pitches are more suitable for tents that do not require electricity. On a hillside deep in the countryside of the Parc Regional du Morvan, with views of pastureland and surrounding hills, you can sit back and relax.

Facilities

At top of site, a fair distance uphill from some of the pitches. Traditional buildings with modern WCs and a heated family/disabled room (although site is not ideal for wheelchair users). More recently fitted washrooms opposite provide modern, bright facilities including good showers and some washbasins in cubicles. Washing machine and dryer. Shop. Bar and restaurant (1/5-30/9). Lake swimming. Fishing. Playgrounds. Caravan storage. American RVs not accepted, site not really suitable for large units. Off site: Riding 2 km. Shops and bank 7 km.

Open: 1 May - 30 September.

Directions

St Léger de Fougeret is about 10 km. south of Château-Chinon. From Château-Chinon take D27 south for 3 km, then fork right on D157 for 5.5 km. to St Léger. Continue through village following signs for another 2 km. to site. GPS: N47:00.394 E03:54.292

Charges 2006

Per unit incl. 2 persons	€ 12,50
child (0-16 yrs)	€ 2,30 - € 2,60
electricity	€ 3,00

187

FR58050 Airotel Château de Chigy

Chigy, F-58170 Tazilly (Nièvre)

Tel: **03 86 30 10 80**. Email: **reception@chateaudechigy.com.fr**

This very spacious site (20 ha. for pitches and another 50 ha. of fields, lakes and woods) lies just at the southern tip of the Morvan Regional Natural Park. The château houses the reception and apartments for rent. Most of the facilities are nearby, and behind are 54 good sized, shaded pitches, with electricity and water supply near. There is a large woodland area with paths, next to which are 100 or so more pitches, some of up to 150 sq.m. They are open and vary from level, terraced, slightly sloping and some are bumpy. All have electrical connections and there are enough water taps.

Facilities

Two toilet blocks contain British style WCs, washbasins in cubicles, and showers. A 'portacabin' has 4 cubicles, each with toilet, washbasin and shower (can be hired as private in July/August). Facilities for disabled people and babies. Laundry facilities. Gas supplies. Shop. Bar, restaurant and takeaway (July/Aug). Two outdoor pools, one with paddling pool (15/5-30/9). Swimming in lake. Playground. Minigolf. Boules. Off site: Luzy 4 km. Riding 9 km.

Open: 29 April - 30 September.

Directions

From Luzy (34 km. southwest of Autun via the N81) take the D973 towards Bourbon Lancy. After 4 km. the site is signed to the left.

Charges 2006

Per person	€ 5,00 - € 7,00
child (2-7 yrs)	€ 4,00 - € 6,00
pitch incl. electricity	€ 9,50 - € 11,50

Reductions during certain periods, for age 55+, and for longer stays.

FR58060 Domaine Naturiste de la Gagère

F-58170 Luzy (Nièvre)

Tel: **03 86 30 48 11**. Email: **info@la-gagere.com**

At this spacious, attractive, well equipped campsite, you will receive a really good welcome from the enthusiastic founders of Naturocamp. There are 120 good sized level grassy pitches, some shaded, some open, of which 105 are available for tourers. Many are arranged around three sides of rectangles between hedges. There is an electricity supply to 84 pitches, 6 of which are fully serviced, but some will need leads of up to 40 m. There are plenty of water points. In high season there are organised activities and entertainment and a children's club meets twice per week.

Facilities

Three modern unisex heated toilet blocks contain British style WCs, washbasins and pre-set showers. En-suite facilities for disabled people. Motorcaravan services. Laundry facilities. Shop (31/5-15/9). Bar. Restaurant with snack bar and takeaway (1/5-15/9). Satellite TV. Two heated swimming pools (one all season, the other 15/5-15/9). Sauna and health suite. Playgrounds. Boules. Bicycle hire. Only gas barbecues permitted. Off site: Fishing 5 km. Luzy 10 km. Riding 10 km.

Open: 1 April - 1 October.

Directions

Luzy is 34 km. southwest of Autun, on the N81. Travel northeast from Luzy towards Autun. After 6 km. site is signed to the right, then reached by 3 km. of winding (often narrow) road.

Charges 2007

Per person	€ 6,00
child (0-12 yrs0	€ 3,00
pitch incl. electricity	€ 15,50 - € 17,00

Less 10-30% outside July/Aug.
Admin fee for stays of 3 nights or less (€ 5).

FR71010 Camping Municipal Mâcon

RN 6, F-71000 Mâcon (Saône-et-Loire)

Tel: **03 85 38 16 22**

Always useful and well cared for, this site is worth considering as a stopover or for longer stays as it is close to the main route south. The 250 good sized pitches, 190 with 6 A electricity and 60 with fresh and waste water points, are on mown, flat grass, accessed by tarmac roads. Gates closed 10.00-06.30 hrs. but large units note – the security barrier has a 3.8 m. height restriction so watch those top boxes! There is a generally bright and cheerful ambience. The bar/restaurant is open all year and seems to be a favourite haunt for the locals at lunchtime.

Facilities

Sanitary facilities in three well maintained units, are fully equipped with British and Turkish style WCs, and washbasins in cubicles. A fourth block is modern. Facilities for disabled visitors. Washing machine and dryer. Motorcaravan service point. Shop/tabac. Bar. Takeaway and restaurant. Heated swimming and paddling pools (campers only, 15/5-15/9). Good TV lounge. Playground. Off site: Supermarket nearby. Centre of Mâcon 3 km.

Open: 15 March - 31 October.

Directions

Site is on northern outskirts of Mâcon on main N6, 3 km. from the town centre (just south of A40 autoroute junction).

Charges guide

Per unit incl. 2 persons	€ 11,60
with electricity (5A)	€ 14,10
extra person	€ 3,10
child (under 7 yrs)	€ 1,65

FR71030 Camping Municipal Saint Vital

Rue des Griottons, F-71250 Cluny (Saône-et-Loire)

Tel: 03 85 59 08 34. Email: cluny-camping@wanadoo.fr

Close to this attractive small town (300 metres walk) and next to the municipal swimming pool (free for campers), this site has 174 pitches. On gently sloping grass, with some small hedges and shade in parts, electricity is available (long leads may be needed). Some rail noise is noticeable during the day but we are assured that trains do not run 23.30 - 07.00 hrs. In high season, on Friday evenings, there is a presentation of local produce in the 'salle de reunion'.

Facilities

Two sanitary buildings provide British and Turkish style WCs, some washbasins in cubicles and controllable showers. Dishwashing and laundry sinks. Washing machine, dryer and ironing board. Chemical toilet disposal. Shop. Off site: Fishing and bicycle hire 100 m. Riding 1 km. Wine routes, chateaux, churches. The excellent traffic free cycle path from Cluny to Givry is highly recommended.

Open: 1 May - 30 September.

Directions

Site is east of town, by the D15 road towards Azé and Blanot.

Charges guide

Per person	€ 3,35
child (under 7 yrs)	€ 1,94
pitch	€ 2,05
vehicle	€ 2,05
electricity	€ 2,66

FR71020 Le Village des Meuniers

F-71520 Dompierre-les-Ormes (Saône-et-Loire)

Tel: 03 85 50 36 60. Email: levillagedesmeuniers@wanadoo.fr

In a tranquil setting with panoramic views, the neat appearance of the reception building sets the tone for the rest of this attractive site. It is an excellent example of current trends in French tourism development. This is a super site, tastefully landscaped, with a high standard of cleanliness in all areas. The main part has 113 terraced, grassy pitches, some with hardstanding, are all fairly level, each with electricity and ample water points. Of these, 75 also have waste water outlets. A second section, used only in high season contains 16 standard pitches. All pitches enjoy stunning views.

Facilities

Sanitary facilities mainly in an unusual, purpose designed hexagonal block, with modern fittings, of high standard. Smaller unit in the lower area of the site, plus further toilets in the main reception building. Motorcaravan service point in car park. Café (high season). Bar, shop and takeaway. Swimming pool complex with three heated pools and toboggan run (1/6-31/8). Children's activities organised in high season. Football. Minigolf. Internet access (credit card or telephone card). Bicycle hire. Off site: Village 500 m. for all services (banks and some shops, closed Sun/Mon). Fishing 1.5 km. Riding 10 km.

Open: 1 May - 30 September.

Directions

Town is 35 km. west of Mâcon. Follow N79/E62 (Charolles, Paray, Digoin) road and turn south onto D41 to Dompierre-les-Ormes (3 km). Site is clearly signed through village.

Charges 2006

Per person	€ 5,50 - € 7,50
child (2-13 yrs)	€ 3,50 - € 4,50
pitch	€ 6,50 - € 9,00
electricity	€ 3,50 - € 4,50
dog	€ 1,50

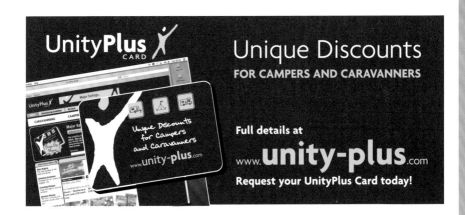

FR71070 Castel Camping Château de l'Epervière

Mobile homes ▶ page 468

F-71240 Gigny-sur-Saône (Saône-et-Loire)

Tel: 03 85 94 16 90. Email: domaine-de-leperviere@wanadoo.fr

Peacefully situated on the edge of the little village of Gigny-sur-Saône, yet within easy distance of the A6 autoroute, this site nestles in a woodland area near the Saône river. There are 135 pitches, 75 for touring, nearly all with 10A electricity. The site is in two distinct areas. The original part, close to the château and fishing lake, has semi-hedged pitches on part-level ground with shade from mature trees, The centre of the second area has a more open aspect, with large hedged pitches and mature trees offering shade around the periphery. A partly fenced road across the lake connects the two areas of the site (care is needed with children). The managers, Gert-Jan and Francois, and their team enthusiastically organise a range of activities for visitors that includes wine tastings in the cellars of the château and a Kids' Club in July/Aug. You may need earplugs in the mornings because of the ducks.

Facilities

Two well equipped toilet blocks include washbasins in cabins, dishwashing and laundry areas. Washing machine and dryer. Basic shop (1/5-30/9). Château restaurant with a French menu (1/4-30/9). Second restaurant with basic menu and takeaway. Converted barn houses attractive bar, large TV and games room. Unheated swimming pool (1/5-30/9) partly enclosed by old stone walls. Smaller indoor heated pool, Jacuzzi, sauna, paddling pool. Play area. Outdoor paddling pool. Bicycle hire. Off site: Riding 15 km. Golf 20 km.

Open: 1 April - 30 September.

Directions

From N6 between Châlon-sur-Saône and Tournus, turn east on D18 (just north of Sennecey-le-Grand) and follow site signs for 6.5 km. From A6, exit Châlon-Sud from the north, or Tournus from the south.

Charges 2006

Per person	€ 5,40 - € 6,90
child (under 7 yrs)	€ 3,30 - € 4,80
pitch	€ 7,90 - € 10,20
dog	€ 2,20 - € 2,90
electricity	€ 2,20 - € 2,90

Camping Cheques accepted.

kawan-villages.com **tel: 00 333 59 59 03 59** ━━━ **kawan** VILLAGES CAMPING

FR71140 Camping du Pont de Bourgogne

Rue Julien Leneveu, Saint Marcel, F-71380 Chalon sur Saône (Saône-et-Loire)

Tel: 03 85 48 26 86. Email: campingchalon71@wanadoo.fr

This is a well presented site, useful for an overnight stop or for a few days if exploring the local area and you want a simple site without the frills. It does get crowded in the third week of July during the Chalon street theatre festival. There are 93 fairly small pitches with 6/10A electricity, 10 with a gravel surface. The new owners of the site plan to replace or improve the facilities in the near future, but when we visited there was a bar/restaurant with an outdoor terrace and serving a good selection of simple, inexpensive meals. Although alongside the Saône river, the site is well fenced. The staff are friendly and helpful.

Facilities

Three toilet blocks, two centrally located amongst the pitches and traditional in style and fittings, the third new and modern, alongside the reception building (including facilities for disabled visitors). Dishwashing facilities but no laundry. Modern bar/restaurant. No shop but essentials kept in the bar (bread to order). Simple play area. Bicycle hire arranged. Off site: Municipal swimming pool 300 m. Golf 1 km. Riding 10 km.

Open: 1 April - 30 September.

Directions

From A6 exit 26 (Chalon-Sud) bear right to roundabout and take N80 (Dole) straight on to roundabout at St Marcel. Turn left (fourth exit) and fork right into Les Chavannes. At central traffic lights turn right and under modern river bridge to site entrance.

Charges 2006

Per person	€ 3,10 - € 3,80
child (under 7 yrs)	€ 1,90 - € 2,50
pitch	€ 3,90 - € 4,70
electricity	€ 2,90 - € 3,50

Domaine
du Château de l'Epervière

Castel Camping ★★★★

Bourgogne du Sud

FRANCE

CAMPING ★★ DU Pont de BOURGOGNE

Chalon sur Saône - Bourgogne du Sud

CH 03107

FRANCE

FR71050 Camping Moulin de Collonge

F-71390 Saint Boil (Saône-et-Loire)

Tel: **03 85 44 00 32**. Email: **millofcollonge@wanadoo.fr**

This well run, family site offers an 'away from it all' situation surrounded by sloping vineyards and golden wheat fields. It has an instant appeal for those seeking a quiet, relaxing environment. There are 57 level pitches, most with electrical hook-ups although long cables may be required. Flower arrangements are in abundance and, like the shrubs and grounds, are constantly being attended. Beyond the stream that borders the site are a swimming pool, patio and a pizzeria (also open to the public all year). A new lake, 1.8 m. deep, has been created for leisure activities.

Facilities

Well kept toilet facilities housed in a converted barn. Laundry and dishwashing sinks. Washing machine and dryer. Freezer for campers' use. Bread each morning. Basic shop (1/6-3/9). Pizzeria, snack bar (1/7-31/8). Swimming pool covered - walls can be opened in good weather. Playgrounds. Bicycle hire. Table tennis. Fishing. Pony trekking. Off site: Riding 4 km. 'Voie Vert', 117 km. track for cycling or walking near the site.

Open: 15 March - 30 September.

Directions

From Chalon-sur-Saône travel 9 km. west on the N80. Turn south on D981 through Buxy (6 km). Continue south for 7 km. to Saint Boil and site is signed at south end of the village.

Charges 2006

Per person	€ 4,50 - € 5,50
child (under 7 yrs)	€ 2,29 - € 3,50
pitch incl. electricity	€ 8,50 - € 11,50

Camping Cheques accepted.

kawan-villages.com **tel: 00 333 59 59 03 59** *kawan* VILLAGES CAMPING

FR71060 Camping Caravaning Château de Montrouant

F-71800 Gibles (Saône-et-Loire)

Tel: **03 85 84 51 13**. Email: **campingdemontrouant@wanadoo.fr**

A small, pretty site beside a lake in the grounds of an imposing chateau, in a steep valley in the Charolais hills. There is shade from mature trees and the 45 pitches (12 used by tour operators) are on reasonably flat grassy terraces, mainly separated by small hedges. All have electrical connections. Some pitches overlook the lake and some are next to a field. This site is probably best for smaller units as the access roads are very steep and not in very good condition (towing is available).

Facilities

The sanitary facilities, not too well designed and with variable maintenance, are housed in a part of the château. They include washbasins in cabins. Dishwashing and laundry facilities. Basic supplies available at reception. Small open-air bar/restaurant/takeaway for evening barbecues (only open certain evenings). Swimming pool (1/6-10/9). Half-court tennis. Fishing. Torches useful. Off site: The village of Gibles 2 km. Riding 10 km.

Open: 1 June - 4 September.

Directions

Site is to the west of Mâcon and can be reached from A6 (Mâcon Sud) via the N79 to Charolles (55 km). Take exit for Trivy - Dompierre-les-Ormes and D41 towards Montneland and Gibles.

Charges 2006

Per person	€ 5,50
child (under 7 yrs)	€ 3,50
pitch incl. electricity (6A)	€ 10,00

Camping Cheques accepted.

FR71080 Camping de L'Etang Neuf

L'Etang Neuf, F-71760 Issy-l'Évêque (Saône-et-Loire)

Tel: **03 85 24 96 05**. Email: **info@camping-etang-neuf.com**

This tranquil campsite overlooking a lake, with views of a forest and the 19th century Château de Montrifaut, is a real countryside haven for relaxation. Separated by low hedges, the 61 marked, grass pitches have 6A electricity and a small hardstanding area for a car. Young trees offer a little shade. There is a separate area for tents. There is no organised entertainment but a play area, fenced swimming and paddling pools and plenty of space will keep children happily amused. Many walks and mountain bike trails start from the site with free maps available.

Facilities

Two very clean sanitary blocks includes washbasins in cabins. Dishwashing and laundry sinks. Washing machine, ironing board and baby room. Separate shower and toilet rooms for disabled people are in the lower block. Motorcaravan services. Bar/restaurant. Bread and croissants to order. Boules. TV and games room. Internet access (WiFi). Off site: Minigolf just outside site entrance. Riding 500 m. Nearest shop 1 km. in Issy l'Évêque.

Open: 28 April - 16 September.

Directions

From D973 (Luzy - Bourbon-Lancy) turn left onto D25 (west of Luzy) and continue for about 12 km. Turn right, D42 in centre of Issy l'Évêque, signed to site. The road narrows slightly, entrance on right.

Charges 2007

Per unit incl. 2 persons	€ 16,50 - € 18,00
with electricity	€ 16,50 - € 21,00
extra person	€ 3,00 - € 4,50

Camping Cheques accepted.

192

FR71090 Camping Intercommunal du Lac de Saint-Point

F-71520 Saint-Point (Saône-et-Loire)

Tel: **03 85 50 52 31**. Email: **camping.stpoint@wanadoo.fr**

This site is situated just below a small reservoir on the side of a valley and forms part of an amenity complex for a group of communes. It is managed by a husband and wife team. The lake offers lake swimming, fishing and pedaloes. Situated 25 km. from the A6, this could be a useful resting place if travelling north or south. The area is renowned for its wine and cheese as well as Roman churches, abbeys and châteaux. There are 39 reasonably level, serviced touring pitches, mostly separated by low hedges, and 46 tent pitches on a sloping and partly terraced field behind. There are lifeguards at the lake in July and August and the communes organise many events during the year. When we visited there was a large competition for model speed boats.

Facilities

Two sanitary blocks, provide all the usual facilities and a washing machine. Shower and toilet/washbasin in separate cabins for campers with disabilities. Bar and snacks (1/6-30/9). Play area. Volleyball, basketball and badminton. Table tennis. Games room. Boules pitch. Mountain bike hire. Off site: Nearest shop 300 m. Tennis 4 km. Organised walks on Wednesdays 4 km. Riding 5 km.

Open: 1 April - 31 October.

Directions

Leave A6 at junction 29 and take the N79 west as far as the Cluny exit (20 km). Turn left and follow signs to Saint-Point (6 km). Site is on the south side of the village on the right.

Charges 2006

Per unit incl. 2 adults, 2 children	€ 11,50 - € 12,50
with electricity	€ 14,50 - € 19,00
extra person	€ 2,00 - € 2,50
extra child (up to 7 yrs)	€ 1,50 - € 1,70
dog	€ 1,50 - € 1,70

No credit cards.

Camping du lac de Saint-Point Lamartine ★

Very comfortable campsite
Near Beaujolais and Mâconnais vineyards,
Cluny (romanesque abbey)
An excellent location by a lake
Quiet, shady, family atmosphere
Bathing, fishing, hiking, Mountain biking,
playground, sportsground, games room, snack-bar...
Chalets for hire
For reservations please contact Chalets Découverts: 0033 (0) 4 73 19 11 11
Open 1st April - 31st October
Le Lac - 71520 Saint-Point
Tel: 0033 385 50 52 31 - Fax: 0033 385 50 51 92
E-mail: camping.stpoint@wanadoo.fr
http://perso.wanadoo.fr/camping.stpoint
Southern Burgundy

FR71110 Camping du Lac

Mobile homes ▶ page 468

Le Fourneau, F-71430 Palinges (Saône-et-Loire)

Tel: **03 85 88 14 49**. Email: **camping.palinges@hotmail.fr**

Camping du Lac is a very special campsite and it is all due to Monsieur Labille, its owner who thinks of the campsite as his home and every visitor as his guest. The campsite contains 45 good sized grass touring pitches, each with a small hardstanding. All but 8 of the pitches have two 10A electricity connections, and 20 have water and waste points. The campsite is adjacent to a lake with a beach and safe bathing. Guests can also use the washing machine and fridge free of charge.

Facilities

The central sanitary block provides all necessary facilities including those for campers with disabilities. Washing machine and fridge. Bread and croissants to order. Boules. Play area. TV room. Sports field. Lake beach and swimming adjacent. Bicycle and pedalo hire in July/Aug. Motorcaravan services. Off site: Bar/snack bar outside entrance (weekends only outside 1/7-31/8). Riding 200 m. Palinges is within walking distance, cycle and walking routes, museums, cruises on canals, chateaux, 'museographical' complex.

Open: 1 April - 30 October.

Directions

Palinges is midway between Montceau les Mines and Paray le Monial. From Montceau take N70, then turn left onto D92 to Palinges. Follow campsite signs. Site is also well signed from D985 Toulon-sur-Arroux to Charolles road.

Charges 2006

Per unit incl. 2 persons with electricity	€ 16,00

No credit cards.

FR71120 Camping la Heronnière

Lac de Laives, F-71240 Laives (Saône-et-Loire)

Tel: **03 85 44 98 85**. Email: **camping.laives@orange.fr**

Camping la Herronière is a quiet relaxing site on the edge of a leisure lake in pleasant rolling woodland countryside. The 90 touring pitches are good sized, grassy and level. About half have shade, with electrical connections for 81 and there are plenty of water points. The site is within easy reach of Chalon-sur-Saône, Tournus and the Chalonnais vineyards and wine route. Cluny and the former industrial towns of Le Creusot and Montceau-les-Mines are each about 40 km. away.

Facilities

Well equipped modern sanitary block includes facilities for campers with disabilities. Snack bar (June - Aug). Covered area outside reception, with bread, drinks, ice cream, basic provisions and French breakfast. Heated outdoor pool. Volleyball. Table tennis. Boules. Bicycle hire. Fishing. Marquee with TV, board games. Playground. Off site: Lake swimming, grass area, beach, bar and restaurant 300 m. Exercise circuit, canoeing, windsurfing, pedaloes. Golf 15 km. Riding 10 km. Cluny, Châlon, Le Creusot and Montceau-les-Mines. Shops, etc. at Laives 4 km.

Open: 1 May - 15 September.

Directions

Leave N6 (Châlon-sur-Saône - Mâcon) at Sennecy-le-Grand (about 18 km. south of the centre of Châlon), taking D18 west to Laives (4 km). Site signed from Laives, initially along the D18, 4 km. to the northwest.

Charges 2007

Per person	€ 4,20
child (0-7 yrs)	€ 2,90
pitch incl. car	€ 7,40
electricity (6A)	€ 4,00

No credit cards.
Camping Cheques accepted.

FR89060 Camping les Ceriselles

Route de Vincelottes, F-89290 Vincelles (Yonne)

Tel: **03 86 42 50 47**. Email: **camping@cc-payscoulangeois.fr**

A distinctive, modern site, Les Ceriselles was created in 1998 on land adjacent to the Canal du Nivernais and is owned by a group of communities. A very level site, it has 84 pitches on grass (70 for touring), all with electricity and 38 with full services. There are also 14 mobile homes. Staff live on site and the gates are locked 22.00 - 07.00 hrs. Cars are now parked on pitches which can make the site seem more crowded in high season. Double axle caravans are not accepted.

Facilities

Four small heated toilet blocks each provide 1 WC, 2 washbasins in cubicles and 2 showers per sex, with a unit for disabled visitors in block one (nearest reception). A further block has a baby room, WCs and laundry. Restaurant (all season, hours vary acc. to demand). Clubroom with TV. Playground. Bicycle hire. Fishing. Boules. Volleyball. Basketball. Archery, canoeing and kayaking on certain days in high season.
Off site: Supermarket and restaurant within walking distance. Cycle path along canal for 8 km. in either direction.

Open: 1 April - 30 September.

Directions

Vincelles is about 10 km. south of Auxerre. From A6 take 'Auxerre Sud' exit and follow N65 towards Auxerre. After 4 km. turn south on N6 towards Avallon and after 10 km. turn left on D38. Site entrance is on left just before canal.

Charges 2006

Per person	€ 2,75 - € 3,00
child (3-10 yrs)	€ 1,25 - € 1,50
pitch	€ 5,00 - € 9,00

Reductions for longer stays.

MAP 9

Located to the south of Alsace, the historic province of Franche Comté boasts a varied landscape ranging from flat plains to dense woodlands, rugged dramatic mountains and limestone valleys.

Franche Comté

DÉPARTEMENTS: 25 DOUBS, 39 JURA, 70 HAUTE-SAÔNE, 90 TRE. DE BELFORT

MAJOR CITY: BESANÇON

Franche Comté is really made up of two regions. The high valley of the Saône is wide, gently rolling farmland with a certain rustic simplicity, while the Jura mountains are more rugged with dense forests, sheer cliffs, craggy limestone escarpments and torrents of clear, sparkling water gushing through deep gorges. It is for this thrilling scenery that Franche Comté is best known. Nature lovers can climb, bike and hike in the mountains or explore the hills honeycombed with over 4,000 caves. The streams and lakes provide world-class fishing. The spa towns of Salins les Bains and Besançon offer relaxation and a chance to 'take the waters'.

The region has a rich architectural heritage dating from many different periods, including medieval abbeys and châteaux and a poignant chapel in memory of the war. Roman remains, fortresses perched on cliff tops and elegant spa towns can all be explored at leisure. The region's position, bordering Switzerland and close to Germany, is reflected in its culture and also the great diversity of architectural style in the many fine buildings.

Places of interest

Arbois: Pasteur Family Home and Museum, Museum of Wine and Wine Growing.

Belfort: sandstone lion sculpted by Bartholdi; Memorial and Museum of the French Resistance.

Besançon: citadel with good views over the city.

Champlitte: Museum of Folk Art.

Dole: lovely old town, Louis Pasteur's birthplace.

Gray: Baron Martin Museum.

Luxeuil-les-Bains: Tour des Echevins Museum.

Ornans: Gustave Courbet birthplace, museum.

Ronchamp: Chapel of Notre-Dame du Haut de Ronchamp designed by Le Corbusier.

Salins-les-Bains: Salt mines and tunnels.

Sochaux: Peugeot Museum.

Cuisine of the region

Freshwater fish such as trout, grayling, pike and perch are local specialities. The region has a rare wine known as *vin de paille* as well as *vin jaune* (deep yellow and very dry) and *vin du jura*, Jura wine.

Brési: water-thin slices of dried beef; many local hams.

Gougère: hot cheese pastry based on the local *Comté* cheese.

Jésus de Morteau: fat pork sausage smoked over pine and juniper.

Kirsch: cherry flavoured liqueur.

Pontarlier: aniseed liqueur.

Poulet au vin jaune: chicken, cream and *morilles* cooked in *vin jaune*.

FR25000 Castel Camping le Val de Bonnal

Bonnal, F-25680 Rougemont (Doubs)

Tel: 03 81 86 90 87. Email: val-de-bonnal@wanadoo.fr

This is an impressive, generally peaceful, well managed site in a large country estate, harmoniously designed in keeping with the surrounding countryside, well away from main roads and other intrusions. The site itself is very busy, with a wide range of activities and amenities. The 350 good sized, landscaped pitches (190 for touring) with electricity (5A) are separated by a mixture of trees and bushes. A newer area has pitches of 200-250 sq.m. but are less secluded. The main attraction must be the variety of watersports on the three large lakes and nearby river.

Facilities

Four clean toilet blocks include washbasins in cabins, suites for disabled visitors and facilities for children and babies. Dishwashing and laundry facilities. Riverside restaurant, snack bar/takeaway, bar and terrace, shop (all 20/5-8/9). Swimming pool complex with slides. Well equipped play areas. Sport facilities including boules, bicycle hire, and water sports. Fishing on the river and lake. Fitness suite. Internet access. Off site: Rougemont 3.5 km. Golf 6 km. Day trips to Switzerland.

Open: 4 May - 4 September.

Directions

From Vesoul take D9 towards Villersexel. After about 20 km. turn right in Esprels signed Val de Bonnal. Continue for 3.5 km, site is on left. From autoroute A36, exit Baume-les-Dames; go north on D50, then D486 to Rougemont and follow site signs.
GPS: N47:30.211 E06:21.116

Charges 2006

Per pitch with electricity, incl. 2 persons	€ 34,00
extra person	€ 8,50
child (2-10 yrs)	€ 4,00

FR25030 Camping du Bois de Reveuge

F-25680 Huanne-Montmartin (Doubs)

Tel: 03 81 84 38 60. Email: info@campingduboisdereveuge.com

Bois de Reveuge has 340 pitches including 150 mobile homes located in woodland to one side of the site. The terraced pitches have good views across the surrounding countryside and lead down to two lakes which may be used for fishing and canoeing. 190 pitches available for tourers have water and electricity and some are extra large (150 - 180 sq.m.). There is a good solar heated swimming pool which can be covered in cool weather and another pool with four water slides and paddling pool, supervised in high season.

Facilities

Four modern sanitary blocks with all necessary facilities (only two blocks open in low season). Facilities for disabled visitors, children and babies. Dishwashing and laundry facilities. Kiosk for basics, restaurant/pizzeria (1/5-15/9). Swimming pools. Play areas. High season 'baby club'. Video screen, music and other entertainment. Bowling alley. Shooting range. Pony club. BMX track. Aqua gym. Groups may request activities such as orienteering. Package deal includes use of canoes, archery, fishing, bicycle hire and pedaloes.

Open: 23 April - 17 September.

Directions

Site is well signed from the D50. From A36 autoroute south of the site, take exit for Baume-les-Dames and head north on D50 towards Villersexel for about 7 km. to camp signs.
GPS: N47:26.472 E06:20.352

Charges 2006

Per unit incl. 2 persons and electricity	€ 17,00 - € 36,00
extra person	€ 3,00 - € 6,00
child (2-5 yrs)	€ 2,00 - € 4,00
Camping Cheques accepted.	

FR25050 Camping Municipal de Saint Point-Lac

8 rue du Port, F-25160 Saint Point-Lac (Doubs)

Tel: 03 81 69 61 64. Email: camping-saintpointlac@wanadoo.fr

A good example of a municipal campsite in which the village takes a pride, this site is on the banks of a small lake with views to the hills. The 84 level, numbered pitches are on grass and 60 have electricity (16A). It is worth making a detour from the Pontarlier - Vallorbe road or for a longer stay. The village shop and restaurant are an easy 200 m. walk. Units over 7 metres are not accepted.

Facilities

Well maintained, older style central sanitary block (partly refurbished) has British style WCs and free hot water. Suite for disabled visitors. Dishwashing and laundry facilities. Hot snacks and takeaway in high season (July/Aug). Fishing. Off site: Lakeside walk. Motorcaravan services opposite. Beach and swimming area. Pedalo hire. Bicycle hire 5 km.

Open: 1 May - 30 September.

Directions

From north, take D437 south of Pontarlier and keep on west side of the lake to the second village (Saint Point-Lac); from south exit N57 at Les Hopitaux-Neufs and turn west to lake.
GPS: N46:48.709 E06:18.186

Charges 2006

Per pitch incl. 2 persons	€ 5,30 - € 9,60
with electricity	€ 12,20 - € 13,80
extra person	€ 2,00 - € 2,50
child (4-10 yrs)	€ 1,00 - € 1,25

FR25080 Camping les Fuvettes

F-25160 Malbuisson (Doubs)

Tel: 03 81 69 31 50. Email: lesfuvettes@wanadoo.fr

Mobile homes ▶ page 469

High in the Jura and close to the Swiss border, Les Fuvettes is a well-established family site with a fine, lakeside setting on Lac Saint Point. The lake is large – over 1000 hectares and a wide range of watersports are possible from the site, including sailing, windsurfing and pedaloes. Most equipment can be hired on site. Pitches here are grassy and of a reasonable size, separated by hedges and small trees. The new swimming pool is impressive with water slides and a separate children's pool. The site's bar/snack bar is housed in an attractive, steep roofed building and offers panoramic views across the lake. Walking and mountain biking are popular pursuits and many trails are available in the surrounding countryside. The Château de Joux is a popular excursion and the nearby Mont d'Or offers fine views towards the Alps. In high season, the site runs an entertainment and excursion programme, including a children's club. Mobile homes and chalets for rent.

Facilities

Three toilet blocks include facilities for babies and disabled people. Shop. Bar and snack bar. Swimming pool with waterslides and jacuzzi. Paddling pool. Play area. Minigolf. Archery. Beach volleyball. Bicycle hire. Sports pitch. Fishing (permit needed). Boat and pedalo hire. Games room. TV room. Children's club in peak season. Entertainment and excursion programme (July and August). Off site: Sailing school. Tennis. Cycling and walking trails. Restaurants, cafes and shops in nearby Malbuisson (walking distance).

Open: 1 April - 30 September.

Directions

From Besançon, head south on the N57 and join the D437 beyond Pontarlier signed Lac St Point and Mouthe. This road runs long the easten shores of the lake and passes through Malbuisson. Site is at the end of the village on the right.

Charges 2006

Per unit incl. 2 persons	€ 14,00 - € 21,00
extra person	€ 3,00 - € 4,90
child (under 7 yrs)	€ 1,50 - € 2,70
electricity (6A)	€ 3,90

CAMPING LES FUVETTES

F-25160 Malbuisson
France

Tél.: 03 81 69 31 50
Fax: 03 81 69 70 46

les-fuvettes@wanadoo.fr

FR25070 Domaine le Chanet

9 chemin du Chanet, F-25290 Ornans (Doubs)

Tel: 03 81 62 23 44. Email: contact@lechanet.com

Located in the heart of the Jura, in the Loue valley on the edge of historic Ornans, this site is on a fairly steep slope that may not appeal to everyone. The area has plenty of outdoor activities, canoeing and kayaking, mountain biking and caving, with a fishing supplies shop just inside the site entrance. With 95 pitches (70 for tourists), some terraced, there are 50 with electric hook-ups (3-16A), including 13 with multi-services and 5 with hardstanding for motorcaravans. There are also 25 mobile homes, caravans or tents to rent on the site and some gites.

Facilities

Two blocks, one at the rear of reception building, a smaller one further up the site. The main block, recently refitted and very bright and cheerful, includes a baby bath and a small children's unit with small facilities. Shop (all season). Café, bar and takeaway (1/6-5/9). Heated outdoor pool and paddling pool (1/5-15/9). Washing facility for caving suits and equipment. Safety deposit boxes. Internet terminal and WiFi. Games room. Play area. Fishing. Bicycle hire. Off site: Fishing adjacent. Golf 20 km. Free admission to the town swimming pool (400 m.) in July/Aug. Buses from town run to Besancon or Pontarlier.

Open: 20 March - 5 November.

Directions

From Besancon take D67 to Ornans. At first and second roundabouts continue straight on towards town centre. Take first right on D241 (Chassagne St Denis), cross river, follow signs and turn right by school. Continue for 0.5 km. and then fork right, site is on left. GPS: N47:06.033 E06:07.677

Charges 2006

Per unit incl. 2 persons	€ 12,00 - € 16,00
extra person	€ 3,70
child (3-9 yrs)	€ 2,70
electricity (3-10A)	€ 3,00 - € 3,50

FR70020 Camping International du Lac

Avenue des Rives du Lac, F-70000 Vesoul-Vaivre (Haute-Saône)

Tel: **03 84 76 22 86**. Email: **camping-dulac@yahoo.fr**

This is one of the better examples of a town site and is part of a leisure park around a large lake. The campsite does not have direct access to the lake as it is separated by a security fence, but access is possible at the site entrance. There are 160 good sized, level, grass pitches, all with electricity (10A). Access is from hard roads and pitches are separated by shrubs and bushes. There is a large area in the centre of the site with a children's playground.

Facilities

Three good quality toilet blocks, one heated, are well spaced around the site and provide a mix of British and Turkish style WCs, washbasins and showers. Baby room. Two superb suites for disabled visitors. Washing machines and dryers. Motorcaravan service point. Baker calls daily (July/Aug); bread ordered from reception at other times. Animation (July/Aug). Bicycle hire. TV and games room. Boules. Internet access. Off site: Bar and restaurant adjacent. 9 km. velo-rail nearby. Riding 4 km.

Open: 1 March - 31 October.

Directions

On road D457 to west of Vesoul on route to Besançon, well signed around the town. GPS: N47:37.812 E06:07.70

Charges 2006

Per person	€ 3,30
child (under 7 yrs)	€ 1,40
pitch	€ 3,25
incl. electricity	€ 5,25

FR39010 Camping la Plage Blanche

3 rue de la Plage, F-39380 Ounans (Jura)

Tel: **03 84 37 69 63**. Email: **reservation@la-plage-blanche.com**

Situated in open countryside, along the banks of the River Loue, this site has 220 good sized, marked pitches on level ground, 194 of which are for touring and all have electricity (6A). Trees provide both fully shaded and semi-shaded pitches. Approximately a kilometre of riverside and beach provides the ideal setting for children to swim and play safely in the gently flowing, shallow water – inflatables are popular and there is a canoe/kayak base. The site also has a swimming pool and paddling pool.

Facilities

Modern, well kept sanitary facilities in three unusual blocks. Dishwashing facilities. Launderette. Motorcaravan service area. Bar/restaurant with terrace (1/5-30/9). Shop (15/6-30/9). Pizzeria and takeaway (all season). TV room. Library. Swimming and children's pools. Play area. River fishing. New fishing lake. Table tennis. Entertainment and activities in July and August. Internet access. Off site: Bicycle hire 200 m. Riding 700 m. Golf, paragliding and hang-gliding 10 km.

Open: 1 April - 15 October.

Directions

Ounans is 20 km. southeast of Dole. From autoroute A36, exit Dole, then D405 to Parcey, N5 to Mont Sous Vaudrey (8 km) then D472 towards Pontarlier. Site signed in Ounans. GPS: N47:00.177 E05:39.823

Charges 2007

Per person	€ 5,50
child (1-7 yrs)	€ 3,50
pitch incl. electricity	€ 11,00
Camping Cheques accepted.	

FR39030 Camping Domaine de Chalain

F-39130 Doucier (Jura)

Tel: **03 84 25 78 78**. Email: **chalain@chalain.com**

Doucier lies east of Lons-le-Saunier among the wooded hills of the Jura and rather away from the main routes. This large, park-like site (804 pitches with 476 for touring) is on the edge of the Lac de Chalain surrounded by woods and cliffs. Large areas are left for sports and recreation. The lake shelves gently but then becomes deep quite suddenly. The site also has an attractive, well equipped pool complex. There are 476 touring pitches, all with electrical connections (7A) but with little shade. 46 also have water and drainage. Maximum length of caravan or motorcaravan is 6.5m.

Facilities

Nine well equipped sanitary blocks with facilities for babies and disabled people. Shops (15/5-15/9). Restaurant. Bar. Takeaway, snacks (20/6-31/8), community room. Pool complex with heated indoor pool, outdoor pools with slide, sauna and spa. Children's playgrounds. Fishing. Pedalo and bicycle hire. Wide range of sports activities including rock climbing, archery, aquagym. TV room. Disco, entertainment, organised activities. Dogs not permitted on lake beach. Off site: Signposted walk starts at edge of site. Riding 2 km. Golf 25 km.

Open: 1 May - 20 September.

Directions

Site is best approached from the east. Leave the N5 north west of Geneva at St Laurent-en-Grandvaux. Take N78 and D39 west. GPS: N46:39.849 E05:48.848

Charges 2006

Per unit incl. 3 persons	€ 19,80 - € 30,30
extra adult	€ 5,00 - € 8,00
child (4-15 yrs)	€ 3,00 - € 4,95

10% discount for couples over 60 staying more than 6 nights in low season.

FR39050 Yelloh! Village Fayolan

B.P. 52, F-39130 Clairvaux-les-Lacs (Jura)

Tel: 03 84 25 26 19. Email: reservation@rsl39.com

This modern site, backed by wooded hills, is situated on the shores of Le Petit Lac about a mile from the town of Clairvaux-les-Lacs amid the lakes and forests of the Jura. The neat, tidy site is in two parts, with pitches from 80-100 sq.m. either on terraces overlooking the lake or on the flatter area near the shore. There are electrical connections (6A) and 200 pitches fully serviced. The upper part has little shade as yet but there is some on the lower section. Used by tour operators (130 pitches).

Facilities

Four modern well equipped toilet units. Baby room. Washing and drying machines. Ironing facilities. Shop. Restaurant. Bar. Snack bar/pizzeria and takeaway. Two good attractive swimming pools (heated from mid-May) and a smaller one for children (trunks, not shorts). Playground. Organised activities include archery, a fitness trail, walks, games, competitions, children's club and dancing. Fishing. Entertainment. Internet access. Off site: Bicycle hire 800 m. Riding 4 km.

Open: 16 May - 2 September.

Directions

Clairvaux-les-Lacs is on the N78 between Lons-le-Saunier and Morez. In Clairvaux follow signs for 'Lacs Campings' and Fayolan.
GPS: N46:33.866 E05:45.367

Charges 2006

Per unit incl. 2 persons	
and electricity	€ 16,00 - € 27,00
extra person	€ 5,00 - € 6,50
child (3-11 yrs)	€ 2,00 - € 4,00
serviced pitch	€ 4,00

FR39040 Camping la Pergola

1, rue des Vernois, F-39130 Marigny (Jura)

Tel: 03 84 25 70 03. Email: contact@lapergola.com

Close to the Swiss border and overlooking the sparkling waters of Lac de Chalain, La Pergola is a neat, tidy, terraced site set amongst the rolling hills of the Jura. It is very well appointed, with 350 pitches, 127 for touring, mainly on gravel and separated by small bushes, all with electricity, water and drainage. Arranged on numerous terraces, connected by steep steps, some have shade and the higher ones have good views over the lake. The bar/restaurant terrace leads to a landscaped waterfall area next to the three swimming pools and entertainment area. Awaiting discovery as it is not on the main tourist routes. A tall fence protects the site from the public footpath that separates the site from the lakeside but there are frequent access gates. The entrance is very attractive and the work that Mme. Gicquaire puts into the preparation of the flower-beds is very evident. The terrace features grape vines for welcome shade and a colourful array of spectacular flowers.

Facilities

Latest sanitary block serving the lower pitches is well appointed. Slightly older blocks serve the other terraces. Facilities for disabled visitors on lower terraces. Shop (1/6-18/9). Bar. Restaurant. Pizzeria/takeaway. Pool complex (two heated). Play areas and children's club. Archery, boules and volleyball. Windsurfing, pedaloes, canoes and small boats for hire. Organised programme in high season, evening entertainment. Disco twice weekly. Internet access. Off site: Hang-gliding 2 km. Riding 3 km.

Open: 15 May - 18 September.

Directions

Site is 2.5 km. north of Doucier on D27 next to Lake Chalain. It is signposted from Marigny.
GPS: N46:40.621 E05:46.851

Charges 2006

Per unit incl. 2 persons	
and electricity	€ 20,00 - € 36,00
extra person	€ 4,40 - € 6,50
child (2-7 yrs)	free - € 5,50

Camping Cheques accepted.

FR39060 Camping la Marjorie

640 boulevard de l'Europe, F-39000 Lons-le-Saunier (Jura)
Tel: **03 84 24 26 94**. Email: **info@camping-marjorie.com**

La Marjorie is a spacious site set on the outskirts of the spa town of Lons-le-Saunier. Bordering one area of the site are open fields and woodlands. . It is a former municipal site with 200 level pitches, 185 for tourists. Mainly on hardstanding they are separated by well trimmed hedges interspersed with tall trees which gives privacy plus a little shade at some part of the day. There are 130 pitches with electricity (6/10A) and 37 are fully serviced. There is a cycle path from the site into town (2.5 km) and a mountain bike track behind the site.

Facilities

Three well maintained toilet blocks, two modern and heated, Baby baths, facilities for disabled people. Small shop (15/6-31/8). Small bar with takeaway meals (all 15/6-31/8). TV room, table tennis, small play area, boules pitch, volleyball and football field. Archery, canoeing and riding. Motorcaravan service point (charge). Off site: Swimming pool 200 m. Bus stop 400 m. Restaurants 500 m. Bicycle hire 1.5 km. Fishing 3 km. Riding 5 km. Golf 6 km. Caves and waterfalls 17 km.

Open: 1 April - 15 October.

Directions

Site is off N83 Lons-le-Saunier - Besancon road. From south site signed from first roundabout on the outskirts of Lons. Approaching from Bescancon on N83, follow signs Club Nautique (outskirts of Lons). Take care entering site. GPS: N46:41.053 E05:34.096

Charges 2006

Per unit incl. 2 persons	€ 12,25 - € 14,90
with electricity (6A)	€ 14,00 - € 17,40
tent pitch incl. 2 persons	€ 10,00 - € 13,20
extra person	€ 2,80 - € 3,80

FR39080 Camping du Domaine de l'Epinette

15, rue de l'Epinette, F-39130 Chatillon (Jura)
Tel: **03 84 25 71 44**. Email: **info@domaine-epinette.com**

It is set in charming wooded countryside on land sloping down to the river Ain, which is shallow and slow moving. There are 150 grassy pitches, 126 are available for touring units, some slightly sloping. These are arranged on terraces and separated by hedges and young bushes and trees, about half being shaded. Nearly all have electricity hook-ups, although some long leads are needed. There is an attractive swimming pool, paddling pool and surrounds. An activity club for children takes place in July/August. Guided canoe trips on the river start and finish at the campsite. This quiet site has the same owners as FR39040, but is more recently established and less than half the size. Four hard standing pitches.

Facilities

Two modern toilet blocks. Unit for disabled visitors. Baby bath. Dishwashing and laundry sinks. Washing machine and dryer. Small shop for basics. Snack bar and takeaway (evenings). New reception, bar, TV room and shop. Playground. Table tennis under marquee. Boules. Direct access to river for swimming and canoeing. Off site: Riding 6 km. Golf 25 km. Shops, etc. in Doucier 6 km.

Open: Mid-June - mid-September.

Directions

From Lons-le-Saunier take D471 eastwards towards Champagnole. After about 8 km. fork right onto D39 towards Doucier. After about 11 km. at Chatillon turn right onto D151 south towards Blye. Site is less than 2 km. on the left.

Charges 2006

Per unit incl. 2 persons and electricity	€ 16,00 - € 26,50
extra person	€ 2,00 - € 4,00
child (2-7 yrs)	free - € 2,50

Less 10% for 10 days or longer.
Camping Cheques accepted.

kawan-villages.com tel: **00 333 59 59 03 59**   kawar

FR39090 Camping les Bords de Loue

Chemin du Val d'Amour, F-39100 Parcey (Jura)

Tel: **03 84 71 03 82**. Email: **contact@jura-camping.com**

This spacious campsite, beside the river Loue, enables canoeing, boating and fishing to be enjoyed direct from the site. It is also at the western end of the Val d'Amour, where the attractive country-side and villages make for pleasant walking and cycling. The site has 284 grass pitches, 216 are for touring. Some are undulating and/or slightly sloping, and only a few have shade. All have electricity (6A), some long leads. Some pitches at the western end of the site are some distance from the nearest water tap. In July/August there are organised events and activities, including pony rides.

Facilities

Three modern toilet blocks with all the necessary facilities, including those for disabled people. Motorcaravan services. Washing machines and dryers. Gas supplies. Bar (all season). Snack bar and takeaway (July/Aug). Satellite TV. Swimming pool and paddling pool (1/5-1/9). Playground. Tennis (free outside July/Aug). Archery. Volleyball. Boules. Off site: Parcey 1 km. with shops, bar, ATM. Golf 1.5 km. Riding 4 km. Bicycle hire 7 km.

Open: 15 April - 10 September.

Directions

Parcey is 8 km. south of Dole. From north, leave A39 exit 6 (Dole). Go southwest for 1 km. on N75/N5 (Beaune and Châlon-sur-Saône). At roundabout, turn left (southeast) (N5) to Parcey. Site well signed.

Charges 2007

Per person	€ 4,30
child (0-7 yrs)	€ 2,00
pitch	€ 4,90
electricity (6A)	€ 2,40

FR39120 Camping Beauregard

F-39130 Mesnois (Jura)

Tel: **03 84 48 32 51**. Email: **reception@juracampingbeauregard.com**

A hillside site on the edge of a small village with views of the rolling countryside, Beauregard has 192 pitches. A fenced oval swimming pool and a circular children's pool provide the main attraction on sunny days. Mobile homes and tents for rent leave around 155 for tourists, all with 6A electricity (long leads may be necessary). The tarmac roads are narrow in places, and many pitches are compact and could be more level. Larger outfits may have difficulty fitting everything on the pitch and with levelling, although the newer pitches on the lower level could be more suitable (but no shade). There are two adventure style playgrounds and bouncy castles for children, plus tennis and boules courts. Just across the road from the site entrance (and under the same ownership) is a good restaurant serving regional dishes, bar and takeaway.

Facilities

Three toilet blocks fairly evenly distributed around the site make a good provision, although the newest one on the lower section is only opened in peak season. Generally modern facilities, some Turkish toilets. The WCs at the block nearest the pool suffer from overuse by unsupervised children. Baby room and facilities for disabled campers. Outdoor pool (mid June - end August). Play areas. Off site: Restaurant bar and takeway (1/4-30/9) adjacent to site. Fishing 500 m. Riding 5 km. Boat launching 2 km. Other shops, bank and ATM and services in Pont de Poitte 2 km.

Open: 1 April - 30 September.

Directions

From Lons-le-Saunier (easily accessed from A39) take N78 southeast towards Clairvaux-les-Lacs. After about 17 km. in Thuron (before Pont-de-Poitte) turn left on D151 to Mesnois. Site is 1 km. on left by road junction. GPS: N46:35.980 E05:41.293

Charges 2006

Per unit incl. 2 persons	€ 16,80 - € 21,00
extra person	€ 3,20 - € 4,00
child (2-8 yrs)	€ 2,00 - € 2,50
electricity	€ 2,80
Less 20% in low season.	

Camping Beauregard

2 • Grande Rue • F-39130 • France • Tél.: 03 84 48 32 51 • Fax: 03 84 48 32 51

FR39100 Camping Trélachaume

Lac de Vouglans, F-39260 Maisod (Jura)

Tel: **03 84 42 03 26**. Email: **info@camping-trelachaume.com**

This spacious campsite is situated in an attractive part of the Jura. The site has 180 pitches of varying sizes up to large, of which 153 are for touring units. Of these, 85 (the ones with the most shade) have electricity (6A), long leads needed. There is no restaurant or bar, etc. on the site, but a good bar with snacks and a takeaway operates 20 metres from the site entrance (1/6-31/8). In high season there are events and activities, many of them in the municipal 'salle des fêtes' on the edge of the site.

Facilities

Three modern toilet blocks contain British style WCs, washbasins and pre-set showers. En-suite facilities for disabled people. Baby bathing room. Washing machine, spin dryer and ironing board. Shop for basics (1/6-31/8). Gas supplies. Paddling pool (20/6-31/8). Playground. Table tennis. Boules. Bicycle hire. Only gas barbecues are permitted (available for hire). Off site: Boating, canoeing, sailing and fishing 1 km. Bus stop 2 km. Riding 3 km.

Open: 22 April - 10 September.

Directions

From the south, at the north end of the A404 motorway, continue north towards Orgelet and Lons-le-Saunier on the D31, D436, D27, and D470. Just before Charchilla go left on D301 to Maisod and follow site signs.

Charges 2006

Per unit incl. 2 persons	€ 11,80 - € 13,20
extra person (over 4 yrs)	€ 3,20
electricity	€ 2,70

FR39110 Camping le Moulin

Patornay, F-39130 Clairvaux-les-Lacs (Jura)

Tel: **03 84 48 31 21**. Email: **contact@camping-moulin.com**

Patornay is a pleasant village, just by the river Ain where it starts to widen on its way to the Lac de Vouglans. This well equipped 5 ha. campsite lies right on the river bank, with direct access for boating, canoeing and fishing. Of the 160 touring pitches, 120 are between well trimmed hedges and trees, with electricity (6A), and water taps very near. The other 40 are in a more natural area, where there is no electricity and water taps are a bit further apart. In July/August the site arranges activities and events for children and for all.

Facilities

Two modern heated toilet blocks. Facilities for disabled people. Baby room. Motorcaravan services. Washing machines and dryers. Basic shop. Bar, snack bar, takeaway and terrace (29/5-31/8). Satellite TV. Internet. Games room. Swimming pool with slides and flume, paddling pool (29/5-31/8). Playground. Sports field. Table tennis. Volleyball. Boules. Off site: Pont-de-Poitte (200 m) with supermarket, shops, restaurants, bars, takeaway, ATM, bus stop. Bicycle hire 1 km. Riding 4 km. Sailing 10 km. Golf 17 km.

Open: 20 May - 17 September.

Directions

From Lons-le-Saunier, take the N78 in a southeasterly direction to Pont-de-Poitte. After about 17 km. in village, cross bridge over River Ain, towards Clairvaux-les-Lacs. After 100 m., turn left at site sign and immediately fork left.

Charges 2006

Per unit incl. 2 persons	€ 18,00 - € 26,00
extra person	€ 5,00
child (2-13 yrs)	€ 2,50 - € 3,00

FR90000 Camping L'Etang des Forges

11 rue Béthouart, F-90000 Belfort (Tre.-de-Belfort)

Tel: **03 84 22 54 92**. Email: **contact@campings-belfort.com**

Belfort (known as the City of the Lion) is a historic fortified town with much history. Although 178 pitches are marked out, this very spacious site only uses 90 of them, and you should always be able to find room here. The pitches are all on level, mostly open ground divided by bushes. A few trees around one end give a little shade to some pitches and there are electricity hook-ups (6A) to all pitches and a good supply of water taps. The reception building also contains a small shop and cafe.

Facilities

A single modern sanitary building (heated in cool weather) provides washbasins in cubicles, a suite for disabled people, dishwashing and laundry sinks, a washing machine and dryer. Motorcaravan services. Outdoor swimming pool (10/6-9/9). Volleyball. Table tennis. Small playground. TV Room. Shop and café (1/7-31/8). Internet terminal. Off site: Large supermarket is on edge of town on the Mulhouse road.

Open: 7 April - 30 September.

Directions

Site is northeast of town centre towards Offemont, adjacent to the lake and sports facilities (well signed). GPS: N47:39.200 E06:51.866

Charges 2007

Per person	€ 3,50 - € 3,80
child (4-9 yrs)	€ 2,50 - € 3,10
pitch	€ 7,50 - € 8,50
electricity	€ 3,00
Camping Cheques accepted.	

MAP 9

Deep valleys dividing mountain slopes, covered in lush alpine pastures and evergreen woods - this is the Savoy Alps bordering Switzerland. Further south you'll come across the Dauphiné Alps which, although they can appear harsh and forbidding, offer spectacular scenery.

Savoy & Dauphiny Alps

DÉPARTEMENTS: 38 ISÈRE, 73 SAVOIE, 74 HAUTE-SAVOIE

MAJOR CITY: GRENOBLE

Lying between the Rhône Valley and the Alpine borders with Switzerland and Italy are the old provinces of Savoie and Dauphiné. This is an area of enormous granite outcrops, deeply riven by spectacular glacier hewn and river etched valleys. One of the world's leading winter playgrounds there is also a range of outdoor activities in the summer. Despite development, great care has been taken to blend the old with the new and many traditional villages still retain their charm and historical interest. For many, it is an opportunity to escape the crowds and enjoy some clean air, unusual wildlife, stunning views, hidden lakes and sometimes isolated villages in spectacular mountain settings.

From Chambéry, north to the shores of Lac Léman (Lake Geneva) are many towns and villages that, since Roman times, have attracted visitors to take the waters. Aix-les-Bains, Evian and Annecy were three major lakeside spa resorts of the Victorians; while Chamonix and Grenoble attracted the 19th century travellers who pioneered modern skiing and 'alpinism'. To the north is the region of Chartreuse famous for its monastery and liqueur!

Places of interest

Aix-les-Bains: spa resort on the Lac du Bourget, boat excursions to the Royal Abbey of Hautecombe.

Albertville: 1992 Winter Olympics, museum, now has an active night-life!

Annecy: canal-filled lakeside town, 12th century château, old quarter.

Bourg-St-Maurice: centre of Savoie café society.

Chambéry: old quarter, Dukes of Savoie château, Savoie museum.

Chamonix: site of first Winter Olympics in 1924, world capital of mountain climbing.

Evian-les-Bains: spa and casino on Lake Geneva.

Grenoble: University city, Fort de la Bastille.

Cuisine of the region

Plat gratiné applies to a wide variety of dishes; in the Alps this means cooked in breadcrumbs.

Farcement (Farçon Savoyard): potatoes baked with cream, eggs, bacon, dried pears and prunes.

Féra: a freshwater lake fish.

Fondue: hot melted cheese and white wine.

Gratin Dauphinois: potato dish with cream, cheese and garlic.

Gratin Savoyard: another potato dish with cheese and butter.

Lavaret: a freshwater lake fish, like salmon.

Longeole: a country sausage.

Lotte: a burbot, not unlike an eel.

Tartiflette: potato, bacon, onions and Reblochon cheese.

FR74010 Camping les Deux Glaciers

Route des Tissiéres, Les Bossons, F-74400 Chamonix (Haute-Savoie)

Tel: **04 50 53 15 84**. Email: **glaciers@clubinternet.fr**

The site has 135 terraced pitches, 110 for touring, with electricity (2-10A) available for 100 pitches. Rock pegs are advised. It is pleasantly laid out with trees and floral displays. Access may be difficult for large outfits. There are magnificent views of Mont Blanc Range and the Aiguille-de-Midi. With a good position and adequate amenities, the site becomes full in July/Aug. The temperature drops as soon as the sun sets and it can be quite cold at night. There is significant road noise. Reservations are not taken in summer, so arrive early. Not ideal for those with walking difficulties.

Facilities

Two small, heated, sanitary blocks, have dated facilities. Facilities for disabled visitors. Washing machine and drying room. Restaurant/takeaway (all year). Mobile traders call. Room (for winter use only). Small play area. WiFi. Off site: Shop 500 m. Fishing, bicycle hire or riding 2 km. Golf 4 km. Chamonix, hang-gliding, cable cars, ski lifts, funicular railway 3 km. Fantastic skiing in winter.

Open: All year.

Directions

From Geneva (N205) take second exit for Les Bossons; site shortly on right. From Chamonix turn right at sign for Les Bossons, left at T-junction and pass under the main road; site shortly on right.

Charges guide

Per unit incl. 2 persons	€ 12,70
extra person	€ 4,80
electricity (2-10A)	€ 2,30 - € 6,70

FR74030 Camping Belvédère

8 route du Semnoz, F-74000 Annecy (Haute-Savoie)

Tel: **04 50 45 48 30**. Email: **camping@ville-annecy.fr**

This municipal site is the nearest campsite to Annecy which can be reached in 15 minutes by a quiet, but steep footpath. There are 120 good sized pitches with electricity (10A) including 80 with part hardstanding and fully serviced plus 50 grass pitches for tents (rock pegs essential). Space may be limited if the site is busy. Tall pines and a steep hillside to the west provide a backdrop to the site and a variety of trees provide decoration and some shade. This site is ideally placed for visiting Annecy but is not suitable for large units.

Facilities

Three modern toilet blocks, one heated in cold weather, with washroom for visitors with disabilities. Laundry. Small shop, bar and restaurant (June-Aug). Games/wet weather room. Playground. Bicycle hire. Communal area for barbecues. Sporting activities. Bus to Annecy in July/Aug. Off site: Boat launching 600 m. Lakeside beach 800 m. Swimming pool 800 m. Boat trips. Lakeside cycle track. Hang-gliding and canyoning.

Open: 4 April - 10 October.

Directions

Leave A41, Annecy Sud, take N508 to Annecy. After some traffic lights descend a hill looking for 'H' and 'Silence' signs. Turn right up hill, signed Le Semnoz. Fork right, then turn left, signed Camping, site is shortly on right.

Charges guide

Per unit incl. 2 persons	€ 10,00 - € 17,80
extra person	€ 3,90 - € 4,70
electricity (10A)	€ 2,50

FR74040 Camp de la Ravoire

Bout-du-Lac, route de la Ravoire, F-74210 Doussard (Haute-Savoie)

Tel: **04 50 44 37 80**. Email: **info@camping-la-ravoire.fr**

De la Ravoire is a high quality site, some 800 m. from Lake Annecy, noted for its neat and tidy appearance and the quietness of its location in this popular tourist region. The 112 numbered and level pitches are on well mown grass with some shade and separated by small shrubs and some hedging. The 90 pitches for touring units (21 with water and drain) have electricity connections (5-15A). Those looking for a quiet campsite in this most attractive region without the 'animation' programmes that so many French sites feel are necessary will find this a peaceful base.

Facilities

Very good toilet block, facilities for disabled people, laundry room, washing machines, dryers and irons. Bar, snack bar, takeaway. Shop. Outdoor pool, water slide and paddling pool. All open all season. Good play area. Sports areas. Off site: Fishing, boat launching, bicycle hire 1 km. Riding 6 km. Golf 8 km. Good restaurants on the lakeside, shops in Doussard and Annecy. Cycle track (20 km) almost to Annecy passes close by. Canyoning and hang-gliding close. Boat trips.

Open: 15 May - 15 September.

Directions

Site signed from N508 Annecy - Albertville road, just north of Bout-du-Lac. About 2 km. south of traffic lights in Brédannaz turn right (west, site signed) and then shortly left. Site on left in about 1 km. GPS: N45:48.147 E06:12.579

Charges 2007

Per unit incl. 2 persons	
and electricity (5A)	€ 29,30 - € 33,40
extra person	€ 6,00
electricity (10/15A)	€ 2,20 - € 3,30
Camping Cheques accepted.	

FR74060 Camping la Colombière

Saint Julien-en-Genevois, F-74160 Neydens (Haute-Savoie)
Tel: 04 50 35 13 14. Email: la.colombiere@wanadoo.fr

La Colombière, a family owned site, is on the edge of the small residential village of Neydens, a few minutes from the A40 autoroute and only a short drive from Geneva. It is an attractive site with only 104 pitches (82 for touring), all reasonably level and separated by fruit trees, flowering shrubs and hedges. Neydens makes a good base for visiting Geneva and the region around the lake. It is a very pleasant site where you may drop in for a night – and stay for several days! English is spoken.

Facilities

Good sanitary blocks (one heated) include facilities for disabled people. Motorcaravan services. Fridge hire. Gas supplies. Good bar/restaurant (all season) and terrace overlooking the pool (15/5-15/9). New heated, indoor spa pool. Internet (WiFi). Games room. Organised visits and activities (all season). Bike hire. Archery, volleyball and boules. Playground. Off site: Fishing 2 km. Riding 3 km. Golf 6 km. Tennis. St Julien-en-Genevois (5 km). Switzerland 3 km.

Open: 1 April - 15 October.

Directions

Take exit 13 from A40 autoroute south of Geneva, and then N201 towards Annecy. After 2 km. turn left into village of Neydens and follow campsite signs to site in just over 1 km. GPS: N46:07.213 E06:06.323

Charges 2007

Per unit incl. 2 persons	€ 16,00 - € 25,50
extra person	€ 3,70 - € 5,70
child (2-7 yrs)	€ 3,50 - € 4,50
electricity (5/6A)	€ 4,70

Camping Cheques accepted.

FR74070 Camping Caravaning L'Escale

Famille Baur, F-74450 Le Grand-Bornand (Haute-Savoie)
Tel: 04 50 02 20 69. Email: contact@campinglescale.com

The 149 fairly sunny pitches (142 for touring with electricity) are of average size (some now 100 sq.m.), clearly marked with a part grass, part gravel surface and separated by trees and shrubs, 86 being fully serviced. Rock pegs are essential. The village (200 m.) has all the facilities of a major resort with ongoing activity for summer or winter holidays. In summer a variety of well signed footpaths and cycle tracks provide forest or mountain excursions of all degrees of difficulty. In winter the area provides superb facilities for down-hill and cross-country skiing and après-ski entertainment.

Facilities

Good heated toilet blocks have all the necessary facilities. Drying room for skis and boots. Superb complex with interconnected indoor (all season) and outdoor pools and paddling pools (10/6-31/8). Bar/restaurant (all season). Play area. Tennis, table tennis. Torches essential. WiFi. Off site: Village (5 minutes walk), shops, bars, restaurants, archery, paragliding, hang-gliding. 150 km. of signed walks. Activities organised. Ice skating, ice hockey in winter. Bicycle hire 200 m. Riding and golf 3 km.

Open: 15 December - 22 April, 20 May - 24 September.

Directions

From Annecy follow D16 and D909 roads towards La Clusaz. At St Jean-de-Sixt, turn left at roundabout on D4 signed Grand Bornand. Just before village turn right signed Vallée de Bouchet and camping. Site in 1 km. GPS: N45:56.261 E06:25.416

Charges 2006

Per unit incl. 2 persons	€ 17,50 - € 22,00
extra person	€ 4,90 - € 5,60
electricity (2-10A)	€ 3,80 - € 8,40

Camping Cheques accepted.

FR74090 Camping le Plan du Fernuy

Route des Confins, F-74220 La Clusaz (Haute-Savoie)
Tel: 04 50 02 44 75. Email: info@plandufernuy.com

This neat and open site has separate summer and winter seasons. It has 80 average sized, stony, grassy, pitches, 58 for tourists with electricity and 22 fully serviced. There are good mountain views but little shade, rock pegs essential. The site's crowning glory is an excellent indoor heated pool with large windows looking out on to the mountains. This is a good site for skiing in winter.

Facilities

Very good heated sanitary provision. Baby room. Facilities for disabled visitors. Washing machine and dryer. Drying room for ski clothing and boots. Motorcaravan services. Small shop and bar, snacks, takeaway. Games, TV room. Heated indoor pool and paddling pool. Skiing from site and ski excursions organised. Off site: Shops and restaurants in village 2 km. Riding 800 m. Golf, bicycle hire and fishing 1.5 km.

Open: 4 June - 4 September, 18 December - 24 April.

Directions

From Annecy take D909 to La Clusaz and at roundabout turn towards Les Confins. Site is on right after 2 km. (well signed). It is best to avoid using D909 from Flumat. GPS: N45:54.567 E06:27.114

Charges 2006

Per pitch incl. 2 persons	€ 17,00 - € 20,50
with electricity (4-13A)	€ 20,70 - € 27,70
extra person	€ 5,00

Winter prices are higher - may be quoted per week.

FR74110 Camping le Taillefer

1530 Route de Chaparon, F-74210 Doussard (Haute-Savoie)

Tel: **04 50 44 30 30**. Email: **info@campingletaillefer.com**

This excellent, small site is family run and friendly. It is only 1.5 km. from Lake Annecy, yet it offers a quiet, very relaxing and beautiful environment all at a very good price. This site is terraced and abounds with flowers, shrubs and small trees. It only has 32 average to good sized, grassy, level and sunny pitches, 28 with electricity (6A). Those at the bottom of the site are reserved for tents. In high season the site is quiet as there are no organised events, although there are plenty on and around the lake close by.

Facilities

Modern toilet block with facilities for disabled visitors. Small shop selling bread, drinks and ices etc. Small bar in high season. Playground. Small club/TV room. Torches needed (no site lighting). Off site: Doussard, shops, bank. Lake Annecy with beaches (2 km), restaurants, snack bars, fishing and many water sports. Lake Annecy with minigolf, bicycle hire, boat launching, small nature reserve. Canyoning, hang-gliding. Boat trips. 20 km. cycle ride passes site. Golf 8 km. Riding 7 km.

Open: 1 May - 30 September.

Directions

From Annecy take N508 signed Albertville. At traffic lights in Brédannaz turn right and left. Site on left in 1.5 km. Do not turn in by reception (this is a dead end) – wait in road until directions are received. GPS: N45:48.141 E06:12.339

Charges 2007

Per unit incl. 2 persons	€ 14,00
extra person	€ 3,20
child (under 10 yrs)	€ 2,50
electricity	€ 3,40

FR74130 Camping de la Plage

304 rue de la Garenne, F-74500 Amphion-les-Bains (Haute-Savoie)

Tel: **04 50 70 00 46**. Email: **info@camping-dela-plage.com**

This very good, family run site is small, quiet and friendly. It has a very long season and is only a few hundred metres from Lake Geneva and the village of Amphion making it an excellent centre to relax and explore this wonderful region. The 53 fully serviced pitches, only a few used by mobile homes, are level, medium to large and separated by trees. In addition to the very small pool on the site there is an adjacent large aqua park plus an excellent spacious playground. The site does not accept large unit or double-axle caravans.

Facilities

Excellent toilet facilities, heated off season. Washing machine, dryer, iron. Small bar and takeaway (high season). Small heated swimming pool, covered in cool weather. Sauna. Small playground for young children. Table tennis, boules. TV room. Exercise room with play area. Wifi. Off site: Lake Geneva, beaches, restaurants, snack bars, fishing, water sports. Ferry service around lake to Geneva and Lausanne. Small shops, restaurants, supermarket within walking distance. Golf 3 km.

Open: All year excl. 2 November - 24 December.

Directions

Site is between Thonon les Bains and Evian les Bains. Turn north off the N5 at Amphion les Bains (at roundabout with statue and fountains) and follow site signs – site is a few hundred metres on the right. GPS: N46:23.589 E06:31.958

Charges 2006

Per unit incl. 2 persons	€ 16,50 - € 22,00
extra person	€ 6,10 - € 6,50
child (under 8 yrs)	€ 3,00 - € 3,20
electricity (2-6A)	€ 2,00 - € 4,20

FR74150 Camping de la Mer de Glace

200 chemin de la Bagna, Les Praz, F-74400 Chamonix (Haute-Savoie)

Tel: **04 50 53 44 03**. Email: **info@chamonix-camping.com**

This attractive site is convenient for Chamonix but is in a tranquil setting away from its hustle and bustle. Set in a large level clearing, with a view of the Mont Blanc range, it has been kept as natural as possible without a pool, restaurant, bar or disco, etc. and is well suited to those looking for quiet and relaxation. The area is rich in trails for walking and mountain biking, and many pass nearby. There are 150 pitches of varying sizes, 75 have electricity connections (3-9A) generally used for caravans and camper vans, the others used for tents.

Facilities

Three sanitary blocks with facilities for disabled visitors. Washing machine, dryer. Motorcaravan services. Bread. Pizza van twice weekly in July/Aug. Meeting room, snack room. Small playground for young children. Free internet and WiFi access. Off site: Fishing and golf 500 m. Bicycle hire 1 km. Riding 5 km. Shops, etc. 700 m. in Les Praz or 1.5 km. Chamonix 1.5 km.

Open: 28 April - 1 October.

Directions

From Chamonix take N506 northeast towards Les Praz. After 1 km. site signed to right. NOTE: the first two signs direct you under a 2.4 m. high bridge. Wait until a small roundabout at entrance to Les Praz, turn right and follow signs.

Charges 2007

Per person (over 3 yrs)	€ 5,50 - € 6,30
pitch incl. electricity (3A)	€ 8,00 - € 9,80

FR74140 Camping les Dômes de Miage

197 route des Contamines, F-74170 Saint Gervais-les-Bains (Haute-Savoie)

Tel: 04 50 93 45 96. Email: info@camping-mont-blanc.com

Saint Gervais is a pretty spa town in the picturesque Val-Monjoie valley and this site is 2 km. from its centre. It is 22 km. west of Chamonix and centrally located for discovering this marvellous mountain region. Nestled among the mountains, this sheltered, well equipped site provides 150 reasonably sized, flat grassy pitches. About half have shade and there are 75 with electricity points (3-10A). The remainder on terraced ground are used for tents. Third generation hosts, Stéphane and Sophie, will welcome you to the site and their passion for this area at the foot of Mont Blanc is infectious. There is no on-site entertainment programme, but a wealth of information about the area and activities available nearby is provided at reception where they will help you plan your itinerary. The region is good for walking and there is a bus service into Saint Gervais, from where there is a frequent shuttle bus to its spa and a tramway to the Mont Blanc range. There is also good public transport between the town and Chamonix.

Facilities	Directions
Two sanitary blocks, one heated and all toilets recently renovated, with a suite for disabled visitors and baby room. Washing machines, dryer. Motorcaravan services. Small basic shop. TV room, library, ironing board. Excellent playground. Playing field with table tennis, volleyball, basketball, goal net. New motorcaravan service point. Off site: Fishing 100 m. Bicycle hire 1 km. Riding 8 km. Shops, etc. and outdoor swimming pool in St Gervais.	From St Gervais take D902 towards Les Contamines and site is on left after 2 km. GPS: N45:52.400 E06:43.200

Open: 12 May - 23 September.

Charges 2007

Per unit incl. 1 or 2 persons	€ 16,50 - € 20,50
extra person	€ 3,00 - € 4,00
child (2-10 yrs)	€ 2,50 - € 3,50
electricity (3/6A)	€ 2,90 - € 3,90

Camping Cheques accepted.

Les Dômes de Miage
CAMPING

A new way to discover the mountains...
A campsite in the middle of untouched nature, in a quiete location at the foot of Mont-Blanc, in the center of many hiking paths. A wide choice of activitities and services, sports centre with swimming pool, tennis etc... at 800 yards.

Aiguille du Midi, Mer de glace & Chamonicix 15 miles, St-Gervais 1,2 miles, Megève 7 miles.

Camping Qualité

La Clef Verte

197 ROUTE DES CONTAMINES
F-74170 SAINT-GERVAIS-LES-BAINS
TÉL. 33(0)4 50 93 45 96
FAX 33(0)4 50 78 10 75
WWW.CAMPING-MONT-BLANC.COM
CAMPING.ST-GERVAIS@WANADOO.FR

FR74100 Village Camping Europa

1444 route Albertville, F-74410 Saint Jorioz (Haute-Savoie)

Tel: **04 50 68 51 01**. Email: **info@camping-europa.com**

You will receive a friendly welcome at this quality, family run site. The flowers, shrubs and trees are lovely and everything is kept neat and tidy. There are 210 medium to large size pitches (110 for touring) on level stony grass. Rock pegs are advised. All pitches have electricity (6A) close by and 18 have water and drainage. The static units are separated from the touring section by high hedges giving the impression that you are on a small site. There may be some noise from the adjacent main road. This is a good base from which to tour the Lake Annecy area. Europa should suit those families who like to make their own entertainment although there are some activities for children and a weekly soirée (high season) and a pool complex with slides, jacuzzi, cascade and paddling pool.

Facilities

Two very good toilet blocks, recently modernised to a high standard, have all the necessary facilities including some large cubicles with both showers and washbasins. Motorcaravan service point. Good bar and restaurant (1/6-31/8). Swimming pool complex (entry bracelet € 2 each). Volleyball. Basketball. Football. Bicycle hire. Internet access. Mini-club. Some musical evenings. Off site: Fishing 300 m. Boat launching 500 m. Lakeside beach 2 km. Riding 3 km. Golf 8 km. Lakeside bike ride (40 km. long). St Joriz. Canyoning and hang-gliding nearby. Boat trips.

Open: 6 May - 12 September.

Directions

From Annecy take N508 signed Albertville. Site is well signed on the right on leaving Saint-Jorioz. GPS: N45:49.48 E06:10.55

Charges 2006

Per unit incl. 2 persons and electricity	€ 18,50 - € 30,50
serviced pitch	€ 22,50 - € 34,50
extra person	€ 4,50 - € 5,80
child (2-6 yrs)	€ 2,50 - € 5,00
dog	€ 2,00 - € 3,00

Village Camping EUROPA

Charming site, 400 meters from the lake of Annecy – 1 heated swimming pool, 1 water complex (with 5 water slides, waterfalls, children's games, jacuzzi, lagoon) – Restaurant with specialities of the Savoy region Quality installations – Chalets and mobile homes to let – Bikes for hire – Situated next to a cycling track.

Village Camping EUROPA
1444, route d'Albertville 74 410 ST – JORIOZ
Tel. 33 (0) 4 50 68 51 01 Fax. 33 (0) 4 50 68 55 20
E-mail : info@camping-europa.com
www.camping-europa.com

FR74160 Camping l'Ile des Barrats

185 chemin de l'Ile des Barrat, F-74400 Chamonix (Haute-Savoie)

Tel: **04 50 53 51 44**

l'Ile de Barrats is a delightful neat, tidy, small and tranquil site,. It is within easy walking distance of the beautiful town of Chamonix, although there are bus and train services close by if needed. There are 53 slightly sloping, grassy pitches all for touring mostly separated by small hedges and a variety of trees offering some shade. All have electricity (5/10A) and 32 have water and a drain. This is an ideal site for those wishing to roam the mountain trails and for those seeking a peaceful and relaxing holiday in a most superb setting. No twin axle caravans.

Facilities

A modern, clean toilet block offers all necessary facilities, including those for disabled visitors. Covered picnic area with table and benches, ideal for those with small tents. Motorcaravan services. Store room for mountaineers. Mobile shop in July/Aug. No organised activities. Off site: Baker 500 m. Chamonix 800 m, high class summer and winter resort with colourful Saturday market. Hang gliding, funicular railway, cable cars and chair lifts.

Open: 15 May - 1 October.

Directions

On entering Chamonix from Geneva, turn left at first roundabout after turn off for the Mont Blanc Tunnel (follow signs for Hospital). Shortly turn left, at next roundabout and site is on right opposite hospital. GPS: N45:54.855 E06:51.689

Charges 2006

Per person	€ 6,20
pitch incl. car	€ 5,00
electricity	€ 3,20 - € 4,20

FR74170 Camping Moulin Dollay

206 rue du Moulin Dollay, F-74570 Groisy (Haute-Savoie)

Tel: 04 50 68 00 31

This spacious site is a gem with only 30 pitches, all for touring. The friendly and enthusiastic owner has worked hard to develop this site to a high quality over the last few years. The large to very large, level, grass pitches are partially separated by hedging and a variety of trees provide some shade. All pitches have 6A electricity and 15 also have sole use of a tap and a drain. Rock pegs are recommended. As there are only a few activities organised for youngsters on site it is perhaps better suited to independent couples and young families. Nestling between Annecy (15 km.) and Geneva (35 km.) this site is suitable for those seeking a peaceful site in a parkland setting alongside a rushing stream. You will discover beautiful countryside with its mountains, waterfalls, woods, birds, animals and flowers. It is a good base for touring the interesting Haute Savoie by car or bicycle, or on foot. The small adjacent river is ideal for fishing and paddling and has a picturesque track alongside suitable for walking and biking. Many marked walks and bike rides to suit all abilities. Small villages with churches, châteaux, museums and markets.

Facilities

Spacious, well appointed, heated toilet block, including facilities for disabled visitors and a baby room. Washing machine, dryer. Motorcaravan services. Bar, TV corner. Large open play and sports area, volleyball and table tennis. River fishing. Off site: Shops, restaurants, bank and supermarkets at Groisy 1 km. Interesting little town of Thorens-Glières with its 11th century château 5 km. Riding 4 km. Golf 6 km.

Open: 1 May - 30 September.

Directions

Site about 12 km. north of Annecy. Heading north on N203 Annecy - Bonneville road, turn left on D2d at Groisy le Plot. Cross river and go under road bridge and immediately turn right and then left, following site signs. GPS: N46:00.146 E06:11.45

Charges 2007

Per unit incl. 2 persons	€ 13,00 - € 16,00
extra person	€ 4,00
child (under 7 yrs)	€ 2,00
electricity	€ 3,00

206 rue du Moulin Dollay
74570 GROISY
Tél./Fax 04 50 68 00 31

Annecy Haute-Savoie

FR74180 Camping International le Lac Bleu

Route de la Plage, F-74210 Doussard (Haute-Savoie)

Tel: 04 50 44 30 18. Email: lac-bleu@nwc.fr

This lakeside site has its own beach and jetty and a short walk brings you to the lake ferry. The site has breathtaking views, a swimming pool and 220 pitches divided by privet and beech hedges. This site is perfect for walking, cycling or sailing and in low season provides a tranquil base for those just wishing to relax. In high season it will be busy and popular. The proximity of the public lakeside area which is often used as a festival venue could be either a source of noise or an exciting place to be depending on your point of view.

Facilities

Three toilet blocks are of a high standard with free showers. Good provision for babies and disabled visitors. Bar (15/5-15/9) and integral small shop. Takeaway. Swimming pool (15/5-15/9). Bicycle hire. Boat launching (sailing lessons and boat hire nearby). Private beach. Off site: Small supermarket 100 m. Hypermarket 4 km. Village close with bars and restaurants. Fishing 100 m. Golf 4 km. Riding and bicycle hire 7 km.

Open: 1 April - 25 September.

Directions

Site is 16 km. south of Annecy on Route d'Albertville, well signed.
GPS: N45:79.042 E06:21.778

Charges 2006

Per unit incl. 2 persons	€ 16,00 - € 25,70
extra person (over 3 yrs)	€ 4,00 - € 5,70
child (0-3 yrs)	free
electricity (8A)	€ 3,80

FR74210 Camping des Iles de Passy

245 chemin de la Cauettaz, F-74190 Passy (Haute-Savoie)

Tel: **04 50 58 40 36**. Email: **info@campingterreoceane.com**

This Alpine site is approached by a lakeside road with mountains to the left and with unrivalled views of Mont Blanc straight ahead. Set in an area with oak trees giving shade, there are 260 very good touring pitches which are all large and divided by 1.2 m. high, well trimmed beech hedges. A small, high season takeaway is located beside the play area allowing relaxed child supervision. An electric railway may cause some noise. This is an ideal site for Alpine lovers, a perfect base for walking and cycling, while the municipal water sports area in which the site is set offers a whole range of water based activities.

Facilities

Two toilet blocks, screened by attractive hedges, are not modern but are acceptable and include hot showers and a WC/shower for disabled visitors. Laundry facilities. Basic takeaway in high season. Chalets to rent. Off site: Site is in the centre of a large municipal water sports complex. Fishing 500 m. Riding 10 km. Golf 20 km. Excellent centre for walking and cycling. Passy 2 km.

Open: 22 May - 26 September.

Directions

Site is west of Passy. From the A40 take exit 21 (Chamonix) and drive through Passy to site (signed).

Charges 2006

Per person	€ 3,60 - € 4,20
child (4-12 yrs)	€ 1,90 - € 2,30
pitch	€ 2,80 - € 3,30
electricity (8A)	€ 2,60

Les Iles De Passy **
Hautes Savoie - France

+334 99 57 20 25
www.village-center.com/iles
iles@village-center.com

Documentation on request

Villagecenter
la vie plein air

FR74200 Camping l'Idéal

715 route de Chaparon, F-74210 Lathuile (Haute-Savoie)

Tel: **04 50 44 32 97**. Email: **camping-ideal@wanadoo.fr**

For panoramic views of mountains and the lake, this family run site is excellent. Trim and neat, the site is well cared for and the welcome is warm. The 150 pitches are generally large and well drained, some with small hedges but mostly open and with 6A electricity. These pitches share the site with chalets which are located at the top of the site well away from the tourers. L'Idéal is far enough from the lake to avoid the noise and crowds but close enough to take advantage of the facilities there. From the site you can cycle downhill to the Annecy cycle route.

Facilities

Three very well designed toilet blocks include excellent facilities for babies and disabled visitors. A further new block is planned. Laundry facilities. Shop (June - Sept). Bar (no smoking). Restaurant, snack bar and takeaway (June - mid-August). Two swimming pools. Tennis. Paragliding lessons. Bicycle hire. Play area. Children's club. Activities and excursions in high season. Off site: Lake 900 m. Golf and riding 5 km.

Open: 8 May - 5 September.

Directions

Lathuile is 18 km. southeast of Annecy and site is well signed in the village.

Charges 2006

Per unit incl. 2 persons and electricity	€ 18,50 - € 24,50
extra person	€ 3,50 - € 5,00
child (2-7) yrs	€ 2,30 - € 4,00

FR38020 Camping Ser Sirant

Lac de Laffrey, Petichet, F-38119 St Théoffrey (Isère)

Tel: **04 76 83 91 97**. Email: **campingsersirant@wanadoo.fr**

This small lakeside site, a few kilometres from La Route Napoléon, has 93 touring pitches (6A reverse polarity) and 6 chalets, set on a level, partly terraced, grassed area. There is a pleasant lakeside terrace just outside the bar and reception, whilst about 70 metres up the lakeside there is a sailing school for you to improve (or start) your sailboarding skills. On site there are kayaks for hire and fishing on the lake. This is a picturesque site with the minimum of extras which will appeal especially to water lovers.

Facilities	Directions
A single toilet block is at one end of the site. Equipped to basic standards it could be under pressure at peak times. Half the WCs are Turkish style. No facilities for children or disabled people. Launderette. Small bar with shop for basic supplies in July/Aug. and bread and milk at all times. Takeaway at weekends in July/Aug. Kayak hire. Fishing. Chalets to rent. Off site: Shops and restaurants within 1 km. Riding and bicycle hire 5 km.	Petichet is on the Route Napoléon between Grenoble and La Mure. Site is well signed and easy to find by the lake.

Open: 1 May - 30 September.

Charges 2006

Per unit incl. 2 persons and electricity	€ 14,80 - € 19,90
child (2-7 yrs)	€ 3,50
dog	€ 2,50

FR38030 Camping la Cascade

Route de l'Alpe d'Huez, F-38520 Bourg-d'Oisans (Isère)

Tel: **04 76 80 02 42**. Email: **lacascade@wanadoo.fr**

La Cascade has a long season and it is within sight and sound of the waterfall from which it takes its name. It is only 2 km. from Bourg d'Oisans which lies in the Romanche valley 725 m. above sea level surrounded by high mountains. The area is a sun trap and gets very hot in summer. The site has 133 individual grassy pitches, 106 for touring units on mainly flat ground and of varying size. Although most are quite adequate, larger units are best near the entrance as the pitches and roads do become narrow. All have 16A electricity.

Facilities	Directions
Two heated sanitary blocks are of good quality with mainly British style toilets, washbasins in cabins and showers. Laundry and dishwashing facilities. Bar and snack bar (25/6-30/8). Heated swimming pool and paddling pool (1/6-30/9). Sunbathing area. TV in bar. Off site: Supermarket or fishing 500 m. Bicycle hire or riding 1 km. Bourg d'Oisans 1 km. Ski resorts of Alpe d'Huez 13 km. and Les Deux Alpes 25 km.	From Grenoble take N91 to Bourg d'Oisans, cross river bridge, after 730 m. turn left on to D211, signed Alpe d'Huez. Site is on right in 600 m. GPS: N45:03.832 E06:02.362

Open: 20 December - 30 September.

Charges 2006

Per unit incl. 2 persons	€ 16,30 - € 23,30
extra person (over 5 yrs)	€ 4,40 - € 5,80
electricity	€ 3,90

FR38040 Camping la Rencontre du Soleil

Route de l'Alpe d'Huez, F-38520 Bourg-d'Oisans (Isère)

Tel: **04 76 79 12 22**. Email: **rencontre.soleil@wanadoo.fr**

The Isère is an attractive and popular region with exceptional scenery. Bourg d'Oisans lies in the Romanche valley 725 m. above sea level surrounded by high mountains. This compact site, pleasant, friendly and family run, nestles between two impressive mountain ranges, at the base of France's largest National Park, Le Parc des Ecrins. Only 2 km. from Bourg d'Oisans, it has 73 level, hedged pitches, most of average size, with mature trees offering good shade (43 for touring). Electricity is available (2, 6 or 10A). Rock pegs are advised. A 'Sites et Paysages' member.

Facilities	Directions
Heated toilet block provides all the usual amenities, but no facilities for disabled people. Washing machine and dryer. Motorcaravan services. Bread to order. Restaurant and takeaway (all season). Room with TV, children's play room. Small, sheltered swimming pool (all season). Play area. Activities in high season include walking, mountain biking, children's club. Off site: Supermarket 1 km. Fishing 5 km. Bicycle hire, riding 2 km. Canoeing, rafting, riding, hiking, climbing. Cable car at Alpe d'Huez.	Leave Bourg d'Oisans on N91 towards Briancon. Shortly on a sharp right hand bend, turn left on D211 signed Alpe d'Huez. Site is on left just beyond Camping la Piscine. Entrance is on a sharp bend - take care. GPS: N45:03.940 E06:02.381

Open: 5 May - 16 September.

Charges 2007

Per unit incl. 2 persons	€ 15,00 - € 24,80
extra person	€ 5,10 - € 6,20
child (2-5 yrs)	€ 3,45 - € 4,65
electricity (2/10A)	€ 3,10 - € 4,30
Camping Cheques accepted.	

FR38010 Le Coin Tranquille

F-38490 Les Abrets (Isère)

Tel: **04 76 32 13 48**. Email: **contact@coin-tranquille.com**

Les Abrets is well placed for visits to the Savoie regions and the Alps. It is an attractive and well maintained site of 192 grass pitches (178 for touring units), all with electricity. They are separated by well maintained hedges of hydrangea, flowering shrubs and a range of trees to make a lovely environment doubly enhanced by the rural aspect and marvellous views across to the mountains. This is a popular, family run site with friendly staff (English spoken) that makes a wonderful base for exploring the area, especially in low season. Set in the Dauphiny countryside north of Grenoble, Le Coin Tranquille is truly a 'quiet corner', especially outside school holiday times, although it is still popular with families in high season. The Chartreuse caves at Voiron are well worth a visit. Used by a tour operator (17 pitches). A 'Sites et Paysages' member.

Facilities

Three well appointed sanitary blocks are well kept, heated in low season. Facilities for children and disabled people. Busy shop. Excellent restaurant. Swimming pool and paddling pool (15/5-30/9; no Bermuda style shorts) with sunbathing areas. Play area. TV/video room, games room and quiet reading room. Weekly entertainment for children and adults (July/Aug) including live music (not discos). Bicycle hire. Off site: Riding 6 km. Fishing 8 km. Golf 25 km. Les Abrets with shops and supermarket 2 km.

Open: 1 April - 31 October.

Directions

Site is east of Les Abrets. From roundabout in town take N6 towards Chambery, turning left in just under 2 km. (signed Restaurant and Camping). Follow signs along country lane for just over 1 km. and entrance is on right. GPS: N45:32.482 E05:36.489

Charges 2007

Per pitch incl. 2 persons and electricity	€ 16,30 - € 30,00
extra person	€ 4,00 - € 6,50
child (2-7 yrs)	€ 2,50 - € 4,50

Camping Cheques accepted.

kawan-villages.com **tel: 00 333 59 59 03 59** *kawan*
VILLAGES CAMPINGS

FR38050 Camping Caravaning le Temps Libre

F-38150 Bouge-Chambalud (Isère)

Tel: **04 74 84 04 09**. Email: **camping.temps-libre@libertysurf.fr**

You will receive a warm welcome at this spacious, family run site which is close to the A7 motorway, between Lyon and Valence. There are 199 pitches, with 90 available for tourers. Mobile homes and seasonal pitches are in a separate section. The medium to large, party sloping, grassy pitches are mostly separated by high hedges and trees giving privacy and some shade. All have 9A electricity and water close by. Most are in cul-de-sacs, in groups of 8, and a few have tricky access. A 'Sites et Paysages' member.

Facilities

Three toilet blocks, two for tourers, providing all the necessary facilities. Motorcaravan service point. Good shop (1/5-31/8), bar/restaurant and takeaway (all 1/7-31/8). Large pool complex (15/5-30/9, no Bermuda style shorts). Two playgrounds. Club/TV room. Football Volleyball. Boules. Tennis. Fishing. Minigolf. Organised activities. Pony cart rides (July and Aug). Internet access point. Off site: Canoeing. Shops. Supermarket. Lafuma factory shop at Anneyron 8 km. Golf and riding 10 km.

Open: 1 April - 30 September.

Directions

From A7 motorway take exit 12 (Chanas) or from N7 take D510 east towards Grenoble for about 7 km. to Bougé Chambalud. Turn right in village. Site is a few hundred metres (signed).

Charges 2006

Per unit incl. 2 persons	€ 14,00 - € 20,00
extra person	€ 4,00 - € 6,50
electricity (9A)	€ 4,00

Camping Cheques accepted.

FR38060 Domaine les Trois Lacs du Soleil

La Plaine, F-38460 Trept (Isère)

Tel: **04 74 92 92 06**. Email: **info@les3lacsdusoleil.com**

Les 3 Lacs is situated on the edge of three lakes in flat, open country in the north of Dauphine. The camping area is on one side of the largest lake with tall trees on one edge and views of distant mountains. The 200 good sized pitches, with 180 for tourists, are well spaced and separated by trees and hedges. All have 6A electricity. There is plenty of activity on offer including fishing in one lake, swimming and boating in the other two and, for the more energetic, roller blading.

Facilities

Two fully equipped toilet blocks are in the centre of the camping area. Toilets for children. Baby changing and laundry room. Small shop (July/Aug). Bar/restaurant. Snack bars. Outdoor pool (all June-Sept). Lakeside beach and water slide. Discos and entertainment in high season. TV and sports hall. Roller blade hire. Walking. Fishing. Gas barbecues only. Off site: Riding 500 m. Trept 2 km.

Open: 1 May - 10 September.

Directions

From A43 take exit 7 on to D522 north. Turn left after 7 km. on to D65 then after 5 km. turn right on to D517. Site is 2 km. east of Trept. Signs in village.

Charges 2006

Per unit incl. 2 persons and electricity	€ 15,50 - € 31,00
extra person	€ 3,00 - € 7,00

Camping Cheques accepted.

FR38070 Camping L'Oursière

F-38250 Villard de Lans (Isère)

Tel: **04 76 95 14 77**. Email: **info@camping-oursiere.fr**

This friendly, family run site is ideally situated within easy walking distance of the attractive resort of Villard de Lans which provides a very wide range of activities. It is ideal for those who prefer a peaceful site in a more natural setting. The good sized grass and stone pitches are slightly uneven but have magnificent views over the surrounding mountains. There are 186 marked pitches, 155 for touring, most have electricity (6/10A). A variety of trees offer some shade. Rock pegs are essential. Because the town of Villard de Lans offers so much entertainment, little is organised on site.

Facilities

Clean, heated toilet blocks with all necessary facilities including those for disabled campers, ski store and drying room. Motorcaravan services. Single building houses reception, bar (July/Aug), cosy lounge with open fireplace. TV room. Snack bar (July/Aug). Internet access. Play area. Trout fishing. Off site: Bus to Autrans and Grenoble. Free bus to ski resorts (winter). Supermarket 1 km. Bicycle hire 1 km. Riding 2 km. Golf 5 km.

Open: All year excl. October and November.

Directions

Northwest of Grenoble, leave Autoroute A48 exit 13 or 3A. Follow N532 to Sassenage, at roundabout take D531. Entering Villard de Lans (25 km), fork left signed Villard Centre, site is shortly on left. GPS: N45:4.655 E05:33.37

Charges 2006

Per unit incl. 2 persons	€ 13,50 - € 15,75
extra person	€ 3,80 - € 4,50
electricity	€ 3,00 - € 6,00

FR38080 Camping Caravaning Au Joyeux Réveil

Le Château, F-38880 Autrans (Isère)

Tel: **04 76 95 33 44**. Email: **camping-au-joyeux-reveil@wanadoo.fr**

The small town of Autrans is set on a plateau, 1,050 m. high, in the Vercors region. The well organised site is run by a very friendly family (English is spoken). It is on the outskirts of the town, set below a ski jump and short lift. There are 111 pitches with 80 for touring, electricity 2-10A. They are mainly on grass, in a sunny location with fantastic views over the surrounding wooded mountains with small trees giving little shade. There is a new swimming pool area.

Facilities

The new toilet block is very well appointed, with under-floor heating and all the expected facilities. Another new building houses a bar with terrace, snack bar/takeaway (July and August). New pool area with two pools, toboggan for children, sunbathing area and a separate paddling pool. Small play area. TV room. Internet point. Off site: Autrans with a few shops 500 m. Villard de Lans, supermarket, shops, restaurants, bars, ice rink and other activities 16 km. Short ski lift near site and a shuttle bus runs (in winter) to the longer runs (5 km). Fishing, bicycle hire, riding 300 m. Bus to Villard de Lans and Grenoble.

Open: 1 December - 31 March, 1 May - 30 September.

Directions

Exit A48, northwest of Grenoble at junction 13 (going south) or 3A (going north). Follow N532 to Sassenage, turn west at a roundabout on D531 to Lans en Vercors. At a roundabout turn right on D106 (Autrans). Entering Autrans turn right at roundabout and very shortly right again. Site on left. The only route recommended. GPS: N45:10.515 E05:32.87

Charges 2006

Per unit incl. 1 or 2 persons	€ 16,50 - € 26,00
extra person	€ 5,00
electricity (2-6A)	€ 2,00 - € 6,00

Camping Cheques accepted.

FR38090 Camping Caravaning Belle Roche

F-38930 Lalley (Isère)

Tel: 04 76 34 75 33. Email: gildapatt@aol.com

Belle Roche is a good, spacious, family run site. The level site is only a few years old, so is rather open at present with very little shade, but it is nonetheless neat and well maintained throughout. There are 57 large, slightly uneven and slightly sloping pitches, many part grass with a gravel hardstanding, partially delineated by shrubs and young trees. Rock pegs are necessary. All have 10A electricity (long leads may be necessary) and there are ample water points.

Facilities

Two modern, well equipped and clean toilet blocks. Facilities for disabled visitors. Laundry and dishwashing. Motorcaravan services. Bar/TV room, terrace serving simple meals (all season). Bread. Swimming pool (mid-May-Sept.) with large sunbathing area and sun beds. Very large play area. Off site: Village shop 400 m. Many marked cycling, walking and climbs to suit all capabilities. Bicycle hire 8 km. Riding 15 km.

Open: 1 April - 15 October.

Directions

Follow N75 south from Grenoble (about 65 km.) turn left onto D66, signed Lalley, Mens and campsite, and then follow camping signs through the village. The campsite is on the right just beyond the village. GPS: N44:45.295 E05:40.736

Charges 2006

Per unit incl. 2 persons	€ 11,50 - € 14,50
extra person	€ 3,50
electricity (10A)	€ 3,20

FR38100 Camping Belledonne

Rochetaillée, F-38520 Bourg-d'Oisans (Isère)

Tel: 04 76 80 07 18. Email: belledon@club-internet.fr

This extremely neat and spacious site, takes its name from the nearby Belledonne mountain range. The 180 well drained, level, generous, grassy pitches, 148 for touring have electricity (3/6A). There is some road noise for a few pitches. Beech hedges and abundant mature trees provide ample privacy and shade. A bar/restaurant with terrace (open all season) is next to an attractive pool complex, comprising two swimming pools, one paddling pool and sunbathing space surrounded by well tended gardens and grass spaces. In July and August the site becomes quite lively.

Facilities

Two well appointed sanitary blocks with baby room and facilities for disabled visitors. Shop. Bar/restaurant and takeaway (all open all season). TV/games room. Swimming and paddling pools. Tennis. Table tennis. Volleyball. Good play area, large meadow with fitness course. Bicycle hire (July/Aug). Off site: Allemont, shops 2 km. Bourg d'Oisans (Saturday market) 8 km. Hiking, mountain biking, white water rafting, canoeing, bungee jumping, paragliding. Cable car (high season).

Open: 15 May - 9 September.

Directions

Site is 8 km. west of Bourg d'Oisans. From Grenoble take N85 to Vizille and then N91 towards Bourg d'Oisans. In Rochetaillée branch left (site signed) onto D526, signed Allemont. Site is 250 m. on right. GPS: N45:06.854 E06:00.459

Charges 2007

Per pitch incl. 2 persons	€ 15,70 - € 23,60
extra person	€ 3,00 - € 6,00
electricity (3-6A)	€ 3,00 - € 4,00
Camping Cheques accepted.	

FR38110 Camping le Champ du Moulin

Bourg d'Arud, F-38520 Venosc (Isère)

Tel: 04 76 80 07 38. Email: christian.avallet@wanadoo.fr

Le Champ du Moulin lies on the floor of the narrow Vénéon valley. It has generous stone and grass pitches that are part-shaded by large trees with electricity (up to 10A). Rock pegs are essential. When the mountain snows melts in late May/early June, the river beside the site changes from its winter trickle to an impressive torrent. Parents with small children need to be especially vigilant. On the edge of the Ecrins National Park with stunning scenery and miles of marked cycling and walking trails, it is an ideal site for active outdoor families rather than those seeking late-night revelry.

Facilities

Heated, well equipped toilet block. Drying racks for clothes. Baby room. Facilities for disabled people. Motorcaravan services. Chalet restaurant/bar with home cooking. Small shop sharing reception with bread. Play area. TV room. Internet access. Fishing. Off site: Municipal heated outdoor pools and flume next door (in summer), playground, tennis, tree-top adventure park. Discounted ski passes. Riding 0.5 km, golf 3 km. (both summer only).

Open: 15 Dec. - 30 April and 1 June - 15 Sept.

Directions

From Grenoble, pass through Bourg d'Oisans on the N91, signed Briancon. After 3 km. turn right on D530 signed Venosc. In 8 km. pass the telecabin on left. Site on right in 400 m. GPS: N44:59.182 E06:7208

Charges 2007

Per unit incl. 1 or 2 persons	€ 13,00 - € 18,50
extra person	€ 3,80 - € 4,70
child (3-7 yrs)	€ 2,30 - € 2,90
electricity (3/6/10A)	€ 3,00 - € 7,50

FR38140 Camping le Colporteur

Le Mas du Plan, F-38521 Bourg-d'Oisans (Isère)

Tel: 04 76 79 11 44. Email: info@camping-colporteur.com

The site is within a few minutes level walk of the attractive market town making this an ideal spot for motorcaravanners. The owners have recently put in much effort to improve this site. There are 150 level grassy pitches, 130 for touring, mostly separated by hedging and a variety of mature trees that offer some shade. All pitches have 15A electricity and rock pegs are advised. Although there is no pool on the site, campers are given free entry to the adjacent municipal pool. In July and August the attractive bar/restaurant is the focal point for evening activities. At over 700 metres above sea level, Bourg d'Oisans is in the largest national park in France. It is surrounded by high mountains making it a real suntrap and can be very hot in summer. The area is revered by serious cyclists as several mountain roads close by are regularly used by the Tour de France. This is an ideal base for exploring this scenic region with its abundance of wild flowers, old villages and rushing waterfalls; by car, on foot or by bike.

Facilities

Large well equipped, modern, airy toilet block has all the necessary facilities including washbasins in cabins, a baby room and an en-suite room for disabled campers. Games room. Boules. Table tennis. Volleyball. Small play area. Organised family activities (July/Aug). Off site: Shops, bars, restaurants in town and supermarket 500 m. Cycling, mountain biking, hiking, rafting, canoeing, climbing, riding, hang-gliding, Parc des Ecrins, cable cars (July/August) and many mountain passes. Bus services.

Open: 1 May - 30 September.

Directions

Site is in Bourg d'Oisans. From Grenoble follow the N91 into town and shortly after the road bears left in the town centre and just beyond a petrol station, turn right (site signed). Follow signs to site, a few hundred metres. GPS: N45:03.156 E06:02.13

Charges guide

Per unit incl. 2 persons	€ 20,00
extra person	€ 5,00
child (0-10 yrs)	€ 1,80 - € 2,90
electricity	€ 3,60

Camping le Colporteur

chalets for rent

5 minutes walk from the town. Grassy touring pitches. Complete tranquility. Views of Alpe d'Huez.
Le Mas du Plan - F-38520 Bourg-d'Oisans - France
Tel.: +33 (0)4 76 79 11 44 - Fax: +33 (0)4 76 79 11 49
info@camping-colporteur.com - www.camping-colporteur.com

FR38130 Camping Belvédère de l'Obiou

Les Egats, F-38350 Saint Laurent en Beaumont (Isère)

Tel: 04 76 30 40 80. Email: info@camping-obiou.com

This very good, small Alpine site with just 45 pitches is in the centre of the Ecrins National Park. It is therefore ideal for walkers and cyclists looking to take advantage of the well marked trails. It has most things a good site should have, with its restaurant (high season), heated pool and sitting room with TV and library. The welcoming owners will even supply you with breakfast. The views from the terraced pitches are spectacular and there is a wealth of activities in the area ranging from bungee jumping to beaver watching by the Lac du Vallon. Bicycles are available to hire.

Facilities

Two modern toilet blocks, one part of the main building, the other 'Portacabin' style, are immaculate and can be heated. High standard facilities for disabled visitors. Excellent laundry. Motorcaravan services. Restaurant (high season) with Savoyard menu, high quality takeaway and breakfast. Small family run shop with ice cream and soft drinks. Swimming pool (June - Sept). Bicycle hire. Good play area. Off site: Fishing 3 km. Walking, cycling and mountain activities.

Open: 1 April - 15 October.

Directions

From Grenoble take the RN85 to 7 km. south of Mure. Site is clearly signed on the left.

Charges 2006

Per unit incl. 2 persons	€ 14,50 - € 18,50
extra person	€ 3,50 - € 4,50
child (2-10 yrs)	€ 2,00 - € 3,00
electricity (4-10A)	€ 3,00 - € 5,00
Camping Cheques accepted.	

FR38150 Camping Caravaning la Daxia

Route de Péage (CD4), F-38370 Saint Clair du Rhône (Isère)

Tel: **04 74 56 39 20**. Email: **info@campingledaxia.com**

Set in the Rhône Valley, a virtually unspoilt area rich in history, this family owned site has 116 pitches and a new swimming pool. The pitches all have electricity and vary in size from 100 sq.m. to larger and are clearly marked by hedges or bushes. Many mature trees give excellent shelter and shade. Larger units should phone ahead as some of the pitches are not easily accessed, although there are some very large places available. This is a quiet country site, not in the top grade but relaxing and close to the attractions of the area.

Facilities

Two unisex toilet blocks, one new are both tiled and clean. Some Turkish style WCs. Facilities for babies and for disabled visitors. Launderette. Motorcaravan services. Good takeaway (weekends only outside July/Aug). Excellent large swimming pool with slide. Minigolf. Barbecue area. Off site: Two small lakes. Shop 1 km.

Open: April - September.

Directions

Take the RN86 to Condrieu, then D4 to St Clair du Rhône. Site is 2 km. southeast of the village. GPS: N45:42.40 E04:78.23

Charges 2006

Per person	€ 3,30 - € 3,50
child (0-7 yrs)	€ 2,30 - € 2,45
pitch incl. electricity	€ 8,65 - € 9,65

FR38160 Camping de Martinière

Route du Col de Porte, F-38380 Saint Pierre de Chartreuse (Isère)

Tel: **04 76 88 60 36**. Email: **brice.gaude@wanadoo.fr**

Chamechaude, the 2,082 metre Eiger-like peak, presides benevolently over the 96 touring pitches at this beautiful, high alpine site open from April to September for the summer season. The 96 large touring pitches, with electricity available (2-10A), have some shade and are slightly sloping. The site has a heated pool in the open air so that not a moment of the views is lost. This well run, family owned enterprise, set around a traditional Savoyard farmhouse, is a peaceful centre for walking, climbing, cycling or just soaking up the ambience. It is in the centre of the Chartreuse National Forest.

Facilities

Two heated toilet blocks, one at each end of the site provide excellent, clean facilities. Facilities for babies but not for disabled visitors. Laundry facilities. Shop (1/6-15/9). Bar (10/6-5/9) with snacks (1/7-1/9). Heated swimming and paddling pools (1/6-5/9). Play area. Indoor sitting area for poor weather. Extensive paperback library (NL. IT, Fr, UK). Off site: Restaurant 50 m. from site entrance. Bicycle hire 5 km. Skiing 6 km. Walking, cycling and mountain activities.

Open: 29 April - 17 September.

Directions

From St Laurent du Pont (north from Voiron or south from Chambery), take D512 signed St Pierre de Chartreuse. Site is well signed in the village (the road south from St Pierre d'Entremont is not recommended for towing).

Charges 2006

Per unit incl. 2 persons	€ 13,50 - € 17,00
extra person	€ 4,50 - € 5,20
child (0-7 yrs)	€ 2,50 - € 3,20
electricity (2-6A)	€ 2,00 - € 3,90

FR38180 Camping Caravaning le Château

Chemin de Bouthean, Rochetaillée, F-38520 Bourg-d'Oisans (Isère)

Tel: **04 76 11 04 40**. Email: **jcp@camping-le-chateau.com**

Set in the grounds of the small château, with spectacular views, this site has recently been upgraded to provide high quality amenities. The grounds are shared with chalets and tents to rent, with these in a separate area. There are 96 touring pitches, all with 6/10A electricity hook-ups on level areas (some large) separated by hedges and trees. The site has an excellent heated swimming pool, a fitness room, sauna, bar/restaurant and takeaway food together with a small shop with bread and basic groceries. The site is in the centre of an area ideal for walkers, cyclists and climbers.

Facilities

Three very good toilet blocks are colourful and very clean. Shower room with facilities for babies. Excellent, spacious facilities for disabled visitors. Small launderette with ironing. Freezer space. Shop (1/6-15/9). Bar, snacks, takeaway and separate restaurant (all 1/6-15/9). Swimming pool. Sauna, fitness room and jacuzzi. Climbing wall. Daily activities for children (July/Aug). Guided mountain walks and other activities. Fishing. Safe hire. Barbecue area. Internet and Wi-Fi. Off site: Many mountain activities. Riding and bicycle hire 4 km.

Open: 20 May - 15 September.

Directions

Site is signed from the N91, just north of Rochetaillée.

Charges 2006

Per unit incl. 2 persons	€ 15,50 - € 22,80
extra person	€ 4,50 - € 5,70
child (0-9 yrs)	€ 3,00 - € 3,80
electricity (6/10A)	€ 3,70 - € 4,20

FR38190 Camping le Champ Long

F-38350 La Salle en Beaumont (Isère)

Tel: 04 76 30 41 81. Email: **champ.long@tiscali.fr**

Set at the entrance to the Ecran National Park and overlooked by the great Obiou massif, this site has been carved from a hilly forest. It provides 97 pitches (8/10A electricity) arranged in glades between mature trees. The setting is such that it is hard to see other units around you, yet the mountain views through trees are wonderful. The site is terraced and hilly and the winding access tracks need adequate power in reserve for towing. Very large outfits are best near the entrance as distant pitches could be difficult to get to. There are some steep paths to the sanitary blocks.

Facilities

Two sanitary blocks, one at reception, the other high on the steep terraces provide British and Turkish style WCs, washbasins in cabins and unexceptional showers. Facilities for babies. Laundry facilities. Motorcaravan service point. Milk, bread and a few staples kept 1/4-15/10. Bar. Good restaurant and takeaway (1/5-15/10). Heated outdoor pool (1/5-31/8). Play area. Barbecues to rent. Caravan storage. Off site: Riding and bicycle hire 6 km.

Open: All year excl. 15 October - 15 November.

Directions

From the RN85 turn off at sign for La Roche which is close to La Salle en Beaumont. Site is signed.

Charges 2006

Per unit incl. 2 persons	€ 13,00 - € 15,00
extra person	€ 3,50 - € 3,80
child (0-7 yrs)	€ 2,50 - € 2,80

FR73020 Camping Caravaneige le Versoyen

Route des Arcs, F-73700 Bourg-Saint Maurice (Savoie)

Tel: **04 79 07 03 45**. Email: **leversoyen@wanadoo.fr**

Bourg-St-Maurice is on a small, level plain at an altitude of 830 m. on the River Isère, surrounded by mountains. Le Versoyen attracts visitors all year round (except for a short time when they close). The site's 205 unseparated, flat pitches (180 for touring) are marked by numbers on the tarmac roads and all have electrical connections (4/6A). Most are on grass but some are on tarmac hardstanding making them ideal for use by motorcaravans or in winter. Trees give shade in some parts, although most pitches have almost none. Duckboards are provided for snow and wet weather.

Facilities

Two acceptable toilet blocks can be heated, although the provision may be hard pressed in high season. British and Turkish style WCs. Laundry. Motorcaravan services. Outdoor and covered pools (July/Aug). Small bar with takeaway in summer. Free shuttle in high season to funicular railway. Off site: Fishing or bicycle hire 200 m. Riding 1 km. Golf 15 km. Cross country ski track.

Open: All year excl. 2 Nov.-14 Dec. and 2-25 May.

Directions

Site is 1.5 km. east of Bourg-St-Maurice on CD119 Les Arcs road. GPS: N45:37.324 E06:47.010

Charges 2006

Per unit incl. 2 persons	€ 10,20 - € 15,60
extra person	€ 3,50 - € 5,55
child (4-13 yrs)	€ 1,60 - € 4,85
electricity (4-10A)	€ 4,30 - € 7,55

FR73030 Camping les Lanchettes

F-73210 Peisey-Nancroix (Savoie)

Tel: **04 79 07 93 07**. Email: **lanchettes@free.fr**

A natural, terraced site, it has 90 good size, reasonably level and well drained, grassy/stony pitches, with 80 used for touring units, 70 having electricity (3-10A). Because it is very cold in winter and quite cold on some spring and autumn evenings (warm bedding necessary) there are no outside taps. For those who love walking and biking, the wonderful scenery, flora and fauna, this is the site for you. In winter it is ideal for the serious skier being close to the famous resort of Les Arcs (via free bus service and cable car). Underpowered units not advised.

Facilities

Well appointed heated toilet block. Motorcaravan services. Restaurant, takeaway (July/Aug. and winter). Playground. Club/TV room. Large tent/marquee used in bad weather. In winter a small bus (free) runs to all the hotels, bars, ski tows. Off site: Walks in National Park. Riding next to site. Peisey-Nancroix, restaurants, bars and shops 3 km. Les Arcs winter sports centre 6 km. Outdoor swimming pool and bicycle hire 6 km. Golf and indoor pool 8 km.

Open: 15 December - 15 October.

Directions

From Albertville take N90 towards Bourg-St-Maurice, through Aime. In 9 km. turn right on D87, signed Peisey-Nancroix. Follow a winding hilly road (with hairpin bends) for 10 km. Pass through Peisey-Nancroix; site on right about 1 km. beyond Nancroix. GPS: N45:31.882 E06:46.536

Charges 2006

Per unit incl. 2 persons	€ 11,60 - € 13,10
extra person	€ 4,00 - € 4,40
electricity (3-10A)	€ 3,00 - € 7,30

Camping Cheques accepted.

Mobile homes ▶ page 469

TRAVEL SERVICE SITE
TO BOOK CALL 0870 405 4055
Advice & low ferry-inclusive prices

FR73040 Camping Municipal le Savoy

Avenue du Parc, F-73190 Challes-les-Eaux (Savoie)

Tel: **04 79 72 97 31**. Email: **camping73challes-les-eaux@wanadoo.fr**

This attractive municipal site is surrounded by mountains and only a few hundred metres from the centre of Challes-les-Eaux. There are 100 level pitches, mostly for touring and 91 with electricity (5-10A). Some are separated by beech hedges and mature trees offer some shade. There are 12 pitches for motorcaravans, 47 part hard standing super pitches with the remainder on grass. Rock pegs are advised. This site is a very good base for touring this scenic region and makes an ideal stop over for those on route to the Fréjus Tunnel and Italy.

Facilities

Two well equipped toilet blocks with all the necessary facilities. Facilities for disabled visitors. Bar, snacks and a meal every Friday (15/6-30/8). Good sized playground. Boules, table tennis and table football. Off site: Small park with lake for swimming, tennis and volleyball courts adjacent. Challes-les-Eaux, with shops, banks, bars, restaurants, spar, casino and minigolf, a few hundred metres. Interesting old town of Chambery 6 km. Fréjus Tunnel 96 km. and Bardonecchia (Italy) 110 km.

Open: 1 May - 30 September.

Directions

Leave autoroute A43 at exit 20 and head towards Challes-les-Eaux. Site is on the N6 at the northern edge of the town, just before a small park and lake. Turn right at traffic lights, site well signed. GPS: N45:33.094 E05:59.036

Charges guide

per person	€ 3,10
child (0-12 yrs)	€ 1,30
pitch	€ 3,55 - € 4,00
electricity	€ 2,50 - € 5,05

FR73050 Camping les Trois Lacs

D916a Les Chaudannes, F-73330 Belmont Tramonet (Savoie)

Tel: **04 76 37 04 03**. Email: **info@les3lacs.com**

If you would enjoy a site surrounded by lakes with views of the distant mountains, then this is ideal for you. The site takes 180 touring units on large, well spaced pitches separated by hedges in a park with mature trees. This rural site has excellent facilities for fishing and boating and there is a hall with lots of entertainment ranging from pool to electronic games. Well away from the pitches, this hall also hosts music and discos in the evenings in high season. The more adventurous visitor can hire roller blades and explore the 26 hectares of the park.

Facilities

Three sanitary blocks are supplemented by small units with WCs around the site. Well equipped showers. Special new block for children. Excellent facilities for disabled visitors. Laundry facilities. Shop, bar and restaurant (by the large lake, full menu in high season) and takeaway (all 1/6-15/9). Small swimming pool (1/5-15/9; unheated). TV and sports hall. Entertainment in high season. Chalets and rooms to rent. Direct access to all three lakes.

Open: 1 May - 28 September.

Directions

From the A43 take exit 11 (St Genix-sur-Guiers) onto D916. Site is 2 km. GPS: N45:33.560 E05:40.490

Charges 2006

Per unit incl. 1 or 2 persons	€ 11,00 - € 22,00
extra person	€ 3,50 - € 6,50
child (1-7 yrs)	€ 2,50 - € 5,00
electricity (6/10A)	€ 3,50 - € 4,50

FR73060 Camping Caravaneige l'Eden

F-73210 Landry (Savoie)

Tel: **04 79 07 61 81**. Email: **info@camping-eden.net**

L'Eden is open almost all year round (it is closed for three weeks in May). Beside the Iser river and set in beautiful woodland glades, it is perfect for winter skiing and summer walking and cycling. The site is set in a valley with the Alpine peaks as a backdrop. The 132 good, spacious pitches all have 10A electrical hook-ups and individual water supplies (available when no frost is likely). The pristine, modern sanitary blocks are heated in colder weather and include a large drying room. There is a pool for summer lounging, a bar and a welcoming communal area with bar, TV and internet access.

Facilities

Two heated toilet blocks include drying rooms, good facilities for disabled visitors and for babies. Small launderette. Communal area with bar, TV and internet. Snack bar and takeaway (July/Aug). Swimming pool (13.5 x 5 m; June - Sept). Games room. Play area. Fishing. Ski passes for sale on-site. Off site: Shops and restaurants in village. Many leisure pursuits including rafting, paragliding, cycle and cross country ski tracks. Riding 10 km. Golf 15 km.

Open: All year excl. 1-23 May.

Directions

From the RN90 take D87 towards Landry. Site is on left after 250 m. and is well signed from the RN90.

Charges 2006

Per unit incl. 2 persons	€ 10,70 - € 21,40
extra person	€ 2,90 - € 5,70
child (0-7 yrs)	€ 2,30 - € 4,50
electricity (10A)	€ 2,00 - € 6,00

MAP 10

Endless shimmering beaches, huge sand dunes, watersports aplenty, fragrant pine forests, the fine wines of Bordeaux, and the chic city of Biarritz: it's easy to see the allure of the Atlantic Coast.

THE COASTAL DÉPARTEMENTS OF THE OFFICIAL REGION OF AQUITAINE, STRETCHING FROM BORDEAUX IN THE NORTH TO THE PYRÉNÉES AND THE SPANISH BORDER ARE INCLUDED IN OUR 'TOURIST' REGION: 33 GIRONDE, 40 LANDES, 64 PYRÉNÉES ATLANTIQUES

The Atlantic Coast stretches north from Biarritz to Arcachon. The most notable features are the uninterrupted line of vast sandy beaches, over 100 miles long, and the endless pine woods in the hinterland - this is Europe's largest man-made forest. There are also many lakes to see, ideal for watersports activities.

The département of the Gironde covers the area from the Bassin d'Arcachon, famed for its oysters and Europe's highest sand dune, to the Gironde estuary and Bordeaux. The vineyards of Bordeaux are world famous and especially well known for their Médoc, Sauternes, and St Emilion wines.

The Pays Basque area in the southwest corner is much influenced by Spain. The most famous Basque towns are Biarritz, Bayonne and the picturesque old port of St-Jean-de-Luz. Further inland and nearer the Pyrénées is the attractive town of St-Jean-Pied-de-Port on the pilgrims' route to northern Spain and Santiago de Compostela, close to the forest of Iraty with its lakes and ski runs.

Places of interest

Bayonne: old streets and fortifications; Basque Museum.

Bordeaux: 14,000 piece Bohemian glass chandelier in foyer of the Grand Theatre, 29 acre Esplanade des Quinconces.

Pau: famous motor racing circuit on (closed) public highway; stadium for the Basque game of *pelota*.

St Emilion: visit the castle ramparts or drink premier cru St Emilion at pavement cafés.

St Jean-de-Luz: seaside resort and fishing village.

St Jean-Pied-de-Port: ancient city with citadel, bright Basque houses in steep streets.

Cuisine of the region

Seafood is popular, local specialities include carp stuffed with foie gras and mullet in red wine.

Chorizos: spicy sausages.

Chou farci: stuffed cabbage, sometimes *aux marrons* (with chestnuts).

Foie Gras: specially prepared livers of geese and ducks, seasoned and stuffed with truffles.

Gâteau Basque: shallow custard pastry with fillings.

Jambon de Bayonne: raw ham, cured in salt and sliced paper thin.

Lamproie: eel-like fish with leeks, onions and red Bordeaux wine.

FR33010 Camping de la Dune

Route de Biscarrosse, F-33115 La Pyla-sur-Mer (Gironde)
Tel: **05 56 22 72 17.** Email: **reception@campingdeladune.fr**

La Dune is an informal, friendly site, with a range of amenities. From its situation at the foot of the enormous dune (the highest in Europe) you can reach the beach either by climbing over the dune or driving round. The 325 pitches, some sloping, some terraced but level, vary considerably in size are hedged with shade from pine trees. Nearly half are caravan pitches with electricity and water. Some of the site roads are quite narrow and sandy. English is spoken. This is a busy site with good security.

Facilities

Modern, well equipped sanitary blocks. Motorcaravan services. Small supermarket. Pleasant bar, restaurant, takeaway - (opens June, all other facilities are all season). Medium-size swimming pool. Children's playground, mini-club. Open-air theatre, sports and tournaments organised July-end Aug. Purpose built barbecue (only gas individual ones are allowed). Fridge hire. Off site: Riding 2 km. Fishing 3 km, Golf 10 km.

Open: 1 May - 30 September.

Directions

The D259, signed from the N250 to Biscarrosse and Dune du Pilat, just before La Teste, avoids Pyla-sur-Mer. At end of new road turn left at roundabout on D218 coast road. La Dune is second site on right.

Charges 2006

Per pitch incl. 2 persons	€ 14,50 - € 28,00
with electricity	€ 17,00 - € 32,00
extra person	€ 4,00 - € 8,00
child (under 10 yrs)	€ 2,50 - € 5,50

FR33020 Camping Caravaning Fontaine-Vieille

4 boulevard du Colonel Wurtz, F-33510 Andernos-les-Bains (Gironde)
Tel: **05 56 82 01 67.** Email: **contact@fontaine-vieille.com**

Fontaine Vieille is a large, traditional site that has been operating for over 50 years. The site stretches along the eastern edge of the Bassin d'Arcachon under light woodland in the residential area of the small town of Andernos. Popular with the French, it has nearly 700 individual pitches, of which 520 are touring pitches (about 400 with electricity). On flat, grassy or sandy ground, they are marked by stones in the ground or young trees. Some pitches have excellent views of the Bassin, but a premium is charged for these.

Facilities

Seven adequate sanitary blocks with facilities for people with disabilities and children. Shop (1/6-15/9). Bar, terrace, takeaway and restaurant (15/5-15/9). Swimming pool complex. Tennis. TV room. Play areas for little ones and adventure area for older children. Minigolf. Boats, sailboards. Sports organised (high season). Internet access. Communal barbecue areas (only gas may be used on pitches). Off site: Grocery shop and bakery 1 km. Town centre 2.5 km. Golf 3 km. Riding 5 km.

Open: 1 April - 30 September.

Directions

From A63 at exit 22, take A660 towards Arcachon. Turn off A660 at exit 2 towards Facture then take RD3 north along edge of the Bassin. Site signed to left as you enter Andernos.

Charges 2006

Per unit incl. 2 persons	€ 13,30 - € 20,40
with electricity (5A)	€ 16,30 - € 24,50
extra person	€ 3,10 - € 5,10
child (2-6 yrs)	free - € 3,00

FR33030 Camping Club Arcachon

5 allée Galarie, B.P. 46, F-33312 Arcachon (Gironde)
Tel: **05 56 83 24 15.** Email: **info@camping-arcachon.com**

The Camping Club of Arcachon enjoys a situation well back from the hustle and bustle, where nights are quiet and facilities are of a high standard. Caravans, motorcaravans and tents all have their own area. The latter have pitches of varying sizes on neatly formed terraces. There are 250 pitches, with 150 for touring, electricity (6/10A). The site enjoys good security with day and night time 'guardians'. The site restaurant is well thought of, and in season the outdoor pool with its slide is open all day.

Facilities

Three sanitary blocks with the usual facilities. Motorcaravan services. Washing machine, dryers. Fridge hire. Shop (15/6-15/9). Bar, restaurant, snack bar, takeaway (April - Oct). Swimming pool (1/6-30/9). Bicycle hire. Play area. Games room. Children's club (15/6-15/9). Entertainment for all age groups (15/6-15/9). Barbecues are only permitted in communal areas. Off site: Beach 1.8 km. Arcachon 2-3 km. Riding 1 km. Golf 2 km.

Open: All year excl. 12 November - 12 December.

Directions

Approaching Arcachon on bypass (from Bordeaux) take exit for 'Hopital Jean Hameau'. Cross over bypass following signs for hospital, then signs for Abatilles. At next roundabout follow signs for 'Camping'. Take care as the route travels through suburban housing. GPS: N44:39.078 W01:10.445

Charges 2006

Per person	€ 3,50 - € 6,50
child (4-10 yrs)	€ 1,00
pitch	€ 3,00 - € 15,00
electricity	€ 3,00 - € 4,00

FR33040 **Camping la Pinède**

Route de Cazaux, F-33260 Cazaux La Teste de Buch (Gironde)

Tel: **05 56 22 23 24**. Email: **info@campinglapinede.net**

La Pinede has recently undergone much reconstruction and will reopen its doors in 2007. It is a popular, family site with an attractive forest setting, close to the Dune de Pyla. The work includes a brand new swimming pool complex. In addition to mobile homes and chalets, there are 200 pitches here, mostly well shaded and with electrical connections. The site is just 3 km. from the very large Lac de Cazaux where there are many watersport activities. It also has direct access to a river with mooring opportunities.

Facilities	Directions
Sanitary buildings. Restaurant, bar and takeaway food. Shop. Swimming pool. Games room. Playground. Table tennis. Volleyball. Canoe hire. Mobile homes for rent. Off site: Hiking and cycling trails through the Landes forest. Lac de Cazaux (fishing and watersports) 3 km. Nearest beach 7 km.	From Arcachon head south towards Cazaux on the D112. Site is located north of the village. GPS: N44:33.30 W01:09.04

Open: 1 May - 30 September.

Charges 2006

Per person	€ 3,50 - € 4,50
child (1-6 yrs)	€ 2,50 - € 3,50
pitch	€ 7,00 - € 12,00
electricity	€ 3,00 - € 4,50

CAMPINGS
FranceLoc

Domaine de la Pinède

Pitches, mobile homes and chalets, swimming pools, waterslides. Ideally situated between the Arcachon basin and Lake Cazeaux and near la Dune du Pyla.

Route de Cazaux
33260 La Teste de Buch
Tél. 0033(0)5 56 22 23 24
Fax. 0033(0)5 56 22 98 03
www.campings-franceloc.com

Aquitaine

FR33050 **Camping les Ourmes**

Avenue du Lac, F-33990 Hourtin (Gironde)

Tel: **05 56 09 12 76**. Email: **lesourmes@free.fr**

Located only 500 metres from the largest fresh water lake in France, only 10 minutes drive from the beach and with its own pool, this is essentially a holiday site. Of the 270 pitches, 240 are for tourers, marked but in most cases not actually separated, and arranged amongst tall pines and other trees which give good shade. All have electricity connections. The site's amenities are arranged around a pleasant entrance courtyard with an evening entertainment programme in season. This site has a busy, cosmopolitan feel, with visitors of many different nationalities.

Facilities	Directions
Three refurbished toilet blocks. Washing machine, dryer. Small shop (1/6-15/9). Bar/restaurant with outdoor tables, takeaway snacks and reasonably priced meals (1/7-31/8). Medium sized swimming pool, paddling pool (1/5-15/9). Large leisure area, play area, volleyball, basketball, table tennis. TV, games rooms. Boules. Off site: Watersports and fishing possible on the lake, with bicycle hire, tennis and riding within 500 m.	Follow Route du Port (Ave du Lac) from the town centre and site is signed on left. GPS: N45:10.926 W01:04.566

Open: 1 April - 30 September.

Charges 2006

Per unit incl. 2 persons	€ 11,00 - € 19,50
incl. electricity	€ 14,00 - € 22,50
extra person (over 2 yrs)	€ 2,00 - € 4,00
dog	€ 2,00

No credit cards.

FR33080 Domaine de la Barbanne

Route de Montagne, F-33330 Saint Emilion (Gironde)
Tel: **05 57 24 75 80**. Email: **barbanne@wanadoo.fr**

La Barbanne is a pleasant, friendly, family-owned site in the heart of the Bordeaux wine region, only 2.5 km. from the famous town of St Emilion. With 174 pitches, most for touring, the owners have created a carefully maintained, well equipped site. The large, level and grassy pitches have dividing hedges and electricity (long leads necessary). Twelve pitches for motorcaravans have tarmac surrounded by grass. The site owners run a free minibus service twice a day to St Emilion and also organise excursions in July and August to local places of interest, including Bordeaux. The original parts of the site bordering the lake have mature trees, good shade and pleasant surroundings, whilst in the newer area the trees have yet to provide full shade and it can be hot in summer. La Barbanne has an attractive entrance and reception area with ample space for parking or turning. A 'Sites et Paysages' member.

Facilities

Two modern, fully equipped toilet blocks include facilities for campers with disabilities. Motorcaravan services. Well stocked shop. Bar, terrace, takeaway, restaurant (1/6-20/9). Two swimming pools, one heated with water slide (15/4-22/9). Enclosed play area with seats for parents, children's club (from 1/7). Evening entertainment (from 1/7). Tennis, boules, volleyball, table tennis, minigolf. The lake provides superb free fishing, pedaloes, canoes and lakeside walks. Bicycle hire. Off site: St Emilion and shops 2.5 km. Riding 8 km.

Open: 1 April - 22 September.

Directions

Site is 2.5 km. north of St Emilion. Caravans and motorhomes are forbidden through the village of St Emilion and they must approach the site from Libourne on D243 or from Castillon leave D936 and take D130/D243. GPS: N44:54.997 W00:08.513

Charges 2006

Per unit incl. 1 or 2 persons	€ 15,50 - € 23,90
extra person	€ 5,00 - € 7,50
child (under 7 yrs)	€ 3,50 - € 6,30
animal	free - € 2,50

Camping Cheques accepted.

kawan-villages.com tel: **00 333 59 59 03 59**

kawan
VILLAGES CAMPING

Domaine de la Barbanne

The only camp site in Saint-Emilion!!

Route de Montagne - F-33330 Saint-Emilion - France
Tel: [33] 5 57 24 75 80 - Fax: [33] 5 57 24 69 68
barbanne@wanadoo.fr - www.camping-saint-emilion.com

FR33120 Camping la Cigale

Route de Lège, F-33740 Arès (Gironde)
Tel: **05 56 60 22 59**. Email: **campinglacigaleares@wanadoo.fr**

La Cigale is an attractive little site with charm and ambience where the owners extend a very warm welcome. Small and beautifully maintained, it is set amid pine trees and M. Pallet's floral displays. The 95 level, grassy pitches, most with electricity and of 100 sq.m. in size, are divided by hedges and flower borders. The majority have shade from the pine trees. There are two small swimming pools in a pleasant setting and under the ample shade of a large plane tree, where drinks, meals and snacks are served on the bar terrace.

Facilities

The well equipped toilet block includes a family room with two showers. Facilities for disabled visitors. Washing machine and dryer. Motorcaravan services. Simple shop. Bar, terrace, meals, snacks. Pizza takeaway (all 17/6-10/9). Two small swimming pools (15/5-12/9). Small play area. Off site: Site is convenient for a wide choice of beaches. Village centre 800 m. Fishing or riding 1 km.

Open: 29 April - 2 October.

Directions

Leave Bordeaux ring road at exit 10 (D213) or exit 11 (D106) and continue direct to Arès. Turn into Arès following road to church. Turn right (signs for Cap Ferret). Site is 800 m. GPS: N44:46.366 W01:08.537

Charges guide

Per unit incl. 1 or 2 persons	€ 17,00 - € 24,00
extra person	€ 4,20 - € 4,90
child (7 yrs)	€ 2,60 - € 2,90
electricity (4/6A)	€ 5,00

FR33090 Camping le Pressoir

Petit Palais et Cornemps, F-33570 Lussac (Gironde)

Tel: 05 57 69 73 25. Email: camping.le.pressoir@wanadoo.fr

The 100 large pitches are arranged on either side of a gravel road leading up a slight hill. Most are shaded by attractive trees, but almost all are sloping. They are over 100 sq.m. and equipped with electricity (blue EC plugs) and interspersed with five Trigano type tents for hire. The old barn has been converted into a stylish bar and a really charming, separate restaurant. A quiet, family site, Le Pressoir provides a comfortable base for a holiday in this area famous for good food and wine. Buried in the famous wine producing countryside of the Lussac, Pomerol and St Emilion area north of Bordeaux, Le Pressoir is surrounded by fields of vines. The manicured entrance featuring attractive trees, shrubs and flowers, together with preserved equipment from its former role as a wine farm, welcomes one to the site.

Facilities

Fully equipped toilet block with facilities for disabled visitors, and washing machine. Bar and restaurant (all season). Swimming pool (15/5-15/9, no Bermuda shorts). Playground with timber equipment. Petanque, volleyball and table tennis. Gates locked 22.00 - 08.00 hrs. Off site: Tennis nearby. Fishing 5 km. Riding and bicycle hire 10 km.

Open: 25 March - 1 October.

Directions

From N89 Bordeaux - Périgueux at Saint Médard de Guizières turn south towards Lussac (D21). From Castillon-la-Bataille on D936 Libourne-Bergerac road, south of site, take D17 north towards St Médard then D21 through Petit Palais. Site signed. GPS: N44:59.824 W0:03.801

Charges 2007

Per person	€ 6,25
child (2-6 yrs)	€ 4,00
pitch incl. 6A electricity	€ 10,00

Camping Cheques accepted.

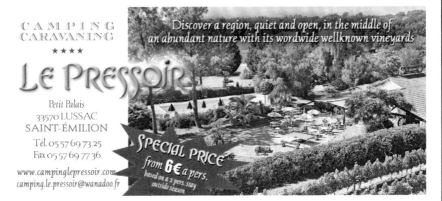

FR33140 Camping le Grand Pré

Route de Casteljaloux, F-33430 Bazas (Gironde)

Tel: 05 56 65 13 17. Email: legrandpre@wanadoo.fr

In a rural position, where the owners stated philosophy of tranquillity is realised. There are only 30 grass pitches, separated by flowering shrubs and bushes. There are plans to expand and four pitches are occupied by mobile homes. All have electricity (6-16A), water and drainage. Reception facilities and a bar are in a very tastefully converted old barn, where you may have breakfast or collect bread. There is a traffic free footpath from the site to the town, which we can recommend. A new cycle path runs from Bazas to the Atlantic coast (on 80 km. of old railway track).

Facilities

The high quality toilet block may not be adequate for demand, but we are told more units will be built. Washing machine and dryer, baby room, facilities for disabled persons. Motorcaravan services. Unusual swimming pool and paddling pool. Sunbathing area. Small playground. Volleyball, boules. B&B nearby at the Château. By prior arrangement touring motorcaravans may park overnight here (with electricity) when the site is closed. Off site: Shops, bars, restaurants, gas supplies available in Bazas, 1.5 km.

Open: 1 April - 30 September.

Directions

Bazas is around 55 km. southeast of Bordeaux, and 15 km. south of Langon. From Bazas centre take the D655 east towards Casteljaloux, and the site entrance is about 1 km. on your right (well signed).

Charges 2006

Per unit incl. 1 or 2 persons	€ 7,90 - € 18,90
incl. 3 persons	€ 9,50 - € 22,00
electricity (6-16A)	€ 3,20 - € 4,75
extra person over 10 yrs	€ 2,40 - € 3,50
dog	free - € 3,00

Discounts for longer stays.

FR33110 Airotel Camping de la Côte d'Argent

Mobile homes ▶ page 469

F-33990 Hourtin-Plage (Gironde)

Tel: **05 56 09 10 25**. Email: **info@camping-cote-dargent.com**

Côte d'Argent is a large, well equipped site for leisurely family holidays. It makes an ideal base for walkers and cyclists, with over 100 km. of cycle lanes. Hourtin-Plage is a pleasant invigorating resort on the Atlantic coast and a popular location for watersports enthusiasts, The site's top attraction is its pool complex with wooden bridges connecting the pools and islands, with sunbathing and play areas plus indoor heated pool. There are 550 touring pitches, not clearly defined, under trees with some on soft sand. Entertainment takes place at the bar near the entrance (until 12.30). Spread over 20 hectares of undulating sand-based terrain and in the midst of a pine forest. There are 48 hardstandings for motorcaravans outside the site, providing a cheap stop-over, but with no access to site facilities. The site is well organised and ideal for children.

Facilities

Very clean sanitary blocks include provision for disabled visitors. Washing machines. Motorcaravan service points. Large supermarket, restaurant, takeaway, pizzeria bar. Four outdoor pools with slides and flumes. Indoor pool. Massage. Astronomy once a week. Tennis. Pool tables. Play areas. Mini-club, organised entertainment in season. Fishing. Riding. Bicycle hire. Internet. ATM. Charcoal barbecues are not permitted. Off site: Path to the beach 300 m. Golf 30 km.

Open: 12 May - 16 September.

Directions

Turn off D101 Hourtin-Soulac road 3 km. north of Hourtin. Then join D101E signed Hourtin-Plage. Site is 300 m. from the beach.
GPS: N45:13.381 W01:09.868

Charges 2006

Per unit incl. 2 persons	€ 25,00 - € 39,00
tent incl. 2 persons	€ 19,00 - € 29,00
extra person	€ 3,00 - € 6,00
child (2-10 yrs)	€ 2,00 - € 5,00
electricity (6A)	€ 5,00

Camping Cheques accepted.

FR33150 Camping Municipal les Gabarreys

Route de la Rivière, F-33250 Pauillac (Gironde)

Tel: **05 56 59 10 03**. Email: **camping.les.gabarreys@wanadoo.fr**

An attractive, small site with well tended flower beds, Les Gabarreys is surrounded by vineyards of the Médoc region. An excellent site, it has 59 pitches, 41 with hardstanding for motorcaravans or caravans (so pegging out awnings could be a problem), 14 grass pitches for tents and 6 mobile homes, all with electric hook-ups (5/10A, some may require long leads). The 'Maison du Tourisme et du Vin' should be your first port of call. The surrounding area is well supplied with wine caves, and being fairly level you could perhaps cycle to some of them.

Facilities

Two immaculate toilet blocks provide open and cubicle washbasins and excellent facilities for disabled people. Motorcaravan services. General room with satellite TV, fridge-freezer and a small library. Minigolf (free) and volleyball.

Open: 3 April - 9 October.

Directions

Pauillac lies NNW of Bordeaux. From Bordeaux take D1 to St Laurent, then D206 to Pauillac. At the roundabout turn right to Pauillac Guais, then straight ahead at next roundabout and turn right before the Maison du Tourisme. GPS: N45:11.098 W00:45.524

Charges 2006

Per unit incl. 1 person	€ 8,00 - € 8,50
incl. 2 persons	€ 11,80 - € 12,80
extra person	€ 4,00 - € 4,40
child (2-7 yrs)	free - € 3,00

Airotel Camping Caravaning
Côte d'Argent
★★★

POOL COMPLEX OF 3500 M² WITH WATERSLIDES, JACUZZI AND COVERED HEATED SWIMMING POOL

Special low season offers (not in July and August)
14 = 11 and 7 = 6
campsite or accommodations

ifi - hotel - shops - restaurant - bar - provisions - animation (sports) - tennis - orse riding - archery - mini club - games room - sailing (4 km) - surfing (300 m)

Hourtin Plage - Aquitaine - Atlantique Sud

La Côte d'Argent is a beautiful sloping park of 20 ha in the heart of a pine tree forest. At 300 m of a long winding sandy beach at the Atlantic Ocean.
A site in the lee of dunes and the forest, this holiday village enjoys an ideal climate for enjoying relaxing nature holidays.

Sun, Life and fun

Airotel Camping Caravaning de la Côte d'Argent
33990 Hourtin Plage
Tél : 00033 (0)5.56.09.10.25
Fax : 0033 (0)5.56.09.24.96
www.camping-cote-dargent.com - www.cca33.com -
www.campingcoteouest.com

FR33160 Euronat

F-33590 Grayan et l'Hopital (Gironde)

Tel: 05 56 09 33 33. Email: **info@euronat.fr**

Euronat is really a large naturist town with extensive facilities, direct access to beach and a Thalassotherapy centre. The caravan and camping sites are in two areas separate from the chalets and mobile homes. A variety of fair sized fairly flat pitches, includes some suitable for large units. The 'town centre' is superb with two supermarkets, an organic supermarket, butcher, fish shop, bakery, restaurants including fish, Chinese, brasserie, pizzeria/crêperie, and a takeaway with a selection of hot and cold dishes and desserts which you can eat in the 'square' at picnic tables.

Facilities

Sanitary blocks are well maintained with some heated. Facilities for people with disabilities. Launderette. Motorcaravan services. Shops, restaurants. Swimming pool, flumes, children's pool. Activities and workshops, archery, pony club, horse riding, tennis, petanque, volleyball, table tennis, children's activities, handicrafts. TV rooms, video/games centre. Library. Dances, film nights, music evenings, sports activities. No barbecues.

Open: 23 March - 3 November.

Directions

From Bordeaux ring road take exit 7, then RN215 to Lesparre and Vensac, then follow (large) signed route.

Charges 2006

Per pitch incl. 2 persons	€ 15,00 - € 40,50
extra person	€ 3,00 - € 6,00
Camping Cheques accepted.	

FR33170 Camping les Acasias

44, route de Saint Vivien, F-33590 Vensac (Gironde)

Tel: 05 56 09 58 81. Email: **contact@les-acacias-du-medoc.fr**

Les Acacias is a medium sized, family run site in a lovely, rural location on the edge of the pretty little village of Vensac. This attractive site has been owned by the Gomes family for 16 years, and they offer a very warm welcome in the chalet-style reception. The mixed woodland setting, with lots of flowering shrubs, makes a welcome change from the ubiquitous pines on the coast. There are 175 pitches (141 for touring units).

Facilities

Maintenance and cleaning of the attractive toilet block is of a high standard. Facilities for disabled visitors. Mother and baby room with good facilities. Washing machines and dryers. Small shop (1/7-30/8). Bar, café and takeaway (1/7-30/8). Swimming and paddling pools (unheated, 1/6-4/9). Pool table, table tennis, minigolf (all free). Play area. Mobile homes to rent. Off site: Fishing and riding 5 km. Bicycle hire in St Vivien 3 km. Nearest beach 12 km.

Open: 1 April – 24 September.

Directions

From Bordeaux ring-road take exit 8 towards St Medard, then a right-left onto D1 (Castelnau). Continue on D1 as it becomes the N215, past Lesparre-Medoc. After 15 km. ignore first left turn to Vensac, take second and site is on left in 200 m. From the north, take ferry from Royan to Le Verdon then N215 south and turn to Vensac (about 20 km).

Charges 2006

Per unit incl. 2 persons	€ 11,00 - € 20,00
extra person	€ 3,20

FR33180 Camping la Rotonde

Chemin de Bécassine, F-33990 Hourtin Lac (Gironde)

Tel: 05 56 09 10 60. Email: **la-rotonde@wanadoo.fr**

A former equestrian centre, this site has been developed and expanded with a heavily Wild West theme. There are totem poles and large wooden carvings around the site, the buildings have clapboard fronts, the toilet block is the old stables, the restaurant serves Tex-Mex food and the entertainment, in high season, consists of line-dancing, calf-roping, country and western concerts and western style riding lessons. Probably all great fun, as long as you visit in July or August and bring your stetson, chaps and high boots. But outside the limited French holiday season, it's just a normal campsite with some unusual features and no amenities open, apart from the bar.

Facilities

Three toilet blocks, but only one open outside July/Aug. (not the old stables). These are adequate with washbasins in cubicles and push-button showers. Washing machine. Bar (all season). Swimming pool (all season). Tex-Mex restaurant and takeaway (July/Aug). Entertainment for children (Club Papoose), western-style fun and games (all July/Aug. only). Electronic games room (aka City Marshal's Office). Off site: Riding adjacent. Hourtin Lac with watersports 400 m. Beach 10 km.

Open: 1 April - 30 September.

Directions

From north, take Royan - Le Verdon ferry then N215 south to Lesparre, then D3 to Hourtin (c. 40 km. in total). In Hourtin follow signs to Hourtin Port and site is about 2 km. on left. From south take exit 8 from Bordeaux ring-motorway then D3 to Lacanau. Here go right to Carcans, then to Hourtin and as above.

Charges 2006

Per person	€ 4,80 - € 5,00
child (3-9 yrs)	€ 3,96 - € 4,13
pitch incl. electricity (6A)	€ 6,05 - € 13,45

FR33130 Yelloh! Village les Grands Pins

Mobile homes ▶ page 470

Plage Nord, F-33680 Lacanau-Océan (Gironde)
Tel: 05 56 03 20 77. Email: reception@lesgrandspins.com

This Atlantic coast holiday site with direct access to a fine sandy beach, is on undulating terrain amongst tall pine trees. A large site, with 600 pitches, 470 of varying sizes for touring units. One half of the site is a traffic free zone (except for arrival or departure day, caravans are placed on the pitch, with separate areas outside for parking). There are a good number of tent pitches, those in the centre of the site having some of the best views. This site is popular and has an excellent range of facilities available for the whole season. Especially useful for tenters are safety deposit and fridge boxes which are available for rent. The large sandy beach is a 350 metre stroll from the gate at the back of the site.

Facilities

Four well equipped toilet blocks, one heated, including baby room and facilities for disabled people. Launderette. Motorcaravan services. Supermarket. Bar, restaurant, snack bar, takeaway. Heated swimming pool (lifeguard in July/Aug) with sunbathing surround. Jacuzzi. Free fitness activities. Games room. Fitness suite. Tennis. Two playgrounds. Adventure playground. Bicycle hire. Organised activities. Entrance barrier with keypad access. Only gas barbecues are permitted. Off site: Fishing, golf, riding and bicycle hire 5 km.

Open: 15 April - 23 September.

Directions

From Bordeaux take N125/D6 west to Lacanau Ocean. At second roundabout, take second exit: Plage Nord, follow signs to 'campings'. Les Grand Pins signed to right at the far end of road. GPS: N45:00.664 W01:11.602

Charges 2006

Per unit incl. 2 persons	
and electricity	€ 16,00 - € 38,00
extra person	€ 5,00 - € 9,00
child (2-12 yrs)	free - € 6,00

Directly on the beach and in the heart of an extensive pine forest, this village is an ideal choice for family holidays, where you can relax and unwind in the open air. Discover Lacanau, the well-known surfing spot, play golf, ride a bike on one of the nice cycle tracks or chose a canoe trip between the lakes. For a full-day excursion, visit a Chateau in the world famous Médoc wine growing area, take a boat trip on the Bassin d'Arcachon or do some shopping in the majestic town of Bordeaux.

Yelloh! Village ★★★★ Les Grands Pins

Camping and Mobile-homes 350m from the beach

Yelloh ! Village LES GRANDS PINS   F 33680 Lacanau Océan
Tél. + 33 (0)5 56 03 20 77   Fax. + 33 (0)5 57 70 03 89
www.lesgrandspins.com   www.yellohvillage-les-grands-pins.com
E-mail : info@yellohvillage-les-grands-pins.com

yelloh! VILLAGE

FR33190 Pyla Camping

Grande Dune du Pyla, F-33115 Pyla sur Mer (Gironde)

Tel: 05 56 22 74 56. Email: info@pyla-camping.com

Pyla Camping is set on quite steeply sloping ground in pinewood between the Biscarosse road and the 110 metre Dune de Pyla. A major attraction here is paragliding and the site has its own launch platform above the beach. The unserviced pitches closest to the beach are very popular with paragliders. In late May there is a festival which attracts flyers from all over Europe (at festival time the music goes on well into the night). The site's 450 pitches are on terraces, 120 used for mobile homes for rent (mostly new, but a few quite old and scruffy). Of the touring pitches, 100 have 10A electricity.

Facilities

Four adequate toilet blocks (one with underfloor heating when needed). Washing machines and dryers. Very well-stocked shop. Large bar/restaurant with takeaway food (all season) and terrace. Large heated swimming pool and paddling pool. Games room. Bicycle hire. Volleyball, basketball, football (tournaments organised in July/Aug). Entertainment in high season. Off site: Golf and riding 4 km. Fishing (sea) from beach below site.

Open: 1 April - 30 September.

Directions

From A63 (north or south) take A660 towards Arcachon. At La Teste turn off towards Dune de Pyla and at the Dune car park roundabout take left turn towards Biscarosse. Site is about 3 km. on right.

Charges 2006

Per unit incl. 2 persons and electricity	€ 16,00 - € 32,00
extra person	€ 4,00 - € 8,50
child (0-7 yrs)	€ 2,00 - € 4,00

FR33210 Sunêlia la Pointe du Medoc

Route de la Pointe de Grave, F-33123 Le Verdon-sur-Mer (Gironde)

Tel: 05 56 73 39 99. Email: info@camping-lapointedumedoc.com

This site has 267 pitches, with around half for touring (6A electricity and many fully serviced). It is situated roughly equi-distant between the sandy Atlantic beach (accessed by a pleasant walk through the forest opposite the site) and that of the Gironde estuary, both around 1 km. away. Pitches are generally large. Some are in full sun but those towards the rear of the site offer much more shade. A large office has recently been converted to provide a library with internet access and a full size billiard table.

Facilities

Two modern toilet blocks are maintained to a high standard, with good hot showers and washbasins in private cabins. Pleasant bar and restaurant with takeaway. Heated swimming pool, small waterfalls, paddling pool. Massage room. Beach volleyball. Minigolf. Multisport terrain. Bicycle hire. Communal barbecues. Organised entertainment and children's club (ages 4-11) all season. Small farm and children's garden. Activities for teenagers in July/Aug. Off site: Sea fishing 1 km. Riding 5 km.

Open: 9 April - 30 September

Directions

Site is on the RN215 just south of Le Verdon and can be accessed either from the south (Bordeaux or the Blaye ferry), or from the north using the regular Royan - Pointe de Grave car ferry.

Charges 2006

Per unit incl. 1 or 2 persons	€ 13,00 - € 20,00
with electricity	€ 16,00 - € 24,00
with water and drainage	€ 18,00 - € 26,00
extra person (over 1 yr)	€ 3,00 - € 6,00

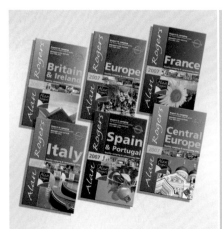

Check real time availability and at-the-gate prices...

www.alanrogers.com

FR33220 Sunêlia le Petit Nice

Mobile homes ▶ page 470

Route de Biscarosse, F-33115 Pyla-sur-Mer (Gironde)

Tel: 05 56 22 74 03. Email: info@petitnice.com

Le Petit Nice is a traditional seaside site, just south of the great Dune de Pyla (Europe's largest sand dune, and a genuinely remarkable sight). It is a friendly, if relatively unsophisticated, site with direct (steep) access to an excellent sandy beach. The 225 pitches are for the most part terraced, descending towards the sea. Many are quite small, with larger pitches generally occupied by mobile homes. For this reason it is likely to appeal more to campers and those with smaller motorcaravans and caravans. Most pitches are shaded by pine trees but those closest to the sea are unshaded. Unusually, the site also has a private hang-gliding and paragliding take-off strip (very popular activities here).

Facilities

Two refurbished toilet blocks include washbasins in cubicles, baby rooms and facilities for disabled people. New, very smart bar/restaurant. Well stocked shop. Games room. Attractive swimming pool with small slide, children's pool and jacuzzi. Good fenced play area. Tennis, table tennis and boules court.

Open: 1 April - 30 September.

Directions

The site is on the D218 (Arcachon - Biscarosse) south of the Dune de Pyla and is the fifth site you pass after the Dune. GPS: N44:34.339 W01:13.255

Charges 2006

Per pitch incl. 2 persons	€ 14,00 - € 28,00
with electricity (6A)	€ 17,00 - € 32,00
extra person	€ 4,00 - € 7,00
child (2-12 yrs)	€ 2,00 - € 6,00
Camping Cheques accepted.	

FR33230 Camping International le Truc Vert

Route du Truc-Vert, F-33950 Lège-Cap Ferret (Gironde)

Tel: 05 56 60 89 55. Email: truc-vert@tiscali.fr

Relaxing amidst the tall pines of this 10 hectare hillside site is pleasant, but if you are looking for more activity there are many cycle ways and walks to enjoy in the lovely local countryside. The site provides over 480 pitches (280 with 6A electricity) with trees giving shade. Some pitches are level but for many you will need levelling blocks. Some site roads are a little steep so care is needed and also while travelling on the local main roads through the woods (keep to speed limits) as the occasional wild boar ventures out onto the roads.

Facilities

Seven toilet blocks (not all open all season) spread well around the site offer satisfactory facilities with showers and washbasins in cubicles, facilities for disabled people (although some may find the roads on site a little steep). Motorcaravan service area. Laundry and dishwashing. Bar/brasserie (1/5-30/9). Restaurant (1/6-30/9). Internet access. Shop. Play area. Volleyball. TV/games room. Some evening entertainment in season. Off site: Riding 500 m. Fishing and beach 600 m.

Open: 1 May - 30 September.

Directions

From Bordeaux take D106 towards Lège-Cap Ferret. Continue on D106 through town and in Les Jacquets, just before village sign for Le Petit Piquey, turn right. Follow through residential area and woods for about 4 km. Site is on left.

Charges 2006

Per unit incl. 2 persons	€ 12,50 - € 18,50
extra person	€ 3,00 - € 4,20
child (2-12 yrs)	free - € 4,20
electricity (6A)	€ 3,05

FR33240 Camping Airotel de L'Océan

F-33680 Lacanau-Océan (Gironde)

Tel: 05 56 03 24 45. Email: airotel.lacanau@wanadoo.fr

Its location on the Atlantic coast, 600 metres from a lovely sandy beach makes this site extremely popular. Set in 10 hectares of wooded sand dunes, the site offers the total holiday experience with 550 pitches set amongst pine trees with areas for peace and quiet and areas for those who want to be on top of it all. Some pitches are quite spacious, some level and others requiring blocks. At the time of our visit everywhere was very dry and there was very little grass. There is a large swimming pool complex, a bar and soundproofed disco.

Facilities

Six toilet blocks provide spacious facilities including a room for disabled visitors in each block (although the site is quite hilly), baby rooms, washing machines. Motorcaravan services. Supermarket. Bar, restaurant, takeaway. Large leisure pool complex. Various sports facilities. Fitness gym. TV, games rooms. Internet access. Bicycle hire. Barbecue area. Off site: Beach 600 m. Shops 1 km. Many cycle routes through the woods.

Open: 9 April - 25 September.

Directions

From Bordeaux take D106 then onto D3 to Royan and through the wooded areas of the Atlantic coast. At Lacanau join D6 to Lacanau Ocean. At the roundabout before village turn right and site is 800 m. on the right. GPS: N45:00.511 W01:11.544

Charges 2006

Per unit incl. 2 persons	€ 12,00 - € 26,50
with electricity	€ 12,00 - € 29,50
extra person	€ 3,00 - € 7,50
child (under 10 yrs)	free - € 4,00

FR33250 Camping Parc du Val de l'Eyre

8, route du Minoy, F-33770 Salles (Gironde)

Tel: 05 56 88 67 03. Email: levaldeleyre2@wanadoo.fr

This comfortable, reasonably-priced site, while perhaps not having enough attractions to warrant a whole holiday, makes a good base for a few days to explore the Atlantic coast with its superb beaches. Set in 13 hectares of mature oak woodland, the 4 hectares for camping are mainly taken up by mobile homes of varying age and condition. Most of the 69 pitches for tourers (40 with 6A electricity) are set in an open, flat area in the centre of the site (therefore no natural shade here), with a few smaller pitches under the trees. Access is straightforward.

Facilities

Two smartly refurbished toilet blocks have good facilities (including seats in the shower cubicles). Shower/toilet room for disabled people (key access). Bar and restaurant (July/Aug). Unheated swimming pool. Play area and games field. Minigolf. Fridge hire. Electronic games in marquee near the pool. Off site: Supermarket 50 m, town shops, etc. 5 minutes. Bus to Biscarosse from outside site. Riding 5 km. Bicycle hire in Salles. Beaches 12 km.

Open: 1 April - 15 October.

Directions

From A63 take exit 21 to town of Salles (2 km). Follow signs to Biscarosse in town and site is a left turn opposite the Champion supermarket. Ignore 'Camping 4 km' signs – that's a different site.

Charges 2006

Per unit incl. 2 persons	€ 13,00 - € 21,00
extra person	€ 3,00 - € 4,00
child (2-7 yrs)	€ 2,30 - € 3,60
electricity (6A)	€ 3,50

FR33260 Camping le Braou

Route de Bordeaux, F-33980 Audenge (Gironde)

Tel: **05 56 26 90 03**. Email: **info@camping-audenge.com**

The present owners, M. and Mme. Gharbi, were the wardens of this simple, former municipal site and now lease it from the town. They have funded several developments since they took over in 2003 including a small pool, a snack bar, play area and new electrical hook-ups. The site is flat with easy access, and the pitches are in avenues, separated by newly-planted small shrubs. There is no natural shade. The new electric hook-ups (on 116 of the 148 pitches) are 10A. Outside high season this is a pleasant, reasonably priced place to stay while exploring the Bassin d'Arcachon with its bird reserve, oyster-beds, way-marked walks and cycle tracks. As with many French sites nothing much happens here until the beginning of July. Audenge (800 m.) is a lovely little town with a good choice of shops and restaurants. The Gharbis are very proud of their site, and this shows in the welcome and the high standard of maintenance.

Facilities

The small toilet block would be stretched when the site is full, but adequate in low season. Washbasins are in cubicles on the ladies side, open for men. Showers are controllable for temperature, push-button operated. Shop for basics. Bar and snack-bar (July/Aug). Small unheated swimming pool (1/6-31/8). Play area. Internet access. Motorhome service point and overnight pitches outside site. Mobile homes to rent. Off site: Town facilities 800 m. Beach and fishing 1.5 km. Riding 2 km. Golf 5 km.

Open: 1 April - 30 September.

Directions

From A63 take exit 22 onto A660 towards Arcachon. From A660 take exit 2 towards Facture, then D3 through Biganos to Audenge. Site is signed 'Camping Municipal' at lights in town.

Charges 2006

Per unit incl. 2 persons	€ 8,50 - € 15,00
extra person	€ 3,00 - € 4,50
child (0-13 yrs)	€ 2,00 - € 4,50
electricity	€ 3,00 - € 3,50

Camping le Braou

33980 Audenge - Tél. 00 33 556 269 003 - Fax 00 33 556 269 003
info@camping-audenge.com - www.camping-audenge.com

FR33270 Camping Municipal la Grigne

35 avenue de l'Océan, F-33680 Le Porge Océan (Gironde)

Tel: **05 56 26 54 88**. Email: **campingduporge2@wanadoo.fr**

La Grigne must be one of the largest municipal sites around, with 700 pitches, all available for touring units, except 18 occupied by mobile homes for hire. The main attraction here is the long sandy beach which is a 500 m. walk through the pines. Set on undulating, sandy grassland under mature pines, the pitches are large and informally laid out, marked by numbered concrete posts. Access is good even for larger units. This is a quiet site for a few days break perhaps, but for a seaside holiday there are sites nearby that are both closer to the beach and with better facilities.

Facilities

Eight good, if small toilet blocks, all of which can be heated in cold weather. They may be under pressure in peak times. Washing machines and dryers. Shop outside gate (15/6-15/9). Play area. Games room outside site gates. Off site: Snack bars and cafés in Le Porge Océan 800 m. Golf and riding 20 km. Beach 500 m. Le Porge 9 km.

Open: 1 April - 30 September.

Directions

From Bordeaux ring-motorway D660 take D106 (Cap Ferret). After about 25 km. turn off the D106 to Lege. Drive through Lege to Le Porge and in village turn left towards Le Porge Océan. Site is 9 km. on the left. Site is signed all the way from the D106.

Charges 2006

Per person	€ 2,85 - € 4,40
child (3-10 yrs)	€ 1,68 - € 2,20
pitch	€ 3,77 - € 10,15
electricity	€ 3,90

FR33280 Sunêlia la Forêt

Route de Biscarrosse, F-33115 Pyla sur Mer (Gironde)

Tel: **05 56 22 73 28**. Email: **camping.foret@wanadoo.fr**

Camping de la Forêt is one of a number of sites in this area that is dominated by the massive Dune de Pyla. The dune has to be negotiated in order to get to the beach (either over it or around, which is about 3 km), and the virtual wall of bright sand is all you have by way of a view to the east. This is a very well kept site with good facilities, easy access for all types of unit, and plenty of attractions for adults and children. Set on a gentle slope, mixed pine and oak trees give shade on most pitches. There are 24 pitches on hardstanding for motorcaravans, and all of the remaining touring pitches (on well-kept grass) have good access to water and electricity. A large area nearest to the dune has un-serviced pitches for tents. Modern mobile-homes for hire have their own area. The pool is perhaps a little basic, being a simple rectangular affair with no loungers, and no separate paddling area for the little ones. However the other facilities are very good, with a large bar and terrace with takeaway food available, and a separate more up-market restaurant. For more active campers there are quite good sports facilities on site, and nearby a network of cycle paths, GR walks, horse riding and (for the really brave) para-gliding. Dances and games evenings are on offer in high season.

Facilities

Six unisex toilet blocks (not all open in low season) have good facilities. No special facilities for babies. Facilities for disabled visitors (key from reception). Washing machines and dryers. Motorcaravan service area. Well stocked mini-market. Bar, takeaway and restaurant (1/5-30/9). Swimming and paddling pools. Two tennis courts (free except in July/Aug). Minigolf. Boules. Bicycle hire. Large play area. Children's club (with clowns) in July/Aug. Off site: Bus (infrequent service in low season) from outside site to Biscarrosse and on to Bordeaux. Golf, riding and sailing all within 5 km.

Open: 7 April - 5 November.

Directions

From A63 (north or south) take A660 towards Arcachon. At La Teste turn off towards Dune de Pyla and at Dune car park roundabout take left turn towards Biscarosse. Site is about 2 km. on the right.

Charges 2006

Per unit incl. 2 persons	€ 14,00 - € 28,00
incl. electricity	€ 16,00 - € 32,00
extra person	€ 5,00 - € 8,00
child (under 7 yrs)	€ 2,00 - € 4,50

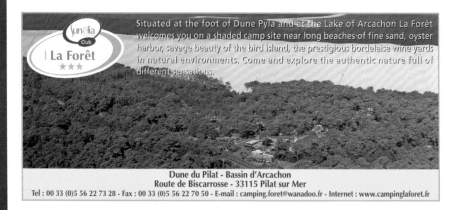

Situated at the foot of Dune Pyla and at the Lake of Arcachon La Forêt welcomes you on a shaded camp site near long beaches of fine sand, oyster harbor, savage beauty of the bird island, the prestigious bordelaise wine yards in natural environments. Come and explore the authentic nature full of different sensations.

Dune du Pilat - Bassin d'Arcachon
Route de Biscarrosse - 33115 Pilat sur Mer
Tel : 00 33 (0)5 56 22 73 28 - Fax : 00 33 (0)5 56 22 70 50 - E-mail : camping.foret@wanadoo.fr - Internet : www.campinglaforet.fr

FR33300 Domaine Residential Naturiste la Jenny

Mobile homes ▶ page 471

F-33680 Le Porge (Gironde)

Tel: **05 56 26 56 90**. E-mail: **info@lajenny.fr**

FR33310 Yelloh! Village Panorama du Pyla

Grande Dune du Pyla, route de Biscarrosse, F-33260 Pyla-sur-Mer (Gironde)

Tel: 05 56 22 10 44. Email: mail@camping-panorama.com

Many campsites set amongst pine trees have a rather untidy look, but Panorama is different. Here the entrance is inviting with well tended flower beds and a pleasant, airy reception. There is a steep climb up to the first of the touring pitches, passing the swimming pool and play area. Some pitches are suitable for caravans and motorcaravans and others suitable for tents. The touring pitches are on terraces amongst the tall pines and most have electricity (3-10A). The sea views from almost all pitches are stunning. Access to the toilet blocks may involve a steep climb (the site is probably not suitable for people with disabilities). All potentially noisy activities – pool, play areas, shop, discos, concerts, bar and takeaway – are grouped on the entrance side of the dune, away from the pitches. A track leads down to the beach with a staircase and right next door is Europe's largest dune, the Dune de Pyla, a favourite with parascenders. The area is a maze of off road cycle tracks. There are many activities and entertainments organised in high season, even classical concerts.

Facilities

Seven toilet blocks (only two open in low season) are clean and well maintained with baby rooms and facilities for disabled people. Fridge hire. Laundry facilities. Motorcaravan services. Restaurant with panoramic view of the ocean. Three heated swimming pools and jacuzzi. Adjacent play area. Tennis. Minigolf, table tennis. Paragliding. Sub-aqua diving. Organised entertainment in high season for all ages. Library and internet access in reception. Off site: Riding and golf 10 km.

Open: 1 May - 30 September.

Directions

From N250, just before La Teste, take D259 signed Biscarrosse and Dune de Pyla. At roundabout at end of road turn left (south) on D218 coast road signed Biscarrosse and Dune de Pyla. Site is 4 km. on right. GPS: N44:34.359 W01:13.232

Charges 2006

Per person	€ 4,00 - € 8,50
child (under 12 yrs)	€ 2,00 - € 3,00
pitch	€ 8,00 - € 17,00
electricity (3-10A)	free - € 5,00

FR33320 Camping Talaris Vacances

Route de l'Océan, F-33680 Lacanau-Océan (Gironde)

Tel: 05 56 03 04 15. Email: talarisvacances@free.fr

It is located near a large lake and just 6 km. from the Atlantic coast at Lacanau Océan, so there are opportunities for swimming in either lake or sea, for surfing, water-skiing or sailing. On site, there is plenty going on for youngsters – the many activities take place in front of the bar, restaurant and swimming pool area, so it is probably not the place for parents to relax! However, the part of the campsite allocated to the 150 tourist pitches is amongst mature trees at the far end of the site, so is surprisingly peaceful and relaxed.

Facilities

Two similar toilet blocks, but the one in the camping/caravanning area is adequate. Washing machines and dryers. Baby room and facilities for disabled people. Shop (July/Aug). Bar/restaurant and takeaway with covered terrace (1/5-13/9). Swimming pools (1/5-13/9). Off site: Lake 1 km. Riding 1 km. Golf 3 km. Sea beach 6 km.

Open: 7 April - 17 September.

Directions

From Bordeaux, take N125/D6 west to Lacanau and continue on D6 towards Lacanau Océan. Site is on right in about 4 km. GPS: N45:00.288 W01:06.443

Charges 2007

Per unit incl. 2 persons	€ 16,50 - € 28,50
extra person	€ 3,00 - € 6,00
child (4-10 yrs)	free - € 4,00
animal	€ 3,00 - € 3,00
electricity (6A)	€ 3,50

FR40020 Camping les Chênes

Bois de Boulogne, F-40100 Dax (Landes)

Tel: **05 58 90 05 53**. Email: **camping-chenes@wanadoo.fr**

Les Chênes is a well established site, popular with the French themselves and situated on the edge of town amongst parkland (also near the river) and close to the spa for the thermal treatments. The 176 touring pitches are of two types, some large and traditional with hedges, 109 with electricity, water and drainage, and others more informal, set amongst tall pines with electricity if required. This is a reliable, well run site, with a little of something for everyone, but probably most popular for adults taking the 'treatments'. Dax is not a place that springs at once to mind as a holiday town but, as well as being a 'spa', it promotes a comprehensive programme of events and shows during the summer season.

Facilities

Two toilet blocks, one new and modern with heating, washbasins in cubicles, facilities for disabled people, babies and young children. The older block has been refurbished. Laundry and dishwashing facilities. Shop also providing takeaway food (1/4-28/10). Swimming and paddling pools (6/5-16/9). Play area. Field for ball games. Table tennis. Boules. Bicycle hire. Mini-club for children (July/Aug). Occasional special evenings for adults. Charcoal barbecues are not permitted. Off site: Restaurant opposite. Riding, fishing and golf all within 100 m. Beaches 28 km.

Open: 25 March - 5 November.

Directions

Site is west of town on south side of river, signed after main river bridge and at many junctions in town - Bois de Boulogne (1.5 km). In very wet weather the access road to the site may be flooded (but not the site). GPS: N43:42.721 W01:04.385

Charges 2006

Per pitch incl. 2 persons and electricity (5A)	€ 13,20 - € 15,80
with water and drainage	€ 15,70 - € 18,40
extra person	€ 5,00
child (0-12 yrs)	€ 3,00

Camping Les Chênes ★★★★

Hôtel de plein air
du Bois de Boulogne
4 0 1 0 0   D A X
Tel. 0033 558 90 05 53
Fax 0033 558 90 42 43

FR40030 Les Pins du Soleil

Départementale 459, F-40990 Saint Paul-lès-Dax (Landes)

Tel: **05 58 91 37 91**. Email: **pinsoleil@aol.com**

This site will appeal to families, particularly those with younger children, or those who prefer to be some way back from the coast within easy reach of shops, cultural activities, etc. and well placed for touring the area. The site has 145 good sized pitches, 99 for touring units of which 59 have electricity and drainage. The site benefits from being developed in light woodland so there is a fair amount of shade from the many small trees.

Facilities

Modern sanitary facilities include provision for babies, disabled visitors and laundry. Small supermarket. Bar. Takeaway (2/6-15/9). Attractive, medium sized swimming pool with café (both 2/6-15/9). Playground and children's miniclub in high season. Bicycle hire. Off site: Fishing 1 km. Riding 3 km. Bus to the thermal baths.

Open: 10 March - 10 November.

Directions

From west on N124, avoid bypass, follow signs for Dax and St Paul. Almost immediately turn right at roundabout onto D459 and follow signs. Site shortly on left. It is well signed from town centre, north of river. GPS: N43:43.224 W01:05.64

Charges 2006

Per pitch incl. 2 persons	€ 8,00 - € 17,50
incl. electricity, water and drain	€ 15,00 - € 23,50
extra person	€ 6,00
child (4-10 yrs)	€ 3,50
Camping Cheques accepted.	

FR40050 Sunêlia le Col-Vert

Lac de Leon, F-40560 Vielle-St Girons (Landes)

Tel: 05 58 42 94 06. Email: contact@colvert.com

There are some 800 pitches in total, the 380 for touring being flat and covered by light pinewood, most with good shade and many along the lake side. They are of around 100 sq.m, only partly separated and some 120 have water and electricity points. Activities are organised in season: children's games, tournaments, etc. by day and dancing or shows in the evenings. Used by tour operators (80 pitches). The site has a supervised beach in July and August, sail-boarding courses are arranged in high season and there are some boats and boards for hire.

Facilities

Four toilet blocks, one heated. Washing machines, dryer, dishwasher, facilities for disabled people. Motorcaravan services. Shops (8/4-10/9). Bar/restaurant, takeaway. Two pools (all season, supervised), one covered and heated. New play area. TV room, table tennis .Games room. Sports areas, boules, tennis, volleyball. Fitness centre and sauna. Jogging tracks. Safety deposit boxes. Bicycle hire, sauna, tennis, minigolf. Fishing. Riding. Sailing school (15/6-15/9). Communal barbecues. Off site: Walking and cycle ways in the forest. Beaches 5 km. Golf 10 km.

Open: 31 March - 23 September.

Directions

Site is off D652 Mimizan-Léon road, 4 km. south of crossroads with D42 at St Girons. Road to lake and site is signed at Veille. GPS: N43:54.190 W01:18.631

Charges 2006

Per unit incl. 2 persons	€ 11,00 - € 44,90
extra person	€ 2,00 - € 6,00
child (3-13 yrs)	€ 1,50 - € 5,00
electricity (3/10A)	€ 3,80 - € 5,00
dog	€ 1,00 - € 4,00

Camping Cheques accepted.

FR40040 Camping Village la Paillotte

F-40140 Azur (Landes)

Tel: 05 58 48 12 12. Email: info@paillotte.com

La Paillotte, in the Landes area of southwest France, is a site with a character of its own. It lies beside the Soustons Lake only 1.5 km. from Azur village, with its own sandy beach. This is suitable for young children because the lake is shallow and slopes gradually. All 310 pitches at La Paillotte are mostly shady with shrubs and trees. The 132 pitches for touring vary in price according to size, position and whether they are serviced. La Paillotte is an unusual site with its own atmosphere which appeals to many regular clients. The campsite buildings (reception, shop, restaurant, even sanitary blocks) are all Tahitian in style, circular and constructed from local woods with the typical straw roof (and layer of waterproof material underneath). Some are now being replaced but still in character. For boating the site has a small private harbour where you can keep your own non-powered boat (of shallow draught).

Facilities

Modern, well equipped toilet blocks. Washing machines, dryers. Motorcaravan services. Shop (1/6-29/9). Good restaurant with terrace overlooking lake, bar, takeaway (all 13/4-26/9). Swimming pool complex (13/4-26/9). Sports, games and organised activities. 'Miniclub' room, with 'mini' equipment. TV room, library. Fishing. Bicycle hire. Table tennis. Sailing, rowing boats and pedaloes for hire. Torches useful. No dogs are accepted. Off site: Riding 5 km. Golf 10 km. Atlantic beaches 10 km.

Open: April - September.

Directions

Coming from the north along N10, turn west on D150 at Magescq. From south go via Soustons. In Azur turn left before church (site signed). GPS: N43:47.229 W01:18.570

Charges 2006

Per unit incl. 2 persons	
with 10A electricity	€ 15,00 - € 35,00
with electricity and water	€ 17,00 - € 37,00
pitch by the lake	€ 20,00 - € 43,00
extra person (over 4 yrs)	€ 3,00 - € 7,00

FR40070 Yelloh! Village Lous Seurrots

Contis Plage, F-40170 Saint Julien-en-Born (Landes)
Tel: **05 58 42 85 82**. Email: **info@lous-seurrots.com**

Lous Seurrots is only a short 300 metre walk from the beach and parts of the site have views across the estuary. There are 610 pitches, mainly in pine woods on sandy undulating ground. They are numbered but only roughly marked out, most have good shade and over 80% have electrical hook-ups. The site's pool complex (two heated) is in a superb setting of palm trees and flower beds and the paved sunbathing areas have wonderful views out to the estuary and the sea. For all its size, Lous Seurrots is a family site with the emphasis on peace and tranquillity (no discos).

Facilities

Six well kept, modern toilet blocks, baby rooms and facilities for disabled people. Laundry facilities. Motorcaravan services. Large shop (15/5-15/9). Bar, restaurant (15/5-15/9). Takeaway (1/7-30/9). Swimming pool complex (2/4-30/9) and a Jacuzzi (July/Aug). Tennis. Minigolf. Canoeing. Bicycle hire. Fishing. Miniclub for younger children. Evening entertainment twice weekly in high season in open-air auditorium. Only gas barbecues are permitted. Off site: Riding 3 km.

Open: 2 April - 30 September.

Directions

Turn off D652 on D41 (15 km. south of Mimizan) to Contis-Plage and site is on left as you reach it. GPS: N44:05.347 W01:18.990

Charges 2007

Per unit incl. 2 persons and electricity	€ 16,00 - € 35,00
extra person	€ 4,00 - € 6,00
child (3-7 yrs)	free - € 4,00
animal	€ 3,00

FR40060 Camping Club International Eurosol

Route de la Plage, F-40560 Vielle-Saint Girons (Landes)
Tel: **05 58 47 90 14**. Email: **contact@camping-eurosol.com**

The site is on undulating ground amongst mature pine trees giving good shade and the pitches on the slopes are mainly only suitable for tents. The 405 pitches for touring units are numbered (although with nothing to separate them, there is little privacy) and 209 have electricity with 120 fully serviced (86 with mobile homes). A family site with entertainers who speak many languages, many games and tournaments are organised and a beach volleyball competition is held each evening in front of the bar.

Facilities

Four main toilet blocks and two smaller blocks, facilities for babies and disabled people. Motorcaravan services. Fridge rental. Well stocked shop and bar (12/5-15/9). Restaurant, takeaway (1/7-31/8). Stage for live shows (mainly performed by the versatile staff) in July/Aug. and finishing by midnight. Outdoor swimming pool (12/5-15/9). Tennis. Multi-sport court for basketball, handball and football. Bicycle hire. Charcoal barbecues are not permitted. Off site: Riding school opposite. Fishing 700 m.

Open: 12 May - 15 September.

Directions

Turn off D652 at St Girons on D42 towards St Girons-Plage. Site is on left before coming to beach (4.5 km). GPS: N43:57.100 W01:21.087

Charges 2006

Per unit incl.1 or 2 persons	€ 12,00 - € 25,50
with electricity	€ 15,00 - € 30,00
with water and drainage	€ 15,00 - € 33,00
extra person (over 4 yrs)	€ 3,00 - € 4,00
dog	€ 2,50

FR40110 Camping Caravaning Sen Yan

Le Village Tropical, F-40170 Mézos (Landes)
Tel: **05 58 42 60 05**. Email: **reception@sen-yan.com**

This exotic family site is about 12 km. from the Atlantic coast in the Landes forest area, set just outside the village. There are 310 pitches marked with hedges, 190 with electricity (6A), and with ample water points. Some mobile homes and tour operator pitches are in a separate 'village'. The reception, bar and pool area is almost tropical with the luxuriant greenery of its banana trees, palm trees, tropical flowers and its straw sunshades. A new slide is planned for 2007. Activities and evening entertainment include a disco twice a week in high season.

Facilities

Three toilet blocks with good quality fittings have showers and washbasins in cabins and some British style WCs. The newest block is especially suitable for low season visitors with a section for babies. Facilities for disabled people. Shop (from 15/6). Bar, restaurant and snacks (1/7-31/8). Outdoor pools (1/7-30/8). Heated indoor pool (1/6-15/9). Practice golf. Bicycle hire. Only gas barbecues permitted. Off site: Fishing 500 m. Riding 6 km. Beach 12 km.

Open: 1 June - 15 September.

Directions

From N10 take exit 14 (Onesse-Laharie), then the D38 Bias/Mimizan road. After 13 km. turn south to Mézos from where site is signed. GPS: N44:04.337 W01:09.38

Charges 2007

Per person	€ 5,00 - € 6,00
child (under 7 yrs)	free - € 5,00
pitch with 6A electricity	€ 24,00 - € 34,00

FR40080 Airotel Club Marina – Landes

Rue Marina, F-40200 Mimizan (Landes)

Tel: 05 58 09 12 66. Email: contact@clubmarina.com

Well maintained and clean, with helpful staff, Club Marina-Lande would be a very good choice for a family holiday. Activities include discos, play groups for children, specially trained staff to entertain teenagers and concerts for more mature campers. There are numerous sports opportunities and a superb beach nearby. A nightly curfew ensures that all have a good night's sleep. The site has 445 touring pitches (279 with 10A electricity) and 128 mobile homes and chalets for rent. The pitches are on firm grass, most with hedges and they are large (mostly 120 sq.m. or larger). If ever a campsite could be said to have two separate identities, then Club Marina-Landes is surely the one. In early and late season it is quiet, with the pace of life in low gear – come July and until 1 September, all the facilities are open and there is fun for all the family with the chance that family members will only meet together at meal times.

Facilities

Five toilet blocks (opened as required), well maintained with showers and many washbasins in cabins. Facilities for babies, children and disabled visitors. Laundry facilities. Motorcaravan services. Fridge hire. Shop (freshly baked bread). Bar and restaurant. Snack bar, pizzas and takeaway (1/7-27/8). Covered pool. Outdoor pool (1/7-27/8). Minigolf. Table tennis. Tennis. Volleyball and basketball. Bicycle hire. Play area. Internet access. Entertainment and activities (high season). Gas or electric barbecues only. Off site: Beach and fishing 500 m. Bus service 1 km. Riding 1 km. Mimizan 8 km. Golf 7 km.

Open: 27 April - 17 September.

Directions

Heading west from Mimizan centre, take the D626 passing Abbey Museum. Straight on at lights (crossing D87/D67). Next lights turn left. After 2 km. at T-junction turn left. Follow signs to site. GPS: N44:12.234 W01:17.472

Charges 2006

Per unit incl. 3 persons	€ 14,00 - € 36,00
incl. electricity	€ 17,00 - € 39,00
extra person (over 3 yrs)	€ 3,00 - € 6,00

237

FR40100 Camping du Domaine de la Rive

Mobile homes ▶ page 470

Route de Bordeaux, F-40600 Biscarosse (Landes)

Tel: **05 58 78 12 33**. Email: **info@camping-de-la-rive.fr**

Surrounded by pine woods, La Rive has a superb beach-side location on Lac de Sanguinet. It provides mostly level, numbered and clearly defined pitches of 100 sq.m. all with electricity connections (6A). The swimming pool complex is wonderful with pools linked by water channels and bridges. There is also a jacuzzi, paddling pool and two large swimming pools all surrounded by sunbathing areas and decorated with palm trees. An indoor pool is heated and open all season. There may be some aircraft noise from a nearby army base. This is a friendly site with a good mix of nationalities. The latest addition is a super children's aqua park with various games. The beach is excellent, shelving gently to provide safe bathing for all ages. There are windsurfers and small craft can be launched from the site's slipway.

Facilities

Five good clean toilet blocks have washbasins in cabins and mainly British style toilets. Facilities for disabled visitors. Baby baths. Motorcaravan service point. Shop. Propane gas. Restaurant. Bar serving snacks and takeaway. Games room. Pool complex (supervised July/Aug). Play area. Tennis. Bicycle hire. Hand-ball, basketball. Table tennis, boules, archery and football. Fishing. Water skiing. Watersports equipment hire. Tournaments (June-Aug). Skateboard park. Trampolines. Mini-club for children. No charcoal barbecues on pitches. Off site: Golf 8 km.

Open: 1 April - 30 September.

Directions

Take D652 from Sanguinet to Biscarosse and site is signed on the right in about 6 km. Turn right and follow new tarmac road for 2 km. GPS: N44:27.607 W01:07.808

Charges 2006

Per pitch incl. 2 persons and electricity	€ 20,00 - € 38,00
with water and drainage	€ 23,00 - € 41,00
extra person	€ 3,40 - € 7,00
child (3-10 yrs)	€ 2,30 - € 5,50

Camping Cheques accepted.

FR40120 Domaine Naturiste Arnaoutchot

F-40560 Vielle-Saint Girons (Landes)

Tel: **05 58 49 11 11**. Email: **contact@arna.com**

'Arna' is a large naturist site with extensive facilities and direct access to the beach. Even with 500 pitches, its layout in the form of a number of sections, each with its own character, make it quite relaxing and very natural. These sections amongst the trees and bushes of the Landes provide a variety of reasonably sized pitches, most with electricity (3/6A), although the hilly terrain means that only a limited number are flat enough for motorcaravans. The centrally located amenities are extensive and of excellent quality. American motorhomes not accepted.

Facilities

Heated sanitary facilities include the usual naturist site type of blocks with communal hot showers and also a number of tiny blocks. Motorcaravan services. Supermarket, other shops. Bar/restaurant, pizzeria and tapita (fish) bar. Pizza. Heated indoor swimming pool with solarium, whirlpool and slide. Outdoor pool, sunbathing area. Spa, sauna, steam, whirlpool, massages. TV, games rooms. Cinema. Library. Cash point. Internet point. Bicycle hire. Fishing. Torches useful. Gas and electric barbecues. Off site: Riding or golf 5 km.

Open: 1 April - 25 September.

Directions

Site is signed off the D652 road at Vielle-Saint-Girons. Follow D328 for 3-4 km. GPS: N43:54.449 W01:21.866

Charges 2006

Per unit incl. 1 person	€ 9,90 - € 33,90
extra person (over 3 yrs)	€ 2,00 - € 6,90
electricity (3/6A)	€ 3,70 - € 5,20
animal	€ 1,20 - € 3,00

Special offers available.
Camping Cheques accepted.

Domaine de La Rive

a Paradise for Children

ww.larive.fr

Pool complex and a covered heated swimming pool

FR40140 Camping Caravaning Lou P'tit Poun

Mobile homes ▷ page 471

110 avenue du Quartier Neuf, F-40390 Saint Martin de Seignanx (Landes)

Tel: **05 59 56 55 79**. Email: **contact@louptitpoun.com**

The manicured grounds surrounding Lou P'tit Poun give it a well kept appearance, a theme carried out throughout this very pleasing site. It is only after arriving at the car park that you feel confident it is not a private estate. Beyond this point an abundance of shrubs and trees are revealed. Behind a central sloping flower bed lies the open plan reception area. The avenues around the site are wide and the 168 pitches (99 for touring) are spacious. All have electricity (6/10A), many also have water and drainage and some are separated by low hedges. A 'Sites et Paysages' member. The jovial owners not only make their guests welcome, but extend their enthusiasm to organising weekly entertainment for young and old during high season.

Facilities

Two unisex sanitary blocks, maintained to a high standard and kept clean, include washbasins in cabins, a baby bath and provision for disabled people. Dishwashing sinks and laundry facilities with washing machine and dryer. Motorcaravan service point. Small shop (1/7-31/8). Café (1/7-31/8). Swimming pool (1/6-15/9). Play area. Games room, TV. Half court tennis. Table tennis. Off site: Bayonne 6 km. Fishing or riding 7 km. Golf 10 km. Sandy beaches of Basque coast ten minute drive.

Open: 1 June - 15 September.

Directions

Leave A63 at exit 6 and join N117 in the direction of Pau. Site is signed at Leclerc supermarket. Continue on N117 for 3.5 km. and site is clearly signed on right. GPS: N43:31.451 W01:24.730

Charges 2006

Per pitch incl. 1 or 2 persons	€ 10,40 - € 23,50
with 6A electricity	€ 13,50 - € 27,00
with water and drainage	€ 20,50 - € 31,50
extra person	€ 5,10 - € 6,50
child (under 7 yrs)	€ 2,10 - € 4,30

Lou P'tit Poun ★★★

At 10 km from the ocean, a friendly welcome awaits you at this quality campsite between Les Landes and the Basque country.

CAMPING LOU P'TIT POUN
40390 ST MARTIN DE SEIGNANX
Tél : 05 59 56 55 79   Fax : 05 59 56 53 71
E-mail : contact@louptitpoun.com
LANDES - AQUITAINE - FRANCE

Rental of bungalows and mobil-homes

FR40160 Camping les Vignes

Route de la Plage du Cap de L'Homy, F-40170 Lit-et-Mixe (Landes)

Tel: **05 58 42 85 60**. Email: **contact@les-vignes.com**

Les Vignes is a large holiday site close to the Atlantic coast with 450 pitches, of which 262 are occupied by a mix of mobile homes, bungalows and tents, most of which are for rent. The 188 tourist pitches are relatively level on a sandy base, all serviced with electricity (10A) and water, some with waste water drains. The site's amenities, including a supermarket, restaurant and bar, are located at the entrance to the site. The rather stylish swimming pool complex includes a six lane water slide. A wide range of activities is provided and during July and August a great variety of entertainment options for both adults and children, some of which take place in the new entertainment 'Big Top'.

Facilities

Four sanitary units with washing machines, dryers, facilities for babies and disabled people. Large supermarket (15/6-10/9). Restaurant, bar (15/6-10/9). Takeaway (July/Aug). Swimming pool complex (1/6-15/9). Tennis. Table tennis. Golf driving range. Minigolf. Volleyball, basketball. Pétanque. Kids club and playground. Bicycle hire. Internet access. Barrier closed 23.00-07.00 hrs. Off site: Golf course, canoeing, kayaking, surfing, riding. Many cycle tracks.

Open: 1 June - 15 September.

Directions

Lit-et-Mixe is on the D652 20 km. south of Mimizan. Turn west on D88 1 km. south of town towards Cap de l'Homy for 1.5 km. where site entrance is on left. GPS: N44:01.375 W01:16.787

Charges 2006

Per pitch incl. 2 persons, electricity and water	€ 16,00 - € 45,00
extra person (over 5 yrs)	€ 4,00 - € 6,00
child (under 5 yrs)	€ 2,00 - € 4,00

FR40180 Camping le Vieux Port

Plage sud, F-40660 Messanges (Landes)
Tel: 01 72 03 91 60. Email: contact@levieuxport.com

Mobile homes ● page 472

A well established destination appealing particularly to families with teenage children, this lively site has 1,406 pitches of mixed size, most with electricity (6/8A) and some fully serviced. The camping area is well shaded by pines and pitches are generally of a good size, attractively grouped around the toilet blocks. There are many tour operators here and well over a third of the site is taken up with mobile homes and another 400 pitches are used for tents. The heated pool complex is exceptional boasting five outdoor pools and three large water slides. There is also a heated indoor pool. The area to the north of Bayonne is heavily forested and a number of very large campsites are attractively located close to the superb Atlantic beaches. Le Vieux Port is probably the largest and certainly one of the most impressive of these. At the back of the site a path leads across the dunes to a good beach (500 m). A little train also trundles to the beach on a fairly regular basis in high season (small charge). All in all, this is a lively site with a great deal to offer an active family.

Facilities

Nine well appointed toilet blocks with facilities for disabled people. Motorcaravan services. Good supermarket and various smaller shops in high season. Several restaurants, takeaway and three bars (all open all season). Large pool complex (no Bermuda shorts) including new covered pool and Polynesian themed bar. Tennis, football, multi-sport pitch, minigolf. Bicycle hire. Riding centre. Organised activities in high season including frequent discos and karaoke evenings. Only communal barbecues are allowed. Off site: Fishing 1 km. Golf 8 km.

Open: 1 April - 30 September.

Directions

Leave RN10 at Magescq exit heading for Soustons. Pass through Soustons following signs for Vieux-Boucau. Bypass this town and site is clearly signed to the left at second roundabout.
GPS: N43:47.863 W01:23.959

Charges 2006

Per unit incl. 2 persons	€ 12,00 - € 35,00
extra person	€ 3,50 - € 6,00
child (under 10 yrs)	€ 2,50 - € 4,00
electricity (6/8A)	€ 4,00 - € 6,50
animal	€ 2,00 - € 3,50

Camping Cheques accepted.

Check real time availability and at-the-gate prices...
www.alanrogers.com

FR40190 Le Saint Martin Airotel Camping

Mobile homes ▶ page 472

Avenue de l'Océan, F-40660 Moliets-Plage (Landes)

Tel: 05 58 48 52 30. Email: contact@camping-saint-martin.fr

A family site aimed mainly at couples and young families, Airotel St Martin is a welcome change to most of the sites in this area in that it has only a small number of mobile homes (85) compared to the number of touring pitches (575). First impressions are of a neat, tidy, well cared for site and the direct access to the beach is an added bonus. The pitches are mainly typically French in style with low hedges separating them plus some shade. Electric hook ups are 10-15A and a number of pitches also have water and drainage. Entertainment in high season is low key (with the emphasis on quiet nights) – daytime competitions and a 'miniclub' and the occasional evening entertainment, well away from the pitches and with no discos or karaoke. With pleasant chalets and mobile homes to rent, and an 18 hole golf course 700 m. away (special rates negotiated), this would be an ideal destination for a golfing weekend or longer stay.

Facilities

Seven toilet blocks of a high standard and very well maintained, have washbasins in cabins, large showers, baby rooms and facilities for disabled visitors. Motorcaravan service point. Washing machines and dryers. Fridge rental. Supermarket. Bars, restaurants and takeaways. Indoor pool, jacuzzi and sauna (charged July/Aug). Outdoor pool area with jacuzzi and paddling pool (15/6-15/9). Multi sports pitch. Play area. Internet access. Electric barbecues only. Off site: Excellent area for cycling, bicycle hire 500 m. Golf and tennis 700 m. Riding 8 km. .

Open: Easter - 31 October.

Directions

From the N10 take D142 to Lèon, then D652 to Moliets-et-Mar. Follow signs to Moliets-Plage, site is well signed. GPS: N43:51.145 W01:23.239

Charges 2006

Per unit incl. 1 or 2 adults, 1 child	€ 17,50 - € 31,50
with electricity	€ 21,00 - € 35,50
with services	€ 24,00 - € 39,00
extra person	€ 3,20 - € 5,50
dog	€ 3,00

Prices are for reserved pitches.

★ ★ ★ ★

Saint Martin

Airotel Camping Caravaning

Avenue de l'Océan
40660 Moliets-Plage

Tél : (33) 05.58.48.52.30
Fax : (33) 05.58.48.50.73

www.camping-saint-martin.fr
contact @camping-saint-martin.fr

FR40170 Siblu Camping la Réserve

Gastés, F-40160 Parentis-en-Born (Landes)

Tel: 05 58 09 74 79. Email: lareserve@siblu.fr

La Resérve, now run by Haven Europe, is a large site set in a pinewood. It has access to a large lake with a beach and small harbour and the Atlantic beaches are nearby (20 km). The lake shelves very gradually so is good fun for children and there are good facilities for windsurfing and sailing; powered boats for water ski-ing are also permitted here. The 700 numbered pitches (200 for touring) are of above average size (mostly 120 sq.m.) set on mainly flat ground and marked by stones in the ground. Most have electricity.

Facilities

Five adequate toilet blocks. Washing machines. Supermarket. Restaurant, bar with entertainment all season. Swimming pool complex with water slides, paddling pools, etc. (lifeguards on duty). Children's club. Two tennis courts (floodlit in the evening), minigolf, table tennis and volleyball. Boat hire, windsurfing courses and water ski-ing. TV room, general room and amusement machines. Fishing. Bicycle hire. Dogs are not accepted. Off site: Atlantic beaches 20 km.

Open: 29 April - 23 September.

Directions

Turn west off D652 Gastes - Mimizan road on southern outskirts of Gastes by campsite sign, then 3 km. to site. GPS: N44:18.801 W01:10.140

Charges guide

Per pitch incl. 2 persons	€ 12,00 - € 54,00
with electricity	€ 14,00 - € 39,00
extra person	€ 3,00 - € 6,00

FR40200 Yelloh! Village le Sylvamar

Mobile homes ▶ page 472

Avenue de l'Océan, F-40530 Labenne Océan (Landes)

Tel: **05 59 45 75 16**. Email: **camping@sylvamar.fr**

Less than a kilometre from a long sandy beach, this campsite has a good mix of tidy, well maintained chalets, mobile homes and touring pitches. The 556 pitches (212 for touring) are level, numbered and mostly separated by low hedges. Most have electricity (10A), many also have water and drainage and there is welcoming shade. The swimming pool complex is superbly set in a sunny location. The pools are of various sizes (one heated, one not) with a large one for paddling. With four toboggans and a fast flowing channel for sailing down in the inflatable rubber rings provided, this is a haven for children. All are surrounded by ample sunbathing terraces and overlooked by the bar/restaurant.

Facilities

Four modern toilet blocks (one recently refurbished) have washbasins in cabins, and facilities for babies and disabled visitors. Washing machines. Shop. Bar/restaurant and takeaway. Play area. TV room. Mini-club (July/Aug). Fitness centre. Tennis. Bicycle hire. Library. Extensive entertainment programme for all ages, incl. evening shows in the outdoor amphitheatre. Fridge hire. No charcoal barbecues. Internet access. Off site: Beach 900 m. Fishing, riding 1 km. Golf 7 km.

Open: 14 April - 25 September.

Directions

Labenne is on the N10. In Labenne, head west on D126 signed Labenne Océan and site is on right in 4 km. GPS: N43:35.742 W01:27.383

Charges 2006

Per unit incl. 2 persons and electricity	€ 15,00 - € 36,00
extra person (over 7 yrs)	€ 3,00 - € 7,00
extra person (3-7 yrs)	free - € 5,00
dog	free - € 4,00

Le Sylvamar

Avenue de l'Océan F-40530 - Labenne Océan - France
T [33] 05 59 45 75 16 - F [33] 05 59 45 75 16 - sylvamar@wanadoo.fr

Nestled in a 37-acre (15 hectares) pine forest, this village is paradise for nature lovers, beachgoers and marine activities. Located on the southern coast of France's Landes region, Sylvamar is right next to Basque country and Spain, between Biarritz and Hossegor. It's up to you to choose wether you'd like an active or relaxing vacation, with plenty of clean, fresh air to make the best of it.

A DREAM COME TRUE - THE AQUATIC AREA IS AT YOUR DISPOSAL:
Blue lagoon, quiet green, luxurious vegetation, natural surroundings. For aquatic fun, there are 2 heated pools, a play river and triple waterslide. For relaxation, use deck chairs to soak up sun, stroll about on bridges and whatever you feel like. It's all designed around games, having fun and taking it easy. Smiling children and parents and all in complete safety, with on-duty lifeguards

FR40220 Camping les Acacias

Route d'Azur, Quartier Delest, F-40660 Messanges (Landes)

Tel: **05 58 48 01 78**. Email: **lesacacias@lesacacias.com**

Close to the Atlantic beaches of Les Landes, this small family run site is quiet and peaceful. There are 79 large, generally flat touring pitches separated by trees and shrubs, with chalets and mobile homes ranged unobtrusively on two sides of the site. There are also some seasonal caravans. All the touring pitches have electricity (5/10A) but water is only available at the toilet block. Pitches are easily accessed by tarmac internal roads. M and Mme Dourthe are constantly improving the site and the facilities and services show the care taken in design.

Facilities

One modern, clean and well designed toilet block with facilities for disabled people. Washing machines, dryer and ironing board. Motorcaravan services. Fridge hire. Shop (15/6-15/9). Takeaway (high season). Games room. Small play area. Football. Volleyball. Table tennis. Boules. Bicycle hire. Off site: Bus service 1 km. Beach 2 km. Fishing 3 km. Riding 1.5 km. Golf 4 km. Supermarket 2 km.

Open: 25 March - 25 October.

Directions

Site is signed off the D652, turning inland (east) 2 km north of Vieux-Boucau; 3 km south of Messanges.

Charges 2007

Per unit incl. 1 or 2 persons	€ 8,90 - € 13,50
extra person	€ 2,60 - € 3,40
child (0-7 yrs)	€ 1,80 - € 2,30
electricity	€ 2,70 - € 4,00
animal	€ 0,80 - € 1,60

FR40250 Camping les Grands Pins

Mobile homes ▶ page 473

1039 avenue de Losa, F-40460 Sanguinet (Landes)

Tel: 05 58 78 61 74. Email: info@campinglesgrandspins.com

Approached by a road alongside the lake, this site is set amongst tall pine trees. The gravel pitches are of average size, mostly level and shaded. Hedges divide those available for tourers and these are set amongst the many mobile homes. Large units may find manoeuvring difficult. There may be some aircraft noise at times from a nearby army base. A central pool complex includes a covered heated indoor pool, an outdoor pool, water slide and flume. In early and late season this is a very quiet site with very few facilities open. However, there are plenty of walks, cycle rides and the lake to enjoy. The poolside bar, restaurant and shops are only open in July/August. In July and August the site becomes busy, offering watersports, minigolf, a children's club, boat trips and organised activities. All four sanitary blocks are open for July and August. Fishing is also available. The charming small village of Sanguinet is 2 km. away with shops, bars, restaurants and an archaeological museum.

Facilities

Four toilet blocks include washbasins in cabins, showers and British style toilets (not all open in low seasons). Baby bath and provision for disabled visitors. Laundry facilities. Motorcaravan service point.Shop, bar, restaurant and takeaway (1/7-31/8). Indoor pool (all seson). Outdoor pool complex (1/7-31/8). Play area. Games room and TV in bar. Tennis. Bicycle hire (July/Aug). Pets are not accepted in July/Aug. Barbecues are not allowed (dedicated area provided). Off site: Beach 30 m. Fishing 2 km. Golf and riding 15 km. Boat launching 1 km.

Open: 1 April - 31 October.

Directions

Enter Sanguinet from the north on the D46. At one way system turn right. Do not continue on one way system but go straight ahead toward lake (signed) on Rue de Lac. Site is 2 km. on left.
GPS: N44:29.038 W01:05.383

Charges 2006

Per unit incl. 2 persons and electricity	€ 13,00 - € 33,50
extra person	€ 2,50 - € 4,00
child (3-10 yrs)	€ 2,00 - € 3,00

FR40260 Camping les Chevreuils

Route de Vieux Boucou á Hossegor, F-40510 Seignosse (Landes)

Tel: 05 58 43 32 80. Email: contact@chevreuils.cegeteldsl.com

Set in a mature pine and oak forest, 1.2 km. from the beach, this campsite has randomly spaced, well shaded pitches of a variety of sizes. Sandy ground and tree roots can make for uneven ground. Little evening entertainment is organised, as the emphasis here is on peace and quiet. This site is ideal for couples and families with small children who wish to stay in natural surroundings reflecting the traditional style of camping. The site is not recommended for people with disabilities due to the uneven, sandy ground. Two swimming pools are set in a sunny area with plenty of space for sunbathing.

Facilities

Three clean toilet blocks are traditional in style. Facilities for disabled visitors (but see above). Motorcaravan service point. Laundry facilities. Fridge box hire. Shop (15/6-2/9). Bar (1/6-15/9). Restaurant (8/6-15/9). Children's club (5-12 yrs) in July/Aug. Barbecues are not allowed (communal area supplied). Off site: Disco 800 m. Fishing 3 km. Golf 5 km. Riding 7 km. Beach 1.5 km. Sailing 3 km. Bus service to Bayonne, Leon and Dax.

Open: 1 June - 15 September.

Directions

From N10 take exit 11 and D116 to Soustons. Head west on D652 towards Vieux-Boucau. Turn left on D79 heading south and site is 6 km. on the left.

Charges 2006

Per unit incl. 2 persons	€ 14,00 - € 20,00
extra person	€ 4,00 - € 5,60
child (4-12 yrs)	€ 3,30 - € 4,70
electricity	€ 4,00 - € 5,00

FR40240 Camping Mayotte Vacances

Mobile homes ▶ page 473

368 chemin des Roseaux, F-40600 Biscarrosse (Landes)

Tel: 05 58 78 00 00. Email: mayotte@yellohvillage.com

This appealing site is set amongst pine trees on the edge of Lac de Biscarrosse. Drive down a tree and flower lined avenue and proceed toward the lake to shady, good sized pitches which blend well with the many tidy mobile homes that share the area. Divided by hedges, all the pitches have electricity (10A) and water taps. There may be some aircraft noise at times from a nearby army base. The pool complex is impressive, with various pools, slides, chutes, jacuzzi and sauna, all surrounded by paved sunbathing areas. The excellent lakeside beach provides safe bathing for all ages with plenty of watersports available. A comfortable restaurant and bar overlook the pool. A new, fully equipped gym is available free of charge. Children of all ages are catered for with organised clubs, play and sports areas and a games room. This well managed, clean and friendly site with helpful multilingual staff in reception should appeal to all and the facilities are open all season.

Facilities

Four good quality, clean toilet blocks (one open early season). Good facilities for visitors with disabilities. Unusual baby/toddler bathroom. Motorcaravan services. Laundry. Supermarket. Boutique. Rental shop (July/Aug). Restaurant. Swimming pools (one heated; supervised July/Aug. and weekends). Play area. Further children's area (extra cost) with trampolines, inflatables and a small train. Bicycle hire. Fishing. Watersports. Organised activities and entertainment (July/Aug). Clubs for toddlers and teenagers (July/Aug). Charcoal barbecues not permitted. Hairdressers (seasonal). ATM. Internet access. Off site: Golf 4 km. Riding 100 m. Beach 10 km. Town 2 km.

Open: 30 April - 24 September.

Directions

From the north on D652 turn right on D333 (chemin de Goubern). Pass through Goubern and Mayotte Village. Take next right (signed to site) into chemin des Roseaux. GPS: N44:26.097 W01:09.303

Charges 2006

Per unit incl. 2 persons	€ 18,00 - € 29,00
extra person	€ 3,50 - € 5,00
child (3-7 yrs)	free - € 2,50
dog	€ 3,00 - € 5,00

Mayotte Vacances

'On the banks of lake Biscarrosse, you are gently swathed so that you unwind and relax. The surface of the water ripples with the breeze as mooring ropes tug in rhythm and the drifting sand whispers over you. The snell of the sea spray and the pine trees tell you the ocean and the forest are not far away. You let go of time. Here, nature has a special kind of healing power and is waiting for you to savour its benefits'

368, Chemin des Roseaux - 40600 Biscarrosse - France
Tel: 0033 (0) 558 78 00 00 - Fax: 0033 (0) 558 78 83 91
camping@mayottevacances.com - www.mayottevacances.com

FR40280 Airotel Lou Puntaou

Au bord du Lac, F-40550 Léon (Landes)

Tel: 05 58 48 74 20. Email: reception@loupuntaou.com

Set between Lac de Léon and the nature reserve park of Huchet, this site offers plenty for young families. The level pitches are mainly grass, hedged and have electricity (15A). Trees offer reasonable shade. In July and August only, there may be some noise from the lake car park and activities. In July and August a full range of activities is organised on the site with sports and clubs for children and activities and evening entertainment for adults. A number of tour operators use the site.

Facilities

Three traditional style toilet blocks include facilities for disabled visitors and children. Laundry facilities. Motorcaravan service point. Simple shop at site entrance. Bar, restaurant and takeaway (all season). TV and games rooms. Tennis. ATM. Internet. Only electric barbecues are permitted (communal area available). Off site: Village 500 m. with shops restaurants and bars. Bus to village (July/Aug). Lake 200 m. Beach 7 km. Golf 7 km.

Open: 1 April - 30 September.

Directions

From N10 take exit 12 towards Castets. Take the D142 to Léon and at island take first exit 'Centre Ville'. At T-. junction turn left on D652. After 300 m. turn left at sign for site and lake. After 500 m. the site is on left.

Charges 2006

Per person	€ 3,00 - € 6,00
child (2-13 yrs)	free - € 4,00
pitch incl. electricity	€ 9,00 - € 27,00

FR40300 Camping Aurilandes

FR40200 Aureilhan (Landes)

Tel: 05 46 55 10 01. Email: contact@village-center.com

In the heart of the Landes forest and five minutes from the popular resort of Mimizan, this site offers 440 pitches, mostly shaded and some with views over the Etang d'Aureilhan. A new pool complex has recently been added, and incorporates a sauna, spa, solarium and gym. This site has been recommended by our French agent and we plan to undertake a full inspection in 2007.

Facilities

Snack bar. Shop. Swimming pool, paddling pool, solarium and fitness area (sauna, spa, gym). TV room. Volleyball. Play area and children's miniclub. Facilities for disabled visitors. Entertainment in peak season. Off site: Fishing. Golf. Parachuting. Riding. Watersports. Hiking trails. Fitness trail. Cycle routes.

Open: 13 May - 16 September.

Directions

Aureilhan is on the D626 (Labouheyre - Mimizan road). Site is well signed from this road.

Charges 2006

Per pitch including 2 persons and electricity	€ 17,00
extra person	€ 3,15
child (under 12 yrs)	€ 2.50

Les Vignes ★★★★
Landes - France

+334 99 57 20 25
www.village-center.com/vignes
vignes@village-center.com

Documentation on request

Aurilandes ★★
Landes - France

+334 99 57 20 25
www.village-center.com/aurilandes
aurilandes@village-center.com

Villagecenter
la vie plein air

FR40290 Yelloh! Village Punta Lago

Avenue du Lac, F-40550 Léon (Landes)

Tel: 00 33 55 84 49 24 40. Email: contact@camping-puntalago.com

Five hundred metres from the charming village of Léon, this site offers above average size, level, grass pitches (some sandy). Most have electricity, water and drainage and they are separated by hedges. Shade is welcome from the tall oak trees. Whilst the pitches would be considered typical for the region, the buildings are a mix of old and new, the old being the sanitary block, in good order, clean and with all the usual facilities including a lovely new children's bathroom and facilities for disabled visitors. The new encompasses an indoor pool, a room serving as a gym and a TV room.

Facilities

The single toilet block is old, but kept clean and well maintained. Facilities for children and disabled visitors. Laundry facilities. Large shop. Restaurant and takeaway. Bar. Heated indoor and outdoor pools. Bicycle hire. Play area. Fridge hire. Entertainment and activities (July/Aug). Barbecues are not permitted. Off site: Lake 300 m. with sailing, windsurfing, kayak, swimming and fishing. Léon 500 m. with market at every day (June/Sept). Beach 7 km. Golf 8 km. Riding 5 km.

Open: 18 April - 24 September.

Directions

From N10 take exit 12 towards Castets. Take the D142 to Léon and at island take first exit to 'Centre Ville'. At T-junction turn left on D652 and after 300 m. turn left at sign for site and lake. After 500 m. site is on the left.

Charges 2006

Per unit incl. 2 persons and electricity	€ 16,00 - € 33,00
incl. water	€ 18,00 - € 35,00
extra person (over 3 yrs)	€ 2,00 - € 5,50

FR64020 Camping Barétous Pyrénées

Quartier Ripaude, F-64570 Aramits (Pyrénées-Atlantiques)

Tel: 05 59 34 12 21. Email: atso64@hotmail.com

Located on the edge of the Pyrénées, this quiet site is well away from the tourist bustle, particularly in early or late season. It has a rural location, yet is close to the town. This is a wonderful location for exploring the region and offers a peaceful haven for those wishing to stay in quiet surroundings. The shady, grass pitches are attractive and of a good size. With hedges they offer both water and electricity (10A). The welcoming reception (English spoken) sells local produce and organic food. The heated swimming and paddling pool area is overlooked by a small sun terrace with a café/bar.

Facilities

Two sanitary blocks, one old, one modern, offer clean facilities with unisex toilets and showers. Facilities for disabled visitors. Café/bar with hot and cold meals (July/Aug). Heated swimming and paddling pools (April - Sept). Communal room with TV, games, library and drinks. Small shop selling organic food. Boules. Small play area with sandpit. Off site: Town with supermarket and ATM 250 m. Fishing 50 m. Riding 3 km Skiing 25 km.

Open: 28 January - 15 October.

Directions

From Oloron Sainte Marie, head southwest on the D919 to Aramits. Through village bear right on D918. Cross river and immediately turn right at campsite sign. GPS: N43:07.284 W0:43.939

Charges 2006

Per unit incl. 2 persons	€ 12,75 - € 17,50
extra person	€ 3,50 - € 4,50
electricity	€ 3,50 - € 6,50

No credit cards.

FR64030 Camping Ametza

Boulevard de l'Empereur, B.P.19, F-64700 Hendaye (Pyrénées-Atlantiques)

Tel: 05 59 20 07 05. Email: ametza@meuf.fr

With a beautiful long sandy beach and the town of Hendaye only 900 metres away (a 20 minute walk) this well cared for, family run campsite, offers plenty for everyone. Attractively laid out, the grass pitches are flat and shady, most having electricity (6A). We found the railway line running nearby was not intrusive. There is a pleasant bar and restaurant together with an excellent pool area (comfortable and with good quality sunbeds). The beach at Hendaye is popular for surfing, particularly for beginners. Having shallow water, it offers safe bathing and many other watersports.

Facilities

Two clean and bright sanitary blocks have good facilities with a new (2006) laundry and facilities for disabled people. Excellent bathroom for children. Shop (w/ends only in early season). Bar and restaurant. Swimming pool (from May). TV room. Small playground. Entertainment and activities (July/Aug). Electric barbecues not permitted. Shuttle bus to beach (July/Aug). Off site: Beach and town 900 m. Bicycle hire 1 km. Fishing 5 km. Golf 10 km.

Open: 8 April - 31 October.

Directions

From the A63 exit 2 (St Jean de Luz Sud) take the D913 signed Hendaye. At roundabout turn left on coast road D912. In 6 km. turn left on D358 (San Sebastian) Cross railway bridge and site is on left. GPS: N43:22.379 W01:45.351

Charges 2006

Per unit incl. 2 persons	€ 16,30 - € 20,80
extra person	€ 4,10 - € 4,80
electricty	€ 3,80

FR64060 Camping le Pavillon Royal

Avenue du Prince de Galles, F-64210 Bidart (Pyrénées-Atlantiques)

Tel: **05 59 23 00 54**. Email: **info@pavillon-royal.com**

Le Pavillon Royal has an excellent situation on raised ground overlooking the sea, with good views along the coast to the south and to the north coast of Spain beyond. There is a large swimming pool and sunbathing area on site. The site is divided up into 303 marked, level pitches, many of a good size. About 50 are reserved for tents and are only accessible on foot. The remainder are connected by asphalt roads. All have electricity and most are fully serviced. Much of the campsite is in full sun, although the area for tents is shaded. Beneath the site – and only a very short walk down – stretches a wide sandy beach where the Atlantic rollers provide ideal conditions for surfing. A central, marked section of the beach is supervised by lifeguards (from mid-June). There is also a section with rocks and pools. Reservation in high season is advisable.

Facilities

Good quality toilet blocks with baby baths and unit for disabled people. Washing facilities are closed at night except for two single night units. Washing machines, dryers. Motorcaravan services. Shop (including gas). Restaurant, takeaway (from 1/6). Swimming and paddling pools. Sauna. Playground. General room, TV room, games room with table tennis, films. Fishing. Surf school. Dogs are not accepted. Barrier card with deposit (€ 20). Off site: Riding 1 km. Bicycle hire 3 km. Sailing 5 km.

Open: 15 May - 25 September.

Directions

From A63 exit 4, take the N10 south towards Bidart. At roundabout after the 'Intermarché' supermarket turn right (signed for Biarritz). After 600 m. turn left at campsite sign. GPS: N43:27.275 W01:34.562

Charges 2006

Per unit incl. 2 persons, electricity and water	€ 25,00 - € 41,00
tent pitch incl. 1 or 2 persons	€ 18,00 - € 31,00
child (over 4 yrs)	€ 6,00 - € 8,00

Le Pavillon Royal
camping caravaning **** NN

64210 BIDART
Tél: 05.59.23.00.54
Website: www.pavillon-royal.com
E-mail: info@pavillon-royal.com

1 Right by a sandy beach with direct access

1 On the outskirts of Biarritz

1 Very peaceful situation

1 Sanitary installations of really exceptional quality

FR64040 Camping des Gaves

F-64440 Laruns (Pyrénées-Atlantiques)

Tel: **05 59 05 32 37**. Email: **campingdesgaves@wanadoo.fr**

Set in a secluded valley, Camping Des Gaves is a clean, small and well managed site, open all year, with very friendly owners and staff. It is set high in Pyrennean walking country on one of the routes to Spain and is only 30 km. from the Spanish border. There are 101 pitches including 50 level grassed touring pitches of which 38 are fully serviced, numbered and separated (the remainder are used for seasonal units). Mature trees provide plenty of shade.

Facilities

The very clean toilet block can be heated in cool weather and has modern fittings. Washbasins for ladies in curtained cubicles and one shower in ladies' suitable for showering children. Dishwashing and laundry sinks. Laundry room. No shop but baker calls daily (July/Aug). Small bar with large screen TV, pool and video games (July/Aug). Larger bar with table tennis. Small play area. Boules. Volleyball. Fishing. Card operated barrier (€ 20 deposit). Off site: Bicycle hire 800 m. Shops, restaurant and bars 1 km.

Open: All year.

Directions

Take N134 from Pau towards Olorons and branch left on D934 at Gan. Follow to Laruns and just after town, turn left following signs to site. GPS: N42:58.929 W00:25.057

Charges 2006

Per person	€ 2,90 - € 3,70
child (under 10 yrs)	€ 1,90 - € 2,40
pitch	€ 4,50 - € 9,60
electricity (3-10A)	€ 2,50 - € 4,00

FR64050 Camping Itsas Mendi

Acotz, F-64500 Saint Jean de Luz (Pyrénées-Atlantiques)

Tel: **05 59 26 56 50**. Email: **itsas@wanadoo.fr**

This large campsite is ideal for families. Set close to the beach (400 metres), it boasts two swimming areas. Both fenced, one is overlooked by a terrace and has a jacuzzi and the other is made for children with a paddling pool, whirlpool, water slides and plenty of grassed sunbathing area. During July and August entertainment, activities and excursions are organised. Together with surfing, scuba and children's clubs, rafting and mountain bike trails, there is something for all ages. All pitches are of medium size, shaded with electricity (10A). May be difficult for large vehicles to manoeuvre and have full choice of pitches.

Facilities

Five sanitary blocks (not all open early season) are clean and one has facilities for disabled visitors. Laundry facilities. Motorcaravan service point. Fridge hire. Bar and restaurant (1/6-15/9). Tennis. Football field. TV room. Internet access. Off site: Large supermarket 1 km. Bus (50 m.) runs every hour to St Jean de Luz. Fishing 1 km. Golf, riding and bicycle hire 4 km.

Open: 1 April - 30 September.

Directions

From the A63 take exit 3, then the N10 toward Bayonne. Turn second left signed 'Acotz Campings Plages'. At T-junction turn right and site is on left. GPS: N43:24.822 W01:37.007

Charges 2006

Per unit incl. 2 persons	€ 11,00 - € 30,00
extra person	€ 3,40 - € 5,50
child (2-10 yrs)	€ 2,00 - € 3,40
electricity (10A)	free - € 3,00

FR64070 Castel Camping le Ruisseau des Pyrénées

Route d'Arbonne, F-64210 Bidart (Pyrénées-Atlantiques)

Tel: **05 59 41 94 50**. Email: **francoise.dumont3@wanadoo.fr**

This pleasant, busy site, just behind the coast, is about 2 km. from Bidart and 2.5 km. from a sandy beach. It has two swimming pools with slides on the main site and an indoor heated pool and new spa complex. Pitches on the main campsite are individual, marked and of a good size, either on flat terraces or around the lake. The terrain is wooded so the great majority of them have some shade. There are 330 here with a further 110 on a second area where shade has developed and which has its own good toilet block. Electrical connections are available throughout.

Facilities

Two main blocks and some extra smaller units. Washing machines. Motorcaravan service point. Shop. Large self-service restaurant with takeaway and bar with terraces, and TV (all 15/5-12/9). Outdoor swimming pools, indoor pool and spa complex (15/5-12/9). Sauna. Large play area. Two tennis courts (free outside July/Aug). Fitness track. TV and games rooms. Minigolf. Fitness room. Bicycle hire. Fishing. Internet access. Off site: Riding and golf 2 km.

Open: 20 May - 17 September.

Directions

Site is east of Bidart on a minor road towards Arbonne. From A63 autoroute take Biarritz exit (no. 4), turn towards St Jean-de-Luz and Bidart on N10. After Intermarche turn left at roundabout and follow signs to site. GPS: N43:26.207 W01:34.068

Charges 2006

Per unit incl. 2 persons	€ 15,00 - € 28,00
extra person	€ 5,00 - € 6,50
child (under 7 yrs)	€ 2,50 - € 3,50
electricity	€ 3,00 - € 4,00

FR64080 Camping les Tamaris Plage

Quartier Acotz, F-64500 Saint Jean-de-Luz (Pyrénées-Atlantiques)

Tel: **05 59 26 55 90**. Email: **tamaris1@clubinternet.fr**

This is a small, pleasant and well kept site. It is situated well outside the town but just across the road from a sandy beach with 79 numbered pitches, 45 with electricity, including some mobile homes and bungalows. They are of very good size and separated by hedges, on slightly sloping ground with some shade. It becomes full for nearly all July and August with families on long stays, so reservation then is advisable. There is no shop, but bread is available daily across the road.

Facilities

Single toilet block of superb quality and unusual design and should be ample provision for the site with facilities for disabled people and washing machine. New covered terrace with views of the sea. TV room for adults and children's room with TV and games. Playground. Not suitable for American motorhomes or twin axle caravans. Off site: Fishing 30 m. Bicycle hire or golf 4 km. Riding 7 km.

Open: 1 April - 30 September.

Directions

Proceed south on N10 and 1.5 km. after Guethary take first road on right (before access to the motorway and Carrefour centre commercial) and follow camp signs. GPS: N43:25.077 W01:37.429

Charges 2006

Per unit incl. 2 persons and electricity (5A)	€ 24,00 - € 31,00
tent pitch	€ 19,00 - € 26,00
extra person (over 2 yrs)	€ 4,00 - € 6,00

FR64110 Sunêlia Col d'Ibardin

F-64122 Urrugne (Pyrénées-Atlantiques)

Tel: 05 59 54 31 21. Email: info@col-ibardin.com

Mobile homes ▶ page 473

This family owned site at the foot of the Basque Pyrénées is highly recommended and deserves praise. It is well run with emphasis on personal attention, the friendly family and their staff ensuring that all are made welcome and is attractively set in the middle of an oak wood. Behind the forecourt, with its brightly coloured shrubs and modern reception area, various roadways lead to the 191 pitches. These are individual, spacious and enjoy the benefit of the shade (if preferred a more open aspect can be found). There are electricity hook-ups (4/10A) and adequate water points. From this site you can enjoy the mountain scenery, be on the beach in 7-10 km. or cross the border into Spain in approximately 14 km.

Facilities

Two toilet blocks, one rebuilt to a high specification, are kept very clean. WC for disabled people. Dishwashing and laundry facilities. Motorcaravan service point. Shop for basics and bread orders (15/6-15/9). Catering, takeaway service and bar (15/6-15/9). Heated swimming pool. New paddling pool. Playground and club (adult supervision). Tennis courts, boules, table tennis, video games. Bicycle hire. New multi-purpose sports area. Not suitable for American motorhomes. Off site: Supermarket and shopping centre 5 km. Fishing and golf 7 km. Riding 20 km.

Open: 1 April - 30 September.

Directions

Leave A63 autoroute at St Jean-de-Luz sud, exit no. 2 and join RN10 in direction of Urrugne. Turn left at roundabout (Col d'Ibardin) on D4. Site on right after 5 km. Do not turn off to the Col itself, carry on towards Ascain. GPS: N43:20.035 W01:41.077

Charges 2007

Per unit incl. 2 persons and electricity	€ 16,50 - € 34,00
extra person	€ 3,00 - € 6,00
child (2-7 yrs)	€ 2,00 - € 3,00

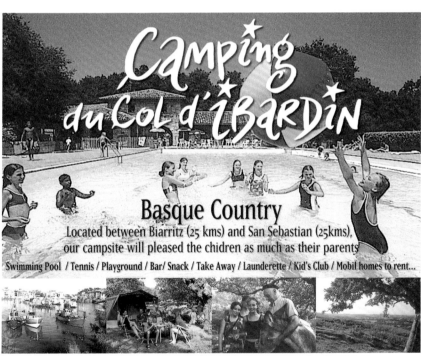

Camping du Col d'Ibardin

Basque Country

Located between Biarritz (25 kms) and San Sebastian (25kms), our campsite will pleased the chidren as much as their parents

Swimming Pool / Tennis / Playground / Bar/ Snack / Take Away / Launderette / Kid's Club / Mobil homes to rent...

Tél. : (00 33) 559 54 31 21 • Fax : (00 33) 559 54 62 28 • 64122 Urrugne
www.col-ibardin.com • info@col-ibardin.com

FR64100 Camping Etche Zahar

Allée de Mesplès, F-64240 Urt (Pyrénées-Atlantiques)

Tel: 05 59 56 27 36. Email: info@etche-zahar.fr

Although this attractive site is small, the hardcore roads give access to remarkably large grass pitches separated by small hedges. The larger pitches have little shade but at the far end an area of trees offers smaller shaded pitches for tents.There are also 12 immaculate mobile homes and 3 chalets. Electricty (10A) is available for 15 pitches. The site is 'Tourisme & Handicap' approved and offers one chalet and facilities specifically for disabled visitors. The English speaking owner is justly proud and offers a warm welcome to her eco-friendly site. Quietly positioned, it is ideal for those who wish to enjoy relaxed rural pursuits. A charming reception serving as library, shop, and tourist information is housed in an old farmhouse, together with a communal room used for occasional theatre, talks, visitor participation and low key entertainment. A ten minute walk to the village provides a supermarket, restaurants, bars and shops.

Facilities

The single sanitary block was very clean when we visited. Laundry facilities. Meals (July/Aug).Swimming pool (June - Oct). Small Library. Motorcaravan grey water point (hose required). Some play equipment. Bicycle hire. Internet facilities. Wi-fi. Pets not accepted 1-20 Aug. Off site: Town with supermarket, shops, restaurants and bars 10 minute walk. Fishing 1 km. Boat launching 1 km. Sailing 10 km. Golf 20 km. Beach 22 km.

Open: 20 March - mid-November.

Directions

From Bayonne go east on D1 and join the A64. Take exit 4 turning right on D936. Turn left on D123 to Urt. Follow 'Toute Directions' to D257. Turn right at fire station to site on the left.
GPS: N43:29.494 W01:17.792

Charges 2006

Per person	€ 3,50
child (0-10 yrs)	€ 2,50
pitch	€ 8,00 - € 11,00
electricity (10A)	€ 3,20

Family owned sites - Less than 130 pitches

YOU ARE IN THE RIGHT PLACE

Ascain
Camping d'Ascain ★★
Tél.: 05 59 54 40 61
www.camping-ascain.com

Hendaye
Camping Dorrondeguy ★★
Tél.: 05 59 20 26 16
www.camping-dorronodeguy.com

Camping les 2 Jumeaux ★★
Tél.: 05 59 20 01 65
www.camping-des-2jumeaux.com

Mauleon
Camping Uhaitza le Saison ★★★
Tel.: 05 59 28 18 79
www.camping-uhaitza.com

Saint Jean de Luz
Camping Merko Lacarra ★★★
Tél.: 05 59 26 56 76
www.merkolacarra.com

Sare
La Petite Rhune ★★★
Tél.: 05 59 54 23 97
www.gite64.com/la-petite-rhune

Urt
Camping Etche Zahar ★★★
Tél.: 05 59 56 27 36
www.etche-zahar.fr

Ascarat
Camping de la Truite ★★
Tél.: 05 59 37 31 22
www.camping-delatruite.com

www.lescampingsdecharme.com

FR64140 Sunêlia Berrua

Rue Berrua, F-64210 Bidart (Pyrénées-Atlantiques)

Tel: 05 59 54 96 66. Email: contact@berrua.com

Berrua, 1 km. from the sea, is an ideal location for visiting the beaches in southwest France. A neat and tidy site, it has 270 level pitches (120 for touring units) set amongst trees. Most have electricity (6A) and some are fully serviced. The focal point of the site is an excellent swimming pool complex with several pools, slides and paddling pools which is surrounded by sun beds for sunbathing. Organised activities and entertainment for both adults and children in high season, guided walks, dances, sporting competitions, bingo and karaoke. A member of the Sunêlia group.

Facilities

Toilet facilities are good (unisex) consisting of two blocks with washbasins in cabins, baby rooms, facilities for disabled visitors, washing machines and dishwashing sinks (cold water only). Motorcaravan services. Shop (July/Aug). Bar/restaurant and takeaway (15/4-15/9). New pool complex. Games room. Play area (3-10 yrs only). Bicycle hire. Archery. Boules. Off site: Fishing 1 km. Golf and riding 3 km. Beach 1 km.

Open: 6 April - 5 October.

Directions

From A63 exit 4, take N10 south towards Bidart. At roundabout after the 'Intermarché' supermarket, turn left. Bear right then take next right (site signed). GPS: N43:26.293 W01:34.942

Charges 2006

Per unit incl. 2 persons	€ 16,10 - € 29,00
extra person	€ 3,20 - € 5,90
child (2-10 yrs)	€ 2,30 - € 3,70
electricity (6A)	€ 2,90 - € 4,70

Camping Cheques accepted.

Check real time availability and at-the-gate prices...

www.alanrogers.com

FR64120 Camping Beau Rivage

Allée des Maronniers, F-64190 Navarrenx (Pyrénées-Atlantiques)

Tel: **05 59 66 10 00**. Email: **beaucamping@free.fr**

Cross the picturesque river and follow the old town walls to discover this well cared for family owned campsite (English). The site is tiered and the large, well maintained grass pitches are surrounded by mature hedges offering a peaceful and relaxed setting. Currently torches may be needed. The attention to well cared for detail is carried into the two sanitary blocks. Projects to be completed for 2007 include a heated swimming pool, low key entertainment area (wine tasting, barbecues, etc), additional chalets, hardstandings and a baby room, adding to an already impressive campsite. The welcoming owners are using their experience to enhance roadway lighting, redesign facilities for disabled visitors, improve laundry facilities, add serviced pitches, a motorcaravan drainage point and more electrical points. With plenty of walks, cycling, kayaking and sightseeing, this site offers plenty for everyone. A walk through the fortified town and along its walls, rewards with superb views across the countryside.

Facilities

Two very clean sanitary blocks with good separate facilities for ladies and men include provision for disabled visitors. Laundry facilities in top block. Playground for small children (rubber matting). Play field for games. Off site: Shop at end of road. Town is five minutes walk for further shops, bars, restaurants, ATM and bicycle hire. Fishing 200 m. Riding 15 km.

Open: 15 March - 15 October.

Directions

From the north take D936 to Navarrenx. Turn left at first roundabout on D115 into Navarrenx. Turn left at T-junction, go over bridge and follow walls of town all the way around. At next island turn right on the D947 and site is signed from here.

Charges 2006

Per unit incl. 2 persons	€ 12,00 - € 19,00
incl. electricity	€ 15,50 - € 22,50
extra person	€ 3,50 - € 5,00
child (0-7 yrs)	€ 2,00 - € 3,00

FR64160 Camping Merko-Lacarra

Plage d'Acotz, F-64500 Saint Jean de Luz (Pyrénées-Atlantiques)

Tel: **05 59 26 56 76**. Email: **contact@merkolacarra.com**

Positioned 50 metres from the beach, scattered with pretty Tamaris trees and enjoying views of the surrrounding coutryside, this beautifully cared for campsite offers everything for a relaxing stay. The proud owners maintain the campsite to a high standard with a light, clean toilet block and well kept, tidy garden areas. The site is sloping but the pitches are mainly level and are all of grass. All have electricity (16A, French connectors; adaptors not available). There is little shade. Tidy mobile homes are on the boundaries of the site. There may be some railway noise but we did not find this intrusive.

Facilities

The single toilet block is well kept and clean. Facilities for disabled visitors. Baby room. Laundry facilities. Motorcaravan service point (charged). Small shop and snack bar (10/6-17/10). Excellent play area. Electric barbecues are not permitted. Off site: Limited public transport July/Aug. Beach and fishing (sea) 50 m. Golf 5 km. Bicycle hire 5 km. Riding 12 km. Mountains (8 km) for walking and cycling.

Open: 1 April - 30 October.

Directions

From A63 exit 3, take N10 toward Bayonne. Turn second left signed 'Acotz Campings Plages'. At T-junction turn right and follow signs for site. However this right turn leads to a low bridge with a height restriction of 3.5 m. To avoid the bridge, turn left at T-junction and continue along road to site on the right. GPS: N43:25.116 W01:37.389

Charges 2006

Per person	€ 3,00 - € 6,00
child (2-13 yrs)	free - € 4,00
pitch incl. electricity	€ 9,00 - € 27,00

253

FR64150 Airotel Residence des Pins

Mobile homes ▶ page 474

Avenue de Biarritz, F-64210 Bidart (Pyrénées-Atlantiques)

Tel: **05 59 23 00 29**. Email: **lespins@free.fr**

This is a very pleasant, reasonably priced site which will appeal greatly to couples and young families. Set on a fairly gentle hillside, the top level has reception and the bar. Slightly lower are the paddling and swimming pools in a sunny location with sun-beds. Next comes the well stocked shop, tennis courts and the rest of the pitches. Some pitches are behind reception and others, lower down, some slightly sloping, are under trees and separated by hydrangea hedges. Some have electricity (long leads required). There is a varied entertainment programme in July and Aug. The site is not suitable for American motorhomes. It is used by tour operators and there are mobile homes around the outer edges of the site. Buses pass the gate. There is a little day-time road noise but not intrusive.

Facilities

The two toilet blocks have some washbasins and showers together. Washing machines, dryers, ironing boards and facilities for disabled people. Motorcaravan services. Shop and bar open all season, restaurant and takeaway (20/6-15/9). Pool open all season. Games room. Table tennis. Tennis (charged in July/Aug). Play area (3-8 yrs). Bicycle hire. Off site: Lake 600 m. with fishing (no licence required). Golf 1 km. Riding 1 km. Beach with lifeguard 600 m.

Open: 14 May - 30 September.

Directions

Heading south on the A63 towards Spain, take exit J4 onto the N10 towards Bidart. At the roundabout straight after Intermarche turn right towards Biarritz. The site is on the right after 1 km. GPS: N43:27.185 W01:34.425

Charges 2006

Per unit with 2 persons	€ 13,50 - € 20,80
extra person (over 2 yrs)	€ 3,20 - € 5,70
electricity	€ 3,20 - € 5,00

Camping Cheques accepted.

FR64230 Camping Municipal de Mosqueros

F-64270 Salies de Béarn (Pyrénées-Atlantiques)

Tel: **05 59 38 12 94**

In scenic surroundings convenient for the A64, this 3 star municipal site is worthy of its grading and is attractively located in a parkland situation 1 km. from the pretty little town of Salies de Béarn. It has an immaculate appearance, welcoming wardens and very clean facilities. Tarmac roads lead from the entrance barrier (locked at night), past reception to spacious, numbered pitches. Most have electricity (10A), many have water taps and all are separated by tall shrubs and hedges giving privacy. Salies de Béarn, with its old houses overhanging the river and its thermal baths, is only minutes away.

Facilities

The fully equipped toilet block is in a central position and maintained to a high standard. Dishwashing and laundry area with sinks, washing machine, dryer and iron. TV and recreation room. Off site: Swimming pool (special rates for campers) and tennis court adjacent. Golf and riding 2 km.

Open: 15 March - 31 October.

Directions

Site is well signed in the town and is on the D17 Bayonne road, west of the town. GPS: N43:28.51 W00:56.282

Charges guide

Per person	€ 2,60
child (1-7 yrs)	€ 1,60
pitch	€ 2,70 - € 5,30
electricity	€ 2,55

MAP 11

The Dordogne is an historical region of great beauty, full of pretty golden-stoned villages and ancient castles. Home to delicacies such as foie gras, truffles and walnuts, plus Roquefort cheese and Cognac, it is one of the gastronomic centres of France.

Dordogne & Aveyron

TO FORM 'THE DORDOGNE' WE HAVE USED DÉPARTEMENTS FROM THESE OFFICIAL REGIONS: FROM AQUITAINE: 24 DORDOGNE AND 47 LOT-ET-GARONNE, FROM MIDI-PYRÉNÉES: 12 AVEYRON, 46 LOT, FROM POITOU-CHARENTES: 16 CHARENTE

The Dordogne's history goes back many thousands of years when man lived in the caves of Périgord and left cave paintings at sites such as Les Eyzies and Lascaux. Aquitaine was ruled by the English for 300 years following the marriage of Eleanor of Aquitaine to Henry Plantagenet, who became King of England in 1154.

The villages and castles of the area bear evidence of the resulting conflict between the French and English, and today add charm and character to the countryside. Monpazier is the best example of the 'bastides' (fortified towns) and is set in a diverse region of mountains, vineyards, and fertile river valleys. The rolling grasslands and dense forests include the beautiful valleys of the Dordogne and Vézère.

South of the cultivated fields and cliff-side villages beside the river Lot lie the higher, stony lands of the Quercy Causse and the rocky gorges of the Rivers Aveyron and Tarn. Centred around Millau, there are tortuous gorges and valleys, spectacular rivers, underground caves and grottes, and thickly forested mountains.

Places of interest

Agen: rich agricultural area, famous for its prunes.

Angoulême: Hill-top town surrounded by ramparts, cathedral, Renaissance château.

Cognac: the most celebrated *eau de vie* in the world, cellars, Valois Castle.

Cordes: medieval walled hilltop village.

Monflanquin: well preserved fortified village.

Rocamadour: cliffside medieval pilgrimage site.

Saint Cirq-La Popie: medieval village perched on a cliff.

Sarlat: Saturday market.

Cuisine of the region

Local specialities include the fish dishes: carp stuffed with foie gras, mullet in red wine and *besugo* (sea bream), plus *cagouilles* (snails from Charentes).

Cassoulet: a hearty stew of duck, sausages and beans.

Cèpes: fine, delicate mushrooms; sometimes dried.

Chou farci: stuffed cabbage, sometimes aux marrons (with chestnuts).

Confit de Canard (d'oie): preserved duck meat.

Foie Gras: specially prepared livers of geese and ducks, seasoned and stuffed with truffles.

Magret de canard: duck breast fillets.

Mouclade: mussels cooked in wine, egg yolks and cream, served with Pineau des Charentes.

FR12000 Camping Caravaning de Peyrelade

Route des Gorges du Tarn, F-12640 Rivière-sur-Tarn (Aveyron)

Tel: 05 65 62 62 54. Email: **campingpeyrelade@wanadoo.fr**

The 130 touring pitches (100-150 sq.m) are terraced, level and shady with 6A electricity hook-ups (long leads may be required for the riverside pitches). There are also 43 mobile homes. The site is ideally placed for visiting the Tarn, Jonte and Dourbie gorges, and centres for rafting and canoeing are a short drive up the river. Other nearby attractions include the Caves of Aven Armand, the Chaos de Montpellier, Roquefort (of cheese fame) and the pleasant town of Millau. Many of the roads along and between the Gorges are breathtaking for passengers, but worrying for drivers who won't like looking down! Situated at the foot of the Tarn gorges on the banks of the river, this attractive site is dominated by the ruins of the Château de Peyrelade. Bathing from the pebble beach is safe and the water is clean.

Facilities	Directions
Two well equipped toilet blocks. Young children are catered for, also people with disabilities. Washing machines, dryer. Bar, restaurant, pizzeria, takeaway (all from 1/6). Paddling pool, attractive heated swimming pool (proper swimming trunks, no shorts). Good playground. Games room, mini-club. Fishing. Off site: Bicycle hire 100 m. Riding 3 km. Nearby leisure centre can be booked at reception at reduced charges. Millau, hypermarket, shops, night markets but note road to/from Millau can be jammed at peak hours.	Take autoroute A75 to exit 44-1 Aguessac then onto D907 (follow Gorges du Tarn signs). Site is 2 km. past Rivière sur Tarn, on the right - the access road is quite steep.

Open: 15 May - 15 September.

Charges 2006

Per unit incl. 2 persons	€ 14,00 - € 22,00
extra person	€ 3,50 - € 5,00
child (under 5 yrs)	€ 2,00 - € 3,00
electricity (6A)	€ 3,00

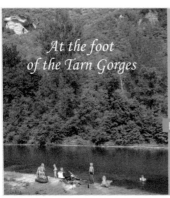

At the foot of the Tarn Gorges

Peyrelade ★★★★

Swimming • Canoe • Potholing • Fossil collecting •
Tennis • Fishing • Activities • Children's club •
Evening entertainment • Horse rides • Walks...

RENT of MOBILE-HOMES and FURNISHED BUNGALOW TENTS

12640 Rivière sur Tarn
Tel. 0033 565 62 62 54 - Fax: 0033 565 62 65 61
Email:campingpeyrelade@wanadoo.fr
www.campingpeyrelade.com

FR12060 Camping Beau Rivage

Lac de Pareloup, route de Vernhes, F-12410 Salles-Curan (Aveyron)

Tel: 05 65 46 33 32. Email: **camping-beau-rivage@wanadoo.fr**

This family run, immaculate site has a wonderful position alongside the beautiful Lac de Paraloup. There are 80 level, grassy pitches (60 for touring) attractively arranged on terraces, separated by neat hedges and a variety of small trees offering little shade. All have electricity (6A). A range of watersports is available on the lake (mostly July and August) and many activities are organised both in high season. On arrival at the site, park outside and go to reception. The site entrance is narrow and quite steep and tractor assistance is available. Once on site access to pitches is easy.

Facilities	Directions
Two well equipped and clean toilets blocks provide all the necessary facilities, including those for disabled visitors. Washing machines. Bar, snacks, terrace, takeaway (July/Aug) . Small shop (July/Aug). Swimming pool. Games rooms. TV room. Pool table, table tennis. Volleyball. Play area. Fishing, boating, lake bathing. Off site: Salles Curan (4 km), shops, bars, restaurants. Boat ramp 200 m, watercraft for hire (July/Aug). Bicycle hire 2 km. Tennis 3 km. Riding 3 km. Golf 35 km. Canoeing, rafting, paragliding, caving, windsurfing.	From D911 Rodez - Millau road turn south on D993 signed Salles Curan. In 7 km, just after bridge over the lake, turn right on D243 (site signed). Entrance is on right in just over 1 km. Park outside gate. GPS: N44:12.55 E02:46.376

Open: 1 May - 30 September.

Charges 2007

Per unit incl. 2 persons	€ 11,50 - € 26,00
extra person	€ 3,00 - € 6,00
child (2-7 yrs)	€ 1,50 - € 4,00
electricity (6A)	€ 13,50 - € 29,00

FR12010 Camping le Val de Cantobre

F-12230 Nant-d'Aveyron (Aveyron)

Tel: 05 65 58 43 00. Email: info@valdecantobre.com

This very pleasant terraced site has been imaginatively and tastefully developed by the Dupond family over the past 30 years. Most of the 200 touring pitches (all with electricity and water) are peaceful, generous in size and blessed with views of the valley. A unique activity programme at Val de Cantobre is supervised by qualified instructors in July and August, some arranged by the owners and some at a fair distance from the site. The terrace design provides some peace and privacy, especially on the upper levels and a warm welcome awaits. Rock pegs are advised. The pool surrounds are bedecked by flowers and crowned by a large urn which dispenses water into the paddling pool. The magnificent carved features in the bar create a delightful ambience, complemented by a recently built terrace. Passive recreationists appreciate the scenery, especially Cantobre, a medieval village that clings to a cliff in view of the site. Nature lovers will be delighted to see black vultures wheeling in the Tarn gorge alongside more humble rural residents. Butterflies in profusion, orchids, huge edible snails, glow worms, families of beavers and the natterjack toad all live here.

Facilities

Fully equipped toilet block is beautifully appointed. Fridge hire. Small shop with wide variety of provisions; including many regional specialities. Attractive bar, restaurant, pizzeria, takeaway (some fairly steep up and down walking from furthest pitches to some facilities). Three swimming pools. Minigolf. Table tennis. Play area. River rafting, white water canoeing, rock climbing, paragliding. All weather sports pitch. Torch useful. There are some fairly steep climbs between the levels on the site. Off site: Fishing 4 km. Riding 15 km. Bicycle hire 25 km.

Open: 5 May - 9 September, with all facilities.

Directions

Site is 4 km. north of Nant, on D991 road to Millau. From Millau direction take D991 signed Gorge du Dourbie. Site is on left, just past turn to Cantobre.

Charges 2006

Per unit incl. 2 persons and 4A electricity	€ 19,00 - € 31,50
extra person (4 yrs and over)	€ 4,00 - € 7,00
dog	free - € 3,00

Camping Cheques accepted.

Pitches with stunning views... Facilities full of character... An area with fabulous scenery

LES CASTELS ★★★★

Castel-Camping Val de Cantobre ★★★★
www.valdecantobre.com

Camping Cheque

FR12040 Camping les Tours

F-12460 Saint Amans-des-Cots (Aveyron)

Tel: 05 65 44 88 10. Email: camping-les-tours@wanadoo.fr

This impressive campsite is set in beautiful countryside close to the Truyère Gorges, Upper Lot valley and the Aubrac Plateau. Efficiently run, it is situated on the shores of the Lac de la Selves. There are 275 average sized pitches with 6A electricity, some bordering the lake, the rest terraced and hedged with views of the lake. About 100 pitches also have water points. The site has a spacious feel, enhanced by the thoughtfully planned terraced layout and it is well kept and very clean. There is some up and down walking to the facilities, especially from the upper terraces. Used by tour operators (70 pitches).

Facilities

Four very well equipped toilet blocks. Attractive central complex housing the amenities. Restaurant, bar. Swimming pools. Shop (with gas), Takeaway. Play area. Volleyball, tennis, football and table tennis. Varied programme of daytime and evening activities, with mini-club, archery and tree climbing (all supervised). Lake activities include canoeing, pedaloes, windsurfing, water ski-ing and provision for launching small boats. Internet terminal. Off site: Riding and golf 8 km.

Open: 20 May - 9 September.

Directions

Take D34 from Entraygues-sur-Truyère to St Amans-des-Cots (14 km). In St Amans take D97 to Colombez and then D599 to Lac de la Selves (site signed, 5 km. from St Amans).

Charges guide

Per unit incl. 2 persons	€ 20,80 - € 26,50
extra person	€ 4,40 - € 5,50
child (under 7 yrs)	€ 3,00 - € 3,80
electricity	€ 2,40 - € 3,00
Camping Cheques accepted.	

FR12020 Camping Caravaning les Rivages

Mobile homes ▶ page 474

Avenue de l'Aigoual, route de Nant, F-12100 Millau (Aveyron)

Tel: 05 65 61 01 07. Email: campinglesrivages@wanadoo.fr

Les Rivages is a large, well established site on the outskirts of the town. It is well situated, being close to the high limestone Causses and the dramatic gorges of the Tarn and Dourbie. Smaller pitches, used for small units, abut a pleasant riverside space suitable for sunbathing, fishing or picnics. Most of the 314 pitches are large, and well shaded. A newer part of the site has less shade but larger pitches. All pitches have electricity (6A), and 100 have water and drainage. The site offers a very wide range of sporting activities close to 30 in all (see facilities). Don't miss the night markets, but don't eat before you get there – there are thousands of things to taste, many of them grilled or spit roasted. Millau is a bustling and pleasant town with easy access via a footpath from the site. The gates are shut 11 pm.- 8 am, with night-watchman.

Facilities

Four well kept modern toilet blocks have all necessary facilities. Special block for children. Small shop (1/6-15/9). Terrace, restaurant and bar overlooking swimming pool, children's pool (from 10/5). Play area. Entertainment, largely for children, child-minding, mini-club. Impressive sports centre with tennis (indoor and outdoor), squash and badminton. Table tennis. Boules. River activities, walking, bird watching, fishing. Off site: Rafting and canoeing arranged. Bicycle hire 1 km. Riding 10 km. Hypermarket in Millau.

Open: 1 May - 30 September.

Directions

From Millau, cross the Tarn bridge and take D991 road east towards Nant. Site is about 400 m. from the roundabout on the right, on the banks of the Dourbie river.

Charges 2007

Per pitch incl. 2 persons and electricity	€ 18,00 - € 26,00
with water and drainage	€ 20,00 - € 28,00
extra person (over 3 yrs)	€ 3,00 - € 4,50
pet	free - € 3,00

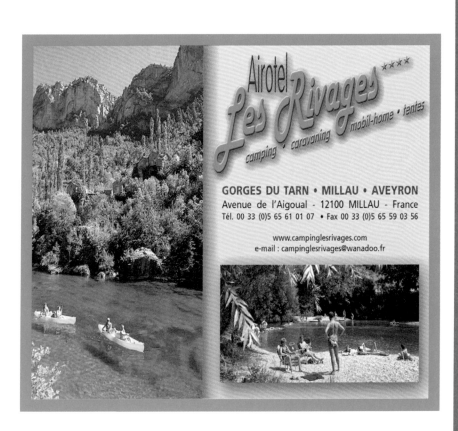

Airotel
Les Rivages ★★★★
camping • caravaning • mobil-home • tentes

GORGES DU TARN • MILLAU • AVEYRON
Avenue de l'Aigoual - 12100 MILLAU - France
Tél. 00 33 (0)5 65 61 01 07 • Fax 00 33 (0)5 65 59 03 56

www.campinglesrivages.com
e-mail : campinglesrivages@wanadoo.fr

FR12050 Camping les Terrasses du Lac

Route du Vibal, F-12290 Pont-de-Salars (Aveyron)

Tel: **05 65 46 88 18**. Email: **campinglesterrasses@wanadoo.fr**

A terraced site, it provides 180 good sized, level pitches, 130 for touring, with or without shade, all with electricity. Some pitches have good views over the lake which has direct access from the site at two places – one for pedestrians and swimmers, the other for cars and trailers for launching small boats. This site is well placed for excursions into the Gorges du Tarn, Caves du Roquefort and nearby historic towns and villages. Although there are good facilities for disabled visitors, the terracing on the site may prove difficult. At an altitude of some 700 m. on the plateau of Le Lévézou, this outlying site enjoys attractive views over Lac de Pont de Salars. The site seems largely undiscovered by the British, perhaps as it is only open for a short season.

Facilities

Four toilet blocks with adequate facilities. Fridge hire. Shop. Bar/restaurant with a lively French ambience serving full meals (high season) snacks (other times), takeaway (all 1/7-31/8). Heated swimming pool, children's pool (1/6-30/9). Solarium. Playground. Volleyball, pétanque, table tennis, billiards. Games, TV rooms. Activities high season. Barbecue area. Off site: Tennis 3 km. Riding 5 km. Golf 20 km.

Open: 1 April - 30 September.

Directions

Using D911 Millau - Rodez road, turn north at Pont de Salars towards lake on D523. Follow camp signs. Ignore first site and continue, following lake until Les Terraces (about 5 km). GPS: N44:18.281 E02:44.098

Charges 2007

Per pitch incl. 2 persons	€ 10,00 - € 21,00
extra person	€ 3,95 - € 4,95
child (2-7 yrs)	€ 3,30 - € 3,95
electricity (6A)	€ 3,95

FR12070 Camping la Grange de Monteillac

F-12310 Sévérac-l'Eglise (Aveyron)

Tel: **05 65 70 21 00**. Email: **info@la-grange-de-monteillac.com**

La Grange de Monteillac is a modern, well equipped site in the beautiful, well preserved small village of Sévérac L'Église. A spacious site, it provides 105 individual pitches, 70 for touring, on gently sloping grass, separated by flowering shrubs and mostly young trees offering little shade. All pitches have electricity (6A, long leads may be required), and 24 have water and waste water connections. There are 35 chalets, mobile homes and tents for rent in separate areas.

Facilities

Modern toilet block with facilities for babies and disabled people. Washing machine, dryer. Shop (1/7-31/8). Poolside restaurant/snack-bar serving pizzas, grills etc, takeaway (1/7-31/8). Music or groups feature in the bar (July-Aug). Two swimming pools (1/6-15/9). Spacious, well equipped playground. Organised activities include children's club, bicycle hire, archery. Off site: Fishing 1 km. Shops in village 3 km. Riding 9 km. Golf 25 km. Many marked walks and bicycle rides, canoeing, rafting, canyoning, rock climbing and hang gliding.

Open: 1 May - 15 September.

Directions

Site is on the edge of Sévérac L'Église village, just off N88 Rodez - Sévérac Le Château road. From A75 use exit 42. At Sévérac L'Église turn south onto D28, site is signed. Site entrance is very shortly on left. GPS: N44:21.911 E02:51.086

Charges 2006

Per unit incl. 2 persons and electricity	€ 16,50 - € 23,50
extra person	€ 2,90 - € 4,20
child (under 7 yrs)	€ 2,00 - € 3,00
Less 30% outside July/Aug.	

FR12150 Camping Marmotel

F-12130 Saint Geniez-d'Olt (Aveyron)

Tel: 05 65 70 46 51. Email: info@marmotel.com

Mobile homes ▶ page 475

The road into Marmotel passes various industrial buildings and is a little off-putting – persevere, as they are soon left behind. The campsite itself is a mixture of old and new. The old part provides many pitches with lots of shade and separated by hedges. The new area is sunny until the trees grow. These pitches each have a private sanitary unit, with shower, WC, washbasin and dishwashing. New and very well designed, they are reasonably priced for such luxury. All the pitches have electricity (10A). A lovely restaurant has a wide terrace with views of the hills and overlooking the heated swimming and paddling pools. These have fountains, a toboggan and sun beds either on grass or the tiled surrounds. The Lot river runs alongside the site where you can fish or canoe. A 'Sites et Paysages' member.

Facilities

Good sanitary facilities include baby baths and facilities for disabled visitors. Washing machines. Bar/restaurant, takeaway (all season). Swimming pools. Small play area. Multi-sports area (tennis, volleyball, basketball). Entertainment July/Aug. including disco below bar, cinema, karaoke, dances, mini club for 4-12 yr olds. Bicycle hire. Fishing. Canoeing. Off site: Large supermarket 500 m. Riding 10 km. Bicycle tours and canoe trips on the Lot and rafting on the Tarn are organised.

Open: 10 May - 10 September.

Directions

Heading south on autoroute 75 (free) take exit 41 and follow signs for St Geniez d'Olt. Site is at western end of village. Site is signed onto D19 to Prades d'Aubrac, then 500 m. on left.

Charges 2006

Per unit incl. 1 or 2 persons, 10A electricity	€ 17,30 - € 30,00
extra person	€ 2,05 - € 5,80
child under 4 yrs	€ 1,00 - € 3,00
animal	free - € 1,60

Less 30% outside July/Aug.
Camping Cheques accepted.

awan
ES CAMPINGS

tel: 00 333 59 59 03 59   *kawan-villages.com*

Marmotel
Camping-Village

"VERY COMFORTABLE, VERY NATURAL"
5 ha in the Lot Valley, by the riverside. 180 pitches, 42 of which have individual toilet. Chalets and Mobile homes for hire. 350 sqm swimming pools, waterslides, multi sports area, animations, kids club, bar, restaurant.
Open 12/05 – 12/09 2007
www.marmotel.com

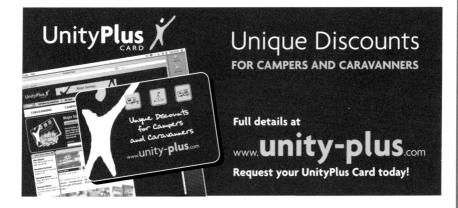

FR12080 Camping Club les Genêts

Lac de Pareloup, F-12410 Salles-Curan (Aveyron)

Tel: 05 65 46 35 34. Email: contact@camping-les-genets.fr

The 162 pitches include 102 grassy, mostly individual pitches for touring units. These are in two areas, one on each side of the entrance lane, and are divided by hedges, shrubs and trees. Most have electricity (6A) and many also have water and waste water drain. The site slopes gently down to the beach and lake with facilities for all watersports including waterskiing. A full animation and activities programme is organised in high season, and there is much to see and do in this very attractive corner of Aveyron. The site is not suitable for American style motorhomes.

Facilities

Two sanitary units with suite for disabled people. Refurbishment of the older unit is planned. Baby room. Laundry. Well stocked shop. Bar, restaurant, snacks (main season). Swimming pool, spa pool (from 1/6; unsupervised). Playground. Minigolf, volleyball, boules. Bicycle hire. Red Indian style tee-pees. Pedaloes, windsurfers, kayaks. Fishing licences available.

Open: 31 May - 11 September.

Directions

From Salles-Curan take D577 for about 4 km. and turn right into a narrow lane immediately after a sharp right hand bend. Site is signed at junction.

Charges 2006

Per unit incl. 1 or 2 persons	
and 6A electricity	€ 11,00 - € 29,00
lakeside pitch	€ 11,00 - € 36,00
extra person	€ 4,00 - € 7,00

FR12120 Camping du Rouergue

Avenue de Fondiès, F-12200 Villefranche-de-Rouergue (Aveyron)

Tel: 05 65 45 16 24. Email: campingrouergue@wanadoo.fr

A spacious and well appointed site in the Vallée de L'Aveyron, Camping du Rouergue is adjacent to the municipal sports facilities. Run by the Rouergue Tourisme Service, the managers are friendly and welcoming. The site has 98 grassy individual pitches of varying sizes, served by tarmac roads, and all serviced with electricity (16A), water and drain. Some pitches are shady. There are reduced rates for campers at the municipal swimming pool and shops and restaurants are within walking distance along the riverside foot and cycle path.

Facilities

The modern spacious sanitary unit includes washbasins in cubicles. Facilities for babies and disabled persons. Dishwashing and laundry sinks. Washing machine. With two identical sections to the block, only one is open during low season. Motorcaravan service point outside campsite entrance. Small bar (June-Oct). TV room. Well equipped playground. Bicycle hire. Off site: Fishing 1 km. Riding 5 km.

Open: 15 April - 15 October.

Directions

Villefranche de Rouergue is about midway between Cahors and Rodez. Site is 1 km. southwest of town on D47 towards Monteils, follow signs from D911 to campsite and 'Stade'.

Charges 2007

Per pitch incl. 2 persons	€ 11,00 - € 14,00
extra person (over 10 yrs)	€ 2,50
child (4-10 yrs)	€ 1,50
electricity	€ 3,00

FR12190 Camping les Calquières

17 avenue Jean Moulin, F-12150 Sévérac le Château (Aveyron)

Tel: 05 65 47 64 82

This site is ideally situated, 3 km. from the free A75 autoroute making an excellent short stay for those on route to the south and a good base for those wishing to visit the Cévennes National Park with its beautiful and rugged scenery. This quiet, neat, family run site nestles below the old village close to the lower part of the town, all within easy walking distance. There are spectacular views from the Château, floodlit at night. There are 97 good sized, level, grassy pitches, with electricity (6A), mostly separated by hedges with maturing trees providing some shade.

Facilities

Two good toilet blocks contain all the necessary facilities, including those for disabled visitors, and were very clean when visited. New snack bar. Off site: Municipal swimming pool (July/Aug), tennis, free to campers. Sévérac le Château (1 km), small range of shops, restaurants and bank. Old, upper part of the town, with the Château is a similar walking distance but involves a good climb. Riding 1 km. Fishing 800 m. Cévennes National Park, Gorge du Tarn and Valley du Lot. Caves.

Open: 1 April - 30 September.

Directions

From A75 exit 42 take N9 signed Sévérac le Château. Shortly hard right (N88), at crossroads straight on, signed Centre Ville. At station roundabout turn left, follow road beside railway through town. Turn left at site sign, immediately left again and site is on right. GPS: N44:19.100 E03:3.833

Charges 2006

Per unit incl. 2 persons	€ 11,10 - € 14,10
extra person	€ 3,00 - € 3,50
electricity (6A)	€ 3,00

FR12160 Camping Caravaning les Peupliers

Mobile homes ▶ page 475

Route des Gorges du Tarn, F-12640 Rivière-sur-Tarn (Aveyron)

Tel: 05 65 59 85 17. Email: lespeupliers12640@wanadoo.fr

Les Peupliers is a friendly, family site on the banks of the Tarn river. Most of the good-sized pitches have shade, all have electricity, water and a waste water point and are divided by low hedges. It is possible to swim in the river and there is a landing place for canoes. The site has its own canoes (to rent). In a lovely, sunny situation on the site is a swimming pool with a paddling pool, sun beds and a new slide, all protected by a beautifully clipped hedge and with a super view to the surrounding hills and the Château du Peyrelade perched above the village. Some English is spoken. A treat for us at dusk was to watch beavers playing and swimming on the far river bank. We were told this happens nearly every day. The site is near the village of Rivière-sur-Tarn and the mouth of the Gorges du Tarn. It is 10 km. from the town of Millau, now famous for its spectacular bridge designed by Norman Foster that carries the A75 over the Tarn valley.

Facilities

Large, light and airy toilet facilities, baby facilities with baths, showers and WCs, facilities for disabled visitors. Washing machines. Shop (1/6-30/9). Bar, TV. Internet. Snack bar, takeaway (1/5-30/9). Swimming pool (from 1/5). Games, competitions July/Aug. Fishing. Volleyball. Football. Badminton. Play area. Weekly dances July/Aug. Canoe hire. Off site: Village with shops and restaurant 300 m. Riding 0.5 km. Bicycle hire 2 km. Golf 25 km. Rock climbing, canyoning, cycling and walking.

Open: 1 April - 30 September.

Directions

Heading south from Clermont Ferrand to Millau on the A75 autoroute take exit 44-1 signed Aguessac/Gorges du Tarn. In Aguessac turn left and follow signs to Riviere sur Tarn (5 km.) and site is clearly indicated down a short road to the right. GPS: N44:11.061 E03:07.402

Charges 2006

Per unit incl. 2 persons	€ 16,00 - € 24,00
extra person	€ 5,00 - € 7,00
child (under 7 yrs)	€ 2,00 - € 4,00
electricity (6A)	€ 4,00

Camping Cheques accepted.

awan
GES CAMPINGS

tel: 00 333 59 59 03 59 *kawan-villages.com*

Camping Caravaning - Mobil-home rental
Canoë-Kayak
Open from april to september

12640 RIVIERE SUR TARN
Tél. : +33 (0)5 65 59 85 17
Fax : +33 (0)5 65 61 09 03
www.campinglespeupliers.fr

Gorges du Tarn   AVEYRON
PAYS D'EMOTIONS

FR12170 Sunêlia le Caussanel

Lac de Pareloup, F-12290 Canet-de-Salars (Aveyron)

Tel: 05 65 46 85 19. Email: info@lecaussanel.com

The site has 235 large, fairly level, grassy pitches, 135 for touring. Most have 6/10A electricity but very long leads may be necessary, and 33 are fully serviced. The pitches are defined by a tree or boulder in each corner and offer little privacy but many have wonderful views over the lake. Most pitches have little shade, a few having good shade. The site has swimming pools with toboggan and slides and a large paddling pool for children with small slides. The adjacent lake offers a large area, 1 km. long, for swimming and all the usual watersports. This large, extremely spacious site on the banks of Lac de Pareloup is greatly improved. It is ideal, in low season, for those seeking a tranquil holiday in a beautiful region of France or in high season, for those seeking an active holiday. One tour operator takes 20 pitches.

Facilities

Modern toilet blocks have all the necessary facilities. Motorcaravan services. Shop. Bar. Restaurant, takeaway (all June-1 Sept.)). Swimming pool complex from June. Large play area. Boules. Tennis. Football. Volleyball. Table tennis. TV room, clubhouse. Organised activities(July/Aug). Fishing. Bicycle hire (July/Aug). Motor boat launching. Water sports (July/Aug), swimming in lake. Internet access. Off site: Paths around lake (24 km). Other marked walks and cycle rides. Shops, banks, restaurants 8 km. Riding 10 km. Golf 30 km. Canoeing, rafting, paragliding caving, windsurfing.

Open: 12 May - 15 September.

Directions

From D911 Rodez - Millau road, just east of Pont de Sellars, turn south on D993 signed Salles-Curan. In 6 km. at crossroads turn right on D538 signed Le Caussanel. Very shortly turn left and continue to site. GPS: N44:12.877 E02:45.995

Charges 2006

Per unit incl. 2 persons	€ 13,20 - € 25,30
extra person	€ 3,50 - € 6,50
child (2-7 yrs)	€ 2,60 - € 4,60
incl. electricity	€ 16,30 - € 29,30
incl. electricity, water and drain	€ 18,70 - € 32,70

Camping Cheques accepted.

FR12200 Camping la Romiguière

Lac de la Selve, F-12210 Montpeyroux (Aveyron)

Tel: 05 65 44 44 64. Email: campinglaromiguiere@wanadoo.fr

A small, rural, well maintained, family run site, La Romiguiere is located beside a man-made lake. It is a peaceful place for lovers of nature. There are 62 slightly sloping, good sized pitches, 40 for touring units. Many are separated by hedges and shaded by mature trees, and all have electricity (10A), water and a drain. There is a small stony beach for bathing in the lake and there are many marked walking and cycling routes around it. Access to the site is by fairly steep, twisting, narrow lanes and is not suitable for large underpowered units.

Facilities

Two modern toilet blocks with all the necessary facilities including excellent facilities for those with disabilities. Motorcaravan service point. Small shop. Bar/restaurant with takeaway. Games room with TV. Heated swimming pool (1/6-15/9). Play area. Family entertainment in high season. Boat ramp. Lake fishing and bathing. Off site: Golf and riding 6 km. Many marked walks and cycle routes. St Amans des Cots with a few small shops, bar, bank 8 km.

Open: 1 May - 15 September.

Directions

Site is about 50 km. southeast of Aurillac. From Aurillac take D920 south for 40 km. to Entraygues. In the town turn left on D34 for 16 km. to St Amans des Cots. Site is signed in the village – take D97 and shortly turn left on D599 and follow the steep narrow lane around the lake to the site (about 9 km). GPS: N44:39.334 E02:42.262

Charges 2006

Per unit incl. 2 persons	€ 11,00 - € 18,00
extra person	€ 4,00 - € 5,00
electricity (10A)	€ 3,00

FR12240 Camping Saint-Pal

Route du Gorges du Tarn, F-12720 Mostuéjouls (Aveyron)

Tel: 05 65 62 64 46. Email: saintpal@wanadoo.fr

Saint Pal is ideally situated on the approach road to the Gorges du Tarn, so access to the site is easy. This small, very neat site is run by a very friendly family and is aimed at those who prefer peace and quiet and less in the way of organised activity. Beside the Tarn river, the site is arranged in the open valley and is fairly flat. There are 74 large, level, grassy pitches, with 64 for touring. Separated by hedging, most are shaded by mature trees and 6A electricity is available. Some pitches are alongside the attractive river. This is a wonderful area for touring, cycling, mountain biking, flowers and birds of prey. Activities such as canoeing, rafting, caving, walking in the trees, rock climbing and bungee jumping are possible..There is a lot to see and do in this area including the new Millau viaduct, designed by Norman Foster and the Observatory for Vultures at Gorges de la Jonte.

Facilities	Directions
One very clean, modern toilet block with good facilities includes a room for babies and campers with disabilities. Motorcaravan service point. Small shop (1/6-15/9). Bar/restaurant and takeaway (1/7-31/8). Small swimming pool (all season). Play area, TV/games room. River bathing, boating and fishing. Organised walks and low key entertainment in July/Aug but no musical events. Off site: Bicycle hire 500 m. Riding 5 km. Le Rozier 1 km. Millau 20 km. **Open:** 19 May - 15 September.	Leave A75 at exit 44, north of Millau. Take N9 south for 14 km. to Aquessac. Turn left on D907 and site is on right in 14 km just before village of Le Rosier. GPS: N44:11.751 E03:11.983

Charges 2006

Per unit incl. 2 persons	€ 11,00 - € 18,00
extra person	€ 3,00 - € 4,50
child (under 5 yrs)	€ 2,00 - € 3,20
electricity	€ 3,00

FR12210 Camping la Source

Presqu'île de Laussac, F-12600 Therondels (Aveyron)

Tel: 05 65 66 27 10. Email: info@camping-la-source.com

This extremely spacious, steeply terraced site borders the long and narrow Lac de Sarrans with its steep wooded sides. The site is run by a very friendly family and is better suited for the younger family wanting to 'get away from it all'. All the facilities are first class, although the layout of the site means that pitches may be some distance and a steep climb away. The owners prefer to provide tractor assistance for caravans. There are 100 medium to large, slightly sloping, grassy pitches with 74 for touring, all with 6/10A electricity, water and a drain.

Facilities	Directions
Two large, well appointed and clean toilet blocks with all the necessary facilities including those for babies and campers with disabilities. Shop (1/7-31/8). Bar with TV (15/5/10/9). Restaurant and takeaway (24/6-31/8). Swimming pool with toboggan and paddling pool (15/5-10/9, heated 1/6-31/8). Play area. TV room. Activities in high season for all the family. Lake fishing. Off site: Boat ramp 500 m. Golf 6 km. Riding and bicycle hire 15 km. **Open:** 5 May - 10 September.	Leave the A75 at exit 28 or 29 (St Flour). Go through town and take D921 towards Chaudes-Aigues. After 12 km. turn right on D990 to Pierrefort and 3 km. after village turn left on D34, signed Laussac. Follow narrow twisting lanes down to site (about 9 km). GPS: N44:51.223 E02:46.263

Charges 2006

Per unit incl. 2 persons	€ 12,00 - € 20,50
extra person	€ 3,00 - € 4,50
child (0-7 yrs)	free - € 3,20
electricity (6/10A)	free - € 5,00
Camping Cheques accepted.	

FR12280 Camping du Viaduc

121 avenue de Millau Plage, F-12100 Millau (Aveyron)

Tel: **05 65 60 15 75**. Email: **info@camping-du-viaduct.com**

Run by a young French couple, this site is situated on the banks of the Tam, across the river from Millau. Of medium size, the site has 237 pitches of which about 200 are for touring units and the rest for chalets. Being close to the town it has access to its services but there is also easy access for discovering the beauty and nature of the gorges. The pitches are flat, of average size, shaded under tall trees and have adequate water and electric points. The site is on the banks of the shallow Tam, where a sandy beach has been created. The site has a rectangular pool with a paved sunbathing terrace close to the reception, a well stocked shop and a bar/restaurant and takeaway. The bar opens out onto a terrace where there is a small stage for animation in high season. Millau was infamous for its tortuous route across the Tam valley, but is now internationally famous for the spectacular viaduct which carries the A75 over the Tam valley, designed by British architect Norman Rogers. Natural sites in the area include the regional park of the grand causes, the Tarn, Dourbie and Jonte gorges.

Facilities	Directions
One large, centrally situated sanitary block with the usual facilities and covered dishwashing areas. Bar with restaurant and takeaway. Swimming pool and children's pool. Shop (all season). Laundry area. Entertainment in July and August. Free children's club in high season. Play area. Fishing and river bathing. Off site: Bicycle and canoe hire 200 m. Hypermarket in Millau and all services of a large town.	Follow signs for 'campings' from Millau centre across the Tam to the east side. At roundabout take last exit signed Paulhe (D187) to second campsite on the left in a short distance.

Open: 1 May - 25 September.

Charges 2006

Per unit incl. 2 persons	€ 12,00 - € 21,00
extra person	€ 2,50 - € 4,50
child (under 5 yrs)	€ 1,60 - € 3,20
electricity (6A)	€ 3,00

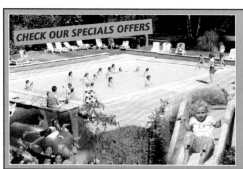

FR12250 Camping du Lac de Bonnefon

L'Etang de Bonnefon, F-12800 Naucelle (Aveyron)

Tel: **05 65 69 33 20**. Email: **email-camping-du-lac-de-bonnefon@wanadoo.fr**

This small family run site, popular with French campers, lies in a picturesque region waiting to be discovered, with rolling hills, deep river valleys, lakes and many old fortified villages. This site is more suitable for those seeking a quieter holiday with less in the way of entertainment. There are 112 good sized, grassy, slightly sloping pitches with 74 for touring (50 with 10A electricity). Some are separated by hedging with others more open and maturing trees give a little shade. The new enthusiastic owners have extended the site and refurbished the facilities to a high standard.

Facilities	Directions
Two toilet blocks include some washbasins in cabins and good facilities for disabled visitors. No shop but bread to order. Bar with TV (all season). Snack bar (July/Aug), other times on demand). Swimming and paddling pools (1/6-30/9). Playground. Archery. Good lake fishing but no bathing. Activities for all the family in July/Aug. Off site: Riding 500 m. Small village of Naucelle with a few shops and large heated pool complex (1 km).	Site is just off the N88 about halfway between Rodez and Albi. From Naucelle Gare take D997 towards Naucelle. In just over 1 km. turn left on D58 and follow signs to site in just under 1 km. GPS: N44:11.283 E02:20.896

Open: 1 April - 31 October.

Charges 2006

Per unit incl. 2 persons	€ 14,00 - € 19,00
extra person	€ 2,00 - € 4,00
child (2-10 yrs)	€ 1,00 - € 2,50
Camping Cheques accepted.	

FR12260 Camping du Val de Saures

Village de gîtes 'Les Bastie', F-12140 Entraygues sur Truyère (Aveyron)

Tel: 05 65 44 56 92. Email: **info@camping-valdesaures.com**

Camping Le Val de Saures is a well presented, value for money site only five minutes across a river bridge from the old town of Entraygues. Situated at the confluence of the rivers Lot and Truyère, it is a good base for relaxing and exploring this beautiful area of Aveyron. There are 110 good sized level grassy pitches (6A electricity) separated by shrubs and trees with varying amount of shade. Many overlook the river. The site has no shop, bar or restaurant but these are available in the town.

Facilities

Three very clean and well appointed toilet blocks with all the necessary facilities including facilities for campers with disabilities. Motorcaravan service point. TV/games room. Playground. River fishing but no bathing. Off site: Fortified town of Entraygues (400 m. by footbridge) with a good range of shops, banks, bars and restaurants. Swimming pool (free), tennis courts and large playground close by. Watersports excursion 400 m. Riding 3 km.

Open: 1 May - 24 September.

Directions

Entraygues sur Truyère is 42 km. southeast of Aurillac on the D920. At southern end of Entraygues on the D920 turn right (site signed), over river bridge onto the D904 and immediately right again. Just past the tennis courts fork right and follow lane down to site. GPS: N44:13.209 E01:58.134

Charges 2006

Per unit incl. 2 persons	€ 8,00 - € 15,00
extra person	€ 2,50 - € 4,00
electricity	€ 3,00

FR16020 Castel Camping les Gorges du Chambon

Eymouthiers, F-16220 Montbron (Charente)

Tel: 05 45 70 71 70. Email: **gorges.chambon@wanadoo.fr**

A welcoming and friendly, family site in pretty, rolling Périgord Vert countryside, Gorges du Chambon is arranged around a restored Charente farmhouse and its outbuildings. It provides an attractive, spacious setting with 140 large, marked pitches of which 90 are for touring units. All have electrical connections (6A) and 4 have water and drainage. On gently sloping grass and enjoying extensive views over the countryside, the pitches are arranged in two circular groups with a sanitary block at the centre of each. The pitches for mobile homes and tour operator tents are not obtrusive. The site is in an area noted for nature trails and bird watching, and information boards abound. It also offers canoe hire on the river and a footpath has been created to the river with two beaches where swimming is possible. A converted barn provides an interesting gallery arrangement in the restaurant/bar. The site owners are very helpful and there is even a herb garden for use by campers.

Facilities

Traditional style blocks include facilities for disabled people. Washing machine, dryer. Basic shop. Bar, restaurant (May - Sept). Takeaway (all season). Swimming pool, children's pool. Children's play area. Games room, TV, table tennis. Tennis, archery, minigolf. Bicycle and canoe hire. Organised activities July/Aug, children's club, youth disco, teenagers' corner. No pets. Off site: Private fishing (free) 6 km; with licence 200 m. Golf 6 km. Riding 10 km. Sailing 20 km. Visits are organised to local producers and day trips (low season).

Open: 1 April - 31 October.

Directions

From N141 Angoulême - Limoges road at Rochefoucauld take D6 to Montbron village. Follow D6 in direction of Piegut-Pluviers and site is signed to the north on D163 just as you enter Tricherie. GPS: N45:39.588 E0:33.460

Charges 2007

Per person	€ 3,80 - € 6,80
child (1-7 yrs)	€ 1,55 - € 3,40
pitch incl. electricity (6A)	€ 8,70 - € 11,65
car	€ 1,55 - € 2,20

Camping Cheques accepted.

Check real time availability and at-the-gate prices...

www.**alanrogers**.com

FR16030 Camping le Champion

F-16230 Mansle (Charente)

Tel: 05 45 20 31 41. Email: ot.pays-manslois@wanadoo.fr

Le Champion is a convenient stop-over from the N10 or a good base to explore the northern Charente area. Beside the Charente river, the site has a cool, relaxing atmosphere created by its attractive location and the 'hippodrome' provides open grassy space on the other side. The site, with 116 average sized and separated touring pitches, is mostly open with little shade. All pitches have electricity (10A) and 15 have water points. Groups are welcome and there is a dedicated area with a second toilet block at the back of the site for groups of more than ten caravans.

Facilities

Modern, well appointed sanitary block is well maintained and provides facilities for disabled people. Washing machine. An additional smaller, older block is in the tenting area at the rear of the site. Motorcaravan service point at entrance. Minigolf. Volleyball. Basketball. Petanque. English spoken. Off site: Restaurant and snacks outside site. Town with its Roman bridge. Tourist office 500 m. Swimming pool in town (discount for campers), recreation area next to the site.

Open: 15 May - 15 September.

Directions

From N10, 30 km. north of Angoulême, take exit for Mansle. From the south, follow signs for Centre Ville, continue past town centre and church, and site is on right, immediately after crossing river. Site is well signed. GPS: N45:52.692 E00:10.891

Charges 2006

Per person	€ 2,20
child (under 7 yrs)	€ 1,20
pitch incl. car	€ 2,80
electricity	€ 2,80

FR16040 Camping Devezeau

F-16230 St Angeau (Charente)

Tel: 05 45 39 21 29. Email: bookings@campingdevezeau.com

Camping Devezeau is open all year and provides a pleasant stopping place on the way to and from the south. It is also within easy reach of Cognac. The site has recently (2004) been taken over by British owners who are working hard to upgrade what is already an attractive site. There are just 39 pitches (34 for touring units) mainly on grass and separated by immature shrubs, although there are four hardstandings for motorcaravans. Most have electricity. The swimming pool is an added attraction for such a small site.

Facilities

The toilet block in a converted barn provides single sex facilities, facilities for disabled people, laundry and dishwashing sinks, and a washing machine. Gas supplies. Swimming pool (12 x 12 m; 1/5-30/9). Play area. Off site: Shop and bar in village 1.5 km. Fishing 2 km.

Open: All year.

Directions

From north, N10 exit for Mansle. Turn left (east) at lights onto D6 for St Angeau. After 9 km, at junction with D15, turn south onto D15, signed for Tourriers. Take first left, after 300 m, site signed, site is 150 m.

Charges 2006

Per unit incl. 2 persons	€ 10,00 - € 17,00
extra person	€ 4,00 - € 6,00
child	€ 1,00 - € 2,00
electricity	€ 2,00 - € 5,00

FR16050 Camping Municipal de Cognac

Boulevard de Châtenay, route de Sainte-Sévère, F-16100 Cognac (Charente)

Tel: 05 45 32 13 32. Email: info@campingdecgnac.com

This area is a must for lovers of brandy, with abundant vineyards and little roadside chalets offering tastings of Pineau (a Cognac based aperitif) and a vast range of Cognacs. This municipal site by the Charente river is convenient as a night stop or longer stay to visit the area, and for sleeping off the effects of the 'tastings' – you probably won't even notice the slight noise from the nearby road! The 168 large touring pitches, all with electricity (5/6A), are neatly laid out and separated by shrubs and trees. A few mobile homes are discreetly positioned along one boundary.

Facilities

Two well equipped, fairly modern toilet blocks (access by steps) include children's toilets and a washing machine. Separate ground level facilities for disabled visitors. Motorcaravan services. Small swimming pool on site (municipal pool nearby). Shop, snack bar, takeaway and entertainment (15/6-15/9). Fishing. Volleyball. Table tennis. Play area on grass. Off site: Bicycle hire 2 km. Riverside walks. Restaurants, bars and shops in the town (2.3 km). Golf 5 km. Riding 6 km.

Open: 1 May - 15 October.

Directions

Site is signed from N141 Saintes - Angoulême road following signs for town centre. It is to the north of the town beside the river on the D24 to Boutiers and Ste-Sévère. GPS: N45:42.544 W00:18.759

Charges guide

Per pitch incl. 2 persons	€ 6,00 - € 10,90
extra person	€ 3,00 - € 3,30
child (0-2 yrs)	free
Less for stays over 3 days.	

FR16060 Camping Marco de Bignac

Lieudit 'Les Sablons', F-16170 Bignac (Charente)

Tel: 05 45 21 78 41. Email: camping.marcodebignac@wanadoo.fr

The small village of Bignac is set in peaceful countryside not too far from the N10 road, north of Angoulême. This mature site is arranged alongside an attractive lake on a level, grassy meadow. The 85 large touring pitches are marked by a trees so there is shade, most have electricity (3/6A). There is a hedged swimming pool and plenty of grassy space for ball games. This site is popular with British visitors and is a peaceful, relaxing location for couples or young families. There is no noisy entertainment and all the activities are free of charge.

Facilities

Two traditional style, functional toilet blocks have functional facilities. Washing machine. Bar, snack bar (1/6-31/8). Small shop, baker calls (high season). Swimming pool (15/6-31/8, unsupervised). Football, badminton, tennis, table tennis, pedaloes, minigolf, boules, fishing, all free. Library. Play area. Pets' corner. Organised activities in high season. A torch may be useful. Off site: Local markets. Riding 5 km. Golf 25 km.

Open: 15 May - 15 September.

Directions

From N10 south of Poitiers, 14 km. north of Angoulême, take D11 west to Vars and Basse. Turn right onto D117 to Bignac. Site is signed at several junctions and in village (Camping Bignac). GPS: N45:47.850 E00:03.831

Charges 2007

Per pitch incl. 2 persons	€ 15,00 - € 21,00
extra person	€ 3,00 - € 5,00
child (2-7 yrs)	€ 1,50 - € 2,50
electricity (3/6A)	€ 2,00 - € 3,00

FR24020 Camping Caravaning les Granges

Mobile homes ▶ page 476

F-24250 Grolejac-en-Perigord (Dordogne)

Tel: 05 53 28 11 15. Email: lesueur.francine@wanadoo.fr

Situated only 500 metres from the village of Groléjac, Les Granges is a lively and well maintained campsite set on sloping ground in woodland. There are 188 pitches, of which 100 are available for touring units. The pitches are marked and numbered on level terraces, and most receive good shade from mature trees and shrubs. All pitches have electricity (6A) and water either on the pitch or close by. The site has a good sized swimming pool and a large shallow pool for children. A bridge connects these to a fun pool with water slides. Regular entertainment is organised in high season, along with a children's club every weekday morning. Around 88 pitches are used by tour operators.

Facilities

The toilet blocks are of a very high standard with good facilities for disabled visitors. Bar/restaurant and snack bar also providing takeaway food (15/05-15/09). No shop, but bread and milk can be ordered. Play area. Table tennis, volleyball, basketball, minigolf, climbing wall. Canoe and bicycle hire. Off site: Shops in the nearby village of Groléjac and hypermarkets of Sarlat or Gourdon are not far away. Golf and riding 6 km.

Open: 5 May - 15 September.

Directions

In centre of village of Groléjac on main D704 road. Site signed through a gravel parking area on west side of road. Drive through this area and follow road around to T-junction. Turn right, under railway bridge, and immediately left (site signed). Site is just along this road on left.

Charges guide

Per unit incl. 2 persons	€ 15,00 - € 22,50
extra person (over 5 yrs)	€ 6,40
electricity (6A)	€ 3,50

269

FR24010 Camping Château le Verdoyer

Mobile homes ▶ page 475

Champs Romain, F-24470 Saint Pardoux (Dordogne)
Tel: **05 53 56 94 64**. Email: **chateau@verdoyer.fr**

The 26 hectare estate has three lakes, two for fishing and one with a sandy beach and safe swimming area. There are 135 good sized touring pitches, level, terraced and hedged. With a choice of wooded area or open field, all have electricity (5/10A) and most share a water supply between four pitches. There is a swimming pool complex and in high season activities are organised for children (5-13 yrs) but there is no disco. This site is well adapted for those with disabilities, with two fully adapted chalets, wheelchair access to all facilities and even a lift into the pool. Le Verdoyer has been developed in the park of a restored château and is owned by a Dutch family. We particularly like this site for its beautiful buildings and lovely surroundings. It is situated in the lesser known area of the Dordogne sometimes referred to as the Périgord Vert, with its green forests and small lakes. The courtyard area between reception and the bar is home to evening activities, and provides a pleasant place to enjoy drinks and relax. The château itself has rooms to let and its excellent lakeside restaurant is also open to the public.

Facilities

Well appointed toilet blocks include facilities for disabled people and baby baths. Serviced launderette. Motorcaravan services. Fridge rental. Shop with gas. Bar, snacks, takeaway and restaurant, both open all season. Bistro (July/Aug). Two pools the smaller covered in low season, slide, paddling pool. Play areas. Tennis. Volleyball, basketball, badminton, table tennis, minigolf. Bicycle hire. Small library. Off site: Riding 15 km.

Open: 16 April - 15 October.

Directions

Site is 2 km. from Limoges (N21) - Chalus (D6bis-D85) - Nontron road, 20 km. south of Chalus and is well signed from main road. Site on D96 about 4 km. north of village of Champs Romain.

Charges 2006

Per unit incl. 2 persons and electricity	€ 18,00 - € 29,00
full services	free - € 4,50
extra person	€ 5,00 - € 6,00
child (under 2-8 yrs)	free - € 4,00

Camping Cheques accepted.

kawan-villages.com **tel: 00 333 59 59 03 59**

kawar VILLAGES CAMPING

Château ★★★★ Le Verdoyer

Dordogne Périgord vert

Accommodation
Restaurant
Camping
★★★★
F 24470
Champs
Romain

Tél.+ 33 5 53 56 94 64
Fax.+ 33 5 53 56 38 70
E mail :
chateau@verdoyer.fr

www.verdoyer.fr

FR24030 Camping les Périères

Rue Jean Gabin, F-24203 Sarlat-la-Canéda (Dordogne)

Tel: 05 53 59 05 84. Email: les-perieres@wanadoo.fr

Les Périères is a good quality small site set on an attractive hillside within walking distance of the beautiful medieval town of Sarlat. The 100 pitches are arranged on wide terraces around the semi-circle of a fairly steep valley, overlooking a central leisure area that includes indoor and outdoor swimming pools and two tennis courts. The pitches are of a very good size, all equipped with electricity (6A), individual water and drainage points and many have dappled shade from the numerous walnut trees on the site (the walnuts can be bought in the campsite shop). Reservations are advised for high season, when the site becomes busy. The site has a refreshingly spacious and open feel, quite free from overcrowding, even at busy times.

Facilities

Good toilet blocks with facilities for disabled visitors, baby bathroom, washing machines, dryers. Motorcaravan services. Small shop. Pleasant bar. Small snack bar/takeaway (July/August). Outdoor swimming pool (no shorts), paddling pool, indoor spa pool and sauna (all season). Tennis, table tennis, football, fitness track. Stone cottages to rent. No electric barbecues allowed. Off site: Bicycle hire 1 km. Fishing 5 km. Riding, golf 7 km.

Open: Easter - 30 September.

Directions

Site is on the east side of Sarlat, on the D47 to Ste Nathalene (negotiating Sarlat town centre is best done outside peak hours).

Charges 2006

Per unit incl. 2 persons	€ 19,20 - € 30,00
with electricity	€ 23,00 - € 33,90
extra person	€ 6,25
child (under 7 yrs)	€ 4,20

Credit cards accepted with 2% fee.

Camping Les Périères

24200 SARLAT, DORDOGNE - PÉRIGORD

The 4-star site in a natural amphitheatre of woods and meadows. A peaceful oasis in the heart of Black Périgord, yet only half a mile from the medieval town and gastronomic centre of Sarlat.

LARGE INDIVIDUAL PITCHES
EXCELLENT TOILET BLOCKS
SWIMMING POOLS, one covered and heated
SAUNA - TENNIS COURTS
VOLLEYBALL - TABLE TENNIS
LOUNGE BAR - SHOP - LIBRARY

FR24040 Castel Camping le Moulin du Roch

Route des Eyzies - Le Roch, D47, F-24200 Sarlat-la-Canéda (Dordogne)

Tel: 05 53 59 20 27. Email: moulin.du.roch@wanadoo.fr

The site has 199 pitches, of which 104 are for touring units. Pitches are mostly flat (some slope slightly) and grassy and all have electricity (6A). Pitches on the upper levels have plenty of shade, whilst those on the lower level near the amenities and the fishing lake are more open. Entertainment and activities are organised from June to September, with something for everyone from craft workshops and sports tournaments to canoeing and caving for the more adventurous. An excellent multi-lingual children's club runs in July and August. Walking and mountain biking lead from the site through surrounding woodland.

Facilities

Modern, well maintained, clean toilet blocks. Washing machines, dryers. Good shop (all season). Bar, terrace (1/6-31/8). Takeaway (2/5-16/9). Superb restaurant (13/5-9/9). Attractive swimming pool, paddling pool, sun terrace (all season). Fishing lake, tennis, table tennis, boules, volleyball, playground, discos twice weekly in high season. Pets are not accepted. Off site: Supermarkets, banks, etc. at Sarlat 10 km. Bicycle hire and riding 10 km. Golf 15 km.

Open: 28 April - 15 September.

Directions

Site is 10 km. west of Sarlat la Canéda, on south side of D47 Sarlat - Les Eyzies road. GPS: N44:54.516 E01:06.883

Charges 2007

Per pitch incl. 2 persons	€ 15,00 - € 27,00
with electricity	€ 19,00 - € 31,00
with full services	€ 23,00 - € 35,00
extra person	€ 4,00 - € 7,80
child (4-9 yrs)	free - € 3,00

Camping Cheques accepted.

awan

tel: 00 333 59 59 03 59 *kawan-villages.com*

FR24060 Camping le Paradis

Saint Léon-sur-Vézère, F-24290 Montignac (Dordogne)

Tel: 05 53 50 72 64. Email: le-paradis@perigord.com

Le Paradis is a well maintained riverside site, halfway between Les Eyzies and Montignac. Well situated for exploring places of interest in the Dordogne region, the site is very well kept and laid out with mature shrubs and bushes of different types. It has 200 individual pitches of good size on flat grass, divided by trees and shrubs (146 for touring units). All have electricity, water and drainage, and there are some special pitches for motorcaravans. At the far end of the site, steps down to the Vézère river give access for canoe launching and swimming. The site welcomes a good quota of Dutch and British visitors, many through a tour operator. Organised games, competitions and evening events are aimed at maintaining a true French flavour. English is spoken. This is a site of real quality, which we thoroughly recommend.

Facilities

High quality, well equipped, heated toilet blocks (unisex), baby baths and toilets,. Well stocked shop (with gas). Good restaurant, takeaway. Good pool complex heated in low season, paddling pool. Tennis, football, BMX track, volleyball, table tennis and pool activities. Multisport court. Canoe hire. Fishing. Bicycle hire. Quad bike and horse riding excursions. Playground. Off site: Riding 2 km. Various trips organised to surrounding area.

Open: 1 April - 25 October.

Directions

Site is 12 km. north of Les Eyzies and 3 km. south of St Léon-sur-Vézère, on the east side of the D706.

Charges 2006

Per unit incl. 2 persons	€ 17,50 - € 25,50
extra person	€ 5,00 - € 7,00
child (3-12 yrs)	€ 4,00 - € 6,00
electricity (10A)	€ 3,00

Low season reductions.
Camping Cheques accepted.

Camping Le Paradis

Camping Le Paradis - 24290 St. Leon sur Vézère
tel.: 05 53 50 72 64 - fax: 05 53 50 75 90 - le-paradis@perigord.com - www.le-paradis.com

FR24070 Camping Lestaubière

Pont Saint Mamet, F-24140 Douville (Dordogne)

Tel: 05 53 82 98 15. Email: lestaubiere@cs.com

The site is just off the main N21 road near Pont St Mamet, mid-way between Bergerac and Perigueux. There are 104 large pitches, most are flat, shaded and wooded, some on more sloping open meadow with views across the valley and others on flat ground beside the lake. Pitches are marked and all have electricity (4/10A), some requiring long leads. The swimming pool and small lake with diving platform and beach encourage longer stays. A pleasant, shaded patio terrace under vines and maples leads to a general room with a bar and a separate room for young people with amusement machines (July/Aug).

Facilities

Three toilet blocks include baby baths, large family room and facilities for disabled visitors. Ample dishwashing and laundry sinks. Washing machine and dryers. Small shop. Bar. Library. Swimming pool (unsupervised) and paddling pool. Excellent adventure style play area. Volleyball. Boules. Fishing. Children's club and organised activities in July/Aug. Off site: Tennis 500 m.

Open: 1 May - 1 October.

Directions

Site is 19 km. north east of Bergerac. From N21 Bergerac - Perigueux road take exit for Pont St Mamet. Site is 500 m. north of the village, on the eastern side of the road, and is well signed.

Charges 2006

Per person	€ 4,80 - € 5,90
child (under 7)	€ 2,80 - € 3,60
pitch	€ 5,90 - € 9,50
electricity (4/10A)	€ 3,00 - € 4,25

FR24080 Camping Caravaning le Moulin de David

Gaugeac, F-24540 Monpazier (Dordogne)

Tel: 05 53 22 65 25. Email: **info@moulin-de-david.com**

Set in a 14 hectare wooded valley, it has 160 pitches split into two sections, 102 are available for touring vans – 33 below the central reception complex in a shaded situation, and 69 above on partly terraced ground with varying degrees of shade. All pitches have electricity (3-10A). Spacing is good and there is no crowding. The site has been attractively planted with a pleasing variety of shrubs and trees and combined with the small stream that runs through the centre of the site they create a beautiful and tranquil setting. Owned and run by a French family who continually seek to improve it, this pleasant and attractive site is one for those who enjoy peace, away from the hustle and bustle of the main Dordogne attractions, yet sufficiently close for them to be accessible. There is a delightful wooded walk via a long distance footpath (GR 36) to Château Biron, about 2-3 km. distance. A 'Sites et Paysages' member.

Facilities

Three good toilet blocks include facilities for disabled visitors and babies. Laundry room. Good shop. Bar/restaurant with shaded patio, takeaway. Swimming pool and children's paddling pool, freshwater pool with waterslide. Play area. Boules, half-court tennis, table tennis, volleyball, basketball, trampoline, football. Library. Bicycle hire. Events, games and canoe trips. Off site: Small supermarket and cash point in Monpazier 2.5 km.

Open: 20 May - 9 September.

Directions

From Monpazier take the D2 Villeréal road. Take third turning left (after about 2 km), signed to Moulin de David and 'Gaugeac Mairie'. Site is about 500 m. along this road on the left.

Charges 2006

Per person (over 2 yrs)	€ 3,80 - € 6,80
normal pitch	€ 5,25 - € 9,85
large pitch incl. water and drain	€ 8,20 - € 12,70
electricity (3/10A)	€ 3,45 - € 5,85
animal	€ 1,50 - € 2,90

FR24090 Camping Soleil Plage

Mobile homes ▶ page 476

Caudon par Montfort, Vitrac, F-24200 Sarlat-la-Canéda (Dordogne)
Tel: **05 53 28 33 33**. Email: **info@soleilplage.fr**

This site is in one of the most attractive sections of the Dordogne valley, with a riverside location. The site has 199 pitches, in three sections, around 104 are for touring units. The smallest section surrounds the main reception and other facilities. There are 59 mobile homes. 20 chalets and 17 bungalow tents. The site offers river bathing from a sizeable pebble or sand bank. All pitches are bounded by hedges and are of adequate size. Most pitches have some shade and have electricity and many have water and a drain. Various activities are organised during high season including walks and sports tournaments, and daily canoe hire is available from the site. Once a week in July and August there is a 'soirée' (charged for) usually involving a barbecue or paella, with band and lots of free wine – worth catching! The site is busy and reservation is advisable. Used by UK tour operators (42 pitches). English is spoken. The site is quite expensive in high season and you also pay more for a riverside pitch, but if you like a holiday with lots going on, you will like this one.

Facilities

Toilet facilities are in three modern unisex blocks (only two open). You will need to hire a plug (€5) for the baby bath. Washing machines and dryer (charged for). Motorcaravan service point. Pleasant bar with TV. Restaurant. Well stocked shop. Very impressive main pool, paddling pool, spa pool and two water slides. Tennis. Minigolf. Playground. Fishing. Canoe and kayak hire. Bicycle hire. Small library. Off site: Golf 1 km. Riding 5 km.

Open: 1 April - 30 September.

Directions

Site is 8 km. south of Sarlat. From A20 take exit 55 (Souillac) towards Sarlat. Follow the D703 to Carsac and on to Montfort. At Montfort castle turn left for 2 km. down to the river.

Charges 2007

Per person	€ 4,50 - € 7,00
child (2-9 yrs)	€ 2,50 - € 4,50
pitch with electricity	€ 9,00 - € 15,50
with full services	€ 12,00 - € 23,00

FR24100 Camping le Moulinal

F-24540 Biron (Dordogne)
Tel: **05 53 40 84 60**. Email: **lemoulinal@perigord.com**

A rural, lakeside site in woodland, Le Moulinal offers activities for everyone of all ages. Of the 280 grassy pitches, only around 62 are available for touring units and these are spread amongst the site's own mobile homes, chalets and a small number of British tour operator tents. All pitches are flat, grassy and have electricity (6A), but vary considerably in size from 75 sq.m. to 100 sq.m. The five-acre lake has a sandy beach and is suitable for boating (canoe hire available), swimming and fishing. Ambitious, well organised animation is run throughout the season including children's club.

Facilities

Toilet facilities, built to harmonise with the surroundings, include facilities for disabled people and babies. Washing machines, dryers. Motorcaravan services. Excellent restaurant. Bar. Snack bar/takeaway. Large, heated swimming pool with Jacuzzi and children's pool. Rustic play area. Multisport court. Boules. Tennis. Archery. Mountain bike hire. Off site: Riding and climbing 5 km. Monpazier, Villeréal and Monflanquin 15 km.

Open: 1 April - 16 September.

Directions

From D104 Villeréal - Monpazier road take the D53/D150 south. Just before Lacapelle Biron turn right on D255 towards Dévillac, (site signed), site is 1.5 km. on the left. GPS: N44:35.988 E00:52.249

Charges guide

Per pitch incl. 2 persons and electricity	€ 17,00 - € 42,00
extra person	€ 4,00 - € 9,00

Camping Cheques accepted.

kawan-villages.com **tel: 00 333 59 59 03 59**

kawan VILLAGES CAMPING

FR24130 Camping les Grottes de Roffy

Mobile homes ▶ page 476

Sainte Nathalène, F-24200 Sarlat-la-Canéda (Dordogne)

Tel: **05 53 59 15 61**. Email: **roffy@perigord.com**

A pleasantly laid out site, about 5 km. east of Sarlat, Les Grottes de Roffy has 162 clearly marked pitches, some very large. Set on very well kept grass terraces, they have easy access and good views across an attractive valley. Some have plentiful shade, although others are more open, and all have electricity (6A). The reception, bar, restaurant and shop are located within converted farm buildings surrounding a semi-courtyard. The campsite shop is well stocked with a variety of goods and a tempting charcuterie section (prepared on site) with plenty of ideas for the barbecue. Various entertainments and excursions are organised during high season. Conveniently located for Sarlat and all other Dordogne attractions, this is a good site for families. Used by tour operators (64 pitches).

Facilities

Two toilet blocks with modern facilities are more than adequate. Well stocked shop. Bar and restaurant with imaginative and sensibly priced menu. Takeaway (all amenities from 6/5). Good swimming pool complex comprising two deep pools (one heated), a fountain, children's pool and heated jacuzzi. Tennis and badminton courts. Games room. Play area. Off site: Fishing 2 km. Bicycle hire 7 km. Riding 10 km. Golf 15 km.

Open: 28 April - 15 September.

Directions

Take D47 east from Sarlat to Ste Nathalène. Just before Ste Nathalène the site is signed on the right hand side of the road. Turn here, and the site is about 800m along the lane.

Charges 2006

Per person	€ 5,45 - € 6,80
child (2-7 yrs)	€ 4,00 - € 4,80
pitch	€ 7,05 - € 8,70
with electricity	€ 9,60 - € 12,00
with full services	€ 11,00 - € 13,50

les
Grottes
de
Roffy
c a m p i n g
c a r a v a n i n g
★ ★ ★ ★

Sainte-Nathalèle • 24200 Sarlat • France
E-mail roffy@perigord.com Tél. +33 (0)5 53 59 15 61 • Fax +33 (0)5 53 31 09 11

FR24110 Camping Caravaning Aqua Viva

Route Sarlac-Souillac, Carsac-Aillac, F-24200 Sarlat-la-Canéda (Dordogne)

Tel: **05 53 31 46 00**. Email: **aqua_viva@perigord.com**

This shaded woodland site is ideally situated for visits to Rocamadour and Padirac, as well as exploring the Dordogne region, including the medieval town of Sarlat, only 7 km. away. The site is divided into two sections, separated by a small access road. Pitches are flat, mainly on grass, divided by shrubs and they vary from average to large size. Many have shade from the numerous trees. All have electricity (6–10A). A wide range of organised activities, children's clubs and entertainments run throughout the season, making this site popular with families, especially those with pre-teen and younger teenage children.

Facilities

Each part of the site has a modern toilet block, with facilities for disabled people and babies. Bar, restaurant/takeaway with terrace. Good shop. Heated swimming pool, children's pool. Small fishing lake. Minigolf. Half tennis, table tennis, volleyball, badminton. Good under 7's play park. Floodlit boules pitch and multi-sports court. Bicycle hire. Off site: Aerial woodland assault course 500 m. Riding and golf 5 km.

Open: 14 April - 25 September.

Directions

Site is 7 km. from Sarlat south of the D704A road from Sarlat to Souillac. From Souillac, the access road to the site is just around a left hand bend, not easy to see.

Charges 2006

Per person	€ 3,90 - € 6,80
child (0-7 yrs)	€ 2,60 - € 4,90
pitch	€ 4,80 - € 9,90
electricity (6/10A)	€ 3,50

275

FR24150 Camping les Deux Vallées

F-24220 Vézac (Dordogne)

Tel: **05 53 29 53 55**. Email: **les2v@perigord.com**

This site is enviably situated almost under the shadow of Beynac castle in the heart of the Dordogne. There are 96 flat marked touring pitches, most of a good size, some large, and with electricity (6/10A). There is plenty of shade and the general feel is of unspoilt but well managed woodland. There is a small fishing lake on site and it is only a short distance to the Dordogne river for bathing or canoeing. The site is being steadily upgraded by its Dutch owners who provide a warm and friendly welcome. English is spoken. This site would be ideal for those wanting a quiet and relatively inexpensive base from which to visit the Dordogne region, particularly in low season, as the site has the advantage of being open all year.

Facilities

The modern unisex, clean toilet blocks (one heated) have facilities for disabled visitors. Shop, bar/restaurant (both 1/6-30/9) meals to take away, eat inside or on the terrace. Good sized pool, children's pool (from mid May). Bicycle hire. Volleyball, basketball, minigolf, boules, table tennis, table football. Quiz nights and barbecues are a regular feature in the main season. Facilities may open earlier than stated if demand is sufficient. Off site: Riding 2 km. Golf 8 km.

Open: All year.

Directions

Site is on the northwest side of the D57 Beynac-et-Cazenac - Sarlat road, about 2 km. from Beynac. From Beynac follow D57, under railway bridge, second left and then first left over bridge. Turn immediately left to site.

Charges 2006

Per person	€ 3,20 - € 5,20
child (3-7 yrs)	€ 2,20 - € 3,20
pitch	€ 4,00 - € 6,75
electricity (6A)	€ 3,50

Camping Les Deux Vallées

OPEN ALL YEAR

Our small and friendly Dutch owned 3 star campsite nestles in the heart of the glorious Dordogne Valley. With all the top class facilities you would expect at a price you thought was a thing of the past. Situated just 500m from the river and within gentle cycling distance of five of the region's major Châteaux "Les Deux Vallees" is the ideal base to explore the delights of this wonderful area. Low season and long stay discounts. Special rates for Rallies. Accommodation Rental. And above all a holiday you will remember with pleasure.

Annemarie & Ruel, Kathalÿn & Maartje, Les Deux Vallées, 24220 Vezac, France Phone: 00 33 553 29 53 55. Fax: 0033 553 31 09 81 E-mail: les2v@perigord.com - Web Site: www.les-2-vallees.com

FR24140 Camping Bel Ombrage

F-24250 Saint Cybranet (Dordogne)

Tel: 05 53 28 34 14. Email: belombrage@wanadoo.fr

Bel Ombrage is a quiet, well maintained site located in a pretty location by the little River Céou, with a pebble beach that is safe and clean for bathing. The site has a good pool complex, but otherwise there are few on site facilities. The 180 well shaded, good sized and flat grass pitches are marked by trees and bushes and all with electricity. The quiet and tranquil setting makes the site particularly popular with couples. Bel Ombrage is very close to Domme and Castelnaud and would make an ideal and inexpensive base for visiting the southern Dordogne area.

Facilities

Two modern toilet blocks are kept spotlessly clean, with facilities for disabled visitors and babies. Laundry facilities. Bread van. Large swimming pool with sun terrace, children's pool. Paddling pool. Play area. Games room. Fishing. Excursions can be booked at reception. Off site: Pizzeria next door. Tennis and canoeing close. Riding and bicycle hire 3 km. Golf 6 km. More shops at Cénac.

Open: 1 June - 5 September.

Directions

Site is about 14 km. south of Sarlat, on the east side of the D57 Castelnaud-la-Chapelle - St Cybranet road, about 1 km. north of the junction with the D50.

Charges 2006

Per person	€ 5,20
child (under 7 yrs)	€ 3,20
pitch incl. electricity (10A)	€ 10,40

No credit cards.

FR24160 Camping le Grand Dague

Atur, F-24750 Périgueux (Dordogne)

Tel: 05 53 04 21 01. Email: info@legranddague.fr

Le Grand Dague is close to Périgueux, in a rural and tranquil setting. Built on a hillside, the site is clean, attractive and very spacious and 68 of the 93 pitches are for touring units. The pitches are only slightly sloping and are divided by tall, mature hedging (electricity 6A). There is a large field suitable for large motorhomes. Those with disabilities might find the roads quite steep. Open grassy areas and a good range of equipment in the play area makes this an ideal site for young families.

Facilities

Excellent, part heated sanitary facilities include a baby room and facilities for people with disabilities. Small shop (15/6-15/9). Bar, attractive restaurant with appetising menu and takeaway (both from June). Swimming pool, water slide and paddling pool (from early May). Football, volleyball, badminton, petanque, minigolf and table tennis. Play area. Fishing. Off site: Paintball outside gate. Riding 5 km. Bicycle hire 8 km. Golf 10 km.

Open: 28 April - 15 September.

Directions

From the Bordeaux - Brive inner ring road in Périgueux take D2 south, signed Atur. Campsite signed. Turn east at roundabout just before entering Atur. Site is in 3 km. GPS: N45:08.880 E00:46.657

Charges 2007

Per person	€ 4,25 - € 6,50
child (0-7 yrs)	€ 2,75 - € 4,25
pitch with electricity	€ 8,45 - € 11,75
animal	€ 1,75

FR24170 Camping le Port de Limeuil

F-24480 Allés-sur-Dordogne (Dordogne)

Tel: 05 53 63 29 76. Email: didierbonvallet@aol.com

At the confluence of Dordogne and Vézère rivers, opposite the picturesque village of Limieul, this delightful family site exudes a peaceful and relaxed ambience. There are 90 marked, grassy, flat pitches, some spacious and all with electricity (5A). The buildings are in traditional Périgourdine style and surrounded by flowers and shrubs. A sports area on a large open grassy space between the river bank and the main camping area adds to the feeling of space and provides an additional recreation and picnic area (there are additional unmarked pitches for tents and camper vans along the bank here).

Facilities

Two clean, modern toilet blocks provide excellent facilities. Bar/restaurant with snacks and takeaway (all 20/5-5/9). Small shop. Swimming pool with jacuzzi, paddling pool and children's slide (1/5- 30 /9). Badminton, football, boules and volleyball. Mountain bike hire. Canoe hire - launched from the site's own pebble beach. Off site: The pretty medieval village of Limeuil 200 m. Riding 1 km. Golf 10 km.

Open: 1 May - 30 September.

Directions

Site is 7 km. south of Le Bugue. From D51/D31E Le Buisson to Le Bugue road turn west towards Limeuil. Just before bridge into Limeuil, turn left (site signed), across another bridge. Site shortly on the right. GPS: N44:52.878 E00:53.444

Charges 2007

Per pitch incl. 2 persons	€ 14,00 - € 24,90
extra person	€ 4,50 - € 5,50
child (under 10 yrs)	€ 2,50 - € 3,50
electricity (5A)	€ 2,50 - € 3,50

277

FR24220 Camping Domaine des Chênes Verts

Route de Sarlat, F-24370 Calviac en Périgord (Dordogne)

Tel: 05 53 59 21 07. Email: chenes-verts@wanadoo.fr

This peaceful countryside family campsite is set in a beautiful area of the Dordogne valley, and is complemented by the renovated Périgourdine farm buildings which house the amenities at the centre of the site. The spacious grounds which contain many trees provide 168 pitches on either side of the main buildings, of which 68 are for touring units. Most of the good sized, grassy pitches are shaded, and all are separated by hedging. There is electricity (6A) to all pitches, and water points nearby. The majority of pitches are large and level but some are gently sloping. The owners, who speak some English, are very helpful and friendly, and in high season they organise a range of entertainments and activities from wine tasting to canoeing expeditions, and of course the obligatory boules tournaments.

Facilities

Two fully equipped unisex toilet blocks include washbasins in cabins, dishwashing and laundry areas. Washing machine. Small shop (fresh bread daily), bar and snack bar (takeaway in high season). Motorcaravan service point. Fridge hire. Gas supplies. Medium sized swimming pool with large sunbathing area (15/6-15/9), covered, heated pool (1/4-20/9) and a paddling pool. Play area. Multisport court. Animation for children. TV and games room. Charcoal barbecues provided. Off site: Forest walks and cycle tracks lead from the site.

Open: 7 April - 22 September.

Directions

From D704 Sarlat - Gourdon road turn east on D704A towards Souillac and Calviac (this turning is about 3.5 km. from Sarlat). Site is about 5 km. along this road on the left.

Charges 2007

Per person	€ 3,75 - € 4,20
child (under 7 yrs)	€ 2,15 - € 2,70
pitch incl. electricity	€ 11,70 - € 20,90
dog	€ 1,75 - € 2,20

Domaine des Chênes Verts

Route de Sarlat F-24370 Calviac en Périgord
Tel.: (33) 5 53 59 21 07 Fax: (33) (0)5 53 31 05 51

Email: chenes-verts@wanadoo.fr
www.chenes-verts.com

FR24180 Camping Caravaning Saint Avit Loisirs

Le Bugue, F-24260 Saint Avit-de-Vialard (Dordogne)

Tel: 05 53 02 64 00. Email: contact@saint-avit-loisirs.com

Although Saint Avit Loisirs is set in the middle of rolling countryside, far from the hustle and bustle of the main tourist areas of the Dordogne the facilities are first class, providing virtually everything you could possibly want without the need to leave the site. This makes it ideal for families with children of all ages. The site is in two sections. One part is dedicated to chalets and mobile homes, whilst the main section of the site contains 199 flat and mainly grassy, good sized pitches, 99 for touring, with electricity (6A), arranged in cul-de-sacs off a main access road.

Facilities

Three modern unisex toilet blocks provide high quality facilities, but could become overstretched (particularly laundry and dishwashing sinks) in high season. Shop, bar, restaurant, cafeteria. Outdoor swimming pool, children's pool, water slide, 'crazy river', heated indoor pool with jacuzzi, fitness room. Sound-proofed disco. Table tennis, minigolf, boules, dirt bike track, tennis, volleyball, play area. Canoe trips on the Dordogne and other sporting activities organised. Good walks from site. Off site: Sarlat and Périgeux for markets and hypermarkets.

Open: 31 March - 30 September.

Directions

Site is 6 km. north of Le Bugue. From D710 Le Bugue - Périgueux road, turn west on narrow and bumpy C201 towards St Avit de Vialard. Follow road through St Avit, bearing right - site in about 1.5 km. GPS: N44:57.082 E00:50.825

Charges 2006

Per person	€ 3,70 - € 8,60
child (under 4 yrs)	free
pitch	€ 5,80 - € 12,50
with electricity	€ 9,50 - € 17,10
with water and drainage	€ 12,10 - € 20,40

FR24230 Camping le Moulin de Paulhiac

F-24520 Daglan (Dordogne)

Tel: 05 53 28 20 88. Email: Francis.Armagnac@wanadoo.fr

You will be guaranteed a friendly welcome from the Armagnac family, who are justifiably proud of their well-kept and attractive site, built in the grounds surrounding an old mill. The 150 shady pitches (98 for touring) are separated by hedges and shrubs, all fully serviced. Many pitches are next to a stream that runs through the site and joins the River Ceou along the far edge. A tent field slopes gently down to the river, which is quite shallow and used for bathing. This site will appeal especially to families with younger children. Used by a tour operator (44 pitches).

Facilities

Two clean toilet blocks provide modern facilities, including those for disabled visitors. Good shop, restaurant, takeaway. Main pool, heated and covered by a sliding roof in low season, children's pool, a further small pool and two slides. Volleyball, table tennis, badminton, boules. Bicycle hire. Canoe trips organised on the Dordogne. Organised evening activities. Children's club in high season.

Open: 15 May - 15 September.

Directions

Site is about 17 km. south of Sarlat, and is on the east side of the D57, about 5 km. north of the village of Daglan.

Charges 2006

Per person	€ 5,20 - € 6,50
child under 10 yrs	€ 3,80 - € 4,75
child under 2 yrs	€ 2,00 - € 2,80
pitch	€ 7,35 - € 9,20

Special offers in low season.

FR24240 Camping les Bo-Bains

F-24150 Badefols-sur-Dordogne (Dordogne)

Tel: 05 53 73 52 52. Email: info@bo-bains.com

Offering a limited number of touring pitches, but with a good range of facilities and activities, Les Bo-Bains is a well kept site in an attractive location alongside the Dordogne river. The flat, grassy and good sized pitches are all set along the river bank, with beautiful views across the Dordogne. Pitches are divided by hedges, shrubs and bushes of different varieties and they have plenty of shade. All pitches have electricity, with water taps and drainaway points between each pair. Canoeing can be arranged from reception and there are places to launch one's own small craft.

Facilities

Good quality toilet blocks with baby rooms and laundry facilities. Small shop. Bar (all season), restaurant, takeaway (15/5-15/9). Swimming pool, another shallower one, three slides. Small play areas. TV room. Multi-gym, football, minigolf, archery, trampoline, badminton, basketball. Organised events in high season. Quad bike and bicycle hire. Riding. Canoeing excursions. Off site: The small village of Badefols is within easy walking distance.

Open: 15 April - 30 September.

Directions

Site is on D29 Bergerac - Sarlat road, about 4 km. east of Lalinde, on the north side of the road.

Charges 2006

Per pitch incl. 2 persons and electricity (5A)	€ 13,00 - € 28,00
extra person over 7 yrs	€ 3,00 - € 7,50

FR24250 Camping les Tourterelles

F-24390 Tourtoirac (Dordogne)

Tel: 05 53 51 11 17. Email: les-tourterelles@tiscali.fr

This is a well maintained, Dutch owned site with its own equestrian centre that will appeal to lovers of the countryside, in an area that is ideal for walking or horse riding, yet is within easy reach of Pèrigueux and the better known sights of the Dordogne. There are 125 pitches in total, but the site has some chalets, bungalows and mobile homes which leaves around 88 grassy pitches for tourists. These are on several different levels most with good shade from mature trees and all have electricity hook-ups (6A). In low season the site can organise tours to local walnut farms, dairies etc. Rallies are welcome and themed programmes can be arranged.

Facilities

Three good, fully equipped toilet blocks include facilities for disabled visitors and a baby unit. Laundry. Bread to order. Bar/restaurant serving good value meals, with takeaway. Freezer pack service. Swimming pool (20 x 10 m.) and paddling pool. Riding. Tennis. Volleyball. Badminton. Children's club and comprehensive activity and entertainment programme in main season. Off site: Shop at Tourtoirac 1 km. Supermarket at Hautefort 6 km. Fishing 1 km. Bicycle hire 6 km.

Open: 16 April - 30 September.

Directions

Site is 46 km north east of Périgueux. From Périgueux, take D5 east to Tourtoirac. Turn north onto D67 on entering village (site signed) and shortly fork left on D73 towards Coulaures; site is on left in 1 km. GPS: N45:16.833 E01:02.913

Charges 2006

Per person	€ 3,80
child (under 10 yrs)	€ 3,20
pitch incl. electricity	€ 12,35 - € 14,25

Low season discounts for over 55's. No credit cards.

FR24280 Camping de Barnabé

Rue des Bains, F-24750 Périgueux (Dordogne)

Tel: 05 53 53 41 45. Email: contact@barnabe-perigord.com

A 1936 Art Deco style building houses the reception, bar, restaurant and games room, complete with terrace overlooking the River L'Isle. This site has 42 touring pitches, hedged and shaded by mature trees, all with electricity (4/6A) and 12 are fully serviced. The entrance and access roads are narrow (larger units take great care). The ground may be rather firm for tent pegs and it occasionally floods in winter. The only site in Périgueux itself, Barnabé is a memorable site in a unique setting. The bar has its own Wurlitzer juke box and you will find games tables in the old ballroom.

Facilities

Six sanitary buildings around the site (one on the far side of the river). Not modern, but functional, simple and clean with spacious shower cubicles. Unisex facilities, with both British and Turkish style toilets. One heated block is open in winter. Bar (1/4-15/10). Fishing. Off site: Périgueux 2 km. Golf 7 km. Riding 10 km.

Open: 1 March - 3 October.

Directions

Approaching from the east of Périgueux on the N221, at roundabout with N2089, take exit for Périgueux 'centre ville'. After about 3 km. turn right at traffic lights at town boundary. Site well signed. GPS: N45:11.207 E00.44.515

Charges 2006

Per person	€ 3,80
child (under 7 yrs)	€ 2,50
pitch incl. electricity (4/6A)	€ 6,00 - € 8,50

FR24290 Camping le Moulin du Bleufond

Avenue Aristide Briand, F-24290 Montignac (Dordogne)

Tel: 05 53 51 83 95. Email: le.moulin.du.bleufond@wanadoo.fr

Built on flat ground around a 17th century mill, this former municipal site has its own pool and is nearby town sporting facilities. The 84 pitches (66 for touring units) are marked and divided by mature hedges, all have electricity and most have some shade. Pitches vary considerably in size. The small town of Montignac is only 5 minutes walk, with shops, restaurants and bars. The site is separated from the river by a reasonably quiet road; there is a sizeable bank for fishing. This is an ideal base from which to visit a fascinating and beautiful part of the Perigord.

Facilities

Modern, clean. heated sanitary facilities are well cared for. Bread and a few essentials available at reception. Bar, snack bar, terrace restaurant (all season). Heated swimming pool, paddling pool. Games room with table football, pool, table tennis and giant TV. Canoe trips and bicycle hire. Musical evenings weekly in high season. Off site: Shops, supermarkets, bars and a range of restaurants in the town only 5 minutes walk away.

Open: 1 April - 15 October.

Directions

Site is just south of Montignac, on D65 to Sergeac. Just after crossing stone bridge on one way system in centre of town turn sharp right (allow for a wide sweep!) The site is 750 m. on left.

Charges 2007

Per person	€ 3,82 - € 5,10
child (2-8 yrs)	€ 2,48 - € 3,32
pitch	€ 4,57 - € 6,10
electricity (10A)	€ 3,00

FR24300 Camping la Rivière Fleurie

Saint Aulaye de Breuilh, F-24230 Saint Antoine de Breuilh (Dordogne)

Tel: 05 53 24 82 80. Email: info@la-riviere-fleurie.com

This quiet and pleasant campsite is close to the vineyards of Pomerol and St Emilion, and not far from the extensive shopping of St Foy la Grande and Bergerac. The 60 pitches are all spacious, divided by shrubs and maturing trees are beginning to provide shade. All pitches have electricity (4/10A) There are no tour operators, but 12 pitches are used for site owned mobile homes, and there are also studio apartments to let throughout the year. The site has a tranquil and peaceful ambience, suitable for anyone looking for a quiet and relaxing holiday.

Facilities

Sanitary facilities are plentiful and modern (no toilet paper). Bar and terrace restaurant serving a range of basic meals. Swimming pool (100 sq.m) and toddlers' pool. Football, volleyball, table tennis, table football and TV room. Weekly 'soirées' where the owners host an evening of French food and entertainment. Canoe trips arranged. Off site: Municipal tennis court adjacent (free to campers). Fishing 100 m. Riding 4 km. Bicycle hire 8 km.

Open: 1 April - 30 September.

Directions

Site is in St Aulaye, about 3 km. south of D936 Bordeaux - Bergerac road. 6 km east of Lamothe-Montravel turn south on local roads and follow signs to site 150 m. from river. GPS: N44:49.743 E00:07.343

Charges 2006

Per unit incl. 2 persons	€ 13,60 - € 17,00
extra person	€ 4,00 - € 5,00
child (under 7 yrs)	€ 2,80 - € 3,50
electricity	€ 2,90 - € 4,00

FR24320 Camping les Peneyrals

Mobile homes ▶ page 477

Le Poujol, F-24590 Saint Crépin-Carlucet (Dordogne)

Tel: **05 53 28 85 71**. Email: **camping.peneyrals@wanadoo.fr**

Within easy reach of all the attractions of the Périgord region, M. and Mme. Havel have created an attractive and friendly family campsite at Les Peneyrals. There are 199 pitches, 80 of which are for touring. The pitches at the bottom of the hill tend to be quieter as they are further from the main facilities, but are all level and grassy (some on terraces), with electricity (5/10A), and most have some shade. An attractive bar and restaurant with terrace overlook the excellent pool complex and at the bottom of the site is a small fishing lake. The site is set on a wooded hillside, with flowers in abundance (thanks to the dedication of Mme. Havel's mother). In July and August activities are organised including archery, various sports tournaments, aqua gym, discos and a children's club. It is used fairly unobtrusively by a UK tour operator (70 pitches).

Facilities	Directions
Two modern, unisex toilet blocks provide good quality facilities, including provision for babies and disabled visitors. Motorcaravan services. Good value shop, excellent restaurant and takeaway. Pool complex with two large pools (one heated), paddling pool and four water slides with splash pool. Indoor heated pool. Bicycle hire. Minigolf, tennis court (charged). Football. Badminton, volleyball and table tennis. Play area. Games room, TV room and small library. Off site: Supermarkets, banks, etc. in Sarlat (11 km).	Site is 11 km. north of Sarlat. From D704 Sarlat - Montignac road turn east on D60 towards Salignac-Eyvigues. After 4 km. turn south on D56 towards St Crépin-Carlucet. Site is about 500 m. along this road on the right.

Open: 15 May - 15 September.

Charges 2006

Per person	€ 4,60 - € 7,30
child (under 7 yrs)	free - € 4,80
pitch	€ 6,70 - € 10,40
electricity (5/10A)	€ 2,00 - € 3,10

FR24310 Camping Caravaning la Bouquerie

F-24590 Saint Geniès-en-Périgord (Dordogne)

Tel: **05 53 28 98 22**. Email: **labouquerie@wanadoo.fr**

La Bouquerie is a well maintained site, situated within easy reach of the main road network in the Dordogne, but without any associated traffic noise. The main complex is based around some beautifully restored traditional Périgordin buildings. It includes a shop and a bar and restaurant (excellent varied menu and reasonably priced) overlooking the pool complex, with a large outdoor terrace for fine weather. Of the 180 pitches, 91 are used for touring units and these are of varying size (80-120 sq.m.), flat and grassy, some with shade, and all with electrical connections (5A).

Facilities	Directions
Three well maintained toilet blocks with facilities for disabled visitors and baby rooms. Washing machines and covered drying lines. Small shop (15/05-15/09), takeaway food. Bar, restaurant (both 15/05-15/09). Paddling pool, large shallow pool (heated), large deep pool, sunbathing areas with loungers. Carp fishing in lake on site. Bicycle hire. Riding. Off site: Shops and restaurants, etc. in the nearby village of St Geniès.	Site is signed on east side D704 Sarlat - Montignac, about 500 m. north of junction with D64 St Geniès road. Turn off D704 at campsite sign and take first left turn signed La Bouquerie – site is straight ahead.

Open: 15 April - 23 September.

Charges 2006

Per person	€ 4,60 - € 6,50
child (under 7 yrs)	€ 3,20 - € 4,50
pitch	€ 6,30 - € 9,00
electricity	€ 3,00

(281)

FR24330 Camping de l'Etang Bleu

F-24340 Vieux-Mareuil (Dordogne)

Tel: **05 53 60 92 70**. Email: **marc@letangbleu.com**

There are 169 pitches, 151 for touring, with the remainder taken up by site owned mobile homes for rent. The pitches are a good size, flat and grassy, with mature hedging and trees providing privacy and plenty of shade. All pitches have water and 90 have electricity (10/16A). At the bottom of the site is a fishing lake stocked with carp (permit required) and various woodland walks start from the campsite grounds. The bright and cheerful 'bistro bar' provides good value food and drinks, and becomes a focal point for evening socialising on site.

Facilities

Modern well maintained toilet block provides facilities for babies and disabled people. Laundry. Small playground, paddling pool. Swimming pool, sun terrace. Bar with terrace (all season), restaurant (1/6-30/9), poolside bar. Takeaway (1/6-30/9). Small shop. Table tennis, boules, volleyball, badminton. Canoe and bicycle hire. Entertainments, sporting activities, excursions in high season. Off site: Restaurant 'Auberge de L'Etang Bleu' adjacent to campsite, small supermarket, post office etc. in Mareuil (7 km).

Open: Easter/1 April -18 October.

Directions

Site is between Angoulême and Périgueux. Leave D939 in Vieux Mareuil, take D93, and follow narrow road. Just after leaving village site signed on right, just past Auberge de L'Etang Bleu. Turn right, follow signs to site.

Charges 2006

Per person	€ 3,75 - € 5,50
child (2-7 yrs)	€ 1,25 - € 2,00
pitch and car	€ 5,75 - € 7,25
with electricity	€ 7,75 - € 11,50

FR24340 Camping le Val de la Marquise

F-24260 Campagne (Dordogne)

Tel: **05 53 54 74 10**. Email: **val-marquise@wanadoo.fr**

This well kept little campsite, between Le Bugue and Les Eyzies, is an ideal base to explore the châteaux and prehistoric sites of the Perigord region. The 104 pitches (88 for touring) are flat, grassy and all of a good size. The pitches are divided by shrubs and some have shade from mature trees, whilst others are more open. Most have electricity (15A). Reception stocks a range of basic groceries including bread and croissants made freshly on site every morning. Weekly entertainment and excursions are organised in high season. The site retains a relaxed peaceful air and is an ideal retreat after a busy day of sightseeing in the area.

Facilities

Clean toilet block provides first-rate facilities, baby bath. Smaller block near reception houses good facilities for disabled visitors. Washing and drying machines. Good bar (1/6-15/10), snack bar/takeaway (1/7-30/8), terrace. Swimming pool, sun terrace, paddling pool. Small fishing lake. Off site: Bars and restaurants in the village of Campagne 500 m. Supermarket in Le Bugue 5 km.

Open: 1 April - 15 October.

Directions

Site is 5 km. southeast of Le Bugue. Take D703/D706 Le Bugue - Les Eyzies road. At Campagne take D35 south east towards St Cyprien (there is a peculiar 'Y' junction with 3 roads). Site is about 500 m. on right.

Charges 2007

Per person	€ 3,10 - € 4,70
child (2-10 yrs)	€ 2,10 - € 3,50
pitch	€ 4,90 - € 7,50
electricity (15A)	€ 4,00

FR24350 Camping RCN le Moulin de la Pique

F-24170 Belvès (Dordogne)

Tel: 05 53 29 01 15. Email: info@rcn-lemoulindelapique.fr

Set in the grounds of a converted former mill and iron foundry, this impressive and well managed site offers something for every member of the family. The 135 touring pitches are flat, grassy and extremely spacious (most well over 100 sq.m.) and most have electricity (6A), water and drainage. Some pitches border the lake which can be used for both fishing and boating. The 11th century fortified town of Belvès is only 2 km. away and the campsite is well located for access to the many other attractions of the Dordogne valley.

Facilities	Directions
Modern good quailty toilet blocks provide facilities for disabled visitors. Washing, drying machines. Bar, restaurant, snack bar, shop (open all season), Swimming pool (heated), paddling pool, water slides, 'lazy river'. Playing field. Volleyball. Table tennis. Tennis. Boules. Minigolf. Play areas. TV, games room. Toddler's playroom. Library. Internet. Off site: Bars, restaurants and shops in the village of Belvès 2 km.	Site is 35 km. southwest of Sarlat on the east side of the D710, about 7 km south of Siorac-en-Périgord.

Open: 14 April - 6 October.

Charges 2007

Per pitch incl. up to 6 persons incl. electricity and water	€ 26,50 - € 49,50
incl. 2 persons	€ 13,50 - € 20,50

FR24360 Camping le Mondou

F-24370 Saint Julien de Lampon (Dordogne)

Tel: 05 53 29 70 37. Email: lemondou@camping-dordogne.info

This quiet and peaceful site mid-way between Sarlat and Souillac is ideally situated for exploring the Dordogne and Lot departments. It is set amongst countryside at the edge of the small village of St Julien and only 2 km. from the Dordogne river. The 62 grassy pitches are of medium to large size, divided by shrubs and with some shade from a wide variety of trees. All have electricity (6A). The friendly and helpful owners, John and Lia, organise regular evening entertainment during high season and they work hard to ensure that everyone enjoys their stay at Le Mondou.

Facilities	Directions
Two sanitary blocks provide basic facilities, including facilities for disabled visitors, baby baths, washing machine, ironing board and iron. Terrace bar and snack bar with reasonably priced menu. Large swimming pool with sun terrace and children's paddling pool. Rustic style play area and large playing field. Boules and badminton. Off site: Bar, restaurant and small shop in the village of St Julien-de-Lampon about 1 km. away.	Site about 12 km. southwest of Souillac. From D703, at Rouffillac, turn south across the river Dordogne (D61 signed St Julien-de-Lampon). Entering village turn left (D50, signed to Mareuil). Site in 500 m. beyond village.

Open: 1 April - 15 October.

Charges 2006

Per person	€ 4,40
child (under 7 yrs)	€ 2,00
pitch	€ 6,90 - € 7,90

FR24380 Camping BleuSoleil

Domaine Touvent, F-24580 Rouffignac Saint Cernin (Dordogne)

Tel: 05 53 05 48 30. Email: infos@camping-bleusoleil.com

Camping BleuSoleil is delightfully located in the countryside and has excellent views. It comprises 70 acres and, at present, has 110 pitches, 95 for touring and 15 used for wooden chalets. Set in an open, woody, and hilly area, some of the pitches have partial shade from well sited trees and hedges. There is some terracing. You will receive a warm welcome at BleuSoleil and a comfortable stay. The village of Rouffignac-St Cernin-de-Reilhac, is 1 km. away and is within walking distance. There you will find small bars, restaurants and other amenities. A good sized supermarket is less than 5 km.

Facilities	Directions
Three modern unisex sanitary blocks are clean, well maintained and adequate for the number of pitches. En-suite toilet for disabled visitors. Baby room with bath. Enclosed laundry area with two washing machines and dryer. Shop, small bar with TV, and restaurant (high season) Large 200 sq.m. swimming pool and paddling pool. Boules. Small play area and a pen with donkeys and goats. Off site: Village facilities 1 km. Fishing 2 km. Riding 4 km.	From Périgueux take N89 east for 17 km. to Thenon, then D31 south signed Balou. Continue from Balou for 3 km. to the outskirts of Rouffignac-St Cernin-de-Reilhac and look for site sign on the left. Turn off main road to site (less than 1 km).

Open: 3 April - 30 September.

Charges 2006

Per person	€ 3,00 - € 4,20
child (under 10 yrs)	€ 1,80 - € 4,20
pitch	€ 4,90 - € 6,90
electricity (10A)	€ 2,70

FR24390 Camping le Vézère Périgord

Route de Montignac, F-24620 Tursac (Dordogne)

Tel: **05 53 06 96 31**. Email: **info@levezereperigord.com**

Camping Le Vézère Périgord is a small secluded campsite set in a wooded and hilly area in the country. It has a total of 107 pitches, 86 for touring and 21 mobile homes. Most pitches have partial shade from well sited trees and bushes, and are terraced. The site has a large 200 m open air swimming pool and a small paddling pool. The river Vézère is 300 m away (accessed through a wooded path on the campsite and across a road). There are several small villages nearby, and the larger towns of Montignac (17 km.) and Périgueux (25 km).

Facilities

Three modern unisex sanitary blocks (only two are open low season) are clean, well maintained, serviced, and adequate for the number of pitches. En-suite toilet for disabled people (not easily accessible). Baby room with bath and sink. Laundry room with drying area. Small bar with TV and shop. Restaurant. Boules. Trampoline. Tennis. Play area. Off site: Canoe hire (arranged by site). Riding 5 km.

Open: 15 April - 31 October.

Directions

Head west on the N89 Brive - Périgueux road and turn southwest on D704 to Montignac. At Montignac take D706 southwest signed Les Eyzies-de-Tayac; 1 km. before Tursac look for sign to site.

Charges 2006

Per person	€ 3,00 - € 6,00
child (0-4 yrs)	€ 2,00 - € 4,00
pitch	€ 5,00 - € 7,00
electricity (6A)	€ 3,00

FR24420 Camping les Valades

D703, F-24220 Coux-et-Bigaroque (Dordogne)

Tel: **05 53 29 14 27**. Email: **camping.valades@wanadoo.fr**

Sometimes we come across small but beautifully kept campsites which seem to have been a well kept secret, and Les Valades certainly fits the bill. Set on a hillside overlooking countryside between the Dordogne and Vezère rivers each of the 49 touring pitches is surrounded by variety of flowers, shrubs and trees. Pitches are flat and grassy, mostly on terraces, all with electricity (10A) and most with individual water and drainage as well. At the bottom of the hill, away from the main area, is the swimming pool, a good sized lake for carp fishing, swimming or canoeing (free canoes). From the moment you arrive you can see that the owners, M. and Mme. Berger, take enormous pride in the appearance of their campsite, with an abundance of well tended flowers and shrubs everywhere you look. There are also a few well shaded 'woodland' camping pitches.

Facilities

The clean modern toilet block includes facilties for disabled people. Washing machine. Main reception building houses bar, snack bar (both July/Aug), enlarged terrace overlooking valley. Swimming pool, sun terrace, paddling pool (all season). New play area near the lake and pool. Off site: Small shop, bar, restaurant in Coux-et-Bigaroque 5 km. Supermarket at Le Bugue 10 km. Riding and bicycle hire 5 km. Golf 6 km.

Open: 1 May - 15 October.

Directions

Site is signed down a turning on west side of D703 Le Bugue - Siorac-en-Perigord road, about 3.5 km. north of village of Coux-et-Bigaroque. Turn off D703 and site is 1.5 km. along on right.

Charges 2006

Per person	€ 4,60
child (0-7 yrs)	€ 3,30
pitch	€ 6,20
electricity (10A)	€ 3,00

No credit cards.

24220 Coux et Bigaroque
FRANCE

www.lesvalades.com

FR24410 Camping Caravaning Le Bois du Coderc

Route des Gaunies, F-24420 Antonne et Trigonant (Dordogne)

Tel: **05 53 05 99 83**. Email: **coderc-camping@wanadoo.fr**

Located in the scenic Perigord region, 10 km. from Périgueux, Les Bois du Coderc is a calm, picturesque, part wooded, riverside site, ideally situated for visiting many interesting places. There are 35 touring pitches (there are no individual markedout pitches) and a mobile home spaced out over a field and woodland, with 32 electricity hook-ups (10A) and water points. This campsite has a calm, relaxing atmosphere. However, it is well placed near the historical town of Perigueux which is rich in history and culture and full of charm and character, with cobbled streets, various squares with restaurants, bars and shops. It is a good base for exploring the Perigord region.

Facilities

One male and female sanitary block with pre - set showers (no charge) clean and well maintained (only one toilet and a shower are open in winter). Baby changing area. Dishwashing area. Laundry facilities, small shop. Snacks and takeaway. Bar/games room. Small play area. The river Isle runs through the campsite and is suitable for paddling.

Open: All year.

Directions

Heading north on the N21 Limoges - Perigueux road, 0.5 km. north of Antonne et Trigonant turn right at Routier Restaurant (near km. marker 49). Continue along this country road following signs. Travelling south from Limoges direction turn is on left 3 km. south of Sarliac sur L'Isle.

Charges 2007

Per person	€ 2,50 - € 3,00
child (3-11 yrs)	€ 1,30 - € 1,50
pitch incl. electricity	€ 7,50 - € 10,00

FR24440 Camping les Acacias

Bourg de la Canéda, F-24200 Sarlat-la-Canéda (Dordogne)

Tel: **05 53 31 08 50**. Email: **camping-acacias@wanadoo.fr**

Only 2.5 kilometres from the historic medieval town centre of Sarlat, and yet surrounded by peaceful countryside, this campsite is well suited to those seeking a relaxing and peaceful site within easy reach of the major attractions of the Dordogne. The 110 grassy pitches are mostly flat, divided by hedges or trees, with plenty of shade, and all have electricity (6A). The small but welcoming bar and terrace are the focal point for daily events and entertainment during high season, with activities for both adults and children. A bus service runs six times daily into Sarlat centre.

Facilities

Two toilet blocks provide clean and comfortable showers, washbasins in cabins, British style toilets, facilities for disabled people, baby bath and children's shower, toilet and washbasin. Laundry facilities. Bar serving snacks and takeaway food (May - Sept). Bread to order from reception (no shop, but large supermarket only 1.5 km). Swimming pool and paddling pool (10/5-20/9), with sun loungers and parasols. Football. Play area. Bicycle hire. Canoe excursions arranged. Off site: Supermarket, restaurant, pizza takeaway all 1.5 km. River fishing 3 km.

Open: 1 April - 30 September.

Directions

From Sarlat follow directions for Souillac and Cahors. Pass under an impressive stone railway viaduct, then take the second turn right, signed La Canéda. Follow this road until a small sports field and stadium on your left, bear right here into village of La Canéda. Site is signed about 500 m. along on the right.

Charges 2007

Per unit incl. 2 persons	€ 10,40 - € 13,50
extra person	€ 3,20 - € 4,00
electricity	€ 2,80

FR24450 Camping Maisonneuve

Vallée du Céou, F-24250 Castelnaud la Chapelle (Dordogne)

Tel: **05 53 29 51 29**. Email: **contact@campingmaisonneuve.com**

This family run site is beautifully situated in the Céau Valley, in the Perigord. There are 140 spacious touring pitches, all with 6/10A electricity. Some are well separated whilst others are on an open field. Most pitches have shade. The site's facilities are grouped around the old farmhouse. Swimming, diving, fishing and canoeing are all possible in the Céou river which borders the site and can be accessed directly. There are also swimming and paddling pools on site and in high season entertainment is organised several evenings each week.

Facilities

Three sanitary blocks are kept clean and tidy. Facilities for babies and disabled visitors. Laundry. Shop with bread. Snack bar. Bar. Swimming and paddling pools. Minigolf. Play areas. TV room. Games room. Dance evenings. Karaoke. Sport tournaments.

Open: 31 March - 13 October.

Directions

From A20 take exit 55 on the D703 towards Sarlat and Beynac. Follow signs for D57 (Castelnaud la Chappelle). Site is well signed.

Charges 2006

Per person	€ 3,50 - € 5,10
child (0-5 yrs)	€ 2,45 - € 3,50
pitch incl. electricity (6/10A)	€ 7,35 - € 11,10

285

FR24460 Camping le Temps de Vivre

F-24590 Salignac-Eyvigues (Dordogne)

Tel: 05 53 28 93 21. Email: contact@temps-de-vivre.com

Le Temps de Vivre is situated in the centre of the Périgord Noir, in the countryside and lies about 250 m. above sea level. The area of the campsite covers about 4.5 acres in total, with 1.5 acres in use at present. It is a small, friendly, family run site with 50 pitches, 30 of which are for touring and 20 for mobile homes. The pitches are wide and terraces separate some of them. All have electricity connections available (10A) and you will find a variety of trees and bushes often as a natural separation. This is a delightful and peaceful rural site.

Facilities

One modern unisex sanitary block, very clean, well maintained, serviced, and adequate for the number of pitches. En-suite toilet for disabled visitors. Baby room with bath. Covered laundry area. Small shop all season in the reception area. Small bar, restaurant and takeaway (July/Aug). Two swimming pools (one for children). Boules. Play area. Off site: Shops and restaurants, etc. within walking distance in the nearby village of Salignac-Eyvigues.

Open: 15 April - 15 October.

Directions

From Brive-La-Gaillarde heading south on the A20 continue for 30 km. to exit 55 signed Souillac. Take D62/D15 northwest for 12 km. until Salignac-Eyvigues. As you drive through the town centre look for blue sign for site. Follow the sign off the main road for about 2 km.

Charges 2006

Per unit incl. 1 person	€ 6,00 - € 11,00
extra person	€ 3,00 - € 5,00
child (3-13 yrs)	€ 2,00 - € 3,50
electricity (10A)	€ 3,00

FR24470 Camping les Nauves

Le Bos Rouge, F-24170 Belvès (Dordogne)

Tel: 05 53 29 12 64. Email: campinglesnauves@hotmail.com

Les Nauves is a pretty and well maintained site, 4 km. from the beautiful medieval village of Belvès in the Périgord Noir region of the Dordogne. The site consists of 100 pitches, 59 for touring and 40 dedicated to mobile homes, chalets and bungalow tents. There are some pitches that are separated and shaded by mature trees, while others are open with good views of the surrounding countryside. The ground on most of the pitches is soft, sandy soil and may cause some difficulty for large vehicles in wet weather. The owners are very dedicated to providing a quality site.

Facilities

The single sanitary block is clean and well maintained. Facilities for disabled visitors. Baby room (with adult shower). Laundry area with one washing machine. Good shop. Bar/restaurant with patio, and takeaway on request. Swimming pool and children's paddling pool. Good play area. Boules. Library (French and Dutch books). Games room. Riding. Off site: Fishing 2 km. Golf 10 km. Bicycle hire 4 km.

Open: 29 April - 23 September.

Directions

From Belvès take D53 southwest towards Monpazier. Site is 4 km. from Belvès on the left hand side. Follow signs and site is 800 m. off the main road.

Charges 2006

Per person	€ 3,65 - € 4,60
child (0-7 yrs)	€ 2,20 - € 2,90
pitch	€ 5,10 - € 6,00
electricity (6A)	€ 3,00

FR24480 Camping les Tailladis

Marcillac Saint Quentin, F-24200 Sarlat (Dordogne)

Tel: 05 53 59 10 95. Email: indo@taillabis.com

Les Tailladis is a well situated, mature campsite of some 17 hectares of woodland, owned by the same Dutch and French family for over 42 years. It is about 12 km. from Sarlat, Eyzies and Montignac-Lascauax, and 35 km from Souillac. Four hectares of the total provides medium to large pitches which are grassy, terraced and partially shaded, with electricity (6A), and water points close by. The hosts are welcoming and you will be greeted with a drink and warm, friendly service. Greater emphasis is placed on serving the customer and friendliness than you will find on well managed, tidy pitches.

Facilities

One heated sanitary block is well sited for all pitches. Toilet for disabled visitors. Baby bath and changing area. Laundry room. Motorcaravan service point. Large shop (fresh bread and milk can be ordered). Restaurant, bar with TV. Library. Swimming pool and paddling pool. Play area with trampoline. Activities organised during high season. Internet access (charged for). Off site: Riding 3 km. Bicycle hire 12 km. Golf or boat launching 25 km.

Open: All year.

Directions

From Sarlat-la-Canéda, take D704 heading north. After 10 km, look for signs on the left for Marcillac St Quentin. Take this road heading northwest, and site is less than 3 km. after Marcillac St Quentin on the left hand side. Access and site roads are narrow for large units.

Charges 2006

Per person	€ 3,75 - € 5,00
pitch incl. electricity (6A)	€ 8,28 - € 9,90

FR24490 Camping les Pialades

F-24250 Nabirat (Dordogne)

Tel: **05 53 28 52 28**. Email: **michelsains@aol.com**

Camping Les Pialades is located in a calm and verdant area of the Périgord Noir, just 14 km. from the historic village of Sarlat and 3 km. from the Valley of the Dordogne. Covering 2.5 hectares, the site has 75 pitches – 49 for touring, 26 mobile homes and chalets, and 3 gîtes. Of a good size and mostly shaded, the touring pitches all have electricity and water. Access to the site is via a short single track road with some overhanging trees, and some of the roads around the site are narrow, which may cause difficulties for larger units.

Facilities

One well maintained sanitary block. En-suite toilet for disabled people. Laundry room. Shop. Bar and snack bar with TV. Swimming pool and paddling pool. Play area. Games room. Boules. Minigolf. Three stone barbecues. Off site: Riding 5 km. Canoe and kayak hire 3 km.

Open: 1 June - 15 September.

Directions

From Gourdon take D704 northwest for 8 km. Look for signs to site on the left. Turn left at signs and follow the secondary road for some 3 km. to site. You will pass through Liaubou Bas.

Charges 2006

Per person	€ 3,50 - € 3,80
child (0-7 yrs)	€ 1,80 - € 2,00
pitch	€ 5,00 - € 5,50
electricity (10A)	€ 2,80

FR24510 Camping les Trois Caupain

Le Port, F-24260 Le Bugue (Dordogne)

Tel: **05 53 07 24 60**. Email: **info@camping-bugue.com**

A superb, mature, ex-municipal site, Les 3 Caupain is less than 1 km from Le Bugue, which has a range of supermarkets and tourist attractions. The site carefully blends mobile homes and camping pitches and fruiting plum trees abound on the site. The well marked pitches are neat, level and mostly shaded, with water and electricity hook ups close by. The current owners, the three Caupain family members, will do all they can to make your stay a pleasant one. The campsite is less than fifty metres away from the river. Popular with tourists, Le Bugue is a delightful town where you can get a coffee, beer, quality meal, or just stroll around looking at the sights, including the lovely river La Vézerè. Sarlat-la-Canéda is less than 10 km.

Facilities

Two clean and well maintained sanitary blocks include toilet and shower for disabled people. Excellent dishwashing and laundry room. Baby room with bath. Motorcaravan service point. Small shop selling local produce all season. Bar with pool table and TV. Restaurant with terrace (high season). Swimming pool and paddling pool. Play area. Boules. Fishing. Bicycle hire. Animation and twice weekly entertainment in high season. Off site: Riding 3 km. Golf 8 km. Cash point and three supermarkets in Le Bugue.

Open: 1 April - 30 October.

Directions

From Le Bugue, take D703 heading southeast and site is less than 1 km. from the town centre, well signed. Turn right off the main road and site is less than 800 m. along this road on the left.

Charges 2006

Per unit incl. 2 persons	€ 12,40 - € 16,50
extra person	€ 3,50 - € 4,50
child (2-12 yrs)	€ 1,90 - € 3,20

Camping Les Trois Caupain

Le Port
24260 · LE BUGUE
France

tél: 05 53 07 24 60
fax: 05 53 08 72 66

e-mail: info@camping-buque.com

Check real time availability and at-the-gate prices...

www.**alanrogers**.com

FR24500 Camping les Ombrages

F-24370 Rouffillac (Dordogne)

Tel: **05 53 28 62 17**. Email: **ombrages@peligord.com**

Les Ombrages is a small site situated between the D703 Souillac to Sarlat road, and the Dordogne river. Just around the corner you will find the small village of St Julien-de-Lampon. The site has 80 pitches most of which are used for touring. The pitches are level, adequate in size and have electricity and water. Shade is provided by mature trees, and some pitches are located by the river. The river is suitable for bathing but has a fast current and children will definitely need to be supervised. The road and bridge nearby carry traffic and the noise can be intrusive in some places.

Facilities

Two sanitary blocks are well maintained and clean. Facilities for disabled visitors. Washing machine in each block. Small bar with TV in a converted mobile home which serves a limited range of snacks. Small children's play area. Tennis court. Boules. Fishing. Canoe, kayak, and bicycle hire. Off site: Riding 5 km. Golf 10 km.

Open: 1 April - 31 October.

Directions

Take the D703 from Souillac heading west towards Sarlat. Follow this road for 13 km. until Rouffilac. Site is well signed just before the bridge on the left side.

Charges 2006

Per person	€ 3,30 - € 4,00
child (2-7 yrs)	€ 2,00 - € 2,50
pitch incl. electricity (10A)	€ 7,30 - € 8,00

FR24520 Camping le Perpetuum

F-24250 Domme (Dordogne)

Tel: **05 53 25 35 18**. Email: **luc.parsy@wanadoo.fr**

Located alongside the Dordogne river, this is a small and friendly, family run site. Attractive and mature, the site is in an ideal location where you can make the most of the river and the Périgord region. The French owners are dedicated to providing a comfortable site and are warm and welcoming, particularly to families with young children. The river has two bathing areas, pebble and sand, and there are canoes to hire. Access to the site is narrow, and some of the roads around the site are narrow with overhanging trees, which may cause some difficulties for larger units.

Facilities

Three well maintained sanitary blocks. En-suite toilet for disabled visitors. Toilet, shower, washbasins for children. Baby room. Laundry room. Motorcaravan service point. Well stocked shop available high season with fresh bread and milk. Bar and snack bar with TV (high season). Swimming pool and paddling pool. Two play areas. Covered games area. Canoeing on the river. WiFi internet access (reasonable cost). Animation and entertainment most days (high season). Off site: Sarlat less than 3 km. Golf 2 km. Tennis 2 km. Riding 3 km.

Open: 1 May - 10 October.

Directions

Take D703 to Vitrac. At Vitrac, head south for several hundred metres and take the bridge over the river, onto the D46e. Follow for 1.5 km. until crossroads at the end. Turn right following signs to site. It is less than 1 km from the crossroads on the right side.

Charges 2006

Per person	€ 4,00 - € 5,00
child (0-7 yrs)	€ 2,00 - € 3,00
pitch	€ 4,00 - € 6,00
electricity (10A)	€ 3,00

FR24530 Camping Port Vieux

1 rue de la Paix, F-24700 Montpon Ménestérol (Dordogne)

Tel: **05 53 80 30 98**. Email: **eto.montpon@wanadoo.fr**

Port Vieux was originally a municipal site established over 25 years ago, but for the last two years, it has been managed by the Terre Océane group. There are 120 pitches, of which 115 are used for touring pitches, most with partial shade and separated by well established hedges. Three mobile homes and two bungalow tents are available to rent. The beautiful river Isle runs through the site, which is within walking distance of the town of Montpon Ménestérol with its many amenities. Within walking distance there is a large, tree lined recreational park with a man-made river beach for swimming and paddling.

Facilities

Two sanitary blocks are clean, well maintained and adequate for the number of pitches. En-suite toilet for disabled visitors. Laundry area with washing machine. Bread ordering service, ice-cream and cold drinks vending machine. Bar open in the evening with TV. Small play area. Boules. Fishing. Canoe hire. Off site: Boat hire 0.5 km. Bicycle hire 0.5 km. Lake beach and large play area 0.5 km. Good supermarkets less than 1 km. Riding 10 km. Golf 20 km.

Open: 15 May - 16 September.

Directions

From N89 (Périgueux – Bordeaux) exit 12, head north to Montpon Ménestérol on the D708. Look for signs to site, which is just over the river bridge. Entrance to site is on a sharp steep bend to the right.

Charges 2006

Per unit incl. 2 persons	€ 5,00 - € 9,00
extra person	€ 2,10 - € 3,00
child (2-12 yrs)	€ 1,70 - € 2,50
electricity	€ 3,00

FR24570 Camping La Palombière

Sainte Nathalène, FR24200 Sarlat (Dordogne)

Tel: **05 53 59 42 34**. Email: **lapalombiere@wanadoo.fr**

This is a spacious site, set in a peaceful valley east of the town of Sarlat, with a quiet and tranquil atmosphere. It has 177 well shaded woodland pitches, some fully serviced, delineated by trees and bushes. A large recreation area provides high quality sports facilities and a range of amenities are arranged on a various terraced levels. This is an ideal site for families where children are at an age where they need a wide range of activities, but it nevertheless preserves a relaxed ambience and general tranquility.

Facilities

Two very clean modern toilet blocks include facilities for babies and disabled people. Laundry. Well stocked shop Bar and restaurant complex, with good range of meals. Good sized, heated swimming pool and children's pool. Play area. Boules pitches, small football pitch, tennis and volleyball courts. Minigolf. Bicycle hire. Canoe trips reserved at reception. Sports competitions and evening activities are organised in season, including talent shows, weekly disco, cabaret and even international scrabble! Off site: Fishing 3 km, riding or golf 10 km.

Open: 27 April - 15 September.

Directions

Take D47 east from Sarlat to Ste Nathalène. Site is signed from village and is reached by taking a left turn just beyond it.

Charges 2007

Per person	€ 4,70 - € 7,10
child (1-12 yrs)	free - € 7,10
pitch: simple	€ 6,90 - € 10,10
with services	€ 11,50 - € 14,80
electricity	€ 2.80 - € 3.00

Camping-Résidences-Loisirs

LA PALOMBIERE

Ste. Nathalène - 24200 SARLAT

Tel: 0033 553 59 42 34

Fax: 0033 553 28 45 40

- A free kids club (from 4 to 12 years old)
- Heated swimming pool
- Tennis, mini-golf, volley...
- Grocery shop, bar, snack, restaurant and cooked dishes

E-mail: la.palombiere@wanadoo.fr   Internet: www.lapalombiere.fr

FR24540 Camping le Peyrelevade

Avenue André Maurois, F-24310 Brantôme (Dordogne)

Tel: **05 53 05 75 24**

Le Peyrelevade is a quiet and peaceful site in the Périgord Vert region. Of a very good standard, it comprises 165 spacious and well kept touring pitches and 5 mobile homes. The site is set in an area that is part open, part wooded and most pitches have partial shade from well sited trees and hedges. The beautiful village of Brantôme on an island surrounded by a river, is close by and there you will find small bars, restaurants and other amenities. You can also relax on a river boat trip. This same river runs through the rear of the site and this adds to its charm. There is a 3.5 tonne weight restriction on the main road through the village.

Facilities

Two modern unisex sanitary blocks are clean, well maintained and adequate for the number of pitches. En-suite toilet for disabled visitors. Baby changing area with bath. Laundry facilities. Bread ordering service, ice-cream and cold drinks vending machine. Open air swimming pool. Play area (3-10 yrs). River is suitable for paddling. Fishing. Bicycle hire. Off site: Boat trips.

Open: 1 May - 16 September.

Directions

Take D939 south from Angoulême, or north from Périgueux. Brantôme is around 35 km. north of Périgueux. Drive through town and look for site sign – about·1.5 km. north outside Brantôme. There is a 3.5 tonne weight restriction on main village road.

Charges 2006

Per unit incl. 2 persons	€ 5,00 - € 13,00
extra person	€ 1,90 - € 4,00
electricity	€ 3,00

FR24560 Domaine le Cros Magnon

Allas-les-Mines, F-24220 St Cyprien (Dordogne)

Tel: **05 53 29 13 70**. Email: **contact@domaine-cro-magnon.com**

Le Cro Magnon is pleasantly situated in the heart of the Dordogne valley in the Périgord Noir. The 160 spacious, mostly shady pitches are divided in two different types: tent pitches without electricity and serviced pitches (6A electricity hook up, water and waste water drain). The site also offers various accommodation for rent. The swimming complex includes two pools, one heated, water slides, a jacuzzi and a sauna. Near the entrance of the site are a snack bar, pizzeria, bar, a well stocked shop and the reception. From a viewpoint on the site there are incredible views over the Dordogne valley.

Facilities

Two toilet blocks provide the usual facilities including facilities for disabled visitors. Washing machines. Motorcaravan services. Shop. Bar with TV. Snack bar and takeaway. Swimming pools with slides, jacuzzi and sauna. Multisport court. Boules. Play area. Off site: Canoeing, walking and cycling. Fishing.

Open: 11 May – 30 September.

Directions

From the A20 (Limoges - Brive) take exit 55 for Souillac and Sarlat. In Sarlat take D57 to Vézac, then D703 to St Cyprien. In St Cyprien follow D703, then D50 (left) to Berbiguières and follow signs for site.

Charges 2006

Per person (over 4 yrs)	€ 3,20 - € 6,80
pitch	€ 5,00 - € 10,10
incl. services	€ 8,10 - € 13,60

FR46030 Camping les Pins

F-46350 Payrac-en-Quercy (Lot)

Tel: **05 65 37 96 32**. Email: **info@les-pins-camping.com**

Set amongst four hectares of beautiful pine forest, Camping Les Pins is well situated for exploring the historical and natural splendours of the Dordogne region, as well as being a convenient overnight stop when heading north or south. There are 125 clearly marked, level pitches (100 sq.m), of which 75 are for touring units. The pitches are well marked and separated by small shrubs or hedges. Many have shade from the abundant pine trees and all have 10A electricity connections. There is a bar and a good value restaurant with a terrace overlooking the pool area.

Facilities

Three toilet blocks (heated April and May), well maintained and include washbasins in cabins and good baby bath facilites. Dishwashing and laundry sinks, washing machines and dryer (with plenty of drying lines). Motorcaravan service point. Shop with basics (1/6-31/8). Bar with T.V. Restaurant and takeaway. Heated swimming pool (1/5-15/9). Three water slides and smaller paddling pool. Tennis. Small library. Some entertainment in season, including family discos. Walking routes. English and Dutch spoken. Off site: Fishing 7 km. Riding 10 km.

Open: 8 April - 15 September.

Directions

Site entrance is 16 km. from Souflas on western side of the N20 just south of the village of Payrac-en-Quercy.

Charges 2006

Per person	€ 3,75 - € 6,30
child (under 7 yrs)	€ 1,50 - € 4,20
pitch	€ 5,50 - € 9,00
with electricity	€ 8,50 - € 12,00
Special low season family price.	

FR46010 Castel Camping Domaine de la Paille Basse

Mobile homes ▶ page 477

F-46200 Souillac-sur-Dordogne (Lot)

Tel: 05 65 37 85 48. Email: paille.basse@wanadoo.fr

Set in a rural location some 8 km. from Souillac, this family owned site is easily accessible from the N20 and well placed to take advantage of excursions into the Dordogne. It is part of a large domain of 80 hectares, all available to campers for walks and recreation. The site is quite high up and there are excellent views over the surrounding countryside. The 262 pitches are in two main areas - one is level in cleared woodland with good shade, and the other on grass without shade. Numbered and marked, the pitches are a minimum 100 sq.m. and often considerably more. All have electricity (3/6A) with about 80 fully serviced. The site is well placed to take advantage of excursions into the Dordogne. A wide range of activities and entertainment are organised in high season. The site can get very busy in high season and is popular with three tour operators. If you like a livelier type of site, you will enjoy La Paille Basse.

Facilities

Three main toilet blocks all have modern equipment and are kept very clean. Laundry. Small shop. Restaurant, bar, terrace, takeaway. Crêperie. main swimming pool, a smaller one, paddling pool (unheated), water slides. Sun terrace. Sound-proofed disco (three times weekly in season). TV (with satellite). Cinema below the pool area. Tennis (charged), football, volleyball, table tennis. Play area. Library. Massage. Off site: Golf 4 km.

Open: 15 May - 15 September.

Directions

From Souillac take D15 and then D62 roads leading northwest towards Salignac-Eyvignes and after 6 km. turn right at camp sign and follow steep and narrow approach road for 2 km.

Charges 2007

Per person	€ 5,40 - € 7,00
child (under 7 yrs)	€ 3,80 - € 5,00
pitch	€ 7,80 - € 10,80
incl. water and drainage	€ 9,80 - € 13,00

Camping Cheques accepted.

FR46040 Camping Moulin de Laborde

F-46700 Montcabrier (Lot)

Tel: **05 65 24 62 06**. Email: **moulindelaborde@wanadoo.fr**

Based around a converted 17th century watermill, Moulin de Laborde has been created by the Van Bommel family to provide a tranquil and uncommercialised campsite for the whole family to enjoy. Bordered by woods, hills and a small river, there are 90 flat and grassy pitches, all of at least 100 sq.m. with electricity (6A). A variety of pretty shrubs and trees divide the pitches and provide a moderate amount of shade. A gate at the back of the site leads walkers onto a 'Grand Randonée' footpath which passes through the village of Montcabrier, 1 km. away. A small lake with rafts and rowing boats and an adventure-type play area with rope bridges and 'death slide' will keep children amused, whilst parents can relax in the charming courtyard area which houses the bar and restaurant.

Facilities

Well designed, clean toilet block, unit for disabled people. Washing machine, dryer. Basic shop (all season). Small bar, restaurant, takeaway. Swimming pool, sunbathing area, paddling pool (all season). Play area. Small lake, free rafts and rowing boats. Fishing. Volleyball. Badminton. Boules. Covered recreation area. Table tennis. Mountain bike hire. Rock climbing. Archery. No dogs. Off site: Riding 5 km. Golf 8 km. Tennis nearby and canoeing on the Lot. The Château of Bonaquil 6 km. Fumel 12 km.

Open: 28 April - 8 September.

Directions

Site is on the north side of the D673 Fumel - Gourdon road about 1 km. northeast of the turn to village of Montcabrier.

Charges 2007

Per person	€ 6,00
child (under 7 yrs)	€ 3,30
pitch	€ 8,40
electricity (6A)	€ 2,60

Less 20% outside July/August. No credit cards.

Moulin de Laborde

F-46700 Montcabrier - France - Tél: 05 65 24 62 06 - Fax: 05 63 36 51 33
moulindelaborde@wanadoo.fr - www.moulindelaborde.com

FR46050 Camping le Rêve

F-46300 Le Vigan (Lot)

Tel: **05 65 41 25 20**. Email: **info@campinglereve.com**

Le Rêve is a peaceful site situated in the heart of rolling countryside where the Perigord runs into Quercy. You are assured of a warm reception from the Van Lersels, a Dutch couple who have been providing a friendly and hospitable welcome to their clients for the past 17 years. The 56 flat and grassy touring pitches are all of good size, with access to electricity (6A) and divided by shrubs. A few of the pitches are situated at the edge of the forest and provide plenty of shade.

Facilities

The modern toilet block includes an enclosed area for cooler weather. Washbasins in cabins, special cubicles for disabled people and a baby room. New dishwashing and laundry section. Small shop for basics (bread, milk etc.), pleasant bar, restaurant and takeaway (all open all season). Small, clean, solar heated swimming pool and large paddling pool with 'mushroom' fountain. Play area. Boules. Table tennis and volleyball. Off site: Riding 2 km. Fishing 5 km. Golf 20 km.

Open: 25 April - 15 September.

Directions

From D820 Souillac - Cahors road turn west onto D673 3 km. south of Payrac. After 2 km. site signed down lane on west side of road. Turn here, follow signs, site in 2.5 km.

Charges 2006

Per person	€ 4,20
child (under 7 yrs)	€ 2,60
pitch	€ 6,25
electricity (6A)	€ 2,60

Less 20-30% outside July/Aug. No credit cards.

FR46070 Camping de la Plage

F-46330 Saint Cirq-Lapopie (Lot)

Tel: 05 65 30 29 51. Email: camping-laplage@wanadoo.fr

The site is situated next to the River Lot and is a good base for those who want an active holiday, with many sporting activities available either on site or in the immediate area. It does attract organised groups of young people and can be quite lively at times. The site is a rental base for canoeing and kayaking (lifejackets and all equipment included in hire charge). The campsite has 120 pitches including 109 for touring pitches, all with electricity, a few fully serviced and some hardstandings. Most are on a very slight slope and have good shade from mature trees and bushes.

Facilities

Two practical sanitary blocks, clean and well maintained, both have dishwashing and laundry sinks. Facilites for disabled people. Laundry facilities (charge for). Motorcaravan services (and toilet block, charged for) outside at the rear of site on the river bank. Bar/café at entrance with internet terminal. Play area. Children's room for animation. Canoeing, kayaking and swimming (lifeguard July/Aug). Off site: Riding, rock climbing, caving and canyoning. Bicycle hire 5 km. Riding 9 km.

Open: All year.

Directions

From Cahors take D653 east to Vers, then take D662 for 17 km. to Tour de Faure. Cross river on narrow bridge and site entrance is on right by bar/restaurant. Do not approach via Saint-Cirq-Lapopie.

Charges 2006

Per person	€ 5,00
child (under 7 yrs)	€ 3,00
pitch	€ 4,00 - € 6,00
electricity (6/10A)	€ 3,00 - € 4,00

FR46080 Camping Château de Lacomté

F-46500 Carlucet (Lot)

Tel: 05 65 38 75 46. Email: chateaulacomte@wanadoo.fr

Château de Lacomté is close to Rocamadour, just a 15 minute drive along a back road. A little further on is the Gouffre de Padirac with its underground rivers and concretions. The main camping field is quietly located down a slope to one side of the bar area. The first section contains pitches marked out on slightly sloping ground, most with flat areas, and six with hardstanding. The majority of pitches on this upper terrace have good shade, although most pitches on the extensive lower field are still relatively open. All pitches have electricity, water and drainage.

Facilities

The good, clean toilet block is well equipped and includes laundry facilities. Fridge hire. Small shop (15/6-15/9). Restaurant (with a good reputation). Bar. Large swimming pool (from 1/6) with paddling area. Playground. Tennis court. Table tennis. Torches useful. Off site: Fishing 6-10 km. Close to Gramat and Cahors for supermarkets and other shops.

Open: 15 May - 15 October.

Directions

From A20 take exit 56, at second roundabout take third exit onto D807 direction Gramat. After approx 1.5 km. take D32 direction Rocamadour/Carlucet. After 2.5 km. left fork and follow signs to site. If approaching from Gramat direction (N140, D807) do not turn left at Le Bastit onto D50, but continue for 5 km, and turn left onto D32. The D50 is totally unsuitable for all types of caravan.

Charges 2006

Per person	€ 8,00
child (under 6 yrs)	€ 3,35
pitch incl. electricity	€ 15,00

FR46110 Camping du Port

F-46600 Creysse (Lot)

Tel: 05 65 32 20 82. Email: contact@campingduport.com

Set off the beaten track this small, unassuming riverside campsite provides an unusual combination of peace and tranquillity alongside a range of sporting activities to occupy even the most adventurous of people. Pitches are mostly flat and of a large size, with plenty of shade from the abundant trees, but no dividing hedges or fences. 70 of the 92 touring pitches have electricity (4/6A). The campsite owner runs daily activities including canoeing, caving, climbing, canyoning, cycling, walking and woodland assault course through the trees, all under qualified supervision.

Facilities

Basic, well cleaned toilet block with washbasins (cold water only) both open and in cubicles. Washing machine. Small shop (15/6-15/9). Open air bar, terrace (15/6-15/9), small snack bar/takeaway (July-Aug). Attractive swimming pool, terrace (no paddling pool). Off site: Bar/restaurant in the pretty medieval village of Creysse, about 500 yds.

Open: 1 May - 30 September.

Directions

Site is about 15 km. east of Souillac. From the village of Martel on the D703 take the D23 south to Creysse. The site is signed on the left just before you enter the village.

Charges 2006

Per person	€ 4,00
pitch with electricity	€ 7,00

(293)

FR46170 Campéole les Reflets du Quercy

Mas de Bastide, F-46150 Crayssac (Lot)

Tel: 05 65 30 00 27. Email: cplquercy@atciat.com

Set in the west of the Lot department, about 16 km. from the large town of Cahors, this site is owned by the Campéole group and is classed as a holiday village. Located on a hill with good views of the surrounding countryside, the pitches are hilly and terraced. Most are partially shaded with Quercy oak trees and some are set apart by small Crayssac stone walls. Almost half of the touring pitches are located on good, level hardstanding. At the rear of the site is a large independent mobile home area and residents here also have access to the campsite facilities. The site has a good 25 metre swimming pool overlooked by the terrace of the bar and snack bar. The site is managed by a very friendly French couple and a welcoming Campéole team.

Facilities

Three clean and well maintained sanitary blocks (not all open outside high season). Facilities for disabled visitors. Baby room with bath. Laundry facilities. Motorcaravan service point. Shop (July/Aug). Bar and snacks (July/Aug). Swimming and paddling pool (July/Aug). TV and games room. Boules. Tennis court. Play area with large bouncy castle. Animation in high season. Off site: Fishing and riding 7 km. Bicycle hire 15 km. Good shops 16 km.

Open: 14 April - 24 September.

Directions

From Cahors on the RN20, follow D911 northwest towards Puy-l'évêque, Mercuès and Prayssac. Several kilometres after Labarthe, take D23, on the left near Crayssac. Site is well signed from Crayssac.

Charges 2006

Per unit incl. 2 persons	€ 13,00 - € 18,90
extra person	€ 4,00 - € 6,10
child (2-5 yrs)	free - € 3,90
electricity (10A)	€ 3,90

Mas de Bastide - 46510 - Crayssac (Lot)
Tél.: 05 65 30 00 27
Fax: 05 65 30 01 43
www.camping-lot.info

FR46140 Club de Vacances Duravel

Mobile homes ▶ page 477

Port de Vire, F-46700 Duravel (Lot)

Tel: 05 65 24 65 06. Email: clubduravel@wanadoo.fr

This quality site is beautifully situated on the banks of the Lot River, only 35 km. from the historic town of Cahors. The site has 300 clearly defined, large pitches all with electricity. Some of these are fully serviced with water and drainage, and private sanitary facilities. The reception, bar, restaurant, snack bar and the shop are all located beside the river and from the terrace you can enjoy lovely views over the water. The pool complex offers two large pools (one is heated) with water slides and a children's pool. Duravel is a holiday destination which would suit all ages.

Facilities

Two clean toilet blocks include facilities for disabled people, baby rooms, laundry facilities and chemical disposal points. Serviced pitch facility provides a toilet, shower and sink (with hot water; cleaning charge € 13,50 per stay). Well stocked shop. Restaurant. Bar. Pizzeria and takeaway. Two tennis courts. Multi-sports area. Play area. Fishing. Boat ramp. Wifi access.

Open: 28 April - end September.

Directions

From Paris A10 towards Orleans and A71 towards Vierzon. Follow A20 and take exit 57 to Villeneuve sur Lot. Take the D811 to Cahors, Puy l'Evêque and the D58 to Duravel. Site is well signed.

Charges 2006

Per person	€ 4,30 - € 6,15
pitch	€ 6,85 - € 9,75
with individual sanitary facilitiy	€ 14,75 - € 17,50
electricity	€ 3,50

FR46220 Camping les 3 Sources

Peyratel, F-46190 Calviac/Sousceyrac (Lot)

Tel: 05 65 33 03 01. Email: info@les-trois-sources.com

This rural site is beautifully situated in the hilly surroundings of the Lot region, only 20 km. from the Dordogne river. The site offers 120 well maintained pitches in an attractive, wooded area. There are also 16 chalets and 20 mobile homes for rent. The pitches are numbered and have 6/10A electricity connections and water points within easy reach. Following a fire in 2005 when the site's facilities burned down, and at the time of our visit, the reception and snack bar were housed in chalets on what was the terrace of the restaurant. A new restaurant, shop and reception are promised for 2007. The pool complex with an outdoor pool, a paddling pool and double waterslides is situated at the bottom of the site. A lake provides opportunities for fishing and a trim trail located on an island.

Facilities

Two toilet blocks provide good facilities including washbasins in cabins. Facilities for babies and disabled visitors. Laundry facilities including ironing. Snack bar (to be replaced by new bar and restaurant). Swimming and paddling pools. Games room. Trim trail on island in the lake. Fishing. Play area. Activities and entertainment including children's club. Off site: Riding 15 km. Lake beach 17 km.

Open: 29 April - 17 September.

Directions

From A20 (Chateauroux, Limoges, Brive) follow D8/D20 towards Vayrac and Bretenoux. Do not go through Martel. Follow signs for St Cère and Sousceyrac (D673) and turn left to Calviac after 6 km. (towards Lamativie). After 2 km. site is on right hand side.

Charges 2006

Per unit incl. 2 persons and electricity	€ 5,62 - € 9,57
extra person	€ 1,88 - € 4,13

Camping Caravaning

46190 Calviac

France

fax: +33 (0)5 65 33 03 01

info@les-trois-sources.com

Tel: +33 (0)5 65 33 03 01 - Site internet: www.les-trois-sources.com

FR46150 Camping la Truffière

F-46330 Saint Cirq-Lapopie (Lot)

Tel: 05 65 30 20 22. Email: Contact@camping-truffiere.com

Set in 4 hectares of mature oak woodland, only 2.5 km from the cliff top village of St Cirq-Lapopie, La Truffière is well suited to those seeking a peaceful countryside holiday amongst the stunning natural scenery of the 'Parc naturel régional des Causses de Quercy'. The 90 terraced touring pitches are of varying sizes and on a mixture of grass and gravel (larger units should reserve pitches in advance). All pitches have electricity (6A) and most have shade from the abundant trees. There are various walks and mountain bike trails in the area and you can hire bikes on site.

Facilities

Two well appointed, clean, modern toilet blocks (one heated) include facilities for disabled visitors. Motorcaravan services. Fridge hire. Bar/restaurant (15/5-30/9), terrace overlooking pool and playing field. Snack bar (15/5-30/9). Swimming pool, paddling pool, sun terrace (April – Sept). Small shop (open all season). Playing field, volleyball, basketball, football. Adventure style play area. Table tennis. Trampolines. Boules. English spoken. Off site: Small shop in village, hypermarkets 36 km. in Cahors. Riding 3 km. Fishing (in the River Lot) 3 km.

Open: 1 April - 30 September.

Directions

From D911 Cahors - Rodez road, turn north on D42 at Concots (signed St Cirq-Lapopie). Site about 5 km. on right. Approaching from north on D42 via St Cirq-Lapopie not recommended due to extremely tight left turn in village.

Charges 2006

Per person	€ 5,00
child (0-7 yrs)	€ 3,00
pitch	€ 5,50
electricity	€ 3,00
dog	€ 1,50

Camping Cheques accepted.

FR46200 Camping les Chênes

F-46500 Padirac (Lot)

Tel: **05 65 33 65 54**. Email: **les_chenes@hotmail.com**

Les Chênes is situated in the heart of the Quercy Causses natural regional park and on the route de Gouffre. With a total area of 4.5 hectares, the hilly site is terraced and well shaded with trees and hedges. The 120 touring pitches are of medium size and not all are well levelled. Some larger vehicles may have trouble negotiating the site due to narrow paths and closely planted trees. During the months of July and August, campers have free access to the Padirac Aqua park, just 500 m. from the campsite and under the same ownership.

Facilities

The three sanitary blocks are clean and well maintained. Facilities for disabled people. Baby room with bath. Two washing machines and dryer. Shop. Bar with TV. Restaurant and takeaway. Swimming pool. Boules. Minigolf. Play area. Games room with electronic games. Animation in high season. Off site: Aquatic park 500 m. Fishing 4 km. Riding 10 km.

Open: 15 April - 30 September.

Directions

From A20 exit 54, take N140 southeast to Gramat. Turn onto D807 northeast to Lavergne, then D11 to Thégra and follow signs for Padirac. Follow D90 northwest for 2 km. and the site is on the left.

Charges 2006

Per person	€ 3,80 - € 6,50
child (under 8 yrs)	€ 2,60 - € 4,80
pitch incl. electricity (6A)	€ 7,50 - € 12,00

FR46190 Camping Domaine de la Faurie

F-46240 Séniergues (Lot)

Tel: **05 65 21 14 36**. Email: **contact@camping-lafaurie.com**

A stunning array of tended shrubs and thoughtful flower plantings is spread throughout this very pretty site which is located on a hilltop with wide open views of the surrounding hills and valleys. Although hidden away, it is an excellent base for exploring the Lot and Dordogne regions. The site is separated into two distinct areas, an open, lightly shaded front section and a much more densely shaded area with tall pine trees all around the pitches. The pitches are large and most are at least 100 sq.m. The owners will tell you that they consider the three hectacre site their personal garden.

Facilities

The single sanitary block is clean and well maintained. Facilities for disabled visitors. Washing machine. Motorcaravan service point. Excellent gift shop selling regional wines, pâtés, specialist tinned meats, and local produce (bread available). Bar, restaurant and takeaway. Swimming pool and paddling pool. TV and games rooms. Bicycle hire. Play area. Small library. Weekly soirées in high season. Off site: Fishing 3 km. Golf 8 km. Riding 15 km.

Open: 7 April - 30 September.

Directions

From A20 exit 56, take D2 towards Montfaucon. Site is 5 km further on.

Charges 2006

Per person	€ 4,00 - € 4,80
child (2-10 yrs)	€ 3,00 - € 3,20
pitch	€ 5,50 - € 6,00
electricity (6A)	€ 3,20

kawan-villages.com **tel: 00 333 59 59 03 59**

kawan VILLAGES CAMPING

FR46180 Camping le Ventoulou

Ventoulou, F-46500 Thégra (Lot)

Tel: **05 65 33 67 01**. Email: **contact@leventoulou.com**

Le Ventoulou is a small, well kept and peaceful site on the Périgord 'walnut' route, at the heart of the Quercy Causses natural park. The site is based around an ancient farmhouse located between the quaint villages of Padirac and Thégra. Of just over half a hectare, the site is compact, yet because of careful spacing of pitches does not seem crowded. You will receive a warm welcome from the French owners. During the months of July and August visitors receive free access to the Padirac Aqua park, just 3 km. away. There is a weekly soirée during the high season.

Facilities

One very well equipped sanitary block is clean and well maintained. Good facilities for disabled visitors. Baby room with bath. Laundry facilities. Shop. Bar with TV. Restaurant and takeaway. Swimming pool and paddling pool. Bicycle hire. Boules. Play area with two trampolines. Games room and library. Off site: Fishing and riding 10 km. Golf 15 km.

Open: 3 April - 30 September.

Directions

From A20 south exit 54 follow the N140 southeast to Gramat. Take the D807 northeast to Lavergne, then the D11 to Thégra and look for signs to the site which is less than 2 km.

Charges 2006

Per unit incl. 2 persons	€ 8,75 - € 12,35
extra person	€ 2,80 - € 5,85
electricity (10A)	€ 2,00 - € 4,30

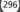

FR46230 Camping des Arcades

Moulin de Saint Martial, F-46800 Saint Pantaléon (Lot)

Tel: **05 65 22 92 27**. Email: **info@des-arcades.com**

Recently taken over by an enthusiastic, young Dutch couple, Camping des Arcades is situated in the hilly surroundings of the Lot Valley. There are 80 level, grass pitches with 6A electricity hook ups. The heated swimming pool is small but provides plenty of fun during hot summer days. Those who enjoy fishing can enjoy lazy afternoons on the banks of the site's lake (the lake is unfenced). The site's facilities such as the reception, the bar and the restaurant are housed in a 13th century watermill. Entertainment and excursions are organised all season. The D653 road runs beside the site, which may cause some nuisance.

Facilities

Two toilet blocks provide good facilities with facilities for disabled visitors in one block. Laundry facilities. Shop for basics in high season (bread available all season). Bar, restaurant and takeaway. Swimming pool. Fishing. Activities and entertainment. Off site: Canoeing, walking, cycling and riding nearby.

Open: 28 April - 30 September.

Directions

From the A20 take the N20 to Cahors. Continue until roundabout (Atrium), then take D653 towards Agen and Montcuq. Site is on left after 10 km.

Charges 2006

Per person (over 4 yrs)	€ 5,00
pitch	€ 7,00 - € 10,00
electricity	€ 3,00
dog	€ 1,50

FR47030 Camping le Château de Fonrives

Rives, F-47210 Villeréal (Lot-et-Garonne)

Tel: **05 53 36 63 38**. Email: **chateau.de.fonrives@wanadoo.fr**

Le Château de Fonrives is situated in Lot-en-Garonne. The site is set in pretty part-farmed, part-wooded countryside. It is a mixture of hazelnut woodland with lake and château (mostly 16th century). An attractive avenue leads to the barns adjacent to the château which have been converted. There are 200 pitches, 96 of which are for touring units, with electricity. Pitches near the woodland receive moderate shade, but elsewhere there is light shade from hedges and young trees. Former barns have been converted to provide a restaurant with covered terrace and bar with an open terrace overlooking the outdoor pool.

Facilities

One sanitary block. Shop. Restaurant, snacks and takeaway. Bar with disco area and terrace. Covered swimming pool (April-Oct), outdoor pool, water slides, paddling pool. Small play area. Small field for volleyball and football. Library. Minigolf Bicycle hire (all charged). Activities organised in season, including excursions and walks. Caravan storage. Off site: Riding 8 km.

Open: 4 May - 14 September.

Directions

Site is about 2 km. northwest of Villeréal, on west side of the D14/D207 Bergerac - Villaréal road.

Charges 2006

Per unit incl. 2 persons	€ 16,00 - € 24,00
extra person	€ 4,00 - € 4,20
child (under 6 yrs)	€ 2,00 - € 2,20
electricity (6A)	€ 4,50

FR47050 Camping Moulin de Campech

F-47160 Villefranche-de-Queyran (Lot-et-Garonne)

Tel: **05 53 88 72 43**. Email: **campech@wanadoo.fr**

This well shaded, pretty site is run by Sue and George Thomas along with Sue's parents, Dot and Bob Dunn. At the entrance to the site, a trout lake with graceful weeping willows feeds under the restored mill house which is home to the owners as well as housing the bar and restaurant. Children will need supervision around the lake and at the pool which is on an elevated area above the mill house. The 60 large-sized pitches are mostly divided by hedges, with electricity (6A, long leads may be necessary in places, but can be borrowed free of charge).

Facilities

The single, rather ordinary toilet block has modern fittings. Washing machine and tumble dryer. Bar, restaurant. Terraced swimming pool. Open grassy games area. Board games and English library. Boules. Barbecue, gourmet nights in high season. Fishing (discounted rate for campers - no permit required). Torch useful. Off site: Watersports, bicycle hire, golf (discounted rate for campers) or riding 10 km. Markets every day in villages and towns around the region.

Open: 1 April - 22 October.

Directions

Take A10 south to Bordeaux. Join A62 for Toulouse and take exit 6 for Damazan. Follow D8 to Mont de Marsan, at Cap du Bosc turn right onto D11 for Casteljaloux. Site is signed, 5 km. on right.

Charges 2007

Per person	€ 3,70 - € 5,45
child (under 7 yrs)	€ 2,80 - € 3,70
pitch	€ 7,30 - € 10,00
electricity (2/6A)	€ 3,80

FR47010 Camping Caravaning Moulin du Périé

Mobile homes ▶ page 478

F-47500 Sauveterre-la-Lemance (Lot-et-Garonne)
Tel: 05 53 40 67 26. Email: **moulinduperie@wanadoo.fr**

Set in a quiet area and surrounded by woodlands this peaceful little site is well away from much of the tourist bustle. It has 125 reasonably sized, grassy pitches, all with 6A electricity, divided by mixed trees and bushes with most having good shade. All are extremely well kept, as indeed is the entire site. The attractive front courtyard is complemented by an equally pleasant terrace at the rear. Two small, clean swimming pools overlook a shallow, spring water lake, ideal for inflatable boats and paddling and bordering the lake, a large grass field is popular for games. The picturesque old mill buildings, adorned with flowers and creepers, now house the bar and restaurant where the food is to be recommended, as is the owner's extensive knowledge of wine that he is pleased to share with visitors. A quiet, friendly site with regular visitors – reservation is advised for July/Aug. Bergerac Airport is an hour away so would suit those choosing a mobile home or bungalow tent and wanting to travel light. A 'Sites et Paysages' member.

Facilities

Two clean, modern and well maintained toilet blocks include facilities for disabled visitors. Motorcaravan services. Fridge, barbecue, chemical toilet hire (book in advance). Basic shop. Bar/reception, restaurant, takeaway. Two small swimming pools (no Bermuda-style shorts). Boules, table tennis, outdoor chess. Playground. Trampoline. Small, indoor play area. Bicycle hire. Organised activities in high season; including canoeing, riding, wine tasting visits, sight seeing trips, barbecues, gastronomic meals. Winter caravan storage. Off site: Fishing 1 km. Small supermarket in village and larger stores in Fumel.

Open: 12 May - 21 September.

Directions

From D710, Fumel - Périgueux, turn southeast into Sauveterre-le-Lemance. Turn left (northeast) at far end on C201 signed campsite, Château Sauveterre and Loubejec. Site is 3 km. on right.

Charges 2006

Per unit incl. 2 persons	€ 12,70 - € 21,20
with electricity	€ 16,50 - € 25,00
extra person	€ 4,10 - € 6,30
child (under 7 yrs)	€ 1,75 - € 3,35
animal	€ 2,10 - € 7,30

Camping Cheques accepted.

kawan-villages.com tel: 00 333 59 59 03 59

FR47100 Camping Municipal Le Robinson

RN 113 Robinson, F-47400 Tonneins (Lot-et-Garonne)

Tel: 05 53 79 02 28

Close to the River Garonne, this small site has a rather formal charm with flower beds, well mown lawns and an extremely well cared for appearance. With a small reception, the Gardien based on site and a security barrier, it only has 32 pitches plus a meadow for additional camping. All with electricity (15A), the pitches are of a reasonable size, separated by small trees providing a little shade. There is some road and rail noise at times. A good stopping off point or base from which to explore the area.

Facilities

Sanitary facilities are roomy but of fairly old design, they are adequate rather than luxurious. Washing machine. No proper chemical disposal point. Ice and cold drinks available. Under cover area with fridge, freezer, tables and chairs. Small play area, sandpit, table tennis. Torch useful. Off site: 1.5 km to Tonneins town centre, with a full range of supermarkets, bars and restaurants.

Open: 1 June - 30 September.

Directions

Take either exit 5 from autoroute to Marmande then the N113 south or exit 6 to Aiguillon (avoid town) and follow N113 north. Site on west side of N113 just south of Tonneins.

Charges 2006

Per pitch incl. 1 person	€ 5,50
incl. 2 persons	€ 8,00
extra person	€ 3,00
electricity	€ 3,50
No credit cards.	

FR47130 Camping des Bastides

Terre Rouge, F-47150 Salles (Lot-et-Garonne)

Tel: 05 53 40 83 09. Email: info@campingdesbastides.com

Attractive and well maintained, this 6.5 hectares is hilly and terraced with good views from the top of the site. Although the terrain is hilly, most of the 90 medium sized touring pitches are fairly level and moderately shaded. The friendly Dutch owners of 11 years are warm and welcoming. Tight turns with narrow gravel paths and overhanging trees may cause some difficulties for larger units. Reception keeps information on a variety of local walking and cycling routes. Weekly trips are arranged to one of the wine growing châteaux in the region.

Facilities

Two modern, clean and well maintained sanitary blocks can be heated. Facilities for disabled visitors. Excellent children's facilities with baby bath and child-size facilities. Private en-suite facilities for hire. Shop. Bar/reception and snack restaurant (and takeaway). Swimming pool complex with slides, and two paddling pools. Play area. Indoor play area with TV and library. WiFi. Animation (high season) including excursions and barbecues. Off site: Fumel 8 km. Fishing 1 km. Riding and bicycle hire 10 km. Golf 25 km.

Open: 1 May - 15 September.

Directions

From Fumel, take D710 north towards Cuzorn. Before reaching Cuzorn, turn northwest on D162 and site is 6 km on the right hand side (well signed).

Charges 2006

Per unit incl. 2 persons and electricity (6A)	€ 16,50 - € 25,00
extra person	€ 4,10 - € 6,30
child (under 7 yrs)	€ 1,75 - € 3,35

FR47120 Camping la Vallée de Gardeleau

F-47410 Sérignac-Péboudou (Lot-et-Garonne)

Tel: 05 53 36 96 96. Email: valleegardeleau@Wanadoo.fr

Camping La Vallée is a delightful, small, family run site established over 12 years ago. It is well hidden and private, some 9 km. from civilization and deep in the countryside of Lot-et-Garonne, very close to the border of the Dordogne and 150 km. from the Atlantic coast. It has a total of 33 pitches, 22 for touring, 7 mobile homes, and 4 bungalow tents. The medium sized pitches are well laid out, all with hedges and some shade, some with views. The owners Pierre and Marie-Madeleine Pécheux are very conscientious and work extremely hard to keep the site clean and well maintained.

Facilities

Two sanitary blocks are well sited and clean. Facilities for disabled visitors. Baby room. Washing machine. Shop with daily deliveries of fresh bread. Bar with snack bar and TV. Restaurant (high season). Swimming pool. Large boules area (need to bring own boules). Small play area. Communal barbecue. Library in reception. Animation for children (high season). Off site: Fishing and riding 2 km. Bicycle hire 9 km. Golf 20 km. Atlantic coast 150 km.

Open: 27 May - 16 September.

Directions

From Castillones on the N21 find the D254 to Sérignac-Péboudou and follow this. Some 10 km along this road, look for signs to site which is on the left hand side.

Charges 2006

Per person	€ 2,50 - € 3,90
child (under 7 yrs)	€ 1,50 - € 2,35
pitch	€ 3,80 - € 6,00

FR47150 Domaine de Guillalmes

Mobile homes ▶ page 478

F-47500 Fumel (Lot-et-Garonne)

Tel: 05 53 71 01 99. Email: info@guillalmes.com

Pitches at Domaine de Guillalmes are exclusively for mobile homes and chalets, although in the near future the site may also provide for touring units.

Domaine de Guillalmes

Nestled on the banks of the River Lot, Domaine de Guillalmes is ideally situated for touring the beautiful Lot et Garonne region of South West France.

Domaine de Guillalmes - Condat - 47500 Fumel - France
info@guillalmes.com - www.guillalmes.com

FR47140 Camping Naturiste Domaine Laborde

Paulhiac, F-47150 Monflanquin (Lot-et-Garonne)

Tel: 05 53 63 14 88. Email: domainelaborde@wanadoo.fr

Ideally situated on the border of Lot et Garonne and Dordogne, Domain Laborde is a naturist site of outstanding quality, with sweeping views from many of the higher pitches. This hilly and terraced site has 120 well maintained touring pitches, many shaded, some partially shaded and all surrounded by woodland. Electricity (6A) is available, although some need long leads. There are also 25 chalets for rent. The site has something for everyone and even in low season it is very popular. If you are new to naturist sites, then this is a must. The ambience is good and you will make new friends.

Facilities

Three sanitary blocks are well sited and clean. Washing machines and dryer. Shop with daily deliveries of fresh bread and milk. Bar with TV. Snack bar serving pizzas. Restaurant. Large swimming pool, whirlpool, children's pool and indoor heated pool. Two play areas. Boules. Giant chess board. Communal stone barbecue. Animation for children (high season). Various excursions and other activities for adults and children are organised. Off site: Riding 2 km, golf 30 km.

Open: 1 April - 1 October.

Directions

From Monflanquin take D272 towards Monpazier. About 10 km. along the road look for the signs to site. It is very well signed at regular intervals and will read 'Laborde FFN'.

Charges 2006

Per person	€ 4,00 - € 5,00
child (under 6 yrs)	€ 4,00
pitch	€ 8,00 - € 10,00
electricity (6A)	€ 3,50

MAP 12

These two quiet and deeply rural provinces are right in the centre of France and are surrounded by the tourist regions of the Loire Valley, the Dordogne and the Auvergne. Unknown to many, it is often 'forgotten territory' but by some it's considered close to paradise.

Limousin & Auvergne

WE HAVE COMBINED TWO OFFICIAL REGIONS: LIMOUSIN WITH DÉPARTEMENTS 19 CORRÈZE, 23 CREUSE, 87 HAUTE-VIENNE; AND AUVERGNE, 03 ALLIER, 15 CANTAL 43 HAUTE-LOIRE, 63 PUY-DE-DÔME. ALSO INCLUDED IS 48 LOZÈRE, PART OF THE OFFICAL REGION OF LANGUEDOC-ROUSSILLON

This is the home of Limoges porcelain and Aubosson tapestry, of exceptional Romanesque and Gothic churches and fairytale Renaissance châteaux. Limousin is an unspoilt, thinly populated region on the western side of the Massif Central. With hills and gorges and lush green meadows, numerous ancient village churches dot the landscape as well as more imposing abbey churches and fortresses. The many lakes and rivers of the Limousin provide endless possibilities for canoeing, sailing, wind-surfing and other watersports. To the south, fortified cities cling to mountain sides, home to many religious events and legends.

The Auvergne, set in the heart of the Massif Central, was formed by a series of volcanic eruptions and is a dramatic region of awe-inspiring non-active volcanoes, lakes, sparkling rivers, green valleys and forests. There are also numerous underground streams that have carved out extensive and fantastic cave systems, for which the region is famous. It is a wonderful destination for nature lovers, those who enjoy active outdoor pursuits or for people who want to relax at spa resorts.

Places of interest

Aubusson: long tradition of tapestry making, Hotel de Ville tapestry collections.

Clermont-Ferrand: old city centre, 11th and 12th century Notre Dame du Port Basilica, 13th century cathedral; known as *ville noire* for its houses built in local black volcanic rock.

Limoges: porcelain, enamel and faience work, château, church of St Michel-de-Lions, cathedral of St Etienne.

Vichy: spa, natural spring park.

Cuisine of the region

Limousin is known for a thick soup called *bréjaude* and its beef, which is extremely tender and full of flavour. Local specialties in the Auvergne include ham and andouille sausages, stuffed cabbage, and bacon with lentil and *cèpes* (mushrooms). Le Puy is famed for its lentils and *Vereine du Velay* – yellow and green liqueurs made from over 30 mountain plants.

Aligot: purée of potatoes with Tomme de Cantal cheese, cream, garlic and butter.

Friand Sanflorin: pork meat and herbs in pastry.

Jambon d'Auvergne: a tasty mountain ham.

Perdrix à l'Auvergnate: partridge stewed in white wine.

Potée Auvergnate: a stew of vegetables, cabbage, pork and sausage.

FR03010 Camping de la Filature

Ile de Nieres, F-03450 Ebreuil (Allier)

Tel: **04 70 90 72 01**. Email: **camping.filature@libertysurf.fr**

Near the spa town of Vichy and beside a fine fly fishing river, this traditional touring and camping site makes a good base to explore the Auvergne including the nearby river gorges, châteaux, mountains and lakes. There are 80 spacious, grassy pitches, most with shade from mature trees and many directly by the river. The river is clean, shallow and pleasant to play in with a deeper swimming area 500 m. away. Most pitches have electricity (3/6A). You will receive a warm welcome from the English owners (the takeaways are good value and very popular). The quiet country roads are ideal for walking and cycling, especially mountain biking and touring by car. Bird watching and rare wild flowers are additional attractions.

Facilities
Very clean sanitary facilities are in individual cubicles. Fully equipped, they include mostly British type toilets, a bathroom and a room for disabled visitors. Laundry facilities. Small shop for essentials (1/5-30/9). Baker calls. Bar (1/6-30/9). Excellent takeaway (1/6-30/9). Barbecues and pizza nights organised in high season. River bathing and fishing. Play area. Bicycle hire. Minigolf. Off site: Riding, canoeing and tennis nearby. Ébreuil with shops and restaurants 1 km.

Open: 31 March - 1 October.

Directions
Site is well signed from exit 12 of A71 autoroute to Clermont Ferrand in the direction of Ébreuil. It is about 6 km. from the A71 and 1 km. west of Ébreuil beside the river on the D915 towards the Chouvigny gorges. GPS: N46:06.526 E03:04.403

Charges 2006

Per unit incl. 2 persons	€ 16,00
extra person	€ 5,00
child (under 16 yrs)	€ 2,50
electricity (3/6A)	€ 2,00 - € 3,00
Discounts in low season.	

Don't wait to die to go to heaven, come to: ★ ★ ★ ★

CAMPING DE LA FILATURE DE LA SIOULE

03450 EBREUIL, FRANCE

See us on website www.campingfilature.com

- Very clean facilities and a bathroom
- Really hot water ● Excellent take away with pizza and barbecue evenings in high season ● Bar and terrace
- Low season bargains for long stays
- Children up to 16 charged child rate
- Near to exit 12 of A71 for stopover or long stay

Tel: 0033 (0)4 70 90 72 01 Fax: 0033 (0)4 70 90 79 48
E-mail: camping.filature@libertysurf.fr

FR03020 Camping Château de Chazeuil

F-03150 Varennes-sur-Allier (Allier)

Tel: **04 70 45 00 10**. Email: **camping-de-chazeuil@ifrance.com**

This spacious site is set in the attractive parkland surrounding a château. Here you will be surrounded by beautiful plants, flowers and bird song (if you are lucky, you will hear the nightingale). The 60 large, marked pitches are laid out on a well maintained lawn and all have electricity (although long leads may be necessary). Mature trees provide some pitches with shade. Although the entrance is adjacent to the main N7, traffic noise should be no problem as the site is set up a long drive. A one-way road system operates to ensure a safe exit from the site.

Facilities
The modern sanitary block provides washbasins and showers in cabins, a washing machine and dishwashing and laundry sinks. It is maintained to a satisfactory level. Very pleasant unheated swimming pool and sunbathing area. Play area. Table tennis. Reading/information room. Off site: Shops, restaurants, etc. in Varennes 2 km. Fishing and canoeing in River Allier 2 km. Marked walks and cycle rides.

Open: 15 April - 15 October.

Directions
Site is 25 km. south of Moulins and just north of Varennes on eastern side of N7. Entrance is at traffic lights at D46 turning for St Pourçain.

Charges 2006

per person	€ 4,95
child (under 7 yrs)	€ 3,00
pitch incl. electricity (6A)	€ 17,90
animal	€ 1,00

FR03030 Camping Beau Rivage

Rue Claude Decloître, Les Berges de L'Allier, F-03700 Bellerive-sur-Allier (Allier)

Tel: 04 70 32 26 85. Email: camping-beaurivage@wanadoo.fr

This well maintained, compact, urban site beside the River Allier is on the outskirts of the famous spa town of Vichy. It has recently been completely refurbished by the enthusiastic new owners (good English and Dutch spoken). Some of the 80 medium sized, reasonably level pitches have delightful views across the river to the beautiful Parc Napoléon beyond. They are separated by flowering shrubs and hedging, and mature trees offer some shade; 10A electricity is available and 12 are fully serviced. Almost 50% of the pitches are occupied by mobile homes and chalets to rent. There are swimming and paddling pools and a separate toboggan. Family entertainment including discos and karaoke finishes at 23.00. Vichy offers a wealth of attractions, spas, theatre, cinema, a racecourse, many sports opportunities and numerous shops, bars and restaurants. There is a simple overspill site adjacent.

Facilities	Directions
Very clean, modern airy sanitary facilities in individual cubicles in pleasantly decorated buildings. Fully equipped, they include mostly British type toilets and a baby room. Washing machine and ironing facilities. Motorcaravan service point. Small bar with snacks (May - Sept). River fishing. Play area. Bicycles and pedalos. Minigolf. Archery. Internet including Wi-fi. Off site: Riding, canoeing and tennis nearby. Very close to the site are several bars and restaurants. Hypermarket complex within 1 km. Vichy 2 km.	Well signed in Bellerive on the west bank of the River Allier. Leave A71 autoroute at exit 12 (Vichy). After about 15 km. turn right at large roundabout with fountains and follow signs, Berges des Allier, Campings and Baurivage (3 km).

Open: 4 April - 30 September.

Charges 2006

Per person	€ 3,50 - € 4,90
child (0-7 yrs)	€ 2,50 - € 3,50
pitch	€ 3,50 - € 5,00
electricity (10A)	€ 3,00

BEAU RIVAGE Airotel
CAMPING★★★★

In the AUVERGNE where you can find volcano's, at 3mn distance from the city centre.
Pitches, chalets and mobil homes
"RIVIERA" for rent situated along the water site.

Great view over the parks of VICHY. Beautiful and peaceful park with lots of shade. Activities all for free: **pedalo, canoeing, swimming-pool, aqua-toboggan.** 03700 BELLERIVE

Web site: www.camping-beaurivage.com   Tel: 0033 (0)470 32 26 85

FR03050 Camping Caravaning la Petite Valette

Sazeret, F-03390 Montmarault (Allier)

Tel: 04 70 07 64 57. Email: la.petite.valette@wanadoo.fr

Originally a working farm, La Petite Valette has been transformed by its hard working Dutch and German owners into a very attractive and peaceful, secluded campsite. There are 55 level grassy pitches of good size, many with rural views, each with an electricity point (6A). They are separated by flowering bushes and trees giving some shade and privacy and many have pleasant, rural views. A small lake in one of the lower fields is stocked with fish for anglers. Ponies and small livestock (rabbits, chickens and ducks) keep the farm feeling alive.

Facilities	Directions
Good toilet facilities in outbuildings. Unit for disabled people, families and babies. Laundry. Bread. Meals, snacks (to order). Takeaway. Small swimming, paddling pools, sunbathing areas. Play area with seating. Table tennis, mountain bike hire, organised activities in July/Aug. Off site: Tennis, riding and sailing in the area. Small town of Montmarault 6 km. for shopping needs.	Leave A71 exit 11. First roundabout take D46 signed St Pourcain. Turn left at next roundabout onto D945 signed Deux-Chaises and La Valette. After 2.5 km. turn left at site sign, follow lanes to site (just under 2 km). GPS: N46:32.568 E02:59.581

Open: 1 April - 30 October.

Charges 2006

Per person	€ 3,95 - € 4,95
child (0-8 yrs)	€ 2,90 - € 3,85
pitch	€ 6,05 - € 7,50
electricity (6A)	€ 2,85
For one night stay 1/7-31/8, plus 10%.	

FR03170 Camping Municipal
F-03290 Dompierre-sur-Besbre (Allier)

Tel: **04 70 34 55 57**

This immaculate and attractive site has 68 level, partly shaded, individually hedged, grassy pitches, all with easy access. It is located next to the municipal sports fields and is ideal for motorcaravans being within easy walking distance of the town centre and supermarket (700 m). There are 70 pitches, some very large, with only a few long stay units, leaving about 65 for tourists; 60 have electricity (10A) and most have full service facilities. The warden is very proud of his efficiently run, value for money site and its award-winning floral displays.

Facilities

Modernised, heated toilet blocks, very clean with all necessary facilities including provision for disabled visitors. Some washbasins in curtained cubicles for ladies. Washing machine. Excellent Motorcaravan services. Off site: The small town has shops, restaurants, Saturday market. Vallée de la Besbre has a wealth of activities, several rivers and small lakes nearby for fishing. Cycle tracks, footpaths, equestrian centres. Le Pal theme park and zoo 8 km.

Open: 15 May - 15 September.

Directions

Dompierre is 35 km. east of Moulins. Leave N79 at eastern end of Dompierre bypass, turn southwest on N2079 towards town. Entrance to sports complex and campsite is on left beyond D55 before the river bridge and town centre. GPS: N46:31.052 E03:41.24

Charges 2006

Per person	€ 2,00
child (5-14 yrs)	€ 1,10
pitch	€ 1,70 - € 2,00
electricity	€ 1,80

FR15050 Camping La Siauve
FR15270 Lanobre (Cantal)

Tel: **04 72 40 31 85**. Email: **contact@village-center.com**

This campsite has been recommended by our French agent and we intend to undertake a full inspection in 2007. La Siauve enjoys a fine location between the Auvergne and the Limousin and is a good choice for those wishing to explore this lesser known part of France.

Facilities

Snack barand pizzeria. Multisports field. Playground. TV room. Mountain bike hire. Laundry room. Off site: Swimming lake, pedalos 300 m. Tennis 2 km. Fishing 3 km. Boat and surfboard hire 4 km.

Open: 16 June - 15 September.

Directions

Site is located south of Lanobre. Take the D922 (Bort-les-Orgues-Clermont-Ferrand) and the site is well signed from Lanobre.

Charges 2007

Per unit incl 2 persons and electricity	€ 7,00 - € 14,00
extra person	€ 1,50 - € 3,25
child (under 7 yrs)	€ 1,30 - € 2,75

FR15030 Camping Caravaning le Val Saint Jean

F-15200 Mauriac (Cantal)

Tel: 04 71 67 31 13. Email: info@camping-massifcentral.com

La Val Saint-Jean is set beside a lake in the heart of the département of Cantal. The campsite has 100 generously sized, slightly sloping, touring pitches (with 10A electricity), many with good views. It is organised for the maximum of privacy and you are never far from a sanitary block. Most of the activities are situated by the lake where you can use all the facilities of the leisure club (high season) including cycling, canoeing, kayaking and pedaloes. This less well known region is well worth exploring and the local gastronomy can be experienced in the village of Mauriac with its attractive architecture typical of the area. Salers, one of the most beautiful French towns is 20 km.

Facilities

The two toilet blocks are well equipped with hot water throughout, providing some washbasins in cabins, dishwashing sinks and a laundry room. Facilities for people with disabilities. Limited shop. Bar, snack bar and restaurant (all May - Sept). Play area, playing field and table tennis. Activities organised for children in July/Aug. Off site: Sandy beach. Lake fishing and swimming. Swimming pool (1/6-15/9). Golf course. Guided walks. Mauriac village 1.6 km. Riding 3 km.

Open: 1 May - 18 September.

Directions

Mauriac is around 120 km. south west of Clermont-Ferrand. Leave A89 autoroute at junction 23 (Ussel West), take D979 (Bort-les-Orgues) for 5 km. Turn right onto D982 (Mauriac) for 40 km. Follow site signs in town. GPS: N45:13.120 E02:18.953

Charges 2006

Per unit incl. 2 persons	€ 11,00 - € 18,50
extra person	€ 4,30 - € 5,30
child (2-7 yrs)	free - € 3,20
electricity (10A)	€ 3,50

FR19020 Camping les Aubazines

F-19110 Bort les Orgues (Corrèze)

Tel: 05 55 96 08 38. Email: email.lesaubaz@aol.com

Owned by a group of several communes, this very spacious site is set out on wide terraces over looking a lake on the River Dordogne, although a short distance from it. Wide but steep site roads give good access to the 113 pitches. Slightly sloping, the grassy pitches (77 for touring) are mostly separated by flowering shrubs and hedging with some shade provided by trees. Most pitches have 10A electricity and a few have drains. This site is not suitable for those with walking difficulties as access to the facilities will often involve a long and steep climb. The owners are trying to keep this a quiet and relaxing site.

Facilities

Three clean modern toilet blocks have all the necessary facilities but access to them is not easy (see above). Bread (July/Aug). Large bar/restaurant (all season) between entrance and lakeside beach. Games/TV room. Play area. Tennis. Boules. Family activities and excursions (July/Aug). Off site: Lakeside beach adjacent to site with large play area and pedaloes and canoes for hire (July/Aug). Boat ramp. Bort-les-Orgues with a good range of shops, bars, restaurants, large swimming pool and magnificent rock formations 4 km.

Open: 17 June - 10 September.

Directions

Bort-les-Orgues is 80 km. southwest of Clermont Ferrand. Leave A89 at exit 23, signed Ussel West. Take D979 signed Bort-les-Orgues for 25 km. Site is on the left 4 km. before the town. GPS: N45:24.964 E02:28.818

Charges 2006

Per unit incl. 2 persons	€ 7,00 - € 13,50
extra person	€ 2,80
child (2-10 yrs)	free - € 1,50
electricity (10A)	€ 2,60

FR19050 Camping la Rivière

Route du Camping Louis Madrias, F-19270 Donzenac (Corrèze)

Tel: **05 55 85 63 95.** Email: **mairie-donzenac@wanadoo.fr**

The Corrèze is less well known than the Dordogne to the immediate south, but it is a beautiful area deserving more attention. Donzenac is an attractive small town with a variety of shops, restaurants, etc. This former municipal site is situated on the outskirts, just under a mile from the centre (an uphill walk). The site is small and neat with 77 fairly large pitches on level grass, the majority with electricity (10A). A variety of trees and shrubs give some shade. The site is next door to the town tennis courts and swimming pool (July/Aug, free to campers).

Facilities

Modernised sanitary facilities are very good and include a laundry room with washing machine and microwave. Baker calls at site in July/Aug. Table tennis, boules and minigolf. Fishing. Double axle caravans are not accepted. Off site: Riding 4 km. Golf 10 km.

Open: 1 June - 30 September.

Directions

At roundabout at southern end of Donzenac (D920) turn southwest onto D170 signed Ussac and La Rivière. Entrance to site is shortly on the right. GPS: N45:13.126 E01:31.122

Charges 2006

Per person	€ 4,20 - € 4,60
child (4-14 yrs)	€ 2,20 - € 2,60
pitch incl. electricity (10A)	€ 7,50

FR19060 Castel Camping Domaine de Mialaret

Route d'Egletons, F-19160 Neuvic (Corrèze)

Tel: **05 55 46 02 50.** Email: **info@lemialaret.com**

Mialaret is 4 km. from the village of Neuvic and only 6 km. from the Dordogne river. It is set in the grounds of a 19th century château, now a hotel and restaurant with a good reputation for fresh lobster and with a special evening menu for campers. Most pitches are set in a sunny, gently sloping meadow type situation. Some are level and separated by small bushes, most have some shade and 6A electricity. Entertainment in high season is quite low key with a mini club, some games, tournaments or an evening sing-along around a campfire, also musical evenings.

Facilities

Refurbished sanitary blocks give an adequate provision, one heated, facilities for disabled people, washing machines. Motorcaravan services. Shop with bread. Bar, snacks, takeaway. Dinner at hotel. Play areas. Tennis. Table tennis. Fishing. Volleyball, football. Bicycle hire. The original swimming pool is an example of art-deco design. No paddling pool but a new swimming pool is planned. Off site: Village with shops and lake 4 km. Golf 4 km. Canoeing, cycling and riding trips organised.

Open: 1 May - 31 October.

Directions

From Clermont-Ferrand take N89 or A89 southwest, at Ussel, take D962 to Neuvic. In Neuvic take D982 signed Egletons. Turn right (D991) signed Egletons and La Mialaret. Site in 4 km. D991 Egletons - Neuvic road is only suitable for small units.

Charges 2006

Per person	€ 5,50 - € 6,50
child (2-8 yrs)	free - € 3,00
pitch incl. electricity	€ 8,50 - € 11,00
Camping Cheques accepted.	

FR19070 Camping Château de Gibanel

Saint Martial Entrayguis, F-19400 Argentat (Corrèze)

Tel: **05 55 28 10 11.** Email: **contact@camping-gibanel.com**

This slightly terraced campsite is located in a beautiful estate, dominated by the 16th century château, on the banks of a very clean lake in this lesser known part of the Dordogne valley. The very friendly family ensures that everything is of a very high standard. Nearly all of the 250 grassy pitches are used for touring units. All have electricity (6A) and are separated by a variety of mature trees giving varying amounts of shade. Many of the trees have low branches making access to most pitches rather difficult for large motorcaravans.

Facilities

Four modern, spacious and very clean toilet blocks include many large cubicles with a shower and washbasin. Good provision for disabled visitors. Washing machine and dryer. Good shop for basics. Bar, restaurant and takeaway (July/Aug). Swimming and paddling pools. Range of family activities in July/Aug, including dance evenings, folklore events, watersports, walking and cycling. Bicycle hire (July/Aug). TV room. Table tennis. Boules. Volleyball. Off site: Argentat 5 km.

Open: 1 June - 9 September.

Directions

Site is 5 km. northeast of Argentat. Take D18, signed Eggletons, and after 4 km. alongside the lake, fork right at site sign. Follow lane down to site. GPS: N45:06.650 E01:57.536

Charges 2006

Per person	€ 3,88 - € 4,85
child (2-7 yrs)	€ 1,96 - € 2,45
pitch	€ 4,68 - € 5,85
electricity	€ 3,10
dog	€ 1,20 - € 1,50

FR19080 Camping le Vianon

F-19160 Palisse (Corrèze)

Tel: 05 55 95 87 22. Email: camping.vianon@wanadoo.fr

You will receive a very warm welcome from the Dutch owners of this spacious and peaceful site and they speak excellent English. The site is tucked away in the lesser known, very beautiful Corrèze region yet it is only a few kilometres from the river Dordogne. This region is reputed to have the purest air in France. The grassy, slightly sloping pitches are of a good size in a natural woodland setting with tall trees offering shade and all have 6A electricity. The bar, restaurant and terrace overlook the swimming pool and sunbathing area and are open all season.

Facilities

Modern toilet blocks with all the necessary facilities. Unit for disabled visitors. Bar. Restaurant, takeaway. Shop. Boules. Table tennis. Volleyball. Spacious play area. Bicycle hire. Lake fishing. Off site: Small town Neuvic (9 km) with shops, restaurants. Large lake with water sports, swimming. Canoeing in the Dordogne (30 minutes). Riding and golf course at Neuvic. Marked walks and cycle rides.

Open: 12 April - 12 October.

Directions

Leave A89 southwest of Ussel and take N89 towards Egletons. In about 7 km, just before Combressol, turn left on D47 signed Palisse and Camping le Vianon. Site entrance is on the left in 7 km. GPS: N45:25.607 E02:12.350

Charges 2006

Per person	€ 4,50 - € 6,10
child (3-9 yrs)	free - € 3,90
pitch	€ 5,00 - € 7,50
electricity (6A)	€ 3,50

FR19090 Camping le Vaurette

Monceaux-sur-Dordogne, F-19400 Argentat (Corrèze)

Tel: 05 55 28 09 67. Email: info@vaurette.com

You are assured of a warm welcome at this immaculate site, beautifully situated beside the shallow river Dordogne and just a few kilometers from Argentat. There are 120 large, gently sloping grass pitches, 118 for touring. Separated by a large variety of beautiful trees and shrubs offering varying amounts of shade, all have 6A electricity and many have good views over the river Dordogne as the pitches nearest the river are slightly terraced. The owners run an active campsite for all the family whilst maintaining an air of tranquillity (no radios). Excellent English and Dutch is spoken. The ancient barn at the far end of the site houses the bar and a large TV room (large screen) and the terrace overlooks the good sized and attractive, but unheated, swimming and paddling pools (all season).

Facilities

Two very clean traditional toilet blocks offer all the expected facilities, including facilities for disabled people. Further facilities are near the bar and pool. Motorcaravan service point. Shop and takeaway (July/Aug). Football. Volleyball. Badminton. Boules. Table tennis. Tennis. Fishing. River bathing. Accompanied canoe trips, walks and mountain bike rides. Organised activities for all the family (July and Aug) but no late night discos etc. Off site: Argentat (9 km.) with shops and watersports centre. Riding 15 km.

Open: 1 May - 21 September.

Directions

Leave Argentat on the D12 heading southwest, signed Beaulieu. Site is 9 km. on the left. GPS: N45:02.739 E01:53.058

Charges 2006

Per unit incl. 2 persons	€ 14,00 - € 20,00
extra person (over 2 yrs)	€ 3,10 - € 4,80
electricity (6A)	€ 3,10
dog	€ 1,50 - € 3,00

Camping ★★★★ *Le Vaurette*

Vallée de la Dordogne
19400 Argentat

Tél. +33 5 55 28 09 67   Fax +33 5 55 28 81 14   www.vaurette.com

307

FR19100 Sunêlia Au Soleil d'Oc

Monceaux-sur-Dordogne, F-19400 Argentat (Corrèze)

Tel: **05 55 28 84 84**. Email: **info@dordogne-soleil.com**

You will be assured of a very warm welcome throughout the long season at this attractive family run site set amongst a variety of tall trees on the banks of the river Dordogne. The 120 large, level, grass pitches, 80 for tourists, all with 6A electricity, are mostly separated by neatly trimmed shrubs and hedges. They are set out on two levels; the lower level nearer the river, with fewer static pitches, being some distance from the toilet facilities and sports area. It is not recommended for very large outfits due to the narrow, winding site roads and hedges. The shop, bar, restaurant and swimming pools are near the entrance and just across the little road is the large sports area. This site should appeal to lovers of water and other sports, particularly in July and August when there are many activities for all the family.This region is famous for its prehistoric caves, castles and ancient villages and their markets.

Facilities

Two unisex toilet blocks offer all the facilities one would expect. Baby facilities. Shop. Bar. Restaurant and takeaway (1/6-30/9). Outdoor pool (1/5-15/10). New indoor pool planned for 2007. Motorcaravan service point. Bathing in the river Dordogne. Canoe hire and organised trips. Volleyball, football, table tennis, pool table and electronic games. Archery. Minigolf. Fishing. Bicycle hire. Guided walks and bike rides. Entertainment programme (July/Aug). Wi-fi. Off site: River Dordogne. Argentat 4 km. Riding 15 km.

Open: 31 March - 15 November.

Directions

Leave Argentat on D12 heading southwest (Beaulieu). In 3.5 km. turn left across a single track bridge spanning the river Dordogne. Immediately turn left and site is a few hundred metres on left. GPS: N45:04.514 E01:55.025

Charges 2006

Per unit incl. 2 persons	€ 12,50 - € 19,80
extra person	€ 3,00 - € 5,80
child (2-13 yrs)	free - € 3,90
dog	free - € 2,00
electricity (6A)	€ 3,50 - € 5,00

Camping Cheques accepted.

Sunêlia Au Soleil d'Oc★★★★

Sun, Nature, Patrimony, Activities.

Our ingredients for a lovely holiday at the borders of the Dordogne River.

Open from 1st of April - 1st of November

Sunêlia Au Soleil d'Oc - 19400 Argentat - tél. +33 (0) 555 28 84 84
info@dordogne-soleil.com - www.dordogne-soleil.com

Camping Cheque

Camping Qualité

FR23030 Creuse Nature

Route de Bétête D15, rue Jean Galein, F-23600 Boussac (Creuse)

Tel: **05 55 65 18 01**. Email: **creuse.nature@wanadoo.fr**

This is a very spacious and well maintained naturist site set in the beautiful Limousin region in the centre of France. The 100 large grassy pitches, some slightly sloping, are laid out in an open wooded parkland setting. The 80 touring pitches all have electricity (10A) and are mainly positioned around the perimeter of the site or the small fishing lake. A central feature is the swimming pool, bar and restaurant complex. Various activities are organised for all the family and there are many footpaths to enjoy around the borders of the site.

Facilities

Four modern, very clean toilet blocks with the usual facilities (open-plan, so little privacy). Facilities for disabled visitors. Dishwashing and laundry facilities. Small shop (baker calls). Indoor (heated) and outdoor pools. Paddling pool. Sauna. Bar (all season). Restaurant (July/Aug). Archery (high season). Volleyball. Boules. Bicycle hire. Lake fishing. Internet access. Gas barbecues only on pitches. Off site: Boussac 5 km. Other towns, villages and châteaux.

Open: 1 April - 31 October.

Directions

Boussac lies 35 km. west of Montluçon, midway between the A20 and A71 autoroutes. In Boussac, site is well signed. Take D15 west for about 3 km. Site is on right.

Charges 2006

Per person	€ 3,50 - € 5,50
child (0-11 yrs)	free - € 3,50
pitch	€ 9,00 - € 11,00
electricity (10A)	€ 3,50

Route de la Châtre, B.P.12, F-23600 Boussac-Bourg (Creuse)

Tel: 05 55 65 02 21. Email: **info.camping-de.poinsouze@wanadoo.fr**

Le Château de Poinsouze is a well established site with pitches arranged on the open, gently sloping, grassy park to one side of the Château's main drive – a beautiful plane tree avenue. It is a well designed, high quality site. The 150 touring pitches, some with lake frontage, all have electricity (6-25A), water, drain and 66 have sewage connections. The site has a friendly family atmosphere, there are organised activities in main season including dances, children's games and crafts, family triathlons and there are marked walks around the park and woods. All facilities are open all season. This is a top class site with a formula which should ensure a stress-free, enjoyable family holiday. Boussac (2.5 km) has a market every Thursday morning. The massive 12/15th century fortress, Château de Boussac, is open daily all year. The Château (not open to the public) lies across the lake from the site. Exceptionally well restored outbuildings on the opposite side of the drive house a new restaurant serving superb cuisine, other facilities and the pool area.

Facilities	Directions
High quality, sanitary unit, washing machines, dryer, ironing, suites for disabled people. Motorcaravan services. Well stocked shop. Takeaway. Bar, internet, two satellite TVs. Library. Restaurant with new mini-bar for low season. Heated swimming pool, slide, children's pool. Fenced playground. Table tennis, petanque, pool table, table football. Bicycle hire. Free fishing in the lake, boats and lifejackets can be hired. Football, volleyball, basketball, badminton and other games. No dogs (7/7-21/8).	Site entrance is 2.5 km. north of Boussac on D917 (towards La Châtre). GPS: N46:22.356 E02:12.157

Open: 12 May - 15 September.

Charges 2006

Per pitch incl. 2 persons	€ 13,00 - € 22,00
with 6A electricity, water, drain	€ 18,00 - € 27,00
10A electricity, water, drain, and sewage connection	€ 24,00 - € 29,00
extra person	€ 3,00 - € 5,50

Camping Cheques accepted.

FR43030 Camping du Vaubarlet

Vaubarlet, F-43600 Sainte-Sigolène (Haute-Loire)

Tel: 04 71 66 64 95. Email: camping@vaubarlet.com

This peacefully located, spacious riverside family site has 131 marked, level, grassy, open pitches, with those around the perimeter having shade, all having electricity (6A). With 102 pitches for tourists, the remainder are occupied by site owned tents or mobile homes. Those who really like to get away from it all can use a small 'wild camping' area on the opposite side of the river with its own very basic facilities. This area is reached either by footbridge or a separate road access. The main site is separated from the river (unfenced) by a large field used for sports activities.

Facilities	Directions
Good, clean toilet blocks, baby room, washing machine, dryer. Two family bathrooms are also suitable for disabled people. Small shop, bread. Takeaway, bar (all season). Attractive swimming pool, children's pool. Bicycle hire. Boules, volleyball and games area. Playground. Activities in season. Fishing. Birdwatching. Off site: Ste Sigolène 6 km. Riding 15 km. Walks and cycle tracks from site. **Open:** 1 May - 30 September.	Site is 6 km. southwest of Ste Sigolène on the D43 signed Grazac. Keep left by river bridge, site signed. Site shortly on right. GPS: N45:12.936 E04:12.766

Charges 2006

Per unit incl. 2 persons	€ 17,00
extra person	€ 3,00
electricity	€ 3,00
Camping Cheques accepted.	

kawan-villages.com tel: 00 333 59 59 03 59 *kawar*

FR48000 Camping Caravaning le Champ d'Ayres

Route de la Brèze, F-48150 Meyrueis (Lozère)

Tel: 04 66 45 60 51. Email: campinglechampdayres@wanadoo.fr

This is a traditional family run site, set in the heart of the Cevennes Champ d'Ayres. Neat, tidy and well kept, it is run with young families in mind (teenagers might be bored). The site is slightly sloping with 85 grass pitches, 68 for touring, the majority hedged with well trimmed bushes and most with some shade. All have electricity (6/10A) but some may require long leads. The area is surrounded by mountains and gorges and some of the roads are not for those with large and under-powered units.

Facilities	Directions
The excellent toilet block is kept very clean and has all the necessary facilities. Baby room. Facilities for disabled visitors. Small bar (15/6-15/9). Shop (15/5-15/9). Takeaway (20/5-15/9). New swimming and paddling pool (20/5-15/9). Play area. Games room. Off site: Meyrueis 500 m. Fishing 100 m. Bicycle hire 500 m. Riding 3 km. **Open:** 8 April - 23 September.	From N9 at Aquessac (5 km. north of Millau) take D907 (Gorge du Tarn). At Rozier turn right on D996 (Meyrueis). Site is 500 m east of town. GPS: N44:10.860 E03:26.135

Charges 2006

Per unit incl. 2 persons	€ 12,00 - € 18,00
electricity (6A)	€ 3,00

FR48020 Camping de Capelan

F-48150 Meyrueis (Lozère)

Tel: 04 66 45 60 50. Email: camping.le.capelan@wanadoo.fr

The Lozère is one of France's least populated départements but offers some truly spectacular, rugged scenery, wonderful flora and fauna and old towns and villages. Meyrueis is accessible from the campsite via a riverside walk, marking the start of the Gorges de la Jonte, with the better known Gorges du Tarn running a little to the north. Le Capelan is a friendly family site with English and Dutch spoken. It has 120 grassy pitches strung out alongside the river, most with some shade and all with electrical connections (6/10A). The site has direct river access and trout fishing is popular.

Facilities	Directions
Well maintained toilet blocks, facilities for disabled visitors. Three bathrooms for rent. Small shop (from 1/6). Bar (from 1/6), satellite TV, internet, pool table. Takeaway (from 1/7). Swimming, paddling pools, sunbathing terrace (from 1/6), access via 50 steps. Multi-sports terrain. Play area. Leisure activities including supervised rock climbing. Fishing. Communal barbecue area, only gas and electric barbecues. Off site: Town centre 1 km. Bicycle hire 1 km. Riding 3 km. Canoeing. Cévennes national park. Caves. **Open:** 29 April - 16 September.	From Clermont Ferrand on the A75 take exit 44-1 Aguessac-le Rozier towards Meyrueis. The site is 1 km. west of Meyruels on the D996, the road to La Jonte. It is well signed from the centre of the town. GPS: N44:11.150 E03:25.193

Charges 2007

Per unit incl. 2 persons and electricity	€ 13,00 - € 19,00
extra person	€ 3,00 - € 4,10
Camping Cheques accepted.	

kawan-villages.com tel: 00 333 59 59 03 59 *kawa*

FR48060 Camping les Terrasses du Lac de Naussac

Lac de Naussac, F-48300 Langogne (Lozère)

Tel: **04 66 69 29 62**. Email: **naussac@club-internet.fr**

With friendly, family owners, this spacious campsite and hotel complex is on the side of a steep hill at nearly 1,000 m. altitude (nights can be cold). There are 180 good size, grassy, sloping pitches, often with part hardstanding (165 for touring). All have 6A electricity and many have panoramic views over the lake and surrounding hills. There are small trees on site offering some shade on a few pitches. There is a small pool and various other leisure amenities, with plenty of room for children to play, although the facilities are widely spaced around this hilly site.

Facilities

Three modern and well maintained toilet blocks. Small shop (1/5-30/9). Restaurant (1/4-30/9). Small swimming pool (1/6-30/9). Lively 'animation' programme in peak season including children's club but no discos. Play area. Communal barbecue area. Bicycle hire. Gas and electric barbecues only. Off site: Disco 300 m. All kinds of water sports with equipment for hire on lake. Bike ride around lake of 30 km. Langogne (shops, restaurants, Stevenson trail etc.) 2 km. 9 hole golf course 3 km. Riding 3 km.

Open: 15 April - 30 September.

Directions

Leave N88 (Le Puy - Mende) road southwest of Langogne. Turn on D26 towards Lac de Naussac, pass by Naussac and follow signs to site. Stop in parking area beside lake and just before hotel. Reception inside hotel. GPS: N44:44.042 E03:50.130

Charges 2006

Per pitch incl. 2 persons	€ 12,50 - € 13,50
extra person	€ 3,50
child (2-6 yrs)	€ 1,50
electricity	€ 2,50
dog	€ 1,00

Camping Cheques accepted.

FR87020 Castel Camping le Château de Leychoisier

1 route de Leychoisier, F-87270 Bonnac-la-Côte (Haute-Vienne)

Tel: **05 55 39 93 43**. Email: **contact@leychoisier.com**

You will receive a warm welcome at this beautiful, family run 15th century château site. It offers peace and quiet in superb surroundings. It is ideally situated for short or long stays being only 2 km. from the A20/N20 and 10 km. north of Limoges. The large, slightly sloping and grassy pitches are in a parkland setting with many magnificent mature trees offering a fair amount of shade. Of the 90 pitches, 85 are for touring, 80 have 10A electricity and many have a tap, although long leads and hoses may be necessary. Explore the grounds and walk down to the four hectare lake. The lake provides free fishing, boating, canoeing and a marked off area for swimming.

Facilities

The toilet block is very clean, but perhaps cramped at busy times. Some washbasins in cabins with good provision for disabled visitors. Washing machine. Basic food provisions. Restaurant (from 10/5). Bar, TV room and snack bar. Small swimming pool with sunbathing area (proper trunks, no shorts). Lake. Play area. Bicycle hire. Tennis and boules courts (in need of repair when we visited), volleyball and bar billiards. Torch useful. Off site: Mini-market 2 km. Supermarket 5 km. Riding 7 km. Golf 20 km.

Open: 15 April - 20 September.

Directions

From A20, north of Limoges, take exit 27 (west) signed Bonnac-La-Côte. In village turn left and follow signs to site. GPS: N45:55.958 E01:17.404

Charges 2006

Per person	€ 6,00 - € 7,00
child (under 7 yrs)	€ 4,00 - € 4,80
pitch	€ 8,00 - € 9,00
electricity	€ 4,00
dog	€ 0,80

No credit cards.

FR63020 Camping Municipal Saint Eloy

F-63630 Saint Germain l'Herm (Puy-de-Dôme)

Tel: **04 73 72 05 13**. Email: **info@camping-massifcentral.com**

This spacious and attractive municipal site is set on two terraces overlooking the nearby village of Saint Germain. There are 84 good sized, slightly sloping, grassy pitches, 63 for touring. Set away from 10 privately owned mobile homes, the touring pitches are separated by some neat conifer hedging and maturing trees offering limited shade. All have water and electricity (6-10A) close by. Barbecues not allowed but there are three communal areas. In July and August a few activities are organised.

Facilities

Two well maintained and clean toilet blocks offering all the necessary facilities plus some further limited facilities next to a large games/TV room. A few snacks are available to order. Good play area. Off site: Village 500 m, with mini-market, restaurant, bank, bicycle hire, riding and tennis. Lake fishing 1 km. Many marked footpaths.

Open: 3 June - 16 September.

Directions

Saint-Germain-l'Herm is 60 km. southeast of Clermont Ferrand. Leave A75 at exit 13 (Issoire) and take D996 east for 3 km. Turn right on D999 signed Saint-Germain-l'Herm for 29 km. From village continue on D999 for just under 1 km. to site on right. GPS: N45:27.412 E03:32.884

Charges 2006

Per person	€ 2,60 - € 3,10
pitch incl. electricity (8A)	€ 11,70 - € 15,80

FR63030 Camping Caravaning de l'Europe

Route de Jassal, F-63790 Murol (Puy-de-Dôme)

Tel: **04 73 39 76 66**. Email: **europe.camping@wanadoo.fr**

L'Europe is, in high season, a lively site, dominated by its mobile homes, on the edge of the little town of Murol. The site is 800 m. from the Lac de Chambon which boasts a sandy beach and range of water sports. There are 219 level grassy pitches, 59 for touring, of good size and offer reasonable shade. It has a busy animation programme including evening entertainment. The bar/restaurant overlooks the pool complex and is the site's focal point and entertainment centre. The surrounding area offers many walking and cycling opportunites, and the site organises a number of popular excursions.

Facilities

Sanitary facilities include washbasins in cabins and showers and provision for disabled visitors. Laundry facilities. Bar, restaurant and takeaway (1/7-3/9). Swimming pool with toboggan and paddling pool. Tennis. Archery. Boules. Football. Aqua gym. Water polo. Play area and large sports area. Internet access and WiFi. Off site: Fishing and bicycle hire 300 m. Riding 5 km. Golf 20 km. Murol 1.5 km. Lac Chambon 2 km. St Nectaire 6 km. Le Mont Dore 20 km.

Open: 27 May - 3 September.

Directions

Site is approx. 40 km. south west of Clermont Ferrand. Leave A75 autoroute at exit 6 (St Nectaire). Take D978 to Murol (34 km). At far end of village turn left onto D5. In 300 m. turn right onto D618 (Jassat). Site on left in 300 m.

Charges 2006

Per unit incl. 1 person	€ 11,00 - € 16,00
extra person (over 5 yrs)	€ 3,20 - € 5,30
child	€ 2,60 - € 4,35
electricity	€ 4,70 - € 5,50

FR63040 Château Camping la Grange Fort

Les Pradeaux, F-63500 Issoire (Puy-de-Dôme)

Tel: **04 73 71 02 43**. Email: **chateau@lagrangefort.com**

This site has good, modern facilities, yet is oozing with character. It is very popular with the Dutch. The new reception is well stocked with tourist information and an internet access point. The cosy bar still has the old stable stalls and hay racks. The 120 pitches (90 for touring units) are of average size, mostly on grass but with some crushed stone hardstandings, and they are connected by rather narrow roads with limited play space for children. Some of the smaller pitches are in sunny fields around the castle, others in bays with hedges and trees. All have 6A electricity.

Facilities

Refurbished sanitary blocks have facilities for disabled visitors and a 'hydra shower'. Laundry room. Bread. Restaurant (1/5-15/9), bar (15/6-15/9), takeaway (1/5-15/9). Small indoor pool with sliding glass doors, sauna, massage table (15/4-15/10). Two outdoor pools (15/6-1/10), grass sunbathing areas. Play area, games room. Internet. Minigolf. Football. Organised activities in season. Torches useful. Off site: Fishing 250 m. Riding 8 km. Good touring area with magnificent scenery. The Parc des Volcans and the Vulcania exhibition are a must.

Open: 10 April - 15 October.

Directions

From A75 autoroute take exit 13 onto D996 east towards Parentignat. At first roundabout take first exit on D999 new road (St Remy, La Vernet). At next roundabout take first exit (D34) and follow site signs.

Charges 2006

Per person	€ 4,20 - € 5,50
child (under 7 yrs)	€ 3,20 - € 3,30
pitch	€ 6,20 - € 9,70
electricity	€ 3,00
Camping Cheques accepted.	

FR63050 Sunêlia la Ribeyre

Jassat, F-63790 Murol (Puy-de-Dôme)

Tel: **04 73 88 64 29**. Email: **laribeyre@free.fr**

This charming site with fantastic views over the wooded mountains is about a kilometre from Murol, dominated by its ancient château. A large aqua-park opened for 2006. Many young trees have been planted to add to those already on site and a man-made lake at one end provides facilities for water sports. There is a picturesque reception area, with a fountain and prize winning floral decorations. The site provides 400 level, grassy pitches, of which 260 have electricity (6A) and 110 have individual electricity, water and drainage. Although not normally advertised, there are 10A outlets for those who ask. The friendly Pommier family, originally farmers, have put much personal effort in constructing the site. The surrounding area has some superb scenery, from mountains rising to over 6,000 ft, to steep valleys, lakes and caverns. This site is a great centre, only 6 kilometres from St Nectaire and about 20 kilometres from Le Mont Dore, a starting point for the Puy de Sancy, the highest peak in the area. This is a wonderful area for walking and cycling. Visit in May or June for fields of beautiful wild flowers and in September for the autumn colours.

Facilities

Six excellent, very clean modern toilet blocks with facilities for disabled persons. Washing machines, dryers. Snack bar in peak season (1/6-1/9). Heated pool complex. TV, games room. Tennis, volleyball, fishing. Play area. Small campsite lake provides swimming, canoeing, surf boarding (lifeguard in July/Aug). Off site: Riding 300 m. Bicycle hire 1 km. Further shops and restaurants and a large Wednesday market (high season) at Murol, 1 km. Fishing, boating and sailing at Lac Chambon 3 km.

Open: 1 May - 15 September.

Directions

From A75, take exit 6, signed St Nectaire and continue to Murol. Several sites signed in town. Turn left up a hill and then, opposite Syndicat d'Initiative, turn right. La Ribeyre is second site on the left. GPS: N45:33.770 E02:56.377

Charges 2006

Per unit incl. 2 persons	€ 15,60 - € 20,90
services	€ 7,10 - € 8,90
extra person	€ 4,50 - € 5,70
child (under 5 yrs)	€ 3,30 - € 4,50
electricity (6A)	€ 4,30 - € 4,90

No credit cards. Camping Cheques accepted.

SUNÊLIA LA RIBEYRE

heated pool complex with 4 slides, river splash and indoor pool

400 pitches with 64 Grand Confort on 10 ha.

To Rent on-site: 70 Mobile Homes, 10 Chalets.

JASSAT 63790 MUROL - Tel: 0033 473 88 64 29 - Fax: 0033 473 88 68 41 - Mail: laribeyre@free.fr - www.camping-laribeyre.com

FR63060 Camping le Clos Auroy

Rue de la Narse, F-63670 Orcet (Puy-de-Dôme)

Tel: **04 73 84 26 97**. Email: **info@campingclub.info**

You are assured a friendly welcome at Le Clos Auroy. It is a very well maintained and popular site, 300 metres from Orcet, a typical Auvergne village just south of Clermont Ferrand. Being close (3 km) to the A75, and open all year, it makes an excellent stopping off point on the journey north and south but you may stay longer. The 90 good size pitches are on level grass, separated by very high hedges, offering privacy but little shade. All have electricity (5/10A) and 25 are fully serviced.

Facilities

High quality, very clean toilet blocks. Washing machine, dryer. Motorcaravan services. Small shop, takeaway (1/7-15/9). Heated pool, jacuzzi, large pool for children (15/5-30/9), terrace near bar (15/5-30/9). Playground. Coffee mornings. Tennis. Children's activities. Off site: Playground and riverside walk. Village with shops and three wine 'caves' 300 m. Fishing and canoeing 500 m. Parc des Volcans. Walking and cycling.

Open: All year.

Directions

From A75 take exit 4 or 5 towards Orcet and follow campsite signs. It is just before the village. GPS: N45:42.030 E03:10.154

Charges 2006

Per unit incl. 2 persons	€ 16,80
extra person	€ 4,20
electricity (5/10A)	€ 3,00 - € 4,50

Less for longer stays in low season. No credit cards.

Check real time availability and at-the-gate prices...

www.**alanrogers**.com

FR63070 Camping le Pré Bas

Mobile homes ▶ page 479

Lac Chambon, F-63790 Murol (Puy-de-Dôme)

Tel: **04 73 88 63 04**. Email: **prebas@campingauvergne.com**

Le Pré Bas is especially suitable for families and those seeking the watersports opportunities that the lake provides. Level, grassy pitches are divided up by mature hedging and trees and, with 63 mobile homes for rent, around 120 pitches are available for tourists, all with electricity (6A). A gate leads to the lakeside, where in high season there is windsurfing, pedaloes, canoes and fishing, and 50 m. away is a beach with supervised bathing and a snack bar. The site has a new pool complex with heated swimming pools (one covered), a large slide and a paddling pool. The site is in the heart of the Parc des Volcans d'Auvergne, beside the beautiful Lac Chambon with its clear, clean water, The cable car ride up to the Puy de Sancy, the highest peak in the area, provides superb views offering an excellent opportunity for trekking and mountain bike rides. Superb scenery abounds; wooded mountains rising to over 6,000 feet, flower filled valleys and deep blue lakes.

Facilities

Refurbished toilet building with facilities for disabled guests plus four smaller units. Washing machines, dryers, ironing, baby room. Motorcaravan services. Snack bar (10/6-10/9 and some weekends in low season). Three pools of different depths (20/5-10/9, lifeguard in July/Aug). Watersports, fishing in lake. Games room, table tennis, table football, pool, TV, library. Adventure style playground, football, basketball. Organised activities. Off site: Lakeside bars, restaurants, shops. Murol 4 km. St Nectaire famous for cheese. Puy de Dome, hang gliding, Vulcania Exhibition.

Open: 1 May - 30 September.

Directions

Leave A75 autoroute at exit 6 and take D978 signed St Nectaire and Murol, then D996. Site is located on left, 3 km, west of Murol towards Mont Dore, at the far end of Lac Chambon.
GPS: N45:34.513 E02:54.854

Charges 2006

Per pitch incl. 2 persons	€ 9,10 - € 14,70
extra person	€ 3,90 - € 5,20
child (5-10 yrs)	€ 2,50 - € 5,20
electricity (6A)	€ 4,10 - € 4,40

CAMPING LE PRE BAS
AT THE BANKS OF LAKE CHAMBON
Camping du Pré Bas ★★★
WWW.LEPREBAS.COM
Lac Chambon - 63790 Chambon sur Lac - France
Tél.: +33 (0) 4 73 88 63 04 - Fax: +33 (0) 4 73 88 65 93

FR63090 Camping les Domes

Les Quatre Routes de Nébouzat, F-63210 Nébouzat (Puy-de-Dôme)

Tel: **04 73 87 14 06**. Email: **camping.les-domes@wanadoo.fr**

A popular site, it is ideally situated for exploring the beautiful region around the Puy de Dôme. The site has 65 small to medium sized pitches, most for touring, 50 with 10A electricity, separated by trees and hedges. Some pitches have a level, paved area ideal for caravans and motorcaravans. Rock pegs are advised. The attractive reception area comprising the office, a small shop for essentials (high season only) and a meeting room has lots of local information and interesting artefacts. An added small attraction is a heated, covered swimming pool, which can be opened in good weather.

Facilities

Well appointed, clean toilet block, no special facilities for disabled visitors. Basic shop (baker calls). Breakfast, snacks. Boules, pool table, table football, table tennis, giant chess, drafts. Small play area. TV and games room. Off site: Fishing 100 m. Restaurant 200 m. Nebouzat 1.3 km. Riding 6 km. Hang gliding and parascending 8 km (Puy de Dôme). Vulcania exhibition. Watersports 9 km. Golf 10 km. Clermond Ferrand with hypermarkets (18 km). Many marked walks and cycle routes.

Open: 1 May - 15 September.

Directions

Site is 18 km. southwest of Clermont Ferrand and is well signed from the roundabout at the junction of the N89 and the D941A. It is a few hundred metres from the roundabout along the D216 towards Orcival. GPS: N45:43.537 E02:53.403

Charges 2007

Per unit incl. 2 persons	€ 9,50
extra person	€ 6,00
child (under 5 yrs)	€ 3,00
electricity (10A)	€ 4,00

FR63080 Camping le Moulin de Serre

D73, Vallée de la Burande, F-63690 Singles (Puy-de-Dôme)

Tel: **04 73 21 16 06**. Email: **moulin-de-serre@wanadoo.fr**

Off the beaten track, this spacious and well maintained site is set in a wooded valley beside a river where one can pan for gold. It offers a good base for those seeking quiet relaxation in this lesser known area of the Auvergne. The 90 large pitches (55 for touring) are separated by a variety of trees and hedges giving good shade. Some pitches have hardstanding and all have electricity (3-10A), long leads may be necessary. Access around the site is easy but the narrow lanes leading to it are twisting which might prove difficult for larger units.

Facilities

Well appointed. clean toilet blocks, one heated having excellent facilities for disabled people and babies. Heated swimming pool, terrace (8/6-28/9). Takeaway (19/5-16/9), bar/restaurant (July/Aug). Bread (19/5-16/9). Washing machine, dryer. Motorcaravan services. Large play area. Tennis. Canoe hire in high season. Organised activities (July/Aug). Off site: Lake for fishing 2 km. Château de Val 20 km. Spa town of La Bourboule 25 km. Barrage de Bort les Orgues offers watersports. Many marked walks and cycle tracks. Riding.

Open: 13 April - 16 September.

Directions

Site is about 25 km. southwest of La Bourboule. Turn west off the D922 just south of Tauves at site sign. Follow site signs along the D29 and then the D73 for about 10 km. GPS: N45:32.584 E02:32.557

Charges 2007

Per unit incl. 2 persons	€ 9,95 - € 16,60
extra person	€ 2,90 - € 4,10
child (under 10 yrs)	€ 1,95 - € 2,85
electricity (3-10A)	€ 3,00 - € 4,60

Friendly atmosphere in a delightful setting in the heart of the upper Dordogne valley

Long heated swimming-pool! Campsite open from 14/06 to 17/09

www.moulindeserre.com

LE MOULIN DE SERRE ★★★
63690 Singles (France)
Tel +33 (0)4 73 21 16 06
Fax +33 (0)4 73 21 12 56

FR63130 Camping le Repos du Baladin

Groire, F-63790 Murol (Puy-de-Dôme)

Tel: **04 73 88 61 93**. Email: **reposbaladin@free.fr**

Recommended by a reader, this is a lovely small and friendly campsite that offers an alternative to the larger sites in this area. The owners are aiming for a quiet, relaxing site, attracting nature lovers who want to spend time walking, cycling or touring in this beautiful region rather than creating a holiday park with everything on site. Attractively and well laid out, there are 62 good sized pitches, 49 for touring (5A electricity), and many with good privacy. They are separated by neat conifer hedges with mature trees offer varying amounts of shade. Murol with its ancient castle is 1.5 km.

Facilities

One excellent, very clean and central toilet block provides all the necessary facilities. TV/games room in same block. Small shop (15/6-15/9). Bar with TV (1/6-15/9). Restaurant with snacks and takeaway (1/6-15/9). Heated swimming pool and sunbathing area (1/6-15/9). Large play area. Boules. Off site: Murol 1.5 km. Fishing, bicycle hire and boat launching at Lac Chambon, 2 km.

Open: 1 May - 15 September.

Directions

Site is 40 km. southwest of Clermont Ferrand. Leave A75 at exit 6 (St Nectaire) and take D978 beyond St Nectaire to Murol (34 km). At far end of the village turn left up hill on D5. In 800 m. turn right on D146, signed Groire and site. Entrance on right in 900 m. GPS: N45:34.437 E02:59.449

Charges 2006

Per unit incl. 2 persons	€ 13,50 - € 16,80
extra person	€ 3,50 - € 3,80
child (0-5 yrs)	€ 2,00
electricity (5A)	€ 3,80

FR63120 Camping Indigo Royat

Route de Gravenoire, F-63130 Royat (Puy-de-Dôme)

Tel: **04 73 35 97 05**. Email: **royat@camping-indigo.com**

This is a spacious, well tended and attractive site sitting high on a hillside on the outskirts of Clermont Ferrand, but close to the beautiful Auvergne countryside. It has nearly 200 terraced pitches on part hardstanding. There are 150 available for touring units, all with 6/10A electricity (long leads may be needed). The pitches are informally arranged in groups, with each group widely separated by attractive trees and shrubs. The bar overlooks the irregularly shaped swimming pool, paddling pool, sunbathing area, tennis courts and play areas. Although very peaceful off season, it could be lively in July and August. This site would be ideal for those who would like a taste of both the town and the countryside.

Facilities

Five well appointed toilet blocks, some heated. They have all the usual amenities but it could be a long walk from some pitches. Small shop. Bar, takeaway. Internet. Attractive swimming, paddling pools, sunbathing area. Tennis. Boules. Table tennis. Bicycle hire. Two grassy play areas. Organised entertainment in high season. Off site: Royat 20 minutes walk but bus available every 30 minutes. Clermont Ferrand, Puy de Dôme, Parc des Volcans, Volcania exhibition.

Open: 6 April - 28 October.

Directions

From A75 exit 2 (Clermont Ferrand) follow signs for Bordeaux (D799). At third roundabout take third exit (D3) signed Beaumont. In 800 m. turn left (D777) signed Beaumont. At T-junction (traffic lights) turn left (N89) signed Ceyrat. Turn right up the hill (D767) signed Royat. At T-junction turn right (D941C) signed Royat and Puy de Dôme. At top of hill turn left (D5, Route) site signed. Entrance 800 m. GPS: N45:45.526 E03:03.308

Charges 2006

Per person	€ 4,00 - € 4,70
child (2-7 yrs)	€ 2,50 - € 3,00
pitch	€ 4,70 - € 11,50
electricity (6/10A)	€ 4,30 - € 6,00

FR63140 Camping les Loges

F-63340 Nonette (Puy-de-Dôme)

Tel: **04 73 71 65 82**. Email: **les.loges.nonette@wanadoo.fr**

This is a pleasant, spacious, rural site bordering the River Allier. There are 126 good sized, level, grassy pitches offering plenty of shade, 100 for touring and all with 6A electricity. This site would suit those seeking a quieter holiday without too much organised activity. The river is ideal for bathing and canoeing and there are many walks and bike rides in the area. It is also well placed to explore the beautiful Auvergne countryside, the extinct volcanoes and the attractive old towns and villages.

Facilities

Modern toilet blocks contain all the usual facilities. Small shop (July/Aug). Bar (June-Aug). TV room. Simple takeaway (all season). Heated swimming pool with slide, paddling pool (June-Sept). Volleyball. Table tennis. Play areas, play room. River fishing, bathing. Sunday evening dances in high season. Canoe trips. Off site: Walking and cycling routes. Riding 10 km. Small village of Nonette 3 km. Small range of shops at Saint Germain 5 km. Larger range of shops, restaurants etc in Issoire 13 km. Parc des Volcans, Volcania Exhibition.

Open: Easter - 8 October.

Directions

From A75 exit 17 (south of Issoire), turn left (D214) signed Le Breuil and Jumeaux. Bypass Le Breuil, turn left (D123) signed Nonette. Cross the river, turn left then immediately very hard left - take care (site signed). Entrance is 1 km.

Charges 2006

Per person	€ 3,40 - € 4,40
child (0-7 yrs)	€ 3,50
pitch	€ 4,70 - € 7,20
electricity	€ 3,50
dog	free - € 1,50

MAP 13

Rhône Valley

With such a rich and varied landscape, the Rhône Valley offers a spectacular region of craggy gorges and scented hills, ideal for life at a leisurely pace - easy to do when there are so many stunning views to take in.

DÉPARTEMENTS: 01 AIN, 07 ARDÈCHE, 26 DRÔME, 42 LOIRE, 69 RHÔNE

MAJOR CITY: LYON

The region's 2,000 year history as a cultural crossroads has blessed the area with a rich blend of customs, architecture and sights of interest. The city of Lyon was developed by the Romans as a trading centre, and was once the capital. It is now the second largest city of France. The Place de la Terreur in the centre of the city is where the guillotine was placed during the French revolution – until it wore out through over-use. Not far from Lyon lies the Dombes, the land of a thousand lakes, and the medieval village of Pérouges and Roman ruins of Vienne.

The Rhône valley holds areas of great interest and natural beauty. From the sun-baked Drôme, with its ever-changing landscapes and the isolated mountains of the Vercors to the deep gorges and high plateaux of the Ardèche, studded with prehistoric caves and lush valleys filled with orchards; and encompassing the vineyards of the Beaujolais and the Rhône Valley. For the energetic there are cycling, horse riding and even white water rafting opportunities, while for the more leisurely inclined, the remote areas are a haven for bird watching and walking.

Places of interest

Beaujolais: vineyards and golden-stone villages.

Bourg-en-Bresse: church of Notre-Dame, craft shops, museum of Ain.

Dombes: lakes, ornithological park.

Lyon: Gallo-Roman artifacts, Renaissance quarter, historical Fabric Museum, silk museum.

Pérouges: medieval village, Galette de Pérouges.

St Etienne: museum of Modern Art.

Vallon-Pont d'Arc: base from which to visit Gorges de l'Ardèche; canoe and rafting centre.

Vienne: Gothic style cathedral, 6th century church St Pierre.

Cuisine of the region

The poultry, cheese, freshwater fish and mushrooms are superb. Local wines include Beaujolais, Côte Rotie, St Julien, Condrieu, Tain-Hermitage, Chiroubles and Julienas.

Bresse (Poulet, Poularde, Volaille de): the best French poultry, fed on corn and when killed bathed in milk; flesh is white and delicate.

Gras-double: ox tripe, served with onions.

Poulet au vinaigre: chicken, shallots, tomatoes, white wine, wine vinegar and a cream sauce.

Poulet demi-deuil (half-mourning): called this because of thin slices of truffle placed under the chicken breast.

Rosette: a large pork sausage.

Sabodet: Lyonnais sausage of pig's head, pork and beef, served hot.

FR01010 Camping la Plaine Tonique

Base de Plein Air, F-01340 Montrevel-en-Bresse (Ain)

Tel: **04 74 30 80 52**. Email: **plaine.tonique@wanadoo.fr**

This excellent site, ideal for active families, belongs to a syndicate of several local villages. It is a very well maintained, large site with 560 marked and numbered pitches, all with 10A electricity. The majority are of a good size, hedged and on flat grass, with reasonable shade in most parts. The site is very spacious and broken up into sections by trees and hedges. It is on the edge of an attractive, 320-acre lake with its own beach and adjacent public beach. A separate area of the site is used by Dutch tour operators (100 pitches).

Facilities

Very clean sanitary facilities are in eleven blocks and include some washbasins in cabins, baby rooms and washing machines. Motorcaravan service point. Restaurant, bar (all season) and shop (July/Aug) next to site. 'Aquatonic' centre with five pools (reduced charge for campers, no Bermuda shorts). Watersports and fishing. Minigolf. Tennis. Adventure play area. Games and TV rooms. Archery, bicycle hire and roller skating. Fitness trail. Off site: Montrevel town 300 m. walk. Riding 2 km.

Open: 14 April - 22 September.

Directions

Montrevel is 20 km. north of Bourg-en-Bresse and 25 km. east of Macon. The site is on the D28 500 m. east of town towards Etrez and is well signed. GPS: N46:20.249 E05:08.188

Charges 2007

Per pitch incl. electricity and 2 persons	€ 13,70 - € 22,60
extra person	€ 3,20 - € 5,30
child (3-7 yrs)	€ 2,00 - € 3,00
pet	€ 1,50 - € 2,00

FR01020 Camping de l'Ile Chambod

F-01250 Hautecourt (Ain)

Tel: **04 74 37 25 41**. Email: **camping.chambod@free.fr**

This small rural site has had many improvements made by its current owners. It has two modern toilet blocks, a swimming pool and small café. The 110 medium-sized, slightly sloping, grassy pitches (many with views of the surrounding wooded hills) are separated by low hedges and most have some shade. They all have access to water and electricity (5/10A) although some may need long leads. A lakeside beach is 300 m. (charged for in high season) offering simple watersports and minigolf.

Facilities

Two modern toilet blocks include some washbasins in cabins, dishwashing, laundry and vegetable preparation sinks. Washing machine and dryer. Both blocks have facilities suitable for disabled visitors and one has a baby room. Bread available to order. Small shop and takeaway (June, July and Aug). Swimming pool (May to end Aug). Small play area. Activities organised in high season for all the family. Off site: Close to the spectacular gorges of the River Ain.

Open: 29 April - 1 October.

Directions

Site is 23 km. southeast of Bourg-en-Bresse via the D979. It is well signed from the crossroads in Hautecourt, and is a further 4 km. southeast down the lane. GPS: N46:07.666 E05:25.691

Charges 2006

Per person	€ 4,60
child (2-12 yrs)	€ 3,10
pitch incl. vehicle	€ 5,70
electricity 5-10A	€ 2,60 - € 3,60

FR01030 Camping les Ripettes

Chavannes-sur-Reyssouze, F-01190 Pont de Vaux (Ain)

Tel: **03 85 30 66 58**. Email: **info@camping-les-ripettes.com**

Recently taken over by an enthusiastic and hardworking English couple, this spacious site is situated in quiet, flat countryside near the pleasant small town of Pont-de-Vaux. The 2.5 hectare (6 acre) site has 54 large (over 100 sq.m. to 400 sq.m.) level grassy pitches, 51 of which are available to tourists. Nearly all are separated by hedges and about half are shaded by the many trees on the site. All but two have electrical connections (10A), and there are ample water points.

Facilities

Two well appointed, small sanitary blocks contain a suite for disabled visitors. Washing machine. Limited range of food stocked and wine, ice cream, meat for barbecues at reception. Two swimming pools. Small play area, sandpit. Areas for ball games, volleyball, badminton, table tennis, boules. Board games, books. Bicycle hire. Off site: Riding 2 km. Fishing 4 km. Golf 15 km. Restaurant 1 km. Shops, etc., in Pont-de-Vaux 4 km.

Open: 1 April - 30 September.

Directions

Leave N6 at Fleurville (14 km. south of Tournus). Go east on D933A to Pont-de-Vaux (5 km). Take D2 east towards St Trivier-de-Courtes. After 3 km turn left after water tower, left again at next junction (100 m). Site is 300 m. GPS: N46:26.402 E04:58.487

Charges 2007

Per person	€ 3,50
child (0-10 yrs)	€ 2,50
pitch incl. electricity	€ 5,00 - € 7,50

No credit cards.

FR01080 Camping Etang du Moulin

F-01240 Saint Paul de Varax (Ain)

Tel: **04 74 42 53 30**. Email: **moulin@campingendombes.fr**

This extremely spacious and well run campsite, which is owned by several villages, lies within a larger leisure complex which will be very busy at weekends. The major attraction here is one of the largest swimming pools in Europe – 5,500 sq.m. It is irregularly shaped, has shallow areas all around, two large toboggans and eight lifeguards always on duty – ideal for all the family and free for campers. The 165 very large, level grassy pitches include 156 for touring, with 4 hardstandings for motorcaravans. All have 6A electricity and are separated by hedges, with shade provided by a variety of trees. The reception, bar, restaurant and entertainment centre is at the entrance well away from the pitches. There is an extensive entertainment programme in high season. There is also a 13 hectare, well stocked fishing lake and large spaces set aside for sporting activities. This site would be Ideal for those active families seeking a campsite based holiday. No animals are accepted.

Facilities

Two very clean and well maintained toilet blocks, functional rather than luxurious, have all the necessary facilities including those for disabled visitors. Motorcaravan service point. All facilities open all season. Bar, TV room, restaurant and takeaway. Large swimming pool with toboggans and pebble sunbathing beach near to entrance. Marquee for entertainment. Bicycle hire. Large area for games. Off site: In adjacent leisure complex – fishing, tennis, minigolf. Bourg-en-Bresse (20 km) has a wide range of shops, bars/restaurants/banks/market.

Open: 24 May - 3 September.

Directions

Site is about 20 km. southwest of Bourg-en-Bresse. Leave the N83 at St Paul de Varax and turn southeast on the D17. In 3 km. turn right down the bumpy lane, signed Base de Loisirs. Site is 1 km. GPS: N46:05.206 E5:09.122

Charges 2006

Per person	€ 3,70
child (3-12 yrs)	€ 2,20
pitch incl. 6A electricity	€ 7,50
vehicle	€ 2,20

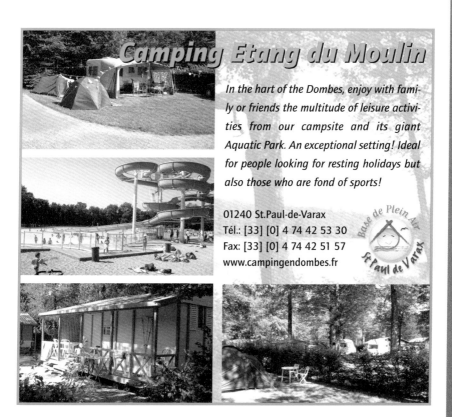

Camping Etang du Moulin

In the hart of the Dombes, enjoy with family or friends the multitude of leisure activities from our campsite and its giant Aquatic Park. An exceptional setting! Ideal for people looking for resting holidays but also those who are fond of sports!

01240 St.Paul-de-Varax
Tél.: [33] [0] 4 74 42 53 30
Fax: [33] [0] 4 74 42 51 57
www.campingendombes.fr

Base de Plein Air
St Paul de Varax

FR01040 Camping Lac du Lit du Roi

La Tuillière, F-01300 Massignieu-de-Rives (Ain)

Tel: **04 79 42 12 03**. Email: **acamp@wanadoo.fr**

This attractive and well cared for, family run site is ideal for those seeking an active holiday in a peaceful setting. This superb, picturesque area offers wonderful opportunities for exploration by foot, bicycle, car and boat. Take time to sample the wines and other local produce on offer. Of the 120 pitches (electricty 10A), 90 are available for touring, all being close to the lake and many having wonderful views over the lake and the wooded hills beyond. The slightly sloping, grassy pitches are set on low terraces and are partly separated by hedging and a variety of trees give some shade.

Facilities

Two modern toilet blocks offer all necessary facilities with provision for disabled visitors. Washing machines. Motorcaravan services. Bar, snack bar, terrace. Bread. Small heated swimming pool (all season). Tennis. Volleyball. Table tennis. Play area beside lake. Grassy beach, pedaloes, canoes, surf bikes for hire. Bicycle hire. Lake fishing. Winter caravan storage. Off site: Belley 8 km. Lac du Bourget (watersports, boat hire). Nature reserve. Cycle tracks and walks. Golf 8 km. Riding 15 km.

Open: 16 April - 2 October.

Directions

Site is about 8 km. east of Belley. Turn east off N504 at roundabout (Champion supermarket) on D992 signed Culoz and Seyssel. After 4 km. turn right over bridge, D37 signed Massignieu. Follow signs to campsite (2 km). GPS: N45:46.122 E05:46.92

Charges 2006

Per unit incl. 2 persons	€ 17,00 - € 22,00
extra person	€ 5,00 - € 6,00
electricity	€ 3,00

Camping Cheques accepted.

FR01050 Camping des Gorges de l'Oignin

Rue du Lac, F-01580 Matafelon-Granges (Ain)

Tel: **04 74 76 80 97**. Email: **camping.lesgorgesdeloignin@wanadoo.fr**

This family run, terraced site (English spoken) offers lovely views across the lake to the hills beyond. There are 132 good sized pitches, 70 for touring, separated by young trees and flowering shrubs and with a choice of grass or hardstanding. About half have their own water point and all have 10A electricity. Twin axle caravans are not accepted. The reception, bar/restaurant and the pool complex are at the top of the site with a steep road down to the terraces and the rest of the campsite. At the bottom of the site is a grassy area next to the lake for sunbathing and activities.

Facilities

Two modern, well equipped and clean toilet blocks with all the usual facilities excepting facilities for disabled people. Bar/restaurant, takeaway and TV room (July/Aug). Swimming pool, paddling pool and new Lazy River (1/6-30/9). Playground. Swimming, fishing and boating on lake (no motorboats). Off site: Golf 2 km. Riding 2 km. Matafelon 800 m. Thoirette 6 km. Oyonnax 10 km.

Open: 1 April - 30 September.

Directions

Matafelon is 40 km. east of Bourg-en-Bresse. Leave autoroute A404 at Oyonnax, exit 11 and head west on D13 to Matafelon (10 km). On entering village and opposite the Mairie turn left, signed camping, and descend to site (800 m).

Charges 2006

Per unit incl. 2 persons	€ 12,00 - € 16,40
electricity (10A)	€ 2,00 - € 2,60

FR01060 Camping Ile de la Comtesse

Route des Abrets, F-01300 Murs-et-Gélignieux (Ain)

Tel: **04 79 87 23 33**. Email: **camping.comtesse@wanadoo.fr**

A very pleasant, family run, lakeside site, there are 100 medium to large, level grassy pitches here. With 69 for touring, many are separated by low hedges and tall poplar trees offer some shade. All have 6A electricity (but very long leads may be necessary) and most have views over the lake and craggy hills beyond. High season activities are aimed mainly at younger children and the family. Fishing, sailing, canoeing and bathing are possible on the lake that borders the site. There is plenty of space around the lake for leisure activities, including marked walks and cycle trails.

Facilities

Traditionally styled, modern and well appointed toilet block with all the necessary facilities. Facilities for disabled visitors. Motorcaravan service point. Small bar/restaurant with takeaway and small shop. Large marquee used for TV and organized activities. Swimming and paddling pools. All facilities open all season. Daily programme of activities in high season. Bicycle hire. Off site: Restaurant adjacent. Aost with shops, etc. 5 km. Walaibi Theme Park 10 km. Riding 10 km. Golf 20 km.

Open: 16 May - 1 September.

Directions

From the A43 (Lyon – Chambery) autoroute, take exit 10 and go north on D592 for about 10 km. After crossing the lake turn right on the D992 and site is shortly on the right. GPS: N45:38.407 E5:38.948

Charges 2006

Per unit incl. 2 persons	€ 18,50 - € 23,50
extra person	€ 5,90 - € 7,50
child (under 7yrs)	€ 3,50 - € 5,40
electricity (6A)	€ 3,00 - € 3,50

Check real time availability and at-the-gate prices...

www.**alanrogers**.com

FR07020 Camping Caravaning L'Ardéchois

Le Chambon, Gluiras, F-07190 St Sauveur-de-Montagut (Ardèche)
Tel: 04 75 66 61 87. Email: ardechois.camping@wanadoo.fr

This site has 106 pitches (83 for touring) laid out on steep terraces, of varying sizes and many separated by trees and plants. Some are alongside the small, fast-flowing stream, while the rest (60%) are on higher, sloping ground nearer the restaurant/bar and pool. All 83 touring pitches have electricity (10A). The main site access roads are tarmac but are quite steep and larger units may find access to some terraces difficult. There are two entrances to the site so, on arrival, park outside on the road and go to reception on foot.

Facilities

Two good sanitary blocks include facilities for people with disabilities. Dishwashing and laundry rooms. Motorcaravan services. Shop, bar/restaurant, takeaway (1/5-25/9). New restaurant. Swimming pool (heated 1/5-25/9), adjacent bar, snack bar, terrace, paddling pool. TV. Table tennis. Volleyball. Bicycle hire, archery, fishing. Comprehensive entertainment programme. Off site: Canyoning, climbing, river walking and canoeing trips organised.

Open: Easter - 31 October.

Directions

From Valence take N86 south for 12 km. At La Voulte-sur-Rhône turn right onto D120 to St Sauveur de Montagut (site well signed), then take D102 towards Mézilhac for 8 km. to site.

Charges 2007

Per unit incl. 2 persons and electricity	€ 28,30 - € 47,50
extra person	€ 5,50 - € 8,50
child (2-13 yrs)	€ 4,00 - € 6,70

Camping Cheques accepted.

FR07030 Yelloh! Village Soleil Vivarais

Sampzon, F-07120 Ruoms (Ardèche)
Tel: 04 75 39 67 56. Email: info@soleil-vivarais.com

A large, lively, high quality site bordering the River Ardèche, complete with beach, Soleil Vivarais offers much to visitors, particularly families with children. Of the 350 pitches, 88 generously sized, level pitches are for tourers, all with 10A electricity. Rock pegs are advised. Many are shaded and 30 have full services. During the day the proximity of the swimming pools to the terraces of the bar and restaurant make it a pleasantly social area. A new section beyond the beach houses good quality chalets, and a very attractive new pool complex, which all may use.

Facilities

Modern, clean, well equipped toilet blocks, facilities for people with disabilities. Washing machines, dryers. Motorcaravan services. Small supermarket. Bar/restaurant, takeaways and pizzas. Heated pool, paddling pool. Water polo, aqua-aerobics, pool games. Tennis. Fishing. Boules. Animation programme in June, July and August. Off site: Riding 2 km. Golf 10 km. Mountain biking, walking, canoeing, rafting, climbing, caving.

Open: 8 April - 16 September.

Directions

Turn off N86 at Montélimar, take N102 west through Villeneuve-de-Berg.(disregard first sign Vallon-Pont-d'Arc), continue for 5 km, turn left on D103 (Vogué), left on D579 through Ruoms. Follow Vallon-Pont-d'Arc signs (Sampzon 3 km. Turn right over bridge.

Charges 2006

Per unit incl. 2 persons and electricity	€ 16,00 - € 41,00
extra person	€ 4,50 - € 7,80

FR07050 Sunêlia le Ranc Davaine

Saint Alban-Auriolles, F-07120 Ruoms (Ardèche)
Tel: 04 75 39 60 55. Email: camping.ranc.davaine@wanadoo.fr

Le Ranc Davaine is a quite large, busy, family oriented site set in two areas separated by a reasonably quiet road. The larger area provides all the entertainment facilities and most of the 430 pitches. The 113 touring pitches are mostly scattered between static caravan and tour operator pitches on fairly flat, stony ground under trees giving much needed shade (electricity 6/10A), very long leads needed, leads may cross roads. Rock pegs are advised. Sunbathing areas surround the pool complex, overlooked by the terrace of the restaurant, providing very pleasant surroundings.

Facilities

Fully equipped toilet blocks include facilities for disabled visitors. Washing machines, dryers. Large shop. Bar/restaurant, pizzeria, takeaway (all season). Swimming pool, covered pool (heated), two small square pools, slide. Play area. Tennis. Achery, minigolf, fishing. Extensive activity and sports programme. Discos (enclosed, until 3 am). Off site: Canoe hire for excursions down the River Ardèche. Rafting. Bicycle hire 2 km. Riding 6 km. Karting.

Open: 23 March - 14 September.

Directions

From Ruoms go south on the D111. Just before Grospierres turn right on D246, cross the river bridge (2.5 m. width restriction) and then left on D208 (Chandolas) to site. GPS: N44:24.848 E04:16.374

Charges 2006

Per unit incl. 2 persons	€ 20,40 - € 35,70
with electricity	€ 25,50 - € 39,80
extra person	€ 6,30 - € 9,50

Camping Cheques accepted.

FR07070 Camping les Ranchisses

Route de Rocher, F-07110 Largentière (Ardèche)

Tel: **04 75 88 31 97**. Email: **reception@lesranchisses.fr**

The site has been developed from an original 'camping á la ferme' into a very well equipped modern campsite. There are 165 good-sized, level, grassy pitches, 88 for tourists with electricity (10A) include 42 fully serviced pitches. They are in two distinct areas, the original site which is well shaded and the lower part with less shade. The site runs parallel to the road and there may be background traffic noise in some areas. There is a small lake providing opportunities for bathing, fishing or canoeing (free life jackets) with one part of the bathing area quite safe for youngsters.

Facilities

Comprehensive toilet buildings include facilities for babies and disabled persons. Laundry. Motorcaravan services. Small shop, takeaway, bar, terrace (all season), new restaurant. Two large pools (both heated), paddling pool. Adventure style playground. Organised amusements for children in high season. Minigolf. Table tennis. Boules. Canoeing. Tennis. Skate park. Off site: Canoe, kayaking arranged (mid -June - end Aug). Medieval village, Largentière (1.5 km.) with Tuesday market.

Open: 7 April - 16 September.

Directions

Largentière is southwest of Aubenas best approached using D104. After 16 km, just beyond Uzer turn northwest on D5. After 5 km. at far end of Largentière, fork left downhill signed Valgorge. Site on left in about 1.8 km.

Charges 2007

Per unit incl. 2 persons	€ 24,00 -	€ 35,00
serviced pitch	€ 26,00 -	€ 37,00
extra person (over 1 yr)	€ 4,50 -	€ 7,50

Camping Cheques accepted.

kawan-villages.com **tel: 00 333 59 59 03 59** — *kawa* VILLAGES CAMPING

FR07080 RCN la Bastide en Ardèche

RD111, route d'Alès, Sampzon, F-07120 Ruoms (Ardèche)

Tel: **04 75 39 64 72**. Email: **info@rcn-labastideenardeche.fr**

Though more expensive than some, this site is maintained to a high standard and this is evident as soon as you drive in, with its neat and tidy appearance and flowers everywhere. This is a pleasant site with good sized pitches, all with some shade and bordered by trees and bushes. All have electricity 3A, and 86 are fully serviced with 5A. Canoe trips are arranged down the Gorge d'Ardèche and in mid-June a section of the river bank next to the site is cleared of boulders and sand put down.

Facilities

Two toilet blocks, one new and one old, with baby room and facilities for disabled people. Shop. Restaurant, pizzeria and bar (mid June to end Aug). Heated pool. Play area. Boules. Tennis. Fishing. Organised activities in July/Aug Only gas barbecues. Off site: Riding, bicycle hire 3 km. Golf 6 km. Ruoms 4 km. Vallon-Pont-d'Arc 7 km.

Open: 1 April - 25 November.

Directions

Going south from Ruoms on the D579, after 2.5 km. at roundabout, turn right on D111 signed Alès. Cross river bridge and site is 200 m. on the left. GPS: N44:25.375 E04:19.297

Charges 2006

Per unit incl. 2 persons	€ 20,00 -	€ 43,50
incl. 3-6 persons	€ 25,50 -	€ 48,50

FR07090 Camping le Domaine des Plantas

F-07360 Les Ollières-sur-Eyrieux (Ardèche)

Tel: **04 75 66 21 53**. Email: **plantas.ardeche@wanadoo.fr**

A good quality site in a spectacular setting on the steep banks of the Eyrieux river, Old, original buildings house the reception, restaurant and bar. The terrace provides a stunning viewpoint. The 162 pitches (90 for touring) are steeply terraced and shaded with electricity (10A, long leads may be needed). Much up and down walking is required making this site unsuitable for those with walking difficulties There is a sandy beach beside the quite fast-flowing, but fairly shallow, river (used for bathing) and a swimming pool and paddling pool. Narrow twisting approach road.

Facilities

Two excellent well equipped toilet blocks (one heated). There are some facilities which will certainly please the very young. Washing machine. Motorcaravan services. Small shop, bar, restaurant, disco. Heated swimming pool, paddling pool. Adventure play area. High season children's activities, discos for 14-18 year olds held in cellar (strictly no alcohol). Many activities and excursions. Only gas and electric barbecues. Off site: Riding 15 km. Mountain biking, canoeing, canyoning, riding and walking.

Open: 12 April - 15 September.

Directions

Leave A7 exit 15 (Valence Sud). Turn right to Valence centre, follow signs to Montélimar via N7 for 7 km. Turn right towards Charmes to Beauchastel. Then follow signs to Ollieres sur Eyrieux. Cross river and follow signs (3 km). GPS: N44:48.520 E04:38.125

Charges 2006

Per unit incl. 2 persons and electricity	€ 19,00 -	€ 30,00
extra person over 3 yrs	€ 4,00 -	€ 7,50

Camping Cheques accepted.

FR07110 Domaine le Pommier

Route Nationale 102, F-07170 Villeneuve-de-Berg (Ardèche)

Tel: **04 75 94 82 81**. Email: **info@campinglepommier.com**

Domaine Le Pommier is an extremely spacious Dutch owned site of 10 hectares in 32 hectares of wooded grounds. The site is steeply terraced (a tractor is available for assistance) and has wonderful views over the Ardèche mountains and beyond. There are 400 pitches with 275 for tourists. They are grassy/stony, of good size and well spaced. Separated by young trees and hedges, some have little or no shade. All have access to electricity and water is close by. The site is not recommended for large units. Recent developments include a mini-farm, including llamas, goats and ponies, and an unusual pancake restaurant. This serves an excellent range of pancakes of various flavours. The site has first class facilities, including the most up-to-date toilet blocks, a very good bar/restaurant and one of the best swimming and paddling pool complexes we have seen – ideal for all the family.

Facilities

Four excellent toilet blocks, one with under-floor heating, provide all the necessary facilities. Comprehensive shop. Bar/restaurant. Swimming pool complex with slides, paddling pools, etc. Everything opens from the end of April. Boules. Minigolf. Activities including games in the woods, archery, water polo and tug of war. Bridge and water colour classes. Tennis. Sound proof disco. Very extensive programme of events on and off site. Off season excursions. Off site: Villeneuve de Berg 1.5 km. River Ardèche 12 km. Potholing, rock climbing, canoeing, canyoning, mountain biking, walking or riding.

Open: 1 May - 30 September.

Directions

Site is west of Montélimar on the N102. The entrance is adjacent to the roundabout at the eastern end of the Villeneuve-de-Berg bypass. GPS: N44:34.350 E04:30.669

Charges 2006

Per unit incl. 2 persons	€ 14,00 - € 29,50
extra person over 4 yrs	€ 4,00 - € 6,50
electricity	€ 4,00
dog	free - € 4,00

Max. 6 persons per pitch.
Special offers for longer stays in low season.

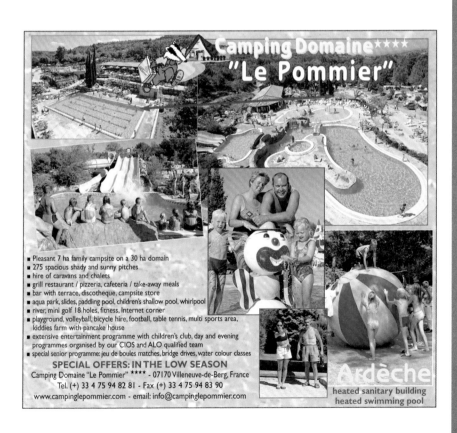

Camping Domaine ★★★★ "Le Pommier"

- Pleasant 7 ha family campsite on a 30 ha domain
- 275 spacious shady and sunny pitches
- hire of caravans and chalets
- grill restaurant / pizzeria / cafeteria / take-away meals
- bar with terrace, discotheque, campsite store
- aqua park, slides, paddling pool, children's shallow pool, whirlpool
- river, mini golf 18 holes, fitness, Internet corner
- playground, volleyball, bicycle hire, football, table tennis, multi sports area, kiddies farm with pancake house
- extensive entertainment programme with children's club, day and evening programmes organised by our CIOS and ALO qualified team
- special senior programme: jeu de boules matches, bridge drives, water colour classes

SPECIAL OFFERS: IN THE LOW SEASON
Camping Domaine "Le Pommier" ★★★★ - 07170 Villeneuve-de-Berg, France
Tel. (+) 33 4 75 94 82 81 - Fax (+) 33 4 75 94 83 90
www.campinglepommier.com - email: info@campinglepommier.com

Ardèche

heated sanitary building
heated swimming pool

FR07100 Camping la Garenne

Chemin de la Garenne, F-07800 Saint Laurent-du-Pape (Ardèche)

Tel: **04 75 62 24 62**

This spacious, family orientated site is within easy reach of the A7/N7 south of Valence and only a short stroll from the village. It has a long season. Owned and run by Dutch couple, Tim and Halka Martojo, guests are predominantly Dutch but all are made welcome and English is widely spoken. The 120 grassy/stony pitches (rock pegs advised), some terraced and some sloping, are of 80-100 sq.m. Some are separated by hedges and all have electricity, but only 4A (some need long leads). The amount of shade varies from none to quite heavy. Visitors' pursuits have been carefully considered resulting in a variety of family activities. People with diverse interests are therefore attracted throughout the season – for example, bridge evenings are organised during May, June and September. Accompanied walks are organized throughout the season, as well as a lively activity and entertainment in peak season. Barbecues are not permitted.

Facilities	Directions
Excellent and very clean, modern toilet blocks provide all necessary facilities including those for children and disabled visitors. Small shop for basics, Bar, restaurant and takeaway (all 15/5-15/9). Swimming pool and sunbathing terrace (20/5-15/9). Paddling pool. Games room. Volleyball. Off site: The village is close by. Fishing 1 km. Riding 2 km. Bicycle hire 3 km. Walking, biking, canoeing, canyoning and exploring the Ardèche region. Some off site activities run from site.	From A7 exit 16 (Loriol) take N304 west over the river to Le Pouzin. Immediately turn right on N86 to la Voulte sur Rhône. Go through Voulte following signs for St Laurent du Pape and then turn left on D120. In St Laurent cross the river and turn left. Shortly, just before La Poste, turn right (site signed), to site shortly on left. GPS: N44:49.574 E04:45.732

Open: 1 March - 1 November.

Charges 2006

Per unit incl. 2 persons	€ 16,40 - € 29,50
extra person	€ 5,50

Camping *La Garenne****
- Ardèche -
... Where Alps, Provence and Massif Central meet ...

• between Valence and Montélimar
• at entrance of beautiful Eyrieux Valley
• at five minutes walk from the village centre

Family camp site (120 pitches) under Dutch ownership with large swimming pool, toddlers pool, bar/restaurant, shop and recreation room.

low season: bridge - jeu de boules - walking
high season: extensive recreation program

07800 St. Laurent-du-Pape • Ardèche
www.lagarenne.org

FR07130 Camping les Coudoulets

Pradons, F-07120 Ruoms (Ardèche)

Tel: **04 75 93 94 95**. Email: **camping@coudoulets.com**

For those who prefer a more intimate, peaceful campsite beside the river Ardèche, only a short distance away from the main centre, then this well cared for site is for you. There are 125 good sized, grassy and well shaded pitches, separated by trees and shrubs. There are 112 for touring, all with 6A electricity. Organised events in July/August for all the family include the occasional evening event such as barbecues and musical evenings (no discos). The river is an ideal spot for canoeists, etc.

Facilities	Directions
Good, clean, recently fefurbished block has all the necessary facilities including excellent facilities for disabled people. Motorcaravan services. Bar, TV, terrace (May - Sept) bread, ices, drinks. Snacks July/Aug. Butcher calls in high season. Small heated swimming pool, paddling pool (May - Sept). Fishiing. Off site: Shop 300 m. Ruoms 4 km. Canyoning, rafting on the river Ardèche. Riding 2 km. Accompanied walks, canoe trips, visits to a wine cellar.	Leave Montélimar westwards on N102 towards Aubenas. After passing Villeneuve de Berg turn left on D103 towards Vogüé for 5 km. Turn left on D579 towards Ruoms, site on right in about 10 km. on entering Pradons. GPS: N44:28.598 E04:21.514

Open: 1 May - 10 September.

Charges 2006

Per unit incl. 2 persons	€ 13,00 - € 21,00
extra person	€ 3,70 - € 5,00
electricity (6A)	€ 3,60

FR07120 Camping Nature Parc L'Ardéchois

Mobile homes ▶ page 479

Route touristique des Gorges, F-07150 Vallon-Pont-d'Arc (Ardèche)

Tel: **04 75 88 06 63**. Email: **ardecamp@bigfoot.com**

This very high quality, family run site is within walking distance of Vallon-Pont-d'Arc. It borders the River Ardèche and canoe trips are run, professionally, direct from the site. This campsite is ideal for families with younger children seeking an active holiday. The facilities are comprehensive and of an extremely high standard, particularly the central toilet block. Of the 244 pitches, there are 197 for tourers, separated by trees and individual shrubs. All have electrical connections (6/10A) and 125 have full services. Forming a focal point is the bar and restaurant (good menus), with a terrace and stage overlooking the attractive heated pool. There is also a large paddling pool and sunbathing terrace. For children, there is a well thought out play area plus plenty of other space for youngsters to play, both on the site and along the river. Activities are organised throughout the season; these are family based – no discos. Patrols at night ensure a good night's sleep. Access to the site is easy and suitable for large outfits. Member of Leading Campings Group.

Facilities

Two well equipped toilet blocks, one superb with 'everything' working automatically, the other to be upgraded for 2007. Facilities are of the highest standard, very clean and include good facilities for babies, those with disabilities, washing up and laundry facilities. Four private bathrooms to hire. Washing machines. Shop. Swimming pool and paddling pool (no Bermuda shorts). Play area. Internet access. Organised activities, canoe trips. Off site: Vallon-Pont-d'Arc 800 m.

Open: Easter - 30 September.

Directions

From Vallon-Pont-d'Arc (western end of the Ardèche Gorge) at a roundabout go east on the D290. Site entrance is shortly on the right.
GPS: N44:23.873 E04:23.929

Charges 2007

Per pitch incl. 2 persons and electricity	€ 28,30 - € 47,50
extra person	€ 5,50 - € 8,50
child (2-13 yrs)	€ 4,00 - € 6,70

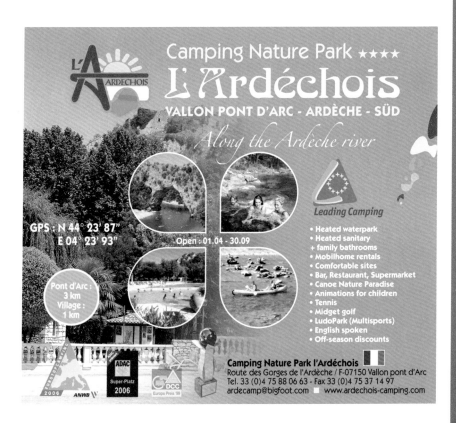

FR07150 Camping Domaine de Gil

Mobile homes ▶ page 480

Route de Vals-les-Bains, Ucel, F-07200 Aubenas (Ardèche)

Tel: **04 75 94 63 63**. Email: info@domaine-de-gil.com

This very attractive and well organised, smaller site in a less busy part of the Ardèche should appeal to couples and families with younger children. The 80, good sized, level pitches, 43 for touring, are surrounded by a variety of trees offering plenty of shade. All have 5-10A electricity with European type connectors. The focal point of the site is formed by the very attractive swimming pool, paddling pool and large sunbathing area, with the bar, restaurant and well appointed children's play areas all adjacent. A spacious sports area and shady picnic/play area are alongside the river Ardèche – an ideal spot to cool off on a hot day. You will receive a warm welcome from the enthusiastic and friendly, new Dutch owners (who speak excellent English).

Facilities

Modern well appointed toilet block, washing machine and iron. Motorcaravan services. Basic shop. Bar/restaurant, takeaway (from June). Heated swimming pool, paddling pool. Two play areas. Volleyball, boules, minigolf, football, tennnis. Canoeing, boating, fishing. Organised activities in high season. Only gas and electric barbecues. Off site: Shops at Vals-les-Bain 1.5 km. Interesting old town of Aubenas with larger range of shops, restaurants, bars 3 km. Organised canoe trips, canyoning on river Ardèche. Bicycle hire, riding 4 km.

Open: 14 April - 16 September.

Directions

Site north of Aubenas. From southeast (N102), after tunnel, turn right, roundabout (signed Privas), cross river into Pont d'Ucel. Bear right and at roundabout, last exit (signed Ucel). Shortly turn left (signed Ucel D18), then right (Ucel D578B). Site is 2 km. GPS: N44:38.558 E04:22.775

Charges 2006

Per unit incl. 2 persons	€ 14,00 - € 27,50
extra person	€ 3,50 - € 5,50
child (under 9 yrs)	free - € 4,00
electricity	€ 3,80

On the banks of the river Ardèche
Heated Swimmingpool
Rent of Mobilhomes

07200 Ucel-Aubenas - Ardèche
Tel. +33 4 75 94 63 63 (english spoken)
www.domaine-de-gil.com
e-mail: info@domaine-de-gil.com

FR07140 Camping les Lavandes

Le Village, F-07170 Darbres (Ardèche)

Tel: **04 75 94 20 65**. Email: sarl.leslavandes@online.fr

Situated to the northeast of Aubenas, in a quieter part of this region, Les Lavandes is surrounded by magnificent countryside, vineyards and orchards. The enthusiastic French owners, who speak good English, run a site that appeals to all nationalities. The 70 pitches (58 for touring) are arranged on low terraces separated by a variety of trees and shrubs that give welcome shade in summer. Visit at the end of May to see the campsite trees laden with luscious cherries. There is no problem with electricity, most pitches having 6A but a few have 10A. Water taps are not so abundant.

Facilities

Comprehensive and well maintained facilties, baby room, excellent facilities for disabled people. Washing machine. Small shop (1/7-31/8). Bar, terrace (1/6-31/8). Restaurant (1/7-31/8). Takeaway (14/4-31/8). Swimming pool, paddling pool, sunbathing areas, all with super views. Two small play areas for younger children. Table tennis, table football, pool table, billiard room, open air chess. No electric barbecues. Off site: Fishing 1 km. Bicycle hire 3 km. Tennis 5 km. Canoeing, walking, cycling, riding, carting nearby. Caves, historical villages. Wonderful area for birds (Golden Orioles and Bonellis eagle).

Open: 15 April - 30 September.

Directions

Site best approached from south. From Montélimar take N102 towards Aubenas. After Villeneuve, in Lavilledieu, turn right at traffic lights on D224 to Darbres (10 km). In Darbres turn sharp left by post office (care needed) and follow site signs.

Charges 2006

Per unit incl. 2 persons	€ 11,50 - € 16,50
extra person	€ 2,80 - € 3,50
child under 8 yrs	€ 1,00 - € 2,60
electricity	€ 3,50
dog	€ 1,50 - € 2,50

Check real time availability and at-the-gate prices...

www.alanrogers.com

FR07170 Ludocamping

F-07170 Lussas (Ardèche)

Tel: 04 75 94 21 22. Email: info@ludocamping.com

This is a quiet family campsite offering a really wide range of activities. From mid-July - early August, only families with children under 14 yrs are accepted which allows the activities to be focussed on this age group. The 160 grassy pitches, all for touring, 5-10A electricity, are in two areas. The upper area has large super pitches with wonderful views but little shade. The lower area, closer to the small river, has pitches set naturally amongst the trees and they have good shade. There is an attractive swimming pool (heated all season), good sized paddling pool and large sunbathing area.

Facilities

Clean, good quality toilet blocks offering all necessary facilities. Bar (all season), takeaway (from 1/5), terrace overlooking the valley. Play area. Volleyball. Table tennis. Recreational area next to river. Fishing, Bike hire. Club for over 6/7 yr olds offering a very wide range of activities. Off season club for older children. Seniors excursions in campsite coach. Only gas and electric barbecues. Off site: Lussas (few shops, restaurant, bar) 600 m. Riding 6 km. Gliding, hang-gliding, canoeing, speed boating.

Open: 1 April - 15 October.

Directions

From Montélimar take N102 west towards Aubenas, pass around Villeneuve, at traffic lights in Lavilledieu turn right onto D224 towards Lussas. Site entrance is on right just before village (about 4 km. from N102). GPS: N44:36.299 E04:28.247

Charges 2006

Per unit incl. 2 persons	€ 11,00 - € 25,00
extra person	€ 2,00 - € 6,00
child (0-7 yrs)	€ 2,00 - € 3,00
electricity (6A)	€ 3,00

No credit cards.

FR07190 Camping le Chambourlas

F-07360 Les Ollières-sur-Eyrieux (Ardèche)

Tel: 04 75 66 24 31. Email: info@chambourlas.com

The 75 grassy, slightly sloping pitches (72 for touring, electricty 10A) are set on low terraces, separated by an interesting variety of trees with excellent views over the wooded hills. The reception, bar/restaurant and shop are in one building accessed by 28 steps. There is a wide range of family orientated activities, especially in July and August, but these do not extend late into the night. Although there are special facilities, this is not an ideal site for those with walking difficulties. It is not ideal for very large units due to the narrow and steep roads in the vicinity. Tucked away up a steep and winding country road in a beautiful setting, in the hills above Privas, this small, neat and tidy family owned site (Dutch and English spoken) is popular with Dutch visitors.

Facilities

One modern toilet block with all the necessary facilities including those for disabled visitors. Bar, restaurant and takeaway (all 15/5-28/8). Small shop (July/Aug). Swimming pool, paddling pool and sunbathing area (15/4-30/9). Play area. Volleyball. Table tennis. Boules. Good range of activities, some in low season, No discos. River fishing. Off site: Many walks and bike rides. Excursions. Village of les Ollières sur Eyrieux 6 km. Privas 19 km. Cévennes Regional Mountain Park.

Open: 1 April - 1 October.

Directions

At traffic lights in Privas take D2 north, signed Le Cheylard. Follow road over two river bridges. Site entrance is on right about 12 km. after traffic lights. Take care – this is a fairly tortuous climb. GPS: N44:46.870 E04:37.016

Charges 2006

Per unit incl. 2 persons	€ 15,00 - € 28,00
extra person	€ 4,50 - € 5,50
child (2-10 yrs)	€ 4,00 - € 5,00

Camping Cheques accepted.

Check real time availability and at-the-gate prices...

www.**alanrogers**.com

FR07180 Ardèche Camping

Boulevard de Paste, F-07000 Privas (Ardèche)

Tel: **04 75 64 05 80**. Email: **jcray@wanadoo.fr**

This spacious, family run site is on the southern outskirts of Privas and would be a good base for exploring the lesser known parts of the Ardèche. Bus and coach trips are available to explore these areas. The site has 166 large, grass, reasonably level pitches, of which 153 are for tourers. A wide variety of trees provide reasonable shade and electricity (6/10A) should now be available on most pitches. Two tour operators use the site. Recent additions include new heated swimming and paddling pools. There is a play area for children and a mini-club, but no provision for teenagers.

Facilities

Two toilet blocks, only one open in low season. Facilities for disabled people. Motorcaravan service point. Bar and restaurant (1/5-30/9). Volleyball. Boule. Table tennis. Play area. Mini-club. Entertainment (high season). Only gas barbecues are permitted. Tents (4) for rent. Off site: Swimming pool and tennis courts adjacent. Supermarket 100 m. Bicycle hire 2 km. Riding 5 km.

Open: 1 April - 30 September.

Directions

At traffic lights in the centre of town take D2, signed Montélimar. Descend the winding road for about 1 km. then at roundabout (near Intermarché) turn right and then shortly left, signed Espace Ouvéze. Entrance is straight on. GPS: N44:43.569 E04:35.898

Charges 2006

Per unit incl. 2 persons	€ 14,00 - € 18,00
extra person	€ 3,50 - € 5,00
electricity (6A)	€ 3,50
Camping Cheques accepted.	

kawan-villages.com **tel: 00 333 59 59 03 59** *kawan* VILLAGES CAMPING

FR07200 Camping L'Oasis

Le Peliet Chaleat, F-07370 Eclassan (Ardèche)

Tel: **04 75 34 56 23**. Email: **oasis.camp@wanadoo.fr**

This is a small but spacious, steeply terraced and rural site in a lesser known area of the northern Ardèche. Immaculately kept, it is run by the enthusiastic and friendly Faure family (English is spoken). The level, grassy pitches are very large, well spaced and most have views. There are 63 pitches with 45 for touring, some on shady terraces with shrubs and trees and others being more open and sunny. All have 3/6A electricity. Due to the very steep site roads, it is unsuitable for large outfits or for those with walking difficulties. Caravans are taken by tractor from the entrance onto the pitches.

Facilities

Two very clean toilet blocks offer excellent facilities, including washbasins in cabins, some showers and toilets with washbasins, and two baths. Facilities for disabled visitors (but see above). Shop (closed Monday). Bar/restaurant and takeaway. Swimming pool and pools for children (heated May - mid Sept). Play area. Minigolf. Bicycle hire. Programme of entertainment (no discos). Off site: Eclassan 4 km. Ardoix 7 km. by road, 20 minutes walk. St Vallier 10 km. Riding 4 km. Golf 15 km.

Open: 15 April - 30 September.

Directions

From A7 autoroute south of Lyons take exit 12 (from north) or exit 13 (from south). Cross River Rhône and take N86 to Sarras. In town turn west on D6, signed St Jeure. Follow winding road up hill for 8 km. Turn right just before quarry (site signed) and site is 4 km. along narrow lane. GPS: N45:10.756 E04:44.374

Charges 2007

Per pitch incl. 2 persons and electricity	€ 14,00 - € 18,50
extra person	€ 3,90

FR07210 Camping L'Albanou

Quartier Pampelonne, F-07000 Saint Julien-en-St Alban (Ardèche)

Tel: **04 75 66 00 97**. Email: **camping.albanou@wanadoo.fr**

This small neat site is enthusiastically run by the welcoming Pougalan family (English spoken). It is situated in the beautiful northern Ardèche region with its many old villages, markets and museums – well worth exploring. The site's 60 large, level and easily accessible pitches (59 for touring) are in groups separated by tall hedges, all with electricity (6A). An attractive modern building houses the reception and a small bar with a terrace. Snacks are available to order. In high season.

Facilities

Refurbished toilet block has all the necessary facilities including those for disabled visitors. Small shop (all season). Bar, snacks, takeaway (all season). Good swimming pool, paddling pool (mid May - mid Sept). Motorcaravan services. Off site: St Julien (shop, bar/restaurant) 2 km. Pouzin 4 km. Supermarket 5 km. Fishing 300 m. Bicycle hire 10 km. Riding 15 km.

Open: 28 April - 22 September

Directions

From A7 autoroute take exit 16 for Loriol, head west across the Rhône to Le Pouzin. At roundabout take N104, signed Aubenas, follow road up hill. Turn left in 4 km. just before St Julien. Site is signed. GPS: N44:45.435 E04:42.722

Charges 2006

Per unit incl. 2 persons	€ 14,00 - € 16,00
electricity (6A)	€ 3,50

Check real time availability and at-the-gate prices...

www.alanrogers.com

FR07220 Camping le Merle Roux

Le Roux Est, F-07210 Baix (Ardèche)

Tel: **04 75 85 84 14**. Email: **lemerleroux@hotmail.com**

It is ideal for those looking for an active holiday based around the campsite. It has a very good swimming pool complex and a large but cosy bar/restaurant and terrace offering an excellent menu and takeaway service. There are 180 irregularly shaped pitches on steep terraces, 130 for touring, 6A electricity and many fully serviced. Most have good views and some shade from a variety of small trees, The steep roads and terracing may make access difficult for larger and under-powered units on some pitches. Rock pegs are essential. In July/August there is an extensive activity programme.

Facilities	Directions
Modern toilet blocks with all necessary facilities including facilities for babies and for those with disabilities, although they are a long distance from some pitches. Bar/restaurant, takeaway (all season). Shop (all season). Three swimming pools, toboggans, paddling pool. Boules. Table tennis. Basketball. Play area. Only gas barbecues. Off site: Pouzin with shops, bars, restaurants, supermarket 5 km. Villages of Baix, Braine and Chomerac close by. Fishing 1.5 km. Bicycle hire 10 km. Riding 15 km.	Leave A7 autoroute, exit 16 for Loriol. Go west across river to Le Pouzin. At roundabout take N86 (south), cross river, just before railway crossing turn right on D22a (site signed). In 500 m. turn left to site in 2 km. GPS: N44:42.313 E04:44.284

Open: 1 April - 31 October.

Charges 2006

Per unit incl. 2 persons	€ 13,00 - € 24,00
extra person	€ 2,50 - € 4,50
child (2-7 yrs)	€ 1,25 - € 2,25
electricity (6/10A)	€ 3,00

FR07230 Domaine Arleblanc Camping

Domain Arleblanc, F-07260 Rosières (Ardèche)

Tel: **04 75 39 53 11**. Email: **info@arleblanc.com**

The word 'bustling' would describe this site admirably. Open for a long season (20 March - 20 Oct), activities are organised on the Ardèche river for much of that time. The site owns its own canoes for hire and after a trip down the gorges you will be met and brought back to the site. Canyoning is organised, as are walks of varying degrees of strenuousness. There are 117 touring pitches and whilst maybe not the tidiest site in France, Arleblanc is certainly welcoming and good value. The staff are very helpful, and the site would appeal to families with young children and teenagers.

Facilities	Directions
Three toilet blocks, one old and with Turkish style WCs is due for replacement by 2007. The other blocks are good. Facilities for disabled visitors. Well stocked shop. Bar, restaurant and good snack bar with takeaway. Large, heated swimming pool (well fenced). Fenced and gated play area. Special meeting room for large groups. Large screen TV. Fishing. Mobile homes for rent. Off site: Bicycle hire and riding 10 km.	Travelling south on D104 Aubenas – St Ambroix road, after passing through Rosieres, take left hand slip road (large Intermarché). Site is signed from here, about 600 m. GPS: N44:27.808 E04:16.337

Open: 20 March - 20 October.

Charges 2006

Per unit incl. 2 persons	€ 12,00 - € 22,00
extra person	€ 2,50 - € 3,40
child (0-9 yrs)	€ 1,60 - € 2,20
electricity	€ 2,50 - € 3,70

FR07250 Yelloh! Village la Plaine

F-07120 Ruoms (Ardèche)

Tel: **04 75 39 65 83**. Email: **info@yellohvillage-la-plaine.com**

One of the 'all singing, all dancing' type of campsite, La Plaine is quiet in low season, but in high season with all-day and evening activities for both teenagers and adults, and a mini-club each day, there is no reason to feel bored! There are 212 pitches of moderate size (52 used for mobile homes), of which 160 have electricity. They are protected from the sun and marked by many trees. A stage and sound equipment are in use most nights and might cause some noise problems. This is a young family site for people with lots of energy, perhaps not for a quiet holiday in high season!

Facilities	Directions
Three sanitary blocks, clean and modern provide all facilities under cover. Young children's toilet facilities. Good facilities for disabled visitors. Excellent laundry room. Fridge hire. Shop, restaurant, bar and takeaway (all season). Heated swimming pool complex (all season). Games room and TV. Boules. Small football field. Play area (unfenced). Fitness room. Activity and entertainment programme day and evening. Miniclub (5-12 yrs). Fishing. River beach. Off site: Town 3 km. Bicycle hire, riding 2 km.	Exit Ruoms south on the D579 and at junction 2 km, south, take D111 signed St Ambroix. Site is on the left. GPS: N44:25.624 E04:20.137

Open: 1 April - 17 September.

Charges 2006

Per unit incl. 2 persons and electricity (6A)	€ 16,00 - € 36,00
extra person	€ 4,00 - € 6,00
child (0-7 yrs)	free - € 5,00

329

FR07290 La Domaine d'Imbours

F-07220 Larnas (Ardèche)

Tel: **04 75 54 39 50**. Email: **info@domaine-imbours.com**

This large site is part of a holiday complex with many mobile homes (99), chalets (41), hotel and 200 camping pitches. These are on scrub grass, not marked, with some shade from mature trees and 6A electricity (long leads may be helpful). For those looking for more or less everything organised for them in high season, this complex may suit. Out of season it is different, with not much happening. The complex is dominated by the hotel which is about 1 km. from the camping area along a descending site road. Around the hotel is a large and well designed pool complex. In high season there are evening shows and dancing, again at the hotel. Here too one can play tennis on one of four courts. To use the laundry one needs to transport washing to the hotel complex, where there are machines. There are quad bikes for hire which seem to be driven round the camping area with some speed As the complex of 270 hectare is rather remote, there is a well stocked, small supermarket and even a cash machine on site. For those who wish to visit towing a caravan – please do use the recommended route – other roads are not suitable.

Facilities

Good sanitary blocks with well designed showers and hot and cold water for washing (in cubicles) Facilities for children and disabled visitors. Laundry. Small but well stocked supermarket (the site is quite remote). ATM.. Bar and restaurant. Takeaway (1/6-31/8). Swimming pool complex (outdoor pools heated 1/430/9, indoor pool all season). Play area on sand. Tennis. Volleyball. Bicycle and quad bike hire. Archery. Riding. Activity clubs and entertainment (high season). Barbecues are not permitted.

Open: 24 March - 6 October.

Directions

From the N86 Bagnols - Aubanas road, exit onto the D4 at Bourg St Andeo to Remeze (a good road). Turn right at entrance to village on the D362 towards Larnas and site is on the right in Imbours. Do not attempt other routes with a caravan.

Charges 2007

Per person	€ 4,20 - € 7,00
child (0-7 yrs)	€ 2,30 - € 4,20
pitch (low season)	€ 4,20
pitch with 3 persons (high)	€ 26,00 - € 29,00

Domaine d'Imbours

Le Domaine d'Imbours offers a large choice of facilities: pool complex with heated indoor pool, outdoor pools, paddling pools and many activities.

Le Domaine d'Imbours
07220 Larnas
Tél. 0033(0)4 75 54 39 50
Fax. 0033(0)4 75 54 39 20
www.campings-franceloc.com

Ardèche

FR07260 Camping Caravaning les Cruses

Ribes, F-07260 Joyeuse (Ardèche)

Tel: **06 75 39 54 69**. Email: **les-cruses@wanadoo.fr**

High in the quiet hills of the southern Ardèche, among the sweet chestnut trees, this small site is carefully terraced. There are 45 pitches and 8 mobile homes and chalets for hire. Pitches are of various sizes, some on grass and some gravel. M. and Mme. Rouvier are very keen to further develop the site but insist that it is to remain a quiet family one. They feel that personal contact with their guests is important. M. Rouvier is the local mayor and will willingly tell you of the history and interesting things to see and do locally.

Facilities

The toilet block is up to date and clean with pre-set showers and a few en-suite shower, toilet and basin cabins. Baby room. Facilities for disabled visitors. Laundry room. Bar, restaurant and pizzeria providing good food (weekends only in low season). Swimming pool (1/5-30/9). Fishing. Play area. Activities arranged. Good air conditioned chalets for rent. Barbecues are not permitted. Off site: Riding 3 km. Golf 7 km.

Open: Easter - 30 September.

Directions

From Joyeuse the road to Ribes is signed. The site is signed on the left some 1 km. before the village. GPS: N44:29.545 E04:12.436

Charges 2006

Per unit incl. 2 person	€ 15,70 - € 19,20
extra person	€ 4,50
child (1-7 yrs)	€ 3,70
electricity (6A)	€ 3,60

FR07280 Camping les Arches

Route de Mirabel, F-07580 Saint Jean le Centenier (Ardèche)

Tel: **04 75 36 75 49**. Email: **pgaschet@clubinternet.fr**

The ever popular Ardèche region does have some quieter places and Les Arches is one of them. Situated behind a row of 19th century arches, now only used to support the track of a tourist train line, the owner has developed a site which shuns all the razzmatazz of many holiday sites. Although on a gentle hill, each well proportioned pitch blends into the terrain. All have access to 10A electricity and many have shade and good views. There is no swimming pool, but by the simple expedient of damming the river which runs by the site, a ready-made one is created.

Facilities

Two toilet blocks (only open in low season). While not the most modern, they are kept very clean and tidy. Baby room. Facilities for disabled visitors. Laundry facilities. Bread is available in high season from reception. Bar (15/6-15/9). Small restaurant (1/7-31/8). Well constructed play area. Table tennis. Boules. Fishing. River swimming. Chalets (10) for rent (plus 2 gites at the farm). Off site: Village with shop, restaurant and bar 2 km. Riding and bicycle hire 4 km.

Open: 1 May - 30 September.

Directions

From Aubenas take the N102- towards Montélimar (18 km) and take exit for St Jean le Centenier. Go under main road and at Citroen garage turn left on D458 signed Mirabel. Site is 500 m. on right. From Montélimar (20 km.) take exit for Mirabel and right at Citroen garage. Do not enter village while towing.

Charges 2006

Per unit incl. 2 persons	€ 11,00 - € 15,50
extra person	€ 3,50
electricity	€ 3,00 - € 3,50

FR07310 Camping la Roubine

Route de Ruoms, F-07150 Vallon Pont d'Arc (Ardèche)

Tel: **04 75 88 04 56**. Email: **roubine.ardeche@wanadoo.fr**

This site on the bank of the Ardèche has been in the same family ownership for some 30 years. During this time there has been constant upgrading and it must now be considered one of the best sites in the area. There are 114 touring pitches, all with electricity (6A) and quite spacious. Well tended grass, trimmed hedging and mature trees and smart tarmac roads create a calm and well kept atmosphere. Much attention is given to cleanliness – the toilet blocks are cleaned three times a day. A variety of sporting facilities are available on the site. The pool complex is heated when necessary throughout the season. There is a bar and restaurant of most modern design which, together with a mini-market, are open throughout the season. The campsite also caters for their young visitors with children's club in high season complete with an adventure playground and an amphitheatre. There is an internet room for visitors. The proprietors, M. Moulin and Mme. Van Eck like to welcome their guests and are available to help during the day – they are rightly proud of their well run campsite.

Facilities

Several small sanitary blocks include washbasins in cubicles. The main toilet block has showers, washbasins in vanity units, a baby bathroom and facilities for disabled visitors. Laundry. Swimming pool. Tennis. Boules. Fishing. Barbecues only permitted on three communal sites. River beach. Off site: Bicycle hire and riding 1 km. Footpath to town (700 m). Supermarket in town.

Open: 23 April - 15 September.

Directions

From Vallon take the D579 towards Ruoms. Site is well signed on left about 400 m. from town. From west (Ruoms) site signed on right near Vallon town sign. If missed proceed to roundabout at entrance to Vallon, go around and return 400 m. (see above).

Charges 2006

Per unit incl. 2 persons	€ 18,00 - € 31,00
extra person	€ 3,00 - € 6,70
child (0-13 yrs)	free - € 6,70
electricity	€ 4,00

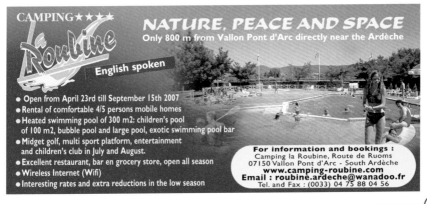

331

FR07300 International Camping

Salavas, F-07150 Vallon Pont d'Arc (Ardèche)

Tel: **04 75 88 00 99**. Email: **inter.camp@wanadoo.fr**

This urban site is situated on the banks of the Ardèche river, on the outskirts of the ancient town of Vallon. For those wishing to explore the country along this famous river, the site offers 110 smallish (80 sq.m) grass, hedge lined and shaded pitches, all with electricity (6A). There is an access gate (locked at night) to a small beach at the river's edge. Although the town's facilities are close to hand, a small restaurant with takeaway is available during the season, together with a mini-market. There may be some road noise, but the site is well placed for the explorer!

Facilities

Sanitary facilities are plentiful, modern and clean, including washbasins in cubicles. Facilities for people with disabilities. Baby room. Laundry facilities. Motorcaravan service point. Small shop for basic essentials. Small restaurant, snack bar and takeaway. Torches may be useful. Off site: Golf, riding and bicycle hire 1 km.

Open: 15 May - 15 September.

Directions

Site is very well signed at south end of the only road bridge across the river on the D579 at southern end of town. GPS: N44:23.851 E04:22.939

Charges 2006

Per unit incl. 2 persons and electricity	€ 19,00 - € 24,00
extra person	€ 6,00
child (0-10 yrs)	free - € 5,00

FR07320 Camping des Gorges

Chemin de Sauze, F-07700 Saint Martin d'Ardèche (Ardèche)

Tel: **04 75 04 61 09**. Email: **info@camping-des-gorges.com**

Situated just outside the extremely attractive village of Saint Martin d'Ardèche, this site is on the north bank of the river, right at the end of the gorge. From here one can explore this unique river and indeed the attractive, small villages on the banks. With a total of 145 pitches (119 for tourists), nearly every pitch has some shade, which is helpful in this region of hot summers. The pitches are of average size on grass, all with 5A electricity (French plugs) and 8 with full services. This family run site is associated with Camping La Roubine at Vallon Pont d'Arc. Although the village is a ten minute walk, there is a surprisingly large and well stocked shop on the site. The site does cater for children – there is an underground games room, pony rides and games, and activities are organised. The modern swimming pool has a section for young children. Teenagers are asked to enjoy themselves at a disco in the village, not on site! As ever, boules are played regularly. There is a barrier at night.

Facilities

The sanitary blocks are modern and very clean with washbasins in cabins. Facilities for disabled people. Laundry room. Good shop. Bar, restaurant and takeaway. Swimming pool and large sunbathing area. Organised activities. Games room. Pony rides. Boules. Barbecues are not permitted. Off site: Fishing 200 m. Riding 4 km. Bicycle hire 8 km. ATM and internet access in village.

Open: 1 April - 15 September.

Directions

From the N86 Aubenas - Bagnols road take road signed St Martin d'Ardèche at the roundabout at St Just. Site is signed on the Sauze road out of the village, about 800 m. on the left.

Charges 2006

Per unit incl. 2 persons	€ 15,00 - € 25,00
extra person	€ 3,00 - € 5,80
child (0-13 yrs)	free - € 5,80
electricity	€ 4,00

* Swimming pool of 200 m2
* Rental of mobile homes
* Bar restaurant
* Grocery store
* Canoe and kayak rental
* Mini club and entertainment in the high season
* Children's playground
* Special rates in the low season

FOR INFORMATION AND BOOKINGS
Camping des Gorges ***
07700 St. Martin d'Ardèche
Tel/Fax : 00 33 4 75 04 61 09
Email: info@camping-des-gorges.com
Internet: www.camping-des-gorges.com

FR07340 Domaine du Cros d'Auzon

Saint Maurice d'Ardèche, F-07200 Vogüé Gare (Ardèche)

Tel: **04 75 37 75 86**. Email: **camping.auzon@wanadoo.fr**

Mobile homes ▶ page 480

This site can be described with the word 'immaculate'. The 55 pitches on well cut grass, are all of a very generous size and all have water, drainage and electricity. On the banks of the Ardèche, the site is part of a holiday complex which includes a hotel and conference centre, separated by a 300 m. driveway. Out of season it is very quiet, but in July and August a newly built bar, takeaway and restaurant together with an 'animations' building, become the focal point of the evenings. There are 55 mobile homes for hire (some tour operators). The hotel complex has an outdoor pool of a modern design which is available to camping customers at no cost, as are minigolf and tennis. Canoe hire is possible on the river. In season there is a shop attached to the bar complex. Out of season the village is about 500 m. with the usual shops and an ATM machine. Although there is no need to dress for dinner, this site has an air of formality which will appeal to some readers.

Facilities

Two excellent, modern toilet blocks of an unusual design are kept very clean. Well equipped laundry room. Fridge hire. Bar, takeaway, restaurant and shop (July/Aug). At the hotel: swimming pool (1/5-15/9), minigolf and tennis. Children's playground of generous size. Charcoal barbecues are not permitted. Bicycle hire. Internet access. Off site: Golf nearby. Riding 10 km.

Open: 1 April - 15 September.

Directions

The D579 between Ruoms and Aubenas passes through the village of Vogue. At the only roundabout take road to the southwest. Site is signed from the roundabout (about 800 m).

Charges 2006

Per unit incl. 2 persons	€ 14,00 - € 24,00
extra person	€ 4,00 - € 6,50
child (0-6 yrs)	€ 2,00 - € 4,50
electricity (6A)	€ 3,50 - € 4,20

FR07360 Camping le Petit Bois

87 rue du Petit Bois, F-07120 Ruoms (Ardèche)

Tel: 04 75 39 60 72. Email: vacances@campinglepetitbois.fr

Situated only 800 metres from the ancient town centre of Ruoms, and yet within an area of trees and rocky outcrops, this site offers a centre for those wishing to explore this part of the Ardèche valley. The 118 pitches are of irregular shape and size and are a mix of stone and grass (76 are used for mobile homes). There is some shade. The site is now thirty years old and is needing some restoration, which is now underway. Some standpipes have coils of tubing attached. Perhaps these should not be used for domestic water purposes. A 'Sites et Paysages' member. There are three toilet blocks, although only one is open in low season (including facilities for disabled people). However there may be some difficulty with some of the stone paths. By local decree the use of barbecues is restricted to April, May and June. Shortly after our inspection a new multisport facility was due to be installed.

Facilities

Three toilet blocks (only one open in low season) were in need of some maintenance when we visited. Cleaning appeared somewhat erratic. Bar. Restaurant and takeaway (1/7-31/8). Modern swimming pool, covered outside July/Aug. Playground. Games and TV rooms in season. Fishing. Entertainment organised in high season. Off site: Town with shops, etc. 300 m. Riding and bicycle hire 1 km.

Open: 1 April - 30 September.

Directions

Approaching Ruoms on the D579 from Vallon Pont d'Arc go straight on at first (Super U) and second roundabouts. At third roundabout turn left (southwest) signed Largentier (site is signed). GPS: N44:27.638 E04:20.240

Charges 2006

Per unit incl. 2 persons	€ 13,00 - € 19,00
extra person	€ 3,50 - € 5,50
child (1-6 yrs)	€ 2,00 - € 3,50
electricity	€ 3,80

CAMPING ***
ESPACE AQUATIQUE CHAUFFÉ ET COUVERT
TOBOGGAN - PATAUGEOIRE LUDIQUE
RIVIÈRE - LOCATIONS
ANIMATIONS
Le Petit Bois
SITES & PAYSAGES DE FRANCE
07120 RUOMS
TÉL : 04 75 39 60 72 - Fax : 04 75 93 95 50
Internet : www.campinglepetitbois.fr - Courriel : vacances@campinglepetitbois.fr

FR07330 Camping la Digue

Chauzon, F-07120 Ruoms (Ardèche)

Tel: 04 75 39 63 57. Email: info@camping-la-digue.fr

Perhaps not the smartest campsite in the Ardèche, La Digue is certainly one with a warm welcome from its resident owners who are looking to introduce their visitors to a great family atmosphere. There are plenty of outdoor activities available, both on and off the site. M. Elne and his small team organise many activities, including canoeing and fishing on the River Ardèche which flows past the site, mountain biking, hill walking and caving. The 74 touring pitches are on grass and of a good size, with 6-10A electricity available to all. La Digue is open for an unusually long season (1/4-3/11).

Facilities

The newly built toilet block is kept in excellent condition. Facilities for disabled visitors. Good laundry room. Well stocked shop. Restaurant and takeaway (1/4-30/9). Swimming pool (heated in season). Fishing. Pony riding. Bicycle hire. Winter caravan storage. Off site: Golf 6 km. Riding 8 km. River beach 200 m.

Open: 1 April - 30 November.

Directions

From the D579 Vallon Pont d'Arc - Ruoms road, turn left immediately on entering village of Pradon, signed Chauzon. Site is signed from here. After crossing river, in about 400 m. take new ring road on left around the village (advised as village itself is very narrow). GPS: N44:29.091 E04:22.379

Charges 2006

Per unit incl. 2 persons	€ 13,90 - € 21,00
extra person	€ 4,00 - € 5,00
child (2-6 yrs)	€ 2,00 - € 4,00
electricity	€ 3,80 - € 4,00

FR07370 Mondial Camping

Route des Gorges de l'Ardèche, F-07150 Vallon Pont d'Arc (Ardèche)

Tel: 04 75 88 00 44. Email: reserv-info@mondial-camping.com

Mondial Camping is one of many along the banks of the Ardèche river. As with the others, Mondial arranges canoe trips downstream with minibuses provided for the return trip. This is a large site of 240 pitches, of which 21 are used for mobile homes. There is a small tour operator presence. The pitches are of normal size on grass, which does get barren by the end of the season. There are 32 'grand comfort' pitches, providing water, drainage and electricity. The site has a good pool complex with a pool for swimming, one for children and another with water slides.

Facilities

Three modern toilet blocks are tiled, very clean and heated in low season. Facilities for disabled customers. Laundry facilities. Shop, bar, restaurant and takeaway (all season). Gas and electric barbecues only. Swimming pools (all season and heated until 15/6). Canoe and kayak hire. Fishing (permit required). Off site: Town facilities 1 km. Riding 100 m. Bicycle hire 500 m.

Open: 1 April - 30 September.

Directions

From Vallon Pont d'Arc take the Route Gorges d'Ardèche.(D290). Site is 1 km. on the right. GPS: N44:23.04 E04:24.088

Charges 2006

Per unit incl. 2 persons	€ 18,00 - € 37,00
extra person	€ 5,50 - € 7,50
child (1-13 yrs)	€ 4,00 - € 6,50
electricity (10A)	€ 4,50

FR07380 Camping le Provençal

Route des Gorges, F-07150 Vallon Pont d'Arc (Ardèche)

Tel: 04 75 88 00 48. Email: camping.le.provencal@wanadoo.fr

Le Provençal is a large, well laid out and well equipped campsite on the banks of the Ardèche. We were impressed with the size and quality of the 178 hedged, grass touring pitches (8A electricity available). There are also 22 pitches used for mobile homes to rent. The excellent fittings and cleanliness in the three modern toilet blocks demonstrate that this is a well cared for site. The bars, takeaways and restaurant are clean and attractive and the pool layout is well planned. Altogether, this site should appeal to those who enjoy the Ardèche area and all that it has to offer.

Facilities

Sanitary facilities are excellent and clean, with heating in low season. Facilities for children and visitors with disabilities. Laundry facilities. Good shop (all season) Bar, restaurant and takeaway. Good swimming pools, heated when necessary. Play area. Tennis. Volleyball. Fishing. Canoe hire. Charcoal barbecues are not permitted. Off site: Riding and bicycle hire 1 km. Golf 10 km.

Open: 10 April - 20 September.

Directions

From Vallon Pont d''Arc take the Route Gorges d'Ardèche (D290). Site is about 1 km. on right. GPS: N44:23.880 E04:23.992

Charges 2006

Per unit incl. 2 persons	€ 20,00 - € 30,00
extra person	€ 5,00 - € 6,70
child (under 4 yrs)	€ 3,50 - € 4,50
electricity (8A)	€ 3,80

FR07390 Camping la Résidence

Rue de la Bateuse, F-07700 Saint Remèze (Ardèche)

Tel: 04 75 04 26 87. Email: mail@campinglaresidence.net

At an altitude of some 370 metres (over 1,200 feet) and set in a village of great charm, this site is run by a young, welcoming and enthusiastic husband and wife team who arrange many outdoor activities. These include hill walking, climbing, mountain biking and canoe trekking amongst others. The views from parts of the site are superb. In the low seasons work continues to develop the site and this is producing more facilities each year. With some terracing, a total of 60 pitches (40 with 5A electricity) are on grass with small acacia and cherry trees to mark them and give some shade.

Facilities

The toilet block is adequate, tiled and clean (again there are plans to extend the existing block with further facilities for disabled visitors and a new area for children). Laundry room. Motorcaravan car service point. Bar, restaurant and takeaway (all season). Unheated, deep swimming pool. Torches useful. Only gas and electric barbecues are permitted. Bicycle hire. Off site: Fishing and riding 8 km. Restaurants and shops in village.

Open: Easter - 30 September.

Directions

From Vallon Pont d'Arc take D4 road, signed St Remeze. After about 13 km. enter village, where site is signed on right. GPS: N44:23.535 E04:30.273

Charges 2006

Per unit incl. 1 person	€ 9,00
extra person	€ 7,00
child (2-14 yrs)	€ 4,75
electricity (5A)	€ 4,00

FR26030 Sunêlia le Grand Lierne

B.P. 8, F-26120 Chabeuil (Drôme)

Tel: **04 75 59 83 14**. Email: **contact@grandlierne.com**

In addition to its obvious attraction as an overnight stop, fairly convenient for the A7 autoroute, this site provides a pleasant base to explore this little known area between the Ardèche and the Vercors mountains and the Côte du Rhône wine area. It has 161 marked, stony pitches, 76 for touring units, mainly separated by developing hedges or oak trees. Many have good shade, some are on flat ground and all have electricity (6/10A). A more open area exists for those who prefer less shade and a view of the mountains, but this area contains many mobile homes. The site has an attractive pool complex with several pools and surrounded by terraces with loungers for sunbathing. One pool is covered in poor weather. English and Dutch are spoken. The site is used by tour operators (30%).

Facilities

Two sanitary blocks with facilities for disabled people. Washing machines, dryers. Motorcaravan services. Shop/restaurant, terrace (1/7-31/8). Bar/takeaway (1/5-8/9). Fridge rental. Three pools 15/5-31/8, one very small, covered and heated (open all season). Paddling pool, water slide. Playgrounds. Mini-tennis, minigolf, table tennis, volleyball, archery football. Bicycle hire. Library. Extensive entertainment programme. Only gas and electric barbecues. No pets (8/7-18/8). Off site: Golf 3 km. Bicycle hire 4.5 km. Fishing 5 km. Riding 7 km. Canoe/kayak near. Vercors mountains. Chabeuil 5 km.

Open: 28 April - 9 September, with all services.

Directions

Site signed from Chabeuil about 11 km. east of Valence. Best approached from south side of Valence via Valence ring road. D68 to Chabeuil. Site is off D125 to Charpey, 5 km. from Chabeuil, well signed. GPS: N44:54.951 E05:03.907

Charges 2006

Per unit incl. 2 persons	€ 16,70 - € 29,60
extra person	€ 7,10 - € 8,30
child (2-7 yrs)	€ 3,60 - € 6,00
electricity (6/10A)	€ 4,30 - € 5,70

Le Grand Lierne

BP 8 - F 26120 CHABEUIL
Tél : 33 4 75 59 83 14
Fax : 33 4 75 59 87 95
www.grandlierne.com
contact@grandlierne.com

Motorway A7,
exit Valence Sud,
direction Grenoble
and then
Chabeuil

Sunêlia
open style

Water slide

Heated pool

Restaurant Boutique

Miniclub

Entertainment

FR26060 Camping Municipal

F-26190 Saint Nazaire-en-Royans (Drôme)

Tel: **04 75 48 41 18**

The pretty village of St Nazaire-en-Royans is to be found on the western perimeter of the Parc Régional du Vercors and is distinguished by its impressive bridge which straddles the Isère river. The municipal site is only 500 m. from the village and is fronted by the municipal tennis courts and boules area. With a well laid out, tidy and organised appearance, the 75 grass pitches are of a good size, all with electricity (3/6A) and separated by hedges. A few overlook the river and trees give some shade. A convenient base for exploring this scenic area.

Facilities

The basic sanitary block is in good condition and clean. It provides British and Turkish style WCs, some curtained washbasin cabins, facilities for disabled visitors, dishwashing and laundry sinks, plus a washing machine. Very small play area with grass base. Fishing. Security gate (locked 10 pm.-7 am). Gas and electric barbecues only. Off site: St Nazaire-en-Royans 500 m. Vercors mountains.

Open: 1 May - 30 September.

Directions

Exit autoroute A49 (Valence - Grenoble) at junction 8. Take N532 east for 3 km. to St Nazaire-en-Royans. Site is clearly signed 500 m. east of village just off D76 (St Jean-en-Royans). The site is a left turn on the brow of a hill on a corner – take care.

Charges 2006

Per unit incl. 2 persons	€ 8,10
extra person	€ 3,10
child (3-12 yrs)	€ 1,60 - € 1,80
electricity (3/6A)	€ 2,60 - € 3,50

FR26040 Camping le Couspeau

Mobile homes ▶ page 480

F-26460 Le Poët Célard (Drôme)

Tel: 04 75 53 30 14. Email: info@couspeau.com

The site has 127 pitches with 87 for touring. Access to the 62 touring pitches on the older section of the site (6A electricity) is reasonably easy, although levelling blocks may be handy. Mature trees provide some shade. The 30 fully serviced pitches on the lower section are large, separated by small hedges with little shade. Access is via a steep road but tractor assistance is available. Rock pegs are advised. The site has a good restaurant/bar and terrace with panoramic views. In July and August there is weekly live music and a themed meal. As one approaches this site a magnificent landscape of mountains and valleys unfolds and the overall impression is one of beauty and tranquillity. Those seeking to unwind and relax should appreciate the delightful scenery and setting of this medium sized site. The most direct approach to the site is via a steep road, and with several hairpin bends to negotiate, care is required (underpowered units not advised). For many people the views are reward enough, for others there is an alternative, easier route via Bourdeaux.

Facilities

Three sanitary blocks. Washing machines, dryer. Facilities for disabled campers (but site is not ideal with steep roads and steps. Shop (15/4-14/9). Bar (20/6-14/9). Restaurant and takeaway (25/6-25/8). Pool (1/6-30/8) and small, heated, covered, toddler's pool (14/4-14/9). Play area, organised activities. Tennis, table tennis, volleyball. Bike hire. Rafting, canoe trips (on River Drôme), riding, paragliding. Off site: Riding, fishing 5 km. Ideal area for the serious cyclist, mountain biker and hiker. Medieval towns and villages, markets and châteaux. Crest, Poët-Laval. Vercors mountains.

Open: 15 April - 14 September.

Directions

From A7, exit 16, take D104 to Crest. At traffic lights, turn right, D538 towards Bourdeaux. Before Bourdeaux turn right over bridge, D328B, signed Le Po't Célard. Climb for 1.5 km. to T-junction, turn right. D328. Before Le Poët Célard turn left, D328A to site. GPS: N44:35.744 E05:06.680

Charges 2006

Per unit incl. 2 persons	€ 18,00 - € 26,00
extra person	€ 4,00 - € 6,00
child (under 7 yrs)	free - € 4,00
electricity (6A)	€ 3,00

Camping Cheques accepted.

FR26090 Camping les Truffières

Lieu-dit Nachony, F-26230 Grignan (Drôme)

Tel: 04 75 46 93 62. Email: info@lestruffieres.com

This is a delightful small site in a rural setting within walking distance of the picturesque ancient village of Grignan with wonderful views and providing peace and tranquillity. The 85 good sized pitches are level and fairly stony with 79 for touring units. Shaded by oak trees and separated by rosemary or laurel hedging, each pitch has electricity. The Croze family is most welcoming and achieves high standards of cleanliness and order while maintaining a friendly, relaxed atmosphere.

Facilities

Good toilet block provides all necessary facilities. Washing machine and ironing board. Snack bar, takeaway (June - Sept). Swimming pool, smaller pool for children. Volleyball, table tennis, boules. Little in the way of on site entertainment but many off site activities can be booked. No dogs.

Open: 20 April - 1 October.

Directions

From N7 (or A7 autoroute exit 18) south of Montélimar, take D133 (changes to D541) signed Grignan. After 9 km, just before entering Grignan, take D71 towards Charamet and site is shortly on the left. GPS: N44:24.714 E04:53.433

Charges 2006

Per unit incl. 2 persons	€ 13,50 - € 16,50
electricity (10A)	€ 4,20

No credit cards.

337

FR26100 Camping Le Sagittaire

Pont de Mirabelle, F-26110 Vinsobres (Drôme)

Tel: **04 75 27 00 00**. Email: **camping.sagittaire@wanadoo.fr**

Recommended by our agent in France, Le Sagittaire is beautifully situated in the heart of the Côte du Rhône region and we intend to carry out a full inspection in 2007. The site is 2 km. from the wine village of Vinsobres and 6 km. from Nyons, which is well known for its olives and its microclimate. The site provides 230 pitches which are spacious and well shaded, all with water and electricity and bordered by hedges. In the centre of the site is an aquatic area of 700 sq.m. with water slides and a spa. A one hectare lake is surrounded by a sandy beach. Leisure activities for all ages are catered for in July and August – sports during the day and karaoke, disco, barbecues and live shows at night.

Facilities

Heated toilet blocks. Supermarket and gift shop. Two bars. Snack bar and takeaway. Pool complex with slides, jacuzzi, 'wild river' and covered pool. Lake with sandy beach. Tennis courts. Minigolf. Boules. Giant chess. Junior Club (3-12 yrs). Off site: Vaison la Romaine, the Castles of Grignan and Suze la Rousse. Mediterranean beaches 1.5 hours away.

Open: All year.

Directions

From Lyon on the A7 exit at Montpellier Sud, towards Nyons-Gap. In Nyons follow signs for Suze la Rousse. Site is signed.

Charges 2006

Per unit incl. 3 persons	€ 28,00
extra person	€ 7,05
child (under 7 yrs)	€ 4,05
electricity (3/6A)	€ 3,55 - € 4,60

Domaine du Sagittaire

3 hectares of relaxation with a 7600 m² waterpark parc and lake, tennis, Californian mini golf, volleyball. New in 2007 200 m² swimming pool.

Vinsobres 26110 Nyons
Tél. 0033(0)4 75 27 00 00
Fax. 0033(0)4 75 27 00 39
www.campings-franceloc.com

FR26110 Les 4 Saisons Camping de Grâne

Route de Roche-sur-Grâne, F-26400 Grâne (Drôme)

Tel: **04 75 62 64 17**. Email: **camping.4saisons@wanadoo.fr**

This small, terraced site, open all year, nestles in the hillsides of the lower Drôme valley. With its 80 pitches (73 for touring units), it provides mainly overnight accommodation but it is worth a longer stay. The modern main building houses reception on the top floor, with other facilities below, and provides commanding views across the valley towards Crest and the Vercors. The pitches are level and stony, of variable size, cut out of the hillside and reached by a one-way system on tarmac roads. All pitches have electricity (6/16A), some with water and drain. This is an excellent base for exploring the Drôme valley and the Vercors mountains.

Facilities

Good sanitary facilities, heated in low season, include, baby room, en-suite facilities for disabled visitors (but site is very sloping and not suitable for wheelchairs). Washing machine. Bar, TV room, snacks (15/4-15/9). Small swimming pool (1/6-15/9). Play area. Bicycle hire. Off site: Village nearby with shops catering for most needs. Fishing 1 km. Riding 3 km.

Open: All year.

Directions

From A7 exit 17, or the N7 at Loriol, take the D104 towards Crest. After 8 km. in Grâne take D113 south. Site is on left about 600 m. beyond the village. GPS: N44:43.622 E04:55.618

Charges 2006

Per unit incl. 2 persons	€ 13,00 - € 15,00
extra person	€ 3,00 - € 5,00
child (0-10 yrs)	€ 2,00 - € 4,00
electricity	€ 4,00

FR26120 Gervanne Camping

Bellevue, F-26400 Mirabel et Blacons (Drôme)

Tel: **04 75 40 00 20**. Email: **info@gervanne-camping.com**

This spacious, riverside family run site with 174 pitches, 162 for touring, is in two sections either side of a road and connected via an underpass. One section is adjacent to the bar, restaurant and superb swimming pool with mountain views. The pitches are of average size with some shade and are separated by a few small shrubs and trees. The other section, closer to the river, is less formally laid out with mature trees offering plenty of shade. All pitches have easy access to electricity (4 or 6A) and there are water points around the site.

Facilities

Two well appointed, very clean toilet blocks with the usual facilities and a baby room. Laundry. Large en-suite unit for disabled people. Bar/restaurant (1/6-15/9) with simple menu, takeaway service and internet terminal. Heated swimming pool (1/5-20/9). Small play area. Football pitch. Boules. Bicycle hire. Electric and gas barbecues only. Motorcaravan service point. Off site: Supermarket next door. Fishing, canoeing and bathing in the River Drôme. Riding 5 km. Golf 13 km.

Open: 1 April - 1 November.

Directions

Site is about 22 km. east of the A7 autoroute (exit 16). Take D104 and then D164 bypassing Crest. After 6 km, turn left onto D164A and cross river into Mirabel-et-Blacons, left at roundabout and follow site signs. GPS: N44:42.666 E05:05.409

Charges 2006

Per unit incl. 2 persons	€ 12,10 - € 17,20
extra person	€ 3,40 - € 5,10
child (up to 7 yrs)	€ 1,70 - € 2,60
electricity (4/6A)	€ 2,80 - € 3,40

FR26140 Camping la Chataigneraie

Route de Mantaille, F-26140 Anneyron (Drôme)

Tel: **04 75 31 43 33**. Email: **contact@chataigneraie.com**

Small and neat, La Chataigneraie is a family run, terraced site (English spoken) tucked away in the countryside and will suit those seeking a quieter, relaxing family orientated site. It is not ideal for those with walking difficulties. There are 71 medium sized, slightly sloping, grassy pitches, 30 for touring away from the static units. They are separated by a variety of hedges and young trees provide varying degrees of shade and all have 6/10A electricity. The Drôme is a beautiful area to explore with many old towns and villages with their markets and museums. Enjoy the local produce and the wines of the Rhône valley.

Facilities

The single toilet block at the top of the site is a good, modern building kept very clean. Bar and small shop. Good restaurant/takeaway with full menu at weekends and high season, otherwise a 'menu de jour'. Swimming and paddling pools (15/5-15/9). Short tennis. Two small play areas, TV and games room. Bicycle hire. Farmer's market twice a week. Entertainment for children and adults (July/Aug). WiFi internet access near bar. Only electric barbecues can be used. Off site: Marked walks and cycle tracks in the hills around. Fishing and golf 3 km. Riding 8 km.

Open: 1 April - 30 September.

Directions

Leave A7 south of Lyons at exit 12 and go south on the N7 for 7 km. Turn left on D1 to Anneyron. In the village turn right on D161 signed Mantaille and in 3 km. turn right on D301, signed Albon. Site is shortly on the right, is well signed. GPS: N45:15.282 E04:54.191

Charges 2006

Per unit incl. 2 persons	€ 13,50 - € 16,00
extra person	€ 3,90 - € 4,90
child (3-14 yrs)	€ 2,00 - € 3,60
electricity (6/10A)	€ 3,70 - € 4,40

FR26150 Camping Lac Bleu

Quarter la Touche, F-26410 Chatillon en Diois (Drôme)

Tel: **04 75 21 85 30**. Email: **info@lacbleu-diois.com**

This spacious and peaceful site is run by a very friendly family who have made many improvements to the site with many more in the pipeline. It lies in a beautiful valley surrounded by mountains, south of the Vercors National Park. The 90 pitches (78 for touring) are large, level, with rough grass, slightly bumpy and separated by a variety of trees offering some shade (rock pegs advised). All have electricity (6-10A). At the centre of the site is a lake of 2.5 hectares with warm clean water fed by springs making it ideal for swimming and fishing. A good bar, restaurant and terrace overlook the lake and there is plenty of space for children to play. An evening stroll around the lake is recommended. The site is near the very small River Bez and not far from the interesting and ancient small town of Die, the home of the famous Clairette de Die – a sparkling wine mentioned in dispatches by the Romans around 40 AD. It is a good site for exploring this picturesque part of France, yet to completely unwind and enjoy the views, the sunset over the mountains and the very clean air.

Facilities

Two clean toilet blocks one new, the other refurbished for 2007, with all the necessary facilities including baby room and facilities for disabled campers. Motorcaravan service point. Small shop. Bar/restaurant. Takeaway. TV and games room. Play area bordering the lake. Large sports/play area. Bicycle hire. Lake bathing and fishing. Pedaloes. Internet point. Only gas and electric barbecues allowed. Off site: Medieval villages (Châtillon 2 km).

Open: 1 April - 30 September.

Directions

Head southeast from Die on the D93, signed Gap. After about 5 km. turn left on D539 signed Châtillon-en-Diois. After 4.5 km. bear right onto D140, site signed. Follow signs to site, shortly on left. GPS: N44:40.947 E05:26.799

Charges 2006

Per unit incl. 2 persons € 9,90 - € 16,50

Quartier la Touche - 26410 Châtillon en Diois - France
Tel.: 0033 (0)4 75 21 85 30 - Fax: 0033 (0)4 75 21 82 05
E-mail: info@lacbleu-diois.com - www.lacbleu-diois.com

FR26130 Camping L'Hirondelle

Bois de Saint Ferreol, F-26410 Menglon (Drôme)

Tel: **04 75 21 82 08**. Email: **contact@campinghirondelle.com**

This natural, spacious and peaceful site is run by a very friendly family and you are assured a good welcome. It lies in a beautiful valley, south of the Vercors mountains and the Vercors National Park, beside the River Bez, a tributary of the River Drôme which is also close by. In natural openings in woodland, the 100 large to very large pitches all have electricity (3/6A) and are stony and slightly bumpy (rock pegs advised). There are 64 for touring units. The large pitches are separated by a wide variety of trees and the 1.5 km. of river bank on one side. A 'Sites et Paysages' member.

Facilities

Two large toilet blocks offer all the necessary facilities. Very good bar/restaurant and takeaway. Small range of supplies from the bar. Swimming pool, plus new excellent pool complex with small slide, paddling pool, jacuzzi and Lazy river (1/5 -17/9). Playground. Club/TV room. Internet access. Fishing. Boules. Archery. Organised events. Advice on activities and bookings made. Occasional evening events. Off site: Riding and bicycle hire 3 km.

Open: 28 April - 17 September.

Directions

From Die follow D93 southwards and after 5 km, at Pont de Quart, turn left on D539 signed Châtillon. After approx. 4 km. turn right on D140, signed Menglon. Site entrance is on the right just after crossing a small river. GPS: N44:40.885 E05:26.846

Charges 2006

Per pitch incl. 2 persons	€ 16,20 - € 24,30
electricity (3-6A)	€ 3,15 - € 4,20

Camping Cheques accepted.

kawan-villages.com **tel: 00 333 59 59 03 59**

FR26170 Camping L'Or Vert

Aubres, F-26110 Nyons (Drôme)

Tel: 04 75 26 24 85. Email: camping-or-vert@wanadoo.fr

This very friendly, well cared for, family run, site with a long season will appeal to those who seek less in the way of on-site entertainment. It is an ideal base to tour the beautiful region of northern Provence, famous for its wines, lavender and olives. There are 78 small to medium sized pitches with 73 for touring. Most are gravelly but a few have some grass (6A electricity is available). Some pitches are laid out irregularly under trees with good shade and others, alongside the river, are separated by hedges and have less shade. Rock pegs are essential.

Facilities

Although not the most modern, the toilet block is kept very clean and has all the usual facilities but no provision for babies and those who are handicapped. Small bar and snack bar (July/Aug). Games/TV room. Fridge hire. Boules. Fishing and bathing in adjacent river. Animals not accepted in July and August. Only electric and gas barbecues permitted. Off site: Riding and bike hire 5 km. Aubres shop, baker and restaurant 500 m. Nyons 3 km.

Open: 1 April - 1 October.

Directions

From Nyons head northeast on the D94 for 3 km. towards Gap. Turn right at traffic lights just before entering Aubres, site signed. Entrance 200 m. GPS: N44:22.326 E05:09.774

Charges 2006

Per person	€ 3,90 - € 4,00
child (0-7 yrs)	€ 2,20
pitch	€ 4,30 - € 5,30
electricity (6A)	€ 3,60

FR26210 Camping Les Bois du Chatelas

Mobile homes ▶ page 481

Route de Dieulefit, F-26460 Bourdeaux (Drôme)

Tel: 04 75 00 60 80. Email: contact@chatelas.com

Located at the heart of the the Drôme Provencale, Les Bois du Chatelas is a smart, family run site which has undergone many recent improvements. The site is just 1 km. from the delightful village of Bourdeaux which offers a good range of shops, cafés, etc. There are 120 pitches here of which 44 are occupied by mobile homes. Although situated on a hillside, the pitches are level and of a good size. They all offer electricity, water and drainage. Les Bois du Chatelas is a particularly good choice for those seeking an active holiday. Member of Sites et Paysages de France. The long distance GR9 footpath passes through the site and there are very many walking and cycle routes close at hand. A popular aquagym is organised in the large outdoor pool in peak season. In the high season, a lively entertainment programme is organized as well as a number of cycling and walking excursions.

Facilities

Two heated toilet blocks (on upper and lower levels) with facilities for babies and disabled people (note: the site is hilly and may be unsuitable). Shop. Bar. Restaurant/pizzeria. Indoor swimming pool. Outdoor pool with water slide, waterfall and jacuzzi. Sports pitch. Archery. Play area. Bicycle hire. Entertainment and excursion programme (July/Aug). Mobile homes for rent. Off site: Rafting and canoe trips. Riding 5 km. Fishing 1 km. Very extensive walking and cycle (mountain bike) opportunities. Vercors mountain range. Many stunning mediaeval villages.

Open: 15 April - 1 October.

Directions

From the north, leave A7 at exit 16 and join the eastbound D104 to Crest. Upon reaching Crest take D538 south to Bourdeaux and continue towards Dieulefit. Site is on the left 1 km. beyond Bourdeaux and is well signed.

Charges 2006

Per unit incl. 2 persons	€ 13,00 - € 23,00
extra person	€ 4,00 - € 4,50
child (1-7 yrs)	€ 2,50 - € 2,60
electricity (10A)	€ 4,20 - € 4,50

Camping Les Bois du Chatelas

Route de Dieulefit - F-26460 Bordeaux - T l.: (33) 4 75 00 60 80 - Fax (33) 4 75 00 60 81
E-mail: contact@chatelas.com - www.chatelas.com

FR26180 Camping de la Pinéde

Quartier du Pont Neuf, F-26150 Die (Drôme)

Tel: **04 75 22 17 77**. Email: **pinedeclub@infonie.fr**

Situated on the edge of the Vercors National Park in the narrow Drôme valley, this site is within walking distance of the historical market town of Die, famous for its Clairette de Die sparkling wines. There are 160 pitches with 105, good to large sized, level, stony pitches for touring. Laid out under pine trees offering some shade, all have 6/10A electricity, although long leads may be necessary. The site is not suitable for large outfits. There is a full programme of events for all the family in July/Aug.

Facilities

Two good sized, clean and modern toilet blocks have all the necessary facilities including good sized cubicles and rooms for babies. Facilities for disabled visitors. Shop. Bar, restaurant and takeaway. TV/games room. Large play area. Tennis. Minigolf. Bicycle hire. Fishing. River bathing. Internet point. Only electric and gas barbecues allowed. Communal barbecue area. Off site: Die with shops, supermarket, banks, restaurants and bars. Riding 2 km. Golf 20 km.

Open: End April - mid September.

Directions

Site is 50 km. east of the A7 exit 16. Head east to Die and on entering town, just after first campsite on right, turn right. Follow signs down narrow lane, under low bridge (2.95 m) and across narrow river bridge (2.75 m) to site. To avoid low bridge continue past first right turn, turn right (Gap) and shortly right again. Follow signs over level crossing and narrow river bridge (2.75 m). GPS: N44:45.434 E05:21.210

Charges 2006

| Per unit incl. 2 persons | € 13,00 - € 29,00 |
| electricity (5/10A) | € 3,50 - € 5,00 |

FR42030 Camping Bel' Epoque du Pilat

Route de Malleval, F-42410 Pelussin (Loire)

Tel: **04 74 87 66 60**. Email: **premilleuxb@aol.com**

This is a peaceful, family run site located within the relatively little known Pilat Regional Park and close to the pretty town of Pélussin. There are fine views over the Rhône Valley and the distant mountains from many of the site's 70 pitches. These are generally level and of a good size with reasonable shade, the majority with electrical connections (6A); 20 pitches are occupied by mobile homes. The site is well maintained with an attractive pool and small bar and snack bar (only open in July and August). The surrounding area offers very many superb walking and cycling opportunites, with over 700km of marked trails.

Facilities

Well appointed toilet block with facilities for disabled visitors. Small shop in reception. Bar, snack bar, and takeaway meals. Swimming pool (May - Sept). Tennis. Play area, Limited entertainment in peak season. Mobile homes for rent. Off site: Golf 12 km. Fishing and riding 5 km. Vienne (Roman town). Safari park at Peaugres. Excursions to Côtes du Rhone vineyards. Lyon (50 km. to the north).

Open: 1 April - 30 September.

Directions

From the north, leave A7 autoroute at exit 10 and join southbound N86. Continue through Condrieu to Chavanay and then take the westbound D7 sign Pélussin. Shortly before reaching the village centre bear left to follow 'camping' signs. Site is 1.5 km.

Charges 2006

| Per unit incl. 2 persons and electricity | € 15,50 - € 19,50 |
| extra person | € 4,50 |

FR69020 Camping Municipal la Grappe Fleurie

La Lie, F-69820 Fleurie (Rhône)

Tel: **04 74 69 80 07**. Email: **camping@fleurie.org**

With easy access from both the A6 autoroute and the N6, this site is ideally situated for night stops or indeed for longer stays to explore the vineyards and historic attractions of the Beaujolais region. Virtually surrounded by vineyards, but within walking distance (less than 1 km.) of the pretty village of Fleurie, this is an immaculate small site, with 85 separated touring pitches. All are grassed and fairly level with the benefit of individual access to water and electricity (10A).

Facilities

Sanitary facilities in two blocks have British and Turkish style toilets and very satisfactory shower and washing facilities (showers closed 22.00-07.00 hrs). Facilities for disabled visitors. Two cold showers are provided for those wishing to cool down in summer. Washing machine and tumble dryer. Outdoor swimming pool (15m by 7m). Small playground. Table tennis, tennis and volleyball Off site: Fishing 10 km. Fleurie 600 m.

Open: End of March - End of October.

Directions

From N6 at Le Maison Blanche/Romanech-Thorins, take D32 to village of Fleurie from where site is signed.

Charges 2006

Per unit incl. 2 persons and electricity	€ 10,00 - € 13,00
extra person	€ 4,00 - € 5,00
child (5-10 yrs)	free - € 3,30

FR69010 Camping International de Lyon

Porte de Lyon, F-69570 Dardilly (Rhône)

Tel: **04 78 35 64 55**. Email: **lyon@huttopia.com**

Camping International is a modern overnight site just off the A6 autoroute. Kept busy with overnight trade, reception and the café (in main season) open until quite late. There are 177 separate numbered plots. Many have electricity (10A), water and waste water drainage. Those for caravans are mostly on hardstandings on a slight slope, with another small grassy part, while those for tents are on a flatter area of grass. A very large commercial centre has been developed just outside the site, with eight hotels, restaurants, a supermarket, petrol station, etc. There is some road noise. Lyon is a very attractive city, especially noted for the excellence of its food, and well worth a visit. A bus stop for the centre (8 km.) is nearby (timetables in reception).

Facilities

Three heated sanitary blocks have free hot water (solar heated) and washbasins in cabins. Dishwashing and laundry sinks. Baby changing facilities and washing machines. Motorcaravan service point. Unheated swimming and paddling pools (15/6-31/8, supervised and free). Playground. TV room. Games room. Reading room (books and local information). Table tennis. Boules. Volleyball. Picnic and barbecue area.

Open: All year.

Directions

Travelling south, do not take A46 motorway around Lyon, continue on A6, take exit Limonest, Dardilly, Porte de Lyon. About 8 km. north of Lyon tunnel; turn left for Porte de Lyon (well signed).

Charges 2006

Per person	€ 3,10 - € 3,72
child (7-15 yrs)	€ 2,40 - € 2,88
motorcaravan or 1 axle caravan	€ 8,20
caravan, 2 axle	€ 16,80

FR69030 Camping les Portes du Beaujolais

Chemin des Grandes Levées, F-69480 Anse (Rhône)

Tel: **04 74 67 12 87**. Email: **campingbeaujolais@wanadoo.fr**

Being just off the main motorway south to the Mediterranean, this campsite would make a good overnight stop. Also the good public transport from Anse means that it could be used as a base for visiting Lyon. However, despite some noise from the motorway and the main line railway, there is much more to it than that. The well run site has good facilities and modern buildings of traditional design and materials. Its 150 formal pitches are shady, level, numbered and marked, with neatly trimmed grass and hedges, and electrical connections (6A). There are 20 fully serviced pitches.

Facilities

Modern toilet blocks, facilities for disabled people. Baby changing room. Motorcaravan services. Washing machines. Shop (all season). Gas supplies. Bar, restaurant, takeaway (1/6-15/9). Games room. Internet. Swimming pool, paddling pool (1/5-30/9) Playground. Playing field. Tennis. Minigolf. Boules. Free loan of barbecues. Off site: Anse 1 km, supermarket, shops, restaurants, bars, takeaway, ATM, bus stop. Narrow gauge railway at exit. Fishing 200 m. Boat launching 500 m. Bicycle hire 1 km. Riding 1.5 km. Sailing 1.5 km. Golf 2 km.

Open: 1 March - 31 October.

Directions

Anse is on N6, 6 km. south of Villefranche-sur-Saône, 21 km. north of Lyon. Site signed from northern and southern ends of village. From southern height limit of 3.1 m. GPS: N45:56.418 E04:43.596

Charges 2006

Per unit incl. 2 persons, electricity	€ 16,90 - € 18,67
incl. services	€ 18,45 - € 21,63
extra person	€ 4,33 - € 4,80
child (2-7 yrs)	€ 3,38

MAP 14

This is a corner of France
that evokes dreamy images
of lazy afternoons amongst
sleepy village squares, sunny
vineyards and beautiful lavender
fields basking under the dazzling blue
of the sky.

ONLY THE DÉPARTEMENTS FROM THE
MOUNTAINOUS REGION OF PROVENCE HAVE BEEN
INCLUDED IN THIS SECTION: 04 ALPES-DE-HAUTE-
PROVENCE, 05 HAUTES-ALPES, 84 VAUCLUSE

Provence is a region of magical light,
bleached landscapes, olive groves,
herb-scented garrigue, vineyards and
Roman and medieval antiquities. The river
valleys provide natural routes through the
mountain barrier. Roman monuments can
be seen at Orange, and Vaison-la-Romaine,
where a 2,000 year old bridge is still in use.
Avignon was the site of the papal court
and the Palais des Papes at Avignon
is a spectacular construction.

The Hautes-Alpes will reward with stunning
vistas, peace and quiet. Briançon is the
highest town in Europe and many of the
high passes are not for the faint-hearted.
The Vaucluse, where in the late spring the
southern slopes of the Montagne du
Luberon are a mass of colour with wild
flowers. The extinct volcanic cone of Mont
Ventoux provides dramatic views. The
scents, the colours and an amazing intensity of light have encouraged artists and
writers to settle amidst the sleepy villages,
with narrow streets and ancient dwellings
topped with sun-baked terracotta tiles,
where the air is fragrant with the perfume
of wild herbs and lavender.

Places of interest

Avignon: ramparts, old city, Papal Palace,
old palace, Calvet museum.

Mont Ventoux: near Carpentras, one of the
best known stages of the classic Tour de
France annual cycle race.

Orange: Roman city, gateway to the Midi,
Colline St Europe.

St Vaison la Romaine: Roman city,
the French Pompei.

Cuisine of the region

Influenced by the Savoie area to the north
and the Côte d'Azur to the south, with
emphasis on herbs and garlic, and fish.
The wine region is mainly known for its dry,
fruity rosé wines: Bandol, Bellet, Palette,
Cassis. Red wines include Côtes du Rhône
and Châteauneuf-du-Pape.

Aigo Bouido: garlic and sage soup with
bread (or eggs and cheese).

Farcement (Farçon Savoyard): potatoes
baked with cream, eggs, bacon, dried pears
and prunes.

Pissaladière: Provencal bread dough with
onions, anchovies, olives.

Ratatouille: aubergines, courgettes, onions,
garlic, red peppers and tomatoes in olive oil.

Tartiflette: potato, bacon, onions and
Reblochon cheese.

FR04010 Sunêlia Hippocampe

Mobile homes ▶ page 481

Route de Napoléon, F-04290 Volonne (Alpes-de Haute-Provence)

Tel: **04 92 33 50 00**. Email: **camping@l-hippocampe.com**

Hippocampe is a friendly family run, 'all action' lakeside site, with families in mind, situated in a beautiful area of France. The perfumes of thyme, lavender and wild herbs are everywhere and the higher hills of Haute Provence are not too far away. There are 447 level, numbered pitches (243 for touring units), medium to very large (130 sq.m.) in size. All have electricity (10A) and 220 have water and drainage, most are separated by bushes and cherry trees. Some of the best pitches border the lake. The restaurant, bar, takeaway and shop have all been completely renewed. Games, aerobics, competitions, entertainment and shows, plus a daily club for younger family members are organised in July/August. A soundproof underground disco is set well away from the pitches and is very popular with teenage customers. Staff tour the site at night ensuring a good night's sleep. The site is, however, much quieter in low season and, with its good discounts, is the time for those who do not want or need entertaining. The Gorges du Verdon is a sight not to be missed and rafting, paragliding or canoe trips can be booked from the site's own tourist information office. Being on the lower slopes of the hills of Haute-Provence, the surrounding area is good for both walking and mountain biking. All in all, this is a very good site for an active or restful holiday and is suitable for outfits of all sizes. Used by tour operators (20 pitches). English is spoken.

Facilities

Toilet blocks vary from old to modern, all with good clean facilities that include washbasins in cabins. Washing machines. Motorcaravan service point. Bread available (from 28/4). Shop, bar, restaurant, pizzeria (all 1/5-15/9). Large, pool complex (heated in early and late seasons). Tennis. Fishing. Canoeing. Boules. Several sports facilities (some with free instruction). Charcoal barbecues are not permitted. Off site: Village of Volonne 600 m. Bicycle hire 2 km. Riding 6 km. Various sporting opportunities.

Open: 4 April - 30 September.

Directions

Approaching from the north turn off N85 across river bridge to Volonne, then right to site. From the south right on D4, 1 km. before Château Arnoux. GPS: N44:06.366 E06:00.933

Charges 2007

Per unit with 2 persons	
simple pitch:	€ 13,00 - € 27,00
with electricity	€ 16,00 - € 32,00
with water/drainage 100 sq.m.	€ 16,00 - € 34,00
with water/drainage 140 sq.m.	€ 20,00 - € 39,00
extra person (over 4 yrs)	€ 3,00 - € 6,50

Special low season offers.
Camping Cheques accepted.

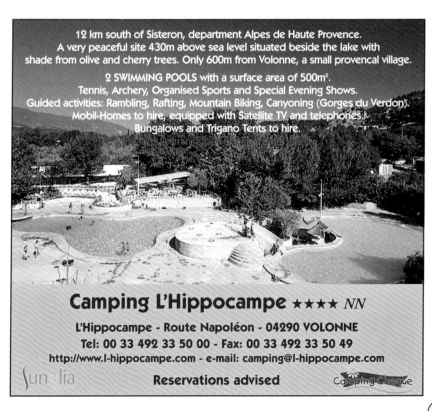

FR04020 Castel Camping le Camp du Verdon

Mobile homes ▶ page 482

Domaine du Verdon, F-04120 Castellane (Alpes-de Haute-Provence)

Tel: **04 92 83 61 29**. Email: **contact@camp-du-verdon.com**

Close to the 'Route des Alpes' and the Gorges du Verdon. Two heated swimming pools and numerous on-site activities during high season help to keep non-canoeists here. Du Verdon is a large level site, part meadow, part wooded, with 500 partly shaded, rather stony pitches (390 for tourists). Numbered and separated by bushes, they vary in size, have 6A electricity, and 120 also have water and waste water. They are mostly separate from the mobile homes (63) and pitches used by tour operators (110). Some overlook the unfenced river Verdon, so watch the children. This is a very popular holiday area, the gorge, canoeing and rafting being the main attractions, ideal for active families. One can walk to Castellane without using the main road. Dances and discos in July and August suit all age groups – the latest finishing time is around 11 pm. (after that time patrols make sure that the site is quiet). The site is popular and very busy in July and August.

Facilities

Refurbished toilet blocks include facilities for disabled visitors. Washing machines. Motorcaravan services. Restaurant, terrace, log fire for cooler evenings. New supermarket. Pizzeria/crêperie. Takeaway. Heated swimming pools, paddling pool with 'mushroom' fountain (all open all season). Organised entertainments (July and August). Playgrounds. Minigolf, table tennis, archery, basketball, volleyball. Organised walks. Bicycle hire. Riding. Small fishing lake. ATM. Room for games and TV. Internet access. Off site: Castellane and the Verdon Gorge 1 km. Riding 2 km. Boat launching 4.5 km. Golf 20 km. Water sports.

Open: 15 May - 15 September.

Directions

From Castellane take D952 westwards towards Gorges du Verdon and Moustiers. Site is 1 km. on left.

Charges 2006

Per unit with 2 or 3 persons incl. 6A electricity	€ 17,00 - € 30,00
	€ 21,00 - € 34,00
extra person (over 3 yrs)	€ 7,00 - € 11,00
dog	€ 2,50

Camping Cheques accepted.

FR04100 Camping International

Mobile homes ▶ page 481

Route Napoleon, F-04120 Castellane (Alpes-de Haute-Provence)

Tel: **04 92 83 66 67**. Email: **info@camping-international.fr**

Camping International has very friendly, English speaking owners and is a reasonably priced, less commercialised site situated in some of the most dramatic scenery in France with good views. The 274 pitches, 130 good sized ones for touring, are clearly marked, separated by trees and small hedges, and all have electricity and water. The bar/restaurant overlooks the swimming pool with its sunbathing area set in a sunny location, and all have fantastic views. In high season English speaking young people entertain children (3-8 years) and teenagers. Access is good for larger units. On some evenings the teenagers are taken to the woods for campfire 'sing-alongs' which can go on till the early hours without disturbing the rest of the site. There are guided walks into the surrounding hills in the nearby Gorges du Verdon – a very popular excursion, particularly in high season. The weather in the hills here is very pleasant without the excessive heat of the coast.

Facilities

Small toilet blocks are of an older design. One newer block has modern facilities, including those for disabled visitors. Washing machines and dryer. Motorcaravan services. Fridge hire. Shop. Restaurant/takeaway (May-Sept). Swimming pool (1/5-30/9). Club/TV room. Children's animation, occasional evening entertainment (July/Aug). Play area. Boules. Internet access. Off site: Riding 800 m. Castellane (1.5 km.), with river, canyon and rapids, ideal for canoeing, rafting and canyoning etc. Walking, biking. Boat launching 5 km.

Open: 31 March - 1 October.

Directions

Site is 1 km. north of Castellane on the N85 'Route Napoleon'. GPS: N43:50.50 E06:30.42

Charges 2006

Per unit incl. 2 persons	€ 14,00 - € 21,00
extra person	€ 3,00 - € 5,00
electricity (6A)	€ 3,00 - € 5,00
dog	€ 2,00 - € 3,00

Camping Cheques accepted.

kawan-villages.com **tel: 00 333 59 59 03 59**

kawa

Check real time availability and at-the-gate prices...

www.**alanrogers**.com

Camping International
Route Napoléon
04120 Castellane
Tél : +33 492 836 667
Fax : +33 492 837 767
mail : info@campinginternational.fr
www.campinginternational.fr

Castel Camping Caravaning
Domaine du Verdon
04120 Castellane
Tél : +33 492 836 129
Fax : +33 492 836 937
E-mail : contact@camp-du-verdon.com
www.camp-du-verdon.com

LES CASTELS
N°209

Provence
Castellane
Canyon du Verdon

3 SEASONS
ELITE

Camping Cheque

FR04060 Camping Caravaning le Haut-Verdon

RD 908, F-04370 Villars-Colmars (Alpes-de Haute-Provence)

Tel: 04 92 83 40 09. Email: campinglehautverdon@wanadoo.fr

For those seeking a quiet, family site set in most spectacular scenery, Camping Le Haut-Verdon is ideal. It is on the banks of the Verdon, an excellent trout river, which flows through the spectacular gorge. Surrounded by the majestic peaks of the Alpes-de-Haute-Provence, it is on the doorstep of the Mercantour National Park. Set amongst the pines, the 87 pitches are mostly on the large size but are rather stony. With 73 for touring units, all have electricity (6/10A) but some require long leads. There is a small village near, and the town of St André is 23 km.

Facilities

Refurbished, heated toilet block. Washing machines. Freezer for ice packs, room for tenters for inclement weather. Motorcaravan services. Small shop. Bar/restaurant, takeaway. Barbecue areas (portable ones banned). Heated swimming, paddling pools (from 1/6). Play area. Volleyball. Basketball. Giant chess. Boules. Skittle alley. TV room. Organised games, competitions. Fishing. Off site: Bicycle hire and riding 10 km.

Open: 1 May - 30 September.

Directions

Follow D955 north from St André les Alpes towards Colmar. After 11 km. road number changes to D908. Site on right at southern edge of Villars-Colmars. Caravans not advised to use the D908 from Annot or Col d'Allos from Barcelonnette.

Charges 2006

Per person over 6 yrs	€ 3,00 - € 4,00
child (2-6 yrs)	€ 1,50 - € 2,50
pitch incl. electricity	€ 10,00 - € 16,00

FR04080 Camping Caravaning L'Etoile des Neiges

F-04140 Montclar (Alpes-de Haute-Provence)

Tel: 04 92 35 01 29. Email: contact@etoile-des-neiges.com

This attractive, family run site near the mountain village and ski resort of St Jean Montclar is open most of the year. Being at an altitude of 1,300 m. the nights can get quite cold in summer. The 130 shady terraced pitches, with 70 for touring, are separated by small shrubs and alpine trees. All pitches are close to electricity and water points. An attractive bar and restaurant overlooks the two swimming pools, with the shallow pool having a water slide ideal for children. The site has no shop but local shops are only a few minutes walk away. A 'Sites et Paysages' member.

Facilities

Central toilet block (heated in winter) and facilities for disabled visitors. Two washing machines. Motorcaravan services. Bar/restaurant. Swimming pool (all amenities open 15/5-9/9). Tennis, table tennis, boules. Two play areas. Rafting, walking (July/Aug). Off site: Shops in the village a few minutes walk. Bicycle hire and riding in village. Fishing 1.5 km. Watersports and beach at Lac Serre Ponçon 7 km.

Open: 15 May - 30 September.

Directions

Site is 35 km. south of Gap via D900B. Beyond Serre Ponçon, turn right, D900 signed Selonnet, St Jean Montclar. Entering St Jean Montclar turn left, pass chalets, shops, fork right to campsite. Approach roads are steep and icy in winter.

Charges 2006

Per unit incl. 2 persons	€ 12,50 - € 22,00
extra person	€ 4,00 - € 5,00
electricity (6A)	€ 3,00 - € 4,00
Camping Cheques accepted.	

FR04110 Yelloh! Village Verdon Parc

Domaine de la Paludette, F-04800 Gréoux Les Bains (Alpes-de Haute-Provence)

Tel: 04 92 78 08 08. Email: info@yellohvillageverdon-parc.com

Friendly and family run, this very spacious site borders the River Ardèche and is close to the attractive spa town of Gréoux les Bains. The 280 medium to very large, stony or gravel pitches (180 for tourists) are in two sections. The main part of the campsite has large pitches laid out in rows separated by poplar trees. Along the river bank the larger, more natural pitches are scattered amongst the trees and are of irregular shape and size. These have very pleasant views across the river to the town beyond. Electrical connections (10A) and water taps are reasonably close to most pitches.

Facilities

Several toilet blocks (one heated in low season) are clean and to a high standard. Facilities for disabled visitors. Laundry room. Motorcaravan service point. Small shop. Bar. Restaurant and takeaway (May-Sept). TV. Internet point. Large play area. Miniclub (high season). Evening entertainment. Dogs are not accepted in high season. Gas and electric barbeques only. Off site: Gréoux les Bains 1 km. Riding, bicycle hire 1 km. Small lake beach 8 km.

Open: 1 April - 30 October.

Directions

Leave A51 autoroute at Manosque and take D907 southeast towards Gréoux les Bains. Turn right on D4, then left on D82 to Gréoux les Bains. Follow main road downhill through town to roundabout with fountain. Take second right (D8 St Pierre) and descend for 700 m. Cross river and turn left.

Charges 2006

Per unit incl. 2 persons	€ 13,00 - € 25,00
extra person	€ 2,00 - € 5,00

FR04030 Camping Moulin de Ventre

Niozelles, F-04300 Forcalquier (Alpes-de Haute-Provence)

Tel: **04 92 78 63 31**. Email: **moulindeventre@aol.com**

This is a friendly, family run site in the heart of Haute-Provence, near Forcalquier, a bustling small French market town. Attractively located beside a small lake and 28 acres of wooded, hilly land, which is available for walking. Herbs of Provence can be found growing wild and flowers, birds and butterflies abound – a nature lovers delight. The 124 level, grassy pitches for tourists are separated by a variety of trees and small shrubs, 114 of them having electricity (6A; long leads may be necessary). Some pitches are particularly attractive, bordering a small stream. English is spoken. A 'Sites et Paysages' member. The site is well situated to visit Mont Ventoux, the Luberon National Park, the Gorges du Verdon and a wide range of ancient hill villages with their markets and museums etc.

Facilities

Refurbished toilet block. Facilities for disabled people. Baby bath. Washing, drying machines. Fridge hire. Bread. Bar/restaurant, takeaway (all season), themed evenings (high season). Pizzeria. Swimming pools (15/5-15/9). New playground. Fishing, boules. Some activities organised in high season. No discos. Only electric or gas barbecues. Internet access. Off site: Shops, local market, doctor, tennis 2 km. Supermarket, chemist, riding, bicycle hire 5 km. Golf 20 km. Walking, cycling.

Open: 1 April - 30 September.

Directions

From A51 motorway take exit 19 (Brillanne). Turn right on N96 then turn left on N100 westwards (signed Forcalquier) for about 3 km. Site is signed on left, just after a bridge 3 km. southeast of Niozelles. GPS: N43:56.1 E05:52.52

Charges 2006

Per unit incl. 2 persons	€ 13,00 - € 20,00
incl. electricity	€ 16,00 - € 25,00
extra person (over 4 yrs)	€ 3,50 - € 5,50
child (2-4 yrs)	€ 2,00 - € 3,00
dog	€ 1,50 - € 3,00

No credit cards.
Camping Cheques accepted.

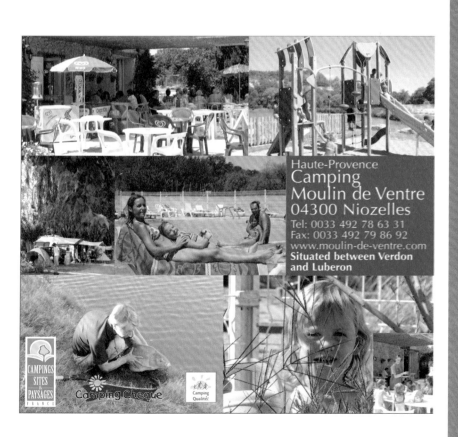

FR04120 Camping Indigo Forcalquier

Route de Sigonce, F-04300 Forcalquier (Alpes-de Haute-Provence)

Tel: **04 92 75 27 94**. Email: **forcalquier@camping-indigo.com**

Although Camping Indigo is an urban site, there are extensive views over the surrounding country-side where there are some excellent walks. The pitches are on grass and are of good size, all with electricity, 10 fully serviced. The site is secure, with an electronic barrier (card deposit required) and there is no entry between 22.30 and 07.00. Local guides lead tours of the historic town and areas. This is an excellent base for visiting Forcalquier, a 15th century fortified hill town and the Monday market (the best in Haute Provence). Since this site has acquired new owners, an extensive modernisation programme has been put into effect.

Facilities

Two refurbished toilet blocks with washbasins in cubicles and excellent facilities for disabled visitors. They are cleaned twice daily. Bar. Snack bar and takeaway (1/7-1/9). Play area. Heated swimming and paddling pools. Off site: All shops, banks etc. available in town centre, 200 m.

Open: 31 March - 30 September.

Directions

From town centre, follow 'Digne - Sisteron' for 400 m. and turn sharp left onto Sigonce road after Esso petrol station, then first right and site is 200 m. on the right. Well signed from town.
GPS: N43:57.660 E05:47.226

Charges 2006

Per person	€ 4,50 - € 5,20
child (2-7 yrs)	€ 3,00 - € 3,50
pitch	€ 3,70 - € 10,00
animal	€ 2,80 - € 3,30

camping Indigo
Forcalquier ★★★

Mobile-homes, tents and chalets to rent

Heated swimming-pool, bar restaurant, brand new bathrooms, sporting activities, hiking...

Route de Sigonce - 04300 Forcalquier
tel: 33 4 92 75 27 94

Close to the Luberon Regional Park, in the middle of Provence ...

www.camping-indigo.com

FR04130 Domaine Naturiste Les Lauzons

Limans, F-04300 Forcalquier (Alpes-de Haute-Provence)

Tel: **04 92 73 00 60**. Email: **leslauzons@wanadoo-fr**

This naturist site is set deep in the countryside, right in the heart of Haute Provence at an altitude of 450 metres and on an estate of 60 hectares, offers peace and tranquility. The owner of this very pleasant naturist site, M. Guy-Claude Loreille does everything to make his guests feel welcome and the facilities are impeccably kept. The 150 pitches are large enough for bigger caravans (although the access is rather narrow). You can chose between open pitches on a grassy hill with views over the surrounding area or more sheltered places with enough shade. Even camping in the wild is possible on this large site.

Facilities

Four toilet blocks are well spaced around the site (one is heated). Some washbasins in cabins and simple showers. Baby room. Facilities for disabled visitors. Laundry. Shop. Bar, restaurant and takeaway. Swimming pool (second planned for 2007). Gym. Play area. Bicycle hire. Entertainment and activities in high season. Walking trips. Communal barbecue area. Off site: Riding and boat launching 5 km.

Open: 1 April - 30 September.

Directions

Site is 2 km. south of village of Limans-en-Provence. From A51 (Sisteron - Aix en Provence) take exit 19. In La Brillane take D100 towards Forcalquier, then N100 towards Avignon. At Folcarquier take D950 towards St Etienne les Orgues. Site is signed on right side of the road, 100 m. before Limans, then 500 m. to site.

Charges 2006

Per unit incl. 2 persons	€ 12,00 - € 24,00
extra person	€ 4,00 - € 7,00
child (3-11 yrs)	free - € 5,00
electricity	€ 3,50

FR04140 Camping les Prairies

Haute-Greyere, F-04140 Seyne les Alpes (Alpes-de Haute-Provence)

Tel: **04 92 35 10 21**. Email: **info@campinglesprairies.com**

Les Prairies lies in a beautiful part of the French Alps, at the foot of the Grand Puy (1,800 m.) and at the entrance to the once fortified town of Seyne. This quiet site is run by a brother and sister team who grew up on a campsite on the French Riviera. With lovely views of the mountains and the river running beside the site, there are 91 good grass pitches (with 10A electricity) and 17 mobile homes. There is a pleasant swimming pool and a bar forming part of the reception area. A few picnic tables have been provided for travellers with tents. Although only small, Seyne is the main centre of the region. Walking through this historical jewel alone is worth a stay at Les Prairies. The surrounding region offers numerous possibilities for walking, mountain biking and climbing. The nearby airfield provides opportunities for glider flying and there is paragliding from the slopes of the Grand Puy.

Facilities

The two toilet blocks near the pool are immaculate and regularly kept that way. Pre-set showers are quite small. Facilities for disabled visitors and babies. Laundry room. Bar and snack bar (15/6-20/8). Swimming pool (1/6-15/9). Petanque. Occasional entertainment in high season. Fishing. Off site: Riding adjacent. Bicycle hire 5 km.

Open: 15 April - 16 September.

Directions

Site is southeast of Gap and north of Digne-les-Bains. From Gap take D900B and turn right at T-junction where it joins the D900. Cross Col de St Jean and go through Seyne to small airfield on the left. Turn right, following signs to site (do not take an earlier sign as road is very narrow). Coming from Digne, turn left at the airfield.

Charges 2006

Per unit incl. 2 persons	€ 13,00 - € 21,00
extra erson	€ 4,00 - € 5,00
child (2-6 yrs)	€ 3,00
electricity (10A)	€ 3,50

FR05000 Camping des Princes d'Orange

F-05700 Orpierre (Hautes-Alpes)

Tel: **04 92 66 22 53**. Email: **campingorpierre@wanadoo.fr**

This attractive, terraced site, set on a hillside above the village has been thoughtfully developed. The genuine, friendly welcome means many families return year upon year, bringing in turn new generations. Divided into five terraces, each with its own toilet block, all its 120 generously sized pitches (96 for tourists) enjoy good shade from trees and wicker canopies and have electricity connections (4/10A). In high season one terrace is reserved as a 1-star camping area for young people. Orpierre also has an enchanting maze of medieval streets and houses, almost like a trip back through the centuries.

Facilities

Six well equipped toilet blocks. Baby bath. Laundry facilities. Bread. Bar, takeaway (1/7-31/8). Heated swimming pool, paddling pool (15/6-15/9). Play area with trampoline with safety net. Boules. Games room. Fridge hire. Only gas barbecues are permitted. Off site: Orpierre with a few shops and bicycle hire 500 m. Fishing 7 km. Nearest shopping centre Laragne 12 km. Riding 19 km. Hanggliding, parascending. Gorges de Guil.

Open: 1 April - 25 October.

Directions

Turn off N75 road at Eyguians onto D30 – site is signed on left at crossroads in centre Orpierre village. GPS: N44:18.675 E05:41.801

Charges 2006

Per unit incl. 2 persons	€ 19,50
incl. 3 persons	€ 21,00
extra person	€ 4,00
electricity	€ 3,00

Less 25% in low season. No credit cards.

FR05060 Camping la Pause

F-05260 Saint Léger les Mélèzes (Hautes-Alpes)

Tel: **04 92 50 44 92**. Email: **valerie-portier@wanadoo.fr**

Camping La Pause is situated amongst some of the most impressive scenery in France with breathtaking views and friendly and helpful owners. There are 80 spacious grassy pitches, with 44 for touring, including some good sized ones for larger units. They are clearly marked and separated by trees and small hedges, some with electricity and water. Access is good for larger units. The weather in these mountains is very pleasant without the excessive heat of the coast. There are guided walks into the surrounding mountains – a very popular excursion, particularly in high season.

Facilities

The heated toilet block in the main building is quite basic with pre-set showers. Baby room. Washing machines, dryer and irons. Motorcaravan service point. Restaurant and takeaway. Swimming pool during summer. Sauna and gym. Club/TV room. Children's animation and evening entertainment in July/Aug and during the ski season. Play area. Free internet access. Off site: Riding 100 m. Ideal area for canoeing, rafting and canyoning etc. Good area for walking and cycling. Ski and trim trail from site.

Open: All year.

Directions

From the A51 (Aix-en-Provence - Gap) take exit 24 and continue north via N185. After Gap and Col de Bayard, turn right on D944 to Laye and Le Cros. From here via D14 to Forrest-St Julien and on via D13 to St Leger-les- Mélèzes. Site is signed at the entrance to the village.

Charges 2006

Per person	€ 4,00 - € 6,00
child (under 5 yrs)	€ 2,00
pitch	€ 4,00 - € 6,00
electricity per amp	€ 1,00
Camping Cheques accepted.	

FR05070 Camping Les Cariamas

Fontmolines, F-05380 Châteauroux-Les-Alpes (Hautes-Alpes)

Tel: **04 92 43 22 63**. Email: **p.tim@free.fr**

Set 1,000 metres up in the stunning scenery of the Alps, Les Cariamas is at the gateway to Ecrin National Park and within easy reach of the Serre-Ponçon lake and the Rabioux-Durance river. The 140 pitches, which all have electrical connections, are pleasantly shaded and many offer beautiful views of the surrounding countryside. There are some mobile homes and chalets to rent. There is an outdoor heated pool on site.

Facilities

Small shop. Takeaway. Laundry. Swimming pool. Play area. Mountain bike hire. Volleyball. Off site: Golf. Riding. Canoeing. Climbing. Fishing. Hiking. Mountain biking. Rafting. Tennis courts.

Open: 1 April - 31 October.

Directions

From Gap follow signs to Embrun Briançon. Take turning for Châteauroux-les-Alpes at first roundabout after Embrun. Shortly (800 m.) before the village turn right and follow signs to site.

Charges 2006

Per person	€ 4,50
child (under 7 yrs)	€ 2,10
pitch	€ 5,50
electricity	€ 3,15

352
Check real time availability and at-the-gate prices...
www.alanrogers.com

FR84040 Domaine le Jantou

535 chemin des Coudeliéres, F-84250 Le Thor (Vaucluse)

Tel: **04 90 33 90 07**. Email: **accueil@lejantou.com**

Le Jantou has been expanded over the years from an 18th century farm and farmhouse. It is bordered by a small river said to be good for trout fishing. The 160 level, small to medium sized, fairly stony pitches (rock pegs advised) are in small groups separated by tall hedges and mature trees giving heavy shade to many. All have electricity (3-10A). About half of them are used for touring with most of them in a separate section. There is a large pool, children's pool and paddling pool surrounded by paved and grass sunbathing areas. In July and August, activities for children are arranged and once a week there is evening entertainment for the family.

Facilities

Two central toilet blocks partially refurbished with all the necessary facilities, include washbasins in cabins, a baby room and facilities for disabled visitors (key access, deposit required). Washing machine and dryer. Motorcaravan service point. Small bar/restaurant with takeaway (July/Aug). Small shop with basic provisions. Swimming pools. Play area. Large sports area including, football and volleyball. Fishing. Bicycle hire. Small games room with TV and internet access. Barbecues are not allowed (four central barbecues each with picnic table and benches). Barrier key € 15 deposit. Off site: Riding 5 km. Supermarket 1 km. Thor 2 km. Isle sur la Sorgue (antiques and Provencal markets) 5 km.

Open: 1 April - 31 October.

Directions

Site is just west of Le Thor. Leave A7 autoroute at Avignon north (exit 23) onto D942 signed Carpentras. Shortly turn south on D6 and in 8 km. turn east on N100, signed Le Thor. Just before bridge turn left on D1 and shortly left again to site entrance. GPS: N43:55.764 E4:58.989

Charges guide

Per unit incl. 2 persons	€ 13,00 - € 18,50
extra person	€ 4,50 - € 5,75
child (2-12 yrs)	€ 2,40 - € 3,10
electricity	€ 2,60 - € 5,15
animal	€ 1,00 - € 1,10

FR84020 Domaine Naturiste de Bélézy

Mobile homes ▶ page 482

F-84410 Bédoin (Vaucluse)

Tel: **04 90 65 60 18**. Email: **info@belezy.com**

At the foot of Mt Ventoux, surrounded by beautiful scenery, Bélézy is an excellent naturist site with many amenities and activities and the ambience is relaxed and comfortable. The 238 marked pitches are set amongst many varieties of trees and shrubs. Electricity points (12A) are plentiful but long leads are necessary. So far as naturism is concerned, the emphasis is on personal choice, the only stipulation being the requirement for complete nudity in the pools and pool area. An area of natural parkland with an orchard, fishpond and woodland has a good range of sports facilities.

Facilities

Sanitary blocks differ – newer ones are excellent, with showers and washbasins in cubicles, others have hot showers in the open air, screened by stone dividers. One block has a superb children's section. Shop (26/3-30/9). Excellent restaurant and takeaway. Two swimming pools. Sauna. Tennis. Adventure play area. Activities in low season. Archery. Guided walks. Children's club. Hydrotherapy centre (1/4-30/9). Barbecues are prohibited. Pets are not accepted. Off site: Bédoin 1 km.

Open: 20 March - 6 October.

Directions

From A7 autoroute or RN7 at Orange, take D950 southeast to Carpentras, then northeast via D974 to Bédoin. Site is signed in Bédoin, being about 1.5 km. northeast of the village. GPS: N44:08.011 E05:11.247

Charges 2007

Per unit incl. 2 persons	€ 14,50 - € 35,00
extra person	€ 5,50 - € 10,00
pitch	€ 4,60 - € 5,30
Camping Cheques accepted.	

FR84050 Camping Caravaning la Sorguette

Route d'Apt, F-84800 L'Isle sur la Sorgue (Vaucluse)

Tel: **04 90 38 05 71**. Email: **sorguette@wanadoo.fr**

This popular, well organised site is well placed, 1.5 km. from Isle sur la Sorgue. Arranged in groups of four, the 164 medium sized level pitches (124 for touring) all have electricity (4-10A). Each group is separated by tall hedges and most have a little shade during the day. In high season a few competitions are organised (boules or volleyball), plus some children's entertainment, but this is quite low key. Running alongside the site, the river Sorgue is only 6 km. from its source in the mountains. It is still very clear and used for canoeing, swimming or fishing.

Facilities

Well maintained toilet blocks, washing machines. Units for disabled people. Baby room. Motorcaravan services. Fridge hire. Shop, bar, snacks (1/7-25/8). Entertainment in July/Aug. Play area, volleyball, tennis, basketball. Canoe and bicycle hire. Internet. Off site: Swimming pools 2 km. Fishing, riding 5 km. Walking and cycling. Canoeing on River Sorgue.

Open: 15 March - 15 October.

Directions

Site is 1.5 km. east of L'Isle sur la Sorgue on the N100 towards Apt. It is well signed from the town. GPS: N43:54.893 E05:04.655

Charges 2006

Per unit incl. 2 persons	€ 15,40 - € 19,20
extra person (over 7 yrs)	€ 5,20 - € 6,60
child (1-6 yrs)	€ 2,60 - € 3,30
electricity (4/10A)	€ 3,50 - € 4,60

FR84060 Camping l'Ayguette

CD 86 Faucon, F-84110 Vaison-la-Romaine (Vaucluse)

Tel: **04 90 46 40 35**. Email: **info@ayguette.com**

Set in the beautiful region of north Provence, surrounded by vineyards and wooded hills, the 99 slightly sloping pitches, all for touring, are widely spaced out on terraces amongst pine and oak trees giving plenty of dappled shade, only a few suitable for large units. All have 10A electricity (long leads necessary) but some are a considerable distance from the amenities, not ideal for those with walking difficulties. Rock pegs are essential. The reception building houses a bar, snack bar, small shop and terrace. Close by is an attractive swimming pool (heated all season) and sunbathing area.

Facilities

Well equipped toilet blocks, one heated. Room for disabled campers or families with young children. Washing machines. Heated swimming pool, terrace (all season). Bar, snack bar, takeaway (July/Aug). Small shop. Volleyball, badminton. Playground. Occasional entertainment, some activities for children. Only gas and electric barbecues. Off site: No public transport. Faucon. Vaison la Romaine 4 km. Nyons 15 km. Mont Ventoux 35 km. Fishing and bicycle hire 5 km. Riding 7 km.

Open: 1 April - 30 September.

Directions

From Vaison-la-Romaine take the D938 towards Nyons. Shortly turn right on the D71, signed St Romain-en-Viennois. Drive through village and then turn right on D86. Site is well signed, on the right. GPS: N44:15.732 E05:07.748

Charges 2007

Per unit incl. 1 or 2 persons	€ 13,00 - € 20,50
incl. electricity	€ 15,50 - € 23,00
extra person	€ 4,00 - € 5,30

FR84080 Camping Caravaning la Simioune

F-84500 Bollène (Vaucluse)

Tel: **04 90 30 44 62**. Email: **la-simioune@wanadoo.fr**

This unsophisticated, rural site is a peaceful and inexpensive base, especially for those who love horses and it is open all year. Off the beaten track it is amongst tall pines on sandy, undulating ground, bordered, by a vineyard. This is a riding school, campers can hire horses by the hour. The favourite is the day-long guided trek with a river crossing and picnic lunch. The 80 unmarked and uneven pitches, many used for long stay caravans, are of varying size and shape, most with electricity (6A). Long leads and rock pegs are needed. The site is not recommended for large units.

Facilities

Basic toilet block, quite old but clean with room for disabled people although the site is difficult for wheelchairs and those with walking difficulties. Washing machine. Small bar, simple meals mid June to mid Sept. Takeaway all year. Small unheated swimming and paddling pools (June - Sept). Excellent riding (30 horses) next to the site. Central barbecue area (individual ones not permitted).Chalets for rent. Off site: Tennis, fishing, walking and canoeing nearby. Shops and restaurants at Bollène 5 km.

Open: All year.

Directions

From A7 exit 19 (Bollène). At first roundabout, third exit signed Suze la Rousse (site signed). After traffic lights, before river, turn left, site signed (Rue Alphonse Daudet), follow signs for about 5 km. (windy, narrow, bumpy lane). GPS: N44:17.811 E04:47.245

Charges 2006

Per person	€ 3,40
child (under 7 yrs)	€ 1,50
pitch incl. electricity (6A)	€ 5,30 - € 5,40

No credit cards.

FR84070 Camping Club International Carpe Diem

Route de St Marcellin, B.P. 68, F-84110 Vaison-la-Romaine (Vaucluse)

Tel: **04 90 36 02 02**. Email: **contact@camping-carpe-diem.com**

Carpe Diem is a new site, attractively themed with Greek statues and an amphitheatre surround to its main pool. This is a good site for active families seeking all day entertainment and the situation is quite impressive with magnificent views over one of the most beautiful parts of France, yet only 800 m. from the fascinating town of Vaison-la-Romaine. There are 232 pitches with 152 small to medium sized, grass touring pitches all with electricity and many with some degree of shade. A new terraced area has mobile homes, chalets and unshaded touring pitches. The main pool is impressive with its tiered seating, plants, etc. It is used as a theatre for evening entertainment. A simple square pool with grass surrounds is near the play area. Organised activities off the site include canoeing, riding, climbing, walking and mountain biking.

Facilities

Central toilet block with fountain and super children's facilities. Washing machine. Motorcaravan services. Reception, small shop (25/3-1/11). Bar (3/6-2/9) , pizzeria (14/4-30/9). TV. Swimming pools (3/4-21/10). Play area. Minigolf, archery, volleyball, football, basketball. Mountain bike hire. Mini-club. Extensive entertainment programme. Barbecues for hire. Off site: Fishing 1 km. Riding 2 km. Golf 20 km. Organised canoeing, riding, climbing, walking, mountain biking. Vaison-la-Romaine (800 m.), magnificent Roman ruins, shops, restaurants, market.

Open: 25 March - 1 November.

Directions

Leave Vaison-la-Romaine on D938 heading south towards Carpentras. 1 km. beyond the 'Super U' roundabout turn left on D151, signed St Marcellin. Site entrance is on the left immediately after the junction. GPS: N44:14.064 E05:05.381

Charges 2006

Per pitch incl. 1-3 persons	€ 16,00 - € 27,00
extra person	€ 4,00 - € 6,00
child (2-10 yrs)	€ 2,50 - € 5,00
electricity (6/10A)	€ 3,20 - € 4,70

Camping Cheques accepted.

CAMPINGS FranceLoc

Domaine Le Carpe Diem

Pitches, mobile homes, swimming pool and paddling pool in a Roman setting. New in 2007: waterslide, heated and covered swimming pool.

B.P. 68 84110 Vaison la Romaine
Tél. 0033(0)4 90 36 02 02
Fax. 0033(0)4 90 36 36 90
www.campings-franceloc.com

Covered swimmingpool planned for 2007

Vaucluse

FR84090 Camping du Pont d'Avignon

10 chemin de la Barthelasse, Ile de la Barthelasse, F-84000 Avignon (Vaucluse)

Tel: **04 90 80 63 50**. Email: **info@camping-avignon.com**

This is a city site, yet it is in a quiet location and only a short walk or ferry ride from the town. There are 300 level pitches, some on grass and some with hardstanding. 118 with electricity (10A). All have some shade but those with electricity are well shaded. A good play area, tennis courts and volleyball pitch are in the centre of the site separating the tent pitches on one side and the electric pitches on the other. Many pitches are separated by hedges. The restaurant, bar and terrace overlook the attractive pool.

Facilities

Well maintained and clean toilet blocks, facilities for disabled visitors. Washing machines, dryer. Motorcaravan services. Well stocked shop (1/4-30/9). Bar/restaurant, takeaway (1/4-30/9). Swimming pool, paddling pool (15/5-15/9). Play area with new climbing frame. Tennis (free). Volleyball. Bicycle hire (July/Aug). Internet. Off site: Avignon with famous bridge and Pope's Palace. Ferry to town centre.

Open: 19 March - 27 October.

Directions

Site is on an island in River Rhône. Well signed from roads into Avignon, ring road has complex junctions. Accessed from Pont Daladier towards Villeneuve via Avignon. Just after crossing first section of river fork right, site signed, site about 1 km. GPS: N43:57.092 E04:48.116

Charges 2006

Per unit incl. 2 persons	€ 10,00 - € 33,20
extra person	€ 2,85 - € 4,20
electricity	€ 2,55 - € 3,05

Camping Cheques accepted.

Provence

FR84100 Camping le Soleil de Provence

Route de Nyons, F-84110 St Romain en Viennois (Vaucluse)

Tel: **04 90 46 46 00**. Email: **info@camping-soleil-de-provence.fr**

The site has been developed to a high standard. The 162 average sized pitches, 140 for touring are separated by hedges and a variety of young trees offering only a little shade (10A electricity). The excellent pool, surrounded by a sunbathing terrace, and overlooked by the bar, is an unusual shape with an island in the centre. Although there is no paddling pool one end of the pool is very shallow. There is some organised entertainment in July and August but the emphasis is on a quiet and peaceful environment and is an ideal site for relaxing and unwinding.

Facilities

Modern well appointed, heated toilet blocks, facilities for disabled visitors, baby room. Washing machine, dryer. Motorcaravan services. Small shop for bread, open on demand. Bar, snack bar, all season. Swimming pool. Small play area. Volley ball, table tennis, boules. Off site: Tennis 1 km. Vaison la Romaine 4 km. Rafting, hiking, cycling, mountain biking 4 km. (Mont Ventoux is a real challenge). Bicycle hire 5 km. Fishing 15 km. Medieval villages, market towns. vineyards, wine tasting.

Open: 15 March - 31 October.

Directions

Site is 4 km. north of Vaison-la-Romaine on the D938 road to Nyons. Turn right, signed St Romain-en-Viennois (site signed) and take first left to site. GPS: N44:16.141 E05:06.358

Charges 2006

Per person	€ 3,50 - € 5,50
child (0-7 yrs)	€ 2,50 - € 3,00
pitch	€ 3,00 - € 4,00
car	€ 3,00 - € 4,00
electricity (10A)	€ 2,50
No credit cards.	

FR84140 Camping Beauregard

Route d'Uchaux, F-84550 Mornas (Vaucluse)

Tel: **04 90 37 02 08**. Email: **beauregard@wanadoo.fr**

Just a kilometre off the D7 and near an A7 exit, this site may appeal to those needing a night stop when travelling to or from the Mediterranean coast. Although there are many mobile homes, there are 89 pitches available for tourists. The pitches are under large pine trees and are rather sandy. Firm pegging might be difficult. They are of various shapes and sizes, mainly about 90 sq.m. Efforts are being made to upgrade what was an old fashioned campsite. There is a new and attractive pool complex including a covered pool (heated from April) – the pools are used by some local people. Entertainment is organised for high season evenings. A good sized shop sells the essentials.

Facilities

Two toilet blocks, one of which is heated when necessary, with washbasins in cabins. Facilities for disabled visitors (access by key). Laundry facilities. Shop (April - Oct). Bar, restaurant and takeaway (April - Sept). Swimming pools, one covered. Volleyball. Tennis. Play area. Boules. Quad bike hire. Fitness trail. Entertainment (high season). Barbecues are not permitted. Off site: Fishing and riding 5 km. Golf 12 km.

Open: 25 March - 4 November.

Directions

From the A7 take exit for Bollene, then the N7 towards Orange. At north end of Mornas village, turn left on D74-signed Uchaux. Site is on left after 1.7 km.

Charges 2006

Per unit incl. 2 persons	€ 14,80 - € 21,00
extra person	€ 4,60 - € 6,60
child (under 7 yrs)	€ 2,50 - € 4,00
electricity	€ 4,40

MAP 15

Rolling fields of yellow sunflowers, the Armagnac vineyards and crumbling, ancient stone buildings amidst the sleepy villages make this colourful region popular with those who enjoy good food, good wine and a taste of the good life.

DÉPARTEMENTS: 09 ARIÈGE, 31 HAUTE-GARONNE, 32 GERS, 65 HAUTES-PYRÉNÉES, 81 TARN, 82 TARN-ET GARONNE. WE HAVE LEFT OUT THE DÉPARTEMENTS OF AVEYRON (12) AND LOT (46), WHICH ARE IN OUR DORDOGNE/AVEYRON REGION

Still a relatively unknown region, the Midi-Pyrénées is the largest region of France, extending from the Dordogne in the north to the Spanish border. It is blessed by radiant sunshine and a fascinating range of scenery. High chalk plateaux, majestic peaks, tiny hidden valleys and small fortified sleepy villages, which seem to have changed little since the Middle Ages, contrast with the high-tech, industrial and vibrant university city of Toulouse.

Lourdes is one of the most visited pilgrimage sites in the world. Toulouse-Lautrec, the artist, was born at Albi, the capital of the département of Tarn. Much of the town is built of pink brick which seems to glow when seen from a distance. In the east, the little town of Foix, with its maze of steep, winding streets, is a convenient centre from which to explore the prehistoric caves at Niaux and the Aladdin's Cave of duty-free gift shops in the independent state of Andorra. The Canal du Midi that links Bordeaux to the Mediterranean was commissioned by Louis XIV in 1666 and is still in working order.

Places of interest

Albi: birthplace and Museum of Toulouse-Lautrec, imposing Ste Cécile cathedral with 15th century fresco of 'The Last Judgement'.

Auch: capital of ancient Gascony, boasts a fine statue of d'Artágnan.

Collonges-la-Rouge: picturesque village of Medieval and Renaissance style mansions and manors.

Conques: 11th century Ste Foy Romanesque church.

Cordes: medieval walled hilltop village.

Foix: 11th/12th century towers on rocky peak above town; 14th century cathedral.

Lourdes: famous pilgrimage site where Ste Bernadette is said to have spoken to the Virgin Mary in a grotto and known for the miracles said to have been performed there.

Cuisine of the region

Food is rich and strongly seasoned, making generous use of garlic and goose fat, and there are some excellent regional wines. Seafood such as oysters, salt-water fish, or piballes from the Adour river are popular.

Cassoulet: stew of duck, sausages and beans.

Confit de Canard (d'oie): preserved duck meat.

Grattons (Graisserons): a mélange of small pieces of rendered down duck, goose and pork fat.

Magret de canard: duck breast fillets

Poule au pot: chicken simmered with vegetables.

Ouillat (Ouliat): Pyrénées soup: onions, tomatoes, goose fat and garlic.

Tourtière Landaise: a sweet of Agen prunes, apples and Armagnac.

FR09020 Camping L'Arize

Mobile homes ▶ page 482

Lieu-dit Bourtol, F-09240 La Bastide-de-Sérou (Ariège)

Tel: 05 61 65 81 51. Email: **camparize@aol.com**

The site sits in a delightful, tranquil valley among the foothills of the Pyrénées and is just east of the interesting village of La Bastide-de-Sérou beside the River Arize (good trout fishing). The river is fenced for the safety of children on the site, but may be accessed just outside the gate. The 70 large pitches are neatly laid out on level grass within the spacious site. All have 3/6A electricity and are separated into bays by hedges and young trees. An extension to the site gives 24 large, fully serviced pitches and a small toilet block.

Facilities

Toilet block includes facilities for babies and disabled people. Laundry room, dryer. Motorcaravan services. Small swimming pool, sunbathing area. Entertainment, high season, weekly barbecues and welcome drinks on Sundays. Fishing, riding and bicycle hire on site. Off site: Golf 5 km. The nearest restaurant is at the national stud for the famous Merens horses just 200 m. away and will deliver takeaway meals to your pitch.

Open: 10 March - 6 November.

Directions

Site is southeast of the village La Bastide-de-Sérou. Take the D15 towards Nescus and site is on right after about 1 km. GPS: N43:00.109 E01:26.723

Charges 2006

Per pitch incl. 2 persons and electricity	€ 16,40 - € 23,70
extra person	€ 4,00 - € 5,20
child (0-7 yrs)	€ 3,00 - € 3,60

FR09050 Camping Municipal la Prade

F-09110 Sorgeat (Ariège)

Tel: 05 61 64 36 34. Email: **meciriesotseat@wanadoo.fr**

Superbly situated high on the mountainside overlooking a valley, this site has magnificent views, with a river 300 m. and a lake 2 km. A small site, it provides just 40 pitches on terraces, some of which are occupied by long stay units, (electricity 5-10A). Well supervised, with the warden present at varying times, the site is kept very clean. A small stream tinkles through the edge of the site and the attractive hills towering above it reverberate with the sound of goat bells. A separate area has permanent brick barbecues for use by campers. A most reasonably priced campsite.

Facilities

The original, rather small sanitary block has only two showers and two WCs in each half. However, a second block has now been added and standards are very high. Hot water is provided for dishwashing. Facilities for the disabled are also very good with special washbasin and a very large shower suite. Chemical disposal and waste water point. Washing machine. Small play area. Off site: Fishing 0.5 km. Riding and bicycle hire 5 km.

Open: All year.

Directions

From Ax-les-Thermes take D613 towards Quillan for 4 km. Turn onto D52 and continue for 1 km. Follow site signs. Bear left at first junction up through Sorgeat village to site. Mountain roads may be difficult for large units. GPS: N42:43.974 E01:51.234

Charges guide

Per person	€ 2,90
pitch	€ 1,60 - € 1,80
electricity (5/10A)	€ 2,70 - € 5,20

FR09080 Camping du Lac

RN 20, F-09000 Foix (Ariège)

Tel: 05 61 65 11 58. Email: **camping-du-lac@wanadoo.fr**

Du Lac is a traditional, urban lakeside site just 3 km. north of the very pretty town of Foix. There is road and rail noise (the site is alongside the old N20). There is space to manoeuvre at the entrance. The site is informally divided into four areas, one for mobile homes. The other areas are generally flat or slightly sloping with some shade under mature trees. There are 135 pitches, most with electricity (8-13A). Access to the lake is through a gate which is locked at night and the fence is secure. Children will need supervision in this area.

Facilities

Adequate but cramped, toilet blocks of varying ages, facilities for disabled campers, baby room. Cleanliness variable. Washing machine. Reception sells basic goods. Snack bar, bar/drinks stall close to pool. Small swimming pool, separate paddling pool. Play areas. Watersports, fishing, canoe instruction (hire charges apply). TV room, electronic games. Tennis, boules. Organised activities (high season). Torches are necessary. Off site: Cycling and walking tours, riding, golf or even white water rafting.

Open: All year.

Directions

From the north leave the N20 at exit 10 and take the old road towards the town. Site is well signed on the left, 3 km. north of the town centre (avoid new bypass and tunnel). GPS: N42:59.366 E01:36.942

Charges guide

Per unit incl. 2 persons and electricity	€ 13,00 - € 35,00
extra person	€ 2,00 - € 5,00
dog	€ 0,50 - € 1,50
Camping Cheques accepted.	

FR09060 Camping le Pré Lombard

F-09400 Tarascon-sur-Ariège (Ariège)

Tel: 05 61 05 61 94. Email: leprelombard@wanadoo.fr

This busy, good value site is located beside the attractive river Ariège near the town. There are 180 level, grassy, pitches with shade provided by a variety of trees (electricity 10A). At the rear of the site are 69 site-owned chalets and mobile homes. A gate in the fence provides access to the river bank for fishing. Open for a long season, it is an excellent choice for early or late breaks, or as a stop-over en-route to the winter sun destinations in Spain. This region of Ariège is in the foothills of the Pyrénées and 85 km. from Andorra. Didier Mioni, the manager here follows the town motto S'y passos, y demoros – 'if you wish to come here, you will stay here' in his aim to ensure your satisfaction on his site. At Tarascon itself you can visit the Parc Pyrénéen de l'Art Préhistorique to view prehistoric rock paintings, or the really adventurous can take to the air for paragliding, hang gliding, or microlighting.

Facilities

Five toilet blocks of varying age, facilities for disabled people. Laundry. Motorcaravan services. Bar and takeaway. Shop. Restaurant, entertainment, dancing (15/5-15/9). Heated swimming pool (15/5-15/9). Playgrounds for toddlers and older children. Video games machines. Boules. Multicourt sports. Fishing. Internet. Satellite TV. Entertainment (high season), nightclub, children's club, sports tournaments. Activity programmes for small groups. Off site: Supermarket 300 m. Town 600 m. Archery, kayaking and fishing nearby. Riding 5 km. Golf 30 km. Skiing 20 km.

Open: 29 January - 11 November.

Directions

Site is 600 m. south of town, adjacent to the river. From north, turn off main N20 into the town, site well signed. From south (Andorra) site signed at roundabout on town approach. GPS: N42:50.391 E01:36.720

Charges 2007

Per unit incl. 2 persons and 6A electricity	€ 15,00 - € 30,00
extra person (over 2 yrs)	€ 5,00 - € 9,00

Camping Cheques accepted.

FR09090 Naturiste Camping Millfleurs

Le Tuilier Gudas, F-09120 Varilhes (Ariège)

Tel: 05 61 60 77 56. Email: ag.kos@wanadoo.fr

Millfleurs is a quiet site in a secluded location for naturists. It is peaceful with some 70 acres of woods and meadows providing guided naturist walks in total privacy. The site has 40 large, flat, mostly terraced pitches (26 with 4/8A electricity), long leads if pitching off the terraces. There are also very secluded pitches in wooded areas with shade, or you can pitch a tent in the meadows if you prefer. There are few leisure facilities here and the site is aimed at the more mature naturist camper.

Facilities

An excellent toilet block, facilities for disabled campers. Bread available to order in high season. Guests dine together in the 'salle de reunion' within the farmhouse two nights a week or just meet friends for a drink. Refrigerator with drinks. Petanque, guide book for walks and cycle rides. Torches essential. Pick ups from airports and stations arranged. Off site: The coast is 1.5 hours.

Open: 15 April - 30 September.

Directions

From Varilhes, 8 km. south of Pamiers on D624 (parallel to N20). Take D13 for Dalou and Gudas cross railway and N20. The site is 2 km. past Gudas, on right. GPS: N42:59.566 E01:40.731

Charges 2006

Per person (all ages)	€ 4,45 - € 5,25
pitch incl. electricity	€ 7,05 - € 7,85

No credit cards.

FR09100 Parc d'Audinac les Bains

Montjoie - Audinac, F-09200 St Girons (Ariège)

Tel: **05 61 66 44 50**. Email: **accueil@audinac.com**

Remnants of an old thermal springs can be found on the site at Parc d'Audinac les Bains, a tranquil haven with wonderful views of the surrounding mountains. Owned by a charming French couple, Olivia and Jérôme Barbry, you are guaranteed a friendly welcome on this site which has 90 touring pitches and 25 chalets for rent. The terraced touring pitches are mostly level, although some do have a slight slope. They are on well drained grass and each has 10A electricity supplied (the older part of the site via French sockets). Water supplies are conveniently located as are the sanitary facilities.

Facilities

Two small modern toilet blocks (one unisex) with hot and cold water to showers and washbasins. British and Turkish style WC's. Washing machines. Motorcaravan service point. Outdoor swimming pool and paddling pool with WCs, showers and changing facilities. Small shop for drinks and ice creams (July/Aug) adjacent to the pool. Children's club (July/Aug). Tennis. Boules. Sports area. Off site: St Girons 3 km. Many outdoor activities.

Open: 1 May - 30 September.

Directions

From St Girons take D117 towards Foix. Turn left on D627 signed St Croix and Merigon. Site is on the right just after Audinac-les-Bains.

Charges 2006

Per unit incl. 2 persons	€ 11,50 - € 16,00
extra person	€ 4,00 - € 6,00
child (0-6 yrs)	€ 3,00 - € 5,00
electricity (10A)	€ 3,50

FR09110 Camping le Pas de l'Ours

F-09310 Aston (Ariège)

Tel: **05 61 64 90 33**. Email: **contact@lepasdelours.fr**

In the small town of Aston, which is located in the heart of the scenic Vallées d'Ax in the Haute-Ariège region, you will find the secluded campsite of Le Pas de l'Ours. With panoramic views of the mountains, this charming site has a total of 57 pitches, although only 30 of these are for tourers, as the rest are taken up by chalets to rent. Six of the smaller touring pitches are reserved for tents and have no electricity, but the other 24 grassy and mainly level pitches are well kept and attractively laid out, separated by shrubs and bushes and have 6A electricity (French sockets).

Facilities

Two modern sanitary blocks are well equipped and include pre-set showers. Large en-suite room for disabled visitors. Motorcaravan service point. Bakers van calls every morning in July/Aug. Communal covered purpose built barbecue area with picnic tables. Small play area. Tennis courts. Off site: Heated outdoor swimming pool in village adjacent to site. Skiing 16 km. Golf 30 km. Riding 20 km. Shops, restaurant and bars 4 km.

Open: 1 June - 15 September (chalets all year).

Directions

From N20 between Ax-Les-Thermes and Tarascon take exit to Les Cabannes on D522a signed Verdun and Aston. After 1.8 km. turn left on D520 to Château Verdun and Aston. Site is well signed. GPS: N42:46.337 E01:40.293

Charges 2006

Per unit incl. 2 persons	€ 12,00 - € 15,00
extra person	€ 3,00 - € 4,00
electricity (6A)	€ 3,00

FR09120 Camping Ascou la Forge

F-09110 Ascou (Ariège)

Tel: **05 61 64 60 03**. Email: **mountain.sports@wanadoo.fr**

The Dutch owners of Ascou La Forge will give you a warm, friendly welcome at their oasis in the mountains of the Pyrenees, close to the borders of Andorra and Spain. The site is 3,500 feet above sea level but is easily accessible for motorhomes and caravans. Lying alongside the Lauze river, there are 50 pitches. In low season 44 mainly level, grass touring pitches with electricity are available, but this number reduces to 20 in July and August to allow more room for the large influx of campers with tents. There are also 2 chalets available to rent.

Facilities

Modern, bright, sanitary block is fully equipped including facilities for disabled visitors which double as a family shower room with a baby bath. Shop. Bar with large screen for major sports events and films about the local flora/fauna. Play area. Maps and walking routes are available from reception. Free WiFi internet access. Off site: Restaurant next door to site (all year). Restaurants, bars and shops in Ax-les-Thermes 7 km.

Open: 1 May - 16 October.

Directions

From Ax-Les-Thermes take D613 signed Quérigat, Quillan and Ascou-Pailhéres. After 3.6 km. turn right on D25 to site on right after 3.4 km.

Charges 2006

Per person	€ 3,00 - € 3,80
child (0-7 yrs)	€ 2,20 - € 2,60
pitch	€ 3,00 - € 7,10
electricity (4A)	€ 3,00

FR09130 Camping du Lac
F-09400 Mercus-Garrabet (Ariège)

Tel: 05 61 05 90 61. Email: info@campinglac.com

Situated in the small town of Mercus just one kilometre from the N20 between Foix and Andorra, this is a lovely campsite on the shores of a lake, devotedly run by Jacky and Martine Podvin. The site has 70 pitches (40 for touring and 18 chalets and mobile homes to rent). The grassy pitches are attractively laid out, level and partially shaded by mature trees. Each has electricity (6/10A; Europlug) adjacent and all are reasonably close to the modern sanitary blocks. There is some background road noise and also several trains run alongside the site throughout the day between 06.00-22.00.

Facilities

Two modern sanitary blocks are well equipped. One also has facilities for disabled visitors and a family shower room with a baby bath. Motorcaravan service point. Bread, sandwiches and pizzas (July/Aug). Heated swimming pool. Play area. Off site: Watersports (July/Aug). Shops, restaurant and bar 1 km. Riding 5 km. Golf 7 km.

Open: 8 April - 10 October.

Directions

From the N20 (Foix - Andorra) take exit 14 to Mercus which is only 1 km. Site is signed in Mercus and is on the right 300 m. after the town centre.

Charges 2006

Per unit incl. 2 persons	€ 12,00 - € 23,00
extra person	€ 3,50 - € 6,00
electricity (6/10A)	€ 3,00 - € 4,50

FR32010 Le Camp de Florence
Mobile homes ▶ page 483

Route Astaffort, F-32480 La Romieu (Gers)

Tel: 05 62 28 15 58. Email: info@lecampdeflorence.com

Camp de Florence is an attractive site on the edge of an historic village in pleasantly undulating Gers countryside. The 183 large, part terraced pitches (95 for tourers) all have electricity, 10 with hardstanding and 25 fully serviced. They are arranged around a large field (full of sunflowers when we visited) with rural views, giving a feeling of spaciousness. The 13th century village of La Romieu is on the Santiago de Compostela pilgrim route. The Pyrénées are a two hour drive, the Atlantic coast a similar distance. There are 20 tour operator pitches. It is run by the Mynsbergen family who are Dutch (although Susan is English) and they have sympathetically converted the old farmhouse buildings to provide facilities for the site. The collegiate church, visible from the site, is well worth a visit (the views are magnificent from the top of the tower), as is the local arboretum, the biggest collection of trees in the Midi-Pyrénées.

Facilities

Two toilet blocks. Washing machine, dryer. Motorcaravan services. Air-conditioned restaurant (open to the public) 1/5-30/9, barbecue. Takeaway. Bread. Swimming pool area with water slide. Jacuzzi, protected children's pool (open to public in afternoons). Adventure playground, games and pets areas. Games room, tennis, table tennis, volleyball, petanque. Bicycle hire. Video shows, discos, picnics, musical evenings. Excursions. Internet and WiFi. Off site: Shop 500 m. in village. Fishing 5 km. Riding 10 km. Walking tours, excursions and wine tasting arranged.

Open: 1 April - 8 October.

Directions

Site signed from D931 Agen - Condom road. Small units turn left at Ligardes (signed), follow D36 for 1 km, turn right turn La Romieu (signed). Otherwise continue until outskirts of Condom and take D41 left to La Romieu, through village to site. GPS: N43:58.975 E00:30.091

Charges 2007

Per unit incl. 2 persons and electricity	€ 16,00 - € 30,90
extra person	€ 3,50 - € 6,90
child (4-9 yrs)	€ 2,60 - € 4,80
Camping Cheques accepted.	

FR32020 Camping du Lac

F-32230 Marciac (Gers)

Tel: 05 62 08 21 19. Email: camping.marciac@wanadoo.fr

Set in the rolling countryside of the beautiful Gers region, Camping Du Lac is on the edge of the ancient fortified town of Marciac. Rob and Louise Robinson, the English owners since 2002, offer a friendly welcome and a quiet, relaxing stay. The well shaded site has 95 pitches, including 15 used for having mobile homes and chalets for rent. There are 60 touring pitches with electricity connections (6/10A, Europlug) on the lower, reasonably level area of the site, including 5 with hardstanding for motorcaravans. On an informal, slightly sloping terraced area giving a 'back to nature' feeling are 20 pitches without electricity mainly used for tents. There is a small swimming pool with sun loungers and a play area for children. Facilities for petanque and table tennis are available and a small meeting room provides tourist information and a library with English books.

Facilities

The centrally situated sanitary block uses solar energy to help to heat water. Washbasins in cubicles. Facilities for disabled visitors are planned. Washing machine. Motorcaravan service point. Bar. Bread delivered daily (order at reception). Swimming pool. Small library and reading room. Play area. Internet access. Off site: Shops, restaurant and bars 1 km. Major international jazz festival in Marciac (first 2 weeks in August) 1 km. Fishing, watersports, sailing and riding 300 m. Golf 7 km. Walking (maps at reception).

Open: 16 March - 30 October.

Directions

From Auch take the D943 west towards Bassoues and Marciac. Just before Marciac turn left opposite the floating restaurant on the lake (site is signed). Site is 200 m. on the left.

Charges 2006

Per unit incl. 2 persons and electricity (6A)	€ 11,00 - € 20,00
extra person	€ 2,50 - € 5,00
child (4-16 yrs)	€ 1,50 - € 3,00

Camping du Lac, Marciac (32230 Gers)*

British owned, calm campsite with swimming pool and snack-bar set in the beautiful rolling country-side of Gascony, yet only 1km from the historic town of Marciac (with shops and restaurants) and 300m from a splendid lake. Shaded touring pitches and modern mobile homes for rent. Hard-standings and service point for motor homes and ARVs. Booking essential in first two weeks of August (Marciac Jazz Festival)

Tel/Fax: +33 (0)5 62 08 21 19
E-mail: camping.marciac@wanadoo.fr
Web: www.camping-marciac.com

FR32060 Yelloh! Village le Lac des Trois Vallées

F-32700 Lectoure (Gers)

Tel: 05 62 68 82 33. Email: lac.des.trois.vallees@wanadoo.fr

This is a large 140 hectare site with many facilities. It is a large holiday complex and good for families with young children or teenagers. The large lake provides the opportunity for canoeing, swimming, diving and there are four water slides. There is a large safe paddling area and a separate fishing lake. The impressive heated pool complex complete with gymnasium and jacuzzi also has paved areas for sunbathing and a large paddling pool. Of the 500 pitches, over 200 are well situated for touring on shaded or open ground, all with electricity (10A). Used by tour operators (100 pitches).

Facilities

Eight modern sanitary blocks each with baby bathing facilities. Provision for disabled visitors. Laundry facilities. Motorcaravan services. Mini-market. Restaurants and bars. Lakeside snack bar and drinks kiosk. Heated swimming pool complex. Lake complex. Multisports pitch. BMX/skateboard area. Fishing. Tennis. Minigolf. Video games room. Disco. Cinema. Children's club. Off site: Golf 10 km. Riding 20 km. Walking and mountain bike trails. Quad bikes. Hot air balloon rides.

Open: 15 May - 12 September with all facilities.

Directions

Take N21 south from Lectoure for 2 km. Site is well signed and is a further 2 km. after turning left off the N21.

Charges 2006

Per unit incl. 2 persons and electricity	€ 16,00 - € 39,00
with electricity and water	€ 17,00 - € 40,00
extra person	€ 5,00 - € 7,50

FR32030 Camping la Plage de Verduzan

Rue du Lac, F-32410 Castéra Verduzan (Gers)

Tel: 05 62 68 12 23. Email: contact@camping-verduzan.com

This is a pleasant site situated 500 metres from the small village of Castéra Verduzan where there are restaurants, bars, shops, a casino and thermal baths. The site is on the shores of a small lake and access to its sandy beach is free for site customers. Here there is a water slide, pedaloes and a small sailing school. The 56 touring pitches at the site are on level grass, hedged with bushes and ornamental trees and all have electricity hook-up (3/10A). There are also a few mobile homes to rent.

Facilities

Two toilet blocks with facilities for disabled people and mixed laundry and dishwashing sinks with one hot tap. Washing machine. Chemical disposal. New play area. Motorcaravan services planned. Small bar, snacks, low key entertainment, games and competitions (open July/Aug). Table tennis. Fishing from the far side of the lake. Off site: Village shops and restaurants. Golf 25 km. Riding 5 km.

Open: 23 March - 31 October.

Directions

Castéra Verduzen is on the D930, 20 km. south of Condom. Site is on south side of village and well signed. GPS: N43:48.485 E00:25.848

Charges 2007

Per unit incl. 2 persons	€ 11,00 - € 15,50
extra person	€ 3,50 - € 5,00
child (3-8 yrs)	€ 3,00 - € 4,00
electricity (6A)	€ 2,00 - € 3,00

Camping La Plage de Verduzan ★★★

Dreaming of.....Nature, quiet and tradition.......
Welcome to "La plage de Verduzan"!!!
For your comfort, we propose you pitches each 100m2 with electricity.
200 meters from the village center, you will find full range of shops, supermarket, doctors and also a play CASINO.
Sport and leisure : supervised swimming, water slide, aquatic gym, windsurfing, rambling,.... dancing, theme dinners.
Near the camping : horse riding, canoe, mountain bike, boat, fishing.
Booking advisable for rent in summer.

Rue du Lac 32410 Castera Verduzan
Tél : +33(0)5 62 68 12 23
fax : +33 (0)5 62 68 18 95
contact@camping-verduzan.com

SPECIAL RATES OUT OF SEASON. www.camping-verduzan.com

FR32080 Camping le Talouch

F-32810 Roquelaure (Gers)

Tel: 05 62 65 52 43. Email: info@camping-talouch.com

Although enjoying a quiet location it is only 10 km. drive from the region's capital, Auch, The entrance is fronted by a parking area with reception to the right and the bar and restaurant facing. Beyond this point lies the top half of the touring area with generous pitches of at least 120 sq.m. located between mature trees and divided by hedges, some with chalets. There are 118 pitches, with electricity (4A). The rear half of the site has unshaded pitches in a more open aspect, and chalets have been built on the hillside to one side of the site.

Facilities

Two immaculate toilet blocks, the larger refurbished. The smaller block is more modern. Baby room, used by people with disabilities. Small shop (1/5-30/9). Two swimming pools, new pool, 'jetstream'. Bicycle hire. Two play areas, volleyball, tennis, basketball. 9 hole golf course. Organised entertainment, high season.

Open: 1 April - 30 September.

Directions

From Auch take N21 for 8.5 km. north and turn west onto D272 to village of Roquelaure. Then follow signs to site 2 km. south of village on D148.

Charges 2006

Per unit incl. 2 persons	€ 14,00 - € 22,05
with electricity	€ 15,90 - € 29,15
extra person	€ 4,15 - € 6,65
child (3-7 yrs)	€ 3,40 - € 5,40
animal	€ 1,50 - € 2,20

Discounts for longer stays.
Camping Cheques accepted.

FR32100 Camping les Lacs de Courtés

F-32240 Estangs (Gers)

Tel: **05 62 09 61 98**. Email: **contact@lacs-de-courtes.com**

This small site has been owned and managed by a friendly French couple for the last 24 years. It is situated on a hillside overlooking a lake and has 114 pitches neatly arranged on terraces. There are 50 level touring pitches each with adjacent 6A electricity supply (French sockets), the remaining pitches being used for 64 mobile homes and chalets of which 29 are to rent. The touring pitches are mainly grassed and are well separated by hedges and mature trees which provide shade. Some are situated alongside a private lake that is used for fishing and canoeing. There is a full programme of organised sports competitions and entertainment for children and adults in July and August, including dancing, karaoke, fancy dress and social evenings with local speciality meals. There is also a mini-market each week in July and August when local producers of wine, foies gras etc. bring their products to site for tasting and sale.

Facilities

Centrally situated toilet block with showers, WCs, washbasins and covered dishwashing and laundry sinks. Separate facilities for disabled people at entrance to site. Laundry room. Motorcaravan service point Bar and small restaurant (1/7-31/8) with covered entertainment area. Two outdoor pools and paddling pool. Play area. Private lake for fishing and canoeing. Off site: Shops, restaurant and bars in Estang 200 m. Golf 18 km. Riding 12 km. Barbotan-Les-Thermes thermal spa 11 km.

Open: Easter - 30 September.

Directions

From Condom take D931 to Eauze then N524 west to Cazaubon. After 4 km. take D30 to Estang. Site is on left as you enter the village of Estang.

Charges 2006

Per unit incl. 2 persons	€ 13,80 - € 23,00
extra person	€ 3,00 - € 5,00
child	€ 1,50 - € 2,50
electricity (6A)	€ 3,00

FR32090 Camping le Pardaillan

27 rue Pardaillan, F-32330 Gondrin (Gers)

Tel: **05 62 29 16 69**. Email: **camplepardaillan@wanadoo.fr**

In the heart of the Armagnac region of the Gers between Condom and Eauze make a stop at the village of Gondrin and stay at the attractive, family run campsite of Le Pardaillan. Neatly manicured and well laid out, the site has 115 pitches arranged on four separate terraced areas; 51 of these are for tourers, the remainder used for chalets (to rent all year). Level and grassy, the touring pitches are small to average in size, separated by tidy hedges and partially shaded by mature trees. Each has 6/10A electricity and 30 also have water and waste water points.

Facilities

Three toilet blocks include WCs, hot showers and washbasins in cubicles. Facilities for disabled visitors. Heated family shower room. Washing machines, dryers, and ironing board. Bar, restaurant and takeaway (all season). WiFi internet access. Play area. Children's club and excursions (July/Aug). Fishing lake. Off site: Shops, restaurant and bars 500 m. Leisure centre 200 m. Golf 6 km. Riding 15 km.

Open: 1 April - 16 October.

Directions

From Condom take D931 to Eauze. Site is in village of Gondrin and is signed.

Charges 2006

Per unit incl. 2 persons and electricity (6A)	€ 12,00 - € 21,00
extra person (over 4 yrs)	€ 3,00 - € 5,15
10A electricity	€ 1,50

FR32110 Camping du Lac de l'Uby

Barbothan les Thermes, F-32150 Gaubazon (Gers)

Tel: 05 62 09 53 91. Email: balia-vacauces@wanadoo.fr

Camping du Lac de l'Uby is a large, mature site set alongside a lake and close to the thermal spa town of Barbotan-Les-Thermes in the Gers Gascogne region. The site is well shaded by mature trees in most areas and has 280 pitches with 240 available for tourers, the remainder taken up with mobile homes and chalets to rent. The mixture of large and average sized pitches are on level grass and gravel, all having 5/10A electricity (French sockets).

Facilities

Five well distributed sanitary blocks include facilities for disabled visitors and a separate baby room. Two blocks have been recently refurbished and the others will be done in next year. Laundry room. Motorcaravan service point. Shop. Play area and covered entertainment area. Fishing. Bicycle hire. Off site: Shop, restaurant and bar 50 m. (1/6-30/9). Leisure centre with pool, beach, and large play area 500 m. Golf 20 km.

Open: 15 March - 30 November.

Directions

From Condom take D931 to Eauze then head west on N524 to Cazaubon. From Cazaubon continue on the N524 towards Barbotan-Les-Thermes, sight is signed on right after 2 km.

Charges 2006

Per person	€ 3,00 - € 5,00
child (3-10 yrs)	€ 2,50 - € 3,70
pitch incl. electricity	€ 4,40 - € 10,00

FR32120 Camping de l'Arros

Allée des Ormeaux, F-32160 Plaisance du Gers (Gers)

Tel: 05 62 69 30 28. Email: infos@plaisance-evasion.com

The village of Plaisance is in the Gascogne region of the Gers and the small and friendly Camping de l'Arros is just on the edge of the village, alongside the river. The site is well shaded and has 82 pitches, with 50 available for touring units, all with 6A electricity. The remainder are taken up with mobile homes and chalets for rent. The large pitches are level, grassy and well separated by hedges and mature trees which provide good shade. Traffic noise is noticeable on some areas of the site. There is a large municipal swimming pool just 100 m. away from the site.

Facilities

Two sanitary blocks with WCs, hot showers and washbasins in cubicles. Washing machines, dryers, iron and ironing board. Shop with local produce. Bar, restaurant and takeaway (July/Aug). Free WiFi internet access. Play area. Children's club (July/Aug). Canoeing. Communal evening meal. Off site: Shops, restaurant and bars 500 m. Outdoor pool 100 m. Minigolf 500 m. Golf 20 km. Riding and tennis 500 m. Major international jazz festival in Marciac (first 2 weeks in August) 14 km.

Open: 1 April - 30 September.

Directions

From Auch take N21 towards Tarbes then after village of Miélan turn right on D3 towards Marciac and Plaisance. At Plaisance turn left on D946, site is signed on left.

Charges 2006

Per person	€ 3,00 - € 5,00
child (3-10 yrs)	€ 2,50 - € 3,70
pitch	€ 2,40 - € 8,00
electricity (6A)	€ 2,00

FR31000 Camping le Moulin

F-31220 Martres-Tolosane (Haute-Garonne)

Tel: 05 61 98 86 40. Email: info@campinglemoulin.com

Set in a 12 hectare estate of woods and fields, Camping Le Moulin is a family run campsite in the foothills of the Pyrénées, close to the interesting medieval village of Martres-Tolosane and situated on the site of an old mill on the bank of the River Garonne. There are 94 pitches (60 available for tourers) all of which have electrical connections. Most pitches are level and grassy, of a good size and with shade from mature trees. A number of very large (150-200 sq.m.) 'super' pitches are also available and there are 34 chalets/mobile homes for rent.

Facilities

Large modern sanitary block with showers and washbasins in cubicles. Separate heated area for disabled visitors with shower, WC and basin. Baby bath. Laundry and dishwashing facilities. Motorhome services. Outdoor bar with WiFi. Snackbar and takeaway (July/Aug). Daily bakers van (except Monday). Heated swimming pool (July/Aug). BMX track. Playground. Games room. Entertainment programme and children's club (high season). Off site: Martres-Tolosane 1.5 km.

Open: Easter - 30 September.

Directions

From the A64 motorway (Toulouse-Tarbes) take exit 21 (Boussens) or exit 22 (Martres-Tolosane) and follow signs to Martres-Tolosane. Site is well signed from village.

Charges 2006

Per person	€ 4,20 - € 6,00
child (2-7 ys)	€ 2,10 - € 3,00
pitch	€ 5,25 - € 11,50
electricity (6/10A)	€ 2,45 - € 5,00

Less 20% outside July and August.

Check real time availability and at-the-gate prices...

www.alanrogers.com

FR65010 Domaine Naturiste L'Eglantière

Aries-Espenan, F-65230 Castelnau-Magnoac (Haute-Pyrénées)

Tel: 05 62 39 88 00. Email: info@leglantiere.com

Alongside a small, fast flowing river, in woods it comprises 12 hectares for camping and caravanning, with a further 32 for walking and relaxing. The river is suitable for swimming and canoeing, with fishing nearby. The 83 traditional, varying size, grassy, level pitches have 10A electricity (long leads). The older secluded ones are separated by a variety of tall trees and bushes, the newer ones more open. There is a tenting area across the river. The site has a medium sized swimming pool with sunbathing areas and a children's pool, overlooked by the clubhouse and terrace.

Facilities

Two toilet blocks in typically naturist style, providing under cover, open plan, facilities. Small block has individual cubicles. Shop (July-Aug). Clubhouse, bar (all season), small restaurant (June-Sept), pizzeria, takeaway (July-Aug), internet. Soundproofed activities/disco area, play room for younger children. Swimming pool (all season). Play area, children's entertainment in season. Volleyball, badminton, table tennis, petanque, archery. River activities. Canoe, mountain bike hire. Trekking, cross country cycling. No barbecues. Torches useful. Off site: Restaurants in village.

Open: Easter - October.

Directions

From Auch take D929 south towards Lannemezan. After Castelnau-Magnoac continue past aerodrome and turn onto the D9 towards Monleon-Magnoac. Take the first left towards Ariès-Espénan and follow site signs. GPS: N43:15.829 E00:31.252

Charges 2006

Per pitch incl. 2 persons	€ 11,00 - € 31,70
extra person	€ 2,00 - € 5,90
child (3-8 yrs)	free - € 4,80
animal	€ 2,20 - € 3,90

Camping Cheques accepted.

FR65020 Sunêlia les Trois Vallées

Avenue des Pyrénées, F-65400 Argelès-Gazost (Haute-Pyrénées)

Tel: 05 62 90 35 47. Email: 3-vallees@wanadoo.fr

This is a large, ever-expanding site on the road from Lourdes into the Pyrénées. It has an unprepossessing entrance and pitches near the road suffer from noise, but at the back, open fields allow views of surrounding mountains on all sides. Amenities include an indoor pool, two jacuzzis and an enormous play area that seems to have everything! The site has 483 flat, grassy pitches of reasonable size, 200 are for tourers, all with 3 or 6A electricity, some fully serviced. The site is popular with young people and could be quite lively at times.

Facilities

The toilet blocks are a little dated, facilities for disabled people. Cleaning can be variable and facilities could be under pressure at peak times. Bread. Bar/disco. Café, takeaway. Swimming pool complex (from 15/5), paddling pool, two water slides. TV room. Good playground. Entertainment in high season. Off site: Supermarket. Bicycle hire 50 m. Fishing 500 m. Riding 3 km.

Open: 1 April - 30 September.

Directions

Argelès-Gazost is 13 km. south of Lourdes. From Lourdes take the new N21 (Voie rapide) south and leave at the third exit. Site entrance is directly off the next roundabout. GPS: N43:00.726 W00:05.871

Charges 2006

Per pitch incl. 2 persons	€ 11,00 - € 25,00
incl. electricity	€ 12,00 - € 30,00
extra person	€ 4,50 - € 9,00

FR65030 Airotel Pyrénées

46 avenue du Barége, F-65120 Esquieze Sere (Haute-Pyrénées)

Tel: 05 62 92 89 18. Email: airotel.pyrenees@wanadoo.fr

It is located on the main road into the mountains, south from Argelès-Gazost and surrounded by the high peaks (some pitches will have daytime road noise). There are 163 level pitches, with 85 for touring units, all with electricity and 90 fully serviced. They are on terraced ground and separated by bushes. Lighting runs through the site and across some pitches. The layout of the pitches with the mobile homes can give a rather crowded feel. In high season a programme of activities is arranged, from walking and mountain bike trips to rafting. There are tour operator pitches.

Facilities

Fairly modern, well appointed, toilet blocks (one heated), facilities for disabled people also doubling as a baby room. Bottled water is advised for drinking and cooking. Motorcaravan services. Small shop (1/7-31/8), bread 15/5-15/9. Outdoor pool (15/6-15/9). Indoor pool, balneotherapy pool, sauna, fitness room (1/12-30/9). Water slides. Practice climbing wall, tennis, boules, table tennis. Small playground. Off site: Skiing 10 km.

Open: All year, excl. 1 October - 30 November.

Directions

Take N21 (Voie rapide) south from Lourdes past Argelès-Gazost towards Luz-St-Sauveur. The site is on left at Esquièze-Sere, just before Luz-St-Sauveur. Site is on left immediately after Camping International. GPS: N42:52.749 W00:00.610

Charges 2006

Per unit incl. 2 persons	€ 15,50 - € 23,00
extra person	€ 5,00
electricity (3/10A)	€ 3,50 - € 6,50

FR65040 Camping International

F-65120 Luz St Saveur (Haute-Pyrénées)

Tel: **05 62 92 82 02**. Email: **reception@international-camping.fr**

Located in the foothills of the Pyrénées, Camping International is an attractive, family run site with 180 pitches, most are on the fairly level lower section. There are 146 grassy pitches for tourists all with electricity (2/ 6A), many divided by hedges and some with a little shade. Around 40 pitches (more for tents) are on terraces on the mountainside at back of the site, all accessed by tarmac roads and with stunning views. However some fairly steep up and down walking will be necessary.

Facilities	Directions
Well equipped toilet blocks (one heated), facilities for babies and disabled campers. Shop. Snack bar, takeaway. Heated swimming pool (1/6-30/9). Bar (20/6-10/9). Half court tennis. Boules. Minigolf. Playground. Organised activities, main season. Off site: Luz St Saveur Jazz Festival in July, Internet (free). Paragliding near Barèges, cable car to the Pic du Midi observatory. Climbing, rafting, walking, winter skiing. Fishing 0.5 km. Bicycle hire 1 km. Riding 7 km. Golf 30 km.	From Lourdes take new N21 (Voie rapide) south, pass Argeles Gazost continuing towards Luz St Sauveur on D921. Site is on left at Esquièze-Sere (just before Luz). Site entrance is well signed but congested at peak times. GPS: N42:52.961 W00:00.806

Open: 1 June - 30 Sept; 15 December - 15 April.

Charges 2006

Per unit incl. 1 or 2 persons	€ 18,00
incl. 3 persons	€ 21,00
extra person	€ 4,00 - € 4,70
electricity	€ 1,85 - € 4,90

FR65060 Castel Camping Pyrénées Natura

Route du Lac, F-65400 Estaing (Haute-Pyrénées)

Tel: **05 62 97 45 44**. Email: **info@camping-pyrenees-natura.com**

Pyrénées Natura, at an altitude of 1,000 metres, on the edge of the National Park is the perfect site for lovers of nature. The 60 pitches (46 for tourists), all with electricity, are in a large, level, open and sunny field. Around 75 varieties of trees and shrubs have been planted – but they do not spoil the fantastic views. The reception and bar are in a traditional style stone building with an open staircase. The small shop in the old water mill is left unmanned and open all day and you pay at reception.

Facilities	Directions
First class toilet blocks include facilities for disabled visitors and babies. Washing machine and airers (no lines allowed). Motorcaravan services. Small shop, takeaway (15/5-15/9). Small bar (15/5-15/9), lounge area. Lounge, library, TV (mainly used for videos of the National Park). Sauna, solarium (free between 12.00-17.00). Music room. Play area for the very young. Small 'beach' beside river. Table tennis, boules, giant chess. Weekly evening meal in May, June and Sept. Internet. Off site: Village restaurants.	From Lourdes take N21 towards Argelès-Gazost. Exit 2, N2021/D21, into Argelès. Approaching town turn onto D918 towards Aucun. After 8 km, turn left, D13 to Bun, cross river, right on D103 to site (5.5 km). Narrow road, few passing places. GPS: N42:56.451 W00:10.631

Open: 1 May - 20 September.

Charges 2007

Per unit incl. 2 persons and electricity (3A)	€ 24,00
extra person	€ 5,00
child (under 8 yrs)	€ 3,50

FR65080 Camping du Lavedan

Lau-Balagnas, F-65400 Argelès-Gazost (Haute-Pyrénées)

Tel: **05 62 97 18 84**. Email: **contact@lavedan.com**

Camping du Lavedan is an old established and very French site set in the Argelès-Gazost valley south of the Lourdes. It is beside the main road so there is some daytime road noise. The 105 touring pitches are set very close together on grass with some shade and all have electricity (2-10A). The area is fine for walking, biking, rafting and of course, in winter, skiing. There is a swimming pool which can be covered in inclement weather and events are organised in high season.

Facilities	Directions
Acceptable toilet block. Baby room. Facilities for disabled visitors. Washing machines and dryer in separate block heated in winter. Restaurant with takeaway and terrace (1/5-15/9). Bar, TV (all year). No shop, bread delivery (1/5-15/9). Swimming pool (with cover), paddling pool. Excellent play area. Internet (July/Aug). Boules, table tennis. Off site: Fishing or bicycle hire 1 km. Supermarket or rafting 2 km. Riding 5 km. Golf 15 km.	Lau-Balagnas, 15 km. south of Lourdes. From Lourdes take the N21 south, exit 3 (Argelès-Gazost). Take N2021, D921 or D21 towards Luz St Saveur for 2 km. to Lau Balagnas. Site is on right, southern edge of town. GPS: N42:59.293 W00:05.340

Open: All year.

Charges 2006

Per unit incl. 2 persons	€ 15,00 - € 19,00
electricity (2A)	€ 2,00 - € 6,00
Camping Cheques accepted.	

Midi-Pyrénées

FR65090 Camping Soleil du Pibeste

Mobile homes ▶ page 483

16 avenue du Lavedan, F-65400 Agos Vidalos (Haute-Pyrénées)

Tel: **05 62 97 53 23**. Email: **info@campingpibeste.com**

Soleil du Pibeste is a quiet, rural site with well tended grass and flower beds. It has 67 pitches for touring, all having electricity (3-15A) with some shade. The Dusserm family welcomes all arrivals with a drink and they are determined to ensure that you have a good stay. There is no shop but the supermarket is only 5 km. and ordered bread is delivered to your door daily. The swimming pool is on a terrace above the pitches, with sun beds, a paddling pool and waterfall and has the most magnificent view of the mountains.

Facilities

Two heated toilet blocks. Baby room. Facilities for disabled visitors (key). Cleaning can be variable. Washing machine, dryer. Motorcaravan services. Bar, snacks, piano, internet. Room for playing cards or reading. Swimming, paddling pools. Small play area. Boules. Bicycle hire. Tai Chi and other relaxation classes. Off site: Fishing 800 m. Golf 10 km. Rafting 2 km. Skiing 2 km.

Open: 1 May - 30 September.

Directions

Agos Vidalos is on the N21, 5 km. south of Lourdes. Leave express-way at second exit, signed Agos Vidalos and continue to site, a short distance on the right. GPS: N43:02.134 W00:04.256

Charges 2006

Per unit incl. 2 persons and 3A electricity	€ 15,00 - € 22,00
extra person	€ 3,00 - € 5,00

FR65100 Camping le Moulin du Monge

Avenue Jean Moulin, F-65100 Lourdes (Haute-Pyrénées)

Tel: **05 62 94 28 15**. Email: **camping.moulin.monge@wanadoo.fr**

A well organised, family run site with a friendly welcome, Moulin du Monge has a convenient location for visiting Lourdes, only 3 kilometres away. There will be some traffic noise from the nearby N21 and railway line. This attractive garden-like site has 57 grassy pitches in several different areas and on different levels. Some are in a level orchard area and are closest to the main road. A few pitches are on a little woodland knoll behind reception, with the remainder on a higher level at the back of the site. All have electricity hook-ups (2-6A).

Facilities

The heated toilet blocks have all necessary facilities, including washing machine, dryer, sauna. No facilities for disabled campers. Motorcaravan services. Well stocked shop. Heated swimming pool, sliding cover (1/5-20/9), paddling pool. Games/TV room. Barbecue, terrace. Table tennis. Sauna. Boules. Playground, trampolines. Off site: Transport links to city centre with its famous grotto. Fishing 3 km. Golf 4 km. Bicycle hire 0.5 km.

Open: 1 April - 15 October.

Directions

Site is just off the N21 on northern outskirts of Lourdes. From north, on N21 (2 km. south of Adé) be prepared to take slip lane in centre of road. Turn left into Ave. Jean Moulin. Site shortly on left. GPS: N43:06.931 W00:01.895

Charges 2007

Per unit incl. 2 persons	€ 13,80
incl. electricity (2-6A)	€ 15,80 - € 17,80
extra person	€ 4,60

FR65110 Camping Cabaliros

F-65110 Cauterets (Haute-Pyrénées)

Tel: **05 62 92 55 36**. Email: **info@camping-cabaliros.com**

After driving up a steady incline through a sheer sided, tree lined valley, the terrain opens up just before you reach the town of Cauterets. Here you will find the delightful Camping Cabaliros where you will receive a warm and friendly welcome. With wonderful views, the site is owned by Jean and Chantal Boyrie and has been in the family since it was opened in 1959. There are 4 chalets for rent, 36 pitches without electricity (mainly for tents) and 60 pitches with 6A electricity (French sockets) for tourers. All of the touring pitches are on well manicured grass and those around the perimeter of the site are reasonably level with some shade provided by mature trees.

Facilities

Sanitary block near to site entrance with WCs, hot showers and washbasins in cubicles. Dishwashing and laundry sinks with cold water only. Washing machine and dryer. Motorcaravan service point. Large library (mainly French) and excellent meeting room with television. Play area for over 7s. Fishing. Off site: Restaurant (July/Aug) 50 m. Supermarket 1 km. Shops, restaurants and bars 2 km. Riding 10 km. Pont d'Espagne 9 km.

Open: 1 June - 30 September.

Directions

From Lourdes head south on the N21 to Argelès-Gazost then take D921 followed by the D920 to Cauterets. Site is on right 1 km. after 'SHOPI' supermarket just before Cauterets.

Charges 2006

Per unit incl. 2 persons	€ 10,80 - € 12,00
extra person	€ 3,80 - € 4,20
child (0-6 yrs)	€ 2,00 - € 2,20
electricity (2-10A)	€ 3,80 - € 4,20

FR65130 Camping Pyrenevasion

Route de Luz-Ardiden, Sazos, F-65120 Luz St Sauveur (Haute-Pyrénées)

Tel: 05 62 92 91 54. Email: camping-pyrenevasion@wanadoo.fr

In the heart of the Pyrénées, Camping Pyrenevasion is at a height of 830 metres on a picturesque hillside with panoramic views of the mountains and the town of Luz-St-Sauveur in the valley below. This family run site, where you will receive a warm and friendly welcome, has 60 well laid out, tidy touring pitches. On level, grassy terraces on the hillside which are partially shaded by young trees, each pitch has electricity (French socket) adjacent and all are reasonably close to the modern heated sanitary block. There are 12 modern, comfortable chalets for rent (all year).

Facilities

Heated sanitary block with showers, WCs, washbasins (cubicles and open area). Facilities for disabled visitors. Baby bath. Washing machine and dryer. Motorcaravan services. Bread can be ordered at reception for next morning delivery. Bar (all year). Takeaway service (1/6-1/10). Heated swimming and paddling pools (15/5-1/10). Small play area (up to 6 yrs). Sports area. Off site: Shops, restaurant and bar 2 km. Fishing 200 m. Riding 10 km. Golf 30 km. Skiing 10 km. Jazz festival in Luz-St-Sauveur in early July. Col de Tourmalet and Pic du Midi mountain top observatory 22 km.

Open: All year.

Directions

From Lourdes take N21 south to Pierrefit-Nestalas then the D921 to Luz-St-Sauveur. Follow signs from Luz-St-Sauveur to Luz-Ardiden (D12). Site is on right as you enter the village of Sazos.

Charges 2006

Per unit incl. 2 persons	€ 12,00 - € 16,00
extra person	€ 5,00
child (2-6 yrs)	€ 3,00
electricity (3-10A)	€ 3,50 - € 11,50

FR81020 Camping le Moulin de Julien

F-81170 Cordes-sur-Ciel (Tarn)

Tel: 05 63 56 11 10

Close to the picturesque fortified old town of Cordes-sur-Ciel, in a secluded valley location in the heart of the Tarn region, this traditional style site has 130 spacious pitches. The grass pitches are arranged around a fishing lake with good shade in some areas and all with electricity hook-ups (5A). The area has magnificent scenery to enjoy and the fortified towns of the region to discover, including medieval Cordes (1 km). This site is full of character with a charming, friendly owner.

Facilities

Two rather elegant, well maintained sanitary buildings provide open and curtained washbasins, dishwashing and laundry sinks, a washing machine, plus facilities for disabled people. Well fenced swimming pool (1/6-30/9) and splash pool with water slide (July/Aug). Minigolf, table tennis, TV room and boules. Fishing. Gates locked 22.00-08.00 hrs. Off site: Shops, bars and restaurants within 1 km. Bicycle hire 3 km.

Open: 1 May - 30 September.

Directions

Cordes is 25 km. northwest of Albi. From D600 just east of Cordes take D922 south, and within 0.5 km. the site is signed at a minor road junction to your left.

Charges guide

Per unit incl. 2 persons	€ 15,00 - € 19,00
incl. 3 persons	€ 19,00 - € 23,00
extra person	€ 5,00 - € 6,00
electricity (5A)	€ 4,00

FR81030 Camping Municipal de Gourjade

Route de Roquecourbe, F-81100 Castres (Tarn)

Tel: 05 63 59 33 51. Email: contact@campingdegourjade.com

Camping de Gourjade is a family run site set in a country park which belongs to the town of Castres. It has the river running along one side and the country park on the other. There are 100 level pitches (88 for tourers), all with electricity (6A) and separated by well trimmed hedges, and some with shade. Those nearest the river are sloping and can be soft. There is a barrier at the entrance and a night watchman for security. A play area caters for children of 3-12 yrs and there is a small swimming pool.

Facilities

The two well appointed toilet blocks have facilities for disabled visitors and baby room. Maintenance and cleaning are variable. Washing machine, dryer. Motorcaravan services. Small shop, bread. Attractive restaurant (all season). Small swimming pool. Bicycles kept at reception for the free use of campers. Barrier card deposit €15 (main season). Off site: Country park adjacent. Supermarket 1 km.

Open: 1 April - 3 October.

Directions

Castres is 42 km. south of Albi. Site on D89 in Parc de Gourjade north of city. Follow signs to Roquecourbe until roundabout with supermarket, then signs to 'Rive droite', camping. After 1 km. turn left at T-junction, site is 300 m. GPS: N43:37.240 E02:15.247

Charges 2007

Per person	€ 3,00 - € 4,00
pitch and vehicle	€ 8,50 - € 13,50
electricity	€ 2,50 - € 3,50

369

FR81040 Camp Municipal des Auzerals

Route de Grazac, F-81800 Rabastens (Tarn)

Tel: 05 63 33 70 36. Email: camping-rabastens.com

Camping des Auzerals is a small, reasonably priced site with 38 pitches. These are near the lake where fishing is possible. There are walks from the site (leaflets from the tourist information office in the town). This is a perfect site for couples seeking peace and quiet, especially in May, June and Sept. All the pitches are on grass, hedged with neat bushes and all with water, drainage and electricity (10A). The local swimming pool is adjacent and the village is only 2.5 km. away. There is no shop (ices from the reception) but a baker calls in July/Aug.

Facilities

The sanitary block is basic but very clean, with mainly Turkish style WCs, good adjustable showers and some washbasins in cubicles. Dishwashing and laundry sinks with hot water. Washing machine. Freezer available in the telephone room. Baker calls. Off site: Village 2.5 km.

Open: 1 May - 30 September.

Directions

Site northeast of Toulouse. Heading south leave A20, exit 66, take D930 south. Road changes to D630 (23 km). Follow until sign for Albi on D988. Rabastens is 8 km. Site is signed to left on entry to village.

Charges 2007

Per unit incl. 2 persons	€ 7,40 - € 8,80
incl. electricity	€ 8,40 - € 9,90

FR81060 Camping les Clots

F-81190 Mirandol-Bourgnounac (Tarn)

Tel: 05 63 76 92 78. Email: campclots@wanadoo.fr

Les Clots is a very rural, simple site in the heart of the countryside with 62 touring pitches and 12 used for canvas tents, chalets and caravans for rent. The 2.5 km. road from the nearest village of Mirandol is quite narrow. The site has been carved out of a steep hillside giving variously sized terraces taking from 1 to 10 units. Nearly all pitches have electricity (6A). A few pitches, mainly for tents, are set well away from the others giving lots of seclusion. Being amongst the trees there is enough shade.

Facilities

Toilet blocks are kept very clean. Baby bath. Facilities for disabled visitors. Washing machines. Bar (July/Aug). Shop with basic provisions incl. bread (July/Aug). Simple swimming and paddling pools (1/7-30/9) with grass sunbathing area. Table tennis. Minigolf. In July/Aug a local comes twice weekly to prepare an evening meal (to order). Fishing. Leaflets for walks in the area. Site is not suitable for American style motorhomes. Off site: Riding 15 km.

Open: 1 May - 1 October.

Directions

Heading south on N88 from Rodez, just before reaching Carmaux turn right onto the D905 towards Mirandol. The site is 5.5 km. north of Mirandol.

Charges 2006

per unit incl. 3 persons	€ 19,00 - € 22,00
extra person	€ 4,50 - € 4,60
child (under 8 yrs)	€ 2,80 - € 2,80
electricity (6A)	€ 2,70 - € 2,80
Low season reductions.	

FR81100 Camping de la Rigole

Route de Barrage, F-81540 Les Cammazes (Tarn)

Tel: 05 63 73 28 99. Email: mary@campingdlr.com

A pleasant, traditional site with 64 pitches in a countryside location, La Rigole is partly wooded, and gives a friendly reception. A slightly sloping site, most of the 43 touring pitches are on small terraces and many have quite deep shade. All have electricity (4-13A). There is a small bar and a snack bar. One evening each week in main season a regional meal is organised. Small children are well catered for with play areas for tiny tots and under 7s, and a delightful children's farm with animals. The site is totally unsuitable for American RVs.

Facilities

Fairly modern toilet block. Baby room. Facilities for disabled campers (althought the slopes might be difficult). Washing machines, dryer. Small shop. Bar. Takeaway. Swimming pool. All open 15/4-15/10. Table tennis. Badminton. Volleyball. Boules. Small animal farm. Off site: Lac des Cammazes with its dam 400 m. Lac de St Ferréol 5 km., with large sandy beach. Fishing 0.4 km. Riding 1.5 km.

Open: 15 April - 15 October.

Directions

Les Cammazes is 25 km. northeast of Castelnaudary, 10 km. southeast of Revel. From Revel take D629 to Cammazes, continue on D629 through village, after 1 km. turn left towards Barrage (site signed), site entrance 200 m. on right.
GPS: N43:24.472 E02:05.196

Charges 2007

Per unit incl. 2 persons	€ 14,60
incl. electricity	€ 17,10
extra person	€ 4,50
child (0-7 yrs)	€ 2,60

FR81070 Camping Indigo Rieu Montagné

Lac du Laouzas, F-81320 Nages (Tarn)

Tel: 05 63 37 24 71. Email: rieumontagne@camping-indigo.com

Rieu Montagné is a delightful site in the heart of the Haut Languedoc Regional park and at the corner of the départements of the Tarn, Aveyron and Hérault. There are 118 touring pitches, mostly on broad terraces with reasonable shade, all with electrical connections (6/10A) and 47 fully serviced. A heated swimming pool overlooks the lake and is used for occasional aqua gym. In high season there is a varied entertainment programme, and a number of guided walks. Most leisure facilities are available at the lakeside complex. Lakeside facilities include tennis, a play area, sailing and other water activities. This site is on a fairly steep slope. The site is a member of the Indigo group and lies close to the Lac du Laouzas where a wide range of sporting activities can be enjoyed.

Facilities

The two toilet blocks, comprehensively refitted in 2005, provide mostly British style toilets, washbasins in cubicles and facilities for disabled people and babies. Laundry. Shop with basic provisions (July/Aug). Bar and snack bar with takeaway. Swimming pool (18/6-18/9). Entertainment programme (high season). Chalets, tents and mobile homes to let (68). Off site: Lakeside leisure complex.

Open: 16 June - 15 September.

Directions

Nages about 80 km. southeast of Albi. From Albi, D999 east towards St Affrique. 11 km. after Albon right, D607, to Lacaune. At T-junction left, D622, for 6.5 km. Right, D62, 2 km. South of town left over bridge, D162. First left uphill to site. GPS: N43:38.877 E02:46.888

Charges 2006

Per person	€ 4,80 - € 5,50
child (2-7 yrs)	€ 3,00 - € 3,50
pitch	€ 4,20 - € 17,50
electricity (6/10A)	€ 4,00 - € 6,00

FR81110 Camping Saint Martin

F-81540 Soréze (Tarn)

Tel: 05 63 50 20 19. Email: mary@campingsaintmartin.com

There are 48 individual tourist pitches with 10A electricity and six wooden chalets for rent. The pitches are all on grass, some divided by newly planted hedging and there are some mature trees for shade. Six pitches are reserved for motorcaravans, although these are rather compact. A small swimming pool is well fenced and gated. Reception has a small bar and snack bar and can also provide basic supplies including drinks, sweets, speciality foods and snacks. However, you are only 100 metres from the town centre shops.

Facilities

Sanitary unit is well built, Facilities for disabled visitors. Covered dishwashing and laundry sinks plus a washing machine. Small shop. Bar with TV. Snack bar. Swimming pool. All amenities open 15/6-15/9. Table tennis. Boules. Volleyball. Communal barbecue. Small playground. Entertainment in high season. No pets. Off site: Municipal leisure and sports facilities including tennis courts adjacent.

Open: 15 June - 15 September.

Directions

Soréze is on the D85 about 25 km. southwest of Castres, 5 km. east of Revel. The site is well signed within the town. GPS: N43:27.271 E02:04.175

Charges 2007

Per unit incl. 2 persons	€ 14,60
incl. electricity	€ 17,10
extra person	€ 4,50
child (0-7 yrs)	€ 2,60

FR81120 Camping le Rouquié

Lac de la Raviège, F-81260 Lamontélarié (Tarn)

Tel: **05 63 70 98 06**. Email: **contact@campingrouqie.com**

Le Rouquié, a family run campsite, is on the edge of Le Lac de Raviège, deep in the heart of the 'parc naturel régional Haut-Languedoc'. The 97 level pitches (79 for tourers) are of varying sizes between 80 and 130 sq.m. They are grassed and arranged on terraces which slope quite steeply to the edge of the lake. All the pitches have superb views over the lake, They are separated by small trees and are partially shaded, with electricity (6A; Europlug) available near each one. A separate section of the site has 12 wooden chalets to rent.

Facilities

Separate ladies and gents sanitary facilities provide hot and cold water to showers and washbasins. Washing machines. Small shop (July/Aug). Bar and snack bar with takeaway (1/6-31/10). Play area. Fishing. Limited English spoken. Off site: Nearest supermarket 8 km. Watersports. Riding 8 km. Golf 30 km.

Open: 1 April - 31 October.

Directions

From Castres take N112 towards Bezier. At Lacabarède turn north on D52 to Anglès. Continue on D52 towards Lac de Raviège and cross bridge at the dam. Keep on the D52 for 1.5 km. then right on D62 toward Salvetat-sur-Agout. Site is on right after another 1.4 km. GPS: N43:35.815 E02:36.434

Charges 2006

Per unit incl. 2 persons	€ 11,04 - € 13,80
extra person	€ 3,04 - € 3,80
electricity (6A)	€ 2,80 - € 3,50

FR81130 Camping l'Amitié

Vallée du Tarn, F-81340 Trébas (Tarn)

Tel: **05 63 55 84 07**. Email: **amitie@trebas.net**

A winding road with wonderful views of the surrounding countryside leads down to the small unspoilt village of Trébas in the Vallée du Tarn, and there on the banks of the Tarn river lies the small friendly site of Camping L'Amitié. There are 60 level, well drained and manicured grass pitches, 49 of which are available for tourers. A few wooden chalets are also available to rent. All with electricity (French sockets), the pitches are on terraces which slope gently towards the riverbank and most have partial shading although some are in the open area close to the river.

Facilities

The toilet block is near the site entrance with Turkish and British style toilets, hot showers and washbasins in cubicles (cold water only). No shop. Bar/restaurant (1/5-15/9). Swimming pool (1/6-31/8). Play area. Some activities and entertainment in high season. Off site: Site is in small village with mini-supermarket, pharmacy, baker and butcher. Bar/restaurant 250 m. (July/Aug. only).

Open: 1 April - 15 September.

Directions

From Albi take D999 east (signed Millau). At Alban take D53 north to St Andre and Trébas. Cross river at Villeneuve sur Tarn to Trébas, the site is in the village and signed. GPS: N43:56.521 E02:28.902

Charges 2006

Per unit incl. 2 persons	€ 9,15 - € 10,15
extra person	€ 2,65 - € 2,95
child (2-7 yrs)	€ 1,62 - € 1,80

FR82010 Camping les Trois Cantons

F-82140 St Antonin-Noble-Val (Tarn-et-Garonne)

Tel: **05 63 31 98 57**. Email: **info@3cantons.fr**

Les Trois Cantons is a well established and very friendly family run with 100 pitches (85 for tourers) set among mature trees that give dappled shade. The pitches are of average size, reasonably level and all have electricity connections. The swimming pool is covered and heated in early and late season, with activities organised there in July and August. There are also walks, archery and boules, clay modelling plus wine tastings and a weekly dance. When the trees are bare early in the season, there could be a little road noise when the wind is in a certain direction.

Facilities

The two sanitary blocks include British and Turkish style WCs, showers, washbasins (some in cubicles) and facilities for disabled visitors. Laundry and dishwashing facilities. Very limited shop (bread daily). Bar serving snacks and takeaways. Swimming pool (heated from 15/5-30/9) and paddling pool. Games/TV room. Play area. Small farm area. Tennis. Volleyball. Boules. English spoken. Off site: Riding 4 km, fishing 7 km. Many pretty medieval villages to visit.

Open: 15 April - 30 September.

Directions

From A20 or N20 at Caussade, take D926 signed Caylus and Septfonds. Site is signed to right 5 km. after Septfonds. Do not take the D5 towards St Antonin-Noble-Val as it involves 5 km. of narrow road.

Charges 2006

Per pitch and 2 people	€ 14,00 - € 18,75
extra person	€ 4,45 - € 5,75
electricity (2-10A)	€ 2,05 - € 6,70
Camping Cheques accepted.	

Languedoc and Roussillon form part of the Massif Central. With its huge sandy beaches the mountainous Languedoc region is renowned for its long sunshine records, and the pretty coastal villages of Roussillon are at their most beautiful at sunset erupting in a riot of colour.

Mediterranean West

THIS SECTION COVERS THE SOUTH WEST COASTAL REGION OF THE MEDITERRANEAN, DÉPARTEMENTS: 11 AUDE, 30 GARD, 34 HÉRAULT, 66 PYRÉNÉES-ORIENTALES.

Once an independent duchy, the ancient land of Languedoc combines two distinct regions: the vineyards of the Corbières and Minervois and the coastal plain stretching from the Rhône to the Spanish border. Much of the region is rugged and unspoilt, offering opportunities for walking and climbing.

There is ample evidence of the dramatic past. Ruins of the former Cathar castles can be seen throughout the region. The walled city of Carcassonne with its towers, dungeons, moats and drawbridges is one of the most impressive examples of medieval France.

Today, Languedoc and Roussillon are wine and agricultural regions. Languedoc, with considerable success, is now a producer of much of the nation's better value wines. But above all, vast hot sandy beaches and long hours of sunshine make this a paradise for beach enthusiasts. La Grande Motte, Cap d'Agde and Canet, are all being promoted as an alternative to the more famous Mediterranean stretches of the Côte d'Azur.

Places of interest

Aigues-Mortes: medieval city.

Béziers: wine capital of the region, St Nazaire cathedral, Canal du Midi.

Carcassonne: largest medieval walled city in Europe.

Limoux: medieval town, Notre Dame de Marseilla Basilica, St Martin church.

Montpellier: universities, Roman sites; Gothic cathedral.

Nîmes: Roman remains, Pont du Gard.

Perpignan: Kings Palace; Catalan characteristics, old fortress.

Pézenas: Molière's home.

Villeneuve-lés-Avignon: Royal City and residence of popes in 14th century.

Cuisine of the region

Cooking is Provençal, characterised by garlic and olive oil with sausages and smoked hams. Fish is popular along the coast. Wines include Corbières, Minervois, Banyuls and Muscat.

Aïgo Bouido: garlic soup.

Boles de picoulat: small balls of chopped-up beef and pork, garlic and eggs.

Bouillinade: a type of *bouillabaisse* with potatoes, oil, garlic and onions.

Boutifare: a sausage-shaped pudding of bacon and herbs.

Cargolade: snails, stewed in wine.

Ouillade: heavy soup of *boutifare* leeks, carrots, and potatoes..

Touron: a pastry of almonds, pistachio nuts and fruit.

FR11020 Camping Aux Hamacs

Route des Cabanes, F-11560 Fleury (Aude)

Tel: **04 68 33 22 22**. Email: **info@campingauxhamacs.com**

If you are looking for sun, sea and sand, Aux Hamacs is a good venue. It is situated adjacent to the Aude river with the attractive village of Fleury nearby and a good beach less than 2 km. away. It is also well located for exploring Cathar country with its amazing hill top castles and attractions such as the Canal du Midi. The site is well away from the frenzy associated with some of the resorts in this region but near enough to visit for an evening out. With 253 large pitches, there are 122 for touring with 6A electricity and some fully serviced (10A electricity plus water and waste water). The remaining pitches are used for a range of chalets and mobile homes to rent. This is a peaceful site but without much shade, although there is a relaxing pool and an interesting range of activities.

Facilities

One fully equipped new toilet block is opened for the main season. A small older one which can be heated is open all season (with plans to rebuild). All facilities are unisex. Baby room and facilities for disabled visitors (key). Washing machine. Shop, bar, restaurant and takeaway (all fully operational 15/6-7/9). Swimming pool (15/6-7/9). Play areas. Activities and entertainment (high season). Off site: Riding 5 km.

Open: 1 April - 30 September.

Directions

From A9 autoroute take exit 36 Beziers Ouest. Follow directions for Lespignan, Fleury and Les Cabanas (D718). Site is on right before village. It is possible to approach from Vendras and Valras Plage by bridge just a little up river from Grau de Vendras.

Charges 2006

Per unit incl. 2 persons	€ 14,30 - € 23,70
extra person	€ 3,50 - € 5,20
child (2-7 yrs)	free - € 3,10

FR11030 Camping Municipal la Pinède

Avenue Gaston Bonheur, F-11200 Lézignan-Corbières (Aude)

Tel: **04 68 27 05 08**. Email: **reception@campinglapinede.fr**

Within walking distance of the town and only 35 km. from Narbonne Plage, La Pinède is set on terraces on a hillside, with good internal access on made-up roads. The 90 individual, level pitches vary in size and are divided up mainly by various trees and shrubs with 6A electricity (16 mobile homes). The guardian sometimes organises local wine tasting and he also has a vegetable patch in one corner of the site where you can sample really fresh vegetables (charged). Outside the gates are a municipal swimming pool (July/Aug), a disco, restaurant and tennis courts.

Facilities

Three sanitary blocks of good quality are fully equipped and recently refurbished. Not all blocks are opened outside high season. Washing machine. Small shop with gas. Pleasant bar also providing decently priced hot food (all July/Aug). A new barbecue facility functions here in season (private barbecues are not permitted). Torches are necessary. Caravan storage. Off site: Bicycle hire 1 km. Riding 3 km. Fishing 4 km.

Open: 1 March - 30 October.

Directions

Access is directly off the main N113 on west side of Lézignan-Corbières. From A61 (to avoid low bridge) exit at Carcassonne or Narbonne onto N113 and follow to site.

Charges 2006

Per person	€ 3,20 - € 4,30
child (under 10 yrs)	€ 2,00 - € 3,20
pitch	€ 5,80 - € 7,50
animal	€ 1,50
No credit cards.	

FR11040 Camping le Martinet Rouge Birdie

F-11390 Brousses-et-Villaret (Aude)

Tel: **04 68 26 51 98**. Email: **martinet.bv@free.fr**

Le Martinet Rouge provides a peaceful retreat in the Aude countryside to the north of Carcassonne. It is a small site where the owners have been working hard to improve the facilities. The most striking features of the site are the massive granite boulders (outcrops of smooth rock from the last ice age). The site offers 50 pitches for touring units, all with electricity (3/6A), in two contrasting areas – one is well secluded with irregularly shaped, fairly level, large pitches amongst a variety of trees and shrubs, while the other is on a landscaped gentle hill with mature trees.

Facilities

Four sanitary blocks of various ages, including facilities for disabled visitors, baby bathroom, laundry facilities. Swimming pool (15/6-15/9). Small shop (no others locally). Bar, terrace, TV (1/7-15/9). Snack bar (1/7-31/8). Barbecue area. Fitness room. Croquet, volleyball, half court tennis, table tennis, small play area. Internet access. Off site: Visit the paper mill in the village. Tennis, riding and fishing quite close.

Open: 1 April - 15 October.

Directions

Site is south of Brousses-et-Villaret, 20 km. northwest of Carcassonne. Best approached via D118, Carcassonne - Mazamet road. Turn onto D103 15 km. north of Carcassonne to Brousses-et-Villaret. Western outskirts of village turn south to site (signed) in 50 m. GPS: N43:20.350 E02:15.127

Charges 2007

Per pitch incl. 2 persons	€ 12,50 - € 15,50
with electricity	€ 15,00 - € 18,00
extra person	€ 3,50 - € 5,50
child (0-10 yrs)	€ 2,00 - € 5,00

No credit cards.

FR11060 Yelloh! Village Domaine d'Arnauteille

Mobile homes ⊳ page 483

F-11250 Montclar (Aude)

Tel: **04 68 26 84 53**. Email: **Arnauteille@mnet.fr**

Enjoying some beautiful and varied views, this site is ideal exploring the little known Aude Département and for visiting the walled city of Carcassonne. However, access could be difficult for large, twin axle vans. The site is set in farmland on hilly ground with the original pitches on gently sloping, lightly wooded land and newer ones of good size with water, drainage and electricity (5/10A), semi-terraced and partly hedged. The facilities are quite spread out with the swimming pool complex, in the style of a Roman amphitheatre, set in a hollow basin surrounded by fine views. The reception building is vast; originally a farm building, with a newer top floor being converted to apartments. This is a developing site so be aware of on-going building work. Some very steep up and down walking between the pitches and facilities is unavoidable. A 'Sites et Paysages' member.

Facilities

Toilet blocks, one with a Roman theme. Laundry, facilities for disabled people and a baby bath. Motorcaravan services. Small shop (15/5-30/9). Restaurant in converted stable block, takeaway (15/5-30/9). Four pools including children's pool. Games court. Boules. Play area. Table tennis, volleyball. Riding (1/7-31/8). Day trips. Library, internet, games room, TV. Off site: Fishing 3 km. Bicycle hire 8 km. Golf 10 km. Rafting and canoeing near, plus many walks with marked paths.

Open: 7 April - 25 September.

Directions

D118 from Carcassonne, pass Rouffiac d'Aude. Before the end of dual carriageway, turn right to Montclar up narrow road (passing places) for 2.5 km. Site signed then sharp left up hill before village. GPS: N43:07.636 E02:15.571

Charges 2007

Per pitch incl. 2 persons	€ 14,00 - € 29,00
with 6A electricity	€ 18,00 - € 33,00
with electricity, water and drain	€ 21,00 - € 37,00

Camping Cheques accepted.

Domaine d'Arnauteille ★★★★

11250 Montclar (close to Carcassonne)

Tel: 0033 468 26 84 53 - Fax: 0033 468 26 91 10

Arnauteille@mnet.fr - www.arnauteille.com

New waterpark with 4 pools in a Greek-Roman style.

Check real time availability and at-the-gate prices...

www.**alanrogers**.com

FR11070 Camping les Mimosas

Mobile homes ▶ page 484

Chaussée de Mandirac, F-11100 Narbonne (Aude)

Tel: 04 68 49 03 72. Email: info@lesmimosas.com

Six kilometres inland from the beaches of Narbonne and Gruissan, this site benefits from a less hectic situation than others by the sea. The site is lively with plenty to amuse and entertain the younger generation whilst offering facilities for the whole family. A free club card is available in July/August to use the children's club, gym, sauna, tennis, minigolf, billiards etc. There are 250 pitches, 150 for touring, many in a circular layout of very good size, most with electricity (6A). There are a few 'grand confort', with reasonable shade, mostly from 2 m. high hedges. There are also a number of mobile homes and chalets to rent. This could be a very useful site offering many possibilities to meet a variety of needs, on-site entertainment (including an evening on Cathar history), and easy access to popular beaches. Nearby Gruissan is a fascinating village with its wooden houses on stilts, beaches, ruined castle, port and salt beds. Narbonne has Roman remains and inland Cathar castles are to be found perched on rugged hill tops.

Facilities

Refurbished high standard sanitary buildings. Washing machines. Shop and 'Auberge' restaurant (open all season). Takeaway. Bar. Small lounge, amusements (July and Aug). Landscaped heated pool with slides and islands (open 1 May), plus the original pool and children's pool (high season). Play area. Minigolf. Mountain bike hire. Tennis. Volleyball. Sauna, gym. Children's activities, sports, entertainment (high season). Bicycle hire. Multisports ground. Off site: Riding. Windsurfing/sailing school 300 m. Gruissan's beach 10 minutes. Lagoon, boating fishing via footpath (200 m).

Open: 24 March - 31 October.

Directions

From A9 exit 38 (Narbonne Sud) take last exit on roundabout, back over the autoroute (site signed from here). Follow signs La Nautique and then Mandirac and site (6 km. from autoroute). Also signed from Narbonne centre.

Charges 2007

Per pitch incl. 1 or 2 persons	€ 13,50 - € 21,00
pitch with electricity	€ 17,00 - € 27,00
with electricity, water and waste water	€ 21,20 - € 31,00
extra person	€ 4,00 - € 5,90

Camping Cheques accepted.

kawan-villages.com tel: 00 333 59 59 03 59

kawan
VILLAGES CAMPING

Check real time availability and at-the-gate prices...

www.alanrogers.com

FR11080 Camping la Nautique

Mobile homes ▶ page 484

La Nautique, F-11100 Narbonne (Aude)

Tel: **04 68 90 48 19**. Email: **info@campinglanautique.com**

This extremely spacious site is situated on the Etang de Bages, where flat water combined with strong winds make it one of the best windsurfing areas in France and it is owned and run by a very welcoming Dutch family. La Nautique has 390 huge, level pitches, there are also six or seven overnight pitches with electricity in a separate area. The flowering shrubs and trees give a pleasant feel. Each pitch is separated by hedges making some quite private and providing shade. All have electricity (10A) and water. Each pitch has an individual toilet cabin. Entertainments are organised for adults and children in July/Aug, plus a sports club for supervised surfing, sailing, rafting, walking and canoeing (some activities are charged for). The unspoilt surrounding countryside is excellent for walking or cycling and locally there is horse riding and fishing. English is spoken in reception by the very welcoming Schutjes family. This site caters for families with children including teenagers. The site is fenced off from the water for the protection of children and windsurfers can have a key for the gate (with deposit) that leads to launching points on the lake.

Facilities

Each cabin has a toilet, shower, washbasin. Pitches for disabled people. Laundry. Shop. Bar/restaurant, terrace, TV. Takeaway. All 1/5-15/9. Snack bar 1/7-31/8. Swimming pools, paddling pool, slide. Play areas, miniclub. Tennis, minigolf, boules. Teenagers' disco (high season). Recreation area. Internet. Only electric barbecues. Torch useful. Off site: Large sandy beaches at Gruissan (10 km.) and Narbonne Plage (15 km). Narbonne is only 4 km. Canoeing, sailing and windsurfing on the Etang.

Open: 15 February - 15 November.

Directions

From A9 take exit 38 (Narbonne Sud). Go round roundabout to last exit and follow signs for La Nautique and site, then further site signs to site on right in 3 km.

Charges 2006

Per person	€ 4,20 - € 6,00
child (1-7 yrs)	€ 2,20 - € 4,50
pitch incl. electricity, water and sanitary unit	€ 8,50 - € 20,00
dog or cat	€ 1,50 - € 3,50

Camping La Nautique Narbonne France

www.campinglanautique.com

Private Sanitary facilities on every pitch.
Open from 15/02 till 15/11
☎ (+33) 04 68 90 48 19

FR11110 Camping Val d'Aleth

F-11580 Alet-les-Bains (Aude)

Tel: **04 68 69 90 40**. Email: **camping@valdaleth.com**

In the gateway to the upper Aude valley, open all year round, this popular small site is run by Christopher and Christine Cranmer who offer a warm welcome. The mellow medieval walls of Alet les Bains form one boundary of the site, while on the other and popular with anglers, is the River Aude (fenced for safety). Beyond this is the D118 and a railway which produces noise at times. The 37 mainly small, numbered pitches, around half of which are on hardstandings, all have electricity hook-ups (4-10A) and are separated by hedges and mature trees which give shade.

Facilities

New reception and toilet blocks opening March 07 with heated shower block and full facilities for the disabled. Reception has small shop, drinks, wine, beer, use of freezer. Small play area. Mountain bike hire. Internet. Off site: White water sports nearby. The area is very popular with walkers and mountain-bikers. Bus and train services to Carcassonne and Quillan. Some shops and restaurants in town, full range at Limoux (10 km. north).

Open: All year.

Directions

From Carcassonne take D118 south for 32 km. Ignore first sign to Alet (to avoid narrow stone bridge) and after crossing the river, turn into town. Site is 800 m. on the left (signed). GPS: N42:59.682 E02:15.333

Charges 2007

Per unit incl. 2 persons	€ 12,00
electricity	€ 2,50
No credit cards.	

FR11050 Camping Rives des Corbières

Avenue du Languedoc, F-11370 Port Leucate (Aude)

Tel: **04 68 40 90 31**. Email: **rivescamping@wanadoo.fr**

Port Leucate is part of the major Languedoc development which took place during the sixties and seventies and it is now a thriving resort. The campsite is on the old coast road into Port Leucate between the Etang de Salas and the beach, 800 m. from the centre of the town and port and only 150 m. from the beach. A mixture of tall poplars and pine trees provide reasonable shade for the 305 pitches. On good-sized sandy plots, all have 6A electricity. About 90 are used for mobile homes.

Facilities

Four toilet blocks opened as required. Two have mainly Turkish toilets. Facilities for disabled people. Laundry room. Small supermarket, bar and takeaway (July/Aug). Swimming pools. Play area. Daytime games and tournaments and in the evening, live music, karaoke and dancing. Off site: Beach 150 m. Port 800 m.

Open: 1 April - 30 September.

Directions

From the A9 take exit 40 and follow signs for Port Leucate on D627 (passing Leucate village) for 14 km. Exit the D627 into Port Leucate village. Go right at roundabout into Avenue du Languedoc and site is on right after 800 m. GPS: N42:50.009 E03:02.004

Charges 2006

Per unit incl. 2 persons	€ 13,10 - € 16,20
extra person	€ 3,40 - € 4,30
electricity (6A)	€ 2,70 - € 3,50

FR30000 Camping Domaine de Gaujac

Boisset-et-Gaujac, F-30140 Anduze (Gard)

Tel: **04 66 61 80 65**. Email: **gravieres@club-internet.fr**

The 293 level, well shaded pitches include 175 for touring with electricity (4-10A) with 22 serviced. Access to some areas can be difficult for larger units due to narrow winding access roads, trees and hedges. Larger units should ask for lower numbered pitches (1-148) where access is a little easier. In high season this region is dry and hot, thus grass quickly wears off many pitches leaving just a sandy base. There are 12 special hardstanding pitches for motorcaravans near the entrance.

Facilities

Heated toilet blocks include facilities for disabled visitors. Washing machines, dryer. Motorcaravan services. Good shop (2/6-27/8). Newsagent. Takeaway/crêperie (15/4-15/9). Bar, restaurant (15/4-15/9). New heated swimming, paddling pool (lifeguard 5/7-15/8) and jacuzzi. Playground, sports field. Tennis. Minigolf. Only gas and electric barbecues. Off site: Fishing 70 m. Bicycle hire 5 km. Riding, golf 8 km. River beach 70 km.

Open: 1 April - 30 September.

Directions

From Alès take N110 towards Montpellier. At St Christol-les-Alès fork right on D910 towards Anduze and in Bagard turn left on D246 to Boisset et Gaujac (5 km). GPS: N44:02.148 E04:01.455

Charges 2006

Per unit incl. 2 persons	€ 14,00 - € 22,00
extra person	€ 4,00 - € 4,70
electricity (4-10A)	€ 3,00 - € 3,50
Camping Cheques accepted.	

kawan-villages.com **tel: 00 333 59 59 03 59**

FR30100 Camping Naturiste de la Sablière

Mobile homes ▶ page 484

Domaine de la Sablière, St Privat de Champclos, F-30430 Barjac (Gard)

Tel: **04 66 24 51 16**. Email: **contact@villagesabliere.com**

Spectacularly situated in the Cèze Gorges, this naturist site with a surprising 497 pitches, 240 for touring, tucked away within its wild terrain offers a wide variety of facilities, all within a really peaceful, wooded and dramatic setting. The pitches themselves are mainly on flat stony terraces, attractively situated among a variety of trees and shrubs (some with a low overhang). Many are of a good size and have electricity (6/10A), very long leads may be needed. Nudity is obligatory only around the pool complex. You must expect fairly steep walking between the pitches and facilities.

Facilities

Six good unisex sanitary blocks have excellent free hot showers in typical open plan, naturist style, washbasins (cold water), baby baths and facilities for people with disabilities. Laundry. Good supermarket. Bar (1/4-22/9). Restaurant and takeaway (1/4-22/9). Small café/crêperie. Swimming pool complex. Activity programme. Barbecues are not permitted. Off site: Bicycle hire 8 km.

Open: 1 April - 1 October.

Directions

From Barjac take D901 east for 3 km. Turn right at site sign just before St Privat-de-Champclos and follow site signs along winding country lane to site entrance in 4 km. GPS: N44:16.021 E04:21.125

Charges 2006

Per pitch incl. 2 persons	€ 13,00 - € 32,55
extra person	€ 3,00 - € 6,50
Camping Cheques accepted.	

FR30020 Yelloh! Village la Petite Camargue

B.P. 21, F-30220 Aigues-Mortes (Gard)

Tel: **04 66 53 98 98**. Email: **petite.camargue@yellohvillage.com**

This is a large, impressive site (553 pitches) with a huge swimming pool complex and other amenities to match, conveniently situated beside one of the main routes across the famous Camargue. The busy road is an advantage for access but could perhaps be a drawback in terms of traffic, although when we stayed overnight in season it was virtually silent. It offers a variety of good sized pitches, regularly laid out and with varying amounts of shade. There are 70 touring pitches (with 6 or 10A electricity) interspersed amongst more than 300 mobile homes and 145 tour operator pitches.

Facilities

Three toilet blocks provide modern facilities including many combined showers and washbasins. Laundry facilities. Motorcaravan service point. Range of shops, bar/restaurant with pizzeria and takeaway. Hairdresser and beauty centre. L-shaped swimming pool complex. Play area, and children's club. Riding at adjoining large stables. Volleyball, basketball, tennis and table tennis. Bicycle hire. Quad bikes. Disco. Off site: Fishing 3 km. Golf 8 km. Nearest beach 3.5 km. with free bus service July/Aug.

Open: 24 April - 19 September (with all services).

Directions

From A9, exit 26 (Gallargues), towards Le Grau-du-Roi, site 18 km. Continue past Aigues-Mortes on D62, site is 2 km. on the right, just before large roundabout for La Grand-Motte and Le Grau-du-Roi junction.

Charges guide

Per unit incl. 1 or 2 persons and electricity	€ 15,00 - € 38,00
extra person	€ 5,50 - € 7,50

FR30060 Camping Domaine des Fumades

Les Fumades, F-30500 Allègre (Gard)

Tel: **04 66 24 80 78**. Email: **domaine.des.fumades@wanadoo.fr**

Domaine des Fumades is a pleasant, busy site with a friendly atmosphere near the thermal springs at Allègre. The entrance as a whole has a very tropical feel with its banana plants and palm trees. The 230 pitches, 80 for touring, are large and level, all with 4A electricity. A variety of trees add privacy and welcome shade. Three pleasantly landscaped swimming pools have ample sunbathing space and bridges and new Jacuzzis. This is a good area for walking, cycling, riding, climbing and fishing. Used by tour operators (80 pitches). Reception at the site is a joy to behold. Set in an attractive courtyard, within the farmhouse, it has a central fountain and masses of tubs and baskets of colourful flowers.

Facilities

Well appointed sanitary blocks, facilities for disabled people. Laundry. Well maintained but cleaning variable. Shop. Bar, restaurant, snack bar, takeaway. Barbecue areas. Swimming pools, sunbathing space. Large, well equipped and fenced playground. Games room, tennis, volleyball, table tennis and boules. Well planned animation and entertainment programme, designed to appeal to families. No barbecues. Off site: Riding 2 km.

Open: 14 May - 2 September.

Directions

From Alès take D16 through Salindres, continue towards Allègre, until signs for Fumades (and the thermal springs) on the right.

Charges 2007

Per unit incl. 2 persons and electricity	€ 16,00 - € 30,00
extra person	€ 3,00 - € 7,00
child (under 7 yrs)	€ 2,50 - € 4,00

FR30030 Camping Abri de Camargue

320 route du Phare de l'Espiguette, Port Camargue, F-30240 Le Grau-du-Roi (Gard)

Tel: **04 66 51 54 83**. Email: **contact@abridecamargue.fr**

This pleasant site has an attractive pool area overlooked by the bar with its outdoor tables on a pleasant sheltered terrace. The larger outdoor pool has surrounds for sunbathing and the smaller indoor one is heated. With 277 level pitches, there are 139 for touring units, mainly of 100 sq.m (there are also smaller ones). Electricity and water are available on most, and the pitches are well maintained and shaded, with trees and flowering shrubs, quite luxuriant in parts. Recent additions include an air-conditioned cinema room and a club for children in high season.

Facilities

Well appointed toilet blocks, facilities for disabled people. Motorcaravan services. Shop. Bar, TV, restaurant, takeaway (all open all season). Heated indoor pool, outdoor pool. Cinema. Entertainment programme. High quality play area. Volleyball. Table tennis. Children's club. Petanque. Off site: Tennis 800 m. Riding, bicycle hire 1 km. Fishing 2 km. Golf 5 km. Nearest beach Port Camargue 900 m. L'Espiguette is 4 km. (free bus passes the gate – July/Aug). Boat, surfboard hire nearby.

Open: 1 April - 30 September.

Directions

Site is 45 km. southwest of Nimes. From A9 autoroute, exit 26, Gallargues to Le Grau-du-Roi. From bypass follow signs Port Camargue and Campings. Then follow Rive gauche signs towards Phare l'Espiguette. Site is on right opposite Toboggan Park. GPS: N43:31.350 E04:08.947

Charges 2006

Per unit incl. 1 or 2 persons	€ 25,00 - € 49,00
incl. 3-5 persons	€ 29,00 - € 53,00
extra person or extra car	€ 6,00 - € 9,00
Campsite access card deposit of € 15.	

FR30070 Castel Camping le Château de Boisson

Boisson, F-30500 Allègre-Les Fumades (Gard)

Tel: **04 66 24 82 21**. Email: **reception@chateaudeboisson.com**

Château de Boisson is a quiet family site within easy reach of the Cévennes, Ardèche or Provence. Reception at the entrance is new, light and cool, built from the stone in the local style. The site is hilly so the pitches are on two levels, many of which slope slightly and all have 5A electricity. Five have personal bathrooms. Rock pegs are essential. Trees provide some shade. The large attractive swimming pool with a toboggan and paddling pool is at the castle in a sunny location and there is also an indoor pool (all season) of excellent quality. The restaurant in the castle is cool and elegant with tables also available outside on the shady terrace. It is set in the grounds of the château, beside the small medieval village of Boisson.

Facilities

Refurbished, clean and well maintained toilet blocks. Washing machines, baby room, facilities for disabled visitors. Small shop. Good restaurant, bar, snacks (all season). Internet, WiFi. Play area. Indoor (all season) and outdoor pools (1/5-29/9). Bridge tournaments in low season. Painting classes. Tennis, boules, volleyball, basketball. Animation in July and Aug for 4-12 yr olds, outdoor competitions for adults. No dogs. No barbecues. Appartments to rent in the castle.

Open: Easter - 29 September.

Directions

From Alès take D16 northeast towards Salindres and Auzon. After Auzon turn right across river, immediately left, signed Barjac and site. Shortly turn right, site signed. Only route for trailers and motorcaravans. Do not drive through the village of Boissons. GPS: N44:12.551 E04:15.400

Charges 2007

Per unit incl. 2 persons and electricity	€ 19,00 - € 33,00
with water and drainage	€ 22,00 - € 37,00
with own sanitary unit	€ 25,00 - € 40,00
dog (not allowed 7/7-18/8)	€ 3,20

Castel Camping Château de Boisson

F - 30500 Allegre les Fumades
Tel : +33 (0) 466 248 561
www.chateaudeboisson.com

FR30040 Camping Mas de Mourgues

Gallician, F-30600 Vauvert (Gard)

Tel: **04 66 73 30 88**. Email: **info@masdemourgues.com**

This is an English-owned campsite on the edge of the Petite Camargue region, popular with those who choose not to use the autoroutes. It can be hot here, the Mistral can blow and you may have some road noise, but having said all that, the previous owners and the present owners, the Foster family, have created quite a rural idyll. There are 80 pitches with 70 for touring and 62 with 10A electricity. Originally a vineyard on stony ground, some of the vines are now used to mark the pitches, although many other varieties of trees and shrubs have been planted.

Facilities

Two small toilet blocks provide for all needs. Facilities for disabled visitors. Washing machine. Motorcaravan service point. Chips and panini to takeaway. Reception keeps essentials. Bread to order (evening before). Communal barbecue but gas or electric are allowed. Apartments, mobile homes and tents to rent. Off site: Fishing 2 km. (licence not required). Riding 8 km. Golf 20 km. Bicycle hire and boat launching 25 km. Beach 27 km.

Open: 1 April - 30 September.

Directions

Leave A9 autoroute at exit 26 (Gallargues) and follow signs for Vauvert. At Vauvert take N572 towards Arles and St Gilles. Site is on left after 4 km. at crossroads for Gallician.

Charges 2006

Per unit incl. 2 persons	€ 11,00 - € 13,00
extra person	€ 3,00 - € 4,00
child (0-10 yrs)	€ 1,50 - € 2,00
electricity	€ 2,50

FR30080 Camping le Mas de Reilhe

F-30260 Crespian (Gard)

Tel: **04 66 77 82 12**. Email: **info@camping-mas-de-reilhe.fr**

This is a comfortable family site nestling in a valley with 95 pitches (76 for tourers), most have electricity (6/10A) and some of the upper ones may require long leads. The large lower pitches are separated by tall poplar trees and hedges, close to the main facilities and may experience some road noise. The large terraced pitches on the hillside are scattered under mature pine trees, some with good views, more suited to tents and trailer tents but with their own modern sanitary facilities. The heated swimming pool is in a sunny position and overlooked by the attractive bar/restaurant. A 'Sites et Paysages' member. There are no shops in the village, the nearest being at the medieval city of Sommières 10 km. away (and well worth a visit). From here you can explore the Cevennes gorges, enjoy the Mediterranean beaches, visit the Petite Camargue or Nimes with its Roman remains from le Mas de Reilhe.

Facilities

Good toilet facilities with washbasins in cabins and pre-set showers. Dishwashing and laundry sinks. Washing machine. Reception with limited shop (bread can be ordered). Bar (6/4-23/9), takeaway and restaurant (1/6-15/9). Small play area on grass. Table tennis. Volleyball. Pentaque. Heated swimming pool (all season). Internet access. Off site: Tennis 0.5 km. Fishing 3 km. Riding 5 km. Bicycle hire 10 km. Golf 25 km. The sea and the gorges are approx 30 km. and Nîmes 25 km.

Open: 6 April - 23 September.

Directions

From the A9 take exit 'Nimes ouest' signed Alès, then onto the D999 towards Le Vigan. The site is on the N110 just north of the junction with the D999 at the southern end of the village of Crespian.

Charges 2006

Per unit incl. 2 persons	€ 13,00 - € 19,00
extra person	€ 3,40 - € 5,20
child (2-6 yrs)	€ 1,80 - € 3,00
electricity (6/10A)	€ 3,30 - € 4,00

Camping Cheques accepted.

Check real time availability and at-the-gate prices...

www.**alanrogers**.com

FR30140 **Camping la Soubeyranne**

Route de Beaucaire, F-30210 Remoulins (Gard)

Tel: **04 66 37 03 21**. Email: **soubeyranne@franceloc.fr**

Recently acquired by the group FranceLoc, this site is well positioned for visiting the Pont du Gard, Nîmes and Uzès, famed for their Roman connections. It is approached by a short tree-lined avenue which leads to reception. The 200 pitches offer extremely generous amounts of shade and keeping the 6 hectares watered involves over 5 km. of hose pipe. Pitches are large, level, numbered and separated, with 100 having 6A electricity connections. An animation programme (July/Aug) is aimed mainly at young children (teenagers may find the site rather quiet). Whilst quiet in some respects, train noise both by day and night can be an irritant.

Facilities

Two well appointed, unisex toilet blocks are basic but clean give more than adequate facilities and include washbasins in cubicles. Provision for dishwashing, laundry, water and refuse points is equally generous. Motorcaravan service point. Fridges for hire. Small shop selling basics. Restaurant, bar and takeaway (all from 15/6) - menu not extensive but adequate and moderately priced. Heated swimming pool complex (1/4-30/9) with 20 x 10 m. pool and smaller toddlers' pool (unsupervised), and partly shaded. Play area. Tennis. Bicycle hire. Off site: Fishing 1 km. Remoulins 1.5 km.

Open: 31 March - 6 October.

Directions

From Uzès take D981 to Remoulins, turn right at lights over river bridge, left at roundabout, then left (signed D986 Beaucaire). Site is 1.5 km. further on left. GPS: N43:55.582 E04:33.866

Charges 2007

Per unit incl. 2 persons	€ 14,80 - € 24,00
electricity	€ 4,00
extra person	€ 4,60 - € 7,00
child (under 7 yrs)	€ 2,50 - € 4,20
animal	€ 4,15 - € 4,30

Camping Cheques accepted.

CAMPINGS FranceLoc

Domaine de La Soubeyranne

Shady pitches, mobile homes, heated indoor pool, waterslides, paddling pool, volleyball, table tennis, boules, mountain biking, entertainment.

Route de Beaucaire
30210 Remoulins
Tél. 0033(0)4 66 37 03 21
Fax. 0033(0)4 66 37 14 65
www.campings-franceloc.com

Gard

FR30110 **Camping du Mas de Rey**

Arpaillargues, F-30700 Uzès (Gard)

Tel: **04 66 22 18 27**. Email: **info@campingmasderey.com**

A warm welcome from the English speaking Maire family is guaranteed at this small, unsophisticated 70 pitch site. The owners are hopng to increasingly make the site 'green' with ecologically aware measures (for example, solar heating). Most of the large (150 sq.m.) pitches are separated by bushes, many are shaded and all have 10A electricity. Due to the wonderful climate, grass can at times be hard to find. The reception, bar, restaurant and shop are in the same large airy building. The owners are always willing to give advice on the numerous things to see and do in the area.

Facilities

Two well maintained unisex toilet blocks, one quite new with solar heating, facilities for disabled visitors, baby room and en-suite family cubicles. Dishwashing and laundry sinks. Washing machine and iron. Shop (high season only but bread to order all season). Bar serves a simple 'menu of the day' most evenings (1/7-31/8). Small circular swimming and paddling pools (1/5-15/10, closed lunch-times). Off site: Riding 5 km, golf or fishing 3 km. and canoeing 10 km. Nîmes, Avignon and the Pont du Gard all near.

Open: 10 April - 15 October.

Directions

From D981 in Uzès take the D982 westwards signed Arpaillargues, Anduze, Sommieres, Moussac. Site is 3 km. on the left, well signed. GPS: N43:59.903 E04:23.055

Charges 2006

Per unit incl. 2 persons	€ 17,00
extra person	€ 4,60
child (under 7yrs)	€ 3,00
electricity	€ 3,00

Less 10-20% outside July/Aug.
Special senior tariff in low season.
Credit cards accepted in July/Aug. only

FR30150 Camping les Sources

Route de Mialet, F-30270 Saint Jean-du-Gard (Gard)

Tel: **04 66 85 38 03.**. Email: **camping-des-sources@wanadoo.fr**

This is a lovely, small, family run site situated in the foothills of the beautiful Cévennes. There are 92 average to good sized, slightly sloping pitches on small terraces with 80 used for touring units, all with electricity (6/10A). They are separated by a variety of flowering shrubs and trees offering good shade. Near the entrance is the attractive reception, bar, restaurant and terrace overlooking the swimming pools and children's play area. In May, June and September a pottery and stone polishing workshop can be arranged locally. The emphasis here is on a quiet family holiday with little organised activity. Nearby one can walk in the footsteps of Robert Louis Stevenson (Travels with a Donkey), ride on a picturesque steam train, explore deep underground caverns, visit a giant bamboo forest and explore the region by foot, on bike or by car.

Facilities

Two well appointed, modern toilet blocks with washbasins in cabins and special facilities for babies and disabled visitors. Washing machine. Motorcaravan service point. Bar/restaurant with takeaway (good menu) and small shop (all open all season). Good swimming and paddling pools (from late May). Games/TV room. Play area. Barbecues are not permitted. Occasional children's activities and family evening meals. Off site: St Jean-du-Gard 1.5 km. Bus service to Nîmes and Alès a few times daily. Fishing and bathing 1.5 km. Riding 12 km. Bicycle hire 14 km. Golf 20 km.

Open: 1 April - 30 September.

Directions

From Alés take D907 through Anduze to St Jean du Gard. Take the ring road (autre directions) towards Florac. Turn right at traffic lights on D983, then right onto D50 (site signed). Very shortly, on sharp right hand bend, fork right (site signed) and descend to site. Take care not to overshoot the entrance, as access is impossible from the north.

Charges 2006

Per unit incl. 2 persons	€ 12,60 - € 18,00
incl. electricity	€ 14,00 - € 22,00
extra person	€ 3,20 - € 4,30
child (0-7 yrs)	€ 2,00 - € 3,10

FR30170 Camping la Sousta

Avenue du Pont du Gard, F-30210 Remoulins (Gard)

Tel: **04 66 37 12 80**. Email: **info@lasousta.com**

With a long season, La Sousta is a former municipal site set under tall trees and with a ten minute walk of the famous Pont du Gard, a World Heritage site. The 300 pitches (including 60 mobile homes to rent) are mainly level and numbered, but are not very clearly defined. The reception office provides plenty of tourist information and coach trips are organised in high season to various places of interest. A large swimming pool set in a sunny location has surrounding grassy areas for sunbathing. A footpath leads to a private beach on the river.

Facilities

The four toilet blocks are quite basic but give clean facilities with mainly British style WCs, baby bath and showers, and facilities for disabled people. Washing machines and dryer. Bar. Snack bar and takeaway. Swimming and paddling pools. Various play areas. Volleyball, tennis and football field. Bicycle hire. Weekly disco in July/Aug. Entertainment and canoes trips organised. Communal barbecue areas.

Open: 1 March - 31 October.

Directions

Site is signed from the centre of Remoulins. From N100 follow signs for Beaucaire and Nimes, then site signs. Site is beside the D981, just before Pont du Gard.

Charges 2007

Per unit incl. 2 persons	€ 11,60 - € 19,50
incl. electricity	€ 15,80 - € 22,50
extra person (over 7 yrs)	€ 3,00 - € 6,30

FR30160 Camping Caravaning le Boucanet

B.P. 206, F-30240 Le Grau-du-Roi (Gard)

Tel: **04 66 51 41 48**. Email: **contact@campingboucanet.fr**

On the beach between La Grande Motte and Le Grau-du-Roi. Many trees have been planted and are growing but as yet most are not tall enough to give much shade. As to be expected, the 458 pitches are sandy but level. The 317 for touring are separated by small bushes, most with electricity (6A). Plenty of flowers decorate the site and the pleasant restaurant (open lunchtimes and evenings) overlooks the large pool (heated at beginning and end of season). An excellent shopping arcade provides groceries, fruit, newspapers, a butcher and cooked meats, rotisserie and pizzas. In July and August organised activities include games, competitions, gymnastics, water polo, jogging and volleyball for adults. There is access to the river for fishing and horse riding on the white horses of the Camargue is to be found within a few kilometres.

Facilities

The toilet blocks include facilities for disabled people. Baby rooms. Washing machines, dryers, irons and fridge hire. Motorcaravan services. Range of shops. Restaurant (1/5). Takeaway (June to end Aug). Bar, snacks. Large swimming pool, paddling pool. Play area on sand, miniclub in July/Aug. Table tennis, tennis. Bicycle hire. No dogs. Off site: Riding 500 m. Golf 1.5 km. Shops, restaurants and bars within 3 km.

Open: 7 April - 7 October.

Directions

Site is between La Grande Motte and Le Grau-du-Roi on the D255 coastal road, on the seaward side of the road.

Charges 2007

Per unit incl. 2 persons	€ 17,00 - € 34,00
electricity	€ 3,50 - € 3,70
pitch on first row of beach, plus	€ 5,00 - € 6,00
extra person	€ 6,00 - € 8,70
child (under 7 yrs)	€ 4,50 - € 7,70
Camping Cheques accepted.	

FR30180 Camping Mas de la Cam

Route de St André de Valborgne, F-30270 Saint Jean-du-Gard (Gard)

Tel: **04 66 85 12 02**. Email: **camping@masdelacam.fr**

Camping Mas de la Cam is rather unusual in that all the pitches are used for touring. It is a very pleasant and spacious site with well trimmed grass and hedges and a profusion of flowers and shrubs. Lying alongside the small Gardon river, the banks have been left free of pitches giving neat grass for sunbathing and some trees for shade, whilst children can amuse themselves in the water (no good for canoes). Slightly sloping, the 200 medium to large pitches are on level terraces, some with varying amounts of shade, electricity (6A). There is no evening entertainment.

Facilities

High quality toilet blocks provide a baby bath, facilities for disabled visitors. Washing machines. Bar/restaurant, terrace. Small shop. Attractive large swimming (heated) and paddling pools. Huge play and sports areas, multisports court for football, volleyball and basketball. Club, used in low season for bridge, in high season as games room. Fishing. Off site: St Jean-du-Gard (3 km.) with shops, market. Bus twice a day. Riding 5 km. Bicycle hire 15 km.

Open: 28 April - 20 September.

Directions

Site is 3 km. northwest of St Jean-du-Gard in direction of St André de Valborgne on D907, site signed, fork left, descend across a narrow unfenced bridge to site. Site entrance not accessible from north.

Charges 2006

Per unit incl. 2 persons	€ 14,00 - € 21,00
with electricity	€ 17,00 - € 24,50
extra person	€ 3,30 - € 4,75
child (under 7 yrs)	free - € 3,65
dog	€ 2,10 - € 2,65

FR30190 Camping International des Gorges du Gardon

Chemin de la Barque Vieille, F-30210 Vers-Pont-du-Gard (Gard)

Tel: **04 66 22 81 81**. Email: **camping.international@wanadoo.fr**

Probably the main attraction in the Gardon area of France is the Pont du Gard, an amazing Roman aqueduct built around 50AD. It provides 200 level, mostly good-sized pitches, 180 for touring. Many are on stony terraces in a woodland setting offering good shade while others are more open, all with electricity (10-15A). Rock pegs are essential. There is direct access to the river where swimming is permitted, although in summer the water level may be a little low. Attractive, heated swimming and paddling pools (unsupervised) provide an alternative. The owners, Joseph and Sylvie Gonzales speak a little English, and visitors will always receive a warm and friendly welcome. Joseph previously owned a restaurant and we highly recommend his site restaurant. Tourist information is in the reception (open all day) and Sylvie will share her local knowledge if you need any additional help. There are other attractions worthy of a visit, such as the medieval village of Castillon-du-Gard perched on a rocky peak with narrow cobbled streets, and Collias at the bottom of the gorge from where you can hire canoes.

Facilities

Two toilet blocks provide facilities for disabled visitors. Baby room. Washing machine, dishwashing and laundry sinks. Bar and good restaurant (table service and takeaway). Heated swimming, paddling pools (unsupervised). Play areas. Games room and TV. Organised family entertainment during July/Aug. Canoeing arranged. Off site: Many old towns and villages with colourful markets. Historic cities of Nîmes and Avignon.

Open: 15 March - 31 October.

Directions

Exit A9 at Remoulins, then take D981 towards Uzès. About 4 km. after Remoulins, just after the junction for the Pont du Gard, turn left, site signed and follow signs to site (a few hundred metres).

Charges 2006

Per unit incl. 2 persons	€ 12,00 - € 17,00
extra person	€ 3,50 - € 6,00
child (under 7 yrs)	€ 2,50 - € 3,50
electricity	€ 3,10

FR30200 Camping Cévennes-Provence

Corbés-Thoiras, F-30140 Anduze (Gard)

Tel: **04 66 61 73 10**. Email: **marias@camping-cevennes-provence.fr**

Whenever a new guest arrives at this spectacular and family owned site, one of the seven members of the family takes time to drive the visitors around to enable them to choose what suits their particular needs. From a place on river bank, to the highest pitch some 330 feet higher, the emphasis is on calmness and tranquility. There are 250 pitches on the various levels, 200 with electricity (2-15A). The river is very popular for swimming and in a separate section for enjoying the rough and tumble of a small 'rapids'. There are no activities arranged on site.

Facilities

The 10 toilet blocks are excellent with modern equipment and are kept exceptionally clean. Good facilities for disabled visitors. Large and well equipped shop. Restaurant, takeaway and bar (1/5-10/9). Comprehensive play area. Minigolf. Volleyball. River bathing and fishing. Many activities off site willingly arranged at reception. Internet point including WiFi. Off site: Bicycle hire 3 km. Riding 4 km. Golf 10 km. Adventure and discovery park on opposite bank of river offering many sports facilities.

Open: 20 March - 5 November.

Directions

From Anduze on the D907 take D284 alongside the river. Site is signed on right about 3 km. from the town. Take care on the approach – there is a narrow lane for 100 m. and then a narrow bridge to cross, but visibility is good.

Charges 2006

Per unit incl. 2 persons	€ 12,50 - € 18,00
extra person	€ 3,00 - € 4,30
child (2-6 yrs)	€ 2,00 - € 2,90
electricity (3-10A)	€ 2,00 - € 3,80

385

FR30210 Camping de l'Arche

Porte des Cévennes, F-30140 Anduze (Gard)

Tel: **04 66 61 74 08**. Email: **campingarche@wanadoo.fr**

Camping de l'Arche is situated in the valley of the Gardon river, in the beautiful Cevennes National Park. An attractive pebble river beach runs the length of the site. The 250 large pitches are shady and mostly divided by hedges, with 222 used for touring units, all with electricity (6/10A). In the centre of the site are a bar and restaurant with a terrace for outdoor dining. An innovative new pool complex integrates indoor and outdoor swimming areas, outdoor slides and spa facilities, together with another bar. In cooler periods, the indoor pool can be closed off and heated.

Facilities

Six toilet blocks are spread around the site. Facilities include washbasins in cabins and controllable showers. Baby rooms. Facilities for disabled people. Motorcaravan service point. Shop (20/5-9/9). Bar/restaurant (25/5-9/9). Swimming pool complex (all season). Entertainment and activities organised in high season. Hairdresser. Play area. Bicycle hire. Gas or electric barbecues only. WiFi internet access. Off site: Bus 500 m. Golf and riding 10 km.

Open: 1 April - 30 September.

Directions

From Alès via N110 towards Montpellier. In St Christol-les-Alès turn on D910 to Anduze. Turn right after bridge over the Gardon river and follow river for 3 km. Turn left to site at Hotel des Cèvennes.

Charges 2006

Per unit incl. 2 persons	€ 12,10 - € 22,00
incl. electricity and services	€ 12,10 - € 26,20
extra person	€ 2,80 - € 5,50
child (2-9 yrs)	€ 1,90 - € 3,60

FR30220 Camping les Genêts d'Or

Route de Carmignan, F-30200 Bagnols sur Cèze (Gard)

Tel: **04 66 89 58 67**. Email: **info@camping-genets-dor.com**

Les Genêts d'Or is situated where the two regions of the Cèvennes and the Ardèche meet. The site is in woodland on the banks of the river Cèze, surrounded by forested hills and vineyards. The site has its own pebble river beach and, if you prefer, a good swimming pool. There are 105 pitches (95 for touring), all with 3-10A electricity and plenty of shade. The site owners are the Quarre family. Mme. Quarre speaks Dutch and English and runs the reception and a very good restaurant. The Cèze offers good fishing and the hilly countryside is ideal for mountain biking or walking.

Facilities

Two modern toilet blocks provide good, comfortable facilities including controllable showers and washbasins in cabins. Facilities for disabled people. Baby room. Shop (20/5-15/9). Bar and outdoor restaurant (10/5-15/9). Snack bar (10/5-15/9). Swimming pool (10/4-30/9). Play area. Weekly disco for children (high season). Fishing. Only gas and electric barbecues permitted. Dogs are not accepted July/Aug. Off site: Riding and bicycle hire 2 km.

Open: 1 April - 30 September.

Directions

From A7 autoroute (Montelimar - Valence) take exit 19 (Bollene), then D994 towards Pont St Esprit and on to Bagnols via the N86. Entering Bagnols, turn left just before Total service station and turn left for Carmigan. GPS: N44:10.424 E04:38.205

Charges 2006

Per unit incl. 2 persons	€ 21,20
extra person	€ 4,35
electricity (3/8A)	€ 2,86 - € 3,70

FR34030 Camping International le Napoléon

Avenue de la Méditérranée, F-34450 Vias-Plage (Hérault)

Tel: **04 67 01 07 80**. Email: **reception@camping-napoleon.fr**

Le Napoléon is a smaller, family run site situated in the village of Vias-Plage bordering the Mediterranean. Vias-Plage is hectic to say the least in season, but once through the security barrier and entrance to Le Napoléon, the contrast is marked – tranquillity, yet still only a few yards from the beach and other attractions. It has a Californian style pool, amphitheatre for entertainment and other new facilities, but thoughtful planning and design ensure that the camping area is quiet. With good shade from trees, the 240 mainly small, hedged pitches (135 for touring), most have electricity.

Facilities

Sanitary blocks are of a reasonable standard. Baby bath. Facilities for disabled people. Laundry. Motorcaravan services. Fridge hire. Supermarket. Bar. Restaurant/pizzeria. Heated swimming pool with lively piped music. Gym/fitness room. Sauna, sun room. Bicycle hire. Tennis, archery, volleyball, basketball, boules. TV. Rooms for young campers. Children's club. Amphitheatre, wide range of entertainment until midnight. Disco outside site (Easter-Sept). Off site: Shops, restaurants, and laundry etc. adjacent. Fishing nearby. Riding 1 km. Golf 5 km.

Open: 7 April - 30 September.

Directions

From autoroute take exit for Vias. From town, take D137 towards Vias-Plage. Site is on the right near the beach; watch carefully for turning between restaurant and shops. GPS: N43:17.508 E03:24.991

Charges 2007

Per unit incl. 2 persons and electricity	€ 15,00 - € 37,00
extra person (over 4 yrs)	€ 5,00 - € 6,00
dog	€ 3,50 - € 4,00

FR34020 Camping le Garden

44 Place des Tamaris, F-34280 La Grande Motte (Hérault)

Tel: **04 67 56 50 09**

Le Garden is a mature site, situated 300 m. back from a fine sandy beach and with all the choice of sports, entertainment and other facilities of the popular holiday resort of La Grand Motte. With space for 86 caravans and 118 mobile homes, the 100 sq.m. pitches are hedged with good shade on sandy/grass base. All have electricity (6A), water and waste water drains. The fine sandy beach and port are only 300 m. away, with a shopping complex, bar and restaurant next to site.

Facilities

Three well situated toilet blocks, smartly refurbished in Mediterranean colours, include washbasins in cabins and baby bath. Dishwashing and laundry sinks. Washing machines. Unit for disabled people. Shop to one side of the site with groceries, cigarettes, newspapers, boutique, etc., restaurant, bar and takeaway service (from 15/5). Swimming pool and paddling pool (from 15/5). Children's play area. Table tennis. Off site: Tennis courts, a riding club, a casino and a nightclub nearby.

Open: 1 March - 31 October.

Directions

Entering La Grande Motte from D62 dual-carriageway, keep right following signs for 'campings' and petite Motte. Turn right at traffic lights by the Office de Tourism and right again by the Bar Le Garden and site almost immediately on right. GPS: N43:33.793 E04:04.367

Charges 2006

Per unit incl. 1-3 persons	€ 26,00
with electricity, water and drainage	€ 36,00
extra person	€ 8,50

Bracelet required for pool € 10.

FR34040 Camping Lou Village

B.P. 30, Chemin des Montilles, F-34350 Valras-Plage (Hérault)

Tel: **04 67 37 33 79**. Email: info@louvillage.com

Valras is perhaps smarter and is certainly larger than nearby Vias and it has a good number of campsites. Lou Village is a well kept, family owned site with direct access to a sandy beach. A busy site with lots of facilities and quite competitive prices, it does becomes crowded in high season as this is a popular area. There are 580 pitches (380 for touring), 100 with electricity (10A). Away from the beach there is good shade with grass pitches, partly separated by tall trees. Nearer the beach they are smaller, sandy and separated by bushes and bamboo hedges.

Facilities

Modern, reasonable, refurbished toilet blocks, facilities for disabled visitors and babies. Maintenance seemed satisfactory. Supermarket, bakery, bazaar, a boutique for gifts. Bar, restaurant. Takeaway. Swimming pools (one heated), water slides, paddling pool. Playground, children's club, football field. Tennis. Volleyball. Minigolf. Bicycle hire. Sailing, windsurfing. Entertainment programme. Gate to beach closes at 21.00. Off site: Riding 500 m. Jet skiing. Paragliding on beach. Canoe kayaking and river fishing 1 km. Golf 12 km.

Open: 28 April - 9 September.

Directions

Site is south of Béziers. From A9, exit Béziers-Ouest to Valras-Plage, 14 km. Follow 'Casino' signs. Site is 1 km. south of centre of Valras-Plage in direction of Vendres, signed to the left between Valras-Plage and Vendres-Plage.

Charges 2006

Per unit incl. 2 persons and electricity	€ 19,50 - € 38,50
extra person	€ 4,00 - € 6,90
child (under 7 yrs)	free - € 3,60
dog	€ 3,00 - € 4,00

Pool complex bracelet € 5.50 (once only payment).

FR34070 Yelloh! Village le Sérignan Plage

Mobile homes ▶ page 485

Le Sérignan Plage, F-34410 Sérignan (Hérault)
Tel: **04 67 32 35 33**. Email: **info@leserignanplage.com**

A large, friendly, family-orientated site with direct access to superb sandy beaches, including a naturist beach. Those looking for 'manicured' sites may be less impressed, as its situation on 'the littoral' close to the beach makes it difficult to keep things neat and tidy. It has 450 mainly good sized, level touring pitches, including some (with little shade) actually alongside the beach, coupled with perhaps the most comprehensive range of amenities we've come across. Perhaps the most remarkable aspect is the cluster of attractive buildings which form the 'heart' of this site with courtyards housing many of the amenities. The hugely enthusiastic owners, Jean-Guy and Katy, continually surprise us with new ideas and developments. New for 2004 was a superb 1,800 sq.m. 'Spa Water Fitness centre' with more new pools, a fitness centre and jacuzzi. The amenities are just too extensive to describe in detail, but they include a pool complex, with slides surrounded by large grassy sunbathing areas with sun loungers and another indoor pool. Sérignan Plage exudes a strongly individualistic style which we find very attractive.

Facilities

Several modern blocks of individual design, with good facilities, including showers with washbasin and WC. Facilities for disabled people. Washing machines. Maintenance variable. Supermarket, bakery, newsagent, ATM. Poissonnerie, boucherie (7/6-8/9). Launderette. Hairdresser. Bars, restaurant, takeaway (all 7/4-10/9). Children's activities, evening entertainment. Heated indoor and outdoor pool with lifeguards in the main season (April - Sept). Sporting activities organised. Bicycle hire. Off site: Riding 2 km. Golf 10 km. Bicycle hire. Sailing and windsurfing school on beach (lifeguard in high season).

Open: 6 April - 24 September.

Directions

From A9 exit 35 (Béziers Est) follow signs for Sérignan, D64 (9 km). Before Sérignan, turn left, Sérignan Plage (4 km). At small sign (blue) turn right. At T-junction turn left over small road bridge and after left hand bend. Site is 100 m.

Charges 2007

Per unit incl. 1 or 2 persons and 6 A electricity	€ 17,00 - € 43,00
extra person	€ 4,00 - € 8,00
pet	€ 3,00

Low season offers.
Camping Cheques accepted.

FR34080 Camping le Sérignan Plage Nature

F-34410 Sérignan (Hérault)
Tel: **04 67 32 09 61**. Email: **info@leserignannature.com**

Benefiting from many improvements, Sérignan Plage Nature is a characterful family-orientated site beside a superb sandy naturist beach. At present it has some 260 good sized touring pitches, on level grass and with plenty of shade except for those beside the beach. A friendly bar and restaurant are housed in the Romanesque style buildings which form the 'heart' of the site, including the setting for evening entertainment.There are some ambitious plans for both their sites, which may involve significant developments on Sérignan Plage Nature in particular, including a new 'aqua-village' with pools, fitness centre, Jacuzzi, etc. In recent years the site has been developed by Jean-Guy and Katy Amat, but was originally owned by Jean-Guy's father, who retains an interest and who has been the mastermind behind the award-winning environmentally friendly irrigation system which serves both this site and Camping Sérignan Plage, the adjoining 'textile' site whose extensive range of facilities are also available to visitors here. These developments will probably take a couple of years to complete, so it may be worth checking out the latest state of play before you book or visit. Member 'France 4 Naturisme'.

Facilities

The toilet blocks of differing designs have all been refurbished, and all offer modern facilities with some washbasins in cabins and both British and Turkish style WCs. All is clean and well maintained. Washing machines. Supermarket. Market for fresh fruit and vegetables, newsagent/souvenir shop and ice cream kiosk. Small bar-café. Evening entertainment. Children's disco. Off site: Riding 2 km.

Open: 6 April - 24 September.

Directions

From A9 exit 35 (Béziers Est) towards Sérignan, D64 (9 km). Before Sérignan, take road to Sérignan Plage. At small sign (blue) turn right for 500 m. At T-junction turn left over bridge, site is 75 m. immediately after left hand bend (the second naturist site).

Charges 2006

Per unit incl. 1 or 2 persons and electricity	€ 17,00 - € 38,00
extra person	€ 5,50 - € 6,50
child (under 7 yrs)	free - € 6,50
dog	€ 3,00

Special discounts in low season.
Camping Cheques accepted.

Le Sérignan Plage

The magic of
the Mediterranean

Passerelles

Imagine – hot sunshine, blue sea, vineyards, olive and eucalyptus trees, alongside a sandy beach – what a setting for a campsite – not just any campsite either !

With three pool areas, one with four toboggans surrounded by sun bathing areas, an indoor pool for baby swimmers plus a magnificent landscaped, Romanesque spa-complex with half Olympic size pool and a superb range of hydro-massage baths to let you unwind and re-charge after the stresses of work.

And that's not all – two attractive restaurants, including the atmospheric "Villa" in its romantic Roman setting beside the spa, three bars, a mini-club and entertainment for all ages, all add up to a fantastic opportunity to enjoy a genuinely unique holiday experience.

Le Sérignan-Plage - F-34410 SERIGNAN
Tel: 00 33 467 32 35 33 - Fax: 00 33 467 32 26 36
info@leserignanplage.com - www.leserignanplage.com

FR34050 Camping Naturiste le Mas de Lignières

Cesseras-en-Minervois, F-34210 Olonzac (Hérault)

Tel: **04 68 91 24 86**. Email: **lemas1@tiscali.fr**

A naturist site hidden in the hills of the Minervois, only 3 km. from the medieval town of Minerve. There are marvellous views to the Pyrénées, the Corbières and the coast at Narbonne. The owners Jeanne and Gilles, offer a warm welcome and promote an enjoyable family atmosphere. The site has 50 large pitches (electricity 6A), and 25 super pitches. Mainly on level grass, separated by mature hedges giving considerable privacy. Some smaller pitches are available for tents, with cars parked elsewhere. There is natural shade and a variety of fauna and flora including four types of orchid.

Facilities

Clean toilet block has open wash basins and showers, facilities for disabled people. Washing machine. Simple shop. Bread (15/6 -15/9). Bar (15/7-15/8). Swimming pool, sliding cover for use when cold. Paddling pool. Room for general use with TV, library, separate provision for young people. Playground. Tennis, volleyball, boules. Torch useful. Only gas barbecues. Off site: Sailing, riding and canoeing nearby – Lac de Jouarres. Canal du Midi.

Open: 1 April - 2 October.

Directions

From A61 take exit for Lézignan-Corbières, D611 to Homps, then D910 to Olonzac. Through village following signs to Minerve (D10). Continue. 4 km. Turn left to Cesseras (D168). At Cesseras follow signs Fauzan for 4 km. (site signed) on right, narrow, winding road.

Charges 2006

Per pitch incl. 2 persons	€ 18,90 - € 24,50
extra person	€ 3,60 - € 4,00

FR34060 Hotel de Plein Air L'Oliveraie

Chemin de Bedarieux, F-34480 Laurens (Hérault)

Tel: **04 67 90 24 36**. Email: **oliveraie@free.fr**

Situated at the foot of the Cevennes, L'Oliveraie has many attractive features and is open all year. Don't assume that the extensive range of sport and recreation available here means that it is all hectic activity – it is surprisingly peaceful. Most of the 116 hedged pitches are large and all have electricity (6/10A). Arranged in rows on two levels, those on the higher level are older and have more shade from mature trees (mainly olives). The ground is stony. The large leisure area is slightly apart from the pitches on the lower area, overlooked by the bar.

Facilities

Smart, modern toilet block, baby bathroom, washing machine. Small, well stocked shop. Bar/restaurant, pizzas, salads, etc. Indoor bar, used for films and activities for younger children (all 1/7-31/8). Good sized pool, children's pool (1/6-30/9). Tennis with practice wall. Volleyball, basketball, minigolf. Bicycle hire. Play area for under 13s. Barbecue area. Archery. Off site: Laurens 1 km. Gorges d'Heric and the Cirques de Navacelles well worth visiting.

Open: All year.

Directions

Site is signed 2 km. north of Laurens off the D909 (Béziers - Bédarieux) road.
GPS: N43:32.080 E03:11.235

Charges 2006

Per unit incl. 1 or 2 persons	€ 9,00 - € 26,80
extra person	€ 5,00
electricity (6-10A)	€ 3,20 - € 4,60
dog	free - € 2,00

FR34090 Camping Caravaning Domaine de la Yole

B.P. 23, F-34350 Valras-Plage (Hérault)

Tel: **04 67 37 33 87**. Email: **layole34@aol.com**

A busy happy holiday village with over 1,100 pitches could seem a little daunting. There are 590 pitches for touring. Most pitches are of a good size, all are level, hedged and have electricity, water and waste water points and, very importantly for this area, they all have shade. The extensive pool area is attractive with lots of sunbathing areas and the impressive activities are located in a central area. The beach, a long stretch of beautiful sand, is 500 m. and here is trampolining, paragliding and jet-skis. This is a busy site with something for all the family.

Facilities

Well maintained toilet blocks include baby rooms. Facilities for families or disabled visitors. Washing machines, dryers. Motorcaravan service points. Refrigerators for hire. Shops. Restaurant, terrace, amphitheatre for entertainment (in season). Two pools, paddling pool, all supervised. Multisports court. Play areas. Children's club. Minigolf. Doctor calls (high season). Internet. Off site: Fishing, riding 1 km. Beach 500m.

Open: 29 April - 23 September.

Directions

From A9 autoroute take Béziers Ouest exit for Valras-Plage (13-14 km.) and follow Casino signs. Site is on left, just after sign for Vendres-Plage.

Charges 2006

Per unit incl. 2 persons	€ 16,85 - € 34,90
extra person	€ 5,35 - € 5,90
child (7-16 yrs)	free - € 3,50
child (under 7 yrs)	free - € 1,80
dog	free - € 3,30

FR34110 Yelloh! Village le Club Farret

Mobile homes ▶ page 485

F-34450 Vias-Plage (Hérault)

Tel: **04 67 21 64 45**. Email: **farret@wanadoo.fr**

Well maintained and with welcoming, helpful staff, everywhere is neat and tidy. It is a large, busy site but the atmosphere is very relaxed. There are 756 good size, level, grassy pitches, with 370 for touring with 6A electricity. and there is some shade from many trees. The large heated pool has lots of sunbathing room. The safe beach is alongside the site so some pitches have sea views. There is a wide range of entertainments and the activities include an extensive art programme. The restaurant is high above the pool with views of the sea, everything is open all season. This superb site of excellent quality has been developed by the Giner family with love and care over the last 40 years. There is no advance booking for the touring pitches – they say that they rarely turn anyone away and will give details of availability. If you wish you can try your hand at catamaran sailing or windsurfing – free of charge for one hour. Activities include pottery, silk painting, mosaics and water colours. The mobile home areas are very smart, and have been attractively landscaped, with African or Balinese themes. Tour operators occupy 14% of the pitches.

Facilities

Very clean toilet blocks, children's toilets, baby rooms, facilities for disabled customers. Washing machines. Dog shower. Well stocked supermarket. Hairdresser. Bars with pizzas, snacks, takeaway. Restaurant. Heated swimming pool complex with lifeguard all season. Play areas. Miniclub (5-10 yrs). Teenagers' club (11-15 yrs). Tennis, table tennis, archery, volleyball, football, programme of games. Multisports court. Bicycle hire. Off site: Riding 1 km. Golf 5 km. Sailing and windsurfing on beach.

Open: 6 April - 23 September.

Directions

Site is south of Vias at Vias-Plage. From N112 (Béziers - Agde) take D137 signed Vias Plage. Site is signed on the left. GPS: N43:17.462 E03:25.147

Charges 2006

Per unit incl. 1 or 2 persons	€ 16,00 - € 42,00
extra person	€ 6,00
extra tent	€ 3,00
pet	€ 3,00

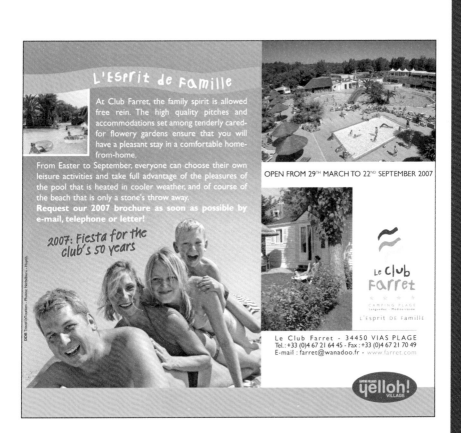

FR34100 Camping le Mas du Padre

4 chemin du Mas du Padre, F-34540 Balaruc les Bains (Hérault)

Tel: **04 67 48 53 41**. Email: **contact@mas-du-padre.com**

The Durand family took over this site a few years ago and have made many alterations and improvements. Madame Durand speaks excellent English. It is a small site, just 2.5 km. from Balaruc-Les-Bains, near the Lake of Thau and is unusually situated in a residential area that has obviously developed around it over the years. Its 116 secluded pitches of varying sizes are enclosed by hedges and mature trees, some on a very gentle slope and 98 have electricity (6/10A).

Facilities

Fully equipped toilet blocks include baby changing area, facilities for disabled campers, washing machines. Reception sells basic provisions. Two small circular pools, one for children (13/5-16/9). Tennis half-court,. Mini-adventure playground. Sports programme, tournaments, aquarobics, animation for children (all in high season). Torch useful. Off site: Fishing or riding 2 km. Golf 20 km.

Open: 31 March - 14 October.

Directions

From A9, exit Sete, follow N800 to Balaruc le Vieux, first roundabout (D2), second roundabout both following Balaruc les Bains/Sete. After 50 m. right for Balaruc les Bains, immediately left across road, double back down it (50 m). Immediately right, on Chemin Mas du Padre. GPS: N43:27.325 E03:41.280

Charges 2006

Per unit incl. 2 persons and electricity	€ 13,50 - € 33,90
extra person (over 13 yrs)	€ 2,90 - € 4,20

FR34130 Camping le Neptune

Route du Grau, F-34300 Agde (Hérault)

Tel: **04 67 94 23 94**. Email: **info@campingleneptune.com**

Camping Neptune is a rare find in this area. This small, family run site with only 165 pitches makes a delightful change. The pitches are mostly separated by flowering bushes, with some shade, most with 6A electricity. The Fray family are welcoming and, even though in a busy area, this site is an oasis of calm, suited to couples and young families. Alongside the D32 there may be a little daytime road noise. The swimming pool is in a sunny position overlooked by the bar. The only entertainment is in high season and is a twice weekly miniclub for children.

Facilities

Two toilet blocks provide roomy pre-set showers, washbasins in cabins, three cold showers for hot weather. Laundry and dishwashing sinks. Two washing machines, dryer. Small shop, bar (both 15/5-30/9). Heated swimming pool heated, bracelets required. Table tennis, field for sports. Boat mooring facility on the River Hérault across the road. Only one dog allowed. No barbecues. Off site: Beach 1.5 km. Golf and riding 1.5 km.

Open: 1 April - 30 September.

Directions

From A9 exit 34, N312, Agde, join N112. Cross river bridge, exit Grau d'Agde, top of exit road over road bridge turn left (roundabout), left at next roundabout, straight over next roundabout, towards river. Left at next roundabout signed Grau d'Agde, D32, parallel to river. Site on left. GPS: N43:17.882 E03:27.377

Charges 2006

Per unit incl. 2 persons	€ 16,00 - € 25,90
extra person	€ 4,50 - € 5,30
Camping Cheques accepted.	

kawan-villages.com **tel: 00 333 59 59 03 59** ━━━━ *kawa*

FR34140 Siblu Camping la Carabasse

Route de Farinette, F-34450 Vias-sur-Mer (Hérault)

Tel: **04 67 21 59 90**. Email: **reservations@lacarabasse.fr**

La Carabasse, a Haven Europe holiday park, is on the outskirts of Vias-Plage, a popular place with lots of shops and restaurants, very much orientated to British visitors. There are lots of activities for young families and teenagers. and the bars and restaurant provide live music in the evenings and entertainment. There are 950 pitches, 50 for touring, with many mobile homes and a good number of tour operator pitches. The touring pitches are set amongst tall poplar and birch trees on level hard ground, all have electricity and partial shade. Some have private sanitary facilities.

Facilities

Varying, fully equipped, toilet blocks. Some pitches with private cabin providing a WC and shower (extra charge). Bars, restaurant, swimming pools. Beach club for windsurfing, pedaloes. Wealth of daytime activities. Children's clubs and multisports unit. Evening entertainment . Off site: Modern resort of Cap d'Agde nearby with Aqualand and golf course (18 holes).

Open: 15 April - 19 September.

Directions

Site is south of Vias. From N112 (Agde - Beziers) road turn right at signs for Vias-Plage (D137) and site (on the left).

Charges guide

Per pitch incl. up to 6 persons and electricity	€ 11,00 - € 37,00
with private sanitary cabin	€ 12,00 - € 43,00

FR34150 Yelloh! Village Nouvelle Floride

F-34340 Marseillan Plage (Hérault)

Tel: **04 67 21 94 49**. Email: **info@nouvelle-floride.com**

Marseillan Plage is a small, busy resort east of Cap d'Adge and it enjoys a super position immediately beside a long gently shelving sandy beach. It is a good quality site set under tall trees with neat hedges separating the 520 pitches (370 for tourers), on sandy soil all having water and electricity (6A). Many newer pitches and the hardstanding pitches have little shade. Amenities and facilities are generally of excellent quality and include a strikingly attractive bar area overlooking the beach with a raised stage for entertainment. This is a well run, family owned site with lots to offer.

Facilities

Impressive toilet blocks, including some en-suite showers and washbasins, facilities for disabled visitors, dog shower. Motorcaravan services. Bar, restaurant. Shop all season. Pool complex, slides, Jacuzzi, paddling pools (all season). Play area, fitness centre, multi-purpose ball court. Water sports. Table tennis. Weekly films, variety of organised games, competitions, dances, discos. Miniclub in school holidays. Bicycle hire. Off site: Shops at Charlemagne across the road. Riding, bicycle hire 500 m. Golf 5 km.

Open: 30 March - 29 September.

Directions

From A9 autoroute exit 34, follow N312 to Agde then take N112 towards Sete. Watch for signs to Marseillan Plage from where site is well signed. GPS: N43:18.522 E03:32.501

Charges 2007

Per unit incl. 2 persons, water and electricity	€ 17,00 - € 44,00
extra person (over 1 yr)	€ 6,00 - € 8,00
animal	€ 4,00

FR34160 Yelloh! Village Charlemagne

F-34340 Marseillan Plage (Hérault)

Tel: **04 67 21 92 49**. Email: **info@charlemagne-camping.com**

The site boasts a large range of amenities, the large supermarket, bakery, takeaway/fast food, bar, restaurant and disco, are open to the public and are consequently well stocked, well equipped and open for the whole season. The site is traditionally laid out under the shade of tall trees providing 480 level pitches, 270 are for touring, neatly hedged and all with electricity (6A) and water. Access to the beach is by a footpath but the site also has a super pool complex complete with 'Niagara Falls'. This site caters for all ages with a wide range of activities.

Facilities

Many toilet blocks, washing machine, some Turkish style toilets. Motorcaravan service point. Fridge hire. Full range of shops, bar/cafe, restaurant, takeaway and disco, all open all season. Pool complex (all season). Fenced play area. Miniclub (May-Sept). Evening entertainment – concerts, cabarets, dances and discos. Off site: Tennis, golf, karting, riding, bicycle hire and water sports.

Open: 31 March - 29 September.

Directions

From A9 exit 34, follow N314 to Agde then take the N112 towards Sete and watch for signs to Marseillan Plage from where site is well signed.

Charges 2007

Per unit incl. 1-2 persons, water and electricity	€ 17,00 - € 44,00
extra person (over 1 yr)	€ 6,00 - € 8,00
dog	€ 4,00

FR34170 Camping Caravaning les Mimosas

Port Cassafières, F-34420 Portiragnes Plage (Hérault)

Tel: **04 67 90 92 92**. Email: **les.mimosas.portiragnes@wanadoo.fr**

Les Mimosas is quite a large site with 400 pitches – 200 for touring units, the remainder for mobile homes – in a rural situation. The level, grassy pitches are of average size, separated and numbered, all with 6A electricity (long leads may be required), some have good shade others have less. The pool area, a real feature of the site, includes a most impressive wave pool, various toboggans, a large swimming pool and a paddling pool (seven pools in all) with lots of free sun beds. This is a friendly, family run site with families in mind.

Facilities

Modern toilet blocks, baby rooms, children's toilets, good facilities for disabled people (whole site wheelchair friendly). En-suite facilities on payment. Washing machines and dryers. Motorcaravan services. Large well stocked shop. Bar, snacks all season, restaurant (from 1/6). Swimming pool complex (early June), lifeguards all season. Play area. Boules. Gym and sauna. Multisports court. Bicycle hire. No barbecues. Off site: Fishing and riding 1 km. Portiragnes Plage 2 km. Golf 10 km.

Open: 20 May - 9 September.

Directions

From A9 exit 35 (Béziers Est) take N112 south towards Serignan (1 km). Large roundabout follow signs for Cap d'Agde, watch carefully for D37, Portiragnes (1-2 km), follow signs for Portiragnes Plage. Site well signed before Portiragnes Plage (5 km). GPS: N43:17.492 E03:22.409

Charges 2006

Per unit incl. 2 persons	€ 22,00 - € 30,00
with electricity	€ 25,00 - € 34,00
extra person	€ 4,50 - € 8,00

FR34180 Camping la Borio de Roque

Route de la Salvetat, F-34220 Saint Pons-de-Thomières (Hérault)

Tel: **04 67 97 10 97**. Email: **info@borioderoque.com**

La Borio de Roque is a peaceful site in a very rural location hidden in a wooded valley 4 km. from St Pons. It lies at the end of a 1.5 km. rough track but it is well worth the effort and it is set around a lovely restored farmhouse with the outbuildings made into four very attractive gites. The 25 large, individually shaped, terraced pitches have 10A electricity and some shade. Some are private to which the owners will escort you. When the site was developed, many different varieties of trees were planted which has created a very attractive environment.

Facilities

Toilet block, baby bath. Use of large freezer. Bread all season. Local wine, home produced goat's cheese, honey, cherry jam for sale. Set menu four times weekly (to order) in high season and eaten with the family in the bar/barn, a very popular event. Swimming pool (from 1/6), small fishing lake. Small grassy play area. Barbecue areas. Not suitable for American motorhomes. Off site: Bicycle hire 5 km. Golf and riding 20 km. Beach 50 km.

Open: 15 May - 15 September.

Directions

St Pons de Thomières is on the N112 northwest of Béziers. Site is 4.5 km. north of the town on the D907 signed Salvaetat, on the right on a bend, then 1.5 km. on a rough track (signed). GPS: N43:30.656 E02:44.789

Charges 2007

Per person	€ 3,50 - € 4,50
child (under 7 yrs)	€ 2,50 - € 3,50
pitch incl. electricity	€ 10,75 - € 12,00
vehicle	€ 2,00 - € 2,25
No credit cards.	

FR34200 Camping Club Californie Plage

Côte Ouest, F-34450 Vias-Plage (Hérault)

Tel: **04 67 21 64 69**. Email: **californie.plage@wanadoo.fr**

With the benefit of direct access to a sandy cove, with a few, much sought-after pitches overlooking the sea, this is a fairly typical holiday-style campsite with a range of good quality facilities. These include a covered pool on the site and situated across the road in the grounds of its sister site is a superb tropical swimming pool complex with the inevitable toboggans etc and even a naturist swimming pool (1/7-31/8). All are mainly on level sandy ground, separated by low hedging, electricity (3-10A) and there is a fair amount of shade from poplars. The site is traditionally laid out, with mobile homes to one side of the central road and touring pitches to the other. Both sites are located away from Vias-Plage, on the Côte Ouest and thereby enjoy a degree of tranquillity in this bustling resort area, Pitches are mostly of 100 sq.m. with shade from tall trees, although those close to the beach are slightly smaller with less shade.

Facilities

Good standard sanitary facilities. Washbasins in cabins, baby rooms, facilities for disabled visitors. Washing machines, dryer. Shop. Bars. Restaurant, takeaway. Beach café, tapas, fish dishes. Covered pool (1/4-30/10). Range of pools on sister site across road (1/7-31/8). Bicycle hire. Games room. Children's play area. Sports nets. Archery. Entertainment programme, children's activities in July/Aug. Off site: Minigolf 2 km. Riding 3 km. Golf 9 km.

Open: Easter - 30 October.

Directions

From N112 Béziers-Agde road take D137 Vias-Plage turn. Watch for signs to 'Cote Ouest' and follow campsite signs thereafter. GPS: N43:17.40 E03:23.89

Charges 2006

Per unit incl. 1 or 2 persons and 6A electricity	€ 16,50 - € 33,00
extra person (4 yrs and over)	€ 3,00 - € 5,00
child (2-4 yrs)	free - € 2,00
10A electricity	€ 3,00

MOBIL HOME air conditioned 6 pers. : **26** € / night*

PITCH 2 persons : **12,50** € / night* *See conditions "Prices".*

35 years / Special Offer

w w w . c a l i f o r n i e - p l a g e . f r

Côte Ouest - F-34450 Vias-Plage - ℭ (0033)4 67 21 64 69 - californie.plage@wanadoo.fr

FR34190 Camping Caravaning les Champs Blancs

Route de Rochelongue, F-34300 Agde (Hérault)

Tel: **04 67 94 23 42**. Email: **champs.blancs@wanadoo.fr**

Les Champs Blancs is set in high trees, 2 km. from Agde and 2 km. from the sea in a shady environment. The 169 level, sandy, touring pitches are bordered with bushes and plenty of trees, all with 10A electricity and 60 have private sanitary cabins. The pool area has been augmented by a super irregular pool, with toboggans, cascade, Jacuzzi, bridges and palms but retaining the original pool and paddling pool. Games, shows and competitions are arranged in July and August. The area nearest the road is bordered by trees to deaden possible road noise.

Facilities

Refurbished toilet blocks, unit for disabled visitors, 60 en-suite private cabins containing WC, shower and washbasin with outside sink for dishes. Washing machines, dryers. Motor caravan services. Well stocked shop in high season, only bread low season. Bar (from 1/6). Restaurant (20/6-15/9). Swimming complex (from 8/4 depending on weather – bracelet required € 5). Good play area, minigolf, table tennis, tennis, basketball. Multicourt. Off site: Riding 1 km. Golf 1.5 km. Beach 2 km.

Open: 8 April - 30 September.

Directions

From A9 exit 34, follow N312 for Adge, joins the N112 Béziers - Sète road. Cross bridge over river, take first turning signed Rochelongue, turn right, next left, then next left (signed Adge). Site on left before another bridge back over N112. GPS: N43:17.821 E03:28.528

Charges 2006

Per pitch incl. 2 persons	€ 18,00 - € 39,00
with individual sanitary facilities	€ 20,00 - € 45,00
extra person	€ 5,00 - € 10,00

Camping Cheques accepted.

FR34220 Camping la Creole

74 avenue des Campings, F-34340 Marseillan-Plage (Hérault)

Tel: **04 67 21 92 69**. Email: **campinglacreole@wanadoo.fr**

This is a surprisingly tranquil, well cared for small campsite in the middle of this bustling resort that will appeal to those seeking a rather less frenetic ambience typical of many sites in this area. Essentially a family orientated site, it offers around 110 good-sized, level grass pitches, all with 6A electricity and mostly with shade from trees and shrubs. It also benefits from direct access to an extensive sandy beach and the fact that there is no swimming pool or bar actually contributes to the tranquillity. It may even be seen as an advantage for families with younger children. The beach will be the main attraction here no doubt, and the town's extensive range of bars, restaurants and shops are all within a couple of minutes walk.

Facilities

Toilet facilities are housed in a traditional building, modernised inside to provide perfectly adequate, if not particularly luxurious facilities including some washbasins in private cabins, a baby room and dog shower. Small play area. Table tennis. In high season beach games, dances, sangria evenings etc, are organised, all aimed particularly towards families. Barbecue area. Bicycle hire. Off site: Local market day Tuesday. Riding 1 km.

Open: 2 April - 10 October.

Directions

From A9 exit 34 take N312 towards Agde, then N112 towards Sète keeping a look-out for signs to Marseillan-Plage off this road. Site is well signed in Marseillan-Plage. GPS: N43:18.765 E03:32.779

Charges 2006

Per unit incl. 2 persons	€ 13,00 - € 24,50
extra person	€ 2,50 - € 4,50
electricity	€ 2,70
dog	€ 2,00

FR34210 Camping les Berges du Canal

Promenade les Vernets, F-34420 Villeneuve-les-Béziers (Hérault)

Tel: **04 67 39 36 09**. Email: **contact@lesbergesducanal.com**

There are surprisingly few campsites which provide an opportunity to enjoy the rather special ambience for which the Canal du Midi is renowned, so we were really pleased to discover this delightful campsite right alongside the canal at Villeneuve-les-Béziers. The campsite has 75 level pitches on sandy grass of average size, mostly with 10A electricity, in a peaceful and shady situation, separated from the canal by an access road. There is a pleasant pool complex, one of the two pools being fitted with a Jacuzzi-style facility, but there are no slides or toboggans thereby ensuring that it is relatively peaceful.

Facilities

A fully equipped toilet block has mainly British-style WCs and some Turkish style, and some washbasins in cabins. Facilities for disabled visitors (with key) and children. Beauty therapist visits weekly. Washing machine, laundry and dishwashing sinks. Motorcaravan service point. Two swimming pools. Bar/snack-bar (serving breakfast too). Small restaurant attached to site. Evening entertainment during high season. Off site: Attractive old village centre of Villeneuve-les-Béziers. Beach at Portiragnes Plage. Riding 5km. Canal du Midi.

Open: 15 April - 15 September.

Directions

From A9 exit 35, follow signs for Agde, at first roundabout take N112 (Béziers). First left onto D37 signed Villeneve-les-Béziers and Valras Plage. Pass traffic lights, left at roundabout and follow site signs (take care at junction beside bridge). GPS: N43:18.99 E03:17.08

Charges 2006

Per unit incl. 2 persons	€ 14,00 - € 19,00
with electricity	€ 16,00 - € 23,00
extra person	€ 2,50 - € 4,50
animal	€ 3,00

FR34240 Camping le Castellas

Route Nationale 112, F-34200 Sète (Hérault)

Tel: **04 67 51 63 00**. Email: **camping.lecastellas@wanadoo.fr**

One would expect a campsite beside a beachside main road and a railway to be noisy, whereas once within the confines of this site it is surprisingly peaceful offering everything one could want. It is situated across the road from a superb sandy beach, with the Etang du Thau behind, yet within a short drive of Sète, Marseillan Plage or Agde. There are 994 pitches with 680 for touring. The large, sandy, hedged pitches, most have 6A electricity. There is a sports area under pine trees along with a restaurant and bar, all well managed. Pitches are accessed by hard roads with a variety of shade – the sorts of shrubs that will grow by the sea. Because of its situation security is tight. There is an emphasis on entertainment with all ages being provided for, although families with younger children are likely to be the most appreciative. It is a large site but is very well organised. 307 pitches used for mobile homes or chalets.

Facilities

Well equipped toilet blocks, en-suite showers and basins. Laundry. Provision for disabled people. Fridge hire. Large supermarket, range of smaller shops and café open to public as well. Restaurant, bars, snack bars. Swimming pool with lifeguards. All open all season. Tennis. Multisports court. Sports field. Play area, bouncy castles. Hairdresser. Masseurs. Internet. ATM. Wide range of entertainment. Off site: Bus for Sète daily in July/Aug.

Open: 1 May - 20 September.

Directions

Site is beside the RN112 which links Marseillan Plage and Sète (nearer to Marseillian Plage). This road can get very busy indeed in main season. GPS: N43:20.431 E03:34.949

Charges 2006

Per unit incl. electricity (6A)	€ 20,00 - € 35,00
extra person	€ 4,00 - € 8,00
extra car	€ 2,00 - € 5,00
dog	€ 4,00

FR34230 Sunêlia le Plein Air des Chênes

Route de Castelnau, F-34830 Clapiers (Hérault)

Tel: **04 67 02 02 53**. Email: **pleinairdeschenes@free.fr**

Situated just outside the village of Clapiers, about 5 km. from the interesting city of Montpellier, yet merely 15 km. from the beach, this is one of few campsites which provides something for everyone, especially for those who prefer to spend their holidays without ever leaving the campsite. There are 130 touring pitches (some large with individual toilet cabin), all in a shaded terraced setting. The site boasts an amazing swimming pool complex, with multi-lane toboggan, four pools and surrounding bars and restaurants. It is also open to the public and obviously very popular and noisy.

Facilities

Three well equipped modern toilet blocks of circular design provide washbasins in cabins and facilities for disabled people. Three washing machines. Shop (July/Aug). Restaurant open to the public (all year), bar, pool side bar, café (June-Sept). Hot food/takeaway (June-Sept). Swimming pools (1/6- 12/9). 4 tennis courts. Multi-sports court. Play area. Miniclub, evening entertainment in main season. Off site: Golf 10 km. Beaches 15km. Fishing 15km. Historic city of Montpellier 5 km.

Open: All year.

Directions

Site is north of Montpellier, 8 km. from A9. Exit 28 on N113 toward Montpellier passing Vendargues. Right on N110, shortly left, D65 for Clapiers circling north of Montpellier. Follow signs for village then site.

Charges 2006

Per unit incl. 2 persons and electricity	€ 23,00 - € 37,00
with water and drainage	€ 18,00 - € 45,00
extra person	€ 3,50 - € 6,50

Camping Cheques accepted.

FR34250 Camping des Sources

F-34700 Soubes (Hérault)

Tel: **04 67 44 32 02**. Email: **jlsources@wanadoo.fr**

This is a 'real' campsite tucked into the side of a small valley with views of the mountains, yet very easily accessible from the A75 autoroute. The level, part grass pitches of variable size, are tucked into bays, all with 6A electricity. There are natural spring water pools large enough for children to splash around in or cool your drinks (the water is drinkable). You can also clamber down to the river to cool off or relax. It is a marvellous natural playground for children, although there is a play area on site.

Facilities

The central traditionally built toilet block is fully equipped including some washbasins in cabins and a washing machine. Simple snack bar. Small pool fed by spring water. Play area. Table tennis. Communal barbecues. Dogs are not accepted. Off site: Village of Soubes 10 minute walk across the river. Lodève 5 km. Montpellier and Mediterranean within one hours drive.

Open: 15 May - 15 September.

Directions

Site is 3 km. north of Lodève. Soubes is signed from A75, exit 52. Take first right towards Fozieres and follow site signs (about 1 km).
GPS: N43:45.733 E03:21.400

Charges 2006

Per unit incl. 2 persons	€ 14,00
extra person	€ 4,50
electricity	€ 2,50

FR34260 Camping Beau Rivage

F-34140 Méze (Hérault)

Tel: **04 67 43 81 48**. Email: **reception@camping-beaurivage.fr**

Beau Rivage is situated on the inland shore of the 4.5 km. by 19.5 km. Etang du Thau. This inland salt lake, lying parallel to the Mediterranean and separated by a very narrow strip of land, is well know for its oyster beds. It also popular for fishing, diving and watersports. The campsite on the edge of the town is within easy walking distance in the direction of Sète. The site has 150 level, sandy-grass pitches all with 6A electricity, plus 35 with mobile homes. The main features of the site are a pleasant pool and paddling pool with a bar and snack restaurant for the high season. Sète is well worth visiting with colourful houses overlooking its many canals, its fish market and 'water jousting'.

Facilities

One fully equipped small toilet block is open all season and a larger block for the main season. Baby bath. Facilities for disabled people. Washing machine. Motorcaravan service point. Bar providing snacks and simple takeaway food (July/Aug). Heated swimming and paddling pools. Play area. Volleyball. Activities in July and August. Communal barbecues. Off site: Restaurant 300 m. Supermarket 200 m. Beach 500 m. Town is within easy walking distance. Tennis and bicycle hire 1 km.

Open: 7 April - 22 September.

Directions

From A9 autoroute take exit 33 for Sète. Follow RN113 for Poussan, Bouzigues and Mèze. Continue for 5 km. to outskirts of Mèze and site is on left just after a petrol station. The entrance is between the petrol station and a pottery (not too easy to see).

Charges 2006

Per unit incl. 2 persons	€ 17,00 - € 32,00
extra person	€ 4,00 - € 7,00
child (0-4 yrs)	free
dog	€ 3,00

FR34290 Yelloh! Village Mer et Soleil

Route de Rochelongue, F-34300 Cap-d'Agde (Hérault)

Tel: **04 67 94 21 14**. Email: **contact@camping-mer-soleil.com**

Close to Cap d'Agde, this is a popular, well equipped site with many facilities. The pool area is particularly attractive with large palm trees, a whirlpool, slides and a gym. An upstairs restaurant overlooks this area and the entertainment stage next to it. There are 500 pitches, around half taken by mobile homes and chalets (some to let, some privately owned). The touring pitches are hedged and have good shade, all with 6A electricity. A path from the back of the site leads to a 1 km. long path leading to the white sandy beach at Rochelongue.

Facilities

One large toilet block plus three smaller ones are fully equipped. Attractive units for children with small toilets, etc. Units for disabled visitors. Motorcaravan service point. Washing machine. Shop. Bar and restaurant. Swimming pools. Gym. Tennis. Archery. Sporting activities and evening entertainment. Off site: Beach 1 km. Riding 1 km. Sports complex opposite site.

Open: 8 April - 15 October.

Directions

From A9 exit 34, follow N312 for Agde. It joins the N112 Béziers - Sète.road. Cross bridge over Hérault river and turn right for Rochelongue. Turn left at next roundabout and site is a little further on the right. GPS: N43:17.171 E003:28.68

Charges 2006

Per unit incl. 2 persons	€ 16,00 - € 39,00
extra person	€ 3,00 - € 6,50
child (2-10 yrs)	€ 1,20 - € 3,50
dog	€ 3,00 - € 3,50

FR34310 Camping Europ 2000

960, avenue des Campings, F-34340 Marseillan Plage (Hérault)

Tel: **04 67 21 92 85**. Email: **contact@camping-europ2000.com**

Europ 2000 is good value option set a little way away from the hectic centre of Marseillan Plage. It has access to the beach by a short, 100 metre path. With 167 pitches of which only 24 are taken by mobile homes, it is a comfortably sized, quiet touring site. The older part of the site has pleasant shade from mature trees with grassy, level pitches of a good size. The new pitches nearer the beach are large and sandy with less shade but with hedging. They all have access to 5/10 amp electricity.

Facilities

Traditional toilet block provides all necessary facilities. Washing machine. Shop and takeaway (15/6-20/9). Play area. Off site: Beach 50 m. Riding, bicycle hire and boat launching 1 km. Fishing 3 km.

Open: 1 April - 20 October.

Directions

From A9 exit 34, follow N312 then N112 towards Sète past turnings for Agde. At first roundabout turn right and at next roundabout in Marseillan Plage village turn right again along Ave des Camping. Continue almost to end and site is on left. GPS: N43:18.4 E03:32.3

Charges 2006

Per unit incl. 2 persons	€ 21,00 - € 23,00
incl. elecricity	€ 16,50 - € 24,50
extra person	€ 3,00 - € 3,50
child (under 5 yrs)	€ 2,00

Widely regarded as the 'Bible' by site owners and readers alike, there is no better guide when it comes to forming an independent view of a campsite's quality. When you need to be confident in your choice of campsite, you need the Alan Rogers Guide.

☑ **Sites only included on merit**

☑ **Sites cannot pay to be included**

☑ **Independently inspected, rigorously assessed**

☑ **Impartial reviews**

☑ **40 years of expertise**

Check real time availability and at-the-gate prices...

www.**alanrogers**.com

FR34370 Camping Blue Bayou

Vendres Plage Ouest, F-34350 Valras Plage (Hérault)

Tel: 04 67 37 41 97. Email: bluebayou@infonie.fr

A very pleasant site, Blue Bayou is situated at the far end of Vendres Plage near Le Grau Vendres (the port of Vendres). It is therefore in a much quieter location than many other sites, away from the more hectic, built-up areas of Vendres and Valras Plage The beach is 300 metres across sand dunes and there are open views from the site creating a feeling of spaciousness. There are 256 pitches, all with 10A electricity, with 74 privately owned mobile homes and 92 to let, including some chalets. The level, grassy touring pitches are large, some with their own sanitary arrangements. Light shade is provided by a mixture of trees. The restaurant and bar area is very attractive, overlooking two swimming pools, one with a toboggan, joined by a bridge where lifeguards station themselves. The site is under new ownership with all the family involved and you are made to feel very welcome. The site would make a very good choice for couples and families.

Facilities

Individual toilet units for about half the touring pitches. Two separate blocks are fully equipped. Baby bath. Facilities for disabled people. Laundry. Bar, restaurant and takeaway (open on demand in early season). Swimming pool (heated all season). Multisport court. Play area. Bicycle hire. Off site: Fishing, boat launching and riding 1 km. Golf 25 km.

Open: 8 April - 30 September.

Directions

From A9 exit 36 (Béziers Ouest) follow directions for Valras Plage and Vendres Plage over four roundabouts. At fifth roundabout (Port Conchylicole) follow sign for Vendres Plage Ouest and site is 500 m. on the left past the Ranch and tourist office. GPS: N43:13.630 E003:14.29

Charges 2006

Per unit incl. 2 persons	€ 19,00 - € 38,00
with private sanitary facility	€ 23,00 - € 49,00
extra person	€ 5,00 - € 9,00

FR34350 Camping la Plage et du Bord de Mer

Route de Vendres, F-34350 Valras Plage (Hérault)

Tel: 04 67 37 34 38. Email: info@campinglaplage.com

A very impressive entrance leads you to this large site beside the beach, yet close to all the amenities of Valras Plage with its own 'centre commercial'. There 670 level pitches on rough sandy grass with very little shade, 500 with electricity (6A/10A) and a further 60 with water and drain. There are just 20 private mobile homes which makes a pleasant change in this day and age. This is very much a seaside site, busy in high season, with three gates to the beach. It also has a good sea food restaurant that is popular with the public. A swimming pool is planned for 2007.

Facilities

Six fully equipped toilet blocks with facilities for disabled visitors and babies. Laundry. Motorcaravan service point. Range of shops, bar and restaurant. Takeaway (1/7-8/9). Tennis. Minigolf. Play area. Entertainment (July/Aug). No dogs or barbecues allowed. Off site: Fishing and boat launching 2 km. Riding 5 km. Golf 20 km.

Open: 1 June – 8 September.

Directions

From A9 exit 36 (Béziers Ouest) follow D64 for Valras then pick up signs for Valras Plage and 'Campings Ouest'. Site is then signed. GPS: N43:14.080 E003:16.12

Charges 2006

Per unit incl. 2 persons	€ 28,00
extra person	€ 5,00
child (2-12 yrs)	€ 4,00
6A electricity	€ 3,00
No credit cards.	

FR34380 Camping le Clos Virgile

F-34410 Sérignan Plage (Hérault)

Tel: **04 67 32 20 64**. Email: **le.clos.virgile@wanadoo.fr**

This good value, family site is set some 400 metres back from a wide sandy beach, but also boasts two pools, one covered and heated, the other with a toboggan and paddling pool. Family entertainment is provided from late June to the end of August from a new stage area beside the pools. In all, there are 299 regularly laid out pitches, with half being taken by mobile homes and chalets (some private, some to let). Tall trees provide shade and the ground is level, but sandy, with 6A electricity to most pitches. Clubs for children are organised with morning sessions for 5-10 year olds and afternoons for teenagers.

Facilities

Three fully equipped toilet blocks include showers with washbasins and facilities for children, babies and disabled people. Shop, bar, restaurant and takeaway (15/6-15/9). Swimming pools (6/5-15/9). Play area. Table tennis. Sports activities. Family entertainment every night (27/6 -23/8). Gas barbecues for hire.

Open: 6 May - 15 September.

Directions

From A9 exit 35 (Béziers Est) follow signs for Sérignan, then Sérignan Plage (D64, about 10 km). Site is almost opposite the 'Horse Ranch' on the left. GPS: N43:16.204 E003:19.87

Charges 2006

Per unit incl. 2 persons	€ 12,00 - € 32,00
incl. electricity	€ 15,00 - € 35,00
extra person	€ 3,00 - € 6,00

FR34390 Camping Village Aloha

F-34410 Sérignan Plage (Hérault)

Tel: **04 67 39 71 30**. Email: **info@yellohvillage-aloha.com**

A well run, orderly site beside the beach at Sérignan Plage, Aloha offers a wide range of good quality facilities all open when the site is open. There are 472 pitches with over 170 mobile homes for hire in attractively landscaped settings. The 295 pitches for touring units are of good size, regularly laid out on level, sandy grass. Easily accessed from tarmac roads, all have 10A electricity. Half are on one side of the small beach road with the swimming pools and other facilities, the other half are somewhat quieter with more grass but less shade across the road.

Facilities

Seven toilet blocks, including three large ones, offer all modern facilities and are well equipped for children. Laundry. Motorcaravan service point. Supermarket including fresh produce market. Bakery, newsagent, bazaar, hairdresser. Bar, restaurant, snack-bar, pizzeria, takeaway. Large heated pool and fun pools. Playground. Tennis. Multisports facility. Beach and sailing club. Bicycle hire. Range of activities. Evening entertainment. Off site: Riding 800 m. Boat launching 8 km. Golf 20 km.

Open: 29 April - 17 September.

Directions

From A9 exit 35 (Béziers Est) follow signs for Sérignan then Sérignan Plage (D64, about 10 km). Site is signed to right after the 'Horse Ranch'. GPS: N43:16.40 E003:20.90

Charges 2006

Per unit incl. 2 persons and electricity	€ 16,00 - € 42,00
extra person	€ 4,00 - € 6,00
child (4-7 yrs)	free - € 6,00

FR34410 Camping le Méditerranée Plage

Côte Ouest, F-34450 Vias (Hérault)

Tel: **04 67 90 99 07**. Email: **contact@mediterranee-plage.com**

Set beside the beach in a quiet part of the coast, this site is somewhat different from the majority of beach sites. It has a most impressive entertainment complex situated to one side of the site with very comfortable outdoor seating, a large stage for entertainment and a very smart bar and restaurant. The colourful furnishings and modern design reflect its Mediterranean setting. The site is very well cared for, with 490 pitches (some 290 used for touring units). Either grassy with a degree of shade or, as you get nearer the beach, more sandy with less shade, all have 6A electricity.

Facilities

Two large toilet blocks are modern, one very impressive with a special nursery unit. Two small ones are more traditional. Facilities for disabled visitors. Laundry. Motorcaravan service point. Smart restaurant and bar. Supermarket. Snack bar. Hairdressers. TV room. Play area. Games room. Tennis. Archery. Windsurfing possible from beach. Activity programme, children's entertainment, circus school, evening shows and dancing. Internet access. Off site: Riding 1 km. Canal du Midi. Luna Park at Vias.

Open: 31 March - 23 September.

Directions

From A9 exit 35 (Béziers Est) follow directions for Agde and Sète on N112. After 4.2 km. turn for Portiragnes. Pass village and continue for 2.5 km. over Canal du Midi then turn left and follow site signs. GPS: N43:16.949 E003:22.26

Charges 2006

Per unit incl. 2 persons	€ 20,50 - € 34,00
extra person	€ 5,00 - € 6,00
child (2-10 yrs)	€ 3,40 - € 4,50

FR34400 Camping les Sablons

F-34420 Portiragnes Plage (Hérault)

Tel: **04 67 90 90 55**. Email: **les.sablons@wanadoo.fr**

Les Sablons is an impressive and popular site with lots going on. Most of the facilities are arranged around the entrance with shops, a restaurant, bar and a large pool complex with no less than five slides, three heated pools and large stage for entertainment. There is also direct access to the white sandy beach at the back of the site close to a small lake. There is good shade on the majority of the site, although some of the newer touring pitches have less shade but are nearer the gate to the beach. On level sandy grass, all have 6A electricity. Of around 800 pitches, around half are taken by a range of mobile homes and chalets (many for hire, some by British tour operators). A wide range of sporting activities, and evening entertainment is arranged with much for children to do. In fact, this is a real holiday venue aiming to keep all the family happy.

Facilities

Well equipped, modernised toilet blocks include large showers some with washbasins. Baby baths and facilities for disabled visitors. Supermarket, bakery and newsagent. Restaurant, bar and takeaway. Pool complex. Entertainment and activity programme with sports, music and cultural activities. Beach club. Tennis. Archery. Play areas. Electronic games. ATM Internet access. Bicycle hire. Off site: Riding 200 m.

Open: 1 April - 30 September.

Directions

From A9 exit 35 (Béziers Est) follow signs for Vias and Agde (N112). After large roundabout pass exit to Cers then take exit for Portiragnes (D37). Follow for about 5 km. and pass over Canal du Midi towards Portiragnes Plage. Site is on left after roundabout. GPS: N43:16.8 E03:21.8

Charges 2006

Per unit incl. 2 persons	€ 16,00 - € 42,00
extra person (max. 6)	€ 4,00 - € 8,00
child (0-4 yrs)	free - € 4,00

DIRECT ACCESS TO THE SANDY BEACH

OPEN FROM 01/04 UNTIL 30/09

ALL FACILITIES ON PLACE...
Restaurant, supermarket, fresh bakery...

LES SABLONS
VILLAGE CLUB CAMPING
★★★★
www.les-sablons.com

WEEK-ENDS' SPECIAL PRICES

FRANCE

Check real time availability and at-the-gate prices...

www.**alanrogers**.com

FR34430 Camping l'Occitanie

B.P. 29, F-34350 Valras Plage (Hérault)

Tel: **04 67 39 59 06**. Email: **campingoccitanie:wanadoo.fr**

L'Occitanie is a good value site, particularly for low season visits, and is within walking distance of Valras Plage. The site is virtually a straight road from the autoroute exit (12 km). On arrival, don't be put off by the entrance (it could be more inspiring). You can find a more open pitch in the higher part of the site which is lightly wooded with some views of the surrounding countryside, or choose the lower area with plenty of shade which French visitors seem to do. A right of way divides the site into two parts. The bar, restaurant and pool make a nice social area in the higher part. There are 400 pitches with 30 privately owned mobile homes and 58 for hire. All pitches have 6A electricity and are of reasonable size on level rough grass. The town is a 20 minute walk and the beach 1 km. It is therefore a relatively peaceful location and seems to attract a mix of visitors.

Facilities

Five toilet blocks are fully equipped and opened as required. En-suite unit with ramped access for disabled visitors .Baby bath. Washing machine. Motorcaravan service point. Bar, restaurant and takeaway. Swimming and paddling pools. Play area. Minigolf. Day time activities for children and sports for adults in high season and some evening entertainment.

Open: 27 May - 9 September.

Directions

From A9 exit 35 (Béziers Est) follow signs for Valras Plage (12 km). Continue straight on at roundabout beside McDonalds and Hyper U and again at next one towards Valras. Then turn immediately left into site. GPS: N43:15.424 E003:17.15

Charges 2006

Per unit incl. 2 persons and electricity	€ 15,25 - € 24,00
extra person	€ 2,00 - € 3,50

Camping L'Occitanie ★★★

Mobil-homes and tents rental

Le bonheur comme on aime

Camping l'Occitanie
B.P 29 34350 Valras Plage
Tél : + 33 (0)4 67 39 59 06
Fax : +33 (04 67 32 58 20
www.campingoccitanie.com
E-mail : campingoccitanie@wanadoo.fr

bar, restaurant, swimming-pool, entertainment (july, august)

May, june and september
21 days = 14
14 days = 10

FR34420 Camping les Romarins

Route du Grau, F-34300 Agde (Hérault)

Tel: **04.67.94.18.59**. Email: **contact@romarins.com**

A small family campsite beside the River Hérault, Les Romarins is only 1 km. from a wide sandy beach and 800 metres from the village. With 120 level pitches separated by shrubs, 50 are available for touring units, the rest are taken by mobile homes and chalets (80 to let) Electricity (6A) is available on all pitches, some of which have more shade than others. The site was bought by the Schwartz family seven years ago and is gradually being improved. A pleasant walk beside the river and past the fish quay, takes you to the shops, restaurants and beach of Le Grau.

Facilities

Two modern toilet blocks are fully equipped. Good facilities for babies and disabled people. Bar with snacks (from 1/5). Bread can be ordered. Heated pool (all season). Large playing field and play area at the back of the site (closed at night). Archery. Bicycle hire. Sports activities and evening entertainment in season. Off site: Beach 900 m. Shops/restaurants 700 m. Boat launching 50 m. Riding 2 km. Golf 3 km. Cap d'Agde and Aqualand 3 km.

Open: 15 April - 25 September.

Directions

From A9 exit 34, follow N312 towards Cap d'Agde picking up the N112. Cross the river and take exit for Grau d'Agde and Rochelonge. Turn left over bridge, left at next roundabout by Hyper U, and straight over next two roundabouts towards river. Left at roundabout beside river following sign 'Campings les Berges du Hérault' along riverside (one way). Site is third on left opposite fish quay.

Charges 2006

Per unit incl. 2 persons	€ 11,70 - € 20,55
extra person	€ 3,90 - € 6,30
child (2-13 yrs)	free - € 4,60
electricity	€ 4,00

FR34440 Camping les Tamaris

140 avenue d'Ingril, F-34110 Frontignan Plage (Hérault)

Tel: **04.67.43.44.77.** Email: **les-tamams@wanadoo.fr**

This is a super site, unusually situated on a strip of land that separates the sea from the étang (or inland lake), and therefore Fontignan Ville from Fontignan Plage. The design of the site is unusual which adds to its attractiveness. The pitches are laid out in hexagons divided by tall hedging and colourful shrubs. In total, there are 250 pitches with 100 taken by mobile homes which are let by the site. All have 10A electricity and are on level sandy grass. Direct access to the sandy beach is possible.

Facilities

Three modern toilet blocks with en-suite showers and washbasins. Excellent facilities for childen. Unit for disabled visitors. Motorcaravan service point. Shop. Bar, restaurant and takeaway (all season). Swimming pool (from 1/5). Hairdresser. Gym. Play area. Miniclub. Archery. Bicycle hire. Internet access. Entertainment for all ages. Off site: Riding 150 m. Sailing 1 km. Boat launching 2.5 km. Golf 15 km.

Open: 1 April - 22 September.

Directions

From the north on the A9 take exit 32 and follow N112 towards Sète and Frontignan. After 16 km. ignore sign for Frontignan town and contine to Frontignan Plage following site signs along the road between the sea and étang. From the south use exit 33 and follow N300 to roundabout beside the port of Sète (11 km). Turn left on N112 and take second exit for Frontignan Plage.

Charges 2006

Per unit incl. 2 persons	€ 22,00 - € 36,00
extra person	€ 4,00 - € 8,00

FR66000 Camping Caravaning de Pujol

Route du Tamariguer, F-66700 Argelès-sur-Mer (Pyrénées-Orientales)

Tel: **04 68 81 00 25**

Le Pujol is an attractive, well cared for site. There are various loud open air discos and activities in the area until the early hours. Pujol may be the best chance of avoiding the hectic seaside sites in otherwise attractive Argelès. There are 310 very large flat, grassy pitches, most with electricity (6A). The site's pride and joy is a delightful pool complex with semi-tropical shrubs and fountains. The bar is for the family, not overrun by youngsters. They are catered for in a covered meeting area opposite. There is some road noise near the entrance to the site.

Facilities

Well kept fully equipped toilet blocks. Baby bath. Washing machines. Small supermarket (1/6-15/9). Good restaurant, friendly family bar (1/6-15/9). Large L-shaped swimming pool, children's pool, spa pool (1/6-15/9). Table tennis. Small multi-gym. Boules. Minigolf. Playground. Games room. Gas or electric barbecues only. Off site: Riding 500 m. Fishing, bicycle hire 1 km. Argelès Plage and quiet resort of Racou short distance.

Open: 1 June - 15 September.

Directions

From autoroute take Perpignan-Nord exit and follow N114 from Perpignan and use exit 10 for Argelès, Cross first roundabout onto Chemin de Neguebous (avoiding town). Turn left at second roundabout and site is 200 m. on right opposite Tour de Pujol.

Charges guide

Per pitch incl. 2 persons	€ 21,00
with electricity	€ 24,00
No credit cards.	

FR66010 Camping L'Etoile d'Or

Route de Taxo á la Mer, F-66701 Argelès-sur-Mer (Pyrénées-Orientales)

Tel: **04 68 81 04 34.** Email: **info@aletoiledor.com**

L'Etoile d'Or is a large family site in the popular resort of Argelès-sur-Mer (home to more campsites than any other resort in France). Many flowering shrubs and trees provide a very comfortable environment with pitches attractively situated amongst the greenery. With 428 pitches in total, over 200 are taken by privately owned mobile homes which accounts for some individuality in pitch layout. A further 128 are available to let, leaving 68 available for touring units (with 4/8A electricity). Activities are available in high season including a children's club and evening entertainment.

Facilities

Two large toilet blocks provide for all needs. Laundry. Supermarket (10/6-20/8). Bar, restaurant and takeaway (1/5-20/9). Swimming pool (1/6-30/9). Multisports court and tennis court. Playground. Games room. Children's club. Entertainment and activity programme Excursion programme. Off site: Nearest beach 2.5 km. Spanish border 30 minutes away.

Open: 15 March - 30 September.

Directions

From the A9 motorway (heading south) take the Perpignan Sud exit and follow signs to Argelès sur Mer on the N114. Take exit 10 signed Taxo d'Avall and Taxo d'Amont, then Plages Nord and St Cyprien. Site is 1 km. further down this road.
GPS: N42:34.12 E003:44.61

Charges 2006

Per unit incl. 2 persons	€ 19,00 - € 25,00
extra person	€ 6,00 - € 8,00
electricity (4A)	€ 4,00

FR66030 Camping Cala Gogo

Avenue Armand Lanoux, Les Capellans, F-66750 Saint Cyprien-Plage (Pyrénées-Orientales)

Tel: **04 68 21 07 12**. Email: **camping.calagogo@wanadoo.fr**

This is an excellent, well organised site and it is agreeably situated by a superb sandy beach with a beach bar and boat launching. There are 450 average sized, level, pitches for touring, electrical connections (6A) everywhere and some shade. The site has a most impressive pool complex carefully laid out with palm trees in ample sunbathing areas. The large bar complex becomes very busy in season and dancing or entertainment is arranged on some evenings on a large stage recently built alongside the bar. A feature of the site is the provision of special beach buggies for the handicapped. A large Aquapark, reputed to be amongst the best in southern France, is nearby. Used by tour operators (148 pitches). There are 50 chalets and mobile homes to rent.

Facilities

High standard, fully equipped toilet blocks. Good supermarket, small shopping mall. Sophisticated restaurant with excellent cuisine, self-service restaurant, simple menu, takeaway. Bar, small beach bar, high season. Disco. TV. Three adult pools plus one for children, water-jets, Jacuzzi, waterfall. Children's play area, remote control cars for children. Tennis, table tennis, playground. Events and sports organised in season. Torches useful. Off site: Fishing, riding, bicycle hire and golf within 5 km. Boat excursions and courses in skin-diving, windsurfing or sailing nearby.

Open: 12 May - 22 September.

Directions

Using D81 (southward) avoid St Cyprien-Plage and continue towards Argelès. Turn right at roundabout signed Le Port and Aquapark and pick up site signs. Site is just past the Aquapark.

Charges 2007

Per person (over 5 yrs)	€ 8,20
pitch	€ 12,00
electricity (6A)	€ 3,30
dog	€ 3,70

FR66040 Camping le Soleil

Route du Littoral, F-66702 Argelès-sur-Mer (Pyrénées-Orientales)

Tel: **04 68 81 14 48**. Email: **camping.lesoleil@wanadoo.fr**

Le Soleil has direct access to the sandy beach. It is a busy, popular, family owned site which has grown recently into a small village. It has over 800 pitches of ample size, and around 550 are used for touring units, on sandy/grassy ground and with a mixture of trees and shrubs providing some shade, all with electricity (6A). Access for caravans sometimes needs care on the narrow access roads. The site has a wide range of amenities, including an impressive pool complex, all facilities open when the site is open. Spain and the Pyrénées are near enough for excursions. There are over 200 pitches used by tour operators and 70 occupied by mobile homes. English is spoken and there is a comprehensive reservation system (advised for most of July/Aug).

Facilities

Seven toilet blocks of the type with external access to individual units. Some family cabins with washbasins, showers. Washing machines. Supermarket, general shop, press, tabac, restaurant, takeaway. ATM machine. Internet. Bar with disco (July/Aug), beach bar. California type swimming pool complex and entertainment area. Adventure playground. TV room. Tennis. Riding in high season (charge). No dogs. Off site: Fishing and mooring boats on the adjacent river. Golf 5 km.

Open: 13 May - 23 September.

Directions

Site is at north end of the beach, about 1 km. from Argelès-Plage village.

Charges 2007

Per person (over 5 yrs)	€ 8,20
pitch	€ 12,30
electricity (6A)	€ 3,30

Less 20% outside July/Aug.
Swimming pool deposit € 15.24 per pitch.

FR66020 Camping Caravaning Ma Prairie

Route de St Nazaire, F-66140 Canet-en-Roussillon (Pyrénées-Orientales)

Tel: **04 68 73 26 17**. Email: **ma.prairie@wanadoo.fr**

Ma Prairie is an excellent site and its place in this guide goes back over 30 years. Then it was simply a field surrounded by vineyards. The trees planted then have now matured, more have been planted, along with colourful shrubs providing a comfortable, park-like setting with some 260 pitches, all with electricity and 35 with water and drainage. It is a peaceful haven some 3 km. back from the sea but within walking distance of Canet village itself. The Gil family still provide a warm welcome and reception boasts an impressive international collection of hats, helmets and uniform caps.

Facilities

Fully equipped toilet blocks, baby bath. Laundry facilities. No shop but bread can be ordered. Snack bar and takeaway. Air-conditioned bar and restaurant. Adult pool, children's pool. Play area. Tennis. Bicycle hire. Volleyball. TV. Billiards. Amusement machines. Dancing three times weekly, busy daily activity programme in season. Caravan storage. Off site: Supermarket 400 m. Riding 600 m. Golf 6 km. Canet Village within walking distance. Bus/tram services to the busy modern resort of Canet Plage.

Open: 5 May - 25 September.

Directions

Leave autoroute A9 at Perpignan North towards Barcarès. Site access is from the D11 Perpignan road (exit 5), close to the junction with D617 in Canet-Village. Go under bridge, right at roundabout the left to site.

Charges 2007

Per unit incl. 2 persons	€ 17,00 - € 30,00
extra person	€ 4,00 - € 7,00
electricity (10A)	€ 4,00 - € 5,00

Camping Cheques accepted.

kawan-villages.com **tel: 00 333 59 59 03 59** ━━━━━━ *kawa*

FR66050 Camping le Haras

Domaine Saint Galdric, F-66690 Palau del Vidre (Pyrénées-Orientales)

Tel: **04 68 22 14 50**. Email: **haras8@wanadoo.fr**

A distinctly 'French' style site, Le Haras is midway between the coast (about 8 km.) and the Pyrénées, in quiet countryside away from the bustle of the coastal resorts. Le Haras has 75 pitches with electricity, 18 fully serviced, arranged informally in bays of four, in the grounds of an old hunting lodge. A mixture of trees, shrubs and flowers provides colour and shade. Some access roads are narrow. There is an attractive pool complex with a bar and a courtyard area beside the restaurant and large function room. Rail noise is possible, although this is screened by large trees.

Facilities

Fully equipped toilet blocks, Renovation of smaller block near the pool planned. Covered dishwashing and laundry sinks. Washing machines. Fridge hire. Bar. Restaurant, open to the public (all year). Takeaway. Swimming pool (1/5-15/9). Play area. No charcoal barbecues. Internet access. Off site: Beaches 10 minutes drive. Fishing 500 m. Riding 2 km. Bicycle hire 6 km. Golf 7 km.

Open: 20 March - 20 October.

Directions

From A9, exit 43 (Le Boulou) follow D618 towards Argelès for 13 km. Bypass St André, turn left, Palau-del-Vidre (D11). Bear right through village, on D11 towards Elne. Site at end of village, before bridge.

Charges 2007

Per pitch incl. two persons	€ 14,00 - € 24,50
electricity (5A)	€ 4,00

Camping Cheques accepted.

kawan-villages.com **tel: 00 333 59 59 03 59** ━━━━━━ *kawa*

FR66080 Camping les Fontaines

Route de St Nazaire, F-66140 Canet en Roussillon (Pyrénées-Orientales)

Tel: **04 68 80 22 57**. Email: **campinglesfontaines@wanadoo.fr**

If you are looking for a different experience more in tune with nature you will perhaps enjoy Les Fontaines. The present owners have spent much money, time and energy on improving it. The site itself borders 'La Réserve Naturelle de l'Etang de Canet-St Nazaire and is set amongst open fields with views of the Canigou and other mountains. The 160 pitches are large and level with 10A electricity but lack shade, although much planting has been carried out.

Facilities

An unusual white castellated houses a fully equipped sanitary block. Baby bath. Facilities for disabled people. Washing machine. Swimming pool with paddling pool (1/6-30/9). Bar. Communal barbecues (only gas or electric on pitch). Play area. Farm. Some mobile homes to rent. Off site: Beach, fishing and boat launching 4.5 km. Riding 5 km. Bicycle hire 3 km. Golf 11 km. St Nazaire and Elne.

Open: 1 May - 30 September.

Directions

Leave A9 at Perpigan Nord and follow directions for Canet for about 20 km. Pick up the D11 Perpigan road and take first exit (5) for Canet village. Go under bridge and continue for about 1.5 km to site.

Charges 2006

Per unit incl. 2 persons	€ 10,00 - € 22,00
extra person	€ 2,00 - € 5,00
electricity	€ 3,50

FR66070 Yelloh! Village le Brasilia

Mobile homes ▶ page 486

B.P. 204, F-66141 Canet-en-Roussillon (Pyrénées-Orientales)

Tel: **04 68 80 23 82**. Email: **camping-le-brasilia@wanadoo.fr**

An impressive family site beside the beach and well managed, Le Brasilia is pretty, neat and well kept with an amazingly wide range of facilities. There are 826 neatly hedged pitches all with electricity varying in size from 100 to 150 sq.m. Some of the longer pitches are suitable for two families together. With a range of shade from pines and flowering shrubs, less on pitches near the beach, there are neat access roads (sometimes narrow for large units). Over 100 of the pitches have mobile homes or chalets to rent. A 'Yelloh Village' member. Member of Leading Campings Group. The sandy beach here is busy, with a beach club (you can hire windsurfing boards) and a naturist section is on the beach to the west of the site. There is also a large California type pool, with sunbathing areas bounded by an attractive mosaic wall and bar. The village area of the site provides bars, a busy restaurant, entertainment (including a night club) and a range of shops. In fact you do not need to stir from the site which is almost a resort in itself also providing a cash dispenser, exchange facilities, telephone, post office, gas supplies and even weather forecasts. It does have a nice, lively atmosphere but is orderly and well run – very good for a site with beach access.

Facilities

Ten modern sanitary blocks are very well equipped and maintained, with British style WCs (some Turkish) and washbasins in cabins. Good facilities for children and for disabled people. Laundry room. Hairdresser. Bars and restaurant. Swimming pool with lifeguards (heated). Play areas. Sports field. Tennis. Sporting activities. Library, games and video room. Internet café. Daily entertainment programme. Bicycle hire. Fishing. Torches useful. Off site: Riding 5 km. Golf 12 km.

Open: 29 April - 30 September.

Directions

From A9 exit 41 (Perpignan Centre/Rivesalts) follow signs for Le Barcarès/Canet on D83 for 10 km, then for Canet (D81). At first Canet roundabout, turn fully back on yourself (direction Sainte-Marie) and watch for Brasilia sign almost immediately on right.

Charges 2006

Per unit incl. 2 persons and electricity (6A)	€ 16,00 - € 42,00
extra person	€ 4,60 - € 6,50
child (1-4 yrs)	free - € 4,00

LE BRASILIA, YOUR PENINSULA, YOUR SECRET

Enjoy this site with water at your feet, an eye-full of blue skies, a floral rainbow and a beach. Oh how lucky you are! But hush... it's your secret, a secret hidden amongst a 15-hectare pine wood with a heated swimming pool, tennis courts, fields for a multitude of sports, entertainment for both adults and children, shops, restaurant-bar, cabaret and discotheque. For your ultimate well being, mobile homes and homes with a garden await you.

Camping Village Le Brasilia
BP 204 - 66141 Canet-en-Roussillon Cedex
tel. 00 33 (0)4 68 80 23 82
fax 00 33 (0)4 68 73 32 97
e-mail : camping-le-brasilia@wanadoo.fr
www.brasilia.fr

FR66090 Camping Mar Estang

Route de St Cyprien, F-66140 Canet en Roussillon (Pyrénées-Orientales)

Tel: **04 68 80 35 53**. Email: **marestang@wanadoo.fr**

Le Mar Estang is a large, 'all singing all dancing' site with something for everyone. Situated on the edge of Canet, between the Etang (part of the Réserve Naturelle de Canet/ St Nazaire) and the sea, there is access to the beach from the site by a tunnel under the road. If you don't fancy the beach, there are four swimming pools to choose from, complete with fun pool, water slides and a heated covered pool. There are 600 pitches, some 200 used for mobile homes or Bengali tents, with 5A electricity, some degree of shade and on sandy ground.

Facilities

Nine well equipped sanitary blocks are well placed around the site. Facilities for babies. Laundry. Motorcaravan service point. Shop, bars, restaurant and takeaway all open when site is open. Swimming pools, Jacuzzi and solarium. Fitness club. Entertainment. Disco. Communal barbecue. Sailing club. Tennis. Bicycle hire. Play areas. Direct access to beach. Off site: Riding nearby. Canet 500 m. with train in high season. Perpignan 10 km.

Open: 29 April - 23 September.

Directions

Take exit 41 from A9 autoroute and follow signs for Canet. On outskirts of town follow signs for St Cyprien/Plage Sud. Site is very clearly signed on southern edge of Canet Plage. GPS: N42:40.542 E03:01.881

Charges 2006

Per unit incl. 2 persons	€ 15,00 - € 30,00
extra person	€ 7,00 - € 12,00
electricity (5A)	€ 5,00 - € 7,00

FR66100 Camping Caravaning la Pergola

F-66478 Sainte Marie la Mer (Pyrénées-Orientales)

Tel: **04 68 73 03 07**. Email: **info@campinglapergola.com**

La Pergola is an attractive tranquil campsite with 180 pitches which include 140 for tourers, all with 10A electricity. It is located in a mainly residential area of this up-and-coming and, at times, quite lively, seaside resort. Family-run, and orientated towards family holidays, it offers a choice of mainly large pitches, some with lots of shade and some with less. It has a very pleasant ambience, a nice quiet pool area (with no noisy slides or toboggans) and it will undoubtedly appeal to families with younger children in particular. It is about five minutes walk from the beach.

Facilities

Three modern toilet blocks include facilities for babies and disabled visitors. Bar (mid June-Aug). Takeaway (July/Aug). Swimming and paddling pools (mid June-Aug; no toboggans). TV. Play Area. Some evening entertainment in high season. Off site: Beach 500 m.

Open: 1 June - 30 September.

Directions

From A9 take exit 41 and follow signs towards Canet via the D83 and D81 until a roundabout signed Ste Marie-la-Mer Plage. Turn left into Ste Marie Plage and follow campsite signs.

Charges 2006

Per unit incl. 2 persons	€ 19,60 - € 24,50
incl. electricity	€ 22,00 - € 27,50
extra person	€ 5,20 - € 6,50
child (0-4 yrs)	€ 3,20 - € 4,00

FR66110 Camping le Dauphin

Route de Taxo-d'Avall, F-66701 Argelès-sur-Mer (Pyrénées-Orientales)

Tel: **04 68 81 17 54**. Email: **info@campingledauphin.com**

Near Taxo in the quieter, northern part of Argelès (a somewhat frenzied resort in season), this family owned site on flat, grassy parkland with plenty of tall trees enjoys good views of the Pyrénées from the terrace area surrounding its excellent complex of swimming pools. There are 310 level, grassy well shaded pitches, all with 10A electricity and some with individual sanitary units. Located some 1.5 km. from the town and beach, there is a regular connecting 'road train' service to and fro throughout the day and evening until midnight. There are 150 pitches taken by mobile homes and chalets either privately owned or for rent. Tour operators use 70 of the pitches.

Facilities

A central sanitary block, although mature, provides all essential facilities including washbasins en-suite. One third of the pitches have their own fully equipped individual sanitary unit. Shops. Bar/restaurant, pizzeria with takeaway (all 1/6-15/9). Two large swimming pools and paddling pool (small charge). Two play areas. Tennis courts. Minigolf. Multisport court, sports ground and games room. Entertainment programme in high season. Torches useful in some areas. Off site: Riding 1 km. Fishing 2 km.

Open: 20 May - 24 September.

Directions

Site is on north side of Argelès. From autoroute take exit Perpignan-Nord for Argelès and follow directions for Plage-Nord and Taxo-d'Avall (similarly from the N114).

Charges 2007

Per unit incl. 2 persons and electricity	€ 18,00 - € 29,40
Individual sanitary unit	€ 4,00 - € 8,00
water and drainage	€ 3,00 - € 4,10
extra person	€ 4,00 - € 6,20

FR66130 Hotel de Plein Air L'Eau Vive

Chemin de St Saturnin, F-66820 Vernet-les-Bains (Pyrénées-Orientales)

Tel: 04 68 05 54 14. Email: info@leauvive.com

Enjoying dramatic views of the Pic du Canigou (3,000 m.), this small site is 1.5 km. from the centre of Vernet-les-Bains in the Pyrénées. It is approached via a twisting road through a residential area. The 70 tourist pitches, with electricity (4/10A) and 45 fully serviced, are on a slight slope, part hedged and some terraced, with a separate tent field. Most pitches have some shade. There is no swimming pool, but the site has a natural pool with water pumped from the nearby stream, with a small beach.

Facilities

First class toilet facilities and provision for disabled people. Washing machine. Bread, main season. Bar/reception, pool table, library. Snack bar, takeaway (15/5-15/9). A 'meal of the day' can be ordered. Play area. Natural pool for children. Sports field. Basketball. Bicycle hire. Off site: Fishing 200 m. Swimming pool, thermal centre in village 1 km. Nearby medieval, walled town of Ville Franche de Conflent, Grottes des Canalettes, Fort Libena with its many steps are well worth visiting. Organised rafting, canoeing, hydrospeed trips.

Open: 16 December - 25 October.

Directions

Following N116 towards Andorra. At Villef Fanche, turn south, D116, for Vernet-les-Bains. After 5 km. keep right avoiding town. Turn right over bridge towards Sahorre. Immediately turn right, Ave de Saturnin for about 1 km. beyond houses, site signed.

Charges 2007

Per unit incl. 2 persons	€ 12,50 - € 21,50
incl. electricity	€ 15,00 - € 25,00
extra person (over 4 yrs)	€ 1,50 - € 2,50
animal	€ 1,50 - € 2,50

Discounts for weekly stays. Credit cards accepted 15/6-15/9 only. Camping Cheques accepted.

FR66140 Camping les Acacias

Avenue du Général de Gaulle, F-66700 Argelès sur Mer (Pyrénées-Orientales)

Tel: 04 68 81 27 88. Email: campacacias@free.fr

Les Acacias is a simple site but it is an oasis in the midst of the hectic holiday resort of Argelès. There are 85 pitches with 76 used for touring units and 9 with mobile homes to rent. Level and semi-grassy, the pitches have good shade and 6/10A electricity connections are available. You can walk easily to the beach and to bars, shops and restaurants. With everything so easily on hand, who needs a swimming pool?

Facilities

The well equipped toilet block is of traditional design with mostly Turkish toilets. Baby bath. Washing machine. Communal barbecue. Play area for under 5s. Table tennis. Off site: All the delights of Argelès by foot or tourist train. Beach 200 m. Fishing 300 m. Sailing 500 m. Bicycle hire 500 m. Riding 2 km.

Open: 1 May - 30 September.

Directions

From A9 take exit 42 (Perpignan Sud) and follow N114 towards Argelès. At exit 10 follow sign for Pujols, then signs for 'Centre Plage' to Avenue General de Gaulle. Site is on the left between two others, well signed but the entrance is a bit tight. GPS: N42:33.019 E03:02.579

Charges 2006

Per unit incl. 2 persons	€ 13,70 - € 20,20
incl. electricity	€ 17,60 - € 23,70
extra person	€ 4,50 - € 5,80

FR66150 Camping les Criques de Porteils

RD 114, route de Coullioure, F-66701 Argelès sur Mer (Pyrénées-Orientales)

Tel: 04 68 81 12 73. Email: criquesdeporteils@wanadoo.fr

This is an amazing site situated on the cliff top with views across the sea to Argelès, set against a backdrop of mountains and close to Collioure, the artist's paradise. What more could you ask? Under new ownership, the facilities are being renovated and some of the pitches being redesigned for easier access. There are around 275 of varying sizes and shapes due to the nature of the terrain, level in places up and down in others. Most have sea views and 5A electricity available. There are three small coves of grey sand accessed by steep steps (gated).

Facilities

Two renovated toilet blocks, fully equipped with super children's room, all small equipment and colourful. Laundry room with internet point. Motorcaravan service point. Shop. Bar. Restaurant with takeaway. Swimming pool. Play area. Sports field. Off site: Collioure 5 mins.

Open: 1 April - 9 September.

Directions

Exit A9 at Perpigan Sud or Le Boulou. Head for Argelès to pick up signs for 'Collioure par la Corniche'. Watch for site signs coming into a bend as you come down a hill by hotel. GPS: N42:32.000 E03:04.001

Charges 2006

Per unit incl. 2 persons	€ 17,00 - € 31,00
extra person	€ 6,00 - € 8,00
electricity	€ 5,00 - € 7,00

FR66160 Camping la Palmeraie

Boulevard de la Plage, F-66440 Toreilles Plage (Pyrénées-Orientales)

Tel: **04 68 28 20 64**. Email: **info@camping-la-palmeraie.com**

La Palmeraie is a very attractive, top quality campsite situated some 600 metres from the beach at Torreilles-Plage. Arguably the prettiest campsite in the area, there is an abundance of foliage, including a variety of trees and flowering shrubs which provide ample shade – unusual in a situation on the littoral and so close to the sea. The site is a credit to the owners. The 110 touring pitches (out of a total of 240 in all) are generally on the large side. All the facilities, including a pool and sunbathing area, are of a good quality and lend an air of elegance to this excellent campsite.

Facilities

Three well equipped, modern sanitary blocks are traditional in style with modern fittings. Facilities for disabled visitors and children. Laundry facilities. Fridge hire. Shop. Bar, restaurant and takeaway (all open when site is open). Swimming and paddling pools. Play area. Games room. Multisport court. Safety depost. Internet access. Evening entertainment and organised sports activities in July/Aug. Children's club (6-12 yrs). Off site: Beach 600 m. Riding 500 m.

Open: 27 May - 30 September.

Directions

From A9 take exit 41 and follow signs for Canet via D81 and D83. Once on D83 look for signs for Torreilles Plage. Site is on right hand side as you approach from the roundabout on the D83.

Charges 2006

Per unit incl. 2 persons	€ 15,70 - € 24,50
extra person	€ 5,00 - € 7,50
child (3-7 yrs)	€ 4,00 - € 5,50
electricity (5/10A)	€ 3,50 - € 6,60

FR66170 Village Camping Spa Marisol

Boulevard de la Plage, F-66440 Torreilles (Pyrénées-Orientales)

Tel: **04 68 28 04 07**. Email: **marisol@camping-marisol.com**

Good quality sites with direct access to the beach are hard to find and Marisol is a useful option. It is a fairly large site with 377 pitches with a significant number of mobile homes, but with 170 available for touring. These are sandy grass pitches of good size with some shade. All have electricity (10A). There is a beauty centre where you can enjoy a sauna, Turkish or spa bath. This is essentially a 'holiday' site with all the popular facilities and an extensive entertainment programme, fitness courses and children's club throughout the main season.

Facilities

Fully equipped toilet blocks, baby bath. Washing machine. Small supermarket. Bar. TV. Restaurant, takeaway. Heated swimming pool, water slide, children's pool. Play area. Tennis. Archery. Fitness room. Beauty centre. Football, volleyball. Access to path across dunes to sandy beach. Watersports activities. Off site: Sea fishing, watersports. Horse riding, minigolf 0.5 km. Microlights, karting 1.5 km. Bicycle hire 2 km. Golf 10 km. Diving, water skiing 4 km.

Open: 1 April - 30 September.

Directions

From A9 take exit 41 (Perpignan Nord) towards Le Barcarès for 9 km. Then south on D81 towards Canet for 3 km. before turning to Torreilles Plage. Site is signed. GPS: N42:47.059 E03:01.974

Charges 2007

Per unit incl. 2 persons and electricity (10A)	€ 15,00 - € 39,00
extra person (over 4 yrs)	€ 5,30 - € 8,10
child (under 4 yrs)	free - € 5,50

FR66180 Mas Llinas Camping

F-66160 Le Boulou (Pyrénées-Orientales)

Tel: **04 68 83 25 46**. Email: **info@camping-mas-llinas.com**

This is a simple, peaceful and well maintained site with a relaxed feel and helpful, friendly owners. The highest terraces on this campsite have commanding views over the valley and to the surrounding mountains. The roads up to the level, terraced, hillside pitches (100) are paved. Some are large, some grassy and a few hedged for privacy, many with outstanding views and lovely trees (electricity 5/10A). Rock pegs advised. The reception is near the bar/café that serves a very limited range of snacks and some local produce, including the wine of the region.

Facilities

One clean and modern toilet block, the other rather small, basic and cramped. Facilities for disabled campers. Washing machine. Motorcaravan services. Limited bar/café (mid June to end Sept). Bread (July/Aug). Small swimming pool (mid May - Oct). Games room. Electronic games. Torches necessary. Riding. Bicycle hire. Only gas barbecues. Off site: VTT with guide. Fishing 5 km. Golf 25 km. The site is close to the border.

Open: 1 March - 30 November.

Directions

Le Boulou is 26 km. north of Spanish border. South from Perpignan, A9 or N9 to Le Boulou (30 km). Site well signed from town, on northern outskirts, approached via light commercial area. Follow road uphill for about 2 km. GPS: N42:32.50 E02:50.05

Charges 2007

Per person	€ 4,20 - € 5,20
child (under 10 yrs)	€ 2,70
pitch incl. electricity	€ 8,30 - € 11,20

FR66190 Sunêlia les Tropiques

Boulevard de la Méditerranée, F-66440 Torreilles-Plage (Pyrénées-Orientales)

Tel: **04 68 28 05 09**. Email: **contact@camping-les-tropiques.com**

Les Tropiques makes a pleasant holiday venue, only 400 metres from a sandy beach and also boasting two pools. There are 450 pitches with 200 given over to mobile homes and chalets. Pleasant pine and palm trees with other Mediterranean vegetation give shade and provide an attractive environment. Activities are provided for all including a large range of sports, caberets and shows but an identity bracelet for entry to the site is obligatory in high season (small payment required).

Facilities

Modern, fully equipped sanitary facilities, provision for disabled visitors. Launderette. Shop and bar (1/5-15/9), restaurant, takeaway, pizzeria (all 1/6-15/9). Heated pool, all season, another pool (15/5-30/9), paddling pool. Tennis. Archery (1/7-31/8). TV, billiards room. Play area. Disco (every evening), club for 6-12 year olds in July/Aug. Bicycle hire (15/6-15/9). Off site: Windsurf board hire, sea fishing 400 m. Riding 400 m. Microlights, karting 1.5 km. Diving, water-skiing 4 km. Golf 15 km.

Open: 31 March - 7 October.

Directions

From A9 exit Perpignan Nord, follow D83 towards Le Barcarès for 9 km. Take D81 south towards Canet for 3 km. turn left at roundabout for Torreilles-Plage. Site is the last but one on left.

Charges 2007

Per unit incl. 2 persons	
with electricity	€ 17,00 - € 35,50
extra person	€ 3,70 - € 8,20
child (0-13 yrs)	€ 2,50 - € 5,80
Camping Cheques accepted.	

FR66200 Camping les Marsouins

Avenue de la Retirada, F-66702 Argelès-sur-Mer (Pyrénées-Orientales)

Tel: **04 68 81 14 81**. Email: **marsouin@campmed.com**

Les Marsouins is a large site situated on the beach road out of Argelès. There are 587 pitches. The 430 good size, grassy, level pitches, electricity (5A), for touring are divided by hedging and tall trees give some shade. An outdoor entertainment area is located at the entrance beside the bar and restaurant (for high season entertainment). The lagoon style heated pool and paddling pool (no water slides) have ample space for sunbathing. The site is well situated for easy access to the good sandy beach, with activities like windsurfing and sea kayaking possible (free 15/5-30/9).

Facilities

Fully equipped toilet blocks provide facilities for the handicapped. Washing machine and iron. Motorcaravan services. Shop (26/5-8/9). Bar, self-service restaurant (16/6-5/9), takeaway (1/4-30/9). Mini-market (8/6-7/9). Heated swimming pool (15/04-29/9). Large play area. Children's club, organised activities (24/6-1/9). Tennis. Evening entertainment (30/5-30/8). Off site: Beach 800 m. Riding next door. Boat launching 2 km. Golf 7 km.

Open: 9 April - 22 September.

Directions

From A9 autoroute take Perpignan Sud exit. Follow signs for Argelès (RN114) exit junction 10 and follow Pujols at roundabout then Plage Nord at next roundabout. Site is 1.5 km. on left. GPS: N42:33.827 E03:02.044

Charges 2007

Per unit incl. 2 persons	
and 5A electricity	€ 14,00 - € 29,00
with water and drainage	€ 15,50 - € 30,50
extra person (over 5 yrs)	€ 4,00 - € 5,50

FR66210 Chadotel Camping le Roussillon

Chemin de la Mer, F-66750 Saint Cyprien (Pyrénées-Orientales)

Tel: **04 68 21 06 45**. Email: **info@chadotel.com**

This a comfortable site, although perhaps somewhat lacking in character. It is part of the Chadotel Group and has a quiet situation on the edge of St Cyprien village, some 2 km. from the beach. A bus service runs in the main season. The site benefits from having a good sized, traditionally shaped swimming pool, with the added attraction for children of a water slide, and plenty of sunbathing areas for adults. There are 166 pitches with only 25 well-kept, grassy, level touring pitches. Of a good size, they all have 16A electricity.

Facilities

Two toilet blocks (one older but refurbished, one more modern) provide modern facilities including a baby bath, laundry and facilities for disabled visitors. Bar/snack-bar with terrace and entertainment in season. New takeaway. Play area on grass.

Open: 1 April - 24 September.

Directions

From D81 southwards (don't enter St Cyprien Plage), follow signs for Argelès. At roundabout ('Aqualand' signed to the left) turn right towards St Cyprien village. Bear right, site is indicated by large Chadotel sign on the right.

Charges 2006

Per pitch incl. 2 persons	€ 14,50 - € 23,50
incl. electricity	€ 19,00 - € 28,00
extra person	€ 3,80 - € 5,80

(411)

FR66230 Camping Caravaning le Romarin

Route de Sorède, Chemin des Vignes, F-66702 Argelès-sur-Mer (Pyrénées-Orientales)

Tel: **04 68 81 02 63**. Email: **contact@camping-romarin.com**

In an area dominated by 'all-singing, all-dancing' holiday sites, we were pleased to discover, almost by accident, this charming little gem of a site tucked away some 2 km. behind the busy resort of Argelès. Essentially a site for families with younger children, or for adults seeking peace and quiet, it provides 110 good sized touring pitches, with electricity (6-10A) set among pine, eucalyptus, oak and mimosa trees. Ideal for exploring this area, especially the Albères range of Pyrénéen mountains and the ancient city of Perpignan.

Facilities

Good, large toilet block provides a mix of British and Turkish WCs, showers, washbasins in cabins, washing machine. Snack bar (mid June - end Sept). Swimming pool (mid June - mid Sept). Play area. Table tennis. Some traditional (local) family entertainment in high season. Off site: Riding and bicycle hire 2 km. Fishing 4 km. Golf 8 km. Within reach of shops, supermarket (2 km.), all the attractions of Argelès, both village and Plage.

Open: 15 May - 30 September.

Directions

From A9 exit 42 (Perpignan Sud), N114 towards Argelès for 25 km, exit 11a. At roundabout, signed St André, for 300 m. Acute left turn (site signed). After 2 km, at T junction, turn left, D11. Shortly take third left (site signed), follow lane to site.

Charges 2006

Per unit incl. 2 persons	€ 11,00 - € 14,00
extra person	€ 2,00 - € 4,20
child (2-5 yrs)	free - € 2,50
electricity	€ 2,00 - € 3,00

CAMPING LE ROMARIN

Great pleasure in a small camping site, in the middle of olive groves, between the sea and the mountain, you will enjoy your stay in natural surroundings. Welcome to the Romarin

Route de Sorède - Chemin des Vignes - F-66702 Argelès-sur-Mer - France
Tél.: 04 68 81 02 063 - Fax: 04 68 81 57 43
Email: contact@camping-romarin.com - www.camping-romarin-com

FR66220 Camping du Stade

Avenue du 8 Mai 1945, F-66702 Argelès-sur-Mer (Pyrénées-Orientales)

Tel: **04 68 81 04 40**. Email: **info@campingdustade.com**

Quieter and more peaceful family orientated sites are rare in this immediate area, so we were pleasantly surprised to discover one in a pleasant shady setting midway between the village and the beach resort – less than 1 km. from both. The 180 good sized pitches, (most with electricity) are in green surroundings with plenty of shade. This traditionally French campsite, could be a quiet haven for those who want to relax at the end of the day without the distraction of a noisy pool and bar, but who want to be close to all the various attractions offered by this resort.

Facilities

With so much within easy walking distance the site itself has few facilities, but it does have two good quality, part modern, part traditional, well-maintained toilet blocks with good sized showers, washbasins in cabins, etc. Unit for disabled people, facilities for babies, covered dishwashing area and washing machine. Snack-bar and takeaway (high season only). Adventure-style play area. Table tennis. Off site: Beach, shops, bars and restaurants all within walking distance.

Open: 1 April - 30 September.

Directions

From A9 exit 42 (Perpignan Sud) take N114 towards Argelès, then exit 10 for Pujols and Argelès. Follow signs towards Centre, Plage. First roundabout straight on (Ave Molliere). At next small roundabout turn left, site immediately on left.

Charges 2006

Per unit incl. 2 persons and electricity	€ 16,80 - € 22,45
extra person	€ 3,50 - € 5,00
child (0-5 yrs)	€ 2,25 - € 3,20

FR66240 Chadotel Camping le Trivoly

Route des Plages, F-66440 Torreilles-Plage (Pyrénées-Orientales)

Tel: **04 68 28 20 28**. Email: **info@chadotel.com**

The popularity of Torreilles derives mainly from its huge sandy beach and for off-site nightlife, shopping, etc. but for smarter resorts one really needs to visit Le Barcares or Canet a few kilometres distance in either direction. Le Trivoly (a member of the French Chadotel Group) is about 500 m. gentle stroll from the beach, in a fairly tranquil setting. It has 170 good size, well shaded and hedged pitches with electricity (6A) and 100 mobile homes. It perhaps offers a rather more peaceful situation than do the other sites here.

Facilities

Four toilet blocks, although not new, provide modern facilities, including washbasins in (rather small) cabins, and were all clean and well cared for when we visited. Small shop (June- mid Sept). Snack-restaurant and takeaway (June-mid Sept). Reasonably sized pool with water slide and paddling pool. Play area. Bicycle hire. Table tennis. Basketball. Entertainment programme in high season. Off site: Centre Commercial 300 m.

Open: 1 April - 24 September.

Directions

From A9 exit 42 (Perpignan Nord) towards Le Barcarès for 9 km. then turn south on D81 towards Canet. After 3 km. turn left at roundabout, signed Torreilles Plage. Site is on left in 500 m.

Charges 2006

Per unit incl. 2 persons	€ 12,00 - € 23,50
with electricity	€ 16,50 - € 28,00
extra person	€ 5,80
child (under 13 yrs)	€ 3,80

FR66260 Camping la Massane

25 avenue Molière, F-66702 Argelès sur Mer (Pyrénées-Orientales)

Tel: **04 68 81 06 85**. Email: **camping.massane.infonie.fr**

Set a little bit back from the seafront, La Massane is one of the traditional older sites with good views of the Canigou and a pool open for a longer season. With 184 pitches and only 26 taken by mobile homes, it could make a good, quiet and relaxing choice. In July and August it will be a little more hectic (as is the whole resort) with a bar and some family entertainment. Other amenities are within walking distance. Pitches are divided, level and semi-grassed with a mixture of shade from tall trees or shrubs. Electricity (6/10A) is available.

Facilities

Two toilet blocks, one large and modernized with a baby room and facilities for disabled visitors. A smaller, traditional block is used early in the season. Laundry room. Swimming pool (heated April – Sept.) with paddling pool. Shop, bar, takeaway and entertainment July/Aug. only. Play area. Charcoal barbecues not permitted. Off site: Village of Argelès. Beach 1 km. Bicycle hire 1 km. Spain, Collieure and the Pyrénées within driving distance.

Open: 15 March - 15 October.

Directions

From the A9 take exit 42 (Perpignan Sud) and follow N114 for Argelès to exit 10.for Pujols. At first roundabout take 'Centre Plage'. Pass school on left and site is almost immediately on left.
GPS: N42:33.043 E03:01.876

Charges 2006

Per unit incl. 2 persons and electricity	€ 11,00 - € 29,00
extra person	€ 2,50 - € 5,00
child (0-4 yrs)	free - € 2,00

FR66270 Village Camping la Roseraie

Taxo d'Avall, F-66702 Argelès sur Mer (Pyrénées-Orientales)

Tel: **04 68 81 17 03**. Email: **info@camping-la-roseraie.fr**

La Roseraie is a mature, well-run site, popular with both the Dutch and English. Do not be put off by its situation beside the N114. The leisure area beside the entrance screens it with pools, shops, bar and restaurant and is also very attractive looking towards the mountains. Various trees and shrubs give a 'park' like feel and colourful wooden chalets blend in along with mobile homes, many privately owned and very pretty. There are 375 pitches in total with 221 for touring units on level grass and with good shade and 6A electricity.

Facilities

With four toilet blocks the provision is good. Two are modern and larger, two smaller, traditional ones are being updated. Baby bath. Laundry. Shop. Bar. Restaurant and takeaway. Heated swimming pool. Play areas. Minigolf. Children's club (high season). Bicycle hire. Off site: Beach 4 km. Riding 3 km. The Pyrénées, Collioure and Spain all within easy driving distance.

Open: 1 April - 10 October.

Directions

From autoroute take exit 42 (Perpigan Sud) and follow N114 south towards Argelès. Take exit 10 and then Taxo d'Avall road at roundabout, then almost immediately left back on yourself. to site which is approx. 500 m. on the right.

Charges 2006

Per unit incl. 2 persons	€ 13,50 - € 24,00
extra person	€ 2,60 - € 5,30
child (3-7 yrs)	€ 1,50 - € 3,10
electricity (6A)	€ 2,00 - € 4,00

413

FR66290 Camping Club le Floride et l'Embouchure

Route de Saint Laurent, F-66423 Le Barcarès (Pyrénées-Orientales)

Tel: **04 68 86 11 75**. Email: **campingfloride@aol.com**

Essentially a family run enterprise, Le Floride et L'Embouchure is really two sites in one – L'Embouchure the smaller one with direct access to the beach and Le Floride on the opposite side of the fairly busy road into Le Barcarès village. Apart from having some very unusual accommodation to rent (the 'Bungahomes') and a few pitches with their own individual sanitary facility, the sites are fairly unremarkable, albeit within a very friendly family-centred environment, very popular with Dutch visitors. In total there are 632 pitches, all with 10A electricity. The site is relatively inexpensive, especially outside the July/August peak period. It offers a comfortable, if unpretentious, holiday opportunity with reasonably sized pitches (300 for touring units) and ample shade. In the case of L'Embouchure, there is direct access to a popular beach, but Le Floride has the pool complex complete with toboggan.

Facilities

Four fully equipped toilet blocks on Le Floride and two on L'Embouchure where 50 pitches near the beach have individual facilities. Shop, bar, restaurant and takeaway (all 15/6-5/9). Three swimming pools (one heated outside July/Aug). Play area. Entertainment programme (July/Aug). Charcoal barbecues are not permitted. Off site: Fishing 1 km. Riding 1.5 km. Bicycle hire 3 km. Beach 100 m.

Open: 1 April - 30 September.

Directions

From A9 take exit 41 (Perpignan Nord) and follow signs for Canet and Le Barcarès via D83. At J9 follow D81 (Canet) then next left into Le Barcarès Village. Site is 1 km. on the left and right sides of the road.

Charges 2006

Per unit incl. 2 persons and electricity	€ 12,00 - € 33,00
incl. individual sanitary facility	€ 16,00 - € 42,00
extra person	€ 2,50 - € 6,00
child (1-4 yrs)	free - € 3,50

Tel. 0033 (0)4 68 86 11 75
Fax 0033 (0)4 68 86 07 50
www.floride.fr

FR66280 Camping le Palais de la Mer

Avenue de Las Illes, F-66470 Sainte Marie la Mer (Pyrénées-Orientales)

Tel: **04 68 73 07 94**. Email: **contact@palaisdelamer.com**

This is an attractive, typically French campsite, and if you're looking for something different to the usual seaside sites used by British tour operators this could well be of interest. It has a relaxed, informal atmosphere and a very informal layout amongst a variety of trees and flowering shrubs. There is plenty of seclusion, ample shade and easy access direct to the beach along a footpath past a small farm. The facilities of this 181 pitch site (74 are for mobile homes; all have 10A electricity) are functional rather than luxurious, and the pool area near the entrance has a relaxed and comfortable, typically French ambience.

Facilities

Four traditional style toilet blocks are fully equipped. Washing machine. Bar, restaurant and takeaway (July/Aug). Swimming pool. Gym. Large play area. Sports ground. Tennis. Entertainment programmes in high season. Small farm. Fishing. Charcoal barbecues not permitted. Off site: Beach adjacent.

Open: 13 May - 23 September.

Directions

From the A9 take exit 41 and follow signs towards Canet via the D83 and D81 until a roundabout signed Ste Marie la Mer Plage. Turn left into Ste Marie Plage and follow campsite signs.

Charges 2006

Per unit incl. 2 persons and electricity	€ 17,00 - € 31,00
extra person	€ 5,00 - € 7,50
child (0-6 yrs)	€ 3,00 - € 4,50

FR66310 Camping le Rotja

F-66820 Fuilla (Pyrénées-Orientales)

Tel: **04 68 96 52 75**. Email: **campinglerotja.ellenetwim@wanadoo.fr**

La Rotja is a pretty, Dutch-owned site, set up a little valley above the fortified old town of Villefranche-de-Conflent and watched over by the impressive, snow-capped Pic d'Canigou. The older part of the site is semi-wooded with wonderful silver birches, whilst the newer part further up the hill is more open and terraced. There is room for 100 fairly level pitches of which 80 have 6/10A electricity and one can chose shade or not. A small pool at the top of the site is very welcome in high season. Trips are organized into the mountains, along with barbecue evenings. A small bar doubles as reception and a rustic outside area allows 'al fresco' enjoyment of the daily menu. The site has a wonderful situation and whilst having all 'mod cons', the naturalness of the area has been retained. The spa town of Vernet-le-Bains in the next valley is worth visiting, as is the celebrated Fort Libéria, or walk around the walls of Villefranche-de-Conflent or even enjoy a jaunt on the Petit Train Jaune to enjoy the magnificent scenery.

Facilities

Two toilet blocks, both fully equipped. The older one beside the bar area can be heated, a larger, more modern one is in the new area. Facilities for disabled visitors and babies. Bar, outside restaurant (15/5-30/9). Swimming and paddling pools (1/5-30/9). Gas barbecues only. Bicycle hire. Off site: Tennis 100 m. Fishing 300 m. Riding 7 km. Beach 55 km. Rafting, canyoning, hydro-speed and 'parc-aventure' possible with trained guides. Walking, VTT.

Open: 1 April - 31 October.

Directions

Follow the N116 from Perpignan (route to Andorra). After about 50 km. bypass Prades and continue to Villefranche-de-Conflent. Follow around and past it to take left turn signed Fuilla and Sahorre. After 2 km. turn right at village to site.

Charges 2006

per unit incl. 2 persons	€ 13,00 - € 15,40
incl. electricity	€ 15,00 - € 18,00
extra person	€ 2,43 - € 3,20
child (0-6 yrs)	€ 1,60 - € 2,20

CAMPING LE ROTJA

Away from the traffic noise awaits camp site Le Rotja you in the nice Apple Valley

Activities:
- Historical sight seeing
- Hiking
- Mountain biking
- Fishing
- Horse riding
- Rafting
- Crayoning

34, Avenue de la Rotja - 66820 Fuilla
Tél.: 0033 (0) 4 68 96 52 75
Email: camping@camping-lerotja.com
www.camping-lerotja.com

FR66300 Yelloh! Village le Pré Catalan

Route de St Laurent, F-66420 Le Barcarès (Pyrénées-Orientales)

Tel: **04 68 86 12 60**. Email: **info@precatalan.com**

The green foliage from the mixed trees and the flowering shrubs makes the site very attractive and an avenue of palms is particularly spectacular. There has been a camping site on the spot since 1960 but the present owners, the Galidie family, took over in 1982 and the site is now run by their son Francois and his English wife Jenny. With 250 pitches in total, there are 180 taken by mobile homes and chalets, half to let and half privately owned. These are mixed amongst the touring pitches which are on level, sandy ground, clearly divided by hedging and with 10A electricity.

Facilities

Good modern facilities include small showers for children. Laundry. Small shop. Bar, restaurant and takeaway (all season). Heated swimming pool and paddling pool. Excellent play area. Tennis. Archery. Internet access. Library. Activities for children with miniclub and evening entertainment (July/Aug). Only gas barbecues. Off site: Beach 900 m. River fishing 1 km. Riding 1.5 km. Boat launching 3 km. Nearby La Réserve Africaine de Sigean and Le Château de Salses.

Open: 29 April - 16 September.

Directions

From A9 exit 41 (Perpignan Nord), follow signs for Le Barcarès and Canet (D83). At junction 9 take D81 (Canet), then first left to Le Barcarès (D90). Site is on left after 500 m. next to Le California. Follow narrow lane to site entrance. GPS: N42:46.5 E03:01.3

Charges 2006

Per unit incl. 2 persons	€ 12,00 - € 30,00
extra person	€ 4,00 - € 7,50
child (3-6 yrs)	€ 2,00 - € 4,00
electricity	€ 4,00

MAP 15 & 16

Bathed in sunshine from early spring to late autumn surrounded by stunning scenery, cosmopolitan towns and superb sandy beaches, no wonder this is one of France's most sought-after destinations.

THIS SECTION COVERS THE EASTERN COASTAL REGION OF THE MEDITERRANEAN. WE INCLUDE TWO DÉPARTEMENTS FROM THE OFFICIAL REGION OF PROVENCE AND THE REGION OF CÔTE D'AZUR: 13 BOUCHES-DU-RHÔNE, 83 VAR, 06 ALPES-MARITIME

The glittering Côte d'Azur, perhaps better known as the French Riviera, is a beautiful stretch of coast studded with sophisticated towns such as the famous Monte Carlo, Nice, and Cannes, not forgetting the other famous and arguably the most glamorous resort of St Tropez. With its vast expanses of golden sandy beaches and long lazy hours of sunshine, this is a paradise for sun worshippers and beach enthusiasts. It's a spectacular coast of rugged coves, sweeping beaches and warm seas.

The quaint harbours and fishing villages have become chic destinations, now full of pleasure yachts, harbour-side cafés and crowded summertime beaches. Further up in the hills are quieter tiny medieval villages with winding streets and white-walled houses with terracotta roofs, which have attracted artists for many years. In St Paul-de-Vence visitors browse through shops and galleries set on narrow winding cobblestone streets and inland Grasse is the perfume capital of the world, surrounded by the Provencal lavender fields and shady olive groves which pervade the air with a magical scent at certain times of the year.

Places of interest

Aix-en-Provence: old town with 17th-18th century character, Paul Cézanne and Tapestry museums.

Cannes: popular for conventions and festivals, Cannes Film Festival, la Croisette, old city.

Monte Carlo: main city of Monaco, casinos, gardens, Napoleon Museum. motorsport circuit.

Cuisine of the region

Aigo Bouido: garlic and sage soup.

Bouillabaisse: fish soup.

Rouille: an orange coloured sauce with peppers, garlic and saffron.

Bourride: a creamy fish soup.

Pissaladière: Provençal bread dough with onions, anchovies and olives.

Pistou (Soupe au): vegetable soup bound with *pommade*.

Pommade: a thick paste of garlic, basil, cheese and olive oil.

Ratatouille: aubergines, courgettes, onions, garlic, red peppers and tomatoes in olive oil.

Salade Niçoise: tomatoes, beans, potatoes, black olives, anchovy, lettuce, olive oil and tuna fish.

FR06010 Camping Domaine Sainte Madeleine

Route de Moulinet, F-06380 Sospel (Alpes-Maritimes)

Tel: **04 93 04 10 48**. Email: **camp@camping-sainte-madeleine.com**

Domaine Sainte Madeleine is an attractive, peaceful site, with swimming pool, in spectacular mountain scenery. It is about 20 km. inland from Menton, and very near the Italian border. The approach to this site is not for the faint-hearted, once there the effort is worthwhile. Situated on a terraced hillside with mountain views towards Italy, manoeuvring within the site presents no problem as the pitches are on level, well drained grass. The lower ones have shade but those higher up on the hill have none. Electricity is available to 70 of the 90 pitches.

Facilities

Good quality toilet block. Hot water (often only warm) for dishwashing and laundry sinks drawn from single tap. Washing machines. Motorcaravan services. Gas supplies. Bread can be ordered. Swimming pool (140 sq.m. and heated in spring and autumn). Off site: The attractive small town of Sospel is only 4 km. with many restaurants, bars, cafés and shops. Tennis, riding and a centre for mountain biking. Fishing 1 km.

Open: 31 March - 30 September.

Directions

From A8 take Menton exit towards Sospel from where you turn onto the D2566 (route de Moulinet). Site is 4 km. north of Sospel on the left.

Charges 2006

Per unit incl. 2 persons	€ 19,00
extra person	€ 4,00
child (under 6 yrs)	€ 2,40
electricity (10A)	€ 2,90

Less 15% outside July/Aug. No credit cards.

FR06020 Camping le Vallon Rouge

Route de Gréolières, F-06480 La Colle-sur-Loup (Alpes-Maritimes)

Tel: **04 93 32 86 12**. Email: **auvallonrouge@aol.com**

In the valley of the Loup river, a pleasant holidaying area, this small site is close to the Côte d'Azur, but away from all the bustle of the Mediterranean coast. There is the opportunity for total relaxation amongst the cork, oak, pine and mimosa. The three hectare site is quite flat with many Mediterranean umbrella pines for shade, with 103 separated pitches for touring caravans and tents. An average of 80 sq.m. in size, all have electricity, with those in one area also having water and drainage. Some pitches are on the banks of the Loup.

Facilities

Two toilet blocks are kept clean and include washbasins in cubicles and spacious showers. Facilities for disabled people and babies. Laundry areas and washing machines. Small shop. Bar/restaurant and takeaway. New pool complex (1/4-30/9). Playground. Electronic games. Fishing. Only gas barbecues are permitted. Off site: Riding or golf 4 km. Beach, Cros de Cagnes 7 km.

Open: 31 March - 13 October.

Directions

Leave A8 at exit 47 on D6 towards Grasse. Follow signs and site is on the right. Larger units should stop at the top access gate and ask for assistance.

Charges 2006

Per person	€ 3,00 - € 4,30
child (5-18 yrs)	€ 3,00 - € 3,20
pitch incl. electricity	€ 13,20 - € 23,20

Camping Cheques accepted.

FR06030 Camping Caravaning Domaine de la Bergerie

1330 chemin de la Sine, F-06140 Vence (Alpes-Maritimes)

Tel: **04 93 58 09 36**. Email: **info@camping-domainedelabergerie.com**

La Bergerie is a quiet, family owned site, situated in the hills 3 km. from Vence and 10 km. from the sea at Cagnes-sur-Mer. This extensive, natural, lightly wooded site is in a secluded position about 300 m. above sea level. Most of the pitches are shaded and all are of a good size. There are 450 pitches, 300 with electricity (2/5A) and 65 also with water and drainage. Because of the nature of this site, some pitches are a little distance from the toilet blocks. There are no organised activities and definitely no groups allowed.

Facilities

Refurbished toilet blocks, excellent provision for disabled people (pitches near the block are reserved for disabled people). Good shop, small bar/restaurant, takeaway (all 1/5-30/9). Large swimming pool, paddling pool, spacious sunbathing area (1/5-30/9). Playground. Bicycle hire. Table tennis, tennis courts, 12 shaded boules pitches (lit at night) with competitions in season. No barbecues. Off site: Riding 6 km. Fishing 10 km. Golf 12 km. Hourly bus service (excl. Sundays) from site to Vence.

Open: 25 March - 15 October.

Directions

From A8 exit 47 take Cagnes-sur-Mer road towards Vence. Site west of Vence - follow 'toutes directions' around town, join D2210 Grasse road. In 2 km. at roundabout, turn left, follow site signs, 1 km. Site on right in light woodland.
GPS: N43:42.421 E07:05.258

Charges 2006

Per unit incl. 2 persons	€ 14,50 - € 20,00
with electricity	€ 17,50 - € 30,00
extra person	€ 4,90

Camping Cheques accepted.

FR06050 Camping la Vieille Ferme

296 boulevard des Groules, F-06270 Villeneuve-Loubet-Plage (Alpes-Maritimes)

Tel: **04 93 33 41 44**. Email: **vieilleferme@bigfoot.com**

Open all year, in a popular resort area, La Vieille Ferme is a family owned site with good facilities. It has 131 level gravel-based pitches, 106 fully serviced and the majority separated by hedges. Some are only small, simple pitches for little tents. There is also a fully serviced pitch on tarmac for motorhomes. There are special winter rates for long stays with quite a few long stay units on site. The entrance to the site is very colourful with well tended flower beds. English is spoken at reception and the whole place has a very friendly feel to it.

Facilities

Modern, heated, well kept toilet blocks children's toilets, baby room, units for disabled people. Motorcaravan services. Washing machines, dryer. Shop (Easter - Sept). Machine with drinks, sweets, ices in TV room. Gas, bread, milk to order. Refrigerator hire. Swimming pool, children's pool, heated and covered for winter use (closed mid Nov-mid Dec), Jacuzzi. Internet. Games, competitions organised in July/Aug. Off site: Fishing 1 km, golf 2 km.

Open: All year.

Directions

From west, A8, exit 44 Antibes, D35, 3.5 km. Left towards Nice, N7. After 3.5 km. turn left for site between Marine Land and Parc de Vaugrenier. Site is 150 m. on right. Avoid N98 Route du Bord de Mer.

Charges 2006

Per unit incl. 2 persons and electricity (10A)	€ 23,00 - € 34,00
extra person	€ 3,70 - € 5,00
child (under 5 yrs)	€ 2,50 - € 3,00

FR06070 Domaine Naturiste Club Origan

F-06260 Puget-Theniers (Alpes-Maritimes)

Tel: **04 93 05 06 00**. Email: **origan@wanadoo.fr**

Origan is a naturist site set in the mountains behind Nice, at a height of 500 m. The access road is single track and winding with a few passing places, so arrival is not recommended until late afternoon. The site's terrain is fairly wild and the roads stony and it is not suitable for caravans longer than six metres due to the steep slopes, although the site will assist with a 4x4 vehicle if requested. The 100 touring pitches, in three areas, are of irregular size and shape with good views. Electricity connection (6A) is possible on most pitches (by long cable). Member 'France 4 Naturisme'.

Facilities

Sanitary facilities, are clean and of a standard and type associated with most good naturist sites - mostly open plan hot showers. Laundry facilities. Shop (1/6-30/8). Bar/restaurant. Takeaway. Heated swimming pools. Jacuzzi and sauna. Disco. Tennis. Fishing. Bicycle hire. Organised activities for all (high season). Only gas or electric barbecues are permitted. Torches advised. Off site: Nearby town of Puget-Theniers. Steam train.

Open: 15 April - 30 September.

Directions

Heading west on the N202, just past the town of Puget-Theniers, turn right at camp sign at level crossing; site is 1 km.

Charges 2006

Per unit incl. 2 persons	€ 16,00 - € 27,50
incl. electricity	€ 20,00 - € 31,50
extra person	€ 4,00 - € 6,00
Camping Cheques accepted.	

FR06090 Camping Caravaning les Gorges du Loup

965 chemin des Vergers, F-06620 Le Bar sur Loup (Alpes-Maritimes)

Tel: **04 93 42 45 06**. Email: **info@lesgorgesduloup.com**

Les Gorges du Loup is situated on a steep hillside above Grasse. The one kilometre lane which leads to the site is narrow with passing places. The 70 pitches are on level terraces, all with electricity and many have stupendous views. Some pitches are only suitable for tents and the site roads are quite steep. A quiet family site, there is no organised entertainment. Grasse (9 km.) is surrounded by fields of lavender, mimosa and jasmine and has been famous for the manufacture of perfume since the 16th century. The very friendly and enthusiastic owners provide 4x4 assistance.

Facilities

Clean toilet blocks, dishwashing and laundry sinks have only a single hot tap. Washing machine and iron. Reception, small shop, bread. Small bar/restaurant with terrace, takeaway (July/Aug). Swimming pool, small slide, diving board, but no pool for small children. Boules. TV room, board games, library. Children's climbing frame, slide. No charcoal barbecues. Chalets, mobile homes for hire. Off site: Bar-de-Loup with its few shops, restaurants is only a 500 m. walk.

Open: 1 April - 30 September.

Directions

From Grasse, D2085 Nice road. D3 briefly to Châteauneuf Pré du Lac. D2210 to Pont-de-Loup, Vence. Site signed on right. Pass Bar-sur-Loup on left. After sharp right turn, take narrow access road 750 m (passing places). GPS: N43:42.148 E06:59.726

Charges 2006

Per unit incl. 2 persons	€ 14,50 - € 23,80
extra person	€ 4,00
electricity (4/10A)	€ 3,00 - € 4,00
No credit cards.	

FR06080 Camping Caravaning les Cigales

Mobile homes ▶ page 485

505 avenue de la Mer, F-06210 Mandelieu-la-Napoule (Alpes-Maritimes)

Tel: **04 93 49 23 53**. Email: **campingcigales@wanadoo.fr**

It is hard to imagine that such a quiet, peaceful site could be in the middle of such a busy town and so near Cannes. The entrance (easily missed) has large electronic gates that ensure that the site is very secure. There are only 115 pitches (40 mobile homes) so this is quite a small, personal site. There are three pitch sizes, from small ones for tents to pitches for larger units and all have electricity (6A), some fully serviced. All are level with much needed shade in summer, although the sun will get through in winter when it is needed. The site is alongside the Canal de Siagne and for a fee, small boats can be launched at La Napoule, then moored outside the campsite's side gate. Les Cigales is open all year so it is useful for the Monte Carlo Rally, the Cannes Film Festival and the Mimosa Festival, all held out of the main season. English is spoken.

Facilities

Well appointed, clean, heated toilet blocks. Facilities for babies and disabled visitors. Washing machine. Motorcaravan services. Restaurant and takeaway (April - Oct). Heated swimming pool and large sunbathing area (April - Oct). Small play area. Table tennis. Two games machines. Canal fishing. Off site: Beach 800 m. The town is an easy walk. Two golf courses within 1 km. Railway station 1 km. for trains to Cannes, Nice, Antibes, Monte Carlo. Hypermarket 2 km. Bus stop 10 minutes.

Open: All year.

Directions

From A8, exit 40, bear right. Remain in right hand lane, continue right signed Plages-Ports, Creche-Campings. Casino supermarket on right. Continue under motorway to T-junction. Turn left, site is 60 m. on left opposite Chinese restaurant.

Charges 2006

Per person	€ 5,50
child (under 5 yrs)	€ 2,75
tent	€ 11,50 - € 18,50
caravan or motorcaravan	€ 14,00 - € 28,50

FR06100 Camping les Pinèdes

Route du Pont de Pierre, F-06480 La Colle-sur-Loup (Alpes-Maritimes)

Tel: **04 93 32 98 94**. Email: **camplespinedes06@aol.com**

Les Pinèdes is seven kilometres inland from the busy coast, at the centre of all the attractions of the Côte d'Azur, yet far enough away to be a peaceful retreat at the end of a busy day. It is terraced on a wooded hillside where olives and vines used to grow, All the level pitches have electricity (3-10A), most also with water and they are separated by low bushes. Due to the nature of the terrain there are no facilities for wheelchair users. The restaurant at the site entrance has an excellent reputation. In May the evenings are alive with fireflies. A 'Sites et Paysages' member.

Facilities

Refurbished, clean, well maintained toilet blocks, a baby room. Shop, bakery. Bar, restaurant, takeaway. Swimming pool. Two small play areas. Field for volleyball, basketball, football, archery, boules. Entertainment for young and old, July/Aug. Weekly walks in the hills June - September (light breakfast carried by the donkeys). Off site: River fishing 50 m. Village 1 km. with tennis, riding school, leisure park, keep fit course, antiques quarter. St Paul de Vence is 15 minutes away.

Open: 15 March - 30 September.

Directions

From A8 take D2 towards Vence. At Colle sur Loup roundabout take D6 signed Grasse, site on right in 3 km. at large sign after the restaurant entrance.

Charges 2007

Per tent incl. 2 persons	€ 14,00 - € 24,50
caravan or motorcaravan	€ 16,00 - € 27,00
extra person	€ 4,00 - € 5,00
electricity (3-10A)	€ 3,20 - € 4,50

419

FR06120 Camping Green Park

Mobile homes ▶ page 486

159, Vallon des Vaux, F-06800 Cagnes-sur-Mer (Alpes-Maritimes)

Tel: 04 93 07 09 96. Email: **info@greenpark.fr**

Green Park has many facilities of a high standard and the family owners are justifiably proud. Situated just over 4 km. from the beaches at Cagnes-sur-Mer, Green Park is at the centre of the Côte d'Azur. The newer part of the site keeps all the family occupied with activities for children, teenagers and adults, while on the other side of the road is a quieter, traditional site, with limited facilities. There are 78 touring pitches mainly on grass, with electricity and 24 are fully serviced. The site has two swimming pools, one on each side of the quiet road. Green Park is situated in an area which benefits from a 'micro climate', hot during the day but pleasantly cooler at night. There are 67 mobile homes and chalets.

Facilities

All the toilets are modern and mostly British, with facilities for children and disabled visitors (the disabled facilities are superb). Showers and washbasins are modern and kept very clean. Dishwashing and laundry sinks and three washing machines. Bar, restaurant and takeaway (28/4-24/9). Two swimming pools (all season, one heated 5/5-24/9). Internet point. Games room. Electronic barrier (€5 card deposit) and a gate keeper on duty all night. Off site: Beach 4 km. Golf and riding 9 km.

Open: 31 March - 15 October.

Directions

From Aix, A8, exit 47 onto N7 towards Nice. Straight on at traffic lights, by racecourse, for 2 km. Turn left towards Val Fleuri, Av. du Val Fleuri. Over roundabouts to Chemin Vallon des Vaux, site on right 2 km. Avoid the town centre. GPS: N43:41.355 E07:09.409

Charges 2006

Per unit incl. 2 persons	€ 13,00 - € 33,20
extra person	€ 4,50 - € 5,70
child (7-17 yrs)	€ 3,00 - € 4,20
electricity	€ 4,10 - € 5,20

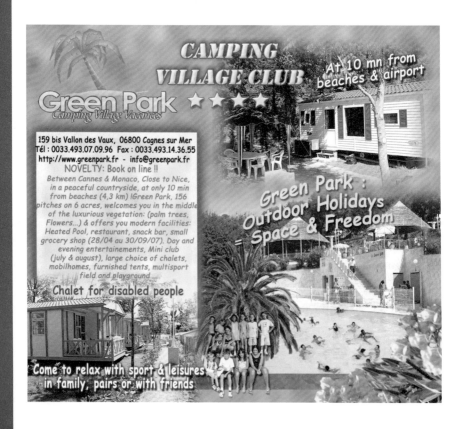

FR06140 Ranch Camping

Chemin Saint Joseph, F-06110 Le Cannet (Alpes-Maritimes)

Tel: **04 93 46 00 11**. Email: **dstallis@free.fr**

Mobile homes ▶ page 486

Ranch Camping is a well run 'French flavoured' site. The ambience here is calm and there is relatively little by way of entertainment or leisure amenities. The site is very well located for the beaches of Cannes just 2 km. away; a regular bus service runs past the site entrance. Despite its urban setting the site enjoys a tranquil position on a wooded hillside. There are 108 touring pitches which are generally level and well shaded, all with 6A electrical connections. The swimming pool is quite small and can be covered in low season. Other leisure facilities are nearby.

Facilities

Principal toilet block has been recently refurbished, whereas the second block is of 'portacabin' style. Both very clean and well maintained. Facilities for disabled people. Washing machines and dryers. Small shop. Swimming pool (covered in low season). Play area. Games room. Mobile homes, rooms to rent. Off site: Beach 2 km. Bus stop at site entrance (regular service to Cannes and beaches). Tennis 200 m. Fishing, bicycle hire 2 km. Golf 4 km.

Open: 1 April - 30 October.

Directions

From A8 exit 42 follow signs to Le Cannet, then L'Aubarède to the right (D809). Follow this road until signs for La Bocca and site is signed from here. GPS: N43:33.883 E06:58.661

Charges 2006

Per unit incl. 1 person	€ 10,00 - € 16,00
extra person	€ 6,00
child (5-10 yrs)	€ 3,00
electricity (6A)	€ 3,00

FR13010 Camping Municipal les Romarins

Route de Saint Remy, F-13520 Maussane (Bouches du Rhône)

Tel: **04 90 54 33 60**. Email: **camping_municipal_maussane.@wannadoo.fr**

A well kept, neat municipal site, Les Romarins has been in the guide for several years and remains popular with readers. Tarmac access roads lead to 145 good sized grassy pitches separated by hedges and bushes, all with electrical connections (4A). The municipal swimming pool (with discounts) is near and shops and restaurants are in the pleasant little town. Les Baux and St Remy-de-Provence are tourist attractions not to be missed, especially St Remy's Roman ruins. Les Romarins is popular and becomes very busy from 1 July - late August.

Facilities

Three toilet blocks, two refurbished, showers (on payment). Baby room, washing machine, laundry and facilities for disabled visitors. An older block open for July and August. Plans for refurbishment. Motorcaravan services. Municipal swimming pool (50 m. from site) free to campers 15/6-31/8. Play area. Free tennis. Reading room. Internet access. Off site: Bicycle hire or golf 1 km. Fishing or riding 3 km.

Open: 15 March - 15 October.

Directions

Site is within the little town of Maussane on the eastern edge.

Charges 2006

Per unit incl. 1 or 2 adults and 1 child	€ 16,00 - € 17,60
extra person	€ 3,70 - € 4,10
child	€ 2,10 - € 2,60
dog	€ 2,50
electricity	€ 3,20

Less 10-20% for longer stays.

FR13040 Camping Monplaisir

Chemin de Monplaisir, F-13210 Saint Rémy-de-Provence (Bouches du Rhône)

Tel: **04 90 92 22 70**. Email: **reception@camping-monplaisir.fr**

Only a kilometre from the centre of St Rémy, in the foothills of the Alpilles mountains, this is one of the most pleasant and well run sites we have come across. Everything about the site is of a high standard and quality. The good impression created by the reception and shop continues through the rest of the site. In all there are 130 level grass pitches with 8 taken by smart mobile homes, with 6A electricity everywhere. Flowering shrubs and greenery abounds, roads are tarmac and all is neat and tidy. There are five toilet blocks strategically placed for all areas, two heated and one larger, but all unisex. The recreation area with a swimming pool (18 x 10 m.), jacuzzi and paddling pool is overlooked by the bar area. Open in July and August, it provides light meals and snacks and some entertainment. St Rémy is a very popular town and the site was full when we visited in mid June.

Facilities	Directions
Five good quality toilet blocks all have some washbasins in cabins. Family rooms and en-suite facilities for disabled people in two. Washing machines. Two motorcaravan service points. Shop with essentials (good cheese and cold meat counter), also providing takeaway pizzas (all season). Bar with snacks (July/Aug). Swimming pool (1/5-3/11). Play area. Table tennis. Boules. Off site: St Rémy 1 km. Les Baux 5 km. Bicycle hire 1 km. Riding 2 km. Fishing 3 km. Golf 15 km.	From St Rémy town centre follow signs for Arles and Nîmes. At roundabout on western side of town take D5 signed Maillane and immediately left by a supermarket. Site is signed and is on the left a little further on.

Open: 1 March - 3 November.

Charges 2007

Per unit incl. 2 persons	€ 13,00 - € 18,20
child (2-7 yrs)	€ 2,20 - € 4,20
electricity	€ 3,40
dog	€ 1,70

CAMPING MONPLAISIR

- Overflowing swimming and paddling pool
- Snack bar in high season, Laundry
- 130 pitches, 2.8 ha of comfort, quietness and garden area
- Boules, children's games, table tennis, grocery
- Chalets & mobile homes to let

CHEMIN MONPLAISIR - F-13210 ST. RÉMY DE PROVENCE - FRANCE
TEL : +33 (0)4 90 92 22 70 - FAX : +33 (0)4 90 92 18 57
www.camping-monplaisir.fr
reception@camping-monplaisir.fr

FR13030 Camping le Nostradamus

Route d'Eyguières, F-13300 Salon-de-Provence (Bouches du Rhône)

Tel: **04 90 56 08 36**. Email: **gilles.nostra@wanadoo.fr**

Only some five kilometres from Salon-de-Provence, near the village of Eyguières, this is a very pleasant campsite with grassy shaded pitches thanks to the many trees which have been preserved here as a result of the imaginative irrigation scheme developed by the owners in the 18th century. The campsite edging the canal was first opened 42 years ago as a farm site but has now been developed to offer 83 hedged pitches including 10 used for mobile homes. There are 20 with full services, the rest having electricity connections (4/6A). This is a family site but having said that the canal is unfenced. You can swim or fish in it or even paddle in the adjoining stream.

Facilities	Directions
One large block with showers and toilets upstairs, and one small toilet block both provide all modern facilities including an en-suite units for babies and children and another for disabled visitors (key). Washing machine (key). Motorcaravan service point. Shop (basic essentials) and bar (1/4-30/10) Takeaway/restaurant (limited in early season). Swimming and paddling pools (15/5-15/9). Play area outside entrance. Table tennis. Volleyball. Petanque. Fishing. Off site: Riding 4 km. Golf 5 km.	From A7 autoroute take exit 26 (Senas) and follow N538 south for 5 km. Then take D175 west and pick up the D17 going south to Salon. Site is at junction of the D17 and CD72 with the entrance off the CD72. From A54 exit 13 go north towards Eyguières and take first right on CD72 (site signed). Entrance is just before the T-junction with the D17.

Open: 1 May - end October.

Charges 2006

Per unit incl. 2 persons	€ 10,00 - € 16,00
child (1-7 yrs)	€ 2,60
electricity	€ 2,90 - € 5,20

FR13050 Camping Mas de Nicolas

Avenue Plaisance du Touch, F-13210 Saint-Rémy-de-Provence (Bouches du Rhône)

Tel: **04 90 92 27 05**. Email: **camping-masdenicolas@nerim.fr**

The site has a very spacious feel to it, due mainly to the central area of gently sloping grass, dotted with shrubs, that is kept clear of pitches and used for leisure and sunbathing. The 140 pitches are separated by hedges, 120 with electricity, water and drainage, and access roads are wide. Some pitches are an irregular shape and some are sloping, but many have views and they are mostly organised into groups of two and four. There is an attractive pool area with new 'Balneotherapie et Remise en form', or as we would call it a spa and gym.

Facilities

Good, modern toilet blocks including baby bathroom. Plans to refurbish one block. Dishwashing and laundry sinks, washing machines. Small bar (May-Sept), occasional Paella evenings. Swimming pool (15/5-15/9). Sauna, steam room, spa bath, gym. Play area. Internet access. Off site: Adjacent municipal gymnasium, tennis, volleyball courts. Bicycle hire, riding 1 km. Fishing 2 km. Golf 15 km. St Rémy has a wide selection of restaurants, Wednesday market.

Open: 1 March - 31 October.

Directions

St Rémy de Provence is located where the D571 from Avignon connects with the D99 Tarascon - Cavaillon road. Site is signed from the village centre on the north side. Leave autoroute A7 at Cavaillon or Avignon-Sud.

Charges 2006

Per unit incl. 2 persons	€ 13,50 - € 17,00
extra person	€ 4,30 - € 5,60
child (under 10 yrs)	€ 2,20 - € 3,50
electricity (6A)	€ 3,00 - € 3,30

FR13060 Camping les Micocouliers

445 Route de Cassoulen, F-13690 Graveson en Provence (Bouches du Rhône)

Tel: **04 90 95 81 49**. Email: **micocou@free.fr**

M. et Mme. Riehl started work at Les Micocouliers in 1997 and they have worked hard to develop a comfortable site. On the outskirts of the town it only some 10 km. from St Rémy and Avignon. A purpose built, terracotta 'house' in a raised position provides all the facilities. The 65 pitches radiate out from here with the pool and entrance to one side. The pitches are on level grass, separated by small bushes, and shade is developing. Electricity connections are possible (4-13A). There are also a few mobile homes. The popular swimming pool is a welcome addition. Bread can be ordered and in July and August a simple snack kiosk operates otherwise Mme. Riehl is most helpful in suggesting places to eat.

Facilities

Unisex facilities in one unit provide toilets and facilities for disabled visitors (by key), another showers and washbasins in cabins and another dishwashing and laundry facilities. Reception and limited shop (July/Aug) are in another. Swimming pool (12 x 8 m. 5/5-15/9). Paddling pool (1/7-31/8). Play area. Table tennis. Volleyball. Off site: Fishing and bicycle hire 1 km. Riding next door. Golf 8 km. Beach 60 km. at Ste Marie de la Mer.

Open: 15 March - 15 October.

Directions

Site is southeast of Graveson. From the N570 at new roundabout take D5 towards St Rémy and Maillane and site is 500 m. on the left.

Charges 2006

Per unit incl. 2 persons	€ 13,50 - € 16,00
extra person	€ 4,40 - € 5,10
child (2-12 yrs)	€ 2,10 - € 4,00
electricity	€ 3,20 - € 5,90

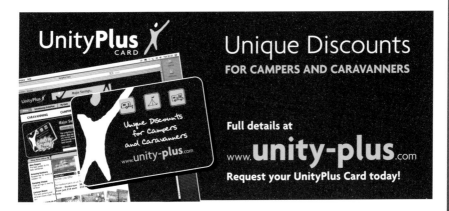

FR83020 Castel Camping Caravaning Esterel

Mobile homes ▶ page 487

Avenue des Golf, F-83530 St Raphaël – Agay (Var)

Tel: **04 94 82 03 28**. Email: **contact@esterel-caravaning.fr**

Esterel is a quality caravan site east of St Raphaël, set among the hills at the back of Agay. The site is 3.5 km. from the sandy beach at Agay where parking is perhaps a little easier than at most places on this coast. It has 230 pitches for tourists, for caravans but not tents, all have electricity and tap, 18 special ones have individual en-suite washroom adjoining. Pitches are on shallow terraces, attractively landscaped with good shade and a variety of flowers, giving a feeling of spaciousness. Some 'maxi-pitches' from 110 to 160 sq.m. are available with 10A electricity. Developed by the Laroche family for over 30 years, the site has an attractive, quiet situation with good views of the Esterel mountains. A member of 'Les Castels' group. Wild boar come to the perimeter fence each evening to be fed by visitors. This is a very good site, well run and organised in a deservedly popular area. A pleasant courtyard area contains the shop and bar, with a terrace overlooking the attractively landscaped (floodlit at night) pool complex.

Facilities

Excellent refurbished, heated toilet blocks. Individual toilet units on18 pitches. Facilities for disabled people. Laundry room. Motorcaravan services. Shop. Gift shop. Takeaway. Bar/restaurant. Five circular swimming pools (two heated), one for adults, one for children, three arranged as a waterfall (1/4-30/9). Disco. Archery. Minigolf. Tennis. Pony rides. Petanque. Squash. Playground. Nursery. Bicycle hire. Organised events in season. No barbecues. Off site: Golf nearby. Trekking by foot, bicycle or by pony in L'Esterel forest park. Fishing, beach 3 km.

Open: 1 April - 6 October.

Directions

From A8, exit Fréjus, follow signs for Valescure, then for Agay, site on left. The road from Agay is the easiest to follow but it is possible to approach from St Raphaël via Valescure.
GPS: N43:27.253 E06:49.945

Charges 2007

Per unit incl. 2 persons,	
standard pitch	€ 23,00 - € 38,00
'maxi' pitch	€ 28,00 - € 47,00
deluxe pitch	€ 32,00 - € 51,00
extra person	€ 8,50
child (1-7 yrs)	€ 6,50

FR83100 Camping de la Plage

Route National 98, F-83310 Grimaud (Var)

Tel: **04 94 56 31 15**. Email: **campingplagegrimaud@wanadoo.fr**

A site on the beach is always in great demand, and Camping de la Plage is no exception, consequently it becomes very crowded. The site is divided into two parts by the N98 although a dangerous crossing is avoided by an underpass. The pitches away from the beach will be the more peaceful. They are mostly of a good size, with the ones over the road having more grass and more shade. There is some traffic noise on the pitches close to the busy road. All pitches have electricity (2-10A) but long leads may be required.

Facilities

Three toilet blocks of varying quality but well equipped and clean. Baby bath. Large supermarket (all season). Bar, restaurant, takeaway (from May). Tennis. Small play area. Off site: Bicycle hire 2 km. Golf and riding 3 km. Boat hire nearby.

Open: Two weeks before Easter - 10 October.

Directions

Site is on N98 main coast road about 6 km. southwest of Ste Maxime. Take care – road is very busy in main season. GPS: N43:16.913 E06:35.159

Charges 2006

Per unit with 2 persons	€ 21,00 - € 25,00
extra person	€ 5,50 - € 6,50
electricity (2-10A)	€ 3,80 - € 8,50

FR83010 Camping Caravaning les Pins Parasols

Route de Bagnols, F-83600 Fréjus (Var)

Tel: **04 94 40 88 43**. Email: **lespinsparasols@wanadoo.fr**

Not everyone likes very big sites and Les Pins Parasols with its 189 pitches is of a comfortable size which is quite easy to walk around. It is family owned and run. Although on very slightly undulating ground, virtually all the pitches (all have electricity) are levelled or terraced and separated by hedges or bushes with pine trees for shade. There are 48 pitches equipped with their own fully enclosed, sanitary unit, with WC, washbasin, hot shower and dishwashing sink. These pitches naturally cost more but may well be of interest to those seeking extra comfort. The nearest beach is the once very long Fréjus-Plage (5.5 km.) now reduced a little by the new marina, and adjoins St Raphaël.

Facilities

Average quality toilet blocks (one heated) providing facilities for disabled people. Small shop with reasonable stocks, restaurant, takeaway (both 15/4-30/9). General room, TV. Swimming pool, attractive rock backdrop, separate long slide with landing pool, small paddling pool (heated). Half-court tennis. Off site: Bicycle hire or riding 2 km. Fishing 6 km. Golf 10 km. Bus from the gate into Fréjus 5 km. Beach 6 km.

Open: 31 March - 29 September.

Directions

From A8 take exit 38 for Fréjus Est. Turn right immediately on leaving pay booths on a small road which leads across to D4, then right again and under 1 km. to site.

Charges 2006

Per unit incl. 2 persons and electricity	€ 17,40 - € 25,50
pitch with sanitary unit	€ 22,00 - € 31,80
extra person	€ 4,40 - € 6,00
child (under 7 yrs)	€ 2,90 - € 3,65

LES PINS PARASOLS CAMPING CARAVANNING ★★★★NN
ROUTE DE BAGNOLS - F-83600 FRÉJUS
Telephone 0033 494.40.88.43
SWIMMING POOL
Supermarket - Snackbar - Individual washing cabins and hot water in all sanitary facilities - Separated pitches (80-100m2) all with electricity. Pitches with individual sanitary facilities (shower, washbasin, sink with hot water, WC) - Children's playground and solarium - Caravan pitches - Water points - Mini-tennis
SUN AND SHADE near the beaches
Fax : 0033 494.40.81.99
Email : lespinsparasols@wanadoo.fr
Internet : www.lespinsparasols.com

FR83600 Sunêlia Holiday Green

Route de Bagnols, F-83600 Fréjus (Var)

Tel: **04 94 19 88 30**. Email: **info@holiday-green.com**

Holiday Green is seven kilometres inland from Fréjus. It is a large, modern campsite with a fantastic view of the red massif of Esterelle – very impressive as you arrive. The site has been developed on a hillside, by reception at the top of hill is a large Californian style heated swimming pool and many other facilities. The rest of the site is terraced into the hillside and almost completely hidden in the 15 hectares of pine woods which absorbs about 500 mobile homes and some 135 touring pitches. Sloping in parts, there is plenty of shade and electricity (6/13A) available.

Facilities

Modern toilet facilities include good hot showers. Laundry. Shopping centre. Bar, restaurant, fast food. Sound proof disco. Swimming pool. Three tennis courts. Archery. Petanque. All open all season. Excursions on foot, on horse-back and on mountain bikes (to hire) offering the chance to explore the countryside. Entertainment programme of dances, concerts and festivals. Playground. Children's club (July/Aug). No charcoal barbecues. Off site: Bus route outside entrance. Beach 8 km. Golf 8 km.

Open: 30 March - 30 September.

Directions

From A8 autoroute exit 38 follow signs for Bagnols-en-Forêt about 2 km. back over the autoroute, and the site is clearly signed at roundabout. GPS: N43:29.138 E06:43.047

Charges 2006

Per unit incl. 2 persons	€ 25,00 - € 45,00
extra person	€ 6,00 - € 9,00
child (under 6 yrs)	€ 4,00 - € 6,00
animal	€ 2,00 - € 3,00

FR83030 Camping Caravaning Leï Suves

Quartier du Blavet, F-83520 Roquebrune-sur-Argens (Var)

Tel: 04 94 45 43 95. Email: camping.lei.suves@wanadoo.fr

Mobile homes ▶ page 487

This quiet, pretty site is a few kilometres inland from the coast, two kilometres north of the N7. Close to the unusual Roquebrune rock, it is within easy reach of St Tropez, Ste Maxime, St Raphaël and Cannes. The site entrance is appealing – wide and spacious, with a large bank of well tended flowers. Mainly on a gently sloping hillside, the 310 pitches are terraced with shade provided by the many cork trees which give the site its name. All pitches have electricity and access to water. A pleasant pool area is beside the bar/restaurant and entertainment area. It is possible to walk in the surrounding woods as long as there is no fire alert. A good number of the pitches are used for mobile homes.

Facilities

Modern, well kept toilet blocks include washing machines, facilities for disabled visitors. Shop. Good sized swimming pool, paddling pool. Bar, terrace, snack bar, takeaway (all 1/4-30/9). Outdoor stage near the bar for evening entertainment, high season. Excellent play area. Table tennis, tennis, sports area. Internet terminal. Only gas barbecues. Off site: Bus stop at site entrance. Riding 1 km. Fishing 3 km. Bicycle hire 5 km. Golf 7 km. Beach at St Aygulf 15 km.

Open: 31 March - 14 October.

Directions

Leave autoroute at Le Muy and take N7 towards St Raphaël. Turn left at roundabout onto D7 heading north signed La Boverie (site also signed). Site on right in 2 km. GPS: N43:28.677 E06:38.324

Charges 2007

Per unit incl. 2 persons	€ 19,00 - € 32,50
incl. 3 persons	€ 21,00 - € 34,50
extra person	€ 4,50 - € 7,30
electricity	€ 4,50

Camping Cheques accepted.

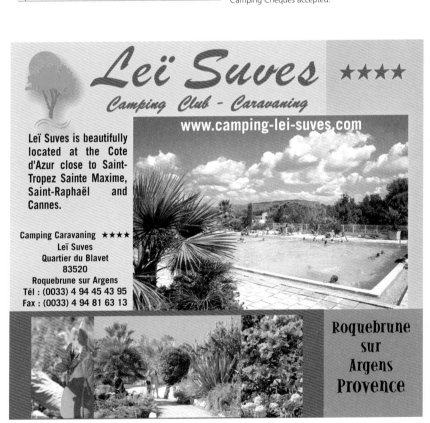

Leï Suves is beautifully located at the Cote d'Azur close to Saint-Tropez Sainte Maxime, Saint-Raphaël and Cannes.

Camping Caravaning ★★★★
Leï Suves
Quartier du Blavet
83520
Roquebrune sur Argens
Tél : (0033) 4 94 45 43 95
Fax : (0033) 4 94 81 63 13

www.camping-lei-suves.com

Roquebrune
sur
Argens
Provence

FR83040 Camping Club la Bastiane

1056, chemin de Suvières, F-83480 Puget-sur-Argens (Var)

Tel: **04 94 55 55 94**. Email: **info@labastiane.com**

With a shady woodland setting, La Bastiane is a well established site with good amenities, well located for exploring the Cote d'Azur and with easy access to nearby beaches. There are 180 pitches here of which 100 are reserved for touring. They are generally of a good size and are all supplied with electrical connections (6A). The terrain is somewhat undulating but most of the pitches are on level terraces. There is a good swimming pool and a range of amenities including a shop, bar and restaurant. The site becomes lively in peak season with a range of activities including sports tournaments, discos, a children's club and excursions to nearby places of interest such as Monaco and the Gorges de Verdon.

Facilities

Four toilet blocks, three of modern construction, one refurbished. Facilities for disabled visitors. Washing machines, dryers. Shop. Bar. Takeaway. Restaurant. Heated swimming pool. Tennis. Multisport terrain. Children's club. Play area. Games/TV room. Bicycle hire. Evening entertainment in peak season. Excursion programme. Only electric barbecues. One dog only. Mobile homes and chalets for rent. Off site: Beach 7 km. Lake beach 8 km. Riding 500 m. Fishing 3 km. Golf 9 km.

Open: 24 March - 21 October.

Directions

Leave A8 at exit 37 (Puget), take right turn at first roundabout (signed Roquebrune), join N7. Turn right, first traffic lights (200 m), then left at T-junction. Site signed from here, on the right 2.5 km. from the motorway.

Charges 2006

Per unit incl. 2 persons,	
electricity	€ 15,34 - € 31,84
extra person	€ 6,20
child (3-13 yrs)	€ 4,10
pet (max. 1)	€ 3,50

Sea Sun Smile

La Bastiane Camping & bungalow ★★★

Heated Swimming pool 25°

35th Anniversary

Between Cannes and St Tropez - A few steps from the big blue
Book on line : **www.labastiane.com** - Tel.: 00.33.494.555.594

FR83260 Camping Château de l'Eouvière

Route de Tavernes, F-83670 Montmeyan (Var)

Tel: **04 94 80 75 54**. Email: **contact@leouviere.com**

This spacious new site is in the grounds of an 18th century château, close to the magnificent hill village of Montmeyan. The swimming pool, bar, restaurant which are in front of the château, have lovely views over the valley and mountains beyond. Many of the terraced pitches, mostly behind the château, have magnificent views. The 80 large touring pitches are part grassy, part stony with varying amounts of shade from mature trees, all have electricity points and most have water nearby. This is a quieter site for those seeking the 'real' France.

Facilities

Main refurbished toilet block has all the necessary facilities including those for disabled visitors. Washing machine, iron. Bar (15/4-15/10), restaurant (15/6-15/10), small shop (1/7-31/8). Swimming pool, sunbathing area. Small play area, paddling pool (some distance from the pool). Entertainment and children's activities in high season. Virtually soundproof disco in the cellars of château. Off site: Montmeyan 1 km. Beach at Lake Quinson (7 km). Other lakes, watersports. Gorges du Verdon. Many interesting towns with their markets and museums.

Open: 15 April - 15 October.

Directions

Leave A8 autoroute at St Maximin and take D560 to Barjols, then D71 to Montmeyan. At roundabout on entering village, take D13 southeast signed Cotignac and site entrance is very shortly on the right.

Charges 2007

Per person	€ 6,00 - € 7,00
child (under 7 yrs)	€ 4,00 - € 5,00
pitch	€ 6,00 - € 9,00
electricity	€ 4,00

FR83050 Camping Résidence du Campeur

D7 (B.P. 12), F-83371 Saint Aygulf (Var)

Tel: 04 94 81 01 59. Email: info@residence-campeur.com

This excellent site near the Côte d'Azur will take you away from all the bustle of the Mediterranean coast. Spread out over ten hectares, there are separate areas for mobile homes and touring caravans and tents, with pitches arranged along avenues. The touring pitches average 100 sq.m. in size, have electricity connections and private sanitary facilities. Unfortunately washbasins double as dishwashing sinks. The bar/restaurant is surrounded by a shady terrace, whilst friendly staff provide an excellent service. A pleasant pool complex is available for those who wish to stay on site instead of going swimming in the nearby lake or from the Mediterranean beaches. Activities are organised daily during the summer season and the site has it's own open air cinema.

Facilities

Private toilet blocks are cleaned at regular intervals and include a washbasin, shower and WC. Laundry area with washing machines. Well stocked supermarket. Bar/restaurant. Takeaway. Good pool complex (1/4-30/9). Three tennis courts. Minigolf. Volleyball. Only gas or electric barbecues are permitted. Off site: Riding, golf and bicycle hire nearby. Beach and St Aygulf 2.5 km. Water skiing nearby.

Open: 31 March - 30 September.

Directions

Leave A8 at Le Muy exit (no. 36) on N555 towards Draguignan then onto the N7 towards Fréjus. Turn right on D7 signed St Aygulf and site is on the right about 2.5 km. before the town.

Charges 2006

Per unit	€ 26,15 - € 43,60

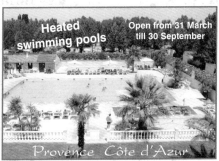
FR83130 Camping le Beau Vezé

Route de la Moutonne, F-83320 Carqueiranne (Var)

Tel: 04 94 57 65 30. Email: info@camping-beauveze.com

Le Beau Vezé is a quiet site, some way inland from the busy resort of Hyères. The owner tries to keep it as a family site with its quiet position, although the superb beaches and hectic coastal areas are within easy reach. On a steep hillside it has terraced pitches and a plateau with more pitches on the top. The 150 pitches are well shaded but unfortunately some will be rather difficult to manoeuvre onto due to over-hanging trees and could be difficult for motorcaravans. There is some road noise on the lower pitches.

Facilities

Reasonable standard sanitary blocks two heated, although maintenance may be variable. Some showers with washbasin. Baby room. Washing machines. Bar/restaurant, takeaway. Bread. Medium sized pool, paddling pool. Play area. Minigolf, table tennis, volleyball, boules, tennis. Bicycle hire. Jetski hire. Walking tours, visits to vineyard. Evening entertainment in restaurant. Off site: Fishing, bicycle hire 2 km. Riding 4 km. The lovely old town of Hyères is only 8 km.

Open: 15 May - 15 September.

Directions

From A57 take exit for Toulon Est and follow D559 between Carqueiranne and Le Pradet. Take D76 northwards signed La Moutonne and site is signed on right of D76.

Charges 2006

Per unit incl. 2 persons	€ 27,00
extra person	€ 6,30
child (under 10 yrs)	€ 4,60
electricity (6A)	€ 4,00
animal	€ 2,50

Camping Cheques accepted.

429

FR83060 Camping Caravaning de la Baume

Mobile homes ▶ page 487

Route de Bagnols, F-83618 Fréjus (Var)

Tel: 04 94 19 88 88. Email: reception@labaume-lapalmeraie.com

La Baume is large, busy site about 5.5 km. from the long sandy beach of Fréjus-Plage, with its fine and varied selection of swimming pools many people do not bother to make the trip. The pools with their palm trees are remarkable for their size and variety (water slides, etc.) – the very large 'feature' pool a highlight. The site has nearly 250 adequate size, fully serviced pitches, with some separators and most have shade. Although tents are accepted, the site concentrates mainly on caravanning. It becomes full in season but one section, with unmarked pitches, is not reserved. Adjoining La Baume is its sister site La Palmeraie, containing self-catering accommodation, its own landscaped pool and providing some entertainment to supplement that at La Baume. There are 500 large pitches with mains sewerage for mobile homes. La Baume's convenient location has its 'downside' as there is some traffic noise from the nearby autoroute – somewhat obtrusive at first but we soon failed to notice it. A popular site with tour operators. An indoor pool and an aquatic play area were added in 2006.

Facilities

Seven refurbished toilet blocks. Supermarket, several shops. Bar, terrace overlooking pools, TV. Restaurant, takeaway. Five swimming pools (heated all season, two covered, plus steam room and jacuzzi). Fitness centre. Tennis. Archery (July/Aug). Organised events, daytime and evening entertainment, some English. Amphitheatre. Discos daily in season. Children's club (all season). Off site: Bus to Fréjus passes gate. Riding 2 km. Fishing 3 km. Golf 5 km. Beach 5 km.

Open: 1 April - 30 September, with full services

Directions

From west, A8, exit 37 Fréjus, take N7 southwest, Frejus, 4 km, turn left on D4. Site 3 km. From east, A8, exit 38 Fréjus, turn right immediately on small road marked Musée, shortly turn right D4. Site is 3 km. GPS: N43:27.992 E06:43.396

Charges 2007

Per unit incl. 2 persons, 6A electricity, water and drainage	€ 18,00 - € 39,00
extra person	€ 4,00 - € 10,00
child (under 7 yrs)	free - € 6,00
dog	€ 4,00 - € 5,00
car	€ 4,00 - € 5,00

Min. stay for motorhomes 3 nights. Large units should book.

FR83110 Camping de la Baie

Boulevard Pasteur, B.P. 12, F-83240 Cavalaire-sur-Mer (Var)

Tel: 04 94 64 08 15. Email: campbaie@club-internet.com

This busy site is only a short walk from the main street of the popular holiday resort of Cavalaire with it's harbour, restaurants and shops. A long, sandy beach runs right round the bay and there are plenty of watersport activities nearby. The site is only 400 metres from the beach, very well positioned for a family holiday. The 253 individual touring pitches are on slightly sloping, sandy ground with terracing and good access roads, and all have electricity hook-ups (10A). Trees give plenty of shade. The remaining 190 pitches are used for mobile homes and chalets. English is spoken.

Facilities

Four main modern toilet blocks include washbasins in cabins, and four smaller units have open washbasins behind. Toilets are mainly British style, with some Turkish. Launderette. Small shop. Restaurant. Bar. Takeaway. Entertainment with dance evenings. Kidney-shaped pool with sunbathing terrace (Easter - end Nov), small paddling pool and new jacuzzi. Playground. Table tennis. TV room. Exchange facilities. Off site: Bicycle hire 200 m. Beach 400 m. Golf 10 km. Riding 12 km.

Open: 15 March - 15 November.

Directions

Take D559 to Cavalaire-sur-Mer (not Cavalière, some 4 km. away). Site is signed by yellow signs from the main street, some 400 m. north of the harbour. GPS: N43:10.176 E06:31.816

Charges 2006

Per unit incl. 1-3 persons	€ 22,00 - € 38,00
extra person	€ 6,00 - € 9,70
child (under 10 yrs)	€ 3,00 - € 5,40
electricity	€ 4,50
animal	€ 2,50 - € 3,80

La Baume ★★★★
Camping - Caravaning

La Palmeraie ★★
Résidence de Tourisme

Fréjus Côte d'Azur

...ated sanitary blocks, marked-out ...ches, 6 swimming pools, 2 covered ...ated swimming pool, 6 water-slides. ...kilometers from the sandy beaches of ...jus and Saint Raphaël.

On going entertainment
Cabaret, Show, Disco,
Children's club during the season

Le Sud Grandeur Nature

Heated swimming pool

1 covered
heated
swimming-pool

Provençal chalet,
Mobil-homes 4/6 persons
and Appartementen 6 of 10 persons
for hire

...ecial rates in low season

Rue des Combattants d'Afrique du Nord   83618 FREJUS Cedex
Tel : + 33 494 19 88 88   -   Fax: + 33 494 19 83 50
www.labaume-lapalmeraie.com   E-mail : reception@labaume-lapalmeraie.com

FR83070 Caravaning L'Etoile d'Argens

Mobile homes ▶ page 488

F-83370 Saint Aygulf (Var)

Tel: **04 94 81 01 41**. Email: **info@etoiledargens.com**

First impressions of L'Etoile d'Argens are of space, cleanliness and calm. This is a site run with families in mind and many of the activities are free, making for a good value holiday. There are 493 level, fully serviced, grass pitches (265 for touring units – 10A electricity), separated by hedges, with five sizes, ranging from 50 sq.m. (for small tents) to 250 sq.m. mainly with good shade. The pool and bar area is attractively landscaped with olive and palm trees on beautifully kept grass. Two heated pools (one for adults, one for children) – both very much with families in mind. Reception staff are very friendly and English is spoken. The exceptionally large pitches could easily take two caravans and cars or one family could have a very spacious plot with a garden like atmosphere. The river runs alongside the site with a free boat service to the beach (15/6-15/9). This is a good family site for the summer but also good in low season for a quiet stay in a superb location with excellent pitches. Tour operators take 85 pitches and there are 175 mobile homes but for a large site it is unusually calm and peaceful even in July.

Facilities

Over 20, well kept, small toilet blocks. Supermarket and gas supplies. Bar, restaurant, pizzeria, takeaway. Two adult pools (heated 1/4-20/6), paddling pool, Jacuzzi, solarium. Floodlit tennis with coaching. Minigolf (both free in low season). Aerobics. Archery (July/Aug). Football and swimming lessons. Boules. Good play area. Children's entertainment (July/Aug). Activity programme with games, dances and escorted walking trips to the surrounding hills within 3 km. Off site: Golf and riding 2 km. Beach 3.5 km.

Open: 1 April - 30 September, with all services.

Directions

From A8 exit 36, take N7, Le Muy, Fréjus. After 8 km. at roundabout take D7 signed Roquebrune, St Aygulf. In 9.5 km. (after roundabout) turn left signed Fréjus. Site signed. Ignore width and height limit signs as site is before limit (500 m). GPS: N43:24.947 E06:42.326

Charges 2006

Per tent pitch (100 sq.m.) with electricity and 2 persons	€ 20,00 - € 45,00
'comfort' pitch (130 sq.m.) incl. 3 persons with water and drainage	€ 32,00 - € 56,00
'luxury' pitch incl. 4 persons 180 sq.m	€ 38,00 - € 64,00
extra person	€ 5,00 - € 8,00
child (under 7 yrs)	€ 4,00 - € 6,00

FR83120 Camp du Domaine

La Favière B.P. 207, F-83230 Bormes-les-Mimosas (Var)

Tel: **04 94 71 03 12**. Email: **mail@campdudomaine.com**

Camp du Domaine, three kilometres south of Le Lavandou, is a large, attractive beach-side site with 1,200 pitches set in 45 hectares of pine woods, although surprisingly it does not give the impression of being so big. Most pitches are reasonably level and 800 have 10A electricity. The most popular pitches are at the beach, but the ones furthest away are, on the whole, larger and have more shade amongst the trees, although many of them are more suitable for tents. The beach is the attraction however and everyone tries to get close. American motorhomes not accepted.

Facilities

Ten modern, well used but clean toilet blocks. Mostly Turkish WCs. Facilities for disabled visitors (but steep steps). Children and baby room. Washing machines. Fridges to hire. Well stocked supermarket, bars, pizzeria (all open all season). Excellent play area. Boats, pedaloes for hire. Wide range of watersports. Games, competitions July/Aug. Children's club. Tennis, table tennis, minigolf. Multisports courts. Barbecues are strictly forbidden. Dogs are not accepted 3/7-31/8. Off site: Bicycle hire 500 m. Riding or golf 15 km.

Open: 1 April - 31 October.

Directions

Just outside and to west of Le Lavandou, at roundabout, turn off D559 towards the sea on road signed Favière. After some 2 km. turn left at site signs. GPS: N43:07.080 E06:21.076

Charges 2006

Per unit incl. 2 persons	€ 18,00 - € 27,00
with electricity and water	€ 26,50 - € 33,00
extra person	€ 5,40 - € 7,10
child (under 7 yrs)	€ 1,00 - € 3,50

2007

L'Etoile d'Argens

✸ ✸ ✸ ✸ *Camping-Caravaning*

ESE COMMUNICATION - DRAGUIGNAN - 04 94 67 06 00

www.etoiledargens.com

E-mail : info@etoiledargens.com

83370 St Aygulf - Tél. +33 4 94 81 01 41

FR83080 Au Paradis des Campeurs

La Gaillarde-Plage, F-83380 Les Issambres (Var)

Tel: **04 94 96 93 55**

Family owned and run, it now has 180 pitches, all with 6A electricity and 132 with water tap and drain. The original pitches vary in size and shape but all are satisfactory and most have some shade. The newer pitches are all large but at present have little shade although trees and bushes have been planted and shade is developing. There is no entertainment which gives peaceful nights. The gates are surveyed by TV (especially the beach gate) and a security man patrols all day. The site has become popular, it is essential to book for June, July and August. Having direct access to a sandy beach (via an underpass) and being so well maintained are just two of the reasons which make Au Paradis so popular.

Facilities

Excellent, refurbished, well maintained toilet blocks, facilities for babies, children, shower at suitable height. En-suite for disabled visitors. Washing machines, dryer. Motorcaravan services. Shop, restaurant, takeaway service, open all season. TV room. Internet and WiFi. Excellent play areas, catering for the under and over 5s, top quality safety bases. Boules. Car wash area. Off site: Bicycle hire 2.5 km. Riding 3 km. Golf 6 km.

Open: 28 March - 16 October.

Directions

Site is signed from N98 coast road at La Gaillarde, 2 km. south of St Aygulf.
GPS: N43:21.956 E06:42.738

Charges 2006

Per unit incl. 2 persons	€ 14,00 - € 22,00
with water and drainage	€ 16,00 - € 26,00
extra person	€ 6,00
child (under 4 yrs)	€ 3,00
electricity (6A)	€ 3,50

FR83160 Parc Camping les Cigales

721 chemin du Jas de la Paro, F-83490 Le Muy (Var)

Tel: **04 94 45 12 08**. Email: **contact@les-cigales.com**

Parc Les Cigales is a pleasant site benefiting from the shady environment of cork umbrella pines, further enhanced by olives, palm trees and colourful shrubs. The terrain is typical of the area with rough, sloped and stony, dry ground but the pitches are of a good size, terraced where necessary and nestling amongst the trees. There are 163 pitches in total with 35 mobile homes to rent. The restaurant/bar area overlooks the attractive pool complex including a children's pool with sloping beach effect. Convenient for the autoroute, this is a spacious family site away from the coast, to be enjoyed.

Facilities

Modern sanitary blocks of varying size, facilities for disabled people. Laundry area, washing machines, ironing boards. Shop (1/5-30/8). Restaurant/bar, patio. Heated pool complex, sunbathing area. Adventure play area. Survival courses. Multisport area. Trampoline. Riding. Canoeing. Hanggliding. Evening entertainment in season, disco twice weekly, daytime activities for children and senior citizens. Internet. No charcoal barbecues. Off site: Le Muy 2 km. Sunday market. Fishing 2 km. Golf 10 km. On bus route, or train at Les Arcs (8 km).

Open: 1 April - 31 October.

Directions

From A8, Le Muy exit, site is signed (west of Le Muy on N7, 2 km). It is necessary to cross the dual-carriageway as you approach the toll booth from Le Muy. Site entrance is well signed.
GPS: N43:27.492 E06:32.728

Charges 2006

Per unit incl. 2 persons	€ 12,00 - € 28,00
extra person	€ 3,00 - € 8,00
child (under 12 yrs)	free - € 4,00
electricity (6-10A)	€ 3,00 - € 5,00
Less 5% for stays over 3 weeks.	

FR83140 Camping les Lacs du Verdon

Domaine de Roquelande, F-83630 Régusse (Var)

Tel: **04 94 70 17 95**. Email: **info@lacs-verdon.com**

In beautiful countryside and within easy reach of the Grand Canyon du Verdon and its nearby lakes, this site is only 90 minutes from Cannes. This bustling and possible noisy campsite is suitable for active families and teenagers. The 30 acre wooded park is divided in two by a minor road. The 480 very stony, but level pitches (rock pegs advised) are marked and separated by stones and trees. 130 pitches are for tourists, many an irregular shape, but all are of average size with 10A electricity (long leads may be necessary). The part across the road is used mainly for mobile homes but has some pitches for tourers, mostly at the far end. There are toilet blocks close by but the pitches are a long way from all the other site facilities. The main site is closer to all the activities. Tour operators and mobile homes, for hire and privately owned, take up nearly three quarters of this site.

Facilities

Modernised toilet blocks have mainly have British style WCs and some washbasins in cubicles. Laundry and dishwashing facilities. Motorcaravan service point. Shop. Bar. Restaurant and pizzeria. TV and teenage games. Discos, dances and theme nights. Excellent swimming pool/paddling pool complex. Artificial grass tennis courts. Volleyball, table tennis and boules. Bicycle hire. Playground. Entertainment programme. Only electric barbecues are permitted. Off site: Régusse 2.5 km. Aups 7 km. Riding 10 km. Fishing, beach, sailing and windsurfing at Saint Croix 15 km.

Open: 29 April - 23 September.

Directions

Leave A8 motorway at St Maximin and take the D560 northeast (Barjols). At Barjols turn left on D71 (Montmeyan), turn right on D30 (Regusse) and follow site signs. GPS: N43:39.612 E06:09.064

Charges 2006

Per pitch incl. 1 or 2 persons	€ 18,00 - € 27,00
extra person	€ 5,00 - € 7,50
child (3-7 yrs)	€ 4,00 - € 6,00
electricity (10A)	€ 4,00
dog	€ 3,00
Camping Cheques accepted.	

FR83180 Camping Caravaning les Rives de l'Agay

Avenue du Gratadis, F-83530 Agay (Var)

Tel: **04 94 82 02 74**. Email: **reception@lesrivesdlagay.fr**

The wide sweep of the beach at Agay is only a 500 metre walk from Les Rives de l'Agay, a quiet site run by the third generation of the Nore family. There are a total of 135 shaded touring pitches, a little smaller than most, but all have 6A electricity. There are also 36 mobile homes. The river runs alongside the site on its way to the sea. This site provides a real taste of France with no entertainment and quiet nights, although trains can be heard during the day.

Facilities

The toilet blocks can be heated and include washbasins in cabins and baby baths. Two washing machines, laundry and dishwashing sinks. Unit for disabled visitors. Well stocked shop. Bar with snacks and takeaway (both 1/4-15/9). Swimming pool. Play area. Fishing. Off site: Beach 500 m. Bicycle hire 1 km. Riding 3 km. Golf 6 km. Agay has bars and restaurants and Wednesday markets. Trains and buses from Agay for Monte Carlo and St Raphael.

Open: 1 March - 2 November.

Directions

From the N98 in Agay take the D100 northwest. Site is 1 km. (on a bad bend). GPS: N43:26.050 E06:51.163

Charges 2006

Per pitch low season incl. 2 persons	€ 15,20
high season incl. 3 persons	€ 31,00
extra person (over 3 yrs)	€ 4,00 - € 5,00
child under 3 yrs	€ 2,00
electricity (6A)	€ 3,20

FR83170 Camping Domaine de la Bergerie

Mobile homes ▶ page 488

Vallée du Fournel, route du Col du Bougnon, F-83520 Roquebrune-sur-Argens (Var)

Tel: **04 98 11 45 45**. Email: **info@domainelabergerie.com**

This excellent site near the Côte d'Azur will take you away from all the bustle of the Mediterranean to total relaxation amongst the cork, oak, pine and mimosa. The 60 hectare site is quite spread out with semi-landscaped areas for mobile homes and, grassy avenues of 200 separated pitches for touring caravans and tents. All pitches average over 80 sq.m. and have electricity, with those in one area also having water and drainage. The restaurant/bar, a converted farm building, is surrounded by shady patios, whilst inside it oozes character with high beams and archways leading to intimate corners. Activities are organised daily and, in the evening, shows, cabarets, discos, cinema, karaoke and dancing at the amphitheatre prove popular (possibly until midnight). A superb new pool complex supplements the original pool adding more outdoor pools with slides and a river feature, an indoor pool and a fitness centre with jacuzzi, sauna, massage and gym.

Facilities

Four toilet blocks (two refurbished) are kept clean and include washbasins in cubicles, facilities for disabled people and babies. Supermarket. Bar/restaurant. Takeaway. Pool complex (1/4-30/9) with indoor pool and fitness centre (body building, sauna, gym, etc). Tennis courts. Archery. Roller skating. Minigolf. Mini-farm for children. Fishing. Only gas barbecues are permitted. Off site: Riding or golf 4 km. Bicycle hire 7 km. Beach, St Aygulf or Ste Maxime 7 km. Water skiing and rock climbing nearby.

Open: 27 April - 30 September.
Mobile homes 15 February - 15 November.

Directions

Leave A8 at Le Muy exit on N7 towards Fréjus. Proceed for 9 km. then right onto D7 signed St Aygulf. Continue for 8 km. and then right at roundabout on D8; site is on the right. GPS: N43:24.547 E06:40.481

Charges 2006

Per unit incl. 2 persons and electricity (5A)	€ 17,00 - € 39,00
3 persons and electricity, water and drainage	€ 22,50 - € 41,00
extra person	€ 4,00 - € 7,30
child (under 7 yrs)	€ 3,00 - € 5,70
electricity (10A)	€ 1,80 - € 2,80

Check real time availability and at-the-gate prices...

www.**alanrogers**.com

F-83520 Roquebrune-sur-Argens (Var)
Tel: 04 94 45 71 25. Email: info@camping-les-pecheurs.com

Les Pêcheurs will appeal to families who appreciate natural surroundings together with many activities, cultural and sporting. Interspersed with mobile homes, the 150 good size, touring pitches (electricity 6/10A) are separated by trees or flowering bushes The Provencal style buildings are delightful, especially the bar, restaurant and games room, with its terrace down to the river and the site's own canoe station (locked gate). Across the road is a lake used exclusively for water skiing with a sandy beach, a restaurant and minigolf. This popular Riviera site has some new spa facilities including steam pool, a sauna and a Turkish bath. Developed over three generations by the Simoncini family, this peaceful, friendly site is set in more than four hectares of mature and well shaded countryside at the foot of the Roquebrune Rock. Activities include climbing the 'Rock' with a guide. We became more and more intrigued with stories about the Rock and the Holy Hole, the Three Crosses and the Hermit all call for further exploration which reception staff are happy to arrange, likewise trips to Monte Carlo, Ventimigua (Italy) and the Gorges du Verdon, etc. The medieval village of Roquebrune is within walking distance.

Facilities	Directions
Modern, refurbished, well designed toilet blocks, baby baths, facilities for disabled visitors. Washing machines. Shop. Bar, restaurant, games room (all open all season). Heated outdoor swimming pool (all season), separate paddling pool (lifeguard in high season), ice cream bar. Spa facilities. Playing field. Fishing. Canoeing, water skiing. Activities for children and adults (high season), visits to local wine caves. Rafting and diving schools. Only gas or electric barbecues. Off site: Bicycle hire 1 km. Riding 4 km. Golf 5 km. (reduced fees).	From A8 take Le Muy exit, follow N7 towards Fréjus for 13 km. bypassing Le Muy. After crossing A8, turn right at roundabout towards Roquebrune sur Argens. Site is on left after 1 km. just before bridge over river.

Open: 31 March - 30 September.

Charges 2007

Per unit incl. 2 persons	€ 17,00 - € 32,50
incl. 3 persons	€ 19,00 - € 34,50
electricity (6/10A)	€ 4,20 - € 5,20
dog (max. 1)	€ 3,00

Camping Cheques accepted.

FR83190 Camping la Presqu'île de Giens

Mobile homes ▶ page 488

153, route de la Madraque-Giens, F-83400 Hyères (Var)

Tel: **04 94 58 22 86**. Email: **info@camping-giens.com**

La Presqu'île de Giens a good family campsite at the southern end of the Giens peninsula. The site is well maintained and extends over 17 acres of undulating terrain. Of the site's 460 pitches, 170 are reserved for touring. These are generally of a good size and well shaded – there is a separate area of smaller pitches reserved for tents. Electrical connections (6/16A) are available on all pitches. In high season this becomes a lively site with a well-run children's club (small charge) and an evening entertainment programme including discos, singers and dancers. Although there is no swimming pool, the site lies between two sandy beaches, and in July and August a free shuttle bus runs to the nearest, 800 metres away. Excursions are organised to the adjacent islands of Porquerolles, Port Cros and Le Levant. There is a beautiful walking trail set out all around the peninsula.

Facilities

Five toilet blocks, two very good new ones (heated in low season), and three refurbished with a higher proportion of 'Turkish' style toilets. All clean and well maintained. Facilities for disabled visitors. Washing machines and dryers. Shop. Bar, restaurant, takeaway food. Play area. Children's club. Evening entertainment. Sports pitch. Diving classes. Sports tournaments. Excursion programme. Only electric barbecues are permitted. Off site: Beach 800 m. Fishing 1 km. Bicycle hire 3 km. Riding 10 km. Golf 15 km. 'Golden islands' excursions.

Open: 31 March - 30 September.

Directions

From the west, leave A57 at Hyères and continue to Hyères on the A570. At Hyères follow signs to Giens - Les Iles (D97). At end of this road, after 11 km. turn right towards Madraque. Site on left side of road. GPS: N43:02.458 E06:08.583

Charges 2006

Per unit incl. 2 persons	€ 12,80 - € 19,20
extra person	€ 3,90 - € 6,10
child (0-5 yrs)	free
electricity	€ 4,50 - € 5,70
pet	€ 2,60

Camping Cheques accepted.

FR83220 Camping Caravaning Cros de Mouton

Mobile homes ▶ page 489

P.O. 116, F-83240 Cavalaire-sur-Mer (Var)

Tel: **04 94 64 10 87**. Email: **campingcrosdemouton@wanadoo.fr**

Cros de Mouton is a reasonably priced campsite in a popular area. High on a steep hillside, about 2 km. from Cavalaire and its popular beaches, the site is a calm oasis away from the coast. There are stunning views of the bay but, due to the nature of the terrain, some of the site roads are very steep – the higher pitches with the best views are especially so. There are 199 large, terraced pitches (electricity 10A) under cork trees with 73 suitable only for tents with parking close by, and 80 for touring caravans. English is spoken by the welcoming and helpful owners. The restaurant terrace and the pools share the wonderful view of Cavalaire and the bay. Olivier and Andre are happy to take your caravan up with their 4x4 Jeep if you are worried.

Facilities

Clean, well maintained toilet blocks have all the usual facilities including those for disabled customers (although site is perhaps a little steep in places for wheelchairs). Washing machine. Shop. Bar/restaurant, reasonably priced meals, takeaways. Swimming and paddling pools with lots of sun beds on the terrace and small bar for snacks and cold drinks. Small play area. Games room.
Off site: Beach 1.5 km. Bicycle hire 1.5 km. Riding 3 km. Golf 15 km.

Open: 15 March - 31 October.

Directions

Take the D559 to Cavalaire-sur-Mer (not Cavalière 4 km. away). Site is about 1.5 km. north of the town, very well signed from the centre.

Charges 2006

Per person	€ 6,00 - € 7,30
child (under 7 yrs)	€ 4,10
pitch	€ 6,00 - € 7,30
electricity (10A)	€ 4,10
dog	free - € 2,00

Camping Cheques accepted.

tel: 00 333 59 59 03 59 *kawan-villages.com*

Mediterranean East

439

FR83210 Yelloh! Village les Tournels

Route de Camarat, F-83350 Ramatuelle (Var)

Tel: **04 94 55 90 90**. Email: **info@tournels.com**

Les Tournels is a large site set on a hillside and pitches have panoramic views of the Gulf of St Tropez and Pampelonne beach. The hillside is covered in parasol pines and old olive trees. The pitches are reasonably level, shady, variable size, most with electricity (long leads). The swimming pool, play area, shop and bar maybe some distance away. Recent additions include a superb new spa centre with gym, sauna and Jacuzzi with an excellent pool alongside, all reserved for over 18s, and a new restaurant with a large terrace. Competitions and shows for adults and children in July/Aug.

Facilities

Well equipped toilet blocks, some heated, baby baths, children's WCs, facilities for disabled visitors. Washing, drying machines, refrigerators to rent. Bar/restaurant (1/4-15/10). Takeaway. Bar, disco away from most pitches. Restaurant. Large heated swimming pool 1/4-20/10. Fitness centre and pool. Good quality play area. Boules. Archery. Miniclub. Only gas barbecues. Off site: Shopping centre 500 m. Golf 6 km. Beach 1.5 km.

Open: All year excl. 11 January - 28 February.

Directions

From A8 exit 36 take D25 to Ste Maxime, then D98 towards St Tropez. On outskirts of St Tropez, take D93 to Ramatuelle. Site is signed on left in 9 km. GPS: N43:12.315 E06:39.043

Charges 2006

Per unit incl. 2 persons	
with electricity and water	€ 22,00 - € 38,00
extra person	€ 5,50 - € 7,80
child (2-7 yrs)	free - € 3,90

FR83230 Domaine du Colombier

Route de Bagnols en Forêt, 1052 rue des Combattants d'AFN, F-83600 Fréjus (Var)

Tel: **04 94 51 56 01**. Email: **info@domaine-du-colombier.com**

Domaine du Colombier is a busy site alongside a main road, some pitches will have some road noise. The majority are down a hillside and pine trees help to deaden the noise. The 408 variable size, level, terraced pitches (268 for touring) with 40 fully serviced, all have electricity. The sunny pool area and snack bar are a long way from many pitches, at the bottom of the site. New planting of attractive trees and shrubs has taken place with gazebos being provided on many pitches to provide shade.

Facilities

Well maintained, fully equipped toilet blocks (two heated), baby rooms, units for people in wheelchairs. Laundry. Well stocked shop. Bar/restaurant, takeaway. Snack bar (from 1/6). Underground disco. Large heated swimming pool, paddling pool. Internet. Two excellent play areas. Games room, miniclub room. Half court tennis. Boules. No barbecues, communal provided. Off site: Bus passes gate.

Open: 8 March - 1 October.

Directions

From A8 exit 38, follow D4 for Fréjus. Site is on left, well signed. GPS: N43:26.750 E06:43.636

Charges guide

Per unit incl. 2 or 3 persons	€ 19,00 - € 43,00
extra person	€ 6,00 - € 7,50
child (under 10 yrs)	€ 4,00 - € 5,50
Camping Cheques accepted.	

kawan-villages.com **tel: 00 333 59 59 03 59**

FR83240 Camping Caravaning Moulin des Iscles

Quartier La Valette, F-83520 Roquebrune-sur-Argens (Var)

Tel: **04 94 45 70 74**. Email: **moulin.iscles@wanadoo.fr**

Moulin des Iscles is a small, pretty site beside the river Argens with access to the river in places for fishing, canoeing and swimming with some sought after pitches overlooking the river. The 90 grassy, level pitches have water and electricity (6A) and a mixture of trees provides natural shade. There is a security barrier which is closed at night. This is a quiet site with little entertainment, but a nice restaurant. Handicapped visitors are made very welcome. It is a real campsite not a 'camping village'.

Facilities

Fully equipped toilet block, plus small block near entrance, ramped access for disabled visitors. Some Turkish style toilets. Washbasins have cold water. Baby bath and changing facilities. Washing machine. Restaurant, home cooked dish-of-the-day. Well stocked shop. Library - some English books. TV, pool table, table tennis. Play area, minigolf, boules all outside the barrier. Internet terminal. Canoeing possible. Off site: Riding and golf 4 km. Bicycle hire 1 km. (cycle way to St Aygulf). Beach 9 km.

Open: 1 April - 30 September.

Directions

From A8, exit Le Muy, follow N7 towards Fréjus for 13 km. Cross over A8 and turn right at roundabout through Roquebrune sur Argens towards St Aygulf for 1 km. Site signed on left. Follow private unmade road for 500 m. GPS: N43:26.708 E06:39.470

Charges 2006

Per unit incl. 2 or 3 persons	€ 19,50
extra person	€ 3,20
electricity	€ 2,70
Camping Cheques accepted.	

FR83250 Camping Douce Quiétude

3435 boulevard Jacques Baudino, F-83700 St Raphaël (Var)

Tel: **04 94 44 30 00**. Email: **sunelia@douce-quietude.com**

Douce Quiétude is five kilometres from the beaches at Saint Raphaël and Agay but is quietly situated at the foot of the Estérel massif. There are 400 pitches, only 70 of these are for touring set in pleasant pine woodland or shaded, green areas. The pitches are of a comfortable size, separated by bushes and trees with electricity (6A), water, drainage and telephone/TV points provided. This mature site offers a wide range of services and facilities complete with a pool complex. It can be busy in the main season yet is relaxed and spacious.

Facilities

Fully equipped modern toilet blocks, facilities for babies and disabled visitors. Launderette. Bar, restaurant, takeaway, pizzeria (3/4-3/9). Shop. Three swimming pools (two heated), water slide, Jacuzzi. Play area. Children's club, activities for teenagers (all July/Aug). Sports area. Games room. Tennis. Minigolf. Archery. Fitness centre, sauna. Evening entertainment (July/Aug). Mountain bike hire. Only gas barbecues. Off site: Bus route 1 km. Golf and riding 2 km. Windsurf hire and sea fishing 5 km.

Open: 3 April - 2 October.

Directions

From A8 exit 38 (Fréjus/St Raphaël) take D100, signed Valescure then Agay. Follow site signs (round the back of Fréjus/St Raphaël). Access via N98 coast road turning north at Agay on D100. Pass Esterel Camping. Site signed. GPS: N43:26.836 E06:48.360

Charges 2006

Per unit incl. 2 persons and electricity	€ 25,00 - € 46,00
extra person	€ 5,00 - € 9,00

Camping Cheques accepted.

tel: 00 333 59 59 03 59 *kawan-villages.com*

FR83290 Camping de Saint Aygulf Plage

270, avenue Salvarelli, F-83370 St Aygulf-Plage (Var)

Tel: **04 94 17 62 49**. Email: **info@camping-cote-azur.com**

This is a large, well run and self-sufficient campsite with a range of good facilities and direct access to the beach. The pitches here are well marked, flat and arranged in long rows, many with good shade from the pine trees. There are 1,100 in total, with 700 for touring units and the remainder used for mobile homes and chalets. Electricity is available on 500 touring pitches. Although there is no swimming pool on site, the direct access to the beach makes this is a fine family holidaying campsite.

Facilities

Four large toilet blocks provide good, clean facilities. No facilities for disabled visitors. Laundry facilities. Supermarket. Bakery. Two restaurants. Bar with stage for discos and entertainmanet. Pizzeria and takeaways. Multi-sports court. Play areas. Boules. First aid. Caravan storage. Beach. Only gas and electric barbecues are permitted. Off site: Bicycle hire 100 m. Riding 1 km. Golf 6 km.

Open: 1 May - 19 September
(chalets, mobile homes 29 March - 25 October).

Directions

From A8 take exits for Puget or Fréjus and RN7 to Fréjus town. Follow signs to sea front and join RN98. Saint Aygulf is 2 km. towards St Tropez. Site signed and is behind Hotel Van der Valk. GPS: N43:23.574 E06:43.608

Charges 2006

Per unit incl. 2 persons	€ 9,50 - € 25,50
incl. electricity	€ 15,00 - € 29,50
extra person	€ 3,00 - € 7,50

FR83300 Camping Clos Sainte Thérèse

Route de Bandol, F-83270 St Cyr-sur-Mer (Var)

Tel: **00 33 4 94 32 12 21**. Email: **camping@clos-therese.com**

This is a very attractive, family run campsite set in hilly terrain four kilometres from the beaches of Saint Cyr. The terraced pitches are level, some with sea views, the friendly owners offering a tractor service if required. There is a good shade from pines, olives, almonds and evergreen oaks. There are 86 pitches for touring units, all with electricity and 26 for chalets or mobile homes. The landscaped pool complex is pretty and well kept, with a small slide, Jacuzzi and a separate paddling pool. This is a friendly, small site, ideal for couples of families with younger children.

Facilities

Clean, well maintained toilet facilities. Fridge hire. Shop (from 1/5). Bar, restaurant (15/6-15/9). Swimming pools (one heated), children's pool. Games room. Table tennis. TV room and library. Boules. Play area. Activities in high season. Off site: Golf course (9 and 18 holes, driving range), tennis courts opposite site. Bicycle hire 2 km. Fishing 4 km. Riding 8 km. Beach 4 km.

Open: 1 April - 1 October.

Directions

From A50 take D559 to Saint Cyr. Continue towards Bandol and site is 3 km. on the left.

Charges 2006

Per unit incl. 2 persons	€ 14,00 - € 20,00
extra person	€ 3,20 - € 4,80
child (3-7 yrs)	€ 2,10 - € 3,10
electricity	€ 2,70 - € 4,80

Camping Cheques accepted.

441

FR83310 Camping l'Argentière

D48 chemin de l'Argentiere, F-83310 Cogolin (Var)

Tel: **04 94 54 63 63**. Email: **campinglargentiere@wanadoo.fr**

This little jewel of a site is in a pleasant setting and the intervening wooded area seems to give it sufficient screening to make the campsite itself quite peaceful. It is only 5 km. from the beach at Gogolin or St Tropez, so its position is handy for one of the showplaces of the Riviera, but away from the hustle and bustle of the beach resorts. There are 150 touring pitches (out of 238 with the others used for mobile homes to rent). Of a good size, all have electricity (3-10A) although long leads may be necessary.

Facilities

Two of three toilet blocks are near the touring pitches and are well kept and clean. Washbasins have warm water (some in cabins) with hot water for dishwashing and laundry. Washing machines (near site entrance). Water has to be taken from the sanitary block. Large swimming pool beside an attractive terrace bar serving snacks. Table tennis. Play equipment. Barbecues are not permitted. Off site: Shops close. Fishing, bicycle hire and riding 2 km. Golf 5 km.

Open: 1 April - 30 September.

Directions

From the A8 (Aix en Provence - Cannes) take exit 36 (Le Muy), then, D25 to Ste Maxime and the coast road N98 towards St Tropez. After Grimaud keep following signs for Cogolin. When near that village follow D48 towards St Maur-en-Collobrière, then signs to site in the suburb of L'Argentière. GPS: N43:15.365 E06:30.744

Charges 2006

Per unit incl. 2 persons	€ 14,00 - € 24,00
extra person	€ 3,00 - € 4,00
electricity (3-10A)	€ 2,00 - € 6,00

FR83320 Campasun Parc Mogador

167 chemin de Beaucours, F-83110 Sanary sur Mer (Var)

Tel: **04 94 74 53 16**. Email: **mogador@campasun.com / campasun@free.fr**

This site in the Mediterranean countryside is very much geared for family holidays with children. Some 20 minutes on foot from the beach, the site has a very large and well kept pool area and a stage for entertainment. Somewhat smaller than other sites of this type, there are 180 good sized pitches (160 for touring units). The ground is mainly level, if rather stony and sandy. Variable shade is available and all pitches have 10A electricity. There are plans to enlarge some of the smaller, 80 sq.m. pitches. The attractive pool, is surrounded by ample paved sunbathing areas.

Facilities

Two large, super de-luxe toilet blocks, one including washbasins and showers in cabins. The high-tech toilets are automatically cleaned and disinfected after every use. Laundry. Motorcaravan services. Restaurant with varied menu (15/5-30/10), also snacks, pizzas and takeaway. TV room. Swimming pool, solarium. Boules. Miniclub and evening entertainment in season. Dogs are not accepted. Off site: Beach 800m. Golf 6 km. Fishing 800 m.

Open: 1 May - 30 October.

Directions

Take Bandol exit 12 from A50 and head for Six Fours on the N 559. Arriving at Sanary-sur-Mer turn left towards Beaucours and site is on left after 100 m.

Charges 2006

Per unit incl. 2 persons and electricity (6A)	€ 27,00 - € 48,00
extra person	€ 5,00 - € 7,00
child (1-7 yrs)	€ 4,00 - € 6,00

FR83340 Camping Bonporteau

RD559 B.P. 18, F-83240 Cavalaire sur Mer (Var)

Tel: **04 94 64 03 24**. Email: **contact@bonporteau.fr**

This terraced site is situated northeast of and above the pleasant and popular holiday resort of Cavalaire where there is a harbour, restaurants and shops. A long, sandy beach runs right round the bay and there are plenty of watersport activities nearby. The site is only 200 metres from the beach, very well positioned for a family holiday, and only a short walk from a very good hypermarket. The 170 individual touring pitches are on sloping, sandy ground with terracing and good access roads, and all have electricity hook-ups (10A). The remaining 70 pitches are for mobile homes and chalets.

Facilities

Three main toilet blocks are modern and include washbasins in cabins, Toilets are mainly British style. Launderette. Small shop. Small but attractive, restaurant (1/4-30/9). Bar. Takeaway. Entertainment with dance evenings. Swimming pool (15/3-30/9) and small paddling pool. Playground. TV and games room. Off site: Beach 200 m. Bicycle hire 800 m. Riding 2 km. Golf 20 km.

Open: 15 March - 15 October.

Directions

Take D559 to Cavalaire-sur-Mer (not Cavalière, some 4 km. away). Site is signed by yellow signs from the main road before entering the town.

Charges 2006

Per unit incl. 1-3 persons	€ 19,00 - € 36,50
incl. services	€ 25,00 - € 52,85
extra person	€ 5,00 - € 9,00
child	€ 2,50 - € 4,50

FR83350 Sélection Camping

12 boulevard de la Mer B.P. 88, F-83420 La Croix Valmer Plage (Var)

Tel: **04 94 55 10 30**. Email: **camping-selection@wanadoo.fr**

This site is only a short walk from the main street of the pleasant and popular holiday resort of La Croix Valmer where there is a harbour, restaurants and shops. There are plenty of watersport activities nearby A sandy beach is only 400 metres from the site, which is a good choice for a family holiday. The 150 individual touring pitches are on sloping, sandy ground with terracing and good access roads, All have electricity hook-ups (10A). There are a further 60 pitches used for mobile homes and chalets. Trees have grown well to give plenty of shade.

Facilities

Three main toilet blocks include washbasins in cabins. Toilets are mainly British style, with some Turkish. Launderette. Shop. Attractive, terraced restaurant (all season), bar and takeaway (form 1/5). Kidney-shaped pool with sunbathing terrace (1/5-1/10) and small paddling pool. Some evening entertainment during July/Aug. Playground. TV in bar. Dogs are not accepted in July/Aug. Only gas or electric barbecues permitted. Off site: Beach 400 m. Bicycle hire 200 m. Riding 1 km. Golf 19 km.

Open: 15 March - 15 October.

Directions

From the A8 (Aix-en-Provence - Fréjus) take exit 36 (Le Muy), then D25 towards Ste Maxime and then N98 towards St Tropez. At roundabout turn right following signs 'Sélection'.
GPS: N43:11.664 E06:33.308

Charges 2006

Per unit incl. 1-3 persons	€ 22,00 - € 31,50
extra person	€ 6,20 - € 9,50
child (under 7 yrs)	€ 3,00 - € 5,50
electricity (120A)	€ 5,00

FR83370 Camping le Fréjus

Route de Bagnols, F-83600 Fréjus (Var)

Tel: **04 94 19 94 60**. Email: **contact@lefrejus.com**

Set on a hillside away from busy Fréjus, this attractively terraced site was developed over 35 years from a farm into a modern, pleasant campsite where there is a warm and genuine welcome. Divided into slightly sloping terraces, its 190 rather small pitches enjoy good shade from trees and have access to 4A electricity. In high season one terrace is reserved as a simple camping area for young people (reservation not required). Whether you choose to drive, walk or cycle, there is plenty of wonderful scenery to discover in the immediate vicinity, whilst not far away beautiful beaches can be enjoyed.

Facilities

Three clean and well positioned toilet blocks have mostly British style WCs and washbasins in cubicles. Baby bath. Laundry facilities. Well stocked shop in high season, bread available from bar at other times. Bar (1/5-31/8) with reasonably priced takeaway service. Swimming pool (15 x 10 m.) and paddling pool (1/5-31/8). Play area. Sports court. Fridge hire. Barbecues are not permitted. Off site: Shops and a restaurant 500 m. Shopping centre Fréjus 6 km. Bicycle hire 3 km. Fishing 6 km. Riding 2 km. Beach and water based activities 6 km.

Open: All year excl. 16 December - 15 January.

Directions

From the A8 (Aix-en-Provence - Nice) take exit 38 onto D4 towards Fréjus. Site lies along this road on the right. GPS: N43:27.877 E06:43.451

Charges 2006

Per unit incl. 2 persons and electricity (6A)	€ 16,00 - € 29,50
extra person	€ 4,50 - € 6,60
child (2-7 yrs)	€ 2,40 - € 3,10

FR83420 Parc et Plage

28 rue des Langoustiers, L'Ayguade, F-83400 Hyeres Les Palmiers (Var)

Tel: **04 94 66 66 77**. Email: **contact@parc-plage.com**

FR83410 Camping Club le Ruou

Les Esparrus RD 560, F-83690 Villecroze-Les Grottes (Var)

Tel: **04 94 70 67 70.** Email: **camping.lervou@wanadoo.fr**

This is a family oriented site in the Provencal countryside, very much geared for family holidays with children. Some 45 minutes by car from the coast at Fréjus, the site has a large and well kept pool area and a mobile stage for entertainment. Smaller than some other sites of this type, there are 110 good sized pitches (52 for touring units). On mainly terraced, rather stony, ground with good shade, all have 6/10A electricity. Some of the pitches for caravans are along a steep path but there is a 4x4 available to assist. The attractive pool complex with three slides is surrounded by a sunbathing area and some shade. Although Le Ruou has all the facilities, activities and entertainment expected of a holiday site, the atmosphere is very relaxed and much less frenzied than some similar sites. Outdoor activities, such as canoeing or wild water rafting are personally arranged for you by the campsite owner.

Facilities

One new super de-luxe toilet block includes washbasins in cabins. Facilities for babies and disabled visitors. Laundry facilities. Snacks and takeaway (15/6-31/8). The main building houses a bar and entertainment room with TV. Area for shows, cabarets, etc. with mobile stage. Two swimming pools. Riding. Tennis. Boules. Miniclub for children and evening entertainment in season.
Off site: Beach 30 km. Riding and bicycle hire 5 km. Fishing 10 km. Golf 17 km.

Open: 1 April - 30 October.

Directions

Directions: Villecroze-les-Grottes is northwest of Fréjus. From the A8 (Toulon - Mandelieu-la-Napoule) take exit 13 onto the N7 towards Le Muy. At Les Arcs turn left on D955 (Draguignan), then onto D557 to Villecroze. Site is on the left side of this road. GPS: N43:33.207 E06:17.879

Charges 2006

Per unit incl. 2 persons	€ 13,00 - € 21,00
extra person	€ 3,00 - € 5,00
child (2-9 yrs)	€ 2,00 - € 4,00
electricity (6/10A)	€ 2,00 - € 3,00

FR83440 Domaine de la Malissonne

F-83740 La Cadière d'Azur (Var)

Tel: **04 94 90 10 60.** Email: **info@domainemalissonne.com**

Surrounded by the famous vineyards of Bandol and only 4 km. away from sandy beaches, Domaine de Malissonne has been recommended by our agent in France. We intend to inspect the site during 2007. The site should be an ideal base for those who would like to explore the Provence region with its small villages with their narrow streets and markets. After a long day exploring, the site's pool will be be refreshing and the bar and terrace will provide the opportunity to enjoy the long summer evenings. Entertainment for children is provided and activities for adults include boules competitons.

Facilities

Bar-restaurant. Pizzeria with takeaway service. Shop. Launderette. Swimming pool and paddling pool. Fitness area. Play area. Children's club. Boules. Archery. Minigolf.

Open: 1 March - 15 November.

Directions

From the A50 take exit 10 (St Cyr-sur-Mer) towards La Cadière d'Azur on the CD66. Site is signed.

Charges 2006

Per unit incl. 2 persons	€ 20,50 - € 27,50
extra person	€ 6,10
child (under 7 yrs)	€ 4,50

444
Check real time availability and at-the-gate prices...
www.**alanrogers**.com

FR83400 Club Holiday Marina

Le Ginestrel - RN 98, F-83310 Grimaud (Var)
Tel: **04 94 56 08 43**. Email: **info@holiday-marina.com**

Owned and operated by an English family this site is an established favourite with British families. It is located in the busy holiday area of the Gulf of St Tropez. The site has a large and well kept pool area and its own adjacent moorings for small yachts. Smaller than many sites in this area, there are 230 good sized pitches of which 49 for touring units. Each of these has its own spacious bathroom with a good shower, washbasin and WC and a shared outdoor sink. On level, rather sandy ground, with variable shade, all have 20A electricity. Cars are parked separately to reduce noise. The roads are paved with flattened cobblestones with lighting built into the roadway. The attractive pool is surrounded by ample paved sunbathing areas with some shade from the trees and a roomy dining terrace with heating for cool evenings in low season. Although having all the facilities, activities and entertainment expected of a holiday site, the atmosphere is very relaxed and much less frenzied than at some similar sites.

Facilities

Private toilet blocks include washbasin, shower and WC, heated in low seasons. Dishwashing sinks. Laundry. Two restaurants with varied and full menu (15/6-31/8). Snacks and takeaway. Separate building houses a bar and games room. TV room. Swimming and paddling pools. Miniclub for children and evening entertainment in season. Fishing in adjacent canal. Off site: Beach 850 m. Golf 4 km.

Open: March - December.

Directions

From the A8 (Aix-en-Provence - Cannes) take exit 36 (Le Muy) and D25 to St Maxime. Follow N98 coast road towards St Tropez and site is 10 km. after very busy roundabout at Grimaud.

Charges 2006

Per unit incl. 2 persons and electricity	€ 15,00 - € 45,00
family rate (2 adults, up to 3 childen)	€ 20,00 - € 55,00
extra person	€ 5,00 - € 15,00

FR83360 La Pierre Verte Camping Village

Route de Bagnols en Fôret, F-83600 Fréjus (Var)

Tel: **04 94 40 88 30**. Email: **info@campinglapierreverte.com**

This attractive, terraced site, set on a hillside under umbrella pines, has been gradually and thoughtfully developed. The genuine, friendly welcome means many families return year upon year, bringing in turn new generations. The site is divided into terraces, each with its own toilet block. All the generously sized pitches (200 for tourists) enjoy good shade from trees and have electricity (6A). For those seeking to 'get away from it all' in an area of outstanding natural beauty, there can be few more tranquil sites, but the many beaches, watersports and excursions the Gulf of St Tropez has to offer can also be enjoyed. For those staying on site, there are two large, heated swimming pools with large sunbathing areas and exciting water slides. Not far away, some exhilarating hanggliding and parascending can be enjoyed.

Facilities

Five toilet blocks with mostly British style WCs and washbasins in cubicles are extremely clean and accessible from all levels. Baby bath. Laundry facilities. Bread available each morning. Bar with reasonably priced takeaway service. Heated swimming pools (25 x 15 m. and 15 x 15m.) and paddling pool. Play area Boules. Games room. Fridge hire. Entertainment and activities in high season. Barbecues are not permitted. Off site: A few shops 2 km. Nearest shopping centre St Tropez 8 km. Riding 1 km. Bicycle hire 5 km. Fishing 8 km. Golf 12 km.

Open: 1 April - 30 Spetember.

Directions

From the A8 (Aix-en-Provence - Nice) take exit 38 onto D4 towards Bagnols-en-Forêt. Site lies along this road past a military camp.

Charges 2006

Per unit incl. 2 persons	€ 17,00 - € 27,00
incl. electricity	€ 23,00 - € 33,00
extra person	€ 5,00 - € 7,00
child (2-6 yrs)	€ 4,00 - € 5,00

La Pierre Verte Camping Village ★★★★

www.campinglapierreverte.com
E-mail : info@campinglapierreverte.com

8 km from the sandy beaches of Fréjus

Rte de Bagnols en Forêt
83600 FREJUS
FRANCE
Tél : 00 33 4 94 40 88 30
Fax : 00 33 4 94 40 75 41

FR83380 Camping des Prairies de la Mer

RN 98 - Quartier St Pons, Les Mûres, F-83310 Grimaud (Var)

Tel: **04 94 79 09 09**. Email: **prairies@riviera-villages.com**

This busy site is in the pleasant and popular holiday resort of Port Grimaud where there is a luxurious harbour, restaurants and shops. A long, sandy beach runs right round the bay. The site is right on the beach and is very well equipped for a family holiday. In fact, it is a complete holiday resort, even including its own amusement park for children. There are 500 individual touring pitches on flat, sandy ground, all with electricity. A further 900 pitches are used for mobile homes and chalets. Trees have grown well to give plenty of shade and but there is no swimming pool.

Facilities

Nine modern toilet blocks with three near the touring pitches include washbasins in cabins. Toilets are all British style, Launderette. Large shopping complex. Bar. Attractive, Italian style restaurant (all season). Good takeaway. Entertainment programme with live music evenings. Play area. Sports ground. TV room. Bicycle hire. Sailing and diving schools. Miniclub. ATM. Excursions. Beach. Off site: Golf 3 km. Riding 2 km.

Open: 1 April - 8 October.

Directions

From the A8 (Aix-en-Provence - Cannes) exit 36 (Le Muy) take the D25 to St Maxime, then the coast road N98 towards St Tropez. Site is 6 km. on the left. GPS: N43:16.628 E06:34.910

Charges 2006

Per unit incl. 2 persons	€ 18,00 - € 42,00
extra person	€ 3,00 - € 7,00
child (5-13 yrs)	€ 2,00 - € 4,00
electricity	free - € 5,00

MAP 16

Corsica

The island of Corsica is both dramatic and beautiful. The scenery is spectacular with bays of white sand lapped by the clear blue waters of the Mediterranean. At certain times of the year the entire island is ablaze with exotic flowers, aided by Corsica's excellent sunshine record.

DÉPARTEMENTS: 2A CORSE-SUD; 2B HAUTE-CORSE

MAJOR CITIES: AJACCIO AND BASTIA

Corsica is regarded by some as the jewel of the Mediterranean islands and is made up of two départements: Haute Corse (upper Corsica) and Corse du Sud (southern Corsica). The island has endured a bloody history, having being much disputed the Greeks, Romans and Lombards. Five hundred years of Italian rule has influenced the look of the island with Italian-style hilltop hamlets and villages developed alongside mountain springs. Many of the villages feature rustic, unadorned churches and also a few Romanesque examples too.

The variety of scenery is spectacular. Across much of the island one can discover dramatic gorges, glacial lakes, gushing mountain torrents and magnificent pine and chestnut forests.You'll also experience the celebrated perfume of the Corsican maquis: a tangled undergrowth of fragrant herbs, flowers and bushes that fills the warm spring and summer air. The highest mountains lie to the west, while the gentler ranges, weathered to strange and often bizarre shapes, lie to the south and a continuous barrier forms the island's backbone.

Places of interest

Ajaccio: a dazzling white city full of Napoleonic memorabilia.

Bastia: historic citadel towering over the headland. The old town has preserved its streets in the form of steps connected by vaulted passages, converging on the Vieux port (the old port). The new port is the real commercial port of the island.

Cuisine of the region

Brocchui: sheeps' milk cheese is used much in cooking in both its soft form (savoury or sweet) or more mature and ripened.

Capone: local eels, cut up and grilled on a spit over a charcoal fire.

Dziminu: fish soup, like bouillabaise but much hotter. Made with peppers and pimentos.

Figatelli: a sausage made of dried and spiced pork with liver. Favourite between-meal snack.

Pibronata: a highly spiced local sauce.

Prizzutu: a peppered smoked ham; resembles the Italian prosciutto, but with chestnut flavour added.

FR20000 Camping U. Farniente

Pertamina Village RN 198, F-20169 Bonifacio (Corse-du-Sud)

Tel: **04 95 73 05 47**. Email: **pertamina@wanadoo.fr**

Irrespective of whether or not you are using the ferry to Sardinia, Bonifacio deserves a visit and it would be difficult to find a more attractive or convenient site than this one to pitch for a night stop or longer stay. The 120 pitches, many with electricity (3A), are partially terraced and are hedged with trees and bushes, providing reasonable shade. They are fairly flat and vary in size, many being well over 100 sq.m. A central feature of the site is the large attractive swimming pool, surrounded by terraces and a bar and a good pizzeria/grill.

Facilities

Two toilet blocks include washbasins in semi-private cubicles, British and Turkish style WCs, washing machines plus drying and ironing facilities. Motorcaravan service point at entrance (public). Shop. Takeaway. Pizzeria/grill serving set meals and á la carte menu at reasonable prices (shorter opening hours in May, June and Oct). Swimming pool. Tennis. Play area. TV room. Off site: Bonifacio 4 km.

Open: Easter - 15 October.

Directions

Site is on the RN198 road, 4 km. north of Bonifacio to the east. Watch for the sign – you come on it quite suddenly. GPS: N41:25.066 E09:10.803

Charges 2006

Per unit incl. 2 persons	
with electricity	€ 18,50 - € 28,50
extra person	€ 6,00 - € 9,00
child (under 8 yrs)	free - € 5,50

Camping Cheques accepted.

FR20050 Camping Naturiste Club la Chiappa

Mobile homes ▶ page 489

F-20137 Porto-Vecchio (Corse-du-Sud)

Tel: **04 95 70 00 31**. Email: **chiappa@wanadoo.fr**

This is a large naturist campsite on the Chiappa peninsula with 220 pitches for tourers and tents, plus 250 bungalows. A few touring pitches have sea views and are taken first in high season. The pitches are informally marked and have a variety of shapes and sizes, some with difficult slopes and access, especially for large units. (75-125 sq.m). Cars are parked separately. Very long electricity leads are necessary here for most pitches (10A) electricity. The beaches are between long rocky outcrops and it is generally safe to swim, or alternatively enjoy the swimming pool by the main beach.

Facilities

The sanitary facilities were tired and in need of refurbishment when we visited. Washing machines. Motorcaravan service point. Well stocked shop. Two bars and restaurants with snacks. Baby sitting service. Swimming pool. Play area for children. Riding. Tennis. Minigolf. Fishing. Diving, windsurfing and sailing schools. Keep fit, yoga, sauna (extra cost). Bistro. Satellite TV. Internet access. Torches essential. Off site: Excursions. Car rental. Bus to La Chiappa once a week (10 persons).

Open: 12 May - 6 October.

Directions

From Bastia, N198 heading south, take Porto-Vecchio bypass (signed Bonofaccio). At southern end, take first left signed Pont de la Chiappa, unclassified road. After 8 km. site signed. Turn left and follow rough track for 2 km. to site. GPS: N41:35 E09:21.40

Charges 2006

Per person	€ 8,00 - € 10,00
child (5-13 yrs)	€ 3,50 - € 4,50
pitch incl. electricity	€ 11,00 - € 13,50

Less for longer stays in low season.

FR20060 Camping la Vetta

Route de Bastia, La Trinité, F-20137 Porto-Vecchio (Corse-du-Sud)

Tel: **04 95 70 09 86**. Email: **info@campinglavetta.com**

This is a site not to be missed in Corsica, the English/French owners Nick and Marieline Long having created a very friendly and peaceful country park setting for their campsite to the north of La Trinité village. The 8.5 hectares of well maintained campsite are part sloping, part terraced with an informal pitch allocation system. It seems to stretch endlessly. The abundance of tree varieties including many cork oaks give shade to 111 pitches which all have 16A electricity. The pool and bar area is delightful and for a campsite of this size, the restaurant is outstanding.

Facilities

Spotless, modern and fully equipped toilet facilities have hot water, include dishwashing, laundry sinks, washing machine. Shop (July/Aug). gas supplies. Excellent restaurant, patio, bar (July/Aug). Swimming pool (all season). Play area. TV. Entertainment in high season. Off site: Beach 1.5 km. Fishing, watersports and boat launching 1.5 km. Riding 4 km. Bicycle hire 5 km. Golf 7 km. Public transport 800 m.

Open: 1 June - 1 October.

Directions

Site is in La Trinité village, off the RN198 (east side), north of Porto-Vecchio.

Charges 2006

Per person	€ 6,00 - € 7,00
child (under 7 yrs)	€ 3,00 - € 4,00
pitch	€ 4,50 - € 6,00

No credit cards.

FR20070 Camping Caravaning Santa Lucia

Lieudit Mulindinu, F-20144 Sainte Lucie-de Porto-Vecchio (Corse-du-Sud)

Tel: 04 95 71 45 28. Email: information@campingsantalucia.com

Camping Santa Lucia is a very small, friendly, family run site in a delightful southern Corsican setting, where little English is spoken. Behind the little reception hut is an unsophisticated restaurant and bar which have a terrace which is pleasant in the evenings when ornamental lamps light up the area. There are 160 pitches, 60 with 6A electrical connections and 18 serviced pitches. Some of the pitches are in enclosed bays which offer privacy. We see this as a transit site, rather than for an extended stay. There were tourers based at this site which is only minutes by car from Porto Vecchio.

Facilities

Two toilet blocks include some washbasins in cubicles, dishwashing and laundry sinks, and a washing machine. Bread to order. Bar (15/6-15/9). Restaurant and takeaway (1/7-31/8). Swimming pool. Play area and high season miniclub for children. Minigolf. Barbecues are only permitted in a specific area. Off site: Beach, fishing and watersports 5 km. Golf 20 km. Supermarket opposite.

Open: 15 May - 10 October.

Directions

Site is at south end of Sainte-Lucie-de-Porto-Vecchio village, off N198 and well signed.

Charges 2006

Per person	€ 5,00 - € 7,35
pitch	€ 5,00 - € 7,05
car	€ 2,00 - € 2,95

FR20220 Camping les Oliviers

F-20150 Porto (Corse-du-Sud)

Tel: 04 95 26 14 49. Email: lesolivierporto@wanadoo.fr

This attractive and modern, resort style campsite is by the Bay of Porto, set alongside a charming river suitable for fishing and swimming. The surrounding area is listed as a World heritage site. It is located on the difficult to access and remote west coast of Corsica and reservations are essential. The 190 pitches are mainly small and terraced, with 64 having electricity (10A), water and drainage. The quality of the pitches reflect the rugged terrain, therefore it is essential to discuss your requirements when making a booking, particularly for owners of large units. A most attractive series of outdoor pools built into the rock are the focal point of the site, together with a sauna and gym.

Facilities

Toilet facilities are in four blocks spread throughout the site. Some washbasins in cubicles, British style WCs. Dishwashing and laundry facilities. Fridge hire. Bread supplies. Restaurant, pizzeria and bar. Swimming pool, gym, sauna and Turkish bath. Play area. Internet access. Fishing. Torches useful. Off site: Supermarket 50 m. Corsican Trek organises sports. Visits to Scandola nature reserve. Bicycle hire 200 m. Golf 1.5 km. Riding 30 km.

Open: 28 March - 30 October.

Directions

When approaching Porto the road crosses a bridge over the river. Les Oliviers is on the right immediately after the bridge. GPS: N42:15 E08:42.51

Charges 2007

Per person	€ 6,50 - € 8,80
child (under 7 yrs)	€ 3,20 - € 4,50
pitch incl. electricity	€ 9,00 - € 14,00

FR20230 Camping le Sagone

Route de Vico, F-20118 Sagone (Corse-du-Sud)

Tel: 04 95 28 04 15. Email: sagone.camping@wanadoo.fr

Situated outside the bustling seaside resort of Sagone, surrounded by protective hills, this campsite which used to be a fruit farm is in an ideal location for exploring Corsica's wild and rocky west coast or its mountainous interior. The large site borders a pleasant river and has 300 marked, shaded pitches, 250 with electricity (6A). There are 90 bungalows offered for rent, which are generally separated. The restaurant/bar and games room overlook the pool and they are the focal point of this well managed site. Animation takes place in the central area by the pool during the high season.

Facilities

Clean, fully equipped toilet blocks. Washbasins in cubicles, washing up, laundry area (cold water only). Facilities for disabled people. Baby baths. Washing machines, dryers. Motorcaravan services. Large supermarket (all year). Restaurant, pizzeria, bar, games room. Swimming pool (May - Sept). Half court tennis. Play area. Sub-aqua experience in pool. Communal barbecues. Satellite TV. Internet. Car wash. New putting and golf practise area. Off site: Riding 500 m. Diving, windsurfing, mountain biking, fishing, bicycle hire, climbing. Tours to local places.

Open: 1 May - 30 September.

Directions

From Ajaccio take the RD81 in direction of Cergése and Calvilby (by coast road). In Sagone take RD70 in the direction of Vico, Sagone can be found on left after 1.5 km. next to supermarket.
GPS: N42:07 E08:42.33

Charges 2006

Per unit incl. 2 persons	€ 14,50 - € 23,00
extra person	€ 4,50 - € 7,70
child (under 12 yrs)	€ 2,25 - € 3,90
electricity	€ 3,00

Camping Cheques accepted.

FR20010 Camping Arinella Bianca

Route de la Mer, F-20240 Ghisonaccia (Haute-Corse)

Tel: **04 95 56 04 78**. Email: **arinella@arinellabianca.com**

Arinella is a lively, family oriented site on Corsica's east coast. The 415 level, grassy, good size, irregular shape pitches (182 for touring units) have a variety of trees and shrubs providing ample shade, 6A electricity (long leads needed). The site is beside a beach of soft sand that extends a long way either side of an attractive complex which, with the pool, forms the hub of this site. A large range of sport and leisure facilities is available nearby. Evening entertainment starts at 22.00 and continues until midnight, unfortunately a local disco goes on until the early hours. This site is a tribute to its owner's design and development skills as it appears to be in entirely natural glades where, in fact, these have been created from former marshland with a fresh water lake.

Facilities

Four open plan sanitary blocks provide showers, (some with dressing area), washbasins in cabins, mainly British style WCs. Open air dishwashing areas. Laundry, washing machines, ironing boards. Motorcaravan services. Shop, bar, terrace, restaurant, amphitheatre, snack bar (all 10/5-15/9). Swimming pool (from 1/5). Windsurfing. Canoeing. Fishing. Tennis. Riding. Children's miniclub. Play area. Disco. Entertainment programme in the main season. Off site: Sailing 0.5 km. Boat launching 2 km.

Open: Mid April - 30 September.

Directions

Site is 4 km. east of Ghisonaccia. From N198 in Ghisonaccia look for sign 'La Plage, Li Mare' (easy to miss coming from south). From south turn is difficult for caravans so continue and turn in garage forecourt to approach from north. Turn east on D144 for 3.5 km. to roundabout. Turn right to site in 500 m. GPS: N41:59.917 E09:26.523

Charges 2007

Per unit incl. 2 persons	€ 21,00 - € 36,00
extra person	€ 7,00 - € 9,80
child (up to 7 yrs)	free - € 5,50
Camping Cheques accepted.	

ARINELLA *Bianca*

Camping Caravaning
20240 Ghisonaccia
Tel: 0033 495 56 04 78 - Fax: 0033 495 56 12 54
www.arinellabianca.com

Camping Cheque

FR20030 Camping Merendella

Moriani-Plage, F-20230 San-Nicolao (Haute-Corse)

Tel: **04 95 38 53 47**. Email: **merendel@club-internet.fr**

This attractive family run site has the advantage of direct access to a pleasant, long sandy beach. It is peacefully situated on level grass with many well tended trees and shrubs providing shade and colour. Level green sites such as this are unusual in Corsica and are ideal for families or those with mobility problems. There are 133 pitches, all with electricity (2/5A, long leads required) and a minimum of 100 sq.m. There is a dedicated night parking area if you arrive late. An excellent bar, restaurant/pizzeria is close to the site entrance (takeaway pizzas are available).

Facilities

Modern blocks, two individual cabin units near the beach. Washbasins in private cubicles. British and Turkish style WCs. Facilities for disabled campers. Dishwashing, laundry areas. Washing machines. Motorcaravan services. Shop. Bar/restaurant, pizzeria. TV room. Games room. Late arrival area. Diving centre. Play area. Torches essential. No pets. Off site: Bus 800 m. from gate. Town 800 m. with usual amenities. Tennis and riding 2 km. Bicycle hire 800 m. All watersports 200 m. along beach from site.

Open: 15 May - 15 October.

Directions

Site is to seaward side of the RN198, 800 m. south of Moriani Plage. GPS: N42:21 E09:31.78

Charges 2006

Per person	€ 6,05 - € 7,15
caravan and car	€ 5,90 - € 6,70
motorcaravan	€ 5,65 - € 6,90
electricity	€ 3,00 - € 4,00

FR20040 Riva Bella Nature Resort & Spa

B.P. 21, F-20270 Alèria (Haute-Corse)

Tel: 04 95 38 81 10. Email: riva-bella@wanadoo.fr

Mobile homes ▶ page 490

This is a relaxed, informal, spacious naturist site alongside an extremely long and beautiful beach. Riva Bella is naturist camping at its very best, with great amenities. It offers a large number and variety of pitches, situated in a huge area of varied and beautiful countryside and seaside. It is difficult to believe that it could become overcrowded. The site is divided into several areas – pitches and bungalows, alongside the sandy beach, in a wooded glade with ample shade, or beside the lake, a feature of this site. Although electricity is available in most parts, a long cable may be needed.

Facilities

Refurbished, high standard toilet facilities, typical of naturist sites, facilities for disabled people and babies. Large shop (25/4-15/10). Fridge hire. Restaurant (all season) with reasonable prices. Snack bar. Watersports, sailing school, fishing, sub-aqua. Therapy centre. Sauna. Volleyball, aerobics, table tennis, giant draughts, archery. Fishing. Mountain bike hire. Half-court tennis. Walk with llamas. No barbecues. Interesting evening entertainment programme. Off site: Riding 5 km.

Open: 8 April - 1 November.

Directions

Site is 8 km. north of Aleria on N198 (Bastia) road. Watch for signs and unmade road to it and follow for 4 km. GPS: N42:09.598 E09:32.64

Charges guide

Per unit incl. 2 persons	€ 17,00 - € 31,00
extra person	€ 4,00 - € 8,50
child (3-8 yrs)	€ 2,00 - € 5,00
electricity	€ 3,80
dog	€ 3,00 - € 3,00

Camping Cheques accepted.

FR20100 Camping Caravaning Santa Barbara

RN 200 route d'Aleria, Aerodrome de Corte, F-20250 Corte (Haute-Corse)

Tel: 04 95 46 20 22

Santa Barbara is a small, uncomplicated campsite in Corsica's mountainous interior. Originally established as a restaurant/bar, the campsite has 25 level touring pitches and 15 mobile holiday homes. The pitches are separated by young shrubs with electricity (12A). A small, inviting swimming pool, alongside the pretty restaurant terrace, is very welcome in this hot terrain and there are impressive mountain views. The area outside the bar and restaurant has several functions. There is a quiet inside area which is good for cooling off and relaxing. There is some noise from the nearby road, runway and microlights.

Facilities

The toilet facilities are dated and tired but kept clean (unisex when seen). Dishwashing and laundry sinks (cold water) and washing machine. Restaurant/bar offers typical menu and snacks. Swimming pool. Basic play area. Table tennis. Pool table. Off site: Corte has all the usual town amenities. Bus 3 km. Bicycle hire 3 km. Riding 10 km. Golf 20 km.

Open: 1 May - 30 September.

Directions

Site is 3 km. southeast of Corte by the N200 Aléria road. GPS: N42:17 E09:11.42

Charges 2006

Per person	€ 6,00
child (under 10 yrs)	€ 2,60
pitch	€ 5,40 - € 5,80

FR20120 Camping le Panoramic

Route de Lavatoggio, Lumio, F-20260 Calvi (Haute-Corse)

Tel: 04 95 60 73 13. Email: panoramic@web-office.fr

Le Panoramic enjoys magnificent views across the Golfe d'Ambroggio. It is a simple family run site with 100 pitches laid out in terraces, shaded by many trees (some 15A electricity - long leads required). The site is on a steep slope and some of the lower pitches have magnificent views. The pool is a pleasant area elevated on a concrete base. Snacks can be obtained from the single building which holds reception and the utilities. Larger units need to telephone ahead to ensure they can be accommodated but no English is spoken here.

Facilities

Well maintained, fully equipped toilet blocks in rough-cast buildings with basic décor. Sinks for dishwashing, laundry (cold water only), washing machines. Chemical disposal can be arranged through reception. Small shop, takeaway, bar (1/6-15/9). Swimming pool. Play area. Caravan storage. Sub-aqua diving introductions, high season. Off site: Scenic drive 5 km. climb to St Antonino, a mountain village on a rocky summit. Riding 3 km. Bicycle hire 4 km. Golf 5 km. Beach 5 km.

Open: 1 June - 15 September.

Directions

From Calvi take N197 towards L'Ile Rousse. Proceed for 10 km. to village of Lumio, then east on D71 and site is 2 km. on the left. GPS: N42:35 E08:50.84

Charges 2006

Per person	€ 4,80 - € 6,20
child (2-7 yrs)	€ 2,40 - € 3,10
pitch incl. car	€ 4,90 - € 6,40
electricity	€ 2,70 - € 3,40

No credit cards.

Check real time availability and at-the-gate prices...

www.alanrogers.com

OVER RECENT YEARS MANY OF THE CAMPSITES FEATURED IN THIS GUIDE HAVE ADDED LARGE NUMBERS OF HIGH QUALITY MOBILE HOMES AND CHALETS. MANY SITE OWNERS BELIEVE THAT SOME FORMER CARAVANNERS AND MOTORCARAVANNERS HAVE BEEN ENTICED BY THE EXTRA COMFORT THEY CAN NOW PROVIDE, AND THAT MAYBE THIS IS THE IDEAL SOLUTION TO COMBINE THE FREEDOM OF CAMPING WITH ALL THE COMFORTS OF HOME.

Quality is consistently high and, although the exact size and inventory may vary from site to site, if you choose any of the sites detailed here, you can be sure that you're staying in some of the best quality and best value mobile homes available.

Home comforts are provided and typically these include a fridge with freezer compartment, gas hob, proper shower – often a microwave and radio/cassette hi-fi too but do check for details. All mobile homes and chalets come fully equipped with a good range of kitchen utensils, pots and pans, crockery, cutlery and outdoor furniture. Some even have an attractive wooden sundeck or paved terrace – a perfect spot for outdoors eating or relaxing with a book and watching the world go by.

Regardless of model, colourful soft furnishings are the norm and a generally breezy décor helps to provide a real holiday feel.

Although some sites may have a large number of different accommodation types, we have restricted our choice to one or two of the most popular accommodation units (either mobile homes or chalets) for each of the sites listed.

The mobile homes here will be of modern design, and recent innovations, for example, often include pitched roofs which substantially improve their appearance.

Design will invariably include clever use of space and fittings/furniture to provide for comfortable holidays – usually light and airy, with big windows and patio-style doors, fully equipped kitchen areas, a shower room with shower, washbasin and WC, cleverly designed bedrooms and a comfortable lounge/dining area (often incorporating a sofa bed).

In general, modern campsite chalets incorporate all the best features of mobile homes in a more traditional structure, sometimes with the advantage of an upper mezzanine floor for an additional bedroom.

Our selected campsites offer a massive range of different types of mobile home and chalet, and it would be impractical to inspect every single accommodation unit. Our selection criteria, therefore, primarily takes account of the quality standards of the campsite itself. However, there are a couple of important ground rules

☑ Featured mobile homes must be no more than 5 years old, and chalets no more than 10 years old.

☑ All listed accommodation must, of course, fully conform with all applicable local, national and European safety legislation.

For each campsite we given details of the type, or types, of accommodation available to rent, but these details are necessarily quite brief. Sometimes internal layouts can differ quite substantially, particularly with regard to sleeping arrangements, where these include the flexible provision for 'extra persons' on sofa beds located in the living area. These arrangements may vary from accommodation to accommodation, and if you're planning a holiday which includes more people than are catered for by the main bedrooms you should check exactly how the extra sleeping arrangements are to be provided!

Charges

An indication of the tariff for each type of accommodation featured is also included, indicating the variance between the low and high season tariffs. However, given that many campsites have a large and often complex range of pricing options, incorporating special deals and various discounts, the charges we mention should be taken to be just an indication. We strongly recommend therefore that you confirm the actual cost when making a booking.

We also strongly recommend that you check with the campsite, when booking, what (if anything) will be provided by way of bed linen, blankets, pillows etc. Again, in our experience, this can vary widely from site to site.

On every campsite a fully refundable deposit (usually between 150 and 300 euros) is payable on arrival. There may also be an optional cleaning service for which a further charge is made. Other options may include sheet hire (typically 30 euros per unit) or baby pack hire (cot and high chair).

INSPECTED CAMPSITES & SELECTED

FR29010 Castel Camping le Ty-Nadan

Route d'Arzano, F-29310 Locunolé (Finistère)   Open: 1 April - 7 September

For our full description of this campsite ▶ see page 27

AR1 – MOBILE HOME – IRM

Sleeping: 2 bedrooms, sleeps 6: 1 double, 1 twin with 2 single beds, 1 double sofa bed, pillows & blankets provided

Living: living/kitchen area, heating, shower & WC

Eating: fitted kitchen with cooking hobs, oven & fridge

Outside: table & chairs, sun loungers & parasol

Pets: accepted

AR2 – WOODEN CHALET

Sleeping: 2 bedrooms, sleeps 6: 1 double, 1 twin with 2 single beds, 1 double sofa bed, pillows & blankets provided

Living: living/kitchen area, heating, shower & WC

Eating: fitted kitchen with cooking hobs & fridge

Outside: table & chairs, sun loungers & parasol

Pets: accepted

Weekly Charge	AR1	AR2
Low Season (from)	€ 357	€ 406
High Season (from)	€ 924	€ 1092

FR29050 Castel Camping L'Orangerie de Lanniron

Château de Lanniron, F-29336 Quimper (Finistère)   Open: 12 May - 15 September

For our full description of this campsite ▶ see page 29

AR1 – MOBILE HOME – Deluxe

Sleeping: 2 bedrooms, sleeps 4-6: 1 double, 1 twin with 2 single beds, 1 double sofa bed, pillows & blankets provided

Living: living/kitchen area, heating, shower & WC

Eating: fitted kitchen with cooking hobs, microwave & fridge/freezer

Outside: table & chairs, sun loungers, parasol & BBQ

Pets: not accepted

AR2 – MOBILE HOME – Comfort

Sleeping: 2 bedrooms, sleeps 4-6: 1 double, 1 twin with 2 single beds, 1 double sofa bed,

Living: living/kitchen area, heating, shower & WC

Eating: fitted kitchen with cooking hobs, microwave & fridge/freezer

Outside: table & chairs, sun loungers, parasol & BBQ

Pets: not accepted

Weekly Charge	AR1	AR2
Low Season (from)	€ 392	€ 280
High Season (from)	€ 616	€ 364

FR29080 Camping le Panoramic

Route de la Plage-Penker, F-29560 Telgruc-sur-Mer (Finistère)   Open: 1 June - 15 September

For our full description of this campsite ▶ see page 30

AR1 – MOBILE HOME – Trigano Elegante 33

Sleeping: 3 bedrooms, sleeps 6: 1 double, 2 single rooms, pillows & blankets provided

Living: living/kitchen area, heating, shower & WC

Eating: fitted kitchen with cooking hobs & fridge

Outside: table & chairs, sun lounger, parasol & BBQ

Pets: accepted

AR2 – MOBILE HOME – Trigano Elegante 25

Sleeping: 2 bedrooms, sleeps 6: 1 double, 2 single beds, sofa bed, pillows & blankets provided

Living: living/kitchen area, heating, shower & WC

Eating: fitted kitchen with cooking hobs & fridge

Outside: table & chairs, sun lounger, parasol, BBQ

Pets: accepted

Weekly Charge	AR1	AR2
Low Season (from)	€ 300	€ 250
High Season (from)	€ 660	€ 580

FR29090 Camping le Raguenès-Plage

19 rue des Iles, Raguenés, F-29920 Névez (Finistère)

Open: 1 April - 16 October

For our full description of this campsite **see page 31**

AR1 – MOBILE HOME – Variante

Sleeping: 2 bedrooms, sleeps 5: 1 double, 1 twin with 2 single beds, 1 bunkbed, pillows & blankets provided

Living: living/kitchen area, heating, shower & separate WC

Eating: fitted kitchen with cooking hobs, oven, microwave coffee maker & fridge/freezer

Outside: table & chairs, parasol

Pets: not accepted (on demand)

AR2 – MOBILE HOME – O'Hara

Sleeping: 2 bedrooms, sleeps 4/5: 1 double, 1 twin with 2 single beds, sofa bed, pillows & blankets provided

Living: living/kitchen area, heating, shower & separate WC

Eating: fitted kitchen with cooking hobs, microwave & fridge/freezer

Outside: table & chairs, BBQ

Pets: not accepted (on demand)

Weekly Charge	AR1	AR2
Low Season *(from)*	€ 320	€ 340
High Season *(from)*	€ 699	€ 740

FR29180 Camping les Embruns

Rue du Philosophe Alain, Le Pouldu, F-29360 Clohars-Carnoet (Finistère)

Open: 7 April - 15 September

For our full description of this campsite **see page 36**

AR1 – CHALET – Campitel

Sleeping: 3 bedrooms, sleeps 6: 2 double, 1 with bunk beds

Living: living/kitchen area, heating, shower & WC

Eating: fitted kitchen with cooking hobs & fridge, mini oven

Outside: covered terrace, table & chairs

Pets: accepted (supplement payable)

AR2 – MOBILE HOME – Embruns

Sleeping: 2 bedrooms, sleeps 4/6: 1 double, 2 single beds, sofa bed

Living: living/kitchen area, heating, shower & WC

Eating: fitted kitchen with cooking hobs, oven & fridge

Outside: terrace, table & chairs, parasol

Pets: accepted (supplement payable)

Weekly Charge	AR1	AR2
Low Season *(from)*	€ 330	€ 330
High Season *(from)*	€ 680	€ 690

FR35000 Camping le Vieux Chêne

Baguer-Pican, F-35120 Dol-de-Bretagne (Ille-et-Vilaine)

Open: 31 March - 22 September

For our full description of this campsite **see page 42**

AR1 – CHALET – Reve Confort

Sleeping: 2 bedrooms, sleeps 6: 1 double, 2 single beds, sofa bed, pillows & blankets provided

Living: living/kitchen area, heating, shower & WC

Eating: fitted kitchen with cooking hobs & fridge

Outside: terrace with table & chairs

Pets: accepted (small supplement)

AR2 – CHALET – Cottage de Bretagne

Sleeping: 2 bedrooms, sleeps 4: 1 double, 2 single beds

Living: living/kitchen area, heating, shower & WC

Eating: fitted kitchen with cooking hobs & fridge

Outside: table & chairs

Pets: accepted (small supplement)

Weekly Charge	AR1	AR2
Low Season *(from)*	€ 320	€ 280
High Season *(from)*	€ 750	€ 650

Check real time availability and at-the-gate prices...
www.**alanrogers**.com

FR44090 Camping Château du Deffay

B.P. 18 Le Deffay, F-44160 Pontchâteau (Loire-Atlantique)

Open: 1 May - 30 September

For our full description of this campsite ▶ **see page 48**

AR1 – MOBILE HOME

Sleeping: 2 bedrooms, sleeps 5: 1 double, 1 single bed, 2 bunk beds in living area, pillows & blankets provided

Living: living/kitchen area, heating, shower & WC

Eating: fitted kitchen with cooking hobs, microwave & fridge/freezer

Outside: table & chairs, sun loungers, parasol & BBQ

Pets: accepted (1 per mobile home)

AR2 – CHALET

Sleeping: 2 bedrooms, sleeps 6: 1 double, 2 bunk beds, 1 double sofa bed, pillows & blankets provided

Living: living/kitchen area, heating, shower & WC

Eating: fitted kitchen with cooking hobs, dishwasher, microwave & fridge/freezer

Outside: table & chairs, sun loungers, parasol & BBQ

Pets: accepted (1 per chalet)

Weekly Charge	AR1	AR2
Low Season *(from)*	€ 205	€ 225
High Season *(from)*	€ 599	€ 699

FR44100 Sunêlia le Patisseau

29 rue du Patisseau, F-44210 Pornic (Loire-Atlantique)

Open: 8 April - 6 November

For our full description of this campsite ▶ **see page 49**

AR1 – CHALET – Chalet 6

Sleeping: 2 bedrooms, sleeps 6: 1 double, 1 twin with 2 single beds, 1 double sofa bed, pillows & blankets provided

Living: living/kitchen area, heating, shower & WC

Eating: fitted kitchen with cooking hobs, microwave, pressure cooker & fridge

Outside: table & chairs, parasol

Pets: not accepted

AR2 – MOBILE HOME – Mobile Home 6

Sleeping: 2 bedrooms, sleeps 6: 1 double, 2 single beds, 1 double sofa bed, pillows & blankets provided

Living: living/kitchen area, heating, shower & WC

Eating: fitted kitchen with cooking hobs, pressure cooker & fridge, microwave

Outside: table & chairs, parasol

Pets: not accepted

Weekly Charge	AR1	AR2
Low Season *(from)*	€ 430	€ 430
High Season *(from)*	€ 889	€ 889

FR44180 Camping de la Boutinardière

Rue de la Plage de la Boutinardière, F-44210 Pornic (Loire-Atlantique)

Open: 31 March - 29 September

For our full description of this campsite ▶ **see page 52**

AR1 – MOBILE HOME – 5 persons

Sleeping: 2 bedrooms, sleeps 4-6: 1 double, 1 twin with 2 single beds & 1 sofa bed

Living: living/kitchen area, heating, shower & WC

Eating: fitted kitchen with cooking hobs & fridge

Outside: table & chairs, parasol

Pets: not accepted

AR2 – MOBILE HOME – 6 persons

Sleeping: 3 bedrooms sleeps 6: 1 double, 2 twins

Living: living/kitchen area, heating, shower & WC

Eating: fitted kitchen with cooking hobs & fridge

Outside: table & chairs, parasol

Pets: not accepted

Weekly Charge	AR1	AR2
Low Season *(from)*	€ 300	€ 330
High Season *(from)*	€ 750	€ 780

FR44190 Camping le Fief
57, chemin du Fief, F-44250 St Brévin-les-Pins (Loire-Atlantique)

Open: 1 April - 15 October

For our full description of this campsite ▶ see page 51

AR1 – MOBILE HOME – Cottage

Sleeping: 3 bedrooms, sleeps 6: 1 double, 2 bedrooms with 2 twin beds

Living: living/kitchen area, shower & WC, sofa

Eating: fitted kitchen with cooking hobs & fridge and microwave

Outside: table & chairs, terrace

Pets: accepted (€ 40 per week)

AR2 – MOBILE HOME – Cottage

Sleeping: 2 bedrooms, sleeps 6: 1 double, 1 twin with 2 single beds

Living: living/kitchen area, shower & WC, sofa bed

Eating: fitted kitchen with cooking hobs, microwave & fridge

Outside: table & chairs, terrace

Pets: accepted

Weekly Charge	AR1	AR2
Low Season (from)	€ 350	€ 350
High Season (from)	€ 847	€ 749

FR44210 Camping L'Océan
44490 Le Croisic (Loire-Atlantique)

Open: 7 April - 30 September

For our full description of this campsite ▶ see page 54

AR1 – MOBILE HOME – Cottage Océan

Sleeping: 2 bedrooms, sleeps 4-6: 1 double, 1 twin with 2 single beds

Living: living/dining area, heating, shower and WC

Eating: fitted kitchen with cooking hobs & fridge

Outside: table & chairs, parasol

Pets: not accepted

AR2 – MOBILE HOME – Ocean Grand Confort

Sleeping: 3 bedrooms sleeps 6: 1 double, 2 twins

Living: living area/kitchen, shower & WC

Eating: fitted kitchen with cooking hobs & fridge

Outside: table & chairs, parasol

Pets: not accepted

Weekly Charge	AR1	AR2
Low Season (from)	€ 340	€ 435
High Season (from)	€ 670	€ 850

FR44220 Parc de Léveno
Route de Sandun, F-44350 Guérande (Loire-Atlantique)

Open: 7 April - 30 September

For our full description of this campsite ▶ see page 54

AR1 – MOBILE HOME – Tradition

Sleeping: 2 bedrooms, sleeps 6: 1 double, 1 twin with 2 single beds and sofa bed

Living: living/kitchen area, shower & WC

Eating: fitted kitchen with cooking hobs & fridge

Outside: table & chairs, parasol

Pets: not accepted

AR2 – COTTAGE – 6 pers

Sleeping: 3 bedrooms sleeps 6: 1 double, 2 twins

Living: living/kitchen area, shower & WC

Eating: fitted kitchen with cooking hobs & fridge

Outside: table & chairs, parasol

Pets: not accepted

Weekly Charge	AR1	AR2
Low Season (from)	€ 245	€ 285
High Season (from)	€ 700	€ 850

FR56280 Airotel les Sept Saints

B.P. 14, F-56410 Erdeven (Morbihan)

Open: 31 March - 23 September

For our full description of this campsite ▶ see page 68

AR1 – MOBILE HOME – Grand Confort

Sleeping: 2 bedrooms, sleeps 6: 1 double, 1 twin with 2 single beds, 1 double sofa bed, pillows & blankets provided

Living: living/kitchen area, heating, shower & WC

Eating: fitted kitchen with cooking hobs & fridge

Outside: table & chairs, parasol & BBQ

Pets: accepted

AR2 – CHALET

Sleeping: 2 bedrooms, sleeps 6: 1 double, 1 twin with 2 single beds, sofa bed, pillows & blankets provided

Living: living/kitchen area, TV, heating, shower & WC

Eating: fitted kitchen with cooking hobs & fridge

Outside: table & chairs, parasol & BBQ

Pets: accepted

Weekly Charge	AR1	AR2
Low Season (from)	€ 285	€ 320
High Season (from)	€ 550	€ 560

FR14070 Camping de la Vallée

88 rue de la Vallée, F-14510 Houlgate (Calvados)

Open: 1 April - 30 September

For our full description of this campsite ▶ see page 71

AR1 – MOBILE HOME– 1

Sleeping: 2 bedrooms, sleep 6: 1 double, 2 single beds, sofa bed

Living: living/kitchen area, shower & WC

Eating: kitchen with sink, cooking hobs & frigde

Outside: table & chairs, sun loungers

Pets: not accepted

AR2 – MOBILE HOME– 2

Sleeping: 2 bedrooms, sleeps 4: 1 double, 2 single

Living: living area/kitchen, shower & WC

Eating: fitted kitchen with cooking hob & fridge

Outside: table & chairs, parasol

Pets: not accepted

Weekly Charge	AR1	AR2
Low Season (from)	€ 370	€ 300
High Season (from)	€ 800	€ 700

FR14160 Camping Bellevue

Route des Dives, F-14640 Villers sur Mer (Calvados)

Open: 1 April - 31 October

For our full description of this campsite ▶ see page 73

AR1 – MOBILE HOME – Oceane Oakley Pacifique

Sleeping: 2 bedrooms, sleeps 4: 1 double, 1 twin with 2 single beds, pillows & blankets provided

Living: living/kitchen area, heating, shower & WC

Eating: fitted kitchen with cooking hobs & fridge

Outside: table & chairs, parasol

Pets: not accepted

AR2 – MOBILE HOME – Tamaris

Sleeping: 3 bedrooms, sleeps 6: 1 double, 2 twin with 2 single beds

Living: living/kitchen area, heating, shower & WC

Eating: fitted kitchen with cooking hobs & fridge

Outside: table & chairs, parasol

Pets: not accepted

Weekly Charge	AR1	AR2
Low Season (from)	€ 315	€ 365
High Season (from)	€ 575	€ 680

Check real time availability and at-the-gate prices...

www.alanrogers.com

FR27060 Domaine de Marcilly

Route de Saint André de l'Eure, F-27810 Marcilly-sur-Eure (Eure)

Open: 1 April - 29 October

Pitches at this campsite are exclusively for mobile homes & chalets

Just between Ile de France and Normandy, less than an hours drive from Paris, Domaine de Marcilly is beautifully situated in a 15 hectare park surrounded by pine trees, oaks and birch trees. The site is distinctive because of its peace and quiet and the agreeable lifestyle. The site also offers full service pitches for motorcaravans.

Facilities

Sanitary blocks providing hot showers, wash basins, laundry room and facilities for disabled people. Heated swimming pool. Tennis. Internet point. TV room. Animation and entertainment during high season. Off site: Local shops 900 m. Fishing lake. Golf 18 holes. Horse riding. Canoe/kayak. Walking and cycling routes.

Directions

From Paris A13, A12 exit onto N12. For Houdan, take exit Goussainville, Havelu then Marcilly.

Reservations

Contact site. Tel: 02 37 48 45 42.
Email: domainedemarcilly@wanadoo.fr

AR1 – MOBILE HOME – O'Phea

Sleeping: 2 bedrooms, sleeps 4/5: 1 double, 1 twin with 2 single beds, pillows & blankets provided

Living: living/kitchen area, heating, shower & WC

Eating: fitted kitchen with cooking hobs, oven & fridge, microwave

Outside: table & chairs, BBQ

Pets: not accepted

AR2 – MOBILE HOME – O'Phea

Sleeping: 3 bedrooms, sleeps 6: 1 double, 1 twin with 2 single beds, 1 double sofa bed, blankets and pillows

Living: living/kitchen area, heating, shower & WC

Eating: fitted kitchen with cooking hobs, oven & fridge, microwave

Outside: table & chairs, BBQ

Pets: not accepted

Weekly Charge	AR1	AR2
Low Season *(from)*	€ 290	€ 320
High Season *(from)*	€ 560	€ 590

FR27070 Camping l'Ile de Trois Rois

FR27700 Les Andelys (Eure)

Open: March - November

For our full description of this campsite see page 78

AR1 – MOBILE HOME

Sleeping: 2 bedrooms, sleeps 4: 1 double room, 1 twin room with 2 beds

Living: living/dining area, heating, shower and WC

Eating: kitchen with 4 gas ring, hob, cooking surface

Outside: table & chairs

Pets: not accepted

Weekly Charge	AR1
Low Season *(from)*	€ 280
High Season *(from)*	€ 410

FR80060 Camping le Val de Trie

Bouillancourt-sous-Miannay, F-80870 Moyenneville (Somme)

Open: 1 April - 31 October

For our full description of this campsite ▶ see page 93

AR1 – MOBILE HOME – Moréva

Sleeping: 2 bedrooms, sleeps 6: 1 double, 1 twin with 2 single beds, 1 double sofa bed, pillows & blankets provided

Living: living/kitchen area, heating, shower & WC

Eating: fitted kitchen with cooking hobs, microwave & fridge/freezer

Outside: terrace with table & chairs, parasol & BBQ

Pets: not accepted

AR2 – MOBILE HOME – Privilege Zen

Sleeping: 3 bedrooms, sleeps 6: 1 double, 2 twin with 2 single beds

Living: living/kitchen area, CD player, shower & WC

Eating: fitted kitchen with dishwasher, cooking hobs, microwave, fridge/freezer

Outside: terrace with table & chairs, sun loungers, parasol & BBQ

Pets: not accepted

Weekly Charge	AR1	AR2
Low Season *(from)*	€ 252	€ 365
High Season *(from)*	€ 595	€ 693

FR80070 Camping la Ferme des Aulnes

1 rue du Marais, Fresne-sur-Authie, F-80120 Nampont-St Martin (Somme)

Open: 1 April - early November

For our full description of this campsite ▶ see page 95

AR1 – MOBILE HOME – Confort

Sleeping: 2 bedrooms, sleeps 5: 1 double, 1 twin with 2 single beds, 1 sofa bed

Living: living/kitchen area, heating, shower & WC, TV

Eating: fitted kitchen with cooking hobs, microwave & fridge/freezer

Outside: table & chairs, sun loungers, parasol & BBQ, terrace

Pets: accepted (supplement € 50 per stay)

AR2 – MOBILE HOME – Privilege

Sleeping: 3 bedrooms, sleeps 6: 1 double, 2 twin with 2 single beds

Living: living/kitchen area, heating, shower & WC, TV (DVD player), safe

Eating: fitted kitchen with cooking hobs, microwave, fridge/freezer, dishwasher

Outside: table & chairs, sun loungers, parasol & BBQ, terrace

Pets: accepted (supplement € 50 per stay)

Weekly Charge	AR1	AR2
Low Season *(from)*	€ 490	€ 590
High Season *(from)*	€ 690	€ 790

FR77020 Camping le Chêne Gris

24, place de la Gare de Faremoutiers, F-77515 Pommeuse (Seine-et-Marne)

Open: 28 April - 27 October

For our full description of this campsite ▶ see page 101

AR1 – MOBILE HOME – Bali

Sleeping: 2 bedrooms, sleeps 6: 1 double, 1 twin with 2 single beds, 1 double sofa bed

Living: kitchen/living area, bathroom with shower & washbasin, separate WC

Eating: four burner gas hob, microwave & fridge/freezer

Outside: covered wooden terrace

Pets: not accepted

AR2 – MOBILE HOME – Tahiti

Sleeping: 2 bedrooms, sleeps 5: 1 double, 1 twin with 2 bunk beds & 1 single bed, 1 single sofa bed

Living: kitchen/living area, 2 bathrooms each with shower, washbasin & WC

Eating: four burner gas hob & fridge freezer

Outside: wooden veranda, picnic table with seating

Pets: not accepted

Weekly Charge	AR1	AR2
Low Season *(from)*	€ 414	€ 450
High Season *(from)*	€ 735	€ 763

FR77060 Le Parc de la Colline

Route de Lagny, F-77200 Torcy (Seine-et-Marne) Open: All year

Pitches at this campsite are exclusively for mobile homes & chalets

Set in the heart of Marne-la-Vallée, with easy access to Paris and Disneyland, Parc de la Colline is in a relatively green area on the outskirts of the capital, situated on a fairly steep slope. There is a childrens' play area and a shop on site, with a supermarket and water park nearby. The site runs a minibus service to the nearest métro station at Torcy, for easy access to Paris or Disneyland, plus trips to Parc Asterix and group visits to central Paris. Reception will advise on the best value travel cards and these can be purchased on site. Reception staff speak English. Note - you are close to a major city environment. Petty crime can be a problem and we recommend the use of the safety deposit boxes.

Facilities

Shop (all year). Snack bar (high season). Several children's play areas, minigolf, basketball and table tennis. Bus service (every 15 minutes between 08.00 and 24.00 with a pause at lunchtime). Off site: Disneyland 10 mins. (métro), central Paris 20 mins (métro), Parc Asterix 30 mins (car). Supermarket and restaurants nearby.

Directions

From Paris and the Péripherique take A4 to the junction with the A104 (Charles de Gaulle - Lille). From A1 Paris - Lille take A104 (Marne la Vallée), leave at exit 10 and head west signed Parc de Loisirs de Torcy to campsite on left in 1 km. GPS: N48:515.10 E02:39.219

Reservations

Contact site. Tel: 01 60 05 42 32. Email: camping.parc.de.la.colline@wanadoo.fr

AR1 – MOBILE HOME – O'Hara

Sleeping: 2 bedrooms, sleeps 6: 1 double, 1 twin with 2 single beds, 1 double sofa bed, pillows & blankets provided

Living: living/kitchen area, heating, shower & WC

Eating: fitted kitchen with cooking hobs & fridge

Outside: table & chairs

Pets: accepted (€ 4.50 per night)

AR2 – CHALET – Neva

Sleeping: 2 bedrooms, sleeps 4: 1 double, 1 twin with 2 bunk beds, pillows & blankets provided

Living: living/kitchen area, heating, shower & WC

Eating: fitted kitchen with cooking hobs & fridge

Outside: table & chairs

Pets: accepted (€ 4.50 per night)

Weekly Charge	AR1	AR2
Low Season (from)	€ 701	€ 687
High Season (from)	€ 785	€ 687

FR52020 Castel Camping la Forge de Sainte Marie

F-52230 Thonnance-les-Moulins (Haute-Marne) Open: 28 April - 14 September

For our full description of this campsite   see page 110

AR1 – MOBILE HOMES – IRM

Sleeping: 2 bedrooms, sleeps 6: 1 double, 1 twin with 2 single beds, 1 double sofa bed

Living: kitchen/living/seating area, bathroom with shower & washbasin, WC

Eating: fitted kitchen

Outside: table & chairs

Pets: accepted

AR2 – GITES

Sleeping: 2 bedrooms, sleeps 6: 1 double, 1 twin with 2 single beds, 1 double sofa bed

Living: kitchen/living/seating area, bathroom with shower & washbasin, WC

Eating: fitted kitchen, dishwasher

Outside: table & chairs

Pets: accepted

Weekly Charge	AR1	AR2
Low Season (from)	€ 240	€ 250
High Season (from)	€ 570	€ 740

FR52030 Camping Lac de la Liez

Peigney, F-52200 Langres (Haute-Marne)

Open: 1 April - 15 October

For our full description of this campsite ▶ see page 111

AR1 – CHALET – Country Lodge

Sleeping: 2 bedrooms, sleeps 6: 1 double, 1 twin with 2 bunk beds, 1 single bed, pillows & blankets provided

Living: lounge, American kitchen, bathroom & WC

Eating: fitted kitchen with cooking hobs, microwave & fridge/freezer

Outside: table & chairs, sun loungers & parasol

Pets: accepted with supplement

AR2 – MOBILE HOME – Zen

Sleeping: 3 bedrooms, sleeps 6: 1 double, 2 twin with 2 single beds

Living: living/kitchen area, TV, heating, shower & WC

Eating: fitted kitchen with oven, microwave, fridge/freezer, cooking hobs

Outside: table & chairs, sun loungers, parasol

Pets: accepted with supplement

Weekly Charge	AR1	AR2
Low Season (from)	€ 350	€ 350
High Season (from)	€ 756	€ 756

FR88040 Camping Club Lac de Bouzey

19 rue du Lac, F-88390 Sanchey (Vosges)

Open: All year

For our full description of this campsite ▶ see page 118

AR1 – MOBILE HOME – ABI

Sleeping: 2 bedrooms, sleeps 6: 1 double, 1 twin with 2 single beds, 1 double sofa bed, pillows & blankets provided

Living: living/kitchen area, heating, shower & WC

Eating: fitted kitchen with cooking hobs, microwave & fridge

Outside: table & chairs, sun loungers, parasol & BBQ

Pets: on demand

AR2 – MOBILE HOME – Zen

Sleeping: 3 bedrooms, sleeps 6: 1 double, 2 twin with 2 single beds, pillows & blankets provided

Living: living/kitchen area, heating, shower & WC

Eating: fitted kitchen with cooking hobs, microwave & fridge/freezer

Outside: table & chairs, sun loungers, parasol & BBQ

Pets: on demand

Weekly Charge	AR1	AR2
Low Season (from)	€ 250	€ 400
High Season (from)	€ 630	€ 840

FR88130 Camping Vanne de Pierre

5, rue du camping, F-88100 St Dié-des-Vosges (Vosges)

Open: All year

For our full description of this campsite ▶ see page 120

AR1 – CHALET – Country Lodge

Sleeping: 2 bedrooms, sleeps 6: 1 double, 1 twin with 2 single beds, 1 double sofa bed,

Living: living/kitchen area, heating, shower & WC

Eating: fitted kitchen with cooking hobs, microwave & fridge

Outside: table & chairs, sun loungers & parasol

Pets: not accepted

AR2 – MOBILE HOME – Zen

Sleeping: 3 bedrooms, sleeps 6: 1 double, 2 twin with 2 single beds

Living: living/kitchen area, TV, heating, shower & WC

Eating: fitted kitchen with cooking hobs, microwave & fridge

Outside: table & chairs, sun loungers & parasol

Pets: on demand

Weekly Charge	AR1	AR2
Low Season (from)	€ 350	€ 300
High Season (from)	€ 840	€ 770

FR85150 Camping la Yole

Chemin des Bosses, Orouet, F-85160 St Jean-de-Monts (Vendée)

Open: 2 April - 28 September

For our full description of this campsite ▶ **see page 141**

AR1 – MOBILE HOME – Louisiane Florès 2

Sleeping: 2 bedrooms, sleeps 4: 1 double, 1 twin with 2 single beds, pillows & blankets provided

Living: living/kitchen area, heating, shower & WC

Eating: fitted kitchen with cooking hobs, microwave & fridge/freezer

Outside: table & chairs, sun loungers & parasol

Pets: not accepted

AR2 – MOBILE HOME – Louisiane Florès 3

Sleeping: 3 bedrooms, sleeps 6: 1 double, 2 twin with 2 single beds, pillows & blankets provided

Living: living/kitchen area, heating, safe, shower & WC

Eating: fitted kitchen with cooking hobs, microwave & fridge/freezer

Outside: table & chairs, sun loungers & parasol

Pets: not accepted

Weekly Charge	AR1	AR2
Low Season *(from)*	€ 395	€ 430
High Season *(from)*	€ 760	€ 795

FR85210 Camping les Ecureuils

Route des Goffineaux, F-85520 Jard-sur-Mer (Vendée)

Open: 1 April - 30 September

For our full description of this campsite ▶ **see page 143**

AR1 – MOBILE HOME – Super Titania

Sleeping: 2 bedrooms, sleeps 6: 1 double, 1 twin, sofa bed, pillows & blankets provided,

Living: living/kitchen area, shower & WC

Eating: fitted kitchen with cooking hob & fridge

Outside: table & chairs, sun loungers

Pets: not accepted

AR2 – MOBILE HOME – Ibiza

Sleeping: 3 bedrooms, sleeps 5: 1 double, 2 twin, sofa bed, pillows & blankets provided,

Living: living/kitchen area, shower & WC

Eating: fitted kitchen with cooking hob & fridge

Outside: table & chairs, wooden terrace

Pets: not accepted

Weekly Charge	AR1	AR2
Low Season *(from)*	€ 460	€ 490
High Season *(from)*	€ 700	€ 750

FR85330 Camping Naturiste Cap Natur'

151avenue de la Faye, F-85270 St Hilaire-de-Riez (Vendée)

Open: 31 March - 14 October

For our full description of this campsite ▶ **see page 147**

AR1 – MOBILE HOME – Mercure

Sleeping: 2 bedrooms, sleeps 4: 1 double, 1 twin with 2 single beds

Living: living/kitchen area, heating, shower & WC

Eating: fitted kitchen with cooking hobs & fridge

Outside: table & chairs, parasol

Pets: accepted (with supplement)

AR2 – APARTMENT – Convives

Sleeping: 2 bedrooms, sleeps 4: 1 double, 1 twin with 2 single beds, all bed linen provided

Living: living/kitchen area, heating, shower & WC

Eating: fitted kitchen with cooking hobs, oven microwave & fridge

Outside: table & chairs, sun loungers & parasol

Pets: accepted (with supplement)

Weekly Charge	AR1	AR2
Low Season *(from)*	€ 174	€ 188
High Season *(from)*	€ 783	€ 846

FR17010 Camping Bois Soleil

2 avenue de Suzac, F-17110 St Georges-de-Didonne (Charente-Maritime) **Open:** 31 March - 4 November

For our full description of this campsite ▶ see page 124

AR1 – MOBILE HOME – O'Hara Cottage Charme

Sleeping: 2 bedrooms, sleeps 4: 1 double, 1 twin with 2 single beds, pillows & blankets provided

Living: living/kitchen area, heating, shower & WC

Eating: fitted kitchen with cooking hobs, microwave & fridge

Outside: table & chairs, parasol

Pets: not accepted

AR2 – MOBILE HOME – Burstner Cottage Confort

Sleeping: 2 bedrooms, sleeps 5: 1 double, 1 twin with 2 single beds, 1 single sofa bed, pillows & blankets provided

Living: living/kitchen area, heating, hair dryer, shower & WC

Eating: fitted kitchen with cooking hobs, microwave & fridge

Outside: table & chairs, parasol

Pets: not accepted

Weekly Charge	AR1	AR2
Low Season *(from)*	€ 238	€ 218
High Season *(from)*	€ 780	€ 720

FR17070 Camping les Gros Joncs

Les Sables Vignier, F-17190 Saint-Georges-d'Oleron (Charente-Maritime) **Open:** All year

For our full description of this campsite ▶ see page 126

AR1 – COTTAGE – O'Hara M36

Sleeping: 2 bedroom, sleeps 6: 1 double, 2 single beds, sofa

Living: living/dining area, shower, washbasin, separate WC

Eating: fitted kitchen with sink, gas hot plate, fridge, crockery, electric coffee-maker, microwave oven

Outside: wooden terrace with set of garden furniture & electrical blind

Pets: contact site

AR2 – CHALET – Paradis

Sleeping: 3 bedrooms, sleeps 6-8: 1 double, 2 single, 3 single beds

Living: living area/kitchen, shower, separate WC, TV Sat, private telephone

Eating: fitted kitchen with sink, gas hot plate, fridge with freeze, microwave

Outside: outdoor terrace sheltered by covering with set of garden furniture

Pets: contact site

Weekly Charge	AR1	AR2
Low Season *(from)*	€ 368	€ 475
High Season *(from)*	€ 824	€ 1110

FR17280 Camping la Grainetière

Route de Saint-Martin, F-17630 La Flotte en Ré (Charente-Maritime) **Open:** 1 April - 30 September

For our full description of this campsite ▶ see page 134

AR1 – CHALET – Confort

Sleeping: 2 bedrooms sleeps 4/5: 1 double, 1 with 2 single beds & a sofa bed

Living: living/kitchen area, shower & WC

Eating: fitted kitchen with cooking hobs & fridge

Outside: table & chairs

Pets: accepted (max 1 small animal)

AR2 – MOBILE HOME – Luxe

Sleeping: 3 bedrooms, sleeps 6: 1 double, 2 twins with 2 single beds, 1 single sofa bed, pillows & blankets provided

Living: living/kitchen area, shower & WC

Eating: fitted kitchen with cooking hobs & fridge

Outside: table & chairs

Pets: accepted (max 1 small animal)

Weekly Charge	AR1	AR2
Low Season *(from)*	€ 220	€ 255
High Season *(from)*	€ 615	€ 615

Check real time availability and at-the-gate prices...
www.alanrogers.com

Bois Soleil

Camping ★★★★
Charente-Maritime

...rounded by pine trees and a sandy beach on the Atlantic ...ast, with one direct access to the beach, Bois Soleil ...poses to you many attractions like tennis, tabletennis, ...ldren playgrounds and entertainment.
...ps, take-away and snack-bar with big TV screen.

Spring and Summer 2007

2, avenue de Suzac - 17110 ST GEORGES DE DIDONNE
Tel: 0033 546 05 05 94 - Fax: 0033 546 06 27 43
...vw.bois-soleil.com / e-mail: camping.bois.soleil@wanadoo.fr

FR85480 Camping Caravaning le Chaponnet

Rue du Chaponnet N-16, F-85470 Brem sur Mer (Vendée)

Open: 1 April - 30 September

For our full description of this campsite ▶ see page 150

AR1 – MOBILE HOME – Classic

Sleeping: 3 bedrooms sleeps 6: 1 double, 2 twin bedrooms

Living: living/kitchen area, shower & WC

Eating: fitted kitchen with cooking hobs & fridge

Outside: table & chairs, parasol, sun loungers

Pets: accepted (with supplement)

AR2 – CHALET – Gitotel

Sleeping: 2 rooms, sleeps 6: 1 twin, 2 single, sofa bed

Living: living/kitchen area, shower & WC

Eating: fitted kitchen with cooking hobs & fridge

Outside: table & chairs, parasol, sun loungers

Pets: accepted (with supplement)

Weekly Charge	AR1	AR2
Low Season *(from)*	€ 275	€ 315
High Season *(from)*	€ 720	€ 770

FR37060 Camping L'Arada Parc

Rue de la Baratière, F-37360 Sonzay (Indre-et-Loire)

Open: 24 March - 1 November

For our full description of this campsite ▶ see page 160

AR1 – CHALET – Samibois

Sleeping: 3 bedrooms, sleeps 6: 2 double, 2 bunk beds, pillows & blankets provided

Living: living/kitchen area, heating, shower & WC

Eating: fitted kitchen with cooking hobs, microwave & fridge/freezer

Outside: table & chairs

Pets: accepted (€ 1.50 per night)

AR2 – MOBILE HOME – Burstner

Sleeping: 2 bedrooms, sleeps 5: 1 double, 1 single bed, 1 bunk bed, 1 sofa bed, pillows & blankets provided

Living: living/kitchen area, heating, shower & WC

Eating: fitted kitchen with cooking hobs, microwave & fridge/freezer

Outside: table & chairs, parasol

Pets: accepted (€ 1.50 per night)

Weekly Charge	AR1	AR2
Low Season *(from)*	€ 345	€ 295
High Season *(from)*	€ 645	€ 595

FR37130 Domaine Résidential Le Parc des Allais

FR37220 Trogues (Indre-et-Loir)

Open: 31 March - 13 October

For our full description of this campsite ▶ see page 165

AR1 – MOBILE HOME – Louisiane Savannah

Sleeping: 2 bedrooms, sleeps 4/6: 1 double, 1 room with 2 single beds, sofa bed

Living: living/kitchen area, shower & WC

Eating: fitted kitchen with cooking hobs & fridge

Outside: table & chairs, parasol

Pets: accepted (€ 30 per week)

AR2 – MOBILE HOME – Louisiane

Sleeping: 3 bedrooms, sleeps 6/8: 1 double, 2 twins with 2 single beds, 1double sofa bed, pillows & blankets provided

Living: living/kitchen area, shower & WC

Eating: fitted kitchen with cooking hobs & fridge

Outside: table & chairs, parasol

Pets: accepted (€ 30 per week)

Weekly Charge	AR1	AR2
Low Season *(from)*	€ 245	€ 294
High Season *(from)*	€ 826	€ 973

FR41020 Castel Camping Château de la Grenouillière

F-41500 Suèvres (Loir-et-Cher) **Open: 1 May - 5 September**

For our full description of this campsite ▶ **see page 168**

AR1 – MOBILE HOME – IRM

Sleeping: 2 bedrooms, sleeps 6: 1 double, 4 single beds

Living: living/kitchen area, heating, shower & WC

Eating: fitted kitchen with cooking hobs & fridge

Outside: terrace with table & chairs, parasol, BBQ

Pets: not accepted

AR2 – CHALET – Gitotel

Sleeping: 2 bedrooms, sleeps 6: 2 double, 2 single beds, sofa bed

Living: living/kitchen area, heating, shower & WC

Eating: fitted kitchen with cooking hobs & fridge

Outside: terrace with table & chairs, parasol, BBQ

Pets: not accepted

Weekly Charge	AR1	AR2
Low Season (from)	€ 400	€ 400
High Season (from)	€ 730	€ 730

FR41070 Camping Caravaning la Grande Tortue

3 route de Pontlevoy, F-41120 Candé-sur-Beuvron (Loir-et-Cher) **Open: 7 April - 24 September**

For our full description of this campsite ▶ **see page 171**

AR1 – MOBILE HOME – IRM

Sleeping: 2 bedrooms, sleeps 6: 1 double, 1 twin with 2 single beds, 1 double sofa bed, pillows & blankets provided

Living: living/kitchen area, heating, shower & WC

Eating: fitted kitchen with cooking hobs & fridge

Outside: table & chairs, sun loungers & parasol

Pets: accepted

AR2 – CHALET – Shelbox

Sleeping: 2 bedrooms, sleeps 6: 1 double, 1 twin with 2 single beds, 1 double sofa bed, pillows & blankets provided

Living: living/kitchen area, heating, shower & WC

Eating: fitted kitchen with cooking hobs, microwave & fridge

Outside: table & chairs, sun loungers & parasol

Pets: accepted

Weekly Charge	AR1	AR2
Low Season (from)	€ 266	€ 371
High Season (from)	€ 343	€ 440

FR49040 Camping de l'Etang

Route de St Mathurin, F-49320 Brissac (Maine-et-Loire) **Open: 15 May - 15 September**

For our full description of this campsite ▶ **see page 175**

AR1 – MOBILE HOME – Willerby

Sleeping: 2 bedrooms, sleeps 6: 1 double, 1 twin with 2 single beds, 1 double sofa bed, Disposable sheets for sale, blankets provided

Living: living/kitchen area, heating, shower & WC

Eating: fitted kitchen with cooking hobs & fridge

Outside: table & chairs, sun loungers, BBQ

Pets: accepted (€ 3 per night)

AR2 – MOBILE HOME – Concorde

Sleeping: 2 bedrooms, sleeps 5: 1 double, 1 twin with 2 single beds, 1 single sofa bed, blankets provided, Disposable sheets for sale

Living: living/kitchen area, heating, shower & WC

Eating: fitted kitchen with cooking hobs & fridge

Outside: table & chairs, BBQ

Pets: accepted (€ 3 per night)

Weekly Charge	AR1	AR2
Low Season (from)	€ 455	€ 350
High Season (from)	€ 650	€ 565

FR86040 Camping le Futuriste

F-86130 St Georges-les-Baillargeaux (Vienne)

Open: All year

For our full description of this campsite ● see page 181

AR1 – CHALET – Fabre

Sleeping: 2 bedrooms, sleeps 6: 1 double, 1 twin with 2 single beds, 1 double sofa bed, pillows & blankets provided

Living: living/kitchen area, TV, heating, shower & WC

Eating: fitted kitchen with cooking hobs, microwave & fridge/freezer

Outside: table & chairs

Pets: not accepted

AR2 – CHALET

Sleeping: sleeps 4

Living: living/kitchen area, TV, heating, shower & WC

Eating: fitted kitchen with cooking hobs, microwave & fridge/freezer

Outside: table & chairs

Pets: not accepted

Weekly Charge	AR1	AR2
Low Season (from)	€ 344	€ 275
High Season (from)	€ 520	€ 370

FR71070 Castel Camping Château de l'Epervière

F-71240 Gigny-sur-Saône (Saône-et-Loire)

Open: 1 April - 30 September

For our full description of this campsite ● see page 190

AR1 – MOBILE HOME – Louisiane Zen

Sleeping: 3 bedrooms, sleeps 6: 1 double, 1 twin with 2 single beds, 1 twin with bunk beds pillows & blankets provided

Living: living/kitchen area, heating, shower & WC

Eating: fitted kitchen with cooking hobs, microwave & fridge

Outside: covered terrace, garden furniture, loungers

Pets: not accepted

AR2 – APARTMENT

Sleeping: 2 bedrooms, sleeps 5: 1 double, 1 twin with 3 single beds, pillows & blankets provided

Living: living/kitchen area, TV, heating, shower & WC

Eating: fitted kitchen with cooking hobs, oven & fridge

Outside: table & chairs, sun loungers

Pets: not accepted

Weekly Charge	AR1	AR2
Low Season (from)	€ 237	€ 349
High Season (from)	€ 690	€ 749

FR71110 Camping du Lac

Le Fourneau, F-71430 Palinges (Saône-et-Loire)

Open: 1 April - 30 October

For our full description of this campsite ● see page 193

AR1 – CHALET – Lavande

Sleeping: 2 bedrooms, sleeps 4: 1 double, 1 twin with bunkbed

Living: living/kitchen area, heating, shower & WC

Eating: fitted kitchen with cooking hobs & fridge

Outside: covered terrace, garden furniture

Pets: accepted (on demand)

AR2 – CHALET – Goéland

Sleeping: 2 bedrooms, sleeps 6/8: 1 double, 2 twins with 2 single beds, 1 sofa bed

Living: living/kitchen area, heating, shower & separate WC

Eating: fitted kitchen with cooking hobs & fridge

Outside: table & chairs

Pets: accepted (on demand)

Weekly Charge	AR1	AR2
Low Season (from)	€ 210	€ 400
High Season (from)	€ 420	€ 600

FR25080 Camping les Fuvettes

F-25160 Malbuisson (Doubs)

Open: 1 April - 1 October

For our full description of this campsite **⊙ see page 197**

AR1 – MOBILE HOME – 800

Sleeping: 2 bedrooms sleeps 4/5: 1 double, 1 with 2 single beds & a sofa bed

Living: living/kitchen area, heating, shower & WC

Eating: fitted kitchen with cooking hobs, fridge & microwave

Outside: table & chairs, parasol

Pets: accepted with supplement

AR2 – CHALET – Chalet

Sleeping: 2 bedrooms, sleeps 5: 1 double 1 twin with 3 single beds

Living: living/kitchen area, shower & WC

Eating: fitted kitchen with cooking hobs, microwave & fridge

Outside: covered terrace with table & chairs

Pets: accepted with supplement

Weekly Charge	AR1	AR2
Low Season (from)	€ 260	€ 295
High Season (from)	€ 350	€ 400

FR73030 Camping les Lanchettes

F-73210 Peisey-Nancroix (Savoie)

Open: 15 December - 15 October

For our full description of this campsite **⊙ see page 217**

AR1 – CHALET

Sleeping: sleeps 4-5: 1double bed, 3 single beds

Living: living/kitchen area shower & WC

Eating: dishwasher, oven, fridge/freezer, cooking hobs

Outside: table & chairs, parasol

Pets: not accepted

AR2 – CHALET – Charlay-Ballario

Sleeping: sleeps 4-6: 1double bed, 4 single beds

Living: living/kitchen area, shower & WC

Eating: fitted kitchen with dishwasher, oven fridge/freezer & cooking hobs

Outside: table & chairs, parasol

Pets: not accepted

Weekly Charge	AR1	AR2
Low Season (from)	€ 300	€ 300
High Season (from)	€ 650	€ 650

FR33110 Airotel Camping de la Côte d'Argent

F-33990 Hourtin-Plage (Gironde)

Open: 12 May - 16 September

For our full description of this campsite **⊙ see page 224**

AR1 – MOBILE HOME – Louisiane Savannah

Sleeping: 2 bedrooms, sleeps 6: 1 double, 1 twin with 2 single beds, 1 double sofa bed, pillows & blankets provided

Living: living/kitchen area, shower & WC

Eating: fitted kitchen with cooking hobs & fridge

Outside: picnic table & chairs, parasol

Pets: not accepted

AR2 – MOBILE HOME – O'Hara

Sleeping: 3 bedrooms, sleeps 6: 1 double, 2 twin with 2 single beds, 1 double sofa bed, pillows & blankets provided

Living: living/kitchen area, shower & WC

Eating: fitted kitchen with cooking hobs & fridge

Outside: picnic table & chairs, parasol

Pets: not accepted

Weekly Charge	AR1	AR2
Low Season (from)	€ 420	€ 476
High Season (from)	€ 889	€ 973

FR33130 Yelloh! Village les Grands Pins

Plage Nord, F-33680 Lacanau-Océan (Gironde)

Open: 7 April - 22 September

For our full description of this campsite ▶ see page 227

AR1 – MOBILE HOME – Premier

Sleeping: 2 bedrooms, sleeps 4: 1 double, 1 twin with 2 single beds

Living: living/kitchen area, heating, shower & WC

Eating: fitted kitchen with cooking hobs, microwave & fridge

Outside: covered terrace, table & chairs, sun loungers & parasol

Pets: accepted (only one)

AR2 – MOBILE HOME – Sunset

Sleeping: 3 bedrooms, sleeps 6: 1 double, 1 twin with 2 single beds, 1 bunk bed, bed linen provided

Living: living/kitchen area, heating, shower & WC

Eating: fitted kitchen with cooking hobs, microwave, dishwasher & fridge

Outside: patio with table & chairs, sun loungers & parasol

Pets: accepted (only one)

Weekly Charge	AR1	AR2
Low Season *(from)*	€ 224	€ 378
High Season *(from)*	€ 826	€ 1113

FR33220 Sunêlia le Petit Nice

Route de Biscarosse, F-33115 Pyla-sur-Mer (Gironde)

Open: 6 April - 30 September

For our full description of this campsite ▶ see page 229

AR1 – MOBILE HOME – Cottage

Sleeping: 2 bedrooms, sleeps 4: 1 double, 1 twin with 2 single beds, pillows & blankets provided

Living: living/kitchen area, heating, shower & WC

Eating: kitchen with crockery & fridge

Outside: terrace with large table & chairs

Pets: one per unit

AR2 – MOBILE HOME – Sunêlia Family

Sleeping: 3 bedrooms, sleeps 6: 1 double, 1 twin with 2 single beds, 1 bunk room with 2 beds, pillows & blankets provided

Living: living/kitchen area, shower & WC

Eating: fitted kitchen with cooking hobs, microwave & fridge

Outside: terrace, table & chairs

Pets: one per unit

Weekly Charge	AR1	AR2
Low Season *(from)*	€ 378	€ 525
High Season *(from)*	€ 686	€ 1036

FR40100 Camping du Domaine de la Rive

Route de Bordeaux, F-40600 Biscarosse (Landes)

Open: 1 April - 30 September

For our full description of this campsite ▶ see page 238

AR1 – MOBILE HOME – Savanah

Sleeping: 2 bedrooms, sleeps 6: 1 double, 1 twin with 2 single beds, 1 double sofa bed, pillows & blankets provided

Living: dining corner convertible into double bed, shower & WC

Eating: fitted kitchen with cooking hobs & fridge, microwave

Outside: table & chairs, parasol

Pets: not accepted

AR2 – MOBILE HOME – Cottage 3

Sleeping: 3 bedrooms, sleeps 6: 1 double, 4 single beds

Living: living/kitchen area, shower & WC

Eating: fitted kitchen with cooking hobs & fridge, microwave

Outside: table & chairs

Pets: not accepted

Weekly Charge	AR1	AR2
Low Season *(from)*	€ 329	€ 364
High Season *(from)*	€ 966	€ 987

FR33300 Domaine Residentiel Naturiste La Jenny

F-33680 Le Porge (Gironde) Open: 20 May - 9 September

Pitches at this campsite are exclusively for chalet accommodation.

Situated at the heart of Europe's largest forest, yet within walking distance of the Atlantic beaches through the forest, La Jenny is a naturist site providing high quality chalets. There are 750 in total of which 600 are privately owned (many let on behalf of their owners) and 150 let by the site. This is an ideal spot for a quiet and peaceful holiday, yet with a great deal on offer for those seeking a more lively holiday. With four pools covering an area of 1,000 sq m, a wide range of sports amenities, including golf, tennis and archery, there is always something to do. There are many activities for children, including a special club in high season, as well as an extensive programme of evening entertainment. The site's 127 hectares stretches along 3 km. of shoreline.

Facilities

Supermarket, boulangerie and fish shop. Launderette. Restaurant and pizzeria. Bar and brasserie. Heated pool complex. Hairdresser. Newsagent. Body care centre. Fitness centre. Sauna. Yoga and aqua gym. Pony club. Tennis (10 full courts, 8 half-courts) with lessons. Short golf course with lessons and clubhouse. Archery. Bicycle hire. Pony club. Diving and instruction courses. Boomerang course. Fully fenced, staffed and gated play area (over 3 yrs). Off site: Fishing and watersports 300 m. Riding 4 km.

Directions

From the Bordeaux ring road take exit 8 signed Lacanau. Follow D107 to Lacanau via Le Temple and La Porge, then towards Lege/Cap Ferret on the D3 to La Jenny (on the right).

Reservations

Contact site. Tel: 05 56 26 56 90. Email: info@lajenny.fr

AR1 – CHALET – Louisiane

Sleeping: 3 bedrooms, sleeps 8: 2 double, 2 bunk beds, 1 double sofa bed

Living: living/kitchen area, shower & WC

Eating: fitted kitchen with cooking hobs, oven, dishwasher & fridge

Outside: table & chairs

Pets: accepted (€ 28 per week)

AR2 – CHALET – Tourterelle

Sleeping: 1 bedroom, sleeps 6: 1 double, 2 single beds on mezzanine, 1 double sofa bed

Living: living/kitchen area, shower & WC

Eating: fitted kitchen with cooking hobs & fridge

Outside: table & chairs

Pets: accepted (€ 28 per week)

Weekly Charge	AR1	AR2
Low Season (from)	€ 1080	€ 700
High Season (from)	€ 1300	€ 800

FR40140 Camping Caravaning Lou P'tit Poun

110 avenue du Quartier Neuf, F-40390 St Martin de Seignanx (Landes) Open: 1 June - 15 September

For our full description of this campsite **see page 240**

see page 240

AR1 – CHALET – Fabre Reve

Sleeping: 2 bedrooms, sleeps 5: 1 double, 1 twin with 2 single beds, 1 single bed

Living: living/kitchen area, shower & WC

Eating: fitted kitchen with cooking hobs, & fridge

Outside: table & chairs, sun loungers

Pets: not accepted

AR2 – MOBILE HOME – IRM Mercure

Sleeping: 2 bedrooms, sleeps 5: 1 double, 1 twin with 2 single beds, 1 single sofa bed

Living: living/kitchen area, shower & WC

Eating: fitted kitchen with cooking hobs & fridge

Outside: table & chairs, sun loungers

Pets: not accepted

Weekly Charge	AR1	AR2
Low Season (from)	€ 285	€ 275
High Season (from)	€ 695	€ 675

FR40180 Camping le Vieux Port

Plage sud, F-40660 Messanges (Landes)

Open: 1 April - 30 September

For our full description of this campsite ▶ **see page 241**

AR1 – MOBILE HOME

Sleeping: 2 bedrooms, sleeps 4: 1 double, 1 twin with 2 single beds, pillows & blankets provided

Living: living/kitchen area, heating, shower & WC

Eating: fitted kitchen with cooking hobs, oven, grill & fridge

Outside: table & chairs, parasol

Pets: not accepted

AR2 – CHALET

Sleeping: 2 bedrooms, sleeps 4/5: 1 double room, 1 twin with 3 single beds, pillows & blankets provided

Living: living/kitchen area, heating, shower & WC

Eating: fitted kitchen with cooking hobs, oven, toaster, grill & fridge/freezer

Outside: table & chairs, sun loungers & parasol
Covered terrace.

Pets: not accepted

Weekly Charge	AR1	AR2
Low Season (from)	€ 285	€ 360
High Season (from)	€ 690	€ 1000

FR40190 Le Saint Martin Airotel Camping

Avenue de l'Océan, F-40660 Moliets-Plage (Landes)

Open: 4 April - 31 October

For our full description of this campsite ▶ **see page 242**

AR1 – CHALET – Duo

Sleeping: studio with 2 beds & a cot, blankets, pillows & sheets provided

Living: living/kitchen area, tables & chairs

Eating: fitted kitchen with cooking hobs & fridge, microwave, coffee machine

Outside: terrace, table & chairs

Pets: accepted (€ 3.50 per night)

AR2 – CHALET – Zephyr

Sleeping: 2 bedrooms, sleeps 5, 1 double, 2 single beds & a single sofa bed, pillows, sheets & blankets provided

Living: living/kitchen area, heating, tables & chairs

Eating: fitted kitchen with cooking hobs & fridge/freezer, microwave, dishwasher, coffee machine

Outside: terrace, table & chairs

Pets: accepted (€ 3.50 per night)

Weekly Charge	AR1	AR2
Low Season (from)	€ 175	€ 527
High Season (from)	€ 500	€ 1180

FR40200 Yelloh! Village le Sylvamar

Avenue de l'Océan, F-40530 Labenne Océan (Landes)

Open: 14 April - 25 September

For our full description of this campsite ▶ **see page 243**

AR1 – CHALET – Montana 4 persons

Sleeping: 2 bedrooms, sleeps 4: 1 double, 1 twin with 2 single beds

Living: living/dining area, heating, shower & WC

Eating: fitted kitchen with cooking hobs, microwave & fridge

Outside: table & chairs, parasol, sun loungers

Pets: not accepted

AR2 – MOBILE HOME – Cottage 5 pers

Sleeping: 2 bedrooms sleeps 5: 1 double room, 1 twin room with bunk beds

Living: living/dining area, shower, washbasin, separate WC

Eating: fitted kitchen with cooking hobs, microwave & fridge/freezer

Outside: table & chairs, parasol, sun loungers

Pets: not accepted

Weekly Charge	AR1	AR2
Low Season (from)	€ 427	€ 350
High Season (from)	€ 1064	€ 875

FR40250 Camping les Grands Pins

1039 avenue de Losa, F-40460 Sanguinet (Landes)

Open: 1 April - 31 October

For our full description of this campsite ▶ **see page 244**

AR1 – MOBILE HOME – Bambi Cosy

Sleeping: 2 bedrooms, sleeps 4: 1 double, 1 twin with 2 single beds

Living: living/kitchen area, shower & WC

Eating: fitted kitchen with cooking hobs & fridge

Outside: table & chairs, parasol

Pets: not accepted (high season)

AR2 – MOBILE HOME – Océane

Sleeping: 3 bedrooms, sleeps 6: 1 double, 2 twin with 2 single beds

Living: living/kitchen area, shower & WC

Eating: fitted kitchen with cooking hobs & fridge

Outside: table & chairs, parasol

Pets: not accepted (high season)

Weekly Charge	AR1	AR2
Low Season (from)	€ 245	€ 350
High Season (from)	€ 672	€ 868

FR40240 Camping Mayotte Vacances

368 Chemin des Roseaux, F-40600 Biscarosse (Landes)

Open: 1 May - 24 September

For our full description of this campsite ▶ **see page 246**

AR1 – MOBILE HOME – Mayotte

Sleeping: 2 bedrooms, sleeps 6: 1 double, 1 twin with 2 single beds, 1 double sofa bed

Living: living/kitchen area, tables & chairs

Eating: fitted kitchen with cooking hobs & fridge

Outside: table & chairs, parasol

Pets: accepted

AR2 – MOBILE HOME – Méditerranée

Sleeping: 2 bedrooms, sleeps 4: 1 double, 1 twin with 2 single beds

Living: living/kitchen area, shower & WC

Eating: fitted kitchen with cooking hobs & fridge

Outside: table & chairs, parasol

Pets: accepted

Weekly Charge	AR1	AR2
Low Season (from)	€ 350	€ 203
High Season (from)	€ 1043	€ 770

FR64110 Sunêlia Col d'Ibardin

F-64122 Urrugne (Pyrénées-Atlantiques)

Open: 31 March - 3 November

For our full description of this campsite ▶ **see page 251**

AR1 – MOBILE HOME – O'Hara

Sleeping: 2 bedrooms, sleeps 5: 1 double, 1 twin with 2 single beds, 1 single sofa bed, pillows & blankets provided

Living: living/kitchen area, heating, shower & WC

Eating: fitted kitchen with cooking hobs, microwave & fridge

Outside: table & chairs, parasol

Pets: not accepted

AR2 – MOBILE HOME – O'Hara

Sleeping: 3 bedrooms, sleeps 6: 1 double, 2 twins with 2 single beds, 1 single sofa bed, pillows & blankets provided

Living: living/kitchen area, heating, shower & WC

Eating: fitted kitchen with cooking hobs & fridge

Outside: table & chairs, parasol

Pets: not accepted

Weekly Charge	AR1	AR2
Low Season (from)	€ 280	€ 399
High Season (from)	€ 602	€ 700

FR64150 Airotel Residence des Pins

Avenue de Biarritz, F-64210 Bidart (Pyrénées-Atlantiques)

Open: 12 May - 29 September

For our full description of this campsite ▶ see page 254

AR1 – MOBILE HOME – O'Hara

Sleeping: 2 bedrooms sleeps 6: 1 double room, 1 twin room with 2 beds & sofa bed

Living: living/dining area, heating, shower & WC

Eating: fitted kitchen with cooking hob & fridge

Outside: table & chairs, parasol, sun loungers

Pets: not accepted

AR2 – CHALET

Sleeping: 2 bedrooms sleeps 5: 2 double rooms, 1 twin room with bunk beds

Living: living/dining area, shower, washbasin, separate WC

Eating: fitted kitchen with cooking hobs & fridge

Outside: table & chairs, parasol

Pets: not accepted

Weekly Charge	AR1	AR2
Low Season *(from)*	€ 287	€ 287
High Season *(from)*	€ 637	€ 651

FR12010 Camping le Val de Cantobre

F-12230 Nant-d'Aveyron (Aveyron)

Open: 14 April - 6 October

For our full description of this campsite ▶ see page 257

AR1 – MOBILE HOME – ABI

Sleeping: 2 bedrooms, sleeps 4: 1 double, 1 twin with 2 single beds. Blankets & pillows provided

Living: living/kitchen area, shower & WC

Eating: fitted kitchen with cooking hobs

Outside: table & chairs, sun loungers, parasol & BBQ

Pets: accepted

AR2 – CHALET FABRE 2012 – Reve

Sleeping: 2 bedrooms, sleeps 5: 1 double 1 single with 2 bunk beds, blankets & pillows provided

Living: living/kitchen area, shower & WC

Eating: fitted kitchen with cooking hobs, fridge, microwave

Outside: table & chairs, sun loungers, parasol & BBQ

Pets: accepted

Weekly Charge	AR1	AR2
Low Season *(from)*	€ 240	€ 309
High Season *(from)*	€ 660	€ 830

FR12020 Camping Caravaning les Rivages

Avenue de l'Aigoual, route de Nant, F-12100 Millau (Aveyron)

Open: 1 May - 30 September

For our full description of this campsite ▶ see page 259

AR1 – MOBILE HOME – IRM

Sleeping: 2 bedrooms, sleeps 4: 1 double, 1 twin with 2 single beds, pillows & blankets provided

Living: living/kitchen area, heating, shower & WC

Eating: fitted kitchen with cooking hobs & fridge

Outside: table & chairs, sun loungers & parasol

Pets: accepted

AR2 – MOBILE HOME – O'Hara

Sleeping: 2 bedrooms, sleeps 4: 1 double, 1 twin with 2 single beds, pillows & blankets provided

Living: living/kitchen area, heating, shower & WC

Eating: fitted kitchen with cooking hobs, microwave & fridge

Outside: table & chairs, sun loungers & parasol

Pets: accepted

Weekly Charge	AR1	AR2
Low Season *(from)*	€ 336	€ 336
High Season *(from)*	€ 600	€ 600

FR12150 Camping Marmotel

F-12130 St Geniez-d'Olt (Aveyron)

Open: 12 May - 12 September

For our full description of this campsite ▶ see page 261

AR1 – MOBILE HOME – Louisiane

Sleeping: 2 bedrooms, sleeps 5/6: 1 double, 1 twin with 2 single beds, 1 single bunk (for children aged 6 to 12 years), 1 double sofa bed; pillows & blankets provided

Living: living/kitchen area, TV, heating, shower & WC

Eating: fitted kitchen with cooking hobs, microwave & fridge

Outside: table & chairs, sun loungers, parasol & BBQ

Pets: accepted (low season only)

AR2 – CHALET – Fabre

Sleeping: 2 bedrooms, sleeps 2/4, 1 twin with 2 single beds, 1 single bunk (for children aged 6 to 12 years), 1 double sofa bed, pillows & blankets provided

Living: living/kitchen area, TV, heating, shower & WC

Eating: fitted kitchen with cooking hobs, microwave & fridge

Outside: table & chairs, sun loungers, parasol & BBQ

Pets: accepted (low season only)

Weekly Charge	AR1	AR2
Low Season (from)	€ 225	€ 225
High Season (from)	€ 660	€ 710

FR12160 Camping Caravaning les Peupliers

Route des Gorges du Tarn, F-12640 Rivière-sur-Tarn (Aveyron)

Open: 1 April - 30 September

For our full description of this campsite ▶ see page 263

AR1 – MOBILE HOME

Sleeping: 2 bedrooms, sleeps 4: 1 double, 1 twin with 2 single beds

Living: living/kitchen area shower & WC

Eating: fitted kitchen with microwave, fridge

Outside: wooden terrace, table & chairs

Pets: accepted

Weekly Charge	AR1	AR2
Low Season (from)	€ 350	€ 000
High Season (from)	€ 650	€ 000

FR24010 Camping Château le Verdoyer

Champs Romain, F-24470 St Pardoux (Dordogne)

Open: 15 April - 15 October

For our full description of this campsite ▶ see page 270

AR1 – MOBILE HOME – Atlas

Sleeping: 2 bedrooms, sleeps 6: 1 double, 1 twin with 2 single beds, 1 double sofa bed, pillows & blankets provided

Living: living/kitchen area, heating, shower & WC

Eating: fitted kitchen with cooking hobs, microwave & fridge

Outside: table & chairs, sun loungers & parasol

Pets: not accepted

AR2 – MOBILE HOME – Burstner

Sleeping: 2 bedrooms, sleeps 7: 1 double, 1 twin with 2 single beds, 1 bunk bed, 1 double sofa bed, pillows & blankets provided

Living: living/kitchen area, heating, shower & WC

Eating: fitted kitchen with cooking hobs, microwave & fridge

Outside: table & chairs, sun loungers & parasol

Pets: not accepted

Weekly Charge	AR1	AR2
Low Season (from)	€ 295	€ 295
High Season (from)	€ 650	€ 650

FR24020 Camping Caravaning les Granges

F-24250 Grolejac-en-Perigord (Dordogne)

Open: 15 May - 15 September

For our full description of this campsite ▶ see page 269

AR1 – CHALET – Rêve-Comfort

Sleeping: 2 bedrooms, sleeps 5: 1 double, 1 twin with 2 single beds, 1 bunkbed

Living: living/kitchen area, heating, shower & WC

Eating: fitted kitchen with microwave

Outside: terrace, chairs, BBQ

Pets: accepted

AR2 – MOBILE HOME – O'Hara

Sleeping: 3 bedrooms, sleeps 6: 1 double, 2 twin with 2 single beds

Living: living/kitchen area, heating, shower & WC

Eating: fitted kitchen with cooking hobs & fridge

Outside: terrace, garden furniture, 2 sun beds, BBQ

Pets: accepted

Weekly Charge	AR1	AR2
Low Season (from)	€ 217	€ 217
High Season (from)	€ 756	€ 840

FR24090 Camping Soleil Plage

Caudon par Montfort, Vitrac, F-24200 Sarlat-la-Canéda (Dordogne)

Open: 1 April - 30 September

For our full description of this campsite ▶ see page 274

AR1 – CHALET – Reve

Sleeping: 2 bedrooms, sleeps 5-7: 1 double & 3 single beds, 1 double sofa bed, blankets & pillows provided

Living: living/kitchen area, TV, shower & WC

Eating: fitted kitchen with cooking hobs & fridge

Outside: table & chairs, sun loungers, parasol & BBQ, covered terrace

Pets: accepted (vaccinated) supp. € 2.50 per day

AR2 – MOBILE HOME – Super Mercure

Sleeping: 2 bedrooms, sleeps 4-6: 1 double, 2 single beds, 1 sofa bed, blankets & pillows provided

Living: living/kitchen area, shower & WC

Eating: fitted kitchen with cooking hobs & fridge

Outside: table & chairs, sun loungers, parasol & BBQ

Pets: accepted (vaccinated) supp. € 2.50 per day

Weekly Charge	AR1	AR2
Low Season (from)	€ 280	€ 250
High Season (from)	€ 690	€ 640

FR24130 Camping les Grottes de Roffy

Ste Nathalène, F-24200 Sarlat-la-Canéda (Dordogne)

Open: 28 April - 15 September

For our full description of this campsite ▶ see page 275

AR1 – MOBILE HOME – O'Hara

Sleeping: 3 bedrooms, sleeps 6/7: 1 double, 2 twin with 2 bunk beds, sofa bed

Living: living/kitchen area, heating, shower & WC

Eating: fitted kitchen with cooking hobs & fridge

Outside: table & chairs, parasol

Pets: not accepted

AR2 – MOBILE HOME – O'Hara

Sleeping: 2 bedrooms, sleeps 6: 1 double, 1 twin with 2 single beds, 1 sofa bed

Living: living/kitchen area, shower & WC

Eating: fitted kitchen with cooking hobs & fridge

Outside: table & chairs, parasol, covered terrace

Pets: not accepted

Weekly Charge	AR1	AR2
Low Season (from)	€ 290	€ 280
High Season (from)	€ 810	€ 740

FR24320 Camping les Peneyrals

Le Poujol, F-24590 St Crépin-Carlucet (Dordogne)

Open: 15 May - 15 September

For our full description of this campsite ▶ see page 281

AR1 – MOBILE HOME – ENEA

Sleeping: 2 bedrooms, sleeps 6: 1 double, 1 twin with 2 single beds, sofa

Living: living/kitchen area, shower & WC

Eating: fitted kitchen with cooking hobs, fridge

Outside: table & chairs, 2 sun loungers

Pets: accepted

AR2 – CHALET – Reve confort

Sleeping: 2 bedrooms, sleeps 7: 1 double, bedroom with 3 single beds

Living: living/kitchen area, shower & WC

Eating: fitted kitchen with cooking hobs & fridge

Outside: garden furniture, table, 7 chairs & 2 sun loungers

Pets: accepted

Weekly Charge	AR1	AR2
Low Season (from)	€ 360	€ 410
High Season (from)	€ 760	€ 780

FR46010 Castel Camping le Domaine de la Paille Basse

F-46200 Souillac-sur-Dordogne (Lot)

Open: 15 May - 15 September

For our full description of this campsite ▶ see page 291

AR1 – MOBILE HOME – Luxe

Sleeping: 2 bedrooms, sleeps 6: 1 double, 1 twin with 2 single beds & third child bed

Living: living/kitchen area, shower & WC

Eating: fitted kitchen with cooking hobs, microwave & fridge

Outside: table & chairs, BBQ, parasol, sun loungers

Pets: not accepted

AR2 – MOBILE HOME – Grand Luxe

Sleeping: 3 bedrooms, sleeps 6: 1 double, 2 single beds, 2 bunk beds, bed linen provided

Living: living/kitchen area, heating, CD player, shower & WC

Eating: fitted kitchen with cooking hobs & fridge

Outside: table & chairs, BBQ, parasol, sun loungers

Pets: not accepted

Weekly Charge	AR1	AR2
Low Season (from)	€ 270	€ 290
High Season (from)	€ 710	€ 810

FR46140 Club de Vacances Duravel

Port de Vire, F-46700 Duravel (Lot)

Open: 1 May - 20 September

For our full description of this campsite ▶ see page 294

AR1 – MOBILE HOME – O'Hara De Luxe

Sleeping: 2 bedrooms, sleeps 6: 1 double, 1 twin with 2 single beds, sofa bed

Living: living/kitchen area, shower & WC

Eating: fitted kitchen with cooking hobs & fridge

Outside: table & chairs, terrace

Pets: not accepted

AR2 – MOBILE HOME – CRL

Sleeping: 2 bedrooms, sleeps 6: 1 double, 1 twin with 2 single beds, sofa bed

Living: living/kitchen area, shower & WC

Eating: fitted kitchen with cooking hobs & fridge

Outside: table & chairs, terrace

Pets: not accepted

Weekly Charge	AR1	AR2
Low Season (from)	€ 295	€ 275
High Season (from)	€ 750	€ 710

FR47150 **Domaine de Guillalmes**

Condat, FR-47500 Fumel (Lot-et-Garonne)

Open: All year

Pitches at this campsite are exclusively for chalet accommodation.

Pitches at Domaine de Guillalmes are exclusively for mobile homes and chalets, although in the near future the site may also provide for touring units. This three hectare park provides a relaxing holiday destination on the banks of the Lot river, close to the village of Fumel. Recently taken over by a pleasant British couple who are welcoming and friendly, the site offers 18 well maintained chalets on 600 sq.m. plots. During the summer guests can enjoy a large number of activities such as tennis, badminton, football and table tennis. The river provdes opportunities for canoeing, fishing, water skiing and many more. After a leisurely day out in the sun you can enjoy a good regional meal in the site's restaurant or an appetizer on the terrace.

Facilities

Restaurant. Pizzeria. Grill. Takeaway. Bar. Ice cream bar. Swimming pool. Jacuzzi. Tennis. Football. Volleyball. Badminton. Watersports on the river. Off site: Cycling and walking routes. Cahors vineyards 2 km. Fumel, Rocamadour and Cahors.

Directions

From Fumel, take D911 following signs to Cahors, then signs to Domaine de Guillalmes. The site is situated between Fumel and Soturac, 150 m. before Soturac (D911).

Reservations

Contact site. Tel: 05 53 71 01 99.
Email: info@guillalmes.com

AR1 – CHALET

Sleeping: 2 bedrooms, sleeps 4/6: 1 double, 1 twin with 2 single beds & sofa bed

Living: living/kitchen area, TV, heating, shower & WC

Eating: fitted kitchen with cooking hobs & fridge

Outside: table & chairs, parasol

Pets: not accepted

Weekly Charge	AR1
Low Season (from)	€ 270
High Season (from)	€ 750

FR47010 **Camping Caravaning Moulin du Périé**

F-47500 Sauveterre-la-Lemance (Lot-et-Garonne)

Open: 15 May - 21 September

For our full description of this campsite ▶ see page 298

AR1 – MOBILE HOME – IRM Super Mercure

Sleeping: 2 bedrooms, sleeps 6: 2 double, 1 twin with 2 single beds, pillows & blankets provided

Living: living/kitchen area, heating, shower & WC

Eating: fitted kitchen with cooking hobs & fridge

Outside: table & chairs, parasol

Pets: not accepted

AR2 – CHALET – Havitat Rêve

Sleeping: 2 bedrooms, sleeps 7: 2 double, 1 twin with 2 single beds, 1 bunk bed, pillows & blankets provided

Living: living/kitchen area, heating, shower & WC

Eating: fitted kitchen with cooking hobs & fridge

Outside: outside

Pets: not accepted

Weekly Charge	AR1	AR2
Low Season (from)	€ 336	€ 378
High Season (from)	€ 658	€ 707

FR23010 Castel Camping le Château de Poinsouze

Route de la Châtre, BP 12, F-23600 Boussac-Bourg (Creuse)   Open: 12 May - 15 September

For our full description of this campsite ▶ see page 309

AR1 – MOBILE HOME – Burstner Natur'Home

Sleeping: 2 bedrooms, sleeps 5: 1 double, 1 twin with 2 single beds, 1 sofa bed, pillows & blankets provided

Living: living/kitchen area, heating, shower & WC

Eating: fitted kitchen with cooking hobs, microwave & fridge/freezer

Outside: table & chairs, sun loungers, parasol & BBQ

Pets: not accepted

AR2 – CHALET – Shelbox Country Lodge

Sleeping: 2 bedrooms, sleeps 5: 1 double, 2 twin with 2 single beds, sofa bed, pillows & blankets provided

Living: living/kitchen area, heating, shower & WC

Eating: fitted kitchen with cooking hobs, microwave & fridge/freezer

Outside: table & chairs, sun loungers, parasol & BBQ

Pets: not accepted

Weekly Charge	AR1	AR2
Low Season *(from)*	€ 230	€ 300
High Season *(from)*	€ 540	€ 620

FR63070 Camping le Pré Bas

Lac Chambon, F-63790 Murol (Puy-de-Dôme)   Open: 15 April - 30 September

For our full description of this campsite ▶ see page 314

AR1 – MOBILE HOME – Confort

Sleeping: 2 bedrooms, sleeps 4: 1 double, 1 twin with 2 single beds

Living: living/kitchen area, shower & WC

Eating: fitted kitchen with cooking hobs & fridge

Outside: table & chairs, terrace

Pets: not accepted

AR2 – MOBILE HOME – Palace

Sleeping: 2 bedrooms, sleep 6: 1 double, 1 twin with 2 single beds, 1 double sofa bed

Living: living/kitchen area, heating, shower & WC

Eating: Fitted kitchen with cooking hobs & fridge

Outside: garden furniture & terrace

Pets: not allowed

Weekly Charge	AR1	AR2
Low Season *(from)*	€ 237	€ 249
High Season *(from)*	€ 690	€ 732

FR07120 Camping Nature Parc L'Ardéchois

Route touristique des Gorges, F-07150 Vallon-Pont-d'Arc (Ardèche)   Open: Easter - 30 September

For our full description of this campsite ▶ see page 325

AR1 – MOBILE HOME – Louisiane Oakley

Sleeping: 2 bedrooms, sleeps 5: 1 double, 1 twin with 2 single beds, 1 bunk bed, pillows & blankets provided

Living: living/kitchen area, heating, shower & WC

Eating: fitted kitchen with cooking hobs & fridge

Outside: table & chairs, sun loungers, parasol

Pets: accepted (low season only)

AR2 – MOBILE HOME – Louisiane Pacifique

Sleeping: 2 bedrooms, sleeps 5: 1 double, 1 twin with 2 single beds, 1 bunk bed, pillows & blankets provided

Living: living/kitchen area, heating, shower & WC

Eating: fitted kitchen with cooking hobs & fridge/freezer

Outside: table & chairs, sun loungers & parasol

Pets: accepted (low season only)

Weekly Charge	AR1	AR2
Low Season *(from)*	€ 360	€ 360
High Season *(from)*	€ 790	€ 790

FR07150 Camping Domaine de Gil

Route de Vals-les-Bains, Ucel, F-07200 Aubenas (Ardèche)   **Open:** 14 April - 16 September

For our full description of this campsite ▶ see page 326

AR1 – MOBILE HOME – IRM or O'Hara	**AR2 – MOBILE HOME – IRM or O'Hara**
Sleeping: 2 bedrooms, sleeps 4-5: blankets & pillows provided	**Sleeping:** 2 bedrooms, sleeps 4-7: blankets, pillows & sheets provided
Living: living/kitchen area, shower & WC	**Living:** living/kitchen area, shower & WC
Eating: fitted kitchen with cooking hobs & fridge	**Eating:** fitted kitchen with cooking hobs & fridge
Outside: terrace & garden furniture	**Outside:** terrace, garden furniture, 2 sun loungers
Pets: accepted	**Pets:** accepted

Weekly Charge	AR1	AR2
Low Season *(from)*	€ 217	€ 266
High Season *(from)*	€ 595	€ 705

FR07340 Domaine du Cros d'Auzon

St Maurice d'Ardèche, F-07200 Vogüé Gare (Ardèche)   **Open:** 31 March - 15 September

For our full description of this campsite ▶ see page 333

AR1 – MOBILE HOME – Jardins d'Auzon	**AR2 – MOBILE HOME – Mobile home Camping**
Sleeping: 3 bedrooms, sleeps 6/8: 1 double, 2 twin with 2 single beds, pillows & blankets provided	**Sleeping:** 2 bedrooms, sleeps 4-5: 1 double, 2 single beds, sofa bed
Living: living/kitchen area, TV, heating, shower & WC	**Living:** living/kitchen area, shower & WC
Eating: fitted kitchen with cooking hobs, microwave & fridge/freezer	**Eating:** fitted kitchen with cooking hobs, microwave & fridge
Outside: terrace & garden furniture	**Outside:** covered terrace, garden furniture
Pets: accepted	**Pets:** accepted

Weekly Charge	AR1	AR2
Low Season *(from)*	€ 310	€ 205
High Season *(from)*	€ 560	€ 480

FR26040 Camping le Couspeau

F-26460 Le Po't Célard (Drôme)   **Open:** 15 April - 14 September

For our full description of this campsite ▶ see page 337

AR1 – CHALET – Néva	**AR2 – MOBILE HOME – Soleil**
Sleeping: 2 bedroom, 5 sleep: 1 double, 2 single beds, sofa bed	**Sleeping:** 2 bedroom, sleeps 5: 1 double, 2 single, sofa bed
Living: living/kitchen area, heating, shower & WC	**Living:** living area/kitchen, shower & WC
Eating: fitted kitchen with cooking hobs & fridge	**Eating:** fitted kitchen with cooking hob & fridge
Outside: covered terrace, garden furniture	**Outside:** covered terrace, garden funiture
Pets: accepted	**Pets:** accepted

Weekly Charge	AR1	AR2
Low Season *(from)*	€ 375	€ 275
High Season *(from)*	€ 623	€ 525

FR26210 Camping Les Bois du Chatelas

Route de Dieulefit, F-26460 Bourdeaux (Drôme) **Open:** 1 April - 1 October

For our full description of this campsite ▶ see page 341

AR1 – MOBILE HOME – Loft 75

Sleeping: 2 bedrooms, sleeps 6: 1 double, 1 twin with 2 single beds, sofa bed

Living: living/kitchen area, heating, shower & WC

Eating: fitted kitchen with cooking hobs & fridge

Outside: covered terrace, table & chairs

Pets: accepted

AR2 – MOBILE HOME – Texas Watipi

Sleeping: 3 bedrooms, sleeps 6/8: 1 double, 2 single rooms each with 2 twin beds, sofa bed

Living: living/kitchen area, heating, shower & WC

Eating: fitted kitchen with cooking hobs & fridge

Outside: covered terrace, garden furniture & parasol

Pets: accepted

Weekly Charge	AR1	AR2
Low Season (from)	€ 265	€ 290
High Season (from)	€ 570	€ 595

FR04010 Sunêlia Hippocampe

Route de Napoléon, F-04290 Volonne (Alpes-de Haute-Provence) **Open:** 4 April - 30 September

For our full description of this campsite ▶ see page 345

AR1 – MOBILE HOME – Watipi Cottage/ Sunelia Family

Sleeping: 3 bedrooms, sleeps 6: 1 double, 2 twin with 2 single beds, pillows & blankets provided

Living: living/kitchen area, heating, shower & WC (air conditioning on request)

Eating: fitted kitchen with cooking hobs, microwave & fridge/freezer

Outside: table & chairs, sun loungers & parasol

Pets: accepted

AR2 – MOBILE HOME – IRM

Sleeping: 2 bedrooms, sleeps 6: 1 double, 1 twin with 2 single beds, pillows & blankets provided

Living: living/kitchen area, heating, shower & WC

Eating: fitted kitchen with cooking hobs & fridge

Outside: table & chairs, parasol, sun loungers

Pets: accepted

Weekly Charge	AR1	AR2
Low Season (from)	€ 274	€ 269
High Season (from)	€ 973	€ 917

FR04100 Camping International

Route Napoleon, F-04120 Castellane (Alpes-de Haute-Provence) **Open:** 31 March - 1 October

For our full description of this campsite ▶ see page 346

AR1 – MOBILE HOME – Shelbox

Sleeping: 2 bedrooms, sleeps 5: 1 double, 2 bunk beds, 1 single bed, pillows & blankets provided

Living: living/kitchen area, heating, shower & WC

Eating: fitted kitchen with cooking hobs, microwave & fridge/freezer

Outside: table & chairs, sun loungers

Pets: accepted

Weekly Charge	AR1
Low Season (from)	€ 190
High Season (from)	€ 620

FR04020 Castel Camping le Camp du Verdon

Domaine du Verdon, F-04120 Castellane (Alpes-de Haute-Provence)   **Open:** 15 May - 15 September

For our full description of this campsite   ▶ see page 346

AR1 – MOBILE HOME – Watipi

Sleeping: 2 bedrooms, sleeps 4: 1 double, 1 twin with 2 single beds, pillows & blankets provided

Living: living/kitchen area, heating, shower & WC

Eating: fitted kitchen with cooking hobs & fridge

Outside: table & chairs, sun loungers

Pets: accepted

AR2 – CHALET – Titom

Sleeping: 2 bedrooms, sleeps 6: 1 double, 1 twin with 2 single beds, 2 bunk beds, pillows & blankets provided

Living: living/kitchen area, heating, shower & WC

Eating: fitted kitchen with cooking hobs & fridge

Outside: table & chairs, sun loungers

Pets: accepted

Weekly Charge	AR1	AR2
Low Season *(from)*	€ 315	€ 350
High Season *(from)*	€ 616	€ 651

FR84020 Domaine Naturiste de Bélézy

F-84410 Bédoin (Vaucluse)   **Open:** 19 March - 6 October

For our full description of this campsite   ▶ see page 353

AR1 – MOBILE HOME – Nautilhome

Sleeping: 2 bedrooms, sleeps 5: 1 double, 1 twin with 2 single beds, 1 single sofa bed,

Living: large living/kitchen area, shower & WC, electric heating

Eating: fitted kitchen with cooking hobs, microwave & fridge/freezer

Outside: teak table & chairs, sun loungers

Pets: not accepted

AR2 – CHALET – Eden

Sleeping: 2 bedrooms, sleeps 5: 1 double, 2 single beds, 1 bunk bed,

Living: living/kitchen/dining area, shower & WC, heating

Eating: fitted kitchen with cooking hobs & fridge/freezer, satellite TV, CD player

Outside: teak table & chairs, sun loungers

Pets: not accepted

Weekly Charge	AR1	AR2
Low Season *(from)*	€ 390	€ 483
High Season *(from)*	€ 861	€ 1001

FR09020 Camping L'Arize

Lieu-dit Bourtol, F-09240 La Bastide-de-Sérou (Ariège)   **Open:** 10 March - 6 November

For our full description of this campsite   ▶ see page 358

AR1 – MOBILE HOME – Willerby

Sleeping: 2 bedrooms, sleeps 6: 1 double, 1 twin with 2 single beds, 1 double sofa bed, pillows & blankets provided

Living: living/kitchen area, heating, shower & WC

Eating: fitted kitchen with cooking hobs & fridge

Outside: table & chairs, parasol & BBQ

Pets: accepted

AR2 – CHALET – Fabre

Sleeping: 3 bedrooms sleeps 8: 1 double, 2 single beds, 2 bunk beds,1 double sofa bed, pillows & blankets provided

Living: living/kitchen area, heating, shower & WC

Eating: fitted kitchen with cooking hobs, microwave & fridge/freezer

Outside: wooden terrace with table & chairs, parasol & BBQ

Pets: accepted

Weekly Charge	AR1	AR2
Low Season *(from)*	€ 353	€ 549
High Season *(from)*	€ 639	€ 729

FR32010 Le Camp de Florence

Route Astaffort, F-32480 La Romieu (Gers)

Open: 1 April - 8 October

For our full description of this campsite ▶ see page 361

AR1 – MOBILE HOME – Willerby/IRM

Sleeping: 2 bedrooms, sleeps 6: 1 double, 1 twin with 2 single beds, sofa bed

Living: sitting area

Eating: sitting/dining area

Outside: table & chairs, covered terrace

Pets: accepted

AR2 – DELUXE MOBILE HOME – IRM

Sleeping: 2 bedrooms, sleeps 6: 1 double, 1 twin with 2 single beds, sofa bed

Living: sitting area

Eating: separate dining room

Outside: table & chairs, covered terrace

Pets: accepted

Weekly Charge	AR1	AR2
Low Season *(from)*	€ 266	€ 280
High Season *(from)*	€ 721	€ 770

FR65090 Camping Soleil du Pibeste

16 avenue du Lavedan, F-65400 Agos Vidalos (Haute-Pyrénées)

Open: 1 May - 30 September

For our full description of this campsite ▶ see page 368

AR1 – MOBILE HOME

Sleeping: 2 bedrooms, sleeps 5: 1 double, 1 twin with 2 single beds, 1 bunk bed, pillows & blankets provided

Living: living/kitchen area, TV, heating, shower & WC

Eating: fitted kitchen with cooking hobs, microwave & fridge/freezer

Outside: table & chairs, sun loungers, parasol & BBQ

Pets: accepted

AR2 – CHALET – Rondins de Bois

Sleeping: 2 bedrooms, sleeps 4-5: 1 double, 2 single beds, 1 bunk bed, pillows & blankets provided

Living: living/kitchen area, TV, heating, shower & WC

Eating: fitted kitchen with cooking hobs, oven, microwave & fridge/freezer

Outside: table & chairs, sun loungers, parasol & BBQ

Pets: accepted

Weekly Charge	AR1	AR2
Low Season *(from)*	€ 300	€ 300
High Season *(from)*	€ 696	€ 696

FR11060 Yelloh! Village Domaine d'Arnauteille

F-11250 Montclar (Aude)

Open: 7 April - 25 September

For our full description of this campsite ▶ see page 375

AR1 – CHALET – Grand Confort

Sleeping: 2 bedrooms, sleeps 6: 1 double, 1 bedroom with 3 single beds, 1 sofa bed, pillows & blankets provided

Living: living/kitchen area, heating, shower & WC

Eating: fitted kitchen with cooking hobs, microwave & fridge/freezer

Outside: table & chairs, sun loungers & parasol

Pets: accepted

AR2 – MOBILE HOME – Louisiane

Sleeping: 3 bedrooms, sleeps 6: 1 double, 2 twin with 2 single beds, 1 sofa bed, all bedding provided

Living: living/kitchen area, heating, shower & WC

Eating: fitted kitchen with cooking hobs, microwave & fridge/freezer

Outside: table & chairs, sun loungers & parasol

Pets: accepted

Weekly Charge	AR1	AR2
Low Season *(from)*	€ 374	€ 463
High Season *(from)*	€ 763	€ 896

FR11070 Camping les Mimosas

Chaussée de Mandirac, F-11100 Narbonne (Aude)

Open: 24 March - 31 October

For our full description of this campsite ▶ **see page 376**

AR1 – MOBILE HOME

Sleeping: 2 bedrooms, sleeps 4: 1 double, 2 single beds, pillows & blankets provided

Living: living/kitchen area, shower & WC

Eating: fitted kitchen with cooking hobs, microwave, coffee maker & fridge

Outside: table & chairs, sun loungers

Pets: accepted

AR2 – CHALET – Cottage

Sleeping: 2 bedrooms, sleeps 6: 1 double, 2 single beds, sofa bed, pillows & blankets provided

Living: living/kitchen area, shower & WC

Eating: fitted kitchen with cooking hobs, microwave, coffee maker & fridge

Outside: table & chairs, sun loungers

Pets: accepted

Weekly Charge	AR1	AR2
Low Season (from)	€ 252	€ 315
High Season (from)	€ 595	€ 707

FR11080 Camping la Nautique

La Nautique, F-11100 Narbonne (Aude)

Open: 15 February - 15 November

For our full description of this campsite ▶ **see page 377**

AR1 – MOBILE HOME – Type VIII

Sleeping: 3 bedrooms, sleeps 6: 1 double, 2 twin, bedlinen provided for stays of 7 nights or more,

Living: living/kitchen area, shower & separate WC

Eating: fitted kitchen with cooking hob & fridge

Outside: terrace with table & chairs

Pets: accepted

AR2 – MOBILE HOME – Type VII

Sleeping: 2 bedrooms, sleeps 6: 1 double, 1 twin, sofa bed, bed linen provided for stays of 7 nights or more,

Living: living/kitchen area, shower & WC

Eating: fitted kitchen with cooking hob & fridge

Outside: terrace with table & chairs

Pets: accepted

Weekly Charge	AR1	AR2
Low Season (from)	€ 301	€ 287
High Season (from)	€ 700	€ 665

FR30100 Camping Naturiste de la Sablière

Domaine de la Sablière, St Privat de Champclos, F-30430 Barjac (Gard)

Open: 24 March - 14 October

For our full description of this campsite ▶ **see page 378**

AR1 – CHALET – Mas

Sleeping: 2 bedrooms, sleeps 6-7: 1 double, 1 room with 3 bunk beds, sofa bed

Living: living/kitchen area, heating, shower & WC

Eating: fitted kitchen with cooking hobs, pressure cooker, microwave, dishwasher & fridge

Outside: table & chairs, sun loungers & parasol

Pets: accepted

AR2 – MOBILE HOME – Amandiers

Sleeping: 2 bedrooms, sleeps 6: 1 double, 2 single beds, 1 sofa bed,

Living: living/kitchen area, heating, shower & WC

Eating: fitted kitchen with cooking hobs, pressure cooker, dishwasher & fridge

Outside: table & chairs, sun loungers & parasol

Pets: accepted

Weekly Charge	AR1	AR2
Low Season (from)	€ 427	€ 301
High Season (from)	€ 791	€ 651

FR34070 Yelloh! Village le Sérignan Plage

Le Sérignan Plage, F-34410 Sérignan (Hérault) Open: 26 April - 23 September

For our full description of this campsite ▶ **see page 388**

AR1 – MOBILE HOME – Cottage

Sleeping: 2 bedrooms, sleeps 6: 1 double, 1 twin with 2 single beds, 1 sofa bed,

Living: living/kitchen area, heating, shower & WC

Eating: fitted kitchen with cooking hobs & fridge, microwave

Outside: terrace with table & chairs, sun loungers

Pets: not accepted

AR2 – MOBILE HOME – VIP

Sleeping: 2 bedrooms, sleeps 5: 1 double, 1 twin with 2 single beds & a bunk bed

Living: living/kitchen area, fan, heating, shower & WC

Eating: fitted kitchen with cooking hobs & fridge, microwave

Outside: terrace with table & chairs, sun loungers, 2 bikes

Pets: not accepted

Weekly Charge	AR1	AR2
Low Season (from)	€ 259	€ 259
High Season (from)	€ 784	€ 875

FR34110 Yelloh! Village le Club Farret

F-34450 Vias-Plage (Hérault) Open: 29 March - 22 September

For our full description of this campsite ▶ **see page 391**

AR1 – MOBILE HOME – Bali

Sleeping: 3 bedrooms, sleeps 6: 1 double, 2 single rooms, pillows & blankets provided

Living: living/kitchen area, air conditioning, shower & WC

Eating: fitted kitchen with cooking hobs & fridge, microwave

Outside: terrace with table & chairs, sun loungers

Pets: not accepted

AR2 – MOBILE HOME – Africa

Sleeping: 2 bedrooms, sleeps 4-6, 1 double, 1 single, sofa bed

Living: living/kitchen area, heating, shower & WC

Eating: fitted kitchen with cooking hobs & fridge, microwave

Outside: terrace with table & chairs & sun loungers

Pets: not accepted

Weekly Charge	AR1	AR2
Low Season (from)	€ 301	€ 259
High Season (from)	€ 1057	€ 966

FR06080 Camping Caravaning les Cigales

505 ave. de la Mer, F-06210 Mandelieu-la-Napoule (Alpes-Maritimes) Open: All year

For our full description of this campsite ▶ **see page 419**

AR1 – MOBILE HOME – O'Hara

Sleeping: 2 bedrooms, sleeps 6: 1 double, 1 twin with 2 single beds, 1 double sofa bed, pillows & blankets provided

Living: living/kitchen area, heating, shower & WC

Eating: fitted kitchen with cooking hobs & fridge/freezer

Outside: table & chairs, parasol

Pets: accepted (max 10kg)

AR2 – MOBILE HOME – Ophea

Sleeping: 2 bedrooms, sleeps 4: 1 double, 1 twin with 2 single beds, pillows & blankets provided

Living: living/kitchen area, heating, shower & WC

Eating: fitted kitchen with cooking hobs & fridge/freezer

Outside: table & chairs, parasol

Pets: accepted

Weekly Charge	AR1	AR2
Low Season (from)	€ 385	€ 385
High Season (from)	€ 750	€ 750

FR66070 Yelloh! Village le Brasilia

B.P. 204, F-66141 Canet-en-Roussillon (Pyrénées-Orientales)

Open: 28 April - 29 September

For our full description of this campsite ▶ see page 407

AR1 – MOBILE HOME – Louisiane

Sleeping: 2 bedrooms, sleeps 5: 1 twin bed, 2 single, 1 sofa bed, blankets & pillows provided; linen on request.

Living: living area/kitchen, heating, shower & WC

Eating: fitted kitchen with cooking hobs, oven & fridge

Outside: table & chairs, sun loungers & parasol

Pets: accepted

AR2 – MOBILE HOME – Okavango

Sleeping: 3 bedrooms, sleeps 6: 1 twin, 4 single, blankets & pillows provided; sheets available on request

Living: living area/kitchen, heating, shower & WC

Eating: fitted kitchen with cooking hobs, oven or microwave & fridge/freezer

Outside: table & chairs, sun loungers & parasol

Pets: accepted

Weekly Charge	AR1	AR2
Low Season *(from)*	€ 259	€ 280
High Season *(from)*	€ 917	€ 1029

FR06120 Camping Green Park

159, Vallon des Vaux, F-06800 Cagnes-sur-Mer (Alpes-Maritimes)

Open: 26 March - 15 October

For our full description of this campsite ▶ see page 420

AR1 – MOBILE HOME – Le Loft

Sleeping: 2 bedrooms, sleeps 6: 1 double, 1 twin with 2 single beds, sofa bed

Living: living/kitchen area, shower & WC

Eating: fitted kitchen with cooking hobs, microwave, fridge/freezer

Outside: garden furniture

Pets: not accepted

AR2 – CHALET – Club Luxe

Sleeping: 2 bedrooms, sleeps 4-5 1 double, 3 single beds including bunk bed

Living: living/kitchen area, shower & WC

Eating: fitted kitchen with cooking hobs, microwave & fridge

Outside: covered terrace, garden furniture

Pets: accepted

Weekly Charge	AR1	AR2
Low Season *(from)*	€ 343	€ 357
High Season *(from)*	€ 595	€ 637

FR06140 Ranch Camping

Chemin Saint Joseph, F-06110 Le Cannet (Alpes-Maritimes)

Open: 1 April - 30 October

For our full description of this campsite ▶ see page 421

AR1 – MOBILE HOME – Mobile home 4

Sleeping: 2 rooms, sleeps 4: 1 twin, 2 single

Living: living/kitchen area, shower & WC

Eating: fitted kitchen with cooking hobs & fridge

Outside: garden furniture

Pets: accepted

AR2 – MOBILE HOME – Mobile home 6

Sleeping: 2 bedrooms, sleeps 6: 1 double, 1 twin with 2 single beds

Living: living/kitchen area, shower & WC

Eating: fitted kitchen with cooking hobs & fridge

Outside: table & chairs

Pets: accepted

Weekly Charge	AR1	AR2
Low Season *(from)*	€ 310	€ 400
High Season *(from)*	€ 580	€ 670

FR83020 Castel Camping Caravaning Esterel

Avenue des Golf, F-83530 St Rapha'l – Agay (Var)

Open: 31 March - 6 October

For our full description of this campsite ▶ see page 424

AR1 – MOBILE HOME – La Suite

Sleeping: 2 bedrooms, sleeps 6: 1 double, 1 twin with 2 single beds, 1 double sofa bed

Living: living/kitchen area, heating, shower & WC

Eating: fitted kitchen with cooking hobs, oven & fridge/freezer

Outside: table & chairs, sun loungers & parasol

Pets: accepted

AR2 – MOBILE HOME – Mini Luxe

Sleeping: 1 bedroom, sleeps 4: 1 twin with 2 single beds, sofa bed

Living: living/kitchen area, shower & WC

Eating: fitted kitchen with cooking hobs & fridge

Outside: table & chairs, sun loungers & parasol

Pets: accepted

Weekly Charge	AR1	AR2
Low Season (from)	€ 400	€ 220
High Season (from)	€ 860	€ 650

FR83030 Camping Caravaning Leï Suves

Quartier du Blavet, F-83520 Roquebrune-sur-Argens (Var)

Open: 31 March - 14 October

For our full description of this campsite ▶ see page 427

AR1 – MOBILE HOME – Type D

Sleeping: 2 bedrooms, sleeps 6: 1 double2 twin with 2 single beds, double sofa bed

Living: living/kitchen area, shower & WC

Eating: fitted kitchen with gas oven

Outside: covered terrace with garden furniture

Pets: not accepted

Weekly Charge	AR1	AR2
Low Season (from)	€ 280	€ 000
High Season (from)	€ 690	€ 000

FR83060 Camping Caravaning de la Baume

Route de Bagnols, F-83618 Fréjus (Var)

Open: 31 March - 29 September

For our full description of this campsite ▶ see page 430

AR1 – CHALET – Bastidon

Sleeping: 1or 2 bedrooms, sleeps 4-6: 1 double, 2 sofa beds (or 2 single beds)

Living: living/kitchen area, WC

Eating: fitted kitchen with cooking hobs & fridge

Outside: covered terrace, table & chairs, 2 sun loungers

Pets: not accepted

AR2 – MOBILE HOME – Phoenix

Sleeping: 2 or 3 bedrooms, sleeps 6: 1 double, 2 (or 4) single beds, 1 sofa bed

Living: living/kitchen area, shower & WC

Eating: fitted kitchen with cooking hobs & fridge

Outside: table & chairs, 2 sun loungers

Pets: not accepted

Weekly Charge	AR1	AR2
Low Season (from)	€ 301	€ 315
High Season (from)	€ 875	€ 890

FR83070 Caravaning L'Etoile d'Argens

F-83370 St Aygulf (Var)

Open: 30 March - 30 September

For our full description of this campsite ► see page 432

AR1 – MOBILE HOME – Watipi

Sleeping: 2 bedrooms, sleeps 6: 1 double, 1 twin with 2 single beds, 1 double sofa bed, pillows & blankets provided

Living: living/kitchen area, heating, shower & WC

Eating: fitted kitchen with cooking hobs, oven & fridge

Outside: table & chairs, sun loungers & parasol

Pets: not accepted

AR2 – MOBILE HOME – IRM

Sleeping: 2 bedrooms, sleeps 4/5: 1 double, 1 twin with 2 single beds, 1 double sofa bed, pillows & blankets provided

Living: living/kitchen area, heating, shower & WC

Eating: fitted kitchen with cooking hobs, oven & fridge/freezer

Outside: table & chairs, sun loungers & parasol

Pets: not accepted

Weekly Charge	AR1	AR2
Low Season (from)	€ 380	€ 280
High Season (from)	€ 950	€ 850

FR83170 Camping Domaine de la Bergerie

Route du Col du Bougnon, F-83520 Roquebrune-sur-Argens (Var)

Open: 15 February - 15 November

For our full description of this campsite ► see page 436

AR1 – MOBILE HOME – IRM

Sleeping: 2 bedrooms, sleeps 4: 1 double, 1 twin with 2 single beds

Living: living/kitchen area, heating, shower & WC

Eating: fitted kitchen with cooking hobs, microwave & fridge/freezer

Outside: patio with table & chairs, sun loungers

Pets: accepted (supplement payable in high season)

AR2 – MOBILE HOME – Rapidhome Loft

Sleeping: 2 bedrooms, sleeps 5: 1 double, 1 twin with 2 single beds, 1 single sofa bed

Living: living/kitchen area, heating, shower & WC

Eating: fitted kitchen with cooking hobs, microwave & fridge/freezer

Outside: table & chairs, sun loungers

Pets: accepted (supplement payable in high season)

Weekly Charge	AR1	AR2
Low Season (from)	€ 343	€ 364
High Season (from)	€ 861	€ 917

FR83190 Camping la Presqu'île de Giens

153, route de la Madraque-Giens, F-83400 Hyères (Var)

Open: 31 March - 30 September

For our full description of this campsite ► see page 438

AR1 – MOBILE HOME – IRM

Sleeping: 2 bedrooms, sleeps 4: 1 double, 1 twin with 2 single beds. Blankets & pillows provided

Living: living/kitchen area, heating, shower & WC

Eating: fitted kitchen with cooking hobs, microwave & fridge/freezer

Outside: covered patio with table & chairs

Pets: accepted

AR2 – CHALET – Gitotel

Sleeping: 3 bedrooms, sleeps 6: 2 double, 1 twin with 2 single beds. Blankets & pillows provided

Living: living/kitchen area, heating, shower & WC

Eating: fitted kitchen with cooking hobs, microwave & fridge/freezer

Outside: covered patio with table, chairs & sun loungers

Pets: accepted

Weekly Charge	AR1	AR2
Low Season (from)	€ 310	€ 360
High Season (from)	€ 650	€ 810

FR83200 Camping Caravaning les Pêcheurs
F-83520 Roquebrune-sur-Argens (Var)

Open: 31 March - 30 September

For our full description of this campsite ▶ **see page 437**

AR1 – MOBILE HOME – Shelbox Paradis'home
Sleeping: 2 bedrooms, sleeps 6: 1 double, 1 twin with 3 single beds, 1 single sofa bed, pillows & blankets but not sheets provided

Living: living/kitchen area, fan, heating, shower & WC

Eating: fitted kitchen with cooking hobs, microwave & fridge/freezer

Outside: table & chairs, sun loungers & parasol

Pets: accepted (supplement payable)

AR2 – MOBILE HOME – Mercure
Sleeping: 2 bedrooms, sleeps 4/6: 1 double, 1 twin with 2 single beds, sofa bed, pillows & blankets but not sheets provided

Living: living/kitchen area, heating, shower & WC

Eating: fitted kitchen with cooking hobs, microwave & fridge/freezer

Outside: table & chairs, sun loungers & parasol, wooden terrace

Pets: accepted (supplement payable)

Weekly Charge	AR1	AR2
Low Season (from)	€ 330	€ 380
High Season (from)	€ 710	€ 765

FR83220 Camping Caravaning Cros de Mouton
P.O. 116, F-83240 Cavalaire-sur-Mer (Var)

Open: 15 March - 4 November

For our full description of this campsite ▶ **see page 439**

AR1 – MOBILE HOME – IRM
Sleeping: 2 bedrooms, sleeps 6: 1 double, 1 twin with 2 single beds, 1 double sofa bed, pillows & blankets provided

Living: living/kitchen area, heating, shower & WC

Eating: fitted kitchen with cooking hobs, microwave & fridge

Outside: table & chairs, parasol

Pets: accepted

AR2 – CHALET – Gitotel
Sleeping: 2 bedrooms, sleeps 6: 2 double, 1 twin with 2 bunk beds, pillows & blankets provided

Living: living/kitchen area, heating, shower & WC

Eating: fitted kitchen with cooking hobs, microwave & fridge

Outside: table & chairs, parasol

Pets: accepted

Weekly Charge	AR1	AR2
Low Season (from)	€ 380	€ 380
High Season (from)	€ 690	€ 680

FR20050 Camping Naturiste Club la Chiappa
F-20137 Porto-Vecchio (Corse-du-Sud)

Open: 12 May - 6 October

For our full description of this campsite ▶ **see page 448**

AR1 – BUNGALOW – Type C
Sleeping: 1 bedroom, sleeps 2: 1 twin with 2 single beds, pillows & blankets provided

Living: living/kitchen area, shower & WC

Eating: fitted kitchen with fridge

Outside: table & chairs

Pets: accepted

AR2 – BUNGALOW – Type B
Sleeping: 1 bedroom, sleeps 2: 1 twin with 2 single beds, pillows & blankets provided

Living: living/kitchen area, shower & WC

Eating: fitted kitchen with fridge

Outside: table & chairs

Pets: accepted

Weekly Charge	AR1	AR2
Low Season (from)	€ 600	€ 420
High Season (from)	€ 1015	€ 700

FR20040 Riva Bella Nature Resort & Spa

B.P. 21, F-20270 Alèria (Haute-Corse)   Open: 8 April - 1 November

For our full description of this campsite ▶ see page 451

AR1 – CHALET – Chalet 4

Sleeping: 2 bedrooms, sleeps 5: 1 double, 1 single bed, 2 bunk beds, all bed linen provided

Living: living/kitchen area, heating, shower & WC

Eating: fitted kitchen with cooking hobs & fridge

Outside: table & chairs, sun loungers & parasol

Pets: accepted

AR2 – CHALET – Chalet 2

Sleeping: 2 bedrooms, sleeps 4: 1 double, 2 bunk beds, All bed linen provided

Living: living/kitchen area, heating, shower & WC

Eating: fitted kitchen with cooking hobs & fridge

Outside: table & chairs, sun loungers & parasol

Pets: accepted

Weekly Charge	AR1	AR2
Low Season (from)	€ 462	€ 203
High Season (from)	€ 1043	€ 553

Naturist Sites

We have had very favourable feedback from readers concerning our choice of naturist sites, which we first introduced several years ago.

Apart from the need to have a 'Naturist Licence' (see below), there is no need to be a practising naturist before visiting these sites. In fact, at least as far as British visitors are concerned, many are what might be described as 'holiday naturists' as distinct from the practice of naturism at other times. The emphasis in all the sites featured in this guide at least, is on naturism as 'life in harmony with nature', and respect for oneself and others and for the environment, rather than simply on nudity. In fact nudity is really only obligatory in the area of the swimming pools.

You may still be required to have a Naturist Licence. These can be obtained in advance from either the British or French national naturist associations, but are also available on arrival at any recognised naturist site (a passport sized photograph is required).

Open All Year

The following sites are understood to accept caravanners and campers all year round. It is always wise to phone the site to check as the facilities available, for example, may be reduced.

Brittany
FR22020 Fleur de Bretagne
FR56150 Du Haras

Normandy
FR27060 Marcilly
FR76090 Etennemare

Paris & Ile de France
FR75020 Bois de Boulogne
FR77060 la Colline
FR91010 Le Beau Village
FR94000 Tremblay

Eastern France
FR57030 Le Felsberg
FR88020 Belle Hutte
FR88040 Lac de Bouzey
FR88050 Champé
FR88090 Lac de la Moselotte
FR88130 Vanne de Pierre

Vendée & Charente
FR17070 Les Gros Joncs

Loire Valley
FR36050 Vieux Chênes
FR37130 Chlorophylle Parc
FR41060 Dugny
FR45040 Hortus
FR79020 Courte Vallée
FR86040 Le Futuriste

Burgundy
FR21060 Les Bouleaux

Savoy & Dauphiny Alps
FR74010 Deux Glaciers

Atlantic Coast
FR64040 Les Gaves

Dordogne & Aveyron
FR16040 Devezeau
FR24150 Deux Vallées
FR24410 Bois du Coderc
FR24480 Les Tailladis
FR46070 La Plage
FR47150 Guillalmes

Limousin & Auvergne
FR63060 Le Clos Auroy

Rhône Valley
FR26100 Le Sagittaire
FR26110 Les 4 Saisons
FR69010 Lyon

Provence
FR05060 La Pause
FR84080 La Simioune

Midi-Pyrénées
FR09050 La Prade
FR09080 Du Lac
FR65080 Lavedan
FR65130 Pyrénevasion

Mediterranean West
FR06050 La Vieille Ferme
FR06080 Les Cigales
FR11110 Val d'Aleth
FR34060 Oliveraie
FR34230 Chênes

Dogs

Since the introduction in 2000 of the Passports for Pets scheme many British campers and caravanners have been encouraged to take their pets with them on holiday. However, Pet Travel conditions are understandbly strict, the procedure is quite lengthy and complicated so we would advise you to check the current situation before travelling. The Passports for Pets website is: http://www.freespace.virgin.net/passports.forpets

For the benefit of those who want to take their dogs to France, we list here the sites which have indicated to us that they do not accept dogs or have certain restrictions. If you are planning to take your dog we do advise you to phone the park first to check – there my be limits on numbers, breeds, or times of the year when they are excluded.

FR01080 Etang du Moulin
FR14090 Brévedent
FR16020 Gorges du Chambon
FR17010 Bois Soleil
FR17020 Puits de L'Auture
FR17040 Bonne Anse Plage
FR20030 Merendella
FR24040 Moulin du Roch
FR27060 Marcilly

FR29140 Kerlann
FR30160 Le Boucanet
FR34140 La Carabasse
FR34250 Des Sources (Soubes
FR34350 La Plage-Bord du Mer
FR34420 Les Romarins
FR40040 La Paillotte
FR40170 La Réserve
FR46040 Moulin de Laborde

FR47150 Guillalmes
FR64060 Pavillon Royal
FR66040 Le Soleil
FR83320 Mogador
FR84020 Bélézy
FR85210 Les Ecureuils
FR85420 Bel

Sites that accept dogs but with certain restrictions:

FR12170 Le Caussanel
FR17080 Le Royan
FR17210 Interlude
FR17280 La Grainetière
FR17290 Les Peupliers
FR23010 Poinsouze
FR24100 Le Moulinal
FR24290 Moulin du Bleufond
FR24470 Les Nauves
FR26030 Grand Lierne

FR26170 L'Or Vert
FR29000 Les Mouettes
FR30070 Boisson
FR30220 Les Gênets d'Or
FR34130 Le Neptune
FR40120 Arnaoutchot
FR40250 Les Grands Pins
FR50030 Lez-Eaux
FR56260 Le Conguel
FR66170 Mar I Sol

FR66210 Le Roussillon
FR66290 Floride-l'Embouchure
FR66300 Le Pré Catalan
FR68080 Clair Vacances
FR83040 La Bastiane
FR83120 Domaine
FR83200 Les Pêcheurs
FR83350 Sélection
FR85030 La Loubine
FR85310 La Trévillière

Travelling

When taking your car (and caravan, tent or trailer tent) or motorcaravan to the continent you do need to plan in advance and to find out as much as possible about driving in the countries you plan to visit. Whilst European harmonisation has eliminated many of the differences between one country and another, it is well worth reading the short notes we provide in the introduction to each country in this guide in addition to this more general summary.

Of course, the main difference from driving in the UK is that in mainland Europe you will need to drive on the right. Without taking extra time and care, especially at busy junctions and conversely when roads are empty, it is easy to forget to drive on the right. Remember that traffic approaching from the right usually has priority unless otherwise indicated by road markings and signs. Harmonisation also means that most (but not all) common road signs are the same in all countries.

Your vehicle

Book your vehicle in for a good service well before your intended departure date. This will lessen the chance of an expensive breakdown. Make sure your brakes are working efficiently and that your tyres have plenty of tread (3 mm. is recommended, particularly if you are undertaking a long journey).

Also make sure that your caravan or trailer is roadworthy and that its tyres are in good order and correctly inflated. Plan your packing and be careful not to overload your vehicle, caravan or trailer – this is unsafe and may well invalidate your insurance cover (it must not be more fully loaded than the kerb weight of the insured vehicle).

Check all the following:

☐ GB sticker. If you do not display a sticker, you may risk an on-the-spot fine as this identifier is compulsory in all countries. Euro-plates are an acceptable alternative within the EU (but not outside). Remember to attach another sticker (or Euro-plate) to caravans or trailers. Only GB stickers (not England, Scotland, Wales or N. Ireland) stickers are valid in the EU.

☐ Headlights. As you will be driving on the right you must adjust your headlights so that the dipped beam does not dazzle oncoming drivers. Converter kits are readily available for most vehicle, although if your car is fitted with high intensity headlights, you should check with your motor dealer. Check that any planned extra loading does not affect the beam height.

☐ Seatbelts. Rules for the fitting and wearing of seatbelts throughout Europe are   similar to those in the UK, but it is worth checking before you go. Rules for carrying children in the front of vehicles vary from country to country. It is best to plan not to do this if possible.

☐ Door/wing mirrors. To help with driving on the right, if your vehicle is not fitted with a mirror on the left hand side, we recommend you have one fitted.

☐ Fuel. Leaded and Lead Replacement petrol is increasingly difficult to find in Northern Europe.

Travelling continued

Compulsory additional equipment

The driving laws of the countries of Europe still vary in what you are required to carry in your vehicle, although the consequences of not carrying a required piece of equipment are almost always an on-the-spot fine.

To meet these requirements we suggest that you carry the following:

- ☐ Fire extinguisher
- ☐ Basic tool kit
- ☐ First aid kit
- ☐ Spare bulbs
- ☐ Two warning triangles – two are required in some countries at all times, and are compulsory in most countries when towing.
- ☐ High visibility vest – now compulsory in Spain, Italy and Austria (and likely to become compulsory throughout the EU) in case you need to walk on a motorway.

Insurance and Motoring Documents

Vehicle insurance

Contact your insurer well before you depart to check that your car insurance policy covers driving outside the UK. Most do, but many policies only provide minimum cover (so if you have an accident your insurance may only cover the cost of damage to the other person's property, with no cover for fire and theft).

To maintain the same level of cover abroad as you enjoy at home you need to tell your vehicle insurer. Some will automatically cover you abroad with no extra cost and no extra paperwork. Some will say you need a Green Card (which is neither green nor on card) but won't charge for it. Some will charge extra for the Green Card. Ideally you should contact your vehicle insurer 3-4 weeks before you set off, and confirm your conversation with them in writing.

Breakdown insurance

Arrange breakdown cover for your trip in good time so that if your vehicle breaks down or is involved in an accident it (and your caravan or trailer) can be repaired or returned to this country. This cover can usually be arranged as part of your travel insurance policy (see below).

Documents you must take with you

You may be asked to show your documents at any time so make sure that they are in order, up-to-date and easily accessible while you travel. These are what you need to take:

- ☐ Passports (you may also need a visa in some countries if you hold either a UK passport not issued in the UK or a passport that was issued outside the EU).
- ☐ Motor Insurance Certificate, including Green Card (or Continental Cover clause)
- ☐ DVLC Vehicle Registration Document plus, if not your own vehicle, the owner's written authority to drive.
- ☐ A full valid Driving Licence (not provisional). The new photo style licence is now mandatory in most European countries).

Travelling continued

Personal Holiday insurance

Even though you are just travelling within Europe you must take out travel insurance. Few EU countries pay the full cost of medical treatment even under reciprocal health service arrangements. The first part of a holiday insurance policy covers people. It will include the cost of doctor, ambulance and hospital treatment if needed. If needed the better companies will even pay for English language speaking doctors and nurses and will bring a sick or injured holidaymaker home by air ambulance.

The second part of a good policy covers things. If someone breaks into your motorhome and steals your passports and money, one phone call to the insurance company will have everything sorted out. If you manage to drive over your camera, it should be covered. NB – most policies have a maximum payment limit per item, do check that any valuables are adequately covered.

An important part of the insurance, often ignored, is cancellation (and curtailment) cover. Few things are as heartbreaking as having to cancel a holiday because a member of the family falls ill. Cancellation insurance can't take away the disappointment, but it makes sure you don't suffer financially as well. For this reason you should arrange your holiday insurance at least eight weeks before you set off.

Whichever insurance you choose we would advise reading very carefully the policies sold by the High Street travel trade. Whilst they may be good, they may not cover the specific needs of campers, caravanners and motorcaravanners.

Telephone **0870 405 4059** for a quote for our European Camping Holiday Insurance with cover arranged through Green Flag Motoring Assistance and Inter Group Assistance Services, one of the UK's largest assistance companies. Alternatively visit our website at **www.insure4campers.com**.

European Health Insurance Card (EHIC)

Important Changes since E111: Since September 2005 new European Health Insurance Cards have replaced the E111 forms .

Make sure you apply for your EHIC before travelling in Europe. Eligible travellers from the UK are entitled to receive free or reduced-cost medical care in many European countries on production of an EHIC. This free card is available by completing a form in the booklet 'Health Advice for Travellers' from local Post Offices. One should be completed for each family member. Alternatively visit www.dh.gov.uk/travellers and apply on-line. Please allow time to send your application off and have the EHIC returned to you.

The EHIC is valid in all European Community countries plus Iceland, Liechtenstein, Switzerland and Norway. If you or any of your dependants are suddenly taken ill or have an accident during a visit to any of these countries, free or reduced-cost emergency treatment is available - in most cases on production of a valid EHIC. Only state-provided emergency treatment is covered, and you will receive treatment on the same terms as nationals of the country you are visiting. Private treatment is generally not covered, and state-provided treatment may not cover all of the things that you would expect to receive free of charge from the NHS.

Remember an EHIC does not cover you for all the medical costs that you can incur or for repatriation - it is not an alternative to travel insurance. You will still need appropriate insurance to ensure you are fully covered for all eventualities.

insure**4**campers.com

Taking your own caravan, motorhome or tent abroad?

European Camping Holiday Insurance

Our specially tailored travel insurance policies provide exactly the right cover for a self-drive camping holiday in Europe at the lowest possible price. Our policies have been adapted to cover the often-unique risks associated with a camping holiday in Europe. For example, policies include cover for valuables stored in your vehicle overnight on a campsite* (loss from unattended vehicles is often excluded from general travel insurance policies).

Specialist insurance for campers and caravanners can include*:

- **Payment towards additional accommodation costs following loss of own tent**
- **Specific tent and camping equipment cover**
- **Reimbursement of caravan insurance excess.**
- **Theft of valuables from an unattended vehicle whilst parked on a campsite.**
- **Increased car hire limits when towing a caravan or trailer (Plus policies)**

* see policy wording for details

Single Trip Policies

Our **Personal Insurance** provides access to the services of Inter Group Assistance Services (IGAS) and Global Excel, two of the UK's largest assistance companies. Experienced multi-lingual personnel provide a caring, efficient service 24 hours a day. They are backed by a medical team who include in-house doctors and nurses headed by specialist medical consultants.

- **24 hour travel advice line and medical assistance**
- **Authorisation of medical costs and payment guarantees**
- **Air ambulance repatriation/evacuation**
- **Repatriation due to serious illness of relatives at home**
- **Medical escorts and regular liaison with overseas doctors providing treatment**

Our **European Vehicle Assistance** cover is provided by Green Flag who, with over 25 years' experience, provide assistance to over 3 million people each year. With a Europe-wide network of over 7,500 garages and agents, you know you're in very safe hands.

Both IGAS and Green Flag are very used to looking after the needs of campsite-based holidaymakers and are very familiar with the location of most European campsites, with contacts at garages, doctors and hospitals nearby.

Green Flag® motoring assistance

Combined Personal and Vehicle Assistance Insurance

PREMIER COUPLES PACKAGE
£57* 18 days cover for motorhome + 2 adults

PREMIER FAMILY PACKAGE
£89* 18 days cover for car + caravan + 2 adults + dependent children under 16

* Based on vehicles under 5 years old

SAVE WITH ANNUAL POLICIES

If you are likely to take more than one overseas holiday in the next 12 months then our Annual multi-trip policies could save you a great deal of money. European self-drive personal cover for a couple starts at just **£69** and the whole family can be covered for just **£89**.

One call and you're covered **0870 405 4059**

kawan
VILLAGES CAMPINGS

83 quality
campsites
in
7 countries

Decidedly Kuality
Decidedly Komfort
Decidedly Konvivial

decidedly Kamping !

kawan-villages.com

free brochure
00333 59 59 03 59

Low Season
Super Savers

Camping Cheque

HOLIDAY CHEQUE

From £24.75 per night in deluxe
chalets and mobile homes

£10.30 per night
for 2 persons per
standard pitch

How do I save miles of driving in

France?

We know a way

Take one of our direct routes to Holiday France from Portsmouth, Poole or Plymouth and save yourself miles of unnecessary driving. You'll find your holiday begins the moment you step on board. And all for less than you'd expect.

Great magazines for touring, holidays and inspirational ideas!

For buying information, top tips and technical help, **Caravan, Motor Caravan Magazine** and **Park Home & Holiday Caravan** are all you need — every month!

3 ISSUES FOR £1

Our practical titles are packed full of holiday tips, technical advice, reader reviews, superb photography…and much more! To subscribe to Practical Caravan or Practical Motorhome *for just £1.*

- **YOU** get your first 3 issues for £1
- **YOU** save 20% on the shop price after your trial
- **RISK-FREE** offer - you can cancel at any time
- **FREE** delivery, straight to your door!
- **EXCLUSIVE** subscriber offers and discounts

CALL 08456 777 812 NOW!

visit **www.themagazineshop.com** quote code ALR07

---

e start my subscription to Practical Caravan. I will pay £1 for the first 3 nd £8.16 every 3 issues thereafter, saving 20% on the shop price.

e start my subscription to Practical Motorhome. I will pay £1 for the sues and £7.68 every 3 issues thereafter, saving 20% on the shop price.

DETAILS BLOCK CAPITALS Please (must be completed)

Ms _____ Name _____ Surname _____

_____

_____ Postcode_____

ne_____

happy to receive offers, news, product and service information from Haymarket and other carefully selected partners via email and SMS, please tick here ☐.

_____

_____

s open to UK residents only and is a Direct Debit only offer. Details of the Direct antee are available on request. For international rates please call +44 (0) 1750 ffer ends 31 March 2007. Haymarket Publishing may contact you by post or n time to time, with special offers and product information. Please tick this box if not receive this information ☐ . Occasionally we may pass your details to carefully artners whose products we think would be of interest to you. Please tick this box er not to receive this information ☐ .

Please return this form to: Practical Caravan/Motorhome
FREEPOST SEA 14716 Haywards Heath RH16 3BR

Sample any of the magazines below for just £1 each for your first three issues

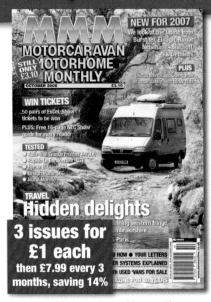

The UK's favourite and best-selling motorcaravan magazine for 40 years

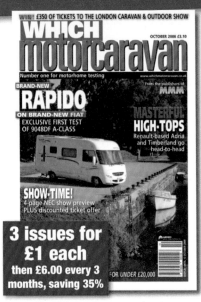

The UK's leading magazine for motorhome buyers

Dedicated to the wonderful world of caravanning, motorcaravanning and camping

Britain's best guide to buying new and used caravans

The UK's only magazine for backpackers and family campers

CALL OUR HOTLINE TODAY ON 01778 391180

quoting ref: ALANROGERS07. Please have your bank details ready when calling
Offers are open to UK residents and close on 31st December 2007

Offers can be used by existing subscribers to renew/extend an existing subscription
Your subscription(s) will start with the next available issue.

Ref: ALANROGERS07

SIXTY GOOD REASONS FOR COMING TO FRANCE

Sites & Paysages DE FRANCE

SITES & PAYSAGES DE FRANCE, 60 QUALITY CAMPSITES
COVERING THE RICH DIVERSITY OF THE FRENCH REGIONS

SITES & PAYSAGES de FRANCE offers campers and caravanners a carefully chosen selection of high quality, 3- and 4-star comfortable campsites across the country. Our 60 campsites are situated in attractively landscaped, tree-shaded environments, with all the amenities for tents, caravans, camping-cars, mobile homes or chalet accommodation.
All are laid out with 'room to breathe' and located in areas of great natural beauty, with masses to do and see, from on-site sport and leisure activities, to nearby heritage visits…
not forgetting the sublime joys of authentic local French cuisine.

inconito Photos : getty images - imagesource

ASK US F
YOUR FR
2007 GUI

information & booking office:
tél. 00 33 820 20 46 46 - www.sites-et-paysages.com
E-mail us at: contact@sites-et-paysages.com

Belle France

Walking & Cycling Holidays

Discover the easy going alternative

It's all on-line

The all-new website gives you all the details, visit

www.**bellefrance.co.uk**

Belle France offers leisurely holidays through the most beautiful and interesting parts of France.

On our walking and cycling holidays your luggage is moved for you whilst you find your own way, at your own pace with our detailed maps and notes.

Relax in the evening in charming family run hotels, offering a good standard of accommodation and a warm and friendly welcome.

Follow suggested routes, stopping where you choose and enjoy complete freedom.

Call now for a **FREE** brochure **0870 405 4056**

Paying too much for your mobile home holiday?

NEW EXTENDED MID-SEASON DATES AVAILABLE

Pay from Just **£24.75** per night
with Holiday Cheque

Holiday Cheque gives you exclusive access to quality mobile homes and chalets on over 100 of Europe's finest campsites - in off peak periods and now closer to high season dates too. You'll find superb family facilities, including sensational pools, great value restaurants, friendly bars and real hospitality. And the kids can have the time of their lives!

All from just £24.75 per night.

HUGE SAVINGS - BUT HURRY

HOLIDAY CHEQUES ARE PRICED AT A SPECIAL PROMOTIONAL RATE, SAVING UP TO 50% OFF CAMPSITE'S STANDARD PRICES. BUT IT'S FIRST COME, FIRST SERVED, SO THERE'S NO TIME TO LOSE IF YOU WANT TO BOOK THE CAMPSITE OF YOUR CHOICE.

HOLIDAY CHEQUE

- ✓ Over 100 top campsites
- ✓ From just £24.75 per nig
- ✓ High quality mobile ho
- ✓ Luxury high specificatio chalets
- ✓ Fully equipped - down the corkscrew!
- ✓ Plus unbeatable ferry p

Call today for your **FREE** brochure
0870 405 4058
IT WILL SAVE YOU £££'S ON YOUR HOLIDAY

www.**holidaycheque**.co.uk

on this map are featured on pages 17-68 of the guide.
e refer to the numerical index (page 532) for exact campsite page references.

Normandy - Map 2

Red text = all year opening
○ Normandy

0   25   50   75 kms

* ST HELIER

CHERBOURG *

50060
50090
50000

50070

50010
50050

MANCHE
50

COUTANCES *

50150
50030
50110
50080

AVRANCHES *

A84

N12

N137

DINAN *
SAINT-MALO *

BRITTANY (Map 1)

N162

LOIRE VALLEY (Map 6)

N12

61040

N176

50100

50140
A84

SAINT-LO *

VIRE *

CALVADOS
14

CAEN *

14130
14020
14030
14150
14170
14060
14010
14190
14070
14200
14160
14180
14090

ARGENTAN *

N158

ORNE
61

14100

61010

N138

ALENCON

LISIEUX *

LE HAVRE *

27020
27010
27030

BERNAY *

EURE
27

27060

DREUX *

EVREUX *

N13

N12

27070

27050

76130 ○
ROUEN *

A29

A13

SEINE-MARITIME
76

76120
76100
76090
76040

DIEPPE *

N27

N31

N14

CHARTRES *

A11

A10

LOIRE VALLEY (Map 7)

PITHIVIERS *

ETAMPES *

A10

PARIS *

PARIS/
ILE DE FRANCE
(Map 3)

N12

N29

A16

CLERMONT *
BEAUVAIS *

MONTDIDIER *

AMIENS *

NORTHERN FRANCE (Map 3)

512

Sites on this map are featured on pages 69-87 of the guide.
Please refer to the numerical index (page 532) for exact campsite page references.

Northern France, Paris & Ile de France - Map 3

Red text = all year opening
- Northern France
- Paris/Ile de France

0   25   50   75 kms

DUNKERQUE

CALAIS
62010
62050
62030
59010
SAINT-OMER
A16
A25
BOULOGNE
A26
LILLE
PAS-DE-CALAIS
62
BETHUNE
NORD
59
LENS
VALENCIENNES
ARRAS
59050
62060
A2
80040
80070
80130
80090
CAMBRAI
AVESNES-
80120
SUR-HELPE
80020
80110
N39
80010
N25
N43
80060
ABBEVILLE
N2
SOMME
80
PERONNE
80100
80030
AMIENS
SAINT-QUENTIN
A29
N29
80080
02000
AISNE
02
MONTDIDIER
LAON
A16
A26
02060
A1
BEAUVAIS
OISE
60
02030
SOISSONS
N31
N31
CLERMONT
N51
REIMS
60010
SENLIS
N14
EPERNAY
95000
VAL-D'OISE
95
A4
78050
CHATEAU
78010
77030
-THIERRY
75020
PARIS
77060
78060
94000
77020
DREUX
N12
77040
N4
77090
78040
A10
91010
SEINE-ET-MARNE
77
A5
91020
77070
ESSONNE
RTRES
91
ETAMPES
TROYES
OIRE VALLEY
(Map 7)
A10
A6
SENS
PITHIVIERS
CHATEAUDUN
N60
MONTARGIS
BURGUNDY
(Map 8)
N77

on this map are featured on pages 88-106 of the guide.
e refer to the numerical index (page 532) for exact campsite page references.

Eastern France - Map 4

Sites on this map are featured on pages 107-121 of the guide.
Please refer to the numerical index (page 532) for exact campsite page references.

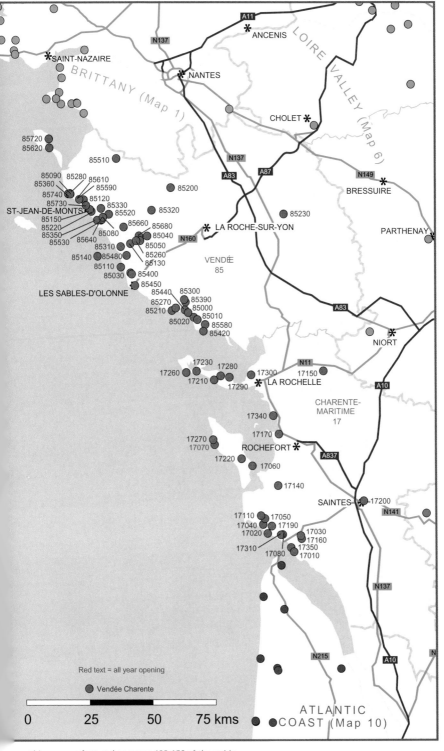

N137

A11

*ANCENIS

*SAINT-NAZAIRE

BRITTANY (Map 1)

*NANTES

LOIRE VALLEY (Map 6)

CHOLET *

N137

N149 *
BRESSUIRE

85720
85620

85510

A83 A87

85090 85280 85610
85360   85590
85740 85120
85730   85330
ST-JEAN-DE-MONTS 85520
85150   85660
85220   85680
85350 85080 85040
85530 85640   85050
85310   85260
85140 85480   85130
85110
85030 85400
85450

85200

85320

*LA ROCHE-SUR-YON

N160

85230

VENDÉE
85

PARTHENAY *

LES SABLES-D'OLONNE

85440 85300
85270 85390
85210 85000
85020 85010
85580
85420

A83

NIORT *

17230 17280
17260
17210 17290
17300 17150
*LA ROCHELLE

N11

A10

CHARENTE-
MARITIME
17

17340

17270 17170
17070
17220
17060

ROCHEFORT *

A837

17140

SAINTES * 17200

N141

17110 17050
17040 17190
17020 17030
17160
17310 17350
17080 17010

N137

N215

A10 N

Red text = all year opening

● Vendée Charente

ATLANTIC
COAST (Map 10)

0   25   50   75 kms

on this map are featured on pages 122-156 of the guide.
se refer to the numerical index (page 532) for exact campsite page references.

Red text = all year opening
● Loire Valley

0   25   50   75 kms

EVREUX ✱

ARGENTAN ✱

N158   N138

DREU

NORMANDY (Map 2)

✱ AVRANCHES

N176

N12

A84

N12

ALENCON ✱

MAYENNE
53

72040   72060

72030   A11

CHATEAUDU

N157

LAVAL ✱

A81

N157   72020

N162

LE MANS ✱

SARTHE
72

CHATEAU-GONTIER

BRITTANY (Map 1)

✱ CHATEAUBRIANT

✱ SEGRE

N138

LOIR-ET-CHE
41

A

37060   41010   41C
41C

37140

ANGERS ✱   TOURS ✱   37030
49000   37010   37110
ANCENIS ✱   A11   49030   37120   INDRE-ET-LOIRE
49110   37
49040   49060   49020   37150
MAINE-ET-LOIRE   49080   LOCHES ✱ 37050
49   SAUMUR ✱   49010
49090   37100   CHINON
✱ NANTES   37070   37090
A87   49070   37130
CHOLET ✱
49120

VENDEE

N149   86010
79020   86030
BRESSUIRE ✱
86090

✱ LA ROCHE-SUR-YON   86040
N160   PARTHENAY ✱   86100   VIENNE   N151
79050   POITIERS ✱   86
DEUX-SEVRES   MONTMORILLON ✱
79

CHARENTE (Map 5)

N11

NIORT ✱
79040   86080

A10   N147

LA ROCHELLE ✱   N10

ROCHEFORT ✱   DORDOGNE/
AVEYRON (Map 11)

Sites on these maps are featured on pages 157-182 of the guide.
Please refer to the numerical index (page 532) for exact campsite page references.

EVREUX

PARIS

NORMANDY (M

PARISILLE DE FRANCE (Map 3)

Red text = all year opening

Loire Valley

0   25   50   75 kms

DREUX

CHARTRES

ETAMPES

EURE-ET-LOIR
28

A5

SENS

PITHIVIERS

28110

CHATEAUDUN

N10

MONTARGIS

N60

A6

AUXERRE

ORLEANS

LOIRET
45

N7

BURGUNDY (Map 8)

45040

N151

LOIR-ET-CHER
41

41020

41040

45030

45010

BLOIS

41090

41030

CLAMECY

41060

41010

41100

COSNE-COURS
-SUR-LOIRE

41070

37030

110

N76

CHER
18

RE-ET-LOIRE
37

VIERZON

37150

N151

CHES

37050

A71

BOURGES

NEVERS

INDRE
36

A20

N7

CHATEAUROUX

SAINT-AMAND-MONTROND

N151

MOULINS

TMORILLON

36050

MONTLUCON

A20

LIMOUSIN/AUVERGNE (Map 12)

N147

N145

VICHY

GUERET

A71

AUBUSSON

RIOM

n these maps are featured on pages 157-182 of the guide.
refer to the numerical index (page 532) for exact campsite page references.

Red text = all year opening

Burgundy

| 0 | 25 | 50 | 75 km |

N4

A26

PARIS / ILE DE FRANCE (Map 3)

A5

TROYES ✳

EASTERN FRANCE (Map 4)

SENS ✳

✳ CHAUMONT

N77

LANGRES ✳

A6

YONNE
89

21070 ○   ○ 21010

AUXERRE ✳

N71

LOIRE VALLEY (Map 7)

○ 89060

✳ MONTBARD

A31

N151

COTE-D'OR
21

AVALLON ✳

A6

DIJON ✳

CLAMECY ✳

COSNE-COURS
-SUR-LOIRE ✳

○ 21000

NIEVRE
58

○ 21040

A39

58030 ○

21030 ○
21020 ○   ○ 21060
21050 ○   BEAUNE

NEVERS ✳

58040 ○

✳ AUTUN

21080 ○   A6

58010 ○

CHALON-SUR-SAONE

N7

N81   58060 ○

N80

○ 71140

58050 ○
○ 71080

71050 ○

○ 71120
○ 71070   N78

SAONE-ET-LOIRE
71

MOULINS ✳

N79

71110 ○

N70

71030 ○

71010 ○

71020 ○   ○ 71090
71060 ○   ✳ MACON

LIMOUSIN/AUVERGNE (Map 12)

BOURG-
EN-BRESSE ✳

✳ VICHY

RHONE VALLEY (Map 13)

ROANNE ✳

VILLEFRANCHE
-SUR-SAONE ✳

A6

A71

N7

RIOM ✳

A72

N89

CLERMONT-FERRAND ✳

THIERS ✳

✳ LYON

Sites on these maps are featured on pages 183-194 of the guide.
Please refer to the numerical index (page 532) for exact campsite page references.

EASTERN FRANCE (Map 4)

Red text = all year opening
● Franche-Comte
○ Savoy/Dauphiny Alps

0   25   50 kms

HAUTE-SAONE
70

TERRITOIRE
-DE-BELFORT
90000   90

MULHOUSE

BASEL

70020 VESOUL

25000

25030

DIJON

BURGUNDY (Map 8)

DOUBS
25

SWITZERLAND

BERN

DOLE
39090   39010

BEAUNE

25070

PONTARLIER

25050
25080

JURA
39
39040
39060   39030
39080
39120   39050
39110
39100

LAUSANNE

CHALON-SUR-SAONE

N78

A6

SAINT-CLAUDE

74130

74180

GEX

HAUTE-
SAVOIE
74

MACON

A39

GENEVE

74060

BONNEVILLE

BOURG-
EN-BRESSE

A41

A40

74150
74160
74010

RHONE VALLEY (Map 13)

VILLEFRANCHE
-SUR-SAONE

74170
74070   74210
74090   74140

ANNECY
74030

74100
74040   74110
74200

LYON

BELLEY

ALBERTVILLE

73020

38150
38060

73060
73030

LA TOUR
DU-PIN

CHAMBERY

73040

73050
38010

SAVOIE
73

VIENNE

A41

A43

SAINT-JEAN
DE-MAURIENNE

38050

ISERE
38

38160

38080

GRENOBLE
38180   38100
38030   38040
38140
38020   38110

38070

BRIANCON
N94

VALENCE

RHONE VALLEY (Map 13)

38130
38190

38090

PROVENCE (Map 14)

N75   N85

ITALY

...es on these maps are featured on pages 195-218 of the guide.
...ase refer to the numerical index (page 532) for exact campsite page references.

519

SAINTES

ANGOULEME

VENDEE CHARENTE (Map 5)

N10

33210

33160
33170

N215
A10

33110
33180   33050   33150

GIRONDE
33

33130
33240   33320

33090
LIBOURNE   33080
BORDEAUX

33300
33270
33120
33230   33020
33010   33030   33260
33280   A63   A62
33190
33220   LANGON
33310   33040   33250
MARMANDE

40250
40240   40100   33140

40170

40080   40300

40070
40160   40110

LANDES
40

40060   N10
40120   40050   N134
40290   40280
40190   40220   MONT-DE-MARSAN
40180   40040
40260   40030
40020
DAX

40200

CONDOM

40140
64060   BAYONNE
64150   40100   64230
64140
64080   64070
64160   64050
64030
64110
64120

PYRENEES-ATLANTIQUES
64

PAU   A64

N134

N21
TARBES

MIDI-PYRENEES (Map 15)

OLORON-
SAINTE-MARIE

64020

64040

DORDOGNE AVEYRON (Map...)

SPAIN

Red text = all year opening

● Atlantic Coast

0   25   50   75 kms

Sites on these maps are featured on pages 219-254 of the guide.
Please refer to the numerical index (page 532) for exact campsite page references.

ATLANTIC COAST (Map 10)

SAINTES

A10

A10

A63

A62

BORDEAUX ✱

LIBOURNE ✱

A89

A10

N10

16050

16060

16030

16040

CHARENTE
16

N10

N10

ANGOULEME ✱

16020

LANGON ✱

47050

MARMANDE ✱
LOT-ET-GARONNE
47
47100

24300

24530

24070

PERIGUEUX ✱
DORDOGNE
24

24330

24540

24010

N21

LIMOGES ✱

N41

N10

47120

47030

47140

47130

47150

47100

24240

24510

24170

24180

24350

24560

24470

24080

24280

24160

24410

24250

N21

N89

AGEN ✱

N21

VILLENEUVE-SUR-LOT ✱

46140

46040

47010

24230

24080

24380

24060

24390

24320

24040

24290

24460

24440

24360

24020

24500

24490

46050

46030

46010

46110

46080

A20

A89

TULLE ✱

USSEL ✱

AUBUSSON ✱

CAHORS ✱

46170

46230

LOT
46

FIGEAC ✱

46150

46070

46200

46180

46220

AURILLAC ✱

LIMOUSIN/AUVERGNE (Map 12)

N140

12260

12250

12120

RODEZ ✱
N88

12050

12170

12080

12070

12060

12190

AVEYRON
12

12040

12200

12150

12210

N122

SAINT-FLOUR ✱

12280

12000

12240

12160

12020

12010

A75

N88

MENDE ✱

N102

MIDI-PYRÉNÉES (Map 1...

A20

1 = 24480
2 = 24310
3 = 24570
4 = 24130
5 = 24030
6 = 24340
7 = 24220

8 = 24110
9 = 24420
10 = 24150
11 = 24450
12 = 24090
13 = 24520
14 = 24140

Red text = all year opening

● Dordogne/Aveyron

0   25   50   75 kms

on these maps are featured on pages 255-300 of the guide.
...se refer to the numerical index (page 532) for exact campsite page references.

Sites on these maps are featured on pages 301-316 of the guide.
Please refer to the numerical index (page 532) for exact campsite page references.

Red text = all year opening
Rhône Valley

0   25   50   75 kms

CHALON-SUR-SAONE

A39

N80

A6

N78

FRANCHE
COMTE (Map 9)

N70

N5

SAINT-CLAUDE ✱

GEX

BURGUNDY (Map 8)

N79

01030

01010

MACON ✱

BOURG-
EN-BRESSE ✱

01050

GENEVE ✱

01020

A40

69020

RHONE
69

A6

VILLEFRANCHE
-SUR-SAONE

A42

AIN
01

01080

ANNECY ✱

VICHY

ROANNE ✱

LOIRE
42

N7

69030

N82

69010

N89

LYON ✱

BELLEY ✱

01040

01060

CHAMBERY ✱

LA TOUR
DU-PIN

ERS ✱

A72

MONTBRISON ✱

A47

VIENNE ✱

SAINT-ETIENNE ✱

42030

A41

BRIOUDE ✱

N102

26140

GRENOBLE ✱

07200

A7

LE PUY-
EN-VELAY ✱

N88

ARDECHE
07

A49

26060

N102

VALENCE ✱

26030

07100

07020

07190

07090

26180

N75

PRIVAS ✱

07210

26110

07180

07220

26120

26150

26130

07150

07140

07170

07280

07110

26040

26210

07070

07340

DROME
26

07260

07130

07330

MENDE ✱

07230

07360

07290

26090

26170

07050

07390

26100

NYONS ✱

07080

07250

07030

07310

07320

07380

07120

N106

07300

07370

ALES ✱

ORANGE ✱

N106

PROVENCE (Map 14)

MEDITERRANEAN WEST (Map 15)

A9

AVIGNON

A7

SAVOY DAUPHINY ALPS (Map 9)

LIMOUSIN/AUVERGNE (Map 12)

on these maps are featured on pages 317-343 of the guide.
se refer to the numerical index (page 532) for exact campsite page references.

Red text = all year opening
● Provence

0   25   50   75 kms

SAINT-JEAN
DE-MAURIENNE
A41
GRENOBLE

SAVOY DAUPHINY
ALPS (Map 9)

BRIANCON

VALENCE

HAUTES-ALPES
05
N94

PRIVAS

N85

N75

05060

05070

GAP

04080

RHONE VALLEY
(Map 13)

04140

A7

NYONS

05000

ALPES-DE-HAUTE-PROVENCE
04

84080

84100   84060

04060

84070

84140

04010   DIGNE-LES-BAINS

ORANGE

84020

MEDITERRANEAN
WEST (Map 15)

VAUCLUSE
84

04130
04120

04030

04100

84090   84040

04020

84050

A51

N85

AVIGNON

04110

A7

GRASSE

ARLES

MEDITERRANEAN EAST (Map 16)

AIX-EN-PROVENCE

A8

BRIGNOLES

MARSEILLE

A57

A50

TOULON

ITALY

Sites on these maps are featured on pages 344-356 of the guide.
Please refer to the numerical index (page 532) for exact campsite page references.

SPAIN

ANDORRA

PYRENEES-ORIENTALES

HAUTES-PYRENEES 65

TARBES

SAINT-GAUDENS

SAINT-GIRONS

HAUTE-GARONNE 31

ARIEGE 09

PAMIERS

MURET

TOULOUSE

AUCH

GERS 32

CONDOM

TARN-ET-GARONNE 82

VILLENEUVE-SUR-LOT

AGEN

MONTAUBAN

ALBI

TARN 81

CASTRES

DORDOGNE/AVEYRON (Map 11)

RODEZ

N88

LODEVE

HERAULT 34

MONTPELLIER

BEZIERS

NARBONNE

CARCASSONNE

AUDE 11

LIMOUX

PERPIGNAN

PRADES

CERET

Red text = all year opening

Midi-Pyrénées

Mediterranean West

0   25   50   75 Kms

s on these maps are featured on pages 357-415 of the guide.
se refer to the numerical index (page 532) for exact campsite page references.

525

Sites on these maps are featured on pages 373-451 of the guide.
Please refer to the numerical index (page 532) for exact campsite page references.

For administrative purposes France is actually divided into 23 official Regions covering the 95 départements (similar to our counties).

However, theses do not always coincide with the needs of tourists (for example, the area we think of as the 'Dordogne' is split between two official regions. We have, therefore, opted to feature our campsites within unofficial 'tourist' regions.

We use the departement numbers as the first two digits of our campsite numbers so, for example, any site in the Manche departement will start with the number 50.

Town and Village Index